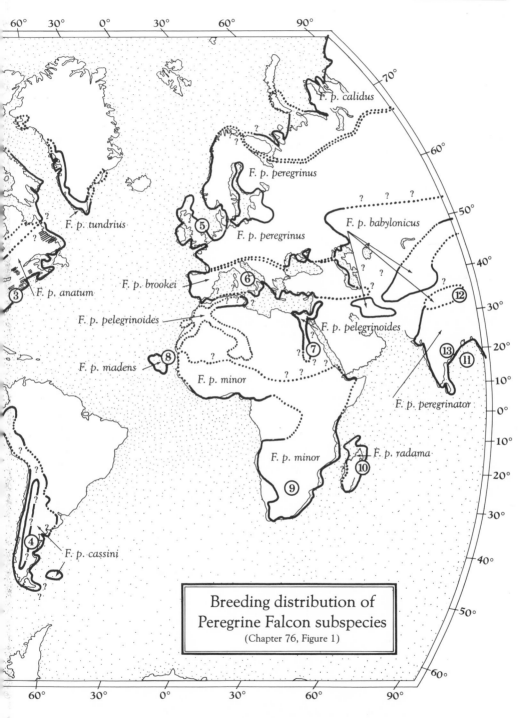

Breeding distribution of
Peregrine Falcon subspecies
(Chapter 76, Figure 1)

PEREGRINE FALCON
POPULATIONS

THEIR MANAGEMENT AND RECOVERY

THE PEREGRINE FUND, INC.

World Center For Birds of Prey
5666 West Flying Hawk Lane
Boise, Idaho 83709

"for the study and preservation of falcons and other birds of prey"

PEREGRINE FALCON
POPULATIONS

THEIR MANAGEMENT AND RECOVERY

Edited by
Tom J. Cade, James H. Enderson,
Carl G. Thelander, and Clayton M. White

The Peregrine Fund, Inc.

ISBN: 0-9619839-0-6
Library of Congress Catalog Card No. 87-063351

Book and Jacket Design: Katie Hart-Thelander
BioSystems Analysis, Inc.
Santa Cruz, California

Typography: Neil Cossman, Douglas Dirks, Lisa Kababek
ASAP Typography
Santa Cruz, California

Printing and Binding: Braun-Brumfeld
San Francisco, California

FOREWORD

The dispassionate brown eyes of the Peregrine, more than those of any other bird, have been witness to our struggle for civilization.

Two thousand years before the Christian era, falconry in Asia, "the oldest sport on earth," provided a means to an end. It meant meat on the table, a method of getting game beyond the range of the swiftest arrow. In the heart of Asia, a hunting eagle was worth from three to ten horses. There they were flown even at wolves.

Marco Polo reported that the Great Khan of Cathay journeyed once a year to the eastern part of his kingdom, riding on a pavilion borne on the backs of four elephants. Ten thousand falconers and their hawks went along, and twelve Gyrfalcons attended by twelve officers rode with the Khan in his pavilion. Men on horseback gave the signal when cranes or other birds appeared overhead. Then the curtains of the pavilion were drawn while the Khan, in sensual splendor, watched the sport from his couch.

The sultan of Bayazid had 7000 hawks, and Frederick II of Hohenstaufen built whole castles for his birds. The kings of the East exchanged their birds with the kings of the West until even the Vikings knew of falconry.

Queens, tsars, and popes flew their birds. A knight was as proud of the falcon on his wrist as of the sword at his side. Bishops carried their birds to the church and down the aisle, releasing them as they approached the altar. Hawking was the pastime of an idle gentry, a pastime destined to decline with the social upheavals of the 17th century.

The Peregrine is the only sharp-winged falcon to span the globe; it is found on all the continents except Antarctica, and on many of the larger islands. The North American bird was originally called the "duck hawk" because Alexander Wilson, the pioneer of American ornithology, did not like the name Peregrine ("traveler"); he believed the Peregrine to be nonmigratory. In recent years we have gone back to the older name, the one that has always been used in England.

The most efficient flying machine, the best-designed bird, the fiercest and fastest bird — all these superlatives have been claimed for the Peregrine. It may well be the swiftest bird, but its ordinary cruising speed is not much greater than that of the pigeons it catches. It is in the "stoop," the plunge when it partially closes its wings and pumps in for the kill, that the Peregrine attains the rocketlike speed for which it is famous.

I still remember the Sunday afternoon nearly 60 years ago when I was shown my first Peregrine eyrie on the palisades of the Hudson River. We scanned the dark cliffs with our glasses for the telltale patch of white that splashed the nesting ledge. On a stub to one side perched the bird, its black mustaches and big yellow feet showing plainly. Many times during those pre-DDT years I watched the Peregrines on the palisades; they were so beautifully cut, like giant swallows.

In those days we always spoke of "the palisades duck hawk." I had no idea there were half a dozen eyries between the Fort Lee Ferry and West Point. The oologists knew them all, but kept them secret. The falconers knew, too, but they had long had an understanding among themselves not to molest the Hudson River Peregrines. It was one of the high points of my birding career to be taken in 1940 to 14 eyries in a weekend, the farthest not more than 100 miles from New York City. I even went overside to examine some of the eggs. It took a great dose of nerve to back off the edge of a 400-foot cliff with nothing but pitons and a half-inch rope for support. The river was so far below!

Formerly a few Peregrines nested in ancient wind-topped trees along the Mississippi. In 1941 I saw such an eyrie in northern Louisiana, 100 miles south of any other known nest in eastern North America. The man who directed me to it was nearly blind. He had dimly beheld the silhouette of a sharp-winged bird circling about a tall cypress stub and protesting. He wondered if it could be a Carolina Parakeet, but added that "it sounded just like the duck hawk we have here in winter." A week later, Doctor Walter Spofford showed me another cypress-top eyrie in Tennessee.

In both Europe and Asia, Peregrines have long nested on cathedrals, temples, and old castles. It was predictably only a matter of time before Peregrines would take up residence in New World cities. In winter, some Peregrines hunted pigeons from the skyscrapers of Boston, Albany, Philadelphia, and Washington, while New York City's "canyons" harbored a dozen or more. Among the favorite command posts for winter Peregrines in New York 50 years ago were the Clason Point gas tank, the George Washington Bridge, the Riverside Church, the New York Hospital, Hearn's Department Store in Greenwich Village, and the Lincoln and Chrysler buildings. The Riverside Church bird fell into disfavor with the rector because it harried the local pigeons.

The main disadvantage of most modern buildings, from the Peregrine's point of view, is that they tend toward simple lines, devoid of gingerbread and suitable niches. When a pair tried unsuccessfully to nest on the Sun Life Building in Montreal, an 18 × 18-inch tray filled with gravel was put out so that the eggs would not roll from the ledge. With this help, the birds reared two young in 1940 and nested there each year until 1952.

Joseph Hickey wrote that "about 400 nesting sites of the Peregrine had been reported east of the Rocky Mountains up to the close of 1940, although several times this number was believed to exist." Most of the latter would have been far to the north. Richard Bond placed the breeding population of western North America at 750 pairs. By all estimates, then, the Peregrine was a rarity, with perhaps not many more than 5000 individuals on the continent. The rather small brotherhood of falconers were not a threat to the birds. Many hawk-shooting sportsmen had been converted by the beauty of a well-trained Peregrine on the wrist of a falconer. Some falconers gave lectures about the birds of prey and took an active interest in protecting nearby eyries, even though they took no birds for training.

In all the long history of falconry, nothing is more bizarre than the short-lived episode that took place at Fort Monmouth, New Jersey, at the outbreak of World War II. Hundreds of requests were sent out asking for live hawks, preferably Peregrines. They were to be trained to intercept enemy pigeons. The idea had possibilities, but it soon got out of hand. Birds were to be trained to dive at airborne troops, slitting their parachutes with knives attached to their breasts!

Soon the unit had three birds: one Red-tailed Hawk, one American Kestrel, and one Peregrine. My friend, Louis Halle, who once kept a pet hawk, was assigned the care of the birds, and an unhappy man he was. Some of his friends who did not fully understand the anatomy of an army seemed to blame him for the whole idea, even though he was only a private at the time and had little choice in the matter. Falconers and ornithologists everywhere protested. They regarded the plan not only as unworkable, but as a threat to the existence of the Peregrine if developed on a large scale. Under pressure, the Pentagon stopped the program.

A grim, long-standing feud aligned another group of Peregrine addicts in an opposite camp. They were the oologists. The rarer the bird, the keener the collector was to acquire its eggs. The challenge was so great that some oologists specialized in Peregrine eggs. One collector in Philadelphia had a cabinet full of Peregrine eggs, drawer upon drawer representing years when some eyries along the Susquehana and elsewhere in eastern Pennsylvania fledged scarcely a single young bird. A Boston oologist was reputed to have 180 sets — more than 700 eggs! Sixty, 80, and 100 sets were frequent.

The oologist claimed he caused less damage than the falconer, because when he took the eggs the bird laid again. This the Peregrines sometimes did; after two weeks or so a smaller clutch was laid, but the "eggers" were often on hand to get those, too. I was shown a cliff in California where a collector pitched his tent before the eggs were laid, so he would be there first. He told me that he had taken the eggs at the eyrie each year for 29 years, "but now due to civilization, this site is no longer occupied."

Egg collecting seems to have died out completely in the United States. How different it was 100 years ago when 30 men climbed one cliff on the same day for a single set of eggs!

Meanwhile, the falconers' star was on the rise. Bitter was their feud with the oologists, who had an advantage: eggs come before chicks. To gain tactical advantage, the falconers climbed the cliffs as soon as eggs were laid and, to make them worthless to oologists, roughed the shells with sandpaper and daubed them with India ink. "The birds don't mind," one of the vigilantes remarked, "they would as soon sit on doorknobs."

The aficionados of the Peregrine had a gentlemen's agreement amongst themselves not to take young from nests along the Hudson River palisades. They insisted that nests near big cities be left strictly alone and took a special interest in seeing the young safely on the wing. Heaven help the egger they caught, particularly on the New York side of the line where the Peregrine was protected by state law. They even enlisted the aid of the park police who patrolled the highway along the cliffs.

But all this had changed by 1960. Shortly after 1950, my friend Richard Herbert, who had shown Joseph Hickey and me all the Hudson River eyries, noticed that although the birds laid eggs, the eggs failed to hatch. At eyrie after eyrie, the birds eventually disappeared. The famous Sun Life birds in Montreal raised their last family in 1952. By 1960 no one knew of a single active eyrie anywhere in the northeastern United States, although passage birds from further north still went through. It was not clear what was wrong, and many explanations were bandied about. Concurrently, the Peregrine population in Europe was also declining precipitously.

In 1965, Joseph Hickey, then teaching wildlife ecology at the University of Wisconsin, called together all those concerned about the Peregrine for a conference at Madison. More than 60 participants and observers from North America and Europe presented papers or took part in discussions. These were published in book form in 1969 under the title *Peregrine Falcon Populations: Their Biology and Decline*. Was it perhaps the requiem of a species? This ecological disaster was explored and a wide variety of adverse factors were examined. The evidence pointed convincingly to the widespread use of chlorinated hydro-carbons such as DDT — residual poisons that were passed upward through the food chain. Obviously, the Peregrine was a casualty of these subtle but deadly biocides.

In the years that followed, this conclusion was confirmed through further intensive work on two continents, and thanks to the banning of DDT in many countries, the environment began to cleanse itself. But what of the Peregrine? It had been completely extirpated as a breeding bird in eastern North America and was much diminished elsewhere.

Thanks largely to one of the Madison participants, Dr. Tom Cade of Cornell, and several others who attended that landmark conference, the Peregrine is now on its way back. By using their knowledge of falconry to raise young from eggs under captive conditions and to hack them out at selected sites, they have saved this critically endangered species. The seed stock of wild breeding Peregrines is now doubling its numbers every year or two in eastern North America, and the species is making a strong recovery in other parts of its range as well.

In November 1985, on the 20th anniversary of the Madison Conference, an even larger get-together of Peregrine aficionados was held in Sacramento, California. It was hosted by The Peregrine Fund, Inc., under the chairmanship of Tom Cade. More than 70 papers were presented, celebrating one of the most remarkable conservation success stories of our time.

This new book, based on the Sacramento conference, tells the fascinating story. Among other things, it shows that avicultural methods can be a very effective tool in saving a species on the brink of extinction. Will it also work for the California Condor? We hope so.

Roger Tory Peterson
Old Lyme, Connecticut

PREFACE

In August 1965, a group of falcon experts met at the University of Wisconsin in Madison to consider a biological phenomenon which conservationists were later to characterize as an ecological disaster: the unprecedented population crashes of Peregrine Falcons in North America and Europe. A book which is now a collector's prize, *Peregrine Falcon Populations: Their Biology and Decline*, edited by Joseph J. Hickey (1969), contains the results of that conference. The Peregrine Fund, Inc. is pleased to offer in this volume the results of a second conference, held 3-6 November at Sacramento, California in 1985, the twentieth anniversary year of the historic Madison Conference. The papers presented at the Sacramento Conference demonstrate the great interest and dedication that the plight of the Peregrine has called forth from an extraordinary array of people who united in their purpose to save this endangered falcon. Their efforts show what can be done through cooperation and good will — and much hard work — to reverse a seemingly hopeless slide toward extinction. We believe that by documenting these efforts and related research, this book will make a lasting contribution to the understanding and conservation of the Peregrine Falcon and will serve, also, as an instructive case history for the preservation of other endangered species.

The Sacramento Conference would not have been possible without the generous financial support of the Raptor Research Foundation, Inc., San Francisco Zoological Society, National Audubon Society, Western Foundation of Vertebrate Zoology in Los Angeles, Hawk Mountain Sanctuary Association, and the U. S. Army Chemical Systems Laboratory at the Aberdeen Proving Grounds, Maryland. The organizing committee for the conference did a superlative job and deserves everyone's thanks: Richard Olendorff (U. S. Bureau of Land Management), Nancy Schofield (San Francisco Zoological Society), David Harlow (U. S. Fish and Wildlife Service), and Patricia Burnham (The Peregrine Fund, Inc.). The program chairmen kept the conference running smoothly and on schedule: we thank Bernd-U. Meyburg, Morlan Nelson, Ian Newton, Ian Nisbet, and David Peakall for their help. Phyllis Dague (The Peregrine Fund, Cornell University) helped with much of the correspondence involved in organizing the conference and in assembling and editing manuscripts.

Support for the publication of this book came from Arthur Weaver, James Weaver, and Daniel Brimm. Publication would not have been possible without their enthusiastic contributions.

BioSystems Analysis, Inc. provided its facilities and staff to design and produce this volume. Special thanks go to Katie Hart-Thelander (Design and Graphic Production), Dana Bland (Assistant Editor), and Douglas Dirks (Typesetting Coordinator); also to David Arora (Associate Editor), who, after editing this book, now claims to know more about Peregrine Falcons than anyone else who has never seen one in the wild.

William J. Beecher (Beecher Research Company, Chicago, Illinois) kindly gave permission to use the original George M. Sutton paintings reproduced on the dust jacket.

Finally, for review of manuscripts and for technical comments on various topics, we acknowledge the special assistance of Jack Barclay, Richard Fyfe, Charles Henny, W. Grainger Hunt, Lloyd Kiff, Ian Newton, Ian Nisbet, David Peakall, Derek Ratcliffe, Robert Risebrough, James Ruos, Kimberly Titus, and F. Prescott Ward.

The Editors
Santa Cruz, California
March 1988

CONTENTS

PART 3

STATUS OF PEREGRINE POPULATIONS SINCE 1965 – EUROPE

PART 4

STATUS OF THE PEREGRINE IN OTHER PARTS
OF THE WORLD

PART 5

DDT AND OTHER CHEMICAL PROBLEMS

PART 8

DYNAMICS AND ECOLOGY OF PEREGRINE
POPULATIONS

PART 9

GEOGRAPHIC VARIATION IN PEREGRINE POPULATIONS

PART 10

HUMANITY AND THE PEREGRINE

SUMMARY AND CONCLUSION

APPENDICES

INTRODUCTION

Tom J. Cade

In November 1985, more than 500 raptor biologists and Peregrine specialists met together in Sacramento, California, for a three-day international conference to discuss Peregrine biology and conservation. The purpose was to assess the worldwide status of the Peregrine Falcon 20 years after the landmark Madison Peregrine Conference in 1965, when world attention focused on the catastrophic population crashes that had occurred simultaneously in Europe and North America owing to the effects of organochlorine pesticides. Held in conjunction with the Raptor Research Foundation's International Meeting and Symposium on the Management of Birds of Prey and sponsored by The Peregrine Fund, the 1985 program involved more than 70 researchers invited from 15 countries. The conference also served as an occasion to celebrate the survival and growing recovery of the Peregrine Falcon in the face of the grave uncertainties which existed 20 years earlier.

The first evening, the conferees heard keynote addresses from three eminent colleagues: Joseph J. Hickey, Derek A. Ratcliffe, and Morlan W. Nelson. As I looked around in the audience, I saw a number of familiar faces, and it was indeed gratifying to note how many of the Madison conferees had themselves survived the intervening 20 years to be present that evening, including the three distinguished speakers. I also saw many less familiar faces which had appeared on the scene since 1965. That was an even more encouraging observation, because it indicated to me that the traditions of research and devotion to the welfare of the Peregrine, so firmly established at the Madison Conference, were being passed into capable hands for the future.

I think it is no exaggeration to say that as a result of the great interest generated by the Madison Conference in 1965, more has been learned about the Peregrine Falcon in the last two decades than in all previous history. As one indication of this fact, a working Peregrine bibliography of some 1500 technical titles has been assembled for publication by The Raptor Information Center of the National Wildlife Federation; the vast majority of these publications post-date the

1

Madison Conference, and most make some mention of the published proceedings (Hickey 1969). In addition to these published sources, large volumes of unpublished information exist in numerous "project reports" of various state and federal agencies, environmental impact statements, theses, and other documents.

It is time for an up-to-date summary and synthesis of all the information that has accumulated about the Peregrine since the Madison Conference, in order to make the best use of this body of knowledge. The Sacramento Conference accomplished this goal for the experts; and this book, the published proceedings, will serve the interests of a wider audience of scientists, managers, conservationists, and devotees of the Peregrine.

Dramatic changes have occurred in the population history of the Peregrine and in its relationship with *Homo sapiens* in the past 20 years. In 1965 many ornithologists and conservationists feared that the Peregrine would become extirpated over most of its vast range in North America and Europe, and, indeed, for a time the numbers of breeding pairs continued to decline over much of continental Europe and the western United States, and even in the subarctic and arctic nesting populations of North America and Eurasia. By 1970, the Peregrine had been officially designated under United States law as an "endangered species" over all of North America except in the Pacific Northwest coastal range of *F. p. pealei*, and since ratification in 1973, the entire species has been on the Appendix I list of the Convention on International Trade in Endangered Species of Wild Fauna and Flora.

Today the downward trends in population have been largely reversed. Great Britain has experienced a dramatic natural recovery of its Peregrines, and some encouraging increases in breeding numbers are beginning to be recorded in parts of continental Europe and the western United States. The northern breeding populations of Alaska, Canada, and Greenland reached their lowest numbers around 1975-76; since then they have shown substantial recovery in numbers of nesting pairs in most parts, an increase that has been especially reflected by the number of fall migrants seen and banded along the Atlantic Coast and Gulf of Mexico. In addition, previously unknown populations have been discovered and studied — tree-nesters in the Pacific Northwest, tundra Peregrines west of Hudson Bay, breeding pairs in northern Peru and Ecuador — and the Peregrines of Australia, Africa, and South America are much better known than they were 20 years ago. Still, there is little information for most of Asia, which encompasses a great portion of the Peregrine's range.

Then, too, the whole pesticide-Peregrine story, which was still vague and incompletely substantiated in 1965, matured into a clear and cogent argument in the years immediately following the Madison Conference and played an important role in securing restrictions on the use of DDT and dieldrin in several western industrialized countries in the 1970s. Even after 10-15 years of the virtual absence of DDT application in North America, there continue to be puzzling, high levels of DDE residues and eggshell thinning in some nesting Peregrines in the western United States and in some prey species. The sources of this contamination, long suspected to be from Latin America, were discussed at the Sacramento Conference.

Finally, the restoration of Peregrine populations by captive propagation and the release of captive progeny into the vacant range has become a worldwide effort with major undertakings in Canada, the United States, West Germany, and Sweden. As a result of these "recovery programs," Peregrines are again nesting in locales where they have been absent for 20-30 years. In addition, released Peregrines have taken up breeding sites in new and unorthodox habitats: on skyscrapers in major metropolitan centers, on bridges, on lighthouses, and on specially constructed nesting towers in coastal salt marshes.

Clearly the range of relationships and adjustments that are possible for Peregrine Falcons in a world populated by *sympathetic* human beings is far greater than anyone could have predicted in 1965. It is time to begin assessing the potentialities and significance of all the new human-falcon relationships that have become possible as a consequence of captive propagation and the successful establishment of breeding pairs in the outdoors by the release of captive-raised birds.

While all conservationists agree about the paramount need to work for the preservation of ecosystems, biomes, and major tracts of "natural" habitat, there is also need to continue focusing attention on work directed at the conservation of single species, such as the Peregrine Falcon and the California Condor. The two approaches should go hand-in-hand. In particular, I feel that the so-called "single species approach," often decried these days as an impediment to ecological holism (e.g., Pitelka 1981, Myers 1986), will actually have much to contribute toward the development of methods for managing the survival of free-living populations in the degraded and seminatural habitats which are going to become — indeed, already are — the predominant environments on earth. In this regard, I think there is much to be learned from the work on the Peregrine Falcon over the past 20 years, knowledge that can be applied not only to other raptors, but to many other kinds of birds and animals as well (Cade 1986a).

The Peregrine Falcon has become a global symbol which has rallied a great diversity of human interests and activities to the cause of biological conservation. As we all know, top predators are especially valuable symbols of environmental concern, because their existence and welfare depend upon the entire web of ecological relationships at all levels of the ecosystem below them. When their populations begin to show signs of stress, it is a clear indication of deeper, underlying troubles in the community of living forms on which they depend. As the most cosmopolitan naturally-distributed avian species in the world and as a top predator in the global ecosystem, the Peregrine Falcon has served as a unique biological monitor of the quality of the world's environments, particularly with respect to chemical contamination by DDT and related organochlorine pollutants. Not only is its reproductive biology sensitive to chemical contamination in its food web, but its many geographical populations also respond to natural changes in the environment, such as climate and food supply.

Finally, the Peregrine Falcon is also the premier example of success in single species conservation. Its recovery both by natural and artificial processes — now well under way on two continents — shows what can be done when human beings are willing to alter their courses of action to benefit the survival of a species. Again, it is important for other species and their environments that we celebrate such success by the kind of international conference that was held in Sacramento.

I can think of no better way for such a conference to have begun than with the three speakers whose keynote addresses follow. Each played a prominent and crucial role at the Madison Conference. Each has a perspective on the Peregrine stretching virtually over his entire lifetime, and each has more than an academic interest in the subject.

I first communicated with Joe Hickey in 1950 when I was a student at the University of Alaska (I still have the correspondence in my files). I was interested in his ideas about "ecological magnetism" expressed in his 1942 paper in *The Auk*, and I sent him some photographs of Peregrine cliffs along the Yukon River. I asked him if he could classify them as to first-class, second-class, and third-class eyries. He kindly wrote back to say that while I had sent him a very interesting series of photographs, he could not classify falcon eyries by pictures alone. I then began to have doubts about "ecological magnetism" and expressed some of them in my 1960 monograph on the falcons of Alaska. But over the years, the Peregrines have proven Joe's insight to be correct. For example, Derek Ratcliffe has reported that when the Peregrine population in Britain began its recovery after 1964, the very same cliffs — often the very same ledges and crannies — that had been used in former times were the ones reoccupied first, even though some of these eyries had been abandoned for one or two decades. Now, we are starting to see the same thing in the eastern United States with captive-produced and released falcons which have no connection, either genetic or traditional, with the historical eyries of the Appalachian region. There is something about specific cliffs which Peregrines can recognize, something which draws them to these special places and not to others. Hickey was right 40 years ago. He is still right today as Professor Emeritus in the Department of Wildlife Ecology at the University of Wisconsin, where he organized and convened the first international Peregrine conference in 1965.

Dr. Derek A. Ratcliffe, Chief Scientist for the Nature Conservancy Council of Great Britain, has also been deeply involved with the Peregrine Falcon for many years. In reading Derek's wonderfully detailed book on the Peregrine, I was struck by the fact that he and I developed our interest in the Peregrine at about the same age and time and in very similar ways. Derek climbed into his first Peregrine eyrie in the Lake District of northern England in the spring of 1945 at the age of 16. I had visited my first nest at Lake Chatsworth in southern California the year before at the same age. Derek found what he was looking for — an active nest with three lovely eggs. I did not, for the Chatsworth eyrie had been robbed of its young only a day or two before I had planned to do the same thing; but I did have a memorable experience with two very angry adult falcons stooping around my head. I also learned that one should not drop over a cliff on a rope without prior training (which I actually received some years later from Morley Nelson).

Derek wrote of his first encounter (Ratcliffe 1980): "My gaze turned quickly from the fleeing falcon to the rock below where, on a grassy shelf, lay three beautiful eggs, reddish brown mottled with white. The intensity of excitement at such moments is perhaps something reserved for youth, but then the young tend to have simple ambitions which can be achieved in a wholly fulfilling way. It was certainly the impetuosity of youth which set me clambering down that sheer wall to reach the eyrie. And there at last was the marvelous bird in life, cruising up and down for me to admire, and filling the dale with its strident chatter . . . There have been many red-letter days in my life as a field naturalist, but none to eclipse this one."

Certainly no name is more closely identified with the British Peregrine, or with unravelling the complicated story of the relationship between the use of organochlorine pesticides and the decline of Peregrine populations, than that of Ratcliffe. It was a great pleasure to welcome Derek back to the United States for the conference.

Morlan W. Nelson traveled with me on the Colville River in arctic Alaska in 1959, and he has been a true friend for 35 years. He has been involved in so many different ventures during a very active life that it becomes difficult to single out one or two accomplishments. He was a decorated soldier of World War II (a "bullet-holed soldier," as he likes to say), snow surveyor for the U. S. Soil Conservation Service, wildlife motion picture photographer, falconer, raconteur, promoter of The Peregrine Fund, but above all an unabashed admirer of the birds of prey. He has done more than anyone to develop public sympathy and appreciation for raptors — particularly in the inter-mountain west and in his home state of Idaho, where he was in-strumental in promoting the establishment of the Snake River Birds of Prey Natural Area.

One of the things I like best about Morley Nelson is that he has a way of looking at situations a little differently than the rest of us. While most scientists are trying to scrutinize things close up and to get it all analyzed in minute detail, Morley likes to stand back at a distance and look at the grander scale of things — at the full sweep of the mountain range, at the flow of the main stream of history and events. While most conservationists today are preoccupied with humanity and its impacts on wildlife and environments, Morley's experience as a snow surveyor and hydrologist have led him to different perspectives on problems — problems which he predicted with some degree of accuracy 20 years ago, but over which we still have no control — the so-called "blind forces of nature," the final arbiters of life on earth.

1 | Keynote Addresses

1 | Some Recollections About Eastern North America's Peregrine Falcon Population Crash

Joseph J. Hickey

It seems appropriate to report at the start that I was more or less seduced into studying the Peregrines around New York City in the 1930s by Walter R. Spofford and the late Richard A. Herbert, who were fantastic Peregrine lovers. As secretary of the Hawk and Owl Society, I set out to learn the current status of the Peregrine east of the Rockies, but with Spofford and Herbert I also participated in an intensive study of the reproductive success of the Peregrine at 19 eyries in the New York City region.

This intensive study should have been published by the three of us, but it got attached to the extensive study which contained confidential reports of eyrie locations in various states east of the Rockies and appeared in *The Auk* (Hickey 1942). The title of the paper submitted to Editor John T. Zimmer did contain the words "Peregrine Falcon" which Zimmer changed to "Duck Hawk" to conform with the American Ornithologists' Union (AOU) Checklist (1931), but I was allowed to use "Peregrine" throughout the rest of the manuscript. Although I certainly did not know all the eyries ever found in this great region, I now had a rough idea of the historical rate of decline sustained there by this species. It was on the order of 11%, and I did come up with a list of 275 known eyries.

THE POPULATION DECLINE IN THE EASTERN UNITED STATES

In 1962 at the 12th International Ornithological Congress at Cornell University, I heard the rumor that not a single Peregrine had fledged that year in the northeastern United States. I think I assumed that falconers — real and would-be — had been very, very busy. I did not realize that most of the eyries in this region had by this time been actually and mysteriously deserted.

9

The real shocker for us in America came in 1963, a year later, when D. A. Ratcliffe published a fine long paper entitled "The Status of the Peregrine in Great Britain" (Ratcliffe 1963) in which he (1) reported wholesale eyrie desertion, and (2) suspected insecticides as the cause. I immediately recalled the rumor at Ithaca in 1962, and promptly wrote Carl W. Buchheister, president of the National Audubon Society, that Peregrines in the United States may be in real trouble. Roland C. Clement, one of Buchheister's assistants, had also caught Ratcliffe's amazing article and called it to Buchheister's attention while my letter was still on the president's desk.

The obvious thing to do was to reactivate in 1964 my earlier extensive study of the Peregrine in the 1930s, at least east of the Mississippi River. One minor problem was that I was scheduled to spend more than half of 1964 in Europe. I first went to Kathleen Herbert, the widow of my old friend Dick Herbert, and told her about this new study which could be a memorial to her husband — if she gave the University of Wisconsin $5000, which she rather promptly did.

I used Kenneth E. Gamble, my teaching assistant, to assemble 250 United States Geologic and Geodetic Survey maps for the eastern United States eyries mentioned in my notebook for the 1942 paper. Ken transcribed terse descriptions of where the eyries were actually located. I had little trouble in persuading Daniel D. Berger, a Milwaukee businessman with Peregrine eyrie experience, to do the actual study in 14 states and one Canadian province. Dan picked Charles R. Sindelar, Jr., as his field partner. The survey team drove over 22,526 km, checked 133 known eyries in the latter part of the 1964 nesting season, and found every single eyrie deserted. There was no way for this team to establish when the decline had started, but they did learn of eyries occupied as late as 1962 in Alabama and Maine (Berger et al. 1969).

In the meantime, I had met a number of Peregrine students in Europe in 1964 and had visited Peregrine eyries in Switzerland with Hans Herren and in Scotland with Derek Ratcliffe. The trip with Derek was a one-day positively harrowing experience as we raced over narrow roads, always, of course, on the *wrong side*, but I did get safely back to the United States in August to start planning for a conference on what had happened to the Peregrine in the United States.

ORGANIZATION OF THE 1965 PEREGRINE CONFERENCE

To some extent I felt intellectually trapped: I had started my own research on the effects of DDT in 1958, and I was now directing a graduate student, J. Anthony Keith, on the contamination by DDT of the whole Green Bay (Wisconsin) ecosystem and nearby Lake Michigan. We were finding DDE, the breakdown product of DDT, in small but detectable amounts at depths of 10-29 m in the lake, and I was tempted to suspect DDT might be a very widespread environmental pollutant. Financial support for the proposed Peregrine symposium should come, I thought, from independent federal agencies and not from the anti-pesticide National Audubon Society. I, therefore, sent funding applications to three federal departments: Agriculture; Interior; and Health, Education and Welfare.

Interior was most sympathetic but felt it had no precedent or authorization to support such a meeting, and it promptly phoned President Buchheister of the National Audubon Society to report its predicament. Agriculture also said "No," much to my surprise. I remember a long eloquent debate I had with its Chief Scientist, a man named Nyle C. Brady, who would concede no responsibility to his department. (The department, however, sent three official observers to the symposium, one of whom later fronted for years for the National Agricultural Chemicals Association.) The National Institutes of Health did give us $10,000, but this was not enough to float the conference. However, in February Buchheister told me that the Board of the National Audubon Society had just voted me $8000 on a motion put to it by Roger Tory Peterson. We were now free to run the conference.

I should relate that Tom Cade had been off Peregrine research for some years and was in 1965 doing field work on other species in Africa. Out there, Tom finally realized that the Peregrine was his number one ornithological love, and he could not bear to miss the Madison Conference. There was no way for me to help Tom with travel expenses with my now-tight budget. He was prepared to attend at his own expense.

I must also tell you about my problem with G. P. Dementiev, the leading ornithologist in the Soviet Union and the authority on the Peregrine in that country. I was strongly advised on the Wisconsin campus not to write him until I had official assurance from the U. S. State Department that it would grant him a travel visa to the United States. Two letters from me to the State Department went unanswered. Finally, in desperation I wrote to S. Dillon Ripley, then head of the Smithsonian Institution, regarding my problem. Ripley, indeed, got the State Department to answer. I had scheduled the Peregrine meeting to take place immediately after the AOU meeting which was being held that year in Columbus, Ohio, and my invitation to Dementiev was to include the suggestion that he take in AOU on his way to Madison. The State Department's reply said it needed a map of the AOU's field trips on which Dementiev would be going. This I was barely able to get from Milton Trautman just before he went on vacation. More silence from the State Department. In midsummer I happened to be in England where I told E. Max Nicholson, head of The Nature Conservancy, about my problems with the State Department. As I recall, we were sitting on a London park bench. We had known each other for years, and my *A Guide to Bird Watching* (Hickey 1943) was inspired by his own *Art of Bird Watching* (Nicholson 1932). "Joe," Max counseled, "you had better give up. The cold war is still on. If the State Department says 'yes,' Moscow will say 'no.' If Moscow says 'yes,' the State Department will say 'no!' It is as simple as that."

I never did hear from the State Department, and in the end I wrote Tom Cade that he was free to use the $1200 that had been initially reserved for Dementiev. Tom did not mind being a substitute for the famous Russian, but we did *not* ask him to report on Peregrines in the Soviet Union, and I still do not know the status of Peregrines in that country.*

CAUSE OF THE DECLINE

Reproductive Failure. — The phenomenon of eyrie desertion is a difficult branch of natural history. The statement that an eyrie is deserted is really a conclusion, and we now know that "abandoned" eyries can be reoccupied after intervals of decades. The actual facts of the matter are the dates a given place was visited, the hours spent watching the site, the absence of "whitewash," and the condition of the nesting ledges along with such supplementary data as the telltale presence or absence of nesting feral pigeons. The 1965 Madison Conference had a lot of reports of eyrie desertion, which, however weak when isolated, were cumulatively impressive because they were consistent and so numerous. It was the British, D. Ratcliffe and I. Prestt, who importantly convinced the conference that the Peregrine population crash was characterized by an extraordinary failure in reproductive success and, even more astounding, that this involved the parent birds breaking and eating their own eggs! Nothing like this breakage had ever been reported in the history of ornithology.

The 1965 Madison Conference was not an anti-insecticide forum. At that moment not a single North American Peregrine had ever been analyzed for a pesticidal chemical. This was quickly changed in the year that followed. The actual eating of the contents of its own eggs by a female Peregrine had been witnessed by G. Harper Hall on Montreal's Sun Life building in 1948 (Hall 1958), but his observation was not

---

*Editors' Note: Not much has changed in Soviet-American relations in 20 years. Two Russian ornithologists were invited to attend the 1985 conference in Sacramento through official communications from the International Affairs Office, USFWS and the Department of State, and also by direct personal contacts. Neither came.

known to us in 1965. Hall, an amateur ornithologist and official biographer of the Sun Life birds, was so shocked that he chose to keep his observation a secret for some years, and it was not mentioned in his initial account of the Sun Life birds (Hall 1955).

Eggshell Thinning. — About a year after the Madison Conference, I received a manuscript for review from Ratcliffe, titled "Egg breakage and disappearance in the Peregrine." In a list of hypothetical causes, he mentioned "defects of the egg" and wrote, "If for some reason, Peregrine eggshells had recently become thinner, an increase in breakage might be expected. I have not measured the thickness of broken eggshells but, allowing for the normal decrease in shell thickness during incubation, none of these appeared to be unusually thin." I returned the manuscript with the following marginal comment: "This hypothesis could be objectively tested; I am told poultry science people here . . . routinely measure shell thickness. I suppose that one would need about 5 shells from pre-1950 collections and 5 modern shells, but the size of n needed would depend on the variance encountered." Meanwhile, D. Nethersole-Thompson had noted the same point, but he suggested to Ratcliffe that since eggshell thickness would be related to eggshell weight, the idea could be easily tested by weighing a large series of old and recent eggs (Ratcliffe 1980).

Derek soon replied that the hypothesis was indeed correct: he had tested it by weighing and measuring a large sample of eggshells in the British Museum and private collections, data which formed the basis of his breakthrough published in *Nature* (Ratcliffe 1967). I then wrote back asking for permission to break this amazing story to my colleagues on our side of the Atlantic. With his permission I immediately relayed the story by phone to Lucille Stickel of the U. S. Fish and Wildlife Service (USFWS) and J. A. Keith of the Canadian Wildlife Service. They took the news very calmly — too calmly for me. I soon asked the USFWS for funds to send a graduate student around the United States to work out the historical thickness in raptor eggshells. There was little suspicion that we might encounter eggs taken in the modern-insecticide era. However, at the start of our study Col. L. R. Wolfe directed us to private egg collectors who were still (to our surprise) collecting raptor eggs. A real piece of good luck ensued when I picked Daniel W. Anderson as the graduate student who would visit public museums and private egg collectors. Dan was and is a *very* friendly human being, and on this job he proved to have the guile and talents of a "confidence man." On innumerable occasions private egg collectors revealed to him their highly illegal prizes. Dan measured 45 Bald Eagle eggs which were actually taken in the DDT era and 73 eagle eggs taken illegally after the Bald Eagle was given federal protection. I finally went to a high federal official in Washington, D. C., and told him that we were learning in confidence about scores of Bald Eagle eggs that had been illegally collected, but we were in no position to reveal any names. The official was a scientist, and he happily did not press us for details or report the matter to his colleagues in law enforcement.

What I did not anticipate in Anderson's survey was that he would find any DDT-era eggs of the Peregrine; but to my astonishment, he found 123, just as Ratcliffe (1980) had been able to do in Britain. Some of these were from strategic places like Massachusetts, New Jersey, and California. Some were taken during critical years, like 1947. The Massachusetts set was even unknown to J. A. Hagar, who was intensively studying Peregrine reproduction in that state at the very time these eggs were secretly and illegally taken from a state park.

Anderson found that a clutch of four Peregrine eggs taken in May 1947 at a sea cliff in southwestern California had dropped only 12% in mean weight, but another clutch of four taken in Ventura County, California, on 6 April 1947 had dropped 23%. In Massachusetts that same year, the mean weight of a clutch of three was down 22%. This clutch and a set of three taken in New Jersey in 1950 were down in weight 25% from normal and 23% in the eggshell-thickness index of Derek Ratcliffe.

Singling Out DDE. — By about 1968 it was generally agreed in the scientific community that DDT was a worldwide pollutant. After all, it had been found to cross the Atlantic on trade winds (Risebrough et al. 1968a), and it was even found in the Antarctic (Risebrough et al. 1968b).

A news item in Britain's serial *The New Scientist* (1966) reported that Soren Jensen of the University of Stockholm had found a new pollutant, PCB, in some 200 pike taken in different parts of Sweden, and in an eagle found dead in the Stockholm Archipelago. In his own family, a five-month-old daughter had the contaminant, and Jensen concluded she got it through her mother's milk. By checking eagle feathers in the Swedish National Museum of Natural History, Jensen was able to trace this compound back to 1944. He did not know its danger, but concluded from reports of its presence in air at London and Hamburg, as well as in seals caught off Scotland, that it must be widespread throughout the world (Anon. 1966).

The real shocker to environmental scientists came a year later when some of Jensen's findings were reviewed (Widmark 1967). On the gas chromatograms, two of the major peaks produced by the chlorinated biphenyls were found to overlap the peaks produced by $p'p'$-DDT and $o'p'$-DDT. In other words, the identification of DDT as an environmental pollutant in earlier years when gas chromatography was so widely used, "wasn't worth a cheesey damn!" A year later, Risebrough et al. (1968b) showed PCBs to be widespread in the global ecosystem.

That same summer, however, Hickey and Anderson (1968) compared eggshell changes in five colonies of Herring Gulls in the north-central United States and on the New England coast. There were indeed marked changes in eggshell thickness, and these statistically correlated with the egg residue levels of DDE, the widespread breakdown product of DDT that was previously regarded as a somewhat innocuous pollutant. The chance of this correlation being a random one was 1 in 1000. This article in *Science* (Hickey and Anderson 1968) was the first to single out DDE as an ecologically significant chemical in our environment.

That fall our Department of Agriculture in Wisconsin asked an ad hoc advisory committee of Wisconsin scientists whether or not it should ban DDT. The committee decided we needed more research despite the bibliography and literature summary I had provided it four days in advance of its meeting. A discouraged Wisconsin Citizens Natural Resources Association now called on the Environmental Defense Fund to petition the Wisconsin Department of Natural Resources for a legal ruling against the use of DDT in the state. This official review lasted about six months, and the ecologists' side was masterminded for the Environmental Defense Fund by R. W. Risebrough and C. F. Wurster, Jr.

At the start, an entomologist spoke on the University of Wisconsin radio and described the coming review by saying it will show that "Hickey doesn't know his stuff!" I did testify for three days, never once mentioned DDT, and confined my pollution remarks to DDE. Months later the chemical industry brought in Dr. Paul Edward Porter of Shell Chemical Company to settle the identification of DDE. Dr. Porter was asked by the industry's lawyer, "Can DDE be safely separated from PCBs on the gas chromatograph?" "Yes," answered Dr. Porter very slowly, "with difficulty." We were home free!

Heath et al. (1969) reported the critical experiment in which a diet of DDE produced significant eggshell thinning in Mallards. Then, in 1970 the scientific community made its most important statement on the effects of pesticides on bird populations. This was at a symposium at the 15th International Ornithological Congress (Voous 1972). Prestt and Ratcliffe (1972), among other things, summarized the residue levels of these pollutants in 78 species of British birds. Anderson and Hickey (1972) reported on thickness measurements of 23,658 eggshells of United States birds, Keith and Gruchy (1972) summarized residue levels in 1039 avian specimens, and Heath et al. (1972) produced the important experimental evidence that low levels of the PCB called Aroclor 1254 in the diet of Mallards and Northern Bobwhite had no measurable reproductive effects.

The demise of DDT in Wisconsin came from the state legislature in

1969, but not at the national level until after an Environmental Protection Agency (EPA) hearing in the Washington D. C. area in 1972. I have little to report about the EPA show. The hearing examiner was a stubborn Irishman — a retired railroad lawyer — named Sweeney who was really hard on the environmentalists. So much so that at one point the USFWS threatened to withdraw all its scientists who were scheduled to be witnesses.

As fellow "bog trotters," Mr. Sweeney and I got along just great. He never challenged a single one of my statements, and I feel sure he never believed any of them. The two hearings are well described in T. R. Dunlap's excellent book *DDT: Scientists, Citizens, and Public Policy* (1981). We should be glad that the final decision on DDT was made by EPA Administrator Ruckelshaus and not by a Boston Irishman.

The comeback of the Peregrine is one of the great stories in modern ecological history, and I am sure we are all looking forward to learning about it at this conference.

ACKNOWLEDGEMENTS

I wish to thank Dr. E. P. Lichtenstein, Department of Entomology, University of Wisconsin, for his friendly and expert bibliographic help in the preparation of this paper.

2 | The Madison Conference and Research on Peregrines

Derek A. Ratcliffe

Joe Hickey has reminisced about the origins of the 1965 Madison Conference. I well remember my first meeting with him, on the lofty eyrie of Edinburgh Castle where, in real American style, he had allocated three whole hours in a tight-packed itinerary to look at Peregrine country and talk about the bird. In between straightening the bends in the road into the hills south of the city, I expounded on the situation revealed by the British Trust for Ornithology's Peregrine Enquiry and the subsequent follow-up by the Nature Conservancy. The bleak facts were a reduction in breeding population to around 44% of the "normal" level of 1930-39 (this was taken as the standard, because recovery from wartime persecution was not quite complete when the new decline began in 1956). Breeding performance was pretty abysmal amongst the remaining population, with a characteristic syndrome of egg-breaking and disappearance, failure of incubated eggs to hatch, death of chicks, small broods, failure to lay, and apparent nonpairing.

Supported by a modest number of analyses of Peregrine eggs and one crucial corpse found in an eyrie, we became convinced that there was a strong circumstantial case for attributing blame to the persistent organochlorine insecticides of agriculture. The Peregrine was not alone: it shared a clear pattern of decline with other predators, notably the European Sparrowhawk, Eurasian Kestrel, Common Barn-Owl and Red Fox revealed by surveys to have occurred in many lowland agricultural districts. The decline correlated with the use of these substances especially as cereal seed dressings. Just before the 1965 Madison Conference, the NATO-sponsored symposium convened at Monks Wood by Norman Moore focused the attention of an international company of scientists on the paramount importance of the persistent organochlorine pesticides as toxic environmental pollutants.

Ian Prestt and I came to Madison with our arguments sharpened by lengthy debate with pesticide apologists back home, though our case for naming these chemicals as the cause of raptor decline was still circumstantial. We were convinced, but we were impressed by Joe Hickey's determination to allow all possible causal hypotheses and points of view to be considered, including one or two that could be described as quaint. His approach was scientific in the best sense: listening fairly to all the available evidence and not prejudging issues. The agrochemical interests were given good opportunity to present their counter-arguments.

The conference went with a great swing. With so many raptor enthusiasts under one roof and such a wealth of experience and interest, the atmosphere became exciting and somewhat charged. There were conjured up visions of the wild and beautiful places of the earth — the great snowy ranges of the Alps, Rockies and Alaska, the barren grounds of arctic Canada, the forest bogs of Finland and the parched buttes and canyons of the arid desert regions. There were scholarly contributions on population dynamics, migration studies, pathogens and parasites, chemistry and physiology. To broaden the perspective, reports on numerous other raptor species around the world were presented. Few of the factors and processes that affect birds of prey were not discussed at some point. And each day after the formal proceedings were over, discussion, argument and anecdote waxed far into the night. It was all very stimulating and informative and, for myself, beyond any doubt the most enjoyable and rewarding scientific meeting I have ever attended.

By the end of the conference, two main points had emerged. One was that Peregrine populations over a large part of both North America and Europe were in serious and evidently increasing trouble; the other was that the weight of evidence and opinion pointed the finger at the persistent pesticides as the primary cause. It was agreed that a great deal more work had to be done. Remaining populations needed to be monitored in as many places as possible; the singular pattern of reduced breeding performance had to be closely studied to find out precisely what happened and to contrast it with mortality as a population decline factor; the contribution of organochlorines and other persistent pesticides to these effects had to be carefully examined, especially experimentally; and thought had to be given to the conservation angle, of how vanished or depleted populations of Peregrines and other raptors might be restored again.

The result of the conference was an enormous and extremely varied spread of research effort by many different people, galvanized into an onslaught on these problems. And I believe that Joe Hickey, in his typically modest way, has underestimated the catalytic effect of his conference in promoting this effort. It focused people's minds and gave them a common sense of purpose. Moreover, Joe continued to act as ringmaster during the marathon task of preparing the conference proceedings for publication, and through his quite heroic efforts as a correspondent. People were kept in touch with events and, having met, they kept in touch with each other. The volume of work on the various fronts continued and grew. The survey and monitoring programs, including residue studies, produced their annual reports and for some years the news from both North America and Europe grew more depressing if anything. Even the remote populations of the arctic regions seemed to be in trouble, with contamination of prey in their southern wintering haunts the main problem. New pieces of evidence kept breaking to reinforce the pesticide hypothesis. I was fortunate enough to land on an explanation for the egg-breaking mystery, as Joe has related, and eggshell thinning blossomed into a whole new field of enquiry. And then the recognition of the PCBs introduced a complicating factor and spread the focus to industrial pollutants.

The eventual outcome was that consensus opinion amongst scientists accepted as proven the cause-effect relationship between organochlorine contamination and decline in breeding performance and/or population in certain raptors, especially Peregrines. The contributions of different chemicals, and the balance between sublethal and lethal effects varied geographically and among species, so that the overall picture was complex. The essential message was nevertheless clear, and increasingly became part of the common knowledge of people everywhere. Peregrines and pesticides were indeed in the forefront of a wave of growing concern over the effects of environmental pollutants which has become such a *cause célèbre* that it is difficult to remember now how little attention it commanded before 1960.

But the most heartening thing of all is that it has led to a return of our bird. This conference, 20 years later, is to hear reports of Peregrine recovery from various regions. The collective effort which identified the organochlorines as prime culprit led, in one country after another, to bans or restrictions on the use of the most damaging compounds. And, resilient species that it is, the Peregrine soon began to respond by increasing and recolonizing lost ground. There are still problems in some places, but in general we can record a success story rare in the annals of nature conservation. And as part of this happier tale, there is the eventual success of the captive breeding projects which began in such earnest in North America after the first conference. With the population extinct in the eastern United States and southeastern Canada, there seemed no other way of bringing Peregrines back to these regions. And so, led by Tom Cade and The Peregrine Fund, Inc., captive breeding was developed as a reintroduction technique. Its successes are now numerous and well-established, vindicating the determination and foresight of its proponents, in the face of numerous vicissitudes and criticisms.

No one will ever know just how much of all these developments can be attributed to the 1965 Madison Conference, but I believe it must be very substantial indeed. We look now to the future with the sense of having won this event, but with a wary eye on what the great contest called "progress" has in store for us.

3 | Continuing Climatic Changes Affecting Peregrines and Humanity

Morlan W. Nelson

Observations on nesting Peregrines begun in 1938 by R. M. Bond, L. L. Schramm and others (including myself) in the northwestern United States are still difficult to interpret. Peregrines were being replaced by Prairie Falcons at a rapid rate. As falconers, we well understood that Peregrines could not be displaced easily from their nesting sites by Prairie Falcons. Peregrines are more powerful birds on the average, and yet traditional Peregrine eyries were being taken over by the other falcons throughout the habitat occupied by both species in the western United States and Canada.

It was estimated in the first publication on this subject (Nelson 1969a) that 80-90% of the known Peregrine eyries in the Northwest had been taken over by Prairie Falcons or were abandoned by 1948. This shift from Peregrines to Prairie Falcons occurred during a period of generally dry years beginning in the 1930s.

There was also a drop in the number of nesting Peregrines in the eastern United States even before the over-use of DDT, but this 10-20% reduction was associated mainly with disturbance or loss of nesting sites on cliffs (Hickey 1942). Research and knowledge resulting from the Madison Peregrine Conference (Hickey 1969) have documented the wonderful ability of the Peregrine to survive around the world, even in the face of unprecedented regional population crashes on two continents caused by human impacts on environments. Publication of Hickey's (1969) book and subsequent work of The Peregrine Fund, Inc., have given humanity the knowledge and concern to save the Peregrine, as well as other endangered species, through the use of scientific techniques.

Data supporting the change in climate which I described at the first Peregrine conference (Nelson 1969a) are now a matter of record. What effect such changes may have on Peregrine numbers in North America and the northern hemisphere needs more study before accurate assessments can be made, but it is likely to be profound.

Updated information from the first table published on land-locked lakes supports the forecast made 20 years ago that a change to a wetter climate began in 1961-63. The data summarized in Table 1 reflect dramatic changes now affecting humanity more than Peregrines, as in the Great Salt Lake region.

The technique of using land-locked lakes to evaluate climatic changes is proposed as a more important method than single measurements of precipitation, snow pack water content, temperature, wind, cloud cover, evaporation and water use because it integrates them all by a measurement for the total size of the drainage basin involved. Furthermore, there are records on these lakes for a longer period of time than for any of the other measurements.

These data can be correlated with tree rings, the stratigraphy of silt deposits and the size of the Greenland ice cap for a hundred years. Such correlations would be useful in forecasting major changes in habitat not only for Peregrines but for almost all other life forms, including agricultural crops and natural vegetation.

The effect of a climatic change on Peregrines, while possibly significant in some areas of North America, is not a limiting factor when considered continent-wide or for the whole northern hemisphere. This point is true because the amount of water on earth has not changed, but shifts geographically, as from one continent to another. Such changes may be a function of periodic variation in energy from the sun. The ability to forecast radio wave interference from the sun provides evidence for this possibility.

The dramatic rise in the size of land-locked lakes was and still is possible to forecast, but the significance for the Peregrine, other wildlife, and humanity is more difficult to interpret. The growth of Great Salt Lake (vertical rise, 5.05 m; area increase, 3496 km^2) since 1961 represents a highly significant change. Other lakes in North America have followed a similar trend, creating problems in some areas and solving them in others.

Ducks and shorebirds have been flooded out of their normal nesting sites in most years of this rise. This is also true of smaller land-locked ponds without records of levels. The birds laying eggs on the periphery of these lakes or ponds have been flooded out before they could hatch their young because of the unusual rise during the nesting season. Once this dramatic trend stops and water levels become more stationary there will be more habitat for these birds, and more food for Peregrines; but so far the rising water has been detrimental to these species.

The issue is further complicated by the fact that an increase in atmospheric carbon dioxide resulting from burning fossil fuels appears to have the opposite effect of that known as "greenhouse" (Idso 1983,

TABLE 1.   Changes in lake sizes in Oregon, Utah and Nevada. Data provided by L. C. Kjelstrom, U. S. Geological Survey, Water Resouces Division.

State and lake	Maximum size		Size in early 1960s		% surface reduction	Size in 1984	
	(km²)	Date	(km²)	Date[b]		km²	% of max. size
Oregon							
Goose	482	1881	ca. 259	(1963)	46	414	86
Malheur and Harney	324		3	1961	99	694	214
Abert	155		Dry[a]	1930	100	168	108
Summer	181		Nearly dry[a]	1961	99		
Silver	39		Dry	(1963)	100	41	107
Utah							
Great Salt	6216	1870	2461	(1961)	60	5957	96
Sevier	324		Dry[a]	(1963)	100		
Nevada							
Pyramid	570	1869	466	1961	18	482	85
Walker	324		277	(1963)	14	171	61
Carson Sink	648		Nearly dry[a]	(1963)	99		
Ruby	96		Nearly dry[a]	(1963)	90		
Winnemucca	466	1882	Dry[a]	(1963)	100		

[a] New irrigation diversions above lakes use nearly all run-off water each year.
[b] Dates not cited by Bue (1963) are in parentheses and represent date of publication.

1984). Quantitative data on effects of CO_2 on cooling snow and water surfaces (Choudbury and Kukla 1979), on earlier accumulation, increase in maximum extent of cover, and later ablation of snow in the northern hemisphere (Dewey and Heim 1982), and other empirical evidence (Kimball and Idso 1983) support this effect, as do data on the land-locked lakes. Also, with increased atmospheric CO_2 the stomata of plants close down, resulting in less transpiration of water and more efficient use of snow and rain moisture by growing plants (Kimball 1983, Rogers et al. 1983, Idso 1984). This effect results in more plant production per volume of water absorbed. A second but equally important result is greatly increased stream flow, which is predicted to increase 40-90% with a doubling in atmospheric CO_2 concentration by the year 2020 (Aston 1984, Idso 1984). The effect of increased carbon dioxide on food supplies for Peregrines and humans appears amazingly good for the future (Idso 1984).

My original point that Peregrines were significantly affected by drought is now supported by work on other species completed by the Bureau of Land Management. In this research period, climate and possibly other factors changed ground squirrel numbers. These prey variations as they affect raptor nesting densities were summarized as follows: "Ground squirrel density was the most important factor, accounting for more than 87% of variation in total number of nesting raptor pairs" (Anon. 1979). The closest approximation to the Peregrine is the Prairie Falcon: "Variation in Prairie Falcon numbers can be explained by the same factors that influence the total number of pairs, with ground squirrels accounting for 86% of the variation and cliff area explaining an additional 10%" (Anon. 1979). Data support the conclusion that in the future Peregrines will vary in numbers with changes in their prey base resulting from man's activity and climate, but the latter will not be the only controlling factors. More significant to the future of raptors is the worldwide work of those who have contributed to the production of large numbers of Peregrines and other raptorial species in captivity, thereby enabling them to remain a part of the environment for the indefinite future. All of these accomplishments were started by Dr. Joseph Hickey whom we are honoring at this meeting for his leadership throughout the world in developing concern, knowledge and success in conserving one of the most inspirational forms of life on this planet — the Peregrine Falcon.

2 | Status of Peregrine Populations Since 1965 — North America

4 | The Greenland Peregrine Falcon Survey, 1972-1985, With Emphasis on Recent Population Status

William G. Mattox and William S. Seegar

No data on Greenland Peregrines were presented at the Madison Conference in 1965 because we had none. Conducted by many field workers, the Greenland survey began in 1972 in West Greenland near the Arctic Circle in the widest part of the ice-free land. The area we hoped to cover extends 170 km from the edge of the inland ice at 49°50′W to the outer coast, and 55 km south to north from 66°45′N to 67°15′N, but we found it impossible to cover the entire area. The northwest quadrant is high and mountainous; we visited only its edges. Likewise, the extreme northeast beyond the impassable Isortoq River was visited only once. Thus, our actual survey area totaled about 2500 km², much less than proposed.

Although mountains in the area exceed 1120 m above mean sea level, all active Peregrine cliffs are between 100-610 m (see Cade 1960 for similar altitudinal limit in Alaska). Mountain ridges and valleys are divided by Søndre Strømfjord, the longest fjord in West Greenland. The area includes nearly 1000 lakes and many connecting streams. Five unnavigable glacial outflow rivers traverse the area and prevent access without air support. One cannot float the rivers as in Alaska. The terrain is rocky, low-arctic tundra including willows, dwarf birches, lichens, mosses, sedges and grasses. Most precipitation falls as rain in June-August. The July-August temperatures vary between 0-15°C. Winter temperatures reach −50°C.

Gyrfalcons, Peregrines and Common Ravens usually nest on cliffs overlooking water. Most Peregrine nest sites have a southerly exposure on the upper half of vertical faces 27-120 m high. Nest ledges are easily accessible only with climbing ropes.

In 1972, after several years of preparation, the survey finally began under the impetus of W. Mattox and R. Graham. Results for 1972-81 are published (Burnham and Mattox 1984). In 1972, four field workers found cliffs occupied by nine pairs, seven of which produced 17 young, 13 of which were banded. In some years following 1972 only two men visited the area, but recent teams have included 12-13 people. This paper concentrates on 1981-85 and occasionally refers to 1972-85.

The main goal was to describe the breeding biology of West Greenland Peregrines and monitor the population. We knew Peregrines bred there, that they were less dense towards the outer coast and northward, and that they were sparse in East Greenland, and perhaps absent in northeast Greenland and Pearyland. Several pairs were reported from the Thule area, but the high-arctic held only Gyrfalcons.

Burnham and Mattox (1984) have published a detailed description of survey methods. Besides yearly population surveys and banding activities, investigators made studies involving close observation at cliffs (Harris and Clement 1975), on Gyrfalcons (Jenkins 1978), post-fledging behavior (Sherrod 1983), brooding behavior (Hovis et al. 1985), trace element analysis of feathers (Parrish et al. 1983), eggshell thickness and pollutant concentrations (Walker et al. 1973a, Springer et al. 1984, O. H. Pattee unpubl. ms.), embryonic abnormality (Pattee et al. 1984), prey densities (R. Meese unpubl. ms., Meese and Fuller unpubl. ms.), nest detritus analysis, habitat analysis, and blood bio-genetics. Burnham (1975) and Burnham and Mattox (1984) also studied prey density, interspecific competition, physical characteristics of nest sites, and general breeding biology.

RESULTS

Period From 1972-80. — Of 28 nest cliffs in the area, 11-25 were visited each year. Burnham and Mattox (1984) reported Peregrines occupied a mean of 60% of the sites annually. The mean minimum distance between eyries was 7.7 km, and nesting density was about one pair per 200 km^2. Productivity was 2.3 young per pair, and 2.8 young per successful pair. Five nest sites were used by both Peregrines and Gyrfalcons but not in the same year. Broods of 4, 3, 2 and 1 young were found in 25%, 44%, 15% and 17% of all nests seen. The male:female ratio of nestlings was 55:45. We banded 161 nestlings, one adult, and one migrant, and recoveries suggested an east coast migration in the United States and wintering in South America. Eggshells were 16% thinner compared with pre-1940 Greenland eggs, but no trends were seen in the study. Contamination with DDE in 1972 eggs was near-critical, and an increase could have endangered the population (Walker et al. 1973a). There was, however, no indication of a decline, and the population appeared stable, perhaps because local prey species carried only low levels of DDE and PCBs. Data on adult population turnover were not obtained.

Period From 1981-85. — The remainder of this paper incorporates the last year of the earlier work (1981) and the 1982-85 seasons. In that period, teams attempted to visit the known Peregrine cliffs throughout the survey area to determine occupancy. Fifty-one participants helped with the survey, some for many seasons. Young were banded and feather samples, addled eggs and eggshell fragments were collected. In 1983 an early team began capture of adults, and recaptures were made in 1984-85.

We have increased the number of known nest cliffs from 29 to 58, and visiting each cliff annually has been a growing problem for recent participants. Using helicopters we found new territories within the usual area and towards the coast. Radios and small aircraft extended our range, communications and aerial reconnaissance. Fixed-wing planes landed teams at an increasing number of places.

We found Peregrines nesting at cliffs occupied before 1972, and at traditional Gyrfalcon cliffs. The number of pairs observed has increased from 14 in 1981 to 38 in 1985. The increase in territories, we believe, reflects both our increased effort and an increase in Peregrines in Greenland. In recent years we sometimes found a third adult, usually male, at nest cliffs. Smaller, less ideal, nest cliffs have been used recently, and we feel the population in Greenland has been stable or perhaps trending upwards.

Occupancy of known cliffs by a defending adult, a pair, or a pair producing young, varied in 1972-80 between 50-64%, and averaged 60%, and in 1981-85 between 65-85% and averaged 70% (Table 1). The annual average number of young per pair on territory varied between 1.8-2.9 and averaged 2.3 in 1972-80. In 1981-85 it ranged between 2.3-2.6 and was 2.4 overall (Table 2). Successful pairs averaged between 2.4-3.3 young annually in 1972-80 and 2.6-3.2 in 1981-85. In the latter period the overall mean was 3.0, and in the former, 2.8, suggesting a slight increase (Figure 1). The production of young per pair or young per cliff visited showed pronounced regular variation in the early years, but not recently.

Brood size changed in the later period, with more four-young broods and fewer one-young nests. Change in four-young broods was not statistically significant, but there was a significant difference ($P=0.0084$) in brood size of one (L. McAllister and M. Fuller pers. comm.). At the same time, the male:female ratio of nestlings overall went from 55:45 in 1972-80 to 51:49 in 1981-85, but there was no significant difference between the two periods.

In 1984, for the first time, Gyrfalcons and Peregrines twice nested simultaneously on the same cliff in Greenland, at widely separated locations. This phenomenon did not occur in 1985, apparently a poor year for Gyrfalcon nesting.

TABLE 1. Occupancy and productivity for Greenland Peregrines, 1972-85.

Year	No. of known eyries	No. checked	No. of lone adults	No. of pairs	% Occ.	No. of pairs with young	Total young	Young/ pair	Young/ productive pair	Young/ territory checked
1972	17	17[a]	1	9	59	7	17	1.9	2.4	1.0
1973	17	17[b]	1	10	65	9	24	2.4	2.7	1.4
1974	21	19	4	6	53	5	15	2.5	3.0	0.8
1975	21	13	2	6	62	5	12	2.0	2.4	0.9
1976	21	11[a]	2	5	64	4	13	2.6	3.3	1.2
1977	21	12[a]	1	5	50	4	9	1.8	2.3	0.8
1978	22	16	2	8	62	8	23	2.9	2.9	1.4
1979	24	22	3	9	55	7	19	2.1	2.7	0.9
1980	28	25	2	14	64	12	36	2.6	3.0	1.4
1981	30	26[a]	3	14	65	12	35	2.5	2.9	1.4
1982	29[c]	29[b]	2	17	65	15	37[d]	2.3	2.6[d]	1.3[e]
1983	33	33	0	22	67	17	51	2.3	3.0	1.6
1984	48	47	10	30	85	22	70	2.3	3.2	1.5
1985	58	58	2	38	69	32	99	2.6	3.1	1.7

[a] 1 cliff occupied by Gyrfalcons.
[b] 2 cliffs occupied by Gyrfalcons.
[c] 1 cliff no longer discernible, and deleted (1982).
[d] 14 broods; 1 had unknown number of young.
[e] 28 territories.

TABLE 2. Comparison of Peregrine (*F. p. tundrius*) breeding successes.

	Young/pair			Young/successful pair		
	North Slope, Alaska[a]	West Greenland	Southwest Greenland[b]	North Slope, Alaska	West Greenland	Southwest Greenland
1972-81		2.3			2.7	
1972-85		2.3			2.8	
1981	1.4(n=28)	2.5(n=14)	1.3(n=13)	2.6(n=15)	2.9(n=12)	2.8(n=5)
1982	1.6(n=32)	2.3(n=17)	1.8(n=11)	2.6(n=20)	2.6(n=15)	3.2(n=5)
1983	2.3(n=28)	2.3(n=22)	1.6(n=13)	3.1(n=21)	3.0(n=17)	2.6(n=8)
1984	1.6(n=39)	2.3(n=30)	1.8(n=11)	2.6(n=24)	3.2(n=22)	2.5(n=8)
1985	1.9(n=37)	2.6(n=38)	1.5(n=10)	2.5(n=28)	3.1(n=32)	2.5(n=6)
Avg.	1.8	2.4	1.6	2.7	3.0	2.7

[a] R. Ambrose pers. comm.
[b] K. Falk, S. Møller pers. comm.

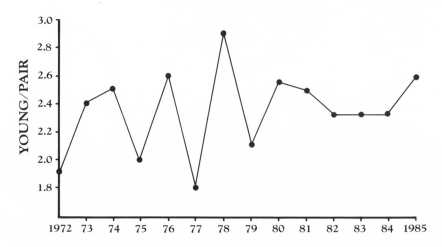

FIGURE 1.   Production of young per pair from 1972-85 in the study area.

Movements of Adults. — We began capturing and banding adult Peregrines at nest cliffs in 1983. Most were trapped on dummy eggs during incubation. We attempted to trap at the same cliffs in 1984 and 1985, and at a few others. The trapping had little effect on production of young; the same result was found in Scotland (Mearns and Newton 1984) and Alaska (R. Ambrose pers. comm.). In fact, in 1983 production was higher where we trapped than at other sites. Twice in 1984-85, however, we found abandoned eggs upon returning to band the young. Trapping may have caused these abandonments.

Females were most often caught because they incubate most. We made 50 captures in all (43 females and 7 males) involving 30 individuals (24 females, 6 males). Although only 1 male was re-captured, at 25 territories where the female was caught in successive years, 18 had the same individual, and at 7 it was a different one (28%). This turnover results from both movement and mortality. Of the 3 females that changed territory, 2 moved to adjacent territories or alternate cliffs in the same territory. One female moved 32 km to nest the next year. Three females used their territories all three years and 11 for at least two years. Of 11 females caught in 1983 in territories where we trapped a female the next year, 9 were on the same territory, and 1 was in a different territory. Maximum loss is therefore 1 female (9%). In 1984, 13 females were caught in territories where females were caught in 1985; 9 were recaptured in the same territory and 1 in a different territory, indicating a possible loss of 3 females (23%). Because two of these females had been banded previously, we knew they reached the ages of four and eight years. We did not recover or see an adult banded as a nestling in our survey area, so we have no information on dispersal, nor do we have information on age at first breeding. No bird banded as an adult was recovered outside Greenland.

Band Recoveries and Migration. — Table 3 lists all recoveries of bands placed between 1972-84. We used red plastic tarsal bands in 1973-81. We used Danish lock-on aluminum bands anodized green in 1984 and red in 1985. Red plastic bands were used in addition to metal ones.

Of 358 Peregrines banded 1972-84, 24 (6.7%) were recovered. Of these, 8 were males and 16 were females. Only 6 of the 24 had been shot or found dead. Our first Cuban recovery was in 1984. The first Peregrine ever banded in Greenland, in August 1941 by L. Meredith, was found dead in Cuba in December of that year.

Most recoveries suggest an autumn migration along the eastern coast of the United States (Table 3). In 1983 one recovery was near the Mississippi River. Two first-year migrant siblings were trapped by T. Nichols near each other on the east coast, but a third sibling was recovered by D. Roosa at McGregor, Iowa! The first spring recoveries were of adults at Padre Island, Texas, and Gunnison, Colorado in April 1985.

Despite the large numbers of fall migrants captured and banded each year at Assateague Island, Maryland/Virginia and Padre Island, Texas, no Greenland bird was caught there until 1982. The only South American recovery was in Ecuador in 1975.

DISCUSSION

Regional Productivity. — In 1981-85, tundra-nesting Peregrines in both Alaska (Colville and Sagavanirktok Rivers) and Southwest Greenland produced 2.7 young per producing pair compared to 3.0 in West Greenland. Except in 1985 the Alaskan data included more pairs than in Greenland (Table 2).

Pollutants and Eggshell Thinning. — Burnham and Mattox (1984) reported a mean DDE level of 14.3 ppm (wet wt) for all Peregrine eggs analyzed 1972-78 ($n=8$), lower than that reported for tundra Peregrines elsewhere. Greenland eggshells from 1972-78 were 16% thinner than pre-1940 eggshells. Both DDE level and eggshell thinning appeared near, but below, critical levels. Analysis by O. H. Pattee of 1981 and 1982 eggs ($n=9$) showed that only two eggshells were more than 20% thinner than normal. We found poor correlation of eggshell thickness with DDE level in egg contents. On the whole, DDE levels in 1981-82 were low, and even the highest (9.1 ppm) was about 50% of that which Peakall et al. (1975) associated with 20% thinning.

TABLE 3. Recoveries of Peregrine Falcons banded in Greenland, 1972-84.

Sex	Date banded	Cliff	Date recovered	Location	Remarks
M	27 July 1974	Dome	13 Oct. 1974	Cape Charles, VA	released
M	29 July 1974	Lone Female	12 June 1975	Egedesminde, Greenland	shot
M	2 Aug. 1974	Icecap	21 Dec. 1975	Ecuador	shot
F	28 July 1978	Icecap	12 Oct. 1978	Cape May, NJ	released
M[b]	26 July 1979	Between Rivers	3-4 Oct. 1979	"Belagorsk", at sea	numbers read
n.d.[b]	n.d.[b]	n.d.[b]	7 Oct. 1979	Cape Sable, NS	sighted color
M	23 July 1980	Icecap	26 Sept. 1980	Democrat Point, NY	released
F	5 Aug. 1981	Between Rivers	12 Oct. 1981	Fisherman's Island, VA	released
F	28 July 1980	Dome	5 Oct. 1982	Chincoteague, VA	released
F	30 July 1981	Gretchen	10 Sept. 1982	Holsteinsborg, Greenland	found dead
F	31 July 1982	Taserssuaq	24 Oct. 1982	Padre Island, TX	released
M	3 Aug. 1982	Wentland	9 Oct. 1982	Democrat Point, NY	released
F	16 July 1983	Hut	2 Oct. 1983	Padre Island, TX	released
F	29 July 1983	Taserssuaq	6 Oct. 1983	Corolla, NC	released
F	29 July 1983	Taserssuaq	11 Oct. 1983	False Cape Pk, VA	released
F	24 July 1983	Between Rivers	11 Oct. 1983	Chincoteague, VA	released
F	29 July 1983	Taserssuaq	19 Oct. 1983	McGregor, IA	released
F	7 Aug. 1982	Myrtle	16 March 1984	Holguin Prov, Cuba	shot
F	8 Aug. 1972	Between Rivers	25 June 1984	Between Rivers[a]	band found
F	10 Aug. 1983	Ringsó	21 Sept. 1984	St. Francis, Quebec	found dead
M	22 July 1984	Taserssuaq	29 Sept. 1984	Corolla, NC	released
F	7 Aug. 1984	Elisabeth	13 Oct. 1984	Chincoteague, VA	released
F	30 July 1984	Mosquito	16 Oct. 1984	Chincoteague, VA	released
F	27 July 1983	Wentland	27 April 1985	Gunnison, CO	found injured
F	23 July 1984	Hut	28 April 1985	Padre Island, TX	released

[a] Study area.
[b] n.d. = no data.

The 1981-82 eggshells do not exhibit the 15-20% thinning that Anderson and Hickey (1972) predicted as population-threatening. In 1972-78 eggshells were 16% thinner than normal. Some thin-shelled eggs did not hatch, but the generally low (<10 ppm wet wt) DDE levels we found suggest pesticide contamination does not now pose a threat to the Greenland population.

Springer et al. (1984) showed that interior Alaska and Greenland tundra Peregrine eggs had similar pollutant levels compared to higher levels in eggs from northern Alaska. They postulated that Greenland Peregrines may winter in a discrete geographic region of South America having lower pollutant levels. Also, prey species in Greenland have less DDE compared with prey that breed in Alaska and winter in South America.

We conclude that the West Greenland Peregrine population continues to be stable or possibly has increased some and that a once critically high level of DDE has decreased over the past several years.

Population Density. — Our survey now measures 3500 km^2, including the fjord and other large water bodies. On that basis, population density in 1985 was one pair per 92 km^2. In 1984, when we searched the same area, we found one pair per 116 km^2.

CONCLUSION

Overall, yearly surveys in West Greenland showed a stable and healthy Peregrine population. Production of young per pair increased in the last five years. A decline in the population might have taken place in the late 1960s and persisted into the early 1970s, when our studies began. After 1980, recovery seems to have been completed; certainly the current population has a high density of nesting pairs and a high rate of reproduction.

ACKNOWLEDGEMENTS

The project for us has been a fascinating and satisfying one. The reasons are obvious — studying this fine bird in a wilderness area in close company with a group of field workers who have no equal anywhere.

This project could not have been carried out without the support and cooperation of many people and agencies. The U. S. Army Chemical Research and Development Center, Aberdeen Proving Ground, Maryland, provided funding and support through the interest of P. Ward and W. Seegar. The Danish Ministry for Greenland and its Commission for Scientific Research issued permits and provided liaison with other Danish agencies (G. Andersen, J. Taagholt, S. Adsersen). We traveled to Greenland with the U. S. Air Force Military Air Lift Command (MAC) and the 109th Tactical Air Group

(New York Air National Guard). Danish and American residents at Søndre Strømfjord Air Force Base helped in many ways. The project's success resulted directly from the hard work under rigorous conditions of 51 participants since 1972. Our Danish colleagues K. Falk and S. Møller have surveyed a coastal area in Southwest Greenland for five years and provided good comparative data and field samples.

Editors' Note: The Greenland Peregrine Falcon survey under the direction of William G. Mattox has continued to record dramatic results in the Søndre Strømfjord study area. In 1986 the field team found 47 pairs and a single bird at 59 cliffs visited; 38 pairs produced a minimum of 106 nestlings (2.8 young per productive pair, 2.3 for all pairs). The 1987 team broke all previous records: they examined 67 cliffs and found 43 pairs and 8 single birds in residence. Production of young was the highest in survey history; 38 pairs had 117 young (3.1 per productive pair), and 90% of all pairs raised young. When will we see the top of this upward trend in the arctic?

5 | Status of the Peregrine Falcon in South Greenland: Population Density and Reproduction

Knud Falk and Søren Møller

We have studied the population of Peregrine Falcons in South Greenland since 1981. Previously the Peregrines in this area had received almost no attention from ornithologists. W. G. Mattox and coworkers have made a long-term study since 1972 in west-central Greenland (Burnham and Mattox 1984) about 850 km north of our study area; however, the differences in climate justified a survey in the archipelago of South Greenland. Our purpose was to collect information on population size and density, reproduction and pesticide contamination. This paper includes these results and a preliminary estimate of eggshell thinning.

STUDY AREA

The investigations were done in the municipalities of Narssaq, Qaqortoq/Julianehåb and parts of Nanortalik, all in the southernmost part of West Greenland (Figure 1). An estimate of population density was made between 60°30'-61°N and 45°-46°18'W, an area of 3768 km². The region is mountainous, yet seldom reaches 1000 m elevation, although peaks in the southernmost parts of the study area exceed 1900 m. Steep cliffs, lakes and marshes are abundant. The land is covered by grasses, and by shrubs belonging to *Salix* and *Betula*; in interior valleys the latter are up to 8 m tall. The land is penetrated by deep fjords, some reaching glaciers near the ice cap where icebergs are produced. Numerous islands and skerries form an archipelago along the outer coast (Figure 1). In spring the waters of South Greenland are periodically blocked by the polar ice drift, causing a cold, foggy, and wet maritime climate. The climate is characterized as low arctic in the coastal region and as subarctic in the inner part of the country (Salomonsen 1981). The mean June, July and August temperatures

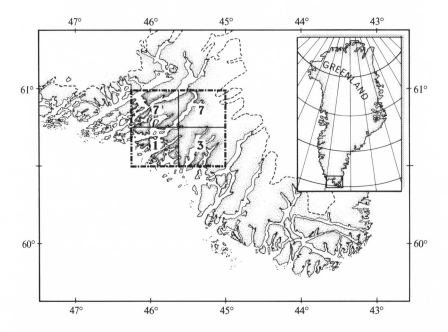

FIGURE 1. The South Greenland region where research was conducted. The dashed
line shows the area for population density estimate. The number of
Peregrine Falcon cliffs occupied after 1970 is shown within each quadrant
of reference area.

and annual precipitation at the two extreme weather stations in the
area are: Narssarssuaq 9.8°C, 696 mm; and Agdluitsup pâ/Sydprøven
4.9°C, 754 mm (Feilberg 1984).

There are only a few widely distributed prey species including: Snow
Bunting, Northern Wheatear, Lapland Longspur, Common Redpoll
and Rock Ptarmigan. The Peregrine feeds almost exclusively on these
five species (Falk et al. 1986). The Black Guillemot is the only alcid
breeding within the study area. A small number of local gull colonies
may also serve as food sources. Shorebirds and ducks are scarce.

The human population in the region totals about 7000; more than
half live in the towns of Narssaq, Qaqortoq/Julianehåb and Nanortalik.
The rest inhabit scattered settlements and sheep farms. The waters of
South Greenland are heavily trafficked by hunters and fishermen, and
on weekends by people on recreational trips. The inland areas are only
occasionally visited by local inhabitants aside from sheep farmers, but
backpacking tourists follow hiking routes, several of which pass below
Peregrine cliffs.

METHODS

Information on potential Peregrine nesting cliffs was collected from local inhabitants, ornithologists and others acquainted with the area. A total of 54 cliffs are listed as potential falcon eyries, but only 30 cliffs have definitely held Peregrines after 1970. This information and our own observations provided the basis for the population survey. Transportation in the study area was in a 16 ft outboard motorboat. Longer backpacking trips to inland cliffs were by teams of 2-3 persons. Fieldwork was carried out from mid-June to late August.

Population density was obtained from the 1983 survey results, which we consider the most complete. The number of occupied territories within the reference area is used. Population density was calculated by dividing the number of 1983 occupied territories by the area we searched (Ratcliffe 1980). The area of the total reference area, excluding the fjords and sea but including lakes, was measured by the aid of a computer. We think the often-used nearest neighbor method for calculating population density (Calef and Heard 1979, Ratcliffe 1980) underestimates the actual density for our area owing to the great amount of sea surface which we discounted.

The number of young reaching two weeks of age was determined by visits to the nesting ledges; during the visits banding was done. However, not all successful nests were visited due either to the near-fledging age of the young or to inaccessibility. In the absence of visits, the number of young was determined by observation of fledged young or by distant views of the nests. Criteria and definitions of occupancy and reproduction are according to Postupalsky (1974). Eggshell thinning was estimated using the method of Odsjö and Sondell (1982). Eggshell fragments collected at 16 active nests were compared with those from 48 eggs collected in Greenland 1879-1930 (Zool. Mus. Copenhagen).

RESULTS

Data on population and reproduction are given in Table 1. Of 10-13 occupied territories found each year, as many as 11, in 1983, were within the reference area (Figure 1). Seawater covers 30% of the area. Thus the density is one known, occupied territory per 240 km^2 based on 2636 km^2 of land area. Eight of these territories held productive nests, yielding one productive nest per 330 km^2. Success at two sites was unknown.

The distribution of Peregrine territories was irregular within the reference area. In Figure 1 the area is divided into four equally sized quadrants, and the number of cliffs known to have been occupied after 1970 is indicated within each quadrant. The inland parts of the area

TABLE 1.   Occupancy rates and reproductive success of Peregrine Falcon territories in
            South Greenland, 1981-85.

	Occupancy			Reproductive success			
Year	No. sites checked	No. occ. territories	Pairs with young	Success unknown	Total young	Young/ occ. cliff[c]	Young/ succ. pair[c]
1981	15	13	5[a]	3	14	1.8	2.8
1982	16	11	5[b]	1	16	1.8	3.2
1983	19	13	8	2	21	1.9	2.6
1984	18	11	8	0	20	1.8	2.5
1985	16	10	6	0	15	1.5	2.5

[a] 2 pairs with undetermined number of young not included.
[b] 1 pair with undetermined number of young not included.
[c] Territories with unknown success omitted from calculations.

were preferred by the Peregrines. The high mountains in the southeastern part may explain the low number of cliffs known to be occupied in this region.

Of visited historical cliffs, 61-87% (average 70%) were occupied in the study period 1981-85, and 60-89% (average 73%) of these were successful (Table 1). The average production in the five years was 2.7 young per successful nest. Mean production per occupied cliff was 1.8 young. The differences in success between years (Table 1) are not significant ($P>0.1$, Mann-Whitney U-test).

Half of the cliffs producing young from 1981-85 are less than 1 km (and often visible) from settlements or other human activities. These pairs did not differ significantly in reproductive success from more distant ones ($P>0.05$, Mann-Whitney U-test, two-tailed). Near pairs fledged 2.6 young per successful nest; farther pairs, 2.8.

During the study period, 45 young and five adults were banded. The only recovery was a juvenile male captured and released in Mexico on 31 October 1981. Eggshells were estimated to be 14.2% thinner than pre-1947 museum specimens. This difference is significant ($P<0.0005$, t-test).

DISCUSSION

Population Density. — Our estimate of about one occupied territory per 240 km² is conservative because the entire study area was not surveyed and additional territories may have been present. The 1983 survey was the most extensive and only a few territories may have been overlooked. At Søndre Strømfjord in West Greenland, Burnham and Mattox (1984) found a population density of one occupied territory per 200 km². The character of territories along the long fjord coastlines might suggest the population is distributed linearly like Peregrines along arctic Canadian and Alaskan rivers (Cade 1960, Fyfe 1969), and that an area-based density estimate is of limited value (Ratcliffe 1980). We think the distributions of suitable cliffs and prey species are not dependent on the morphology of the fjord landscape, and we therefore regard estimates of density based on area as valid.

Reproduction. — We may have overestimated nesting success because young may have died after the visits. In some cases young were counted only a few days after hatching. Usually they were 2-3 weeks old. Burham and Mattox (1984) suggested a high mortality for younger or smaller young just before fledging, due to competition for food. But based on several return visits, nestling mortality appears very low in our area, at least after the young have lived two weeks. The tendency to overestimate reproductive success was offset where counts were of fledged young. Though observations were always carried out for several hours, we were uncertain that all fledged young were recorded. We think that the effect of these two types of error was small.

No significant difference in reproduction between years was detected, though such difference might be expected owing to mortality caused by weather, or through the influence of weather on prey abundance (Newton 1979). Reproductive performance in South Greenland was very similar to that at Søndre Strømfjord, West Greenland (Table 2), and among the highest reported for arctic Peregrine Falcons.

Band Return. — The single band recovery from Mexico is one of the westernmost recoveries of a Peregrine from Greenland. However, a Greenland Peregrine was recently found injured near Gunnison, Colorado (Mattox pers. comm.). Mexico is far west of a route across the Caribbean supposedly followed by these Peregrines (see Burnham and Mattox 1984).

Eggshell Thinning. — Eggshell thinning of about 14% is close to the 16% found in West Greenland. A similar level of DDE may be present in these birds. Burnham and Mattox (1984) found 305 ppm DDE and 323 ppm PCBs (lipid wt) in egg contents from that area.

TABLE 2. Average reproduction of Peregrine Falcons at Søndre Strømfjord, West Greenland (Burnham and Mattox 1984) and in South Greenland.

	Young / successful pair	Young / occupied territory
West Greenland, 1972-81	2.8	1.8
South Greenland, 1981-85	2.7	1.8

Outlook for the Peregrine in South Greenland. — In the short survey period we were unable to determine trends in reproduction or in territory occupancy. Reproduction rates in South Greenland exceed those considered sufficient to maintain a stable population. Lindberg (1977a) gave 1.6-2.3 "young per pair" as the necessary range, and 1.16 young per year from all breeding pairs was suggested by Hickey and Anderson (1969).

Burnham and Mattox (1984) compared Peregrine density near Søndre Strømford with densities in arctic Canada. They concluded the latter is not as high as that found in "optimum nesting habitat" defined by Fyfe (1969), but similar to regions with "limited nesting habitat," a conclusion appropriate to our study area.

The population in South Greenland may be limited by availability of food (Falk and Møller 1986), though shortage of breeding habitat or a reduction owing to the effects of pollutants cannot be disregarded. Eggshell thinning data indicate that the population is vulnerable, but the occupancy and reproductive rates suggest a healthy population.

Human disturbance does not seem to affect the falcons. Successful pairs produced a normal number of young, and no pairs appeared unsuccessful owing to disturbance. Despite disturbance from heavy machinery used in road construction 50 m from a nest, and camping during the entire nestling period about 30 m from another nest, falcons raised their broods. The population may not be seriously affected by increasing tourism and agricultural development, provided the birds are not intentionally persecuted.

Size Estimate of Greenland's Peregrine Population. — Peregrines breed commonly in West Greenland and from Cape Farewell to Disko Bay, and are scarce northwards to Thule. They are rare in East Greenland (Salomonsen 1950). West Greenland has approximately 119,100 km² ice-free land (Trap 1970). Subtracting 10% (high mountains or coast) considered unsuitable for Peregrine Falcons, and using an average population density of one occupied cliff per 220 km², a total of 487 occupied territories per year is estimated. This figure may be too high because some unsurveyed regions probably support fewer Peregrines than the two study areas; 400-500 occupied territories may be the right range.

ACKNOWLEDGEMENTS

This project has been carried out in cooperation with W. G. Mattox, and we are grateful for all his help and inspiration. The project has been funded by The Commission for Scientific Research in Greenland, Det Kongelige Grønlandsfond and Roskilde University Institute of Biology and Chemistry. K. Nielsen, Julianehåb, provided boats as well as valuable assistance in various logistical problems arising during the field seasons. We also thank all who have provided information on falcons in the study area, making this survey possible. J. V. Christiansen and S. M. Bang traversed an inland area in 1984, and P. H. Pedersen assisted in the field in 1985. Thanks are due H. Noer for reviewing early drafts of this paper.

6 Peregrine Falcon Populations in Ungava Bay, Quebec, 1980-1985

David M. Bird and James D. Weaver

Since 1967, the Ungava Bay region of northern Quebec has been surveyed for nesting Peregrine Falcons. Berger et al. (1970) described eggshell thinning and reproductive decline in this population. The results of two surveys in 1970 and 1975 were presented by Cade and Fyfe (1970) and Fyfe et al. (1976a). From 1980-83, surveys were undertaken to determine the occupancy of both previously and newly found eyries, as well as the number of young per nest. The region was again visited in 1985 as part of the national five year censusing program.

METHODS

We attempted to visit four local populations during each year: (1) Koksoak River north of Fort Chimo, (2) Gyrfalcon Islands, (3) Leaf Bay Basin, and (4) Payne-Arnaud River as far inland as the first rapids. Depending on finances, a survey was conducted by canoe, helicopter, or a combination of the two. In 1980, the Koksoak River, Gyrfalcon Islands and Leaf Bay were covered by canoe, and Payne River by helicopter. In 1981, Payne River and the Gyrfalcon Islands were not visited. We surveyed all four areas by canoe in 1982. In 1985, only the Koksoak was canoed; Leaf Bay and Payne River were surveyed by helicopter.

Generally, nests were visited once each year during the last two weeks of July. Cliffs were scanned for whitewash on potential nesting ledges and perching sites. Where necessary, a shotgun was fired to flush falcons from cliffs. Suspected occupancy was investigated by an intensive but brief search of the cliff for signs of nesting. In scrapes with young, nestlings were counted and banded if old enough. Unhatched eggs were collected for later residue analysis.

RESULTS

Occupancy of Peregrine nest sites from 1980-82 and 1985 was compared with those of 1970 and 1975 (Table 1). In 1980, 19 of 27 previously known territories were checked. Two new territories were discovered, one on an inland cliff. Owing to inclement weather, two active territories were likely missed in the Payne River and Peregrine Sound areas. In 1981, only half of the total sites were visited. Eight new active sites were found in 1985, bringing the total known sites to 36 from only 15 in 1970 (Cade and Fyfe 1970).

The numbers of pairs and young from 1980-82 and 1985 are compared with those of 1970 and 1975 in Table 2. Of territorial pairs, roughly 80% had young each year. From 1980 onward, young per successful pair ranged from 2.36-3.21.

Twelve territories were surveyed in all four years (Table 3). Only one territory produced young every year; however, two other territories were attended by at least one adult. Number of young from

TABLE 1.   Occupancy of nest sites by Ungava Bay Peregrine Falcons.

Year	Total known sites	No. checked	No. unoccupied	No. of lone adults	No. of pairs	% occupancy[b]
1970[a]	15	15	3	3	9	80
1975[a]	27	25	14	2	9	44
1980	28	21	11	0	10	48
1981	28	14	4	2	8	71
1982	28	22	8	1	13	64
1985	36	28	5	0	23	82

[a] Data for 1970 and 1975 are from Cade and Fyfe (1970) and Fyfe et al. (1976a), respectively.
[b] No. occupied/no. checked × 100.

TABLE 2.   Reproductive performance of Peregrine Falcons nesting in Ungava Bay.

Year	No. of pairs checked	No. of pairs with young	% total pairs with young	Total young	No. young/ pair	No. young/ successful pair
1970[a]	9	7	78	12	1.33	1.71
1975[a]	9	9	100	16	1.78	1.78
1980	10	10	100	27	2.70	2.70
1981	8	8	100	19	2.36	2.36
1982	13	12	92	30	2.32	2.50
1985	23	19	83	61	2.85	3.21

[a] Data for 1970 and 1975 are from Cade and Fyfe (1970) and Fyfe et al. (1976a), respectively.

these territories ranged from 12 in 1981 to 19 in 1982. The lowest number of young per successful nest was 1.50 in 1981, while the highest was 2.83 in 1985. The percent occupancy of the 12 territories was about 67% over the last three years.

Of three nestlings banded and later recovered during fall migration, two were recovered at Assateague Island, Maryland, and the other in Pennsylvania.

DISCUSSION

The number of new active sites found each year provides strong evidence of a substantial Peregrine population in the Ungava Bay region. Fyfe (1969) classified the southern shores of Ungava Bay as Group 2, i.e., "areas of limited Peregrine nesting habitat where there may be cliffs, cutbanks, or dykes locally, but where they are not extensive enough to warrant classifying in the first group." If Fyfe's group classification still holds, our results argue strongly for a reclassification of this region into Group 1, i.e., "areas that provide optimum nesting habitat for Peregrines, such as cliffs, cutbanks, or dykes, in close association with water." Although we did find three or four active cliffs somewhat inland and away from any substantial body of water over the four survey years, it is doubtful that large numbers of Peregrine pairs are established on inland cliffs in Ungava Bay. In 1985, a helicopter inspection of extensive inland cliffs in the north arm of Leaf Bay Basin revealed no nesting Peregrines.

TABLE 3. Reproductive performance of 12 Peregrine Falcon territories in Ungava Bay during 1980-85.

Territory reference	1980	1981	1982	1985
A	0	2	2	3
B	0	0	0	0
C/D	2	2	2 Adults	3
E/F	0	1	2	0
G	0	0	3	2 Adults
H/I	4	3	0	3
J/K	1	2	0	1
L	3	1 Adult	3	0
M	0	0	0	0
N/O	0	0	2	4
P/Q	3	2	4	3
R	3	1 Adult	3	2 Adults
Total young	16	12	19	17
No. occupied nests	6	8	8	8
% occupancy	50	67	67	67
No. young/ successful nest	2.67	1.50	2.38	2.83

Since the same territories were not checked every year and new active territories were found each year, it is somewhat misleading to compute a percentage occupancy (see Cade and Fyfe 1970) because the newly found active eyries tend to bias the results toward higher apparent occupancy; nevertheless, the calculation does show the expected trend from 1970-75 and reflects antecedent changes in reproductive output. From 1980 onward though, the 12 territories checked each year demonstrate a relatively stable occupancy (Table 3).

One indicator of the health of a Peregrine population is the number of young per successful nest. Compared with both 1970 (Cade and Fyfe 1970) and 1975 (Fyfe et al. 1976a), the number of young per successful nest (Table 2) has risen dramatically from a low of 1.71 in 1970 to 3.21 in 1985, one of the highest figures ever recorded for this species. Minor fluctuations do occur, however, from year to year.

Sources of error need comments. Our figures of numbers of young per pair are based on the assumption that all young in the nest survive to fledging. They most certainly do not. Also, while we are reasonably confident that our results are indicative of the true situation for Peregrines nesting in the area we surveyed, we concede that some active eyries with young may have been missed. Cliffs attended by one or two adults but seemingly without young may have harbored well-hidden nestlings. In some cases, we were fortunate enough to locate a brood on a cliff unattended by either adult during our visit. In one instance with dusk approaching, a female with a brood refused to flush even after several shotgun blasts. Had we not undertaken a foot search, the territory would have been recorded as vacant.

A cliff with a successful pair of Common Ravens seldom, if ever, had a pair of nesting Peregrines. We did, however, find one cliff several hundred meters long, with successful nests of Rough-legged Hawks, Common Ravens and Peregrines. Peregrines also shared cliffs with Gyrfalcons in Ungava Bay region.

When censusing Peregrines, one must consider the use of alternate cliffs from year to year. Table 3 shows six territories with alternate cliff sites within them, either adjacent to the cliff or across the river from it. Whenever one cliff within such a territory had Peregrines, the other invariably had none. The Koksoak River north of Fort Chimo best shows this situation. During no survey from 1980 onwards were there more than three active Peregrine nests on the river. In most cases, the alternate cliff was selected the following year. Whether this behavior is related to disturbance the previous year, some form of hygiene, or some other factor is not known.

The production of young by the Koksoak River pairs is encouraging. Peregrines continue to thrive despite increasing boat traffic up and down the river, as well as growing numbers of cabins constructed near active cliffs. Moreover, there appears to be a favorable change in native attitudes toward falcons, perhaps as a result of well-publicized efforts by foreigners to poach eggs and young for the black market. The appointment of a local Inuk to the post of provincial conservation officer for the region has contributed markedly to improving attitudes.

In conclusion, the record number of young per successful pair in 1985 and the reasonably stable percentage occupancy of the 12 territories visited in each of the four years indicate that the Ungava Bay Peregrine Falcons are demographically healthy and productive.

ACKNOWLEDGEMENTS

We thank the following, for without their assistance the surveys would have been much less successful: R. Bowman, W. Cooper and family, S. and E. Gordon, J. Grist and family, A. Kudluk, M. Lepage and I. Ritchie. Grants were generously provided by the World Wildlife Fund (Canada), the Canadian National Sportsmen's Fund, le Ministére du Loisir de la Chasse et de la Pêche du Québec, and The Peregrine Fund, Inc.

7 | Status of Peregrine Falcons in the Kitikmeot, Baffin, and Keewatin Regions, Northwest Territories, 1982-1985

Robert G. Bromley

From 1982-85, I conducted extensive aerial surveys of the Gyrfalcon in the Kitikmeot (central arctic), and Baffin (eastern arctic) regions, Northwest Territories (Figure 1). During these surveys, observations of territorial and nesting Peregrine Falcons (*F. p. tundrius*) were routinely recorded. Peregrines in the Kitikmeot Region were more intensively studied on the ground in cooperation with Kim Poole, University of Alberta, Edmonton. Summaries for the Keewatin region (west side of Hudson Bay) are from work by Cormack Gates, Department of Renewable Resources, Government of the Northwest Territories, Fort Smith, and Gordon Court, University of Alberta, Edmonton.

METHODS

Except for areas of intensive study, observations resulted from one site visit, usually by helicopter. Timed to coincide with the mid-nestling stage for Gyrfalcons, visits to Peregrine nests occurred during their late incubation or early nestling stages. Thus, data are on numbers of eggs or young per successful pair, unless otherwise stated. Since adult females would usually not leave the nest despite the proximity of the helicopter, I was unable to count eggs or small young in many cases. Owing to time constraints, I did not land the helicopter and enter eyries to check reproduction. Details of methods have been presented elsewhere (Bromley 1983).

HISTORICAL PERSPECTIVE

Kitikmeot Region. — Few historical data are available on Peregrines in the central arctic, Northwest Territories. In the mid-1950s, McEwan (1957) reported Peregrines as "fairly common" in Bathurst

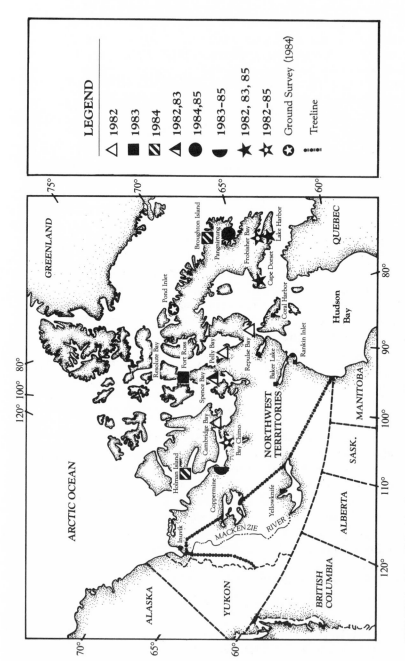

FIGURE 1. Map of the Northwest Territories indicating the location of 13 helicopter surveys and one ground survey for Peregrine Falcons from 1982-85.

Inlet. The Canadian Wildlife Service (CWS) began to check sites in the same area in the 1970s. During the 1975 Peregrine survey, 24 previously known sites were checked and 3 new sites located (Fyfe et al. 1976a). They reported an occupancy rate of 48%. Presumably the three new sites were active, so excluding these an unbiased rate of 42% (10 out of 24 sites) can be calculated.

In 1980, surveys by CWS and LGL Ltd. in the Minto Inlet area of Victoria Island documented the presence of 23 active Peregrine territories (McLaren and Alliston 1981). They did not present their data in terms of density.

The area reported here is overlapped by both Bathurst Inlet and Minto Inlet. Surveys were also conducted by LGL Ltd. on southern Somerset Island and the Boothia Peninsula, Northwest Territories, from 1974-77 (Alliston and Patterson 1978). Of 17 sites located, clutch size averaged 3.24 (SD=±0.9) eggs and brood size averaged 2.86 (±0.68, $n=7$) young during the early nesting period. My surveys in the 1980s overlapped the above areas.

Baffin Region. — Observations on the historical use of south Baffin by nesting Peregrines have been inconsistent. Kumlien (1879) termed them regular breeders in Cumberland Sound, usually in the vicinity of Eider Islands. In northwestern Foxe Basin, Bray (1943) found Peregrines rather common. Based on cumulative records (late 1920s-early 1930s), Soper (1946) considered them rare, nesting "sparingly." Subsequent observations by F. G. Cooch (unpubl. ms.) and MacPherson and McLaren (1959) indicated the Peregrine was a common resident in the 1950s. In 1970, Weaver and Grier (*in* Cade and Fyfe 1970) spent over five weeks scouring south Baffin, locating only five occupied nests (with eggs or young present) and two inactive sites (no adults or young present) during 1900 km of boat travel. Ten years later, G. S. Court and P. Trefry (unpubl. ms.) conducted surveys in the same area along 3050 km of coast. They located only one occupied site, with three young, but of five historical sites none were active in 1980. My study areas overlapped with all areas mentioned above.

RESULTS

Density of Territorial Pairs. — Density of territorial pairs averaged one pair per 186 km^2 in the Kitikmeot region and one pair per 285 km^2 in the Baffin region (Tables 1 and 2). These densities are lower than Fyfe's (1969) estimate of one pair per 52 km^2 for optimal nesting habitat in the Northwest Territories. Of the area covered in the 1980s, approximately 80% lies within Fyfe's zone of "optimal nesting" habitat. Thus, about one pair per 66 km^2 was expected. Observations were consistent with Fyfe's "limited nesting" zone, where densities should

TABLE 1. Density of active territories and reproduction of Peregrine Falcons in the Kitikmeot region, Northwest Territories, 1982-85.

	1982	1983	1984	1985	Overall
Area surveyed (km²)	9926	10,859	7974	9986	38,745
No. of territories	31	30	82	65	208(177[a])
Km²/territory	320	362	97	154	186
No. of territories with known eggs or young[b]		5	25	41	71
Eggs or young/ successful pair		3.6	3.0	2.6	2.8

[a] Represents territories for 1983-85 from which reproduction data were taken.
[b] Pairs only where eggs or young were counted.

TABLE 2. Density of active territories and reproduction of Peregrine Falcons in the Baffin region, Northwest Territories, 1982-85.

	1982	1983	1984	1985	Overall
Area surveyed (km²)	6663	6663	6977	10,201	30,504
No. of territories	22	33	14	38	107(85[a])
Km²/territory	303	202	498	268	285
No. of territories with known eggs or young[b]		17	1	10	28
Eggs or young/ successful pair		2.6	4.0	2.9	2.8

[a] Represents territories for 1983-85 from which reproduction data were taken.
[b] Pairs only where eggs or young were counted.

average about one pair per 259 km². Since little historical data exist for our areas, I suggest that either the Peregrine population is currently depressed or that Fyfe's (1969) estimate of one pair per 52 km² was an overestimate of what optimal nesting habitat can support. One further possibility is that our survey technique, producing a minimum estimate of territorial pairs per unit area, grossly underestimated the actual Peregrine population there. Based on one area in the Kitikmeot region, intensive ground-based studies revealed a density of one pair per 69 km² (Poole and Bromley 1985). This study also had the highest density of Peregrines based on aerial surveys. I concluded that the aerial survey does underestimate populations, but not to an extent sufficient to account for discrepancies between observed and expected densities. Continued surveys are required to identify which of the other two possibilities, a depressed population or an overestimate of what the habitat can support, accounts for densities of territorial Peregrines in the past four years. My subjective impression is that most optimal Peregrine habitat will not support one pair per 52 km^2, although local pockets of such densities occur.

No extensive Peregrine surveys have been recently conducted in the Keewatin Region. Calef and Heard (1979) calculated a density of one pair per 50 km^2 on an area of about 2100 km^2 on the northwest coast of Hudson Bay. More recently, Court (1986) measured an average density of one pair per 19 km^2 for a 450 km^2 area on the west coast of Hudson Bay. Although such densities are known to exist in local situations, more extensive surveys are required to estimate regional densities in Keewatin.

Reproduction. — By late incubation to early nestling stages, successful pairs averaged 2.8 eggs or young for both the Kitikmeot and Baffin regions (Tables 1 and 2). This is very similar to that observed by Alliston and Patterson (1978) in the Kitikmeot region during the mid-1970s. Based on other studies (Ratcliffe 1980, Pruett-Jones et al. 1981a) this average would likely drop about 15% to perhaps 2.4 young per successful pair by fledging. Nevertheless, such productivity compares favorably with other studies of arctic Peregrines (Calef and Heard 1979).

From 1982-85, Court (1986) observed production of 2.4-3.5 young fledged per successful pair and 1.9-2.4 young fledged per territorial pair on the west Hudson Bay coast study area in the Keewatin region. Since these rates are for fledged young, they indicate somewhat higher productivity than I observed in the Kitikmeot and Baffin regions during the same period.

Occupancy Rates. — In order to assess population trends, I examined annual occupancy rates at known Peregrine sites, and re-occupancy rates at individual sites checked in consecutive years. For this discussion I defined occupancy as the presence of one or two territorial adults in a nesting territory.

Occupancy rates of historical sites averaged 44% and 73% in the Kitikmeot and Baffin regions, respectively (Tables 3 and 4). Reasons for the difference in rates between the two are not fully understood. Reoccupancy of individual territories from one year to the next has been similar, 58% for the Kitikmeot region and 65% for Baffin, and comparable to Peregrines (*F. p. anatum*) in the Mackenzie Valley, Northwest Territories (Bromley and Matthews Chapter 8). During the 3-4 years of my surveys, population trends in the Kitikmeot and Baffin regions have not become apparent.

Recent studies have indicated that size, location and density of territories may vary annually in response to various factors such as food supply and habitat saturation by falcons (for discussion regarding

TABLE 3.   Historical nest site occupancy and consecutive year occupancy rates by
            Peregrine Falcons in the Kitikmeot Region, Northwest Territories, 1982-85.

	1982	1983	1984	1985	Overall
No. of historical sites checked	4	14	34	69	121
No. of historical sites active with territorial adults	1	7	11	34	53
% active	25	50	32	49	44
Reoccupancy of sites active in previous year and checked in the following year		7/14	10/13	21/39	38/66
% reoccupancy		50	77	54	60
No. of new sites located[a]	25	27	70	22	144

[a] Most new sites represent active territories located during first-time surveys.

TABLE 4.   Historical site occupancy, occupancy rates, and number of new Peregrine
            Falcon sites in the Baffin region, Northwest Territories, 1983-85.

	1983	1984	1985	Overall
No. of historical sites checked	20	6	37	63
No. of historical sites active with territorial adults	12	5	29	46
% active	60	83	78	73
Reoccupancy of sites active in previous year and checked the following year	12/20	3/4	7/10	22/34
% reoccupancy	60	75	70	65
No. of new sites located[a]	21	9	10	40

[a] Most new sites represent active territories located during first-time surveys.

Eurasian Kestrels see Village 1983; for arctic Peregrines see Court
1986). The implication is that simply monitoring known territories
without completely censusing study areas may give biased results.
Although I attempted to census study areas completely, there remains
some possibility that such biases existed in this study. Monitoring
through intensive ground-based studies will evaluate these biases.

CONCLUSIONS

Extensive aerial surveys have now been conducted in northern regions of the Northwest Territories for four consecutive years. Although population trends were not detected, apparently numerically healthy populations exist in all surveyed areas and are reproducing at normal rates. The lower occupancy rate of Peregrine territories in the Kitikmeot region may indicate a depressed population, relative to former populations with higher occupancy rates in the Baffin region, or simply more dynamic fluctuations in environmental conditions from year to year. Alternatively, but less likely, habitat in the Kitikmeot region may simply be less favorable than that in coastal areas of Baffin. Ongoing monitoring of intensive study areas will address those questions for the Kitikmeot and Keewatin regions, but increased effort is required in the Baffin region.

8 | Status of the Peregrine Falcon in the Mackenzie River Valley, Northwest Territories, 1969-1985

Robert G. Bromley and Steven B. Matthews

Prior to the mid-1960s there were few observations of Peregrine Falcons in the Mackenzie Valley from which to assess population trends (Fyfe 1969). Nesting territories and reproductive success of Peregrines were consistently monitored during the succeeding two decades, but little follow-up work was conducted to monitor pesticide levels in the Mackenzie Valley population. This report documents the changes in number of active territories and reproductive success from 1969-85.

METHODS

Methods of field investigations for 1969-81 are reported elsewhere (Cade and Fyfe 1970, Fyfe et al. 1976a). From 1983-85, two helicopter surveys* with three observers were flown annually, one in mid-June and one in late July or early August. Only some of the Mackenzie Valley territories were checked in 1983 and 1984, while almost all territories were checked in 1985. During these years, most observations were made from the air, without an attempt to land at each site.

Throughout the 1970s (R. Fyfe pers. comm.) and the 1980s, surveys included rigorous searches for new territories as well as visits to known territories. Because of impending large scale development projects, financial and logistic support was seldom limiting.

To determine year-to-year changes in the proportion of active versus inactive territories, we compared data that were available from different locales within the Mackenzie Valley. Thus, the same territories may

*Editors' Note: Aerial surveys from a helicopter are not as accurate as ground surveys. Occupied eyries are more likely to be missed, and particularly the number of young in eyries may be incorrectly counted. Nevertheless, such surveys should be fairly consistent in error and therefore comparable with each other from year to year.

not have been checked each year. To check the validity of trends determined from these data, we examined data for those individual territories that were checked during two consecutive years. For example, if territory "A" was checked in 1971 (year 1) and 1972 (year 2), it was included in the analysis. If it was not checked in 1972, it was excluded from the 1971-72 analysis. A comparison of activity at individual sites should indicate population trend; if more sites are active in year 2 (e.g., 60%) than in year 1 (e.g., 40%), the population is likely to be increasing; if the reverse applies, it is decreasing. Similar activity during both year 1 (e.g., 48%) and year 2 (e.g., 47%) indicates a stable population.

We defined an active territory as one where a single Peregrine or a pair of Peregrines was present when the territory was visited during the breeding season. Definite signs of nesting were not required.

RESULTS

From 13-78 territories were checked annually, except for 1976 and 1982 when little or no work was conducted (Table 1). Based upon the percentage of territories that were active, the Peregrine population apparently declined somewhat in the late 1970s, but subsequently returned to prior levels by the mid-1980s (Figure 1). Although less pronounced, a concurrent drop in the percentage of territorial pairs that were productive was also indicated. A rise in this parameter similarly occurred in the mid-1980s (Figure 1). There was no discernible pattern in annual productivity, measured either as the mean number of young per successful pair or as the mean number of young per territorial pair (Table 1).

We examined changes in the percentage of known territories active with two territorial adults for the period 1969-85. A drop in the Peregrine nesting population of about 35% was indicated, apparently occurring from 1977-81 (Figure 1). This trend was reversed in the 1980s, and an upward trend has continued to date. Continued monitoring is needed to determine whether the population will stabilize at or above the early to mid-1970s level. It is worth noting that for the percent of territories with pairs, all annual fluctuations observed were within the range of variation measured between 1970-71 (Figure 1).

Further evidence of similar population trends was observed in occupancy rates (at least one adult present) of individual territories checked in two consecutive years (see Figure 2). In the early 1970s, the rates of occupancy in year 2 of the comparisons were generally similar to that of year 1. From 1973-74 to 1974-75, the occupancy rate in year 2 declined somewhat, and in 1977-78 the occupancy rate in year 2 was at the lowest level measured relative to year 1. Three years later (1980-81), the trend had reversed. In 1980-81, year 2 was characterized by a much higher rate of occupancy than was year 1, indicating an

TABLE 1. Observations of Peregrine Falcon nesting territories and reproductive success in the MacKenzie Valley, Northwest Territories, 1969–85.

Year	No. territories checked	Occupancy[b]		Successful pairs[c]		No. young per successful pair		Mean no. young for all pairs
		n	%	n	%	$\bar{x}$	n[d]	
1969	21	9	43	6	67	2.7	6	1.8
1970	22	5	23	2	40			
1971	13	8	62	6	75	2.2	6	1.7
1972	30	15	50	10	67	2.6	8	1.7
1973[a]	45	24	53	21	88	2.2	20	1.9
1974	34	18	53	12	67	2.9	12	1.9
1975	49	23	47	16	70	2.6	14	1.8
1977	30	15	50	12	80	2.5	11	2.0
1978	13	3	23	2	67			
1979	21	5	24	4	80	2.8	4	2.2
1980	44	12	27	7	58	2.4	7	1.4
1981	23	6	26	3	50	2.3	3	1.2
1983	15	5	33	5	100	2.3	3	2.3
1984	23	10	43	9	90	2.6	7	2.3
1985[a]	78	40	51	38	95	2.2	26	2.1

[a] During both 1973 and 1985, 17 new territories were located in each of the other survey years. From 0–4 new territories were located with at least 1 young when last observed. Almost all final observations occurred during the "partially fledged" stage although some were during the "large downy" period.

[b] Occupancy = territorial pair present.

[c] Successful pairs were those territorial pairs which had at least 1 young when last observed.

[d] No. sites where young were counted.

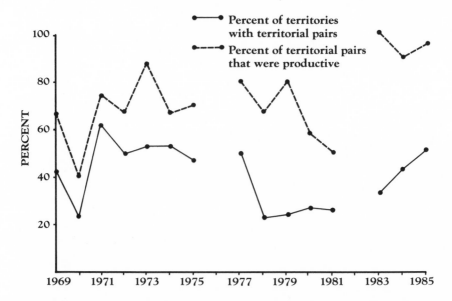

FIGURE 1.   The percent of Peregrine Falcon (*F. p. anatum*) territories that were active
with two adults and the percent of territorial pairs that were productive in the
Mackenzie Valley, Northwest Territories from 1969-85. Sample sizes are
provided in Table 1.

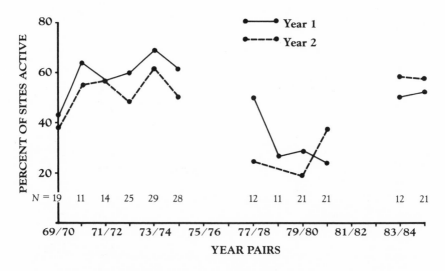

FIGURE 2.   A comparison of the percent of Peregrine Falcon (*F. p. anatum*) territories
that were active (with at least one adult) in year 1 and year 2 of consecutive
pairs of years in the Mackenzie Valley, Northwest Territories, from 1969-85.
Sample sizes are indicated.

increasing population. By 1983-84 and 1984-85, rates for year 1 and year 2 were again similar, indicating a return to a more stable population as characterized by the early 1970s.

DISCUSSION AND CONCLUSIONS

Whether or not the magnitude of the population fluctuation documented here can be termed a "population decline" and "recovery" is questionable. Although few data exist to allow an assessment of population changes prior to 1969, high levels of organochlorine residues in eggs and adipose tissues from the Mackenzie Valley population of Peregrine Falcons in the mid-1960s were not associated with lowered reproduction (Enderson and Berger 1968). Based upon observations in 1966, 1969, and 1970, Fyfe et al. (*in* Cade and Fyfe 1970) concluded that the Mackenzie Valley Peregrines were declining at a fairly constant rate, but they also noted that the number of young produced per successful site was normal. From long-term data (Figure 1), it seems probable that they observed a normal population fluctuation rather than an actual population decline. Alternatively, they may have observed the end of a major decline, and the recovery has yet to occur. Searches for and monitoring of nesting territories from 1969-85 indicate that a slight population decrease may have occurred in the period 1977-81, followed by a rapid "recovery" by 1985. We also found no evidence of a decline in productivity and in the population itself during the early to mid-1970s (Table 1). A decline in the percentage of territories with productive pairs did apparently occur simultaneously with the population decrease of 1978-81. The population decrease must therefore have been a result of either lowered recruitment of breeding adults (despite normal productivity — see Table 1) or increased mortality of adults. Although we believe that lack of adults could reasonably have been the proximate factor leading to the small decline, we are unable to suggest the ultimate cause of these population changes without a review and synthesis of long-term data for this population and others showing similar trends.

ACKNOWLEDGEMENTS

We acknowledge the work of R. Fyfe and associates of the Canadian Wildlife Service, Edmonton. Fyfe's consistent and dedicated efforts provided us with a unique long-term data set with which to work. The Department of Renewable Resources, Government of the Northwest Territories supported surveys from 1983-85, in conjunction with environmental monitoring during pipeline construction.

The report benefited from a detailed review by J. Enderson.

9 | Current Status of Peregrine Falcons in Yukon, Canada

David Mossop

In the Yukon Territory there are five recognizable populations of Peregrine Falcons. One inhabiting the arctic coastal drainages is considered to be the F. p. tundrius race; the others are F. p. anatum. These populations are not separated by great distances, but occupy different drainage basins and are separated by mountain ranges. More importantly, these groups have shown different population dynamics over the years of study (1973-85).

The various groups have been visited repeatedly to monitor population performance. The resulting data are documented in annual reports and in the five-year North American Peregrine Survey (Mossop and Hayes 1980, Mossop and Baird 1985). In 1981 we reported the first evidence of recovery in one F. p. anatum population — that occupying the Porcupine River drainage (Hayes and Mossop 1982). Since that time, a dramatic recovery has been recorded in the Yukon River population. The third F. p. anatum population, occupying the Peel River drainage, has been monitored less effectively, but past evidence has indicated stability only at a depressed level. The fourth (Southern Lakes) population once occupied nesting habitat associated with larger lakes in the southern portion of the Yukon Territory. Visits to historically occupied nest sites have been made periodically, but this population has not been systematically monitored. It has been recorded as extirpated in previous reports (Mossop and Hayes 1980). The fifth (North Slope) group, the F. p. tundrius population, has been visited and surveyed annually. We have reported a drastic decline over the years of study, and in 1981 it ceased to exist as a breeding population.

Recent surveys have included only a small sample of nesting territories in the case of the Peel River and Southern Lakes populations (Table 1). We have no evidence that their status has changed over the last five years — that is, the Peel River population is thought to be stable at a low density and the Southern Lakes population is thought to be extirpated.

TABLE 1.   Recent surveys of Peregrine Falcons in the Yukon Territory, Canada.

Region	Total no. historical sites known	No. sites surveyed	No. sites occupied	No. occ. sites surveyed for productivity	No. productive sites
Peel River					
(F. p. anatum)					
1980	28	26	18	6	0
1985	28	2	2	2	2
Southern Lakes					
(F. p. anatum)					
1980	3	3	0		
Porcupine River					
(F. p. anatum)					
1980	24	22	18	18	7
1985	28	13	11	11	8
Yukon River					
(F. p. anatum)					
1980	14	14	12	12	6
1985	30	30	27	27	16
North Slope					
(F. p. tundrius)					
1980	15	15	2	2	0
1985	16	9	0		

North Slope Population (F. p. tundrius). — Annual surveys since 1980 have covered most of the former range and all known formerly occupied nest sites. No adults have been observed (Table 1). Two observations of fledged young-of-the-year have been made recently by tourists in the area. The source of these birds is unknown. The Yukon government has been carrying out reintroduction of captive-bred young by cross-fostering techniques utilizing Gyrfalcons. To date, 23 young have been released (Mossop and Baird 1985).

Porcupine River Population (F. p. anatum). — Surveys have been conducted annually since 1980. Although in some years the surveys were less complete, coverage is thought adequate to document trend and current status. Generally, occupancy has remained high and productivity, though variable, is probably normal for these high-latitude taiga birds.

Yukon River Population (F. p. anatum). — Surveys have been conducted annually and intensively throughout the breeding season. Since 1980 a strong increase has occurred so that active sites now outnumber former (n=14) known historical sites. Productivity has varied, but has averaged 30-40 young fledged annually over the last three seasons. Our data are complemented by findings on the Yukon River in Alaska (Ambrose et al. Chapter 11).

A more complete analysis of these data and surveys conducted in the period 1980-85 is being prepared for reporting with the 1986 survey results.

10 | Status of Peregrines in the Queen Charlotte Islands, British Columbia

William T. Munro and
Benjamin van Drimmelen

The Queen Charlotte Islands lie about 80 km off the coast of central British Columbia. They became generally known as a major nesting area of the *F. p. pealei* race of the Peregrine as a result of Beebe's (1960) report on the latter's status. This paper summarizes our information gathered on the population up to 1980.

MATERIALS AND METHODS

Data in this paper are from mostly unpublished sources. As the inventory coordinator with our agency, the late Ian Smith compiled the data collected prior to 1975. He used field notes from workers of the provincial museum, maps and reports from falconers, survey data collected by Canadian Ministry of Environment staff for 1965-68 and his own data from annual surveys for 1970-74. Survey data for 1975 were gathered by W. Munro and other Ministry staff including I. Smith. A 1980 survey was done by B. van Drimmelen and other Ministry staff. We have omitted data from Langara Island in this review, an area studied extensively by W. Nelson and reported elsewhere (Nelson 1976, Nelson and Myres 1976).

We were careful in this review to select only historical data that appeared reliable. For example, we did not accept sites marked on maps unless they were accompanied by notations relating to adults or young. Undoubtedly this rigorous screening has excluded some valid information but it seemed necessary for useful comparisons with recent findings.

Extensive surveys were conducted from boats. Cliffs were approached as closely as possible and one or more shots fired from a shotgun or rifle to flush falcons. Defensive flight and vocalization by a pair indicated an occupied site. In the case of a single bird, sites were considered occupied by pairs only if defended persistently; these

69

included less than 5% of occupied sites. Efforts to obtain specimens for museums or young birds for falconry were more intensive but confined to smaller areas. Although Peregrines are known to nest in trees (Campbell et al. 1977) where cliffs are scarce on islands near the British Columbia mainland, tree sites were not investigated on the Queen Charlotte Islands. We assumed the abundant availability of suitable nesting cliffs near all seabird colonies made the use of tree sites unlikely.

We divided the data into four periods for comparison: (1) 1952-69, including mostly data from 1963-69, (2) 1970-74, (3) 1975, and (4) 1980. The most comprehensive surveys were done in 1975 when the whole of the Queen Charlotte Islands was covered, and in 1980 when all but a portion of their southwest coast was covered. Two closely adjacent sites were considered alternates in one territory unless they were occupied simultaneously at least once. Where more than two close sites occurred on each of three widely separated small islands, the number of territories was taken as the maximum number occupied in any year. For example, on one island we knew of nine sites that had been used by nesting Peregrines, but several years of data show that no more than two pairs ever nested on the island in the same year.

RESULTS

We have records of 91 territories used in at least one nesting season, but the number checked in any period varied between 59 and 90, and the occupancy rate ranged from 56-93% (Table 1). Of 56 territories surveyed in each period, occupancy rate ranged from 48-95% (Table 2) while the rates at 79 sites checked in both 1975 and 1980 were 49% and 72%, respectively (Table 3).

Data on productivity were best for the early years where harvest was common, and scanty for more recent years. Production of nestlings has varied from 2.1-3.2 young per nest that produced at least one nestling (Table 4).

TABLE 1. Occupancy by adult pairs of Peregrines at 91 territories on the Queen Charlotte Islands.

Time period	No. checked	No. occupied	% occupied
1952-69	59	55	93
1970-74	69	46	67
1975	90	50	56
1980	80	58	73

TABLE 2.   Occupancy by Peregrines of 56 territories on the Queen Charlotte Islands checked in each time period.

Time period	No. occupied	% occupied
1952-69	53	95
1970-74	39	70
1975	27	48
1980	35	63

TABLE 3.   Occupancy by Peregrines of 79 territories on the Queen Charlotte Islands checked in both 1975 and 1980.

Time period	No. occupied	% occupied
1975	39	49
1980	57[a]	72

[a] $\chi^2 = 7.44$, $P < 0.01$.

TABLE 4.   Productivity of young in successful nests of Peregrines on the Queen Charlotte Islands, 1952-80.

Time period	No. checked	Total young	Young per nest
1952-69	44	101	2.3
1970-74	11	28	2.5
1975	5	16[a]	3.2
1980	7	15	2.1

[a] Includes 2 pipped eggs.

DISCUSSION AND CONCLUSIONS

Combined data from different sources and different years must be interpreted carefully. We believe the occupancy rate of 95% for 1952-69 is higher than for any single year in that period; however, in no single year were enough sites checked to provide a more useful comparison. Similarly, the occupancy rate for 1970-74 is also biased upwards over that in any single year. This bias occurred because several early investigators recorded visits only to territories that were occupied and some sites visited several times in 1952-69 and 1970-74 were listed as occupied if pairs were present only once. Thus comparison of occupancy during those periods with that of 1975 and 1980 must be made cautiously.

The occupancy rates for the 79 territories checked in 1975 and 1980 are reliable, and we conclude that a significant increase in breeding Peregrines occurred in that five-year period. Based on occupancy of 91 known territories, we believe the estimated maximum Peregrine population decreased from 85 pairs in 1952-69 to 61 in 1970-74 to a low of 51 pairs in 1975. The population recovered significantly to a minimum of 66 pairs in 1980. We suggest about 66 pairs in 1980 because, of the 11 sites not checked in 1980, all were occupied in 1975.

Possible causes for the decline and recovery of the Peregrine population on the Queen Charlotte Islands are pesticides, legal harvest, poaching, logging, changes in abundance and distribution of prey species, or a combination of factors (Nelson and Myres 1976). We doubt whether data can now be assembled to reveal the most significant factors.

ACKNOWLEDGEMENTS

We are indebted to the many falconers, museum workers and others who made their notes and maps available to the Ministry, and to the late Ian Smith for his annotated compilation of the pre-1975 material.

11 | Changes in the Status of Peregrine Falcon Populations in Alaska

Robert E. Ambrose, Robert J. Ritchie,
Clayton M. White, Philip F. Schempf,
Ted Swem, and Robert Dittrick

Three subspecies of Peregrine Falcon occur in Alaska: *F. p. tundrius* inhabits the northern tundra region of the state, *F. p. anatum* occurs in the forested interior, and *F. p. pealei* occurs in the coastal regions of the Aleutian Islands, Gulf of Alaska, and southeast Alaska (Figure 1). Both *F. p. tundrius* and *F. p. anatum* are highly migratory, wintering as far south as northern Argentina. *F. p. pealei* is for the most part a year-round resident within its range, but some movement along the west coast of Canada and the United States occurs.

We studied all three Peregrine subspecies in Alaska, but especially the endangered populations of *F. p. tundrius* and *F. p. anatum*. Results of statewide surveys in Alaska were summarized in 1970 (Cade and Fyfe 1970) and again in 1975 (Fyfe et al. 1976a). Since then an intensive survey and banding program in interior and northern Alaska, and extensive surveys in the range of *F. p. pealei*, have occurred. This paper presents the results of surveys between 1979 and 1985, emphasizing areas studied historically for comparison. Different survey methods, different site numbering systems, and different study area boundaries made the results of some surveys difficult to interpret and compare with each other and with recent surveys. For this reason, this paper does not address specific site occupancy, but instead focuses on the numbers of birds present and the numbers of young produced within specific study areas since 1965.

STUDY AREAS AND METHODS

We worked on the Colville and Sagavanirktok rivers in northern Alaska, and on the upper Yukon and Tanana rivers in the interior (Figure 1). The Colville River was studied between the Etivluk River

73

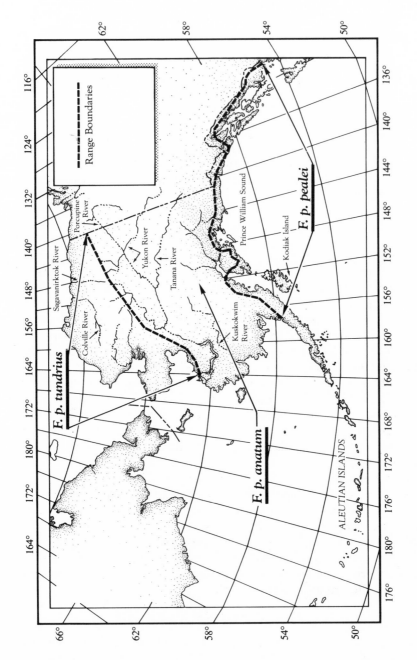

FIGURE 1.   Ranges of the three Alaskan Peregrine Falcon races in the principal survey areas.

and Ocean Point, a distance of 295 km, and the Sagavanirktok River between Slope Mountain and Franklin Bluffs, a distance of 180 km. The upper Yukon River was studied between the Alaska-Yukon Territory border and Circle, Alaska, a distance of 265 km, and the Tanana River between Tanacross and Fairbanks, Alaska, a distance of 375 km. In both northern and interior Alaska, other areas were surveyed, but to a lesser extent than the principal study areas. Surveys of *F. p. pealei* were limited to a few islands in the Aleutian chain and to the outer coast of southeast and south-central Alaska.

In most cases trips were made by raft or boat on each river twice a year: once during incubation to determine the number of birds attempting to breed, and again when young were 3-6 weeks old to determine productivity and to band them. Surveys in the Aleutian Islands were limited to one per year, using boats and helicopters; only boats were used in the surveys of southeast and south-central Alaska.

RESULTS AND DISCUSSION

Northern Rivers. — Peregrine Falcons nesting along the Colville have been studied since the 1950s (Cade 1960, White and Cade 1971, Cade and White 1976, unpubl. U. S. Fish and Wildlife Service (USFWS) reports 1979, 1980, unpubl. Bureau of Land Management (BLM) reports 1981, 1982, 1985), and those along the Sagavanirktok River since 1970 (unpubl. USFWS reports 1970, 1972, 1982, Roseneau et al. 1976a, unpubl. Northwest Alaska Pipeline Co. reports 1981, unpubl. BLM reports 1985). Other drainages were surveyed less frequently, including the Utokok River (Fyfe et al. 1976a, White and Boyce 1978, unpubl. BLM report 1985), tributaries of the Colville and other northwestern Alaska drainages (Roseneau et al. 1976b, White and Boyce 1978) and rivers in northeastern Alaska (Roseneau et al. 1976a, unpubl. USFWS reports 1985). Although some changes in numbers are artifacts of sampling procedures and a few records are suspect because of possible confusion with Gyrfalcons, the results of these surveys offer a good picture of the status of Peregrine Falcons in northern Alaska.

Only the Colville River was surveyed intensively prior to the mid-1960s. Cade (1960) observed 32 pairs and 44 young in 1952, and 36 pairs and 50 young in 1959. A severe decline in the number of young produced and an increase in nesting failure were evident on the Colville River between 1969-71. A survey in 1973 revealed a drastic decline in occupancy and productivity: 14 pairs produced only nine young that year (Cade and White 1976). By 1980, the number of pairs on the Colville had increased to 21 and productivity exceeded 1.0 young per territorial pair for the first time since 1968. Increases continued through 1985 (Table 1). In 1985, 29 pairs and 5 lone adults occupied cliffs along the Colville, and 18 of these pairs produced 50 young.

In 1982-85, an average of 62% of pairs had young, or 2.85 young per successful pair. In 1952 and 1959, 68% of the pairs were successful and averaged 2.04 young. In comparison, 77% of pairs on the upper Yukon were successful in 1981-85, averaging 2.62 young per successful pair, and 84% of pairs were successful in Greenland in 1972-82, averaging 2.8 young per successful pair (Burnham and Mattox 1984). Productivity along the Colville may have been below normal even during the 1950s. Three eggs collected on the Colville by J. W. Bee in 1952 had eggshell indices of 1.45-1.50 (Cade et al. 1971), values generally associated with decreased productivity (Anderson and Hickey 1972).

TABLE 1.   Territory occupancy and productivity of Peregrine Falcons along the Colville River, Alaska, 1952-85.

	Occupancy			Nestling productivity				
Year	No. of pairs	No. of lone adults	% relative occup.[a]	No. of pairs with young	% pairs with young	No. of young[b]	Young/ pair	Young/ succ. pair
1952[e]	32	5	92	21	66	44	1.4	2.1
1959[e]	35	5	100	25	69	50	1.4	2.0
1967[f,g]	27	5	80	18	67	34[c]	1.3	1.9
1968[f,g]	31	1	80	16	52	34	1.1	2.1
1969[f,g]	33	0	83	13	39	26	0.8	2.0
1971[g]	25	5	75	9	36	14	0.6	1.6
1973[h]	14	1	38	4	29	9	0.6	2.3
1975[i]	10	3	33	NC[j]	NC[j]	NC[j]	NC[j]	NC[j]
1978	15	9	60	8	53	14	0.9	1.8
1979	16	5	53	6	38	15	0.9	2.5
1980	21	2	58	12	57	29	1.4	2.4
1981	24	5	73	12	50	31	1.3	2.6
1982	26	3	73	18	69	48	1.9	2.7
1983	26	2	70	16	62	52	2.0	3.3
1984	31	4	88	18	58	47[d]	1.5	2.6
1985	29	5	85	18	62	50	1.7	2.8

[a] $\dfrac{\text{No. of occupied sites in survey year}}{\text{No. of occupied sites in 1959}} \times 100.$

[b] Young 3-6 weeks old.

[c] Eggs (number not reported) collected for pesticide analysis.

[d] 8 eggs collected for pesticide analysis.

[e] Cade (1960).

[f] Cade et al. (1971).

[g] White and Cade (1971).

[h] Haugh (1976) (aircraft used on second survey; occupied sites possibly missed).

[i] Cade and White (1976) (aircraft and ground survey; occupied sites possibly missed).

[j] NC = not checked.

Although we have less information for the Sagavanirktok River than the Colville, probably 5-8 sites were occupied in the pre-pesticide era (USFWS 1982). The number of pairs and productivity had declined by the early 1970s, but at least three pairs occurred there through 1980. Increases were first observed in 1981 and have continued through 1985. In 1985, at least seven pairs were present on the Sagavanirktok and six of these produced 21 young. Although the apparent rate of increase may be attributed partially to differences between surveys, an increase in productivity and a high occupancy rate both indicate a measure of stability not recorded during any survey between 1970-80.

Sections of 11 other rivers in northern Alaska (Canning, Aichillik, Toolik, Chandler, Anaktuvuk, Utokok, Kavik, Etivluk, Jago, Kongakut, and Nigu) historically used by Peregrines were surveyed in 1985. Seven pairs and four lone adults were observed (Table 2), but only portions of some of these rivers were examined. Additional recent sightings of Peregrines on other rivers that were probably used historic-ally attest to an increasing population in northern Alaska. These sightings include three adults at three locations on the Ikpikpuk River in 1982, two pairs on the upper Colville in 1984, two pairs on the Kogosukruk River in 1981, and one pair on the Killik River in 1985.

TABLE 2. Comparisons of Peregrine Falcon use of peripheral drainages on Alaska's North Slope.

River	Largest no. of pairs (year)		
	Historical	Mid-1970s	1985
Aichillik	2 (1966)[a]	0 (1972-75)[a]	1[e]
Canning	3 (1972)[a]	0 (1974)[a]	1[e]
Toolik	2 (1958)[a]	1 (1973)[a]	1
Kavik	1-2 (1947)[a]	?	0[g]
Chandler and Anaktuvuk	6 (1971)[b]	1+2 adults (1975)[b]	1+2 adults[g]
Etivluk	?	1 (1975)[b]	1+1 adults[f]
Nigu	?	0 (1977)[d]	1[f]
Utokok	5 (1953)[c]	0 (1977)[d]	1[f]
Kongakut	3 (1966)[a]	0 (1972-75)[a]	0 (1984)[e]
Jago	?	?	1 adult[e]
Total	22-23 pairs	3 prs.+2 adults	7 prs.+4 adults

[a] Roseneau et al. (1976a).
[b] Cade and White (1976).
[c] Fyfe et al. (1976a).
[d] White and Boyce (1978).
[e] M. Amaral pers. comm. (1985).
[f] J. Silva pers. comm. (1985).
[g] Partial survey.

The Alaska Peregrine Falcon Recovery Team estimated an historical population of 150 pairs for Alaska's tundra regions (USFWS 1982). Earlier, Cade (1960) had estimated 200-250 pairs. That population has been recovering since at least 1980, and we are now seeing the repopulation of some drainages that had been unoccupied or had severely reduced populations in the 1970s. In 1985, 44 pairs were recorded in an area where at least 66 pairs occurred in the 1950s. Therefore, this population has yet to reach historical levels of occupancy.

Interior Rivers. — Biological surveys noted nesting Peregrines along the Yukon River as early as 1898 (Bishop 1900), and along the Porcupine and Tanana rivers in the 1920s (O. Murie, unpubl. field notes, Rasmuson Library, University of Alaska). In the 1950s, Cade (1960) surveyed the upper Yukon River; he also worked there during the 1960s and 1970s (Fyfe et al. 1976a). Surveys since that time have also included the lower Yukon River (below the Yukon Flats), the Porcupine and the Black (unpubl. USFWS reports 1979-85), the Charley and the Kandik (Cade 1976, unpubl. National Park Service (NPS) reports 1980-85), the Fortymile, the Dulbi, the Melozitna, the Gisasa, Beaver Creek and Birch Creek (unpubl. BLM reports 1979-85), the Kuskokwim (Ritchie and Ambrose 1978, Mindell 1983), the Kisaralik (Wier 1982, Mindell pers. comm.), and the Kanektok (unpubl. USFWS report 1985).

In 1898 (Bishop 1900) and 1951 (Cade 1960), 16 pairs were found on the upper Yukon. These surveys were in late July and early August and could have missed unsuccessful pairs or dispersed adults and young. When intensive surveys conducted in 1966 (Cade et al. 1968) again revealed 16 pairs, the population was deemed healthy. More recently, Cade et al. (1976) estimated that the population in 1951 was more likely around 20 pairs. However, in the last three years an average of 26 pairs per year were found, and it seems possible that at least this many pairs were present prior to the 1950s. As already mentioned, the lower number of pairs observed by Cade in 1951 may have been the result of the late date of the survey, or it is possible that the population was already declining.

The population on the upper Yukon declined in the early 1970s, stabilized in 1974-77 (Cade et al. 1976), increased from 1978-83, and has remained stable since 1983 (Table 3). For the past five years, productivity averaged 2.02 young per territorial pair and 2.62 young per successful pair, and 77% of the pairs produced young.

Surveys were incomplete on the upper Tanana River prior to 1970. In 1968, there may have been 12 pairs with 23 young, but in 1970 there were only 6 pairs and 16 young (Haugh 1976). This population then declined further, to a low of 2 pairs in 1974 and 1975 (Haugh

1976). Since 1978, the Tanana population has had 4-5 pairs with 4-12 young each year. Developments such as construction of homes near the river at Delta and Fairbanks may prevent full recovery.

Occupancy and productivity trends of Peregrines along the upper Yukon are likely to be representative of the entire Peregrine population of interior Alaska with the exception of the Tanana River. Although other areas in interior Alaska lack good historical data, surveys since 1979 have revealed increases concurrent with those in the upper Yukon. Including the observations along the upper Yukon and Tanana rivers, 62 pairs and 113 young were recorded in 1979, 76 pairs and 156 young in 1980, 83 pairs and 197 young in 1981, 87 pairs and 159 young in 1982, 103 pairs and 202 young in 1983, 94 pairs and 189 young in 1984, and 106 pairs and 191 young in 1985.

TABLE 3. Territory occupancy and productivity of Peregrine Falcons along the upper Yukon River, Alaska, 1951-85.

	Occupancy			Nestling productivity				
Year	No. of pairs	No. of lone adults	% relative occup.[a]	No. of pairs with young	% pairs with young	No. of young[b]	Young/ pair	Young/ succ. pair
1951[d]	15[i]	2	61	10[i]	67	16	1.1	1.6
1966[d]	15	0	57	12[i]	75	27	1.7	2.3
1967[e]	14	0	50	10	71	14	1.0	1.4
1968[e]	13	3	57	6	46	13	1.0	2.2
1970[f]	12	0	43	7	58	18	1.5	2.6
1973[g]	11	1	43	6	55	16	1.5	2.7
1975[h]	12	0	43	9	75	17	1.4	1.9
1977	12	3	54	9	75	22	1.8	2.4
1978	16	3	68	12	75	28	1.8	2.3
1979	19	0	68	15	79	39	2.1	2.6
1980	17	3	71	16	94	44	2.6	2.8
1981	18	2	71	17	94	54	3.0	3.2
1982	23	2	89	16	70	40	1.7	2.5
1983	27	0	96	21	78	56	2.1	2.7
1984	25	3	100	21	84	48[c]	1.9	2.3
1985	25	2	96	16	64	40	1.6	2.5

[a] $\dfrac{\text{No. of occupied sites in survey year}}{\text{No. of occupied sites in 1984}} \times 100$.

[b] Young 3-6 weeks old.

[c] 8 eggs were collected for pesticide analysis.

[d] Cade et al. (1968).

[e] Cade et al. (1971).

[f] Temple et al. (1970).

[g] Ritchie (1976).

[h] Cade et al. (1976).

[i] Minimum estimate.

Cade (1960) estimated 150-300 pairs in the forested interior of Alaska. Surveys have located nearly 100 pairs each year since 1982; when the population has fully recovered, at least as many pairs may nest outside our study areas. As on the North Slope, the number of pairs has increased since the late 1970s and is now apparently at or near historical levels in most areas; recent surveys of smaller drainages indicate they are being repopulated as well.

The Aleutians and Southeastern Alaska. — We have much less information on Peregrines in maritime Alaska compared to other regions (Table 4). Peregrines were found in coastal areas of southern Alaska in the late 19th century (Dall 1873, Turner 1886), but their distribution and density remained largely undetermined until recently. Data on productivity are too scant to warrant discussion here.

Based largely on the work of Murie (1959) in the 1920s and 1930s, approximately 100 pairs were thought to inhabit the Aleutian Islands as late as 1960 (Cade 1960). Only the Rat Islands group and a few other locations have been adequately surveyed. Based on surveys in the Rat Islands, Agattu, and Buldir, where density was one pair per 10-16 km of coastline, White (1976) estimated a population of 375-580 pairs for the Aleutians, more or less uniformly dispersed but with some local clumping near seabird colonies (such as on Buldir Island).

In 1977-80, USFWS personnel conducted raptor and seabird surveys and found that Peregrine densities were similar in the eastern and western Aleutians (Early 1982). Early estimated 260 pairs for the Aleutians based on one pair per 25 km of coastline, but said there may have been more because he surveyed in July after the young had fledged. Therefore, we estimate 300 pairs for the Aleutians.

TABLE 4.   Survey results for Peregrine Falcons in maritime Alaska.

	Coastline examined (km)	No. of cliffs occupied	Km per occupied cliff	Years studied
Aleutians[a]				
Near Islands	398	12	33	1974-80
Rat Islands	542	54	10	1969-80
Dalarof Islands	147	8	18	1977-80
Western Andreanof Islands	1042	29	36	1977-80
Gulf of Alaska and				
Prince Williams Sound Area	800	10	80	1983
Kenai Peninsula	720	25	29	1985
Southeast Alaska				
(south of Yakutat)	1720	36	48	1981

[a] Aleutian data modified from Early (1982).

The Alaska Peninsula and Kodiak Island region east of the Aleutians has not been adequately surveyed for Peregrines. White et al. (1976) reviewed available literature and tallied 69 recorded eyries for the area.

The Kenai Peninsula coastline (720 km) was surveyed in 1985, and 25 cliffs were occupied by Peregrines (unpubl. USFWS report 1985). In 1983, the Gulf of Alaska and Prince William Sound coastlines (800 km) were surveyed, and 10 cliffs were occupied (unpubl. USFWS report 1983). Surveys in southeast Alaska south of Yakutat in 1981 covered 1720 km of coastline and located 36 occupied cliffs (unpubl. USFWS report 1981). These recent surveys by USFWS personnel located 71 occupied sites on the outer coast, but they did not cover inner coastal areas such as Glacier Bay, Juneau-Admiralty Island, Petersburg-Kupreanof Island, Forrester Island, or Ketchikan. These areas contained at least eight sites listed by White et al. (1976). Additionally, Van Horn et al. (1982) found eight nests in trees and perhaps 3-4 others on cliffs not previously reported.* There are probably more than 140 territories within the region from the Kenai Peninsula to southeast Alaska.

Because historical data are few for this population, and because recent surveys dealt only with portions of its range, the current status of *F. p. pealei* relative to previous levels cannot be projected. However, based on these surveys, we estimate 600 pairs of *F. p. pealei* in Alaska.

SUMMARY

The populations of Peregrines in northern and interior Alaska likely declined during the mid-1960s and may have been declining as early as the 1950s, when Cade (1960) first surveyed the Colville and Yukon rivers. Between the late 1960s and 1985, the number of occupied territories declined approximately 65% for *F. p. tundrius* and 55% for *F. p. anatum*. Both populations reached their lowest levels in the early 1970s, stabilized in the mid-1970s, and started to increase in the late 1970s. This pattern closely parallels that observed in Great Britain, where the Peregrine population declined through 1962 (at which time several European countries restricted the use of dieldrin and DDT), remained stable until 1968, and then increased (Ratcliffe 1980). Northern and interior Peregrine populations in Alaska declined through 1972, when the United States restricted the use of DDT. The populations stabilized and then began to increase in the late 1970s, and have continued to do so.

*Editors' Note: These tree sites are not the same as those reported by Campbell et al. (1977) farther south in Canada. The distance between those reported in Canada and those in Alaska is in excess of 700 km. It is therefore conceivable that there are 20-30 nest sites along this island chain. They are also probably clumped and localized.

ACKNOWLEDGEMENTS

The survey program in northern and interior Alaska was initiated in 1979 by D. Benfield, USFWS in Alaska. P. Bente, L. Craighead, J. Curatolo, D. Mindell, D. Roseneau, and A. Springer conducted surveys for the USFWS on various rivers in Alaska. M. Amaral, M. Ambrose, K. Bollinger, M. Britten, T. Cade, B. Durtsche, G. and J. Edelbrock, R. Hunter, C. McIntyre, T. Nichols, K. Riddle, J. Shryer, J. Silva, D. Toelle, S. Ulvi, and D. Williamson participated in surveys either as agency personnel (USFWS, BLM, or NPS) or as volunteers. The information we present is the result of the efforts of all of these individuals, and we appreciate their help. B. Lawhead and R. Hunter reviewed a draft of this paper.

Editors' Note: The Alaska surveys have continued to reveal increasing numbers of Peregrines (Ambrose pers. comm.). On the Colville River in 1986, 34 pairs produced 53 young; in 1987, 35 pairs produced 60 young, comparable to the best years recorded in the 1950s. On the Sagavanirktok River, 7 pairs produced 16 young in 1986 and 24 young in 1987. On the upper Yukon River, 29 pairs raised 48 young in 1986; in 1987, 31 pairs produced 61 young. The number of pairs nesting on the upper Yukon is now twice the number counted in 1951, and the same situation applies across the border in Yukon Territory (D. Mossop unpubl. ms.). The most depressed population in interior Alaska, along the upper Tanana River, has increased from one known pair in the mid- to late-1970s to seven pairs with 10 young in 1987.

12 | Status of Peregrines in the Rocky Mountains and Colorado Plateau

James H. Enderson, Gerald R. Craig,
and William A. Burnham

At the time of the Madison Conference in 1965, few surveys of breeding Peregrines had been done in the western United States. Prior to their decline, Bond (1946) estimated roughly 350 pairs of Peregrines nested in the western United States, including Baja California. In the Great Basin and in the Rocky Mountains the species was considered rare. In 1964 all available sources yielded 31 records of historical territories in Colorado, Wyoming, and Montana (Enderson 1965). Since that time numerous surveys have been done, and the results collated by the U. S. Fish and Wildlife Service Recovery Team (Craig 1985). In this report we review the present information on the distribution, occupancy and productivity in Idaho, Montana, Wyoming, Utah, Colorado and New Mexico.

METHODS

In general, most Peregrine surveys are spring visits to historical territories and include scrutiny of cliffs for evidence of occupancy. In Wyoming, Colorado and New Mexico the state wildlife agencies have operated thorough searches annually for several years. In 1984-85 The Peregrine Fund, Inc., under contract to the National Park Service, operated surveys in Utah and Colorado using four two-man crews placed by helicopter for 24-hour periods near large cliffs. In this way, otherwise inaccessible habitat was searched for periods long enough to reveal nesting Peregrines.

RESULTS

Territory Occupancy. — The number of known territories increased dramatically in the southern portion of the region after the mid-1970s (Table 1). By 1984 about 204 territories were known, and the number increased to at least 211 by 1985.

TABLE 1.   Territories, occupancy, and natural productivity of Peregrines, 1975-85.

State	No. of known territories			No. of adult pairs		No. young fledged[e]		No. young/ adult pair[e]		No. young/ succ. pair[e]	
	1975	1984	1985	1984	1985	1984	1985	1984	1985	1984	1985
CO	27	44	45	11[c]	12[d]	2	13	0.7	1.9	2.0	2.2
MT	23	25	25	1	1	2		2.0		2.0	
NM	17	42		17		38		2.2		2.9	
UT	29	58[a]	64[b]	22	25	29	31	1.3	1.2	1.9	2.4
WY	18	18	18	1	1	3	3	3.0	3.0	3.0	3.0
ID	17	17	17	1	1	0	2	0	2.0	0	2.0

[a] Includes 2 hack towers.
[b] Includes 3 hack towers.
[c] 3 pairs not augmented.
[d] 7 pairs not augmented.
[e] From eyries not augmented.

The increase in the number of known territories reflects more intensive searches rather than actual increase in population. In Colorado most territories have been visited each year since 1977. Of 29 territories known that year, 11 had adult pairs, and in 1985 only 6 had adult pairs even though none of the 29 territories became useless to Peregrines after 1977. Further, of the 12 territories used by adult pairs in 1985, 5 were found in 1980-85. In 1975, 27 territories were known in Colorado (Table 1) and most of these remain usable; only 4 were used by adult pairs in 1985.

Occupancy of ideal sites probably shows most graphically the poor state of Peregrines in Colorado. Of 11 such territories known prior to 1973, 9 were used in 1973, 4 in 1977, fewer than 2 in 1979-84, and 3 in 1985.

Peregrines were reported widespread on the Colorado Plateau (Porter and White 1973). In 1984-85, J. Enderson and coworkers found a substantial number of occupied territories there (Table 1). Along one watercourse several pairs were separated by regular intervals of about 9 km, and at one upland locality six pairs nested inside an area about 32 km long.

No subadult Peregrines were seen in the 1984-85 survey in Utah. In Colorado we saw up to four subadults each year as members of pairs in recent years. At least four subadult females laid eggs (three sets fertile) and three fledged fostered young.

Productivity. — Most information on recent productivity is from Utah and Colorado; in the latter case fostering of captive-bred young to wild pairs has reduced the pool of pairs reproducing naturally (Table 1). In 1985 the seven adult pairs in Colorado not augmented with nestlings fledged 13 young (1.9 young per pair). When 1984 and 1985 are combined and the pair with a subadult female included, the natural production was 1.4 young per pair on territory ($n=11$) and 2.1 young per successful pair ($n=7$).

On the Colorado Plateau in southern Utah, 13 nesting attempts at territories above 2300 m elevation in 1984 and 1985 combined yielded 1.2 young per pair, and 1.8 young per successful pair. At much lower elevations along the Colorado River drainage, 27 attempts in both years yielded 1.4 and 2.2 young per pair, respectively. Overall, the 40 attempts collectively produced 1.3 and 2.1 young per pair, respectively.

DISCUSSION

A review of the literature indicates that historically about 80-90% of Peregrine territories in a region were occupied in a given year (Enderson and Craig 1974). In Colorado we found about 25% in use in recent years, a value biased upwards slightly by the discovery of a few previously unknown territories each year. A few of the 45 territories in Colorado are now unlikely to be used again by Peregrines because of human disturbance, and a few others were marginally attractive and probably only used infrequently when the population was not depressed. These factors considered, we estimate the Colorado population is about one-third its former size. No tendency to increase was apparent in 1985 (but see Addendum).

We have no longterm data on occupancy for territories in Utah. The present density of Peregrines there suggests the population on the Colorado Plateau is not depressed. Similarly, the population in New Mexico occupies about half of all known territories and appears fairly stable.

Northward in Idaho, Montana, Wyoming, and northern Utah the Peregrine population suffered nearly complete collapse. Very few recent records of nesting have been added since 1975 (Table 1). Only six pairs (including six released birds) now nest in those areas where over 84 historical territories were recorded. Several times that number must have occurred in that region prior to DDT use, and we urge a major effort be made to reestablish that population.

An interesting result of recent surveys on the Colorado Plateau and of nonaugmented eyries in Colorado is the close similarity in reproductive rate. Based on the presence of large feathered nestlings or fledged young, the production rate in both areas was about 1.4 young per pair holding territory or 2.1 young per successful pair. These results compare favorably with means of 1.3 and 2.3, respectively, from 10 Peregrine populations not seriously affected by pesticides (Newton 1979). Peregrines in these areas should be able to maintain themselves in the long run if these rates continue, but they may not reoccupy the many vacant territories in northern Utah, Colorado, and the northern Rockies in the next few decades without supplementation by the release of captive-bred birds.

ACKNOWLEDGEMENTS

We are indebted to L. Hayes, J. Connor, S. Petersburg, J. Hogan, and L. Belli for their help with the field surveys. J. Hubbard has kindly allowed us to use information from New Mexico. Many field workers have participated in this research.

ADDENDUM

In the two years since the 1985 conference, a marked increase in known occupied territories occurred. In 1985, 40 adult pairs were known in the region (Table 1), but by 1987 about 88 adult pairs were present. This increase is due to extensive new surveys in previously unsearched habitat, especially in Utah, and to the reoccupancy of abandoned territories. The 1987 estimate includes pairs seen in 1986 but not actually revisited in 1987. Evidence of an actual increase is best seen in Colorado where 12 adult pairs appeared in 1985, 22 in 1986, and 24 in 1987. The increase of 12 pairs, 1985-87, resulted from reoccupancy of eight known territories and discovery of five previously unknown territories in regions surveyed in recent years. Further, three additional pairs with subadults were found in 1987, and two lone adults were at other localities. A high proportion of Peregrines on territory in Colorado bear bands of fostered or hacked birds.

Productivity in 1987 was good. Young produced per territorial pair averaged 1.6 ($n=22$) in Colorado, and 1.9 ($n=31$) in Utah where a group of nine territories within an 18-km radius produced 25 young; no pair failed.

13 | Distribution, Productivity, and Status of the Peregrine Falcon in Arizona

David H. Ellis

In 1884, Edgar Mearns first documented the Peregrine Falcon breeding in Arizona (Mearns 1890 and unpubl. ms.). From 1885 until 1975, various ornithologists observed pairs of Peregrines at another 20 sites in Arizona (Ellis 1976, Ellis and Monson 1987). About 10 of these were known breeding sites (i.e., locations where eggs, nestlings or fledglings had been observed).

In 1975, my coworkers and I began fieldwork to determine activity at old sites, to locate additional breeding sites, and to evaluate the suitability of all regions of the state as Peregrine Falcon breeding habitat (Ellis 1982). For that study, all of Arizona was surveyed with light aircraft, and all cliff areas were evaluated for suitability as breeding habitat. Thereafter hundreds of locations were visited on the ground during the breeding season to determine occupancy and to provide a statewide population estimate (Ellis and Glinski 1987). During the study, the number of pairs observed in a single season increased from 7 in 1976 to 24 in 1982 and 37 in 1985. By 1985, records were available for 59 locations where Peregrine Falcons were known to have nested sometime in the past (Figure 1). Records were also available for 31 other sites where adults had been seen during the breeding season and likely or reportedly bred in the vicinity. With this historical perspective, the following report outlines reproductive performance for the 1976-85 period and occupancy rates for all sites visited in an intensive survey during the 1984 and 1985 breeding seasons.

STUDY AREA AND METHODS

For purposes of this report, Arizona is defined as the state of Arizona and adjacent portions of Utah and New Mexico which lie on the Navajo Indian Reservation. The sites included in the report are

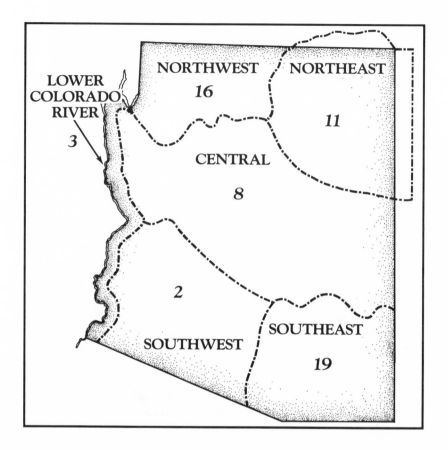

FIGURE 1. Distribution of 59 known or probable Peregrine Falcon breeding sites in Arizona.

either in Arizona (as defined) or are near enough to the border (within 3 km) that hunting adults and dependent young probably visit the state regularly.

In Figure 1, Arizona is divided into six broad geographic zones on the basis of topography and vegetation (see Brown 1982 for details of plant distribution within each zone). The Southeastern Zone is characterized by pine-clad mountain ranges which rise island-like from the surrounding Chihuahuan Desert grasslands. In the Southwestern Zone, elevations are lower and Sonoran Desert plant communities dominate from the valleys to the highest mountain ridges. The Lower Colorado River Zone is Sonoran Desert in the south and Mohave Desert in the north; the defining feature is the Colorado River. The Central Zone is characterized by forested ridges and canyons below the Mogollon Rim.

The Northwestern Zone includes the extensive canyon systems of the Colorado, Virgin, and Paria rivers. The Northeastern Zone consists of elevated valleys dominated by cold-desert plant communities and pine-clad ridges cut by hundreds of canyons.

From 1975-83, new sites located by fieldwork and correspondence were sporadically visited to determine occupancy. The occupancy data presented here, however, are for 1984-85, when we systematically revisited 73 sites and, where practical, determined productivity as well as occupancy.

To determine occupancy, sites were visited at least twice: once during the courtship-incubation period and once when young were most likely to be present. Visits were at least two hours long and usually more than four hours. To maximize the chances of encountering more secretive individuals and pairs that failed to reproduce (and therefore were less conspicuous), we frequently camped near former breeding cliffs. In areas with an abundance of suitable nesting cliffs, we often visited many cliffs in search of Peregrines.

To determine productivity, most sites were visited three times: first, during courtship or early incubation to determine occupancy; second, during the mid- to late nestling period to determine the presence and, if possible, the age of young; and third, during the fledgling period to determine the number leaving the nest. Additional visits were often required for eyries where nestlings were not visible but activities of adults indicated that nestlings were present. A few remote sites were visited only once (during the late nestling or early fledgling period) to document occupancy and, where possible, productivity.

Two biases tend to inflate productivity estimates: (1) until an eyrie location is known, the site is more likely to be discovered in a productive year when noisy nestlings or conspicuous fledglings are present than when a nesting attempt has failed, and (2) estimates of fledging success based only on observations of downy young ignore nestling mortality. To minimize the latter bias, I included in the productivity estimates only birds that had fledged or were within one week of fledging. Nestlings were counted as fledged if their dorsal wing surfaces were mostly brown (i.e., 35 or more days of age). Sites containing chicks younger than 35 days were revisited or deleted from the productivity estimates. A third bias tends to deflate productivity estimates: at eyries found or visited after young are aloft several days, some of the young likely will have already been lost to predation, accidents or dispersal. To minimize this bias, we adjusted the time spent evaluating potential sites according to the stage in the nesting cycle. In general, more time was spent evaluating sites during the courtship and incubation periods, and, when possible, fledgling counts were made shortly before or after the actual fledging date. When all three biases are considered, I believe the fledging success data reported here are conservative and slightly underestimate actual productivity.

RESULTS

Occupancy. — During the intensive occupancy survey (1984-1985), 73 sites were visited during one or both years (Figure 2). For 65 of these sites, a clear determination of occupancy was made. Forty-five of the 65 (69%) were occupied by pairs. Single adults were seen at five other sites that were visited briefly; some of these sites may have actually been occupied by pairs. Because of this uncertainty, only the 65 sites which were thoroughly evaluated are included in Figure 2.

Two factors complicate the reoccupancy data. First, potential nesting habitat at many sites is so vast that it is often impossible, even after

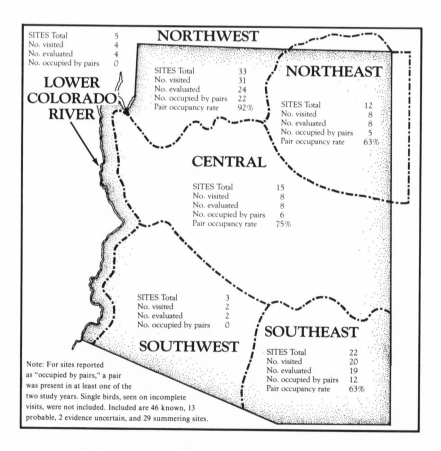

FIGURE 2. Occupancy at Peregrine Falcon breeding or summering sites in Arizona, 1984-85.

extended searching, to be certain that a site is vacant. Second, because occupancy surveys from 1975-85 were not annual, the exact year of reoccupancy is often not known. However, our surveys were frequent enough at most eyries that we can say that the birds likely returned in one of two or three years. At least five sites were reoccupied from 1975-80 and another five from 1981-85. A few other sites, vacant early in the study, were recently reoccupied, but the year of reoccupancy is less certain. At least 14 sites were reoccupied during the 11-year study. In interpreting the reoccupancy figures, one must be aware that 35 of the 45 sites harboring pairs during the 1984-85 survey were located during the 1975-85 study. Some of these were likely reoccupied shortly before discovery. The study area was probably experiencing population recovery throughout the past decade. While some of the 14 reoccupied sites did not have pairs each year, 10 were active in 1984 or 1985 or both.

Productivity. — At the onset of the study in 1975, no active sites were known for Arizona. By 1981, however, we had accumulated records for 68 pair-years (Ellis et al. unpubl. ms.). At the close of the 1985 season, this total was 182. A clear productivity determination was made for 126 pair-years (Table 1). Of these, 92 (73%) fledged 209 young. Productivity averages for the duration of the study were 1.66 young fledged per breeding attempt, 1.70 young fledged per adult attempt, and 2.27 fledged per successful attempt.

In Table 1, productivity figures are compared for the four zones with sizable populations. All four were highly productive, but the percentage of successful nesting attempts was highest in the Northwestern (87%) and Northeastern (95%) zones and lowest in the Southeastern Zone (58%). The number of young fledged per pair per year also decreased from north to south, but the average number of young fledged per successful attempt varied with no north-south trend.

DISCUSSION

High productivity of Peregrine Falcons in Arizona and the trend toward eyrie reoccupancy indicate that unaided population recovery is under way. Natural population recovery has also been dramatically demonstrated during the last decade over most of Great Britain (Ratcliffe 1980 and Chapter 17), parts of Alaska (Cade 1985a, Ambrose et al. Chapter 11), and elsewhere.

High productivity partially explains the reoccupancy trend now under way in Arizona; however, most of the recently reoccupied sites are in the Southeastern Zone where only 58% of the pairs fledge young. This lower fledging success in the expanding portion of the population is owing, in part, to lower reproductive output in young

TABLE 1. Pairing and productivity of Peregrine Falcons by geographical zone in Arizona, 1976-85.

	Northwest	Northeast	Central	Lower Colorado River	Southwest	Southeast	Total
Pairing							
No. pair-years	58[a]	24	36	0	0	64	182[a]
No. adult pair-years[b]	55	23	34	0	0	61	173
No. mixed pair-years[b]	0	1	2	0	0	3	6
Productivity							
No. attempts where outcome known	23	22	29	0	0	52	126
No. successful attempts	20	21	21	0	0	30	92
% success	87	95	72	0	0	58	73
Total no. fledged	40	54	44	0	0	71	209
Mean no. fledged per attempt	1.7	2.5	1.5	0	0	1.4	1.7
No. adult attempts	23	21	28	0	0	50	122
No. fledged (adult attempts)	40	54	44	0	0	71	209
Mean no. fledged per adult attempt	1.7	2.6	1.6	0	0	1.4	1.7
Mean no. fledged per successful attempt	2.0	2.6	2.1	0	0	2.4	2.3

[a] The sum of adult pair-years plus mixed pair-years does not equal the number of pair-years because the age of 1 bird in the Northwest zone was not determined in each of 3 pair-years.

[b] Mixed pair = pair with a juvenile member.

pairs (Newton 1979). Mixed pairs (pairs with an immature member) have not been known to fledge young in Arizona.

Pesticide levels in eggs and prey are treated in another study (Ellis et al. unpubl. ms.). In general, eggshells for Arizona show moderate thinning approaching critical levels (15% thinner than the pre-DDT era) which have resulted in egg breakage (Peakall 1976). However, high DDE levels recently identified in avian prey species in the agricultural zones in southern Arizona (Clark and Krynitsky 1983) may influence birds which breed elsewhere in Arizona. The winter home of the breeding population is unknown. DDE concentrations in European Starlings collected in southern Arizona in 1979 and 1982 were higher than those for any other state (Cain and Bunck 1983, Bunck et al. unpubl. ms.). In Arizona, Peregrine Falcons rarely prey on European Starlings during the breeding season (Ellis et al. unpubl. ms.). However, European Starlings may be important for wintering Peregrines, and other prey species in Arizona may be similarly contaminated.

CONCLUSIONS

Few pairs of Peregrine Falcons have bred historically in the Lower Colorado River and Southwestern zones. Even with the intensive surveys of these areas conducted in 1979, periodic follow-up visits to the historical sites made over the last ten years, and the systematic occupancy survey of 1985, we found no active sites. The other four zones have sizable populations.

The general trend toward higher fledging success (87-95%) in the north, intermediate success (72%) in the Central Zone, and lower success (58%) in the south suggests that chlorinated hydrocarbon residues are differentially influencing local populations. Because of this uncertainty, the favorable statewide productivity values should be viewed with guarded optimism.

The Arizona Peregrine Falcon population is sufficiently large and productive to be expanding into formerly occupied habitat. Nearly all historical sites remain suitable for occupancy. If present trends continue, the population should fully recover without the release of captive-produced young or other enhancement measures. As the environment becomes clean enough to allow for natural population recovery, the Arizona population, together with sizable concentrations in neighboring states, may be sufficient to provide the necessary dispersers to repopulate much of the western United States.

ACKNOWLEDGEMENTS

Through the years many people devoted unsalaried time to the project. I deeply appreciate the following for their energetic help in the fieldwork: J. K. Fackler, W. B. Sloan, Jr., R. Sloan, T. Deecken, J. H. Schnell, J. G. Goodwin, Jr., G. Depner, T. G. Grubb, D. P. Mindell, and my wife, Cathy. R. L. Glinski assisted in the fieldwork and also piloted the aerial surveys without salary.

The following governmental and private agencies financed the work: U. S. Fish and Wildlife Service, Region II (USFWS) and Patuxent Wildlife Research Center (PWRC); Bureau of Indian Affairs (BIA); U. S. Forest Service, Region III (USFS), and Rocky Mountain Forest and Range Experimental Station (RMFRES); U. S. Air Force (USAF); Bureau of Land Management (BLM); U. S. National Park Service; Navajo Fish and Game Branch; Tucson Audubon Society; and Maricopa Audubon Society.

I also thank those who were most instrumental in arranging funds: R. C. Erickson (PWRC), S. Hoffman (USFWS), T. G. Grubb and D. R. Patton (RMFRES), C. Kennedy (USFS), L. Shotton (USAF), D. Siebert (BLM), and E. Olson (BIA).

Editors' Note: While it is most encouraging that there are substantial and increasing breeding populations in Arizona, southern Utah, and New Mexico, it is unknown whether or not these populations can produce "surplus" individuals that will disperse the long distances (many hundreds of kilometers) required to settle and breed in the still largely vacant habitats of the northern Rocky Mountain states (i.e., northern Utah, Idaho, Wyoming and Montana). Data from released Peregrines in California and the Rocky Mountain states indicate that only a few individuals move long distances (mostly females), while the majority settle to breed within 100-200 km of their natal eyries, usually as close as possible. Given enough time (decades) and adaptations to local conditions, the population expansion envisioned by Ellis could occur. See Kleinstäuber and Kirmse (Chapter 20) for a parallel conclusion.

14 | The Status of Peregrines Nesting in California, Oregon, Washington, and Nevada

Brian J. Walton, Carl G. Thelander, and David L. Harlow

As has been the case throughout much of their range, Peregrine Falcons in California, Oregon, Washington, and Nevada occurred in generally stable numbers throughout the 1940s, then declined precipitously during the 1950-70s, and are now experiencing a recovery during the 1980s. Bond (1946) provided a fairly complete summary of the distribution of Peregrines in the western United States. He indicated that some areas were experiencing local declines (mostly associated with direct contact with people), but did not suggest or predict the widespread population decline that occurred in the following decade.

At the 1965 Madison Conference, Ben Glading and Morlan Nelson reported a well-established decline of Peregrine populations throughout the region. Their findings focused on the increasing occurrence of eyrie abandonment and poor reproductive success at the few remaining active sites. But no comprehensive survey was conducted from the time of Bond's work to 1965; the regional summaries presented at the Madison Conference were definitely negative but also poorly supported by conclusive data. Most of the information on Peregrine nest locations and their occupancy or productivity was secreted in the memories and notebooks of a diverse group of Peregrine enthusiasts: falconers, egg collectors, wildlife photographers, and others whose observations were believed trustworthy but whose trust was not easily won.

By 1970, the California legislature passed its Endangered Species Act of 1970, a precursor to the federal Endangered Species Act of 1973. Long-needed efforts to study and protect the Act's list of "endangered species," which included the Peregrine Falcon, finally had the proper authority and funding. In 1970, Steven G. Herman was contracted by the California Department of Fish and Game (CDFG) to survey Peregrine nesting cliffs throughout the state. It was this study (Herman et al. 1970), some 25 years after Bond's pioneering efforts, that set the precedent for what have become almost annual, comprehensive surveys for nesting Peregrines in California. Unfortunately, Peregrines in Oregon and Washington have yet to be surveyed as intensively. Nevada contains very little suitable nesting habitat, and the five historical sites there are relatively easy to survey.

The purpose of this paper is to: (1) briefly review the historical nesting data on Peregrines in each of the four states, (2) summarize the nesting site occupancy and productivity data for 1970-86, and (3) evaluate the current and probable future status of Peregrines in the region.

REVIEW OF PAST SURVEYS

Since the late 1800s, numerous ornithologists and natural historians have recorded observations, collected eggs, or shot museum specimens of Peregrine Falcons in the region. Throughout the 1930s, the late Richard Bond systematically collected most of the available information on Peregrine nesting locations through personal contacts and during his own field work. He was particularly successful since he was a falconer, had numerous friends who were egg collectors, and worked for the U. S. Soil Conservation Service. This profession provided him with ample field time and travel opportunities to pursue Peregrines and contact others who knew where to find them. Bond published his findings (Bond 1946) at the urging of Joseph J. Hickey, who had just a few years previously summarized the status of Peregrines in the eastern United States (Hickey 1942).

As already mentioned, S. G. Herman began a study in 1970 of Peregrine nesting sites in California. He obtained the cooperation of Bond, who was retired and living in the U. S. Virgin Islands. Bond provided his files on individual nesting sites annotated with notes and personal communications from his colleagues. This provided the necessary foundation from which Herman intended to compare historical nesting site occupancy to that of the late 1960s and early 1970s. In addition to Bond's data, Herman, a falconer as well as a trained field ecologist, was able to collect numerous nesting records from the 1950s and 1960s, all of which were essential pieces to the puzzle of understanding the Peregrine's decline.

Herman's survey technique involved traveling to 62 selected historical nesting sites when adults would normally be present and observing each cliff long enough to be reasonably convinced that Peregrines were or were not present. Some regions of the state were flown using a fixed-wing aircraft, mainly to locate suitable cliffs for later ground surveys; helicopter surveys were not used at that time.

Herman's study was continued with funding from the CDFG through 1971 (Herman 1971). In the period 1972-74, he continued to seek incidental data on nesting Peregrines but conducted no systematic searches. The CDFG funded a statewide survey of Prairie Falcons in 1972-73 (Garrett and Mitchell 1973), and numerous investigators were in the field, much of the time in Peregrine habitat.

In 1975 and 1976, the CDFG again funded statewide Peregrine nesting surveys; these were conducted by C. G. Thelander. Herman generously provided his and Bond's Peregrine nesting data so that the same sites could be sampled. By this time, over 200 historical nesting locations were documented. Thelander visited 147 known or potential nesting cliffs throughout California. Meanwhile, numerous other field biologists were searching for Peregrines and other raptors, particularly California Condors, Prairie Falcons, and Golden Eagles, all of which are cliff nesters sympatric with Peregrines. Their findings relating to Peregrines combined with Thelander's survey results were reported in Thelander (1976). Thelander (1977) summarized the historical and current nesting status of Peregrines in California. The Peregrine's decline was well-documented, and management strategies were being developed in California.

During 1970-80, state and federal resource agencies became increasingly interested in finding Peregrines nesting on public lands. The U. S. Forest Service (USFS), the Bureau of Land Management (BLM), and the U. S. Fish and Wildlife Service (USFWS) took an active role, under the mandate of the federal Endangered Species Act of 1973, in attempting to survey all public lands for nesting Peregrines. This resulted in more areas being surveyed each year, some of which had never been searched for Peregrines. Numerous researchers participated and a wide range of methods was employed. Standardization was not maintained, and observer reliability varied. The most significant organized survey efforts in recent years include: Boyce and White (1979), a ground and helicopter survey of Peregrine nesting habitat in Six Rivers and Klamath national forests of northwestern California; Thelander and Walton (1980), a ground and helicopter survey of Angeles, Los Padres, and San Bernardino national forests in central and southern California; the USFWS's Peregrine nest site surveillance program (Monk 1981, Monk and Harlow 1984); a variety of extensive field surveys for nesting sites as part of The Peregrine Fund's nest site manipulation and hacking program under the direction of B. Walton; surveys of Yosemite National Park and adjacent areas by the National Parks Service (Asay and Davis 1984); and a ground and helicopter survey of the BLM's Ukiah District (Monk 1979). The latter survey has continued each year since 1979. It is this region of the state that supports over two-thirds of the active nesting sites (Monk 1980, 1981, Kirven 1982, 1983, 1984, 1985, 1986).

Before 1975, there were no organized surveys of potential Peregrine nest sites in Oregon or Washington. Efforts in Oregon began in 1980 with an extensive field survey of selected areas (Boyce and White 1980, Henny and Nelson 1981, Collins unpubl. report). In Washington, C. Anderson, J. Fackler, and S. G. Herman began to organize and conduct annual Peregrine nesting surveys in the late 1970s, in conjunction with F. Dobler of the Washington Game Department. The five historical nesting sites in Nevada were believed to have been inactive during this entire period and probably for many years prior.

The primary objectives of all of these efforts and those of numerous independent investigators have been to locate active Peregrine nesting cliffs and to quantify productivity to the fullest extent possible. These findings are summarized here. To prepare this summary, we either contacted local experts familiar with the current status of Peregrines in each region, or we reviewed their published findings. The primary contributors are listed in alphabetical order with each regional report.

REGIONAL SUMMARIES

NORTHERN COASTAL RANGES OF CALIFORNIA
M. Kirven, G. Monk, B. Walton

Prior to 1980, little was known about Peregrines in this region. It is mountainous, rugged terrain with relatively limited access. It contains many major river drainages and hundreds of suitable cliff formations. Earlier studies (Herman et al. 1970, Herman 1971, Thelander 1976, 1977) recognized the potential for a large number of pairs but fewer than 10 active sites were found. No doubt others existed, considering the relatively small area of coverage; however, the apparent increase in nest site occupancy from the early 1970s to the mid-1980s was not monitored adequately. The extent to which this region supported a remnant breeding population during the peak of the Peregrine decline will never be known.

From 1980 to the present, the region has been the subject of intensive surveys, mostly by helicopter, of a large percentage of all suitable nesting areas. Net productivity (young produced per pair) was remarkably consistent over the past seven years of study (Kirven 1986). Overall, reproductive output is within the range considered normal for the species in northern temperate regions (1.5 young per breeding pair, Ratcliffe 1980).

Despite these data indicating an apparent recovery, two indices of the population's health are not entirely positive: (1) eggshell thinning continues to average 16% below normal for this region, and (2) the adults failed to hatch their eggs at approximately 30% of the active sites in 1986 (n=53).

Given the apparent increase in the region's number of known breeding pairs and their productivity at near-normal levels, we conclude that this population is in the process of recovery and expansion. This process remains somewhat inhibited, however, by the effects of DDE-induced eggshell thinning. Before this population can be considered recovered and stable, more data are needed on DDE residue levels and their relationship to productivity.

NORTHERN COASTAL CALIFORNIA
B. Walton

Historical records indicate over 30 coastal or insular Peregrine nesting locations from San Francisco to Oregon (Thelander 1977). Despite several intensive surveys in recent years, there are no known nesting attempts (and less than three rumored attempts) since 1971 directly associated with this coastline or its offshore rocks. This is somewhat alarming since the adjacent northern Coast Ranges support the largest number of pairs in the western United States and about 67% of California's nesting Peregrines.

CENTRAL COASTAL AND INTERIOR CALIFORNIA
B. Walton and L. Aulman

The central coastal region contains approximately 65 historical nesting locations. It has a long history of Peregrine activity well-documented by egg collectors and other observers. Intensive surveys since the mid-1970s have resulted in one of the best records of Peregrine nesting attempts, productivity, and eggshell thinning data ever collected (L. Kiff pers. comm.). A single pair of Peregrines persisted at Morro Rock, San Luis Obispo County, through the 1960s and 1970s. Regular management of this failing nesting site permitted young to fledge. As a few additional sites were located, these too were augmented with young. Slowly, new pairs began to appear at previously vacated sites, especially along the Monterey County coastline (Big Sur). By the early 1980s, Peregrine pairs reached nearly historical densities in some areas. Throughout this period, intensive manipulations of eggs and young were conducted to ensure that young fledged from each site each year (Walton and Thelander Chapter 55).

At present, 12 pairs of Peregrines continue to occupy coastal or offshore rock nest sites despite excessive eggshell thinning. Each year, all eggs laid are collected, replaced temporarily with dummy eggs, and hatched at The Peregrine Fund. The young are then replaced into nests throughout the region. Given the abnormally thin eggshells, it is only through artificial means that this population has expanded to nearly historical numbers and persisted.

Peregrines nest in California's interior regions mainly in the river canyons of the Sierra Nevada and Cascade Mountains. Although these regions are poorly surveyed, it is generally believed that nesting densities are relatively low and have always been so. Fewer than six active sites are presently known in montane California. There are at least two pairs in Yosemite National Park.

SOUTHERN CALIFORNIA AND THE CHANNEL ISLANDS
L. Kiff and B. Walton

Peregrines nesting in the southern part of the state (San Diego to Santa Barbara) were nearly or completely extirpated by the mid-1950s (C. Thelander unpubl. data). The species also disappeared from the California Channel Islands, which had once supported 20-30 pairs, by the end of the 1950s (Kiff 1980). Anecdotal accounts by falconers and egg collectors of Peregrine nesting attempts during the late 1940s and early 1950s indicate that the same sorts of reproductive failure, especially egg breakage, occurred there as in the eastern United States (Thelander 1977, Kiff 1980). In fact, Peakall (1974) demonstrated the presence of DDE in museum eggshells of California Peregrines as early as 1948 and in amounts sufficient to account for the observed eggshell thinning in southern California Peregrine eggs measured by Anderson and Hickey (1972).

Fewer than five pairs of Peregrines presently nest in the region. At least two pairs, possibly three, are nesting on large buildings and bridges in the Los Angeles basin. At present, there are no verified active nesting sites on the Channel Islands, though adults are seen more frequently than in past years. Peregrine releases on Santa Catalina and San Miguel islands should yield results in the coming years.

OREGON
D. Fenske and L. Kiff

The historical status of Peregrines in Oregon is unclear. Gabrielson and Jewett (1940) considered it a comparatively rare bird in Oregon, and they knew of only one nesting pair in the state after 1920. No Peregrine egg sets are known to have been taken by collectors, a further indication of the scarcity of the species (L. Kiff pers. comm.).

Henny and Nelson (1981) made a detailed analysis of historical Peregrine sites in Oregon, and they concluded that there was a minimum of 39 pairs in the 1930s. By 1973 there were only 4-5 pairs suspected along the coast and three additional pairs suspected in the eastern part of the state (Craighead et al. *in* Fyfe et al. 1976a). Henny and Nelson (1981) found evidence that most of the abandoned sites were last occupied in the 1950s. D. Fenske recently completed reports that show over 70 historical nest sites in Oregon.

In 1978-79 field surveys, one known breeding pair and a single adult were located (Henny and Nelson 1981). Although the pair produced two young, an unhatched egg from the nest contained 19 ppm DDE (wet wt) and was 19% thinner than normal. By 1980, only this single pair was known.

A portion of the historical decline was attributed to climatic changes, especially those in the drier parts of the state (Nelson 1969a). However, the major loss of birds occurred during the 1950s, or later, and was presumably associated with DDT use (Henny and Nelson 1981).

Following a period of several years without any known Peregrines nesting in Oregon, a recovery seems to be under way. In 1986, D. Fenske found two breeding pairs in south-central Oregon. Four other pairs are known in the state.

WASHINGTON
C. Anderson, F. Dobler, and S. Herman

Historical data on Peregrine Falcons nesting in Washington prior to 1970 are limited to 14 sites. Craighead et al. (*in* Fyfe et al. 1976a) reported two possible active sites in 1975, but these were never verified. A survey of the 14 historical eyries by C. Anderson and J. Fackler in 1976 revealed no active historical nests, although one new active one was found (E-1). A survey in 1980 by F. Dobler and R. Spencer (Washington Department of Game) revealed a second active site (E-2). Since 1981, five historical sites (H-1 through H-5) have been reoccupied and are producing young irregularly. Significant eggshell thinning (16.3%) is still occurring in the Washington population and is probably contributing to some reproductive failure (F. Dobler and S. Sumida unpubl. ms.)

The first active site in the Cascade Mountains (E-3) was reported by a local falconer in 1982. In 1983, E. Cummins found another site (E-4). K. Franklin and J. McNutt, surveying with an ultralight aircraft, discovered two additional eyries in the Cascades (E-5, E-6).

Productivity among several of these pairs has been irregular. Some sites have reportedly been active only a single year. In 1985, only seven young are known to have fledged from three nest sites in Washington. Pairs of adult Peregrines were present at three other eyries. Large areas of suitable habitat remain unsurveyed.

NEVADA
G. Herron and R. Oakleaf

The arid lands of this Great Basin state are more apt to support Prairie Falcons than Peregrines. The five historical Peregrine nesting locations documented for the region are associated with large bodies of water (of which there are few). Lake Tahoe, a shared border with California in the Sierra Nevada, supported up to two pairs in the same year prior to the 1950s. An island in Pyramid Lake, the terminus of the Truckee River, supported a pair in the late 1800s, but there is no evidence of use in recent times.

Nevada's first (and only) active Peregrine nest site in recent years was found in 1985 along the Colorado River. This site is near an artificial reservoir created for flood-control. Its historical use by Peregrines is unknown.

In the few regions of Nevada where suitable prey populations and nesting habitat exist, Peregrine release efforts are under way (see Walton and Thelander Chapter 55).

CONCLUSIONS

The reproductive output and occupancy of nesting cliffs are generally accepted, basic indices of the health of a Peregrine population. In the 1980s, these two measures indicate that the population has partially recovered from the unprecedented lows of the 1950s that warned of the species' possible extinction. It appears that there has not been a significant geographical shift in the relative numbers of nesting Peregrines throughout this four-state region: California by far has the largest nesting population. Oregon and Washington probably always supported relatively lower nesting densities (Bond 1946), and the vast majority of Nevada is marginal habitat for the species. The reasons for the difference in nesting density between California and Oregon or Washington are not clear, despite many habitat similarities within significant portions of the three Pacific states.

The recent increase in the number of known active Peregrine nest sites within California is, in part, the result of increased efforts to find them. In 1970, Herman reported fewer than five active nesting sites; today there are over 80. Of the 200 historical nest sites known to Bond and more recent researchers, only about 35 have been reoccupied. Many seemingly suitable sites remain vacant, and the process of population expansion has been very slow. The most rapid recovery has been in those areas with a nucleus of breeding pairs fledging young, either naturally or by management efforts, for several successive years.

Nesting Peregrines in southern California (south of Point Conception) and on the Channel Islands number fewer than five pairs. Three of these are in urban areas, the result of release programs. Historically, this region probably supported over 40 pairs. Major habitat changes, namely urbanization, have radically altered the mainland from Santa Barbara to San Diego. While it is unlikely that most historical nesting sites remain suitable for Peregrines, some continued expansion into urban habitats is expected in the coming years. The Channel Islands remain relatively undisturbed and seemingly suitable. The recent increase in numbers of Peregrine sightings, and recent release efforts on Santa Catalina and San Miguel islands, indicate that the first breeding attempt on the Channel Islands in more than 25 years is forthcoming.

The largest increases in nesting density have occurred in the northern Coast Ranges and central coastal regions of the state. It is in these regions that the greatest amount of management activity has occurred through manipulations of eggs and young. The results of these management efforts are no doubt a major factor in the Peregrine's rapid recovery. One or both adults at nearly 50% of the known nesting sites passed through The Peregrine Fund facility at Santa Cruz either as eggs or young, as indicated by their blue anodized USFWS bands.

Many questions remain about the Peregrine's historical (pre-1945) status in comparison to the present. Clearly, nest site occupancy has increased and observations during the nonbreeding season are more regularly reported. However, Peregrine eggshell thinning continues at critical or near-critical levels throughout California. Peregrines nesting in the central coastal region are unable to hatch their eggs owing to excessive eggshell thinning and embryo deaths. A relatively large percentage of the dense population in the northern Coast Ranges fails to hatch eggs each year. There are no Peregrines nesting in vast portions of their historical range.

In Washington, there is little indication that the number of breeding Peregrines is increasing. While a few new pairs have been found in recent years, the paucity of comparative historical data or regular and systematic surveys make it difficult to assess the situation. This is also true of Oregon. However, recent and limited field efforts there have revealed several previously unknown pairs. Researchers there are optimistic that densities similar to those in adjacent northern California will be found as more intensive surveys are conducted in the coming years (D. Fenske pers. comm.). In Nevada, it is hoped that Peregrine release efforts will increase the number of nesting pairs. A natural expansion into this region, believed to support a very low density of pairs (Bond 1946), should not be expected to occur rapidly or in significant numbers.

For the four states in question, the absolute number of Peregrine pairs is encouraging and should, based on recent trends, continue to increase in the coming years. The ability of this region's Peregrines to sustain a normal reproductive output, however, remains in question. It appears that many pairs are able to fledge suitable numbers of young to sustain some population growth, but the primary cause of the decline, DDE-induced reproductive failure, is still expressed by a significant portion of the Peregrine population. As the eggshell thinning data indicate that the majority of pairs remain near the threshold at which reproductive failures could once again depress the population, it is certainly premature to declare Peregrines recovered or nonendangered in this region.

ACKNOWLEDGEMENTS

We thank each of the regional contributors, who are truly colleagues in the finest sense of the word, for communicating over the years on a topic of common interest. There are literally hundreds of people regularly contributing bits and pieces to the puzzle. We are reminded of the comprehensive list of cooperators D. A. Ratcliffe acknowledged in his publications of the landmark surveys of the Great Britain in the early 1960s. Unfortunately, we cannot meet that standard. But there are several people who over the years have played one or more extraordinary roles in this region. These people cannot go unmentioned: M. Felton, K. Stolzenburg, R. Roy Ramey III, J. Linthicum, C. Himmelwright, L. Aulman, and D. Boyce, Jr. Also, we thank the personnel of the various state and federal resource management agencies who have cooperated with and encouraged Peregrine research.

15 | Status and Reproductive Performance of Marine Peregrines in Baja California and the Gulf of California, Mexico

Richard D. Porter, M. Alan Jenkins,
Monte N. Kirven, Daniel W. Anderson,
and James O. Keith

This report updates the paper by Banks (1969) on Peregrines in Baja California and the Gulf of California presented at the Madison Conference in 1965. It embraces research undertaken in the region since 1965, including the current population and reproductive status of the species in the area covered by Banks (1969) and Anderson (1976), and on islands off the states of Sonora, Sinaloa, and Nayarit (including the Revillagigedo Islands, where nesting is suspected). It also includes pre-1967 data not given by Banks.

FIELD SURVEYS

Banks' report contained data collected from other observers or incidental to other research in the region. It was the first detailed account of Peregrines in the Baja California region, and stimulated several of us to investigate Peregrines there.

M. Kirven first surveyed the area extensively for Peregrines from 1966-71, covering nearly all of the historical nesting localities on both sides of the Baja peninsula and on the offshore islands. He discovered 15 previously unknown occupied territories in the Gulf of California, and monitored eyries there from 1966-71. Kirven showed the locations of these eyries to D. Anderson and J. Keith in 1971. The middle area of the Gulf of California was surveyed by Anderson (1976) and Keith irregularly from 1971-82, in conjunction with their studies of the Brown Pelican; two new occupied territories were located. Porter, Jenkins, C. Stone, E. Boeker, and others surveyed the area from 1976-84. They checked most of the historical Baja peninsula sites, inland eyrie locations and historical eyries in the middle region of the Gulf of California, but not all of the islands on the western side of the Baja peninsula. In 1976-80 they surveyed over 16,500 km of insular, mainland, and Baja peninsular shorelines along the Gulf of California, from the tip of the Baja peninsula to latitude 30°N, plus several islands in the Pacific. In 1981 Jenkins, accompanied by A. DeAnda, R. Graham, R. Ogilvie and J. Swift, checked the middle area of the Gulf of California, and in 1984 he and R. Ogilvie surveyed 40 previously known breeding territories in the Gulf of California from Puerto Peñasco in the north to La Paz in the south. All but three of the 23 breeding territories known before 1966 were checked from 1976-84.

POPULATION ESTIMATES

Pre-1966 Estimates. — Table 1 gives the number of Peregrine territories where eggs or young were recorded for regions of Baja California, 1800-1984. Through 1965, Banks (1969) reported 38 territories at 21 "localities" on the western side of the Baja peninsula and 17 territories at 14 "localities" on the Gulf of California side. He listed 4 suspected territories (where birds were seen but were not known to have nested) on the western side of the Baja peninsula, 4 in the interior and 5 in the Gulf of California. We discovered 12 additional records of territories unknown to Banks (1969), increasing the number known before 1966 to 42 on the western side of the Baja peninsula, 23 in the Gulf of California, and 2 insular sites off the Pacific coastline of mainland Mexico, for a total of 67 nesting territories (Table 1).

Population Decline. — Banks (1969) was unable to describe a decline in the Peregrine population in Baja California because the data were too meager. Kirven's studies revealed that by 1966-71 there were only 2-3 pairs still nesting on the western side of the Baja peninsula and that productivity appeared low in the Gulf of California. This decline in breeding pairs may have been caused by the effects of high levels of organochlorines, as reported for other areas. Anderson (1976) reported that Peregrines on the west coast of Baja California had either declined drastically or disappeared. We found none there in 1976. An aerial survey by Henny and Anderson (pers. comm.) in March 1977 revealed the presence of a Peregrine at only one of the historical nesting sites along the western coast of the Baja peninsula.

Post-1965 Estimates. — Between 1967-71 Kirven recorded 16 eyries in the Gulf of California. Anderson (1976) reported 19 occupied territories in the middle region of the Gulf of California between 1971-75, and believed that 35-50 was a reasonable estimate for the entire Gulf of California. As a result of our surveys, we now know of

TABLE 1. History and geographic distribution of Peregrine Falcon breeding territories in Baja California, the Gulf of California, and adjoining waters.

Region & Period	No. in the period				
	Occupied territories	With eggs or young	With fledged young	Probably occupied	Estimated occupied territories
Baja California					
Western side					
1800-1965	42	26	5	5	47
1966-1984	6	5	2	1	7
1800-1984	45	28	7	6	51
Sierra[a]	0	0	0	0	0
Gulf of California					
1800-1965	16	3	0	4	20
1966-1984	38	24	16	8	46
1800-1984	42	25	16	8	50
Sonora					
Gulf of California					
1800-1965	7	2	0	3	10
1966-1984	13	9	5	4	17
1800-1984	15	10	5	7	22
Sinoloa, Nayarit[b]					
1800-1965	2	2	0	2	4
1966-1984	0	0	0	1	1
1800-1984	2	1	0	2	4
All regions					
1800-1965	67	33	5	14	81
1966-1984	57	38	23	14	71
1800-1984	104	64	28	23	127

[a] Includes mountains of the Baja peninsula; there were sightings at 3 different localities, but all were post-breeding.
[b] Includes the Revillagigedo Islands.

104 sites where Peregrines have nested in our study area from the 1860s to the present; 57 of these were occupied after 1965 (Table 1). From 1965-84, 51 Peregrine breeding territories were occupied in the Gulf of California, but only 6 were occupied on the western side of the Baja peninsula. Nesting Peregrines were suspected at 23 other sites; 14 were prior to 1966 and 14 after 1965 (5 were common to both periods). Their geographic distribution is shown in Table 1.

REPRODUCTIVE PERFORMANCE

Breeding has been verified at 64 of the 104 nesting territories (62%) by the presence of eggs or young in or near the eyrie (Table 1). Eggs, nestlings, or fledged young were recorded at 33 of 67 territories (49%) prior to 1966 and at 38 of 57 territories (67%) in 1966-84. Before

1966, breeding was recorded at 26 of the 42 territories (62%) known on the western side of the Baja peninsula, 5 of 23 (22%) on the Gulf of California side, and 1 of 2 off the coast of Nayarit. Only four territories on the western side of the Baja peninsula and eight on the Gulf of California side were occupied or were suspected to have been occupied during the 1950-65 pesticide period. After 1965, 33 of 51 Gulf of California territories (65%) are known to have produced eggs or young compared with only 5 territories (100%) on the western side of the Baja peninsula. Known fledging occurred at 23 of 57 territories (40%) from 1965-84, but only 5 of 67 sites (7%) prior to 1966 (Table 1). In the Gulf of California, 21 of 51 territories (41%) are known to have fledged young after 1965 (Table 1). Because productivity data were not obtainable for all territories, the breeding data presented here reflect incompleteness rather than actual reproductive success. Although L. Walker (Banks 1969) reported seeing fledged young prior to 1966, he gave no specifics.

Percent Occupancy. — From 1967-71, Kirven made 50 checks to ascertain occupancy at 16 breeding territories in the Gulf of California and found 82% occupied. Anderson (1976) made 40 checks at 12 breeding territories in the middle region of the Gulf of California from 1971-75 and found 77% occupied. The average occupancy rate in the Gulf of California from 1966-84 was 81% (range: 59-100%, Table 2), based on 17 annual surveys of 51 territories. From 318 checks, 193 territorial pairs and 259 occupied territories (pairs plus lone birds) were seen (Table 2). New territories were included in the tally as they were found. In 1976-84, the average annual occupancy was 80% for 51 territories (range: 59-100%). Based on 80-84% occupancy between 1967-84, we expect that 41-43 territories were occupied annually in the Gulf of California.

Territory occupancy in the Gulf of California fell within ranges reported for other regions. In Great Britain, Ratcliffe (1980) reported about 80-85% of territories in most counties were occupied annually. For 39 territories in the Lakeland and northern Pennines districts of Great Britain in 1936-60, Ratcliffe (1980) reported that 28 (72%) were occupied on every visit. The occupancy rate was more variable in the Gulf of California than that reported by Ratcliffe. Although none of the territories in the Gulf of California were visited in all of the 17 years for which we have records, one territory was occupied 14 years out of 16 checked. Another territory was occupied in each of 13 years visited, and two others were occupied all 10 years they were checked. Three others were occupied consecutively for 13, 12 and 10 years.

Laying Dates. — Banks (1969) cited Howell (1917) and Bancroft (1927), who reported that eggs are laid from mid-March to mid-April on the Los Coronados Islands and the middle Baja peninsula,

TABLE 2. History of occupancy and reproduction at Peregrine Falcon breeding territories (BTs) in the Gulf of California, 1966-84.[a]

	Territories					Breeding success					
Year	No. visited	No. with pairs	No. with lone birds	No. newly found	% occupied	No. pairs with eggs	No. of eggs	No. pairs with nestlings	No. of nestlings	No. of BTs with fledglings	No. of fledglings
1966	1	1	0	0	100	nc	nc	nc	nc	0	0
1967	7	4	2	3	86	1	A	0	0	3	3
1968	14	10	1	4	79	1	3	2	2+, 1+	3	3
1969	14	8	4	5	86	2	2+1+	2	4	1	1
1970	13	10	2	3	92	es	es	1	2	0	0[b]
1971	13	6	3	0	69	nc	nc	1	2	2[b]	3[b]
1972	12	5	5	1	83	en	en	nc	nc	1	2+
1973	12	8	2	0	83	nc	nc	nc	nc	0	0
1974	10	4	5	1	90	nc	nc	nc	nc	1	3
1975	8	3	4	0	88	nc	nc	nc	nc	1	2
1976	27	12	4	1	59	1+1ie	2+ie	1[c]	2	5	7
1977	38	20	6	3	68	1	1	1	4[d]	1	1
1978	44	28	13	11	93	1	2	2+1?	3+3?	6	14
1979	4	3	1	0	100	nc	nc	nc	nc	2	4
1980	33	26	3	1	88	4Ay	12Ay	6Ay	13Ay	6	10+yc
1981	28	19	3	0	79	1	2	9	24+	1	3+1?
1984	40	26	8	2	85	5+1Ay	14[e]+1A	9+1[f]	17[f]	6[f]	8

[a] nc = eyrie not checked for eggs or nestlings; A = addled eggs; Ay = addled egg + 1 nestling in an eyrie; ie = infertile egg; en = BT containing eggshell fragments in eyrie; es = BT containing eggshell fragments on ground below an eyrie; eggs were just hatching at 2 other eyries — one had 2 eggs + 1 hatchling, the other 2 eggs + 2 hatchlings; 8 nestlings were removed from 6 eyries for captive breeding project; yc = young calling in 1 eyrie, but not seen.

[b] Natal down found at another site.

[c] Adults carried food to 3 other sites.

[d] One young seen from below at another site.

[e] Includes clutch of 3 addled eggs which contained high mercury content — all failed. Another eyrie contained 3 eggs on 4 May and 2 young + 1 addled egg on 24 May; an adult at an additional eyrie was seen carrying food to eyrie.

[f] At one BT there were 2 well grown young in the eyrie + 1 flying young.

respectively. Banks (1969) reported that sets in which incubation had just begun, all apparently from the Pacific side of the Baja peninsula, were laid 24 March-19 April. Our data indicate laying on the western side of the Baja peninsula as early as the first week of March. McGregor (1899) wrote that six sets of eggs were taken at Natividad Island the first week of March, confirmed by Beck (1899). McGregor also reported eggs on San Gerónimo Island in the middle of March, and E. Sechrist collected four eggs there (now in the Western Foundation of Vertebrate Zoology) with little incubation on 12 March 1917. A. Anthony collected a 4- or 5-day-old chick on one of the San Benito Islands on 31 March 1897 (K. Parkes and C. M. White pers. comm.); the egg would have been laid about 18 February, the earliest known laying date for the western side of the Baja peninsula. We have only two recent observations on laying dates for the western side. Four eggs were found in an island eyrie off the southern coast of the Baja peninsula. The first hatched about 31 March (B. Reitherman pers. comm.). At a centrally located eyrie on the western coast, a single 17-day-old nestling found on 6 May 1980 is consistent with laying in the middle of March. First-clutches on the western side of the Baja peninsula appeared from about the third week of February through the third week of April and peaked in mid-March.

Only four egg sets are known from the Gulf of California, all collected by Bancroft and now in the collection at the Western Foundation of Vertebrate Zoology. They were collected on 14 April 1925, 18-19 March 1928, and 24 March 1930; the latter two had been incubated a week or less. We found that laying began in the Gulf of California in the first half of February and ended in the first half of April, with the peak in the first two weeks in March. The mean estimated laying date of 30 pre-1947 clutches from North American museums (see Anderson and Hickey 1972) is 17 March ±4 days. Thus, there are no apparent differences between current and historical egg-laying dates on either side of the Baja peninsula.

Clutch Size. — Table 3 compares the size of clutches from California (Thelander 1977) with those from Baja California including those reported by Bond (1946) and Banks (1969). Clutches reported by Bond (1946) averaged 3.30 eggs (n=23), all presumably collected in Baja California. Banks (1969) reported an average clutch size of 3.53 (n=19) in Baja California prior to 1966; two clutches were from an eyrie in the Gulf of California and the remainder from the Pacific coastal areas of northern Baja California.

We have records for 39 first-clutch sets collected from eyries in Baja California between 1897-1941, probably including those reported by Bond and Banks. All but one (collected on 30 April) were taken prior to 21 April. Four sets came from the Gulf of California and a fifth

TABLE 3.   Clutch size comparisons between Baja California, Mexico and California, 1800-1965.

Geographic area	n	1 egg		2 eggs		3 eggs		4 eggs		5 eggs		Mean ± S.E.
		No. of clutches	% of clutches	No. of clutches	% of clutches	No. of clutches	% of clutches	No. of clutches	% of clutches	No. of clutches	% of clutches	
California [a]												
Central coast	93	0	0	3	3	20	22	68	73	2	2	3.74 ± 0.057
Southern	152	0	0	7	5	55	36	89	59	1	1	3.55 ± 0.048
Baja California												
Bond (1946)	23	1	4	3	13	8	35	10	43	1	4	3.30 ± 0.193
Banks (1969)	19	0	0	3	16	3	16	13	68	0	0	3.53 ± 0.177
Baja California [b]												
All clutches	39	0	0	9	23	11	28	18	46	1	3	3.28 ± 0.137
Incub. < 50% [c]	17	0	0	2	12	3	18	12	71	0	0	3.59 ± 0.173
Incub. > 50% [c]	14	0	0	5	36	4	29	5	36	0	0	3.00 ± 0.234

[a] Thelander (1977).
[b] Porter et al. (unpubl. ms.)
[c] These clutches came from the 39 given above; the extent of incubation for the remaining 8 was not given by the collector; those incubated >50% were significantly larger than those incubated <50% ($P<0.05$, $T=2.02$, $df=26$).

from Isabela Island, off the Nayarit coast. The remaining sets came from the western side of the Baja peninsula. The mean clutch size was 3.59 for the fresher 17 egg sets (Table 3). This is comparable to the mean sizes of fresh egg sets reported for Baja California by Banks (1969) and for southern California by Thelander (1977) (Table 3).

A mean of 2.64 eggs per clutch was determined for 14 clutches (exclusive of one-egg clutches) seen in eyries in the Gulf of California from 1967-84 (Table 4). This average is considerably smaller than that of the pre-1967 clutches, but was probably caused by loss of eggs preceding observations, and in some cases by egg loss resulting from contamination. The presence of four eggs at several eyries where laying was typically later supports this hypothesis.

Four probable second clutches, including three collected between 9-21 May 1920 and one taken on 29 April 1923 from localities on the northern Pacific coastline of Baja California, contained a mean of 3.75 eggs. Egg sets had been taken from each of these territories earlier in the season.

Bancroft (1927) believed three eggs were laid more often than four by Baja California Peregrines. Banks (1969), however, reported that most of the 19 records he examined were four-egg sets (Table 3). Our

TABLE 4. Clutch, brood and fledgling frequency distribution, percentages and averages for Peregrine Falcons in the Gulf of California, 1967-84.

| | Clutch or Brood Size | | | | | | | | |
| | 1 | | 2 | | 3 | | 4 | | |
	No. of eyries	% of eyries	No. of eyries	% of eyries	No. of eyries	% of eyries	No. of eyries	% of eyries	Mean ± S.E.
Clutches									
1967-75	2	50.0	1	25.0	1	25.0	0	0	1.75 ± 0.479
1976-84	1	7.7	7	53.8	2	15.4	3	23.1	2.54 ± 0.268
1967-84	3	17.6	8	47.1	3	17.6	3	17.6	2.35 ± 0.242
Nestlings									
1967-75	2	33.3	3	50.0	1	16.7	0	0	1.83 ± 0.307
1976-84	9	31.0	10	34.5	6	20.7	4	13.8	2.17 ± 0.193
1967-84	11	31.4	13	37.1	7	20.0	4	11.4	2.11 ± 0.168
Fledglings									
1967-75	9	69.2	3	23.1	1	7.7	0	0	1.38 ± 0.180
1976-84	12	44.4	11	40.7	3	11.1	1	3.7	1.74 ± 0.156
1967-84	21	52.5	14	35.0	4	10.0	1	2.5	1.63 ± 0.122
All young									
1967-75	11	57.9	6	31.6	2	10.5	0	0	1.53 ± 0.160
1976-84	21	37.5	21	37.5	9	16.1	5	8.9	1.96 ± 0.127
1967-84	32	42.7	27	36.0	11	14.7	5	6.7	1.85 ± 0.105

data support Banks (1969). N. Carpenter told Bond (1946) that sets of two eggs were more frequent in Baja California ($n=39$) than they were in California ($n=245$), and our data also support this conclusion ($P<0.001$, $X^2=93.4$, $df=4$) (Table 3). Among fresh clutches from southern California, 5% were two-egg sets ($n=152$) compared with 12% for two-egg sets among clutches less than 50% incubated ($n=17$) from Baja California ($P<0.001$, $X^2=23.9$, $df=4$), and 36% among those more than 50% incubated. The percentage of four-egg clutches appears to be lower in Baja California than in California (Table 3), possibly a result of the latitudinal phenomenon but more likely caused by the difficulties encountered in collecting before incubation or during early incubation at the more inaccessible Baja California eyries.

Nestlings and Fledglings. — Peregrine productivity in the Gulf of California remained relatively stable from 1976-84 (Table 2). There is an indication that the average number of young reared by successful pairs at Gulf of California eyries was greater during 1976-84 (nestlings 2.17, fledglings 1.74) than it was from 1967-75 (nestlings 1.83, fledglings 1.38), but the differences were not statistically significant (Table 4). The mean difference for all young, however, was significant ($P<0.05$, $t=2.14$, $df=69$) between 1967-75 and 1976-84 (Table 4). Because we were unable to see all of the young at some of the sites, our counts underestimate the actual numbers of young, especially the fledglings. Based on the data available to us, reproductively successful Peregrines in the Gulf of California during the past two decades reared fewer young, on the average, than did Peregrines in the arctic, where Cade (1960) reported an average of 2.45 young (75 broods) and 2.18 fledglings (28 eyries), or Peregrines on Langara Island, Canada, where Beebe (1960) reported an average of 2.78 nestlings (9 eyries) and 2.36 fledglings (25 eyries). The smaller broods of successful nests currently recorded in the Gulf of California may be influenced, in part, by normally smaller clutches, but the inimical effects of chemical pollutants at a few local eyries may also play a role.

On the western side of the Baja peninsula, observations of young at nests have been few. R. DeLong and R. Crossin (unpubl. ms.) saw four Peregrines, two of which were probably fledglings, calling and circling at an historical site on 24 June 1968, and Kirven found two nestlings there in 1971. We saw one nestling at a second historical locality in 1980, R. Wauer (unpubl. ms.) noted two fledglings at a third in 1979, and B. Reitherman (pers. comm.) found a new site in 1981 that fledged two young both in 1981 and 1982.

CONCLUSIONS

A small remnant breeding population is extant on the western side of the Baja peninsula. Not only are most historically known nesting localities in the Gulf of California still occupied, but additional localities and eyries have been discovered. However, because the Gulf of California was never thoroughly surveyed prior to the present study, a comparison between past and present populations is not meaningful. In the Gulf of California, rate of occupancy was normal for breeding territories, but productivity was somewhat less than normal. Although the Gulf of California environment is relatively uncontaminated, low productivity at a few eyries may have been caused by high levels of pollutants acquired from resident storm-petrels (Porter and Jenkins Chapter 40) and migrant prey species.

ACKNOWLEDGEMENTS

We thank R. S. Crossin, R. L. DeLong, and R. H. Wauer for use of their unpublished manuscripts, and B. Reitherman for use of his data. We thank the following individuals and institutions for their contributions: E. Boeker, E. Harrison, L. Kiff, G. Knoder, E. Stahr, C. Stone, the Dirección General de la Fauna Silvestre de México, the U. S. Fish and Wildlife Service (which sponsored the project) including the Denver and Patuxent Wildlife Research Centers, the National Audubon Society, and the Western Foundation of Vertebrate Zoology. We also thank the many other contributors too numerous to mention here.

16 | *Nesting Peregrines in Texas and Northern Mexico*

W. Grainger Hunt, James H. Enderson, Dirk Lanning, Mark A. Hitchcock, and Brenda S. Johnson

When organochlorines were causing the reduction of nesting Peregrines over most of temperate North America, many eyries in the Southwest remained occupied. The eyries may have persisted because (1) much of the region is remote and pastoral so that most eyries are far from pesticide use, and (2) neither Peregrines nor the bulk of their prey leave the breeding areas in winter (Hunt 1977).

This report provides data on eyrie occupancy and productivity of Peregrines in western Texas and northeastern Mexico during surveys conducted from 1973-85. Hunt (1977) reviewed literature on their historical occurrence in this region.

STUDY AREA

Our study area includes the Chihuahuan Desert and its surrounding mountain ranges, principally the Sierra Madre Occidental and Oriental of Mexico (Figure 1). All Texas eyries lie west of the Pecos River. We found Peregrines and Prairie Falcons nesting throughout the region and as far south as Durango and San Luis Potosi in Mexico. We have not surveyed portions of the Chihuahuan Desert in New Mexico and Arizona (see Ellis Chapter 13).

Biotic communities vary with altitude. The low desert is dominated by creosote (*Larea tridentata*) and shrubs such as *Prosopis*, *Acacia* and *Mimosa*. As elevations increase, habitats change to sotol grasslands or short-grass prairies (1100-1400 m above sea level), to juniper-oak associations (1400-1700 m), to pinyon-oak-juniper, and finally to coniferous forests dominated by various pines (*Pinus* spp.) and Douglas fir (*Pseudotsuga menziesii*). Dramatic differences in vegetation depend on slope orientation, and there is an increase in floral and faunal diversity southward in the study area. Webster (1977) found roughly half again as many breeding bird species in the southern Chihuahuan

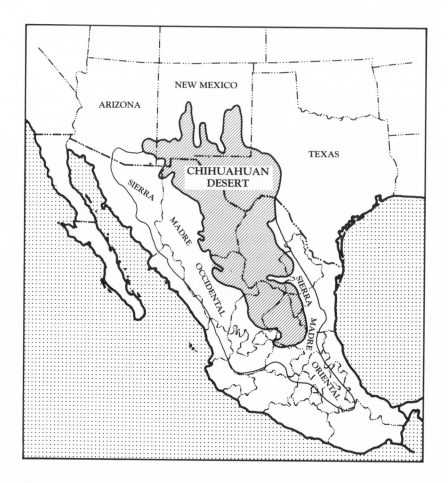

FIGURE 1.   Map of the study area: Chihuahuan Desert and its surrounding mountain
ranges.

Desert compared to the northern. Much of the eastern slope of the
Sierra Madre Oriental has a near-tropical biota. Most of the region is
pastoral and much of it is wilderness, but large irrigated areas of
cotton, sorghum, wheat, orchards, and vegetable farming exist in
western Texas and in the adjacent Mexican states (Hunt 1977).

METHODS

Virtually all data on occupancy and reproduction were obtained
during visits on foot or by boat to territories where we often spent the
night, observing cliffs at dusk and dawn. Many eyries are remote and
only one or two visits per season were possible. Because of the

remoteness and the great sizes of cliffs, we sometimes could only determine a minimum number of young per brood; more young may have been present. Interpretations therefore focus on the presence or absence of broods rather than numbers of fledged young. Methods of prey specimen collection and pesticide analyses are given in Hunt et al. (1986) and Risebrough et al. (1986).

RESULTS AND DISCUSSION

Surveys and Productivity. — During our surveys in Texas and along the Mexican border we found most Peregrines nesting in the Big Bend and Guadalupe Mountains national parks. Seven of 14 territories were along both sides of the Rio Grande river system in Texas and Mexico with the remaining eyries in mountains. One of these was located 16 km from the Rio Grande, but observations suggest that the adults routinely traveled to the river for foraging.

Big Bend has the greatest number of bird species of any national park in the United States (Wauer 1974). Peregrines breeding there and in other parts of the Chihuahuan Desert feed on a large variety of abundant migrant songbirds in April and May. Peregrines throughout the region favor Mourning Doves and other Columbiformes, which we believe are especially vulnerable in xeric conditions where they must go long distances for water.

Territory occupancy and productivity from 1974-85 are shown in Table 1. In 71 nesting attempts for which the presence or absence of broods was determined, 34 (48%) were successful. Of 25 broods with known numbers, 4 had 1 nestling, 9 had 2 nestlings, 10 had 3, and 2 had 4, an average of 2.4 young per successful nest. There was no apparent trend toward improvement in brood size from the 1970s to the 1980s; 1977 and 1978 were the best years when 83% and 75% of the pairs, respectively, produced young.

Hunt reported that Peregrines nesting on the Rio Grande and Rio Conchos rivers from 1973-76 were less successful than mountain eyries elsewhere in the Chihuahuan Desert (Fyfe et al. 1976a). This pattern failed to maintain itself in subsequent years, and overall there was no geographical difference in reproduction.

Three eyries in the Guadalupe Mountains near the Texas-New Mexico border were active in 1975 and 1976. One fledged 14 young in a four-year period through 1978 but failed each year thereafter. The other two territories have been inactive since 1976.

Pesticides in Prey. — Prey available to Peregrines in this region contained DDT residues. A sample of putative prey birds collected by P. Lawson in the Guadalupe Mountains area in 1979 contained significant levels of DDE. A Mourning Dove showed 5.3 ppm (whole

TABLE 1.   Territory occupancy and productivity in nests in Texas and adjacent Mexico.

						Year						
	74	75	76	77	78	79	80	81	82	83	84	85
No. territories visited	4	8	10	9	8	6	5	2	11	8	10	12
No. territories with adult pair	3	7	8	6	6	5	5	2	8	6	7	8
No. territories with lone adult		1	1	1	1					2		1
No. territories with one yearling						1			1	1	1	
No. pairs with young	1	3	4	5	4	3	2		4	1	1	6
No. young per adult pair[a]	0.3	0.9	1.3	2.2	1.7	0.8	0.8		1.1	0.2	0.3	1.5
No. young per pair with young[a]	1.0	2.0	2.5	2.6	2.5	1.3	2.0		2.0	1.0	3.0	2.0

[a] Minimum estimate; ledges not visited.

body, wet wt), a Common Poorwill 3.5 ppm, four Say's Phoebes 7.1 ppm, and a Cassin's Kingbird had 4.6 ppm DDE.

Hunt et al. (1986) reported even higher levels of DDE in farmland songbirds collected in western Texas in 1982-83. The sample pools of 8-10 birds contained some of the highest levels of DDE recorded in North American songbirds, concentrations sufficient to impair Peregrine reproduction and probably also prey reproduction. Red-winged Blackbirds collected in summer at cotton farms near Balmorhea and Pecos, Texas had 74.8 and 60.1 ppm DDE, respectively (whole body, wet wt), and Western Kingbirds from the same localities showed 54.5 and 58.8 ppm. Western Kingbirds at Dell City, Texas, a site probably within the foraging range of Peregrines in the Guadalupe Mountains, had 82.4 ppm DDE. Great-tailed Grackles at four localities in western Texas contained 10.2-24.1 ppm, and a winter (January) sample of this species collected at Balmorhea showed 39.0 ppm DDE, implying a local source. Very low levels in all samples of the parent compound DDT (0.016 ppm and lower) suggest that the pesticide was not recently applied or that the DDE derived from compounds other than DDT (Hunt et al. 1986, Risebrough et al. 1986).

There is some evidence that environmental concentrations of DDE may actually have increased in the late 1970s. The European Starling monitoring program conducted by the U. S. Fish and Wildlife Service (Cain and Bunck 1983) reported the results from six annual collections of 100 pools of 10 individuals per pool. The overall trend for the United States has been one of more or less steady decline in DDE levels. However, at Chaves, New Mexico, not far from the Guadalupe Mountains, DDE concentrations in the pooled samples from 1967-79 were 20.0, 1.5, 3.5, 3.7, 12.0 and 16.0 ppm. This increase was concurrent with eyrie failure and abandonment in the Guadalupe Mountains.

Sierra Madre Occidental. — Hitchcock (1978) found eight occupied territories in the mountains of western Chihuahua and Durango beginning in 1976. Our data include 17 nesting attempts of which 14 (82%) were successful. Nine with known numbers of young averaged 2.1 young per brood.

Agriculture in the region includes cotton and vegetable farming, much of which is in large irrigated areas near the Rio Conchos and Rio Nazas east of the Sierra Madre Occidental on the edge of the desert plateau. There are also dryland corn and wheat monocultures in the large inner valleys of the Sierra Madre. DDT, dieldrin, toxaphene, endrin, aldrin and heptachlor were still being used in the Rio Conchos and Rio Nazas irrigation districts in 1978. Individual Great-tailed Grackles collected in these areas contained 68.0, 46.0, 23.0, 2.9, and 0.9 ppm DDE (whole body, wet wt). There is thus a real threat of

TABLE 2.   Territory occupancy and productivity in the Sierra Madre Occidental and
Sierra Madre Oriental, Mexico.

	1975	1976	1977	1978	1979	1982
No. territories studied	5	12	17	16	4	17
No. territories with adult pair	3	9	11	10	3	10
No. territories with lone adult				2	2	
No. territories with						
one yearling	1	2	2	1	1	3
No. pairs with young	3	7	6[a]	7	1	5
No. young per adult pair[b]	1.7	1.6	1.4[a]	1.2	0.7	0.9
No. young per pair						
with young[b]	1.7	2.0	2.5	1.7	2.0	1.8

[a] Includes 3 young where one parent was a yearling female.
[b] Minimum estimate; ledges not visited.

pesticide contamination to Peregrines that might forage in these regions.

Sierra Madre Oriental. — We found Peregrines nesting at 10 territories in the Sierra Madre Oriental. Six pairs were located within a 12 km radius, apparently the highest known density of nesting Peregrines south of Canada. These six pairs in 1977 were spaced 4.2-8.1 km apart ($\bar{x}$=5.8 km) (Lanning et al. 1985).

Productivity during five nesting seasons in the Sierra Madre Oriental was lower than that in the Occidental. There were 17 broods from 26 nesting attempts by adult pairs (65%) and an additional 8 cases where adult males were paired with yearling females, none of which were known to be successful. About 50% of all attempts were successful. An average of 1.8 young was obtained from six successful nests where exact brood counts were made.

Almost 25% of the pairs in our Sierra Madre Oriental sample consisted of adult males and yearling females, suggesting recent poor productivity. Healthy Peregrine populations contain a substantial proportion of nonbreeding adults that replace those lost (Hunt Chapter 63). Our data suggest that adult females are less numerous than males with territories, and that there are few potential replacements for losses in the breeding population.

DDE levels were present but not exceptionally high in 18 potential prey species collected in the region of high Peregrine density (Lanning et al. 1985). Only two species showed over 1 ppm (whole body, wet wt). A White-throated Swift contained 1.4 ppm and a pooled sample of 20 Lump-nosed Bats (*Plecotus townsendii*) had 5.2 ppm. Both species may eat airborne insects over cotton-farming areas to the east and orchards throughout the higher valleys. The bats also contained 0.57 ppm dieldrin, and four Mourning Doves had 0.27 ppm of this compound. As shown in Figure 1, the Sierra Madre Oriental is much narrower than the Sierra Madre Occidental. In the Oriental the Peregrines and their prey are correspondingly closer to lower elevation agricultural areas and pesticide use.

CONCLUSIONS

We have found 32 Peregrine nesting territories occupied by pairs in western Texas and the highlands of Mexico since the mid-1970s. Our most recent surveys showed continued occupancy by pairs at 71% of these territories. Six of eight eyries in Texas found occupied in 1985 contained young. Pairs were seen at 14 sites in Mexico in 1982, but only 5 broods were counted, and at 3 of the eyries there were yearling females paired with adult males. Territory occupancy and productivity for the Sierra Madre Occidental and Oriental are summarized in Table 2. Continuing high levels of DDE in our songbird samples apparently constitute a threat to Peregrine populations in the Chihuahuan Desert.

ACKNOWLEDGEMENTS

We thank R. Wauer, D. Langowski, T. Cade, S. G. Herman, and W. Burnham for advice and encouragement throughout the study. Field workers included J. Bean, S. Belardo, J. Bulger, T. Conner, R. Enderson, M. Fairchild, G. Falxa, M. Foster, F. Fridrikkson, J. Fryxell, D. Gaddis, B. and L. Hill, P. Lawson, T. McEneaney, B. McKinney, J. and M. Morlock, H. Postovit, R. Skaggs, P. Scott, L. Tynan, D. Sharp, C. Vance, V. Wade, D. Whitacre, and S. Williams. S. G. Herman, R. W. Risebrough (The Bodega Bay Institute), D. H. White, R. DeWeese, and the staff of Patuxent Wildlife Research Center performed the pesticide analyses and evaluations.

Research was supported by the U. S. Fish and Wildlife Service, U. S. National Park Service, Texas Parks and Wildlife Department, National Geographic Society, National Audubon Society, U. S. Boundaries and Water Commission, and the Chihuahuan Desert Research Institute. We thank the Dirección General de la Fauna Silvestre de México for its cooperation and support.

Commentary

Changes in the Status of the Peregrine in North America: An Overview

Lloyd F. Kiff

The Peregrine Falcon has become the principal symbol of the "DDT syndrome" in North America since its unprecedented decline after the late 1940s. Never a particularly common species on this continent, it has nevertheless commanded the attention of a broad array of nature enthusiasts. This paper reviews certain now-familiar aspects of the decline of the Peregrine in North America and summarizes current population trends based on studies reported in this volume and elsewhere.

HISTORICAL STATUS

Although the Peregrine was poorly studied in most parts of North America historically, it is clear that its numbers here rarely approached the high densities found in some other parts of the world, especially the British Isles (Ratcliffe 1980). Indeed, the main thread running through the Peregrine accounts in the older regional bird lists is that the species was nowhere considered to be common when compared with other breeding diurnal birds of prey.

The two most important papers on the former status of the Peregrine in temperate North America are those of Hickey (1942) for eastern North America and Bond (1946) for the western United States. Fortuitously, both papers appeared just prior to the advent of synthetic chemicals, and thus provided baseline data on Peregrine populations in the last decade of the pre-pesticide era. Both papers have had a great influence on later Peregrine enthusiasts although the Bond study has remained somewhat enigmatic because of its tantalizing paucity of specific details. Although both researchers may have included a few spurious sites from faulty information provided by their collaborators, the total numbers of Peregrine nesting territories given in these papers are inevitably on the low side because of the lack of rigorous historical survey efforts.

Estimates of the number of known Peregrine nesting territories in various North American regions are shown in Figure 1. It is difficult to compare these figures except in the very broadest sense. Many of the "historical" sites have come to light only in recent years, as researchers trying to reconstruct the former region-by-region status of the species have scoured the Peregrine literature, field notes of long-dead collectors, and specimen records. There have been steady increases in known nesting territories in most regions, reflecting the great recent increases in our knowledge of the Peregrine in every part of the continent.

A detailed examination of each respected expert's estimates for the number of pairs reinforces the impression that the Peregrine was sparsely distributed in North America except on certain Pacific island groups. The highest known densities of breeding Peregrines on the continent have been reported from the Queen Charlotte Islands of British Columbia (Beebe 1960), Natividad Island off southern Baja California (Lamb 1927), and the Los Coronados Islands off northern Baja California (Kiff 1980), all in association with dense colonies of seabirds. On the mainland, Bond (1946) regarded Peregrines as "common" in areas having densities of slightly more than one pair per 2000 sq mi; in much of the western region (especially the Intermountain Zone), he described the bird's density as less than one known pair per 20,000 sq mi! Cade (1960) gave similar figures for Alaska, although the species has traditionally been regarded as common there. In the Arctic, the density of nesting pairs can be quite high locally, as in the Rankin Inlet area (Court et al. Chapter 70). Hickey (1942) could not arrive at such a generalized estimate for eastern North America because of the discontinuity of the Peregrine's distribution in that region, as well as the lack of specific knowledge about it in many areas.

The principal intent in compiling the estimates shown in Figure 1 was to arrive at an approximate estimate of North America's historical "carrying capacity" for Peregrine nesting territories. Taking the highest credible figure for each region as the best available estimate, one arrives at a total of 3875 known and probable Peregrine nesting territories on the continent and its associated islands, including 2275 south of the arctic and subarctic regions. The Peregrine populations in the temperate portions of North America are the best known, and the latter figure is probably fairly accurate. In contrast, the total for arctic and subarctic regions includes only those areas actually investigated, so the total number of confirmed nesting territories, i.e., about 1600, is surely far too low for such a vast region. Over the years, Cade (1960, 1975, 1982) has ventured several estimates of the breeding population in the Arctic (including Greenland, Alaska, Canada) ranging from 1000-

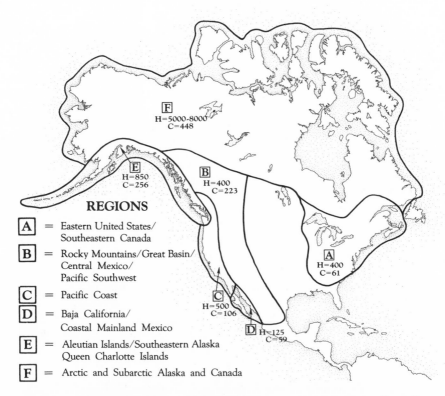

FIGURE 1. Estimated numbers of historical Peregrine nesting territories ("carrying capacity") and current (since 1985) breeding Peregrine pairs in North America. H=historical territories (n=7000-10,000); C=current confirmed pairs (n=1153+).

3500 pairs; Fyfe (1969) offered an estimate of 7548 pairs for northern Canada. More recent figures suggest that the actual number of historical breeding territories is closer to the latter projection, probably falling between 5000-8000 sites for the Alaska-Canada portion of the Arctic. In summary, based on these necessarily broad assumptions, it seems likely that North America supported 7000-10,000 Peregrine nesting territories prior to the modern era. Any estimate of the actual number of pairs of Peregrines extant in a given year depends on the rate of occupancy of available sites in a stable population; this figure is generally accepted to be about 80-90% of the number of available nesting sites in a healthy population (Hickey and Anderson 1969, Ratcliffe 1980).

PERIOD OF DECLINE

There is nothing to suggest that the Peregrine was in a precipitous decline in the early and mid-1940s in North America. Although

Hickey noted that some (10-18%) historical eyries had fallen into disuse for a variety of reasons, he did not apparently regard this as indicative of a major decline in number, although this interpretation has been made by others, including Beebe (1971) and even Berger et al. (1969). Certainly nothing emerged from Hickey's survey that would have predicted the later crash. In fact, Hickey cited numerous instances of rapid replacement of breeding birds or even pairs, suggesting that a healthy floating population of nonbreeding Peregrines existed during that era.

Hickey and Anderson (1969) noted that by 1962 it was rumored that Peregrine productivity was near zero in the northeastern states. Based on general alarm about the welfare of the eastern Peregrine population, Hickey instigated a new study (Berger et al. 1969), which was essentially intended to be a rerun of the earlier survey published in 1942. Not one occupied cliff was reported among 109 historical eyries for which information was obtained. These dramatic results led to the Madison Peregrine Conference in 1965 (Hickey 1969).

Berger et al. (1969) were able to provide little specific information on the dates of the birds' disappearance. It now seems apparent, however, that the decline was under way in many parts of North America by the early 1950s. The actual collapse of the Peregrine population was of an insidious nature, unprecedented in the previous collective experiences of conservationists and not easily recognized as a widespread phenomenon. Furthermore, the actual symptoms of the decline were apparent mostly to those individuals, primarily egg collectors and falconers, least likely to publicize them.

Fortunately, a few dedicated conservationists did carefully record the demise of certain populations. Herbert and Skelton (in Cade 1960) gave a paper in 1953 at the annual meeting of the American Ornithologists' Union (AOU) in Los Angeles referring to the complete reproductive failure of the Hudson River Valley population, formerly one of the healthiest known. (Their report elicited not a single question or comment from the assembled ornithologists!) Along the Hudson River, productivity essentially ceased in 1950, most sites were abandoned by the mid-1950s, and the number of pairs steadily decreased until none were reported by 1961 (Herbert and Herbert 1969). Hagar was noting almost complete reproductive failure of the 14 known Massachusetts pairs at about the same time. In 1965 he summarized as follows: "Sampled reproductive success seemed above normal in 1946, but well below average in 1947 when broken eggs were observed for the first time. By 1951, occupation of the cliffs was spotty, and by 1955-57 only an occasional single bird was left" (Hagar 1969). In Pennsylvania, Rice (1969) felt that a substantial Peregrine population remained in 1946, but productivity declined in the period

1947-52 (from 1.25 young per eyrie to 0.3). At the end of this period only six eyries remained. Low productivity continued, and by 1959 only a single, nonproductive nest was known.

The situation was remarkably similar in many other diverse regions, including southern California, where egg collectors (R. Quigley pers. comm.) and falconers (J. Colton pers. comm.) monitored the gradual loss of many traditional Peregrine eyries in the late 1940s and early 1950s. Successful breeding of the species in this section of the state, once a stronghold, was not verified after the mid-1950s (Herman et al. 1970, Thelander 1977). The once substantial nesting Peregrine population on the adjacent Channel Islands and Los Coronados Islands also became extinct between the mid-1940s and mid-1950s (Kiff 1980). In Alberta, Enderson (1964) concluded that Peregrines last occupied many sites in the 1950s, although a few isolated pairs remained until the late 1960s. R. Stocek (*in* Fyfe et al. 1976a) found that the last report of Peregrine nesting activity in New Brunswick was in 1948, and young were last known to have been produced in Nova Scotia in 1955. Following a more gradual decline in the 1930s and 1940s, the majority of Oregon Peregrine nesting sites were abandoned during the 1950s, although a few persisted through the 1960s and into the 1970s (Henny and Nelson 1981, D. Fenske pers. comm.).

In the more remote Peregrine populations of Alaska and arctic Canada, a decline apparently occurred later, although Ambrose et al. (Chapter 11) suggest that a more gradual decline may have already been under way as early as the 1950s. This matter is now difficult to resolve. The main support for the lack of an earlier decline of major proportions came from the surveys of Enderson and Berger (1968), Enderson et al. (1968), and Cade et al. (1968), which were compared with the earlier data of Cade (1960). However, these authors warned that Peregrines were experiencing major reproductive problems in Alaska and that major population losses could be expected to follow soon. A dramatic collapse did occur in 1970 (Cade et al. 1971) and continued through at least the first half of the decade.

Whatever the specific dates, by the time of the 1965 Madison Conference the Peregrine was essentially extirpated east of the Mississippi in both the United States and Canada south of the boreal forest (Berger et al. 1969), and only 33% of all known eyries in the Rocky Mountains were still occupied (Enderson 1969a).

The actual dimensions of the North American decline were more clearly defined by the findings of subsequent studies which were reported at a follow-up conference held at Cornell University in November 1969. There it was reported that the Peregrine was also gone as a breeding species from the southern part of California and the northern half of Baja California, and major declines had also occurred in other parts of the western United States and in much of southern Canada and even the Northwest Territories. In general, the decline began in more southern regions and spread north in several areas, as documented in California (Herman et al. 1970, Thelander 1977), the upper Mississippi River Valley (Berger and Mueller 1969), Alberta (Fyfe et al. 1976a), and the eastern United States (Berger et al. 1969).

Certain insular Peregrine populations on the Pacific coast of Alaska and Canada evidently remained more or less stable throughout this period. In other areas, e.g., the southwestern United States and mainland Mexico, the historical populations were largely undocumented (and even unsuspected) until after the advent of synthetic chemicals, making it difficult to identify temporally-related trends. However, the fact that certain of these populations have shown marked increases in recent years may be an indication that they are recovering from earlier unrecognized declines.

CAUSES OF DECLINE

In an important "strategy" paper at the outset of the Peregrine management era, Cade (1974) divided the main threats to wildlife, and to birds of prey and the Peregrine in particular, into three categories: (1) "overkill" — direct exploitation or persecution by humans, including shooting, poaching of adults, young and eggs, and poisoning; (2) destruction or degradation of natural habitats; and (3) chemical pollution. Of these, Cade ranked direct killing or molestation by man as the *least* important threat to birds of prey, particularly the Peregrine. He regarded habitat loss as ultimately the most important factor controlling Peregrine populations, and chemical pollution as the most immediately important. The subsequent history of the Peregrine has verified the accuracy of this assessment.

Overkill. — This category includes highly visible mortality factors that have probably existed ever since the Peregrine first came to humanity's attention. There is no evidence to suggest that any such causes were responsible for the rapid decline of the species in the 1950s. While shooting or poaching incidents may be dramatic and deleterious on a local basis, density-independent factors of this type have rarely, if ever, had a significant impact on the overall breeding populations of raptor populations in North America (see also Cade 1968).

Although shooting of all raptors, including the Peregrine, continues in North America to the present time, there is no reason to believe that the intensity of shooting increased dramatically during the late 1940s and 1950s, when the major Peregrine decline occurred. In fact, data based upon banding returns for other diurnal raptors (Henny 1972) suggest that the frequency of shooting of North American raptors probably declined after about 1940. Increased legal protection for such species has presumably contributed to a reduction of shooting (although it has also doubtless reduced the tendency to acknowledge such incidents).

Other traditional mortality factors for the Peregrine include the removal of birds and young for falconry and egg collecting. Hickey (1942), Bond (1946), Banks (1969), Berger et al. (1969), Hickey and Anderson (1969), and Cade (1974) discussed these factors and dismissed the notion that the latter two contributed significantly to the Peregrine's rapid decline in the 1950s. Indeed, at the time of the introduction of DDT in 1947, North American egg collecting was in its twilight years, and falconry was still in its infancy.

Habitat Changes. — Habitat changes are exceedingly important for the Peregrine in the long term. They include those which are human-induced (e.g., the loss of California's wetlands, road building and other construction, shooting, and disturbance from recreational activities) and those which are the result of climatic changes.

Nelson (1969a, Chapter 3) has been the principal proponent of the hypothesis that major habitat changes, primarily a drying effect, caused a general decline of Peregrines in at least the Pacific Northwest and the Great Basin. Beebe (1971) cited such historical declines in southern Alberta and the Okanagan Valley of British Columbia. However, Porter and White (1973) challenged the view that habitat changes were responsible for the Peregrine's decline in Utah; instead they attributed the decline to the use of DDT and other pesticides and to human encroachment on traditional nesting sites and foraging areas.

Habitat changes, from whatever cause, are mediated through changes in food availability, and a general drying effect presumably resulted in a decline of shorebirds, a staple Peregrine food in many regions. Although Peregrine nesting cliffs are still available throughout California, the wetlands that provided foraging habitat for the nesting birds are now gone in many areas.

Nelson (1969a) made the further point that Peregrines (and other species) may have suffered from increased temperatures that have accompanied a general decline in precipitation since the 1870s, especially in western North America. In support of this hypothesis, he contended that Peregrines nesting above 6000 ft (ca. 2000 m) in western North America were managing to survive, but that the birds at lower elevations in xeric habitats had vanished. Nevertheless, the persistence of breeding Peregrines in Arizona, southern Utah, and other hot desert areas at elevations less than 2000 m argues against this point.

Replacement of Peregrines at nest sites by Prairie Falcons has been mentioned for Colorado (Hickey 1942), Alberta (Enderson 1969a),

Utah (Nelson 1969a, Porter and White 1973), the Pacific Northwest (Nelson 1969a), British Columbia (Cowan and Brooks *in* Bond 1946, Brooks *in* Nelson 1969a), and California (Marshall *in* Bond 1946). On the other hand, Phillips et al. (1964) suggested that the Peregrine has increased in Arizona since 1939 at the apparent expense of the Prairie Falcon; there is no reason that both trends could not exist, reflecting differences in local conditions.

It may not be accurate to characterize the shift to Prairie Falcons in some areas as a competitive replacement, as that species is probably merely occupying sites and territories left vacant by Peregrines extirpated for various reasons. Thus, this phenomenon is presumably an effect of other changes, not the cause itself. Thelander (1977) described several instances in central California where both species nested on the same cliff simultaneously. He found that Prairie Falcons nested in the immediate vicinity of at least 12% of the Peregrine nesting locations in the state. Although he gave a number of instances where Prairie Falcons now nest in former Peregrine sites, this replacement is apparently an indication of the Prairie Falcon's ability to fill the void created by the Peregrine's decline. It also probably indicates that the prey base of Prairie Falcons is less contaminated than that of Peregrines, especially considering that Prairie Falcons are apparently more sensitive to DDE than Peregrines (Fyfe et al. Chapter 33)

Beebe (*in* Hickey 1969) suggested that the decline of the Peregrine in the eastern and midwestern United States may have been part of a longterm trend resulting from the demise of the Passenger Pigeon. However, this does not seem sufficient to explain the complete and sudden loss of the Peregrine in the 1950s; nor does it explain the Peregrine's survival at saturation levels in other parts of the northern hemisphere, where food and other conditions are similar to those now existing in the eastern United States, and where a prey base of Passenger Pigeon dimensions is absent.

In summary, as pointed out by Porter and White (1973), Nelson's hypothesis does not answer why the Peregrine declined so abruptly in the late 1940s and early 1950s, but may explain the apparent very gradual population decline in many North American regions owing to pre-pesticide habitat changes, both human-induced and "natural." Environmental "carrying capacity," then, is still the ultimate factor setting the top limit on numbers for any given region.

Chemical Pollution. — Although additional details about the North American decline have emerged since the Madison Conference, no evidence has been forthcoming which suggests that the abrupt crash of the Peregrine in North America resulted from any cause other than chemical contamination, primarily DDE-induced eggshell thinning. Ratcliffe (1967) first recognized a connection between organochlorine pesticides and thinner-shelled eggs, and Hickey and Anderson (1968) related this specifically to DDE in several species, including North American Peregrines. Cade et al. (1971) demonstrated a highly significant negative correlation between eggshell thickness and DDE content in Peregrine eggs, and such a relationship has now been shown for many other Peregrine populations (Peakall and Kiff Chapter 34). Peakall (1974) and Peakall et al. (1976) showed that DDE was present in Peregrine eggs laid shortly after the introduction of DDT in amounts sufficient to explain the eggshell thinning observed in the eggs. Peakall (1976) concluded that 20 ppm DDE wet weight in eggs was correlated with 15-20% eggshell thinning, and a further analysis of various data sets by Peakall and Kiff (Chapter 34) confirms and refines this original estimate. Specifically, Peregrine populations which experience on the average more than 17% eggshell thinning appear invariably to decline. Similarly, no population is known to have increased in numbers until DDE residues in eggs have dropped below an average of 20 ppm wet weight and eggshell thinning has decreased below the 17% threshold.

All Peregrine populations have shown some degree of eggshell thinning during their recent history, although in some areas it has evidently not been severe enough to cause reproductive failure (Peakall and Kiff 1979, Chapter 34). All four Peregrine recovery teams in North America have independently concluded that DDE was the major cause of the declines or extirpations of the species documented in their respective regions.

The evidence that it was DDE, and not dieldrin or other organochlorines, which was responsible for the Peregrine crash in North America (and elsewhere) is discussed at length by Risebrough and Peakall (Section 5 Commentary) and Peakall and Kiff (Chapter 34). Nisbet (Chapter 35) and Newton (Section 8 Commentary), on the other hand, present contrary arguments in favor of a primary role for dieldrin (HEOD) as a mortality factor.

PERIOD OF RECOVERY

Conservation Efforts. — In response to the catastrophic decline of the Peregrine in the 1950s and subsequent documentation of the decline in the 1960s, the races *F. p. anatum* and, later, *F. p. tundrius* were placed on the federal Endangered Species List in 1970. As one way to fulfill its mandate under the Endangered Species Act of 1973, the U. S. Fish and Wildlife Service established a policy to prepare "recovery plans" to assist governmental agencies in protecting and aiding in the recovery of endangered species. Following a 1974 Peregrine conference in Connecticut sponsored by the National Audubon Society (Clement 1974), four recovery teams were named in the

United States to develop regional recovery programs: one for Alaska, one for the eastern states, one for the Rocky Mountain/Southwest region, and the other for west coast populations. Each team has prepared a recovery plan for its respective region.

Captive-releases and direct manipulation of the existing wild populations have been central elements of the recovery efforts in both the United States (particularly the southern states) and Canada. According to Murphy (1987), 710 Peregrines had been released in Canada as of December 1986, but the results were numerically discouraging: only 21 banded birds were known to be occupying territories in 1986. By the summer of 1987, more than 2000 young had been released in the United States, and more than 130 nesting pairs had been reestablished in 20 states (California, Colorado, Delaware, Idaho, Maine, Maryland, Massachusetts, Minnesota, Montana, New Hampshire, New Jersey, New York, North Carolina, Oregon, Pennsylvania, Utah, Vermont, Virginia, Wisconsin, and Wyoming) (T. Cade pers. comm.).

Five-year North American Peregrine Surveys. — A principal recommendation of the 1969 Cornell conference was that a continental survey of North American Peregrine breeding populations should be conducted at five-year intervals, beginning in 1970. The original intent of the surveys was to monitor changes in the population status and reproductive rates of Peregrines. Regrettably, funding limitations and other difficulties prevented the project from being more comprehensive and sustained. However, each of the four survey efforts to date has yielded invaluable information on the Peregrine populations examined. Along with numerous annual surveys conducted by resource agencies in specific regions, they have provided the major bases for the figures and trends summarized in Figures 1 and 2.

1970 Survey. — The 1970 survey documented decimated Peregrine populations throughout North America, and it predicted the possible extirpation of the species on the continent within the decade if the rate of decline was not halted (Cade and Fyfe 1970). Fifteen regions were surveyed, and about 237 known eyries were examined in the ranges of the three subspecies. Only four pairs were found at 82 former *F. p. anatum* eyries in southern Canada, 34 pairs at 64 Canadian and Alaskan *F. p. anatum* taiga eyries, 31 pairs at 53 Alaskan *F. p. tundrius* sites, and 23 pairs at 32 *F. p. pealei* eyries.

1975 Survey. — The 1975 survey involved a check of the species in virtually every part of its North American range. This survey showed a further decline in the North American Peregrine population, particularly in Canada. Specifically, the survey indicated that only 62 occupied eyries of *F. p. anatum* were known in the western United States and Baja California (Fyfe et al. 1976a). The published survey summarized the status of various Canadian populations, and Fyfe

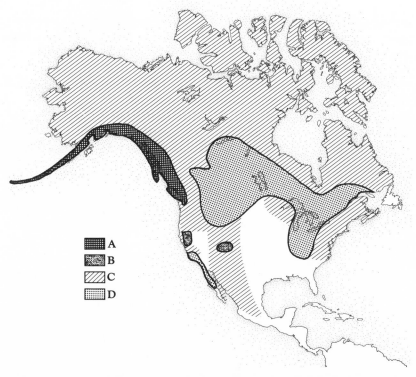

FIGURE 2. Present status of North American Peregrine populations. A=areas where no significant post-DDT decline occurred; B=areas where complete recovery has probably occurred; C=areas where some degree of recovery is underway; D=areas where Peregries are essentially extirpated.

pronounced *F. p. anatum* extinct in eastern Canada (a nesting pair was subsequently discovered in southern Quebec), declining in the prairie provinces, Northwest Territories, and the Yukon, and of unknown status in interior British Columbia. Declines in the populations of *F. p. tundrius* appeared to be accelerating. At that time, only populations of *F. p. pealei* were thought to be stable or in only slight decline. Otherwise, the Peregrine was not recovering anywhere within its North American range. However, it was expected that the populations confined to North America would rebound soon after the banning of DDT in Canada in 1969 and in the United States in 1972.

1980 Survey. — The summary of the 1980 survey was not formally published (C. M. White and R. Fyfe unpubl. ms.). Although the results were made somewhat ambiguous by the severe climatic conditions in the northern regions, this survey revealed a more encouraging picture than the one in 1975. It appeared that a recovery, or at least stabilization, of Peregrine populations had occurred in most parts of North America. The tundra populations, for example, had mostly stabilized, although some further declines were noted, and the boreal forest populations had mostly increased. On the other hand, the situation was still grim in most of southern Canada. The number of known sites in the western United States and adjacent Mexico rose from 62 occupied territories in 1975 to at least 185 in 1980, but most of the increase was probably owing to greater efforts to locate nests, rather than to a major recovery. "Although some populations still carry harmful levels of chlorinated hydrocarbons in their eggs, there appears to have been a major stabilization continent wide, with increases and decreases largely on a local basis" (C. M. White and R. Fyfe unpubl. ms.).

1985-86 Survey. — The results of the 1985-86 survey, which was conducted only in Canada, were even more encouraging (Murphy 1987). In general, the 1985-86 Canadian Peregrine survey showed that Peregrine populations in the Northwest Territories, including both *F. p. tundrius* and *F. p. anatum*, were stable or increasing (Murphy 1987). West coast populations were found to be stable or increasing, and a new high number of nestlings was reported in southern Canada. The survey indicated a continuing recovery, although numbers remained very low in southern Canada. Various ups and downs had occurred on the local level. A total of 18 areas in 7 provinces and the 2 territories were surveyed: 3 in 1985, 13 in 1986, and 2 in both years.

DISCUSSION

The "crash" of North American Peregrine populations was most pronounced during the 1950s, but the decline continued through the 1960s and into the early 1970s in most areas. Cade (1975) speculated that the Peregrine decline in North America bottomed out around 1969-70, but with the perspective of time, it seems to have occurred a bit later, approximately 1973-75, at least in most areas. By the time of the 1975 survey, only 324 nesting pairs of Peregrines could be confirmed in North America (Fyfe et al. 1976a). Since many areas could not be covered, this figure is conservative, but the dimensions of the decline are nevertheless obvious.

It is now apparent that a recovery of the Peregrine has occurred or has been under way in most parts of North America since the late 1970s. In some major areas, however, the species remains essentially extirpated (Figures 1 and 2). Recent (1985 or later) surveys have confirmed the existence of at least 1153 breeding pairs of Peregrines on the continent, and increasing numbers of birds are being reported annually in most regions. Recovery now appears to be complete or nearly so in many arctic and subarctic areas, the Colorado Plateau, and northern California. No populations of the largely sedentary, insular *F. p. pealei* are thought to have suffered significant declines during the post-DDT era. A gradual increase in breeding Peregrines is being documented in the eastern United States, Texas and the Sierra Madre of northern Mexico, Arizona, the Pacific Northwest, and southern Baja California and the Gulf of California region. However, the species is still essentially extirpated in a few arctic (tundra) areas, most of southern Canada, the Rocky Mountains of the northern United States, southern California, and the northern Pacific coast region of Baja California. Recovery has presumably occurred only where DDE residue levels have declined sufficiently to allow for increased recruitment. In fact, a lack of recovery in traditional nesting areas is probably a reliable indicator of still-high DDE levels. Although the incredible persistence of DDE in Peregrines in California and apparently southern Canada remains a vexing and only partially explained problem, it is to be expected that the Peregrine and other species will eventually rebound from DDE pollution. DDT use will almost certainly decrease on a worldwide basis in the future. It is presently used mostly in Third World countries, primarily for malarial control and on cotton. These applications are expected to decline gradually as the compound becomes less effective for agricultural use and as malarial vaccines, now in the experimental stage, are made widely available. Eventually, ambient DDE levels should decline to background noise levels, i.e., to a point where they do not have any particular bearing on the populations of the species affected by eggshell thinning and other aspects of the "DDT syndrome."

On the other hand, certain obvious problems remain. It is of some concern that DDE levels in the birds now recolonizing the eastern United States are so high (Gilroy and Barclay Chapter 39). We still have a very poor understanding of the distribution of DDE and other organochlorines in South America. Presently more disturbing is the high incidence of embryonic deaths from unexplained but presumably biocidal causes in some populations (e.g., in California, B. Walton pers. comm.), because they may be the cause of more reproductive failure than eggshell breakage. This is an area requiring much future work. Nisbet (Chapter 35) calls attention to the continued threat of dieldrin and other cyclodiene pesticides. Where still in use, they may pose a graver danger to birds than DDE. The effects of other classes of pesticides and types of pollutants on Peregrines are still largely uninvestigated.

Until DDE levels do subside in the problem areas, we are involved in a "holding action," marked mainly by intensive captive breeding programs and hands-on management of wild populations. The formidable expense and manpower commitments involved in these efforts

have been criticized by some as being inordinate, artificial, and ultimately doomed to failure (arguments also perennially applied to the
California Condor recovery effort). However, integrated management
efforts have unquestionably been indispensable in maintaining or
reestablishing remnant Peregrine populations in the eastern United
States, eastern Canada, Colorado, and the central coast of California,
as well as in Germany. Captive-releases accounted for 32% of the
Peregrines fledged in Colorado from 1975-85 (Craig et al. Chapter
54). As suggested by Roseneau et al. (*in* C. M. White and R. Fyfe
unpubl. ms.), repopulation of regions where Peregrines persisted
during the crash may occur earlier and more rapidly than repopulation
of regions where Peregrines disappeared entirely. The latter areas and
those where the remnant pairs were widely separated may require
human intervention (see also Ratcliffe 1980), as no unaided (i.e.,
"natural") repopulation has occurred. Thus, it has become clear that
holding on to whatever birds may survive in severely affected areas is
the most important task of all.

Certain major environmental changes that have occurred over the
last few decades in North America, especially major habitat and
climatic changes, make it unlikely that the Peregrine will ever completely regain its historical population densities in some regions.
According to various resource agency estimates, the stretch of California coastline between Morro Bay and the Mexican border has lost
over 95% of its historical wetlands within the past century, and it is
unrealistic to expect Peregrines, which were so closely associated with
the tidal marshes, ever to reoccupy at former levels this now heavily
impacted region. Peregrines formerly occurred in high densities on
Langara Island, British Columbia (Nelson 1976), and on the Los
Coronados Islands off Baja California (Kiff 1980), but the principal
prey, insular seabird colonies, have themselves declined to levels too
low to support large numbers of resident Peregrines.

Inevitably, the relentless growth and concomitant activities of the
human population in many diverse parts of the continent, ranging
from the Hudson River (Herbert and Herbert 1969) to California
(Thelander 1977), Wyoming (Oakleaf and Jenkins *in* C. M. White
and R. Fyfe unpubl. ms.), and even parts of Alaska (Haugh *in* Fyfe et
al. 1976a), have made many former Peregrine nest sites forever
unsuitable, regardless of DDE levels. Habitat changes are equally
important to migratory Peregrines, which spend most of the year on
their migration routes and wintering grounds. Indeed, it is likely that
certain unexplained population fluctuations in arctic and subarctic
Peregrine populations may be the result of deleterious impacts on the
birds in South America (Springer et al. 1984). Ultimately, the quality
of the habitat that we leave for the Peregrine will be the most

important factor controlling its numbers, far more so than the lingering, albeit dramatic, biocidal effects.

The greatest hope for the Peregrine lies in its latent adaptability, as reflected by the great diversity of habitats it occupies even on our single continent. The reoccupancy or fresh occupancy of urban environments by Peregrines in many areas, whether human-aided or spontaneous, is particularly promising. There certainly must be more breeding and wintering Peregrines in North American cities now than historically, possibly reflecting the results of a human-induced form of natural selection, as well as the sheer increase in the area now occupied by urban centers. Hickey and Anderson (1969) summarized the Peregrine's use of artificial structures for nesting around the world, and the list must be much longer now. Virtually every large west coast city now contains Peregrines, at least in the winter months, and most of them have taken up residence there unaided by humans. In Quebec and southern Alberta, the only active nesting sites are in cities (Murphy 1987). It is of interest to recall that Hickey (*in* Clement 1974) suggested that the "Rock Peregrine" of the eastern United States was just beginning to become adapted to city life when it was eliminated by DDT.

Perhaps our own capacity for adaptability can work for the benefit of the Peregrine. In reviewing recent conservation history, one cannot help but marvel with Beebe (1974) and Newton (1976) at the great shift in western society's perception of the Peregrine Falcon. For centuries it was a victim of human persecution, but is now regarded as a virtual media darling in North America. The plight of the species and the ongoing efforts to speed its recovery receive frequent mention in the popular press. Urban releases in North American cities and their attendant publicity have greatly improved the image of the Peregrine and other birds of prey among the population at large.

The Peregrine may ultimately profit as a result of the very adversity it has suffered over the past four decades. It is probable that more money has been spent in the effort to save the Peregrine than on any other endangered species, including even the well-publicized (and oft-criticized) effort on behalf of the California Condor.

SUMMARY

(1) The Peregrine was never particularly common in most parts of North America except on a few Pacific islands where prey species were particularly abundant, and in localized areas of the Arctic.

(2) Although in some regions there was possibly a gradual decline of the species under way in this century owing to habitat changes (both human-induced and natural), a viable Peregrine population existed in North America until the mid-1940s. It is estimated that the continent

contained 7000-10,000 traditional Peregrine nesting territories, of which probably 80-90% were occupied in any given year.

(3) An unprecedented crash of the population, characterized primarily by widespread reproductive failure, followed by the eventual disappearance and nonreplacement of breeding pairs, occurred between the late 1940s and early 1960s in many parts of North America; the Peregrine was completely extirpated as a breeding bird in some major former strongholds. The decline appeared first in the southern parts of the range and moved north. Insular, nonmigratory populations remote from sources of DDT application were least affected. The lowest point in most North American populations was evidently reached by the mid-1970s; by 1975 only 324 nesting pairs of Peregrines could be confirmed on the continent.

(4) Beginning in the late 1970s, recoveries to varying degrees have occurred in many portions of North America, including the arctic and subarctic regions of Alaska and Canada and most of the continental United States and Mexico. Recent surveys have confirmed the existence of at least 1153 breeding pairs on the continent, and many more must exist in unsurveyed portions of Alaska and northern Canada. However, Peregrines are still largely absent from most of Canada south of the boreal forest, the Rocky Mountains of the northern United States, the southern half of California, and the northern Pacific coast of Baja California.

(5) Major trends in Peregrine populations in North America coincide closely with known temporal and geographical patterns of introduction, use, and banning of DDT, respectively. Where the levels of DDE (the metabolite responsible for eggshell thinning) were high, the species vanished or declined greatly. Where they were low, populations remained more or less stable. As DDE levels have subsided in formerly contaminated areas, the species has recovered, aided in many regions by vigorous management and captive breeding programs. Where ambient DDE levels remain high, the species remains in trouble. There seems to be little doubt now that DDE was the principal culprit in causing the decline of the Peregrine in North America. Whether other organochlorines contributed to the decline, and, if so, to what extent, are still unanswered questions (see Nisbet Chapter 35).

(6) As environmental DDE levels eventually drop, the Peregrine can be expected to stabilize in most parts of North America, although at levels generally lower than historical population sizes. The Peregrine should benefit from more enlightened societal attitudes towards raptors, but other factors, especially habitat changes, can be expected to have a largely negative effect on the species throughout the western hemisphere. Nevertheless, there is no reason to believe that we cannot maintain substantial Peregrine populations indefinitely in North America, and widespread utilization of urban nest sites are among the most hopeful signs for the future.

ACKNOWLEDGEMENTS

This manuscript profited greatly from the editorial attentions of D. Arora, C. Thelander, D. Bland, and, especially, T. Cade. R. Ambrose, C. Anderson, D. Bird, C. Bruce, T. Cade, T. Early, D. Ellis, J. Enderson, D. Fenske, J. Hubbard, C. Henny, W. G. Hunt, T. Johnson, R. W. Nelson, R. D. Porter, R. Skaggs, R. Walters, B. Walton, and C. White provided unpublished data on the current status of Peregrine populations in their respective areas. C. White, R. Fyfe, and J. Murphy kindly made the unpublished results of the 1980 and 1985-86 North American Peregrine Surveys available for my use, and I owe a special debt to the army of researchers, technicians, and volunteers who have so effectively monitored Peregrine populations on this continent over the past two decades. J. Fisher, E. Harrison, J. Jennings, J. Kiff, and C. Sumida provided various forms of assistance at the Western Foundation of Vertebrate Zoology, which supported this work.

Commentary

Migration Statistics as Peregrine Population Estimators?

The Editors

Although most estimates of population size of the Peregrine Falcon have been based on breeding season surveys of nesting sites, there has also been some interest in developing estimates based on migration statistics from banding or direct observations on numbers passing through well-known concentration areas (Kruyfhooft 1964, Enderson 1969b). The Atlantic coast of eastern North America, the coastline of the Gulf of Mexico, and the western shoreline of Lake Michigan are three such areas (Ward et al. Chapter 45, Mueller et al. Chapter 46, Hunt Chapter 49). Surveys of nesting populations give accurate data on small samples of the total breeding population, whereas the migration data cover a larger fraction of the total population, but in a less precise manner. The results of the great efforts expended on trapping and banding Peregrines in North America in the last decade, largely owing to the organization and enterprise of F. Prescott Ward and associates, should lend themselves to better estimates of the total size of the northern migratory population (those continental, arctic island, and Greenlandic falcons nesting north of 55°N latitude) than has so far been attempted. This is a problem that ought to challenge the talents of a good biostatistician with a special interest in the Peregrine.

Several students of the Peregrine have broached the subject in the past (Shor 1970a, 1970b, J. L. Ruos unpubl. ms., F. P. Ward unpubl. ms.). For example, there have been attempts to apply the "Lincoln Index" to the banding data. The results of this admittedly crude method of estimating total population from a banded sample have been most thoroughly explored to date by the U. S. Fish and Wildlife Service (USFWS) in its proposal (prepared by J. M. Sheppard) to reclassify *F. p. tundrius* from endangered to threatened (USFWS 1983).

Based on rather small banding and recovery samples for the years 1976-81, the Lincoln Index equation yielded an average of about

13,500 young Peregrines produced in northern North America and Greenland per year. The last three years, represented by larger samples of banded and retrapped Peregrines, averaged more than 20,000 young produced, calculated from the data then available (see Table 1). The Lincoln Index is a crude statistic, and it can be influenced by several kinds of inaccuracies requiring adjustment — for example, the mortality of nestlings before they reach the trapping points in the United States south of Canada might be on the order of 15-20%. Also, a small change in the number of R_2 produces a large change in the calculated value of P.

We have extracted the relevant figures from the computer print-outs of the USFWS Bird Banding Laboratory (with the help of D. Bystrak) and obtained the banding records from the Greenland Peregrine Falcon Survey (W. G. Mattox) for the years of 1982-85, and we also rechecked the numbers for 1980-81 (see Table 1). Note that additional reported recoveries for 1980 and 1981 substantially lower our calculation of P compared to the earlier USFWS report. We expect our

TABLE 1. Lincoln Index figures for migratory Peregrines in the Nearctic.[a]

Year	n_1[b]	n_2[c]	R_2[d]	P[e]
Series A: USFWS (1983)				
1976	23	120	0	2900
1977	88	218	1	9750
1978	71	226	2	5450
1979	148	434	2	21,600
1980	281	216	2	20,400
1981	314	267	3	21,100
Series B: Editors' compilation				
1980	285	249	4	14,300
1981	328	321	5	17,650
1982	306	362	9	11,150
1983	415	456	13	13,550
1984	356	465	6	23,750
1985	406	369	5	24,700

[a] The Lincoln Index can be expressed as: $P = \dfrac{(n_1 + 1)(n_2 + 1)}{(R_2 + 1)} - 1$.

[b] n_1 = total young wild Peregrines banded as nestlings in the above region (includes both USFWS and Danish bands).

[c] n_2 = total Peregrines trapped south of Canada and east of 100° W in their first fall migration.

[d] R_2 = number of Peregrines in n_2 which were banded as part of n_1.

[e] P = total production of fledgling Peregrines in North America (north of 55° N excluding the Gulf of Alaska region) and Greenland; P has been rounded to the nearest 50.

figures for 1984 and 1985 will need to be modified for the same reason in the future.

The Lincoln Index can perhaps be accepted as reflecting the upper limit of plausible estimates for the migratory population. It indicates that 10,000-20,000 young Peregrines have been produced annually in northern North America over the past several years. If we assume an average of 1.5 young produced per territorial pair, these figures translate into 6700-13,000 pairs nesting north of 55°N. If we further assume that there is at least one nonbreeding adult or subadult per pair in the overall population (there could be twice as many), then the total migratory population in the immediate post-breeding season could equal 26,000 breeders, 13,000 nonbreeders, and 20,000 young of the year.

As the USFWS (J. M. Sheppard) noted, however one judges the accuracy of the Lincoln Index, it certainly indicates that several thousand Peregrines are being produced each year in arctic and boreal America by several thousand pairs of adults. On the order of 2000 first-year birds are actually seen and counted during fall passage along the Atlantic and Gulf coasts. If they represent 20% of all the birds, then there are 10,000 young; if 10%, there are 20,000. It seems safe to say that this migratory population has reflected the existence of 5000-10,000 breeding pairs in the last few years. This range nicely brackets Fyfe's (1969) original estimate, based on limited breeding season surveys, of 7500 pairs in northern Canada.

Again, both the breeding surveys of recent years and the migration statistics show clearly that this northern population has been increasing since about 1975. What current estimates mean in relation to "historical" population size, prior to the advent of organochlorine pesticides in the late 1940s, is highly problematical at this juncture in our knowledge of Peregrine population changes. It could well be that the current increase in numbers is taking this northern migratory population to a higher level than existed prior to the 1940s, just as appears to be happening in the British Isles and in some other parts of Europe.

3 | Status of Peregrine Populations Since 1965 — Europe

17 | The Peregrine Population of Great Britain and Ireland, 1965-1985

Derek A. Ratcliffe

In 1965 I reported that the Peregrine breeding population in Great Britain had suffered a dramatic decline, beginning in southern England and spreading rapidly northwards during the next few years (Hickey 1969). By 1963, the national population stood at approximately 44% of the numbers estimated for 1930-39. In southern England and Wales only a handful of pairs remained. Northern England was slightly better, and some parts of Scotland showed only partial decline, but only in the central Scottish Highlands had numbers remained around their normal level.

In most districts there was a characteristic pattern of territory desertion, small broods, failure of eggs to hatch, egg-breaking, non-laying, and unmated birds in nesting haunts. The persistent organochlorine insecticides were suspected as the main cause of this unprecedented population collapse, but largely on circumstantial evidence. Restrictions on use of the most suspect chemicals (dieldrin, aldrin and heptachlor) as seed-dressings for spring-sown cereals in 1962 were followed by an arrest in the decline by 1964 and stabilization in 1965.

In Ireland a parallel decline and accompanying symptoms of population ill-health were reported, but with a less clearcut geographical pattern and a less severe reduction in overall numbers. Decrease appeared to be more marked in the Republic of Ireland than in Northern Ireland (Temple Lang 1968, A. Benington and M. Gilbertson unpubl. ms.).

Research subsequently focused on monitoring the breeding population. Studies of possible causal relationships between organochlorine pesticide contamination and adverse symptoms of Peregrine biology involved in the population "crash" were also undertaken.

THE 1965-1971 PERIOD

Annual sample surveys of the breeding population were made. In 1966, the low numbers reached by 1963 were maintained. There was something of a flux, with gains in reoccupation of territories and improved breeding being roughly balanced by further losses and failures at hitherto occupied or successful eyries. Further voluntary restrictions on the use of aldrin, dieldrin and heptachlor in 1964 gave additional hope that Peregrine recovery would eventually follow, and 1967 saw the first signs of a reverse trend. Northern England showed a new gain of seven reoccupied territories that year. This was a heartening portent, and further slight improvements appeared over the next three years; significance between successive years was dubious, but a slow upward trend seemed to be established.

Ten years after the first national census of the Peregrine population seemed an appropriate time for a full-scale repeat. Efforts of the largely amateur and unpaid force of field workers were mobilized in 1971 under the auspices of the British Trust for Ornithology and Nature Conservancy, with three full-time surveyors on contract. Their collective enterprise showed that of 726 known territories examined, 341 were occupied by Peregrines, representing 54% of the pre-World War II population level (Figure 1). At least 157 eyries with young were seen, representing 46% of occupied territories, but with a success rate of only 25% compared to the number of territories in the total sample which would have been occupied before the war (Ratcliffe 1972).

These data provided evidence of incipient recovery, but the increase was largely restricted to inland districts of Scotland and, to a lesser degree, northern England. To this extent the trend appeared to be a reversal of the pattern of decline, with recovery beginning first in the northern districts where decrease had occurred last and been least severe. Yet coastal districts generally showed no recovery, and it

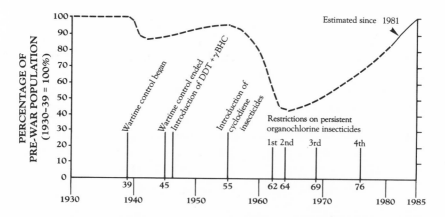

FIGURE 1. Decline and recovery of Peregrine population in Great Britain.

appeared the position was appreciably worse than in 1963 in coastal districts of the Scottish Highlands and nearby islands.

In 1971, 44 known breeding haunts in Northern Ireland were visited, and 34 were found to hold Peregrines (77% occupation), after a sample survey in 1968 had shown a decline to 63% occupation (McKelvie 1973, M. Gilbertson unpubl. data). Partial surveys for the Republic of Ireland during the late 1960s showed that the year of lowest numbers was also 1968, when territory occupation fell to 51%. Afterward there was a slow but continual recovery, and an improvement in breeding performance parallel to that in Britain: in 1971, out of 88 breeding haunts examined, 59 held Peregrines (67% occupation) (J. Temple Lang unpubl. reports 1969-72).

THE 1972-1981 PERIOD

Annual sample surveys were again maintained and showed that recovery was continuing, spreading steadily southwards and into some coastal areas. By the mid-1970s, recovery was marked in both inland and coastal districts of Wales, extending to southwest England, where the breeding places are almost entirely coastal. The census of Great Britain was again repeated in 1981, with the Royal Society for the Protection of Birds (RSPB) taking the lead. By 1981, at least 1078 Peregrine territories were known, representing an estimated pre-1940 population of 820 breeding pairs in an average year. At least 999 territories were examined during the 1981 survey, and 730 were occupied by Peregrines: 651 by pairs and 79 by apparently single birds. The other 79 territories not examined were estimated to hold a further 25 pairs, giving a total estimated territory-holding population of 716 pairs. Numbers had thus risen to about 87% of the pre-1940 population level. There had been a remarkable recovery throughout Wales, in both coastal and inland areas, with numbers completely back to the pre-1940 level, against only 22% of this level in 1971. Southwest England also showed substantial improvement, with numbers up to nearly half the pre-war level (Ratcliffe 1984a).

A different geographical emphasis nevertheless emerged, compared with the period before the crash (Figure 2). Peregrines were still virtually absent from the south coast of England east of Devon, while in many parts of the northern Scottish Highlands and nearby islands numbers were at only 60-80% of the normal level. The strong overall recovery was explained by increases in certain other districts to far higher levels than were ever known before the crash. In inland parts of northern England there were 76 occupied territories in areas for which the pre-war estimate was only 46 — an increase to 165% of former numbers. Other increases were in southern Scotland (inland) 150%, Wales (inland) 125%, southern and eastern Highlands center (inland)

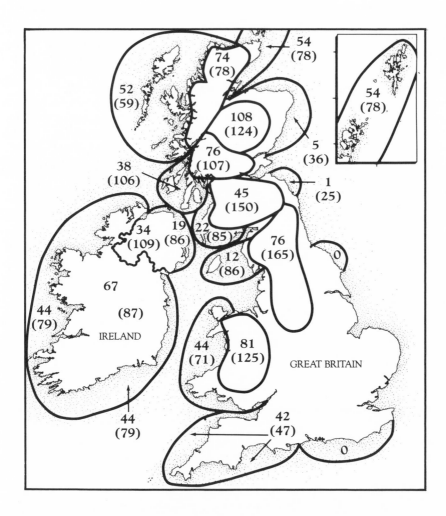

FIGURE 2.   Status of Peregrine Falcon breeding populations in different regions of
             Great Britain in 1981.

*Note: Figures are the number of breeding territories occupied in 1981 in each nesting
region. These are then expressed parenthetically as percentages of the numbers of
breeding territories occupied during the period 1930-39. Figures for Republic of
Ireland are based on a sample survey covering approximately 50% of known
breeding areas.*

124%, Northern Ireland (inland) 109%, southern and eastern Highlands fringe (inland) 107% and southern and eastern Highlands (west
coast) 106%.

What of breeding success? In 1981 an unusually cold and wet spring
caused heavy mortality of chicks at hatching and during the early
nestling stages. The previous five years, 1976-80, had shown better

breeding performance, regarded as more truly indicative of the contemporary situation. The averages of Great Britain for this period were: 56% of territory-holding pairs rearing young, with an average fledged brood size of 2.30 young and productivity of 1.29 young for all pairs. In 1981 the respective figures were 49%, 2.19 young, and 1.07 young, compared to 43%, 2.04 young, and 0.87 young for the period 1961-65. Population recovery has thus been marked by an associated improvement in all aspects of breeding performance, a fact even more pronounced when the data for the previously depleted districts are compared individually in this way.

In Ireland, parallel surveys in 1981 were conducted by the RSPB in Northern Ireland, and by the Forest and Wildlife Service with assistance from the Irish Wildbird Conservancy in the Republic of Ireland. In Northern Ireland, 64 known territories held 52 pairs and one lone adult, against a pre-1940 estimate of 54 pairs, so that recovery in breeding population was regarded as complete (Norris et al. 1982). In the Republic of Ireland, a survey of 15 representative areas covering about half of the Peregrine breeding districts located 111 occupied and 4 probably occupied territories out of an estimated total of 135, yielding an occupancy of 82-85%. The total number of available breeding territories in the country was estimated to be 278, and the total population in 1981 was estimated at 225 pairs. This gave an overall population estimate for Britain and Ireland of 993 pairs. Breeding success in the Republic of Ireland was also lower in 1981 than during the previous few years, the reduction being again attributed to bad spring weather. Data for the Republic of Ireland are from Norris and Wilson (1983).

THE POST-1981 PERIOD

Since 1981, I have information only from sample areas of Britain, but they show a continuing upward trend. In northern England, at least 100 pairs held breeding territories in 1984, a further increase of 24 pairs since 1981, representing 217% of the pre-1940 level. In inland districts of southern Scotland, 56 pairs held territory in 1984, compared with 44 in 1981, or 187% of the pre-1940 level. In Wales, although not all the 1981 nesting places were visited, surveys through all districts in 1984 disclosed at least 40 pairs in places where they were not known in 1981. On the slightly optimistic assumption that none of the 1981 pairs had since dropped out, this increase represents a new high of 124% of pre-1940 numbers.

In these regions there has thus been a possible gain of 76 pairs, though the lack of complete coverage of the 1981 nesting places makes it uncertain that this was the actual net gain. Reports from other regions suggest that there has been a more marginal increase in the south and east Highlands, on the coast of southern Scotland and in southwest England. In 1985, the first successful nest in at least 30 years was reported in Dorset, and the Isle of Wight had one pair in 1986, but there still seems to be an absence of breeding Peregrines from Sussex and Kent. There appears to have been no appreciable improvement since 1981 in those parts, especially coastal, of the northern and western Highlands and nearby islands where numbers and breeding performance have not really improved since 1971.

Thus the overall picture for Great Britain is that further recovery has probably increased the territory-holding population by at least 70 and perhaps by up to 100 pairs, giving a total of 786-816 pairs. The estimated average total breeding population for 1930-39 was 820 pairs, so that recovery may be regarded as virtually complete, especially since reports for 1985 indicate a further slight increase in northern England and southern Scotland (Figure 2). The change of emphases in the distribution pattern reported in 1981 nevertheless persists. While no data for Ireland have been available to me since 1981, it seems almost certain that the breeding population of the country as a whole now approaches and probably exceeds 300 pairs. Numbers for Britain and Ireland combined are thus of the order of 1100 pairs.

THE PRESENT POSITION — AN ASSESSMENT

The Role of Organochlorine Insecticides. — The Peregrine's recovery is not only of considerable satisfaction to wildlife conservation, but also holds much scientific interest. The primary factor in the increase of the Peregrine population since 1963 has been the substantial reduction in exposure to all the organochlorine insecticides. The pattern of decline in this hazard is supported by the monitoring of residues in the tissues and eggs of Peregrines, and in a variety of raptors and fish-eating birds (Cooke et al. 1982). Egg analysis during 1963-69 showed only moderate dieldrin residues (0.54 ppm wet wt, $n=47$), but was limited to northern regions where Peregrines had survived the population crash and began only *after* the first restrictions on this pesticide. Heptachlor epoxide was constantly present up to 1967, but then virtually disappeared. At the end of 1975 dieldrin was finally withdrawn from use as a cereal seed-dressing, but a few permitted uses on other crops remained, and aldrin was still allowed for wireworm control in grassland. There was an upsurge in dieldrin residues in Peregrine eggs in 1976 as stocks were used up. During 1977-84, dieldrin declined to low levels ($\bar{x}=0.29$ ppm wet wt, $n=152$), though it remained present.

Though DDT is still quite widely used in Britain, DDT/DDE levels have also declined greatly. During 1963-69, DDE levels of 20-30 ppm were common in Peregrine eggs, and the arithmetic mean for this period in northern England, southern Scotland, and the southwest Highlands was 13.5 ppm ($n=47$). During 1970-79, few eggs had DDE levels above 10 ppm, and the arithmetic mean for the same districts was 4.3 ppm ($n=145$). For 1980-84, DDE in eggs averaged 3.1 ppm ($n=92$). This trend has been matched by increase in eggshell thickness index for these parts of Britain. From an average during 1963-69 of 19.0% thinner ($n=27$) than pre-1947 in these regions, there was a recovery to 7.0% thinner ($n=129$) during 1970-79 and 5.8% thinner ($n=67$) during 1980-83. Various aspects of breeding performance have shown parallel improvement, but likewise have not yet reached normality.

A point of interest is that population recovery has taken place against reduced but continuing contamination by organochlorine residues. The development of some degree of resistance to these substances is a theoretical possibility, but without supporting evidence. Within the varying spectrum of organochlorine compounds to which Peregrines have been exposed, as reflected in the "cocktail" of residues found in their tissues and eggs, we have always regarded the dieldrin group as the most significant in their population effects in Britain, because they greatly increase adult mortality. Peregrines had been exposed to DDT and gamma-BHC for at least eight years from 1947 onwards, and eggshell thinning had become widespread, but the population crash did not occur until dieldrin, aldrin and heptachlor were introduced into widespread agricultural use around 1956. Similarly, it was the restrictions on the use of these cyclodiene insecticides which so clearly appeared to halt the crash, and the further restrictions of 1964 and 1969 evidently fueled the recovery. DDT probably contributed to the crash and helped to constrain recovery, so that the decline in its use which became noticeable by 1969-70 has most probably contributed to the build-up of population. Recovery certainly coincided with an increase in breeding performance, which had been so markedly depressed during the crash. Yet the increase to unprecedented levels in certain districts has taken place in the face of DDT/DDE contamination still high enough to produce detectable eggshell thinning and associated symptoms. In countries with different exposure patterns, the contribution of the various organochlorines to raptor population effects may be different, for example the much greater importance of DDT in North America.

Failure of Local Populations to Recover. — The lack of Peregrine recovery in certain districts is something of a mystery. Continued absence from the coast of southeast England, when set against the strong recovery in the southwest, points to some substantial adversity.

Despite increased human presence, the lofty and vertical chalk cliffs must remain attractive to Peregrines for they hold some of the most secure nest sites in the country. Since the cliffs mostly back onto rich arable farmland, my suspicion is that pesticidal hazards in this district remain critically high, though I should not like to conjecture which substances might be involved. It seems somewhat suggestive that on the east coast of Britain between Yorkshire and east Ross-shire (which contains scattered pre-war Peregrine seacliff haunts), virtually all of the cliffs abut similarly rich farmland, and the Peregrine has reappeared there somewhat erratically and shows poor breeding performance.

Farther north in Scotland, in Caithness and around the north coast into Sutherland and then west Ross-shire, and in all the island groups including Orkney, Shetland, and the Inner and Outer Hebrides, there is little arable land. Peregrine seacliff nesting places here often back onto wild and barren moorland. Some of them were formerly amidst great seabird colonies which provided a prolific source of food, but others subsisted on more limited abundance of coastal prey and varied this with moorland birds from inland areas. Limited analyses of Peregrine eggs from these northern coastal localities consistently show higher levels of PCBs than those from inland areas ($\bar{x}=25.9$ ppm, $n=25$ compared to 3.5 ppm, $n=289$). The main source of these elevated PCB levels is likely to be marine pollution, with accumulation in Peregrines attributable to ingestion through the food chain. The sea is a gathering ground for all manner of toxic wastes, and PCBs may simply be indicative of exposure to a whole galaxy of residues, most of which pass notice because Peregrine egg and tissue analyses are aimed at detecting only a limited range of organochlorines.

There is another pointer to the probable influence of marine pollutants. Peregrines in these northern coastal districts make the poorest showing where the proportion of seabirds in their diet tends to be highest — in the large breeding colonies of auks, kittiwakes and fulmars. In the main seabird stations very few pairs attempt to breed, and young are seldom reared. Territory occupation and breeding performance are appreciably better on seacliffs where Peregrine prey is more usually a mixture of gulls, terns, waders and moorland species. Another possible factor is that poor winter food supply may cause many of these northern coastal Peregrines to leave for winter quarters where they are exposed to hazardous contamination. And, finally, oiling by aggressive fulmars on the nesting cliffs has been claimed to be a serious mortality factor for these Peregrines. Deaths from this cause certainly occur, but the scale and pattern seem unlikely to be an adequate explanation of the state of this population.

One feature has become clear during the last ten years. Adverse spring weather can so appreciably reduce breeding performance as to resemble the earlier, pesticidally-induced depressions in output of young. The last decade has been notable for cold, backward springs, sometimes also accompanied by unusually heavy rainfall, especially in 1981. Many hatching eggs or broods of small young have perished, and several high elevation Highland eyries in especially bleak settings have become deserted. It is possible, however, that the effects of adverse weather may become accentuated in a Peregrine population still carrying moderate burdens of pesticide residues. Several instances have been found where adult Peregrines undoubtedly ate their own chicks, though whether these had died beforehand could not be discerned (R. Mearns pers. comm.).

Increase in Breeding Density Above Historically Known Levels. — The increase of Peregrines to unprecedented levels in certain regions requires explanation beyond the reduction of exposure to organochlorine pesticides. Other factors have allowed numbers to rise above the pre-war level. One obvious factor is that persecution is much reduced, compared with pre-1940 years, when egg robberies were heavy in many districts, and killing of breeding adults on grouse moors was rife. There is still a good deal of raiding of nests for eggs and young, but the changed climate of opinion, with much increased public concern for bird protection, combined with the surveillance of many nests by the Royal Society for Protection of Birds, local birdwatchers, landowners, foresters, and even gamekeepers, ensures that many pairs rear young successfully every year. Illegal destruction by game preservers is greatly reduced, though it still happens here and there. The work on population turnover reported by Mearns and Newton (1984) for southern Scotland shows a remarkably low mortality amongst established territory holders, and this trend may now be true of several regions. There is clearly a massive output of young birds each year, and the number of sightings in low ground away from nesting haunts suggest that there could be a considerable recruitment pressure tending to push up the breeding population.

The pressure of new birds seeking nesting places, and the relaxation of hostility to Peregrines, could explain the many instances of first-time occupations of nesting places of marginal quality, small cliffs, often close to human presence — third class cliffs (Hickey 1942). At least two instances of genuine ground nesting have occurred; a good many have occurred almost on the ground in "walk-in" sites, and one for two different years in a tree-nest. Several successful nest sites in still-active quarries have been found, and at least three on disused industrial waste tips. The falcons are simply becoming bolder and more adaptable in following their urge to nest in areas where all the suitable crags are already occupied or there are no good cliffs.

Yet it is more difficult to explain the real increase in breeding density which has occurred in Lakeland, north Wales and southern Scotland, involving doubling up in at least 21 territories where cliffs formerly used as alternates by one pair are now occupied by two separate pairs (Figure 3). I am inclined to think that this would not have happened without an increase in food supply, which, in the districts concerned, can only mean an increase in availability of homing pigeons, since this is overwhelmingly the principal prey and other species there contribute little to Peregrine diet. Statistics are hard to obtain on this sensitive subject, but the Royal Pigeon Racing Association (RPRA) quoted the following issues of rings for young birds: 1,540,000 in 1977; 1,813,450 in 1979; and 1,840,000 in 1980. The RPRA states that this is a sport steadily increasing in popularity, especially in northern districts where the enforced leisure of growing unemployment finds suitable outlet in pigeon fancying.

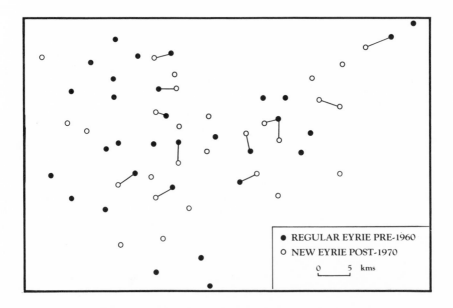

FIGURE 3.   Increase in Peregrine breeding population and density in the Lake District. Connecting lines are where the new eyrie represents an additional pair at a cliff formerly used as an alternate by the regular pair.

CONCLUSION

The Peregrine recovery in Britain is virtually complete in overall numbers, though not in precise distribution or some aspects of breeding performance. The pattern of recovery runs so closely parallel to the reduction in environmental use of persistent organochlorines and resulting reduction in contamination of Peregrines by their residues, as to confirm the original hypothesis that these chemicals were the cause of the post-1955 population "crash". The upward trend in breeding population continues, at least locally, even though toxic chemical effects on the species have evidently not entirely disappeared.

18 | The Peregrine Falcon in Fennoscandia

Peter Lindberg, Peter J. Schei, and Marcus Wikman

The Peregrine Falcon was once widespread in Fennoscandia, breeding in different habitats from cliffs to bogs (Linkola and Suominen 1969, Lindberg 1975, 1977b, Salminen and Wikman 1977). The pattern of decline in the 1950s and the 1960s was essentially the same as reported for many other areas in the northern hemisphere (Hickey 1969, Ratcliffe 1972, 1980). The population probably reached its lowest level in the early and mid-1970s with a possible 95-97% reduction of its pre-World War II size (Lindberg 1985). The main reason for the decline was accumulation of persistent organochlorines and heavy metals affecting reproduction and increasing mortality. Pesticides were accumulated both on wintering grounds in western Europe and on breeding grounds in Fennoscandia. In the late 1970s and the beginning of the 1980s, both the productivity and number of breeding pairs increased in Norway and Finland (Schei 1984, Wikman 1985), probably as an effect of decreasing residue levels in prey species and protection in winter quarters. DDT and several other contaminants were banned in most European countries in the early 1970s. The rate of persecution in the winter quarters also decreased as most raptors in these areas became fully protected in the 1970s (Saurola 1985).

MATERIALS AND METHODS

A Peregrine project, including both management and research, was initiated in 1972 in Sweden by the Swedish Society for the Conservation of Nature. Annual census work started in Finland in 1972 and in Norway in 1976. Monitoring of pesticides, color-ringing, and captive-breeding have been conducted cooperatively among the three countries. Some of the results of this work have been published elsewhere (Lindberg and Odsjö 1983, Lindberg 1985, Lindberg et al. 1985).

Extensive surveys of suitable cliffs throughout Sweden were carried
out in 1972-78. Helicopters were used to check about 1000 cliffs in
rugged low mountain terrain in the three northern counties. Since then
old nest sites have been rechecked annually, mainly in southwestern
and northern Sweden.

In Finland much of the census work has been concentrated in the
bogs in the northern part of the country. Formerly about 34% of the
total land area in Finland was peatland, and in some northern regions
50% or more was bog of some kind. Since 1974 over 1000 bogs have
been searched. Not all of these are suitable for falcons as many have
been drained for forestry or used for the peat industry (Wikman
1985).

The census effort has varied both among years and countries. While
large areas in southern Sweden and northern Finland can easily be
surveyed, the Norwegian coastline is difficult because of its tall, steep
cliffs.

This paper summarizes data on population status and reproduction.
Clutch size is based on early visits to nests to avoid bias owing to
destruction of thin-shelled eggs. The category, "breeding attempt,"
includes all pairs laying eggs, and "successful breeding" involves at
least one fledged young. Figures given on population size and fledged
young are minimum values; however, we believe that the unknown
part of the population does not deviate significantly in reproduction
and trend from the known.

EARLIER DISTRIBUTION AND POPULATION DECLINE

According to the older Fennoscandian ornithological literature the
Peregrine was found in most non-alpine habitats. High density was
locally found in lowland and coastal regions in southern and western
Fennoscandia. In Finland, Merikallio (1958) estimated population size
at about 500 pairs; however, Linkola and Suominen (1969) calculated
the former population to be about 1000 pairs (see also Thomasson
1947). Salminen and Wikman (1977) concluded that the earlier
population size was on the order of no less than 1000 pairs, with
perhaps as much as 50% of them breeding on bogs in northern
Finland, giving an average density for Finland of one pair per 300 km².

Little is known of the earlier status of the Peregrine in Norway.
Hagen (1952) wrote that the species was spread all over the country
with the exception of mountain areas above the tree limit. Willgohs
(1977) mentioned that there were at least several hundred pairs
breeding before the 1950s. Schei (1984) estimated the population to
be between 500-1000 pairs around 1900. In Sweden over 600 old nest
places are known, and Lindberg (1975) estimated the population to be
about 1000 pairs around 1900. The situation for the Peregrine is best

known from southwestern and eastern Sweden, where locally the population reached a maximum density of one pair per 140 km^2. From other parts of Sweden the density was estimated as one pair per 300-600 km^2, which gives a former population size in the range of 900-1400 pairs. The total Peregrine population in Fennoscandia before 1950 is estimated to have been between 2000-3500 pairs (Figure 1).

Local decline mainly owing to heavy persecution (by pigeon fanciers, hunters) was noted in some regions (southwestern Sweden, southern Norway, and southern Finland) in the 1930s and 1940s, but a large-scale decline started in the 1950s.

The pattern of decline varied between regions. In general, Peregrines in the southern parts of the countries (i.e., agricultural and densely populated areas) disappeared first, while northern Peregrines seemed to decline more slowly. The falcons in eastern and central Sweden were gone by the 1970s, and only a small nucleus remained in northern Sweden, as well as a few isolated pairs in southwestern Sweden. In southeastern Norway and southern Finland the Peregrine was extinct by the 1970s. In Figure 2 the rate of decline is given for some studied populations. As the large-scale decline in the mid-1950s was mirrored by many other European Peregrine populations, it is likely that both migrating and resident populations were affected in the same way and to the same extent. The population crash was probably caused mainly by an increased adult mortality (Ratcliffe 1980) owing to the introduction of cyclodienes and by lowered reproduction owing to DDT contamination and eggshell thinning. The use of alkyl mercury in agricultural areas of Scandinavia may also have contributed to increased mortality and hatching failures (Lindberg and Odsjö 1983).

The decline of the British Peregrines and the continental Peregrines stopped shortly after the mid-1960s, when the use of cyclodienes was restricted, and these populations have since recovered partly or fully (Ratcliffe 1980). The Fennoscandian Peregrine population probably reached its lowest level in the mid-1970s; in 1975 a total of 65 pairs was noted (Figure 1). Since then the Peregrine has recovered slightly in northern Finland (Wikman 1985) and Norway (Schei 1984), and the total population in 1985 was estimated at 120-150 pairs.

NEST SITES

Most of the former Peregrine population bred on cliffs, but in regions without suitable rocks they commonly nested in trees and on the ground. Also, in typical "cliff-areas" pairs were occasionally found in stick nests in trees or on the ground on flat skerries. Thomasson (1947) described 95 breeding sites in Sweden, of which 81% were on cliffs, 12% in trees (stick nests of Osprey, White-tailed Eagle, Carrion Crow, Common Raven), and 3% on the ground.

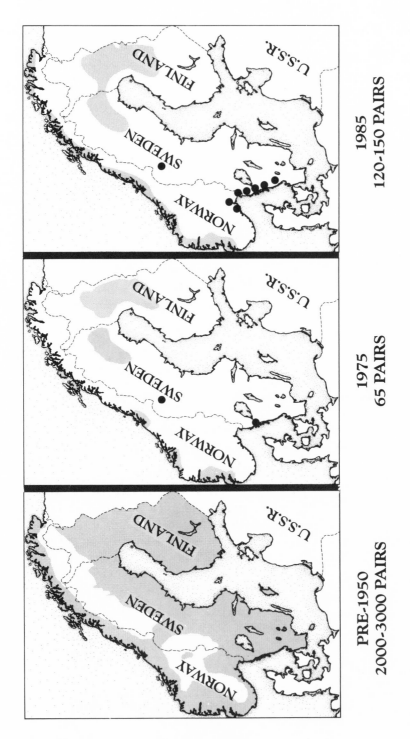

FIGURE 1. Breeding range (shaded areas) and estimated population size of Peregrines in Fennoscandia. Dots = single territorial pairs.

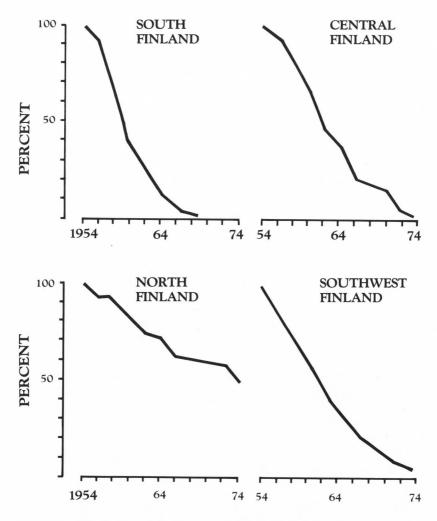

FIGURE 2. The decline of Peregrines in different regions of Finland and Sweden, 1954-74.

The height and topography of the breeding cliffs varied from region to region, with the highest cliffs found along the Norwegian coastline. Average height of cliffs (from base to top) in southwestern Sweden was 50 m ($n=54$, range 10-119 m) with 39% facing west, 22% facing south and 15% facing southeast. Almost all (78%) were situated close to water. A check of these cliffs in 1972 showed that five were still occupied by pairs or single Peregrines. Several of the classic Peregrine rocks have been known for a long time — one of them was first mentioned in the literature in 1756 (Lindberg 1975).

In Finland, Peregrines commonly nested on bogs in the western and northern parts of the country, where cliffs are scarce and large open bogs are numerous. A bog site in Finland, first mentioned in 1864, was still in use in 1985. Nesting in Osprey nests on bogs was also quite common. The highest densities of cliff-nesting Peregrines were found on the Åland Islands and in an area with abundant cliffs in southwestern Finland. In areas with cliffs and bogs, both kinds of nest sites were used, but there are no proven instances of the same birds shifting from one kind of nest site to the other. There are some cases in which cliffs and bog sites close to each other were occupied in alternate years, but it is not known whether a change of birds was also involved. Linkola and Suominen (1969) listed a total of 386 nest sites, with bogs and cliffs in about equal numbers. In 1972 the total of historical sites known was 458 (Aro 1973); most of the added sites were in bogs in northern Finland. Since then more than 50 additional sites have been found, bringing the total to more than 500.

All but two of the Finland nest sites found since 1972 have been bog sites. The three cliff sites known to be occupied in the 1980s are the northernmost sites in Finland. Recently, nesting in trees seems to have become quite rare. At one site, deserted in 1976, the Peregrines regularly used an Osprey nest on a bog. Two other tree eyries were Osprey and Rough-legged Hawk nests. These were only used in one year when snow conditions on the bogs were difficult in May. The year before and the year after, both pairs nested on the ground.

The smallest nest bogs have been little more than 2 km² in size, but the majority of nest bogs have been much larger. Even where the nest bog itself was small, there were usually several adjacent bogs that provided suitable hunting terrain. In those areas where Peregrines are found today, the amount of peat land is usually 40% or more of the total land area.

PRESENT DISTRIBUTION

Figure 1 summarizes the Peregrine's distribution in 1985. In Sweden the main population (estimated at 10-20) is found in the two northern counties (latitude 63°N–66°N). In southern Sweden only one territorial pair was known in the mid-1970s, but since then there has been a slow recovery resulting from management — including double clutching and reintroduction (Lindberg 1985).

The main concentration of breeding Peregrines in Norway is along the coast between latitude 59°N–70°N. The number of breeding pairs has increased, and several old territories in southwestern and southeastern Norway were reoccupied in the 1980s. In 1984 at least 36 territories were occupied by pairs or single birds, and the total population was estimated at well over 50 pairs (Schei 1984).

The main population in Finland is found north of latitude 66°N. A total of 53 nest sites were occupied at least once in 1980-85. A number of new sites have been found each year (Figure 3). At least some might be of recent origin, but many seem to have been occupied for some time before discovery. Most of these "new" nest sites are found in the area where the population is at its densest, thus filling gaps in the distribution. The number of annually occupied sites is considerably smaller than the total known sites. Peregrines are not restricted to nesting at any particular place on a bog, and are often free to choose from a number of equally suitable spots. Thus the birds may shift between three or four different sites. The longest distance between two nests of one female was more than 8 km. There has been a more than fivefold increase in the number of sites to check since the early 1970s. The increase in effort to check these sites has not been of the same order. Thus, there has been a trade-off of efficiency for numbers (Figure 4). This strategy is no longer paying off, as the number of nest sites found occupied each year has leveled off since 1982 (Figure 3).

The breeding density in the central part of the northern areas is about one pair per 330 km². There are probably some sites still to be found in this area; certainly there is room for several more. The closest distances between pairs are 4 km and 5 km; however, these seem to be

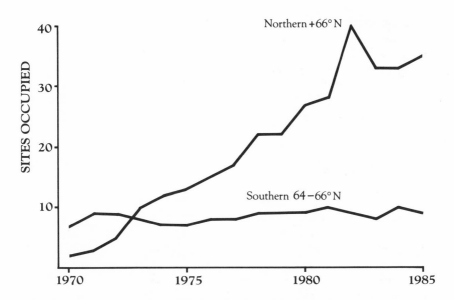

FIGURE 3. The number of nest sites occupied by Peregrines in the southern and northern regions of Finland.

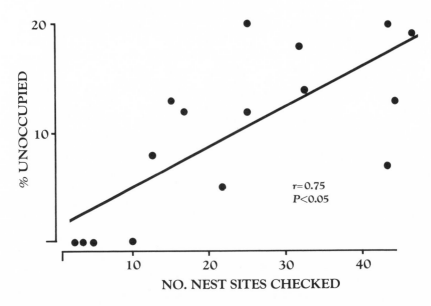

FIGURE 4. Proportion of Peregrine nest sites found "unoccupied" in relation to the number of sites checked in Finnish Lapland, 1970-85.

somewhat exceptional. A distance of some 10 km between nests is more typical.

In the zone between 64°N and 66°N several nest sites were deserted in the early 1970s. Then the rate of decline seemed to level off, and the last desertions were observed in 1976-77. In the 1980s, 12 nests were recorded, but fewer than 10 sites were occupied annually. From the area south of 64°N the Peregrines were gone by 1975. The last sites to be occupied in this zone were bogs in western Finland.

REPRODUCTION

The Fennoscandian Peregrines exhibit the same symptoms as many other pesticide-affected populations, including eggshell thinning and lowered reproduction. Eggshell index for a sample of eggs from Finland and Sweden in 1948-76 was about 17% lower than pre-1945 eggs, and in Norway 23% lower (Odsjö and Lindberg 1977, Nygård 1983). In 1983, eggshell thicknesses of 10 clutches from the wild were measured by beta back scatter technique (Forberg and Odsjö 1983). Ca-index of four clutches (latitude 64°N–66°N) had a mean of 556, and the corresponding figure for six clutches from the area north of 66°N was 613 (Figure 5). The figures would roughly convert to 25% and 13% thinning from the pre-DDT mean, respectively (Linde'n et al.

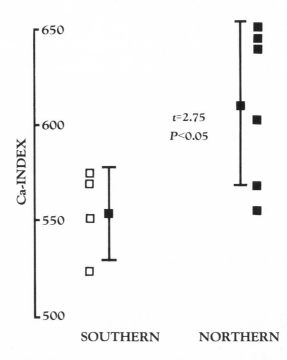

FIGURE 5. Eggshell thickness as revealed by Ca-indices of ten clutches of Peregrine eggs
in Finland, 1983. The means convert to roughly 25% and 13% thinning
compared with pre-DDT shell thickness for the southern and northern
regions, respectively. For details see Linde'n et al.(1984).

1984). Organochlorine analyses of eggs from the 1970s showed that
the Fennoscandian Peregrines were the most contaminated in Europe
(Lindberg 1985).

Reproductive rates varied between years from 0.6-2.9 young per
breeding attempt (Table 1, Figure 6). The rates in the three countries
show similar trends, with poor reproduction in 1976-77 followed by
good years in 1978 and 1980. Reproductive success improved significantly in Finland in the late 1970s. Wikman (1985) estimated the
average annual improvement to be 0.06 young per pair. This improvement has not persisted through the last few years; especially in the
64°N–66°N zone there has been a sharp drop in reproductive success.
The mean for 1981-85 was only 1.0 young per breeding attempt,
lower than the mean for the 1970s. These birds appear to be in
trouble. The reproductive success for the northern population in
Finland has been quite good, averaging 2.1 young per breeding attempt
during 1981-85.

TABLE 1. Number of occupied Peregrine territories in Fennoscandia, 1972-85. "Breeding attempts" means eggs were laid; "breeding successfully" means at least 1 fledged young. Figures are minimum values. Hacked birds are not included.

Year	No. of territories with pairs or lone adults	No. of territories with pairs	No. of breeding attempts	No. of pairs breeding successfully	No. of fledged young	Young/ breeding attempt
Norway						
1976	8	7	6	5	7	1.2
1977	18	12	10	8	19	1.9
1978	13	10	8	8	18	2.3
1979	14	9	7	6	12	1.7
1980	13	9	7	7	20	2.9
1981	22	20	14	14	29	2.1
1982	35	27	17	16	27	1.6
1983	36	25	22	21	46	2.1
1984	36	27	19	12	24	1.3
1985	47	35	24	15	33	1.4
Sweden						
1972	9	9	9	7	16	1.8
1973	9	8	7	5	11	1.6
1974	11	9	8	6	11	1.4
1975	11	8	6	4	9	1.5
1976	11	10	7	4	6	0.9
1977	12	11	11	3	7	0.6

Year						
1978	13	11	11	9	17	1.5
1979	13	11	11	7	12	1.1
1980	11	10	9	6	10	1.1
1981	11	9	9	7	16[a]	1.8
1982	11	8	6	6	19[a]	3.2
1983	11	9	9	7	17[a]	1.9
1984	12	10	6	4	13[a]	2.2
1985	9	7	7	6	16[a]	2.3
Finland						
1972	15	13	10	10	18	1.8
1973	19	18	16	12	25	1.6
1974	19	17	15	11	27	1.8
1975	19	18	16	15	35	2.2
1976	24	23	19	15	29	1.5
1977	27	21	19	14	28	1.5
1978	32	30	29	27	62	2.1
1979	31	28	28	15	39	1.4
1980	36	33	32	26	66	2.1
1981	39	33	33	19	50	1.5
1982	50	47	47	39	100	2.1
1983	41	39	39	30	76	2.0
1984	45	41	41	38	86	2.1
1985	47	36	36	24	59	1.6

[a] Broods were artificially increased in southwestern Sweden.

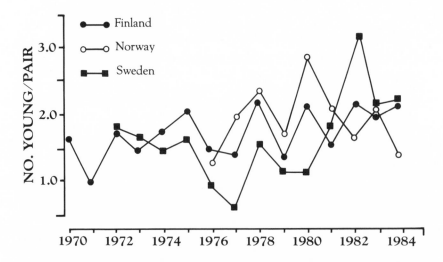

FIGURE 6.   Variation in reproductive rates of Fennoscandian Peregrines in 1970-84 calculated as number of fledged young per breeding attempt (=number of eggs laid). Figures from Sweden after 1980 include artificially increased broods and are thus not comparable with data from Norway and Finland.

Figures from Sweden and Norway are based on smaller sample sizes than those from Finland; those for Sweden include some manipulated clutches which restrict calculations for the 1980s. However, with the exclusion of the manipulated clutches, the positive trend is similar to that of Finland.

Clutch size was rather constant among years and among different populations and did not account for the large variation in reproduction. Average clutch size in Sweden in the period 1865-1939 was 3.35 ($n=79$), not significantly different from 3.29 eggs for a recent sample ($n=28$) in 1972-79 (Lindberg 1983). Linkola and Suominen (1969) reported an average clutch size in Finland of 3.1 ($n=130$) in 1850-1949, and Linde'n et al. (1984) found a rather similar clutch size between 3.2-3.5 ($n=146$) in recent nests.

The annual variation in reproduction may depend on several proximate and ultimate factors such as: (1) weather conditions affecting hatchability and nestling survival, (2) food supply affecting both female condition and brood survival, (3) different accumulation rates of organochlorines affecting eggshell thickness and hatchability, and (4) age structure of the population.

We have observed very few instances of nestling mortality, so the problems are concentrated in the incubation period. Especially in the 1970s, there was a high incidence of broken and addled eggs in the nests. The variation in reproductive output may indicate that the females in certain years were more affected by pesticides than in other years. A poor food supply in the period before egg laying may result in release of more fat-deposited organochlorines affecting eggshell thickness. It is also possible that a change in age structure of females in a population may result in a change in egg quality, assuming that younger females have accumulated less significant levels of organochlorines than older females.

Lindberg (1985) reported that DDE, and possibly PCBs, reduced the productivity of Fennoscandian Peregrines, although this impact varied between populations, depending on wintering quarters and food choice. In the early 1970s the use of organochlorines was reduced in many countries of northern Europe, and residue levels have since decreased in many important prey species. A similar trend was found in a small sample of embryonated Peregrine eggs from northern Sweden. A significant difference in breeding success was found for Finnish Peregrines breeding north and south of latitude 66°N. The southern part of the population had a 50% lower production of young than the northern one; this may indicate that the southern Peregrines winter in more contaminated areas. In 1980-84, the average productivity per breeding attempt in Fennoscandia was about two young. According to Ratcliffe (1980), this figure indicates a stable or increasing population.

CONCLUSION

The present number of Peregrines in Fennoscandia is still far below that of 40 years ago. The main distribution has shifted from southern to northern Fennoscandia, with many pairs breeding on bogs in northern Finland. The bog-nesting population has increased, as has the number of Peregrines breeding along the Norwegian coast. These increases are probably the result of lowered contamination levels and increased productivity, plus increased survival owing to changes in sport-hunting regulations in winter quarters. Local populations and some pairs still exhibit poor reproductive success; these birds may winter in polluted areas. If the positive trends for the bog-nesting and Norwegian coastal breeding populations continue, vacant areas of central Finland, northern Sweden, and southern Norway may be reoccupied by Peregrines.

Editors' Note: The number of pairs at controlled territories in Sweden and Finland has remained about the same since 1985 (see Table 1). Information from P. Lindberg indicates that 9 pairs were at eyries in Sweden in 1986 and 10 in 1987. They raised 21 and 30 young, respectively, owing mainly to the very successful fostering of captive-produced young into wild nests. In Finland, 35 pairs occupied eyries in 1986 and produced 2.2 young per pair; in 1987, 37 pairs produced 1.9 young per pair, so that natural productivity in this population remains high. We have no recent information from Norway.

19 | The Return of the Peregrine Falcon in West Germany

Theodor Mebs

In earlier times — before the post-World War II decline — the Peregrine Falcon was widely distributed throughout most of West Germany, and was a common breeder for a raptor of its size. Two ecologically distinct populations could be recognized: (1) a cliff-nesting population in the southern half of the country — part of a more extensive rock-inhabiting population in adjacent districts of France, Switzerland, Austria, Czechoslovakia, and East Germany, and (2) a tree-nesting population in the northern half of the country — again part of a more extensive arboreal nesting population extending across the north of East Germany, through Poland, and into the Baltic states (Kleinstäuber 1969, Mebs 1969, Schröder 1969, Kumari 1974). In the north German plain, Peregrines nested exclusively in mature pine or beech stands, where they used old stick nests of other raptors or corvids. My purpose in this paper is to summarize the changes in population size since 1950 and to account for the decline and subsequent increase in numbers.

ORIGINAL POPULATION SIZE

In a paper on Peregrine Falcon population trends in West Germany (Mebs 1969) I wrote that in 1950 there were about 320-380 breeding pairs of Peregrine Falcons in West Germany, an apparent underestimate. Another estimate placed the total number in 1950 at about 380-410 pairs (Glutz von Blotzheim et al. 1971). By summarizing all available data, I have recently concluded there may have been as many as 400-430 pairs in 1950. Originally I underestimated the size of the population in the region of the Swabian Alps and Upper Danube. In 1950 there were 103 pairs there instead of the 50-65 pairs cited in my paper (Rockenbauch in Glutz von Blotzheim et al. 1971).

Further, in the region of the Bavarian Alps, where the population of Peregrine Falcons was not known well until recently, about 30-35 pairs nested between 1950-55. In 1965 at least 25-28 pairs persisted (Bezzel 1969, Glutz von Blotzheim et al. 1971, Wüst 1981).

In 1968-69 about 75 pairs remained in West Germany (Glutz von Blotzheim et al. 1971), a decline of about 80% from the approximately 415 pairs of 1950. Surviving populations of about 35 pairs each were living in Baden-Württemberg and in Bavaria; a few pairs persisted also in Rhineland-Pfalz, in southern Hesse and in Westphalia. In the northern half of West Germany, no Peregrines are known to have nested from 1970-80, and the entire tree-nesting population apparently disappeared (reviewed by Cramp and Simmons 1980).

According to Saar et al. (1982), the lowest level of decline was not reached before 1975, when only 40 pairs were left in West Germany, 30 of them in Baden-Württemberg, and 10 in Bavaria and southern Hesse. Again, I suspect the number of Peregrines in Bavaria, especially in the Bavarian Alps, was underestimated and actually might have been twice as large. If so, about 50 pairs of Peregrines were surviving in West Germany in 1975 (Speer 1985).

PESTICIDE CONTAMINATION

The relatively large remnant population of Peregrines that persisted in southern West Germany may suggest that contamination with pesticides there was not as great as farther north. Early chemical analyses of addled eggs and dead Peregrines in Baden-Württemberg indicated very low levels of pesticides — perhaps a result of analytical difficulties (König and Schilling 1970).

In later tests, however, alarmingly high levels of organochlorine contaminants were found, especially of DDE, HCB and PCBs (Conrad 1977). The author came to the conclusion that pesticide contamination in Baden-Württemberg was as high as in other areas of Germany and might have caused some losses there, but that this population was protected in other ways (see Brücher and Wegner Chapter 60).

Presently, the Arbeitsgemeinschaft Wanderfalkenschutz (Working Group for Protection of Peregrines) acknowledges a high pesticide contamination, but they still deny effects on breeding success. Schilling and König (1980) say: "Regarding many disturbances at all nesting sites we finally had no confirmed signs that the development in the population of Peregrines in Baden-Württemberg was recognizably influenced by biocides." They believe that the pesticide-induced decline mainly affected migrant Peregrines, while sedentary populations, such as in Baden-Württemberg, showed no decline of similar extent in spite of contamination.

An example from the Bavarian Alps shows high contamination with biocides and the distinct likelihood of reduced breeding success. A female Peregrine appeared in 1969 as a yearling at a lake site at the edge of the Alps, raised young in 1970 and 1971, but did not succeed from 1972 on in spite of normal breeding behavior. In December

1975 this female died by collision with a high tension cable near the nesting place. The analysis of her liver showed enormously high residues: HCB=1140 ppm (dry weight), DDE=935 ppm, PCBs=3350 ppm, lead=30.6 ppm, and cadmium=0.28 ppm (B. Conrad pers. comm.).

A reduction of DDE and HCB contamination has occurred in recent years (Conrad *in* Brüll 1984). This change might be the result of a complete ban on the use of DDT in West Germany since 1974, and on the use of HCB since 1977. On the other hand, contamination with PCBs appears to be increasing.

PEREGRINE CONSERVATION

In Baden-Württemberg, the Arbeitsgemeinschaft Wanderfalkenschutz (AGW) was founded in 1965 for the purpose of better controlling and more effectively protecting nesting sites. Their aim has been to identify and to remove the real causes of decline. The main activities of the AGW are public education, management of nest sites, and eyrie-watching. Each breeding season about a hundred volunteers watch Peregrine eyries day and night to reduce human disturbance, especially illegal taking of eggs or nestlings. Without this special protection it is estimated that about one-third of all broods might be taken illegally. Eyrie-watching has limited this loss to 3% (Schilling and König 1980).

Losses during breeding caused by natural predators have also been reduced. Aromatic repellent substances and automatic sound-producers were developed and used against martens, which hypothetically might cause loss of about one-third of all broods. In this way losses to martens were reduced to 11% (Schilling and König 1980).

Further, ticks (*Ixodes arboricola*) caused losses of 6%. These were transferred to Peregrines from nesting birds brought as prey. Treatment of affected nestlings and nesting sites largely reduced these losses.

In 1984, an important cause of breeding losses was the Eagle Owl (Meyburg 1985). There was increasing competition for nesting sites also. For several years the AGW has placed artificial nest-boxes on suitable cliffs to attract Peregrines and to divert them from cliffs inhabited by Eagle Owls or frequented by humans.

Another group, Aktion Wanderfalken und Uhuschutz (AWU), has watched endangered eyries of Peregrines in Bavaria, Hesse, Rhineland-Pfalz, and Lower Saxony since the 1960s (Speer 1985).

According to Dietzen and Hassmann (1982), the Landesbund für Vogelschutz (Union for Bird Preservation) established a working group in 1982 for the protection of Peregrines in Bavaria. About 150 volunteers observed nesting sites and in some cases, where necessary, they watched endangered eyries day and night. In 1984 they monitored 28 pairs; 14 of these had successful broods. Ten other sites had single birds. The group reported a newly discovered nesting site in the Bavarian Alps situated at an elevation of about 1430 m (Anon. 1985).

RELEASE OF CAPTIVE-BRED FALCONS

In 1977 some members of the Deutscher Falkenorden (German Falconers' Association) started a reintroduction project after success in propagation. In 1977-85 they released 245 young captive-produced Peregrines. In the first three years only 8, 9 and 13 were released but in the last three years 41, 49, and 54 were liberated (Saar et al. 1985, Saar Chapter 59).

The releases were mainly in northern Hesse, northern Bavaria, and in Berlin. Hacking was most commonly used, mainly on suitable high buildings. The expectation is that young Peregrines released from buildings will later prefer nesting sites on buildings. Because nesting sites on buildings are more secure than those on cliffs, normally the former do not need to be watched for disturbances. Since 1950 Peregrines have nested at ruins of five castles or towers in southern Germany (Kuhk 1969, Mebs 1969). Other hack sites were deserted nesting cliffs, and since 1980, artificial tree-nests were built in the former tree-nesting area in northern Germany. Fostering and cross-fostering were used at eight Peregrine nests, at four Northern Goshawk nests, at two Eurasian Kestrel nests, and at one Common Buzzard's nest. About 85% of all released young Peregrines reached independence (Saar et al. 1982, 1985).

PRESENT STATUS

Baden-Württemberg. — As a result of the untiring activities of the AGW and also because of reduced contamination with DDE and HCB, the Peregrine population in Baden-Württemberg has increased since 1978. In 1966-77 only 30-35 pairs raised a total of 265 young, an average of 22 per year; in 1978-81 more than 40 pairs raised 233 young falcons, an average of 58 per year. No data have been published for 1982-83, but in 1984 the Peregrine population in Baden-Württemberg stood at more than 80 breeding pairs and more than 120 young were produced. Apparently this population has more than doubled within seven years. Ringing results and observations of color-banded Peregrines have revealed dispersion in all directions and re-settlement of deserted nesting cliffs in neighboring areas, but not yet in the former tree-nesting range.

Bavaria. — The exact number of breeding pairs, especially in the Bavarian Alps, is presently unknown because of the difficulty of searches in mountainous regions. The Bavarian Peregrine population is estimated at about 40 pairs and shows an increasing trend. The resettlement of deserted nesting cliffs, especially in the Franconian Jura, should take place within the next few years.

Reintroduction Project. — The first breeding success of re-introduced Peregrine Falcons was observed in 1982 in the Harz Mountains in East Germany, where the cliff-nesting population has been gone since 1974. At least 13 pairs of released captive-produced Peregrines have taken over nesting sites, at least 9 pairs laid eggs, and at least 34 young have fledged (Saar Chapter 59). It is very likely that more pairs exist in the wild, and some falcons may have joined the population in southern Germany. Presently five pairs are living in the Harz Mountains west and east of the German frontier. A pair nested at an old lighthouse in the flats of the North Sea in 1982. The tiercel was captive-raised and released in 1980 in Berlin, about 350 km southeast of the lighthouse (Reilmann 1985). In Frankfurt/Main in 1983 a successful brood was observed at a 300-m high telecommunication tower; the tiercel of this pair was released in 1980 at a high building in Kassel, about 150 km to the northeast (Anhäuser 1985).

CONCLUSION

Presently there are about 140 occupied Peregrine eyries in West Germany, and the number of pairs continues to increase each year, thanks to the efforts of many concerned individuals and organizations and to the government's restrictions on use of DDT and HCB. The Peregrine Falcon is making a comeback in West Germany, as elsewhere in central Europe, particularly in the cliff-nesting portion of its range. Its future in the former tree-nesting range in the north plains of the Baltic region may depend largely on the establishment of captive-produced Peregrines as nesters on buildings in cities and in artificial tree-nests.

20 | Status of the Peregrine Falcon in East Germany, 1965-1985

Gert Kleinstäuber and Wolfgang Kirmse

The German Democratic Republic (East Germany) has an area of approximately 108,000 km^2 and 17 million inhabitants. It has witnessed major changes in ecological conditions and is today a highly industrialized country with intensive land use. The country is divided geographically into the northern flatland with higher Tertiary and Pleistocene remnants and the southern mid-mountain range. Historically this geographical division determined the occurrence of two different breeding populations of the Peregrine Falcon. The forested flatland was occupied by tree-nesting Peregrines, while in the mountainous areas only cliff-nesting Peregrines were found. There are no data to indicate that these populations have ever mixed (Kleinstäuber 1969, Schröder 1969). A line from Magdeburg to Halle to Dresden defines the border that existed between these populations.

STATUS

During the past century the Peregrine Falcon was a common and wide-ranging breeding bird throughout the territory of what is now East Germany. An estimate based on verbal data yields pre-World War II figures of 300-500 breeding pairs. In the southern part of the area the population was probably not more than 100 breeding pairs. This cliff-nesting population was part of the larger population nesting in southern mid-Europe (France, middle and southern West Germany, Switzerland, Austria, Czechoslovakia, southern Poland). In contrast, the tree-nesting population of the flatland of northern mid-Europe was essentially a closed population (northern part of West Germany, middle and northern parts of East Germany and Poland). It is also thought that there was no exchange between this population and the more northern and northeastern nesting Peregrines in Scandinavia and the Baltic states.

In 1950, there were approximately 140-150 active tree-nest territories in East Germany, and 25-30 cliff-nest territories in the mountain areas. In 1960 there were 67 tree-nest territories used in the north and 18 territories (all cliff-nests) in the south. Checks during 1965 showed 25 sites used in the north and 11 in the south; in 1970, 22 in the north and 2 in the south. The year 1974 marks the time when this species almost completely disappeared as a breeding bird in East Germany, except for some single birds and a few broods (2-4) produced in the tree-nesting area until the end of the 1970s.

The repopulation of our area began in 1980, when young captive-raised Peregrine Falcons (Saar et al. 1982, Saar Chapter 59) became established as a territorial pair in the Harz Mountains. The population in 1985 consisted of four breeding pairs in the mountains and one pair in a city.

THE PATTERN OF POPULATION CHANGE AFTER 1964

Cliff-nesters. — The decline of this population appeared to occur in two phases (Figure 1). During the first phase from 1940-55, a large

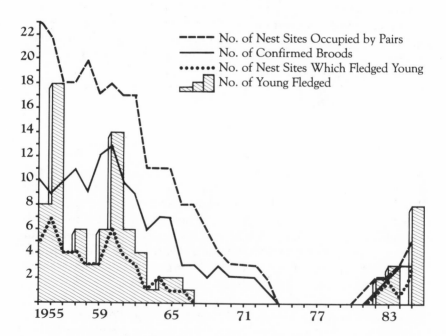

FIGURE 1.   Changes in the Peregrine Falcon cliff-nesting population in East Germany, 1954-85.

portion of the breeding population was lost, perhaps 50%. The decline continued after 1955 at a slower but fairly steady pace with about one breeding pair lost per year. The number of young fledged per occupied territory decreased from 1.1 (K. Kleinstäuber in the Elbsandstein Mountains, 1928-38) to 0.4, and after 1962, to 0.2. The last young fledged in 1966. In the Elbsandstein Mountains, the area of most preferred nesting habitat, only isolated pairs were recorded at the most preferred territories after 1965, until 1972 when the last clutch was abandoned by a pair which had been unsuccessful for years. In widely separated areas in the Thüringer Forest and the Harz Mountains, the most preferred territories remained occupied the longest; pairs bred there for the last time in 1969 and 1973, respectively.

Tree-nesters. — The remaining population of 22 breeding pairs in 1970 was soon reduced, during which time there must have been a high mortality of adults. In contrast to the cliff-nesters, until 1972 there were isolated successful pairs in the northern areas. The last breeding pairs were separated by great distances in the forest area and were located where intensively used agricultural lands were less prevalent. In the Muskauer Heide, the last successful breedings of one pair were reported in 1975 and 1976, although the pair remained present until 1981. A pair southeast of Berlin definitely sighted in 1982 is said to have bred successfully at least from 1979-81. It is not known whether this was an historically occupied site or a newly occupied one, but this pair also disappeared after 1982.

The confirmation of pairs nesting in the forested area is more difficult than for cliff-nesters. Even if some isolated pairs have not been found, they alone would not provide enough of a nucleus to repopulate the depleted areas because they would be so few and too far apart.

EVALUATION OF THE POPULATION COLLAPSE

The timing of the decline and ultimate collapse of the Peregrine Falcon in East Germany was similar to occurrences in countries of northern and middle Europe and North America. Some peculiarities should be noted as follows: (1) Based on data from nests visited in 1928-38 (Kleinstäuber et al. 1938), it is possible to say that signs of a decline were present before DDT came into use. (2) In contrast to other countries, where drastic population declines also occurred but remnant populations remained, East Germany experienced a total extirpation of the breeding population. Even sightings of single birds and occasional pairs since the final collapse will not change this fact. (3) The disappearance of the tree-nesting Peregrine Falcons in East Germany at the same time as their disappearance in middle Europe

(Netherlands, West Germany, Poland) meant that a specialized type of tree-nester was being eliminated forever, unless attempts at captive-breeding and reintroduction prove successful.

Keeping in mind the definite manner in which former territories are being reoccupied, and the significance to wildlife management today and in the future, these three peculiarities require some discussion.

Mortality and Lower Productivity Before the Worldwide Declines Resulting from Environmental Contaminants. — Based on life expectancies calculated from band recoveries during 1920-40, Kirmse and Kleinstäuber (1977) calculated that 1.7 young had to be fledged per breeding pair in order for the cliff-nesting population to remain stable. K. Kleinstäuber ascertained that even during "normal" reproductive times in the Elbsandstein Mountains, only 1.1 young fledged per breeding pair from 97 broods. Thus, even before the impact of environmental contaminants, nest-robbing and other human disturbances reduced productivity to such a degree that it could not compensate for the high mortality of young during migration. In the cliff-nesting area the Peregrine Falcon had already been reduced in numbers owing to human disturbances at nests, independent of sub-sequent reduction in productivity because of environmental con-tamination with pesticides.

This reduction of the population, and specifically in the number of young recruits, resulted in a breeding population with a large percentage of old birds. This unnaturally skewed age distribution, together with the reduction in free-flying pigeons during and immediately after World War II, was probably responsible for the reduced breeding success by Peregrines. (In the mid-mountain area where prey species are few, pigeons were an important prey item when the young were growing.) After 1950, the abnormal breeding behavior noted by Kleinstäuber (1969) further reduced reproduction.

Signs of the Influence of Contaminants During the Decline of the Peregrine Falcon in East Germany. — In 1954 we became aware that embryo deaths were occurring even though there had been no interruption or cessation in incubation. In 1955, for the first time, G. Kleinstäuber verified that eggshell thinning was occurring in a cliff-nest in the Elbsandstein Mountains. After we had heard about data on DDE accumulation in other animals, we were finally able to fit our data into the picture 10 years later. From 1954 until the disappearance of the cliff-nesting population, intensive observations revealed eggshell thinning, unexplainable loss of eggs, and embryo deaths, even with pairs which showed overintensive breeding behavior, such as incubating for a number of weeks after hatching should have occurred. Too many long breaks in incubation behavior, weak attachment to the nesting territory, long-lasting mating behavior without laying of eggs, and other abnormal breeding behavior became more obvious during the last one or two years before the final disappearance of the breeding pair. These symptoms can be interpreted as indicating a pair too old to reproduce (compare with Ebert 1967).

In the time span from 1960-65, a small number of deserted Peregrine Falcon clutches were tested with thin-layer chromatography. The results were negative on grounds of technical shortcomings. No opportunities became available to test for the presence of environmental contaminants using gas chromatography.

In the tree-nesting area after 1960, more and more clutches failed to hatch even though normal clutch sizes and intensive incubating behavior were observed. The early decline noted in the cliff-nesters was less pronounced here. Disturbance during incubation and the taking of young from nests were also less. Because of the often yearly rotation within breeding territories of nest sites up to 2 km apart, the chances of human detection were lower and successful reproduction higher than at the well-known cliff sites in the mountains. A shortage of prey species was never noticeable because pigeons were a less important prey item in this region. Unlike the case of the cliff-nesting falcons in East Germany, in which decline could have taken place without the influence of environmental contaminants, the loss of the more than 100 pairs nesting in the forest area after 1950, in association with the symptoms of reproductive failure, indicate a decided impact of environmental contaminants that resulted in the quick decline and extinction.

ATTEMPTS AT SALVAGING THE SPECIES

Protective Measures for the Last Survivors. — The decline of the Peregrine Falcon population was noted early and observed intensively since 1955. The step-by-step protective measures taken in East Germany did not keep pace with its disappearance and limped along, as in many other countries, despite the efforts by nature organizations and support from the state. The final, dominating cause of the decline, namely DDT contamination of the environment, was not acknowledged early enough to take some wild birds into captivity for preservation and breeding purposes — the remaining population was already too small.

An arrangement as effective as that in the southwestern part of West Germany, where a population of about 20 breeding pairs received unlimited protection and guarding (Brücher and Wegner Chapter 60), could not be done in East Germany. Nevertheless, for many years a high degree of personal sacrifice was involved in the protection of the last remaining Peregrine Falcon broods. Nesting territory protection areas were designated as out of bounds; artificial nest platforms were put up; nests were repaired and protected from weather, plundering, and destruction through falling rocks. Even so, no young birds hatched (Kleinstäuber 1963).

The following advantages in Baden-Württemberg were not available to us in East Germany: (1) a much lower post-nestling mortality rate because the young Peregrines do less south-southwest migrating, (2) the already partial successes of one-year-old Peregrines which added significantly to productivity, (3) the much lower DDE burden owing to less intensive agriculture, and (4) the possibilities of reoccupancy of some of the abandoned territories from the large and growing population in adjacent parts of France.

Artificial Incubation and Rearing Attempts in Captivity. — In 1965, two eggs were taken from each of two Elbsandstein Mountain nests containing three and four eggs, respectively, and incubated artificially. Neither pair had been successful for years. The eggs were thin-shelled, and the embryos died part way through incubation (Ebert 1967). At the same time two eggs of three were taken from a tree-nesting pair which had been unsuccessful for seven years. These eggs were also thin-shelled, and the embryos died.

Finally in 1968, just before the final disappearance of the population, J. Ebert took one young from each of two tree-nests north of Berlin and put them together as a pair. In addition to two Peregrine Falcons from the Tierpark in Berlin, which had already been paired by V. Wachter, these were then the only Peregrine Falcons in captivity in East Germany. Because the falconers in the 1950s had, of their own volition, chosen not to keep any large falcons in captivity, they could not be held responsible for the Peregrine's decline, as claimed in some other countries.

Before any successful breeding occurred, V. Wachter's male and J. Ebert's female died. The two remaining birds, paired by J. Ebert, subsequently produced a total of 26 eggs from first and second clutches from 1972-75. The behavior of the pair was normal except no copulation was seen. Attempts at artificial insemination did not succeed owing to the uncooperativeness of the male. After the loss of the female from an infection, the last living male in East Germany was incorporated into a captive-breeding project by Professor S. Pielowski in Czempin, Poland and Professor Christian Saar in West Berlin. The tiercel lived until 1985. Because of the successful captive-breeding and reintroduction program of Saar and the Peregrine Falcon Protection Group in North Hessen, West Germany, it became the main progenitor of the newly established Peregrine population started in 1980 (Saar Chapter 59).

THE INITIAL REPOPULATION

Summary. — In the fall of 1980 a pair of Peregrines appeared at an historical nesting area in the Harz Mountains. The male had juvenile plumage while the female was an adult. Pair-bonding and the selection of an eyrie progressed normally, but no eggs were laid in the spring of 1981. Colored bands worn by birds confirmed that both were from the captive-breeding program of Christian Saar. The male parent of the female was taken as a juvenile in 1968 from an area north of Berlin in East Germany, and the female parent was from the Vosges Mountains in western West Germany. In 1982 this new pair successfully fledged young. For the first time in 15 years, young Peregrine Falcons were present in the mountain area. At the same time, it was the first known instance of captive-raised Peregrines breeding successfully in the wild in Europe. This pair is still present at the same nest site. It fledged two young in 1982, two in 1983 and three in 1985. In 1984, this pair and two others in the Harz recycled after a snowstorm, but did not hatch any eggs.

The second most favorable Peregrine Falcon territory in the Harz was reoccupied by a pair in 1982. One young was fledged in 1983 and three in 1985. This pair was also captive-raised in Saar's project, and again the male was in juvenile plumage during the pair-bonding and establishment of a territory. The third new breeding pair established itself in East Germany in 1983, also in the Harz. In this area the Peregrine Falcon Protection Group had put up nest platforms on the cliffs, and they were utilized. In 1985 this third pair (again from the reintroduction program carried out in West Germany) fledged two young in such a box.

The oldest living male Peregrine in East Germany is one raised by Saar in 1978; it was one of the first to be released in West Germany, in Hessen. His movements were followed throughout the years in the southern part of the Harz, where he attempted to establish a territory. In 1982-83 he spent four months recovering from an injury and was again released. In the fall of 1984 he acquired a one-year-old female as mate and set up a territory, in the same town as the previous year, occupying an unused chimney of a factory as the nest site. An artificial nest box installed on the chimney at a height of 55 m in the spring of 1985 was accepted; mating and breeding of the new hesitant pair occurred, but no eggs were laid. The female was also definitely captive-raised, but has not been specifically identified.

Finally, since 1984-85 Peregrine Falcons have been noted in the Thüringer Forest in East Germany, at least two of which have been identified by colored bands as originating from the release program in West Germany. No successful breeding has been recorded; however, we are expecting an artificial platform installed on a massive cliff to be occupied in 1986.

There have been no other reports of reoccupied territories in the cliff-nesting area since 1980. North of the mid-mountains, in Berlin, single birds have been seen and confirmed in the area, probably from the building and tree-nest releases carried out in West Berlin. However, up to this time there has been no confirmation of occupied territories in the city or in the forest area.

Some Comments on Reintroduction. — Since 1980, 30 different Peregrine Falcons have been recorded in the cliff-nesting area in East Germany. Of these, 13 have been young fledged from the newly established territories. Ten have definitely originated from the reintroduction program in West Germany and have become breeding birds (bands verified). The origins of seven present for only short times during the breeding season have not been identified. Outside of the mid-mountain area only the pair confirmed breeding until 1982 near Berlin has been noted, along with single birds in the city and surrounding area. No colored bands have been verified on these birds.

From the nesting distribution of these reestablished falcons, their behavior, and the young hatched, we surmise the following 12 points.

(1) The well-established population of Peregrine Falcons in Baden-Württemberg, West Germany has not spilled over into East Germany. All the newly established breeding pairs in East Germany have originated from captive-raised birds.

(2) The captive-raised Peregrines behave normally during and following reoccupation of historical territories. There have been no differences noted in the behavior of these birds from those that existed before the decline in respect to selection of nest sites, perch points, plucking perches, food caches, type of hunting flights, and preference for prey. The reestablished Peregrines are using the same ecological opportunities that the former Peregrines used. The fact that they are less afraid of humans is a positive factor in raising broods successfully. (Direct threat of human persecution is under control now, but disturbance by casual tourists is greater than ever before.)

(3) The occupancy of a city chimney with an artificial nest box is not the result of a misguided captive-raised Peregrine Falcon. This behavior is comparable to the occupancy of masts and towers on the tundra and in the Watten Sea and renews the tradition (less common in earlier times) of broods being raised on city buildings in Europe (Mebs 1969).

(4) The cliff-nest territories are reoccupied in a sequence opposite to that of their abandonment during the decline. This means that Peregrines occupied the breeding territories according to the rank of their ecological suitability. In other words, the top-quality territories were the last to be occupied and the first to be reoccupied. Astonishingly, the captive-raised newcomers accept the same criteria for occupation as did their wild forerunners, a fact which underlines the untouched

inborn site-selection sensitivity of the captive-raised Peregrines. Observations of ringed birds confirm that a vacant, first-class territory even attracts paired owners of second and third class territories in the area.

(5) We do not yet know whether the genetic inclination of the young Peregrine Falcons to migrate has changed (all the young in our previous population migrated south-southwest). However, we do have evidence that two males set up territories in the fall of the same year they were released; they acquired mates and only left their territories briefly in the cold winter months, but remained close by. These two birds did not migrate south-southwest.

(6) The lack of production by first-year birds and the loss of young in 1984 owing to weather lowered the calculated productivity rate for 1981-85 to 1.0 young per breeding attempt ($n=14$). Even so, the figure of 13 young fledged by six successful pairs leaves room for optimism. From 18 eggs, only three did not hatch (not including the weather related losses in 1984). In spite of this good reproduction, the small population cannot yet maintain itself. Further management, such as increasing the productivity by additional releases, must be continued.

(7) The success of our new Peregrine Falcon pairs in mountain areas, where for 15 years no pair had bred successfully, may be an indication that the levels of environmental contamination in the upper reaches of the food chain have now lessened in East Germany. The use of chlorinated hydrocarbons in farming is no longer permitted, and in forestry it is only allowed under special conditions.

(8) Reoccupation by captive-raised Peregrines of historical territories in the Harz Mountains sometimes occurred at distances in excess of 60 km from the release sites in West Germany, leaving closer territories of lesser quality unoccupied. However, these secondary territories seemed to be preferred when there was potential for acquiring a mate in the vicinity. This observation could be important in planning future releases.

Young Peregrines become attached to a particular site faster if they find a mate or assume because of certain signs that they may procure one. Thus, in spite of territorial boundaries and the presence of birds on a territory, there remains a cohesiveness in Peregrine Falcon populations. Therefore, secondary nest sites closer to the productivity center of the population are reoccupied earlier than prime territories far away from the productivity center.

(9) The knowledge of how sites are being chosen for reoccupancy allows biologists to gear future management efforts in formerly occupied nesting areas. In other words, one would expect the repopulation of any territory far away from newly established pairs and release sites — in particular the center of the former cliff-nesting East German population in the Elbandstein Mountains — to take a long time unless proper management strategies are utilized.

(10) The level of productivity could certainly be raised by the installation of nest boxes in preferred places. By this method, breeding pairs would become tied to specific places which could be better protected against weather, human interference, and predation by the marten, but still allow observations to be made without interference (see Brücher and Wegner Chapter 60).

(11) Throughout the forested area in middle Europe, the tradition of nesting in trees in large cliff-free areas otherwise offering the necessary requirements (availability of prey and older stands of trees) to breed and survive successfully, was probably owing to predisposition by imprinting. But this tree-nesting disposition does not preclude the tendency of inexperienced breeders to nest in cliffs. If tree-nesters occur in areas where cliff-nesting is the norm, the cliff-nesting population would tend to absorb the young tree-nesters. This is probably why there were no tree-nesters or only extremely exceptional ones (Ratcliffe 1984b) in the cliff-nesters' area, and why there was an unoccupied corridor about 50-100 km wide between the tree- and cliff-nesting populations in middle Europe.

To achieve the goal of reestablishing the tree-nesting population in the forested areas of middle Europe, it would be desirable to raise young with the imprinted tendency for choosing tree-nests and then release them far from any cliff-nesting areas, so that they could initiate a new tradition of tree-nesting. This would make it possible for young inexperienced Peregrines to find mates within the tree-nesting habitat and not be absorbed by the cliff-nesting population (as is now happening).

(12) With a successful start on rebuilding the Peregrine Falcon population, we have confirmed that captive-rearing and reintroduction are useful methods for preventing an endangered species from disappearing completely, at least until the reason for its decline has lessened or disappeared. It does, however, take some time to acquire the necessary biological background to raise these birds in captivity and reintroduce them successfully; therefore, it is advisable to get an early start with the work while there is still an adequate breeding stock.

If the protectionists involved with the saving of the Peregrine Falcon in Baden-Württemberg reject this method because it presents an excuse for western falconers and raptor smugglers to take Peregrine Falcons from the wild (or even promotes taking them), then we have a special problem with human behavior, not with the method. It is also incorrect to say that such strategies of wildlife management are not necessary to save the Peregrine Falcon, because even in West Germany the Peregrine population declined from about 400 to 20 breeding pairs in a short time. Peregrine Falcon protectionists in East Germany have learned from the Peregrine population changes of the last 30 years that the species would have disappeared from West Germany, East Germany and all neighboring countries, in spite of the personal involvement of nature protectionists, had not a slowing of the decline occurred and the use of DDT and related pesticides been banned or reduced in Europe.

We in East Germany are happy about the small but growing population of Peregrine Falcons, which we protect and support further by intensive management. We especially monitor the activities of the laying females and the hatching of eggs because they are strong indicators of what is occurring in the environment.

Editors' Note: We thank Ursula Banasch, Canadian Wildlife Service, for translating this article from German to English.

21 | Status of the Peregrine Falcon in the Ceskomoravska Vrchovina Highlands and Other Parts of Czechoslovakia

Karel Hudec

During the 1950s and 1960s, a tremendous decline was noted in the Peregrine Falcon population throughout Europe, a decline which, in some areas, constituted an almost complete disappearance (Fischer 1967). This decline also included Czechoslovakia. Biologists looked for various reasons: shooting of Peregrines at nest sites and especially on the wintering range, disturbance of nest sites by rock-climbers, taking of young from the nests by falconers, and the reduction in productivity caused by pesticides.

To trace the decline of the Peregrine in Czechoslovakia is not easy; the breeding places were not checked systematically over long periods, and none of the literature (Jirsik 1935, 1948) gives an overall picture. Therefore, I decided to look at some of the earlier data from a major nesting area in the Moravian part of the Ceskomoravska Vrchovina Highlands (Figure 1), and concentrate on the decline of the Peregrine in this region (Hudec 1972). This paper summarizes my findings in that region and provides some information on the overall situation in Czechoslovakia since 1975 (see also Sládek 1977).

CHARACTERISTICS OF THE NEST SITES

Only cliff-nesting territories are known in the Ceskomoravska Vrchovina Highlands. In many instances these cliffs are in forested areas surrounded by cultivated fields. The nest sites are concentrated in five areas in conformity with the geomorphological characteristics of the Ceskomoravska Vrchovina Highlands. Three areas surround rivers that cut through the high plateau before joining up with the Dyje, Svratka, and Talsenke rivers. Another nesting area is the Moravian Karst, where canyonlike valleys exist from the steady erosion of the limestone by smaller streams. A much different type of nesting area is

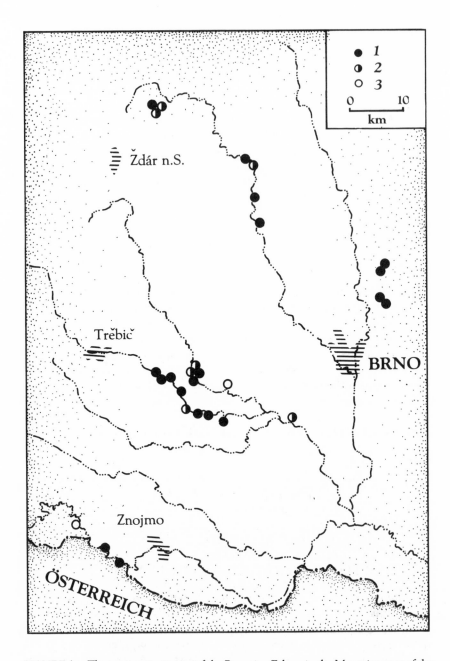

FIGURE 1. The nesting territories of the Peregrine Falcon in the Moravian part of the
Ceskomoravska Vrchovina Highlands: (1) Regularly used territories; (2)
Territories used for a short time; (3) Unoccupied territories.

found in the vicinity of Milovy, where hard stone cliffs (inselbergs) jut up from the flats.

POPULATION CHANGES IN THE HIGHLANDS

Capek (1924) noted an increase in the first survey of the Peregrine Falcon nest sites in Moravia. In the 19th century, data existed for only one pair near Pernstejn. Capek was aware of all ornithological activities in Moravia at the end of the 19th century, so that data concerning large numbers of breeding Peregrines would not have been missed. Additional data concerning breeding Peregrines were first verified after the start of the 20th century, and the numbers of Peregrines steadily increased (Figure 2). Owing to protection by forestry personnel and landowners, the population of the Peregrine Falcon increased just before it was protected by law in 1929. Numbers reached their maximum between 1929-40 or possibly in the following 10 years.

Precisely when population growth leveled off and the decline began is not known. The figures for the 10-year period of 1941-50 suggest the beginning of the downward trend (Figure 2), but one must not necessarily consider these indications as the actual start. During these years, the nesting sites were not checked as systematically as before, and observers tended to estimate population figures using former numbers of breeding pairs.

Nevertheless, between 1941-53 pairs nested at three locations where they had not previously nested or where long-occupied nesting territories had not been known. In contrast, when Fiala surveyed most of the nesting territories in the Jihlavka, Oslava, and Svratka rivers in 1955, most were unoccupied. In territories that were once occupied regularly, three were occupied for the last time in 1949, another three were occupied for the last time in 1957, and for another seven the last occupancy occurred before 1955.

Therefore, the maximum decline in the Moravian part of the Ceskomoravska Vrchovina Highlands occurred from 1950-57. A short time later other nesting sites in Moravia were deserted (Cimburk 1960, Pavlovské 1962) and likewise, in the rest of Czechoslovakia (Cerny et al. 1977).

After this period, only single pairs were recorded, and since 1969 there have been no confirmed nesting attempts of Peregrines in the Ceskomoravska Vrchovina Highlands.

RECENT SITUATION IN CZECHOSLOVAKIA

Sládek (1977) and Cerny et al. (1977) estimated a total population of 10-20 pairs remaining in the early 1970s. Table 1 summarizes the information I have been able to gather from all of Czechoslovakia since

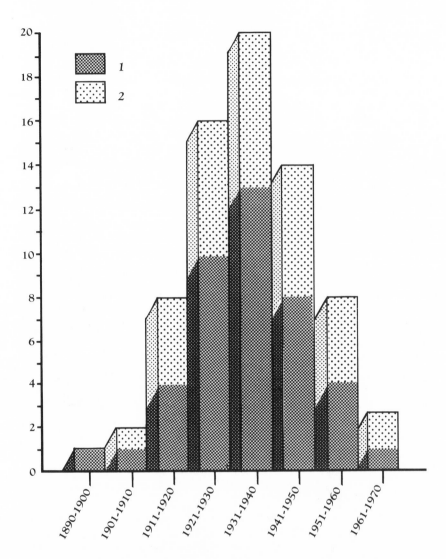

FIGURE 2.   The number of breeding pairs of Peregrine Falcons in the Moravian part of
the Ceskomoravska Vrchovina Highlands: (1) Number of occupied sites;
(2) Probable number of unoccupied sites.

1975. It is difficult to know how closely these figures conform to
reality, because there is secrecy and much rivalry between the nature
protection bureau and the falconers regarding information about
eyries. Nevertheless, it is evident that there has been no strong
rejuvenation of the population as yet. But there is, perhaps, an

TABLE 1. Population estimates of Peregrine Falcons in Czechoslovakia.

Year	No. of nesting pairs			
	Confirmed	Probable	Possible	Total
1975	1	1		2
1976	1			1
1977			2	2
1978			1	1
1979	1		3	4
1980	1		2	3
1981			1	1
1982			1	1
1983		1	1	2
1984		1	2	3
1985		2		2

encouraging sign. The disappearance of the Peregrine in 1950-65 was most noticeable in the western part of the country, while elsewhere in Slovakia isolated pairs remained until 1976-77. From 1978 to the present, all reports of Peregrines have come from Bohmen and Mahren. Possibly a recovery has begun in the west and will spread eastward.

Editors' Note: We thank Ursula Banasch of the Canadian Wildlife Service for translating this paper. Unfortunately, some references were not provided by the author, and are therefore missing from the Literature Cited.

22 | Recolonization of the Swiss Jura Mountains by the Peregrine Falcon

Michel Juillard

Switzerland is a small federal state situated in the center of Europe. Geologically speaking, it is divided into three main regions: the Alps, the Jura Mountains, and the plateau that stretches between them (Herren 1962).

The history of the recolonization of the Swiss Jura Mountains by Peregrine Falcons is related to three main factors: (1) the decrease in use of DDT and some other pesticides in the mid-1960s and 1970s, (2) the wardening of their nesting places, and (3) the management of their breeding biology.

HISTORY

Before the 1950s, the Peregrine Falcon lived in most of the chalk rocks of the Jura, in sandstone cliffs of the plateau, and in some steep valleys of the Alps. The Peregrine population of the whole country was about 150-200 pairs in the best years. Between the 1950s and 1970s the Swiss population of Peregrines decreased to such an extent that there was only one breeding pair left by 1971, plus a few isolated nonbreeding pairs.

BEGINNING OF OUR RESEARCH PROGRAM

In 1969, within the Societe des Sciences Naturelles du Pays de Porrentruy (SSNPP), research began on distribution, density, and reproduction of the Common Raven in the Jura. Walking over the cliffs, we discovered by chance the last pair of breeding Peregrine Falcons by finding prey remains and pellets. Motivated by this discovery, we looked systematically for this bird in the whole of the Jura, and we contacted other ornithologists interested in this species elsewhere in Switzerland to obtain information about its status. At the same time, we contacted other specialists in neighboring countries, and we decided to start a comprehensive research program on the Peregrine.

RESULTS

Nesting Sites. — The Peregrine lives in chalk cliffs situated in transverse valleys or in blind valleys. It is also found in rocks overlooking the rivers of the Jura and their effluents, sometimes in open quarries. The Peregrines breed from the beginning of March to the end of June. They lay their eggs and raise their young on the ground, in holes in the rock, or frequently, in old Common Raven nests.

Problems. — The Peregrine has long fascinated humans, partly because of its use in falconry. On noting the decrease of the population of this raptor in nature, some bird traffickers have exacerbated the problem by taking young birds out of their nests. Having observed several plundered Peregrine nests, we decided to monitor the eyries in association with cantonal hunting services, policemen, customs officers, and plenty of volunteers. The latter were given food and did some camping on the spot. They sometimes had unexpected visitors and spent lonely, unforgettable nights in the Jura in hostile weather.

The control of pesticides and the regular watching of the nests have enabled Peregrines to gradually recolonize the very sites they used to occupy. Consequently, in the Jura region, the population of the Peregrines has increased from one nesting pair in 1971 to more than 50 in 1985 (Figure 1). In all of Switzerland there are now nearly 100 pairs.

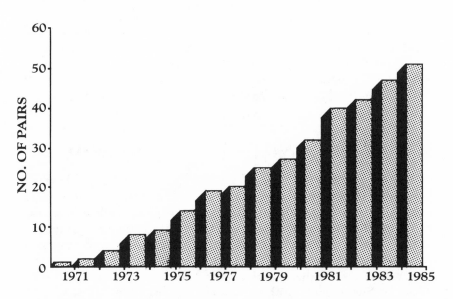

FIGURE 1. Peregrine Falcon populations in the Jura region of Switzerland, 1971-85.

By observing the nesting of the first pairs to resettle, we noted that some showed a high rate of hatching failure. We decided to intervene by taking the eggs at the beginning of incubation and inducing the birds to lay a second clutch. The collected eggs were incubated in a laboratory, and the hatchlings were fed in captivity for a fortnight before being placed into natural nests to make up broods of 3-4 young.

The ringing of the young in the Jura has enabled us to observe their recolonization of the mountains. All the young hatched in the area have been marked: most of them with red rings, some with rings made of aluminum showing a large letter visible through a telescope. In order to observe the Peregrines closely and be able to see the rings better, we have built blinds at the tops of the cliffs and placed perches well in sight from our shelters. In addition to the beautiful observations of the birds and the information on their diet collected at the feeding places, we could also observe the various behaviors of the young after leaving the nest. The results that we have gathered over the last 15 years will soon appear in a Swiss ornithological review.

FUTURE

After the justified fears of the 1970s, we can now say that the Peregrine Falcon is no longer in danger of disappearing in Switzerland. The Jura population is about to reach the saturation level, and Peregrines from the Jura are recolonizing the plateau and several lateral valleys of the Alps. The situation is sound.

The only problem troubling us now is the uncontrolled reintroduction of the Eagle Owl, a known predator of recently fledged Peregrines, near Peregrine eyries in the Jura mountains. A few pairs of these owls, which have successfully nested for about five years, come from zoological gardens or from private people who no longer know what to do with their young because captive-breeding is so successful. They release the owls wherever they can, and most of them starve to death or are killed in accidents after a few days, weeks or months. If we are pleased to observe the reappearance of raptors in areas from which they had entirely disappeared, it would be a great pity, through lack of general agreement and coordination, for the reintroduction of one species of raptor to act negatively upon the recovery of another.

ACKNOWLEDGEMENTS

We achieved our purpose thanks to scientific support by the Station Ornithologique Suisse in Sempach and to the financial contributions from Fonds d'Intervention pour les Rapaces, Organisation Suisse, Ligue Suisse pour la Protection de la Nature,

World Wildlife Federation — Switzerland, Office Federal des Forets, Division de la Protection de la Nature et du Paysage, Fondation Brunette pour la Protection de la Nature, and various associations for protection of birds, namely ALA and Nos Oiseaux.

Editors' Note: This is the second summary of this extremely interesting work to be presented at an international conference; the first was delivered in 1982 at the Second World Conference on Birds of Prey, ICBP World Working Group on Birds of Prey, Thessaloniki, Greece (but was not published in the proceedings). The increase in number of nesting pairs reported for Switzerland from 1971-85 is dramatic, and Peregrine biologists eagerly await publication of the data which will document this recovery and elucidate the factors responsible for it. The population increase in the Swiss Jura is no doubt part of an overall regional expansion also observed in adjacent parts of France and West Germany.

23 | Changes in the Peregrine Falcon Populations of France

René-Jean Monneret

Since the summary given by Terrasse and Terrasse (1969) at the 1965 Madison Peregrine Conference, a great deal of new information has been obtained about the Peregrine Falcon in France (Monneret 1987), and just as in other countries, each region now has a cadre of observers who watch after the species and keep records of its numbers, nesting success, and other details of its biology.

This report consists of two parts: (1) a review of changes in the Peregrine Falcon populations in France during the last 40 years, and (2) a brief analysis of the numerical data specifically involved in changes in the nesting population in the French Jura Mountains during the last 22 years, as an example of the way in which populations over the whole of France have been recovering.

HISTORICAL REVIEW

A brief historical account will set these changes in perspective. As for most raptors, one can distinguish three periods in the recent status of the Peregrine in France: before 1950, from 1950-70, and after 1970. These correspond approximately to the time before wide scale use of DDT and other organochlorine pesticides, the period of heaviest use, and the period of abatement in use. Before the early 1950s, few French ornithologists took an interest in the biology of raptors. Only a few enthusiasts, falconers for the most part, kept alive the knowledge of birds of prey. The small number of observers allowed for only a sketchy understanding of populations. Estimations for the whole of France were based on extrapolations from small, local censuses and were largely inaccurate.

In regard to the Peregrine Falcon, only the nesting populations of the Seine Valley and along the south coast of the English Channel were known with some accuracy. Terrasse and Terrasse (1969) and their colleagues counted 14 pairs between Paris and Le Havre on the chalky cliffs of the Seine Valley and about 40 pairs on cliffs of the Pays de

Cau. As for the rest of the country, except for eyries known traditionally for decades, even centuries, the estimation of actual numbers
remained quite subjective.

Since then, raptors have become the center of interest for a large
number of local studies, which have provided information for determining more precisely the status of the Peregrine in France between
1945-50, and for estimating changes in populations that have taken
place subsequently. Table 1 summarizes the best estimates for number
of breeding pairs by regions for the three historical periods. Before
1950, the total Peregrine population of France was probably between
900-1000 pairs, roughly twice the number first estimated by Terrasse
and Terrasse (1969).

SITUATION IN THE 1960s

By 1955, the Terrasse brothers had noticed that the northwestern
population was declining — gradually at first, but then precipitously
(Terrasse 1969). As there were no thorough scientific studies done, we
could say that hunting, shooting, trapping, or destruction of habitats
were the likely cause of this decline. It was only after the British
studies that a closer look was taken, and it could be confirmed that
chemical pollution had a great share in the eradication of a once
prosperous species (Thiollay 1966). It soon became evident that all the
populations of raptors declined quickly and in an alarming way in the
highly mechanized agricultural plains of the north, and less quickly,
but just as regularly in the areas of traditional family farms.

The last pair of Peregrines disappeared from the Seine Valley in
1963; those from the Pays de Cau disappeared about the same time
(Terrasse and Terrasse 1969). In Burgundy, a well-known wine

TABLE 1.   Population estimates of Peregrine Falcons by region in France.

| | No. of nesting pairs | | |
Region	Before 1950	1950-70	1985
Northwest (Seine, Pays de Cau)	50	0	0-2
Brittany	10-15	0	1-2
Northeast (Lorraine)	20-30	0	0
Burgundy	20-30	5	3
Vosges Massif	20-30	7	10-12
Jura Mountains	110-140	30	90-95
Northern Alps	140-160	30-40	120-130
Southern Alps	140-160	30	100-120
Massif Central	100-120	30-40	90-100
Pyrenees Range	140-160	30-40	100-120
Corsica	100	40-50	60-70

growing region, Formont (1969) had witnessed the spectacular collapse of the effective breeders within a few years: they fell from 19 to 4-5 pairs. In the Vosges, a forested region near the agricultural Alsatian plain, the original 20-30 nesting pairs had declined by 1965 to 10 not very prolific pairs (P. Felder pers. comm.).

From 1960-68 the decline of productive pairs was so rapid in the few regions where the species still remained that complete eradication seemed inevitable. By 1968-69, the Peregrine Falcon no longer nested in the whole northwestern half of France. Only some scattered populations, certainly less than 30% of their original number, remained in the mountainous parts of eastern and southern France. The whole population at that time was probably about 200-250 pairs (Table 1). This total includes the island of Corsica (Thiollay 1968), where the Peregrines belong to the Mediterranean population.

THE PRESENT SITUATION

Around 1970 the decline appeared to cease. Even better, in the early 1970s, we noticed a slight increase in some regions. In spite of a transitory drop in 1972, the reoccupation of the old territories accelerated in mountainous districts, but did not extend into those regions totally deserted for more than 10 years.

In the 1980s we have observed that the number of productive pairs has greatly increased in the regions which remained occupied by the species, and we have started seeing a few sporadic birds during the spring in northwestern France, in the places where nesting Peregrines had disappeared more than 20 years ago. In 1985, the number of territorial pairs was the highest ever counted, with a plausible estimation of between 570-660 pairs for the whole country (Table 1).

These figures show how the nesting population has developed overall, but they say nothing about the demographic phenomena associated with the decrease and, later, with the return of the species to its former territories. Detailed figures and data which I have collected for over 20 years in my studies on Peregrines in the Jura Mountains show the way in which the larger French population has changed through time. This population lives in one of the "refugia" from which the species has begun to recapture lost range in France and bordering districts of Germany and Switzerland.

A TWENTY-TWO YEAR HISTORY OF A PEREGRINE POPULATION IN THE FRENCH JURA

The data that are presented and discussed here are only a provisional outline of the more detailed information which has been collected for 22 years. The detailed figures will require elaborate statistical testing;

however, the long time spent in observation and the large quantity of numerical data recorded give this study a special importance for understanding the demographic phenomena associated with the history of this Peregrine Falcon population.

The Region and Geography. — The districts we have studied consist of the French part of the Jura Mountains, about 160 potential eyries, and the northwest peripheral fringe of the French Alps, about 190 potential eyries. These estimates of potential territories are based on clues such as presence of old prey remains, pellets, whitewash, yellow lichens growing on old roosts, and on historical information from hunters, naturalists, falconers, egg collectors, and pigeon keepers. Only the Jura region is considered here, because data have been recorded more regularly there and are more accurate. Moreover, if we were to compare diagrams showing the development of the Jura population and that of the whole area — Jura and the northern Alps — we would see much similarity between them.

The Jura Mountains are shaped like a thin limestone crescent with low and middle ranges from 400-1500 m high. They stretch out as far as 250 km from north to south and 50-60 km from east to west in the French sector. The mountains act as a border between France and Switzerland, and the high range of the Jura is in the latter country (see Juillard Chapter 22).

Forest vegetation occupies about 60% of the area, the rest being meadows or wasteland. Rainfall is quite high in every season and annually reaches 1000-2000 mm. The temperatures are among the lowest in France: average January temperatures of –10°-0° C and minimums as low as –20° C in winter, which lasts from 3-5 months.

The resident avifauna is numerous and diversified. Due to its geographical situation and orography, the region attracts a great number of northern migrants both in the spring and fall. Suitable limestone cliffs are numerous. Their average height reaches 100 m with a range from 10-250 m.

Observations and Data. — We are only considering the figures collected during the spring in the breeding areas. The number of pairs and of nestlings recorded is probably less than actual, but probably not by more than 5-10%. In some areas we can count the young at all stages of development, whereas in others we cannot. For that reason, in order to have uniformity of numbers for the whole population we only take into account the number of fledglings.

Figure 1 shows the change in total pairs per year and in the number of breeding pairs per year we have observed. Annual fluctuations, largely associated with variations in spring weather, did not conceal the continuing decrease in the numbers of breeding pairs before 1970-71, or the regular increase in number of breeding pairs from 1972-85.

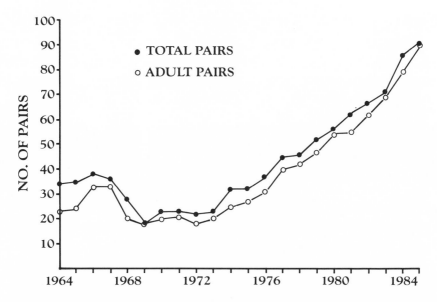

FIGURE 1. Changes in the number of Peregrine pairs per year, 1964-85.

As the rough figures are influenced by the number of observations, which have increased for 15 years as interest in the Peregrine has increased, those figures must be modified by referring them to the number of visited sites (Figure 2a). Figure 2b shows the annual change in the ratio of total pairs per visited site, and the ratio of adult pairs per visited site. The steep negative slope between 1964-72 conforms to the collapse indicated by the examination of gross figures. The increase in the ratios between 1972-82 is not so steep as the one for the decline. There seems to be little or no change after 1982. Just as the rough figures need to be modified, so these ratios must be corrected too by the fact that ornithologists stimulated by the general recovery of the species are now visiting even the least suitable cliffs, making the basis of these ratios less stable. A more detailed account of the studies from the most regularly visited sites should avoid this problem.

Figure 3 shows that the variation of the ratio of breeding pairs to total pairs precedes those of the overall French population. The decline stops, indeed, in 1968-69, about three years before the general recovery. This fact confirms, if need be, the crucial importance of reproduction for the population's increase, and that an average three years are necessary for the maturity of the breeders.

The annual values increased until 1980-81, but appeared to decline after this period. Does this decrease point to a new decline of the population, or is it only a simple variation within normal limits for a

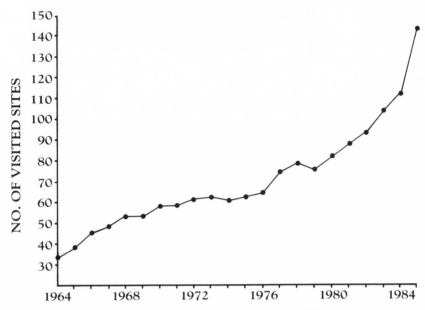

FIGURE 2a. Number of Peregrine nest sites visited per year, 1964-85.

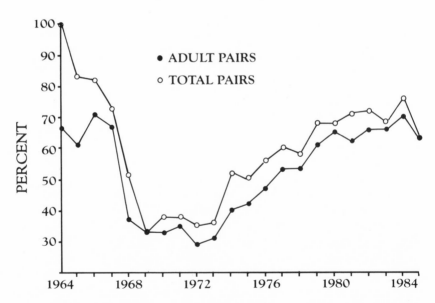

FIGURE 2b.   Changes in the percentage of total pairs and adult pairs present at sites
            visited, 1964-85.

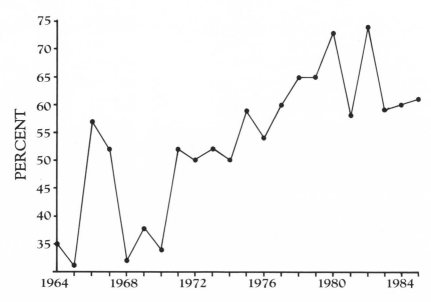

FIGURE 3. Changes in the ratio (%) of breeding pairs to total pairs of Peregrines, 1964-85.

stable population? It is probably too early to draw any final conclusion from these observations.

Figure 4 shows the annual change in ratios of young per breeding pair and young per territorial pair. One can see that these changes occurred in association with legal protection in France (1970), the banning of organochlorine pesticides, and with the campaigns of surveillance over the eyries endangered by the illegal traffic in falcons.

It is noteworthy that between 1.5-1.7 young per breeding pair, or 0.70 young per territorial pair (annual values from 1965-70) have been enough to stabilize and then to increase this endangered population. These figures show that if fledged young are not shot, poisoned, or trapped, a low level of reproduction is sufficient to sustain or increase a natural population (see also Cugnasse 1984).

Between 1972 and 1980-81, the average values increased respectively from 1.51 to 2.29 young per breeding pair, and from 0.71 to 1.55 young per territorial pair, whereas from 1981-82 to 1984-85, the same ratios showed a small decline from 2.29 to 2.11 and from 1.55 to 1.33. It appears that these ratios have followed the similar trend shown in Figure 3, denoting a good correspondence among variables.

Figure 5a shows the change in the ratio of territorial pairs per occupied site, and corroborates the loss of the productive pairs from the territorial population during the period of decline. The corollary ratios of solitary adult males per occupied site and solitary females per

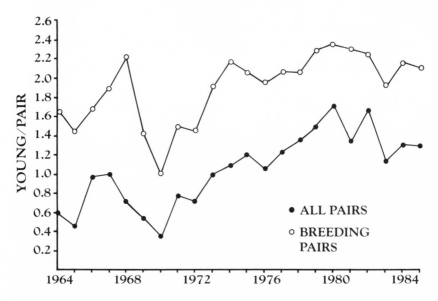

FIGURE 4. Annual fluctuations in the number of young per pair of Peregrines, 1964-85.

occupied site (Figure 5b) show the reverse trend. The latter curves especially show a considerable deficiency of adult females — 2-3 times lower than those of males — suggesting a much higher mortality of the females, or a lesser attachment to territory.

The gap of three years between the peak for single males in 1972 and for the females in 1969 conforms to the usually accepted idea that males are more attached to their territories than females. It could also suggest that females which are tied less to the territory could have filled up vacancies at other eyries causing a readjustment of the number of territorial pairs. The conspicuous relocation of pairs, noticed in some areas, could be related to this postulated phenomenon, if the noticeable move was not one involving both birds but only a female to a solitary male. In any case, this hypothesis does not explain why the number of solitary males was three times higher than that of females from 1967-75. Only an actual deficiency of females fully explains this difference.

This difference suggests a higher mortality of the females after independence or a longevity of males 3-4 years greater than for females. Such a difference between sexes could be a natural, genetic characteristic typical of the population or of the species itself, or it could be the result of a higher accumulation of toxic agents in the female's body, or a higher mortality of females from shooting, accidents, and other causes. A final conclusion cannot yet be reached.

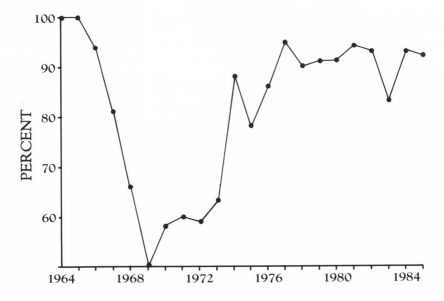

FIGURE 5a. Changes in Peregrine nest site occupancy by territorial pairs, 1964-85.

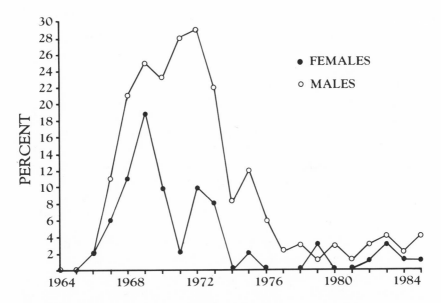

FIGURE 5b. Changes in the occurrence of solitary male and female Peregrines at occupied nest sites, 1964-85.

Figures 6a and 6b show that the increase in breeding pairs was at first (from 1970-76) the result of the filling of sites occupied by solitary adult males by new females. Figure 7 shows that the number of sites occupied by more than one pair — one pair and one female, sometimes one pair and two females or even one pair and another supernumerary pair — increased for about 10 years. This finding corroborates the trend shown in Figure 6b, and it means that the increase in number of pairs depends on the preliminary occupancy of a site by an adult male. It also indicates some degree of reluctance on the part of new birds to occupy fully deserted sites or cliffs, or a preference for settling down on territories already occupied.

The occurrence of extra birds on nesting territories, sometimes associated with positive help when only one extra female is present, seems more often to disturb the life and reproduction of the settled pair. This disruption has occurred more and more often for the last 5-6 years, particularly in cases where two or more extra birds arrive the same spring and trigger aggressive behavior of the resident pair with such high frequency that the normal breeding behavior becomes disturbed. This phenomenon could be a peculiarly effective limiting factor of the species, and it could also explain the smooth decline of the ratios of breeding pairs per territorial pairs (Figure 3), young per breeding pair (Figure 4) and young per territorial pair (Figure 4), found for about the last five years.

CONCLUSIONS

It is too early to draw any definite conclusion from this study about indications of decline over the last five years. The figures may only reflect the disastrous effects of the rainy springs of the last three years. If the trend is confirmed it could mean that the studied population has filled all available territories in suitable habitat. The annual observed figures would then vary up and down from the specific average population size for the region. It is interesting to note that the neighboring populations of the Swiss Jura and Swiss Plateaus, studied by M. Juillard and M. Neuhaus, began their recovery later than in the French Jura and North Alps, suggesting that the Swiss recovery is probably a reflection of the same population expansion. The rate of recovery has been faster in Switzerland, probably because hunting is less developed and much more regulated than in France.

Continuation of this study in the Jura should increase our knowledge of Peregrine population dynamics, the development of which seems important for the recovery of the species in France and adjacent regions. Comparison with data from other populations should also allow distinctions to be drawn between characteristics which are peculiar to the Jura population and those which are normal for the

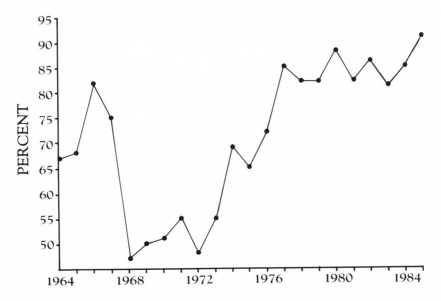

FIGURE 6a. Occurence of adult pairs of Peregrines at occupied nest sites, 1964-85.

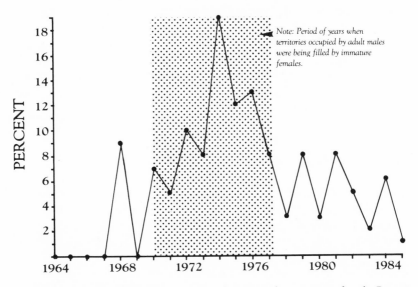

FIGURE 6b. Changes in the occurence of pairs with immature female Peregrines present, 1964-85.

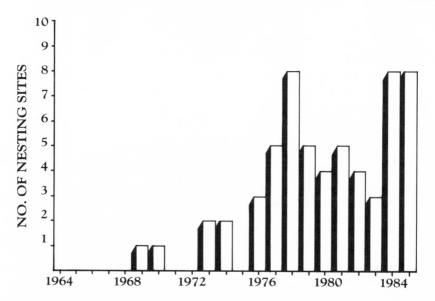

FIGURE 7.   Number of Peregrine nest sites occupied by one pair and 1-2 additional
            females or by two pairs.

species as a whole. In this regard, it is interesting to compare the
figures on density, rate of increase, age structure, and reproductive rate
of the Jura breeding population with those given by Cugnasse (1984)
for the Peregrines in the Massif Central. Despite some differences in
the geomorphological and biotic features of these regions, the population dynamics of the Peregrines nesting in these two areas have been
remarkably similar over the past 10 years, including similar rates of
population growth, high incidence of immature females at eyries and
extra birds at eyries, and relatively low reproductive success associated
with population increase.

ACKNOWLEDGEMENTS

For information on Peregrines in northeastern France I am indebted
to FIR, Alsace-Lorraine, LPO, Haut Rhin and AFRPN, Bas Rhin (D.
Beguin and M. Bertrand); for information from Burgundy,
COPRONAT (B. Bonin and L. Strenna); for the Jura Mountains and
northern Alps, FRIR Jura-Alps, CORA, FRAPNA (Y. Orecchioni,
J. M. Faton, H. Bouvier, D. Baud, B. Gougeon, D. Goy, D. Materac,
L. Weill, R. Le Pennec, P. Joly, R. Ruffinoni, L. Morlet, M. Truche,
J. P. Herold, P. Basset, M. Juillard, P. Roncin, J. C. Robert,
J. P. Cretin, J. Francois); for the Massif Central, CROAP, SEPOL,
SPN, middle Pyrenees (C. O. Auvergne, D. Brugiere, J. M. Cugnasse,
V. Heculme, T. Leblanc, D. Mathieu); for the Pyrenees, OROMP and
SAIAK; and for Corsica (O. Patrimonio and J. C. Thibault).

The research on the Peregrine population in the French Jura, which I started on my own (Monneret 1973), could not have been continued and developed without help from an increasing number of enthusiastic ornithologists. While I cannot list all their names, I must give special recognition to P. Basset, R. Ruffinoni, Y. Orechioni, J. P. Vernet, G. Perrotton, M. Juillard, R. Le Pennec, L. Morlet, J. Michel, J. M. Michelat, D. Goy, B. Goujon, M. Rebetet, Mr. and Mrs. Anay, my colleagues of the Besancon University of Science, my friends of the Regional Intervention Fund for Raptors and, of course, the French Ministry of Environment which, by its financial, logistical, and administrative help, made it possible to carry out this research under the best conditions.

24 | Status and Conservation Problems of the Peregrine Falcon in Italy

Stefano Allavena

As a well-known species with a wide distribution, the Peregrine Falcon was relatively common throughout its range during the 1950s. Since then the catastrophic effects of pesticides on the populations in North America and a part of Europe, as well as the subsequent recovery of the species in parts of those areas, has been reported (Hickey 1969, Cade 1982).

The number of breeding pairs of Peregrines in certain countries of southern Europe — Italy in particular — was poorly known until very recently. Although the presence of a nesting population in Italy was known, published information about the actual numbers was not fully reported. Cramp and Simmons (1980), for example, reported 40 pairs for continental Italy, 110-130 pairs for Sardinia, and scattered pairs for Sicily and nearby islands. Cade (1982) reported 170 or more pairs. Chiavetta (1981a) estimated a population of 250-270 pairs, distributed as follows: 20-40 pairs in the Alps, about 100 pairs in the Apennines from Liguria to Calabria, about 50 pairs in Sicily, about 80 pairs in Sardinia, and 20 pairs in the smaller islands. As a result of recent growing interest in the study of falcons in Italy, it has become possible to obtain a better understanding of the status and distribution of the Peregrine. Information now available shows that the number of pairs in Italy is decidedly greater than was previously thought.

SUBSPECIES

In peninsular Italy and the islands, *F. p. brookei* is the only subspecies. It is the typical race of the Mediterranean area. In the Alps it seems probable that there are individuals belonging to the *F. p. brookei* race, others belonging to *F. p. peregrinus* (Mingozzi 1981), and probably intergrades also. In the past, Peregrines killed in the western Alps belonged to *F. p. peregrinus*. It seems that this race remains predominant there. In any event, this problem in systematics is still being studied.

DISTRIBUTION AND STATUS

Peregrines are present in the Alps, in the Apennine chain, along the coast, in Sicily, in Sardinia, and in the smaller islands. They nest exclusively on cliffs. The distribution is as follows: western Alps, 18-20 pairs; east-central Alps, at least 8-9 pairs; Apennines, 85-95 pairs; the peninsular coast, 40-45 pairs; Sicily and its islands, 130-180 pairs; Sardinia and its islands, 120-170 pairs; and all the other smaller islands, 30-32 pairs. The total Italian population is between 430-550 pairs, of which 67% are in Sicily, Sardinia and the smaller islands. Minimum density is found in the Alps. Reproductive data for several areas since 1971 are given in Table 1.

A comparison of the Italian data with similar data from Scotland, France and Spain (Newton 1979, Meyburg 1981, Schenk et al. 1983) suggests that the Italian population is relatively healthy and stable.

CONSERVATION

Although the Peregrine population may be considered to be in good condition in Italy, it is subject to certain negative impacts, mainly nest-robbing of eggs and young, illegal shooting, environmental degradation, and disturbances of various kinds.

Nest-robbing. — For a number of years nest robbers, especially from West Germany, have been coming to Italy seeking Peregrine eggs and young. Almost all stolen birds are sold abroad. In the last few years security measures against nest-robbing have been taken by the Italian Forest Service as well as by nature conservation groups. They are guarding nesting sites and investigating suspected nest robbers. All raptors, including the Peregrine, have complete legal protection in Italy.

Even though the number of persons available for protecting the Peregrine is limited, efforts have been effective in making nest-robbing more difficult and risky. As a result, in areas where nests were in the past molested, pairs are now reproducing regularly.

Illegal Shooting. — Although protected by law, Peregrines are killed by hunters during every hunting season (18 August-10 March). This is a common practice. It is difficult to estimate the losses, and even more difficult to control the shooting. In certain areas of the south, there is a surviving tradition of shooting young Peregrines as they take their first flight.

Environmental Degradation. — In spite of the fact that the Peregrine is very adaptable to environmental changes, the increasing impact of human activities on the environment will have distinctly negative effects on its survival. In particular, disturbances in the immediate vicinity of nesting sites discourage pairs from remaining there. Road building opens up hitherto remote areas to nest-robbing and other human activities that disturb breeding. In addition, road building often leads to urbanization.

Disturbance of Various Kinds. — In recent years recreational activities have become more common. Some of these can have notable

TABLE 1. Reproductive and demographic values for Peregrines in the areas of Italy surveyed.

Region (Period of study)	No. young per pair	No. young per successful pair	% productive pairs
Western Alps (1978-82)[a]	1.63	2.57	63.6
Northern Apennines (1971-81)[a]	1.19	2.32	51.4
Central Italy (1983-85)	2.14	2.51	87.0
Southern Italy (1983-85)[b]	1.90	2.03	93.3
Sicily (1978-81)[a]	2.05	2.25	91.1
Sardinia (1972-81)[a]	1.72	2.39	71.9
Overall	1.77	2.34	76.4

[a] Data from Fasce and Mingozzi (1983), Chiavetta (1981a), Schenk et al. (1983).
[b] Data from Mirabelli (pers. comm.).

impact on the overall environment and on Peregrines in particular. Nature photography, rock-climbing on cliffs where nesting is taking place, and careless watching and nature observation are all activities that, when uncontrolled, can result in the Peregrines ceasing to breed. What is particularly disturbing for the future is that the trend is towards an increase in these activities.

ACKNOWLEDGEMENTS

I thank the following for furnishing research data, without which it would have been impossible to prepare this paper: G. Angle, M. Chiavetta, L. Corsetti, A. Di Marca, R. Di Mauro, S. Falcone, E. Germi, G. Mezzalira, T. Mingozzi, A. Monni, G. Murgia, M. Panella, P. Pedrini, M. Pellegrini, F. Perco, I. Reichegger, S. Seminara, A. Zocchi, and F. Zunino. I particularly thank T. M. Pasca for assistance in translating this paper into English.

25 | Status, Ecology, and Conservation of the Peregrine Falcon in Spain

Borja Heredia, Fernando Hiraldo,
Luis M. González, and José L. González

Spain, Australia, the islands of the North Pacific and the Bering Sea, and the British Isles are major centers of Peregrine abundance in the world (Cade 1982). The Peregrine is present in every part of Spain where cliffs or manmade structures are available for breeding. *F. p. brookei* is the race which breeds in the Mediterranean districts, but Peregrines in the north and in the Pyrenees may be intergrades with nominate *F. p. peregrinus*. Our knowledge of the Peregrine in Spain is still fragmentary since no monographic study has yet been done. Estimates have been made on the size of the population (Noval 1976, Garzón 1977), and aspects of its biology have been described in general works on birds of prey (Bernis 1966, Valverde 1967, Noval 1976, Morillo 1984). The present paper summarizes a national survey and includes information about distribution, density, productivity, demography, prey and conservation problems.

MATERIALS AND METHODS

Our data come from a general review of the literature, local ornithological atlases (de Juana 1980, Lopez Beiras and Guitian 1983, Muntaner et al. 1984, Alvarez et al. 1985, Elosegui 1985), reports from individual observers and groups around the country plus our unpublished observations. The Canary Islands have not been included; they are inhabited by *F. p. pelegrinoides* (Cramp and Simmons 1980).

The data on status include resident pairs on territory during the breeding season, omitting the wintering population from other European countries (Bernis 1966). The survey included over 80% of the country. The density of breeding pairs was studied in three of the major geotectonic units which form the Iberian Peninsula by comparing the number of National Topographic Map squares in which the species occurred in each of the units. These regions are the hercynian basement, the mesozoic areas, and the tertiary basins (Vegas and Banda 1982). The hercynian basement predominates in the western parts of the country. It includes low-altitude mountain ranges where cliffs are not very abundant; the rocks are granites, gneisses, quartzites and slates. The mesozoic areas are more abrupt, with mountains of higher altitude and plenty of cliffs and crags; the most abundant rock is limestone. The tertiary basins are plains covered with clay, gypsum and other soft deposits; the only available cliffs are found along rivers.

Data on average minimum distance between occupied eyries in the different sample areas have been taken from reports of C. Junco (Palencia), G. Doval and F. Martinez (unpubl. ms.) (Madrid, Segovia and Soria), J. M. Hernandez (Salamanca), Sanchez y Carmona (unpubl. ms.) (Murcia), Parellada and de Juan (1981) (Pyrenees) and our own unpublished data (Huelva, central ranges). Data on productivity and human disturbance come from reports by C. Llandrés and B. Ramos (Madrid, Valladolid and Guadalajara), A. Fernandez-Gil (Burgos) and Garzón and Araujo (1972) (central Spain). Information about food comes from the analysis of pellets and prey remains over the annual cycle. It has been compiled from Valverde (1967) (Valladolid and Madrid), Real (1981, 1983) (Barcelona), Soler et al. (1983) (Granada) and our own unpublished data (Huelva, Guadalajara).

RESULTS AND DISCUSSION

Population, Distribution and Density. — Our survey revealed 1628-1751 pairs. This is probably a conservative estimate as not all areas were searched equally. The amount of suitable habitat for the Peregrine in Spain is great, and some regions are still mostly unsurveyed. The numbers of breeding pairs in the different autonomous communities are given in Table 1. Previous national estimates were 1500 pairs (Noval 1976) and 2000 pairs (Garzón 1977). In both cases the numbers given were only approximate.

The Peregrine is distributed throughout Spain, wherever suitable habitat is available for breeding. It was found in 532 of 1078 (49%) of the squares of the National Topographic Map. The distribution was uneven, with areas of high concentration and others where the species was almost lacking (Figure 1). The highest density was in the mesozoic areas, followed by the basins and the hercynian basement; the differences are significant (Table 2). In the northern basins of the Duero and Ebro rivers the number of breeding pairs was much larger than in the southern basins of the Guadiana and Guadalquivir rivers, where cliffs are practically absent.

TABLE 1.   Breeding pairs of Peregrines in the Spanish autonomous communities.

District	Estimated no. of pairs
Galicia/Asturias/Cantabria	225
Pais Vasco	25-35
Navarra	70
Rioja	30-35
Aragon	208-218
Cataluña	170-180
Madrid	30
Extremadura	30-36
Castilla-Leon	266-291
Castilla-La Mancha	136-163
Valencia	90
Baleares	57-72
Murcia	60
Andalucia	231-246
Total	1628-1751

The average minimum distance between neighboring pairs in the three areas was also different. The shortest distances were found in the basins, followed by the mesozoic areas and the hercynian basement, and the differences are significant (Table 2).

The differences in occupancy and spacing of breeding pairs in the areas studied are probably related to the morphological characteristics of the landscape and the resulting difference in nest-site availability, a factor that can strongly limit Peregrine Falcon populations (Cade 1960). However, the abundance of suitable prey is probably another influencing factor (Ratcliffe 1980, Thiollay 1982).

Breeding Performance and Population Trends. — The average annual breeding success of the Peregrine in Spain has been 1.73 young per territorial pair ($n=262$). In areas densely populated by humans, such as the basins, productivity figures tend to be smaller (1.39 young per territorial pair, $n=212$) than in areas with less human pressure (2.40 young per territorial pair, $n=50$), and the difference is significant ($t=3.38$, $P<0.001$). A similar trend was found in the British Isles in districts where a great amount of egg-collecting was carried out and in others where it was not (Ratcliffe 1980).

In the absence of evidence of reproductive failure related to pesticide pollution, it seems that breeding performance has been reduced in some areas by rock-climbing, egg-collecting and robbing of young. During the years 1970-80 the Spanish Peregrine population seemed to

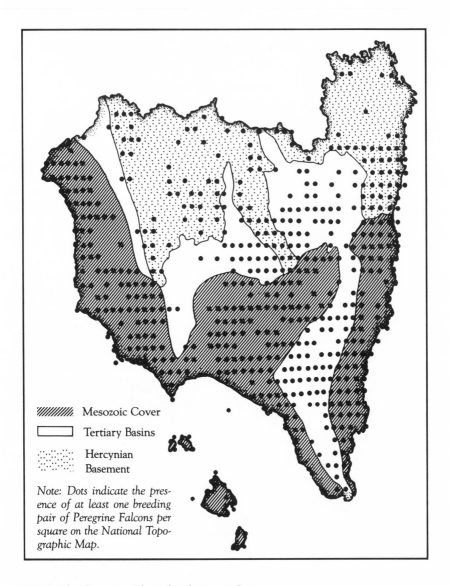

Mesozoic Cover

Tertiary Basins

Hercynian
Basement

Note: Dots indicate the presence of at least one breeding pair of Peregrine Falcons per square on the National Topographic Map.

FIGURE 1.   Peregrine Falcon distribution in Spain.

show symptoms of decline (Garzón 1973, Aragüés and Lucientes 1980, Campos 1982), although the reasons remain unclear. At present this trend seems to have stopped, though in local areas some territories have been recently abandoned on account of nearby human activities. It is difficult to assess the present situation in the whole country, as the limiting factors are perhaps different from one area to another.

TABLE 2. Percentage of National Topographic Map squares where the Peregrine Falcon is present, and average minimum distance between neighboring pairs in the three major geotectonic units of the Iberian Peninsula. Differences between the units are statistically significant for both parameters.

Geotectonic unit	% squares where present (n)	Avg. min. distance (km) between pairs (n)
Hercynian basement (Hb)	36.7 (330)	20.3 (26)
Mesozoic cover (Mc)	62.1 (451)	8.7 (41)
Tertiary basins (Tb)	48.0 (273)	4.9 (35)

[a] For % of squares present: Hb-Mc: $G = 49.78$, $P < 0.001$; Hb-Tb: $G = 7.87$, $P < 0.01$; Mc-Tb: $G = 13.73$, $P < 0.001$; G-test. For average minimum distance: Hb-Mc: $t = 6.57$, $P < 0.001$; Hb-Tb: $t = 8.97$, $P < 0.001$; Mc-Tb: $t = 4.42$, $P < 0.001$; t-test.

Generally, the population appears to be stable, with a tendency to decrease in some areas with great human pressure.

Diet. — The diet of the Peregrine Falcon in four areas of Spain is represented in Figure 2, with a complete list of prey items in Table 3. Columbiform birds are the most preyed upon, but where they are scarce passerines take their place. The latter form the second most frequent group, although the charadriiforms are predominant as secondary prey along coasts. Other significant groups are bats (Chiroptera) and apodiform, coraciiform, and galliform birds. These prey selections are consistent with those found in other areas of Europe (Cramp and Simmons 1980).

Major Threats and Conservation. — The robbing of young has probably been a major factor affecting the Peregrine population in Spain, especially in basin areas where year after year, some birds are taken illegally for falconry or for trade abroad. In 1979-81, 140 young disappeared from 75 eyries in three central districts (Llandrés and Ramos unpubl. ms.).

In Spain the Peregrine was protected by law beginning in 1970, and standard fines for taking eggs and young or killing individuals are about 90,000 pesetas ($600). At present there are no coordinated efforts to put an end to poaching. Shooting also occurs, but the Peregrine is not affected as much as other raptors. Out of 910 birds of prey illegally killed to be stuffed, five were Peregrine Falcons (Costa et al. 1982, Tamame and Barbero 1983). Cases of electrocution or crashing against power lines are infrequent. In some eastern districts, the Peregrine has suffered direct persecution from pigeon fanciers, a factor that could become an important problem.

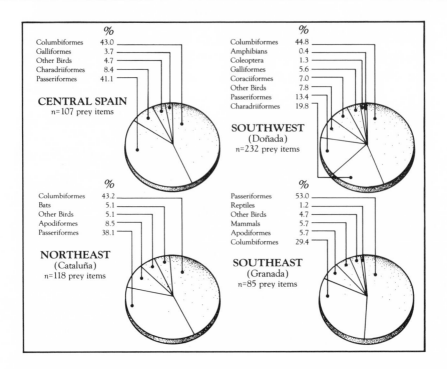

FIGURE 2.   Peregrine Falcon prey utilization in four areas of Spain.

Pesticide pollution reduces Peregrine breeding performance (Peakall and Kiff 1979). The free use of DDT and its derivatives was prohibited in Spain in 1976, but it can still be used locally in so-called emergency situations (Hernández 1982). It remains unclear how this factor has affected the Peregrine population. Analysis of Imperial Eagle eggs from different areas in Spain have shown levels of organochlorine compounds averaging 5.6 ppm (0.4-12.6 ppm, $n=40$) in the years 1972-84. Levels tended to decrease in this period (González and Hiraldo 1985). It is likely some environmental pollutants occur in Peregrines and their eggs, but not in enough quantity to cause reproductive failure.

The Eagle Owl often preys on Peregrines (Mikkola 1976). This owl is a common resident in Spain, but apparently few Peregrines are eaten. In two studies on the diet of this owl, more than 7000 prey items were analyzed but no Peregrine remains were found (Hiraldo et al. 1975, Donázar pers. comm.).*

To promote the conservation of Peregrines in Spain we suggest the establishment of a captive breeding center to provide falconers with

*Editors' Note: Observations on loss of released Peregrines in the eastern United States due to predation by Great Horned Owls indicate that the young falcons frequently are not eaten, or only small portions of them are, so that remains might not show up around owl nests and perches.

TABLE 3. Prey items of the Peregrine Falcon in Spain.

Taxa	n	Taxa	n
Birds	550	Birds (cont.)	
European Sparrowhawk	1	Crag Martin	3
Red-legged Partridge	7	Northern Shrike	2
Common Quail	10	Unidentified Muscicapidae	4
Common Moorhen	1	Blackbird	9
Northern Lapwing	11	Mistle Thrush	3
Unidentified *Limosa*	1	Song Thrush	11
Ruddy Turnstone	1	Unidentified *Turdus*	17
Little Stint	1	Unidentified *Emberiza*	1
Curlew Sandpiper	2	Chaffinch	3
Dunlin	8	Brambling	1
Snowy Plover	6	Citril Finch	1
Unidentified *Tringa*	2	Goldfinch	4
Common Sandpiper	1	Greenfinch	1
Redshank	4	Linnet	3
Wood Sandpiper	2	Red Crossbill	1
Golden Plover	2	Unidentified Fringillidae	4
Jack Snipe	1	House Sparrow	3
Black-winged Stilt	1	Unidentified *Passer*	1
Common Snipe	1	Rock Sparrow	1
Stone-Curlew	2	Spotless Starling	6
Unidentified Charadriiformes	11	European Starling	2
Pintailed Sandgrouse	6	Golden Oriole	5
Wood Pigeon	11	Jay	6
Feral Pigeon (Rock Dove)	34	Chough	1
Stock Dove	1	Azure-winged Magpie	4
Unidentified *Columba*	106	Carrion Crow	4
Turtle-Dove	83	Jackdaw	13
Unidentified Columbiformes	8	Black-billed Magpie	1
European Cuckoo	1	Unidentified Passeriformes	19
Great Spotted Cuckoo	1	Unidentified Aves	11
Little Owl	4	Mammals	12
Red-necked Nightjar	2	Unidentified *Pipistrellus*	6
Common Swift	20	House Rat (*Rattus rattus*)	2
European Bee Eater	4	Common Rabbit	
Common Roller	5	(*Oryctolagus cuniculus*)	4
Hoopoe	7	Insects	3
Green Woodpecker	2	Unidentified Coleoptera	3
Greater Short-toed Lark	1	Amphibians	1
Calandra Lark	5	Unidentified Anura	1
Wood Lark	1	Reptiles	1
Eurasian Skylark	1	Eyed Lizard (*Lacerta lepida*)	1
Unidentified Alaudidae	26		

captive-bred birds. We also urge regular watches in the areas most affected by robberies in order to increase law enforcement. Finally, research should be carried out to determine whether or not environmental pollutants are affecting reproduction and to establish a reliable estimate of the needed "recruitment standard" for replacing losses among the adult breeders, so that an assessment of the "harvestable surplus" can be made.

ACKNOWLEDGEMENTS

The present paper would not have been possible without the collaboration of all persons, groups and institutions listed here (with regions for which they provided information in parentheses): ADENEX, J. J. Ferrero (Extremadura); Agencia de Medio Ambiente, M. Romero (Malaga); ANSAR (Zaragoza); ARCA, G. Palomero (Cantabria); ATHENE, G. Doval, F. Martinez (Madrid); D. Carmona, M. A. Sanchez (Murcia); Diputacion General de Aragon, M. Cabrera, I. Ballarin (Zaragoza); DURATON, J. Saez (Segovia); DALMA, J. J. Calvo (Guadalajara); Dpto. de Zoologia, Univ. of Leon, F. J. Purroy (Leon); E. Errando (Valencia, Castellon); J. Escudero, A. Manzanares (Albacete); A. Fernandez-Gil (Burgos, Vizcaya); R. Heredia (Huesca); GEDEB, J. Bustamante (Burgos); Grupo Zaragoza de Ornitologia (Zaragoza); C. Junco (Palencia); O. del Junco (Cadiz); P. P. Linares (Granada); C. Llandrés, B. Ramos (Valladolid, Madrid, Guadalajara); J. Manrique (Almeria); A. Noval (Asturias); NYCTICORAX, G. Sierra (Valladolid); OTUS, A. Marco (Teruel); J. Real (Cataluña); J. A. Sanchez (Alicante); Servici de Conservacio de la Naturaleza, J. Muntaner (Baleares); Seccio Territorial del Medi Natural, J. Canut, D. Garcia, J. Marco (Lerida); J. M. Hernandez (Salamanca).

To them and to B. Arroyo, V. Garza, F. Ibañez, A. Larramendi, A. Ortega, J. Prada and C. Sansegundo we are most grateful. We also thank T. Cade, who suggested this work as a contribution to the Second International Peregrine Conference.

Commentary

Changes in the Status of the Peregrine Falcon in Europe: An Overview

Ian Newton

The Peregrine has received such widespread attention in recent years that more information is now available on its status and distribution than at any time previously. In this review, I summarize some recent published data from different parts of Europe and examine Peregrine population trends in relation to organochlorine pesticide use. The quality of information varies greatly from one country to another, but for most countries it is sufficient to give some idea of population size and trend and to pinpoint some remaining problems.

ORGANOCHLORINES AND OTHER CHEMICALS

Over much of Europe, DDT came into agricultural use in the late 1940s, and the more toxic cyclodiene compounds, including aldrin and dieldrin, were introduced in the late 1950s. The efficiency of all these compounds led to their rapid and widespread adoption. They were used as general insecticides on practically all common crop species, and the cyclodienes became the main chemicals used in seed treatments. Their use continued unabated for several years; then, owing partly to widespread environmental problems, their use became progressively more restricted during the 20-year period between the early 1960s and early 1980s. In general, restrictions were first imposed in the northern half of Europe and spread to southern countries in later years. The use of DDT and the cyclodienes was banned in the Scandinavian countries in 1969-72; in the Netherlands, cyclodienes were restricted in 1968, and DDT was banned in 1973 (Burgers et al. 1986); in West Germany, DDT was banned in 1972, and dieldrin and some other organochlorines in 1974 (Ellenberg and Dietrich 1981); in Britain, cyclodiene use was reduced by successive (nonbinding) restrictions in 1962, 1965 and 1975; in Spain, DDT was banned in 1977; and in all European Economic Community countries, any remaining uses of DDT and the cyclodienes were banned in 1981-83. In the

Soviet Union, DDT was "excluded from the list of chemicals recommended for pest control" in 1970 (Govortchenko 1983).

Figures on organochlorine use have seldom been made available, but Table 1 lists some figures for several countries that were published in the Food and Agriculture Organization's (United Nations) Production Yearbook for 1983. They confirm substantial use of DDT and aldrin/dieldrin in several countries, notably Italy, in the mid-1970s, and some continued use in a few countries, notably Austria and Portugal, beyond 1980. In addition, the Shell Chemical Company released the following data on their yearly sales (tons) of aldrin/dieldrin in Britain from 1959-73: 362, 458, 371, 368, 386, 229, 172, 88, 72, 93, 83, 71, 56, 41 and 54. These figures reflect both agricultural and industrial uses. In general, therefore, the use of DDT and cyclodiene compounds has been greatly reduced over most of Europe during the last 15-20 years.

The decline in Peregrine numbers became obvious mainly in the late 1950s, soon after the cyclodienes came into use. These highly toxic chemicals affected bird populations mainly by increasing mortality above the natural level. They were associated with many large-scale mortality incidents involving seed-eating birds and their predators. Other chemicals may have contributed to the decline in Peregrine numbers. In particular, DDE (from DDT) has been linked with eggshell thinning and reduced breeding success. The highly persistent

TABLE 1. Estimates of annual organochlorine use in various European countries. Figures show numbers of 100 kg units, and are taken from the United Nations Food and Agriculture Organization's Production Yearbook for 1983. Blanks imply no official usage.

Country	DDT				Aldrin/dieldrin			
	1974-76	1980	1981	1982	1974-76	1980	1981	1982
Austria	109	52	56	64	21	30	38	39
Czechoslovakia	333				70			
Denmark	8	12			9	5		
Finland								
Greece								
Hungary	6							
Italy	15,695				9127			
Malta							8	8
Norway								
Poland	167							
Portugal							167	162
Sweden								
Switzerland	100	20	30	30				
Totals	16,418	84	86	94	9227	210	208	39

hexachlorobenzene (HCB) was used as a fungicide in Germany, Spain and elsewhere in the late 1950s and early 1960s. Its involvement in wildlife mortality incidents was suspected, but not proved, because it always occurred alongside other organochlorines (Dobson et al. 1984). HCB appeared at high concentrations in raptor eggs from Germany (Conrad 1977) and could conceivably have contributed to the reduction in Peregrine numbers there. Likewise, alkyl-mercury fungicides were used in Sweden, and elsewhere, in the late 1950s and early 1960s. They were implicated in many incidents of bird mortality (Borg et al. 1969), and may also have affected Peregrines. Unlike the organochlorines, however, to which all declining Peregrine populations were exposed, HCB and alkyl-mercury were used only in certain countries, so they cannot be held responsible for widespread decline. The industrial polychlorinated biphenyls (PCBs) have also occurred as widespread contaminants in Peregrines, and levels in eggs have not diminished in recent years. Some populations (including Britain's) have partly recovered despite continuing high PCB contamination; it therefore seems unlikely that these chemicals were important in the decline.

As Peregrine populations dwindled, there was a rising demand for eggs and young in Germany and elsewhere, and they became subject to greater human pressures. In Europe as a whole, however, the timing and pattern of decline suggested strongly that the organochlorines were the primary cause, while other chemicals, or other influences, may have contributed in a minor way or in particular regions.

POPULATION DECLINE

Because it was unexpected, the decline in Peregrine populations was not widely noticed until it was well under way. In most regions it became evident in the late 1950s or early 1960s, though poor breeding was noted earlier. In each region, breeding numbers reached their lowest in the 1960s or 1970s, depending partly on patterns of exposure to organochlorines in breeding and wintering areas. In Britain, numbers were lowest around 1963 at about 44% of the pre-organochlorine level (Ratcliffe 1980), in France around 1970 at 25-30% of their former level, in West Germany around 1965 at about 10%, and in Fennoscandia around 1975 at less than 5%. Regional variation was marked in each of these countries, and birds disappeared altogether in some districts. Declines in resident populations were generally least pronounced in areas remote from farmland (e.g., the Scottish Highlands), where the falcons fed mainly on uncontaminated resident prey species, whereas extinctions occurred in the most arable areas, where pesticide use was greatest (e.g., southeast England and northwest France). The extensive tree-nesting population which occupied the mainly agricultural landscape extending across northern and eastern Germany into Poland and the Baltic states was extirpated. Peregrines also disappeared from Belgium, which had only about 35 pairs (Kesteloot 1977), and from Denmark, which held only 2-5 pairs (Dyck et al. 1977, Wille 1977). Declines were acknowledged in other European countries, but without estimates of former numbers, it was impossible to judge their extent. In Spain and Portugal, numbers were said to still be decreasing in the early 1980s, and at least in Portugal the relevant organochlorines were still in use (for Spain see Heredia et al. Chapter 25, for Portugal see Palma 1985).

POPULATION RECOVERY

Following restrictions in organochlorine use, some recovery has occurred in regions where residual populations remained, or where birds were reintroduced. In Britain, numbers had increased by 1981 to more than 90% of their pre-pesticide level (Ratcliffe 1984a), in West Germany to 30% by 1985, in France to 60% by 1985, but in Fennoscandia to only 5% by 1985. Annual rates of increase have varied from 12% in Britain to 16% in West Germany, but within each country there was again much local variation (see Ratcliffe 1980 for Britain).

Only in the Harz Mountains in East Germany was the reestablishment attributable entirely to releases of captive-bred birds. In this area, Peregrines had disappeared altogether by 1974 (Kirmse and Kleinstäuber 1977), and the three pairs found there in 1985 were from releases by C. Saar. Further releases may have contributed to the spectacular increase observed in Bavaria. Releases of captive-bred birds in Sweden may also have helped recovery in Fennoscandia, but they cannot have been wholly responsible. These are the only areas in Europe where releases have been made on any scale, but breeding programs have been started in Poland and Czechoslovakia, where only a few pairs now remain.

In regions where sufficient chemical analyses have been made, population increases have coincided with reductions in organochlorine levels in Peregrine eggs. In Germany, declines were noted in egg levels of DDE, dieldrin and HCB, and in Britain and Fennoscandia, in DDE and dieldrin (Conrad 1977, Ratcliffe 1980, Schilling and Rockenbauch 1985). In Fennoscandia, where population decline continued later than elsewhere, organochlorine levels in eggs were higher in the 1970s than in Britain and Germany during the same period. The Peregrines that breed in Fennoscandia are mainly migratory, and Lindberg (1985) attributed continuing high contamination to their wintering largely on estuaries, where pollutants tend to accumulate. Both in wintering and breeding areas, these Peregrines eat many waders which are contaminated at higher levels than are pigeons and other species which predominate in the Peregrine's diet elsewhere. Declines in organochlorine pesticide levels (especially cyclodienes) have also been noted in eggs and tissues of other predatory birds in Europe, wherever analyses have been made (e.g., Fuchs et al. 1972 for the Netherlands, Conrad 1981 for West Germany, Newton and Haas 1984 for Britain).

PRESENT POPULATIONS

The completeness of population estimates varies greatly among countries, depending on the terrain and effort expended on surveys. At one extreme, the estimates from Britain and Germany are probably accurate to within 10%; in some other countries, such as Yugoslavia and Greece, estimates are little more than informed guesses. However, taking the estimates at face value, Spain held more Peregrines than any other European country, with an estimated 1500-1600 pairs in the early 1980s. Britain was next, with about 900 pairs. Substantial numbers were also found in Italy (including Sardinia and Sicily) and in France (Table 2). Europe as a whole probably held at least 4000 pairs. Considering the extent of declines and the depleted status of populations in several countries, the potential for further increase and spread is great.

These estimates exclude the Soviet Union, for which I know of no recent information. In an earlier review, Cramp and Simmons (1980) gave estimates from Fischer (1967) of 950-1000 pairs for European Russia to the Caucasus, but there are probably fewer now. Estonia is said to have held at least 40 pairs in the early 1950s, but breeding has not been proven since 1971 (Kumari 1974, Cramp and Simmons 1980). Latvia formerly held at least 20-25 pairs, which later disappeared. The species is also said to have gone from Lithuania. In these Baltic states the former population nested mainly on bogs. Peregrines also bred on Cyprus and Malta into the 1970s (Sultana and Gauci 1977, Cramp and Simmons 1980), and may still be present there.

Although reduction in organochlorine pesticide use has almost certainly been the crucial factor permitting population recovery in Europe, extra protection against human nest-robbers has helped to reduce the clutch and brood losses in recent years. This has been particularly true in West Germany and Switzerland, where continued observation of individual nests has been accompanied by various other measures to improve productivity (Brücher and Wegner Chapter 60).

DISCUSSION

In general, the Peregrine's decline followed the introduction of organochlorine pesticides in agriculture, and its recovery followed

TABLE 2. Population estimates (pair numbers) for Peregrines in different European countries.

Country	Pre-DDT population	Lowest level (year)	Recent level (year)	Recent trend[a]	Source
Austria	200	27 (ca. 1980)	40-45 (1985)	I	Karenits unpubl. ms.
Belgium	35	0 (1975)	0	–	Kesteloot 1977
Britain and Northern Ireland	874	385[b] (1963)	784-816 (1985)	I	Ratcliffe 1984a; Ratcliffe Chapter 17
Czechoslovakia	?	1 (1976)	1-2 (1984-85)	?	Sládek 1977; Hudec Chapter 21
Denmark	2-5	0 (1973)	0 (1984)	–	Dyck et al. 1977; Wille 1977
East Germany	120+	0 (1974)	5 (1985)	I	Bijleveld 1974; Kleinstäuber and Kirmse Chapter 20
Fennoscandia	2000-3500	65 (1975)	120-150 (1985)	I	Lindberg et al. Chapter 18
France	900-1000	200-300 (1970)	600 (1985)	I	Monneret Chapter 23
Greece	?	?	150	D?	Hallman 1985
Hungary	10	?	0 (1977)	–	Cramp and Simmons 1980
Ireland	278	?	225 (1981)	I	Norris and Wilson 1983
Italy[c]	?	?	430-550 (1985)	?	Allavena Chapter 24
Malta	?	?	1-2 (1975)	?	Sultana and Gauci 1977
Poland	180+	? (1970s)	1-2 (1978-82)	?	Bijleveld 1974
Portugal	?	?	20-30	D	Palma 1985; Rufino et al. 1985
Spain	2000	?	1588-1698	D?	Garzón 1977; Heredia et al. Chapter 25
Switzerland	50+	1+ (1970)	100+ (1985)	I	Bijleveld 1974; Juillard Chapter 22
West Germany	400-430	75 (1970)	130 (1984)	I	Mebs Chapter 19
Yugoslavia	?	?	60+	D	Vasic et al. 1985

[a] I = increase; D = decrease.
[b] Calculated as 44% (Ratcliffe 1980) of the pre-DDT level given.
[c] Includes Sardina and Sicily, which have substantial numbers.

restrictions in organochlorine use. Regional variations in the timing and extent of population change corresponded with variations in exposure to these chemicals. Declines were least marked in resident populations living in mountain areas away from agricultural land (e.g., the Scottish Highlands), and most marked in populations occurring in farmland (northern Germany) or wintering in farmland and estuaries (Fennoscandia). Although changes have also occurred in the extent of human predation, there is no reason to doubt that changes in the use of organochlorine pesticides have been the major cause of Peregrine population changes. The roles of other chemicals, notably HCB and alkyl-mercury, remain uncertain, but they are no longer used on a large scale.

A remaining uncertainty concerns the relative roles of DDT/DDE and the cyclodienes in the declines. The timing of the decline and the subsequent recovery, plus the known high toxicity of aldrin/dieldrin strongly suggest that cyclodienes were the primary cause of the population changes. The small number of Peregrines found dead and analyzed in recent decades included several with dieldrin residues (from aldrin and dieldrin) thought large enough to have killed them. This conclusion was based on analogy with various nonraptorial birds in captivity, where dieldrin emerged as 12-150 times more toxic than DDT, depending on species (Hudson et al. 1984).

At the same time, DDE has been clearly implicated in eggshell thinning and reduced breeding success (Newton 1979, Ratcliffe 1980). An unresolved question is whether poor breeding success through DDE was, on its own, sufficient to promote some population decline in the absence of extra mortality caused by cyclodienes. The fact that decline was not apparent until after cyclodienes came into use some 8-9 years after DDT does not exonerate DDT in this respect. A lag of several years would be expected before reduced reproduction affected the breeding numbers of such a long-lived bird, initially buffered against decline by a nonbreeding "surplus". However, Peregrine populations can withstand a considerable loss of eggs and young without declining, as shown by the long periods of heavy human nest-robbing which formerly occurred in several European countries. The birds evidently compensated for this loss, either by improved post-fledging survival or by breeding at an earlier age, and thereby maintained their numbers.*

Even the most elementary population model confirms that decline in breeding numbers is more readily brought about by an increase in adult mortality than by a corresponding decline in breeding rate

* Editors' Note: Alternatively, natality may have been sufficiently high even with these losses to maintain a stable breeding population limited by number of territories, with some surplus nonbreeders, without compensatory adjustments in age of first breeding or in survival of birds after leaving the nest. See Hunt Chapter 63 for relevant discussion.

(Young 1969). Where declines were monitored from annual counts, as in parts of Britain and Germany (Kirmse and Kleinstäuber 1977, Ratcliffe 1980), the rates were too rapid to be attributed to poor breeding alone and must have entailed extra mortality (as high as 22% between 1961 and 1962 in northern England).

Little can be learned from the pattern of recovery, because in most countries, DDT and cyclodiene use were restricted at about the same time. Increase in breeding populations has been accompanied by improvements in eggshell thickness and breeding success. What is clear, however, is that recovery has taken place despite continued eggshell thinning and egg breakage, and despite a lower-than-"normal" reproductive rate.

It is therefore plausible that, through their effects on mortality, the cyclodienes were the main cause of the Peregrine's decline (at least in those regions for which information is available). Through its effect on breeding, DDE may well have hastened the speed of the decline and slowed the recovery; its contribution (relative to that of dieldrin) may also have varied in different areas. The evidence for these views is circumstantial, but is paralleled in the European Sparrowhawk, which is shorter-lived than the Peregrine and has been more thoroughly studied in this respect (Newton and Haas 1984, Burgers et al. 1986).

SUMMARY

(1) The widespread decline in Peregrine breeding populations which occurred in Europe, mainly in the late 1950s and 1960s, followed the widespread introduction of organochlorine pesticides in agriculture. The recovery in populations, which began in most countries during the 1970s, followed reductions in organochlorine use.

(2) The population declines were more closely linked with the use of cyclodienes (aldrin and dieldrin) than with DDT, and appear to have resulted mainly from increased adult mortality.

(3) In 1985, the Peregrine population of Europe was probably at least 4000 breeding pairs, with considerable potential for further increase and spread. Numbers were still extremely low in certain countries which formerly held large populations, notably Czechoslovakia, East Germany and Poland.

ACKNOWLEDGEMENTS

I am grateful to T. Cade, J. Dempster and P. Lindberg for helpful comments on the manuscript.

4 | Status of the Peregrine in Other Parts of the World

26 | Distribution and Status of the Peregrine Falcon in South America

J. Weldon McNutt, David H. Ellis,
Cesar Peres Garat, Terry B. Roundy,
W. Guillermo Vasina, and Clayton M. White

The breeding range of the Peregrine Falcon in South America has been typically illustrated to include the southern tip of South America and the Falkland Islands (Brown and Amadon 1968, Hickey 1969, Cade 1982), with scattered records for coastal and central Chile (Johnson 1965, 1967). Based on this supposed distribution and a few recent records for Peru (Ellis and Glinski 1980) and Ecuador (Jenny et al. 1981), Cade (1982) suggested that the population probably consisted of a few hundred pairs. The population and distribution of *F. p. cassini* is now known to be considerably greater than previously indicated. We summarize here the recent observations of the Peregrine Falcon in South America and provide a revised map of its breeding range. Recent fieldwork has revealed that *Falco kreyenborgi*, the "Pallid Falcon," (or previously, "Kleinschmidt's Falcon") is a color morph of *F. p. cassini* (Ellis et al. 1981, McNutt 1981, Ellis and Peres G. 1983, McNutt 1984), and it is included in our consideration of the South American Peregrine.

HISTORICAL REVIEW

In 1932, C. Hellmayr examined a few Peregrine specimens from central Chile and identified them as *F. p. cassini*. Since all were collected during the austral autumn or winter, he asserted that *F. p. cassini* was likely a "winter visitor" from the south. At the time of the Madison Conference in 1965, Johnson (1965) said that *F. p. cassini* was a "relatively common nesting species from the Strait of Magellan to Cape Horn in Chile and from southern Patagonia to Staten Island in Argentina." Because no other recent observations for central Chile were mentioned, this assertion was likely based on the statement by

Olrog (1948) that *F. p. cassini* was "quite common in the northern part of Tierra del Fuego," and the fact that the majority of collected specimens at that time were from the Magellan region. In 1956 W. Partridge (then curator, Museo Argentino) told one of us (White) that he understood there were several pairs along the Santa Cruz River and in Rio Negro Province, Argentina. J. P. Myers (pers. comm. to White) reaffirmed the Santa Cruz information in 1966 when he noted "several" along the river while studying wading birds.

The first data to indicate potential population size and density of Peregrines in South America were provided by Cawkell and Hamilton (1961) for the Falkland Islands, where 28-29 pairs were seen in a 1951-52 census of a portion of the archipelago. They mentioned that two (of more than 200 islands in the archipelago) had 10 eyries collectively. These two islands were both near "big colonies of petrels."

Brown and Amadon (1968) described the range of *F. p. cassini* as: "Breeds in Chile from Atacama south to Tierra del Fuego and the Falkland Islands," but their map includes virtually all of Argentine Patagonia and Tierra del Fuego and none of Chile north of the Straits of Magellan. Apparently the actual distribution was not clearly known in the 1960s, and this subspecies was largely ignored until recently. Apart from a trip in 1971 by F. Hughes to collection localities of *F. p. cassini* and a brief survey which revealed one eyrie in central Chile and one probable eyrie in southern Tierra del Fuego (Walker et al. 1973b), no systematic surveys have yet been undertaken to determine the distribution of the "normal" morph of the South American Peregrine. In contrast, the question raised by Streseman and Amadon (1963) about the correct identity of *Falco kreyenborgi* generated considerable interest and field activity, particularly in the latter part of the 1970s. Anderson and Ellis (1981) reviewed information on *Falco kreyenborgi* through 1980. Most data on breeding density and reproduction of Peregrines in South America are from studies on what is now known to be a pallid morph of the Peregrine Falcon, and pertain mainly to southern Patagonia and Tierra del Fuego.

SOUTHERN CHILE AND ARGENTINA

This region, including the Chilean province of Magallanes, and the Argentine provinces of Rio Negro, Chubut, Santa Cruz and Tierra del Fuego has especially attracted Peregrine surveyors because it was believed to be the home of the "Pallid Falcon," and because the region has been commonly cited as the primary range of *F. p. cassini*. We have studied breeding activities in this region since 1979, and have also relied on observations by C. Anderson and R. Stranek.

Peregrines have been collected at many localities across Tierra del Fuego (Dabbene 1902, Reynolds 1934, Olrog 1948, Humphrey et al.

1970) and frequently observed north of the Strait of Magellan in Magallanes Province (Venegas and Jory 1979) and Chubut Province (J. P. Myers pers. comm.). Several specimens were collected in Rio Negro Province by the Kovac brothers, and some were said to be at breeding sites, but no records of actual eyrie locations appear in the literature. The seasonal and reproductive status of *F. p. cassini* in the putative core of its range remained unknown until the late 1970s.

In northeastern Chubut Province an eyrie was located (Peres) in the 1978-79 breeding season. In November 1979, C. Anderson (pers. comm.) located two nest sites of normally-colored Peregrines in Magallanes Province. In the same season, Roundy filmed a pallid individual in central Chubut Province, and located eyries of normally-colored birds. He also visited the two eyries located earlier in the season by Anderson and obtained data on reproduction. In 1980, 15 other territories with all normal-colored adults, except one male, were found in two studies primarily concerned with locating and studying the "Pallid Falcon" (Ellis et al. 1981, McNutt unpubl. ms.), and a pallid juvenile was seen in a family group of normally-colored Peregrines. In that breeding season, R. Stranek (pers. comm.) found a pair of normally-colored Peregrines at a cliff in the vicinity of Ushuaia, Tierra del Fuego. Their behavior suggested that they were nesting, but no eyrie was located.

In 1981 three independent surveys looking for "Pallid Falcons" found at least 31 more territories in the southern tip of South America, including 16 sites in Magallanes and Tierra del Fuego (McNutt), 12 sites in Rio Negro, Chubut, and Santa Cruz provinces (Ellis), and 3 in Santa Cruz (Peres).

In the 1982 season, reproductive data for 12 nests, including 6 that were previously unknown, were gathered in southern Argentina (Peres). In 1983 nine pairs were studied, and two of these were previously unknown (Table 1) (Peres).

Peregrines are now known to nest in the Andean foothills, along the major rivers which cut through the Patagonian steppe, and along the coast south from southern Rio Negro Province. Surveys of these regions resulted in the location of 64 Peregrine nest sites between 1978-84 and far less than 20% of the range has been searched. Extensive, relatively inaccessible and uninhabited regions along the eastern and western slopes of the Andes and the extensive island archipelago extending over 1500 km south from Puerto Montt, Chile (latitude 42°S) have not been surveyed for Peregrines. Many of these islands and channels are lined by large cliffs suitable for nesting Peregrine Falcons. Large populations of petrels and other marine birds occur in the northern region of the island archipelago (Roundy, Walker et al. 1973b). Given the availability of suitable cliffs and the

TABLE 1. Nest site records and reproductive performance of Peregrines in southern Chile (Magallanes Province) and Argentina (Rio Negro, Chubut, Santa Cruz, and Tierra del Fuego provinces).

Year	No. newly found sites[a]	No. sites checked[b]	No. pairs with young	No. young	No. young per pair	No. young per successful pair
1978 (CPG)	1	1	1	2	2.0	2.0
1979 (C. M. Anderson pers. comm.)	2	0				
(CPG)	0	1	1	3	3.0	3.0
(TBR)	6	6	4	10	1.7	2.5
1980 (JWM)	6	4	3	6	1.5	2.0
(DHE)	9	11	7	20	1.5	2.9
(R. Stranek pers. comm.)	1	0				
1981 (McNutt 1984)	16	15	12	20	1.3	1.7
(Ellis 1985)	12	18	9[c]	27	1.5	3.0
(CPG)	3	3	2	6	2.0	3.0
1982 (CPG)	6	12	8	21	1.8	2.6
1983 (CPG)	2	9	7	14	1.6	2.0
Totals	64	80	54	129		
Average					1.6	2.4

[a] Includes only sites occupied by a pair (cliffs occupied by single adults were not considered new eyrie locations).
[b] Includes previously known sites.
[c] Three more with eggs (2,2,1), hatching and fledging success unknown.

potential for patches of high prey density, we speculate that there is very likely a large population of Peregrines typically associated with marine habitat on the Pacific side south of 42°S. In addition, some pairs likely occur inland on the western slopes of the Andes. This population could conceivably be as large as several hundred pairs.

THE "PALLID FALCON"

The "Pallid Falcon" is a color polymorph of *F. p. cassini* (Stresemann and Amadon 1963, Ellis and Peres 1983, McNutt 1984, Ellis 1985). Most populations of Peregrines show variation in plumage darkness, but the two discrete variants of *F. p. cassini* may be unique among the numerous races. Based on the morph mating frequencies and phenotype frequencies of offspring and assuming normal Mendelian segregation, the pallid morph appears to reflect an autosomal monogenic trait recessive to the normal plumage. Under this assumption the pallid phenotype would be expressed only in those falcons homozygous for the pallid gene. Further, any normal-colored falcon producing a pallid offspring would be heterozygous at the normal/pallid locus. If further data regarding the genetic mechanism of this plumage variation support the monogenic control hypothesis, the pallid morph of *F. p. cassini* could provide a unique opportunity among Peregrine Falcon populations to use a phenotypic marker to investigate gene flow among demes.

At 38 eyries in 1981 in southern Chile and Argentina, 20 of the 76 adults were pallid (26.3%). At only three sites were both adults pallid. The remaining 14 pallid adults were paired with phenotypically normal Peregrines, representing 37% of the 38 pairs. Twenty offspring, 38% of the total produced, were pallid. A steep morpho-ratio cline where the pallid morph is most frequent in the region of the Strait of Magellan appears to correlate with gradients such as temperature and precipitation, suggesting a slight differential selection between the morphs (McNutt 1984). However, given the small population size, it could also be accounted for by random drift or by recent secondary contact between formerly allopatric gene distributions. In any case, the pallid morph of *F. p. cassini* may provide some interesting insights into evolutionary processes operating on the Peregrines in this region and, perhaps, on Peregrine populations worldwide.

THE FALKLAND ISLANDS

The Falkland Islands, lying approximately 400 km east of the eastern mouth of the Strait of Magellan (latitude 52°S, longitude 60°W), have rugged sea cliffs with large sea bird colonies. In 1979 a pair showed aggression toward an observer standing above a cliff on

Bleaker Island and was thought likely to have a nest nearby (R. Stranek pers. comm.). Stranek also related that a resident ornithologist knew of at least two eyries on New Island in 1979. Vasina (1975) described the Falkland Islands as the region of highest density of *F. p. cassini*, probably on the basis of a 1951-52 census by Cawkell and Hamilton (1961). Apart from the Anglo-Argentine conflict over the possession of the islands in April-May 1982, very little has changed with respect to human population size or activity in the past 50 years. Because of limited human activities, the geographic isolation, and the extent of favorable nesting habitat throughout the archipelago, we estimate that the Peregrine population in the Falkland Islands is probably between 50-120 pairs but could be as high as 200 pairs. The pallid morph is not known to occur there.

CENTRAL AND NORTHERN CHILE AND ARGENTINA

Most data from northern central Argentina are from Cordoba Province. W. Vasina and R. Stranek have surveyed the area to some extent, and for several years only one and possibly two eyries were known (Table 2). Several locations were checked in 1980 by C. White, J. Albuquerque and R. Brimm and, while adults were seen at two locations, only one nest was found. Vasina has found most of the 20 eyries now known (Table 2). At least one is in a stone quarry in southern Buenos Aires Province. The success of one pair that attempted to nest on a cathedral in the city of Cordoba is unknown (Vasina and Stranek 1984). The only records from northern Argentina are from two areas within 10 km of each other in Salta Province, where two adults and nesting ledges were present in 1984 (White and Boyce). These were areas where river valleys bisected outlying foothills along the eastern Andean slope. Numerous valleys of a similar ecological configuration occur in northern Argentina and southern Bolivia, and other pairs can be expected. In Salta Province, C. Olrog (pers. comm.) saw many Peregrines that he did not consider to be North American wintering migrants, but he found no eyries.

No systematic survey for Peregrines has been done in Chile north of Magallanes Province. In 1972, Walker et al. (1973b) checked two sites W. Millie located in 1966 (Johnson 1967) on coastal Chile and found them unoccupied. They did, however, locate another coastal site which had three young approximately 12 days old. W. Vasina found nine sites on the coast south of Coquimbo between 1969-74. Roundy surveyed a small coastal region of central Chile in Coquimbo Province in 1975 not far from the sites found by Millie; he found three nest sites from which young had recently fledged (Table 2). In April 1982, McNutt met a falconer in Santiago who reportedly knew of about 15 Peregrine eyrie locations in central Chile from which he typically

TABLE 2. Nest site records and reproductive performance of Peregrine Falcons in central and northern Chile and Argentina.

Year	No. newly found sites	No. sites checked	No. pairs with young	No. young	No. young per pair	No. young per successful pair
Chile						
1966 (Johnson 1967)	2	2	2	6	3.0	3.0
1969-74 (WVG)	9					
1972 (Walker et al. 1973b)	1	1	1	3	3.0	3.0
1975 (TBR)	3	2	2	5	2.5	2.5
Argentina						
1977 (WGV)	1	1	1	4	4.0	4.0
1978 (WGV)	0	1	1	2	2.0	2.0
1979 (WGV)	0	1	1	3	3.0	3.0
1981 (WGV)	0	1	1	3	3.0	3.0
1982 (WGV)	4	5	5	14	2.8	2.8
1983 (WGV)	1	6	6	13	2.2	2.2
1984 (WGV)	3	9	8	18	2.0	2.2
1985 (WGV)	1	9	9	25	2.8	2.8
1982-85 (WGV)	10					
Totals	35	38	37	96		
Average					2.5	2.6

collected six young each year for falconry. The sites were not verified, but video tapes were seen of at least three, one of which was obviously coastal. In addition, he possessed six Peregrines from the 1981-82 season as well as four in adult plumage said to be 2-4 years old. G. F. Edmunds (pers. comm.) found a nest inland on the Andean foothills about 300 km south of Santiago in the 1960s, and F. Jaksic (pers. comm.) found one in the same situation near Santiago in the 1980s. Vast areas of central Chile should be searched, particularly regions of suitable cliffs along the western foothills of the Andes and the coast. Based on the limited data now available on the presence of nesting Peregrines in the coastal desert regions to the north and in the mesic coastal regions of central and southern Chile, we project that more than 100 pairs occupy central and northern coastal Chile and perhaps 200 pairs nest in the western Andean foothills.

PERU AND ECUADOR

Reports of Peregrines in Peru (Morrison 1939, Gochfeld 1977) and Ecuador (Albuquerque 1978) in the past were assumed to be of migrants from breeding areas in southern Chile and Argentina. A record of Peregrines nesting in the Andes north of Quito, Ecuador in 1979 (Jenny et al. 1981) very near the equator greatly expanded the known nesting range in South America. That eyrie has been monitored since (Hilgert Chapter 72). Peregrines may occur in many of the high dry valleys in Ecuador, where some have been seen (S. Temple pers. comm.).

Several sites are known in Peru. In March 1979, Ellis and Glinski (1980) located a probable nest site near Tacna in southern Peru. Although no young were seen, a pair of adults attended the cliff, and the adult female was observed for an extended period in a small cave with much excrement on the floor. Molted feathers and prey remains indicated that the falcons were resident. The following year a single adult was observed on a cliff in northwestern Peru approximately 100 km from the coast (Risebrough et al. unpubl. ms.). In 1980 a pair was reported at this same site but produced no offspring. Two other pairs bred further inland in northern Peru in 1981-82 (Schoonmaker et al. 1985) (Table 3). Although pairs of Peregrine Falcons have been observed in coastal situations in Peru (C. Thelander pers. comm., M. Wallace pers. comm.), no evidence of breeding has been obtained. Nest records for Peru (Ellis and Glinski 1980, Schoonmaker et al. 1985) are all for the western Andean foothills. Perhaps 50-100 pairs nest in similar habitat from southern Ecuador into Chile. The Peregrine eyrie in central Ecuador and observations of pairs in interior Peru (Morrison 1939, Gochfeld 1977) suggest an extensive if not dense population in mid-elevation valleys of the northern Andes.

TABLE 3. Nest site location and reproductive performance of Peregrines in Peru and Ecuador.

Year	No. newly found sites	No. sites checked	No. pairs with young	No. young	No. young per pair	No. young per successful pair
Ecuador						
1979 (Jenny et al. 1981)	1	1	1	2	2.0	2.0
1980 (Jenny et al. 1981)	0	1	0	0		
1981 (Jenny et al. 1983)	0	1	1	1	1.0	1.0
1983 (Hilgert Chapter 72)	0	1	0	0		
1984 (Hilgert Chapter 72)	0	1		4[a]		
1985 (Hilgert Chapter 72)	0	1	1	3	3.0	3.0
Peru						
1979 (Ellis and Glinski 1980)	1	1	0	0		
1980 (Schoonmaker et al. 1985)	1	2	2	2	1.0	1.0
1981 (Schoonmaker et al. 1985)	2	3	2	2	0.67	1.0
1982 (Schoonmaker et al. 1985)	0	1	1	1	1.0	1.0
1984 (Schoonmaker et al. 1985)	0		0	0		
Totals	5	13	8	11		
Average					0.85	1.4

[a] Eggs; young unknown.

DISCUSSION

Breeding Seasons and Distribution. — Peregrines near the equator in Ecuador nest at various times of the year from June to December and seemingly have no precise reproductive season (Hilgert Chapter 72). The three pairs in northern Peru produced young in a breeding season extending from April to September. The Peregrines in Chile, Argentina and the Falkland Islands typically nest from September to January. These data are suggestive of a possible gradient in reproductive seasonality among South American Peregrines. More complete surveys are required to determine latitudinal variation throughout the Peregrine's range in South America.

Although nesting records from northern South American countries are scarce, Peregrines identified as *F. p. cassini* have been recorded for various locations in Chile (Hellmayr 1932), Argentina (Olrog 1948, Vasina 1975), Uruguay (Escalante 1961), Peru (Morrison 1939, Gochfeld 1977, Risebrough et al. unpubl. ms.) and Ecuador (Albuquerque 1978). Most of these sightings, however, have been ascribed to migrants from Fuegia because observations were made during the austral fall and winter. These birds may have been residents because recent evidence for a wide range of nesting dates in Ecuador and Peru decreases the likelihood that a particular falcon can be designated as migrant or resident and because the migratory patterns of South American Peregrines are unknown. In view of recent evidence of breeding Peregrines in South America from Ecuador to Tierra del Fuego, we believe it possible that most Peregrine sightings, excluding North American migrants in central and northwestern South America (e.g., Morrison 1939, Gochfeld 1977), represent resident birds.

Vast areas of South America have not been searched for breeding Peregrines. The few territories outside Argentina and Chile may be a part of an extensive breeding distribution in northwestern South America. Peregrines may even occur in Colombia and western Bolivia because they nest in adjacent parts of Ecuador, Peru and northern Argentina. We cannot speculate on resident Peregrines in the mesic zones from the eastern slopes of the Andes to the Atlantic Ocean. No breeding birds have been found in Brazil where Peregrines were studied for several years (H. Sick pers. comm., Risebrough et al. unpubl ms.), and it is difficult to believe that breeding residents could have been overlooked. Nonetheless, it is curious that the bold granitic monoliths near Rio de Janeiro, Brazil, where North American migrants occur October-March, are devoid of resident Peregrines.

Reproduction and Pesticides. — We have reproductive data for 134 pair-years representing 104 breeding territories in three broad geographic regions of South America (Tables 1, 2, 3). Unfortunately, the data were not gathered uniformly from area to area. Prior to 1975 only the number of downy young is available, not the number of young fledged. Pre-1977 data and, to a lesser extent, data from the year an eyrie was found are biased in favor of successful eyries which are easier to locate. Despite such biases, reproduction was apparently very good for two of the three regions. Ratcliffe (1980) proposed a value of 1.0 young fledged per pair as representing the minimum required to maintain a population, and Newton (1979) proposed the value of 2.0 young fledged per successful pair as representing a healthy rate of reproduction. A high proportion (74%) of the pairs successfully fledged young. Reproduction was also high on the basis of all pairs (1.7 young per pair) and for successful pairs (2.4 young per pair) (Table 4). Lower values were found in Peru and Ecuador but only 13 reproductive attempts were seen. These may reflect the reduced reproductive output commonly found in tropical nesting species and races (Newton 1979).

Concordant with the high reproductive values, pesticide levels were low in two eggs and tissue samples from migrants, and eggshell thickness remained high (Ellis 1985). Jenny et al. (1983) reported extremely low pesticide levels for two Ecuadoran eggs. Eggshells from nine sites in southern Argentina (Ellis 1985) averaged only 2% thinner than the pre-DDT average for California. Pesticides in three eggs from Patagonia were about half the level normally associated with a decline in reproductive performance. Residues in body tissues were recently examined in a small sample of North American migrants and a single resident adult female from Chubut Province, Argentina (Springer et al. unpubl. ms.). Migrant birds contained elevated DDE levels, perhaps from shorebird prey, while the resident adult had low levels. Walker et al. (1973b) also reported low levels in biopsies from two adults taken in central Chile in 1972.

The difference in residue amounts in migrants in South America and residents may be unreliable because of small sample size. If the samples analyzed to date reflect an existing difference, perhaps South American falcons eat prey with lower residue levels compared to

TABLE 4. Summary of reproductive performance of Peregrine Falcons in South America, 1967-85.

Total known sites	104
No. pair-years of productivity data	134
No. successful nesting attempts (%)	99(74)
Total young	236
Mean young, all pair-years	1.7
Mean young per successful pair	2.4

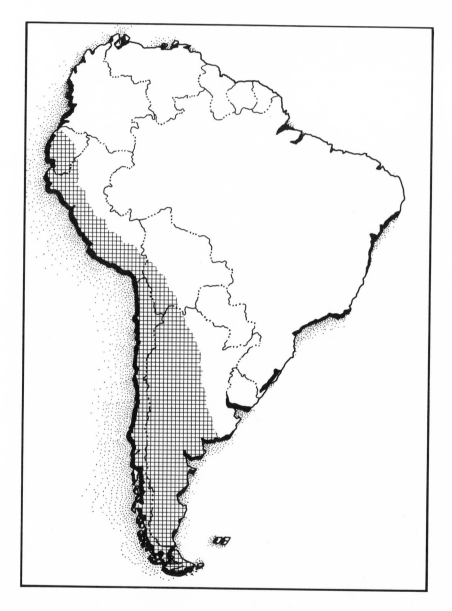

FIGURE 1.   Probable breeding distribution of Peregrine Falcons in South America.

North American Peregrines. Reproductive performance of Peregrines in South America supports this possibility.

CONCLUSIONS

Peregrines breed in South America where there are suitable nesting cliffs, an abundance of potential prey, especially Columbiformes, and relatively open habitat. They are inexplicably absent from coastal Brazil. We predict that resident Peregrines will be found in drier or more elevated regions of Colombia, southern Venezuela, and northern Brazil. Peregrines are now known to breed in Ecuador, Peru, central and southern Chile and central and southern Argentina. On the basis of known densities and available habitat, we doubt that there are fewer than 1000 pairs of Peregrines in South America. In Figure 1, the known breeding distribution plus conservative range extrapolations, based on habitat, are presented. The South American Peregrine population appears healthy and is considerably larger than previously supposed.

ACKNOWLEDGEMENTS

For their contributions of unpublished observations and discussions about Peregrines breeding in South America we gratefully acknowledge J. Albuquerque, C. Anderson, G. Hoy, F. Jaksic, J. Jehl, J. Myers, the late W. Partridge, C. Olrog, R. Sierra, R. Stranek, S. Temple, C. Thelander, and M. Wallace. Support for travel was provided by a fellowship to JWM from the Thomas J. Watson Foundation and grants to DHE from the National Geographic Society, the U. S. Air Force, and the USFWS (Patuxent Wildlife Research Center). Support while writing this manuscript was provided by a Graduate Fellowship to JWM from the University of California at Davis.

Editors' Note: Clifford Anderson and Tom Maechtle, assisted by Guillermo Vasina, located 14 active Peregrine nest sites in southern Argentina from 17 November-22 December 1986 (Chapter 27). A minimum of 32 young (2.3 per site) was produced. The researchers banded 22 individuals (13 nestlings, 9 adults). Pallid-form *F. p. cassini* were present at three of the sites. In these cases, pallid adult females were paired with nonpallid adult males. All young produced at these locations were the nonpallid form.

27 | The Southern Breeding Limit of the Peregrine Falcon

Clifford M. Anderson, Thomas L. Maechtle, and W. Guillermo Vasina

The Peregrine Falcon is the most widely distributed bird in the world (Hickey and Anderson 1969), breeding on every continent except Antarctica (Cade 1982). Because its distribution borders the remote and relatively inaccessible subpolar regions of the planet, both its northern and southern breeding limits are imprecisely known.

Although he did not delineate the latitudes of specific sites, Dementiev and Gladkov (1951) established the general northern range of the Peregrine to be at 78°N, in the area of Novaya Zemlya, Soviet Union. Salomonsen (1950) located the breeding limit more precisely in Greenland near Thule at 76°N.

In the southern hemisphere, the relative lack of continental landmass facilitates the task of establishing the Peregrine's southern breeding limit. The southern terminus of the South American continent is located at approximately 56°S (Tierra del Fuego), considerably closer to Antarctica than either southern Africa (35°S) or Tasmania (44°S); therefore, the southern breeding limit likely occurs in the region of Tierra del Fuego and involves the South American race, *F. p. cassini*.

The type specimen of *F. p. cassini* was described by Sharpe (1873) from an adult male Peregrine (Hellmayr 1932) collected by King in 1827 near Port Famine, Chile, on the Straits of Magellan (Hellmayr and Conover 1949). This specimen is currently in the British Museum of Natural History (Warren 1966). Although it cannot be considered a breeding bird, the falcon was apparently the basis for several authors (Brabourne and Chubb 1912, Peters 1931, Hellmayr 1932, Hellmayr and Conover 1949, Cade 1960, Johnson 1965, Brown and Amadon 1968, Olrog 1968, and Hickey and Anderson 1969) to delineate the Straits of Magellan and Tierra del Fuego region as a breeding area for the species. In fact, no active Peregrine nest sites had been described in the Fuegian area until the late 1970s. For example, Humphrey et al. (1970) stated that although the Peregrine occurred throughout Isla

Grande, "there are no data on breeding," and its "seasonal and reproductive status are unknown."

Further east in the Falkland Islands, Cawkell and Hamilton (1961) documented nearly 30 Peregrine sites; for several years the known southern limit was located there at approximately 52°S (Hickey and Anderson 1969).

In November-December 1979, C. Anderson (unpubl. ms.) located two active *F. p. cassini* nest sites in the Magallanes District of southern Chile, one near Seno Skyring at 52°30'S. This mainland site extended the known range further south than the Falkland Islands.

In 1981-82, McNutt (1984) located 17 pairs of Peregrines, "in the eastern region of the province of Magallanes, Chile, and the northern region of Tierra del Fuego." This presumably included the first breeding record of the Peregrine on Isla Grande, although McNutt was not specific about the latitudes of individual sites.

On 16 December 1986, Anderson and Maechtle (unpubl. ms.) located an active Peregrine nest with a phenotypically mixed pair (one "pallid" morph and one "normal" morph) and three "normal" young on the Atlantic coast of Isla Grande near 53°40'S. To our knowledge, this site represents the southernmost known eyrie at the present time.

Information on several other probable eyries to the south of this location strongly suggests that the documented breeding range will be extended further south in future years. For example, during the breeding season (29 January) of 1967, Keith (1970) observed a Peregrine flying "near the east end of Lago Fagnano" (54°35'S). In December 1972, Walker et al. (1973b) visited the cliffs at Cerro Heunuepen near Keith's sighting and "observed one adult pair and one subadult male . . . although no evidence of breeding was found." Peregrines had previously been reported at this site by the Goodall family of Estancia Viamonte. We (Anderson and Maechtle) visited the same location on 17 December 1986 and found no Peregrines, although a single Andean Condor was present on the cliff.

Approximately 7 km south at Lago Escondido, M. Rumboll (Jehl and Rumboll 1976) observed two adult Peregrines and one flying immature on 27 January 1974, considered at that time to be the "most convincing evidence to date that this species actually nests on Isla Grande."

Peregrines have also been observed in the vicinity of Ushuaia (approximately 54°50'S) on the Beagle Channel (Humphrey et al. 1970). In 1980, R. Stranek (pers. comm.) observed a pair of adults near there, but did not locate an eyrie. We also observed a single adult Peregrine at Mt. Susana, 5 km west of Ushuaia on 17 December 1986, but found no nest.

The islands south of the Beagle Channel (Islas Navarino, Hoste, Wollaston Hermite, and Hornos) have apparently never been visited by raptor biologists. The Cape Horn group, situated near 56°S, has high, vertical cliffs and supports several species of breeding seabirds (A. Goodall pers. comm.), but it is not yet known whether Peregrines breed there.

Two other regional island groups are situated further south than Cape Horn: the Islas Diego Ramirez and the South Sandwich Islands. Both could support breeding Peregrines, and it is perhaps there, at a latitude equivalent to Sitka, Alaska or Edinburgh, Scotland that the southern breeding limit of the Peregrine Falcon will ultimately be found.

ACKNOWLEDGEMENTS

Support and funding for our fieldwork in Patagonia was provided by P. Ward, W. Seegar and W. Mattox. C. White and C. Thelander made several useful suggestions on a draft of this paper.

28 Population Trends, Distribution, and Status of the Peregrine Falcon in Australia

Penny D. Olsen and Jerry Olsen

In Australia the Peregrine (*F. p. macropus*) is, we believe, monotypic. It is a medium-sized subspecies: females average about 900 g, males 600 g, and individuals in warmer areas tend to be smaller than those in cooler areas. They are nonmigratory, and there is no evidence of any significant exchange with Papua New Guinea. The broken chain of islands crossing Torres Strait is used by other raptors but apparently not by Peregrines (cf. Draffan et al. 1983). Peregrines have never been recorded in New Zealand even though the Australian Kestrel and Black Falcon have occasionally reached there.

At one recently deserted Tasmanian Peregrine site, carbon dating extends occupancy back 19,000 years (Bowdler 1984, N. Mooney pers. comm.). Late last century, Peregrines were considered to be widely but sparingly distributed throughout Australia (North 1912). By the early 20th century, North (1912) believed they had become less common around larger cities and more densely settled farming areas owing, at least in part, to shooting because of poultry losses.

More recently, the Peregrine is said to have become more common in former woodland that has since been opened for wheat cultivation. This previously less suitable habitat now supports thinly scattered, stick-nesting populations (e.g., Bush *in* Serventy and Whittell 1976) mainly because of the provision of permanent water, more open vegetation, and the spread of the Galah as a food source. Wells now provide permanent water in inland Australia, and the introduced European Starling and feral pigeon, together with the native Galah, have exploded in numbers over much of the country to provide a larger and more stable food base than existed previously. These three species often make up 75% or more of the Peregrine's diet in southeastern Australia.

The introduced European rabbit (*Oryctolagus cuniculus*) has probably benefited Peregrines indirectly by effecting an increase in eagles and other rabbit-eating stick nest builders on which the Peregrine is dependent for nests in some areas. Rabbits may also have altered the vegetation to the advantage of the Peregrine and its prey.

Negative effects on the Peregrine by human actions include persecution, both inadvertent and deliberate interference at nests, and pesticide use, none of which has had a profound effect on the population as a whole (Olsen 1985, Olsen and Olsen 1985). DDT is now recommended for only a small number of agricultural uses; use has declined in the past three years to between 140,000-400,000 kg annually, less than 10% of that used in 1974 before phasing out began. Although still applied for nonrecommended purposes, its use remains localized and it is probably for this reason Peregrines have not been eliminated from vast areas as they were in the northern hemisphere. Nevertheless, they appear to have declined dramatically in numbers since the 1950s in certain regions where DDT is implicated, such as the intensively farmed Murrumbidgee Irrigation Areas of New South Wales.

Peregrines have been found breeding almost anywhere that there are suitable cliffs. In the deserts of central Australia they are largely confined to ranges and gorges; only rarely do they breed in stick nests in mulga and other acacia shrublands, or in the taller eucalypts lining the inland drainage system. A few breed in the open grasslands where they may be found on the occasional low mesa. Many breed in mallee shrubland, mainly in nests of the Wedge-tailed Eagle, but also on the occasional cliff. Cliffs on coastally draining rivers and other water bodies have the highest densities known in Australia. In the open woodland zone, tree hollows are used in the lowlands of the Murray-Darling drainage system, and stick nests on wooded slopes. Coastal cliffs and islands have moderate densities. Peregrines have not been found breeding in subalpine and alpine areas above 1500 m.

During the nonbreeding season, most Peregrines remain around their nest sites (Jones and Bren 1978, Czechura 1984a, pers. obs.), although some adult pairs may move to regular wintering areas not far away. First-year birds (Emison and Bren 1981), especially females, move farther (mean distance 135 km (n=35) for females, 60 km (n=8) for males), but the greatest movement recorded is only 415 km. Nonbreeding habitat includes coastal flats and inland plains, higher altitudes, and more northerly latitudes, where nesting pairs are scarce or absent.

Peregrines tend to be clumped in groups of more or less regularly spaced pairs around areas with suitable nest sites and stable food supply. Measured densities range from one pair per 28 km² to one pair per 3100 km² (Table 1 and regional reports). Greatest densities

TABLE 1. Density of Peregrine Falcons in different parts of Australia. The minimum known density of a well-searched area is given, except where an estimate has been made. Each study area is centered on the researcher's home base and has not been selected for the Peregrines it contains.

State/Study area	Predominant climate and habitat	Minimum density (km²/pair)	No. pairs	Closest 2 pairs (km)
New South Wales				
Coastal	temperate escarpment	157	10	3
Southern Tablelands	temperate riparian	154	30	2
Victoria				
	mostly temperate riparian, ranges, woodland	650-750[a]		5
South Australia				
Nuriootpa	temperate riparian	650[a]	24	3
Kangaroo Island	temperate sea-cliffs	435[a]	10	5
Adelaide	temperate ranges	201	12	6
Southern Flinders Ranges	semi-arid ranges	227	14	2
Central Flinders Ranges	semi-arid ranges	195	5	6
Eyre Peninsula	semi-arid sea-cliffs, ranges	1825	6	
Tasmania				
Southwest half	wet temperate heath, ranges	3106	11	
Northeast half	temperate riparian	551	62	3

[a] Estimate based on a subsample.

are on permanent river systems, with pairs nesting as close as 1.6 km apart (cf. Paton et al. 1981). The sparsest breeding population yet surveyed inhabits the barren heathlands of southwest Tasmania (Table 1). Breeding density is not tied tightly to climate or general productivity of the land; provided there are nest sites, it mainly depends on topography and the presence of permanent water. High Peregrine densities occur where water bodies, ranges and coastal strips act as refugia for surrounding areas and provide "highways" for movement of birds. If the arid zone supports one pair per 3500 km² and there is one pair per 1000 km² elsewhere, an estimated 4500 pairs of Peregrines currently occupy nest sites in Australia.

Of 609 known nest sites, 81% are cliffs, 11% are stick nests, and 8% are hollows in trees, but the proportion of each varies geographically (Figure 1a, b, c). Ground nesting (n=2) and nesting on "buildings" (one on a dam wall and one, unconfirmed, on a church) are rare occurrences. In general, where there are suitable cliffs they are used almost to the exclusion of other nest site types. Stick-nesting Peregrines predominate in woodland and acacia shrubland, where cliffs are absent or scarce; they usually use nests built by Wedge-tailed Eagles, other

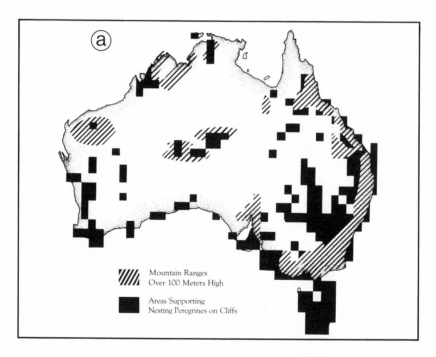

FIGURE 1a. Distribution of Peregrine cliff sites in Australia since 1950 (includes 3 stick nests on cliffs), and mountain ranges over 100 m (indicated by crosshatching). 1 degree latitude × longitude blocks.

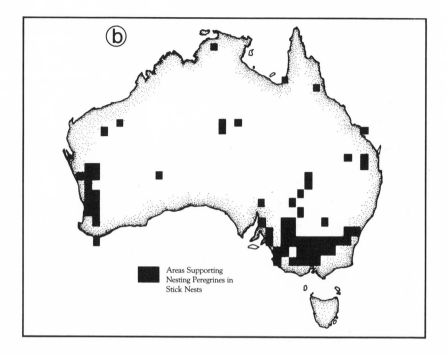

FIGURE 1b. Distribution of Peregrine stick nest sites in Australia since 1950. 1 degree
latitude × longitude blocks.

raptors, or corvids. Nesting in the hollow trunks and spouts of large
red gums, commonly in lowlands subject to flooding, seems a more
restricted habit, most prevalent in the Murray-Darling Basin. Olsen
(1982) found evidence that the eggs from these latter nests were,
before the 1940s, broader than those from other nests and suggested
that these falcons may have been a genetically distinct population.

Before the introduction of agricultural DDT in the late 1940s, clear
latitudinal and temperature related clines in egg size existed; since that
time they are no longer present south of latitude 33°S, where agriculture has been most intensive. DDT may have created voids, and
other farming practices have opened new areas, both of which appear
to have been filled by Peregrines that would normally have nested
elsewhere. These movements could have resulted in genetic "mixing"
of populations and the breakdown of geographic clines in southern
Australia (Olsen 1982). An increased food supply may have facilitated
this process.

In temperate southeastern Australia, breeding success and site
occupancy are higher in drought than in wet years. During an 11-year
study near Canberra (P. Olsen and J. Olsen unpubl. ms.) where nest

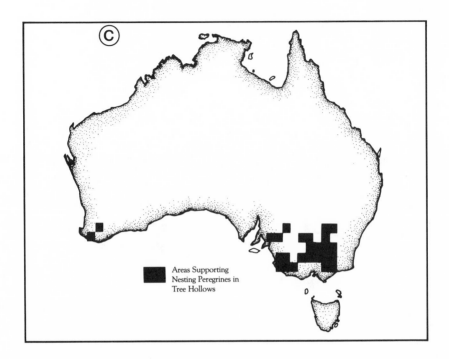

FIGURE 1c. Distribution of Peregrine tree hollow sites in relation to the Murray River region and elsewhere in Australia, post-1950. 1 degree latitude × longitude blocks.

sites were at a premium, the total number of raindays between August and October was correlated with the number of young fledged per pair ($r=-0.576$, $df=10$, $P<0.05$) and the percentage of pairs successfully fledging young ($r=-0.791$, $df=10$, $P<0.01$). Rain significantly affected breeding mainly through its effect on nest sites. In wet seasons, reproductive success was higher in those territories which had at least one alternate nest site than in those with no alternate site, whereas in dry seasons success was similar for the two groups (Table 2). If rain had acted on breeding mainly through its influence on food (food availability, hunting success, and food needs, cf. Newton 1979), then reproductive success should have been less in wet years than in dry at all territories. In wet years some sites were flooded; as a result some clutches failed to hatch, and very young nestlings were killed. More young were fledged from those sites protected from the prevailing inclement weather than from those which were unprotected: 1.76 young per pair ($n=25$) versus 1.25 young per pair ($n=17$) ($F=5.326$, $P<0.05$). In wet years, in 10 territories (of 31) where an alternate nest site was available, the Peregrines used the site less likely to be flooded (more sheltered, better drained) in all except two cases. Moreover, the number of young fledged from territories with alternate nest sites was

TABLE 2. Mean annual nest site occupancy and breeding success of Peregrine Falcons in different parts of Australia. Range (parentheses) and trends during each study are indicated where available. A site is one that was occupied some time during the study. An occupied site is one where a pair or single bird was sighted. A breeding pair is one with young, and a successful pair is one fledging young.

State/Study Area	Occupancy			Nestling productivity		
	Mean annual no. of sites (range)	Mean annual % occupied (range)	Mean annual % of pairs breeding (range)	Mean annual young/pair (range)	Mean annual young/successful pair (range)	Mean annual young/site (range)
Southeast Queensland (1978-84)	6.9 (5-9)	85 (80-89)		2.2	2.2 (only 2 pairs checked)	2.2
Southern Tablelands, New South Wales (1975-84)	23.8 (13-31)	91 (81-100)	64 (53-84)	1.4 (1.1-1.8)	2.1 (2.0-2.6)	1.3 (1.0-1.6)
Agricultural Victoria (1975-84)	66.2 (42-76)	77 (66-84) decline	60 (50-69)	1.2 (0.9-1.6)	2.1 (1.8-2.3)	0.8 (0.6-1.2)
Mallee, Victoria (1975-84)	6.8 (5-10)	71 (12-100)	81 (50-100)	1.5 (0.5-2.0)	1.8 (1-2.5)	0.9 (0.2-1.5)
Nuriootpa, South Australia (1981-84)	16 (9-24)	91 (83-100)	88 (83-91)	2.0 (1.6-2.2)	2.2 (1.8-2.2)	1.8 (1.6-2.0)
Southern Flinders Range, South Australia (1972-84)	6.9 (3-10)	82 (70-100)	61 (25-100)	1.3 (0.5-2.7)	2.1 (1.0-3.0)	1.0 (0.4-1.5)
Central Flinders Range, South Australia (1982-84)	3.3 (2-5)	60 (50-67)	100	1.5 (1.3-2.0)	1.5 (1.3-2.0)	0.9 (0.8-1.0)
Eyre Peninsula, South Australia (1972-84)	3.5 (2-5)	80 (50-100)	72 (0-100)	1.7 (0-2.7)	2.2 (0-2.7)	1.2 (0-2.6)
Tasmania (1973-82)	32 (11-57)	68 (54-79)	75 (57-86) increase	1.9 (1.3-2.3)	2.5 (2.2-3.0)	1.2 (0.8-1.5)

not correlated with raindays whereas that from territories without alternates was (young per pair and August-October raindays, $r=-0.79$, $P<0.01$).

All Australian studies were started in the 1970s or later, after a peak in DDT use in the preceding decade. Nest site occupancy and breeding success were average to high in all populations thus far studied (Table 2). In both Tasmania (Mooney and Brothers 1987) and Victoria (19 of 108 eyries no longer in use, White et al. 1981), the states with the heaviest intensity of agriculture, populations were down to an estimated 80% of former numbers. In Tasmania, eggshell thinning was high, but, more importantly, pigeon racers destroyed greater numbers of Peregrines than were fledged in some years. Today, better protection and enforcement have alleviated the situation, eggshell thinning is low, numbers have recovered to 90%, and the use of nest sites is more regular. Continued persecution of Peregrines at about 10-15% of Tasmanian nest sites is thought, however, to be slowing the recovery. In Victoria, the effects of a decade of eggshell thinning, which averaged 20% and reduced productivity in over half of the state, may have been offset by an increased food supply, recruitment from healthy surrounding populations, and low post-fledging mortality. Nevertheless, in the past two years occupancy of nest sites in Victoria declined about 10%, to about 70% of former numbers, and should be monitored closely for signs of further decline. In the other main study areas, nest site occupancy and breeding success were relatively stable. On the southern tablelands of New South Wales the scarcity of cliffs may prevent expansion of the population.

Annual adult mortality tends to be low in comparison to other (declining) populations (Tables 3 and 4). This apparent low mortality is in keeping with Nelson's (1977) hypothesis that smaller, warm-climate Peregrines have lower mortality and smaller clutches (Australian Peregrines have a mean clutch size of 2.9, Olsen 1982) than do larger, cold-climate Peregrines. Since they were given nationwide protection in 1971, the percent of banded Peregrines that were recovered by shooting decreased to 14%; cars are now responsible for the greatest mortality (21%).

Predators are not a major threat to Peregrines, although the pugnacious Tasmanian Devil (*Sarcophilus harrisii*) consumes between 2.5-5.0% of nestlings in Tasmania. Feral cats climb to stick nests in inland Australia; these and Goannas (*Varanus* spp.) and the Masked Owl may take eggs or nestlings. Competitors are few; the Black Falcon is the only other large, bird-eating falcon. It does not nest on cliffs and prefers more open, featureless country than the Peregrine. Most conflict between the two occurs in autumn when both disperse over flatlands such as coastal plains. Where White-bellied Sea Eagles nest on seacliffs, Peregrines tend to nest elsewhere.

TABLE 3. Comparative annual mortality of Peregrines in five countries and the percentage of recovered banded individuals found shot dead (adapted from Newton 1979 and Ratcliffe 1980).

	Age (years) at mortality			
	0-1 (%)	1-6 (%)	% shot	Source
Sweden	59	32	48	Lindberg (1977)
North America	70	25	45	Enderson (1969b)
Germany	56	28	43	Mebs (1971)
Finland	71	19	78	Mebs (1971)
Southeast Australia	55	5	21	This study

TABLE 4. Life table for Peregrines in southeastern Australia based on recoveries of dead birds banded as nestlings. Date of banding taken as age 0. Most data collected by authors of regional reports for Victoria (n = 374), South Australia (n = 99), Tasmania (n = 213) and New South Wales (n = 224). Because not enough time has elapsed since banding for all recoveries to have been made, the figures are corrected to allow for this bias.

Age interval (years)	No. of recoveries (R)	No. available (A)	Ratio (R/A × 100)	Annual mortality (%)
0-1	33	915	3.61	55
1-2	5	836	0.60	
2-3	4	694	0.58	9
3-4	1	547	0.18	6
4-5	0	427	0.00	
5-6	1	337	0.30	3
6-7	0	275	0.00	
7-8	1	188	0.53	
8-9	1	129	0.78	

The Peregrine has been totally protected in all states since 1971. Falconry is not practiced legally. The public, in general, is becoming more knowledgeable and sympathetic towards birds of prey. An overall lack of interest has helped Peregrines, for they nest, unmolested, along highways and near houses. The remoteness of many pairs from the limited amount of agricultural land in Australia has also aided their survival. Although the techniques of captive breeding have been researched and successfully applied, release of fledglings for the purpose of restocking wild populations is not warranted at present. In conclusion, Australia has a substantial, widespread, and viable population of Peregrines and is, as Cade (1982) pointed out, one of the main centers of concentration in the world.

REGIONAL REPORTS (See Figure 2)

QUEENSLAND
Greg Czechura

Study Area. — The study area — subcoastal, southeast Queensland — has a subtropical climate. The main vegetation is a mosaic of open forest, subtropical rainforest, dry rainforest, and woodland. Queensland as a whole is tropical in the north and subtropical in the south. Habitats range from stony and sandy deserts in the far west and grasslands in the vast interior to woodlands, forests, and rainforests in the east. Main mountain ranges are located mostly in the eastern third of the state. The arid southwest receives less than 250 mm of rain per year, while some areas on the east coast receive over 2000 mm.

Distribution and Density. — The closest two pairs nested 5.1 km apart. The closest 10 sites averaged 24 km apart (range: 0.8-50 km); distance between eight others averaged 26 km (range: 8-60 km). Peregrines are distributed throughout Queensland (Czechura 1984a) but are apparently most common in the highlands of the east where there is abundant water and habitat diversity. The flat, featureless, grassland-dominated plains of central and western Queensland, where permanent surface water is scarce, have the lowest numbers. A few pairs are found on continental islands within 100 km of the mainland (Czechura 1984b). The total breeding population is estimated to be about 950 pairs, or one pair per 1800 km^2.

Nest Sites. — In the study area all known pairs have nested on cliffs. Nest sites were overhung ledges and caves on escarpments, bluffs, isolated cliffs and a river gorge, and on the ground at the crest of a high, steep sand dune (structurally similar to a cliff). Height was between 50-200 m ($\bar{x} = 120$ m). Elsewhere in the state Peregrines used mesas, coastal cliffs and stick nests in open plains or on steep wooded slopes. A report of a pair using a tree hollow in dense riverine vegetation has not been confirmed.

Occupancy and Breeding Success. — No comprehensive study has been undertaken. Results to date suggest that, in some areas, both occupancy and breeding success are high.

Threats and Limiting Factors. — In the southeast, increasing pressures of residential development may disturb some pairs. In central and western Queensland, lack of cliffs may be a major limiting factor, although the increase in permanent surface water created by dams and wells has probably benefited Peregrines. Pesticides may be a problem in intensively farmed areas, largely in the southeast and parts of the northeast. In some areas eggshell thinning has been as high as 38% ($\bar{x} = 4\%$, $n = 31$, Olsen and Olsen 1979), but no comprehensive

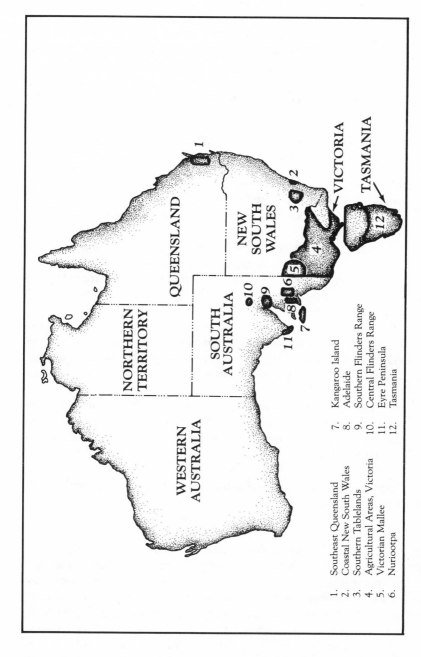

FIGURE 2. Study areas referred to in text and regional reports.

WESTERN
AUSTRALIA

NORTHERN
TERRITORY

SOUTH
AUSTRALIA

QUEENSLAND

NEW
SOUTH
WALES

VICTORIA

TASMANIA

1. Southeast Queensland
2. Coastal New South Wales
3. Southern Tablelands
4. Agricultural Areas, Victoria
5. Victorian Mallee
6. Nuriootpa

7. Kangaroo Island
8. Adelaide
9. Southern Flinders Range
10. Central Flinders Range
11. Eyre Peninsula
12. Tasmania

study has been done. Several pairs breed successfully in such areas. Pigeon racers have interfered with some breeding pairs, and recreation causes disturbance in more populated areas.

Overall Status and Security. — Most pairs occur in thinly settled, inaccessible, remote, pastoral or undisturbed land, and the population is stable. Localized losses may occur, but the overall population is secure. Some pairs are in national parks, state forests, or other reserves; no special measures are taken for the protection of any sites.

SOUTHERN TABLELANDS, NEW SOUTH WALES
Jerry Olsen and Penny Olsen

Study Area. — The 4600 km² study area encompasses the urban Australian Capital Territory and environs. Habitat is temperate savannah woodland and woodland, cleared but with extensive pockets of natural vegetation.

Distribution and Density. — Peregrines were concentrated where there were nest sites, and were regularly spaced there. The closest two pairs nested 2 km apart, and 21 pairs averaged 6.1 km apart (range: 2-22 km, nearest neighbor distance). The area had a minimum of 30 pairs, giving a density of one pair per 154 km². A thoroughly searched subsection of high density had 16 pairs at a mean density of one pair per 28 km². During the 10-year study period, the larger population increased by two pairs; one pair occupied a quarry the season after blasting stopped and the other used a cliff between two pairs 4 km apart.

Nest Sites. — All nest sites but one were on cliffs. A stick nest was used on a lake abundant in birdlife but lacking cliffs. Many sites were riparian; the remainder were on scattered cliffs and rock outcrops usually associated with water. Cliff height averaged about 25 m (range: 10-60 m).

Occupancy and Breeding Success. — Both occupancy and breeding success were high.

Threats and Limiting Factors. — Since the study began, houses have been built near two eyries, one above the eyrie within 100 m, with no apparent ill effects. Young were stolen from one eyrie, pigeon racers are said to have destroyed young at another; the attentions of a photographer in one case, and unknown visitors in other cases may have caused breeding failure. The activities of humans have generally enhanced the area for Peregrines and have not intruded upon their breeding activities. The pattern of land clearing has created new hunting opportunities, introduced prey species abound, and quarries provide nest sites where none existed previously. The major limiting factor is the scarcity of nest sites. Almost all cliffs have been occupied, and only three of 30 pairs were known to use an alternate cliff. Pesticides are a minor problem and eggshell thinning is low. The herbicide 2,4,5-T is thought to have possibly killed a male at one site, following the spraying of blackberries.

Overall Status and Security. — Increasing recreational use of some areas may be a potential problem, but at present does not conflict to any great degree with the needs of Peregrines. The population is saturated, with the potential for further expansion if nest sites become available.

VICTORIA — AGRICULTURAL AREAS
William B. Emison, William M. Bren and Harley F. Archer

Study Area. — Habitat is a diverse mosaic of farmlands, woodlands, rivers, marshes and ranges in or adjacent to agricultural land in temperate Victoria. Peregrines nesting on seacliffs within the study area hunt over farmland and eat mostly landbirds.

Distribution and Density. — Breeding distribution is widespread. White et al. (1981) found pairs nesting as close as 5 km apart on rivers ($\bar{x}=16$ km for 14 eyries). For five areas mean distance between pairs was 12-21 km (range: 5-36 km, $n=6$-14). They estimated the total population of Victoria to be 300-350 pairs, giving a density of one pair per 650-750 km^2.

Nest Sites. — Of the 116 eyries examined, 79 were on natural cliffs, 11 on cliffs in quarries, 20 in hollows of trees, 5 in stick nests made by other birds, and 1 on a man-made structure (dam wall). The average height of 51 cliffs was 29.1 m (range: 4-75 m) (Pruett-Jones et al. 1981a).

Occupancy and Breeding Success. — Over 60 eyries were checked each year (1976-84). The percent occupied was over 70% each year except the last two, when it dropped to 68% (1983) and 66% (1984). Reproductive success changed little over the 10 years.

Threats and Limiting Factors. — Between 1975-77, 35 eggs had a mean level of 17.63 ppm DDE (wet wt); 30 eggs had a mean decrease in shell thickness of 20.4%, and 16 were over 20% thinner than pre-DDT eggs (Pruett-Jones et al. 1981b). This level of contamination has continued.

Overall Status and Security. — Much of the studied population occurs in state parks and reserves surrounded by agricultural land. The large unstudied population in the Victorian high country is probably secure because of its remoteness from agriculture and the ruggedness of the terrain. However, the majority of the population is associated with agricultural land and is showing some indications of a reduction in numbers after a decade of eggshell thinning levels usually associated with population decline. Monitoring of this population by the Fisheries and Wildlife Service ceased in 1984.

VICTORIA — MALLEE
William B. Emison, William M. Bren and Max Arney

Study Area. — Study area was the semi-arid, northwestern corner of Victoria: predominantly mallee scrub with some River Red Gum (*Eucalyptus camaldulensis*) woodlands along the Murray River.

Distribution and Density. — The Peregrine is widely distributed: 13 pairs in a 34,000 km² area, or one pair per 2615 km². However, the area has not been exhaustively surveyed, and many eyries no doubt remain to be found.

Nest Sites. — Of 13 eyries located, 11 were stick nests of other birds, and two were in tree hollows.

Occupancy and Breeding Success. — Between 5-10 eyries were checked each year (1975-84). The number occupied fluctuated widely, ranging from 100% in 1975 (n=10) to 12.5% in 1980 (n=8). Reproductive success also varied greatly from year to year.

Threats and Limiting Factors. — DDT-induced eggshell thinning was low. Four eggs contained a mean level of 2.3 ppm DDE (wet wt) and showed an 8.8% decrease in shell thickness. Tree-clearing and the scarcity of young trees to replace older trees currently used for nesting are probably the biggest threats. Increasing salinity may have longterm adverse effects on nest sites of both the Peregrine and its prey.

Overall Status and Security. — Secure at present; many are in state parks and reserves.

NURIOOTPA, SOUTH AUSTRALIA
Ian Falkenberg

Study Area. — This area encompasses a 100 km radius around Nuriootpa and is generally temperate, with mallee scrub merging into woodland. A major tree-lined watercourse flows through the area.

Distribution and Density. — Along the river the closest two eyries were 3 km apart and the farthest 8 km apart. The mean distance between the 10 closest sites was 4.7 km. Twenty-four sites are known in an area of 31,400 km², or one pair per 1300 km². However, only 50% of the area was exhaustively surveyed. A conservative estimate of total numbers of breeding pairs in the area is 50, giving a density of one pair per 650 km². In neighboring mallee outside the study area, only one pair was found in an equivalent area (13,400 km²), and this pair was nesting in a quarry.

Nest Sites. — Of 24 sites, 19 were ledges or cavities on cliffs, 3 in hollow trees and 1 in an abandoned stick nest. Cliffs were vertical rockfaces usually along the river. They ranged in height from 20-84 m but 17 of the 19 were below 36 m. At one site Peregrines nested for four consecutive years in a stick nest built by a Little Eagle. In 1984 the stick nest was deserted, and a pair used the hollow limb of a dead tree 500 m away. Another tree nest was located 1.5 km from an unused, suitable cliff.

Occupancy and Breeding Success. — Both occupancy and breeding success were high.

Threats and Limiting Factors. — Pesticides do not seem to be a major problem, although the river carries drainage from agricultural areas. Eggs failed to hatch each year at one site; pesticides were implicated. Construction, excavation and housing have each caused desertion of one eyrie; increasing holiday home development along the river is a threat to some sites.

Overall Status and Security. — Most cliffs are occupied and the population is dense and stable.

SOUTHERN FLINDERS RANGES, SOUTH AUSTRALIA
Jerry Olsen, Penny Olsen, and Terry Billett

Study Area. — This study area consists of ranges and gorges in semi-arid South Australia, predominantly savannah woodland. Adjoining plains are extensively grazed.

Distribution and Density. — Nesting pairs were scattered more or less regularly where there were cliffs. The closest two pairs nested 6 km apart. Thirteen pairs nested between 6-32 km apart ($\bar{x}$ distance to nearest neighbor=10.2 km), 13 were less than 14 km apart. Thirteen pairs nested in a thoroughly searched area, including lowland plains where none were found, at a mean density of one pair per 227 km². In the ranges only, density was much higher at around one pair per 65 km².

Nest Sites. — All observed eyries were on cliffs averaging about 35 m (range: 7-52 m). Up to four alternate ledges and two alternate sites were used. The tops of some nest cliffs in gorges were heavily forested; others were sparsely vegetated.

Occupancy and Breeding Success. — Both nest-site occupancy and breeding success fluctuated widely from year to year, possibly because the relatively severe climate limited breeding to fewer pairs in dry years. Breeding success was also reduced in the second consecutive year of drought.

Threats and Limiting Factors. — Human interference was a major problem, both direct (young have been stolen from eyries and rocks have been dropped on eggs and young) and indirect (the area is popular for a number of recreational activities, including gun club and motorcycle club meetings). Contamination by DDE was moderate, with an average decrease in eggshell thickness of 12% (maximum 26%), and the possibility of adverse effects of contaminants emitted from a nearby electrical power station are being considered.

Overall Status and Security. — In general, Peregrines are secure and seem to be at a density that can be supported by the area. Some of the area is a national park, ensuring protection of habitat.

CENTRAL FLINDERS RANGES, SOUTH AUSTRALIA
Tim Fraser

Study Area. — This area is typified by steep, rocky gorges and bluffs of the central Flinders Ranges in semi-arid Australia. The highest peak is 1160 m, but altitude is usually less than 1000 m.

Distribution and Density. — A minimum of five pairs frequented the 790 km^2 area, giving a density of one pair per 158 km^2. The closest two occupied sites were 2 km apart.

Nest Sites. — All known eyries were on nearly vertical cliffs averaging approximately 20-25 m high. Three were on ledges and two in caves or holes, all shaded from the afternoon sun. At least one pair frequented an area devoid of cliffs, but there were several unoccupied Wedge-tailed Eagle nests in which they may have bred.

Occupancy and Breeding Success. — Four or five eyries were checked over three years (1982-84). Six (60%) of 10 sites were occupied. Occupancy was low, but possibly some unknown alternate sites were used. Breeding success of six known pairs, all of which fledged one or two young, was 1.5 young per pair.

Threats and Limiting Factors. — Human interference has been the major problem. Young were removed from one eyrie in two successive years. The eyrie has been abandoned along with another which was interfered with early in the nesting season. The area is becoming increasingly popular with rock-climbers.

Overall Status and Security. — The area is a national park staffed by rangers. Peregrines in the more remote and inaccessible parts of the park are probably secure. Park regulations are currently under review and recommendations have been made that climbing be controlled by permits and, in sensitive areas, restricted to the non-breeding season. Implementation of these regulations and increased vigilance by park staff will give fuller protection than has been possible.

EYRE PENINSULA, SOUTH AUSTRALIA
Jerry Olsen and Jeff Jolly

Study Area. — The area consists of towering coastal cliffs, low ranges, and mallee and eucalypt woodland plains, extensively cleared for grazing, in semi-arid Australia.

Distribution and Density. — Peregrines appear limited to cliffs with areas of natural vegetation around or above them. Pairs were as close as 6.5 km on the sea coast. Five pairs averaged 19.3 km apart (range of nearest neighbor: 6.5-42 km). Six pairs were on the southern part of the peninsula, with a mean density of one pair per 1426 km[2].

Nest Sites. — Sites were all cliffs; two were on small ranges, three were coastal cliffs. The nest site used on one of the latter was the stick nest of a White-bellied Sea Eagle. Cliff height ranged from 25-250 m.

Occupancy and Productivity. — Nest site occupancy and productivity were high; no trends were evident.

Threats and Limiting Factors. — A relatively poor food supply appears to keep this population at a relatively low density. One site was deserted after a road was built along the cliff top allowing greater access to fishermen. Another site became popular for campers and was less successful. The remaining four sites are presently secure owing to their remoteness and inaccessibility.

Overall Status and Security. — The Peregrine's status is secure, but the population is small and may have been affected in the past by clearing and DDT.

TASMANIA
Nick Mooney and Nigel Brothers

Study Area. — Tasmania is a mountainous island of 68,300 km[2] with a broken chain of islands linking it to mainland Australia about 220 km to the north. It has, except for South America, the most southerly population of Peregrines, extending from latitude 40°50'S-43°45'S. The climate is temperate. The eastern half of the island is a complex system of low to high altitude hills and ridges, largely covered by dry sclerophyll forest. Lowland areas are often cleared, and small wetlands are common. The western half is low to high altitude and rugged, with a mosaic of wet sclerophyll forest, temperate rainforest and sedgelands. Here coastal flats are small, and extensive lowlands are only found in the northern midlands.

Distribution and Density. — The closest two sites were 3 km apart and much of the population was clumped in groups of 5-10 regularly spaced pairs separated by areas with little apparent food and few nesting Peregrines. Within high-density areas, mean distances separating pairs ranged from 5.7 km ($n=4$) in an inland gorge to 24 km on a series of remote islands ($n=6$). The mean distance between the closest 10 pairs was 13.8 km (range: 4.5-20 km). Some seabird islands of only 5 ha have breeding Peregrines which often hunt on neighboring islands.

Tasmania has about 73 nesting pairs in any given year, with a density of one pair per 936 km[2]. However, 85% of the population is in the northeastern portion of the state, giving that region a density of one pair per 551 km²; the western half of the state supports only one pair per 3106 km².

Nest Sites. — All nests were on cliffs which ranged from 7-200 m high ($\bar{x}$=49 m). In the past, one pair used a hollow tree. Of 115 cliff sites, 44% were sheltered, 22% were prominent and exposed, 24% of the cliffs were extensive (>1 km long) and 11% were on small (<5 km²) islands.

Occupancy and Breeding Success. — All potential eyries were not used, and only higher cliffs were used regularly. Occupancy was low but increasing. Breeding success was high throughout the study. Breeding population was estimated to have been at 80% of former numbers at the commencement of the study in 1973. By 1982, with a dramatic decline in the use of DDT and, particularly, a lessening of persecution, numbers recovered to 90%.

Threats and Limiting Factors. — Lack of cliffs is considered the major factor limiting the population in only about 2.4% of the state. A further 2.7% of the state is above 900 m, which is considered to be the Peregrine's upper altitudinal nesting limit in Tasmania. Eggshell thinning decreased from around 18% (Olsen and Olsen 1979) to less than 5%. Persecution, mainly by pigeon racers, was probably the greatest limiting factor with about 100 Peregrines, eggs and young destroyed in some years. Since legal protection in 1971, and rigorous attempts by the state wildlife authority to discourage persecution, this has been reduced to around 30 birds per year but is thought to be sufficiently high to slow the Peregrine's recovery. Extensive forest clear-felling has not had a detectable effect on adjacent eyries.

Overall Status and Security. — Approximately 25% of nesting pairs are in national parks and reserves of lesser status where disturbance is minimal. An additional 40% are on crown land or state forest. The remainder are on private land, and it is largely here, near concentrations of the human population, that persecution can be considerable. At present, however, only 10-15% of active pairs are subject to persecution, the species is secure, and the population is slowly expanding. (See Mooney and Brothers (1987) for more details.)

WESTERN AUSTRALIA
G. M. Storr

Study Area. — Western Australia is a vast state, encompassing roughly 33% of Australia. Much of the central part of the state is arid. In the north the climate is tropical, and in the south, Mediterranean. No studies of the Peregrine have been undertaken.

Distribution and Density. — The Peregrine is distributed over the greater part of the state, but is only an autumn-winter visitor in most flatlands. It is mainly found near cliffs and water (fresh or salt), especially in mountainous country and along rocky coasts. In flatlands it was originally almost entirely confined to the vicinity of lakes and river pools fringed with tall eucalypts suitable for nesting corvids and hawks; however, it has recently moved into the wheat belt of the southwest, a waterless flatland now comparatively rich in food (parrots) and nest sites (Australian Raven nests).

Peregrine strongholds are thought to be, in order of importance: the western Kimberley in the far north; the south coast, especially rocky islands from the Archipelago of the Recherche west to St. Alouarn Island; the Stirling Ranges of the southwest; and the mountain ranges of the far eastern interior, which extend into the Northern Territory. The population is estimated to be about 750 pairs, giving a mean density of one pair per 3370 km^2.

Nest Sites. — Most nests were on cliffs; on the plains Peregrines used stick nests. Tree holes were rarely used.

Overall Status and Security. — Peregrines are fully protected in the state, but pigeon fanciers lobby for the repeal of its protection. The effect of pesticides is probably negligible as the bulk of the Peregrine population lives far from agricultural areas. In agricultural areas eggshell thinning was as high as 31% (Olsen and Olsen 1979), but averaged about 4%. Other falcons (Australian Kestrel and Brown Falcon) declined in agricultural areas in the last 25 years, but the greater part of the Peregrine population is remote from centers of human population, and secure.

NORTHERN TERRITORY
Penny Olsen

The monsoonal north of the state is mostly savannah woodland; in the south there are extensive arid plains separated by ranges. Peregrines are thinly scattered along the north coast and islands, and in the escarpments and gorges of Arnhem Land. Their stronghold in the state appears to be the central Australian highlands. Elsewhere they are scarce or absent.

No studies have been undertaken. In two areas extensively and regularly surveyed for other reasons — 250 km^2 around the Mary River and 700 km^2 at Kapalga — no Peregrines were present, even though the latter area has a number of small hilly outcrops of the type that would be used elsewhere (T. Hertog unpubl. ms.). Three northern nest cliffs were 130 m, 180 m and 250 m high and were all near or over permanent water; on one cliff the pair nested in a Wedge-tailed Eagle nest.

In the north, summers are very wet, and many bird species go to more southerly latitudes to breed. This may limit Peregrine numbers.

Inland, aridity is the problem and Peregrines are more or less confined to permanent water, where prey species gather to drink. Much of the population is secure because of its remoteness. Tourism is an increasing threat in some areas. Near population centers, nest sites have been deserted. For example, a monolith at Alice Springs was floodlit, causing immediate desertion (B. Bravington pers. comm.).

ACKNOWLEDGEMENTS

We acknowledge the assistance of G. Caughley, G. Chapman, A. Hertog, D. Mount, S. Neville, T. Outtrim, C. M. White, and the authors of the regional reports. The New South Wales National Parks and Wildlife Service Foundation and the South Australia Conservation Foundation partially supported studies in New South Wales and South Australia.

29 | A Study of Peregrines in the Fiji Islands, South Pacific Ocean

Clayton M. White, Daniel J. Brimm, and Fergus Clunie

The Whitney family, through the auspices of the American Museum of Natural History, sponsored a 12-year collecting expedition to the South Pacific during the 1920s and 1930s. In 1924-25, the Fiji Islands (some of the largest islands lying to the east of the larger island masses of Australia, New Zealand, New Guinea, and the Solomon Islands) were visited, and Peregrine specimens were collected from both the New Hebrides (now Vanuatu) and Fiji. At that time Peregrines had also been reported from the Loyalty Islands and New Caledonia. E. Mayr (1941) subsequently determined that those specimens from New Caledonia and Vanuatu were morphologically distinct from adjacent races in Australia, New Guinea and the Solomon Islands; he named them *F. p. nesiotes* ("the islander"). Fiji Peregrines may also be *F. p. nesiotes*, but not enough individuals have been examined to definitely establish them as such.

Although Mayr was not sure whether Peregrines bred in Fiji, nesting had in fact been recorded as early as 1877, when A. J. L. Gordon (1897-1912) reported that three Peregrine nestlings were eaten by people at Namosi (where we recently found two eyries) in September. Additionally, in 1924 a missionary acquired a young Peregrine which was sent to the New York Zoological Gardens where it subsequently died (Clunie 1980a). Mayr had access to that specimen but was still not certain whether Peregrines bred on Fiji (Mayr 1941). Mayr's uncertainty about breeding status may have been influenced by the statements of H. K. Swann of the British Museum, regarding a Fiji specimen (Wood and Wetmore 1926). Swann thought the specimen may have been an example of *F. p. macropus* from Australia that wandered to Fiji from New Caledonia, the easternmost area where Peregrines were known to occur and where *F. p. macropus* was the presumed race. Mayr (1945) later reported breeding on two islands in

Fiji and suggested that Peregrines occured near cliffs on the larger islands. Based on information available to them, Brown and Amadon (1968) also questioned whether Peregrines bred in Fiji, but recent sources show Peregrines breeding throughout Fiji (Watling 1982, Clunie 1984).

Breeding was clearly confirmed in the late 1960s when Clunie found Peregrines nesting at Joske's Thumb, an andesitic plug near Suva, Fiji's capital. Considerable information has now been published on these Peregrines and others nearby (Clunie 1972, 1976a, 1976b, 1980a, 1980b). Visitors to Suva can see the Thumb from town, and many climb it. C. M. White and M. T. White first visited it in 1974; Brimm visited it with Clunie in 1980 and obtained food remains and eggshell fragments. In October 1985, the three of us undertook a helicopter survey of the two large islands of Vitilevu and Vanualevu and intervening islands of the Koro Sea, gathering data on the distribution and density of Peregrines. In August and September 1986, the three of us climbed into five eyries to obtain reproduction and food data. Many areas could not be examined because of constraints on time and money and because of the timing of the 1985 survey in relation to breeding cycles. Areas not visited included the Yasawa, Kadavu, Yasayasamoala and Lau groups. C. M. Anderson and F. L. Craighead visited most of the Yasawa Group in August 1986. Clunie and D. Watling had many observations from previous years at locations not visited by us, and we were also able to obtain information from native Fijians. The data presented here thus come from a variety of sources: the Whitney Expedition, local Fijians, previous work by Clunie and Watling, work by Anderson and Craighead, and our joint efforts in 1985 and 1986.

Some historical facts will serve to put this information into perspective. The Fijian word for Peregrine is *ganivatu*, literally "duck of the rock." Ducks are among the few conspicuous large land birds in Fiji. As early as 1850, the Fijian dictionary defined *ganivatu* as, "The name of a very large bird, perhaps, fabulous, said to live in holes and eat men" (Hazlewood 1850). Many natives know the Peregrine and there is a rich Fijian folklore surrounding it (Brewster 1922). (As a cautionary note, some natives confuse the Peregrine with other birds and know its name only from folklore, not personal experience.) Islanders of the eastern or Lau Group say the Peregrine arrives each year at planting time (August) and departs after the harvest (February-March), and so it was a seasonal indicator in times past. It was a good omen because as it flew to the rocks it called "ji-ji," which the Fijians say encouraged the roots of the yams to grow. Brimm and White talked to many natives in the rainy, misty Namosi highlands where in the past young have been eaten by people and where we found two eyries. They said *ganivatu* is usually seen when it is hot (October-March), soars on sunny days, is black in color, lives on cliffs, makes a "ka, ka" call, and flies to the sea where it eats fish. The last belief, widespread in Fiji, is built around the mystical power of *ganivatu* and rooted in a folklore too extensive to repeat (see Clunie 1986).

MATERIALS AND METHODS

In 1985, we spent 10 hours in a helicopter examining major cliff areas on Vitilevu and Vanualevu and several smaller islands. Three observers and the pilot examined each cliff closely for nesting ledges with excreta and for falcons. Besides the Peregrine, only the Common Barn-Owl and, exceptionally, the Swamp Harrier use inland cliffs, although along the coast the Eastern Reef Heron and White-tailed Tropicbird use cliffs for nesting and roosting. We thus had confidence in fecal signs ("whitewash") and other circumstantial evidence we found inland, especially where they corresponded to previous information and sightings. At coastal cliffs on Wakaya and Kioa we saw Peregrines, confirming their presence and ruling out confusion of eyries with those of seabirds or herons. Locations were plotted on maps, and the elevation and orientation of each cliff were recorded. Following the 1985 helicopter work, Brimm and White visited two accessible areas on foot and by car. Cliffs visited were recorded as small (<50 m tall), or large (>50 m tall). Figures for the numbers of cliffs examined were somewhat arbitrary, as it was often hard to determine exactly where one cliff ended and another began. Islands known not to have cliffs were not examined. Data on distribution in the Lau Group came mainly from Clunie (northern Lau), from Fijians, and from P. Geraghty of the Fijian Dictionary Project.

In 1986, 6.5 hours were spent in a helicopter examining most eyries on Vitilevu, Wayaka, and Kioa, and some eyries on Vanualevu where Peregrines were seen in 1985. Six eyries were climbed into to confirm reproduction data and gather food remains and eggshell fragments. Parts of at least six eggshells from four eyries were measured for thickness by C. Sumida at the Western Foundation for Vertebrate Zoology. Ten measurements were made on each shell for a total of 60 measurements. Thickness measurements included membranes.

RESULTS

Cliff Size and Distribution. — The route of our 1985 helicopter flight is shown in Figure 1. A large cliffy area in northeastern Vitilevu and major cliffy areas in the east and west of Vanualevu were not checked. On Vitilevu, the largest (10,385 km^2), highest, and most mountainous island, the checked cliffs varied in elevation between

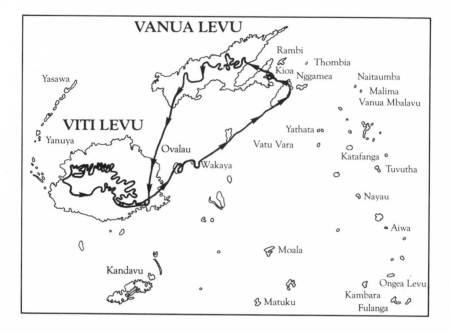

FIGURE 1.   Route flown by helicopter during the 1985 survey. Suva was the starting
point and is located on Viti Levu in the lower right hand portion of the
island.

122-920 m. The mean elevation for a sample of 49 large cliffs was
598 m, and the mean for 49 small cliffs was 483 m. More than half of
the inland cliffs were checked, but small coastal cliffs were not
examined. On Vanualevu (5535 km²), 35 large cliffs and 55 small
cliffs were checked; 6 large and 15 small cliffs were checked on
Ovalau, 1 large and 2 small cliffs on Wakaya, and 3 small cliffs on
Kioa Island. Koro, one of the largest islands of the Koro Sea, was
examined and found to have no suitable cliffs. Low clouds and rain
prevented an effective survey of Taveuni, but no suitable cliffs were
seen on a flight along the forested, windward coast of the island. The
remaining island area of Fiji includes about 2072 km² of land scattered
over a wide expanse of sea.

Among a total of 215 cliffs examined, 124 small and 91 large, 19
Peregrines were seen. We found Peregrines at two small cliffs and five
large cliffs, and we found nesting ledges (but did not flush Peregrines)
at six small cliffs and four large ones. Young had been on the wing for
at least four weeks at one eyrie. We found one young at each of two
locations, and two young at a third. There was no trend in directional
orientation of cliffs examined, or for those occupied by Peregrines.
Likewise there was no apparent preference of habitat inland, with

equal numbers of eyries in the dry, grassy lee as opposed to the wet forested windward side of each large island examined. The presence of eyries on coastal cliffs at Wakaya and Kioa suggests that these may be favored over inland sites in Fiji, especially when compared with Clunie's observations from northern Lau.

The locations of 13 places where Peregrines were reported by Fijians (presumably eyrie sites), 9 locations previously recorded by Clunie and Watling, and 17 found by us are shown in Figure 2. In addition to the site shown for the Yasawa Group, Anderson and Craighead found a Peregrine at another location in the south Yasawas (they checked 21 islands in the Yasawas) and confirmed a pair near one of our 1985 sites (where we saw no Peregrines) on western Vitilevu. These locations probably do not accurately reflect true distribution, but do indicate areas where information is available. For the eastern or Lau Group, most information is from inhabited islands. Interestingly, on flat

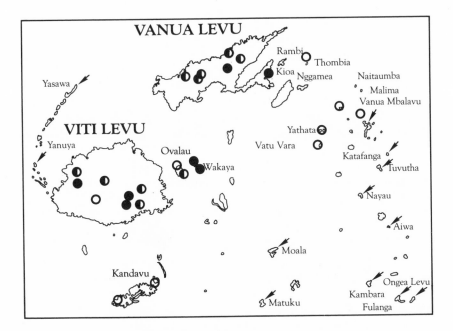

FIGURE 2. Locations of reported and known Peregrine eyries in Fiji.

islands in the Lau Group without cliffs, the Peregrine is not recorded, and the Fijian name is not in the native vocabulary. There are scores of uninhabited and rugged coral limestone islands, many only a few hectares in area, that were uplifted from the sea and have adequate cliffs. Some certainly have Peregrines. Examples range between Vatuvara, 1.6 km across and 343 m high, to the tiny uplifted limestone Kibobo Islets of a few hectares in area, where Clunie found pairs of Peregrines.

The number of islands without adequate cliffs needs to be accurately determined before any semblance of true distribution and density can be known. For example, within the Koro Sea between the two large islands of Vitilevu and Vanualevu, Peregrines were seen at each of two main cliff areas on the little island of Wakaya, while the much larger nearby islands of Nairai and Koro lack any suitable cliffs.

Reproduction. — Prior to 1986, only scattered information was available on reproduction. Gordon (1897) reported that three young were eaten by people at Namosi, and in 1925 W. Belcher of the Fiji Museum wrote that three was the usual clutch size. Clunie observed three young with parents at Joske's Thumb, but elsewhere he noted only 1-2 young per eyrie. He found a completed but abandoned clutch of one egg, but apparently 2-3 eggs are usually laid. We obtained no egg data in 1986, but brood sizes were 2, 2, 3, 3, and 3. On 22 August, most broods were 2-7 days old, except one in the rainforest of the Korombasambasanga Range on inland Vitilevu, where there were two 3-week-old females weighing about 680 g each, with tail feathers 60 mm long from the base. On 23 August, three small young at Kioa Island, about the same age as young in four other eyries, weighed between 200-220 g. By 4 September, five young from four eyries, including the Kioa Island young, weighed 495-550 g.

Most eggs were laid about the third week of July, with the earliest during the first week of July. Egg dates corresponded roughly to dates at similar latitudes in Australia (Czechura 1984). Based on our 1986 data, our 1985 observations, and earlier observations by Clunie, there is a synchrony in egg laying. On both dry lee and wet windward sides of the islands, breeding takes place during the "dry" season when rainfall on the dry side is about 75% less than during the rainy season and that on the wet side about 25% less.

Food and Feeding Habits. — Like many Peregrine populations, the Fiji Peregrines have a diverse diet (see Clunie 1972, 1976a, 1980b). Prior to 1985, food remains were gathered from urban Suva, a rainforest area, and two oceanic islands. In 1986, food remains were gathered from eyries at two rainforest sites, one dry grassland site, and two seacliff sites. Based on size, there are some 94 species (56 land birds, 31 marine or aquatic birds, 7 mammals) that could be captured.

Only 81 of these (43 land birds, 31 marine or aquatic birds, 7 mammals) are readily accessible, however, because of forest canopy or other habitat features. Another 12 are not likely to be captured because of their behavior (some spend their lives on the forest floor), leaving only 69 species (40 land birds, 25 marine or aquatic birds, 4 mammals) of the 94 that are vulnerable to predation. To date, 45 (41 birds, 4 mammals) of the 69 species have been found in prey remains. One reptile has also been found, a large Voracious Gecko (*Gehyra vorax*) that inhabits cliffs or rocky areas and may simply have been a fortuitous catch. The overwhelming majority of the mammals (perhaps 98%) were flying fox fruit bats (*Pteropus* spp.); one rat (*Rattus* sp.) was found. Of the birds, 14 species were marine or aquatic, 6 were doves or pigeons, and 3 were parrots. Of the remaining species, 13 were passerine.

The relative importance of each food type varied considerably between habitats, although *Pteropus* bats occurred in all samples. In an analysis of 50 pellets from one rainforest eyrie, 64% contained parrots, 32% contained doves and 56% contained bats. This sample differed from nonpellet prey remains in the number of parrots and doves. A comparison of prey remain samples from three major habitats for one collection period is shown in Table 1. There are some characteristics of the Fiji Peregrines' feeding habits that depart from patterns recorded elsewhere. In Fiji, Peregrines do not habitually spend the nonbreeding periods in the urban areas of Suva where there is a large food supply of feral pigeons and mynas. The two Peregrines that have resided in the urban area over the past 15 years did not exploit the enormous myna population. As an example of that population, in August 1986 several thousand mynas came to roost in the storage building at the dock area nightly, arriving about one hour before darkness. Scores were at the landfill dump area about 3 km from downtown Suva. Yet, a sample of food remains from the downtown Suva winter roost had 101 feral pigeons, 81 Collared Petrels, 45 Sooty Terns, 76 Wandering Tattlers, 55 Golden Plovers, 22 Many-colored Fruit Doves, and several each of about a dozen other species (Clunie 1980a). Only two mynas were in the sample. At one rainforest eyrie near Suva, the 3.5-week-old young all had empty crops and were ravenous when hand-fed on one visit. On two visits to the same eyrie no adults were seen; presumably they were hunting. Mynas were numerous 2 km away near open rice fields, but only one myna was among the 21 individuals of 11 species found in prey remains. The Fiji Peregrine certainly does not exploit this abundant sturnid as Peregrines in Australia (Pruett-Jones et al. 1981) and elsewhere do other sturnids like the European Starling. Peregrines nesting near the coast are more likely to capture holarctic migrants, but Peregrines

TABLE 1. A comparison of food remains found during one collection period at Peregrine eyries in three distinct habitats, Fiji.

Habitat-eyrie-prey item	n	Habitat-eyrie-prey item	n	Habitat-eyrie-prey item	n
Rain Forest		Dry Grassland		Sea Cliff	
Korombasambasanga eyrie		Koroimaia eyrie		Wakaya Island eyrie	
Fiji Goshawk	1	Fiji Goshawk	3	White-tailed Tropicbird	1
Flying fox fruit bats (*Pteropus*)	15	Collared Lory	1	Pacific Pigeon	1
Rama (Joske's Thumb) eyrie		Polynesian Triller	1	Crimson-crowned Fruit Dove	1
Barking Pigeon	1	Golden Whistler	1	Spotted Dove	1
Golden Dove	1	Unidentified White-eye (*Zosterops*)	1	Collared Lory	1
Collared Lory	1	Red Avadavat	1	White-collared Kingfisher	1
Wandering Tattler	1	Jungle Myna	1	Pacific Swallow	1
White-collared Kingfisher	1	Flying fox fruit bats (*Pteropus*)	2	Vanikoro Broadbill	1
Wattled Honeyeater	1			Unidentified White-eye (*Zosterops*)	1
Polynesian Starling	1			Polynesian Starling	1
Jungle Myna	1			Flying fox fruit bats (*Pteropus*)	1
Red-headed Parrot Finch	1			Vatuvara Island eyrie[a]	
Voracious Gecko (*Gehyra vorax*)	1			Collared Petrel	
Flying fox fruit bats (*Pteropus*)	11			White-capped Noddy	
				Pacific Pigeon	
				Crimson-crowned Fruit Dove	
				Collared Lory	
				White-collared Kingfisher	
				Flying fox fruit bats (*Pteropus*)	

[a] Prey items not tabulated.

wandering away from inland eyries during the nonbreeding season may also be exposed to them.

Food habits on tiny isolated oceanic islets need to be determined, but marine birds are undoubtedly important. *Pteropus* fruit bats (flying foxes) and *Ducula*, *Columba* and *Ptilinopus* pigeons are quite often seen at sea, flying long distances from one island to another, and may also form an important source of food. Flying foxes in particular often camp on small islands in large numbers.

Eggshell Thinning. — Numerous agricultural changes have occurred recently in Fiji. Pesticides are now used on crops in areas that were native forest. Many holarctic migrant birds exposed to agricultural chemicals in the northern hemisphere spend their nonbreeding season in Fiji and are eaten by Peregrines. Therefore, Peregrines in Fiji may obtain agricultural chlorinated hydrocarbons from two sources: local prey and northern hemisphere migrants.

There are no historical eggshell thickness or residue data for Fiji Peregrine eggs, but there are three ways to view the values we have recently obtained. The Fiji Peregrine is about the same size as *F. p. macropus* from Australia, and should have a similar egg size. Anderson and Hickey (1972) determined that the correlation between eggshell thickness and Ratcliffe's thickness indices (RI) are highly significant. RI values are available for pre- and post-DDT eggs of *F. p. macropus*. Pre-DDT Peregrine eggshells from various northern hemisphere areas varied between a thickness of 0.375 mm correlating with an RI of 1.99, and 0.347 mm correlating with an RI of 1.81 (Anderson and Hickey 1972, L. Kiff pers. comm.). The average RI for eight northern hemisphere populations was 1.91. For Australia there were some high average pre-DDT RIs of 2.06 (Olsen and Peakall 1983), but the mean RI for six regions of Australia was 1.93 (n=161) (Olsen and Olsen 1979), corresponding to an eggshell thickness of 0.370 mm.

The overall mean thickness (n=6) from Fiji was 0.327 mm (range: 0.311-0.344). The Fiji value of 0.327 is 12% thinner than the derived pre-DDT Australian value of 0.370. One of the lowest pre-DDT thicknesses was 0.347 mm (n=42) from Greenland (L. Kiff pers. comm.), which is 6% thicker than the Fiji eggs.

DISCUSSION AND CONCLUSIONS

We cannot reliably estimate Peregrine density for Fiji. If the locations reported by Fijians are confirmed as breeding sites, and the remaining islands with cliffs are checked, the number of pairs could be between 50-75. Peregrines are about as frequently seen in Vanuatu as in Fiji (R. Pickering pers. comm.), suggesting that their density there may be similar to Fiji. If cliffs suitable for nesting and food resources are similar on Vanuatu (smaller than Fiji with an area of 14,763 km²),

New Caledonia, and the Loyalty Islands (larger than Fiji with an area of 22,139 km²), then the race *F. p. nesiotes* may not contain more than 200-250 pairs.

While cliff abundance per se would not appear to limit pairs in Fiji, the actual structure or presence of suitable ledges on these cliffs may be limiting. Many cliffs that looked excellent for Peregrines from a distance proved to be composed of highly eroded but smooth or conglomerate rock lacking horizontal ledges. Because mongooses (*Herpestes auropunctatus*) have been introduced to several islands, including Vitilevu and Vanualevu, and have largely eradicated petrel colonies and most other species of ground-nesting birds (Watling 1982, Clunie 1984), it may be that inaccessible ledges are necessary to avoid predation of eggs or young; the Swamp Harrier, however, nests on the ground and seems to do well despite the presence of the mongoose. Also, mongooses have access to a ledge at Joske's Thumb, where Peregrines have successfully fledged young. On one island where Clunie saw Peregrines, an eyrie may recently have been abandoned owing to domestic goats, which have gained access to every cliff ledge over the last seven years.

Food does not outwardly appear to be limiting. Most Peregrine pairs on Vitilevu and Vanualevu could derive a major food source from the two introduced myna species, the Common Myna and the Jungle Myna. Both are abundant in or near human settlements. In forested areas, there are not many available birds other than parrots, doves and pigeons, and a few smaller species that habitually expose themselves in or above the canopy, but the ubiquitous flying fox fruit bats, lumbering over the canopy in daylight, are highly vulnerable.

We think, however, that food may in fact be limiting in some ways. Both adults were frequently gone from eyries, presumably hunting, when young were only 1.5-2 weeks old. The weight category of some prey items suggests that females were hunting rather than remaining at nests as is usual when young are that age. When males arrived at some eyries to defend against our presence, they were immediately driven away by their mates. In one case, we watched the male leave only to continue on a soaring hunting flight. Lack of parental attention might alternatively have evolved as a response to the absence of nest predators. When young were hand-fed, they were absolutely ravenous, and many appeared to be in poor condition. The reduced amount of food remains in eyries with three-week-old young was conspicuous compared to our experience elsewhere.

There are no numerically large food sources other than generally distributed *Pteropus* bats and mynas (see above) or seabird colonies at specific local areas. The seabird resource, however, is not particularly abundant, and even at seacliff eyries, land birds constituted a major portion of the prey remains (Table 1). This condition is reminiscent of most Peregrines nesting on seacliffs in Victoria, Australia (White et al. 1981) where they are sparsely distributed and also use mainly land birds as food. The flying fox fruit bat appears to be to the Fiji Peregrine what seabirds are to Aleutian Peregrines, parrots are to Australian Peregrines, and pigeons and doves are to British, Spanish, and central Argentine Peregrines. The presence of bats in the numbers that they occur may mean the difference between success or failure at many eyries. Most of the Peregrines of the Papuan-western Pacific region may be similarly dependent on flying fox fruit bats.

Assuming there are available cliffs, there is no biogeographical reason why breeding Peregrines should not extend further eastward into the Pacific beyond Fiji (into Tonga, Samoa, etc.) other than the reduced diversity and density of suitable prey. The Lau Group is as close to the Tongan Islands as to Vitilevu, but the bird fauna is much reduced in Tonga over Fiji (Watling 1982). Fiji has 47 species of endemic land birds, Samoa has 32 and Tonga has only 13. The three island groups have 9, 2, and 3 introduced bird species, respectively. New Zealand, which is off the path of dispersing birds, lacks Peregrines as well as *Pteropus* fruit bats and *Ptilinopus* and *Ducula* fruit doves. The islands east of Fiji, on the other hand, form a typical "stepping stone" pathway for island-to-island dispersal which prime Peregrine prey such as the fruit bats and fruit doves have used (Williamson 1981). Peregrines could likewise have followed this dispersal pathway if food in the appropriate density and cliffs were present.

Of 215 cliffs checked during our 1985 Fiji survey, only 17 (8%) were being used by Peregrines. This apparent scarcity of Peregrines in Fiji is very striking. The following five factors may help to explain our findings.

(1) The Peregrine may be a generally uncommon bird in tropical insular situations. E. Mayr (pers. comm.) said that throughout his extensive experiences in southeast Asia and the Pacific he only rarely saw Peregrines. This was especially true when compared to his experience in Europe. The results of the Whitney expedition possibly also influenced Mayr's impressions of the Peregrine's rareness in the tropics. That expedition visited 114 islands in Fiji, and Peregrines were seen at only four (Watling 1985). They even visited the small islands of Kioa, Wakaya, and Vatuvara for a combined total of seven days; although we found eyries there, they did not see any Peregrines. The differences between our findings and those of the Whitney expedition may have been a function of their not having looked specifically for Peregrines.

(2) Some cliffs may have been vacated in recent times. Probable goat disturbance has been mentioned, and the proximity of human

dwellings and activities may be a factor. The human population of Fiji has increased more than five-fold since 1900. Roads have made many formerly remote areas easily accessible, especially during the past 15 years. Indeed, one eyrie we saw on Vanualevu was very close to a new road, and one on Vitilevu was about 250 m from a road. An eyrie known to D. Watling (pers. comm.) in the Sigatoka Valley was vacated around 1975 but reoccupied in 1986 (and incidently now has a road leading nearly to it). Several Fijians questioned by P. Geraghty said that Peregrines "used to be" on various islands, implying that they no longer were.

(3) On the dry leeward sides of the main islands, large-scale grass- and scrub-burning by villagers during the July-September incubation and nestling periods could result in abandonment of sites by Peregrines. Some cliffs were blackened by smoke.

(4) During our 1985 survey, we may have missed pairs owing to their being away from nearly independent young or their lack of reaction to helicopters. Adults were frequently not at cliffs even when young were less than two weeks old. One female left a cliff, made one small circle, then flew immediately to perch in the shelter of the forest canopy. Peregrines in Fiji may be more forest-oriented than we are accustomed to. Clunie, in fact, received an unverified report from Fijian villagers of a pair using a Fiji Goshawk nest along the Wainibuka River on Vitilevu. They claimed that there were young in the nest in August and that they fledged and left during September.

(5) Finally, there may have been some depression of the population locally with the loss of some pairs as a result of deleterious chemical residues acquired from northern hemisphere migrants, notably waders, or as a result of spraying of rice and other crops, especially on Vitilevu and Vanualevu. Both Vitilevu and Vanualevu have extensive tidal flats, and the common waders are certainly taken by Peregrines nearby. Although some eggshell fragments are available, their condition and the possible chemical content of eggs cannot be verified until we have a larger sample.

The low clutch size and fledging rate from a scattered adult population of low density suggests that adults have low mortality rates and long life spans, a notion supported by the very few juveniles Clunie has seen among many sightings of Peregrines. More data on clutch size, fledging rates, and adult replacement at eyries need to be gathered before Peregrine population dynamics can be understood in Fiji.

ACKNOWLEDGEMENTS

We thank I. Simpson and N. Ragg, Pacific Crown Aviation, for their excellent helicopter support. D. Watling spent many hours with us talking about Peregrines and checking his records. R. Mercer provided some information and P. Geraghty generously gave us his data. N. Tabunokawai, Ministry of Primary Industries, facilitated acquiring necessary permits to work. C. M. Anderson and F. L. Craighead freely allowed us to use their data and helped in numerous ways as did G. and I. Watkins, owners of Orchid Island. R. Miller helped obtain permission to visit the private island of Wakaya.

30 | Distribution and Status of the Peregrine in Kenya

Simon Thomsett

Very few data have been collected on the population of Peregrines (*F. p. minor*) breeding in Kenya. Much of Kenya is largely inaccessible, especially those areas ecologically suitable to falcons. Very few observers have the time or the inclination to outfit surveys to look for falcons. There are few falconers or falcon fanatics in Kenya. Scattered reports, therefore, must be checked carefully since the Lanner Falcon is encountered throughout Kenya and may be confused with the Peregrine.

CLIMATIC VARIABLES

To make a complete survey of nesting Peregrines in Kenya would take many years because of regional and climatic factors. On the equator it is difficult to define "spring" (rainy, breeding season), as there are two dry seasons and two rainy seasons. In different parts of Kenya the "short rains" (October-December) are in fact long rains, while in other parts the "long rains" (April-May) are short. In some parts, particularly the coast of Lake Victoria, rain occurs every month of the year, while in others it does not rain for years on end. Peregrines breed in all these areas. Rains are thought to be the only important climatic factor likely to regulate the Peregrine's breeding cycle, as day length is the same throughout the year.

Peregrine distribution seems to have little relationship to rainfall, altitude or other climatic conditions. It has been suggested that large falcons found in areas with more than 10.5 cm annual rainfall are more likely to be Peregrines, and those in areas with 10 cm or less most likely are Lanners (Brown and Amadon 1968). While this separation might occur in some regions, it has too many exceptions to make it a useful guide. The Peregrine is physically capable of living in wet and cold conditions as well as in hot and dry ones. The Lanner with its softer plumage is less likely to thrive in cold, wet regions. The Lanner is well suited to hot, dry areas, but no more so than coinhabiting Peregrines. One would expect Lanners to be absent from cold, wet highlands, but in some cases they are present — for example, on Mount Elgon.

PREY AVAILABILITY

The laying period for Kenya's Peregrines is given as August (Brown and Amadon 1968), and yet I have recorded Peregrines at the same eyrie laying as far apart as June and December. I believe the most important factor that induces breeding is availability of prey species. In some areas it might be beneficial to breed in the dry season when prey are exposed. Sandgrouse, doves, and Red-billed Quelea become easy targets when they flock into isolated drinking holes in the dry weather. It is possible that some Peregrine pairs make heavy use of Palearctic migrant passerines. Other pairs might take advantage of local fluctuations in prey. Still others may feed during the outward return journey of Palearctic migrants. In less hospitable areas, such as the semi-arid deserts, the food source is quite likely to be only passing through on migration. I have, however, been in desolate areas where prey species have been at extremely low densities and seen a male Peregrine leave his cliff and without any apparent effort return some five minutes later with a dove. It is, therefore, difficult to understand the Peregrine's "breeding season." Although not yet recorded, it is conceivable that two broods of young could be raised at the same eyrie in a 12-18 month period.

OTHER ENVIRONMENTAL FACTORS

Inaccessible cliff faces are preferred for nesting, although some eyries are situated in incredibly accessible places. Two Peregrine eyries (one in Tsavo and one in Embu) can be walked into. Both suffer from predation. Baboons roost on cliff faces and regularly destroy falcon eggs and nestlings. At almost every site I know, baboons and mongooses are present. I have seen Peregrines attack both as well as attack leopards. It is therefore important, particularly in Kenya where many species of small carnivores exist, that a successful eyrie be totally inaccessible, as indeed most are. Only two tree-nesting Peregrines are recorded. I do not know whether or not they were successful, but I did observe a male carry food to a *Euphorbia candelabra* tree with an old snake-eagle (*Circaetus* sp.) nest on top. The tree was on a steep hillside with no cliffs and as the tree was among many others and covered with excreta, I think it reasonable to suppose that it was an eyrie. Snake-eagle nests situated on a hillside would make ideal nests for falcons. The other was up a eucalypt (L. Siemens pers. comm.).

The above cases are rare indeed, and the distribution of Peregrines is undoubtedly related mainly to available cliff faces. They must, however, compete with a large number of other raptors for suitable sites, such as Verreaux's Eagles, African Hawk Eagles, Augur Buzzards, African Harrier Hawks, Lanner Falcons, Eagle Owls, vultures and even ravens, all of which nest on cliffs and vigorously defend them.

Although vultures are not aggressive, I have seen a prospecting Lanner land on a ledge and walk into a pothole. Five minutes later, a blundering Ruppell's Griffon flew in and stood in the entrance. The Lanner, after much screaming, pushed past and stooped time and time again until the vulture departed. The Lanners, however, did not use that pothole. I have also witnessed this pair of Lanners harrass a neighboring pair of Peregrines that tried unsuccessfully for three years to breed 2 km away. Although other factors probably disturbed this pair of Peregrines, the Lanners were largely responsible for the Peregrine pair's failure.

CONGENERS

Of the 23 Peregrine eyries and 11 Lanner eyries I know, there are a number that are particularly close to one another. For instance, two pairs of Peregrines nest not more than 1 km from each other on one huge cliff. There is also a pair of Lanners on a smaller cliff about 2 km from the nearest of these Peregrines. At another site (Lukenya), two eyries (one a Peregrine, the other a Lanner) are about 80 m from one another, and both raised young at the same time. It is often supposed that there are areas that are inhabited by Peregrines to the exclusion of Lanners and vice versa, the presumption being that they compete with one another. Peregrines seem more likely to tolerate Lanners that may feed on different prey than other Peregrines that feed on the same food items.

Lanners seem to play an important role in the Peregrine's distribution. I feel that there is no set rule that separates them. The two species are so randomly placed and integrated that it is impossible to generalize. Lanners do, however, occupy some available eyries and defend them from Peregrines, so to some extent they must affect the Peregrine population. A pair of very rare Taita Falcons vigorously attacked my captive Peregrines while they were flying. I have seen these falcons attack wild Peregrines that lived nearby, and they usually drove the Peregrines away. It is possible that the Taitas might compete for eyries. It is significant to note that a suspected Taita eyrie known to me is very close to a Peregrine eyrie, a situation which reportedly occurs in the Zambezi Gorge below Victoria Falls. Where they occur together, pairs of Taitas are often seen attacking the resident Peregrines. However, Taitas are so rare that there is certainly no adverse influence on the Peregrines; the reverse might be true.

Peregrine eyries, if not defended throughout the year, are in danger of being used by ravens or various raptors. At one unsuccessful Peregrine eyrie, the pair returned after a week's absence to find a pair of Fan-Tailed Ravens occupying the eyrie. The same eyrie had been prospected by a neighboring pairs of Lanners and Lesser Kestrels. Although the Peregrines returned regularly to this site, they never bred for a period of three years. During the nonbreeding season some pairs still defend their territories, but others desert for months on end. Lanners reclaimed two Peregrine sites that were originally occupied by Lanners (Hell's Gate and Shaba) in years when Peregrines were absent.

DENSITY ESTIMATES

It has been suggested that in tropical Africa, Peregrine pairs may be 15-25 km apart, though this distribution is probably affected by the availability of suitable breeding sites (Brown and Amadon 1968). This estimate has been remarkably accurate in those areas I have studied. If Peregrines were uniformly distributed without respect to topography, one could triangulate Kenya and deduce a population of about 1200-2400 pairs. This is undoubtedly a very high estimate. However, using the pairs known to Leslie Brown (8 in 300 km^2), the calculation would suggest about 1500 pairs. Subtracting those land masses without cliffs, and with forest, lakes, true deserts, intense farmland and densely populated regions, one would be nearer to the correct number. In exceptional areas eyries are as little as 1.9 km apart or even closer. A classification of areas might be: exceptionally good areas with an average of 10 km between pairs, moderate areas with pairs 25 km apart, poor areas with pairs 40-50 km apart, and areas with none.

The 23 eyries known to me are difficult to arrange in a convenient fashion to make calculations of population densities. These eyries are generally situated near roads or on mountains that have hundreds of other likely nest sites. These latter areas are largely unsurveyed.

About one-third of Kenya (18,750 km^2) can be considered devoid of Peregrines. The remaining 375,000 km^2 would in theory contain about 1000 pairs, as the area for those categories of exceptional, moderate, and poor densities equal out to an average of one pair per 25 km^2.

White splashes on ledges or potholes too small for eagles or vultures are almost certainly signs of a falcon eyrie. These are seen from aerial surveys and abound in many impenetrable habitats, but Peregrine eyries are impossible to separate from Lanner eyries. The ratio of known Peregrine to Lanner eyries is 2:1. Contrary to what one is locally led to believe, the Peregrine appears to be the more common. In contrast, in southern Africa the ratio may be close to 10:1 in favor of the Lanner (Tarboton and Allan 1984). One possible explanation is that the Lanner is far more frequently seen. Road counts in particular tend to bias this ratio in the Lanner's favor. Lanners can be seen many miles from available cliffs. Oddly, the Lanners are usually in their immature plumage, suggesting local migrants. These inter-African migrants can lead one to suppose that the Kenya breeding population of Lanners is larger than the breeding population of Peregrines. Peregrines are seldom seen away from mountains or cliff ranges. Many Peregrines seen in unlikely areas may be Palearctic migrants. However, in the air these are almost impossible to differentiate from the local ones. Without doubt, the sample is too small to make an accurate ratio of Peregrines to Lanners.

The breeding records for Kenya, compiled over a number of years (P. B. Taylor pers. comm.), are from the same sites that I know. Breeding records of the Lanner are also mostly from the same areas. Combining other recorded nests with my own records, there are 26 Peregrine eyries and 16 Lanner eyries. If one concedes to the general opinion that Lanners are more common, then an estimate of 1000 Peregrine pairs is probably too high. From an area estimate, location by location, with combined aerial and ground knowledge of topography, I tally a minimum of 450 sites. I thus estimate the current Peregrine population in Kenya at 450-1000 pairs. Although it is difficult to know how much confidence to place in such estimates, it is certain that the numbers of Peregrines in Kenya and in East Africa generally are much larger than had been supposed on the basis of limited information (see Cade 1982).

DISCUSSION

I have little data on the population dynamics of Peregrines in Kenya. Essentially nothing is known on the numbers of nonbreeders, mean clutch size, fledging rates, ratios of immatures to adults in the population, or other demographic features. My own observations tend to be limited to one visit to each eyrie per year. I have seen clutches of 2, 3, and 4 eggs. I have known of four young being fledged. I have also seen large young dead in eyries of no apparent cause.

Road counts and the separation of juveniles from adults can be misleading, particularly as the resident population seems not to make any obvious movement or migration. Young Peregrines are seen quite frequently, particularly during the heavy rains, perhaps because the storms push the birds to the ground. Peregrines eat flying ants on the wing as do smaller falcons. I suspect that Peregrines may prey on flocks of migratory small falcons. I have seen an immature Peregrine determinedly attack a mixed flock of Lesser Kestrels, Northern Hobbies and Eastern Red-footed Falcons. I felt sure that the Peregrine was going to capture one when they disappeared from view. Immatures are,

I think, mistaken frequently for Palearctic *F. p. calidus*. Most observers believe that local *F. p. minor* is small. I think it is difficult to identify *F. p. calidus* by plumage, and I also think size is difficult to judge in the field.

Coloration among individual African Peregrines is variable. I have a male that has very fine, almost indistinct, bars on the chest, two rufous patches on the back of his head, indistinct bars on the tail and flight feathers, and no white on top of the cere. He is small — weight 480-537 g, wing 280 mm, tail 110 mm, and tarsus 50 mm. I also have a large female with obvious bars on her chest and a fair amount of rufous. The head is totally black with hardly any moustache protruding below the "helmet." Tail and flight feathers have obvious bars and there is no white about the cere. She is stocky and could easily be confused with *F. p. calidus*: weight 764-840 g, wing 344 mm, tail 155 mm, and tarsus 55 mm. I have had other *F. p. minor* that weighed 950 g and a small female that weighed about 660 g. I have seen others with very white undersides and white on top of the cere. Only once did I see *F. p. calidus*, and it was obvious by its size and flight.

Another possible source of confusion in the field, and even a possible breeder in Kenya, is *F. p. pelegrinoides*. I currently have an injured male that was brought in from the foothills of Mt. Kenya at about 2500 m. *F. p. pelegrinoides* might be overlooked, for it can be mistaken for *F. p. minor* or, if seen close enough, for a Lanner. It is certainly not a falcon that most local ornithologists expect to see because most are not aware of its existence in the country as a migrant or possible resident.

Survival of falcons in Kenya is a matter of some concern. The most permanent loss of falcons comes from habitat destruction by humans. Pesticides are at times grossly misused, and direct persecution is a growing problem. Kenya boasts the fastest growing population in the world, and the national policy is to give land to everyone for subsistence farming. Road counts of previously extremely common species of raptors (Augur Buzzards, Black-shouldered Kites, Long-crested Eagles) have fallen in some areas to almost zero. Seed dressing on maize is used very frequently as a way of destroying rodents, especially ground squirrels.

I remember walking in a patch of forest and coming across a dead leopard. The next day in the same area I found dead vultures. I heard that a European farmer had tried to control local hyenas by lacing a dead cow with dieldrin. The carcass was left out until eaten. On another occasion some lions sat in a cattle dip to get out of the heat, then died and were eaten by vultures that also died. Red-billed Quelea control is, I believe, potentially dangerous to raptor populations. I witnessed an operation that led to the total extinction of most raptors (except the Tawny Eagle) on at least an area of some 15,000 hectares. This wheatland was remarkable for its concentration of raptors. Peregrines were particularly obvious taking the large numbers of doves that fed on fallen grain. About four days after the first spray very few raptors were seen and many dead ones were found. The raptor population decreased to almost zero, and Peregrines disappeared. Red-billed Quelea is an important food, particularly when in swarms. The pesticides Parathion and Fenthion, when sprayed on the Red-billed Quelea, are in sufficient concentration to kill by contact with the skin. Sublethal doses that might be carried on feathers of an ailing bird for a number of days may prove fatal to raptors if eaten.

Locust control can also destroy raptors that feed on the locusts. The sale of dangerous chemicals is open and encouraged. The layman wishing to destroy aphids frequently ends up destroying his crop as the majority cannot read the instructions on the can of pesticide.

Whether or not there is any eggshell thinning or reproductive disorder in our local Peregrines in not known. Fortunately about three-fourths of Kenya is barren scrubland that would be impossible for vast numbers of people to live in. Peregrines exist in these areas in stable numbers. They may be threatened by intermittent Red-billed Quelea operations that venture out into barren areas, but I doubt that Peregrines in these areas are in any real danger.

ACKNOWLEDGEMENTS

The author thanks B. Taylor, St. Austins Academy in Nairobi, Kenya, for the use of nest breeding records; C. Gichuki, Department of Ornithology, National Museums of Kenya, for viewing specimens; and D. Sindiyo, Director of Wildlife Conservation and Management.

31 | The Status and Biology of the Peregrine in the Afrotropical Region

John M. Mendelsohn

The African Peregrine (*F. p. minor*) is resident over much of the Afrotropical region, the area south of the Sahara. Its biology and status are comparatively poorly known, but recent studies (Hustler 1983, Tarboton 1984, Tarboton and Allan 1984) provide much useful new data. I review this and other information to provide a modern account of the Peregrine's basic biology and to examine those factors which limit its numbers and distribution in Africa.

A high proportion of published data on African Peregrines should be treated with caution. Few observers have distinguished nonbreeding *F. p. minor* from migrant *F. p. calidus* from the northern Palearctic, and Peregrines may be confused with Northern Hobbys and resident, particularly juvenile, Lanner Falcons.

BASIC BIOLOGY

Morphology. — African Peregrines are one of the smallest races; males weigh about 500 g and females 700-750 g. They are very dark, especially dorsally and on the head. Structural proportions are similar to those of other Peregrines. Sympatric Lanner Falcons are similar in size, but African Peregrines have relatively shorter wings and tails, larger feet and bulkier bodies.

Distribution and Status. — Although Peregrines may be seen anywhere in the Afrotropics, their breeding distribution is discontinuous. Most of Africa is rolling savanna woodland and forest, or to a lesser extent grassland and desert, which generally lack high cliffs with vertical faces 50 m or more in height. Peregrines only breed along deeply incised river valleys and escarpments, on isolated inselbergs and in the few mountain ranges. In southern Africa, for example, the majority of Peregrine breeding sites are in the southwestern Cape Mountains, on isolated hills in Botswana and Namibia, in deep river valleys in the east, along the escarpment in the Transvaal, and in river valleys, on inselbergs, and in the eastern highlands of Zimbabwe. Elsewhere in Africa, breeding populations are known or probably exist in the Ethiopian highlands, isolated mountains in East Africa, inselbergs in Zambia, Malawi, Mozambique, the Ruwenzori Mountains, and on isolated mountains in Angola and West Africa. Several authors (e.g., Steyn 1982, Tarboton and Allan 1984, Thomson 1984a) reported that most breeding sites overlook extensive woodland and are close to rivers or dams.

While widespread, the zones occupied by breeding pairs probably comprise less than 5% of the total area in the Afrotropics. The Peregrine is therefore uncommon, although in certain areas it is probably as abundant as anywhere in the world. Between four and eight pairs breed in 620 km² in the Matopos National Park (MacDonald and Gargett 1984). In the Transvaal, four pairs averaged 6.4 km between their nest sites (Tarboton and Allan 1984) and in Kenya, L. H. Brown found eight pairs in 3200 km² (Cade 1969a). Zimbabwe probably has more resident pairs than any other region, and Thomson (1984a) estimates 200 pairs. The Transvaal, however, is the only large area to be intensively surveyed. Tarboton and Allan (1984) found 14 eyries and estimated a total population of 20-40 pairs in 286,000 km². Considering the comparative suitability of habitats in the Transvaal and elsewhere in Africa, extrapolation leads to a rough estimate of 1000-2000 pairs for the Afrotropical region. Most optimal habitats are remote and seldom visited by ornithologists, and even less likely to be surveyed. For example, there are probably 500-1000 bird watchers in the Transvaal, yet no positive breeding record existed for the area prior to Tarboton and Allan's intensive survey. Furthermore, Peregrines in Africa appear to be rather unobtrusive, especially compared with Lanners. The pair at a nest site I often visit is usually hard to find, yet a nearby pair of Lanners can be readily seen.

Tarboton and Allan's (1984) study over five years is the only systematic survey in Africa. There are thus no comparative data to judge whether the population has changed in recent times. Comparatively few museum specimens were obtained during the heyday of collecting and old regional literature describes the species as rare or uncommon, suggesting that numbers today are similar to those 100 or more years ago. Peregrines may have declined in areas subjected to heavy pesticide contamination since relatively high residues and eggshell thinning have been recorded (Peakall and Kiff 1979, Mendelsohn et al. Chapter 43). Tarboton and Allan (1984) and Thomson (1984a) suggested that clearing of woodlands for crop cultivation has caused the local disappearance of breeding Peregrines, but further information is lacking.

Breeding. — Recorded eyries have been on vertical cliffs, on the structurally similar Kariba Dam wall in Zimbabwe/Zambia, and on a building in Nairobi, Kenya. One nest in a tree in Zimbabwe might have belonged to a Lanner (Steyn 1982), a species that regularly uses old vulture and eagle nests. Most occupied cliffs are particularly tall, and usually higher than surrounding ones. The average cliff height for 14 Transvaal nests was 150 m (range 60-300 m, Tarboton and Allan 1984). Other recorded cliff heights are 30 m (Hustler 1983), 60 m (C. Green SAOS NRC (Southern African Ornithological Society nest records)), 130 m (A.C. Kemp SAOS NRC) and 130 m (pers. obs.). Most, if not all, nest sites in Africa are particularly sheltered, presumably from rain and direct sun. The sites are usually on ledges below large overhanging rocks or deep within potholes or large horizontal cavities, and contrast with the exposed sites often used by Peregrines in the northern hemisphere (Ratcliffe 1980). Old sheltered nests of the Black Stork, African White-necked Crow and Verreaux's Eagle are also often used (Steyn 1982).

In southern Africa, eggs are laid in July ($n=4$), August ($n=7$) and September ($n=2$), much the same period described for East Africa: June to October, with 11 of 16 records in August (Brown et al. 1982), but see Thomsett (Chapter 30). Most authors mention clutches of 2-4 eggs, but four-egg clutches are evidently rare, as I can find no positive record of one. From various published descriptions of nests and SAOS NRCs, there are two records of two eggs and 12 of three eggs in southern Africa, giving a mean clutch size of 2.6 eggs, which is exactly the same as the mean of 10 clutches in East Africa (Brown et al. 1982). Brood sizes in southern Africa were: one young ($n=4$), two young ($n=7$) and three young ($n=8$) ($\bar{x}=2.2$ young per site). I have not seen any reliable measurements of incubation, nestling, or post-nestling periods in the wild, but these are variously estimated to be 31, 35-45, and up to 120 days, respectively (Condy 1973, Brown et al. 1982, Steyn 1982, Hustler 1983).

Three observers recorded eagles either attempting to or probably killing young Peregrines (Hallamore 1972, Hustler 1983, Brooke SAOS NRC). These involved Tawny Eagles, Wahlberg's Eagles and Verreaux's Eagles. While these might be isolated occurrences, they could indicate fairly frequent nestling predation, bearing in mind the paucity of published observations of young Peregrines. Chacma baboons (*Papio ursinus*) frequently clamber around cliffs and readily consume the contents of a nest; both Hustler (1983) and Hallamore (1972) mention interactions or potential predation.

At the only two nests studied intensively (Hustler 1983, Tarboton 1984), the males shared one-third or more of the incubation during daylight, and at one nest the female hunted for herself during the five days of observed incubation. The male fed the female at the other nest.

Hunting and Food. — Observations on hunting have been largely limited to those made around breeding cliffs near wooded areas. Most hunts started from a position high above the potential prey with the falcon then flying and stooping toward a flying bird. High cliff perches and trees above the rock face provided suitable positions from which to scan for prey, but the Peregrines launched most attacks (especially those away from breeding cliffs) while soaring. In woodland areas birds flying above trees or across clearings were attacked, but trees allowed flying prey to gain quick cover. Both Hustler (1983) and Tarboton (1984) recorded apparent "flush" hunting, in which falcons frequently alighted at different spots on a cliff to pursue birds flushed from the area. Neither observer saw prey captured using this method, however. Hallamore (1972) described Peregrines making daily visits to particular areas with aggregations of doves and weavers. They flew in low with the apparent chance of snatching vulnerable prey. Condy (1973) recorded attacks on Red-billed Quelea flocks flying across a river.

African Peregrines feed mostly on birds, although bats (Finch-Davies and Kemp 1982) and termite alates (Hallamore 1972) have been recorded occasionally. Hustler (1983) and Tarboton (1984) provided the only systematic lists of prey attacked or found at eyries. They recorded at least 45 species in a total of 162 items, ranging in weight from 15-600 g with an average of 127 g. Both samples were from areas with extensive surrounding woodlands, so arboreal and other birds dependent on woodland predominated, making up 66.7% of prey numbers or 67.2% of prey weight (Table 1). Most terrestrial species that occurred in open country spent a good deal of their time in woodland, returning there for shelter or to their nests. Doves, pigeons and francolins were the most important taxonomic groups preyed upon, comprising 40.1% of prey numbers and 66.1% of prey weight (Table 2). These groups also provided most of the large prey (>150g): 8 francolins (500-600 g) and 12 pigeons and large doves (250-340 g). The majority (n=45) of doves were relatively small *Streptopelia* spp. weighing 100-150 g, but these contributed to a high proportion of the diet, both by number and weight (Figure 1). The few large birds (>300 g) also formed a significant part of the total prey.

DISCUSSION

Comparative Ecology. — Clutch size should vary latitudinally, but clutches in equatorial East Africa were very similar in size to those in temperate southern Africa. For this whole region, the mean clutch size

TABLE 1. Habitat preferences of 162 birds recorded as prey of Peregrines by Hustler (1983) and Tarboton (1984).

Habitat (no. of species)	No. of birds (%)	% prey by weight
Woodland – terrestrial (10)	68 (42.0)	53.7
Woodland – arboreal (18)	40 (24.7)	13.5
Open ground – terrestrial (5)	25 (15.4)	21.0
Cliffs (3)	12 (7.4)	8.8
Aerial insectivores (9)	17 (10.5)	3.0
Total	162	

TABLE 2. Taxonomic groups of birds recorded as prey of Peregrines by Hustler (1983) and Tarboton (1984).

Family or group (no. of species)	No. of birds (%)	% prey by weight
Columbidae – pigeons (6)	57 (35.2)	45.6
Phasianidae – francolins (2)	8 (4.9)	20.5
Sturnidae – starlings (3)	23 (14.2)	11.5
Coraciidae – rollers (3)	3 (1.9)	1.6
Hirundinidae – swallows (2)	4 (2.5)	0.4
Apodidae – swifts (5)	11 (6.8)	1.9
Other passerines (8)	28 (17.3)	5.0
Near passerines[a] (13)	25 (15.4)	10.3
Other non-passerines[b] (3)	3 (1.9)	3.1

[a] Cuckoos, woodpeckers, hoopoes, kingfishers, bee-eaters, parrots, etc.
[b] Plovers, goshawks, egrets.

of 2.6 eggs ($n=24$ clutches) is small compared with averages ranging from 2.8 eggs (Victoria, Australia) to 3.8 eggs (British Columbia, Canada) (Pruett-Jones et al. 1981a). The only areas with average clutches of less than three eggs are in very different parts of the world: northern Alaska (72°N) (Cade 1960), Australia (Victoria) (36°-38°S), and Africa (0°-30°S), although ecological conditions which determine clutch size might be similar.

Peak laying in August in southern Africa is slightly earlier than the peak September laying period in Victoria, Australia (Pruett-Jones et al. 1981a). This might be attributed to the slightly higher latitude (36°-38°S) of Victoria, in the same way that laying occurs later at higher latitudes in the northern hemisphere. However, Peregrines in East Africa and southern Africa have similar breeding schedules, most eggs being laid in August, suggesting that latitude is not as relevant in determining laying dates as it is elsewhere (but see Thomsett Chapter

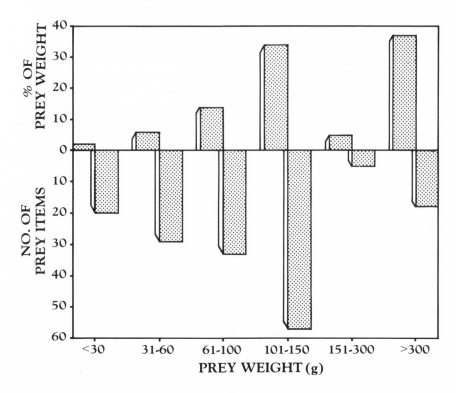

FIGURE 1.   Importance by weight (top) and frequency (bottom) of prey items of
different sizes in the diet of Peregrine Falcons at two nests in southern
Africa. Data from Hustler (1983) and Tarboton (1984).

30 for Kenya). The August laying period is during the dry part of the
year, but by the time young falcons are present, rains have usually
fallen and much of their avian prey is breeding. Futhermore, millions
of migrant birds from the Palearctic arrive in Africa from October
onwards, providing a new food supply for young falcons present at
that time.

Throughout the world, optimal nest sites for Peregrines are on
sheltered ledges or in holes on tall cliffs (Hickey and Anderson 1969,
Ratcliffe 1980, Pruett-Jones et al. 1981a). All unequivocal Peregrine
breeding sites in Africa have been on cliffs, most of which are higher
than 100 m. Compared with cliffs used by Peregrines elsewhere
(Hickey 1942, Cade 1960, Ratcliffe 1980, Pruett-Jones et al. 1981a),
African sites are particularly high, although in many parts of the world
there are fewer really tall cliffs available. However, the value of nesting
on tall cliffs may be enhanced in Africa where primate predators,
especially baboons, are abundant.

Pruett-Jones et al. (1981a) showed that protected nest sites with little horizontal and vertical exposure were more successful than less sheltered ones in Australia. While no measurements of exposure for African sites have been made, the general impression is that nests are placed in particularly protected positions where they would seldom, if ever, be exposed to direct sunlight. In the hot climate over much of Africa, this would protect incubating females and nestlings from potentially lethal overheating (Beecham and Kochert 1975). Tarboton and Allan (1984) found that eyries in southern Africa did not face west, the aspect most exposed to sun at the hottest period of the day. In cool climates, by contrast, eyries are often exposed to the sun, presumably for extra heating (Ratcliffe 1980).

From the analysis of remains found at two eyries, average prey weight was 126 g. Although other prey analyses might show a somewhat different result, it seems likely that prey in Africa is smaller on average than elsewhere. For example, average prey weights in various parts of Europe range between 217-398 g (Cramp and Simmons 1980). While small passerines of less than 50 g make up a significant proportion of prey throughout the range of the Peregrine, high average prey weights in most areas are the result of frequent predation on pigeons, ducks, grouse, large waders, gulls and terns, petrels, ptarmigan, parrots, etc. Many of these birds are associated with water and open country, but at the two African sites, prey in these taxonomic and ecological groups were either comparatively insignificant or absent (Tables 1 and 2). Furthermore, most doves and pigeons killed were relatively small (<150 g). In contrast, the feral pigeon and its allies, which weigh 400 g or more, form a substantial part of the Peregrine's diet in many other regions.

Limiting Factors. — Several authors (Cade 1969a, Finch-Davies and Kemp 1983, Tarboton 1984, Thomson 1984a) have attempted to explain the rarity of Peregrines in Africa. Their explanations made one or more of the following points: nest sites are in short supply, Peregrines are competitively excluded by Lanners, or there is a shortage of appropriate food.

Since there are few tall cliffs in many large areas of Africa, the idea that nest sites are limited has apparent merit. However, nest sites per se cannot limit Peregrine nesting distribution in Africa because there are many low cliffs and old stick nests in trees which could, as in some other parts of the world (Ratcliffe 1980), be used for breeding. Nevertheless, the preferential selection throughout the world of very tall cliffs suggests that, as optimal sites, these might be the only viable nest sites in Africa. If this is true, one would expect nesting pairs to be densely clumped in areas with many tall cliffs. This prediction is not upheld because even where densities are comparatively high, they are much lower than in some other regions where pairs nest less than 1 km from neighbors (Cramp and Simmons 1980).

A similar argument can be used to test the idea that Peregrines are excluded from marginal sites by Lanners. Tarboton (1984) suggested that Lanners, which feed on a greater variety of prey and use many different kinds of nests, are competitively superior where Peregrines do not have the advantages of hunting from very tall cliffs. Aggressive interactions between these species certainly occur (pers. obs.), as they do between conspecifics and other competitors for cliff space, such as Verreaux's Eagles and the Jackal Buzzard. While aggression and the simple presence of nesting falcons may exclude other birds from the immediate vicinity of nests, it should not prevent nesting further, say more than 500 m, away. If anything, conspecific competition should be more intense than interspecific contests, yet pairs of Lanners have nested within 200 m of each other (Tarboton and Allan 1984). Neighboring pairs of Peregrines and Lanners have been found 400 and 1000 m apart (Brown et al. 1982, pers. obs.). Such close proximity between nests is rare, indicating that the availability of nest sites is not a general limiting factor.

Lanners also feed substantially on birds, so there might be some competition for food between the species. To my knowledge, no quantitative analysis of Lanner prey has been done, but they also feed on insects, rodents, lizards, and birds on the ground (Steyn 1982). The two falcons therefore exploit a somewhat different spectrum of prey.

The data suggest that African Peregrines have smaller prey available to them than elsewhere in the world, and their small body size might be attributable to this situation. Many groups of large birds that are important prey in other regions are either poorly represented in Africa or not generally accessible to breeding Peregrines. For example, there are no ptarmigan and grouse, few large parrots, and there are few substantial bodies of water with ducks, waders, gulls and terns. Large doves and pigeons are also relatively uncommon, and over much of Africa feral pigeons are restricted to urban areas, there being few racing pigeon fanciers. As substitutes for these groups, there are large woodland hornbills, rollers and some starlings, but few are ever sufficiently abundant to be dependable sources of food. The hunting of Peregrines, therefore, seems to be more opportunistic than in many other regions, and a general shortage of optimal-sized prey and poor feeding conditions may be a major factor limiting their numbers.

If African Peregrines are largely limited by low prey numbers, they should be restricted to areas in which they can hunt most efficiently. This might help explain their dependence on tall cliffs from which they have an advantage of seeing and stooping at prey. The elevation of a tall cliff may also be more important in woodland areas, since a low cliff only 50 m high would provide a limited vantage point over a 10-30 m high canopy.

The association between Peregrines and woodlands might simply be that most cliffs and permanent water (see below) are in areas with high rainfall. Brown et al. (1982) suggest that woodlands have higher bird densities than open steppes and deserts, so greater availability of food might further contribute to the relative abundance of Peregrines in woodland. The suggested disappearance of Peregrines from areas cleared of woodlands (Tarboton and Allan 1984, Thomson 1984a) could be due to changes in prey populations or the use of pesticides on land cleared for cultivation.

The frequency with which Peregrines bathe, and presumably drink, is well known (Cade 1960), although few authors bother to comment on this habit. There are even two references to bathing (Hallamore 1972, Hustler 1983) in the limited literature on African Peregrines, suggesting that bathing is regular in this population as well. Much of Africa has little permanent water, and if there is a need to drink and bathe regularly, this might be a strong limiting factor. Lanners occur commonly in arid areas of southwestern Africa, and I know of no record of this species drinking or bathing. The abundance of Lanners and the absence of Peregrines in these areas could therefore be attributable to the latter's greater dependence on water. In Arizona, where the annual rainfall at Peregrine nest sites was only about 350-400 mm, Ellis (1982) found that most (35 of 48) nesting cliffs were within 5 km of a permanent stream or pond.

The absence of Peregrines from arid areas, both in Africa and elsewhere (Cade 1982), could also be related to higher temperatures in these regions. The apparent requirement for shaded nests suggests that excessive heat limits their activities. While many stick nests in trees may be unsuitable because of direct exposure to sunlight, nests in trees used by Peregrines in Australia are often well shaded (P. Olsen pers. comm.).

Conservation. — The status of the Peregrine has apparently not changed dramatically during the past 100-200 years, although some decline may have occurred as a result of pesticide poisoning (Mendelsohn et al. Chapter 43) and the clearing of woodlands. In some parts of the world, numbers have increased in response to the introduction of feral pigeons and the European Starling (White et al. 1981). In Africa, however, comparable environmental changes have been insignificant and probably have had no beneficial effect on numbers.

While populations might have been relatively stable so far, it seems likely that numbers will decline in the next few decades. Environmental degradation owing to rapid human population growth, agricultural development and the use of pesticides is inevitable. The chemicals that caused severe declines in the northern hemisphere during the 1950s and 1960s (Newton 1979) are now being applied in Africa, probably in large quantities. Woodlands are cut down to make way for crops and for firewood. The rate of human population growth is higher than elsewhere. African Peregrines have already been bred in captivity (Hartley 1983, Thomson 1984b), so this method of preservation and perhaps the continued existence of a few pairs in the remotest areas are probably the only prospect for continued survival in the next 100 years.

32 | *The Genus* Falco *in Arabia*

Joseph B. Platt

The Peregrine Falcon is one of 40 Falconiformes recorded on the Arabian Peninsula (Table 1). This region is roughly the size of the western United States. It stretches from latitude 13°N-30°N and longitude 35°E-60°E. Within these 3.2 million km² are habitats ranging from barren deserts of dunes to 3000-m high mountain ranges covered with Mediterranean evergreen forests. Jordan and Iraq form the northern boundary while the waters of the Red Sea, Arabian Sea and Arabian Gulf delimit the remaining borders.

Knowledge about the avian community of Arabia is almost solely dependent on Europeans who have birdwatched as a hobby during their work assignments there. Thus, data are clumped around areas where expatriates are employed; the more distant wilderness settings are poorly understood. The Arabs have a heritage closely tied to the land and its wildlife, but their relationship is more as participants than as observers. Species that provide for their needs are well-known; others are of little consequence. Falcons are a significant group. Because of their usefulness as trained hunters, Arabs have learned the falcons' ways and can provide information about their migration, but virtually nothing about the raptors breeding in their midst.

The zoogeography of the Arabian Peninsula is unique in that the region is at the meeting of three zoogeographical realms — the Ethiopian, Oriental and Palearctic. Each of these contribute to the makeup of the bird populations of the Arabian avifauna. Southwest Arabia contains several peripheral breeding populations of African species: Helmeted Guineafowl, Abyssinian Roller and Dark Chanting Goshawk.

To the east, the Oriental realm finds expression in the avifauna of Oman and Musandam Peninsula. Breeding species included the Indian Silverbill, Purple Sunbird, and Indian Roller.

About 515 species of birds have been recorded on the Peninsula; perhaps 100 breed (Gallagher and Woodcock 1980, Jennings 1981a, 1981b). Similarly, of the 40 diurnal raptors recorded, only 17 are breeding species. Ten falcons occur, but little is known about either

TABLE 1.   Raptors recorded on the Arabian Peninsula.

Name	Status[a]	Name	Status[a]
Western Honey Buzzard	PM	Common Buzzard	PM
Black Kite	PM	Long-legged Buzzard	RB
Pallas' Fish Eagle	V	Greater Spotted Eagle	PM
Bearded Vulture	RB	Tawny Eagle	PM
Egyptian Vulture	RB	Imperial Eagle	PM
Griffon Vulture	RB	Golden Eagle	PM
Ruppell's Griffon	RB	Verreaux's Eagle	RB
Lappet-faced Vulture	RB	Booted Eagle	PM
Cinereous Vulture	RB	Bonnelli's Eagle	RB
Short-toed Eagle	RB	Osprey	RB
Bateleur	PM	Lesser Kestrel	PM
Marsh Harrier	PM	Eastern Red-footed Falcon	PM
Northern Harrier	PM	Eurasian Kestrel	RB
Pallid Harrier	PM	Merlin	PM
Montagu's Harrier	PM	Northern Hobby	PM
Dark Chanting Goshawk	RB	Sooty Falcon	RB
Northern Goshawk	PM	Lanner Falcon	RB
Gabar Goshawk	RB	Saker Falcon	PM
European Sparrowhawk	PM	Peregrine Falcon	PM
Levant Sparrowhawk	PM	Barbary Falcon[b]	RB

[a] PM = Passage migrant; RB = Resident breeder; V = Vagrant.
[b] Considered a subspecies of the Peregrine, *F. p. pelegrinoides*, in this book.

their nesting or migratory behavior in Arabia. It may be helpful, then, to discuss what is known about the entire genus *Falco* and from that gain insight into the Peregrine.

BREEDING FALCONS

Of the 17 raptors recorded as breeders, 12 are accipitrids (including 5 vultures), 1 is the Osprey and the remaining 4 are falcons.

The Peregrine Falcon (excluding *F. p. pelegrinoides*) is not known to breed on the peninsula. Cade (1969a) pointed out that the Peregrine has not developed a distinctive desert form throughout its extensive range. *F. p. pelegrinoides* fills the aerial predator niche, capitalizing on the avian fauna of Arabia. It nests in mountainous regions of the west and southeast. Thinly scattered, it produces young in early April, and is thus able to feed its young on the fledging passerines and Palearctic migrants. Its range in Arabia overlaps heavily with the Lanner Falcon. The latter is a medium-sized falcon that occurs in the deserts of Africa and the Middle East. Its selection of prey is broader than that of *F. p. pelegrinoides*, ranging from lizards and insects to doves and songbirds. Lanners have lighter wingloading than Peregrines (Cade 1982), a feature which may aid them in covering the large expanses of desert necessary to find food. It appears that the two species do not breed in the same area within their overlapping ranges. *F. p. pelegrinoides* nests on higher cliffs and in more diverse habitat. The Lanner, with the more catholic diet, is better suited to utilize the sparse food resources of open deserts. In the higher elevations of the Asir Mountains of southwest Arabia and the Tuwaiq Escarpment of central Arabia, *F. p. pelegrinoides* is a regular breeder, but the Lanner does not occur — although it breeds nearby. The Lanner also has not been recorded in the mountains of Oman where *F. p. pelegrinoides* is a regular breeder.

The relationship between these two species in Arabia is reminiscent of the Peregrine and Prairie Falcon in the deserts of the western United States before 1960. Nesting Prairie Falcons and Peregrines occurred in the same desert areas, but Peregrines were dependent on a water course or other feature to sustain their more restricted prey base of small birds (Porter and White 1973). Prairie Falcons fed on birds when available but often captured mammals and reptiles exclusively. Thus, they were able to occupy drier sites. Nelson (1969b) pointed out that as Peregrine nest sites became more xeric through climatic change, they were occupied by Prairie Falcons.

Two other falcons nest in Arabia. The Eurasian Kestrel nests on the fringes of the Peninsula. It selects the relatively cooler mountain regions, especially those near areas modified by farming and land-scaping.

The last nesting falcon is, in many ways, the most interesting. The Sooty Falcon breeds in loose colonies on islands along the east, west and south coasts of the Peninsula (Walter 1979a). Like its close relative, Eleonora's Falcon, the Sooty Falcon nests during the autumn migration of European passerines (Walter 1979a, 1979b). Millions of prey items stream over the islands off Arabia, providing food for the young hatched in early September. Nests in the Arabian Gulf islands are not synchronized. About 15 pairs nest along a 20-km line of islands near Bahrain. The hatching dates of nests can vary by nearly two weeks in the same season. This may ensure survival of some young if the arrival of migrants is delayed or interrupted. Sooty Falcons are present in Arabia at least seven months of the year. They defend nest cliffs in May, lay eggs in August, and disperse in November. Thus, although their prey base is similar, they probably avoid competing with *F. p. pelegrinoides* by being separated in time and nesting habitat.

These four species of falcon exert pressure on nearly all the prey bases utilized by the genus in other locations. Theoretically, only the largest prey class of the genus is not exploited by breeding falcons in

Arabia, but that prey class is poorly represented there during the breeding season.

MIGRANT FALCONS

Twenty-three species of raptors occur on the Arabian Peninsula only as migrants; 17 are accipitrids and the remaining six are falcons.

Bruun (1985) classified migrating raptors into passive and active (passive using thermal updrafts, active seldom doing so). The Arabian Gulf's west shore is flat from Kuwait to the Musandam Peninsula. The Iranian coast of the Gulf, however, is lined by the Zagros Mountains and associated foothills. This higher relief may contribute to the greater number of broad-winged species reported on that coast. More Peregrines and Saker Falcons are also trapped on the Iranian shore than the Arabian side. Peregrines and Sakers cross the southern end of the Gulf near the Strait of Hormuz each year in numbers sufficient to sustain a traditional trapping location on an island between the shores near the Strait.

Millions of raptors skirt the Mediterranean to the east by flying through the Levant to Africa. As on the Arabian Gulf side, they must choose a detour to the southeast using the mountainous coastline of the Red Sea or move west through the flatter terrain of Egypt. Bruun (1985), Lesheim (1985) and others working in the Sinai report seeing hundreds of thousands of raptors each autumn. Only a handful are falcons. But these species, being active migrants, move on a broad front and may cross the Red Sea as well as go around it. Arab falconers trap Peregrines and Sakers on the Saudi coast of the northern Red Sea.

Migrants coming to Arabia from the Oriental realm cross either the Gulf of Oman or the Arabian Sea, making landfall in Oman. Because the Omani people do not practice falconry, the extent of large falcons entering Oman is not known. However, one of the main trapping grounds for large falcons in Pakistan is on the coast, a few hundred kilometers to the northeast.

Six species of falcons migrate into Arabia from the north and east. Migrant Peregrines arrive in the Dhahran-Bahrain area each year between 5 and 25 September. They are seen along coastlines and wetlands until April. No work has been done with marked birds, but indications are that individuals (especially adults) winter along the eastern shores, feeding on the abundant shorebird community. Natural shoreline habitat has been lost in some areas, but farming and sewage lagoons have created new areas for wintering Peregrines and their prey. Workers in Oman report Peregrines wintering along its southern coast. They occur as migrants on the Peninsula's west coast, but their status during the winter is unknown.

Saker Falcons occur during the winter in all parts of the Peninsula except the mountains of the southwest. They appear to winter in eastern Saudi Arabia and Bahrain.

An uncommon visitor is the Merlin. It is occasionally recorded, but is so easily confused with the more common small falcons that its true numbers are unknown.

The rarest falcon is interesting for its scarcity. The Eastern Red-footed Falcon has been sighted less than 12 times and collected perhaps only once (Jennings pers. comm.). This is remarkable because it breeds in eastern China and Russia but winters in India and southern Africa. The species migrates in large flocks and would surely be seen if it regularly visits the Peninsula. It appears that these falcons cross the Indian Ocean south of Arabia.

THE IMPACT OF FALCONRY

Four breeding species and six migrant species of falcons occur on the Arabian Peninsula. No discussion of the status of falcons in Arabia would be complete without addressing their relationship with falconry. I have lived among the Arab people for 10 years. As a raptor biologist and falconer, I have sought to understand the impact of the sport on wild populations. Three species are used: Sakers, Peregrines and Lanners. I estimate that fewer than 3000 falcons are trained for the hunting season lasting from October to April. Less than 1000 are kept for the subsequent seasons; the rest are either lost during the hunt or released in spring. Of the approximately 2000 birds removed from the migrating population, virtually all are females and 80-90% are Sakers (Platt 1983a). All but a handful are birds of the year.

Before oil came in the 1930s, trained falcons augmented scarce meat supplies in the Bedouin camps. Quarry were the Stone Curlew, Houbara Bustard and desert hare and rabbit. As new wealth provided freedom from dependence on the desert and the sea, falconry came to be practiced more for sport than for survival. Today, hares are no longer hunted. Houbara Bustard, a bird larger than the falcons, is the main quarry; it is pursued with female Sakers and female Peregrines. The Stone Curlews are hunted with smaller falcons because of their small size and high maneuverability. Male Sakers and male Peregrines are used against them. Occasionally Lanners are trained for Stone Curlew, but the few that are kept are mostly for the young boys to learn the art of training and keeping falcons.

In the days before oil wealth, the falcons were only trapped locally. Some birds were taken along the northern shore of the Red Sea, but most were caught in the Gulf states, western Iran and Saudi's Eastern Province. Only freshly trapped, untrained birds were bought, so the importation of falcons from distant sources did not come about until the arrival of modern transport.

Today, Peregrines and Sakers for the Arab market are trapped in Syria, Afghanistan, Pakistan, Iran and the Arabian Peninsula countries. In Arabia, falconers or their employees catch them. In the other countries trapping is very much a "cottage industry," with villagers catching a few birds and several middle men getting them to a hawk bazaar.

There are no records kept on numbers trapped or prices paid, so one must depend on interviews with trappers and falconers. This limits the information to less than 50 years of personal experiences. Trappers agree that in the early and mid-1970s Peregrines (but not Sakers) were hard to find in Arabia. At about the same time, new-found wealth made it possible for some individuals to increase the number of falcons they kept. It was for these reasons that the purchase of birds from dealers in Pakistan began. Trapping locally has continued. Trappers say that Peregrines are as available now as they were before the scarcity of the 1970s. Prices paid for Peregrines support this view. In 1981 and 1983 the price of a female Peregrine in perfect feather and health was $5000-$7000. In 1984 it was slightly less. Indications are that 1985 prices will continue in the same range. It is interesting to note that the prices in 1982 were closer to $10,000. Saker Falcons vary in price in relation to their variations in size and color. High quality (but not exceptional) Sakers are the same price as Peregrines (see Platt 1983b).

Even though these large sums are paid for birds, they are seldom kept longer than seven months. They are then released within their normal migratory range. Falcons less than one year old are preferred for training. Thus, fewer than 2000 falcons are removed from the wild populations during their first migration; they are then returned to the wild seven months later in their natural range and most probably fit to survive. Even a cursory look at avian life tables reveals the high (50-70%) death rate of immature raptors. The falcons used in Arab falconry sustain no such mortality.

ACKNOWLEDGEMENTS

I thank H. H. Shaikh Mohammed bin Rashid Al Maktoum for support and ongoing interest in wildlife and the understanding of it. I express appreciation to many people who have contributed their raptor sightings and especially to organizations that compile them: the Dubai Natural History Group, the Bahrain Natural History Society, and the Saudi Arabian Natural History Society. M. Jennings provided data from his unpublished work, the Atlas of the Breeding Birds of Arabia. R. Upton and J. Burchard shared their considerable knowledge about falconry in Arabia, for which I am most grateful.

Commentary

The Status of Peregrines in Asia and the Pacific

Tom J. Cade

There has been a gratifying increase in our knowledge about Peregrines in many parts of the world where the species was little known at the time of the Madison Conference in 1965. This is particularly so in the southern hemisphere regions of South America, Africa, Australia, and even in the remote Fiji Islands, as revealed by the preceding chapters of this section. On the other hand, the status of Peregrines in most of the great Asiatic landmass and associated islands remains virtually unknown to westerners, and judging by the paucity of publications, to the indigenous ornithologists of those regions as well.

The vast tundra and taiga regions of Siberia provide habitat comparable in every respect to similar landscapes in Alaska and Canada (Yegorov 1959), especially because of the numerous large, northward flowing rivers that cut cliffs and bluffs along their courses. However, scant information seems to be available on the status of nesting Peregrines in Siberia in the last 20 years. The Soviet "Red Book" on rare and endangered species (Flint 1978) lists the Peregrine (sapsan) as a *rare* species of special concern, but fewer than a dozen references are provided for documentation, and no population surveys have been systematically repeated over several years. While numbers are said to be reduced from earlier decades, Yelisyeev (1983) estimates that there are several (nyeskol'ko) thousand pairs nesting in the Soviet Union east of the Ural Mountains, including local estimates of 100-200 pairs in the Yamal Peninsula and 200 pairs on the Taimir Peninsula.

Some recent studies have been carried out on *F. p. babylonicus* in the arid regions of the Soviet central Asiatic republics (Stepanyan *in* Flint 1978); it has been listed as a "critically endangered species" with an estimated surviving population of only 35-50 nesting pairs in the Soviet Union (Flint 1978). In other parts of its range in Iran, Afghanistan, and Pakistan, the current status of this falcon is unknown.

313

The Government of India and the World Wildlife Fund-India have expressed concern about the apparent decline in numbers of F. p. *peregrinator* and the Red-necked Falcon, but again few hard data are available. Not only is the numerical status of this forest-adapted Peregrine poorly known, but even its distributional limits in southeast Asia and China are ill defined (White and Boyce Chapter 76).

China is the greatest enigma of all the Asiatic countries as far as the occurrence of Peregrines is concerned. Most world distribution maps of Peregrines (Dementiev and Gladkov 1951, Brown and Amadon 1968, Cramp and Simmons 1980) show a large void in the breeding distribution for the northern half of China, adjacent regions of Mongolia, the Soviet Union and most of Korea. It would be surprising, indeed, if so cosmopolitan a species as the Peregrine is truly absent as a breeder in this region.

Peregrines in the islands of Japan are not well known either. According to some of the old falconers, there used to be several hundred pairs of Peregrines nesting in Japan. Although still widely distributed in the islands, more recent information indicates that fewer exist today. The Tochigi Chapter of the Wild Bird Society of Japan has been investigating the status of the Peregrine in Japan since 1982 (K. Endo and K. Iinuma unpubl. report). They have obtained sight records of Peregrines in 39 prefectures; 2 others recorded none, and 6 provided no information. Breeding records have been obtained in 13 prefectures as follows: Hokkaido, 6-8 pairs; Iwate, about 20 pairs; Akita, 1 pair; Miyagi, 5-7 pairs; Yamagata, 1 pair, Niigata, 1 pair; Tochigi, 1 pair; Ishikawa, 2 pairs; Hyogo, 4-6 pairs; Tottori, 5-7 pairs; Shimane, 5-10 pairs; Huhuoka, 1-2 pairs; Kagawa, 1 pair. Nearly all of these pairs were found at eyries on rocky coastlines. These workers estimate the breeding population for all of Japan to be 54-68 pairs. These figures no doubt represent minimum estimates, but even so it appears that the Peregrine is now decidedly rare in Japan.

In addition to these surveys, Ito (1986) has published a recent, popular book on the Peregrine. It contains what surely is the most superb series of color photographs ever published on the life history of the Peregrine. It will no doubt stimulate much national interest in the Peregrine and lead to better information on the species in Japan in coming years.

North of Japan, the Kuril Islands form a volcanic chain. As they are similar in many ways to the Queen Charlotte Islands, situated at comparable latitudes on the other side of the Pacific, they may well support a large population of Peregrines; likewise, the Komandorski Islands, which are western outliers of the Aleutian Chain, provide habitat for at least 20 pairs of Peregrines (Yelisyeev 1983).

Except for the recent information on the Fiji Islands (White et al. Chapter 29), not much is known about the status of the Peregrine in the western Pacific, other than it is a widely distributed breeding species on many of the islands (Cade 1982). Peregrine population surveys are needed in Formosa, the Philippines, New Guinea, the Solomons, Vanuatu (New Hebrides), and New Caledonia.

5 | DDT and Other Chemical Problems

33 | DDE, Productivity, and Eggshell Thickness Relationships in *the Genus* Falco

Richard W. Fyfe, Robert W. Risebrough,
J. Geoffrey Monk, Walter M. Jarman,
Daniel W. Anderson, Lloyd F. Kiff,
Jeffrey L. Lincer, Ian C. T. Nisbet,
Wayman Walker II, and Brian J. Walton

The hypothesis that organochlorine contaminants in the environment had caused the extinction or decline of local breeding populations of Peregrine Falcons and other raptors was discussed at the Madison Conference in 1965 (Hickey 1969). The supporting evidence, however, consisted of weak correlations between the timing of the population declines and the introduction of the chlorinated hydrocarbon pesticides and between the areas of decline and areas of pesticide use. Since then, convincing support has appeared for the hypothesis that one, several, or a complex of organochlorine compounds have caused reproductive failures, low productivity, population declines and local extinctions of Peregrine populations. There is as yet no agreement on the relative contribution of the individual organochlorines or groups of organochlorines to the extinction process. Some investigators think mortalities induced by the cyclodiene insecticides (principally aldrin, dieldrin and heptachlor) were the major factor; others attach greater importance to the low productivity induced by DDE.

There is, however, agreement that the DDT metabolite DDE (1,1-dichloro-2, 2-bis-(p-chlorophenyl)ethylene) causes eggshell thinning in falcons. Low levels of DDE fed to captive American Kestrels produced eggshell thinning (Wiemeyer and Porter 1970), and four dosage levels produced a significant inverse relationship between DDE levels in the eggs and the degree of thinning (Lincer 1975). Comparable inverse correlations were found in eggs from wild American Kestrels (Lincer 1975), Peregrine Falcons (Cade et al. 1971, Peakall et al. 1975), and

Prairie Falcons (Fyfe et al. 1969, Enderson and Wrege 1973), and in eggs of Bat Falcons and Aplomado Falcons obtained in Mexico during periods of DDT use and now preserved in museums (Kiff et al. 1980). Eggshell thinning and high levels of DDE have also been reported in Merlin eggs (Fox 1971, Temple 1972, Fyfe et al. 1976b, Newton et al. 1982).

In this paper we present data relevant to the following questions on DDE levels, eggshell thickness, and productivity among several species of the genus *Falco*.

(1) Have compounds other than DDE contributed to eggshell thinning in wild populations?

(2) Does the present data base clarify the quantitative relationships between DDE and eggshell thinning?

(3) Are there differences among species of the genus *Falco* in their sensitivity to DDE?

(4) What are the relationships between productivity and eggshell thickness and between productivity and DDE?

(5) Is depressed productivity caused by a reduction in eggshell thickness or by DDE contamination of eggs or adults?

METHODS

Productivity data for Prairie Falcons breeding in Alberta in the period 1967-73 and for Merlins breeding in Alberta in 1969-73 were obtained by counting the number of young fledged from clutches after the collection of a single egg from each clutch shortly after clutch completion (Fyfe et al. 1976b). Eggs were analyzed at the Ontario Research Foundation with methods described by Reynolds (1969), Vermeer and Reynolds (1970), and Reynolds and Cooper (1975). Productivity data for Peregrine Falcons breeding in California in 1976-85 were obtained from counts of young fledged at eyries under observation by various investigators during this period (Walton and Thelander Chapter 55). Sites from which eggs were taken or to which young were placed in manipulation experiments were not included in the data set examined for productivity. Clutch means of thickness indices (Ratcliffe 1967) or eggshell thickness and DDE residues were compared with productivity data to determine relationships among these parameters. Pollutant data from individual eggs were used when Ratcliffe's thickness index was the dependent variable.

Relationships between thickness index as the dependent variable and pollutant concentrations as the independent variables were examined by stepwise regression analyses (Nie et al. 1970) which determine the combination of independent variables resulting in the greatest reduction in the sum of squares of the thickness index. Independent variables included the pollutant concentrations (c_i for the ith pollutant), their logarithms ($\ln c_i$) and variables (S), defined by the equation:

$$S(c_i) = \left(1 + \frac{c_i^2}{A^2}\right)^{-1}$$

In contrast to the logarithm, this function predicts a slow decrease in the dependent variable (thickness index) for low concentrations of independent variables such as DDE. The scale parameter A was selected in each case to yield the best fit (i.e., to maximize the contribution to the explained variance). Additional regression analyses were undertaken with the Interactive Statistics Package of the University of California and the SYSTAT statistical software, version 2.1, on an IBM XT computer.

Estimates of the pre-DDT thickness indices of Prairie Falcon and Merlin eggs were 1.93 and 1.31, respectively; they were derived from unpublished data of D. W. Anderson and L. G. Swartz, respectively (Monk et al. Chapter 37). We used the pre-DDT estimate of 0.365 mm for eggshell thickness of California Peregrine Falcons (Anderson and Hickey 1972); it was derived from a large data set from southern California. This value is assumed to be valid for the areas of the present distribution of the species in California (primarily northern California). A value of 0.369 mm was used by Peakall and Kiff (Chapter 35). Estimates of the pre-DDT eggshell thickness indices of Peregrines in Alaska and California were 1.86-1.89 and 1.94, respectively (Cade et al. 1971, Anderson and Hickey 1972). Pre-DDT estimates of eggshell thickness index (1.06) for the American Kestrel (Lincer 1975) in the northeastern United States are from Anderson and Hickey (1972). Estimates of pre-DDT thickness indices for Bat Falcons and Aplomado Falcons were 1.28 and 1.50, respectively (Kiff et al. 1980).

RESULTS AND DISCUSSION

Contribution of Pollutants Other Than DDE to Eggshell Thinning. — Eggs of the Prairie Falcons and Merlins were analyzed for DDE, PCB, dieldrin, heptachlor expoxide, and total mercury (Tables 1 and 2). Concentrations of each pollutant were not determined in all eggs, hence the variable n in Tables 1 and 2. Moreover, thickness index data were not available for all eggs.

Data for all five pollutant variables and for thickness index were available for 254 Prairie Falcon eggs. These were used in the initial stepwise regression analyses. $S(DDE)$ with $A=32$ provided the greatest reduction in the sum of squares; none of the other pollutant variables or their transformations further reduced significantly the sum of

TABLE 1.   Pollutant concentrations (ppm dry wt) in eggs of Prairie Falcons from
           Alberta, 1967-73. Data from 229 clutches.

Pollutant	n	Arithmetic mean	Standard deviation	Geometric mean
DDE	282	13.4	14.5	8.7
PCBs	258[a]	4.6	5.4	2.8
Dieldrin	279[a]	1.7	3.8	0.73
Heptachlor epoxide	282	2.4	5.2	1.3
Mercury	263[a]	0.71	1.1	0.39

[a] Some eggs not analyzed for this pollutant, or data not available.

TABLE 2.   Pollutant concentrations (ppm dry wt) in eggs of Merlins from Alberta,
           1969-73. Data from 169 clutches.

Pollutant	n	Arithmetic mean	Standard deviation	Geometric mean
DDE	189	78.0	118.1	38.8
PCBs	188[a]	6.8	5.7	5.2
Dieldrin	189	3.1	3.3	1.8
Heptachlor epoxide	189	2.6	3.0	1.7
Mercury	187[a]	1.0	0.99	0.7

[a] Some eggs not analyzed for this pollutant, or data not available.

squares when they were incorporated into the stepwise regression analysis. Significance was determined with a larger set for which both DDE and thickness index data were available ($n=276$); $F_{1,274}=106$; $P<0.001$; $r^2=0.378$; $a=1.262$; $b=0.550$.

Regression analysis of the Merlin data yielded comparable results. S(DDE) with $A=22$ provided the greatest reduction in the variance within the subsample ($n=184$) that was complete for thickness index and all five pollutant variables; no other variable contributed significantly to the explained variance. Repetition of the regression analysis with the slightly larger data set ($n=186$) that contained values of both thickness index and DDE yielded the following parameters: $F_{1,184}=154$, $r^2=0.456$, $a=0.99$, $b=0.267$.

Although a modification of the S function provides a better description of the relationship between thickness index and DDE concentrations (see below), these results provide further support to the conclusion, based upon all available experimental and field data, that no pollutants other than DDE, with the possible exception of other DDT compounds, have had a significant effect on the eggshell thickness of wild populations of sensitive avian species (Risebrough 1986).

Experimental data, however, indicate an apparent PCB effect upon eggshell strength. Feeding of a DDE-PCB mixture to domestic Mallards and to American Kestrels increased the frequency of egg breakage over that of groups fed DDE alone (Lincer 1972, Risebrough and Anderson 1975). A PCB effect on the formation of the organic cores upon which the eggshell material is deposited (Greenburg et al. 1979) might explain a decrease in eggshell strength. Confirmation of these reports is important for an assessment of PCB effects on Peregrines and other avian species.

The DDE–Eggshell Thickness Relationship. — The earlier studies of the relationships between eggshell thickness and DDE concentrations in the eggs of Herring Gulls (Hickey and Anderson 1968), Peregrines (Cade et al. 1971, Peakall et al. 1975), Brown Pelicans (Blus et al. 1972, Risebrough 1972), Prairie Falcons (Enderson and Wrege 1973) and American Kestrels (Lincer 1975) reported a significant relationship between decreasing thickness and the logarithm of DDE concentrations. Thickness decreased more rapidly than DDE concentrations increased. Such a relationship is predicted by a biochemical and physiological model of DDE effects in the eggshell gland that has no surplus of sensitive sites whose action would be blocked by DDE, i.e., calcium transport enzyme systems in the eggshell gland membranes (Miller et al. 1976). Inactivation of transport sites would begin with low concentrations of DDE; as DDE levels increased, the chances of binding between DDE molecules and transport sites would decrease, hence the observed logarithmic relationship.

Published plots, however, of thickness indices and DDE concentrations in the eggs of Peregrine Falcons from Alaska (Peakall et al. 1975) and of an experimental colony and a wild population of American Kestrels in New York State (Lincer 1975) indicate that in these cases there was a range of DDE concentrations with comparatively little effect on eggshell thickness, in the order of 5 ppm and perhaps up to 10 ppm (dry wt) in the Peregrines and American Kestrels. Such an observation is consistent with a physiological model that assumes a surplus of sensitive sites, with a significant reduction in calcium carbonate deposition occurring only after the surplus sites have been blocked. This model furthermore predicts that a logarithmic function would not provide the best description of the relationship between thickness/thickness index and DDE concentrations.

This prediction was confirmed by the stepwise regression analyses of the Prairie Falcon and Merlin data described above; the S function provided a better function than did the logarithm. In biological terms, this implies a low range of DDE concentrations with only a small reduction of thickness.

The values predicted by the S function and the logarithm of DDE in the Prairie Falcon eggs do not differ widely (Figure 1). The S function

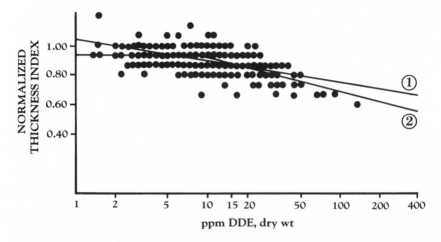

FIGURE 1. Reduction of thickness index of Prairie Falcon eggshells normalized from estimated pre-DDT mean of 1.93, versus DDE concentrations, dry weight. (1) Logarithmic function, thickness index = 1.03119–0.0619 *ln* DDE; (2) "S" function, thickness index =

$$1.262 + \frac{0.55}{1 + \left(\frac{DDE}{32}\right)^2}$$

predicts an intercept of 1.81 at DDE=0 which is too low; the estimated pre-DDT thickness index is 1.93; the predicted index at DDE=1 ppm by the logarithm is 1.99, a value that is too high. The logarithm predicts lower values than the S function in the range 5-20 ppm, but higher values in the range 20-200 ppm DDE. This version of the S function, $a=1.262$, $b=0.550$, $A=32$, predicts that the thickness index will approach a value of 1.262 with increasing DDE, and will not drop below this level, which represents a 35% reduction in thickness index.

Thinning of this magnitude has apparently not been reported in falcon eggs, but eggs of Brown Pelicans with a 95% reduction of eggshell thickness were found on Anacapa Island in 1969 (Risebrough et al. 1971, Risebrough 1972). The S function, while improving the fit at low levels of DDE, cannot therefore be extrapolated to high levels of DDE.

Use of the logarithm of thickness index rather than the thickness index with the S function provides a slightly better fit, explaining 40% of the variance rather than 37.8%: $a=-0.4027$, $b=0.3387$, with standard errors of 0.02154 and 0.02492, respectively; $r^2=0.4028$; $A=32$. Logarithmic transformation of the thickness index variable did not improve the fit of the Merlin data.

The best data set encompassing low, intermediate, and high levels of DDE in eggs correlated with significant thinning appears to be that produced by feeding DDE to a captive group of American Kestrels (Lincer 1972, Lincer 1975). The logarithm of the thickness index versus $S(DDE)$, $A=70$, provided a better fit ($r^2=0.871$, $a=-0.35005$, $b=0.32060$) than did thickness index versus ln DDE ($r^2=0.755$, $a=1.0216$, $b=-0.04986$). The experimental conditions permitted determination of the effect of low levels of DDE on thickness index; there was no substantial reduction over the ranges 1-15 ppm DDE (Figure 2).

Data sets from wild populations rarely have many DDE values in the "no effect" range, hence the relatively good fit to logarithmic functions.

Interspecific Differences in Sensitivity to DDE. — Peakall et al. (1975) concluded that productivity of Peregrine Falcons would be sufficient to maintain population levels if DDE levels in eggs were below 15-20 ppm wet weight, or 75-100 ppm dry weight. However, productivity of Prairie Falcons is almost completely inhibited at DDE levels in the order of 12 ppm dry weight, and productivity of Merlins is severely inhibited at DDE levels above 60 ppm (Fyfe et al. 1976b). Enderson and Wrege (1973) reported that the mathematical relation-

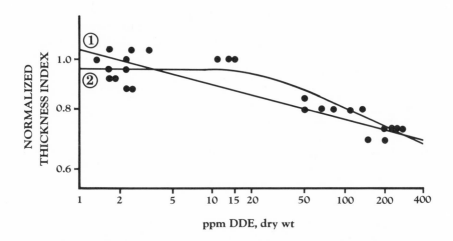

FIGURE 2. Reduction of thickness index of eggshells of American Kestrels, normalized to estimated pre-DDT value of 1.06. Data of J. L. Lincer from field and experimental studies. (1) Logarithmic function, thickness index = 1.0216–0.04986 ln DDE; (2) "S" function, thickness index =

$$-0.35005 + \frac{0.3206}{\left(1 + \frac{DDE}{70}\right)^2}$$

ship between eggshell thinning and DDE residues is similar in Peregrine and Prairie Falcons. How are these apparent discrepancies resolved? We compare the results obtained from analysis of the Prairie Falcon and Merlin data from Alberta with published data in the literature on these and other species of the genus *Falco* (Table 3).

TABLE 3. Eggshell thickness (Th) and thickness indices (In), normalized to estimated pre-DDT values, as a function of the natural logarithm of DDE concentrations in falcon (*Falco*) eggs.

Species	Th or In source	Basis	Intercept (S.E.)	Slope (S.E.)	n
Prairie Falcon	In[a]	dry	1.03119 (0.01212)	-0.06190 (0.00510)	276
	In[a]	lipid	1.07414 (0.01667)	-0.05381 (0.00479)	276
	In[a]	wet	0.92870 (0.00517)	-0.06079 (0.00492)	276
	Th[b]	wet	0.9578	-0.0795	40
Merlin	In[a]	dry	1.02239 (0.01772)	-0.05376 (0.00457)	186
	In[a]	wet	0.93204 (0.01055)	-0.05191 (0.00441)	186
	In[a]	lipid	1.06780 (0.02147)	-0.05256 (0.00447)	186
Peregrine	In[c]	dry	1.11086 (0.02322)	-0.06233 (0.00545)	73
	In[d]	dry	1.026	-0.046	74
	Th[e]	lipid	1.096 (0.036)	-0.049 (0.006)	74
Bat Falcon	In[f]	lipid	1.30912 (0.07292)	-0.10606 (0.01518)	35
American Kestrel	Th[g]	dry	0.92322 (0.03654)	-0.03416 (0.01042)	65
	In[g]	dry	1.07347 (0.03990)	-0.04607 (0.01138)	65

[a] This study.
[b] Enderson and Wrege (1973).
[c] Recalculated from figure of Peakall et al. (1975), using estimated pre-DDE thickness index of 1.86 (Anderson and Hickey 1972). If value of 1.89 (Cade et al. 1971, Peakall et al. 1975) is used, intercept and slope are 1.0932 and -0.06134.
[d] Derived from: (1) California data of D. W. Anderson, thickness index = 0.1258 + 4.97 (thickness), n = 218; and (2) membrane lipid-thickness data of Peakall and Kiff (Chapter 35), assuming ppm lipid = 4 (ppm dry), thickness = 0.375-0.018 (ln DDE, dry).
[e] Data of Peakall and Kiff (Chapter 35).
[f] Data of Kiff et al. (1980).
[g] Data of J. L. Lincer.

Although the function S(DDE) yielded a better fit to the eggshell thickness data for Prairie Falcons and Merlins than the logarithmic transformation, this section uses regressions on ln DDE for interspecific comparisons. The statistical model used is of the form

$$T = a - b \ln DDE$$

where T is eggshell thickness (or thickness index) and a and b are regression parameters to be determined. As described above, this relationship cannot hold for very small values of DDE; the dose-response relationship that is hypothesized is of a "hockey stick" form (see Figure 1) in which T remains constant at the pre-DDT mean level up to a "threshold" value of DDE, denoted by H, and then declines linearly with ln DDE with constant of proportionality b. This simple two-parameter model permits interspecific comparisons of H and b which are easier to interpret than comparisons using the S function.

The only statistically significant difference among species is that the regression coefficient for the Bat Falcon is significantly higher than that for each of the other species ($P<0.05$, Duncan's multiple range test). Among the other species, the reductions of eggshell thickness induced by DDE are equivalent; if small differences exist, they cannot be detected with the present data sets.

The value of DDE predicted by the regression equation when the thickness or thickness index equals the pre-DDT value provides an estimate of the "threshold" concentration, H, below which there is only a slight reduction in DDE-induced eggshell thickness (Table 4). In spite of uncertainties in sampling error in museum collections and in the eggs obtained in recent studies, there appears to be a significant difference between the Prairie Falcon and the Merlin, which both have a very low "threshold" concentration in the order of 1.5 ppm dry weight, and the American Kestrel and the Bat Falcon, which both have a "threshold" concentration in the order of 5 ppm dry weight (Table 4). The "threshold" concentrations for all species are relatively low, however, compared to the ranges of DDE concentrations that have been recorded.

The "threshold" concentration for Peregrine Falcons from Alaska appears to be similar to those of American Kestrels and Bat Falcons, whereas that of Peregrines from California resembles those of Prairie Falcons and Merlins. Initially, 1.86 was used as the estimated pre-DDT thickness index for the Alaska Peregrines (Anderson and Hickey 1972); use of 1.89 (Cade et al. 1971) would reduce the estimated "threshold" level to 4.6 ppm (Table 4). Reduction of H to a level of about 2 ppm in this model would require an estimated pre-DDT thickness greater than 2.0, which appears unrealistic. The observed difference in "threshold" concentrations of DDE between the two Peregrine populations appears, therefore, to be real.

TABLE 4. Estimated approximate "threshold" levels of DDE concentrations derived from regression equations of Table 3, and estimated pre-DDT thickness indices and thicknesses.

Species	Estimated pre-DDT thickness index (or thickness in mm)	"Threshold" level of DDE (ppm dry wt)
Prarie Falcon[a]	1.93[b]	1.6
Merlin[a]	1.31	1.5
Peregrine Falcon, Alaska[c]	1.86[d]	6.0
	1.89[e]	4.6
Peregrine Falcon, California[f]	1.94[d]	1.8
	(0.365 mm[d])	1.8
Bat Falcon	1.28[g]	4.7
American Kestrel	1.06[d]	4.9

[a] This study.
[b] Monk et al. Chapter 36.
[c] Peakall et al. (1975).
[d] Anderson and Hickey (1972).
[e] Cade et al. (1971), Peakall et al. (1975).
[f] Peakall and Kiff (Chapter 34), derivation of thickness index values in Table 3.
[g] Kiff et al. (1980).

Estimates of the degree of thinning at various levels of DDE (Table 5) predict that the Bat Falcon is the most sensitive among the species examined at higher levels of DDE, and the American Kestrel is the least sensitive. The Peregrine Falcon appears intermediate in sensitivity. Because of a higher regression coefficient, the Alaska Peregrines show a response similar to that of California Peregrines at DDE levels in the order of 100 ppm.

The limited number of Aplomado Falcon eggs examined ($n=20$, 11 clutches) had a mean thickness index of 1.098, indicating a reduction of 27% from the estimated pre-1947 mean (Kiff et al. 1980); they had a geometric mean DDE concentration of 260 ppm lipid weight, or an estimated 65 ppm dry weight. This species, therefore, appears to be relatively sensitive to DDE at higher levels; its sensitivity is comparable to that of the Bat Falcon (Table 5).

Productivity-Eggshell Thickness and Productivity-DDE Relationships. — Wiemeyer et al. (1984) reported that both productivity and eggshell thickness in Bald Eagles declined linearly with the logarithm of DDE. This would imply a linear relationship between the degree of eggshell thinning and the degree of reduction in productivity, with no threshold; in other words, productivity would begin to decrease with low degrees of eggshell thinning. We looked for "threshold" degrees of thinning and for "threshold" DDE concentrations in Peregrine Falcon and Merlin eggs by plotting numbers of

TABLE 5.   Percent reduction of thickness index (In) and thickness (Th) as a function of DDE concentrations in species of the genus *Falco*. (Wet wt values approximately 20% of dry wt concentrations.)

DDE (ppm dry wt.)	Prairie Falcon[a] In[a]	Merlin[a] In[a]	Peregrine Falcon In[b]	Peregrine Falcon In[c]	Peregrine Falcon Th[d]	Bat Falcon In[e]	American Kestrel In[f]
5	6.8	6.4	0.0-0.5	4.9	5.2	0.1	0.1
10	11.1	10.1	3.3-4.8	8.1	8.6	8.2	3.3
15	13.7	12.2	5.8-7.3	9.9	10.6	12.5	5.1
20	15.5	13.9	7.5-9.1	11.3	12.0	15.6	6.5
50	21.1	18.8	13.3-14.7	15.5	15.6	25.3	10.7
100	25.4	22.5	17.6-18.9	18.7	20.0	32.6	13.9

[a] This study.
[b] Alaska Peregrine Falcons, Peakall et al. (1975); range related to choice of pre-DDT values, 1.86-1.89.
[c] California Peregrine Falcons, dry wt values determined as in Table 3, Peakall and Kiff (Chapter 34).
[d] Data of Peakall and Kiff (Chapter 34), dry wt values = $\frac{\text{lipid wt}}{4}$.
[e] Kiff et al. (1980).
[f] Lincer (1975).

young fledged versus the normalized thickness indices and their 95%
confidence intervals (Figures 3a and 3b), and versus the logarithms of
DDE concentrations, also with their 95% confidence intervals (Figure
4).

In both species there is clearly a "threshold" level of eggshell
thinning, below which there is no apparent effect on productivity, but
above which productivity rapidly declines. In spite of a similar response
of eggshell thickness to increasing DDE concentrations (see above), the
Prairie Falcon is more sensitive to the effects of thinning than is the
Merlin. The "threshold" level of thinning is in the order of an 8%
decrease in thickness index, and productivity falls to zero when the
decrease in thickness index is about 14% (Figure 3a). The corresponding interval for the Merlins is approximately 15-20% (Figure 3b).

The plots of numbers of young fledged versus DDE concentrations
are similar (Figure 4). In each species there is a range of DDE
concentrations with no detectable effect on productivity, but above the
"threshold" level productivity falls. The "threshold" level of DDE
concentration is 3-5 times higher in Merlins than in Prairie Falcons.

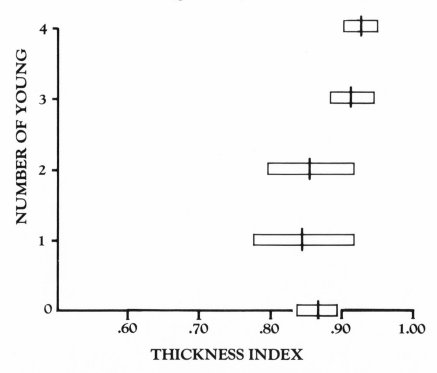

FIGURE 3a. Productivity of Prairie Falcons as a function of normalized eggshell
          thickness index. One egg from each clutch removed for analysis. Means
          of thickness indices with 95% confidence intervals.

In the data set for Peregrine eggs from California compiled through 1985, there were 129 clutches which had both productivity and thickness data and which had not been subjected to manipulation experiments through removal of eggs or addition of young. These came principally from the northern interior, where thinning averaged 16% from 1980-85 (Monk et al. Chapter 37). A reduction of 16% in eggshell thickness corresponds to a 15% reduction of thickness index (data of D. W. Anderson, Table 3). In this sample, mean thinning was 14.5% (0.312 ±0.020 mm) and the mean productivity was 1.88 ±1.18 young fledged per active pair, a level substantially higher than the value of 1.5 compiled by Hickey and Anderson (1969) for healthy populations. Sites producing four young ($n=4$) had a mean thinning of 12.5%, and sites with no productivity ($n=25$) had a mean thinning of 16.5%. There was, however, no significant relationship between thinning and productivity ($r^2=0.0245$, $F_{1,127}=3.2$, $P>0.05$). The sample included very few clutches with greater than 14.5% thinning and low productivity. The mean level of thinning at which productivity is

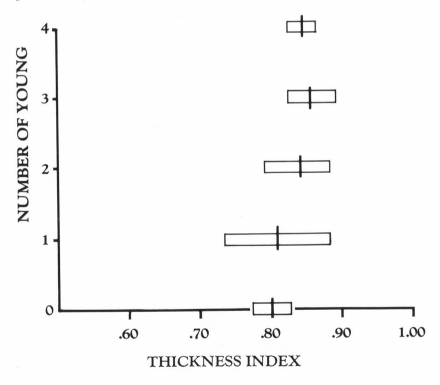

FIGURE 3b. Productivity of Merlins as a function of normalized eggshell thickness index. One egg from each clutch removed for analysis. Means of thickness indices with 95% confidence intervals.

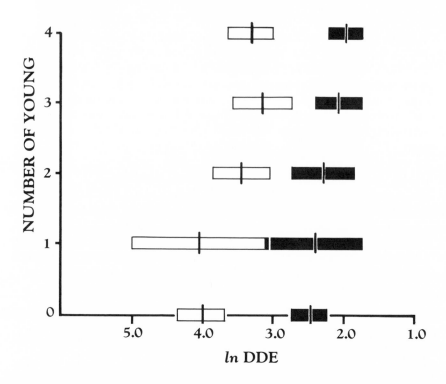

FIGURE 4. Productivity of Prairie Falcons (shaded) and Merlins (nonshaded) as a
function of DDE concentrations in one egg per clutch removed for
analysis. Means of ln DDE concentrations with 95% confidence intervals.

significantly depressed is therefore greater than 14.5%, and is a
minimum estimate of the "threshold" below which there is no appreciable effect on productivity. The existence of such a "threshold" level
of thinning is consistent with the earlier conclusion of Hickey and
Anderson (1968) and Anderson and Hickey (1972) that a level of
thinning in the order of 20% was associated with population declines
of Peregrine Falcons. On the basis of 150-350 ppm DDE in eggs of
Alaska Peregrines, thinning in the range of 19-25%, declining populations, and a declining productivity, Peakall et al. (1975) estimated
that DDE concentrations of 75-100 ppm dry weight in the egg (or
15-20 ppm wet weight) would be a critical level, corresponding to an
eggshell thickness index interval of approximately 15-20% thinning,
above which populations would not be able to sustain themselves.
However, the "critical intervals" determined by Peakall et al. (1975)
are not equivalent to the "threshold" levels estimated in this paper; the
former refer to population decline, the latter to a decline in
productivity.

DDE Contamination Versus Egghell Thinning as the Cause of Reproductive Failure. — A previous analysis of this data set (Fyfe et al. 1976b) showed a significant relationship between the productivity of Prairie Falcons and thickness index, but not DDE; both thickness index and DDE concentrations were significantly associated with productivity of Merlins, with DDE showing a stronger relationship. PCBs were also associated with decreased productivity of Merlins, but levels were relatively low (Table 2) and were strongly correlated with DDE concentrations. A PCB effect in this case is therefore unlikely.

The majority of the Prairie Falcon and Merlin eggs were collected early in the incubation period. Broken eggs, characteristic of populations of other raptors experiencing low productivity such as the European Sparrowhawk (Newton 1974), were generally not observed. Alterations in the eggshell structure which impair gas and water exchange appear to be a plausible explanation for at least some of the depressed productivity associated with increased thinning. Microclimates of individual nests would have particular importance. Peakall et al. (1973) reported a decrease in the number of pores through the eggshells in thin-shelled eggs of American Kestrels, Pekin Ducks, and Ring Doves, although Cooke (1979) found no decrease in the number of pores in thin-shelled Peregrine eggs. Porosity, measured as the rate of passage of water vapor, was decreased in thin-shelled eggs of all four species, contrary to the expected. A further clue to relative sensitivity might come from the observation of Tyler (1966) that Falconiformes have fewer pores through the eggshell than other taxonomic orders so far studied. Interspecific differences in the microstructure of the eggshell might, therefore, account for the observed differences in productivity-thickness relationships.

A number of experimental and field studies (some of them reviewed in Risebrough 1986) have shown that DDE and other organochlorines may alter behavior in ways that would depress productivity. The Merlin showed a significant relationship between low productivity and weak nest defense (Fyfe et al. 1976b), but no such correlation was observed for the Prairie Falcon. The exchange of eggs between healthy and failing populations of Ospreys showed that incubation of eggs from the failing colony by adults of the healthy colony did not improve the hatching rate (Wiemeyer et al. 1975). Factors intrinsic to the egg, either the modification in eggshell structure or lethal levels of pollutants, were responsible.

No significant relationships between embryonic mortality or the incidence of addled eggs and eggshell thickness or pollutant concentrations could be demonstrated from the Merlin and Prairie Falcon data sets (Fyfe et al. 1976b). Since the majority of eggs were collected when fresh, a hypothesis that incidence of embryonic death was related to thinning could not be tested. A hypothesis that the reproductive failures are due principally to embryotoxic effects of DDE receives only weak support. The "threshold" level of DDE concentration in the eggs of Prairie Falcons is about 7 ppm dry weight or 1.5 ppm wet weight, a low level that is frequently encountered in populations of other species. The hypothesis would, therefore, require an exceptional sensitivity to DDE of Prairie Falcon embryos, as well as a 3-5 fold difference in sensitivity between Prairie Falcons and Merlins. Dieldrin has a much higher avian toxicity than DDE, but Common Barn-Owl embryos are not affected by dieldrin levels of 8 ppm wet weight, or about 40 ppm dry weight (Mendenhall et al. 1983).

Taking into account evolutionary considerations, any departure from the normal eggshell structure or thickness might be expected to lower the reproductive potential. The results of this study are consistent with this generalization; small decreases in reproductive potential would remain significant over longer periods of time in an evolutionary context. Within the short term, however, it is the elimination of all reproductive potential above critical levels of eggshell thinning and of DDE concentrations that is more relevant to the future of species and populations.

The relatively low reduction in productivity over a range of thicknesses and of DDE concentrations, and the sharp drop in productivity above "threshold" levels of thinning and of DDE, casts a light on the rapid recovery of Peregrine populations reported in this volume. A small increase in eggshell thickness within the range below the "threshold" would cause productivity to rise from a level that is almost zero to a level not far from normal. DDE concentrations would need to be reduced only to the "threshold" level to achieve a virtually complete recovery. A model using logarithmic relationships between DDE concentrations and productivity would require that DDE levels decline to almost zero before productivity approached normal levels.

A logarithmic relationship between eggshell thinning or productivity and DDE concentrations has provided a good fit in previous studies largely because the data came from a range of DDE concentrations that were associated with rapid decreases in eggshell thickness and productivity. The S function used here also adequately describes this rapid change in thickness or productivity, but also describes much less pronounced changes at low levels of DDE. It is clearly not adequate to describe the relationships at the highest levels of DDE, when productivity drops to zero, or when there is extreme eggshell thinning. Words provide a much more adequate description than the mathematics of what happens at the highest levels; we have not attempted to develop further mathematical relationships between productivity and thickness or between productivity and DDE.

Although some pairs in the Prairie Falcon and Merlin populations we studied were experiencing complete reproductive failure associated with eggshell thinning, the populations have undergone no reduction in numbers of breeding pairs. Net productivity was evidently sufficient to maintain the populations with or without immigrations from other areas. The recorded productivities of nests from which one egg had been removed for residue analysis were 2.3 for Prairie Falcons and 2.0 for Merlins (Fyfe et al. 1976b). The northern California population of Peregrines is currently expanding in spite of the recurrent failure of some pairs; although the mean level of eggshell thinning was 16% in 1980-1985, the mean productivity was high, on the order of 1.9 young fledged per active pair. The models presented here predict a rapid decrease of productivity to zero if there were a relatively small increase in the environmental levels of DDE in northern California.

It is now clear how there can be major differences in sensitivity to DDE among the several species of the genus *Falco* that have been studied here, in spite of similar responses of eggshell thinning to DDE. There are interspecific differences in the "no-effect" range of DDE concentrations, above which eggshell thickness begins to decrease sharply, but these cannot account for the principal differences that are observed. Prairie Falcons are affected by a level of eggshell thinning, or perhaps more accurately, of eggshell change that does not affect Merlins or Peregrines. In turn, productivity of Merlins is decreased by a degree of eggshell changes that apparently does not affect Peregrines.

Our data, and our interpretation of these data, are therefore consistent with a hypothesis that it is the physical changes in the eggshell that are the principal cause of reproductive failure, and that breakage need not necessarily be involved. Scanning electron microscope studies of the eggs of DDE-contaminated American Kestrels, Merlins, Peregrines and Prairie Falcons might provide further support or refutation of this hypothesis.

ACKNOWLEDGEMENTS

Research was supported by the Canadian Wildlife Service, by the National Science Foundation grant GB-36593, and by the Bodega Bay Institute. We thank U. Banasch for preparation of data, H. Armbruster, G. Fox, K. Hodson and L. Kemper for assistance in the field in Alberta, and L. M. Reynolds of the Ontario Research Foundation for the analyses of samples.

34 | DDE Contamination in Peregrines and American Kestrels and its Effect on Reproduction

David B. Peakall and Lloyd F. Kiff

The 1965 Madison Conference first focused our attention on the connection between pesticides and the widespread decline of several populations of the Peregrine. As Cade (1968) put it: "Down through the centuries, not all the falcon trappers, egg collectors, war ministries concerned for their messenger pigeons, or misguided gunmen have been able to effect a significant reduction in the number of breeding falcons. But the simple laboratory trick of adding a few chlorine molecules to a hydrocarbon and the massive application of this unnatural class of chemicals to the environment can do what none of these other grosser, seemingly more harmful agents could do." Twenty years after the first trickle of data, the notion that DDT is responsible for the decline of the Peregrine has become entrenched as conservation dogma.

We examine here the evidence for the relationship between DDE levels and eggshell thinning and the relationship between eggshell thinning and reproductive failure. In addition, we include a brief review of post-DDT Peregrine population trends as related to DDE residue levels and eggshell thinning.

Before examining these points, a few basic facts should be reviewed. DDE is a stable, very persistent metabolite of the pesticide DDT and is the form that occurs most widely in the environment. Except for shortly after spraying, the levels of the parent component DDT are low compared to DDE. DDT was first used as a pesticide on a widespread scale in 1947, and this is the year generally accepted as the cutoff point for eggshell thinning studies. Residue levels can be expressed in three ways: wet (fresh) weight basis, dry weight basis, or lipid weight basis. In general, conversions between these units can be made on a 1:5:25 basis (Peakall et al. 1975). In the case of our work on eggshell membranes, the residue levels are expressed on a lipid weight basis, as only the lipid is extracted.

Finally, eggshell thickness is frequently expressed in terms of the Ratcliffe Index. This index, devised by Ratcliffe (1967) in order to compare museum specimens with newly collected eggs, is the eggshell weight (mg) per length times breadth (mm). It has been shown to be highly correlated with eggshell thickness (Ratcliffe 1970, Anderson and Hickey 1972, Burnham et al. 1984).

RELATIONSHIP BETWEEN DDE AND EGGSHELL THINNING

Risebrough (1986) recently reviewed the evidence that DDE is the only pollutant causing significant eggshell thinning at environmentally realistic concentrations. He cited four lines of evidence to support this statement. First, significant negative correlations between DDE and eggshell thickness have been demonstrated in several families of birds. Second, there is experimental evidence that environmental levels of DDE induce eggshell thinning in the Anatidae, Falconidae and Strigidae. Third, experiments using other pollutants have failed to demonstrate eggshell thinning at environmentally realistic doses. It is obviously impossible to test all chemicals, but so far, no convincing evidence has been produced that any pollutant other than DDE is involved. Fourth, affected populations and eggshell thickness increased after DDT usage ceased in many areas. Although not mentioned specifically by Risebrough, the last point can be expanded to cover the temporal and geographic patterns of decline in several species of raptors, especially the cosmopolitan Peregrine.

The degree of eggshell thinning caused by a given dosage of DDE varies greatly among families and even from species to species within the same family (Peakall 1975). The Galliformes are almost completely resistant to DDE-induced eggshell thinning, other groups such as the Anseriformes and Columbiformes are moderately sensitive, and still others, including the Falconiformes and Pelicaniformes, are highly sensitive. One factor inhibiting laboratory investigations on the eggshell thinning phenomenon has been the fact that the groups which show the most dramatic response are those which are most difficult to maintain in captivity.

In order to avoid problems of species-to-species variation, data on only two species of the genus *Falco*, the Peregrine and the American Kestrel, are considered here. The data on the Peregrine consists entirely of field-collected material, while data on the American Kestrel includes both laboratory-dosed and field-collected samples.

The data relating DDE residue levels in the egg and the degree of eggshell thinning in the American Kestrel are plotted in Figure 1. Two sources of data are used, those given in Lincer (1975) and unpublished data of the Canadian Wildlife Service. Regression analysis supports the

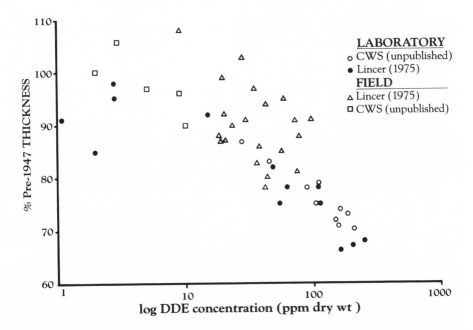

FIGURE 1.   DDE residue levels and corresponding eggshell thinning in American
Kestrels.

original conclusion of Lincer that eggshell thickness is inversely related to the log of DDE concentration and that the relationship is similar for laboratory-dosed and field-collected samples. The correlation coefficient for the combined field sample is $r=0.62$; for the laboratory samples, $r=0.78$; and for all samples combined, $r=0.72$.

The data from Wiemeyer and Porter's (1970) pioneering study on the effect of pesticides on American Kestrels were not included, as they did not give values for individual eggs. However, they demonstrated that eggshell thinning occurred when the birds were exposed to 10 ppm of DDE wet weight, and the mean value from their work lies fairly close to the regression line.

A linear relationship between the eggshell thickness and the log of the DDE concentration was also established for Peregrine eggs collected in Alaska (Cade et al. 1971, Peakall et al. 1975). The regression analysis of these data yields a highly significant relationship ($r=0.72$). Similar correlations have been demonstrated in British Peregrines by Ratcliffe (1970), Australian Peregrines by Pruett-Jones et al. (1981b) and Olsen and Peakall (1983), and in various other *Falco* species (Fyfe et al. Chapter 33). A review of the pollutant literature has indicated that such correlations have been demonstrated for at least 30 species of birds from 11 families (L. Kiff unpubl. ms.).

It should be noted that such an inverse relationship between eggshell thickness and DDE residue levels in the eggs was not found in the Rocky Mountain sample of Enderson et al. (1982) and is weaker for the Canadian data of Fyfe et al. (unpubl. ms.), although the reasons for the departures are not altogether clear. In the case of the Rocky Mountain data set, a basic problem may be the large intraclutch variation (67% of the total variation) encountered in DDE residues compared to an interclutch variation of only 26% (Burnham et al. 1984). This trend of greater intraclutch than interclutch variation is opposite from the findings of several other studies, including those of Lincer (1975) based on the American Kestrel laboratory data, Newton and Bogan (1974, 1978) based on European Sparrowhawks, and Newton et al. (1982) based on Merlins in Great Britain, in which interclutch variation far exceeded intraclutch variation in both eggshell thickness and DDE residues. Most studies on nonraptor species, e.g., those of Potts (1968), Vermeer and Reynolds (1970), and Blus et al. (1974), have likewise shown greater agreement in these parameters between eggs of the same clutch than between eggs of different clutches. If the conclusions of Burnham et al. (1984) are correct for Peregrines, then the usual mode of collecting one egg per clutch for monitoring programs, while perhaps sound from a conservation view-point, may well be decreasing the degree of correlation between eggshell thickness and DDE content.

The problem of biological variation is clearly shown in the early experiments of Wiemeyer and Porter (1970). The range of the control data was larger than the experimental, and, in fact, the thinnest egg was in the control group, a point seized upon by Hazeltine (1972) to criticize the whole eggshell thinning story. Under field conditions there are additional problems involving biological variation. Eggs that are broken will often not be sampled, thus biasing the sampling by excluding those eggs that are thinnest-shelled.

The log normal relationship between DDE content and eggshell thickness explains the rapid onset of eggshell thinning in Peregrines and other species that occurred after the introduction of DDT as an insecticide. The detailed British data (Ratcliffe 1967, 1970) clearly show an abrupt decline in Peregrine eggshell thickness (Ratcliffe Index) in 1947, and then comparatively little further decrease over the next few years. Gunn (1972) attacked the idea that DDT was the cause of the decline of the Peregrine, stating "the thinning must have some other cause, for an effect occurring before its cause is utterly un-acceptable." He continued, "Ratcliffe's work was done ten to twenty years later, so all sorts of tests were excluded and the whole story had to be based on coincidences in the past."

The development of a technique of extracting DDE from the membranes of eggs collected many years before (Peakall et al. 1983) has enabled the relationship between DDE content and eggshell thickness to be established for the critical period after the introduction of DDT (Peakall 1974, Peakall et al. 1976). The membrane extraction technique has been used in studies of Peregrines in California (Kiff et al. unpubl. ms.), Australia (Olsen and Peakall 1983), the arctic (Springer et al. 1984), and elsewhere (Peakall and Kiff 1979), as well as in previous studies on eggs of the California Condor (Kiff et al. 1979), vultures of both the New World and Old World (Kiff et al. 1983), and the Aplomado Falcon and Bat Falcon (Kiff et al. 1980).

As a part of a management program for the endangered California Peregrine population, eggshell quality and associated DDE residues have been monitored since 1975, and the major findings from this study will be reported separately (Kiff et al. unpubl. ms.). Our California sample ($n=302$) for the years 1975-83 includes eggshell thickness data from addled eggs, eggs broken in nests, and eggs hatched both in the wild and in the laboratory. The relationship between DDE levels and eggshell thickness in the California Peregrine sample is shown in Figure 2. A good degree of correlation ($r=0.78$) was found between log DDE and eggshell thickness. The regression shows that eggshell thinning of 20% is associated with 300-400 ppm DDE lipid weight.

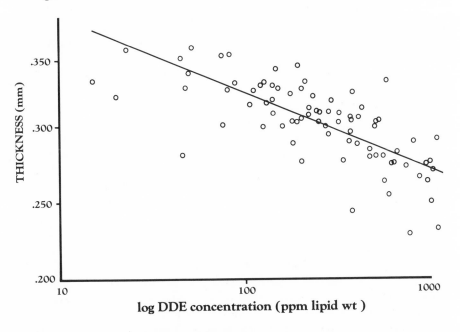

FIGURE 2. Relationship between DDE residue levels and eggshell thickness in California Peregrines.

Regression analysis of the data compiled earlier by Nygård (1983), as well as additional data from other studies on the relationship between eggshell thinning and ppm DDE in various Peregrine populations also shows a value of 300-400 ppm DDE (lipid weight) associated with 20% eggshell thinning. The correlation coefficient for these data is high ($r=0.71$), and therefore the value of 300-400 ppm DDE (lipid weight), or 15-20 ppm DDE (wet weight), can be considered to have a firm basis on both an intra- and interpopulation basis.

RELATIONSHIP OF EGGSHELL THINNING TO REPRODUCTIVE FAILURE

Various forms of avian reproductive failure have been attributed to organochlorines, including failure or inability to breed, addled eggs, and death of embryos or young. However, outright egg breakage as a result of eggshell thinning is the symptom most frequently and specifically related to DDE contamination (Cooke 1975, Newton 1979, Ratcliffe 1980, Risebrough 1986). The increased incidence of egg breakage following the introduction of DDT was clearly demonstrated by Ratcliffe (1970). During the period 1905-50, broken eggs were recorded in only 3 of 100 closely observed clutches, whereas the corresponding figures for 1951-66 were 51 out of 163 clutches and another 30 in which one or more eggs disappeared without trace.

Hickey and Anderson (1968) examined the relationship between eggshell thinning and reproductive performance of raptorial and fish-eating birds and concluded that 19% or more thinning was associated with population declines. This estimate was later refined to 20% (Anderson and Hickey 1972, 1974). Lincer (1975) arrived at a similar figure of 18% from an analysis of data for several raptor species, and Newton (1979) came up with a figure of 16-18% by the same processes. However, because of the variety of responses to DDE contamination by different species mentioned earlier, it is risky to extrapolate from these species to others that have not been studied (Prestt and Ratcliffe 1972). Specifically for the Peregrine, Ratcliffe (1980) concluded, "It is evident that a Peregrine population showing an average eggshell thinning of 20% is inevitably in serious trouble, but the recent British evidence indicates that the critical replacement level of productivity can be exceeded and recovery can take place within populations still showing 6-10% shell thinning."

The data for eggshell thinning against population changes in various Peregrine populations are shown in Figure 3. Declining or extirpated populations were found in every instance where mean eggshell thinning exceeded 17%, except for the managed California population, where thinning has averaged 18%. It should be emphasized that the degree of thinning is a mean figure, since many other factors, including the

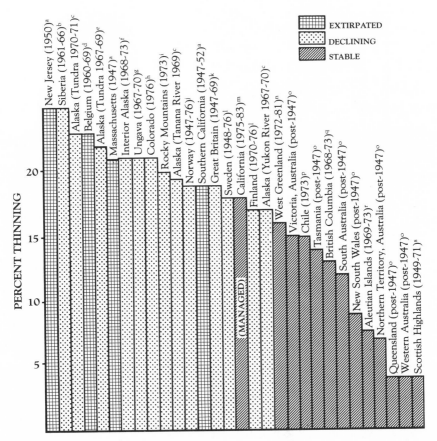

FIGURE 3. Percent eggshell thinning in the Peregrine from throughout its global range. SOURCES: [a]Hickey and Anderson (1968), [b]Peakall and Kiff (1979), [c]White and Cade (1975), [d]Joiris et al. (1979), [e]Cade et al. (1971), [f]Peakall et al. (1975), [g]Berger et al. (1970), [h]Burnham et al. (1978), [i]Enderson and Craig (1974), [j]Nygård (1983), [k]Ratcliffe (1973), [l]Odsjo and Lindberg (1977), [m]Kiff et al. (unpubl. ms.), [n]Burnham and Mattox (1984), [o]Olsen and Olsen (1979), [p]Walker et al. (1973b), [q]Nelson and Myres (1975), [r]White et al. (1973), [s]Ratcliffe (1972).

individual behavior of the birds and the nature of the nest substrate, doubtless influence the rate of egg breakage (Ratcliffe 1973, Nelson 1976). Consequently, there are instances where eggs whose shells were thinned 20% or more have hatched successfully.

For the 1975-83 California sample mentioned earlier, the fate of nesting attempts in relation to eggshell thickness is shown in Figure 4. Decreased reproductive success was associated with thinning of 18% or greater, except for eggs that were hatched in the laboratory. It is clear that artificial incubation of thin-shelled eggs by Brian Walton and

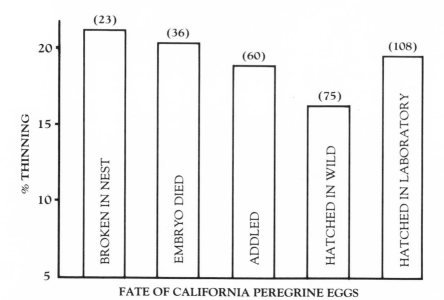

FIGURE 4. Fate of California Peregrine eggs (number of eggs in brackets).

his colleagues at the Santa Cruz Predatory Bird Research Group has resulted in the successful hatching of many eggs that otherwise would have been lost. Similar results have been reported by Enderson et al. (1982) and Burnham et al. (Chapter 53) from The Peregrine Fund's Rocky Mountain facility and by Lindberg (1981) in Sweden.

Peakall et al. (1975), after reviewing their own data and the literature, stated, "a tentative conclusion can be formed: namely that the critical level of DDE in egg content is about 15-20 ppm wet weight. This value corresponds with the suggested critical value of 20 ppm DDE wet weight derived from consideration of the eggshell thinning data." This preliminary value, now widely cited as gospel, is in agreement with the figures derived from our recent work in California. There, eggshell thinning of more than 17%, which leads to egg failure, was associated with DDE residue levels of 300-400 ppm on a lipid basis (or 15-20 ppm wet weight).

Confirmation of the critical residue levels and eggshell thinning associated with population decline in Peregrines thus comes from a comparison of the mean values for individual eggs and a comparison of the mean values for various Peregrine populations. However, it must be emphasized that all these figures are averages and do not apply rigidly to individual eggs.

DISCUSSION AND CONCLUSIONS

Eggshell thinning and DDE residues have been found in every post-1947 Peregrine egg sample so far examined throughout the global range of the species (Peakall and Kiff 1979). Associated population declines, at least on a local level, have been reported from a minimum of 36 countries representing five continents (Bijleveld 1974, Ratcliffe 1980, Newton and Chancellor 1985). The global data we previously presented (Peakall and Kiff 1979) are updated and shown graphically in Figure 5. One minor error in our earlier paper should be mentioned: the unthinned and uncontaminated eggshells attributed to the Celebes, the only post-1947 sample thought to have been devoid of DDE residues and eggshell thinning, were subsequently found to be misidentified. (The collection data had apparently been falsified by an unscrupulous collector.)

While the data are by no means as firm as one would like, there seems to be a difference in the pattern of declines observed in the British Isles and in other parts of the world, especially North America. The decline in the more populated regions of North America seems to have begun immediately after the introduction of DDT, and the evidence, such as it is, supports the hypothesis that eggshell thinning was the major cause (Hickey and Anderson 1968). In Britain, eggshell thinning was observed by 1947, and, for the British Isles as a whole, eggshell thickness remained low (roughly 20% below pre-war) for the period 1947-70, after which significant increase occurred (Ratcliffe 1984a). However, the main population crash of the species apparently occurred during the mid-1950s, concurrent with the introduction of cyclodiene pesticides, to which the crash has been attributed (Newton 1979, Ratcliffe 1980). The relative importance of DDE and the cyclodiene pesticides, particularly dieldrin, in causing the decline of the Peregrine in the British Isles is difficult to assess now, but it is perhaps significant that the recovery of the species there has been paralleled clearly by a decline in DDE residue levels in eggs, rather than by a decline in dieldrin levels (Ratcliffe 1980, Cooke et al. 1982). In any case, with this possible exception, it seems fairly clear that the main pollutant of importance in affecting Peregrine populations has been and continues to be DDE.

Differences in migratory habits and feeding ecology make broad generalizations on the recovery of Peregrines difficult. In looking for common patterns throughout the cosmopolitan range of the species, it appears that the health of various populations reflects their relative exposure to sources of DDE contamination.

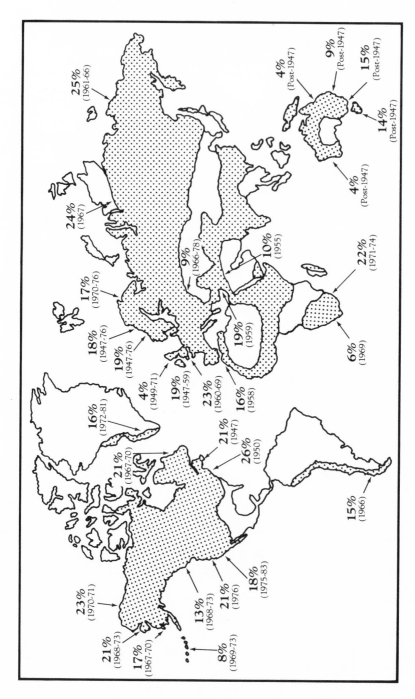

FIGURE 5. Global distribution of eggshell thinning in the Peregrine Falcon. Figures are percent reductions in eggshell thickness using Ratcliffe's Index (years of most extreme thinning in brackets).

Following the banning of DDT usage in temperate North America and most of western Europe, some recovery of Peregrine populations, assisted by management techniques in certain areas, has been reported from western Europe (Chapters 18-25), Great Britain (Ratcliffe 1984a), the eastern United States (Cade and Dague 1980, Cade 1985a), the southern Rocky Mountains (Enderson et al. Chapter 12), northern California (Walton et al. Chapter 14), parts of Canada (Bird and Weaver Chapter 6), much of the Arctic (Springer et al. 1984), and the Pacific coast of Baja California (Porter and Jenkins Chapter 15).

There have apparently been no significant post-DDT declines in the Peregrine populations in western Greenland (Burnham and Mattox 1984), the southwestern United States (Ellis et al. unpubl. ms.), northern Mexico (Hitchcock 1976, Lanning and Lawson 1977), the Gulf of California (Porter et al. Chapter 15), South America (Walker et al. 1973b, Jenny et al. 1983, Ellis 1985) and most of Australia (Olsen and Olsen 1979, 1985). Although significant levels of DDE residues in eggs and eggshell thinning have been reported from each of these areas, they have been below the levels associated with reproductive failure at the population level.

Recovery has not yet occurred in northern Sweden (Wallin 1984, Lindberg et al. Chapter 18), southern Finland, central California (Walton et al. Chapter 14), Oregon (Henny and Nelson 1981), Washington (Dobler et al. unpubl. ms.), most of eastern and southern Canada (Bird and Weaver Chapter 6, Fyfe Chapter 56), the Rocky Mountains of the northern United States (Enderson et al. Chapter 12), and Victoria, Australia (Olsen and Olsen Chapter 28).

The fragmentary information from the Middle East (Peakall and Kiff 1979), the Soviet Union (Galushin 1977, Peakall and Kiff 1979, Yelisyeev 1983), the remainder of the Asian continent (Ratcliffe 1980), and Africa (Tarboton and Allan 1984, Thomson 1984c, Kiff unpubl. ms.) generally suggests that Peregrine populations in these regions are depressed, and that DDE residues in eggs, where data are available, are still high.

Coastal populations of Peregrines have fared worse and recovered more slowly than inland populations in several regions, including the British Isles (Ratcliffe 1984a), California (Walton et al. Chapter 14), Oregon (Henny and Nelson 1981, Walton et al. Chapter 14), Scandinavia (Lindberg et al. Chapter 18), and France (Terrasse and Terrasse 1969, Monneret Chapter 23). This pattern reflects the tendency for coastal Peregrines to feed upon seabirds, which generally contain higher organochlorine residues than terrestrial prey species (Lindberg et al. 1985, Monk and Risebrough pers. comm.). In England, the birds nesting on coastal cliffs are also exposed to heavy pesticide use from the agricultural lands immediately inland (Ratcliffe 1984a).

Sedentary populations in the northern temperate zone are less at risk than migratory ones because DDT use is now greatest in near-equatorial latitudes (Goldberg 1975), and far northern Peregrine populations that feed on migrant prey are more contaminated than those which feed on resident prey. For example, the sedentary Peregrine populations of the Aleutian Islands and Queen Charlotte Islands, which feed mostly on resident prey, have remained stable throughout the post-DDT era, while the migratory populations of the mainland interior have declined during the same period (White et al. 1971, 1973, Nelson and Myres 1975). Nygård (1983) noted differences in eggshell thinning and DDE residue levels in the Fennoscandian populations which may be best explained by differential exposure of migrants on the wintering grounds. The thinnest eggshells reported in the world by Peakall and Kiff (1979) were those of Siberian Peregrines, which presumably obtain the bulk of the contaminants in their winter range. The British Isles provide a classic example: the nearly sedentary Peregrines of the Scottish Highlands are least affected by eggshell thinning and population declines, while the western coastal birds, which are more prone to move around in response to a fluctuating food supply of seabirds, are the most severely affected (Ratcliffe 1969).

Peregrines well-removed from actual DDT usage have also suffered less than those in regions heavily populated by humans. A prime example is seen in Australia, where the least amount of thinning for post-DDT Peregrine populations anywhere in the world has been reported from Queensland (3.6%) and western Australia (4.2%) (Olsen and Olsen 1979). Conversely, the most severe eggshell thinning (and recent population decline) in Australia has occurred in Victoria, where DDT usage has been greatest (Olsen and Olsen 1979, Pruett-Jones et al. 1981b). The partial extirpation of the Peregrine in California may have coincided geographically with patterns of DDT usage in the state (C. Thelander pers. comm.). In Britain, Newton (1974) found that European Sparrowhawks more than 20 km away from a source of DDT application were less contaminated than birds residing closer.

Temporal aspects of exposure are probably as important as geographical ones. The immediate eggshell thinning response following the introduction of DDT occurred in heavily populated areas and agricultural districts in North America and western Europe in the vicinity of actual DDT usage (Hickey and Anderson 1968, Newton 1979, Ratcliffe 1980). Populations more remote from actual DDT usage showed a delayed response, but eventually became thoroughly contaminated as DDT became a global pollutant and, as Newton (1979) has suggested, when DDT usage on their wintering grounds became widespread. Anderson and Hickey (1972) found significant eggshell thinning in eggs from all North American Peregrine populations with the exception of a single clutch from Baja California taken in 1948 and specimens taken from British Columbia in 1947-53; both of the latter areas were remote from early DDT use. Arctic Peregrines did not begin to exhibit severe eggshell thinning until the late 1960s (White and Cade 1977), probably reflecting their lack of exposure to significant amounts of DDT in Latin America before then. Anderson and Hickey (1972) noted: "In species with significant population reserves of nonbreeding subadults, a sustained reproductive failure will not affect the known nesting population for several years." This was thought to be the case with Peregrines and Bald Eagles on the California Channel Islands (Kiff 1980), where evidently unsuccessful breeding pairs of Peregrines survived only until the mid-1950s, while the longer-lived eagles remained (but were unable to breed successfully) for a decade or more after the introduction of DDT. Anderson and Hickey's hypothesis may also explain why British Peregrine populations did not show widespread decline until the mid-1950s, despite the fact that eggshell thinning and reproductive failure were documented on a widespread basis several years earlier.

These temporal and geographic factors are important only insofar as they affect prey utilization, since this ultimately determines the relative exposure of Peregrines to DDT-type contaminants. Numerous studies have indicated a relationship between DDE residue levels in prey and levels in Peregrines and their eggs, including those of Cade et al. (1968), Risebrough et al. (1968b), Lincer et al. (1970), White et al. (1973), Pruett-Jones et al. (1981b), and Enderson et al. (1982). The fact that the Baden-Württemberg population in West Germany has held up well has been attributed partly to the fact that those Peregrines did not feed on waterfowl (Rockenbauch 1971). Springer et al. (1984) suggested that the differences in DDE residue levels within arctic Peregrine populations reflected different prey choice.

Another example can be seen in Sweden. In the southern part of the country, the largely resident Peregrines that feed mostly on resident herbivorous birds are less contaminated than the migratory Peregrines of northern Sweden, which not only feed on highly contaminated waders on their breeding grounds, but also winter in western Europe where organochlorine residues are still high (Lindberg et al. 1985). Recovery is therefore proceeding faster in southern Sweden than in the north, and population trends elsewhere in Scandinavia also reflect migratory habits and prey choice (Nygård 1983, Lindberg et al. 1985, Wikman 1985).

The lack of an earlier general population decline in areas where there was over 17% eggshell thinning, such as sections of the British Isles (Ratcliffe 1970), southern Greenland (Falk and Møller Chapter

5), and Victoria, Australia (Olsen and Olsen 1979), was probably owing to the fact that excess young produced in less affected areas moved into more contaminated regions. This movement compensated, to some extent, for adult losses in contaminated areas and thus dampened the rate of population decline. Based on a breakdown of clines in egg size which existed before 1946, Olsen (1982) suggested that Australian Peregrines may have become more genetically homogeneous during the DDT era. This process may have occurred in many other regions where a mosaic of areas of normal and lowered productivity were created by DDE-induced population disruptions.

As we indicated at the outset of this paper, Peregrines have suffered diverse forms of human-induced mortality from time immemorial, and the number and variety of threats to the Peregrine have increased in our highly technological society. The bans on the use of DDT in a number of countries have unquestionably allowed the recovery of many Peregrine populations. Taken together, these bans represent the single most important conservation measure that could be taken to save the Peregrine and many other bird species.

ACKNOWLEDGEMENTS

We wish to thank D. Bird and J. Lincer for permission to use their data on American Kestrels. The California Peregrine eggshell samples were obtained by field teams under the direction of B. Walton of the Santa Cruz Predatory Bird Research Group, and G. Monk of the U. S. Fish and Wildlife Service, with assistance from V. Apanius, L. Aulman, D. Boyce, P. Detrich, M. Felton, M. Kirven, D. Ledig, W. Lehman, R. Lehman, N. Naslund, J. Pagel, R. R. Ramey, K. Stolzenberg, C. Thelander, B. Woodbridge, J. Yablonsky, and other individuals. All eggshells were measured at the Western Foundation of Vertebrate Zoology by C. Sumida, to whom we owe a particular debt of gratitude. J. Fisher assisted with preparation of the manuscript and many other matters. Finally, we are grateful to the Western Foundation of Vertebrate Zoology and the Canadian Wildlife Service for supporting this study.

35 The Relative Importance of DDE and Dieldrin in the Decline of Peregrine Falcon Populations

Ian C. T. Nisbet

There is now general agreement that persistent organochlorine contaminants were the primary cause of the widespread reproductive failures and regional population declines of many species of birds of prey, including the Peregrine Falcon, that took place between 1947-75 (Ratcliffe 1970, 1980, Cade and Fyfe 1970, Fyfe et al. 1976a, Newton 1986, and chapters in this book). However, differing opinions have been expressed about the relative importance of the various organochlorine compounds. British workers (Ratcliffe 1970, 1972, 1980, Newton 1974, 1986) have identified two major mechanisms of population decline: reproductive impairment, caused primarily or exclusively by DDE, leading to reduced recruitment; and excess mortality of adults, caused primarily or exclusively by dieldrin (see Figure 1). While acknowledging that both mechanisms have contributed to population declines in British Peregrine Falcons and other birds of prey, Ratcliffe and Newton have concluded that adult mortality caused by dieldrin was the more important of the two mechanisms, at least for Peregrine Falcons and European Sparrowhawks. They based their conclusions on the temporal and geographical correlations between the declines and subsequent recoveries of British populations of these two species and on the use and subsequent withdrawal of aldrin and dieldrin, combined with the persistence of the populations at other times and places despite some reproductive impairment.

In contrast, most North American workers have regarded reproductive failure caused by DDE as the exclusive cause of population declines in Peregrine Falcons and other birds of prey (Cade et al. 1971, Fyfe et al. 1976a, 1976b, Peakall 1976, Peakall and Kiff 1979, Chapter 34). Many North American papers either fail to mention dieldrin at all (e.g., Berger et al. 1970, Lincer et al. 1970, Cade et al. 1971, Anderson and Hickey 1972, Henny and Wight 1972, Gilbertson and Reynolds 1973, Walker et al. 1973b, Burnham et al. 1978, Peakall and Kiff

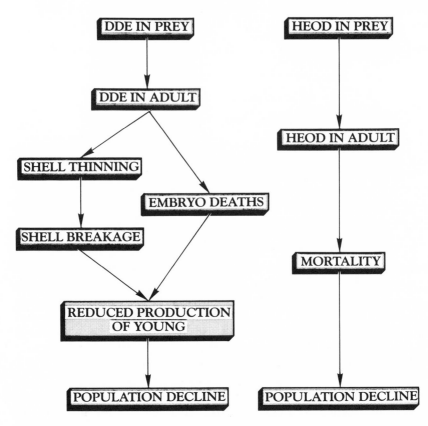

FIGURE 1. Main mechanisms of Peregrine population decline resulting from organochlorine use. From Newton (1986).

1979) or mention it only perfunctorily (Keith and Gruchy 1972,
Jacknow et al. 1986, many chapters in this book). Risebrough (1986)
concluded that pesticide-induced mortality apparently did not significantly affect the population status of any North American raptor
species. Authors from several other countries also have paid little or
no attention to dieldrin (Dyck et al. 1977, König 1977, Lindberg
1981, Pruett-Jones et al. 1981b, Keck et al. 1982, Nygård 1983, Olsen
and Peakall 1983, several other chapters in this book).

Risebrough and Peakall have developed and presented arguments
that reproductive failure caused by DDE could have caused the
population declines and local extinctions of Peregrine Falcon populations in North America. They concluded that increased adult mortality
was a factor in the decline of the Peregrine in eastern North America,
but the decline occurred primarily prior to 1953 and was caused only
by DDT/DDE. However, they did not assess potential exposure to
dieldrin during that period. In this paper, I compile and summarize
information on the extent and intensity of exposure of North American

Peregrine Falcons to dieldrin in the period 1948-72 and discuss whether this exposure was sufficient to have contributed to the population decline. Much of the evidence on both sides is circumstantial, because few reliable measurements of dieldrin levels in the environment are available for the period 1949-63, when the population crash occurred. Two critical issues in the discussion are whether local population crashes took place too rapidly to have resulted from reproductive failure alone (in the absence of excess adult mortality) and, if so, whether the decline coincided with local uses of DDT, dieldrin, or any other biocide.

Discussion of the likely role of dieldrin in contributing to the population decline of North American Peregrine Falcons in no way represents questioning of the conclusion that DDE also played a role in this decline. It is now generally accepted that DDE was the exclusive cause of eggshell thinning in Peregrine Falcons and was the major, if not exclusive, cause of the unusual pattern of reproductive failure (Peakall 1976, Fyfe et al. Chapter 33, Peakall and Kiff Chapter 34). This reproductive failure was in many populations sufficient to lead to failure of recruitment, and would have led to population decline and extinction if it had continued for sufficiently long. The issue addressed in this paper is whether the observed population declines actually took place more rapidly than can be accounted for by failure of recruitment, so that an *additional* effect of excess adult mortality must have occurred.

CHEMICAL TERMINOLOGY

In the remainder of this paper, the terms "dieldrin", "aldrin" and "DDT" are used for the technical insecticide mixtures. Dieldrin contained not less than 85% of HEOD (1,2,3,4,10,10-hexachloro-6,7-*endo*-epoxy-1,4,4a,5,6,7,8,8a-octahydro-*endo-exo*-5,8-dimethano-naphthalene). Aldrin contained not less than 95% of its active ingredient HHDN, which is metabolized in the environment and in animals to yield HEOD. Although many papers report "dieldrin" residues in the environment, what is actually measured is HEOD; such residues are referred to as HEOD in this paper. Use of either aldrin or dieldrin gives rise eventually to residues of HEOD, and these two insecticides will be treated as equivalent in this paper.

Technical DDT contained about 60-70% of p,p'-DDT (1,1,1-tri-chloro-2,2-bis(p-chlorophenyl)ethane), which is metabolized in the environment and in animals to yield p,p'-DDD and p,p'-DDE (1,1-dichloro-2,2-bis(p-chlorophenyl)ethylene). Although p,p'-DDE is a relatively minor product of the metabolism of DDT (Menzie 1969), it is much more stable and more strongly bioaccumulated than the parent material or other metabolites, so that it predominates in most environmental samples. In this paper, the term "DDT" is used to refer to the technical mixture, and "DDE" is used to refer to residues of p,p'-DDE. Although many papers have also reported environmental residues of p,p'-DDD and p,p'-DDT, these residues are not discussed in this paper because these chemicals are thought to contribute little to reproductive failure in birds of prey, and because residues of these chemicals reported prior to 1970 were often confounded with residues of PCBs.

QUANTITIES USED

In Great Britain, DDT was first used on an experimental basis in 1944-45 and then used widely thereafter, whereas aldrin and dieldrin were not introduced until 1956 (Ratcliffe 1970). Table 1 summarizes estimates of the quantities of aldrin, dieldrin, and DDT used for agricultural purposes (i.e., excluding mothproofing and other industrial uses) in Great Britain between 1959-77. The data on domestic sales of aldrin and dieldrin were supplied by the manufacturer (Shell 1974) and are about twice as high as the only previously published estimates (Strickland 1965, 1966, Newton and Haas 1984). Hence, it is possible that Strickland's estimates of usage of DDT, included in Table 1, were also too low. Recognizing this possibility, it appears that the ratio between the total quantities of DDT and aldrin/dieldrin used in Great Britain in the period 1959-69 was between 1:1 and 3:1.

In the United States, DDT was field-tested in 1944 and was widely used from 1945 onwards (Hayes 1959, USEPA 1975). Aldrin and dieldrin were field-tested in 1948-49 and 1949-50, respectively, and were widely used from 1950 and 1951 onwards (Compton 1951, Sloan 1973, Train 1974). Table 2 summarizes data on sales and uses of the three mixtures in the United States between 1949-74. Over this entire period, the ratio between the total quantities of DDT and aldrin/dieldrin used in the United States was about 7:1. However, this ratio was about 30:1 in the period 1950-54. I have not traced any data on usage of these pesticides in Canada.

EARLY PATTERNS OF USE OF ALDRIN AND DIELDRIN

In Great Britain, aldrin and dieldrin were used primarily as soil insecticides or as seed dressings on wheat, sugar beets, potatoes, and brassicas. Other uses that led to significant exposures of waterbirds and scavengers were in sheep-dips and mothproofing (Ratcliffe 1970, Newton and Haas 1984). All these uses were gradually reduced after 1963 as wildlife damage was documented (Table 1).

In North America, aldrin and dieldrin were used for a much wider variety of purposes. Table 3 summarizes the distribution of the principal uses in four years between 1954-71. Between 1949-51, most

TABLE 1. Aldrin, dieldrin and DDT: estimates of quantities (metric tons of active ingredient) used in Great Britain, 1959-77.

Year	Aldrin[a]	Dieldrin[a]	Aldrin and dieldrin[a]	DDT[b] (England and Wales)	DDT[b] (Scotland)
1959	270	92	362		
1960	370	88	458		
1961	300	71	371		
1962	270	90	368		
1963	300	86	386	266[c]	
1964	130	99	229		
1965	100	72	172		58[d]
1966	40	48	88		
1967	62	10	72		
1968	83	10	94		
1969	73	10	83		
1970	62	9	71		
1971	48	8	56		
1972	40	1	41	78[e]	
1973	52	2	54		
1975-77				72	33

[a] Annual listings or sales, excluding industrial uses (Shell 1974).
[b] Estimated usage in agriculture and horticulture (Strickland 1965, 1966, Newton and Haas 1984).
[c] 1962-64.
[d] 1964-66.
[e] 1971-74.

uses of both compounds were on cotton in the southeast, although dieldrin was field-tested for outdoor fly control in at least 25 states in 1949 and 1950 (Compton 1951, Sloan 1973). Large-scale use for grasshopper control, mostly in Plains states, started about 1952, and about 1.6 million ha were treated in 1954. By 1954, major uses had been developed for soil insects on corn, potatoes and peanuts, and for foliage insects on small grains (especially in the Rocky Mountain states) and alfalfa, and on apples (especially in the northeast), and other fruit.

In Illinois, for example, aldrin use increased from 8,000 ha of corn in 1953 to more than 200,000 ha in 1955 (Metcalf 1974). From about 1953, dieldrin was used widely to control mosquitoes and other biting flies, with documented uses in Florida, New York, New Jersey, and Massachusetts. Starting in 1954, dieldrin was used widely in government programs attempting to eradicate introduced pests such as the Japanese beetle, white-fringed beetle, European chafer, imported fire ant, and alfalfa snout beetle; the largest program was for the white-fringed beetle, for which annual usage averaged about 50,000 kg from

TABLE 2.   Aldrin, dieldrin and DDT: estimates of quantities (metric tons of active
ingredient) used in the United States, 1944–76.

Year	Aldrin[a]	Dieldrin[a]	Aldrin and dieldrin[a]	DDT[b]
1944	0	0	0	2000
1945	0	0	0	14,000
1946	0	0	0	20,000
1947	0	0	0	22,000
1948	test	0	test	9000
1949	test	test	test	17,000
1950	662	test	662	26,199
1951	1495	84	1579	33,040
1952	370	341	711	31,851
1953	561	516	1077	28,409
1954	1360	808	2168	20,508
1955	1987	1175	3162	28,091
1956	2952	1652	4604	34,091
1957	1105	1215	2320	32,273
1958	2260	1397	3657	30,318
1959	2530	1367	3907	35,765
1960	3686	1205	4891	31,885
1961	4512	1256	5768	29,122
1962	4948	1359	6307	30,566
1963	5524	1220	6744	27,802
1964	5770	933	6704	22,974
1965	6490	825	7315	24,085
1966	8785	867	9652	21,215
1967	8224	670	8894	18,299
1968	6223	605	6828	14,888
1969	4501	548	5049	13,753
1970	5280	340	4390	11,571
1971	5395	320	5600	8182
1972	5395	336	5731	ca.10,000
1973 (est.)	4682	261	5053	no data
1974	5632	129	5764	no data
1975	ca. 1000	no data	ca. 1000	no data
1976	409	no data	ca. 409	no data

[a] Domestic sales (Sloan 1973, Train 1974, Aspelin 1975, Ackerman 1980).
[b] "Domestic disappearance" for 12-month period ending in middle of year listed
(Stickel 1968, USEPA 1975); figures for 1944-49 are production estimates from
Woodwell et al. (1971).

TABLE 3. Aldrin and dieldrin: end use estimates (metric tons per year) in the United States for four years, 1954–71.[a]

	1954	1964	1968	1971
Aldrin				
Cotton (foliage)	425	9		
Corn (soil)	365	4587	5495	4277
Grasshoppers	216	9		
Potatoes (soil)	131			
Peanuts	37			
Citrus (soil)		16	91	68
Sugar beets		27		
Seed treatment (except rice)	3	36	68	59
Rice seed treatment		107	215	130
Japanese beetles		6		
White-fringed beetles	5			
Dieldrin				
Cotton (foliage)	344	9	1	
Public health (biting flies)	28			
Government programs	60	93	47	
Fruit (foilage)	92	185	99	55
Mothproofing		145	72	
Small grains (foilage)	80	82		
Small packages (home and garden)		103	15	1

[a] Source: Sloan (1973).

1955 until the late 1960s (Sloan 1973). From the late 1950s until 1970, about 120,000 kg were used annually for mothproofing, resulting in substantial discharges into waterways throughout the United States (Benedict 1973). Treatment of rice seeds started in the late 1950s and continued on a large scale until 1974 (Sloan 1973). Treatment of other seeds appears never to have been a major use in the United States (Table 3), although it was significant in the prairie provinces of Canada (Fyfe 1973). I have found no reference to use in sheep-dips in North America.

In summary, both aldrin and dieldrin were in fairly wide use in North America by 1949, seven years earlier than in Great Britain and only four years after the first wide-scale use of DDT. By 1954, both compounds were in use throughout the United States, including many dispersive uses with the potential for significant exposure of wildlife.

EARLY INCIDENTS OF MORTALITY AND RESIDUES IN WILDLIFE

The introduction of aldrin and dieldrin as seed dressings in Great Britain in 1956 was followed immediately by large-scale mortality of wildlife, including pigeons, Ring-necked Pheasants, raptors, and predatory mammals (Turtle et al. 1963, Prestt and Ratcliffe 1972). Similar effects were reported in The Netherlands (Fuchs et al. 1972). In some cases, high residue levels of HEOD were found in the affected birds (e.g., Turtle et al. 1963, Koeman and van Genderen 1966).

In North America, similarly, mortality of wildlife and/or high residue levels of HEOD were reported in a number of incidents during the 1950s and early 1960s. Table 4 summarizes 29 such incidents reported in the United States between 1949-66. Significant incidents of wildlife mortality were reported in at least 21 states, involving all the major uses of aldrin and dieldrin during that period except for uses on corn, cotton, and orchard fruit; significant mortality of birds was reported during this period in both cotton fields and orchards, but was attributed without critical analysis to effects of DDT (e.g., Wilson Ornithological Society (WOS) 1961). Many cases of wildlife poisoning were accompanied by high residues of HEOD in waterfowl or other potential prey of Peregrines (e.g., shorebirds, doves); others involved mortality and severe contamination of species such as fish and crustaceans which serve as food for the prey of Peregrines. A particularly noteworthy report is that of aldrin use on millet and sudangrass grown as food for wild ducks at a state refuge in North Carolina; this led to high residues of HEOD in ducks sampled from flocks of thousands that fed in the treated fields (U. S. Fish and Wildlife Service, Patuxent Wildlife Research Center (USFWS PWRC) unpubl. reports 1960-63). Another noteworthy report is the mortality of thousands of ducks from HEOD poisoning at the Rocky Mountain Arsenal, Colorado, in each year from 1951 until at least 1961 (Finley unpubl. report); dead ducks contained high residues of HEOD, and survivors presumably did so also (Sheldon et al. 1962).

In summary, throughout the period 1949-66, uses of aldrin and dieldrin throughout the contiguous United States led to widespread poisoning and contamination of birds and other wildlife, including species used as prey by the Peregrine Falcon. However, the use that probably led to the greatest exposure of Peregrine Falcons in Great Britain — as a seed dressing on wheat — was not reported to have caused wildlife damage in the United States during this period. Use of aldrin as a seed dressing on rice caused severe damage to birds and other wildlife in Texas, Louisiana, and Missouri, as well as contamination of potential prey of Peregrine Falcons, but this use apparently was not introduced until the late 1950s (Flickinger and King 1972, Sloan 1973).

CONCENTRATIONS OF DDE AND HEOD IN PEREGRINES AND OTHER INDICATOR SPECIES

Concentrations of DDE and HEOD in eggs and tissues of Peregrine Falcons provide information on cumulative exposure in the months

TABLE 4. Reported incidents of bird mortality or other wildlife damage caused by aldrin or dieldrin in the United States, 1949-66.

Year	Location	Target pest or type of use	Application[b] rate (kg/ha)	Animals killed	HEOD[c] in dead birds (ppm)	Reference
1949-50	several states	fly control (field tests)		chickens		Compton 1951
1950-51	MT	grasshopper control	A, 0.14	Red-winged Blackbird		Eng 1952
1950	AR	rice fields	D, 0.11	fish		Hogan in Rudd and Genelly 1956
1951-61	CO	effluent from manufacturing plant	A, D	ducks (2000 per year), American Coots, Ring-necked Pheasants, songbirds, mammals, frogs	3.3-33	Finley unpubl. report, Sheldon et al. 1962
1951	WY	grasshopper control	A, 0.14	merganser, Gray Catbird	4, 63[d]	Post 1952
ca. 1951	ND	lake areas	A, 0.14	ducks, American Coots		Knedel in Rudd and Genelly 1956
1952	CA	rodent fleas	D, 1.3	ground squirrels, rabbits		Ryckman et al. 1953
1953	CA (13 sites)	rice leaf miner	D, 0.57	egrets (hundreds), Mallards, American Coots, shorebirds, Ring-necked Pheasants, doves, fish		Rudd and Genelly 1956
ca. 1954	TX	rice fields	A	fish, crustaceans, reptiles, amphibians		Lehmann and Mauermann 1963

TABLE 4. (continued)

Year	Location	Target pest or type of use	Application[b] rate (kg/ha)	Animals killed	HEOD[c] in dead birds (ppm)	Reference
1954-55	IL	Japanese beetles	D, 2.3	quail, Ring-necked Pheasants, chickens, songbirds, Killdeer, mammals		Scott et. al. 1959
1955	FL	salt marsh sandflies	D, 1.1	fish, crustaceans		Harrington and Bidlingmayer 1958
1955	CA (3 sites)	stink bugs in pear orchards	D, 0.57-1.7	Ring-necked Pheasants, quail, gophers, jack-rabbits, snakes		Rudd and Genelly 1955
ca. 1955	MO	grasshopper control	A	quail		Anon. 1955
ca. 1956	IA	Japanese beetles	D	quail		Sandfort unpubl. report
ca. 1956	CO	Mormon cricket control	A, 0.14	mice		Springer 1956
ca. 1956	NJ	mosquito control	D, 0.14	songbirds		Springer 1956
1956-57	NY	salt marsh tabanids	D, 0.34	fish, crabs		Bryant unpubl. reports
1957-58	GA	fire ants	D, 2.3	quail		Rosene 1958
1957-58	AL	fire ants	D, 2.3	quail	3.3-11.3	Clawson and Baker 1959
1957-59	NC	cinch bugs on waterfowl food plants	A, 2.8	ducks	3.6-5.5	USFWS PWRC unpubl. reports 1960-63

Date	State	Use	Chemical, rate	Species affected	Concentration	Reference
ca. 1957-1959	GA, TX, AL, FL, LA	fire ants	D	ducks, songbirds woodpeckers, mammals, reptiles, amphibians		DeWitt et al. 1960, unpubl. ms.
1958	AL, FL	fire ants	D, 2.3	quail, Blue Jay, Northern Mockingbird	1.1 10.4	USFWS PWRC unpubl. reports 1960-63
1960-62	IL	Japanese beetles	D, 2.3	Ring-necked Pheasants	0.1-15 (5-8, eggs)	Labisky and Lutz 1967
ca. 1960	IL, IA	Japanese beetles	D	songbirds, quail		Bartel in WOS 1961
1960-71	TX, LA	rice seed treatment, rice water weevils	A, 5 g/kg seed	White-faced Ibis, Fulvous Whistling-Ducks, other ducks, Snow Geese, rails, gallinules, shorebirds, Mourning Doves, etc.	1.0-40	Flickinger and King 1972, Flickinger and Meeker 1972
1964	IL	hayfield	D	Red-winged Blackbirds	0.2-5.7 (eggs)	Graber et al. 1965
1966	PA	European chafers	D, 3.4	American Robins, European Starlings, American Woodcocks		Stickel et al. 1969
ca. 1966	TN	white-fringed beetles	D	Eastern meadowlarks, cotton rats, rabbits	2.8-5.5	Stickel et al. 1969

[a] Approximate dates given in cases where precise dates were not reported.
[b] A = aldrin; D = dieldrin; 1 kg/ha = 0.88 lb./acre.
[c] Concentrations of HEOD in whole carcasses or equivalent tissues, wet wt basis.
[d] Reported as aldrin by nonspecific method of analysis.

and years prior to sampling. Concentrations of HEOD in tissues also provide information on the risk of lethal poisoning, because residues of HEOD stored in body fat can be mobilized under conditions of stress, giving rise to lethal concentrations in the brain (Stickel et al. 1969). Concentrations of DDE and HEOD in prey species provide additional information on potential exposure of Peregrine Falcons. Where direct information on exposure or tissue residues of Peregrine Falcons is scanty or lacking, indirect information on exposure can be derived from data on tissue residues in other birds of prey or in other bird species used for environmental monitoring.

This section summarizes the most relevant information available on residues of DDE and HEOD in Peregrine Falcons, their prey, and other surrogate species, during the 1960s. Special attention is given to DDE:HEOD ratios, which provide information on relative exposure, and on data that permit comparisons between measures of exposure in Great Britain and North America. Unfortunately, the available information is limited in several ways. Almost all the residue information dates from 1963 onwards, after the population crash of Peregrine Falcons on both sides of the Atlantic. Although exposure to DDE prior to 1963 has been documented by analyzing extracts from eggs preserved in museums (Peakall 1974, Peakall et al. 1976, Peakall and Kiff 1979), no data on HEOD residues in Peregrines prior to 1961 have been reported.

Monitoring of other birds of prey and of Peregrine prey species began in Great Britain in 1963 and in North America in 1964. Because pesticide use patterns changed rapidly in the 1950s and 1960s (Tables 1-3), residue data collected in the 1960s must be used with caution to infer exposure in the 1950s. No data on residue levels in domestic pigeons, the prey species suspected to be the principal route of exposure of British Peregrine Falcons to HEOD (Jefferies and Prestt 1966), appear to have been reported on either continent. Data on residues in eggs or tissues of living birds provide measures of cumulative, chronic exposure to DDE and HEOD; they generally do not reflect the occasional exposure to highly contaminated prey items which poses the primary hazard of lethal poisoning (Jefferies and Prestt 1966). Data on birds found dead (e.g., Reichel et al. 1969a, 1969b, Coon et al. 1970, Cooke et al. 1982) provide biased information on exposure to HEOD because of the inclusion of birds poisoned by that compound. These factors should be taken into account in evaluating the data summarized in this section.

Tables 5 and 6 summarize data on residues of DDE and HEOD in eggs and livers of Peregrine Falcons in Great Britain, 1961-77. Concentrations of both compounds decreased significantly after 1965 (Cooke et al. 1982), but those of DDE decreased more rapidly, so that the

TABLE 5.   Geometric mean concentrations and ratios of DDE and HEOD in Peregrine Falcon eggs in Great Britain, 1961-77.[a]

Period	n	ppm wet wt ($\bar{x} \pm$ S.E.)		DDE:HEOD
		DDE	HEOD	
1961	1	2.6	1.1	(2.4)
1963-65	23	11.3 (9.9-13)	0.59 (0.49-0.71)	18
1966-71	76	3.6	0.14 (0.11-0.17)	26
1972-75	34	2.0 (1.7-2.3)	0.18 (0.11-0.28)	11
1977	12	2.4 (2.1-2.8)	0.34 (0.25-0.46)	7
All eggs	146	3.6 (3.25-4.02)	0.20 (0.17-0.23)	18

[a] Sources: Ratcliffe (1980), Cooke et al. (1982).

TABLE 6.   Geometric mean concentrations and ratios of DDE and HEOD in livers of Peregrine Falcons in Great Britain, 1963-75.[a]

Period	n	ppm wet wt		DDE:HEOD
		DDE	HEOD	
1963-66	7	12	1.5	7.8
1969-71	7	18	3.2	5.8
1973-75	7	3.7	3.9	0.93

[a] Sources: Jefferies and Prestt (1966), Bogan and Mitchell (1973), Ratcliffe (1980), Cooke et al. (1982).

DDE:HEOD ratio in eggs decreased from about 20 to about 10 (Table 5). DDE:HEOD ratios in livers were generally lower (Table 6), but this was probably owing to the inclusion of birds that died from HEOD poisoning (Cooke et al. 1982).

In the period 1963-74, seven Peregrine Falcons found dead in Great Britain and one found dead in The Netherlands reportedly had HEOD levels in brain and/or liver high enough to be the primary cause of death (Jefferies and Prestt 1966, Bogan and Mitchell 1973, Ratcliffe 1980). Many other terrestrial birds of prey and fish-eating birds in Great Britain and The Netherlands reportedly died from HEOD poisoning in the same period (Jefferies and Prestt 1966, Koeman and van Genderen 1966, Prestt et al. 1968, Koeman et al. 1972, Fuchs et al. 1972, Cooke et al. 1982, Newton 1986). Such mortality was especially severe in bird-eating predators such as the European Sparrowhawk (Koeman et al. 1972, Cooke et al. 1982, Newton 1986).

Table 7 summarizes data on residues of DDE and HEOD in Peregrine Falcons in North America, 1966-70. For this period, data are available only for populations in Canada and Alaska. In these popula-

TABLE 7. Concentrations and ratios of DDE and HEOD in eggs and tissues of Peregrine Falcons in North America, 1966-70.

Area	Year	Sample	n	ppm lipid wt[a]		ppm wet wt (estimated)[a]		DDE: HEOD	Reference
				DDE	HEOD	DDE	HEOD		
Alberta	1966	eggs	8	430	15	19	0.65	29	Enderson and Berger 1968
		adipose	9	330	3.8	39	0.46	86	
Alaska	1966	eggs	2	290	16	12	0.72	17	Cade et al. 1968
		chicks	2	380	8.4	12	0.28	45	
		muscle	4	490	25	23	1.2	19	
Northwest Territories (F. p. tundrius)	1966-70	eggs	4	410	24	18	1.0	17	Fyfe 1972
Canada (F. p. anatum)	1968-71	eggs	15	500	13	22	0.56	39	Fyfe 1972
British Columbia	1969-70	eggs	6	400	15	17	0.67	26	Fyfe 1972
Wisconsin (migrants)	1966	adipose	5	16	0.23	1.6	0.02	70	Enderson and Berger 1968
Wisconsin (migrants)	1969	adipose	10	18	0.40	1.8	0.04	45	Risebrough et al. 1970

[a] Interconversions among dry, wet, and lipid bases assume 74% water in eggs, 68% water in chicks, 74% water in muscle, 86% lipid in adipose tissue, 10% lipid in whole body of migrants (Cade et al. 1968).

tions, DDE:HEOD ratios in eggs were in the range of 17-39, comparable to those in British eggs during the same period (Table 5). Concentrations of HEOD in North American Peregrine eggs in 1966-70 were higher than those in British eggs at the same period and similar to those in British eggs in the period 1961-65, immediately after the population crash. Thus, the data in Tables 5 and 7 provide little evidence for substantial differences in the pattern of contamination of British and North American Peregrines, except that the North American birds may have been exposed to higher levels of DDE; concentrations of both DDE and HEOD decreased earlier in Great Britain.

Two Peregrine Falcons reportedly died in North America with lethal or near-lethal levels of HEOD in their tissues: a migrant in North Carolina in 1973 (Reichel et al. 1974) and a breeding bird in New York City in 1985 (Stone and Okoniewski Chapter 42). Stone and Okoniewski also report several other terrestrial birds of prey dying from apparent HEOD poisoning in New York State in 1982-86. I have found no other reports of terrestrial birds of prey dying from HEOD poisoning in North America, even in the incidents of heavy wildlife mortality associated with early applications (Table 4). However, terrestrial birds of prey that are found dead have not been routinely analyzed in North America; the findings of Stone and Okoniewski suggest that HEOD poisoning in terrestrial birds of prey may have been overlooked in the past. In North America, mortalities of fish-eating birds such as herons (Faber et al. 1972, Ohlendorf et al. 1979, 1981), Bald Eagles (Reichel et al. 1969a, 1969b, Coon et al. 1970, Mulhern et al. 1970), and Ospreys (Wiemeyer et al. 1975, 1980) have frequently been attributed to HEOD poisoning.

Table 8 summarizes residue concentrations of DDE and HEOD in other bird species in Great Britain during the period 1963-68. Other data from this period were published by Moore and Walker (1964), Moore and Tatton (1965) and Cooke et al. (1982). In other raptors, HEOD concentrations were generally higher and DDE:HEOD ratios lower than those of Peregrine eggs during the same period. In Peregrine prey species, HEOD concentrations were generally in the same range as those in Peregrine eggs during the same period, and DDE:HEOD ratios were generally somewhat lower. These comparisons suggest that British Peregrines at this period were less heavily exposed to HEOD than were other birds of prey — perhaps because Peregrines had been eliminated from the most contaminated areas prior to 1963, so that only relatively lightly contaminated birds were sampled after that date (Ratcliffe 1972, 1980).

Table 9 summarizes data on concentrations of DDE and HEOD in other raptors in North America, 1964-73. Compared to the data for

TABLE 8.   Mean concentrations and ratios of DDE and HEOD in eggs of other raptors and in eggs of Peregrine prey species in Great Britain, 1963–68.[a]

Species	Areas	n	ppm wet wt DDE	HEOD	DDE:HEOD
European Sparrowhawk	S.E. England	42	30	4.6	6.5
	northern and western areas	8	11	1.8	6.1
Golden Eagle	W. Scotland	60	0.71	0.75	0.94
	E. Scotland	8	0.11	0.06	1.7
Merlin	all	12	10	2.8	3.8
Eurasian Kestrel	all	29	3.6	0.23	16
Common Buzzard	all	30	0.78	0.72	1.1
Common Raven	all	10	0.95	0.78	1.2
Carrion Crow	all	26	0.34	0.14	2.4
Rook	all	11	0.06	0.13	0.5
Common Murre	all	66	2.12	0.28	7.6
Razorbill Auk	all	49	2.15	0.84	2.6
Black-legged Kittiwake	all	53	0.49	0.09	5.4
Common Black-headed Gull	all	9	1.17	0.27	4.3
Shag	all	43	2.14	1.34	1.6
Golden Plover	all	2	1.53	0.10	15

[a] Sources: Ratcliffe (1970), Prestt and Ratcliffe (1972).

Peregrine eggs in Table 7, the data in Table 9 reflect similar or slightly lower concentrations of HEOD and substantially lower concentrations of DDE, so that DDE:HEOD ratios were substantially lower in eggs of other raptors than in Peregrine eggs. In interpreting these differences, it should be borne in mind that all the samples listed in Table 9 were collected south of the areas where Peregrine eggs were collected during the same period. The samples listed in Table 9 may provide better measures of contamination patterns in the contiguous United States and southern Canada than those in Table 7, at least for the period after 1963.

Compared to the data for British birds of prey in Table 8, the North American data in Table 9 show generally similar levels of DDE, but lower levels of HEOD. However, the British data show much wider variations among species. The only species sampled in both continents were the Merlin, which showed much higher levels of HEOD in Great Britain, and the Golden Eagle, which showed much higher levels of HEOD in west Scotland, but not in east Scotland.

Table 10 summarizes data on concentrations of DDE and HEOD in Peregrine prey species and in other indicator species in North America, 1964-73. The two samples of Peregrine prey species, collected from or near Peregrine eyries in Alberta and Alaska in 1966, had very low levels of HEOD and very high DDE:HEOD ratios. The remaining

TABLE 9. Mean concentrations and ratios of DDE and HEOD in eggs or carcasses of other raptors in North America, 1964-73.

Species	Area	Years	Tissue	n	ppm wet wt DDE	ppm wet wt HEOD	DDE: HEOD	Reference
Prairie Falcon	CO/WY	1967-68	eggs	34	7.1	0.49	14	Enderson and Berger 1972
Prairie Falcon	prairie provinces	1969-73	eggs[a]	161	2.4	0.21[b]	11	Fyfe et al. 1976b
Merlin	prairie provinces	1969-73	eggs[a]	128	9.6	0.46	21	Fyfe et al. 1976b
American Kestrel	NY	1970	eggs	5[c]	11	0.70	15	Lincer 1972
		1971	eggs[a]	6[c]	8.6	0.04	220	Lincer 1975
Cooper's Hawk	AZ/NM	1969-71	eggs	26	3.0	0.08	37	Snyder et al. 1973
Golden Eagle	USA (4 states)	1964-65	carcass	21	0.49[d]	0.09[d]	5	Reichel et al. 1969b
Bald Eagle	USA (20 states)	1964-65	carcass	44	8.4[e]	0.49[e]	17	Reichel et al. 1969b
Bald Eagle	USA (25 states)	1966-68	carcass	69	11[e]	0.55[e]	20	Mulhern et al. 1970
Bald Eagle	USA (3 states)	1966-68	eggs	27	7.4	0.57	13	Krantz et al. 1970
Bald Eagle	USA (4 states)	1969-70	eggs	11	15	0.80	19	Wiemeyer et al. 1972
Osprey	CT	1964	eggs	6	9.9	0.68	15	Wiemeyer et al. 1975
	CT	1968-69	eggs	10	8.9	0.61	15	
	MD	1968-69	eggs	12	2.4	0.25	10	

[a] Converted from dry wt basis assuming 74% water in eggs.
[b] Mean 0.33 ppm in 1967-70 (Fyfe 1973).
[c] Sample size for mean HEOD concentration only; sample size for mean DDE concentration was larger.
[d] Median.
[e] Mean of medians for individual years.

TABLE 10. Mean concentrations and ratios of DDE and HEOD in Peregrine prey species or other indicator species in North America, 1964–79.

Species	Area	Years	Tissue	n	ppm wet wt		DDE: HEOD	Reference
					DDE	HEOD		
Peregrine prey (17 species)	AK	1966	whole body	36	0.90	0.011	78	Cade et al. 1968
Peregrine prey (8 species)	Alberta	1966	whole body	11	0.66	0.01	66	Enderson and Berger 1968
Migratory songbirds (10 species)	FL	1964-66	whole body	7	2.2	0.13	17	Johnston 1974
		1969-70	whole body	14	1.3	0.084	16	
		1972-73	whole body	21	0.75	0.22	2.8	
American Black Duck	Atlantic flyway	1965-66	wing pools	178	0.59	0.058	10	Heath 1969
		1969	wing pools	41	1.4	0.14	10	Heath and Hill 1974
Mallard	Atlantic flyway	1965-66	wing pools	80	0.66	<0.05	>13	Heath 1969
		1969	wing pools	18	1.05	0.05	21	Heath and Hill 1974
	Mississippi flyway	1965-66	wing pools	246	0.17	<0.05	>3	Heath 1969
		1969	wing pools	51	0.40	0.04	10	Heath and Hill 1974
	Central flyway	1965-66	wing pools	130	0.13	<0.05	>2	Heath 1969
		1969	wing pools	49	0.30	0.02	15	Heath and Hill 1974
	Pacific flyway	1965-66	wing pools	237	0.64	0.04	16	Heath 1969
		1969	wing pools	49	0.71	0.02	35	Heath and Hill 1974
European Starling	USA (48 states)	1967-68	whole body pools	360	0.58	0.084	7	Martin 1969
		1970	whole body pools	125	0.36	0.036	10	Martin and Nickerson 1972
		1972	whole body pools	130	0.39	0.035	11	Nickerson and Barbehenn 1975
		1974	whole body pools	126	0.23	0.019	12	White 1976

	Location	Years	Tissue					Reference
Mourning Dove	MO	1970-71	muscle	10	0.22	0.016	14	Kreitzer 1974
	LA	1970-71	muscle	10	0.013	0.002	6	
American Woodcock	LA	1965	carcass	22	1.3	0.09	14	McLane et al. 1971
	USA (23 states)	1970-71	muscle	129	0.22	0.018	12	McLane et al. 1973
	USA (11 states)	1970-71	wing pools	53	0.88	0.031	28	Clark and McLane 1974
	USA (15 states)	1971-72	wing pools	65	0.68	0.13	5	McLane et al. 1978
Herons (4 species)	MD/VA	1969-74	carcass	12	0.75	0.28	2.5	Ohlendorf et al. 1981
	Great Lakes	1970-79	carcass	31	1.7	0.37	4.6	
Herons (7 species)	LA	1969-70	eggs	33	3.8	0.16	24	Faber and Hickey 1973
Fish-eating birds (13 species)	Great Lakes	1969-70	eggs	85	10	0.33	31	Faber and Hickey 1973

samples were all collected in the contiguous United States and represent potential Peregrine prey or appropriate surrrogates. Except for the Mallards and Mourning Doves, the samples listed in Table 10 had residue levels of HEOD in the same range as those listed for potential Peregrine prey species in Table 8. However, the DDE levels and DDE:HEOD ratios were generally higher in the North American samples. The high levels of HEOD in European Starlings, migratory songbirds, American Black Ducks, American Woodcock, and fish-eating birds (including herons, gulls and terns) in the period 1965-71 are particularly noteworthy. All of these samples included potential Peregrine prey, and all were collected to be representative of regional contamination levels. In addition to the systematic regional samples summarized in Table 10, there have been several reports of high levels of contamination of potential Peregrine prey species with HEOD in association with local agricultural uses of aldrin/dieldrin. In addition to those listed in Table 4, these include data on seed-eating birds in the Canadian prairie provinces (Fyfe 1973), bats in Missouri and elsewhere (Clark et al. 1975, 1978, Reidinger 1976, Clark 1981), waterbirds in Texas and Louisiana (Flickinger and King 1972, Flickinger and Meeker 1972, Stickel 1973), shorebirds and waterfowl in California (Rudd and Genelly 1955, Keith and Hunt 1966), and terrestrial birds in Alabama, Mississippi, and New York (Stickel 1968, 1973, Stone and Okoniewski Chapter 42).

Overall, the residue data summarized in this section and in Tables 5-10 are tantalizingly incomplete. Although DDE levels have been measured retrospectively in Peregrine eggs collected as early as 1947, no information is available on exposure of Peregrines to HEOD prior to the population crash. By the mid-1960s, the surviving Peregrine populations in upland Britain and northern North America appear to have been exposed only relatively lightly to HEOD; the North American Peregrines may have been more heavily exposed to DDE than those in Great Britain, and their exposure to both compounds continued for longer. In the southern areas where the Peregrine populations had crashed, the results of monitoring of other species in the mid-1960s suggest that North American birds of prey were generally exposed to higher levels of DDE and lower levels of HEOD than were British birds of prey. However, this generalization is limited by wide variations among species and among geographical areas. The data in Tables 4 and 10 show that local or regional populations of potential Peregrine prey species in many parts of North America were highly contaminated with HEOD during the 1950s and 1960s. Both Peregrines and other birds of prey in North America reportedly died of apparent HEOD poisoning. However, there is no direct information on the exposure of Peregrines to HEOD during the 1950s, either for North America or for Great Britain.

TIMING AND SPEED OF THE POPULATION CRASH

Another approach to the issue raised in this paper is to examine the timing and speed of the declines in the various regional populations of Peregrine Falcons. If reproductive failure were the only proximate mechanism of population decline, then it would be expected that the declines would be relatively slow, and would be delayed initially because of the buffering provided by pools of nonbreeding adults or prebreeding adolescents normally present in healthy populations prior to the onset of reproductive failure (Newton 1979). On the other hand, if excess adult mortality were the proximate mechanism, population declines ought to be more rapid and would coincide more closely with the introduction of the agent causing the excess mortality.

Risebrough and Peakall (in prep.)* have presented population models to support the argument that low productivity alone could account for the disappearance of Peregrine Falcons from eastern North America by 1964, 18 years after the first widespread use of DDT. Their models probably overestimate the rate of population decline, because they assume a constant adult mortality rate of 16.7% and first breeding at age 3; the data of Newton and Mearns (Chapter 62) show that the adult mortality rate can be as low as 10% and that many birds breed at age 2 in a population with vacant breeding sites. Even if Risebrough and Peakall's population parameters are accepted, their models predict gradual population declines in the period 1946-66. Risebrough and Peakall pointed out that the populations in Pennsylvania and Massachusetts had declined more rapidly than their prediction, and concluded that adult mortality was a factor in these declines, but that it had occurred prior to 1953.

Table 11 summarizes reported data on the timing of the declines in 13 regional Peregrine Falcon populations in North America. Although the data on the various populations vary greatly in completeness and precision, wide differences appear in the pattern and timing of the declines. Although several populations persisted into the 1960s, at least five populations (four in the northeastern United States and one in the Midwest) were effectively extirpated by 1957-60, only 10-13 years after the first evidence of reproductive problems. In at least five populations (2 or 3 in the northeast, 2 in the midwest, and that of California), there was evidence of very sharp declines in very short periods between 1954-59. The only data suggesting more rapid decline in a local breeding population prior to 1954 than can be accounted for by lack of recruitment are those from Pennsylvania (Rice 1969).

DISCUSSION AND CONCLUSIONS

The conclusions of Ratcliffe (1980) and Newton (1986) that adult mortality from HEOD poisoning played a major role in the declines of

*Editors' Note: See Commentary, Part V, this volume.

TABLE 11. Timing of reported population declines in regional populations of Peregrine Falcons in North America.

Area	Reported period of decline	Reference
Bonaventure Island, Quebec	3 pairs disappeared about 1960; 1 pair on nearby mainland in 1964	Spofford 1969a
NH, VT, northern NY	19 of 38 eyries active in 1954-55; 19 of 32 active in 1956-57; 1 of 13 active in 1958-59; no birds in 1960 or later	Spofford 1969a
ME	At 3 documented sites, last recorded activity in 1955, 1960 or 1961, and 1962	Berger et al. 1969
MA	26 birds, 8 clutches in 13 sites in 1947; 15 birds, 4 clutches in 10 sites in 1951; 2-3 birds at 4 sites in 1957	Hagar 1969
Hudson River, NY	9 pairs in 1947, 7 pairs in 1950, 5 pairs in 1952, 4 pairs in 1956, 3 pairs in 1957, 0 birds in 1958, 1-2 birds in 1959, 1 bird in 1961; last young raised in 1951; last nesting attempt in 1957	Herbert and Herbert 1969
PA	Occupied sites declined from 16 in 1946-48 to 13 in 1950, 9 in 1951, 6 in 1952, 4-5 in 1953-55, 4 in 1957, 3 in 1958, 1 in 1959, 0 in 1960	Rice 1969
Upper Mississippi River	Sharp decline from 21 birds in 1955 to 8 birds in 1957; slower decline to 4 birds in 1962; last bird in 1964	Berger and Mueller 1969
Niagara Escarpment, MI/WI	4 nests active in 1955-56, all deserted in 1956-58	Berger and Mueller 1969
Alberta	Of 19 documented sites, 6 deserted after 1959, 5 at unknown dates	Enderson 1969a
WY	Of 3 documented sites, 1 deserted after 1950s, 1 after 1958	Enderson 1969a
CO	Of 14 documented sites, 2 deserted in early 1950s, 5 deserted in 1960-65	Enderson 1969a
OR	Of 26 documented sites, 4 last occupied in 1940s, 17 in 1950s, 3 in 1960s	Henny and Nelson 1981
CA	No indication of decline in 1946-50; sharp decline in 1951-60 (especially 1954-59); 1 of 8 sites deserted in 1961-64; no clear evidence of decline in 1965-69	Herman et al. 1970

British populations of Peregrine Falcons and European Sparrowhawks were based in large part on temporal correlations. Both species maintained or increased their populations during the period 1947-55, despite severely impaired reproduction caused by DDE, but they then decreased rapidly in the period 1956-61, following the introduction of aldrin/dieldrin. At least in the case of the European Sparrowhawk, this conclusion was reinforced by the recovery and reoccupation of lost range in coincidence with the progressive reduction in environmental contamination with HEOD (Newton and Haas 1984).

In North America, such temporal and geographical distinctions are more difficult to make. Aldrin/dieldrin were introduced only about four years later than DDT, were used on a similarly wide scale, and were withdrawn only about three years after DDT was banned (Tables 2 and 3). Nevertheless, Table 11 includes several cases in which local or regional populations of Peregrine Falcons appear to have crashed abruptly in the mid-1950s. In the midwestern populations, this crash coincided with the introduction of aldrin as a soil insecticide in the "corn belt" (Sloan 1973, Metcalf 1974), while the crashes in the northeast coincided with the introduction of dieldrin as a foliar spray in apple orchards (Sloan 1973). The Pennsylvania population had shown an earlier sharp decline between 1950-52 (Rice 1969), which was probably too early to have been caused by HEOD poisoning, unless the birds involved had migrated to cotton-growing states in the southeast. This early decline coincided with widespread use of DDT against gypsy moths in the northeast, and may be attributable to DDT poisoning. Data on the California population (Herman et al. 1970) also suggest that the most rapid decline took place in the period 1954-59, coinciding with damaging uses of dieldrin but somewhat later than the introduction of DDT (Rudd and Genelly 1956).

The data compiled and summarized in this paper show that aldrin/dieldrin were widely used throughout the United States by the mid-1950s, and that many uses during that period led to major wildlife damage and contamination of potential Peregrine prey (Tables 3 and 4). Subsequent monitoring of Peregrine Falcons and other species during the 1960s indicated that exposure of Peregrines and certain surrogate species to HEOD in North America was at least comparable to that in Great Britain during the same period (Tables 5-10). Peregrine Falcons and other birds of prey in North America have been diagnosed as having died with lethal or near-lethal tissue levels of HEOD on a number of occasions since 1966. However, wide variations in patterns of contamination among species, among geographical areas, and among time periods make it impossible to draw precise parallels between exposure patterns in Great Britain and North America. Much more aldrin/dieldrin was used in Great Britain relative to DDT than in

North America (Tables 1 and 2). For several species, tissue residues of HEOD were substantially higher in Great Britain (Tables 8-10). For Peregrine Falcons themselves, egg residue levels of HEOD measured in surviving populations were similar in the two areas, while levels of DDE were substantially higher in North America (Tables 5 and 7). Thus, the available data can be used to support the hypothesis that Peregrine Falcons in North America in the 1950s and early 1960s were nearly as much at risk of exposure to HEOD as were those in Great Britain, but that the North American birds may have had substantially higher exposure to DDE. In other words, the exposure data summarized in this paper provide evidence for substantial exposure of North American Peregrine Falcons to HEOD, but do not, by themselves, show whether or not HEOD played a major role in the population crash.

Actual measurements of residues in surviving Peregrine Falcon populations and in their prey during the 1960s suggest that exposure to HEOD was then quite modest (Tables 5, 7-9). Jefferies and Prestt (1966) suggested that HEOD poisoning in Peregrine Falcons and other birds of prey may have resulted from rare encounters with single highly-contaminated prey items, so that the risks would not be reflected in routine monitoring of Peregrine tissues or prey. Although this suggestion is plausible for North America as well as for Great Britain, there is little or no direct evidence to support it. At least in North America, lethal poisoning of Peregrine Falcons might be attributable in some cases to other agents, including DDT itself, DDE, heptachlor epoxide, oxychlordane and endrin. All of these agents have been associated with deaths of other birds of prey in North America (DeWitt et al. 1960, Stickel 1968, Mulhern et al. 1970, Prouty et al. 1982, Blus et al. 1983a, 1983b, 1985a, Henny et al. 1983, Stone and Okoniewski Chapter 42). Even in Great Britain, birds of prey have been reported with liver residues of DDE and PCBs high enough to have caused death (Cooke et al. 1982). Concentrations of heptachlor epoxide were generally higher than those of HEOD in eggs and tissues of British Peregrine Falcons in the period 1963-65 (Ratcliffe 1980), and the former compound may have contributed to adult mortality and reproductive failure in this population.

In conclusion, the declines in some regional populations of Peregrine Falcons in North America were too rapid to have been caused by reproductive failure alone. Excess adult mortality must have occurred in the 1950s in conjunction with reproductive impairment and probably other stresses. Recorded and potential exposure of Peregrine Falcons and their prey to HEOD was sufficiently high and widespread in the mid-1950s to have contributed to excess adult mortality. However, the evidence that it actually did so remains circumstantial for North American as well as British populations. A possible role for other oranochlorine compounds cannot be excluded, even for Peregrine Falcons in Great Britain.

ACKNOWLEDGEMENTS

I thank L. Garret for assistance in tracing obscure references, I. Newton, T. Cade, R. Risebrough, and C. Thelander for helpful discussion, and T. Cade, R. Risebrough, and J. Grier for critical review of an earlier draft.

36 Within-Clutch Variation of Eggshell Thickness in Three Species of Falcons

J. Geoffrey Monk, Robert W. Risebrough,
Daniel W. Anderson, Richard W. Fyfe,
and Lloyd F. Kiff

A reduction in eggshell thickness associated with DDE has been well-documented in several species of the genus *Falco*, including the Peregrine Falcon (Cade et al. 1971, Peakall et al. 1975), the Prairie Falcon (Fyfe et al. 1969, Enderson and Wrege 1973, Fyfe et al. Chapter 33), the Merlin (Fox 1971, Temple 1972, Newton et al. 1982, Fyfe et al. Chapter 33), the American Kestrel (Wiemeyer and Porter 1970, Lincer 1975), the Aplomado Falcon (Kiff et al. 1980), and the Bat Falcon (Kiff et al. 1980). Within a population exposed to variable levels of DDE, the variation in eggshell thickness might be expected to be greater than for pre-DDT era samples. Regression analyses have shown this to be true, with DDE accounting for all or most of the increased variance (Cade et al. 1971, Enderson and Wrege 1973, Peakall et al. 1975, Fyfe et al. Chapter 33).

Highly variable levels of DDE have been recorded among different prey species of the Peregrine Falcon (Cade et al. 1968, Enderson and Berger 1968), and of the Gyrfalcon (Walker 1977); variation in DDE levels within a prey species may also be highly variable (Monk et al. unpubl. ms.). DDE ingestion prior to and during egg laying should vary, therefore, depending upon the prey consumed.

In this paper we examine the hypothesis that the within-clutch variation of eggshell thickness of Peregrine Falcons, Prairie Falcons and Merlins is higher than the pre-DDT condition owing to variable levels of DDE ingestion during egg laying.

METHODS

Almost all of the recent data on eggshells from Peregrine Falcons in California are derived from hatched or broken eggs for which eggshell thickness indices (Ratcliffe 1967) could not be calculated. Therefore, the variation of eggshell thickness within clutches of pre-DDT and post-1946 Peregrine eggshells was examined. The data for Prairie Falcons and Merlins were obtained from intact eggs, and thus eggshell thickness indices (Ratcliffe Index) were used for these two species.

Pre-1947 (pre-DDT era) Peregrine Falcon eggs utilized in this study were collected primarily from southern California (Anderson and Hickey 1972). Eggshells were measured by inserting a micrometer into the hole drilled by the collector at the girth of the shell; four measurements of thickness were made 7 mm from the edge of the hole. These measurements were then averaged to the nearest 0.01 mm for each eggshell. Thickness in each case represented the eggshell itself plus the dried egg membranes. Eggshell thickness indices (Ratcliffe Index) were determined by dividing the weight of the dry eggshell by the product of the length and breadth.

Recent Peregrine Falcon eggs were collected from the mid-coastal and the northern interior regions of California (terminology from Herman et al. 1970), principally for manipulation experiments (Walton et al. Chapter 14). After the eggs failed or were hatched under artificial incubation, eggshell thickness measurements were made at the Western Foundation of Vertebrate Zoology, Los Angeles, with a Federal bench comparator thickness gauge. At least five measurements were taken at the middle latitudes of each whole eggshell. All measurements were made after the eggshell membranes were removed from the samples, and 0.063 mm (the average thickness of Peregrine Falcon eggshell membranes) was added to the mean thickness measurements to permit comparison with historical eggshell thicknesses.

L. G. Swartz (pers. comm.) calculated eggshell thickness indices for 12 clutches of eggs laid by Merlins collected in Saskatchewan and Alberta before 1945 and housed in the museum of the Western Foundation of Vertebrate Zoology. Data from 216 eggs of 47 clutches from Alberta, Saskatchewan, South Dakota, Montana and Wyoming provided information on eggshell thickness of Prairie Falcons before 1945. Single eggs taken from nests soon after clutch completion plus collection of complete clutches that had failed to hatch provided post-DDT samples for Prairie Falcon and Merlin eggs from Alberta (Fyfe et al. 1976b).

Ratcliffe (1980) found that most Peregrine Falcons breeding in Britain lay clutches of 3-4 eggs, but that genuine clutches of two eggs are occasional; incubated single eggs were considered to represent depleted clutches. Because of the frequent loss of eggs from thin-shelled clutches, two-egg clutches in our study were also considered to be depleted clutches, and one-egg and two-egg clutches were not utilized in this study.

The eggshell is a source of calcium for the developing embryo in domestic fowl (Romanoff and Romanoff 1949), and the weight of the eggshell decreases on the order of 5% during incubation (Simkiss 1967). However, changes in thickness and thickness index during incubation were found to be insignificant in several avian species including the American Kestrel (Bunck et al. 1985). The eggshell thickness of Peregrine Falcon eggs was also found not to change during incubation (Burnham et al. 1984). In this study, incubated eggs were considered equivalent to fresh eggs with respect to thickness.

Enderson et al. (1982) and Burnham et al. (1984) treated second clutches of Peregrine Falcons as equivalent to first clutches since eggshell thickness and DDE concentrations did not differ significantly between first and second clutches, although there was an apparent trend toward thinner eggshells after the first clutch, with mean eggshell thickness in the third clutch being significantly lower. Since third clutches of Peregrine Falcon eggs are rarely if ever produced in the wild, we make no distinction in our data between eggs of first and second clutches.

Statistical analyses used SYSTAT statistical software, Version 2.1, on an IBM XT personal computer.

RESULTS

Eggshells of Peregrine Falcons in California from 3-egg, 4-egg and 5-egg clutches over the period 1978-85 (84 clutches, 287 eggs) averaged 18% thinner than the estimated pre-1947 mean of 0.365 mm (54 clutches, 201 eggs) (Table 1). The majority of the recent eggs were obtained from manipulation experiments and were artificially incubated.

Although other studies (Anderson and Hickey 1972) have shown a significant increase in variance* of eggshell thickness in Peregrine Falcon eggs laid in several locations after 1946, the variance of our 1978-85 sample was not significantly greater than that of the pre-1947 samples ($F=1.13$, $P>0.1$, $df=286, 200$). Moreover, the within-clutch

*Editors' Note: The term variance is used in the strictest statistical sense.

TABLE 1. Eggshell thickness of Peregrine Falcon eggs in California, based on whole eggs from 3-, 4-, and 5-egg clutches.

Egg set	Region	No. of clutches	No. of eggs	Clutch means (mm)	Std. dev. all clutches	Means of all eggs (mm)	Std. dev. all eggs
Pre-1947	All regions	54	201	0.365	0.0149	0.365	0.0222
1978-85	Mid-coast	33	116	0.293	0.0194	0.292	0.0244
1979-85	NI[a]	45	151	0.306	0.0145	0.306	0.0209
1978-85	All regions	84	287	0.300	0.0174	0.300	0.0235

[a] NI = Northern interior.

TABLE 2.   Variation in eggshell thickness within and among clutches of California
Peregrine Falcons.

No. of eggs in clutch	Period of collection	Region	Mean squares (df)	
			Among clutches	Within clutches
3	pre-1947	All regions[a]	0.0005062 (13)	0.0002024 (28)
	1978-85	All regions[b]	0.0008834 (49)	0.0003103 (100)
4	pre-1947	All regions[a]	0.0009667 (36)	0.0003782 (111)
	1978-85	All regions[b]	0.0011186 (32)	0.0003229 (99)
3, 4	pre-1947	All regions[a]	0.0009105 (53)	0.0003642 (151)
and 5	1978-85	All regions[b]	0.0010702 (83)	0.0003188 (203)
		Mid-coast	0.0013147 (32)	0.0003246 (83)
		NI[c]	0.0007102 (44)	0.0003222 (106)

[a] Principally southern California.
[b] Principally mid-coast and northern interior regions (designations of Herman et al. 1970).
[c] NI = Northern interior.

variance of the 1978-85 sample (0.0003188, $df=203$) was less than the pre-1947 within-clutch variance (0.0003642, $df=151$), but the differences were not significant ($F=1.14$, $P>0.2$; Table 2).

The 216 eggs from 47 clutches of Prairie Falcons obtained before 1945 in Alberta, Saskatchewan, South Dakota, Montana and Wyoming showed no significant difference in thickness index among the regions ($P=0.17$), and the data were therefore combined (Table 3). The sample of 283 eggs from 230 clutches collected in Alberta and Saskatchewan from 1967-73 showed a mean reduction in eggshell thickness index of 11% over the estimated pre-1945 mean (Table 3). The variance of the recent sample was significantly greater than the variance of the museum eggs ($F=1.98$, $P<0.001$, $df=282, 215$), but

TABLE 3.   Eggshell thickness indices of Prairie Falcon eggs from western Canada and
the northern prairie region.

Period	Region	No. of eggs	No. of clutches	Mean[a]	Variance
Pre-1945	Alberta	13	3	1.91	0.011848
	Saskatchewan	53	11	1.95	0.017577
	South Dakota	17	4	1.91	0.026952
	Montana	63	14	1.94	0.013948
	Wyoming	70	15	1.90	0.013809
	All regions	216	47	1.93	0.015840
1967-73	Alberta and Saskatchewan	283	230	1.72	0.031329

[a] Mean Ratcliffe Index (Ratcliffe 1967) values for all eggs.

the increase in variance was largely owing to an increase in variance among clutches (Table 4). The within-clutch variance had increased in the recent sample, but not significantly so ($F=1.27$, $P>0.05$, $df=53$, 169).

A sample of 190 eggs from 170 Merlin clutches from Alberta obtained from 1969-73 showed a mean reduction of 18% in eggshell thickness index compared to a museum sample of 52 eggs from 12 clutches (Table 5). The variance of the recent sample was significantly increased ($F=2.76$, $P<0.001$, $df=189$, 51). However, the within-clutch variance of the recent sample was less than the within-clutch variance of the museum sample (Table 6).

TABLE 4. Analysis of variation of Prairie Falcon eggshell thicknesses.

Sample	df	Mean squares
Museum group		
Among clutches	46	0.046920
Within clutches	169	0.007381
1967-73		
Among clutches	29	0.066553
Within clutches	53	0.009263

TABLE 5. Eggshell thickness indices of Merlin eggs from Alberta and Saskatchewan.

Period	Region	No. of eggs	No. of clutches	Mean[a]	Variance
Pre-1945	Alberta	37	8	1.32	0.004051
	Saskatchewan	15	4	1.29	0.004051
	Alberta and Saskatchewan	52	12	1.31	0.004785
1967-73	Alberta	190	170	1.08	0.013255

[a] Mean Ratcliffe Index (Ratcliffe 1967) values for all eggs.

TABLE 6. Analysis of variation of Merlin eggshell thicknesses.

Sample	df	Mean squares
Museum group		
Among clutches	11	0.0098
Within clutches	40	0.0034
1969-73 group		
Among clutches	11	0.0484
Within clutches	20	0.0019

DISCUSSION

Feeding studies with captive birds have demonstrated a rapid eggshell thinning response to the ingestion or administration of DDE/DDT. Peakall (1970) found that intraperitoneal injection of 150 mg/kg DDE into Ring Doves within a day before laying reduced the eggshell weight of the following egg. Bitman et al. (1969) fed two groups of Japanese Quail low calcium diets containing 100 ppm o,p'-DDT or p,p'-DDT; in both groups, successive eggs within a clutch showed sharply declining eggshell thicknesses, while a control group laid eggs with only slightly decreasing eggshell thicknesses over time. Peakall et al. (1973) fed 40 ppm DDE to Mallards. Eggshell thickness began to decrease on the second day of feeding. Similarly, Cooke (1975) fed Mallards a daily diet of 24 mg p,p'-DDT per kg body weight; the eggshells of the eggs laid were successively thinner and showed greater variation of thickness than did a control group. These experimental results suggest that populations of *Falco* exposed to variable levels of DDE contamination in their prey during egg laying should show increased within-clutch variation of eggshell thickness.

In Colorado during the 1970s, Enderson et al. (1982) noted that the within-clutch variation of eggshell thickness "was often extreme," but the variation was not quantified. However, Burnham et al. (1984) subsequently found that the within-clutch variation in eggshell thickness of the wild population of Peregrine Falcons in Colorado, expressed as the mean coefficient of variation, was equivalent to that of a captive population on a diet low in DDT/DDE. The wild population showed a mean 16% reduction in eggshell thickness from the estimated pre-DDT mean thickness. This observation, therefore, suggests that this DDE-contaminated population did not show an increased variation in within-clutch eggshell thickness.

Our analyses confirm the finding of Burnham et al. (1984). Comparable variances of eggshell thicknesses in pre-1947 and post-1946 eggs of California Peregrine Falcons are attributed to the overall relatively uniform levels of DDE contamination in recent eggs. Differences between the northern interior region and the mid-coastal region were, however, significant ($P=0.001$, $t=3.495$). Moreover, regression analysis of eggshell thickness versus DDE in egg membrane lipids (Peakall and Kiff Chapter 34) has shown that DDE accounted for a significant portion of the variance in a subsample of the total sample considered here.

The failure to find an increase in the within-clutch variance is surprising. Ingestion of a highly contaminated prey item immediately prior to or during egg-laying may be a sufficiently rare event such that an effect upon the within-clutch variance could not be detected even in the large samples of recent Peregrine Falcon eggs which we examined.

ACKNOWLEDGEMENTS

We thank U. Banasch for compilation of the Prairie Falcon and Merlin data, S. C. Sumida for measuring eggshell thickness of recent Peregrine Falcon eggs, L. G. Swartz for measurements of Merlin eggs, W. Walker II for assistance in computer operations, and B. J. Walton and other personnel of the Predatory Birds Research Group (The Peregrine Fund, Inc.) at Santa Cruz, California for assistance in obtaining Peregrine Falcon eggs and data. Research was supported by the Canadian Wildlife Service and the Bodega Bay Institute.

37 | Organochlorines in Alaskan Peregrine Falcon Eggs and Their Current Impact on Productivity

Robert E. Ambrose, Charles J. Henny,
Robin E. Hunter, and John A. Crawford

Population declines of Peregrines at several locations have been correlated with DDE levels in their eggs, eggshell thinning and hatching failure (Hickey and Anderson 1968, Ratcliffe 1970, Cade et al. 1971, Peakall et al. 1975). In 1966, Cade et al. (1968) first found DDE and the parent compound DDT in eggs of Peregrines and in tissues of young and adult Peregrines from Alaska's interior. Subsequent studies of organochlorines in eggs from Alaska were limited mainly to addled eggs collected from 1968-73 (Peakall et al. 1975).

Alaskan Peregrines declined in the 1960s, stabilized in the mid-1970s, and began to increase in the late 1970s (Ambrose et al. Chapter 11). Those breeding north of the Brooks Range and those on the Seward Peninsula are considered *F. p. tundrius*. Those breeding in interior Alaska south of the Brooks Range are *F. p. anatum* (White 1968a).

Our objectives were to determine: (1) organochlorine residue levels in Peregrine eggs from *F. p. tundrius* and *F. p. anatum* during the late 1970s and early 1980s, and compare these with published information from the late 1960s and early 1970s, (2) whether DDE residues in addled eggs were similar to those in fresh eggs for populations we studied, and (3) whether current levels of organochlorine residues in eggs adversely influenced reproductive success.

METHODS

We evaluated organochlorine residues in addled Peregrine eggs collected in Alaska during the late 1970s and early 1980s and in 20 random eggs collected during the 1984 nesting season (no more than one egg per sampled clutch). We defined addled eggs as those that had not hatched at banding time, whereas random eggs were collected during incubation.

Pairs were located during an initial survey each year. Sample sites were selected randomly once eyrie occupancy was determined. However, eyries difficult to reach, resulting in long disturbance times to the pairs, were not used. In 1984, 10 eggs were randomly collected from both *F. p. anatum* and *F. p. tundrius* populations. Within the *F. p. anatum* population, eight eggs came from the upper Yukon River and two from the Tanana River. Within the *F. p. tundrius* population, eight eggs were taken from the Colville River and two from the Sagavanirktok River. Numbers of eggs collected were based on the average number of breeding pairs in 1982 and 1983, i.e., about 25 pairs each for the Yukon and Colville rivers and five pairs each for the Tanana and Sagavanirktok rivers. Two randomly collected eggs of *F. p. tundrius* were not analyzed owing to mishaps. Addled eggs were collected from 36 eyries between 1979-84 ($n=28$, 1982-84) for organochlorine analyses.

The "sample egg" technique has been used to evaluate reproductive performance in relation to pollutants in several free-living raptors including the Eastern Screech-Owl (Klaas and Swineford 1976) and American Kestrel (Henny et al. 1983). Residues from sample eggs collected in 1984 were evaluated in relation to reproductive success of remaining clutches. We evaluated intraclutch variability of DDE (of primary concern) because low variability is required for the "sample egg" approach to be effective. The number of young produced was determined at banding when young were approximately three weeks old (=fledged in text).

Eggs were analyzed at Patuxent Wildlife Research Center for: p,p'-DDE, p,p'-DDD, p,p'-DDT, dieldrin, heptachlor epoxide (HE), oxychlordane, *cis*-chlordane, *trans*-nonachlor, *cis*-nonachlor, endrin, toxaphene, and polychlorinated biphenyls (PCBs) (Cromartie et al. 1975, Kaiser et al. 1980). In addition, 1979 eggs were analyzed for beta-HCH (beta isomer of hexachlorocyclohexane), and eggs from 1979-80 were analyzed for hexachlorobenzene and mirex. The lower limit of reportable residues was 0.1 ppm for pesticides and 0.5 ppm for PCBs. We calculated geometric means when at least 70% of the samples contained a given contaminant and assigned one-half the lower limit of detection to those samples where no residues were detected. We converted egg contents to an approximated fresh wet weight based on egg volume (Stickel et al. 1973); residues were expressed on a fresh wet weight basis. Eggshell thickness (shell and shell membranes) was measured at three sites on the equator of each egg with a micrometer graduated in units of 0.01 mm; the average was used to represent eggshell thickness.

A paired *t*-test was used to compare DDE residues in addled and random eggs from the same clutch, and an unpaired *t*-test was used to compare DDE residues (log transformed) in random and addled *F. p. anatum* eggs from different clutches in 1984. The same tests with untransformed data were used to evaluate eggshell thickness of random and addled eggs. An unpaired *t*-test was used to compare DDE residues (log transformed) in the combined addled and random eggs of *F. p. tundrius* and *F. p. anatum*. The year-to-year numbers of eggs analyzed for each subspecies were similar, with 68% of *F. p. tundrius* eggs and 77% of *F. p. anatum* eggs collected in 1983-84. Again the same test, but with no log transformation, was used for eggshell thickness. Chi-square tests were used to compare occurrence of DDT between subspecies. We accepted the significance level of 0.05 for all tests.

RESULTS

DDE and DDT in Peregrine Eggs. — Four eyries in 1984 were represented by both a random and an addled egg, and they showed no significant difference in DDE residues ($t=0.88$, $P>0.05$; geometric mean$=8.3$ ppm, random and 8.2 ppm, addled). In addition to the four paired samples in 1984, there were seven random eggs and six addled eggs of *F. p. anatum* which also showed no significant difference (geometric means of 12.5 ppm and 12.6 ppm, respectively; $t=0.04$, $P>0.05$). The random and addled *F. p. anatum* data for all years were combined (if more than one egg was obtained from a clutch, the arithmetic mean residue value was used and treated as one observation) and yielded a geometric mean of 10.6 ppm DDE ($n=31$), whereas combined *F. p. tundrius* eggs yielded a geometric mean of 9.3 ppm DDE ($n=19$) (Table 1), with no significant difference between subspecies ($t=0.67$, $P>0.05$). The combination of all eggs obtained during the study resulted in a geometric mean of 10.1 ppm DDE.

A comparison of *F. p. tundrius* eggs with *F. p. anatum* eggs indicated that a higher proportion (32%) of *F. p. tundrius* eggs had detectable levels of *p,p'*-DDT ≥ 0.1 ppm than the *F. p. anatum* eggs (6%) ($\chi^2_1=5.53$, $P<0.02$). Of special interest were the eight eggs that contained *p,p'*-DDT at levels >0.1 ppm, since they included three of the five highest DDE egg values recorded during the study (46 ppm, 31 ppm, 31 ppm, 27 ppm, 26 ppm); two eggs with DDE residues of 31 ppm contained lower levels of DDT.

Eggshell Thickness. — In 1984, the four eyries represented by both a random and an addled egg showed no significant difference in eggshell thickness (0.328 mm and 0.323 mm, $t=0.50$, $P>0.05$). Likewise, seven random and six addled *F. p. anatum* eggs in 1984 (0.316 mm and 0.307 mm) were not significantly different ($t=0.72$, $P>0.05$). Mean eggshell thickness for random and addled *F. p. anatum* eggs was 0.313 mm, whereas mean eggshell thickness for *F. p. tundrius*

TABLE 1.   The distribution of DDE residues (ppm wet wt), in Peregrine eggs from
           Alaska, the incidence of DDT residues, and mean eggshell thickness and
           percent thinning, 1979-84.[a]

Category	F. p. tundrius	F. p. anatum
No. eggs with ≤ 10.0 ppm DDE	11	16
No. eggs with 10.1-15.0 ppm DDE	4	6
No. eggs with 15.1-20.0 ppm DDE	1	3
No. eggs with 20.1-30.0 ppm DDE	1	5
No. eggs with > 30.0 ppm DDE	2	1
Total no. eggs sampled	19	31
Geometric mean (ppm DDE)	9.3	10.6
No. eggs with ≥ 0.10 ppm DDT	6	2
% eggs with ≥ 0.10 ppm DDT	32	6
Mean eggshell thickness (mm) ±S.D.	0.311 ± 0.026	0.313 ± 0.019
No. eggshells measured	21	34
% eggshell thinning[b]	13.6	13.1

[a] If more than 1 egg was obtained from a clutch, the mean residue value or mean
    eggshell thickness was used and treated as 1 record.
[b] Compared to pre-1947 mean thickness of 0.360 ± 0.007 mm (±95% C.L.) for 53
    eggs from arctic and subarctic Alaska.

was 0.311 mm (Table 1); there was no significant difference between subspecies ($t=0.30$, $P>0.05$). Overall eggshell thickness during the study was 0.312±0.022 mm (mean ± S.D., $n=55$).

Nesting Success and DDE. — Two or more eggs were analyzed at nine eyries and provided examples of generally low DDE intraclutch variability, as follows (in ppm, with semicolons separating clutches): 13, 12 and 11; 15 and 12; 34, 31 and 27; 18, 15, 12 and 12; 10 and 9.4; 4.9 and 4.3; 8.2 and 8.0; 13 and 12; 8.3 and 8.2. The order of egg-laying was unknown in the series.

In 1984, twelve randomly selected eyries with ≤15 ppm DDE in the sample egg produced 1.8 young per eyrie, while six eyries with >15 ppm DDE produced 1.7 young per eyrie (Table 2). However, reproduction values were not adjusted for the one egg collected from each eyrie mentioned above. Addled eggs collected at banding time provided supplementary information on nesting success relative to DDE residues (Table 2). Four of seven eyries were successful when addled eggs contained >15 ppm DDE.

Other Contaminants. — All eggs contained PCBs, and nearly all had detectable levels of HE and dieldrin (Table 3). In 1984, three random eggs contained >1 ppm HE (3.3 ppm, 1.9 ppm, 1.2 ppm), and each eyrie produced two young. Between 1979-83, addled eggs at two eyries contained >0.50 ppm dieldrin; one eyrie (0.70 ppm) produced two young, and one eyrie (1.68 ppm) failed. The four addled eggs at

TABLE 2. Clutch size of Alaskan Peregrines and number of young fledged, arranged according to DDE residue levels (ppm wet wt) in fresh randomly collected and addled eggs.

DDE residues (ppm)	Random sample (1984)[a]					Addled sample (1979-84)[b]				
	No. clutches sampled[c]	Mean clutch size[d]	Mean no. fledged per eyrie	No. eyries	No. successful eyries[e]	No. clutches sampled	Mean clutch size	Mean no. fledged per eyrie	No. eyries	No. successful eyries[e]
≤15.0	12	3.4	1.8	12	9	11	3.6	1.4	25	15
15.1-30.0	4	3.8	2.0	4	4	2	3.5	1.2	6	4
>30.0	2	2.5	1.0	2[f]	1[f]	1	3.0	0.0	1	0
Overall	18	3.39	1.78	18	14	14	3.57	1.31	32	19

[a] 1 egg per clutch was collected for residue analysis.
[b] Includes only those eyries containing an addled egg at banding time (when young were about 3 weeks old), thus probably biased toward less successful eyries. No randomly sampled eyries included, even if addled egg was collected later.
[c] Eyries visited during incubation.
[d] Includes sample egg collected.
[e] Successful eyrie means with at least 1 young at banding time (about 3 weeks old).
[f] Egg from the unsuccessful eyrie contained 31 ppm DDE: egg from the successful eyrie (2 young fledged) contained 46 ppm DDE.

TABLE 3.   Organochlorine contaminants other than DDT-related compounds (ppm wet wt) in Peregrine eggs from Alaska, 1979-84.[a]

Contaminant	F. p. tundrius (19 eggs)[b]			F. p. anatum (31 eggs)[c]		
	Geometric mean	No. eggs with ≥ 0.10 ppm	Highest residue (ppm)	Geometric mean	No. eggs with ≥ 0.10	Highest residue (ppm)
Dieldrin	0.25	16	1.68	0.16	26	0.70
Heptachlor epoxide	0.24	16	1.90	0.33	29	3.32
Oxychlordane	0.12	14	0.28	0.14	22	0.96
Trans-nonachlor	NC[d]	2	0.29	NC[d]	1	0.11
PCBs (estimated)	2.04	19[e]	6.30	2.65	31[e]	28.0

[a] If more than 1 egg was obtained from a clutch, the mean residue value for each contaminant was used and treated as 1 record.
[b] Mirex was found in 4 of 5 eggs analyzed in 1979-80; highest residue was 0.43 ppm. Beta-HCH was found in 1 of 4 eggs analyzed in 1979 (0.22 ppm).
[c] Mirex was found in 3 of 3 eggs analyzed in 1979-80; highest residue was 0.18 ppm; cis-chlordane was found in 1 egg (0.21 ppm) and endrin in 2 eggs (both 0.10 ppm).
[d] NC = not calculated.
[e] No. eggs ≥ 0.50 ppm.

the latter eyrie also contained 14 ppm (wet wt) DDE. Dieldrin above 0.70 ppm was not found in 1984 Peregrine eggs; two of three eyries with egg dieldrin levels of 0.50-0.70 ppm were successful and fledged two and three young, respectively. The egg from the eyrie that failed in 1984 contained not only 0.70 ppm dieldrin, but also 24 ppm DDE, 0.51 ppm HE and 27 ppm PCBs. This eyrie (the Robertson River bluff site, Tanana River) also failed in 1982, when its three addled eggs averaged 0.43 ppm dieldrin, 12 ppm DDE, 1.2 ppm HE and 28 ppm PCBs. The same female occupied this site in 1982 and 1983 (4 young produced in 1983), but a different female was at the site in 1984. Thus, the high levels of PCBs may be unique to the site rather than the individual females. During the study, only one other egg contained PCBs over 7.0 ppm — an addled egg from a Porcupine River eyrie that produced three young in 1982 contained 8.7 ppm PCBs.

DISCUSSION

Peakall et al. (1975) reported in excess of 20% eggshell thinning along the Colville, Yukon and Tanana rivers in the late 1960s and early 1970s and identified a significant relationship between eggshell thickness and DDE levels. Furthermore, Peregrines in interior Alaska were declining in the late 1960s and early 1970s (Cade and Fyfe 1970, Cade et al. 1971, White and Cade 1971), and arithmetic means of DDE in eggs for various river populations were 20-40 ppm wet weight (Peakall et al. 1975). It was tentatively concluded by Peakall et al. (1975) that egg residue levels of 15-20 ppm DDE wet weight in eggs were associated with the Peregrine's inability to maintain population numbers. However, they emphasized that this value was not based on sample eggs and reproductive success from specific eyries, but corresponded with the suggested critical value of 20 ppm DDE derived from eggshell thinning data.

Our analyses of DDE content were based on fresh and addled eggs. We compared our results with previous data obtained mainly from addled eggs. Geometric means of DDE residues in our study were substantially lower than previously reported: *F. p. anatum*=10.6 ppm, *F. p. tundrius*=9.3 ppm; combined geometric mean of 10.1 ppm (n=50 eyries); combined arithmetic mean of 12.6 ppm. Pre-DDT era eggshell thickness for Peregrines from arctic and subarctic Alaska was 0.360 ± 0.007 mm (mean ± 95% C.L., n=53) (Anderson and Hickey 1972). Anderson and Hickey reported 19-23% eggshell thinning in arctic and subarctic Alaska during the period 1952-57 and 1964, based on 11 eggs. Their values were similar to those reported by Peakall et al. (1975) for the same region in the late 1960s and early 1970s. Eggshells during our study showed only 13.3% thinning.

Of the 20 eyries each represented by a randomly collected egg in 1984, 16 (80%) were successful. They produced 37 young, or 1.9 young per pair. We judge this reproduction to be excellent, particularly since one egg was collected from each clutch during early incubation. On the upper Yukon River in 1984, 21 of 25 (84%) *F. p. anatum* pairs were successful and fledged 48 young (eight eggs were collected), or 1.9 young per pair (Ambrose et al. Chapter 11). Production on the upper Yukon River in 1979, 1980, 1981, 1982, 1983 and 1985 was 2.1, 2.6, 3.0, 1.7, 2.1 and 1.6 young per pair, respectively. On the Colville River in 1984, 18 of 31 (58%) *F. p. tundrius* pairs were successful and fledged 47 young (8 eggs were collected), or 1.5 young per pair (Ambrose et al. Chapter 11). In 1984, reproduction on the Colville River was somewhat lower than on the Yukon River; however, the numbers of young per pair on the Colville River in 1982, 1983 and 1985 were 1.9, 2.0 and 1.7, respectively. Prior to 1982, Colville River production was considerably lower (0.9 young per pair in 1979, 1.4 young per pair in 1980, 1.3 young per pair in 1981) than during the last four years (see Ambrose et al. Chapter 11). Some Peregrines in our 1984 study laid eggs containing >15 ppm DDE and produced young. Our data indicate that the cutoff point suggested by Peakall et al. (1975) of 15-20 ppm DDE in eggs should not be construed as so rigid that it can predict the success or failure of individual Peregrine eggs. We believe that a gradual reduction in productivity occurs above a DDE level that is not yet precisely known. A similar pattern was reported for American Kestrels in relation to HE (Henny et al. 1983) and for the Black-crowned Night-Heron in relation to DDE (Henny et al. 1984). It appears that present levels of DDE (see Table 2) have a minimal effect on reproduction in these populations. The above conclusion is not in direct conflict with the statement of Peakall et al. (1975) that inadequate production for population maintenance occurs if the mean (unspecified if arithmetic or geometric) residue for the population is above 15-20 ppm DDE. On a population basis, the DDE residues in Alaskan Peregrine eggs in recent years were below this published critical range, and the population has actually been increasing (Ambrose et al. Chapter 11).

DDE residues in eggs from Alaska (1979-84) were slightly lower than from Greenland (1972-78). Eight addled eggs from Greenland averaged 14.3 ppm DDE (arithmetic mean) or 13.0 ppm DDE (geometric mean) (Burnham and Mattox 1984). The eight eyries were all successful and fledged an average of 2.1 young. The highest DDE egg residue in the series was 22.8 ppm, and eggshell thinning averaged 16%. Burnham and Mattox (1984) reported no indication of a population decline, and production averaged 1.9 young per occupied site during their longterm investigation.

The occurrence of the parent compound DDT in samples has been an indicator of exposure to recently applied DDT (Henny et al. 1982a). Although the DDE residues in *F. p. tundrius* were not significantly different from those of *F. p. anatum*, the increased frequency of measurable DDT in its eggs suggests that *F. p. tundrius* from Alaska and/or its prey species may be wintering in different areas than *F. p. anatum* from Alaska.

Effects of specific levels of other organochlorines on Peregrines are not well understood, and sensitivity differs considerably among avian species. For example, more than 1.5 ppm HE in American Kestrel eggs resulted in reduced reproduction, but did not result in total reproductive failure until egg residues were above 6 ppm (Henny et al. 1983). In contrast, the Canada Goose showed no signs of reduced reproduction until HE egg residues were above 10 ppm (Blus et al. 1984). Henny et al. (1983) found no negative impact on reproduction when dieldrin was in the 2.2-3.9 ppm range in American Kestrel eggs. No obvious relationship to reproductive success was seen between HE and dieldrin residues in Alaska Peregrines. PCBs were generally low with the exception of the eyrie located along the Tanana River at the mouth of the Robertson River.

Peregrine populations in interior Alaska declined to their lowest point in the early 1970s, but have increased steadily since (Ambrose et al. Chapter 11). Reproduction rates at numerous locations in more northern latitudes (Mattox and Seegar Chapter 4, Bird and Weaver Chapter 6) and counts during fall migration (Ward et al. Chapter 45) have been increasing for several years. We believe the impact of DDT/DDE on Peregrines in Alaska at present is minimal, and populations are recovering.

ACKNOWLEDGEMENTS

We appreciate the field help from R. Dittrick, K. E. Riddle, P. F. Schempf and J. B. Silva. We thank O. H. Pattee, R. C. Stendell and S. N. Wiemeyer for preparing eggs for analyses. This study is part of a Co-operative Education Agreement between the U. S. Fish and Wildlife Service and Oregon State University. We thank T. W. Custer for his comments on an early draft of the manuscript, and C. M. Bunck for statistical advice.

38 | Eggshell Thinning and DDE Residues in Rocky Mountain Peregrines

James H. Enderson, Gerald R. Craig, and Daniel D. Berger

Since 1976, an intensive program of nest site manipulation and management has been undertaken with the Peregrine population in Colorado. Sets of eggs were removed from nests prior to the fostering of captive-bred young (Burnham et al. 1978), providing a large sample of eggs for eggshell measurement and DDE residue analysis. We reported early results through 1979 (Enderson et al. 1982). The present paper summarizes data gathered during 1973-85 in Colorado and northern New Mexico, and on the thickness of eggshell fragments collected from 14 territories in Utah in 1985.

METHODS

Most eggs from Colorado and New Mexico were collected as entire sets and incubated artificially. The contents of those failing to hatch in 1973-75 were analyzed for organochlorine residues using techniques described by Peterson et al. (1976) and from 1976 onward, by the method of Cromartie et al. (1975).

In Utah in 1985, we collected eggshell fragments from nest ledges known to have been used in 1984-85. After young fledged, we screened the substrate with a 3.5 mm wire mesh. Fragments found were separated manually into age categories: (1) current-year eggshells with unfaded pigment, or (2) faded (usually white) fragments from earlier years. Some of the latter may have been from the Prairie Falcon, although it is much less common than the Peregrine in the area. Because there is little variation in eggshell thickness for a given egg, but sometimes great variation between eggs (Burnham et al. 1984), we lumped fragments with similar thicknesses and calculated mean thicknesses for such fragment sets. Fragment set means were averaged to yield a clutch mean.

All eggshells were measured optically by an ocular scale calibrated
with a stage micrometer. This technique was accurate to ±0.004 mm.
When entire eggshells were available, three measurements were made
around the equator. Older fragments often lacked eggshell membranes;
0.078 mm, the average membrane thickness of many recent eggs
(Burnham et al. 1984), was added to such measurements.

RESULTS

Eggshell Thickness. — The period 1973-85 yielded 294 eggshells
from 23 localities in Colorado and northern New Mexico. Of these,
34 were from 1973-76, and eggshell thicknesses (some reported in
Enderson and Craig 1974) averaged about 0.301 mm with membranes.
Eggshell thickness of the remaining 260 eggs for 1977-85 are shown in
Figure 1. A few values for eggshells from second clutches, especially
before 1980, are plotted; thickness of eggshells from first and second
clutches were shown not to differ significantly (Burnham et al. 1984).

Because of the great variation in eggshell thickness within clutches,
only the 1977 mean of 0.292 mm was significantly different from
those of later years (*t*-tests, *P*<0.05). The eggshells from 1973-76 were
few and the variation great. After 1977, the yearly averages ranged
from 0.306 mm (1980) to 0.325 mm (1982), but the differences were
not significant. The 1982 mean may have been atypically high because
no drastically thin eggshell was found as in other years.

Recently, the annual average eggshell thickness has been about
0.317 mm, or 12% thinner than the pre-1947 mean of 0.359 mm for

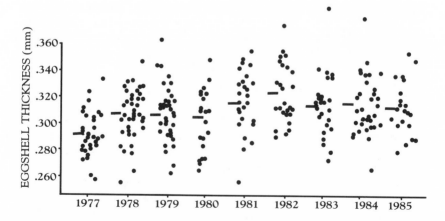

FIGURE 1.   Thickness (mm) of individual Peregrine eggshells collected in Colorado
            and New Mexico, 1977-85. Data for eggshells from each territory are
            aligned vertically; the horizontal bars are annual arithmetic means.

eggshells from this region (Anderson and Hickey 1972). In 1977, only 3 of 32 eggshells measured were thicker than 0.317 mm.

Eggshell fragments from Utah appeared to differ in thickness by year and by habitat (Figure 2). Eggshell fragment sets from eggs laid in desert scrub habitat prior to 1985 averaged 0.341 mm compared to 0.310 for those laid in 1985 (t-test, P<0.001). Similarly, those laid in montane habitat above 2300 m averaged 0.315 mm prior to 1985 and 0.284 mm in 1985 (t-test, P<0.007). About one-third of the pre-1985 group included fragment sets laid in 1984; the remainder may have been laid several years before.

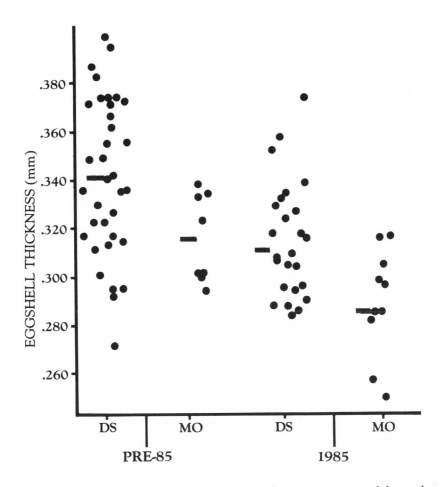

FIGURE 2. Thickness (mm) of Peregrine eggshell fragment sets screened from substrate of eyries in two habitats in Utah, 1985. Data from each territory are aligned vertically, and the horizontal bars are annual arithmetic means. DS=desert scrub; MO=montane.

Fragment sets laid at territories in desert scrub below 1200 m elevation were significantly thicker than those laid in montane habitat. The sets laid prior to 1985 in desert scrub were significantly thicker (*t*-test, P<0.006) than those from higher elevations, and the same is true for the parallel comparison of 1985 fragments (*t*-test, P<0.009). In contrast, there was no apparent pattern between eggshell thinning and elevation or habitat type among the data from Colorado and New Mexico, where most Peregrine territories included several habitat types.

Organochlorine Residues. — The contents of 78 eggs collected during 1973-83 were analyzed for organochlorine residues. Most were incubated artificially and showed no development or had embryos that died before hatching. The DDE (ppm wet wt corrected for desiccation) amounts are shown in Figure 3, where eggs from the same territory and same year are averaged. In a few cases, values for both first and second clutches are also averaged. Very seldom did DDE levels in eggs from the same female in a given year differ by more than a few ppm, and clutch means usually had small standard errors; eggs from second clutches usually had lower DDE levels than first clutches, but not significantly so (Enderson et al. 1982). The geometric means for the years 1973-79 averaged 26 ppm, and for 1980-83, 15 ppm, but the difference was not significant (*t*-test, P=0.15).

Other organochlorine residues detected included PCBs, with a geometric mean of about 2 ppm in 1973-79 (Enderson et al. 1982). After 1979, PCBs seldom exceeded 1 ppm.

Before 1976, egg contents were analyzed for DDE and PCBs only; after 1976, several compounds were quantified. DDT was found above detection limits in 59% of the 69 eggs examined in 1976-83, but seldom exceeded 0.5 ppm. Dieldrin and heptachlor epoxide were detected in most eggs; the former was usually less than 0.25 ppm and the latter less than 0.75 ppm.

There was no statistically significant relationship in our data between eggshell thickness and DDE residues in egg contents. The correlation coefficient for that comparison for 66 first-clutch eggs laid in 1973-83 was very low (*r*=−0.117, P>0.20).

In three instances, residues in egg contents were determined for eggs laid by the same female in different years (Table 1). The identity of the individuals was determined photographically, as described by Enderson et al. (Chapter 12). Except for one instance (SI 1982), the DDE levels were surprisingly similar in eggs laid by the same female up to four years apart.

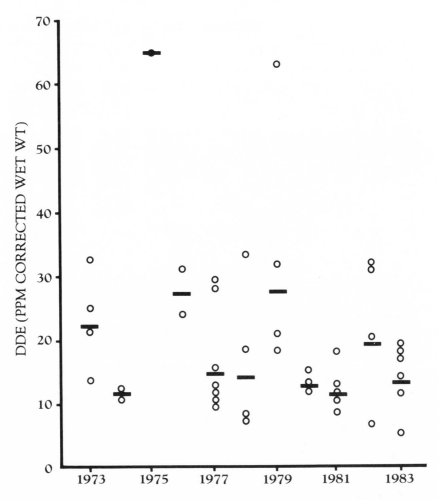

FIGURE 3. DDE values for Peregrine egg contents from different territories arranged by year. Each point is the mean of all eggs collected; bars are geometric means.

TABLE 1. DDE residues in egg contents laid by 3 Peregrines, 1980-83.

Female[a]	DDE residues, ppm corrected wet wt (no. of eggs)			
	1980	1981	1982	1983
No. 1 (HH)	11.6 (4)	13.2 (1)		11.3 (1)
No. 2 (CE)	15.3 (4)		20.4 (3)	18.1 (3)
No. 3 (SI)		11.8 (1)	32.0 (1)	14.3 (1)

[a] The identities of the females were determined photographically. See Enderson et al. (Chapter 12).

DISCUSSION

Eggshells. — Post-1976 eggshell samples in this study were probably not significantly biased because entire clutches were taken from several territories each year in Colorado and New Mexico. We expect that the Utah samples included fragments from thin-shelled eggs that broke prematurely or were broken by hatching, providing the opportunity to collect the actual spectrum in eggshell thickness.

Generally, there has not been an improvement in eggshell thickness in the Rocky Mountain sample since 1981, and probably not since 1978 (Figure 1). The recent average, 12% thinning, is less than the mean level of thinning of 16% in the expanding Peregrine population of northern California (see Monk et al. Chapter 36). Cade et al. (1971) found that Peregrines experiencing about 7% thinning can maintain an apparently stable population, and Enderson and Wrege (1973) found normal production in Prairie Falcons with 10% eggshell thinning. In 1984-85, 11 pairs of Peregrines in Colorado produced 1.4 young per occupied territory (see Enderson et al. Chapter 12); if sustained, the rate is probably adequate to maintain a stable population but inadequate to produce an early recovery in the severely depressed population in the central Rocky Mountains.*

The eggshell fragments collected in Utah clearly show that Peregrines nesting adjacent to desert scrub habitat produce thicker eggshells than their montane counterparts. Pre-1985 samples from desert scrub territories, some of which may be decades old, showed only minor thinning, but the 1985 samples were similar to their recent Colorado counterparts, about 14% thinner than normal. The thinnest sample set we have seen is from montane habitat in Utah, where fragments were 21% thinner than normal; we predict occasional poor reproduction at these Utah territories.

Oganochlorine Residues. — In each of the last several years, the contents of eggs from 3-7 territories have contained an average of between 12-18 ppm DDE, a remarkably narrow range. That range of DDE has been shown to correlate with about 15% eggshell thinning in the Brown Pelican (Blus et al. 1972), Prairie Falcon (Enderson and Wrege 1973), and Peregrines in Alaska (Cade et al. 1971). The 12% thinning we found in this study roughly agrees with those studies.

Our data show no clear relationship between eggshell thickness and DDE in egg contents, possibly because of the relatively narrow range of eggshell thickness and DDE concentrations encountered, combined with high variance.

After 1979, other organochlorines very seldom exceeded 1 ppm in egg contents. Except for PCBs, most were present in amounts below

---

*Editors' Note: For 1985-87 Colorado Peregrine populations, see Addendum to Enderson et al. (Chapter 12).

0.5 ppm. In general, PCB levels appear to have fallen from the 2-5 ppm range of the late 1970s.

In summary, Peregrines of the central Rocky Mountains and the adjacent Colorado Plateau have in recent years experienced a level of eggshell thinning averaging 12-21% thinner than normal. We cannot detect a clear improvement in eggshell thickness or a reduction in the DDE content of eggs, and we predict little change in these conditions in the next several years.

ACKNOWLEDGEMENTS

We are grateful for the interest and cooperation of S. Petersburg, J. Hogan, W. Burnham, L. Hayes, J. Connor, W. Heim, L. Belli, O. Pattee, and the numerous field observers, without whom this work could not have been completed. R. Ramey, C. Neighbors, R. Enderson, and C. Schultz gathered eggshells from Utah.

39 | DDE Residues and Eggshell Characteristics of Reestablished Peregrines in the Eastern United States

Martin J. Gilroy and John H. Barclay

Efforts to reintroduce the Peregrine Falcon in the eastern United States have proven to be effective (Barclay and Cade 1983); the number of breeding pairs in the region is nearly doubling annually (Cade and Dague 1984, Barclay Chapter 51). Longterm success, however, depends in part on the decline of the persistent organochlorines that caused the extirpation of the Peregrine population that inhabited the region historically (Peakall 1976). This study provides a preliminary analysis of contaminant load of Peregrines reestablished in the eastern United States.

METHODS

Personnel of The Peregrine Fund, Inc. collected 39 infertile or addled eggs and eggshell fragments at nine mid-Atlantic coastal and urban breeding sites between 1981-84. Coastal nest sites are on man-made towers from which Peregrines have been released since 1974. One site is on an island in the Chesapeake Bay, Maryland and six are along the Atlantic coast of New Jersey. One of the two urban sites is a 40-story skyscraper in Baltimore, Maryland and the other is a bridge over the Delaware River between New Jersey and Philadelphia, Pennsylvania. Eggs and fragments were collected while banding nestlings or when observations indicated that clutches had been abandoned.

Eggs were shipped to the Patuxent Wildlife Research Center, Laurel, Maryland where they were measured and prepared for chemical analysis by the methods described in Pattee (1984). Egg contents were homogenized and a 10 g aliquot was prepared and organochlorines quantified (Kaiser et al. 1980). Residue levels were corrected for moisture loss following Stickel et al. (1973) and expressed as ppm (lipid). The compounds quantified were: DDE, DDD, DDT, dieldrin, heptachlor epoxide, oxychlordane, cis-chlordane, trans-nonachlor, cis-nonachlor, endrin, toxaphene, and PCBs.

Statistical analyses were performed using the SPSS package on the CDC Cyber computer at George Mason University, Fairfax, Virginia. Only those compounds detected in more than 90% of the eggs were considered in this analysis. Other compounds were detected in 50% or fewer of the eggs; no egg contained detectable quantities of endrin or toxaphene. A value of one-half the detection limit was assigned when no residue was detected (detection limits were 0.1 ppm for pesticides and 0.5 ppm for PCBs). DDT and metabolites are sums of the residues of DDE, DDD and DDT. Arithmetic means are used.

RESULTS

Physical measurements of sampled eggs are summarized in Table 1. Mean eggshell thickness and Ratcliffe Index (Ratcliffe 1967) of the 1981-84 sample were compared to means of pre-1947 eggs of eastern Peregrines reported by Anderson and Hickey (1972) using Student's t-test (Table 2). The mean eggshell thickness of the sample was 0.340 mm, significantly thinner than the 0.375 mm mean of pre-1947 eggs ($t=6.721$; $P<0.05$), a thinning of 9.4%. The Ratcliffe Index of the contemporary sample was 1.75, significantly thinner than the 1.99 mean of the pre-1947 eggs ($t=12.091$; $P<0.05$) by 12.1%. A two-way analysis of variance (ANOVA) comparing year and site means for eggshell thickness and Ratcliffe Index (Table 3) indicated that year and site were independent factors ($P>0.05$), that the means were not significantly different among years ($P>0.05$), but that the means were significantly different among sites ($P<0.05$). Site means varied by 20-25%. Duncan's multiple range test was used to separate the site means (Table 4). Although the results differed slightly between eggshell thickness and Ratcliffe Index, the two urban sites tended toward the thicker end of the range.

Residue levels of the sample eggs are summarized in Table 5. The correlations among the contaminants, eggshell thickness and Ratcliffe Index are shown in Table 6. There were significant ($P<0.05$) negative correlations between eggshell thickness and DDE, between eggshell thickness and DDT and metabolites, and between Ratcliffe Index and all contaminants. There were significant ($P<0.05$) positive correlations among all of the contaminants, indicating that Peregrines acquired them in concert.

A two-way ANOVA comparing year and site means for DDE residues indicates that year and site were not independent factors, but that a given site mean depended on year ($F=38$; $P<0.05$). The same result was found for each contaminant. Since this interaction makes separate treatment of the two factors invalid, the analysis was expanded to compare all year-site combinations with a one-way ANOVA. The year-site means were ranked, and the average site ranks compared for the four years (Table 7). The average ranks, and therefore, the mean residues were lowest in 1983 and highest in 1984.

TABLE 1. Mean physical measurements (standard deviations in parentheses) of Peregrine eggs collected in eastern North America, 1981-84.

Year	Site	n	Length (mm)	Breadth (mm)	Volume (ml)	Eggshell wt (g)	Lipid (g/cc)	Eggshell thickness (mm)	Ratcliffe Index
1981	Baltimore	4	50.55 (0.86)	40.02 (0.83)	41.72 (1.25)	3.80 (0.29)	0.051 (0.003)	0.348 (0.025)	1.878 (0.128)
	Brigantine	2[a]	53.90	42.80	51.40	4.35	0.046	0.364 (0.006)	1.886
	Sea Isle City	1[b]						0.350	
1982	Baltimore	9[c]	49.30 (1.07)	39.39 (0.71)	39.02 (1.24)	3.71 (0.25)	0.044 (0.004)	0.356 (0.023)	1.910 (0.101)
	Brigantine	1	53.76	40.51	35.00	4.10	0.042	0.366	1.883
	Manahawkin	1						0.268	
	Sedge Island	4	50.33	39.42	39.92	2.91	0.054	0.287	1.464
	Sea Isle City	1						0.312	
1983	Baltimore	4	49.97 (1.69)	39.16 (0.40)	39.08 (1.95)	3.75 (0.24)	0.048 (0.002)	0.368 (0.007)	1.914 (0.056)
	Manahawkin	2	54.11 (0.20)	42.32 (0.75)	49.40 (1.56)	3.73 (0.06)	0.016 (0.001)	0.306[d] (0.047)	1.629 (0.047)
1984	Comm. Barry Bridge	2	55.48 (1.07)	44.76 (0.07)	56.65 (0.92)	4.41 (1.20)	0.023 (0.011)	0.372 (0.016)	1.775 (0.080)
	Manahawkin	2	58.02 (1.65)	42.74 (0.45)	54.10 (2.69)	3.78 (0.13)	0.046 (0.005)	0.310 (0.006)	1.522 (0.005)
	Sedge Island	1	53.40	42.90	50.10	3.88	0.022	0.344	1.694
	Sea Isle City	1	54.55	40.10	44.70	3.64	0.052	0.311	1.664
	South Marsh Island	1	49.88	40.94	42.60	3.00	0.052	0.348	1.469
	Swan Bay	1	51.50	41.85	46.00	3.81	0.042	0.383	1.768
	Tuckahoe	2	52.56 (0.86)	43.20 (1.05)	50.10 (3.25)	3.22 (0.19)	0.044 (0.005)	0.305 (0.003)	1.415 (0.265)

[a] 1 whole egg; 1 fragment.
[b] Fragment, only thickness measured.
[c] 2 clutches of 5 and 4 eggs.
[d] Only 1 egg measured.

TABLE 2. Comparison of eggshell thickness and Ratcliffe Index in pre-1947[a] and 1981-84 Peregrine eggs from eastern North America.

	Sample	n	Mean	C.I.[c]	t-value	% change
Eggshell thickness (mm)	pre-1947	94	0.375	0.005		
	1981-84	38	0.340	0.011	6.721[b]	– 9.4
Ratcliffe Index	pre-1947	392	1.99	0.01		
	1981-84	35	1.75	0.07	12.091[b]	–12.1

[a] Anderson and Hickey (1972).
[b] $P < 0.05$.
[c] 95% confidence interval.

TABLE 3. Comparison of year and site means for Peregrine eggshell thickness and Ratcliffe Index with two-way analysis of variance.

Source	Sum of squares	df	Mean square	F-stat	P	Eta²
Eggshell thickness						
Year	0.003	3	0.001	2.328	0.105	0.06
Site	0.026	8	0.003	7.839	0.000	0.69
Year × site	0.001	2	0.000	0.692	0.512	
Residual	0.008	20	0.000			
Total	0.037	33	0.001			
Ratcliffe Index						
Year	0.020	3	0.007	0.719	0.552	0.26
Site	0.816	8	0.102	10.879	0.000	0.83
Year × site	0.029	2	0.015	1.566	0.234	
Residual	0.187	20	0.009			
Total	1.399	33	0.042			

TABLE 4. Comparison of site means (*a posteriori*) for Peregrine eggshell thickness and Ratcliffe Index with Duncan's multiple range test.

Site	Mean	Range[a]
Eggshell thickness (mm)		
(n =38)		
Manahawkin	0.298	
Sedge Island	0.299	
Tuckahoe	0.305	
Sea Isle City	0.324	
South Marsh Island	0.348	
Baltimore	0.357	
Brigantine	0.364	
Comm. Barry Bridge	0.372	
Swan Bay	0.383	
Ratcliffe Index		
(n =35)		
Tuckahoe	1.415	
South Marsh Island	1.469	
Sedge Island	1.510	
Manahawkin	1.576	
Sea Isle City	1.664	
Swan Bay	1.768	
Comm. Barry Bridge	1.775	
Brigantine	1.884	
Baltimore	1.904	

[a] Any pair of means enclosed by the range of any one line is not significantly different.

TABLE 5. Mean contaminant concentrations (ppm wet wt; standard deviations in parentheses) in Peregrine eggs collected in eastern North America, 1981-84.

Year	Site	n	DDE	DDT and metabolites	Heptachlor epoxide	Oxychlordane	PCBs
1981	Baltimore	4	3.4 (0.19)	3.4 (0.19)	0.09 (0.018)	0.20 (0.06)	2.1 (0.10)
	Brigantine	1	6.5	6.6	0.18	0.44	10
1982	Baltimore	8	2.4 (0.38)	2.5 (0.38)	0.12 (0.025)	0.18 (0.020)	2.8 (0.28)
	Brigantine	1	9.6	9.7	0.23	0.47	15
	Sedge Island	4	8.8 (1.05)	9.0 (1.05)	0.08 (0.006)	0.18 (0.013)	4.9 (0.50)
1983	Baltimore	4	1.9 (0.22)	2.0 (0.22)	0.06 (0.025)	0.16 (0.020)	3.3 (0.26)
	Manahawkin	2	5.3 (2.19)	5.4 (2.19)	0.10 (0.007)	0.38 (0.078)	5.8 (1.41)
1984	Comm. Barry Bridge	2	5.7 (0.07)	5.8 (0.07)	0.25 (0.028)	0.26 (0.078)	6.3 (0.14)
	Manahawkin	2	14 (2.62)	15 (2.62)	0.47 (0.014)	0.78 (0.014)	12 (1.56)
	Sedge Island	1	5.4	5.6	0.39	0.41	5.7
	Sea Isle City	1	18	18	0.31	0.62	19
	South Marsh Island	1	14	15	0.36	0.75	8.2
	Swan Bay	1	6.4	6.5	0.09	0.29	7.5
	Tuckahoe	2	12 (0.00)	12 (0.00)	0.46 (0.014)	0.82 (0.007)	6.9 (0.21)

TABLE 6. Correlation coefficients (r) for eggshell thickness, Ratcliffe Index, and contaminant residues in Peregrine eggs from eastern North America, 1981-84.

	Eggshell thickness	Ratcliffe Index	DDE	DDT and metabolites	Heptachlor epoxide	Oxychlordane
Ratcliffe Index	0.862[a]					
DDE	-0.527[a]	-0.715[a]				
DDT and metabolites	-0.529[a]	-0.717[a]	1.000[a]			
Heptachlor epoxide	-0.263	-0.507[a]	0.732[a]	0.731[a]		
Oxychlordane	-0.309	-0.566[a]	0.826[a]	0.824[a]	0.907[a]	
PCBs	-0.215	-0.370[a]	0.826[a]	0.825[a]	0.608[a]	0.709[a]

[a] $P < 0.05$.

TABLE 7. Average rank of site means for contaminant residues in Peregrine eggs from eastern North America, 1981-84.

Contaminant	1981	1982	1983	1984
DDE	5.5	7.0	2.5	9.7
DDT and metabolites	5.5	7.0	2.5	9.7
Heptachlor epoxide	5.0	5.3	3.0	10.4
Oxychlordane	6.5	5.0	4.0	9.7
PCBs	6.0	6.3	4.5	9.3

TABLE 8. Comparison of residue levels (ppm wet wt) in Peregrine eggs from unsuccessful and successful clutches in eastern North America.

Contaminant	Production	No. of clutches	No. of eggs	Mean (S.D.)	P
DDE	unsuccessful	5	10	9.09 (3.15)	
	successful	6	8	10.01 (5.20)	0.65
DDT and metabolites	unsuccessful	5	10	9.25 (3.16)	
	successful	6	8	10.13 (5.22)	0.67
Heptachlor epoxide	unsuccessful	5	10	0.25 (0.16)	
	successful	6	8	0.24 (0.16)	0.91
Oxychlordane	unsuccessful	5	10	0.40 (0.28)	
	successful	6	8	0.52 (0.19)	0.33
PCBs	unsuccessful	5	10	5.99 (1.15)	
	successful	6	8	10.74 (4.60)	0.02

A nested ANOVA was used to compare mean DDE residues of urban versus coastal sites and the sites within each site-type. Mean residues from urban sites were significantly lower ($F=20$; $P<0.05$) than from coastal sites, as were site means within each site-type ($F=4.6$; $P<0.05$). Similar findings were obtained for each of the other contaminants.

Student's t-test was used to compare mean residue levels in eggs from unsuccessful and successful clutches (Table 8). Only PCBs were significantly different ($t=0.02$; $P<0.05$), with the mean from successful clutches nearly twice that of unsuccessful clutches.

DISCUSSION

The data show that contaminant loads in eastern Peregrines have varied widely from site to site. Residue levels at some sites were 8-9 times those at other sites. Eggshell thickness and contaminant levels of eggs at some coastal sites approach those in some Rocky Mountain Peregrines known to have suffered impaired reproduction (Enderson et al. 1982).

In approximately 25% of the eggs, the parent DDT compound, p,p'-DDT, was detected, presumably acquired from migrant prey. Lower residue levels in eggs at urban sites support this indication, as predicted by Peakall (1976), since urban falcons seem to feed less on migrants than do coastal falcons. Eggs were not analyzed for heavy metals or other toxins that may cause problems at urban sites. Three Peregrines have died of strychnine poisoning in Baltimore.

Eggs from both unsuccessful and successful clutches indicate that residue levels and eggshell thinning have not been severe enough to have affected reproduction.

Organochlorine contaminants pose a potential threat to reestablished eastern Peregrines and warrant close monitoring as restoration continues.

ACKNOWLEDGEMENTS

The chemical analyses were performed under the direction of O. H. Pattee, Patuxent Wildlife Research Center. P. Nickerson, U. S. Fish and Wildlife Service, Region 5, and J. Hickey, U. S. Fish and Wildlife Service, Cortland, New York facilitated the chemical analyses. S. R. Taub, George Mason University, Fairfax, Virginia provided statistical guidance.

40 | Pollutants and Eggshell Thinning in Peregrines and Their Prey in the Baja California Region

Richard D. Porter and M. Alan Jenkins

Earlier studies of organochlorine contaminants in the Gulf of California have shown an exceptionally high level of DDE (in the order of 100 ppm wet weight) in an egg of a Peregrine Falcon, and high residues in one of the principal prey species, the Black Storm-Petrel (Risebrough et al. 1968b). The resident Peregrine Falcons breeding on the islands of the Gulf of California were the subject of intensive study by M. N. Kirven over the period 1967-70. Many observations of Peregrines in the area were made by D. W. Anderson and his colleagues during their investigations of Brown Pelicans and other seabirds throughout the 1970s and early 1980s. Our own studies in the Gulf of California and adjacent areas of Baja California were undertaken during 1976-84. We analyzed principal prey items of the Peregrine Falcon for organochlorine pesticides, selected heavy metals, and trace elements. We also determined the thickness of eggshells from 15 eyries in the Gulf of California and one eyrie on the Pacific coast. This report presents the results of our analyses and the implications for the reproductive health of the Peregrine population in the Gulf of California.

METHODS

Data on eyrie site locations were provided by M. N. Kirven and D. W. Anderson. Addled eggs were analyzed for eggshell thinning and chemical residues. Eggshells of 8 eggs from 7 eyries and fragments of 22 eggshells from 13 eyries were measured for thickness. Samples were obtained from nine eyries one year, three eyries two years, and three eyries three years. All measurements included eggshell membranes unless otherwise indicated. Eggs collected in 1980 were analyzed for organochlorines, heavy metals, and other chemical elements by the Patuxent Wildlife Research Center (PWRC) in Laurel, Maryland. Eggs

413

collected in 1984 were analyzed for organochlorines at PWRC and for mercury at the Analytical Bio-Chemistry Laboratories, Inc. (ABC Laboratories). All results of chemical analyses are reported on a wet weight basis unless otherwise indicated.

We collected eight Peregrine prey species (74 individuals) in the central region of the Gulf of California during March-May 1978. These eight species included five examined a decade earlier by Risebrough et al. (1968b). Additional prey remains, mainly muscle, were collected from three eyries and analyzed for heavy metals and other chemicals. Samples of breast muscle from the specimens were preserved in formalin. Breast muscle and fat samples of Craveri's Murrelets (collected by D. Anderson in April 1971) were dehydrated and preserved in sodium sulfate.

Samples for heavy metal analyses were placed in jars which had been previously immersed in about 10% nitric acid, and rinsed separately with de-ionized water. The jars were dried on a neoprene covered rack. Containers for organochlorine pesticide samples were rinsed with 10-20 ml of distilled reagent grade acetone and then twice with distilled reagent grade hexane. Raltech Scientific Services, Inc., analyzed the prey samples for organochlorine residues, and ABC Laboratories analyzed them for heavy metals.

RESULTS AND DISCUSSION

Organochlorine Residues in Prey. — Residues of DDE in several prey species sampled by us were generally lower than in the same species sampled by Risebrough et al. (1968b) in the late 1960s (Table 1). DDE in breast muscle of Black Storm-Petrels (5.2 ppm), Heermann's Gulls (6.1 ppm) and one of five samples of the Eared Grebe (2.1 ppm) (Table 1) may have been sufficiently high to affect reproductive success adversely. DDE residues of these magnitudes produced reproductive effects in captive American Kestrels (Wiemeyer and Porter 1970). Additionally, dietary DDE of 3 ppm, 6 ppm, and 10 ppm resulted in an average thinning of 14.0%, 17.4%, and 21.7%, respectively, in the eggshells of the American Kestrel (Lincer 1975).

All other prey species were relatively low in DDE, ranging from 0.01 ppm in a downy young murrelet to 0.8 ppm in Least Storm-Petrels (Table 1). DDT, DDD, and dieldrin were either not detected or were in low concentrations in our samples. PCBs (polychlorinated biphenyls, primarily penta- and hexa-chlorophenyls) were generally low in pooled samples of breast muscle; 1.7 ppm in Heermann's Gulls and 1.5 ppm in some Black Storm-Petrels. Most samples contained less than 1 ppm (Table 1).

Heermann's Gulls and Black Storm-Petrels contained the highest concentrations of DDE and PCBs found in any of the prey species

TABLE 1.   Organochlorine residues in tissues of Peregrine Falcon prey in the Gulf of California, Mexico, 1967-84. Residue values are geometric means in ppm wet wt. 1967 samples collected by Risebrough et al. (1968b).

Prey species	Year	Tissue	n[a]	DDE ± S.E.	DDT ± S.E.	PCBs ± S.E.
Eared Grebe	1978	Muscle	5 (13)	0.20±0.39	0.0	0.5±0.06
	1967	Whole body	3	0.92±3.64	0.50±0.31	0.0
Black Storm-Petrel	1978	Muscle	1 (10)	5.17	0.67	1.5
	1967	Whole body	8	7.45	1.75	1.0
Least Storm-Petrel	1978	Muscle	1 (4)	0.77	0.06	0.25
	1967	Whole body	3	2.66	0.54	0.35
Red-necked Phalarope	1978	Muscle	1 (2)	0.53	0.0	0.72
Bonaparte's Gull	1978	Muscle	2 (5)	0.36±0.09	0.0	0.15±0.07
Heermann's Gull	1978	Muscle	1 (10)	6.12	0.0	1.67
Craveri's Murrelet	1978	Muscle	5 (9)	0.06±0.10	<0.01	0.02±0.01[b]
	1978	Muscle	5	0.15±0.08	<0.01	0.04±0.03
	1978	Fat[c]	5	6.40±1.69	0.64±0.15	1.33±0.62
	1967	Whole body	2	0.73±0.89	0.13±0.16	0.10±0.11
Fish-eating Bat	1978	Upper torso	1 (11)	0.45	0.05	0.16
(Myotis vivesi)	1967	Whole body	7	0.44	0.27	0.02

[a] The sample (n) refers to number of pools or number of separate individuals analyzed; the number in parentheses refers to total individuals if samples were pooled.
[b] Arithmetic mean.
[c] Samples were dehydrated and preserved in sodium sulfate.

sampled by us (Table 1). Risebrough et al. (1968b) noted especially
high concentrations of DDE and PCBs in Black Storm-Petrels from the
Gulf of California (Table 1). Henny et al. (1982b) reported higher
residues in eggs of Leach's Storm-Petrels than in eggs of several other
species of seabirds. Storm-Petrels are the principal prey of some Baja
California Peregrines. In the Gulf of California, two Peregrine pairs
that preyed heavily on Black Storm-Petrels had long histories of
reproductive failure. At one of their territories (1B), eggs were found
in only 8 of 13 years and young in only 3 years. At the other (1A),
eggs were laid in only 5 of 10 years, and young produced once. Never
was more than one young hatched or fledged at either site in any year.

Organochlorine Residues in Peregrine Eggs. — DDE was much
lower in five eggs sampled by us in the Gulf of California in the 1980s
than in an unhatched 1967 egg (99 ppm DDE) from eyrie 1B
(M. Kirven field notes, Risebrough et al. 1968b, see Table 2 below). An
egg containing 25 ppm came from eyrie 22 where three addled, thin-
shelled eggs were found in 1984 (Table 3). DDE in the other four eggs
was less than 15 ppm (Table 2). Ratcliffe (1980) considered that a
mean level of 14 ppm DDE in eggs of British Peregrines corresponded
with eggshells 21% thinner than normal, whereas Peakall et al. (1975)
believed that 20 ppm DDE corresponded with a reduction in eggshell
thickness of 20%.

Eggshell Thinning. — The eggshells at some Gulf of California
eyries were precariously thin. Only one eggshell out of 40 was greater
in thickness than the pre-1947 mean of 0.348 mm (Table 3, Anderson
and Hickey 1972). Eggshells that were more than 20% thinner than
the pre-1947 mean were present in 5 (20%) of 25 clutches at 16

TABLE 2.   Organochlorine and mercury residues and eggshell thickness in eggs of
Peregrine Falcons in the Gulf of California, Mexico, 1967-84.

Eyrie no.	Wet wt (g)	ppm wet wt			Eggshell thickness (mm)	Percent thinning
		DDE	PCB	Hg		
1[a]		99.0	10.2			
31	9.29[b]	2.4	0.5	0.2	0.293	16
22	34.87[b]	10.5	2.3	1.1	0.295	15
22[c]	10.00[b]	25.0	10.6	2.7		
40	10.00[b]	12.9	3.0	4.2	0.321	8
43	10.00[b]	13.0	2.8	1.9	0.356	+2[d]

[a] From Risebrough et al. (1968b).
[b] Based on corrected wet wt.
[c] Egg was unusally small (48.96 × 38.83 mm and eggshell 0.214 mm thick).
[d] 2% above normal.

TABLE 3. Eggshell thickness and percent (%) thinning of eggs at Peregrine eyries in Baja California, Mexico, 1977-84.

Eyrie no.	Year	Egg 1		Egg 2		Egg 3		Egg 4	
		Thickness (mm)	% thinning	Thickness (mm)	% thinning	Thickness (mm)	% thinning	Thickness (mm)	% thinning
Entire eggshell									
12	1981	0.260[a]	(25)	0.271[a]	(22)				
22	1980	0.295	(15)	0.262	(25)				
22	1984	0.214[a]	(39)						
31	1980	0.293	(16)						
40	1984	0.321	(8)						
43	1984	0.356	(2)						
68[b]	1984	0.251	(+2)	0.239	(31)	0.287	(18)	0.268	(23)
75[b]	1981	0.313	(10)	0.313	(10)	0.282	(19)		
Eggshell fragments									
1B	1984	0.295	(15)						
3	1977-81	0.341	(2)						
15	1981	0.338	(3)						
21	1981	0.345	(0)			0.345	(0)		
22	1980, 84	0.270	(22)	0.284	(18)				
24	1980-81	0.323	(7)	0.303	(13)				
31	1980	0.321	(8)						
35	1984	0.305	(12)						
36	1984	0.300	(14)						
37	1981	0.304	(13)						
43	1978-84	0.273[c]	(22)	0.262	(25)	0.324	(7)		
44	1981, 84	0.301	(14)	0.286	(18)				
68	1980-81	0.319	(8)	0.289	(17)				

[a] Eggs from Eyrie 12 (see Jenkins 1984), and 1 egg from Eyrie 22 unusually small; their thin shells may have been a reflection of their small size.
[b] Island eyrie west side of Baja California; all others in Gulf of California.
[c] Egg membranes absent; 0.079 mm taken as membrane thickness (Burnham et al. 1984).

eyries (Figure 1). Eggshell thinning at two eyries was greater than 20% in two separate years (Table 3). Reductions of 15-20% in eggshell thickness (Anderson and Hickey 1972) are related to negative changes in population and a decrease of 20% or more is associated with population decline (Peakall et al. 1975). The thinnest fragments were from three unusually small eggs (Jenkins 1984) whose shells were 22%, 25% and 39% thinner than average pre-1947 eggs (Table 3). These eggshells may have been thin, in part, because of their unusually small size.

Average eggshell thinning for 25 nestings representing 16 eyries in Baja California (15 in the Gulf of California) was clearly correlated with productivity (Figure 1) but not with year. Our regression analysis (Figure 1) tends to support the hypothesis that eggshell thinning of about 20% results in reproductive failure in Peregrines (Anderson and Hickey 1972, Peakall et al. 1975). This correlation occurred even though we were not always able to ascertain the number of young per

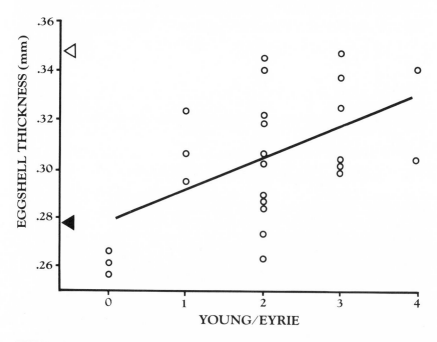

FIGURE 1. Mean eggshell thickness plotted against nest productivity for Baja California Peregrines. Data for 25 nestlings at 16 eyries (some eyries sampled 2 or more years). $y=0.27 + 0.014x$, $r=32\%$, $P<0.01$ (with elimination of 3 unusually small eggs (24 nestlings, 15 eyries) $y=0.28 + 0.012x$, $r=23\%$, $P<0.05$). Open triangle indicates location of pre-1947 mean (Anderson and Hickey 1972); closed triangle shows point of 20% thinning (Peakall et al. 1975).

eyrie at the same stage of the nesting cycle or obtain a sample of each egg laid. Peregrine eggs show a wide variation in eggshell thickness both within clutches and between clutches, and samples based on one egg in a sample or a few fragments may insufficiently represent the average eggshell thickness produced by a female (Burnham et al. 1984). All of our samples were from first clutches, and no clutches collected by us were known to be complete.

Residues of Heavy Metals and Other Chemical Elements in Eggs and Prey. — In the absence of comparative data it is not possible to estimate an anthropogenic component in any of the metal levels recorded in our study. There is as yet no evidence that the concentrations of any of the metals or trace elements in food webs of the Gulf of California have been elevated because of human activities. Levels recorded could therefore be natural. Mercury in various prey parts from the Gulf of California ranged from 0.30-3.15 ppm in the 1970s (Table 4). When Mallards were given a diet containing about 0.6 ppm methylmercury for three generations, the number of sound eggs decreased, duckling mortality increased, and avoidance behavior was altered (Heinz 1976a, 1979). Comparable effects in a species naturally exposed to higher levels of mercury have not been demonstrated.

Four of five eggs from four different eyries in the Gulf of California, two collected in 1980 and three in 1984, contained 1.2-4.2 ppm mercury (Table 2), 2-13 times higher than the 0.32-0.57 ppm which

TABLE 4. Mercury and lead in tissues of Peregrine Falcon prey in the Gulf of California, Mexico, 1972-78. Residue values are geometric means in ppm "wet" wt as received.

Prey species	Tissue	n	Hg	Pb
Eared Grebe	Wing/back[a]	1	1.60	2.70
Black Storm-Petrel	Breast muscle	10(P)[b]		0.48
	Wing	1	3.15	2.10
	Wing[c]	1	1.72	2.30
Least Storm-Petrel	Wing	1	1.03	12.30
	Wing[c]	1	0.51	7.10
Red-necked Phalarope	Wing	1	0.30	
Bonaparte's Gull	Wing	1	1.08	2.80
Heermann's Gull	Breast muscle	10(P)[b]		0.84
Craveri's Murrelet	Wing[c]	1	0.64	4.30
Belted Kingfisher	Head	1	0.95	0.24
Fish-eating Bat	Upper torso	11		0.94

[a] Includes feathers, skin, bones, muscles.
[b] Number of individuals in a single pool (P).
[c] Collected in 1972 by D. Anderson; all remaining samples were collected in 1977-78.

Fimreite et al. (1970) reported in four Peregrine eggs from Canada, and attributed to mercurial seed-dressing. One of the four contaminated Peregrine eggs was unusually small; it contained high levels of DDE, PCBs, and Hg (Table 2). In addition, a small egg without a yolk was found by Kirven in 1969 at eyrie 1B (M. Kirven field notes). Molted primary and contour feathers taken from a successful Gulf of California eyrie (Site 3) contained 25.8 ppm mercury. The sex of the bird or birds from which they molted is unknown. Nevertheless, an average of 2.6±0.9 young per year (1976-81) was produced at this site.

Mercury in these Peregrine feathers was 8-17 times higher than the 1.5-3.1 ppm reported by Parrish et al. (1983) in Alaskan Peregrines. Lindberg and Mearns (1982) believed that levels of 15-20 ppm mercury in Peregrine feathers from northern Fennoscandia were owing to a high proportion of waders in their diet. Henriksson et al. (1966) examined feathers of White-tailed Eagles in Finland and found mercury residues similar to those we found in Peregrine feathers from the Gulf of California.

Lead concentrations in body parts (mostly wings) ranged from 12.3 ppm in a Least Storm-Petrel to 0.24 ppm in a Belted Kingfisher (Table 4). Muscle from a Black Storm-Petrel and a Heermann's Gull contained 0.48 ppm and 0.84 ppm lead, respectively, and a carcass of a Fish-eating Bat (*Myotis vivesi*) contained 0.94 ppm. Pattee (1984) found no adverse effects with respect to survival, egg laying, initiation of incubation, fertility, or eggshell thickness in American Kestrels given a diet of 10 ppm or 50 ppm lead. Molted Peregrine feathers from a Gulf of California eyrie contained 24.6 ppm lead.

Chromium ranged from 2.2 ppm in a pool of five Fish-eating Bats to less than 0.1 ppm in a pooled sample of breast muscle of 10 Black Storm-Petrels.

Nickel in Peregrine prey ranged from 6.7 ppm in the breast muscle of the Eared Grebe pool to less than 0.1 ppm in the breast muscle of some specimens of Craveri's Murrelet. Nickel apparently has little toxic or reproductive effects on birds except at high dietary levels (1200 ppm) (Cain and Pafford 1981, Eastin and O'Shea 1981).

Cadmium was present in amounts less than 0.1 ppm in some Craveri's Murrelets to 7.0 ppm in the breast muscle of the Black Storm-Petrel pooled sample. White and Finley (1978) reported no reproductive effects on Mallards fed a diet of 2 ppm cadmium chloride. Egg production was suppressed only in a group fed 200 ppm; there was a moderate effect on maturation of spermatozoa in a group given 20 ppm in their diet.

Arsenic ranged from a low of 0.03 ppm in the breast muscle of a Craveri's Murrelet to 2.4 ppm in the wing of a Black Storm-Petrel.

Selenium in the pooled breast muscles of prey was 6.8 ppm in Black Storm-Petrels, 3.7 ppm in Eared Grebes and 3.6 ppm in Heermann's Gulls.

SUMMARY AND CONCLUSIONS

An increase in occupied Peregrine breeding territories and in productivity in the Gulf of California since 1967 (Porter et al. Chapter 15) was apparently related to a reduction in residues of organochlorine pesticides in the Peregrine's prey. This conclusion is based on a comparison of the present levels of these contaminants in the Peregrine's prey to those present in the late 1960s. Nevertheless, environmental contamination was still a problem at three eyries where serious eggshell thinning and high levels of contamination were evident. Furthermore, some heavily used prey species such as Eared Grebes, storm-petrels, and Craveri's Murrelets had high residues of several contaminants, especially DDE. Eggshell thinning and DDE residues, however, did not seem sufficient to cause reproductive failure at most eyries; DDE appeared to be a problem at only 3 of the 15 eyries sampled in the Gulf of California.

ACKNOWLEDGEMENTS

We thank the Dirección General de Fauna Silvestre of Mexico for their cooperation, the Western Foundation of Vertebrate Zoology for funding the mercury analyses of the 1984 Peregrine eggs (L. Kiff and E. Harrison assisted throughout our study; S. Sumida measured eggshells) and the U. S. Fish and Wildlife Service for supporting the project (S. Haseltine and O. H. Pattee expedited the chemical analyses of the eggs; with R. Hillen's assistance, the Region 6 office provided funding for the chemical analyses of prey items). O. H. Pattee and C. A. Porter reviewed and offered valuable suggestions on an earlier draft of the manuscript; the reviews of J. Enderson and S. D. Porter were especially helpful and appreciated.

41 Organochlorine Pollutants in Plasma of Spring Migrant Peregrine Falcons from Coastal Texas, 1984

Charles J. Henny, Kenton E. Riddle, and Craig S. Hulse

Peregrine Falcons suffered population declines in much of the northern hemisphere (Hickey 1969, Peakall 1976, Ratcliffe 1980). These declines coincided with the use of DDT and resultant decreases in eggshell thickness. In North America the status of the northern breeding populations was the least understood. We first captured fall-migrant Peregrines and collected blood samples in 1976 (Henny et al. 1982c). The blood plasma was analyzed for organochlorine pesticide residues. Earlier work with humans and birds showed that DDE residues in blood plasma were correlated with exposure and body burden (Henny and Meeker 1981). The blood-sampling approach seemed especially suitable for endangered species research because it is nondestructive. Furthermore, it is relatively inexpensive in comparison to investigations in remote arctic regions where nesting birds are at low density. We think our approach complements the few detailed arctic investigations (Chapters 4-9). While studies from small nesting areas may not be representative, migrants are probably from broad geographical regions. We include here the results from Texas in 1978-80 and 1984.

A spring concentration of migrating Peregrines was first discovered at Padre Island, Texas, in April 1978. Only 4 birds were captured that year, but techniques were improved, and 25 and 82 were captured in 1979 and 1980, respectively. Based upon residues in blood samples from 433 Peregrines captured in fall and spring (1976-80), we concluded that much of the pesticide burden, primarily DDE, in the strongly migratory population sampled was accumulated on wintering grounds in Latin America (Henny et al. 1982c). Also, DDE declined significantly from 1978-79 to 1980 in first-time spring migrants returning from Latin America.

In 1976-79, hatch-year Peregrines were the dominant age class (about 85%) captured and bled during fall migration (Henny et al. 1982c). They were only a few months old and contained low organochlorine residues. Therefore, to evaluate trends in residue levels during the 1980s, we concentrated our effort in the spring when all the birds captured would contain residues of interest. We obtained blood samples from 46 Peregrines between 28 March and 26 April 1984.

METHODS

Field collection, plasma storage, sample preparation, extraction, and clean-up were described by Henny et al. (1982c). Caution is required when interpreting plasma residues, which may be inflated for birds with severe weight loss. However, poor body condition was not encountered with spring migrants. Polychlorinated biphenyl (PCB) levels were estimated and p,p'-DDE, p,p'-DDD, p,p'-DDT, dieldrin, heptachlor epoxide, oxychlordane, cis-chlordane, trans-nonachlor, cis-nonachlor, endrin, toxaphene, and mirex residues were determined in 1984. Silica gel (100-200 mesh, grade 923, Davison Chemical Division, W. R. Grace and Co.) column chromatography was used to collect the pesticides into four fractions to separate dieldrin and/or endrin (Kaiser et al. 1980). All fractions were quantified by electron capture, gas-liquid chromatography using a 1.83 m x 4 mm id glass column packed with 1.5/1.95% SP-2250/2401 on 100/120 mesh supelcoport. Residues in approximately 10% of the samples were qualitatively confirmed by mass spectrometry. Recoveries of pesticides and PCBs averaged 94%. Reported results were not corrected for recovery. The lower limits of quantification were 0.02 ppm for pesticides and 0.10 ppm for PCBs.

Statistical analyses were limited to the 43 females sampled in the spring of 1984. These were second-year (SY) birds known to have hatched in the calendar year preceding the year of capture, and after-second-year (ASY) birds known to have hatched earlier than the calendar year preceding the year of capture. We used two-factor ANOVA with age (ASY and SY) and year (1978-79, 1980, 1984) as factors to evaluate the log-values of DDE residues. Differences found in the ANOVA were quantified with the Bonferroni multiple comparison procedure. If a pesticide or metabolite occurred above the detection limit in at least 25% of the samples for an age class, chi-square tests were used to compare occurrence during the years 1978-79, 1980 and 1984. We used the significance level of 0.05 for acceptance of the null hypothesis.

RESULTS AND DISCUSSION

Source of the Peregrines. — Because Peregrines were rare in mid-February of 1980 on Padre Island, we assumed almost all Peregrines captured there from late March to early May had arrived recently from wintering areas in Latin America (Henny et al. 1982c). We did not distinguish subspecies (see Henny and Clark 1982).

Twenty previously-banded Peregrines captured in the spring of 1984 included: 1 from Rankin Inlet, Northwest Territories, banded as a nestling in 1981; 1 from the middle Yukon River, Alaska, banded as a nestling in 1983; 1 captured and banded as a first-year migrant at Ft. Morgan, Alabama in October 1981; 12 previously captured in the fall at Padre Island (from 1977-83); 6 previously captured in the spring at Padre Island (from 1981-83); and 1 previously captured in the spring and fall of 1981 at Padre Island. Other banded Peregrines captured in earlier years on Padre Island included 2 from the Yukon River, Alaska, 1 from northeastern Keewatin, Northwest Territories, 1 captive-bred bird released by the Canadian Wildlife Service in northern Alberta, and 1 fall migrant banded 24 days earlier at Cape May Point, New Jersey (Henny and Clark 1982). Padre Island birds recovered south of the United States included one each from Mexico (Yucatan), El Salvador, Panama, Brazil, and Argentina (Hunt et al. 1975, Henny and Clark 1982). Another Peregrine from Padre Island was found above the Arctic Circle in Franklin, Northwest Territories. Clearly, migrant Peregrines sampled at Padre Island were from widespread nesting and wintering locations.

Trends in DDE Contamination. — DDE is the primary metabolite of DDT and was detected in 26 of 27 ASY females and all 19 SY males and females in 1984 (Table 1). The two-factor ANOVA

TABLE 1. DDE residues (wet wt) in blood plasma of female Peregrine Falcons captured in the spring at Padre Island, Texas, 1978-84.

Age[a]/Sex	Year	n	Geometric mean DDE (ppm)	High DDE (ppm)
SY F	1978-79	8	1.43	6.3
SY F	1980	19	0.42	3.0
SY F[b]	1984	16	0.43	2.9
ASY F	1978-79	21	0.88	3.8
ASY F	1980	63	0.62	3.1
ASY F	1984	27	0.55	4.3

[a] SY = second year; ASY = after second year.
[b] 3 SY males contained 0.18, 0.58, and 0.20 ppm DDE (geometric mean 0.28 ppm).

TABLE 2.   Organochlorine pesticides (excluding DDE) and PCBs in blood plasma of Peregrine Falcons captured in the spring at Padre Island, Texas, 1978-84.

| Age[c]/Sex/Year | n | DDT | DDD | No. with detectable residues (highest residue)[a,b] | | | | |
				Heptachlor epoxide	Dieldrin	Oxychlordane	Mirex	PCBs
SY F 1978-79	8	2(0.38)	0	4(1.10)	4(0.30)	0	0	NA[d]
SY F 1980	19	0	0	12(0.53)	9(0.20)	0	1(0.05)	NA[d]
SY F 1984[e]	16	0	0	7(0.69)	9(0.22)	1(0.04)	1(0.09)	2(0.29)
ASY F 1978-79[f]	21	4(0.44)	2(0.07)	6(0.44)	9(0.17)	2(0.13)	4(0.08)	NA[d]
ASY F 1980[g]	63	1(0.04)	0	28(0.44)	37(0.65)	11(0.05)	18(0.17)	NA[d]
ASY F 1984	27	1(0.42)	1(0.28)	9(1.40)	15(0.60)	4(0.06)	7(0.16)	12(0.75)

[a] Number of samples with pesticides ≥ 0.02 ppm wet wt, or PCBs ≥ 0.10 ppm wet wt.
[b] Trans-nonachlor not included because not evaluated all years; none detected in 1984.
[c] SY = second year; ASY = after second year.
[d] NA = not analyzed.
[e] 3 SY males were sampled; 1 contained 0.30 ppm heptachlor epoxide.
[f] 1 contained 0.06 ppm cis-chlordane.
[g] 1 contained 0.02 ppm endrin; 1 contained 0.03 ppm hexachlorobenzene; 1 contained 0.05 ppm cis-chlordane.

showed that mean DDE values varied among years (F=5.73, P<0.01) but showed no difference between age classes (F=0.09, NS) and no interaction (F=1.68, NS). Bonferroni comparisons among years indicated that DDE levels were significantly higher in 1978-79 than in 1980 and 1984. The highest DDE residue (4.3 ppm) in an ASY female in 1984 was accompanied by the only occurrence of parent DDT plus DDD (14% of DDTR was DDT and DDD). This residue profile suggests exposure to recently-applied DDT despite the general downward trend in DDE. The decline in DDE residues for ASY females, the largest data set, was about 38% between 1984 and 1978-79.

Other Pesticides and PCBs. — In addition to DDT and its metabolites, the 1984 plasma samples were tested for nine other pesticides or metabolites and PCBs. Dieldrin and heptachlor epoxide were most frequently encountered in both age classes in 1984 and earlier years (Table 2). PCBs were first investigated in 1984 and were detected in 13% of the SY females and 44% of the ASY females. Heptachlor epoxide, dieldrin and mirex showed no significant change in occurrence during the years 1978-79, 1980 and 1984.

ACKNOWLEDGEMENTS

We thank R. Ambrose, M. Haley, J. Hoolihan, R. Hunter, T. Nichols, R. Richie, W. Satterfield, P. Schempf, W. Seegar, R. Whitney, D. Williamson, and M. Yates for trapping assistance on Padre Island in 1984. C. Bunck and E. Burton provided assistance with the statistical analysis. D. J. Hoffman and M. R. Fuller reviewed the manuscript and offered helpful suggestions.

42 | Organochlorine Pesticide-Related Mortalities of Raptors and Other Birds in New York, 1982–1986

Ward B. Stone and Joseph C. Okoniewski

By January 1971, all uses of DDT and toxaphene, and most uses of dieldrin and heptachlor, were prohibited in New York. Chlordane use was restricted to subterranean applications for termites in 1975 and, as of April 1987, totally banned, as were the remaining uses of dieldrin and heptachlor. Nevertheless, residues of these compounds remain in soils, sediment, and biota at levels sufficient to cause lethal intoxication in some species of birds. This article summarizes documented cases of lethal intoxication in New York between May 1982-October 1986 during the course of routine examination of dead or debilitated wildlife specimens submitted directly by the public to the Wildlife Pathology Unit or submitted through regional offices of the New York State Department of Environmental Conservation (DEC). The numbers of Great Horned Owls we examined were augmented by active solicitation in relation to an ongoing study of that species.

METHODS

Brains from birds for which the history, ante-mortem signs, and gross pathology suggested possible organochlorine poisoning were removed, frozen in clean glass jars and shipped to Hazleton Laboratories, Inc. (Madison, Wisconsin) for gas chromatographic analysis. Analyses at Hazleton were conducted according to Smart et al. (1974), Johnson et al. (1976) and AOAC (1984). Screens for organochlorine pesticides and related compounds generally included analyses for DDE, DDD, DDT, dieldrin, alpha-HCH, beta-HCH, gamma-HCH, HCB, endrin, heptachlor, heptachlor epoxide (HE), aldrin, mirex, methoxychlor, toxaphene, cis-chlordane, trans-nonachlor (TNCH), oxychlordane (OXY), octachlorostyrene and polychlorinated biphenyls (PCBs). Gas chromatographic results were confirmed with mass spectrometry in nine cases. All residue data are presented on a wet weight basis.

Residue levels in the brain were compared with the minimum lethal levels found in experimentally poisoned passerines: >4 ppm for dieldrin (Stickel et al. 1969), >20 ppm for DDT equivalents* (Stickel et al. 1970), >9 ppm HE for birds killed with heptachlor (Stickel et al. 1979), >3.4 ppm HE plus >1.1 ppm OXY for birds killed with technical chlordane (Stickel et al. 1979), and >310 ppm PCBs for birds killed with Aroclor 1254 (Stickel et al. 1984).

FINDINGS

Based on gross post-mortem findings and residue levels in the brain, diagnosis of organochlorine pesticide poisoning was made for 39 birds from 31 separate cases (Table 1). Twenty-eight of these cases involved single birds.

OXY and HE derived from chlordane were the principal toxicants, or together with dieldrin were among the principal toxicants, in 30 birds: one Great Blue Heron, two Sharp-shinned Hawks, two Cooper's Hawks, two Eastern Screech-Owls, eight Great Horned Owls, five Blue Jays, three American Robins, one Eastern Bluebird, five European Starlings, and one Common Grackle. In 10 cases, both the HE and OXY levels were above the lower lethal limits experimentally defined by Stickel et al. (1979). OXY levels more commonly exceeded those of HE in the brain. In three Great Horned Owls, two Eastern Screech-Owls and a Blue Jay, OXY and HE appeared to be the principal toxicants despite HE levels below the 3.4 ppm minimum reported by Stickel et al. (1979). Eleven cases (16 birds) were from Long Island locations. Tremors, convulsions, or seizures were reportedly observed in some birds before death. Grossly visible fat reserves were absent in all birds, but marked emaciation was present only in two Cooper's Hawks and one Great Horned Owl. Carcass lipids, when measured, were generally <1%. No birds showed any gross signs of infectious or parasitic disease or serious trauma.

Dieldrin by itself was the principal toxicant in seven cases which included eight birds: one Cooper's Hawk, one Common Barn-Owl, one Eastern Screech-Owl, one Great Horned Owl, three American Robins, and one Blue Jay. Levels of dieldrin in the brain ranged from 3.65-12.3 ppm. Five of the seven cases originated in the northern part of the Finger Lakes region of New York.

DDE (228 ppm), DDT (31.4 ppm) and dieldrin (3.51 ppm) were present in the brain of an adult female Eastern Bluebird found

* $\frac{DDE}{15} + \frac{DDD}{5} + DDT > 20$ ppm

moribund in a recently abandoned apple orchard in the mid-Hudson Valley in May 1985. Levels of these toxicants in soil samples taken beneath the drip zone of two trees in the orchard averaged 49 ppm DDE, 7.2 ppm DDD, 138 ppm DDT and 3.0 ppm dieldrin.

A hatch-year Northern Goshawk was found in a weakened condition at a golf course in Greene County (just north of the Catskill region) in August 1985. The Goshawk died shortly after discovery. In fair flesh at best, its brain contained 6.93 ppm HE and 0.30 ppm OXY, a ratio which identifies the insecticide heptachlor as the parent compound (Blus et al. 1985a). Although the level of HE found in the brain was below the 9 ppm minimum level reported by Stickel et al. (1979), the gross pathology strongly suggested organochlorine poisoning.

Toxaphene at 8.48 ppm in the brain and 22.2 ppm in the liver was found in an adult Great Blue Heron exhibiting severe motor problems and tremors at Fish Creek, the outlet to Saratoga Lake in the upper Hudson Valley, in May 1982. The heron was in fair flesh. Hemorrhagic ovarian follicles and possible low-grade peritonitis were noted. No bacterial pathogens were isolated from the ovary or the feces (cultures performed by the New York State Department of Health).

In addition to the cases summarized in Table 1, there have been others in which organochlorine compounds may have directly contributed to avian mortality to varying degrees (Table 2). In four Great Horned Owls and a Cooper's Hawk, grossly inexplicable emaciation was coupled with some combination of elevated but individually sublethal levels of DDE, dieldrin, HE, OXY and/or PCBs in the brain. Another Great Horned Owl also had a similar residue profile but was in fair flesh. A sixth Great Horned Owl, debilitated by a fractured mandible, died in fair-to-poor flesh with 4.13 ppm OXY in its brain.

The remaining Great Horned Owl in Table 2 (Jefferson County) was found dead at a residence along the upper St. Lawrence River (Thousand Island section) in fair flesh with traces of subcutaneous fat present. There were no signs of infectious or parasitic disease, and trauma was limited to recent lacerations on two toes (possibly bite wounds). Analyses performed at the DEC's laboratory in Hale Creek (the only analyses which were not done at Hazleton Laboratories) revealed PCB levels in the brain and liver of 205 ppm and 467 ppm, respectively. Elevated levels of mirex in these tissues (6.2 ppm, brain; 14.1 ppm, liver) indicated that the owl had preyed upon fauna linked to the Lake Ontario watershed (Kaiser 1978, Norstrom et al. 1980). Although the level of PCBs in the brain was below the 310 ppm lethal minimum reported for Aroclor 1254, organochlorine poisoning appeared to be the most likely cause of death. Unfortunately, no analyses for HE, OXY, dibenzofurans or dibenzodioxins were done, and the contribution of PCBs to this mortality must remain speculative.

TABLE 1. Data on birds from New York (plus 2 birds from Pennsylvania), 1982-86, for which the principal cause of death appeared to be intoxication with organochlorine pesticide residues.

Species	Location (county)	Date of death	Age[a]-sex	Residue levels in the brain (ppm wet wt)									
				DDE	DDD	DDT	PCBs	Dieldrin	HCB	Mirex	HE[b]	OXY[c]	TNCH[d]
Great Blue Heron	Saratoga	05/18/82	AHY-F	22	3.1	0.63	3.92	0.12		8.48[g]		2.37[h]	
	Queens	04/17/85	SY-F	5.8	2.7	0.27	10.0	4.03			0.57	2.29	
Northern Goshawk	Greene	08/18/85	HY-M	0.98			0.62	0.34	0.02	0.02	6.93	0.30	0.03
Sharp-shinned Hawk	Nassau	03/11/85	SY-F	3.3	0.03		3.3	2.09	0.04	0.11	0.07	2.27	1.0
	Suffolk	03/17/86	SY-F	8.9	0.02		4.7	0.16			3.49	4.3	0.32
Cooper's Hawk	Cattaraugus	07/??/83	AHY-F	21	0.23	0.14	13.5	1.97	0.09	2.61	4.34	5.83	1.27
	Monroe	04/09/84	ASY-F	37	0.25	0.10	9.1	8.73	0.09		0.27	1.02	
	Albany	04/30/84	ASY-F	19	0.47		8.09	5.74	0.04	1.01	2.65	1.15	0.24
	Onondaga	08/25/84	HY-M	2.7			0.31	3.65				0.01	
Common Barn-Owl	Putnam	12/20/85	HY-M	2.1	0.08	0.01	34.0	9.74	0.02		0.05	0.74	0.03
Eastern Screech-Owl	Suffolk	07/25/83	HY-M	3.1			1.4	0.09	0.01		1.81	2.64	1.81
	Ontario	07/03/84	HY-?	19		0.18	2.05	5.78		0.02	0.55	1.00	
	PA[i]	06/28/86	AHY-F	16		0.03	2.2	0.04	0.02		1.11	2.07	0.12
Great Horned Owl	Dutchess	04/29/81	AHY-M	27	0.23	0.08	25.1	0.72	0.27	1.72	1.41	5.00	
	Westchester	10/03/83	AHY-F	59			71.0	0.50	0.02	1.92	2.24	8.68	0.23
	Albany	06/21/84	AHY-M	96	0.11	0.17	37.4	0.85	0.10	1.99	1.04	3.98	
	Putnam	04/20/84	AHY-M	26	0.13	0.09	10.97	6.80	0.06	1.51	6.02	5.10	0.50
	Nassau	08/31/84	AHY-M	20			2.83	1.31		0.05	0.12	3.77	
	Ontario	10/14/84	AHY-M	44	0.65	0.07	4.84	9.89	0.02	0.14	0.54	0.98	
	Suffolk	08/18/85	AHY-F	26	0.01		26.1	1.48	0.02	0.03	7.74	4.74	2.29
	PA[i]	10/08/85	HY-F	78	0.19		12.0	1.97	0.07	0.02	2.26	3.85	
	Monroe	07/12/86	AHY-M	13	0.13	0.10	3.2	8.44	0.012	0.02	3.69	3.64	0.60
Blue Jay	Suffolk	07/29/84	AHY-F;HY-M[e]	9.5			1.1			0.01	3.28	3.29	

Species	County	Date	Age										
	Nassau	07/29/84	AHY-F	10			0.8		0.026	3.72	4.85	
	Monroe	06/28/85	HY-?	0.07				12.3	0.03	0.68	0.19	
	Suffolk	07/13/85	HY-F	6.2				2.95		3.57	4.31	
	Suffolk	07/27/86	HY-F	3.5	1.7			0.11		2.08	4.99	2.00
American Robin	Monroe	06/27/83	AHY-2F;1M[f]	2.0	0.15		0.86	10.7	0.17	2.66	1.3	1.9
Eastern Bluebird	Onondaga	08/??/84	AHY-F	1.8				2.66	0.17	2.20	3.00	
	Columbia	05/09/85	AHY-F	228	1.6	31	0.31	3.51				
European Starling	Nassau	07/16/85	HY-F	14			2.2			4.96	7.65	
	Nassau	07/16/85	AHY-M	2.9	0.10			6.00		3.00	2.62	
	Nassau	07/16/85	AHY-F	3.5			2.5	3.67		2.46	4.26	
	Nassau	07/16/85	U-F	6.7			1.1	1.42		4.29	6.38	
	Nassau	07/14/86	HY-F	2.5			0.65	2.47		3.33	2.33	0.52
Common Grackle	Nassau	07/17/84	AHY-M	9.4	0.01		1.3	0.08		9.09	10.8	

[a] HY = hatch year (calendar); AHY = after hatch year; SY = second year; ASY = after second year; U = undetermined.
[b] HE = heptachlor epoxide.
[c] OXY = oxychlordane.
[d] TNCH = *trans*-nonachlor.
[e] 2 birds, brains pooled for analysis.
[f] 3 birds, brains pooled for analysis.
[g] Total is for toxaphene.
[h] Total is for chlordane.
[i] Northampton, Pennsylvania.

TABLE 2. Birds from New York, 1982-86, for which intoxication with one or more organochlorine pesticide residues was probably an important contributing mortality factor.

Species	Location (county)	Date of death	Age[a]-sex	Cond.[b]	Gross pathology	Residue levels in the brain (ppm wet wt)				
						DDE	PCBs	Dieldrin	Heptachlor epoxide	Oxy-chlordane
Cooper's Hawk	Cattaraugus	12/14/83	AHY-M	P	inexplicable emaciation	21.5	13.6	0.44	0.26	1.52
Peregrine Falcon	Brooklyn	06/30/85	AHY-F	U	no trauma/extensive scavenging by fly larvae	(125)[c]	(180)[c]	(5.02)[c]		(4.46)[c]
Great Horned Owl	Onondaga	08/01/83	AHY-M	P	superficial laceration of breast	45.3	20.4	0.90	2.26	1.29
	Schenectady	10/19/83	AHY-M	VP	extreme emaciation; minor puncture wounds and abrasions	83.8	57.5	0.53	0.64	2.44
	Schenectady	03/14/84	AHY-M	F-P	debilitating fracture of right mandible	79.6	72.5	0.46	0.32	4.13
	Niagara	11/24/84	HY-M	F	nonspecific	89.3	67.2	1.37	0.36	1.30
	Albany	08/09/85	AHY-M	VP	inexplicable emaciation	78.9	86.0	0.38	0.60	2.19
	Erie	07/17/86	AHY-M	VP	emaciated; numerous coccidia in lower intestine	128	28.0	0.40	0.41	1.46

[a] HY = hatch year (calendar); AHY = after hatch year.
[b] Assessment of body condition based on size of grossly visible fat reserves (if any) and degree of muscle and organ atrophy: F = fair; P = poor; VP = very poor to emaciated; U = undetermined.
[c] Only muscle available for analysis owing to scavenging by fly larvae.

The Peregrine Falcon in Table 2 was found dead at a nest site on a bridge in New York City. Greatly elevated levels of DDE, PCBs, dieldrin, and OXY were found in its wing muscle. Unfortunately, owing to autolysis and extensive scavenging by fly larvae, the brain was not available for analysis, and a definitive diagnosis could not be made. This Peregrine was a captive-bred female which had been hacked at Sea Isle City, New Jersey in 1980.

The frequency with which these organochlorine poisonings were recorded is shown in Table 3. Only mortalities from Table 1 were used to calculate percent frequencies. The data in Table 3 should be considered as conservative because analyses were usually done only to confirm probable poisonings, to substantiate other tentative diagnoses, or to compile data on a particular species (such as the Great Horned Owl) or locale.

DISCUSSION

Although chlordane has been used as an insecticide since the late 1940s, the first record of wild bird mortality associated with its use did not appear until Blus et al. (1983b) documented the deaths of two

TABLE 3. Percentage of organochlorine pesticide-caused deaths in wild birds submitted for diagnosis in New York State, 1982-86 (excluding roadkills submitted for toxicant analyses).

Species	No. necropsied	No. analyzed for organochlorines		Deaths chiefly caused by organochlorines[a]	
		brain	carcass or liver only	n	%
Great Blue Heron	39	17	7	2	5.1
Northern Goshawk	19	4	1	1	5.3
Sharp-shinned Hawk	24	7	3	2	8.3
Cooper's Hawk	37	20	5	4	10.8
Common Barn-Owl	6	5		1	16.7
Eastern Screech-Owl	28	10	3	3	10.7
Great Horned Owl	176	152	11	9	5.1
Blue Jay	23	7		6	26.1
American Robin	66	7	1	3	4.5
Eastern Bluebird	19[b]	4	8[b]	2	10.5
European Starling	255[c]	14[d]	5[d]	5	2.0
Common Grackle	52[e]	2		1	1.9

[a] Birds from Table 1 only.
[b] Includes 2 nests of young (7 nestlings total).
[c] Represents 26 cases, many involving multiple mortalities caused by cholinesterase inhibitor pesticides and other toxicants.
[d] Includes 2 pools, 5 birds total (brain), and 5 pools, 11 birds total (liver).
[e] Represents 22 cases, many involving multiple mortalities caused by cholinesterase inhibitor pesticides.

Red-shouldered Hawks and a Great Horned Owl. Our findings indicate that chlordane-related bird mortality is far from uncommon in New York and is encountered more frequently than any other type of organochlorine pesticide poisoning. Many of the chlordane-related cases we have documented originated on Long Island where chlordane was used extensively as a termiticide. Prior to 1975, chlordane was also widely applied to lawns, and extensive soil and sediment sampling and analyses are needed to determine the principal source(s) of the HE and OXY found in poisoned birds. At this point at least, it seems that the source(s) of the toxicants are more commonly historical than contemporary in nature. This conclusion is based on the dominance of OXY in many birds, and the relative rarity of less persistent components of chlordane in the residue profiles; e.g., *trans*-nonachlor was detected in less than half of the birds with high levels of HE and/or OXY, and only six of these birds had detectable levels of other less persistent chlordane components such as *cis*-nonachlor, compound C, and compound E.

The hazards of dieldrin to wild birds are well-documented (Clawson and Baker 1959, Scott et al. 1959, Stickel et al. 1969, Ohlendorf et al. 1979, Kaiser et al. 1980). Although more than a decade has elapsed since most uses of dieldrin were banned in New York, this insecticide continues to pose a threat to birds in some areas of the state. Elevated dieldrin levels are often (especially on Long Island) paired with elevated levels of chlordane-related compounds, indicating that both pesticides were previously used in the same areas. Experimental data on the combined effects of these two cyclodiene pesticides are sorely needed.

The DDT-related death of the Eastern Bluebird at a Hudson Valley orchard is surprising only in its singularity. Johnson et al. (1976) recorded little mortality among breeding American Robins in an active Hudson Valley orchard during 1966-68, mainly because earthworms and other prey items were, owing to pesticide levels in the soil, exceedingly scarce within the orchard. The American Robins, therefore, generally foraged outside of the orchard. As years pass, the levels of dieldrin and DDT-related compounds decline in abandoned orchards, and populations of earthworms and other soil-dwelling invertebrates recover. These invertebrates, however, may be expected to harbor pesticide levels which will threaten a variety of insectivorous birds and mammals and their predators. In May 1980, an American Kestrel found dead in neighboring Dutchess County had lethal or near-lethal levels of both DDT and dieldrin in its brain (Stone 1981). Orchards were present near the site where the American Kestrel was collected. Future monitoring of orchard sites is warranted.

The heptachlor and toxaphene intoxications are interesting, if somewhat anomalous. Neither pesticide has reportedly been used in significant quantities in New York. It is believed that the Great Blue Heron acquired the toxaphene somewhere on its winter range or migration route. Where the Northern Goshawk acquired its heptachlor is uncertain, as dispersal from its natal territory may have begun prior to its demise in mid-August. Although heptachlor-related avian mortality is well documented (Smith and Glasgow 1963, Rosene 1965, Kreitzer and Spann 1968, Henny et al. 1983, Blus et al. 1984, 1985a), there are few records of avian mortality associated with toxaphene (Rudd and Genelly 1956, Keith 1966, McEwen et al. 1972). Lethal brain residues for toxaphene have not been determined, but carcasses of birds killed after toxaphene applications on short-grass rangelands to control grasshoppers (McEwen et al. 1972) contained from 0.1-9.6 ppm toxaphene.

In addition to some of the Great Horned Owls in Tables 1 and 2, several other Great Horned Owls examined during this period were found to have high levels of PCBs in their brains. Summaries of our findings relative to mortality and environmental toxicants in this species will be the subject of future papers. To date, the only cases of wild bird mortality in North America which have been attributed to PCBs have been those involving Ring-billed Gulls in southern Ontario (Canada) in 1969 and 1973 (Sileo et al. 1977), and that of a Great Horned Owl found dying along the Hudson River in 1981 (Stone and Okoniewski 1983). Until the toxicity of individual PCB congeners is more fully understood, and capillary chromatography is more frequently used to characterize PCBs in environmental samples, interpretation of the effects of PCBs on birds will remain difficult.

As can be seen in Tables 1 and 2, individual birds often have elevated levels of more than one organochlorine toxicant. These toxicants may act in an isolated, additive, synergistic or antagonistic manner. Stickel et al. (1970) suggested that additivity most nearly reflects the interaction of DDE, DDD and DDT in birds. In Coturnix Quail, Heath et al. (1972) found the effects of DDE and PCBs to be additive. The findings of Stickel et al. (1979) indicate that HE and OXY may act synergistically to some degree. Based on a similar mode of toxic action (Matsumura 1985), these two cyclodiene compounds might be expected to act additively with the other commonly detected cyclodiene insecticide, dieldrin. Experimental data on these and other inter-pesticide relationships are incomplete at best. Nevertheless, combined effects should be considered by diagnosticians, as should species-specific differences in vulnerability to toxicants, and variability in the recovery rates, instrumentation, and methods of analysis.

Most data indicate that levels of organochlorine pesticides in birds in the United States have, in general, declined considerably in the last decade (Spitzer et al. 1978, Ohlendorf 1981, Blus 1982). However, we have shown that individuals of several species of raptors and ground-feeding insectivorous birds are still threatened by DDT, dieldrin, and chlordane in certain areas of New York. Although organochlorine pesticide residues in migratory birds are now frequently attributed to contamination of wintering grounds, e.g., in Central and South America (Lincer and Sherburne 1974, Henny et al. 1982c, Blus et al. 1985b), it seems probable that significant portions of the residue loads in most of the birds discussed in this paper were acquired on the breeding grounds within the state. Nationwide surveys of organochlorine pesticides and PCBs in European Starlings (Bunck et al. 1987) suggest that areas of the south-central and southeastern United States may be significantly contaminated with heptachlor, chlordane, and dieldrin. We suspect that avian mortality linked to these pesticides is probably occurring in those areas today.

The impacts of organochlorine poisonings at the population level are uncertain. Table 3 ignores regional variation, which appears to be considerable. Also to be considered are the effects on reproduction such as eggshell thinning (Ratcliffe 1967, Hickey and Anderson 1968, Wiemeyer and Porter 1970), embryo and post-hatching mortality (Genelly and Rudd 1956, Heath et al. 1969, Porter and Wiemeyer 1969, Longcore et al. 1971, Neill et al. 1971) and aberrant parental behavior (Jefferies 1973).

Considering the amount of mortality which probably occurred during the heyday of organochlorine pesticide use in the United States, published records of such mortalities are few. As attention shifted to the environmental effects of cholinesterase inhibitor pesticides and other toxicants, it is not surprising that current reports of such mortality are scarce. Diagnosticians should be alert for ground-feeding insectivores, raptors, and piscivores which lack fat (but are often in otherwise good flesh), have empty alimentary canals, and grossly appear to be poisoned. Contrary to much contemporary thinking, environmental problems related to persistent organochlorine pesticides have far from disappeared, although they have perhaps lessened.

ACKNOWLEDGEMENTS

We are grateful for the vigilance of wildlife rehabilitators, sportsmen and other environmentally concerned members of the public for submitting the birds discussed in this paper. Valuable comments on an early draft of the manuscript were provided by L. J. Blus. This work was funded by voluntary contributions of taxpayers in New York (Return-A-Gift-To-Wildlife Program).

43 | Organochlorine Residues and Eggshell Thinning in Southern African Raptors

John M. Mendelsohn, Ashley C. Butler, and Ron R. Sibbald

The effects of certain residual organochlorines on survival and reproduction of birds of prey are well known (Newton 1979, 1984). Most research on the effects of these chemicals on raptor populations has been done in western Europe and North America. Because use of DDT, dieldrin and related organochlorines has largely stopped in these regions, many raptor populations are recovering, and concern for the effects of residual poisoning has diminished (Ratcliffe 1980, Newton and Haas 1984, other chapters in this book). Use of organochlorines has now shifted to countries in Central and South America, Africa, and Asia. There is every reason to predict that raptor populations in these areas will decline significantly unless the use of these chemicals is restricted. It is vital to have information on quantities and kinds of chemicals being applied, current health of raptor populations, and levels of residues in raptors. We review data on the latter issue for raptors in southern Africa — the region lying south of the Zambesi, Cunene and Okavango rivers. We also present data on eggshell thinning in this region. Finally, we examine those areas and potential problems most in need of study.

DATA SOURCES AND METHODS

We attempted to extract all original pesticide residue data for wild raptors (excluding migrants) from the following studies: Butler and Sibbald (unpubl. ms.), de Kock and Watson (unpubl. ms.), Kiff et al. (1983), Mundy et al. (1982), Peakall and Kemp (1976, 1980), Robertson and Boshoff (unpubl. ms.), Snelling et al. (1984), Tannock et al. (1983), Thomson (1984c), and Whitwell et al. (1974). The accumulated data consist of 201 samples collected between 1960-84: 180 egg samples and 21 tissue samples from full-grown birds. Results from eggs in the same clutch were pooled. The analytical methods used are described in the publications from which results were drawn, and the unpublished results were obtained using methods described by Butler et al. (1983). Our data are presented on a ppm wet weight basis; results published as "dry wt" were converted by multiplying by 0.25.

Eggshell thickness was measured using the Ratcliffe Index (Ratcliffe 1967) for eggs in the Transvaal Museum (Pretoria), Durban Natural History Museum, and various private collections. Results obtained by Mundy et al. (1982) for Cape Vultures and African White-backed Vultures are included.

RESULTS

Distribution of Residue Samples. — Most samples came from Zimbabwe ($n=105$) and the Transvaal ($n=63$). Those from Botswana ($n=12$) and the Cape Province ($n=14$) were of Cape Vultures. The remaining five samples were collected in Natal. No data were available for Mozambique, Swaziland, Lesotho, Namibia and, in South Africa, the Orange Free State, Venda, Bophuthatswana, Transkei and Ciskei. The data were dominated by two species: Cape Vulture ($n=44$) and African Fish Eagle ($n=54$ from Zimbabwe, $n=3$ from Natal). The only other species represented by more than 10 samples were Black Sparrowhawk ($n=19$) and African White-backed Vulture ($n=12$). The remaining samples were spread between 18 species of diurnal raptors and six species of owls. For certain analyses, samples were pooled according to the preferred diet of the raptor species, as follows: bird predators ($n=40$), fish predators ($n=58$), mammal predators ($n=11$), general vertebrate predators ($n=15$), invertebrate predators ($n=12$) and scavengers ($n=65$).

DDT and Metabolites. — Of 200 samples tested, 198 had detectable residues of DDT or DDE and TDE; the compounds were not detected in an African Crowned Eagle and a Wahlberg's Eagle, both from Zimbabwe. DDE levels were much higher than either DDT or TDE. DDT residues >0.5 ppm, perhaps indicating significant recent contamination, were found in a Cape Vulture egg (1960) from South Africa and six samples from Zimbabwe: a Black Sparrowhawk (1980), three African Fish Eagles (1980, 1980, 1981), a Pel's Fishing Owl (1980) and a Verreaux's Eagle Owl (1972). Bird- and fish-eating raptors were more contaminated than other predators (Figure 1, Table 1). Of 40 samples from bird-eaters, 34 (85%) showed levels >5.0 ppm DDE, 23 contained >10.0 ppm, and 12 had residues >20.0 ppm, the highest being 79 ppm and 118 ppm in Black Sparrowhawks. All bird-eating species were apparently contaminated to a similar degree (Table 1).

Of the 58 samples from piscivores, one was a Pel's Fishing Owl egg containing 27.5 ppm DDE. The other 57 were African Fish Eagles, 46

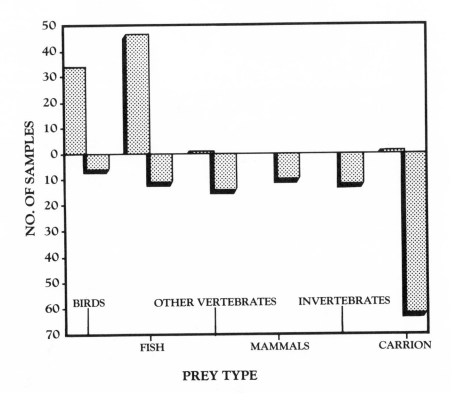

PREY TYPE

FIGURE 1. Comparative levels of DDE contamination in southern African raptors, according to their main prey of birds, fish, mammals, other vertebrates, invertebrates, or carrion. Number of samples containing >5.0 ppm (above) or <5.0 ppm (below) DDE wet wt.

TABLE 1. Frequency of samples showing various levels of DDE contamination (ppm wet wt) in southern African bird- and fish-eating raptors.

Species	>20.0	19.9-10.0	9.9-5.0	<5.0	Total no. of samples
Black Sparrowhawk	8	4	6	1	19
African Goshawk	0	1	0	1	2
Ovampo Sparrowhawk	0	1	4	1	6
Little Sparrowhawk	1	0	0	0	1
Lanner Falcon	1	4	1	2	8
Peregrine Falcon	2	1	0	1	4
African Fish Eagle	7	24	15	11	57
Pel's Fishing Owl	1	0	0	0	1
Total	20	35	26	17	98

(81%) of which contained >5.0 ppm; 31 had >10.0 ppm, and 7 showed levels >20.0 ppm. The highest values of >40 ppm were found in four clutches from Zimbabwe and in muscle samples (56 ppm and 42 ppm) from two birds found dead in Natal. These two birds had liver residues of 140 ppm and 5.5 ppm DDE, respectively, and were perhaps killed by poisoning (especially by dieldrin — see below).

Of the remaining 102 samples, 101 contained <5.0 ppm DDE; 8.9 ppm DDE was found in one Wahlberg's Eagle egg. One Cape Vulture egg had a total DDT/DDE/TDE residue of 6.0 ppm. Kiff et al. (1983) reported a level of 0.6 ppm DDE in a Palm-nut Vulture egg from Zimbabwe. However, this species is unlikely to breed in Zimbabwe (Irwin 1981) so we have excluded his report from our data.

Dieldrin. — Some samples were not analyzed for dieldrin. As with DDE, a higher degree of contamination was found in bird- and fish-eaters than in other predator groups (Figure 2). Seven of 27 samples

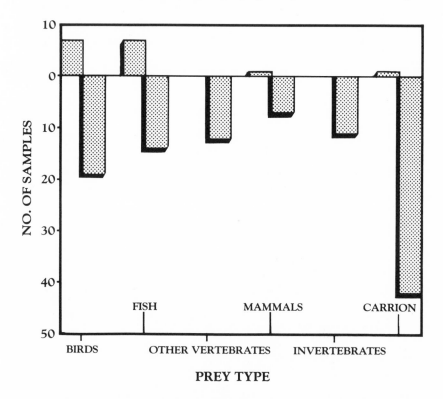

FIGURE 2. Comparative levels of dieldrin contamination in southern African raptors, according to their main prey of birds, fish, mammals, other vertebrates, invertebrates, or carrion. Number of samples containing >1.0 ppm (above) or <1.0 ppm (below) dieldrin wet wt.

from bird predators contained >1.0 ppm; two Black Sparrowhawks from Zimbabwe had high levels of 3.3 ppm and 9.5 ppm. Seven of 21 piscivores had residues >1.0 ppm, high levels of 2.4 ppm and 5.6 ppm being found in Zimbabwe African Fish Eagle eggs. The muscle tissue of the only three African Fish Eagles from Natal contained 3.7 ppm, 14.0 ppm and 14.1 ppm, and their livers contained 23.0 ppm, 7.0 ppm and 1.5 ppm, respectively. Only 4 of 73 samples from other raptors had levels >1.0 ppm: 2.5 ppm in a Cape Vulture egg (Transvaal) and 1.6 ppm in muscle tissue, 2.2 ppm in liver tissue and 67.0 ppm in brain tissue of a Verreaux's Eagle found dead in Natal.

Other Organochlorines. — Some studies reported residues of PCBs and the "HCH" compounds, mainly gamma-BHC or Lindane, but few levels >1.0 ppm were found. PCB residues of >1.0 ppm were detected in the liver of an African Fish Eagle and in the egg of a Lanner Falcon from Natal, and in a Common Barn-Owl and Ovampo Sparrowhawk in the Transvaal; 16 other samples contained <1.0 ppm. Levels of gamma-BHC were generally low, the highest values being 0.1-0.2 ppm. The less toxic isomers, alpha- and beta-BHC, were also found mostly at low levels, although Lanner Falcons (1.2 ppm and 2.8 ppm) and Black Sparrowhawks (1.5 ppm, 3.0 ppm and 31.5 ppm) in Zimbabwe had significant levels.

Eggshell Thickness. — The thickness indices for eggs collected before and during the DDT era were compared for 20 species (Table 2). All had thinner eggshells during the period of DDT use, but differences between the two periods were statistically significant ($P<0.05$) in only seven species: African Fish Eagle (13% thinner), Gabar Goshawk (10% thinner), Western Marsh Harrier (9% thinner), Wahlberg's Eagle (6% thinner), Greater Kestrel (5.5% thinner) and Cape Vulture (3.5% thinner). The data were highly variable, however, and larger samples are probably required to confirm real differences. For example, the very small difference in Cape Vulture eggs was significant because 58 and 76 eggs were available for measurement for the two periods, respectively (Mundy et al. 1982).

The degree of eggshell thinning varied greatly between species, but was not generally related to their diet (Table 2), as expected from differences in DDE contamination (Figure 1). The only Ratcliffe Index value (2.14) for one clutch of Black Sparrowhawk eggs from the pre-DDT period was higher than for all 12 clutches ($\bar{x}=1.76$) collected after 1947. Kiff et al. (1983) reported eggshell thinning in other vultures, but none of the differences between the periods before and after the introduction of DDT were statistically significant. The only eggshell thickness data for African Peregrines (Peakall and Kiff 1979) suggest substantial thinning, although the samples were too small to show significance.

TABLE 2. Indices of eggshell thickness (and number of clutches measured) before and after the first use of DDT (1947) in southern African raptors for which 3 or more clutches were available in each period. Data for Cape and African White-backed Vultures after Mundy et al. (1982).

Species	Main prey	Pre-1947 Index	Post-1947 Index	% reduction
African Fish Eagle	fish	2.93 (6)	2.54 (12)	13.3[a]
Little Sparrowhawk	birds	1.06 (4)	0.95 (6)	10.4
African Harrier Hawk	vertebrates	2.01 (3)	1.81 (3)	10.0
Gabar Goshawk	vertebrates	1.23 (12)	1.11 (3)	9.8[a]
Western Marsh Harrier	vertebrates	1.65 (6)	1.50 (7)	9.1[a]
Verreaux's Eagle	mammals	3.17 (5)	2.91 (4)	8.3
Wahlberg's Eagle	vertebrates	2.08 (36)	1.95 (13)	6.3[a]
Greater Kestrel	insects	1.45 (9)	1.37 (13)	5.5[a]
Rufous-breasted Sparrowhawk	birds	1.35 (6)	1.28 (3)	5.2
Lizard Buzzard	vertebrates	1.37 (34)	1.31 (4)	5.0
Jackal Buzzard	vertebrates	2.16 (7)	2.06 (8)	4.8[a]
Lanner Falcon	birds	1.75 (3)	1.67 (21)	4.6
Shikra	vertebrates	1.18 (47)	1.13 (8)	4.2
African White-backed Vulture	carrion	3.48 (31)	3.35 (50)	3.7
Ovampo Sparrowhawk	birds	1.41 (7)	1.36 (10)	3.6
Cape Vulture	carrion	3.96 (58)	3.82 (76)	3.5[a]
Tawny Eagle	vertebrates	2.89 (3)	2.81 (7)	2.8
Bateleur	vertebrates	3.23 (4)	3.17 (6)	1.9
African Hawk Eagle	vertebrates	2.33 (3)	2.30 (14)	1.1
Black-shouldered Kite	mammals	1.22 (5)	1.21 (8)	0.8

[a] $P < 0.05$.

DISCUSSION

We have attempted to identify patterns of contamination and eggshell thinning. However, because these data are subject to many sources of error and bias, small quantitative differences cannot be given much emphasis. Moreover, the degree of contamination and level of thinning may be exaggerated because many samples were obtained from addled eggs and birds found dead. The degree of bias is hard to estimate because most samples lack information on egg fertility or cause of death. Nevertheless, about 83% of samples from bird- and fish-eaters contained more than 5 ppm DDE (Table 1), a level which may be associated with lowered productivity in sensitive species (Newton 1979). This suggests that a significant proportion of these raptors have depressed reproductive rates. By contrast, the much lower levels of contamination in other raptors suggest their hatching rates are normal.

The high number of eggs with more than 5.0 ppm DDE (Figure 1) suggests that eggshells should have been thinner than those measured (Table 2). This incongruity might be owing to inadequate sample sizes and to the fact that much of the eggshell thickness data was obtained from eggs taken by egg collectors.

Dieldrin residues were also higher in fish- and bird-eating raptors than in other species. Levels above 1.0 ppm in eggs may be associated with reproductive failure in some species, while levels above 5-10 ppm in adult tissues are probably lethal (Ratcliffe 1980, Blus 1982). The frequency of high dieldrin levels suggests that many bird- and fish-eating raptors in southern Africa are affected detrimentally by this chemical. The data on other organochlorines are too inadequate to assess.

Zimbabwe, Transvaal, and Natal are the only areas for which samples from bird- and fish-eating raptors are available, and since the latter are the only species likely to show substantial levels of organochlorine residues (Newton 1984), these areas are the only ones in southern Africa for which data on pesticide contamination has been collected. No useful information is available for the much larger remainder of the region, including such large countries as Namibia, Mozambique and Botswana, and the Cape and Orange Free State provinces of South Africa.

Although some samples are small and differ in species composition, the data suggest that raptors in Zimbabwe and the Transvaal are contaminated to about the same order of magnitude. Those from Natal had amongst the highest DDE, dieldrin and PCB residues and may suffer from greater residues if the five samples are representative. DDT use in the Transvaal and Natal has been limited since 1976 to malaria mosquito control in the eastern and coastal areas. While dieldrin was withdrawn from general use in 1982, there is a continued source from the degradation of aldrin which is still used for certain applications. Zimbabwe uses DDT and dieldrin for a variety of puposes, and rates of application are apparently high (Thomson 1984c).

The data presented here suggest that residues of some organochlorines are sufficiently high to cause reproductive failure and mortality in southern African raptors. However, no information is available on possible demographic effects, largely because few raptor populations have been monitored to any degree during the last two decades. Cape Vultures (Piper et al. 1981) and Verreaux's Eagles (Gargett 1977) have been studied in detail, but are unlikely to show significant effects of residual organochlorines. Some populations may have increased as a result of other environmental changes. For example, African Fish Eagles have occupied newly built dams, Black Sparrowhawks and several other accipiters now breed in plantations over large regions previously lacking suitable nesting habitat, and Lanner Falcons now occupy nest sites on power line structures, buildings, quarries, etc. (Steyn 1982, Tarboton and Allan 1984). These changes may have balanced the negative effects of pesticides on these species. Population declines of other species which have not benefited from recent changes may not have been detected. In a related case of chemical poisoning, reductions in numbers of Bateleurs and Cape Vultures are partly attributable to feeding on strychnine-poisoned meat (Benson and Dobbs 1984, Tarboton and Allan 1984).

There is little information on quantities of organochlorines used in southern Africa. This problem is complicated by the great number of political authorities in each region; there are at least 11 autonomous governments each of which may have its own system of controlling and using pesticides.

We believe the data reviewed here demonstrate that organochlorine residues in southern Africa are high enough to have a significant impact on the dynamics of some raptor populations. More research is needed on the question of pesticide contamination in southern Africa. We see three aspects needing study: (1) There is an urgent need to monitor the health of raptor populations, in particular selected bird- and fish-eating species which could show negative changes attributable to residual poisoning. (2) Pesticide residues should be monitored throughout the region on a sustained and regular basis in selected species so that comparative changes can be detected. The monitoring program should cover as many kinds of residual pesticides as possible, including heavy metals for which virtually no information is currently available. (3) Conservation agencies should gather information on the quantities and application of different pesticides used in southern Africa. These agencies would then be in a position to identify problems of excessive pesticide use in particular areas, and to recommend restrictions.

ACKNOWLEDGEMENTS

Through the courtesy of A. Kemp, R. Dean kindly measured and weighed all the raptor eggs in the collection of the Transvaal Museum. We also thank H. Chittenden, K. Thangavelu, A. Connell and R. Thomson for collecting and providing data. The participation of J. M. Mendelsohn in this conference was made possible by the generosity of The Peregrine Fund, Inc., and the Durban City Council.

Commentary

The Relative Importance of the Several Organochlorines in the Decline of Peregrine Falcon Populations

Robert W. Risebrough and David B. Peakall

At the 1982 Thessaloniki meeting of the International Council for Bird Preservation's World Working Group on Birds of Prey (Newton and Chancellor 1985), discussions on the relative importance of DDE and dieldrin in the population declines of birds of prey revealed a divergence of views. North Americans have generally attributed population declines primarily to decreases in productivity caused by DDE and associated eggshell thinning; Europeans have generally attached greater importance to adult mortality, caused principally by the cyclodiene insecticides, especially dieldrin. Nisbet (Chapter 35) raises the question again and suggests that dieldrin may have contributed significantly to the disappearance of breeding Peregrines from eastern North America in 1946-64 by increasing adult mortality. The scientific need to resolve this issue is evident, but since both DDT and dieldrin are still in use in many countries, their effects on raptor populations remain practical questions. Conservation policies that would restrict or eliminate the use of these pesticides will surely be impeded if this apparent disagreement is not resolved.

Avian mortalities caused by dieldrin occurred in North America (Scott et al. 1959), but less frequently than in Great Britain, the Netherlands, and other areas of western Europe where dieldrin, used as a seed treatment, poisoned birds which were then preyed upon by raptors (Cramp 1962, 1965, 1967, Koeman et al. 1969, Prestt and Ratcliffe 1972). In Britain, these dieldrin-induced mortalities attained wide notoriety. In North America, the massive mortalities of urban songbirds caused by the use of DDT in a futile effort to control the Dutch elm disease attracted the attention of ornithologists (Mehner and Wallace 1959, Hickey and Hunt 1960a, 1960b, Wurster et al. 1965).

The respective fates of Peregrine Falcon populations on the two continents also contributed to divergent views on the probable causes. The extirpation of the breeding populations in eastern North America and parts of western North America, particularly southern California, was a deep shock to the ornithological community, all the more so because it went virtually unobserved until after the fact. The extirpation became indelibly linked to the demonstration that eggshell thinning in the order of 20%, caused by DDE but not dieldrin, was invariably associated with declining populations (Hickey and Anderson 1968, Anderson and Hickey 1972, Peakall et al. 1975). In Britain, however, populations were never completely eliminated, even in southern England where the decline was most severe, and overall reduction was to about 44% of pre-World War II numbers (Ratcliffe 1969, 1972). In spite of the discovery of eggshell thinning, broken eggs, and low productivity, the massive dieldrin-induced mortalities of other birds at the time of the Peregrine decline inevitably linked the two phenomena (Newton 1979, Ratcliffe 1980).

Nisbet's (Chapter 35) suggestion that dieldrin may have been more important than DDE/DDT rests on the conclusion that the decline occurred too rapidly to be explained by low productivity alone, one of the main points also stressed by the Europeans. He has also proposed that heptachlor, in the form of its highly toxic environmental derivative heptachlor epoxide, also contributed significantly to the decline of Peregrines in eastern North America through mortality of adults.

Henny (1972) undertook an extensive analysis of the data available from banding records of 16 species, including the Great Horned Owl, Red-shouldered Hawk, American Kestrel, Osprey, Cooper's Hawk, Common Barn-Owl, and Red-tailed Hawk, but not the Peregrine. He estimated mortalities from the recoveries of banded birds and estimated recruitment from information provided by banders on clutch size and numbers of young fledged per successful nest. A comparison of data from the first 20 years of the pesticide era (1945-65) with data from the previous 20 years revealed a decrease in mortality rates of Cooper's Hawks and American Kestrels, as well as of Great Blue Herons and Brown Pelicans; this decrease was attributed to a decrease in shooting pressure. No increase was found in post-nestling mortality rates during the pesticide years in any of the species examined, although the analysis was not sufficiently sensitive to detect local effects. Evidence was found, however, for lower recruitment rates in the Osprey, Cooper's Hawk, Red-shouldered Hawk, and American Kestrel, as well as for the Brown Pelican. The decline in local populations of the Osprey (Ames and Mersereau 1964, Ames 1966) and Cooper's Hawk (Schriver 1969) in eastern North America was, therefore, attributed primarily to lowered recruitment rather than to an increase in adult mortality. Further studies of the Osprey provided additional support for this conclusion (Henny and Ogden 1970, Henny and Wight 1969, 1972), but also indicated that higher-than-expected adult mortality had occurred in the areas of Gardiner's Island, the Connecticut River, and Rhode Island (Henny 1977).

Newton (1979) compared the patterns of decline of raptor populations in Europe and North America and concluded that slow declines of sensitive species occurred in both areas, but that the declines in western Europe developed into population crashes owing to mortalities caused by the use of cyclodienes in seed dressings. Thus, the European Sparrowhawk disappeared from much of England during a two-year period after 1958. He noted, however, that this distinction between the two continents was not always clear-cut. Dieldrin, for example, was extensively used in North America in areas where it entered the food webs that supported Cooper's Hawks as well as Peregrines (Nisbet Chapter 35).

Henny (1972) concluded that there ". . . is little doubt that the Cooper's Hawk is in serious jeopardy in the northeastern United States." The fate of the Cooper's Hawk in eastern North America appears to have been substantially similar to that of the European Sparrowhawk in England, yet the analysis undertaken by Henny (1972) pointed to lower recruitment as the primary cause of population decline of Cooper's Hawks. In England, on the other hand, the coincidence of dieldrin use in the mid-1950s with the virtual disappearance of European Sparrowhawk populations had suggested that adult mortality was a more important factor (Newton 1979).

If the extinction of breeding populations of Peregrine Falcons in eastern North America can be explained only by an increase in adult mortality, the response of Peregrines to environmental contaminants would appear to be different from that of other North American species. We will examine this issue and assess the relative contributions of individual organochlorine compounds, or more accurately, compound groups, to the extinction of the populations of Peregrine Falcons in eastern North America over the period 1946-64. This assessment includes the PCBs in addition to pesticides and compounds deriving from them. The exposure of Peregrines to PCBs in eastern North America during the period of decline is unknown, but an accumulation of high concentrations of PCBs by eastern Peregrines was likely; high levels were found in California Peregrines in the mid- and late 1960s (Risebrough et al. 1968b).

The organochlorine pesticides and their derivatives included in our analysis are DDT/DDE, aldrin/dieldrin, and heptachlor/heptachlor epoxide. All of these compounds were used in substantial amounts in the areas where Peregrines would have been exposed to them, and all have the potential for causing mortality or a reduction in breeding success. No other synthetic biocide introduced into the North American environment during this interval appears to have been sufficiently toxic and to have been used in sufficient amounts to have had a significant effect on the Peregrine population breeding in the eastern United States and Canada. In the absence of evidence suggesting otherwise, we assume that no other environmental contaminant other than these pesticides and the PCBs could have contributed to population declines in North America.

MODELS OF PEREGRINE POPULATIONS

At the Madison Conference, Young (1969) constructed a model of Peregrine reproduction, recruitment and mortality. He assumed an average productivity of 1.5 fledged young per active pair, consistent with the summary of available information on Peregrine breeding biology compiled by Hickey and Anderson (1969), a yearling mortality of 66.7% per year, and an adult mortality of 20% per year. He concluded that a small increase in adult mortality would be more important in reducing Peregrine populations than a small decrease in reproductive success.

A theoretical demonstration that an increase in adult mortality would be more effective in reducing a population of Peregrines does not constitute proof that the decline was in fact caused by an increase in adult mortality. We therefore address the question of whether or not a decrease in productivity alone could account for the decline.

We feel that the model used by Young (1969) should be revised to conform more closely to population characteristics of Peregrines and to other aspects of breeding biology. Young assumed that all adults breed. Instead, as shown by the rapid replacement of breeding adults that die (Hickey 1942, MacIntyre 1960, Newton 1979, Newton and Mearns Chapter 62, Hunt Chapter 63), and the occasional presence of a second or third female in a territory (Spofford 1969b, Ratcliffe 1980, Monneret Chapter 23, Brücher and Wegner Chapter 60), each year some adults experience early failure or do not breed. The size of the breeding population appears to be limited by a subtle combination of factors, the most important of which are the number of suitable breeding sites and the availability of an adequate food base within each territory (Hickey 1942, Ratcliffe 1962, 1980, Newton 1979, Newton and Mearns Chapter 62, Hunt Chapter 63). The availability of food outside breeding territories is thought not to limit the nonbreeders (Newton and Mearns Chapter 62, Hunt Chapter 63). The size of the total population, and therefore the number which do not hold territories, is largely determined by the balance between productivity and mortality. The size of the nonterritorial component can be a small fraction of the breeding component, or it can exceed the breeding component. The effects of changes in mortality or productivity should therefore be considered with respect to the entire population and not just the breeding component. In the event of lower productivity or higher mortality, it is evident that the presence of a nonterritorial component will delay change in the size of the breeding component as long as nonterritorial individuals can readily fill vacancies in the breeding territories.

Another reality of Peregrine biology should be considered in the construction of a model: the species is highly site-tenacious. The model used by Young, and by many other population biologists, assumes that a bird that has lost a mate finds another. We assume, however, that a bird that has lost a mate remains on its territory and that its chance for remating will depend on its being found by a bird without a territory. For simplification of the calculations, we assume that nonterritorial birds are 100% successful in finding a single bird of the opposite sex on territory. This is more likely to be true in areas of relatively high breeding density such as Great Britain, and less likely to be true in North America, which had a much lower breeding density. A population in the latter region would, therefore, be expected to decline at a more rapid rate than our model predicts.

We used Young's estimate of a mean production of 1.5 fledged young per territorial pair, since it is based on a thorough review of Peregrine biology (Hickey and Anderson 1969). Since Young's level of yearly recruitment of maturing birds to the total adult population could not sustain a nonterritorial component, we initially reduced the estimated adult yearly mortality from 20% to 16.7%. The nonterritorial component would then amount to 25% of the breeding component (Table 1). Rice (1969) recorded a reproductive rate of 0.3 young per active pair in Pennsylvania in 1947-52. Ratcliffe (1972) recorded the following productivity data in England in 1962: 2 broods that hatched at 5 active sites in southern England, 3 broods at 19 active sites in Wales, and 3 broods at 22 active sites in northern England. Using an estimate of 2.5 fledged young per brood, based on estimates of the normal number of young per successful pair (Hickey and Anderson 1969), the mean productivity of the total of the 46 territories would be 0.43. In a stressed population with very low productivity, this figure would likely be somewhat lower. We shall use the figure of 0.3 young produced per active pair that is affected by one or more of the organochlorine contaminants.

These assumptions lead to a prediction (Table 1) that the number of breeding pairs would remain constant until Year 4, but would then fall rapidly (58% by Year 6 (1952), and 37% by Year 8 (1954)). An increasing number of sites would be occupied by single birds. By Year

TABLE 1. Model for the decline of a population of Peregrine Falcons when productivity falls from 1.5 young per active pair to 0.3; adult and yearling mortalities are assumed to be 16.7% and 66.7%, respectively.[a]

Year	No. of breeding pairs	No. of fledglings	No. of 2nd year birds	No. of sites with single adults	No. of floating adults	Total adults
0 – 1946	100	150	50	0	50	250
1 – 1947	100	30	50	0	50	250
2 – 1948	100	30	10	0	50	250
3 – 1949	100	30	10	0	16.7	216.7
4 – 1950	91.7	27.5	10	5.6	0	188.9
5 – 1951	72.0	21.6	9.2	17.1	0	165.7
10 – 1956	23.4	7.0	2.9	36.3	0	83.1
15 – 1961	7.6	2.3	1.0	23.6	0	38.8
18 – 1964	3.9	1.2	0.5	16.3	0	24.0
20 – 1966	2.5	0.7	0.3	12.4	0	17.4

[a] Additional assumptions: (1) nonbreeding birds and birds newly recruited into the breeding population immediately pair with breeding birds that have lost their mates, (2) adults remain in their territories following loss of a mate, and (3) there are no density-dependent factors affecting breeding success, mortality, or size of the pool of nonbreeding birds.

18 (1964), which was the year of the survey undertaken by Berger et al. (1969), there would be only 4% of the original number of breeding pairs. Either a further decrease in productivity or a modest increase in mortality would reduce the number of breeding pairs to approximately 1% by Year 18. Furthermore, the bias in our model arising from the assumption that a nonterritorial bird is 100% successful in finding an unmated bird on territory would further reduce the number of breeding pairs. If productivity fell to zero, fewer than 1% of the breeding pairs would survive by Year 18; if adult mortality increased from 16.7% to 20%, the number of breeding pairs would also be about 1% by Year 18 (Table 2).

Further reduction of mortality estimates in an uncontaminated population from 16.7% to 15% for adults and 66.7% to 50% for first-year birds results in a very large increase in the nonterritorial component, from 50 birds to 225 birds per 100 breeding pairs. These would be expected to "buffer" the impact of either an increase in mortality or a decrease in productivity. Thus, a decrease in productivity from 1.5 to 0.3 would not change the number of breeding pairs at Year 5. At Year 10, 82% of the original sites would still be occupied by breeding birds, but by Year 18 this number would fall to 27% (Table 2). Increases in mortality to 20% and 25% would decrease the number of pairs surviving at Year 18 to 5.5% and 1% of the original, respectively (Table 2). From banding data, including data from birds banded prior to 1951, Enderson (1969b) estimated first-year and adult mortality rates of 70% and 25%, respectively. An adult mortality rate of this magnitude would not maintain a population with a mean productivity of 1.5. Because of the possibility of band losses, these estimates were considered as upper limits.

Predictions of the population model are, therefore, very dependent upon the choice of initial parameters. Nevertheless, two principal conclusions emerge: (1) low productivity alone, considering the bias and a margin of error in the predictions of the model, could account for the disappearance of breeding Peregrines from eastern North America by 1964; the response of the Peregrine to environmental contaminants would be comparable to that of the other North American species studied by Henny (1972), and an additional small increase in mortality could have ensured nearly complete extinction by 1964; (2) in response to an increase in mortality or a decrease in productivity, the number of breeding pairs would remain constant over an initial lag period of at least several years; thereafter there would be a period of rapid decline. The duration of the lag period would depend largely on the initial number of nonterritorial adults.

The rapid decline in Britain, which coincided with the introduction of dieldrin, occurred approximately a decade after the introduction of

TABLE 2. Models of Peregrine populations with different productivities and mortalities, beginning with 100 adult pairs at time 0.

Adult mortality (percent)	First year mortality (percent)	Productivity (young/pair)[d]	No. of breeding pairs Years hence			No. of total adults[e] Years hence			No. of territories with single adults Years hence		
			5	10	18	5	10	18	5	10	18
16.7	66.7	0.3	72	23	4	166	83	24	22	36	16
16.7	66.7	0.0	53	18	1	145	48	14	39	37	13
20.0[a]	66.7	0.3	54	13	1	142	57	11	34	32	9
15.0[b]	50.0	0.3	100	82	27	294	178	82	0	13	28
20.0[b]	50.0	0.3	100	36	6	224	106	26	0	33	16
25.0[c]	50.0	0.3	75	14	1	168	57	8	19	28	8

[a] Adult mortality 16.7% in year 1, 20% therafter.
[b] Adult mortality 15% in year 1, 20% therafter.
[c] Adult mortality 15% in year 1, 25% therafter.
[d] Productivity 1.5 young per territorial pair, indicated value thereafter.
[e] Total adults = breeding pairs × 2 plus nonterritorial adults.

DDT. The pattern of decline in Britain was consistent with the predictions of our model, on the basis of a period of low productivity in the order of a decade and at the level recorded by Ratcliffe in 1962 (Ratcliffe 1972), with or without a simultaneous increase in mortality. Low productivity alone could, therefore, account for the observed performance of the population in Britain as well as in eastern North America. For the initial decade, before the introduction of dieldrin, low productivity would have been caused by DDE/DDT alone, with a possible contribution by the PCBs.

TOXICOLOGY OF THE ORGANOCHLORINES

After a more thorough review of the literature, we have revised our original assumption that mortality is always the more significant effect of dieldrin, heptachlor epoxide, and the related compound endrin, and that sublethal effects on populations are relatively insignificant.

Henny et al. (1983) determined the effects of heptachlor epoxide on a breeding population of American Kestrels in an area of local heptachlor use in Oregon in 1978-81. Levels of heptachlor epoxide in the eggs exceeded 1.5 ppm in 14% of the nestings and were associated with lower productivity rather than mortality.

A diet of 0.75 ppm endrin resulted in a 43% reduction in the fledging success of captive Eastern Screech-Owls without causing mortalities of breeding adults (Flemming et al. 1982); critical levels in the eggs were in the order of 0.3 ppm. A comparable sublethal effect of dieldrin on productivity has not yet been reported. Mendenhall et al. (1983) fed DDE, dieldrin, and a combination of DDE and dieldrin to breeding pairs of captive Common Barn-Owls in doses of 3.0 ppm DDE and 0.5 ppm dieldrin. DDE caused eggshell thinning, egg breakage, embryonic mortality and reduced productivity; dieldrin caused a slight decrease in eggshell thickness, no change in productivity, and three of the birds on the dieldrin diet died. Dieldrin levels in eggs were in the order of 4-9 ppm, higher than concentrations in the few Peregrine eggs analyzed in Britain (Ratcliffe 1972). Henny et al. (1983) reported successful nestings of American Kestrels when dieldrin levels in eggs were in the range 2.2-3.9 ppm wet weight. Depressed productivity of American Kestrels fed combinations of DDT and dieldrin was observed by Porter and Wiemeyer (1969), but the experiment did not determine the relative contribution, if any, of dieldrin.

Newton and Bogan (1978) recorded DDE effects on eggshell thickness, egg breakage, egg addling and hatching failures in European Sparrowhawks. No effects could be attributed to dieldrin, present at mean levels in the order of 19% of DDE concentrations. These several studies have not, therefore, demonstrated a sublethal effect of dieldrin on reproduction, although the sublethal effects of the more toxic compounds, endrin and heptachlor epoxide, would suggest that such effects of dieldrin do occur but have not yet been detected.

Although the primary effect of DDE is clearly on reproduction, both DDT (p,p'-DDT) and DDE (p,p'-DDE) may have contributed significantly to adult mortality of Peregrines. Feeding low levels of DDE to American Kestrels produced mortality (Porter and Wiemeyer 1972). The toxicity of DDT to birds is well documented. In areas of high DDT use, Peregrines may therefore have accumulated lethal levels.

The experiments undertaken both in the field and with captive birds do not always permit an assessment of the contribution of altered parental behavior toward reproductive failure. All failures recorded by Henny et al. (1983) resulted from all eggs not hatching, or the death of all nestlings during the first week. These losses could be attributed either to the toxic effects of heptachlor epoxide on embryos or nestlings, or to sublethal effects on the behavior of adults by inducing abnormal incubation, feeding patterns, or attentiveness. Egg eating and the disappearance of eggs may have resulted from behavioral abnormalities (Ratcliffe 1969) rather than being the natural response of breeding adults to remove damaged eggs.

Abnormal behavior (including abnormal nest defense, courtship and incubation) linked with organochlorines has been reported in a number of bird species, both in the field and under experimental conditions (Milstein et al. 1970, Peakall and Peakall 1973, Snyder et al. 1973, Heinz 1976b, Fyfe et al. 1976b, Haegele and Hudson 1977, Fox et al. 1978, Gesell et al. 1979, Fox and Donald 1980, Kreitzer 1980, Tori and Peterle 1983). Such behavioral changes may be attributed in part to a higher rate of metabolism of steroid hormones following the induction of mixed-function oxidase enzymes (Peakall 1967, 1970, Risebrough et al. 1968b, McArthur et al. 1983). This effect appears to be common to almost all organochlorines, including the PCBs. Other hormonal effects, such as those associated with abnormal thyroid activity, have also been recorded (Jefferies 1969, Jefferies and French 1972, Jefferies and Parslow 1972).

Levels of the several organochlorines in environmental samples are usually correlated with each other (Risebrough et al. 1968b, Newton and Bogan 1978). The American Kestrel feeding experiment with p,p'-DDT and dieldrin showed that the combination of these compounds inhibited reproduction (Porter and Wiemeyer 1972), but the relative or synergistic effects of each were not determined. Mendenhall et al. (1983) recorded no synergistic effects of DDE and dieldrin on the reproduction of Common Barn-Owls. Lincer (1972) found that DDE caused eggshell thinning in American Kestrels, but no thinning was caused by the PCB Aroclor 1254. A combination of DDE and

Aroclor 1254 produced eggshells that were slightly but not significantly thinner than eggshells of those that were fed DDE, but the incidence of egg breakage was much higher in the combination group. Risebrough and Anderson (1975) reported a similar effect with ducks fed DDE, PCBs, or a combination of the two; a higher frequency of broken eggs was recorded in the latter group. Lincer (1972) also reported that the DDE-PCB combination reduced hatching success to zero in a small sample, suggesting enhanced toxicity or modification of eggshell structures as shown by Greenburg et al. (1979).

Recoveries of populations of both Ospreys and Bald Eagles have been associated with a decline of DDE levels, but with no change in PCB levels (Spitzer et al. 1978, Grier 1982); the interpretation was that DDE but not PCBs had been responsible for the earlier population declines. It is possible, however, that the combination was responsible, with levels of both DDE and PCBs exceeding critical values.

Eggshell thinning is now attributed only to DDE, with but a minor contribution if any by other environmental chemicals (Risebrough 1986). Productivity of Prairie Falcons and Merlins in Alberta was found to be closely associated with both increasing DDE levels and decreasing eggshell thickness (Fyfe et al. 1976b). Over a range of low concentrations of DDE, and of decreasing eggshell thicknesses, there was no significant depression of productivity; productivity decreased rapidly, however, beyond a critical level of DDE and a critical level of thinning. The productivity of Prairie Falcons was more sensitive to eggshell thinning than was productivity of Merlins (Fyfe et al. Chapter 33). It is likely that the productivity of Peregrines shows similar relationships with eggshell thickness and DDE. The available California data indicate that the critical level of thinning exceeds 15-16%, and that the Peregrine is less sensitive to eggshell thinning than Merlins or Prairie Falcons (Fyfe et al. Chapter 33). This conclusion is consistent with earlier observations that eggshell thinning in Peregrines of approximately 20% was associated with population declines (Hickey and Anderson 1968, Anderson and Hickey 1972), and with other estimates of a critical range of thinning between 15-20% in Alaskan populations, with corresponding DDE levels of 75-100 ppm dry weight or 15-20 ppm wet weight (Peakall et al. 1975).

CHRONOLOGY OF ORGANOCHLORINE USE

DDT was first used in the United States in 1946; dieldrin was first used in 1951, on cotton in the southeast (Nisbet Chapter 35). DDT use rapidly increased, and we can assume that use was heavy throughout eastern North America by the late 1940s. Dieldrin use had become heavy by the mid-1950s, and heptachlor was widely used by 1960 in the southern states during the fire ant program. We assume that PCBs were used throughout the period in increasing amounts.

Observations Between 1946-52. — The observations of breeding Peregrines were largely casual, but they indicate a significant disruption of populations before dieldrin appeared. In Pennsylvania, 17 territorial pairs produced a mean of 1.25 young in 1946, but by 1952 the number of active eyries had declined to 6, 35% of the 1946 number (Rice 1969). Although the removal of birds for falconry may have had some impact, population characteristics of the Peregrine strongly suggest that a decline of this magnitude should not be attributed to that cause. In Massachusetts, "occupation of the cliffs was spotty" by 1951 (Hagar 1969). These several observations indicate that the decline was well under way in Pennsylvania and Massachusetts by 1952, before the introduction of dieldrin. Since our model did not predict a population decline over such a short period of time without a significant level of adult mortality (Table 2), we conclude that adult mortality was a factor in the decline of the eastern Peregrines, but that until 1952 the mortality was caused solely by DDT/DDE.

Observations After 1952. — By 1955-57, "only an occasional single bird was left" in Massachusetts (Hagar 1969). In Pennsylvania, the "three pairs remaining in 1958 and one in 1959 reared no young in these years, despite lack of any known disturbance" (Rice 1969). Although factors such as disturbance were affecting productivity of the Hudson River birds after 1946, there was no productivity at all at the six sites under observation after 1951. They remained active, however, for a mean interval of 8-9 years thereafter without raising young (Herbert and Herbert 1969). These several observations, particularly those of the Hudson River birds, indicate that extremely low productivity was characteristic of these populations at that time.

Residue Data From Declining Populations. — No residue data are available from the 1950s in either Britain or eastern North America. An egg from Perthshire in 1961 was the first to be analyzed; it contained dieldrin, heptachlor epoxide and DDE in ratios of 1.0:0.56:2.3 (Moore and Ratcliffe 1962). Four Peregrines that were recovered in Britain before 1966 contained 6-70 ppm DDE in the liver. Their ratios of heptachlor epoxide and DDE normalized to dieldrin were: (1) 0.4:18, (2) 0.3:11, (3) 0.05:3.8, (4) 1.4:23 (Jefferies and Prestt 1966). Six eggs from northern England in 1962-66 contained mean levels of 21 ppm DDE (dieldrin: heptachlor epoxide: DDE mean ratio was 1.0:1.7:21); 13 eggs from southern Scotland during the same period averaged 13 ppm DDE with a mean ratio of 1.0:1.4:26 (Ratcliffe 1972). Toxicologically, the residues of heptachlor epoxide may have been more significant than those of dieldrin (Henny et al. 1983).

Six Peregrines found dead or dying in Britain in 1971 contained less heptachlor epoxide than dieldrin; ratios of DDE to dieldrin in the livers were, respectively: 15, 0.55, 17, 13, 11, and 0.94 (Ratcliffe 1972). Some birds were, therefore, being exposed to as much dieldrin as DDE.

Data on the relative exposure to DDE, dieldrin, and heptachlor epoxide of Peregrines in eastern North America are not available; Nisbet (Chapter 35) has based the argument for exposure to dieldrin and heptachlor epoxide mainly on the rapidity of the decline, not on direct evidence. Eggs from Colorado and northern New Mexico in the mid- and late-1970s had DDE:dieldrin ratios in the order of 100:1 (Enderson et al. 1982). In an adult and an immature Peregrine from California in the mid-1960s, when the population had almost disappeared (Herman et al. 1970), the ratios in the carcasses were 44 and 170, respectively (Risebrough et al. 1968b). A female that died in its eyrie in coastal California in 1969 contained 480 ppm DDE and 5.8 ppm dieldrin in yolk lipid, a ratio of 83:1 (Thelander 1977, Risebrough unpubl. data). Adipose tissues of breeding Peregrines in northern Canada in 1966 contained dieldrin, heptachlor epoxide and DDE in the ratios of 1.0:1.3:166 (Enderson and Berger 1968). Cade et al. (1968) recorded DDE:dieldrin ratios of 100:1 in adipose tissues of Peregrines breeding in Alaska in 1966.

In these areas of North America, the pattern of organochlorine accumulation by Peregrines has therefore been characterized by higher DDE:dieldrin ratios than in Britain. The relative importance of dieldrin versus DDE in causing population declines would have been correspondingly less in these areas of North America than in Britain.

CONCLUSIONS

All of the organochlorines considered here are detrimental to Peregrine populations; the degree of harm is dependent upon the level of exposure. With the possible exception of dieldrin, all of them cause depressed productivity at lower levels of exposure; with the possible exception of the PCBs, all of them cause mortalities above critical levels.

In eastern North America, depressed productivity caused only by DDE could have accounted for all or almost all of the population decline by 1964; a small increase in mortality caused by DDT/DDE in conjunction with the depressed productivity would have ensured the disappearance of the population by 1964, without the contribution of other environmental chemicals. The principal effect on the population as a whole of the other chemicals — dieldrin, heptachlor epoxide, and, we believe, the PCBs — was most likely a further reduction of productivity, with the more contaminated individuals succumbing to mortality.

Because of the buffering effect of a nonbreeding component of the population, the effect of depressed productivity in Britain, caused initially by DDE but later by the other chemicals as well, was not detected for at least several years; thereafter the population decline was rapid. The "crashes" of populations can therefore be attributed in part to the delayed effects of depressed productivity in previous years. With no buffering effect of nonbreeding birds, and with a very low replacement through reproduction, additional mortalities, such as those resulting from the use of dieldrin as a seed dressing, would have had a cumulative and, therefore, greater impact upon population size than would otherwise be the case (Newton 1979).

ACKNOWLEDGEMENTS

This study was supported by the Bodega Bay Institute and the Canadian Wildlife Service. J. H. Enderson, T. J. Cade and C. J. Henny provided valuable comments and suggestions.

Commentary

The Role of Organochlorine Pesticides in Peregrine Population Changes

The Editors

Nisbet (Chapter 35) has rightly chastened American scientists for disregarding mortality from dieldrin and other organochlorine intoxication as plausible factors in the decline of Peregrine populations in the 1950s and 1960s. W. Stickel did broach the possibility at the Madison Conference in 1965 (Hickey 1969), and Stone and Okoniewski (Chapter 42) caution us that such mortality may still occur in the United States in the 1980s. Although the evidence is largely circumstantial, we feel that few, if any, careful students of the subject would now disagree with the proposition that organochlorine-induced mortalities did occur in Peregrines both in North America and in Europe. On the other hand, we feel that the Europeans, especially our British colleagues who discovered the phenomenon of eggshell thinning in the first place, have too easily dismissed the role of DDE-induced reproductive malfunction as the cause of the decline in Peregrine numbers.

Everyone is probably willing to agree that both processes were at work to varying degrees in different places and at different times (Newton 1979, Ratcliffe 1980). The only question remaining is which was the more important factor or, better perhaps, how did the two factors interplay in given situations. That question can probably never be answered in a rigorous or entirely satisfactory way 40 years after the fact, and we expect that each researcher will continue to be biased toward one or another explanation depending on his or her individual experiences with the problems created by organochlorine pollution.

Expressing our own bias, the editors of this book continue to view DDE-induced reproductive malfunction as the principal cause of decline in many Peregrine populations around the world in the 1950s and 1960s (and into the early 1970s for some), but we accept as plausible and likely that organochlorine-induced mortality was an additional factor — perhaps the main factor in some local populations and over limited spans of time. This conclusion applies only to the Peregrine Falcon, and not to the European Sparrowhawk (Newton 1986) or any other species of raptor which may have had different exposures to pesticides. Our reasons for this conclusion are based on the following considerations about the two proposed mechanisms.

Organochlorine Pesticide-induced Mortality. — The evidence for a primary role of increased mortality from pesticide intoxication is largely circumstantial and indirect. (1) The disappearance of adult falcons at eyries showed a close temporal and spatial correspondence with the massive application of toxic chemicals — in Britain especially with the use of dieldrin as a seed dressing beginning in 1955, and in the eastern United States with the extensive spraying of DDT for Dutch elm disease and other forest pests in the early 1950s. (2) Locally, but not regionally, the loss of adults at eyries occurred at a rate too high to be explained solely by lack of recruitment from a diminished nonbreeding segment of the population — again, in part of Britain (Ratcliffe 1980), in the cliff-nesting population of East Germany (Kleinstäuber and Kirmse Chapter 20), and perhaps along the Susquehanna River in Pennsylvania, but not along the Hudson River or in Massachusetts (see Risebrough and Peakall Commentary preceding this one). (3) DDT, dieldrin, and other organochlorine pesticides were clearly involved in massive mortalities of many species of birds, including other raptors (especially European Sparrowhawks, Eurasian Kestrels, and Common Buzzards in Europe) and many of the principal prey species of the Peregrine, so that there were, indeed, frequent opportunities for exposure of Peregrines to lethal diets. (4) Recoveries in population began soon after the use of dieldrin or other highly toxic organochlorine pesticides was curtailed or stopped. One problem in interpreting these temporal and spatial correspondences is that cyclodiene use followed closely the pattern of DDT use in most countries. Britain was a notable exception in that DDT use continued after most uses of the cyclodienes had been voluntarily phased out.

On the other hand, direct evidence of pesticide-induced mortality in Peregrines is scant — all the more so in view of the relatively large number of cases reported for other birds of prey (Newton 1979, 1986) — and there is virtually no information to indicate what fraction of total mortality can be attributed to pesticide poisoning for a given population. Ratcliffe's (Table 22 *in* 1980) set of data come the closest, but most of the specimens analyzed were obtained after the heavy use of the cyclodiene pesticides had ended. A tiercel found dead at his eyrie on Lundy Island in 1963 provided the first possible case of organochlorine poisoning (70 ppm DDE, 4.0 ppm dieldrin, 1.5 ppm heptachlor epoxide, and 2.0 ppm HBC in liver, wet wt). Of 21 Peregrine carcasses (livers) analyzed from 1963-75, 3 contained lethal cyclodiene concentrations (minimum of 10 ppm wet wt), and 3 others were close enough to include as likely being lethal. However, if one applies Newton's (1986) figures of 20-40 ppm in liver as lethal, then only one of Ratcliffe's Peregrines died of cyclodiene poisoning. These limited figures suggest that cyclodiene intoxication might have increased mortality by about 33% above the "normal range" during those years, say from 15% per year for adults to 20% per year. Almost certainly, however, the increase would have been higher in the period of heaviest use of cyclodienes before 1964, and in the main areas of cyclodiene use, in which Peregrines were extinct by 1964. It is also worth noting that when Enderson and Berger (1970) fed wild female Prairie Falcons, just prior to laying, as many as eight starlings with near-lethal dieldrin levels, the diet caused no mortality or abandonment of nests.

While residue levels in some prey were no doubt high enough to have killed Peregrines (Nisbet Chapter 35), probably fewer than three North American Peregrines have ever shown residues of chlorinated hydrocarbons approaching lethal concentrations. On the other hand, very few dead or dying Peregrines were ever examined.

DDE-induced Reproductive Malfunction. — We take it as proven that a causal relationship exists between DDE residues in the maternal body and the production of abnormally thin-shelled eggs in Peregrines and many other birds (Risebrough 1986, Peakall and Kiff Chapter 34). We take it as proven that when eggshells reach a certain critical range of thinness, there is an increased likelihood of failure to hatch, either from breakage or addling. Species vary greatly in their susceptibilities to eggshell thinning from DDE and in the degree to which thin-shelled eggs contribute to lowered productivity. The Peregrine Falcon is one of the more sensitive species in both respects.

For example, British Peregrines (Ratcliffe 1980) and European Sparrowhawks (Newton 1986) have some revealing similarities and differences. Both species showed an almost immediate response to environmental DDE residues, with a significant reduction in eggshell thickness in 1947, the same year DDT began to be used on a wide scale in Britain. On a population-wide basis, Peregrine eggs averaged 16% lighter than in the pre-DDT years (all the way back to the 1850s). This general level of reduction continued through 1971, after which there was a partial return to normality, with most eggs showing less than 10% reduction in eggshell index in recent years (see Figure 8 in Ratcliffe 1980). Eggshell thickness in the European Sparrowhawk dropped 17% from the pre-DDT population average. Unlike the Peregrine, however, there was little increase in average thickness in the 1970s, and many eggshells are still thin enough to break easily during incubation (see Figure 81 *in* Newton 1986). Although the European Sparrowhawks experienced a reduction in eggshell index as great as that experienced by the Peregrines, and sustained it over a longer period of years, abnormally thin-shelled eggs have not influenced their productivity as much as they have Peregrines. According to Newton (1986) eggshell thinning and egg breakage accounted for about 12% of all Sparrowhawk nest failures and resulted in about a 25% reduction in normal brood size, not enough to influence recruitment into the breeding population in most years or to prevent a speedy recovery in numbers following the reduction from mortality induced by cyclodiene poisoning. By contrast, brood size in the most affected Peregrine populations in Wales, northern England, and southern Scotland was reduced more than 70% in the worst years (1961-65), and the fraction of pairs rearing young dropped to 25% from a normal range of 55-60% or more. Thus, overall productivity in these populations dropped into the range of only 0.4-0.5 young per pair, compared to the more typical range around 1.5 young per pair for a healthy population. Figure 14 in Ratcliffe's (1980) book clearly shows the close parallel relationships among productivity, brood size, occupied territories, pairs producing eggs, and pairs rearing young during the decline and recovery phases of the population in northwest England (Lakeland and northern Pennines).

Newton (1986, Commentary Section 8) argues that improved survival following reduction in cyclodiene use was more important than improved breeding success in leading to the recovery of raptor populations, because populations have expanded while breeding remained poor and DDE residues continued to be high in eggs. This argument is valid for European Sparrowhawks in Britain, but less so for Peregrines in Britain (Ratcliffe Chapter 17) and even less so for Peregrines elsewhere. The remarkable increase in the British Peregrine population since 1964 has been closely paralleled by a marked decrease in DDE residues measured in egg contents (Figure 15 *in* Ratcliffe 1980), by considerable increase in eggshell thickness in most eggs (Figure 8 *in* Ratcliffe 1980), and by a simultaneous increase in reproductive rate from the low of 0.4-0.5 young per pair to 1.2-1.4 young per pair since 1970 (Table 18 *in* Ratcliffe 1980).

Furthermore, we are unaware of a studied Peregrine population anywhere that has been able to maintain its numbers in the face of sustained eggshell thinning averaging around 20% and corresponding DDE residue levels of 20 ppm wet weight in egg contents, regardless of the presence or absence of other organochlorine contaminants in the food chain (Peakall and Kiff Chapter 34). Also, we are unaware of any Peregrine population that has increased significantly in numbers as long as a high frequency of thin-shelled eggs, high DDE residues in eggs (maternal bodies), and greatly increased egg losses have continued to characterize the breeding condition of the falcons. This implies that, at this high level, DDE alone can cause population decline. It does not, however, exclude the possibility that cyclodienes have also contributed to population decline in certain parts of the Peregrine's range.

The important point emphasized by population modeling (Risebrough and Peakall Commentary preceding this one, J. Grier unpubl. computer simulations) is that the effect of abnormally lowered reproduction (caused by DDE) will not be reflected as a reduction in the adult breeding population until the reserve of nonbreeding adults has been used up by recruitment; this was earlier recognized by Ratcliffe (1980) and Newton (1979 and Commentary Section 8). If the British population of the early 1950s had a large reservoir of nonbreeders, as Ratcliffe (1980) surmised, it would take 8-10 years for lowered productivity to influence the number of breeders negatively, especially as some Scottish populations apparently continued to produce a surplus above local recruitment needs right through the worst years. It is actually easier to construct a model to account for a 55% reduction in Britain's nesting population over the observed span of time, resulting from lowered reproduction without increased mortality, than it is to account for the total extirpation of the eastern North American Peregrines over the time span observed for that event.

We suspect that the eastern North American population was already in a "stressed" condition before the DDT-dieldrin era, not because of high post-nestling mortality, but reproductively through human disturbances at the eyries during egg-laying and incubation. Hickey (1942) pointed out that 19 pairs "around New York" averaged only 1.1 young per pair in the years 1939 and 1940, and Hagar's (1969) 14 eyries in Massachusetts did no better in the 1930s and early 1940s. Depending on mortality rates, this rather low productivity could mean that there were relatively few surplus nonbreeders in the eastern North American population by 1945-46, although reproduction may have been better during the war years. Thus, a further drastic reduction in reproduction would have shown up much sooner as a loss of breeders in eastern North America after the onset of DDT use than was the case in Britain. Also, as the eyries were much more dispersed in North America than in Britain, recruitment from peripheral populations would have been less likely to occur.

Such a population would have gone to near extinction in about 20 years (Risebrough and Peakall Commentary preceding this one), close enough to the actual occurrences to be plausible. It is incorrect to assume that eastern North America's population was entirely extirpated by 1964 simply because Berger et al. (1969) failed to find any birds that year. They did not check all eyries, and their survey was done late in the season well after the incubation period; thus they would have missed the early presence of failed pairs. Further, W. Spofford and J.

H. Enderson (*in* Fyfe et al. 1976a) found a single adult at Willoughby Lake, Vermont in 1970, and a pair is known to have nested off and on throughout most of the 1970s at Lyster Lake just across the border in southern Quebec. The last "wild" (unbanded) tiercel at this eyrie paired with one of Cornell's captive-produced and released falcons, and they raised young in 1980 (Cade and Dague 1980). It seems likely, therefore, that about 5% of the original population could still have been extant in 1964, but mostly as nonreproducing birds.

Finally, no one's considerations have taken into account the effect of reproductive senility, which (based on data from captive-breeders) cuts in at about age 15-16 for females, or the effect of absolute life span (about 20 years). With greatly decreased reproduction, older birds would dominate the population in later years and adult mortality would proceed at a more rapid rate than in a population with normal age distribution.

6 | Migration and Banding Studies

44 Recoveries of Peregrine Falcons Migrating Through the Eastern and Central United States, 1955-1985

Michael A. Yates, Kenton E. Riddle, and F. Prescott Ward

Extensive banding and recovery records available for the Peregrine Falcon provide insights into the movements of fall and spring migrants from various geographic regions, their wintering areas, and survivorship. The east and Gulf* coasts are areas of major autumn concentrations of migrating Peregrines (Enderson 1969c). Respective focal points of these routes are Assateague Island in Maryland and Virginia and North and South Padre Islands, Texas, where most bandings and recoveries have occurred. The study area at Assateague Island has been described by Ward and Berry (1972), and at Padre Island by Hunt et al. (1980) and Weise and White (1980). North and South Padre Islands are also the only known localities in the western hemisphere where northward migrating Peregrines are numerous in spring (Ward et al. 1978). In this analysis we attempted to determine origins, wintering areas, and migration routes of these migrants, to measure their fidelity to migratory routes, to characterize routes southward and wintering areas of Peregrines passing Wisconsin (another area of concentration in autumn), and to estimate age-specific mortality through recoveries of banded Peregrines from records in the Bird Banding Laboratory of the U. S. Fish and Wildlife Service (USFWS).

METHODS

Visits were made during July and August 1985 to the Bird Banding Laboratory, USFWS, and computer listings of bandings and recoveries were obtained. Bandings were available in computer files back to 1955. We only analyzed recoveries since then, because by that time very few resident eastern Peregrines were being banded. We discarded bandings and recoveries of captive-bred Peregrines and their progeny, known

*Editors' Note: Authors' use of "Gulf" refers to the Gulf of Mexico.

eastern *F. p. anatum*, and individuals held in captivity more than one week. Also eliminated were live recoveries of Peregrines in the same study area and same migratory season as banding. All bandings and recoveries were segregated by east coast (ME, NH, VT, MA, CT, RI, NY, NJ, PA, DE, MD, VA, WV, NC, SC, GA, FL), Gulf coast (TX, MS, LA, AL), and Wisconsin, including Peregrines banded elsewhere and recovered on the east and Gulf coasts. Also listed were birds banded in Canada and recovered anywhere south of Canada, and birds banded in Greenland and Alaska which were recovered on the east and Gulf coasts. Finally, records were available for Peregrines banded as nestlings or in their hatching-year and later recovered dead. Because the complete 1984 banding summaries were not yet available, we used the totals on record and added 1984 bandings in NJ, MD, VA, NC, FL, and TX that were not on file but otherwise available to us. We mapped the bandings and recoveries to aid in analysis.

RESULTS AND DISCUSSION

Of 4477 Peregrines banded on the east and Gulf coasts and in Wisconsin, 4.65% were recovered (Table 1). Recoveries of Peregrines

TABLE 1.   Number of Peregrines banded and recovered, 1955-84.[a]

	No. banded	No. recovered	% recovered
East Coast			
MA	5	0	0
RI	1	0	0
CT	4	0	0
NY	64	8	12.5
NJ	274	21	7.7
PA	20	2	10.0
MD	684	32	4.7
VA	897	28	3.1
NC	142	2	1.4
GA	97	7	7.2
FL	215	5	2.3
Total	2403	105	4.4
Gulf Coast			
AL	59	0	0
LA	2	0	0
TX	1703	86	5.1
Total	1764	86	4.9
Wisconsin	310	17	5.5
Total	4477	208	4.65

[a] 1984 banding totals incomplete.

banded as nestlings indicate the Greenland population figures prominently in the fall migration on the east coast (Table 2), as suggested by Shor (1970a). Of 23 Peregrines banded as nestlings and recovered on the east coast, 12 were from Greenland. Origins of the rest were distributed fairly evenly across the Arctic from Quebec westward, but only two came from Alaska (Table 2, Figure 1). Of 105 recoveries of Peregrines banded on the east coast, 48 were recovered elsewhere (Figure 2), including 13 from north of the United States border. Eight of these were in Greenland, two in Keewatin (Northwest Territories), and one each in Manitoba, Saskatchewan and Alaska. The 29 recoveries south of the United States border were from the West Indies and Antilles, Central America, and most of South America to latitude 38°S in Argentina.

Recoveries on the Gulf coast of 29 Peregrines banded as nestlings included 17 from Alaska and only 3 from Greenland. The remaining recoveries were of birds from the Yukon and Northwest Territories, Canada (Table 2, Figure 3). Of 86 recoveries of Peregrines banded on the Gulf coast, only 19 were recorded later outside of Texas (Figure 2). The one recovery north of the United States border was in Franklin, Northwest Territories. The 13 recovered south of Texas included birds from the Gulf coast of Mexico, Central America, and the southern two-thirds of South America to latitude 33°S in Uruguay. East and Gulf coast migrants share many wintering areas, but east coast migrants have not been recovered between Honduras and the United States border. Conversely, Gulf coast migrants have not been recorded in the northeastern one-third of South America or in the Antilles and West Indies.

Banding recoveries indicate that most Peregrines display fidelity to a particular flyway. Despite the fact that many are trapped and banded

TABLE 2.   Peregrines banded as nestlings and recovered on the east and Gulf coasts, January 1955 – June 1985.

Origin	Recovered on east coast		Recovered on Gulf coast	
	No.	%	No.	%
Greenland	12	52.2	3	10.3
Quebec	2	8.7	0	0
Keewatin, NWT	3	13.1	2	6.9
Franklin, NWT	1	4.3	1	3.5
Mackenzie Valley, NWT	1	4.3	4	13.7
Alberta	0	0	1	3.5
Yukon	2	8.7	1	3.5
Alaska	2	8.7	17	58.6
Total	23	100.0	29	100.0

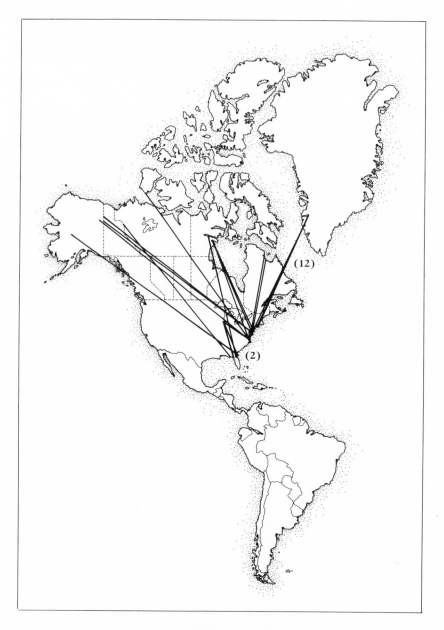

FIGURE 1. Recoveries on the east coast of Peregrines banded elsewhere, January
          1955-June 1985.

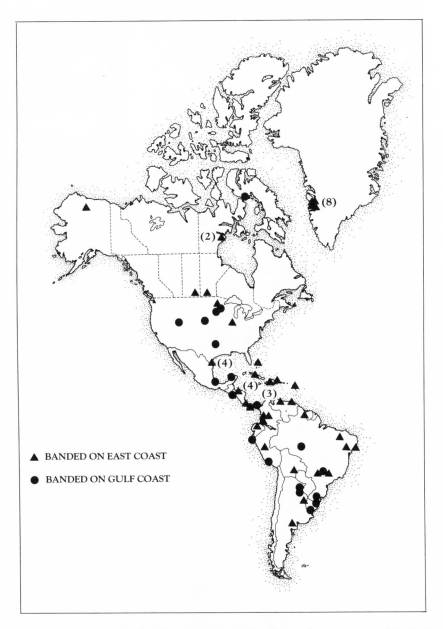

FIGURE 2. Recoveries elsewhere of Peregrines banded on the east coast and Gulf of Mexico coast, January 1955-June 1985.

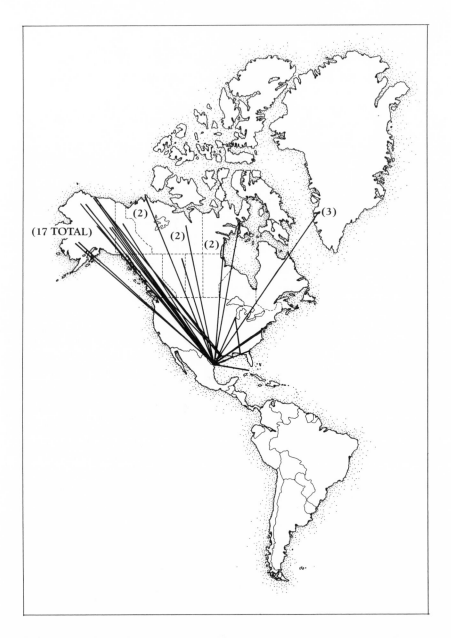

FIGURE 3.   Recoveries on the Gulf of Mexico coast of Peregrines banded elsewhere,
              January 1955-June 1985.

on the east and Gulf coasts, few records of interchange between flyways exist. No Peregrine banded on the Gulf coast has been recovered on the east coast, and only 4 of the 105 recoveries of bands from the east coast occurred on the Gulf coast. Three of these were from birds banded on the east coast in autumn and recovered in Texas on a subsequent spring migration, suggesting that only a small proportion of the east coast sample may participate in a "loop" migration. All data indicate that separate and distinct autumn migratory populations pass through the east and Gulf coasts. Recoveries of Peregrines banded in Canada show association with broad-front migrations south (Figures 4 and 5). The Alaska and Greenland recoveries also indicate variability, because Peregrines from the same natal locale do not always use the same flyway on migration. Indeed, siblings fledged from the same cliff do not always use the same flyway. In 1983, three of four sibling Peregrines in Greenland were recovered on autumn migration, two on the east coast and one in northeastern Iowa (Mattox unpubl. data). Apparently once an individual selects its migratory route, it is unlikely to deviate from it on subsequent migrations. Further support for this conclusion lies in the fact that over half of the subsequent recoveries of east coast-banded Peregrines occurred on the east coast; the Gulf coast figure is over 75%.

Fieldwork at South Padre Island in 1978 disclosed a substantial migration in April and May. Hunt et al. (1981) discovered that Peregrines use the habitat as a staging area during the migration north. Radio telemetry studies indicate that on departure from Padre Island, Peregrines begin a direct course to their northerly destination (W. G. Hunt and J. Chase pers. comm.). There are three records of autumn-banded east coast Peregrines recovered in Texas during spring migration, but data indicate that most spring migrants are probably those passing the Texas coast in the previous fall migration. Fully half the recoveries of Peregrines banded in Texas have come in April-May at Padre Island. Spring work at Assateague Island in 1972-74 and 1976, in Panama in 1973-74, at Dry Tortugas, Florida in 1974-75 and 1983, at Cumberland Island, Georgia in 1976, and at Sandy Hook, New Jersey in 1977-78 resulted in fewer than 15 Peregrine sightings and only one capture (Ward et al. 1978). There is no evidence of a spring concentration of east coast migrants similar to that described for Gulf coast migrants.

Peregrines migrating through Wisconsin in autumn appear to use a separate south to southeast course. Of 17 recoveries of these birds (Figure 6), 1 occurred in Texas and 5 were on the east coast. There were also two recoveries in Ohio, one in Illinois, two in Tennessee, one in Missouri, and one in Alabama. Recoveries south of the United States border totaled four; three of these were in areas where east coast migrants were recovered, but no recovery of a Gulf coast migrant is on

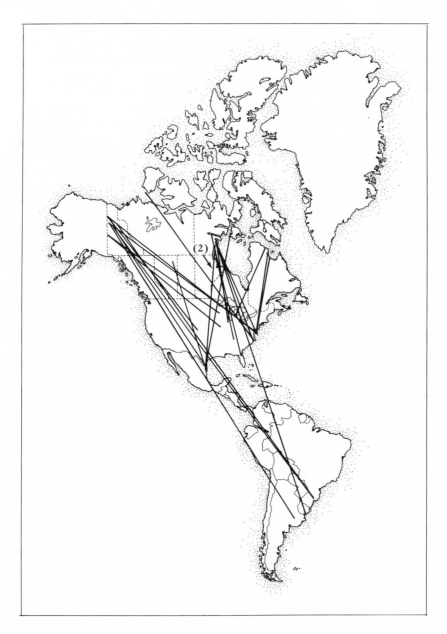

FIGURE 4. Peregrines banded in Canada and recovered south of Canada, January 1955-June 1985 (excluding Mackenzie Valley, Northwest Territories).

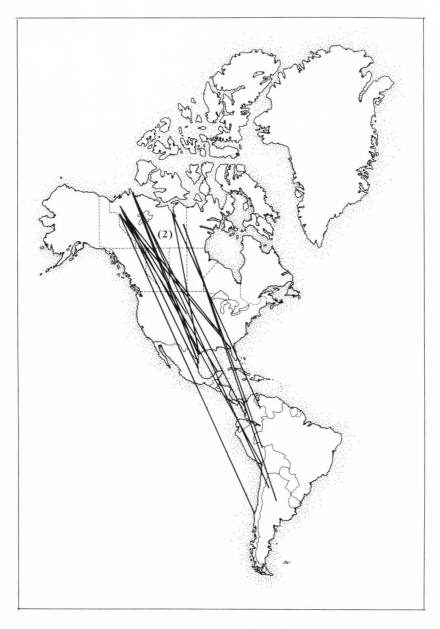

FIGURE 5. Peregrines banded in Mackenzie Valley, Northwest Territories and recovered south of Canada, January 1955-June 1985.

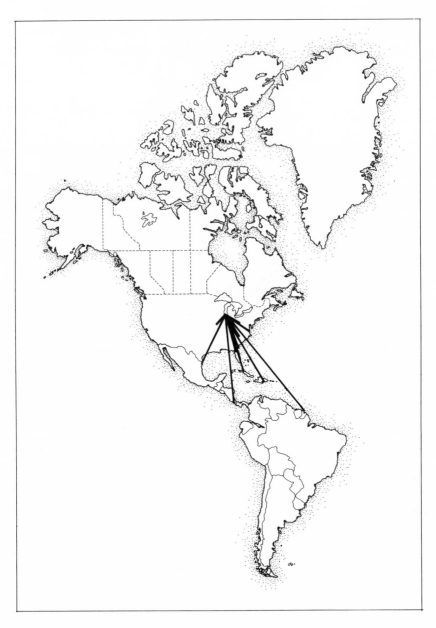

FIGURE 6.   Recoveries elsewhere of Peregrines banded in Wisconsin, January 1955-
          June 1985.

record. In addition, it appears that the Wisconsin migrants sustain higher mortality rates than east or Gulf coast migrants. Only 4 of the 17 recoveries of Peregrines banded in Wisconsin were live, compared to at least 2 of every 3 recovered Peregrines banded on the east and Gulf coasts. Although intense banding efforts on the latter flyways would be expected to account for this difference, it must be noted that the percentage of recoveries is actually higher among the Wisconsin migrants.

Age-specific mortality was ascertained for 88 Peregrines banded as nestlings or hatching-year migrants and later recovered dead. Those banded as adults were not considered because age at death was not always known. For the most part, our method eliminated the biases attendant to estimating mortalities from recoveries discussed by Newton (1979), especially as we did not attempt to establish a yearly mortality rate (non-age-specific) for the entire population and assumed that all mortalities had an equal chance of being found and reported. The potential for overestimating first-year mortality also exists, since future recoveries of more recent bands placed on still-surviving birds cannot be factored into this study. We found that 55 (62.5%) of the 88 individuals did not survive to complete their first northward spring migration. The remaining 33 (37.5%) were recovered dead after their first year (Figure 7).

Because individuals banded as nestlings may endure a higher first-year mortality than those banded on migration, these samples were further separated and analyzed. Only 58% of 38 nestlings were first-year mortalities, while 66% of 50 migrants did not survive. Possible explanations are: (1) during the stressful migration period, less viable individuals are more susceptible to trapping, (2) observed mortality of those banded as nestlings is biased downwards compared to migrants, because the former die before migration to remote areas where discovery is unlikely, and (3) sample size is insufficient for meaningful conclusions. A larger statistical base would enhance accurate representation of yearly mortality beyond the first year.

The recoveries of two Peregrines banded on the Maryland portion of Assateague Island warrant special mention. A female banded as an adult on 7 October 1965 was recovered alive on the Virginia portion of Assateague Island on 2 October 1975; thus she was at least in her 12th year when retrapped. A hatching-year male banded on 25 September 1975 was recovered alive at Nuniluk Bluff, Colville River, Alaska on 15 July 1984 and was later shot and killed in Alagoas State, Brazil in December 1984. In addition to providing two upper longevity records, these returns and others less noteworthy bring us to a final point. We said previously that Peregrines display fidelity to

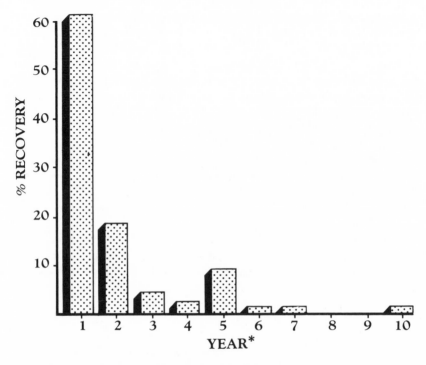

FIGURE 7. Peregrines banded as nestlings or hatching-year birds and recovered dead
         (n=88 records).

*Note: Individual is considered to have survived year if it completes northward
migration to breeding grounds in spring.

their chosen migratory routes. The first individual above made a
minimum of 12 southerly migrations and was captured twice on
migration; the second was captured on southerly migration once in 10
trips. Other recoveries demonstrate the same fact, i.e., individuals
observed and captured on migration constitute a small fraction of the
actual migratory population.

SUMMARY

Most Greenland Peregrines migrate along the east coast in autumn
and constitute a significant proportion of migrants on that flyway; the
same is true of Alaska Peregrines and the Gulf coast. Migrants of any
origin may appear on any flyway and tend to display fidelity to that
same flyway on subsequent southerly migrations. Many wintering areas
are shared by east and Gulf coast autumn migrants, but members of

each group also seem to winter in areas unique to their migratory population. A significant northerly migration occurs along the Texas Gulf coast in spring, but there is no indication of a similar spring concentration on the east coast. Peregrines banded on autumn migration in Wisconsin comprise a separate but not distinct migratory population, which mixes more on wintering grounds with east coast autumn migrants than with Gulf coast counterparts. Recoveries of all banded first-year Peregrines suggest a 63% mortality before completion of their first northward migration. Those banded as nestlings suffered a 58% first-year mortality, but both estimates are subject to bias. Finally, recoveries suggest that only a small fraction of autumn migrants are observed or captured in any given year.

ACKNOWLEDGEMENTS

We gratefully acknowledge the contributions of W. Hunt and B. Johnson, whose initial analysis of recoveries in 1981 was an invaluable resource. K. Klimkiewicz, Bird Banding Laboratory, was extremely helpful and much more receptive to our urgent needs than her busy schedule dictated. M. Fuller provided manuscript review in record time. Assistance in various forms came from J. Chase, K. Titus, and the remainder of the Bird Banding Laboratory staff. Most importantly, we salute those individuals who for decades banded Peregrines and reported recoveries. Among our colleagues in these efforts, we wish to acknowledge by name R. Berry, J. Rice, L. Woyce, D. Berger, W. Clark, T. Nichols, D. Slowe, W. Mattox, R. Ambrose, R. Fyfe and his Canadian collaborators, and J. Weaver. To those not listed, our debt is no less great. And finally, our sincere thanks go to W. Seegar, not only for his banding and recovery contributions but for manuscript review, support, and friendship.

45 | Autumn Migrations of Peregrine Falcons at Assateague Island, Maryland/Virginia, 1970-1984

F. Prescott Ward, Kimberly Titus,
William S. Seegar, Michael A. Yates, and
Mark R. Fuller

Enderson (1969c) raised the possibility of using observations of migrating Peregrine Falcons to estimate population size: "[My purpose] . . . is to call attention to the possibility of developing population indices for Arctic-nesting peregrines by means of systematic counts at certain favorable points where migrants can be readily seen along shorelines in the United States." Newton (1979) corroborated the premise: "Counts over many years at concentration points have revealed long-term population trends . . ." Edelstam (1972), however, pointed out possible problems, particularly when year-to-year variation is high.

Studies during the nesting season across the Peregrine's vast range in North America (e.g., White and Cade 1977, Burnham and Mattox 1984) are quite expensive and logistically difficult to conduct. They sample only a tiny portion of the population, and are often not conducted annually. Migration counts, on the other hand, are usually much easier to implement, and draw their samples from a large area of the breeding range.

Hawk Mountain in eastern Pennsylvania (Nagy 1977) and Cedar Grove, along the western shore of Lake Michigan in Wisconsin (Mueller and Berger 1961), are well-known raptor lookouts that have provided migration data on Peregrines for many years; however, annual counts are generally so low that inferences about population trends are difficult to make (but see Mueller et al. Chapter 46).

Assateague Island, a barrier island off the east coast of Maryland and Virginia, has been known since 1938 as a major focal point for migrating Peregrines in autumn (Shor 1970b, Nye in Ward and Berry 1972). Falconers trapped Peregrines there until the island was declared a national seashore in 1969. Hunting regulations implemented in the summer of 1970 included a prohibition on taking raptors for personal use. That year we initiated a standardized observation and banding study of Peregrines that has continued uninterrupted each autumn since.

Early falconers provided invaluable baselines through their detailed field notes and summaries of numbers of falcons sighted and captured in the early years (B. McDonald unpubl. ms., Nye *in* Ward and Berry 1972). The objectives of our study have been to describe the timing and magnitude of the autumn migration, to observe trends in the numbers of Peregrines over time, and to compare recent migration counts with those from historical accounts.

METHODS

We observed and captured Peregrine Falcons each autumn from 1970-84 at Assateague Island, which is 58 km long. Observation and trapping methods followed those of Ward and Berry (1972) and were consistent for all years. F. P. Ward, M. A. Yates and W. S. Seegar made 92% of all the observations. Annual studies began as early as 17 September and continued as late as 25 October. Two moving vehicles were operated simultaneously from at least the last week in September through the first two weeks in October. A "party" refers to one or more people in one vehicle driving along the beachfront and wash-over areas of the island.

Different marking techniques were used during the 15 years. From 1970-72, trapped birds were marked only with United States Fish and Wildlife Service (USFWS) aluminum bands. Green plastic tarsal bands were also attached from 1973-79 (Ward 1975). In 1980-81, the breast feathers of immature birds were dyed yellow with picric acid, and from 1982-84 every bird trapped was dyed. Falcons were marked with dye so that effort would not be expended retrapping those individuals seen subsequently. Even so, some birds were retrapped.

Since 1981, a resident territorial pair of Peregrines has been present on the Virginia portion of the island (Wash Flats), having been released by The Peregrine Fund, Inc. as part of the effort to reestablish Peregrine Falcons in the eastern United States (Cade and Temple 1977, Cade 1985a). These resident birds were sighted usually once daily, and their counts were removed from all analyses of migrants. Residents were identified by their association with the hack tower, or by territorial behavior, color band or other markings. Other Peregrines released by The Peregrine Fund were also captured as they passed along the island.

Immature birds are Peregrine Falcons in brown juvenile plumage that were hatched in the same calendar year as their capture. The USFWS Bird Banding Laboratory refers to these as hatching-year (HY) birds. Observed birds that completed at least one pre-basic molt and were in a blue-gray plumage are called after-hatching-year (AHY). Peregrine Falcons trapped in the fall that were in their first basic plumage with some juvenile feathers remaining are second-year (SY) birds. Consequently, AHY birds may include SY birds, but an after-second-year (ASY) designation does not.

RESULTS

During the 15 years, 4702 Peregrine Falcons were observed and 1082 were captured as first encounters (Table 1). The capture efficiency for birds caught for the first time at Assateague Island was 23%, and nearly 6% of "new" birds were banded elsewhere or were banded at Assateague during a previous season. Recaptures, sightings of color-banded and color-marked birds, and sightings of the nonmigratory resident pair accounted for another 27% of our encounters. The total study effort comprised more than 6500 party-hours, ranging from a low of 221 party-hours in 1971 to a high of 725 party-hours in 1984.

Timing of Migration. — Ninety percent of the Peregrine Falcons counted at Assateague Island were observed between 21 September-18 October. Migrations by immature and adult birds were temporally similar (paired *t*-test, $n=15$ years, $P>0.05$, Figure 1). Mean capture date was 5 October for both immature and adult Peregrines.

Male Peregrine Falcons migrated before females (paired *t*-test, $n=15$ years, $P<0.05$), although there was substantial overlap and variation among years. Figure 2 is a composite for all years, indicating an overall trend not necessarily apparent in any single year.

Hourly observation and capture rates were rather constant throughout the day (Figure 3). The survey was not always conducted during the first and last hours of a day.

TABLE 1. Status of Peregrine Falcons observed at Assateague Island, 1970-84.

Status	n	%
First capture of unbanded bird	1018	21.7
First recovery of bird with band applied elsewhere or at Assateague in a previous season	64	1.4
Not captured	2324	49.4
Recaptured in the same season (some multiple)	331	7.0
Not captured but number read on color band (some multiple)	73	1.6
Not captured but color band observed	91	1.9
Not captured but yellow dye sighted	500	10.6
Not captured but identified as adult female resident	172	3.7
Not captured but identified as adult male resident	129	2.7
Total	4702	100.0

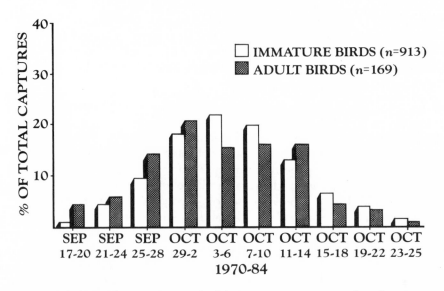

FIGURE 1. Dates that immature and adult Peregrines were captured at Assateague Island, 1970-84.

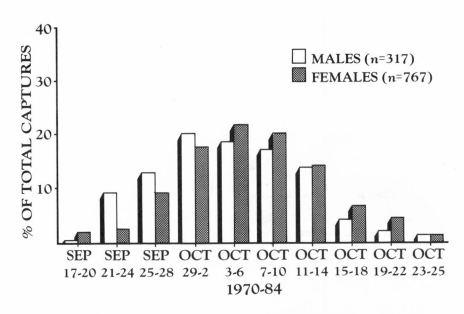

FIGURE 2. Dates that male and female Peregrines were captured at Assateague Island, 1970-84.

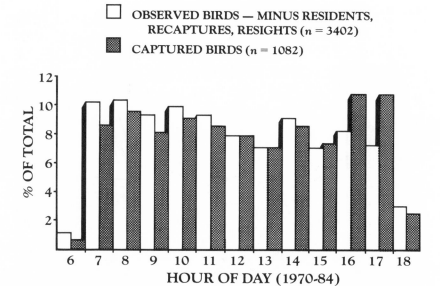

□ OBSERVED BIRDS — MINUS RESIDENTS,
  RECAPTURES, RESIGHTS (*n* = 3402)

▨ CAPTURED BIRDS (*n* = 1082)

FIGURE 3. Hour of day in which Peregrines migrating through Assateague Island were observed and captured, 1970-84.

Trend in Numbers Observed and Trapped. — Numbers of Peregrine Falcons observed and trapped increased markedly near the end of the 15-year period. Numbers observed (minus resightings, recaptures and resident birds) averaged 76 birds per year from 1970-74, 222 birds per year from 1975-79 and 382 birds per year from 1980-84. When the data were standardized to the number of birds seen per 10 man-hours to account for more effort in recent years, the trend was similar (Figure 4). Less erratic observation and capture trends are evident for adult Peregrines (Figure 5), a group (unlike the HY cohort) not influenced by the annual vicissitudes of hatchability and survival in the nest.

After eliminating resightings, recaptures and resident birds, 85.1% of the Peregrines observed from 1970-84 were immature. There was considerable annual variation in the ratio of immatures to adults but no discernible trend (Table 2).

Of the 1082 Peregrine Falcons captured, 55.6% were HY females and 28.7% were HY males. The proportion of immature birds captured (84.5%) was similar to the proportion of immature birds observed (Chi-square with Yates correction = 1.04, $df=1$, $P>0.25$). Of the 169 AHY birds captured, 73 (43.2%) were second-year females, 71 (42%) were ASY females and 18 (10.7%) were AHY females (i.e., discrimination between an SY versus older birds was in doubt). Only seven (4.1%) adult males were captured.

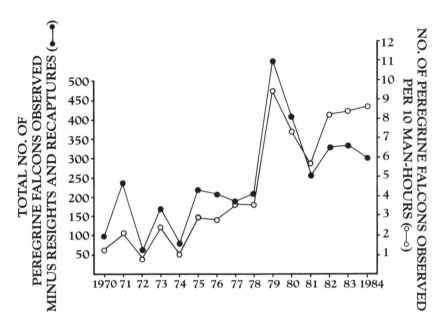

FIGURE 4. Total numbers of Peregrine Falcons observed and captured at Assateague
Island, 1970-84.

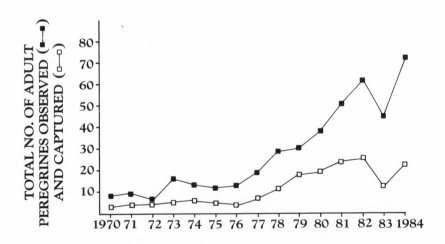

FIGURE 5. Numbers of adult Peregrines observed and captured at Assateague Island,
1970-84.

TABLE 2. Number of Peregrine Falcons observed according to age at Assateague Island, 1970-84, with historical data since 1939[a].

Age		Year														
	39-47[b]	70	71	72	73	74	75	76	77	78	79	80	81	82	83	84
Adult	40	8	9	7	16	13	12	13	19	29	30	38	51	62	45	72
Immature	126	44	93	21	96	35	114	84	134	122	380	275	176	281	269	295
Unknown	309	11	4	11	8	6	19	41	24	28	61	56	55	66	105	65
Total	475	63	106	39	120	54	145	138	177	179	471	369	282	409	419	432
Percent Immature	76	85	91	75	86	73	91	87	88	81	93	88	78	82	86	80

[a] Excludes known resightings, recaptures and resident birds.
[b] Nye (1969) taken from Ward and Berry (1972); numbers are totals for all years from 1939-47.

Of 422 Peregrines recaptured or resighted and identified as individuals (e.g., by reading the number on a colored and numbered tarsal band), 217 (51.4%) were recaptured or resighted on the same day. Some Peregrines were recaptured up to 19 days after their initial capture in Assateague Island (Table 3). Seventy-nine percent of the recaptures or resightings other than on the same day were 1-3 days later.

Comparisons with Historical Data. — Our Peregrine Falcon observations from Assateague Island were compared with those by A. Nye for the period 1939-44. B. McDonald (unpubl. ms.) also provided data on observations of Peregrines on Assateague Island and nearby Virginia barrier islands from 1956-69. Data were converted to the number of Peregrines seen per party per day for the period of 25 September-16 October (Ward and Berry 1972). Nye saw an average of 11.7 Peregrines per day during the peak of migration, and McDonald saw an average of 4.3. Our average from 1970-78 was 3.6. By 1979-84, the numbers observed increased dramatically to an average of 11.8 per party per day (Figure 6). There was a positive correlation between the mean number observed per party per day over time for the 15-year study ($r=0.82$, $n=15$ years, $P<0.001$); i.e., in each successive year more Peregrines were observed.

TABLE 3.   Number of recaptures or identified resightings of Peregrine Falcons within the same season at Assateague Island, 1970-84. Recaptures on the same day and observations of resident adults are excluded.

Day after initial capture	Frequency ($n = 205$)	Percent
1	96	46.8
2	40	19.5
3	26	12.7
4	13	6.3
5	5	2.4
6	4	1.8
7	1	0.5
8	3	1.5
9	3	1.5
10	2	1.0
11	2	1.0
12	1	0.5
13	2	1.0
14	2	1.0
15	1	0.5
16	2	1.0
17	1	0.5
18	0	0.0
19	1	0.5

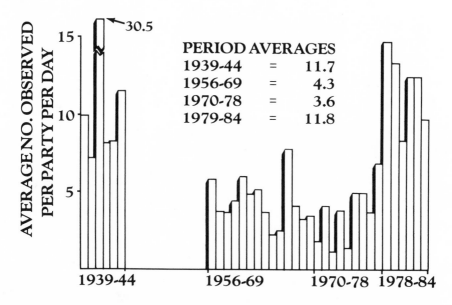

FIGURE 6. Numbers of Peregrine Falcons migrating each year on Maryland/Virginia barrier islands, 25 September-16 October.

DISCUSSION

The results of this study indicate that:

(1) Populations of northern Peregrine Falcons from which Assateague Island draws its sample of autumn migrants decreased substantially from 1956-78 relative to pre-DDT data from the same environs.

(2) Observations of Peregrines from 1979-84 were nearly identical to data from a pre-DDT survey conducted from 1939-44.

(3) Many migrants (about 20%), particularly immature birds, remain on Assateague for a day or more; about 20% of those stay for more than four days.

(4) More than 6% of Peregrines captured for the first time during a season had been banded elsewhere or at Assateague during a previous season (see Yates et al. Chapter 44).

(5) When carried out in a systematic manner, longterm counts of Peregrines at key migration foci do reveal longterm population trends.

Our counts increased substantially during the course of this study, agreeing with the summary by Cade (1982) that Peregrine populations breeding in the American arctic increased in the late 1970s. The low counts we had in the early 1970s also agree with surveys on arctic breeding grounds (Cade and Fyfe 1970); even in 1975 numbers were still considered to be very low (Fyfe et al. 1976a). Interestingly, the trends in our data (Figures 4 and 5) were similar to those presented by Wikman (1985) for Finland, and Speer (1985) for the Federal Republic of Germany for *F. p. peregrinus*. A population recovery in Britain appears to have taken place a few years earlier (Ratcliffe 1980).

By 1979, many of our daily counts during peak migration were similar to historical accounts (1939-44) for peak days. As an example, on 3 October 1979, 61 Peregrine Falcons were observed, 17 by Ward and 44 by Yates. Another example was 1 October 1980, when 75 were observed, 36 by Ward and 39 by Yates.

Unlike many raptors, immature and adult Peregrine Falcons were not temporally separated during fall migration at Assateague Island (Figure 1). Rosenfield and Evans (1980) found that immature Sharp-shinned Hawks peak in their migration a few weeks before adults. Weir et al. (1980) found that female Northern Saw-whet Owls migrated earlier than males in some years. Hunt et al. (1975) reported that adult Peregrine Falcons arrived first during autumn migration along the Texas coast (Chi-square analysis for 20 years pooled, which does not allow for year-to-year variation). They found adult females migrating prior to immature males, followed by immature females. Immature and adult Peregrines migrate by Assateague Island at the same time; however, they generally feed on different prey (Ward and Laybourne 1985).

With many Peregrine Falcons being resighted and recaptured in a season at Assateague, it is difficult to determine the actual number of Peregrines that pass by the island each fall. Because all birds were not captured, we do not know how many individuals were resighted several times, thus inflating counts. However, the field methods remained standardized for 15 years, and data indicate a strong upward trend.

The timing of autumn migration at Assateague Island and Padre Island, Texas is similar (Hunt et al. 1975). This indicates that observers at these concentration points were not counting the same birds, but that both locations are key concentration areas for Peregrine Falcons in autumn. Banding results also indicate little seasonal interchange between these two areas (Yates et al. Chapter 44). Indeed, Assateague Island and Padre Island are the two known major concentration areas for migrant Peregrine Falcons in North America, and data accrued for more years at these two locations will augment tremendously our ability to infer population status based on migration statistics.

ACKNOWLEDGEMENTS

Invaluable tutelage plus excellent field work were generously provided during the first seven years of this study by R. B. Berry.

L. C. Woyce, Jr. substituted for Mr. Berry at times during the 1975 and 1976 seasons, and his field work was no less professional. The list of assistants who accompanied the principal investigators is much too long to recognize (or even to remember completely), but each participant's unselfish contributions are deeply appreciated. Among them, special thanks are due to J. N. Rice, A. G. Nye, Jr., B. B. McDonald, G. Nye, R. A. Whitney, Jr., W. C. Cole, B. Firth, Mr. and Mrs. H. M. Paulson, Jr., J. W. Hanes, Jr., R. Gritman, and G. M. Jonkel.

Several people were instrumental in securing and sustaining political approval and permit authorizations to initiate and continue our 15-year study. They include E. Baysinger, T. Cade, R. Rohm, E. Johnson, R. Fielding, A. Eno, and especially the late L. Glasgow. Among those who manage the various administrative subdivisions of Assateague, many officials of state and federal agencies on the island are due our acknowledgement and heartfelt thanks, including D. F. Holland, R. Rector and M. Olsen; without the personal commitment of these people and many members of their staffs, our research endeavors would have been far more difficult.

Timely computer programming advice was provided by L. Moyer, L. McAllister and particularly D. Jacobs.

Editors' Note: According to information from M. Yates, the number of Peregrines observed and trapped at Assateague Island continued to increase in 1985 and 1986. The team counted 483 falcons and trapped 147 in 1985. The numbers nearly doubled in 1986 to 830 observed and 230 trapped. The number of observed adults reached an all-time high of 109 in 1986 (compare with Figure 5).

46 Population Trends in Migrating Peregrines at Cedar Grove, Wisconsin, 1936-1985

Helmut C. Mueller, Daniel D. Berger, and George Allez

In the proceedings of the Madison Peregrine Conference, Hickey and Anderson (1969) noted the value of counts of migrating Peregrines as indicators of population trends. This paper presents an analysis of counts of migrant Peregrines for 35 consecutive autumns from 1951-85, plus observations from an additional eight autumns from 1935-49.

In 1921, H. L. Stoddard and C. S. Jung noted that migrating hawks were concentrated along the western shore of Lake Michigan east of the village of Cedar Grove, Wisconsin. Occasional observations and attempts to trap hawks culminated in 1935 with the construction of a permanent blind about 200 m from the lakeshore at that locality. O. J. Gromme and other personnel of the Milwaukee Public Museum were responsible for the construction and operation of the station, but many of the routine activities, including observation, were performed by workers provided by the Civilian Conservation Corps. Migrating raptors were observed, trapped, and banded during most of each autumn from 1936 until 1941, when World War II interrupted regular operation. Consistent operation was resumed in 1946, but ceased thereafter, except for 1949, when the Museum provided W. Schultz to assist the volunteer, R. A. Herbert.

METHODS

D. D. Berger and H. C. Mueller occupied the station in 1950, but reasonably regular observation and systematic record-keeping did not begin until 1951. The original blind and adjoining living quarters were destroyed by fire and were replaced by a larger, but similar, structure on the same spot in 1960. At least one of the authors was present at the station for the majority of observation days in all of the 34 years. Berger was present at the station for at least part of the season for 34 of the 35 years, Mueller and Allez for 21 years. We discarded unsupervised observations of other volunteers in those few cases where we had doubts about their accuracy. Two or more observers were present at the station on most days. We usually watched continually from before sunrise until after sunset, although on days with little or no migration, our observation occasionally became sporadic, particularly in the 1950s and 1960s. Observation was suspended completely only in periods of heavy and continuous rain or dense fog. We operated an intensive program of mist-netting of small birds in the years 1958-63 (Mueller and Berger 1967a), an effort that required reduced observation for hawks on some days with little migration. In recent years, the on-duty observer did not leave his post for any reason without first being replaced by another observer. Our vigilance on days with little migration was certainly superior to what it was in the 1950s and 1960s, and, probably, greatly superior to that of museum personnel in the 1930s.

Observations were performed from carefully designed, spacious, and comfortable blinds which offered an extensive view to the north, east and west. The view offered from our blinds probably resulted in the sighting of more southbound migrants than would be seen by an unrestrained observer because it forced the observer to scan continually to the north, east and west. The incentive of possibly trapping a Peregrine was sufficient to maintain the vigilance of most observers in spite of occasional distractions or long hours of little activity. Observations made from the same point, with the same constraints, and with reasonably constant and high motivation were certainly more comparable between years than those obtained by unconstrained bird watchers. The vegetation in the vicinity of the station has changed greatly in the last 35 years. A vigorous program of cutting, pruning and topping of trees has reduced the effects of vegetative growth on our observations.

The data from 1936-49 were taken from the notes of the late C. S. Jung, who extracted the information from the field notes of the Milwaukee Public Museum in preparation for a publication (Jung 1964). Berger and Mueller also browsed through original notes years ago and concluded that most were too inexact for quantitative comparisons with our observations. Many of the records of raptors seen per day are obvious estimates, including two for Peregrines: 28 September 1938, "50-55+"; 7 October 1941, "20+" (in both of these cases, we used the minimum estimate in our analyses). It is not clear how many of the other numbers given for Peregrines were actual counts or merely estimates. Details about when observations began and ended each day, and how much of the day was actually spent in watching for hawks were recorded only incidentally and rarely. We have almost no information on the qualification and diligence of various observers, but we think that at least some, particularly some workers from the Civilian Conservation Corps, were not as skilled, and especially not as dedicated to watch continually from dawn to dusk, as were our observers.

RESULTS AND DISCUSSION

Bias Caused By Unequal Yearly Coverage. — The number of days that the station was in operation varied considerably from year to year. A first step to reduce the bias caused by unequal coverage is to limit the analysis to that part of the autumn when most Peregrines are seen. The median date for Peregrine sightings for the years 1951-84 was 29 September and this date ±13 days includes 88.8% of all Peregrines seen. The data for the calendar interval of 16 September-12 October inclusive, are presented in Table 1. We use a five-year moving average (Table 2) to reduce effects of annual fluctuations, reveal long-term changes, and permit the use of statistics (Table 2). One can obtain two indices of Peregrine abundance from these data: (A) the number of Peregrines seen per year, and (B) the mean number of Peregrines seen per day. Both of these indices are biased when the number of observation days is less than the possible maximum of 27. Index A obviously is an underestimate unless no Peregrines passed on days without observation. Index B is an overestimate because we usually made a greater effort to be at the station on days when the forecast indicated good weather for the migration of raptors. Weather has a considerable effect on the number of raptors seen at Cedar Grove (Mueller and Berger 1961, 1967b). We have not done an analysis of weather and Peregrine migration, but the species is seen in reasonable numbers at Cedar Grove in a greater variety of weather conditions than any other raptor; good days for Peregrines are often relatively mediocre days for other species. Our ability to predict good days for Peregrines is questionable, as is the reliability of weather forecasts. Thus, it is very difficult to judge the magnitude of over-estimation in Index B in years with less than the full 27 days of observation.

The two indices are biased in opposite directions, and we propose that an agreement between the two provides a reasonably valid indicator of changes in the numbers of migrant Peregrines. We further propose that changes are probably real only if differences are statistically significant. We compared peaks (but not high years adjacent to peaks) with all other five-year moving averages, using the randomization test for two independent samples (Siegel 1956). Differences were considered significant where $P<0.05$, two-tailed. Agreement between both indices indicates that: (1) more Peregrines currently are migrating past Cedar Grove than in 1959-63 and 1960-64 and than in any five-year

TABLE 1.   Observations of Peregrines at Cedar Grove, Wisconsin, 16 September-
12 October.

Year	No. of observation days	No. of Peregrines	No. of Peregrines /day
1936	20	36	1.80
1937	27	23	0.85
1938	27	71+	2.63+
1939	27	26	0.96
1940	27	22	0.81
1941	19	55+	2.89+
1946	25	11	0.44
1949	22	28	1.27
1951	5	8	1.60
1952	12	23	1.92
1953	27	37	1.37
1954	20	30	1.50
1955	27	22	0.82
1956	8	7	0.88
1957	19	8	0.42
1958	27	48	1.77
1959	27	26	0.96
1960	27	14	0.52
1961	27	16	0.59
1962	27	13	0.48
1963	27	34	1.26
1964	27	22	0.81
1965	14	20	1.43
1966	12	21	1.75
1967	27	11	0.41
1968	18	29	1.61
1969	27	16	0.59
1970	27	16	0.59
1971	26	35	1.35
1972	25	3	0.12
1973	26	26	1.00
1974	26	13	0.50
1975	27	9	0.33
1976	27	6	0.22
1977	27	19	0.70
1978	27	26	0.96
1979	27	24	0.89
1980	27	37	1.37
1981	27	43	1.59
1982	27	30	1.11
1983	27	26	0.96
1984	27	43	1.59
1985	27	86	3.19

period since 1969, and (2) the number of Peregrines seen in 1937-41 was greater than in the years 1972-76 through 1974-78.

Differences Between the Two Indices of Abundance. — The discrepancies between the two indices warrant examination. Index B indicates that more Peregrines were seen in 1951-55 than in 1959-63, 1960-64 and in the years 1969-73 through 1976-80, but Index A shows that 1951-55 did not differ significantly from any other five years (Table 2). A reasonable resolution of the conflict between the two indices can be obtained by determining: (1) the number of additional Peregrines that must have migrated past, unseen, to increase the annual totals for 1951-55 so that they are significantly greater than those for another five years, and (2) the likelihood that this number of Peregrines passed on those days when there was no observation. The first of these can be determined easily and rigorously. For the second, we propose to use the number of Peregrines seen on the worst n days in the nearest year with a full 27 days of observation in which the total seen is greater than the year for which the estimate is being made (n=number of days with no observation). In 1953, two Peregrines were seen during the worst 15 days and 14 during the worst 22 days, yielding estimates of 22 Peregrines for 1951 and 25 for 1952. The resulting adjusted average for 1951-55 is significantly greater than those for 1972-76, 1973-77 and 1974-78, suggesting that Peregrines were more abundant in the early 1950s than in the 1970s. The lowest five-year moving average is that for 1960-64 (Table 2); 1951-55 would be significantly greater only if 27 Peregrines passed unobserved in 1951, 6 in 1952, and 5 in 1954, suggesting no difference between the 1950s and 1960s.

Index B indicates that more Peregrines were seen in 1964-68 than in 1972-76. Index A would show the same difference only if eight Peregrines passed in the 15 days with no observation in 1966 and if six passed in the 13 days with no observation in 1965. This is unlikely; no Peregrines were seen in the 15 worst days of either 1963 or 1964. It thus appears that the apparent peak of 1964-68 in Index B is an artifact resulting from limited observation and very probably biased sampling during several of the years involved.

Index A shows that significantly more Peregrines were observed in 1981-85 than in the years 1961-65 through 1968-72, but Index B indicates no significant differences. There is thus some question as to whether Peregrine observations showed a small increase somewhere between the obvious lows of 1960-64 and 1972-76. The two most likely five-year moving averages that might not have been significantly different from 1981-85 are 1962-66 and 1963-67. In both cases, the differences would not be significant if two Peregrines passed by during the 13 days of no observation in 1965 and five during the 15 days of

TABLE 2. Five-year moving averages of observations of Peregrines at Cedar Grove, Wisconsin, 16 September-12 October.

Years	$\bar{x}$ Days $\pm$ S.D.	$\bar{x}$ Peregrines $\pm$ S.D.	$\bar{x}$ Peregrines/day $\pm$ S.D.
1936-40	25.6 ± 3.13	35.6 ± 20.55	1.41 ± 0.79
1937-41	25.4 ± 3.58	39.4 ± 22.32	1.63 ± 1.04
1951-55	18.2 ± 9.63	24.0 ± 10.79	1.44 ± 0.40
1952-56	18.8 ± 8.64	23.8 ± 11.17	1.30 ± 0.46
1953-57	20.2 ± 7.79	20.8 ± 13.26	1.00 ± 0.44
1954-58	20.2 ± 7.79	23.0 ± 17.00	1.08 ± 0.55
1955-59	21.6 ± 8.35	22.2 ± 16.68	0.97 ± 0.49
1956-60	21.6 ± 8.35	20.6 ± 17.08	0.91 ± 0.53
1957-61	25.4 ± 3.58	22.4 ± 15.71	0.85 ± 0.55
1958-62	27.0 ± 0	23.4 ± 14.69	0.87 ± 0.54
1959-63	27.0 ± 0	20.6 ± 9.10[d]	0.76 ± 0.34[b,d]
1960-64	27.0 ± 0	19.8 ± 8.67[d]	0.73 ± 0.32[b,d]
1961-65	24.4 ± 5.81	21.0 ± 8.06[d]	0.92 ± 0.41
1962-66	21.4 ± 7.70	22.0 ± 7.58[d]	1.15 ± 0.50
1963-67	21.4 ± 7.70	21.6 ± 8.20[d]	1.13 ± 0.53
1964-68	19.6 ± 7.09	20.6 ± 6.43[d]	1.20 ± 0.57
1965-69	19.6 ± 7.09	19.4 ± 6.66[d]	1.16 ± 0.61
1966-70	18.6 ± 6.91	18.6 ± 6.80[d]	0.99 ± 0.64
1967-71	25.0 ± 3.94	21.4 ± 10.11[d]	0.91 ± 0.53
1968-72	24.6 ± 3.78	19.8 ± 12.52[d]	0.85 ± 0.61
1969-73	26.2 ± 0.84	19.2 ± 12.03[d]	0.73 ± 0.47[b,d]
1970-74	26.0 ± 0.71	18.6 ± 12.30[d]	0.71 ± 0.47[b,d]
1971-75	26.0 ± 0.71	17.2 ± 13.05[d]	0.66 ± 0.50[b,d]
1972-76	26.2 ± 0.84	11.4 ± 8.96[a,d]	0.44 ± 0.35[a,b,c,d]
1973-77	26.6 ± 0.55	14.6 ± 8.02[a,d]	0.55 ± 0.31[a,b,d]
1974-78	26.8 ± 0.45	14.6 ± 8.02[a,d]	0.54 ± 0.30[a,b,d]
1975-79	27.0 ± 0	16.8 ± 8.93[d]	0.62 ± 0.33[b,d]
1976-80	27.0 ± 0	22.4 ± 11.28[d]	0.83 ± 0.42[b,d]
1977-81	27.0 ± 0	29.8 ± 9.88[d]	1.10 ± 0.37
1978-82	27.0 ± 0	32.0 ± 7.91	1.19 ± 0.29
1979-83	27.0 ± 0	32.0 ± 7.91	1.19 ± 0.29
1980-84	27.0 ± 0	35.8 ± 7.67	1.33 ± 0.28
1981-85	27.0 ± 0	45.6 ± 23.84	1.69 ± 0.88

[a] Significantly less than 1937-41 (randomization test for two independent samples, $P < 0.05$, two-tailed).
[b] Significantly less than 1951-55.
[c] Significantly less than 1964-68.
[d] Significantly less than 1981-85.

no observation in 1966. No Peregrines were seen in the worst 15 days of 1963 and 1964, suggesting that 1962-66 and 1963-67 were significantly different from 1981-85.

There is one remaining way to examine our data: restrict the analysis to years in which there were observations on all of the 27 days between 16 September and 12 October (Table 3). This analysis confirms that more Peregrines were seen in the 1940s and 1950s than in the 1970s, and that more Peregrines were seen in the 1980s than in either the 1970s or 1960s.

Pre-DDT and Post-DDT Comparison. — Are Peregrines as abundant now as they were in the 1930s, before the introduction of organochlorine pesticides? We previously suggested that the observations performed by the Milwaukee Public Museum and its helpers might have been less efficient than those of the authors and their volunteers. It is difficult to evaluate this suspicion empirically. We propose to use the numbers seen of a common species that is likely to occur on each of the days in the period 16 September-12 October as an index of observer effort. More Broad-winged Hawks are seen in fall migration than any other species, but most individuals seen in a season usually pass on a few big days. Excluding the Broad-winged Hawk, more than 75% of the Falconiformes seen during 16 September-12 October are Sharp-shinned Hawks, and a day within this period with 100% observation and no sightings of Sharp-shinned Hawks is relatively rare (in 1981-85 this occurred on an average of only 2 of the 27 days). Although the number of Sharp-shins seen per day shows an apparent, consistent increase from the 1930s through the 1980s (Table 3), none of the differences are statistically significant (note the large standard deviations). These counts should not be used as indicators of the abundance of Sharp-shins because portions of the two peaks in seasonal occurrence of the species lie outside of the calendar interval 16 September-12 October (Mueller and Berger 1967b). The annual totals include two sources of error: (1) some years contain days with estimates, instead of actual counts, and more importantly, (2) they are affected by differences in the efficiency of observation. The extremes, rather than the mean are a more instructive way of revealing differences in the efficiency of observation. Peregrines passing through on days on which more than 100 Sharp-shins pass are unlikely to go unnoticed, as the high numbers of hawks should serve to maintain a high level of observer interest and vigilance. Also, errors in estimation are of no consequence as long as the estimate is for more than 100 birds. There is no significant difference between any groups of years with full observation in the number of days on which more than 100 Sharp-shins were recorded (Table 3).

We have arbitrarily chosen days with less than five Sharp-shins recorded as the other extreme. Significantly more of these days were recorded in 1937-40 than in any other group of years (Table 3). Very few, or very many, Sharp-shins were seen on most days in 1937-40, and there is a remarkable paucity of days (22%) on which moderate numbers (5-100) of Sharp-shins were seen. The percentage of days with moderate numbers of Sharp-shins for the other four groups of years ranges from 44-70%. The only reasonable explanation for this great difference between 1937-40 and other groups of years in Table 3 is that the museum personnel were considerably less vigilant than were our observers on days when moderate or low numbers of Sharp-shins were migrating. The decrease in the number of days with fewer than five Sharp-shins recorded from the 1950s through the 1980s (although not statistically significant) is in accord with our estimates of changes in vigilance during the 35 years that we have operated the station.

The data indicate that there is no significant difference between 1937-40 and 1981-85 in the number of Peregrines recorded, but also that there is a considerable difference in observer effort between the two groups of years. The considerably reduced vigilance of observers in 1937-40 on days with less than five Sharp-shins recorded should result in markedly fewer Peregrines observed per day than observed on similar days in 1981-85. This is obviously not true (Table 3), and the only plausible explanation is that more Peregrines migrated past Cedar Grove in the 1930s than in the 1980s. The magnitude of the differences involved (almost three times the number of days per year with fewer than five Sharp-shins in 1937-40 than in 1981-85) suggest that the numbers of Peregrines recorded in 1937-40 may be considerably lower than the number that might have been seen with observation as diligent as that of 1981-85.

The number of Peregrines migrating past Cedar Grove would have been significantly greater in 1937-40 than in 1981-85 if vigilance of observation was sufficiently lax to allow an average of 34% of the Peregrines to pass unobserved. The years 1937 and 1939 would require the largest portion of unobserved Peregrines, 48% and 41%, respectively. These also are the only two years of the 24 included in Table 3 in which more than 50% of the total Peregrines were seen on days with fewer than five Sharp-shins. The high proportion of Peregrines on days presumably with reduced observation suggests that there is a reasonable probability that significantly more Peregrines migrated past Cedar Grove in 1937-40 than in 1981-85.

CONCLUSION

A synthesis of our several approaches to the data shows that the number of Peregrines migrating past Cedar Grove in autumn declined from the 1950s to an extreme low in the early and mid-1970s and then showed a remarkable recovery in the 1980s. Current numbers are as great as they were in the 1950s and possibly as great as in the 1930s. It appears, however, that differences in the intensity of observation between the 1930s and 1980s were sufficiently great so that it is likely

TABLE 3. Some characteristics of groups of years with observations of Peregrines at Cedar Grove, Wisconsin on every day from 16 September-12 October.

Year	$\bar{x}$ Peregrines /day	$\bar{x}$ Sharp-shinned Hawks/day	% of days with > 100 Sharp-shinned Hawks	% of days with < 5 Sharp-shinned Hawks	% of Peregrines on days with < 5 Sharp-shinned Hawks
1937, 38, 39, 40	1.31 ± 0.879 [a]	17.7 ± 17.67	2.8 ± 1.85	75.2 ± 8.22	0.66 ± 0.187
1953, 55, 58, 59, 60	1.09 ± 0.493	24.9 ± 13.41	3.7 ± 5.22	48.1 ± 18.99 [b]	0.61 ± 0.208
1961, 62, 63, 64, 67	0.71 ± 0.343 [d]	28.3 ± 19.56	6.7 ± 6.07	49.6 ± 17.48 [b]	0.08 ± 0.050 [b,c]
1969, 70, 75, 76, 77	0.49 ± 0.206 [b,c,d]	37.0 ± 22.44	8.9 ± 10.00	36.3 ± 9.22 [b]	0.22 ± 0.204 [b]
1981, 82, 83, 84, 85	1.69 ± 0.883	40.2 ± 36.78	3.7 ± 3.70	25.9 ± 13.37 [b]	0.63 ± 0.663

[a] The ± indicates one standard deviation.
[b] Significantly less than 1937-40 (randomization test for two independent samples, $P < 0.05$ two-tailed).
[c] Significantly less than 1953-60.
[d] Significantly less than 1981-85.

that more Peregrines passed Cedar Grove in the 1930s than in the 1980s. The status of Peregrines in the 1960s is unclear because of differences in the vigilance of observation between the 1960s and 1980s. Overall, it appears likely that the Peregrine decline from the 1950s was slow and would not have been recognized until the 1970s even if we had observed with equal diligence throughout the years.

Most Peregrines trapped at Cedar Grove were clearly of the race *F. p. tundrius*, and it is likely that all but a few individuals that passed Cedar Grove in fall were of arctic or subarctic origin. We have captured two Peregrines banded as nestlings: one from Alaska and one from northwestern Hudson Bay. Unequivocal winter recoveries of Peregrines banded at Cedar Grove are all from South America. Geographic patterns of pesticide use offer a reasonable explanation for the decline of this population of Peregrines but do not explain the sudden, dramatic increase in the past few years. An explanation for the increase is as important as is one for the decline. The recent rapid increase in Peregrines is unprecedented and monitoring of numbers should be continued. The most economical and efficient way to monitor arctic and subarctic populations is with counts of birds during migration.

Every effort should be made to standardize the diligence and efficiency of data collection in longterm studies of population changes. Indices based on birds per unit time, per linear unit, or per unit area should be examined carefully for all possible sources of bias between years. Our paper shows some of the problems involved in the interpretation of longterm studies.

ACKNOWLEDGEMENTS

We thank all of those who have aided in various ways in our 35 years at Cedar Grove. We apologize to those "gaboons" who are included in the following list and those who are not: G. Allen, V. Appanius, F. Bentley, E. Berg, E. Bienvenu, S. Conway, R. Eckstein, T. Erdman, F. Fiala, G. Geller, H. Gibbs, F. Hamerstrom, E. Horvath, J. Kaspar, K. Kuhn, H. Meinel, K. Meyer, N. Mueller, J. Oar, F. Renn, W. Robichaud, D. Seal, C. Sindelar, T. Sisk, W. Walker III and C. Whelan. We thank the Wisconsin Department of Natural Resources for permitting us to use land and providing materials for construction and maintenance of our buildings. Prof. J. T. Emlen and the University of Wisconsin at Madison provided invaluable support during our years of affiliation with the University. The National Science Foundation provided financial support for four years.

Plate 1   Painting used courtesy of Terry Draut

1. Painting of an immature Peregrine Falcon that was to have been the cover for *Peregrine Falcon Populations: Their Biology and Decline,* edited by Joseph J. Hickey (1969). In a 30 December 1968 memo to the conference's contributors, Dr. Hickey stated: "The handling of illustrations by the Press was a tale of sheer frustration. My original suggestion for the dust jacket was a magnificent oil (opaque water color) of a Canadian arctic Peregrine generously offered us by James Grier. This was turned down as 'too fierce.' No kidding! What a missed opportunity!" Now, with a more optimistic outlook for the species, we are pleased to present Dr. Hickey's first choice for a cover illustration.

Plate 2   J. Enderson

Plate 3   D. Ellis

2–5. Peregrines in flight.

Plate 4   J. Enderson

Plate 5   J. Enderson

6–9. Peregrines in flight.

Plate 10   C. Thelander

10. A Peregrine nesting cliff overlooking the Napa Valley, California. Several caves near the center of the highest cliff section have been used as nest sites over the years. 11. This Peregrine nesting cliff east of San Francisco, California, was occupied from the late 1800s until the early 1950s, but has since remained vacant. The eyrie is in a cave near the top of the highest peak shown. A photograph by H. Snow of the adult female from this site appeared as Figure 21 in Bond (1946).

Plate 11   S. K. Carnie, 1949

Plate 12

D. Ratcliffe

12. Nesting site in the Lake District, Great Britain, where a Peregrine was seen eating its eggs in 1951.

Plate 13   R. Quigley

13. Morro Rock, a famous Peregrine nesting site on the central California coastline.
14. Portrait of a juvenile female Peregrine from northern Finland.

Plate 14   P. Lindberg

15. Incubating adult female Peregrine using an artificial nesting cavity. This was the last known *F. p. anatum* nesting pair in southern Alberta, Canada.

Plate 15   R. Fyfe, 1972

Plate 16   R. Fyfe, 1975

16. Peregrine eyrie with four lightly-colored eggs laid as a second clutch in northern Alberta, Canada.

17. Peregrine eyrie on a 200 m pillar in central Arizona. The nest site (arrow) is a broad over-hung ledge about 40 m from the column top. 18. A recently-fledged Peregrine at an eyrie in southern Arizona.

Plate 17   D. Ellis

18. A recently-fledged Peregrine at an eyrie in southern Arizona.

Plate 18   D. Ellis

Plate 19   W. Tarboton

19. Adult female Peregrine defending its nest and eggs in an old Black Stork nest in the Transvaal, South Africa. This photo illustrates the large nest cavity and the woodland vegetation below, two common features of Peregrine eyries in Africa.

Plate 20   C. Himmelwright, 1987

20. Adult female Peregrine with two fostered young in 1987 at a coastal cliff in central California. This site was reoccupied after more than 30 years of vacancy.

21. Four eggs in a scrape on the same cliff as photographed by W. M. Pierce on 17 April 1926. In 1896, one of the first sets of Peregrine eggs collected in California came from this site.

Plate 21   W. M. Pierce, 1926

Plate 22   P. McCormick

22. This adult female Peregrine was banded as a nestling in 1981 on the Tanana River, Alaska. In 1985, she was trapped as a breeding adult on the same river some 100 miles from her natal cliff. 23. Adult Peregrine feeding young in South Australia.

Plate 23   J. Jolly

Plate 24   D. Clement

24. Female Peregrine feeding young in Greenland.

Plate 25   C. Anderson

25. Four nestlings banded in Greenland. The male in the foreground was sighted at sea in October of the same year perched on a Russian ship. Seven years later, he was trapped as a breeding adult in Greenland.

26–27. Adult female Peregrines on eggs in Rankin Inlet, Hudson Bay, Canada.

Plate 28   C. Anderson

28. A recently-fledged *F. p cassini* (pallid form) in Santa Cruz Province, Argentina.
29. Nesting cliff of *F. p. cassini* on a volcanic crater rim, Magallanes District, Chile.

Plate 29   C. Anderson

Plate 30   S. Saari

30. Female Peregrine feeding young at a ground-nesting bog site in northern Finland.
31. Adult Peregrine with nestlings in Czechoslovakia.

Plate 31   S. Danko, 1969

Plate 32   P. Lindberg

32. Nestling Peregrines fostered into an eyrie in Sweden where dummy eggs were temporarily incubated. 33. A juvenile female Peregrine in Finland.

Plate 33   P. Lindberg

Plate 35

M. Silvernale, 20 May 1939

34-36. The "Chatsworth" Peregrine nesting cliff (34) near Los Angeles, California, with four young (35) and a defending adult female (36). The nest ledge can be seen running across the middle of the cliff. The site has been vacant for over 30 years.

Plate 36 M. Silvernale, 20 May 1939

Plate 34   M. Silvernale, 20 May 1939

Plate 37   K. Falk

37-39. Peregrine nesting habitat in Greenland (37). Adult female (38) and male (39) Peregrines near their eyrie in Greenland.

Plate 38   K. Falk   Plate 39   K. Falk

Plate 40   J. Weaver, 1968

40. Four nestling Peregrines at a site overlooking the Colville River, Alaska. 41. Four nestlings in a similar nesting situation on Kent Peninsula, Northwest Territories, Canada.

Plate 41   R. Fyfe, 1969

42. Wild female Peregrine with fostered young and three dummy eggs about to be removed. 43. Reintroduced Peregrine nesting in Colorado.

Plate 44

T. Smylie

44. A migrant juvenile female Peregrine trapped, banded, and released on the Dry Tortugas, Florida.

45. A wintering adult female Peregrine on the Skagit Flats, Washington.

Plate 45   C. Anderson

46. Migrant Peregrine resting on a coastal dune on South Padre Island, Texas.

Plate 46   J. Glassburn

Plate 47 J. Enderson

47. "Lil," trained and flown in falconry by James H. Enderson, was the first *F. p. anatum* to lay eggs and raise young in captivity. She lived for 19 years and laid 97 eggs during her lifetime. 48. "Scarlett," a released Peregrine who lived for seven years in downtown Baltimore, Maryland, atop the United States Fidelity and Guaranty Building. She raised 18 fostered young Peregrines before hatching her own brood of four in April 1984, the year she died.

Plate 48 G. Fine

49. A pair of *F. p. peregrinus* at a captive breeding facility in Denmark.

P. Lindberg

Plate 49

Plate 50   The Peregrine Fund, Inc.

50. A baby Peregrine emerges from its eggshell in the laboratory of the "Hawk Barn," Cornell University. 51. A similar scene at the Wainwright breeding facility, Alberta, Canada.

Plate 51   R. Fyfe

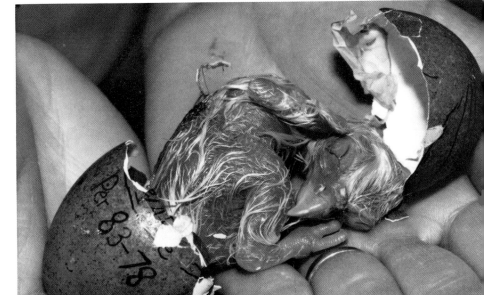

52. A human-imprinted female Gyrfalcon feeding fostered young Prairie Falcons in the laboratory. 53. Hand-feeding young Peregrines at Cornell University. Young are usually hand-reared for 1–2 weeks before being given to parent falcons.

54–56. Brian Walton (54) on the Union Bank Building replacing thin-shelled wild eggs with dummy eggs. Later, young hatched in the laboratory will be placed in the nest. A banded adult (55) near the artificial nest ledge. The Union Bank Building (56) in downtown Los Angeles, California. The artificial nest ledge is situated in the shadow behind the sign on its far left end.

57–58. Young Peregrines (57) just after their release from an urban hack site atop the 688-ft. Multifoods Tower (58) in Minneapolis, Minnesota.

Plate 59   G. Stewart   Plate 60   B. Walton

59. Climbers place young Peregrines in a hack box in Grand Teton National Park, Wyoming. The pipe structure facilitates food delivery to the box from an easily accessible location. 60. A coastal hack site at Muir Beach just north of San Francisco, California. 61. Swedish biologists prepare a hack box.

Plate 61   P. Lindberg

Plate 62   F. Reilmann / C. Saar / Deutscher Falkenórden

Plate 63   F. Reilmann / C. Saar / Deutscher Falkenorden

62. In 1978 and 1982, Peregrines nested in the abandoned living room of this lighthouse on the North Sea. 63. The female Peregrine is visible perched in the window (bottom). Thirty-five pairs of cormorants nested on the roof and balcony.

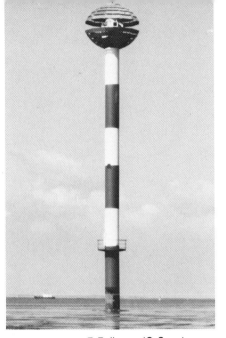

64–66. Peregrines nesting in a lighthouse (64) near Bremerhaven, West Germany. The adults (65) perched near their nest box. The adult female (66) entering the nest box containing two nearly-fledged young.

Plate 67   P. McLain

67-68. An adult female Peregrine (67), banded as a fostered nestling several years earlier, guards her nesting site on a tower in a New Jersey salt marsh (68).

Plate 68   T. Cade

47 New Evidence of a Peregrine Migration on the West Coast of North America

Clifford M. Anderson, David G. Roseneau, Brian J. Walton, and Peter J. Bente

The major migratory routes of the Peregrine Falcon studied thus far in North America occur along the Gulf of Mexico coast in Texas (Enderson 1965), the Atlantic coast (Ward and Berry 1972), the Great Lakes region (Mueller and Berger 1961), and the Canadian prairies of Alberta (Dekker 1979). Peregrine migration on the Pacific coast had been considered nonexistent (Hunt et al. 1975). However, new evidence from band returns and sightings of Peregrines has confirmed that migration does indeed occur along the west coast of North America in both spring and autumn, although the extent of this movement remains largely unknown. Only one report of the Pacific coast Peregrine migration has been published (Herman and Bulger 1981). We present additional information here.

METHODS

We reviewed literature on migrant Peregrines and examined all North American Peregrine band returns on file with the Bird Banding Laboratory, U. S. Fish and Wildlife Service (USFWS), up to and including those from 1984. All west coast recoveries from British Columbia south through Mexico of Peregrines banded in Alaska, Northwest Territories, British Columbia, Washington, Oregon and California were included (Figure 1). We eliminated records of captive-released Peregrines and most reports of short-distance intra-province and intra-state recoveries. We have also included what we judge to be reliable sightings reported by ornithologists, biologists and birders, plus information from the literature.

In 1984-86, C. Anderson studied migrant Peregrines at two locations on the Washington coast. We captured Peregrines with a lurepole and bownet from a stationary blind at Cape Flattery (Clallam County) or

507

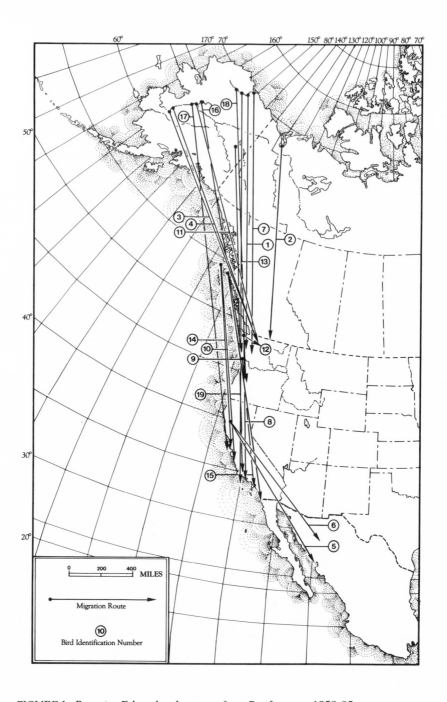

FIGURE 1. Peregrine Falcon band returns from Pacific coast, 1958-85.

with harnessed pigeons released from a vehicle at Long Beach (Pacific County). All captured falcons were weighed (g), measured (wing chord and tail in mm), and banded. We collected samples of feathers (Parrish et al. 1983) and blood (Morizot Chapter 74) from several birds. We determined subspecies of Peregrines by measurements, plumage coloration, and breeding ranges as reported by White (1968b).

RESULTS AND DISCUSSION

Band Returns. — Nineteen Peregrine band returns have been reported from the Pacific coast region of North America (see Supplement). Their geographic distribution is summarized in Table 1. Returns include 16 (84%) birds banded as nestlings and three (16%) banded as autumn migrants. Fifteen (79%) were recovered as immatures (6 females, 8 males, 1 not sexed) and four (21%) as adults (2 females, 2 males). Six were recovered on the west coast during autumn migration (September-October), two in spring (April) and eight in winter (November-March); the remaining three records involved decomposed birds whose specific dates of return are unknown. Among the eight wintering birds, two were reported from southern British Columbia, four from California, and two from northwestern Mexico. These records indicate that all three North American races of Peregrine occur along the Pacific coast as far south as California.

Autumn Sightings. — Further evidence of the west coast Peregrine migration comes from small clusters of sightings reported throughout the Pacific flyway. Roseneau (cf. White 1969a) provided the first report of an autumn passage of Peregrines in the eastern Gulf of Alaska. More recently, Mickelson et al. (unpubl. report) reported 29, 41, and 17 sightings of autumn Peregrines, respectively, in August-October 1978, 1979 and 1980 during studies on the eastern Copper River Delta, Alaska. This area is a major fall staging area for waterfowl

TABLE 1. Geographic distribution of 19 Peregrine Falcon band returns from the west coast of North America.

Where banded	Where recovered	n
Alaska	British Columbia	2
Alaska	Washington	4
Alaska	Oregon	1
Alaska	California	3
Northwest Territories	British Columbia	1
British Columbia	California	3
Washington	Washington	1
Washington	California	2
California	Mexico	2

and shorebirds. Later studies by Swem (unpubl. report) at Sitkagi Beach, Alaska, produced four sightings of migrant Peregrines from 2 September-26 September.

Further south on the Washington coast, migrant *F. p. pealei* have been observed on 27 August at Westport, far south of their known breeding range (D. Paulson pers. comm.). Warburton (1925) collected Peregrines there on 28 August and 7 September. During three studies of the fall migration along the same coast, we observed Peregrines 91 times, including 20 sightings at Cape Flattery in 1984 (21 September-29 October), 38 at Long Beach in 1985 (19 September-15 October) and 33 at Long Beach in 1986 (30 September-15 October). In the Puget Sound basin, small numbers of migrant Peregrines have been seen at San Juan Island (S. Layman pers. comm.) and the Skagit Flats (J. Fackler pers. comm.).

In California, autumn migrant Peregrines were observed at Pt. Diablo, north of San Francisco (Binford 1979). C. Faust (pers. comm.) reported 4 sightings in 1982, 4 in 1983, 18 in 1984, and 13 in 1985. Peregrines have been observed 33 km offshore, in the Farallon Islands, every autumn since the mid-1970s. On four autumn-winter visits to the Farallons from 1977-85, all 11 Peregrines observed by Walton were identified as the larger, darker *F. p. pealei*. In 1982, T. McElroy (pers. comm.) estimated that at least seven Peregrines passed the islands in October.

The Santa Cruz Predatory Bird Research Group has compiled sight records for California since 1975. Of 406 sightings recorded during that period (obvious resident breeders not included), 80 (20%) were during the first week in October when migrants would be predicted to pass through California from more northerly latitudes.

Spring Sightings. — In 1976, Anderson and Fackler (unpubl. ms.) noted a spring movement of Peregrines along the Washington coast; five (2 adults, 3 immatures) were seen at Cape Flattery during 22 March-26 March. Since no active nests existed in the vicinity, it seems likely that these birds were migrants. Nine sightings by R. Paine (pers. comm.) at Tatoosh Island (0.8 km offshore) during the 1980s also indicate that Peregrines passed the Cape Flattery area in March and April. In 1983, Anderson and Fackler observed Peregrines at Cape Flattery on 18 occasions (4 adults, 2 immatures, 12 not aged) from 8 April-5 May. They also discovered that several thousand other raptors were migrating north past Cape Flattery (C. Anderson and J. Fackler unpubl. ms.). During additional studies of this migration in 1985, they saw Peregrines on 23 occasions (3 adults, 10 immatures, 10 not aged) from 5 April-14 May. In the spring of 1986, they observed migrant Peregrines on 48 occasions at Cape Flattery during April-May.

Several were observed flying north until they were well beyond the range of 10X binoculars.

Field studies conducted further south on the Washington coast produced similar results. Herman and Bulger (1981) reported 16 Peregrines (8 adults, 7 immatures, 1 not aged) from 10 April-7 May 1981 at Grays Harbor, an area far from potential Peregrine nesting sites. These sightings were associated with one of the largest spring shorebird migrations in North America. More than one million shorebirds annually stage at Grays Harbor during the last week of April (Herman and Bulger 1981) en route to Alaska. Twenty miles south, at Willapa Bay, P. Meehan-Martin (pers. comm.) reported an additional 27 sightings of Peregrines (11 adults, 6 immatures, 10 not aged) from 3 April-7 May 1983. These observations were also made in a shorebird staging area. Herman and Bulger (1981) and Meehan-Martin (pers. comm.) observed the Peregrines preying exclusively on the spring migrant shorebirds. Gabrielson and Jewett (1940) reported that their latest record of a spring migrant Peregrine in Oregon was 3 May 1931.

Such Peregrines were presumably on their way to northern breeding sites, for they have also been seen in the spring on the coast of Alaska. Swem (unpubl. report) reported 11 Peregrines at Sitkagi Beach near the Malaspina Glacier from 21 April-9 May 1982. Mickelson et al. (unpubl. report) listed four sightings on the Copper River Delta, Alaska for April-May 1979. Roseneau and others also noted a spring passage of Peregrines (about 1 per observer per day) occurring annually through Portage Pass between northwestern Prince William Sound and Turnagin Arm in Cook Inlet in the late 1950s and 1960s (D. Roseneau unpubl. ms.).

Capture Results. — We captured and banded 22 migrant Peregrines on the coast of Washington during 1984-86 (19 in autumn, 3 in spring). Nineteen (86%) were in immature plumage, and three (14%) in adult plumage. Fourteen (64%) were males, and eight (36%) were females. The races of six (including the 3 adults) could not be determined, but we judged the other 16 to be *F. p. pealei*.

DISCUSSION

The autumn Peregrine migration generally begins along the west coast of North America by mid-August (Beebe 1960) and is well under way by mid-September. Warburton (1925) collected migrant Peregrines on the Washington coast in August and September. Kitchin (1930) observed several migrants in the same area between 15 September-19 September. In Oregon, Gabrielson and Jewett (1940) reported that migrant Peregrines begin to appear on the ocean beaches in late August. Their earliest specimen was collected there on 31 August 1923. All 19 autumn migrants we banded in Washington were captured between 19 September-12 October. Dates of the five autumn recoveries of Peregrines from Alaska ranged from 23 September-22 October (see Supplement). Dates from a series of 24 specimens collected along the Washington coast from 1916-63 (C. Anderson unpubl. data) ranged from 25 September-8 November. These data suggest that optimal dates for Peregrine migration along the Washington coast are 1 October-10 October. These dates are rather similar to those reported for Assateague Island, Maryland/Virginia (Ward and Berry 1972) and Padre Island, Texas (Hunt et al. 1975). In California, C. Faust (pers. comm.) reported that a peak in the 1984 Peregrine migration appeared to occur at Pt. Diablo during the last week of October and first week of November (56% of 18 sightings), several days later than the projected peak in Washington.

Based on a small sample of band returns, there appear to be two general autumn migration routes for Peregrines in western Washington, one along the outer coast and one further inland through the Puget Sound basin. The two routes are separated geographically by the Olympic Mountains. Most coastal migrants that we captured or observed appeared to be F. p. pealei. As already mentioned, 16 (73%) of 22 banded in spring and fall were F. p. pealei. Previous information (Swarth 1933) established that this race winters as far south as California. Bent (1938) reported the southernmost limit in North America as Colorado Landing, Baja California. Presumably the autumn F. p. pealei migrants are restricted in passage to coastal Washington, Oregon and California, since this race has seldom been observed away from salt-water environments (White 1972). F. p. pealei apparently wanders well out into the Pacific Ocean (Beebe 1960), and at least one specimen has been taken as far west as the far northwestern part of the Hawaiian Islands (Woodward 1972, C. Anderson unpubl. ms.).

Until 1984, the natal origins of F. p. pealei wintering in California were unknown. The three F. p. pealei recovered in California were banded as nestlings along the northern coast of British Columbia (see Supplement). All three nestlings originated from eyries located within 320 km of each other (lat. 52°-55°N). No F. p. pealei banded as nestlings in Alaska have been recovered as yet on the Pacific coast south of Alaska.

Since adults reportedly remain in the vicinity of their eyries throughout the winter (White 1971, Nelson and Myres 1976), the majority of fall migrant F. p. pealei are presumably immatures. In the fall of 1985, however, we captured two adult female Peregrines that appeared to be F. p. pealei at the Long Beach Peninsula in Washington, some 160 km south of their historical breeding range (Dawson and Bowles 1909), suggesting that more adults may be migrating south than previously suspected.

At present, little is known about the movements of *F. p. tundrius* and northern *F. p. anatum* along the west coast region of North America. Hunt (1966) stated that *F. p. tundrius* was not known to occur along the west coast, and Beebe (1974) stated that *F. p. tundrius* was unrecorded in British Columbia. Prior to these reports, only one banded Colville River Peregrine had been recovered on the west coast of Washington, in 1959 (Enderson 1965). More recently, however, three more Colville birds have been found in Washington and California (see Supplement).

More Alaskan *F. p. tundrius* and *F. p. anatum* certainly occur along the Pacific coast than has been previously suspected. R. Ambrose (pers. comm.) reports that of 1898 Peregrines banded in Alaska since 1952, 37 (1.9%) have been recovered from an area south of Alaska and north of Mexico. Ten (27%) of the 37 were recovered from the west coast region.

There is some evidence to suggest that far northern Peregrines may prefer a more inland (rather than coastal) route through western Washington. Four (67%) of six Alaska-banded Peregrines recovered in British Columbia and Washington were found in the Puget Sound basin (see Supplement), 160 km inland from the Pacific coastline. The migratory routes of these birds beyond Washington are not known. They may continue south along the Pacific shoreline or migrate across the western United States towards Texas. Further study is necessary to clarify these movements.

ACKNOWLEDGEMENTS

We thank F. P. Ward, W. Seegar, and W. Mattox for their encouragement and support of this study. Fieldwork was funded by the U. S. Army Chemical Research and Development Center, Aberdeen Proving Ground, Maryland, The Raptor Education Foundation, and R. and B. Robbins. Banding data were provided by the USFWS Bird Banding Laboratory, the Canadian Wildlife Service, F. P. Ward, and W. G. Hunt. We are also indebted to all of the field biologists who originally banded the birds. Information on Peregrines in British Columbia was supplied by R. Nelson, U. Banasch, W. Munro, D. Wilson, C. Trefry and D. Maynes; in Alaska by R. Ambrose (USFWS); in Washington by S. Herman, J. Bulger, P. Meehan-Martin, E. Cummins, R. Lowell and J. Fackler; and in California by C. Thelander, G. Monk, T. Balgooyen, C. Faust, T. McElroy and A. Fish. J. Fackler and R. Lowell also provided able field assistance during our Washington fieldwork. D. Heiser of the Washington State Parks and Recreation Commission arranged the use of a vehicle during the Long Beach study. J. Blum and the Makah Indian tribe graciously allowed us to conduct our studies on the Makah Reservation. D. Byrne and B. Hockett provided both hospitality and housing at Neah Bay. Most significantly, we have benefited from conversations with other Peregrine researchers over the years, particularly S. Herman, W. G. Hunt, C. Thelander and C. M. White; they have always generously shared with us their hard-won insights on the Peregrine. S. Herman also made many useful suggestions on this manuscript.

SUPPLEMENT

Peregrine Falcon band returns from the Pacific coast of North America, arranged chronologically by dates of return:

(1) A female *F. p. tundrius* (#527-99606) banded as a nestling by T. Cade on 1 August 1959 on the Colville River, Alaska was recovered 11 weeks later on 15 October 1959, near Humptulips, Washington. F. Gossler (pers. comm.) reported that the female captured a Snow Goose and was then killed by a logger. This is the first Alaska-banded Peregrine to be recovered along the west coast of North America, as well as the first record for *F. p. tundrius* in Washington.

(2) A male (#686-01716) banded as a nestling by J. Windsor on 31 July 1974 near Inuvik, Mackenzie District, Northwest Territories was found "well-rotten" on 7 March 1975, 3 km north of Winfield, Okanagan Valley, British Columbia. Although it was recovered on the east side of the Cascade Mountains, the area is still considered to lie within the Pacific flyway.

(3) A male (#987-47120) banded as a nestling by D. Roseneau and P. Bente on 11 July 1980, near Nulato, lower Yukon River, Alaska was found near Burlington, Washington on 23 September 1980, 10 weeks after banding. It had apparently been stunned by a vehicle.

(4) A female in adult plumage (#987-47140) banded as a nestling by D. Roseneau and P. Bente on 16 July 1980 near Grayling, lower Yukon River, Alaska was found shot but alive near Delta, British Columbia on 9 December 1981 (C. Trefry pers. comm.), 17 months after banding. This is the first record of an Alaskan Peregrine in British Columbia and is one of the few examples of a northern migrant wintering in Canada.

(5) A male (#816-49522) banded as a nestling by G. Monk on 4 June 1981 near Leggett, California was recovered in December 1981 within 100 km of its sibling, in Sonora, Mexico. This is the first record of a California-banded Peregrine recovered in Mexico.

(6) A female (#987-55937) banded as a nestling by G. Monk on 4 June 1981 near Leggett (same site as for previous bird) was recovered on 17 January 1982 near Etchojoa, Sonora, Mexico, 1900 km south of its eyrie. This bird and the previous one represent the only California-banded Peregrines to be recovered out of state so far.

(7) A male (#987-30584) banded as a nestling by T. Swem on 28 July 1982 on the lower Colville River, Alaska was found, unable to fly, near Rochester, Washington on 22 October 1982 (E. Cummins pers. comm.), 12 weeks after banding.

(8) An immature female (#987-38116) banded by C. Anderson as a fall migrant on 3 October 1984 near Cape Flattery, Washington was found electrocuted on 11 October 1984, at Pt. Mugu, California (M. Klope pers. comm.). This bird had traveled approximately 1760 km south in eight days, a minimum average of 216 km per day.

(9) A female *F. p. pealei* (#877-01654) banded as a nestling by R. Marshal on 13 June 1984 near Aristazabal Island, British Columbia, was found seven months later stunned on a hotel balcony in San Diego, California on 17 January 1985, approximately 2700 coastal km south of its nesting site. It was banded at a tree-nesting site in the area described by Campbell et al. (1977) and is the first banded *F. p. pealei* to be recovered south of Canada.

(10) A female *F. p. pealei* (#877-64129) banded as a nestling by R. W. Nelson on 8 June 1984 at Langara Island, British Columbia was found dead at Elkhorn Slough, south of Santa Cruz, California on 12 February 1985 (eight months after banding), 2200 coastal km south of its nesting site.

(11) A female in adult plumage (#987-62357) banded as a nestling by P. Bente on 19 July 1983 near Anvik, lower Yukon River, Alaska was found shot 21 months later near Surrey, British Columbia on 16 March 1985 (D. Maynes pers. comm.). The date falls within the known wintering period in that region (Anderson et al. 1980); along with the fourth recovery listed here, it suggests that an unknown number of lower Yukon River Peregrines may be wintering in the Puget Sound basin.

(12) An immature male *F. p. pealei* (#816-36716) banded as a fall migrant by C. Anderson on 5 October 1984 near Cape Flattery, Washington was found seven months later, unable to fly, on 25 April 1985 in Seattle, Washington, 192 km east of the point of banding. Although immature *F. p. pealei* regularly winter in the inland region of western Washington (Beebe 1960), this is the first record of an autumn migrant *F. p. pealei* moving eastward into the Puget Sound basin.

(13) A male in adult plumage (#987-47260) banded as a nestling by T. Swem and R. Dittrick on 23 July 1981 on the Colville River, Alaska was found dead in April 1985 by Don Guthrie at San Miguel Island, California. The bird was presumed to have died sometime in February-March 1985 because the carcass was not observed on an earlier February visit by Guthrie. This represents the first northern migrant adult male Peregrine to be recovered on the west coast, and

the first Alaskan *F. p. tundrius* to be recovered in California. It is currently at the Bean Museum, Brigham Young University.

(14) A male (#877-64130) banded as a nestling by R. W. Nelson on 9 June 1984 at Langara Island, British Columbia was found dead in September 1985, at Richardson Bay near Point Reyes, California, about 2200 coastal km south of its nesting site. The bird was still in immature plumage and was identified from a single green-colored band marked "O.A.P."

(15) An immature male (#816-36706) banded as a fall migrant by C. Anderson on 19 September 1985 at Long Beach, Washington was recovered with a wing injury near La Jolla, California by D. Brimm on 22 February 1986.

(16) A male nestling (#816-46643) banded by P. Bente on 14 July 1986 on the lower Yukon River, Alaska was found dead by S. Wirth on 2 October 1986 near West Twin River, Clallam County, Washington.

(17) T. Balgooyen (pers. comm.) reports that an immature female (#987-70897) banded as a nestling by P. Bente on 16 July 1986 near Anvik, lower Yukon River, Alaska was recovered on 20 November 1986 at San Jose International Airport, San Jose, California. It was struck and killed by a DC-10 aircraft while stooping at a Gyrfalcon.

(18) A Peregrine (#987-70583) banded as a nestling by J. Silva on 26 July 1986 on the Colville River, Alaska was recovered on 21 October 1986 by J. Rosecrans in the Willamette River Valley near Monmouth, Oregon. This is the first record of a banded Peregrine being recovered in Oregon.

(19) An adult male (#987-62460) banded as a nestling by T. Swem on 15 July 1984 on the Charley River (a tributary of the upper Yukon River) in Alaska was found injured in Long Beach, California on 1 April 1987.

48 The Influence of Local Weather on Autumn Migration of Peregrine Falcons at Assateague Island

Kimberly Titus, F. Prescott Ward,
William S. Seegar, Michael A. Yates, and
Mark R. Fuller

Observations of diurnal hawk migration have been well documented in many regions of the world (Richardson 1978, Newton and Chancellor 1985). Many studies of the relationship between counts of migrating hawks and weather have been conducted where migrants become concentrated in the northern hemisphere, including those of Mueller and Berger (1967b) for Sharp-shinned Hawks, Haugh (1972) for a variety of species, Alerstam (1978) for the Common Buzzard, Western Honey Buzzard, and European Sparrowhawk, and Titus and Mosher (1982) for other species. Consequently, we have some understanding of effects of local weather on visible migration of common holarctic raptors. This is not the case for migrant Peregrine Falcons, although they have been counted annually at many locations (Allen and Peterson 1936, Broun 1939, Mueller and Berger 1961, Hofslund 1966, Edelstam 1972, Evans and Lathbury 1973, Dekker 1984). The numbers counted have usually been too few for comparison with weather data; however, at Assateague Island, Maryland/Virginia, Peregrines have been counted in sufficient numbers to allow analyses of the effects of weather on counts.

We studied long-distance migrants from natal areas hundreds of kilometers to the north in the arctic regions of central Canada and Greenland (Yates et al. Chapter 44). Local weather en route probably causes only short-term responses by the migrants but identification of such influences may improve the comparison of counts among sites or years. By understanding and correcting for the influences of local weather on autumn counts, we also gain insight into the utility of these counts as indicators of population levels (Svensson 1978, Hussell 1981).

METHODS

We studied the autumn migration of Peregrines from 1970-84 at Assateague Island, Maryland/Virginia, a barrier island oriented north-northeast to south-southwest. Observation methods following those of Ward and Berry (1972) began as early as 17 September and continued daily as late as 25 October, but the only data used were from 21 September-18 October, when 90% of the migration occurs (cf. Alerstam 1978). Resident Peregrines, resightings and recaptures were eliminated from analyses (Ward et al. Chapter 45). Local weather data and migration counts for 1970-81 were used in analyses. Hourly wind direction, wind speed and cloud cover, and daily rain and temperatures were collected from a weather station on Assateague Island (Table 1). Barometric pressure data were taken from daily weather maps for Salisbury, Maryland.

Daily counts were pooled into three migration intensity categories as follows: (1) 0-1 bird observed per day, (2) 2-10 birds observed per day, and (3) 11 or more birds observed per day. As the numbers observed increased throughout the 12-year study (Ward et al. Chapter 45), we standardized the transformed daily count data to eliminate the year effect by calculating a "Z" score based on the number of birds observed within that year. Two migration intensity categories were created from the standardized counts for categorical analyses: (1) lower-than-average daily count ($Z<0$), and (2) equal-to- or greater-than-the-average daily count ($Z\geq0$). Two sets of analyses were conducted, the first with actual counts and the second with standardized counts. These and other approaches have been used in migration/weather studies (Mueller and Berger 1961, Alerstam 1978, Beason 1978, Richardson 1978, Titus and Mosher 1982).

Spearman rank correlations (Zar 1974) were conducted between the daily counts, transformed daily counts, and all weather variables (Table 1). The cosines of the 16 wind directions were derived according to a standardized scheme so that these variables could be evaluated on a linear scale. We termed these wind direction effect variables. Log-likelihood ratio Chi-square analyses (Zar 1974) were used to compare categorical weather variables with categories of migration intensity. The 16 wind directions were pooled into eight wind directions for log-likelihood ratio analyses. Correlation and log-likelihood ratio Chi-square analyses were also conducted with the daily counts of birds that were flying when first sighted, and also with those that were not flying (e.g., perched, actively hunting, eating). These two sets of analyses were conducted to determine whether local weather might have been associated with active migration (flying) versus any other nonmigratory behavior.

TABLE 1. Summary and definitions of local weather variables available for analysis.

Variable	Method of measurement
Wind direction	Obtained hourly as 16 directions or calm
DMORN	The rounded daily mean of hourly wind directions from 0600 – 1300
DAFTER	The rounded daily mean of hourly wind directions from 1300 – 1900
DDAY	The rounded daily mean of hourly wind directions from 0600 – 1900
DNIGHT	The rounded nighttime mean of hourly wind directions from 2000 – 0600
Wind direction effect	The cosine of the mean wind direction assuming a NNE to SSW migration path (the orientation of the island). This scales the data from –1.0 (opposing winds) to +1.0 (following winds)
DMORNEFF	Same time periods as for wind direction
DAFTEREFF	
DDAYEFF	
DNIGHTEFF	
Wind speed	Obtained hourly in miles per hour
SMORN	Same time periods as for wind direction rounded
SAFTER	to the nearest mile per hour
SDAY	
SNIGHT	
Cloud cover	Obtained hourly according to the following scale:
	0 = clear or less than 0.1 cloud cover
	1 = scattered clouds or 0.1 – 0.5 cloud cover
	2 = mostly or 0.6 – 0.9 cloud cover
	3 = overcast
	4 = fog
CMORN	Rounded to the nearest whole number;
CAFTER	same time periods as for wind direction
CDAY	
CNIGHT	
MAXT	Maximum temperature for the 24 h time period (00 hrs to 2400)
MINT	Minimum temperature for the 24 h time period (00 hrs to 2400)
T1700	Temperature at 1700
RAIN	Measured as inches of precipitation. In 1970-71 taken from daily weather maps, Salisbury, Md; 1972-81 taken from a rain gauge, Assateague State Park
BAR	Barometric pressure in millibars; taken from daily weather maps, Salisbury, Md, 0700 EST
BARHL	Barometric pressure at Salisbury, 0700 EST higher or lower than or the same as at 0400 EST
BARTEND	Barometric pressure tendency at Salisbury, 0700 EST; nine codes as described on standard NOAA weather maps

Stepwise discriminant function analysis (DFA, Hair et al. 1979) was conducted to determine: (1) whether levels of migration intensity could be predicted from some subset of local weather variables, and (2) which variables were most correlated with the data in deriving the canonical variates. Prior probabilities were based on group sample sizes. The test of homogeneity of covariance matrices was set at default ($P<0.10$).

RESULTS

Observations were made on 313 days over the 12-year period. On 62 of these days (19.8%) no Peregrine Falcons were observed. The maximum daily count was 65, and 30 or more Peregrines were observed on only 12 (3.8%) days.

Temperature, wind speed and wind direction effect variables were not correlated with counts of migrants (Table 2). Only two of 14 local weather variables considered in the correlation analyses were significant when all years were pooled. More Peregrine Falcons were observed when rain increased and barometric pressure decreased. The total number of migrants was positively correlated with the standardized number of migrants ($r_s=0.81$, $n=313$, $P<0.001$); the lack of perfect correlation can be attributed to the yearly variation and the increase in

TABLE 2. Spearman rank correlation coefficients among numbers of migrant Peregrine Falcons and local weather variables at Assateague Island, 1970-81.

Weather variables[a]	Total no. of migrants seen daily		Standardized total no. of migrants	
	r	Significance[b]	r	Significance[b]
MAXT	0.012	NS	0.043	NS
MINT	0.057	NS	0.054	NS
TI700	0.005	NS	0.043	NS
RAIN	0.167	**	0.125	*
BAR	−0.270	***	−0.187	***
BARTEND	0.022	NS	0.028	NS
SMORN	0.011	NS	−0.010	NS
SAFTER	0.042	NS	−0.013	NS
SDAY	0.026	NS	−0.015	NS
SNIGHT	−0.029	NS	0.068	NS
DMORNEFF	0.012	NS	−0.047	NS
DAFTEFF	0.006	NS	0.002	NS
DDAYEFF	0.008	NS	−0.016	NS
DNIGHTEFF	0.019	NS	−0.040	NS

[a] Weather variables as in Table 1.
[b] Levels of significance: NS = not significant; * = $P < 0.05$; ** = $P < 0.01$; *** = $P < 0.001$.

annual counts. Of 168 pairwise correlations within years, 13 were significant ($P<0.05$), which was not much more than chance error. In five of the 12 years, no weather variables were correlated with counts from that year. No correlations were significant in one direction one year and then significant in the opposite direction in another year.

Only three of 10 categorical weather variables were statistically related to the total counts of migrants (Table 3). Days with high migration counts occurred more frequently when barometric pressure was lower at 0700 hours than three hours earlier in the morning. Significantly more Peregrine Falcons were observed when cloud cover exceeded 60%. Conversely, fewer falcons were sighted when days were clear to partly cloudy. No significant results were found when the counts were partitioned into flying versus perching or hunting behaviors relative to weather.

Of 12 days when 30 or more migrants were observed, four days each occurred in 1979 and 1980 (Table 4). Local weather conditions were not the same on each date when peak flights occurred. Cloud cover on peak migration days was not different from that typically encountered throughout the study. Barometric pressure on six of these days was falling in the early morning, which was atypical. On 78% of 313 days with data, the barometric pressure was rising. Wind direction showed no apparent pattern with peak flight days. Both following (northeast) and opposing (south and southwest) winds were associated with large counts.

TABLE 3. Log-likelihood ratio Chi-squares among numbers of migrant Peregrine Falcons and local weather variables at Assateague Island, 1970-81.

Weather variables[a]	Total no. seen daily (3 categories)			Standardized total no. of migrants (2 categories)		
	χ^2	Degrees of freedom	Significance[b]	χ^2	Degrees of freedom	Significance[b]
BARHL	13.2	4	*	5.7	2	NS
BARTREND	19.6	16	NS	14.5	8	NS
DMORN	9.9	14	NS	7.3	7	NS
DAFTER	10.1	14	NS	1.6	7	NS
DDAY	5.5	14	NS	5.5	7	NS
DNIGHT	13.5	14	NS	13.0	7	NS
CMORN	15.0	6	*	4.6	3	NS
CAFTER	7.1	6	NS	2.6	3	NS
CDAY	13.7	6	*	3.3	3	NS
CNIGHT	4.7	6	NS	4.6	3	NS

[a] Weather variables as in Table 1.
[b] Levels of significance: NS = not significant; * = $0.01 < P < 0.05$.

TABLE 4. Dates and weather when 30 or more Peregrine Falcons were observed at Assateague Island, 1970-81.

Year	Date	No. observed	Rain (inches)	Mean daily wind speed (mph)	Mean daily cloud cover	Barometric pressure trend	Average daily wind direction
1971	6 Oct.	34	0.19	7	partly cloudy	missing	W
1978	5 Oct.	31	0.00	8	mostly cloudy	rising	E
1978	6 Oct.	34	0.01	5	partly cloudy	falling	SW
1979	3 Oct.	48	0.90	15	mostly cloudy	rising	W
1979	4 Oct.	32	0.00	8	clear	rising	S
1979	7 Oct.	37	0.00	13	cloudy	falling	W
1979	9 Oct.	58	0.15	12	mostly cloudy	falling	SW
1980	30 Sept.	41	0.00	16	mostly cloudy	falling	NE
1980	1 Oct.	65	0.08	11	cloudy	rising	NE
1980	10 Oct.	30	0.00	13	partly cloudy	missing	E
1980	11 Oct.	42	0.00	12	partly cloudy	falling	SW
1981	1 Oct.	36	0.00	12	partly cloudy	falling	S
Mean for all days (n = 313)		6.7	0.10	8	partly to mostly cloudy	rising	S and SW

Eighteen variables were inserted into the stepwise DFA, and five variables were selected by the procedure (Table 5). The covariance matrices were not homogeneous ($P=0.045$), so the procedure used a quadratic DFA. The derived canonical variates were significant, but the canonical correlation values were low. That barometric pressure had the highest correlation with the canonical variates supports the conclusion from univariate testing that high counts of migrants were most associated with low barometric pressure. The other variables were correlated with the canonical variates to lesser degrees. Classification rates were poor (Table 6). Both the low-count and high-count days were more often misclassified as medium-count days. A similar stepwise DFA was conducted with the "Z" score standardized counts that were grouped into low and high categories. The stepwise procedure selected only one variable (barometric pressure), and the results were not significant ($P>0.05$).

DISCUSSION

Significant associations between local weather and counts of Peregrine Falcons at Assateague Island were few. Unfortunately, other detailed studies of the association between weather and counts are lacking for this species. The only weather variable that we found to be consistently associated inversely with the daily counts was barometric pressure. Most notably, counts did not relate to wind direction and

TABLE 5. Results of a quadratic discriminant function analysis attempting to separate low, medium and high Peregrine Falcon migration counts based on local weather variables.

	Discriminant function	
Statistic or variable	I	II
Statistic		
Canonical correlation	0.35	0.23
F-statistic	5.39, P < 0.001	3.86, P < 0.01
Variable[a]		
Barometric pressure	0.89	0.11
Temperature at 1700 hrs.	−0.15	0.64
Afternoon cloud cover	−0.39	0.37
Barometric pressure tendency	−0.32	0.43
Previous night wind speed	0.13	0.09

[a] Within class correlations between the canonical variates and the original variables.

TABLE 6. Classification of low, medium, and high Peregrine Falcon migration count dates from the discriminant analysis of Table 5.

	Predicted group		
Actual Group	Low	Medium	High
Low	27	55	2
Medium	15	122	9
High	13	26	16

Overall percent correctly classified = 57.9%
Percent correctly classified above chance = 22.6%

wind speed. Our results for 12 years do not support the empirical observations of Ward and Berry (1972) over two autumns, that light west winds might be associated with higher counts.

Numerous other raptor migration studies have found wind speed and wind direction to be strongly associated with counts of visible migrants (Ferguson and Ferguson 1922, Allen and Peterson 1936, Rudebeck 1950, Mueller and Berger 1961, 1967b, Haugh 1972, Alerstam 1978, Titus and Mosher 1982). Along the east coast of North America, northwest winds were shown to be strongly associated with peak hawk flights (Trowbridge 1895, Ferguson and Ferguson 1922, Allen and Peterson 1936, Stone 1937). Like Peregrine Falcon migration, Northern Harrier migration was not related to wind direction at Hawk Mountain, Pennsylvania (Haugh 1972), or along the Atlantic coast (Ferguson and Ferguson 1922). Dekker (1979) observed Peregrines migrating under a variety of weather conditions including strong headwinds. Based on a limited number of observations, Slack and Slack (1981) felt that Peregrines may alter their direction of migration depending on local weather.

Despite a lack of strong association between counts and local weather at Assateague Island, Peregrine Falcons did respond differently to small-scale local conditions on the island. Blowing sand on the beaches was a noticeable local effect of wind. Dry sand was blown on the beach at about 35 km per hour, and Peregrines seemed to avoid standing in such areas. This very localized condition only occurred along the beach front, often beginning around mid-morning. In fair weather, wind speed varied greatly on the island. By mid-morning a strong sea breeze was often blowing on the beach while only a light wind was blowing inland, behind the line of sand dunes paralleling the beach. Wind speed at various locations on the beaches was not measured.

We expected a relationship between weather and flying (migrating) versus perching or hunting (nonmigrating) behaviors, but no relationship was found. Peregrine Falcons may not alter their migrating versus nonmigrating behavior because of local weather at Assateague Island, or perhaps we could not detect the differences.

Although the Peregrine Falcons we observed were long-distance migrants, they were seldom observed using soaring flight as other hawks often do in migration. It thus seems logical that local weather would not be as important to Peregrine Falcons as to soaring hawks that depend on thermals. Note, however, that Peregrine Falcons have been detected using soaring and gliding flight in radio-telemetry studies of migration (Cochran 1985). Also, unlike other raptors that are reluctant to migrate over the ocean or will only make water crossings under optimal local weather (Kerlinger 1985), Peregrine Falcons can migrate far out to sea (Cochran 1985).

The weak but significant relationships of our counts with barometric pressure, rain and cloud cover indicates that continental-scale weather may influence Peregrine Falcon migration more than localized conditions. Not all Peregrine Falcons migrate quickly by Assateague Island. Many individuals spend a few days using the island for resting and hunting (Ward et al. Chapter 45), and some Peregrines have been found lingering between bouts of migratory flight. We need to explore the relationships between weather and the large numbers of resightings and retrappings of individuals within a season.

Our counts of Peregrine Falcons may be largely made up of birds exhibiting nonmigratory behavior after they have made landfall at the end of a "dogleg" flight down the Atlantic coast. If many of our counts were of nonmigratory birds, then the lack of association with local weather might be like that of some shorebirds, where radar studies indicate one pattern for migrating birds, but visual counts often associate higher numbers with inclement weather (Richardson 1979).

Examination of daily weather maps provides clues to the possible relationship between peak counts and the location of major weather systems. For example, high counts occurred on consecutive days during 1979 and 1980 (Table 4). On 2 October 1979 (one day prior to a high count day), low pressure systems were in central Canada, over Nova Scotia and over the Ohio Valley, with rain off the New England coast and in the Ohio Valley. On 29 September 1980, a large, low pressure storm was over James Bay, one was over Newfoundland, and another was just off the coast of South Carolina. Rain was present for the next few days as the result of two storm systems, one across eastern Canada, and another in the southeastern United States far out into the Atlantic Ocean. It is possible that inclement weather to the north, south and ocean sides of Assateague Island induces less migratory flight, producing high counts for a few days. These weather systems may not influence local weather at Assateague Island on dates with high counts, hence a lack of correlations between counts and local weather variables.

The passage of cold fronts may also be associated with high count dates, as occurred on 4-5 October 1978, 29 September 1980, and 9-10 October 1980. However, not all cold fronts produced higher counts.

A statistical approach is needed to determine whether broad weather systems are associated with visible counts of Peregrine Falcons. Because weather can influence the detectability of migrants (Evans 1966, Evans and Lathbury 1973, Kerlinger et al. 1985), the development of "correction factors" is needed to understand Peregrine Falcon migratory behavior and to use counts for detecting population trends.

ACKNOWLEDGEMENTS

Field work during the first seven years of this study was conducted by R. B. Berry along with L. C. Woyce, Jr., in 1975 and 1976. We appreciate the help of the numerous assistants: J. N. Rice, A. G. Nye, Jr., B. B. McDonald, G. Nye, R. A. Whitney, Jr., W. C. Cole, B. Firth, Mr. and Mrs. H. M. Paulson, Jr., J. W. Hanes, Jr., R. Gritman, and G. M. Jonkel.

Several individuals were instrumental in securing and sustaining political approval and permit authorizations to initiate and continue our 15-year study. These include E. Baysinger, T. Cade, R. Rohm, E. Johnson, R. Fielding, A. Eno, and especially the late L. Glasgow. We thank those who manage the lands of Assateague Island, especially D. F. Holland, R. Rector, and M. Olson. The staff at Assateague State Park provided the hourly weather data. We also appreciate the reviews by L. R. DeWeese, M. C. Perry, and R. L. Jachowski.

49 | Habitat Selection by Spring Migrant Peregrines at Padre Island, Texas

W. Grainger Hunt and F. Prescott Ward

The annual movements of Peregrines that breed in arctic and boreal North America are gradually being understood through field studies. Winter band recoveries show that most of them go to South America, as far as Argentina, and on their way south in early October they concentrate on the beaches of coastal Texas (Enderson 1965, Hunt et al. 1975) and the Atlantic seaboard (Ward and Berry 1972).

Until recently, little was known of their northward return in the spring. Cade (1960) reported that Peregrines appear in Alaska in May and that North Slope birds arrive later than those nesting in the taiga. Dekker (1979) recorded a spring migration in Alberta from 16 April-30 May with peaks during 4-23 May. White (1969a) observed migrants near Fairbanks, Alaska most frequently in late April and early May.

During the mid-1970s, Ward (unpubl. ms.) searched unsuccessfully for April migrants on the coast of Maryland and elsewhere along the eastern seaboard in areas where they were known to occur in fall; however, in April 1978 he observed substantial numbers of Peregrines at Padre Island, a barrier island on the southern coast of Texas. Since that time, more than 700 Peregrines have been banded there in spring.

In this report, we give results, based on a telemetry study conducted during April-May of 1979 and 1980, which indicate that Peregrines stage in the vicinity of Padre Island and nonrandomly select among a variety of habitats there.

STUDY AREA

The region covered in our routine airplane surveys for telemetered Peregrines included Padre Island from Baffin Bay south to Boca Chica and west to Highway 77 (Figure 1). When necessary we searched for "missing" birds in a wider area extending west to Hebbronville and north to Sinton.

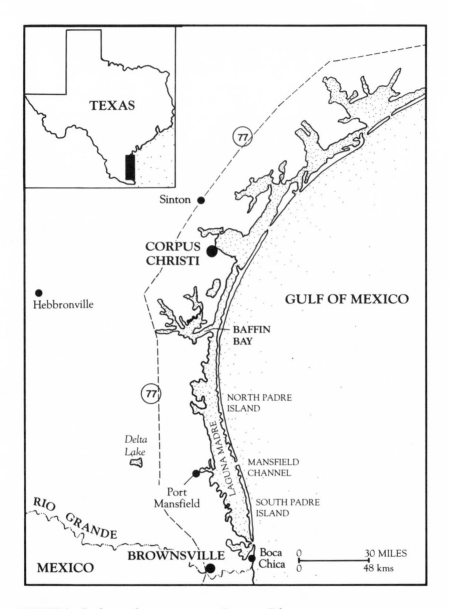

FIGURE 1. Study area for spring migrant Peregrine Falcons.

Padre Island (Figure 1) was formed 2000-3500 years ago by river delta sediment interacting with a rising sea level (Brown et al. 1977, 1980). As a result of continued wave and wind action it is in constant landward retreat. The island is 176 km long and less than 1.5 km wide near its southern end. A shallow bay, the Laguna Madre, separates the island from the mainland. Mansfield Channel, dividing North and South Padre Islands, is identified in this report as a reference location for Peregrine distribution.

Vast unvegetated, featureless expanses of sand and mud called wind-tidal flats form a continuous band along most of the western (leeward) edge of Padre Island and at some locations on the mainland shore (Figure 2). Frequently inundated by wind-driven lagoon waters (hence the term wind-tidal flats), some areas support extensive mats of blue-green algae. Hurricane surge tides erode openings (washover channels) in the dunes through which shell and sand are transported from the Gulf of Mexico to the lagoon side of the island. From the standpoint of useful Peregrine habitat, the washover channels resemble the wind-tidal flats in that they are normally featureless. In Peregrine studies of years past (Hunt et al. 1975), the channels provided the only view of the wind-tidal flats of the inner island to observers driving along the 150-m wide beach strip.

Bordered on the east by beach and on the west by the wind-tidal flats, the dune area, up to 10 m in elevation, is typically vegetated by sparse, salt-tolerant grasses and vines. Among the dune fields are barrier flats of low, grass-covered sand. These contain long, shallow, wind-created deflation troughs which run parallel to the shoreline and which act as passageways for excess lagoon water to return gulfward after hurricanes. Fresh water may collect in these vegetated low areas for up to several weeks after a storm, creating marshlike conditions amidst the dunes. In this report, we refer to these marshes as "dune lakes."

More than 33,000 hectares of Padre Island are designated as national seashore and are administered by the National Park Service. A portion of the delicate island ecosystem within park boundaries is protected by federal regulation, but the predominantly private lands of South Padre Island are a foundation for expanding development, based primarily on tourism.

The mainland adjacent to the island consists of large cattle ranches composed of mesquite chapparal with scattered lakes and dune fields. Large cotton farms, vegetable farms and orchards occur farther inland.

METHODS

Ward tagged 15 Peregrines with radio transmitters on Padre Island in 1979 (10-29 April) and 9 more in 1980 (15 April-1 May). Transmitters (Wildlife Materials, Inc.) weighing about 5 g were affixed to the proximal portion of an outer tail-feather by means of nylon thread and epoxy. The 32-cm long fine-wire antenna was tied and then

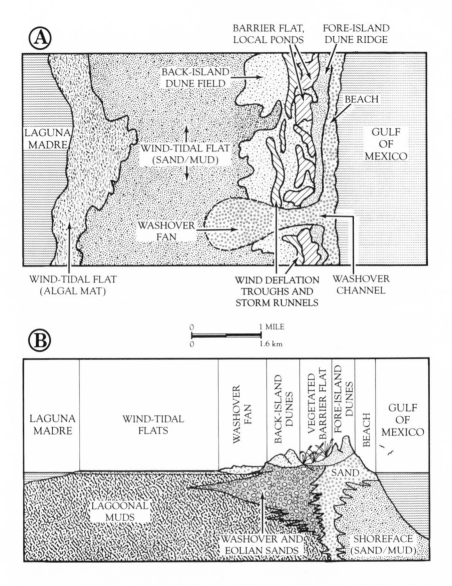

FIGURE 2.   Schematic representation of Padre Island environments, after Brown et al.
(1980). Upper figure (a) shows aerial view of a segment of the island. Lower
figure (b) is a cross-section of the same segment. (Relief features are
amplified for clarity.)

glued along the shaft of the retrix, extending about 12 cm past the tip
of the tail. Transmitters had an expected battery-life of 30 days.

A Cessna Model 172 airplane equipped with two side-facing, four-element yagi antennas on the wing-struts was used for tracking, and we often employed a third, forward-facing antenna. Receiving equipment included an AVM LA-12 and/or a Telonics TR-2 coupled with a TS-1 programmable scanner connected to a switch box for alternating the receiving antennas.

Tracking flights on Padre Island involved flying transects about 450 m above ground level along the length of the island within the study area. By circling at a lower altitude when radio signals were detected, we were normally able to estimate locations of perched Peregrines to within 200 m. To locate "missing" birds, we climbed above 3000 m and scanned while making slow turns.

RESULTS

Our data show that Peregrines staged on Padre Island and its environs before continuing their journeys northward across the continent (Table 1). Spans of telemetry contact with the Peregrines ranged from 3-28 days with a mean of 8.4 days per Peregrine. Actual tenures in the study area were probably longer because birds were present for unknown periods before capture. Data on departures and long-distance migration will be reported elsewhere.

During our surveys, we located the 24 birds during daylight hours in the study area a total of 220 times; there were 163 detections (74%) on Padre Island, 14 (6%) on the Laguna Madre or its mainland shore, and 43 (20%) in rangeland or farmland on the mainland.

From the airplane we visually identified 21 habitat types on Padre Island, the bay (Laguna Madre), and the mainland; for simplicity, we have condensed these into the 10 habitat types shown in Table 1. On the island itself we located radio-tagged Peregrines in six specific habitats: (1) wind-tidal flats ($n=107$ telemetry detections), (2) vegetated dunes with wind-deflation troughs ($n=13$), (3) beach ($n=8$), (4) wind-tidal flats with dunes ($n=11$), (5) unvegetated dunes ($n=5$), and (6) towns (South Padre Island) or paved roads ($n=3$). There were an additional 16 Peregrine detections on Padre Island in which habitats were not identified. Bay habitat designations included islands ($n=2$ detections), the mainland shore ($n=2$), tidal flats on the mainland shore ($n=2$), areas of human habitation ($n=1$), detections of Peregrines flying or soaring over the bay ($n=3$), and undesignated ($n=4$). Mainland habitats included rangeland ($n=5$), sand dunes ($n=13$), rangeland lakes ($n=5$), cultivated fields ($n=10$), farmland lakes ($n=8$), and trees in farmland ($n=2$).

The occurrence of radio-tagged Peregrines on wind-tidal flats on Padre Island represented about 72% of the total detections on the island. To test whether Peregrines tended to select wind-tidal flats nonrandomly, we measured the area of each island habitat within

TABLE 1. Frequency of detections of 24 radio-tagged Peregrines in 10 habitat types in the study area. Birds 1-15 were telemetered in 1979 and birds 16-24 in 1980. All were females except birds 19 and 24.

| | | | | No. of detections | | | | | | | | | |
| | | | | Padre Island habitats | | | | | Mainland habitats | | | | |
Bird	Age	Date tagged	Tenure[a]	Flats	Dunes	Beach	Other	Bay	Range	Dunes	Lakes	Fields	Trees
1	imm	10 Apr	28	3	4	3	3	3	3	6	3		
2	adult	13 Apr	7	1		1					8	10	2
3	imm	14 Apr	24	1	1								
4	adult	17 Apr	15	15		2	2						
5	adult	17 Apr	4	4	1		2						
6	imm	20 Apr	18	4	4	1	5	3		2	1		
7	adult	20 Apr	4	2			3	1					
8	imm	22 Apr	3	2			1						
9	adult	23 Apr	9	7	1			2		1	1		
10	adult	24 Apr	5	4	1		1		1				
11	adult	25 Apr	4	3	1								
12	adult	27 Apr	5	4	1								
13	adult	27 Apr	6	2	2								
14	imm	27 Apr	4	4		1							
15	imm	29 Apr	8	3			1						
16	adult	17 Apr	6	1			1						
17		19 Apr	5	3	1								
18		19 Apr	12	13									
19	imm	20 Apr	9	11	1			3					
20		20 Apr	4	8									
21		27 Apr	7	11						1			
22	imm	28 Apr	6	8						2			
23	adult	1 May	4	2				2	1	1			
24	imm	1 May	4	2									

[a] Number of days from capture to last detection.

16 km of the Mansfield Channel. The information for these measurements was obtained from the environmental maps of the Bureau of Economic Geology (Brown et al. 1977, 1980). In this portion of the island, wind-tidal flats (including washover fans) made up 77.5% of the land, dune areas formed 20.6%, and beach 1.9%.

Pooling the data for both years, we found no significant departure from a random distribution of Peregrines over the three habitat types ($X^2=1.29$, $df=1$); however, we found a highly significant difference between the two years of study in the frequency with which Peregrines used wind-tidal flats: 59% in 1979 as compared with 93% in 1980 ($X^2=20.9$, $df=1$, $P<0.001$, $n=55$ detections). Moreover, in 1979 the Peregrines occurred more frequently in the dune areas than expected by chance ($X^2=13.1$, $df=1$, $P<0.005$), while in 1980 they occurred disproportionately in the tidal flats ($X^2=6.0$, $df=1$, $P<0.025$ with Yates' correction for small samples, $n=40$ detections). Because the data for the two years were skewed in opposite directions, no overall tendencies toward habitat selection could be detected in the pooled sample.

The reason Peregrines favored dune areas in 1979 and wind-tidal flats in 1980 may have been the greater numbers of prey birds attracted by freshwater on the island during the 1979 study period. The wind deflation troughs in the dune areas on the surf side of the island contained numerous lakes to which White-winged Doves, Mourning Doves, waterfowl and other water birds were attracted (K. Riddle pers. comm.). The lakes were particularly abundant in the area 13-24 km north of Mansfield Channel. In 1980, there were very few of these dune lakes in evidence.

The radio-tagged Peregrines appeared also to be distributed non-randomly along the length of Padre Island. Despite surveys covering 95 miles of the island, 94% of the detections were made within a central 64-km stretch extending from 16 km south to 48 km north of Mansfield Channel (see Figure 1). Not surprisingly, we found that the distribution of wind-tidal flats corresponded with that of the Peregrines: 82% of the total area of wind-tidal flats on Padre Island occurred within the 64-km area of Peregrine concentration.

Data on the diet of spring migrant Peregrines on Padre Island are similar to those reported for the fall migration by Hunt et al. (1975). Prey items identified in fall included 60% land birds, 29% shorebirds, 9% waterfowl, and 2% mammals. In spring, the proportions were 61% land birds, 25% shorebirds, 9% waterfowl, and 5% other.

When we looked for telemetered Peregrines at night we found them roosting on the island; in eight detections where habitat could be determined, the Peregrines were on tidal flats.

Radio detections of Peregrines on mainland portions of the study area also indicated habitat selection. Near the Laguna Madre, Peregrines frequented sand flats and dune fields and avoided chaparral, by far the most abundant habitat. Bird No. 3 left Padre Island soon after tagging (14 April) and frequented farmlands and orchards around a large lake about 72 km inland. It attacked doves and shorebirds from atop a 70-m high series of radio towers and roosted at least seven nights in trees on the edge of the lake. Violent thunderstorms with heavy winds prevailed on the night of 29 April, and the next morning we found the bird back on Padre Island near the capture site where it remained for up to six days. It subsequently returned to the radio towers by 7 May.

DISCUSSION

The importance of wind-tidal flats to Peregrines was recognized by Hunt et al. (1975), who likened them to the broad flood plains of arctic rivers near which Peregrines commonly nest (see photos in Cade 1960). These flats, occurring in abundance on Padre Island, provide no cover for prey birds, which can escape only by outflying pursuing falcons. Along with the surrounding bodies of water over which land birds can be caught (see Walter 1979a, Thiollay Chapter 67) and the occurrence of prey-attracting wetlands in some years, these flats create conditions of extraordinary prey vulnerability.

Another important factor influencing the occurrence of Peregrines on Padre Island is prey abundance. The appearance of Peregrines in spring coincides with the migrations of millions of passerines and shorebirds (Stevenson 1957, Gauthreaux 1971). As these birds pass over the island they may be attacked by Peregrines hunting under far more advantageous circumstances than in most other habitats. Impressed with the enormous numbers of migrants so vulnerable to attack by Peregrines, C. M. Anderson (unpubl. ms.) metaphorically described Padre Island as ". . . a giant bird trap."

The preference of arctic Peregrines for featureless and unvegetated terrain has also been observed during winter. C. G. Thelander and P. Bloom, while banding North American Peregrines in the Atacama Desert of coastal Peru in 1980, found them wintering in barren habitat similar in character to the wind-tidal flats of Padre Island.

It is important to understand that no assemblage of spring migrant Peregrines has yet been noted elsewhere. We speculate that spring migrants follow the middle-American stem from South America; when the coast turns eastward at the northern end of Padre Island, the Peregrines cannot continue a northward course without leaving the prime coastal foraging habitat. We speculate that they delay their migrations until favorable winds and/or the passing of the hosts of migrant songbirds, shorebirds and waterfowl facilitate their journeys across the continent. Females no doubt utilize the Padre Island staging area to amass fat and mineral stores for the making of eggs and for incubation in the cold northern temperatures. Newton et al. (1983) have demonstrated that female European Sparrowhawks lose considerable amounts of weight during breeding because they give priority to the feeding of their young. In Alaska, R. E. Ambrose and K. Riddle (unpubl. ms.) found adult female Peregrines weighing 20-25% less than their normal (pre-laying) weight during late stages of the chick cycle, particularly when large broods were present.

Padre Island, and possibly the similar habitats along the northeastern coast of Mexico, may figure importantly in Peregrine conservation. At the time of this writing, much of the area frequented by Peregrines is in private hands and much is scheduled for "development." Given the need of females to amass fat and the probability that a significant proportion of the arctic Peregrine population visits the island in spring, deterioration of those habitats on Padre Island that influence foraging success may have latent effects on Peregrine productivity. Specifically needing preservation are the featureless wind-tidal flats, especially in the middle portion of the island, and the water-holding potential of wind-deflation troughs within the dune areas.

ACKNOWLEDGEMENTS

The work was supported by the U. S. Fish and Wildlife Service and the U. S. Department of the Army. We are particularly grateful to B. Johnson, who helped with the fieldwork and many other aspects of this study. Others who assisted were: G. Vose, C. Anderson, C. Porpor, W. Cochran, R. Lindsey, A. Raim, C. Hunt, T. Nichols, K. Riddle, W. Seegar, and J. Bullock. W. Cochran designed and built the transmitters, gave valuable advice, and was helpful in the field. We thankfully acknowledge the logistical support of the Laguna Atascosa Wildlife Refuge. We thank T. Cade for comments on the manuscript.

7 | Captive Propagation, Reintroduction, and Management

50 The Breeding of Peregrines and Other Falcons in Captivity: An Historical Summary

Tom J. Cade

The breeding of falcons and other raptors in captivity has become a worldwide enterprise since 1965 and continues to increase in scope and intensity. In 1983-84 I tried to survey the effort and came up with some figures on the species and numbers of diurnal raptors that have been bred in captivity (Cade 1986b). Precise figures are no longer possible for many species because of poor record-keeping or failure to keep records at all. Because some reported cases are bogus, it is not always easy to distinguish the true records from the false. Nevertheless, I think the major features of captive propagation are clear, and my purpose here is to summarize briefly the historical events that have led to all this activity.

Only 15 species of diurnal raptors (Falconiformes in the traditional sense) are recorded as having produced and raised young in captivity before 1950, and the total had increased to only 23 species by 1965. To date, at least 83 species have been bred successfully one or more times in confinement; some of them have produced hundreds of progeny, and at least two — the American Kestrel and the Peregrine Falcon — have produced thousands. Breeding has been taken to the F_2 generation or beyond for at least seven species, and the total number of raptors produced in captivity now exceeds 11,500 birds, possibly by another 1000 or more (Cade 1986b).

Twenty-three species of falcons (genus *Falco*) have reproduced in confinement. We added a new one to the list at Cornell in 1985 — the neotropical Orange-breasted Falcon. The list includes the captive production of approximately 100 Red-headed Falcons, more than 100 Laggars, more than 300 Gyrfalcons, some 400 Lanners, over 500 Prairie Falcons, nearly 1000 Eurasian Kestrels, about 3000 American Kestrels, and 4000-4500 Peregrines. The latter include at least the following "subspecies": *F. p. tundrius* of the American arctic, *F. p. anatum* of North America, *F. p. pealei* of the American Pacific

Northwest, *F. p. cassini* of South America, *F. p. peregrinus* of Europe, *F. p. brookei* of the Mediterranean, *F. p. minor* of Africa, *F. p. peregrinator* of India, *F. p. macropus* of Australia, and both *F. p. babylonicus* and *F. p. pelegrinoides*, if they are included as subspecies of *F. peregrinus*.

HISTORY OF EARLY ATTEMPTS TO BREED FALCONS

What were the historical events which led to the successful propagation of falcons and other raptors? We will probably never know who first bred falcons in captivity, and it does not much matter, except as an item of scholarly curiosity, because whoever it was worked in historical isolation and had no influence on later developments. We do know that the ancient and medieval falconers were not interested in propagation because there was a plentiful supply of wild falcons and hawks to be taken for training and because they held young falcons or eyasses in low regard for hunting, much preferring to trap fully wild passage or haggard birds.

There is one curious reference to the captive breeding of falcons in a late 15th or early 16th century English manuscript on falconry (Loft 1978). In a section titled "How to Ordere a Place to Brede Hauks," the unknown author gives a set of directions so explicit and detailed for propagating a pair of Lanner Falcons as to imply that he wrote from experience. He even included the proper caution that bars for the cage should be vertical rather than horizontal, to prevent the birds from clinging to the sides and marring their feathers. Otherwise there is little in the older European literature on the subject.

Aviculturists and zoological gardens showed little interest in propagating falcons either. In Britain in the late 1800s there were a few gentlemen who combined an interest in falconry and aviculture. Men like Colonel Meade-Waldo, St. Quintin, and the Fourth Lord Lilford kept up a lively correspondence about attempts to pair and breed various kinds of raptors in captivity (Trevor-Battye 1903). Lilford had a famous estate where he kept a free-flying pair of Bearded Vultures and where he successfully bred Little Owls brought over from continental Europe (Turk 1981). Even these men who had such a keen interest in the Peregrine for falconry (see Fisher 1901) seem not to have considered seriously the possibility of propagating the species.

Quite by accident, one of their countrymen almost succeeded in doing so in 1852. A. G. Johnstone, in a communication to *The Naturalist* (1853) from Dumfries, Scotland, mentioned a pair that, after having been kept in confinement for some years, laid two fertile eggs. Both male and female incubated faithfully for 12 days, until put off by some kind of human disturbance. There are few details, except that the eggs proved to be fertile on examination. Yarrell (1871) in his book *A History of British Birds* cites this record, but no one else seems to have paid any attention to it, until it caught Steve Herman's eye a few years ago and he mentioned it to me.

There is also one early American record of some interest. A data card with a set of Peregrine eggs in the collection of the Western Foundation of Vertebrate Zoology bears the following information: "Collector, C. Nichols for C. Littlejohn, Redwood City; Locality, Sea Shore, West of Pescadero, California; Date, 21 March 1897. In 1896 four young were taken from the same nest and kept in confinement, when grown two were given liberty and one of the remaining two laid at least two eggs in the house in which they were confined. I did not learn the exact date but it was about the same time the old birds deposited this set." If the dates are correctly recorded, the captive bird laid in her first year. No other information exists. (I am indebted to Carl Thelander for calling attention to this record.)

These early results remained isolated and unknown to the group of falconers and breeders who later became obsessed with the desire to breed Peregrines in captivity.

EFFORTS IN THE PERIOD 1940-1965

The first widely reported and accepted case of successful breeding of Peregrines came from Germany during World War II. Renz Waller (1895-1979), a highly renowned wildlife artist and one of the principal architects of the rebirth of falconry in Germany in the 1920s (Awender 1980), kept a pair of Peregrines in an old mews at his place in Dusseldorf. The female was a 12-year-old eyass when she laid eggs in 1942; the male was a wing-injured passage bird which had also been in captivity for many years and could not fly. These two birds produced fertile eggs and reared one young each year, while allied bombs were falling all about the neighborhood. Waller (1962) has given a full account of the parents and their offspring in his book *Der Wilde Falk ist mein Gesell* (see also, Kendall 1968). While some of the details involving this case have become confused with time and some later critics have even cast doubt on whether Waller's birds really produced their own young, there is no substantive reason to deny Waller's claim. It has been independently corroborated by other observers present at the time and is internally consistent in all its details (see Kenward 1972).

Waller's story, which became known to the international falconry community only some years after World War II, stimulated a few other enthusiasts to try the same thing. The British falconer, Ronald Stevens, who is best known for his charming books *Laggard* (1953) and *The Taming of Genghis* (1956), kept Peregrines paired together for a number of years in the late 1950s and 1960s at his place in Ireland but without results (Stevens 1964, 1967). Later he and John Morris were the first to produce hybrid offspring by natural mating between a female Peregrine and a male Saker (Morris and Stevens 1971). A little later another well-known British falconer, Philip Glasier, became interested in breeding birds of prey in captivity at his Falconry Centre in Newent. While he never had success with Peregrines, he did produce offspring from Eurasian Kestrels and a variety of other raptors beginning in the 1960s (Glasier 1978).

In North America, Morlan Nelson (1969c) had a famous eastern *F. p. anatum* Peregrine named "Blackie," which some boy scouts had taken as a young eyass from a nest in Virginia. In the 1950s she began laying eggs in her mews, and she readily reared young Prairie Falcons, providing an early demonstration of the potential for using human-imprinted falcons in propagation.

The younger generation of German falconers paid some attention to Waller's results, and one in particular, Prof. Christian Saar, began experimenting in the late 1950s with methods to breed Peregrines in captivity. Like the rest of us, he had many frustrating years of watching his females lay infertile eggs each season. Later, fertile eggs were lost before hatching (Saar 1970). He did not give up, however, and he learned from his mistakes, as the results he has achieved in recent years admirably attest (Saar 1985, Chapter 59).

The first falcon to be bred in significant numbers was the American Kestrel, beginning in the early 1960s. My former student, Ernest J. Willoughby, and I called attention to the ease of breeding this species for scientific studies on reproduction (Willoughby and Cade 1964), and about the same time Amelie Koehler (1968), working with just two pairs in her lab at Freiburg, produced 106 eggs and 61 young between 1962-68, and an additional 6 young from 2 F_1 pairs. In 1964, pesticide researchers at the Patuxent Wildlife Research Center of the United States Fish and Wildlife Service (USFWS) established a breeding colony of American Kestrels. After some initial problems, this colony grew to large size under the scientific management of Richard D. Porter and Stanley A. Wiemeyer and provided birds for significant experimental research on the effects of DDT and other organochlorine pesticides on eggshell thinning and related behavioral and physiological problems (Porter and Wiemeyer 1969, Wiemeyer and Porter 1970). Porter and Wiemeyer also demonstrated the feasibility of managing a large captive population of falcons and of achieving large scale production of young, including reproduction by F_1 progeny (Porter and Wiemeyer 1970).

These impressive results with American Kestrels served to encourage those who were beginning to make major efforts to propagate Peregrines in captivity. Then, in 1968, Henry Kendall (1968), an American falconer in St. Louis, raised three young Prairie Falcons from a captive pair of trained birds, and interest in achieving consistent success with Peregrines and other large falcons heightened.

RESULTS OF BREEDING SINCE 1965

North American efforts to breed Peregrines in captivity became organized on a continent-wide scale following the first International Peregrine Conference at Madison, Wisconsin in 1965. At the end of the conference a group of attending falconers and biologists met to discuss the possibility of breeding the Peregrine in captivity as a measure for saving the species from possible extinction, to consider ways in which different parties and interests could cooperate, and to develop plans for obtaining the needed wild stock for breeding. Those attending this meeting were: Don Hunter from South Dakota, serving as chairman; Frank Beebe from British Columbia; Richard Fyfe, then from New Brunswick; Fred and Fran Hamerstrom from Wisconsin; David Hancock from British Columbia; Steve Herman from California; Hans Herren from Switzerland; Grainger Hunt from Texas; Morlan Nelson from Idaho; Joe Simonyi from Ontario; and Lucile and William Stickel from Patuxent, Maryland (USFWS) (see Hunter and Harrell 1967).

From the beginning it was clear that a continent-wide effort would develop in North America involving both institutional programs and private projects. It was also obvious that there were two intimately interwoven motives behind these efforts to breed Peregrines. One was the desire of falconers to ensure a continuing source of Peregrines available for training and hunting; the other involved the conservationists' goal to preserve the Peregrine as a wild species and if possible to repopulate vacant range by releasing captive-produced falcons. Regardless of how one evaluates the first motive, it is highly unlikely that the conservationists' objective could have been achieved without the intensely personal and essentially selfish desire of falconers to be able to continue possessing and using Peregrines in their sport, because this drive, more than anything else, was responsible for the successful breeding of Peregrines in captivity.

The group that met after the Madison Conference recognized the need for some kind of organization to coordinate efforts to obtain suitable breeding birds, to establish bona fide breeding projects, and to disseminate information quickly on methods of breeding. The formation in 1966 of The Raptor Research Foundation, Inc. was a direct outgrowth of these perceived needs. Originally headquartered in Vermillion, South Dakota, incorporated by Donald V. Hunter, Jr., Byron E. Harrell, and Paul F. Springer, and soon joined by George Jonkel (the four served as the first officers), the foundation began publishing *Raptor Research News* (now *The Journal of Raptor Research*). It was a valuable clearinghouse of information on the developing raptor propagation projects from 1967-74, especially through the quick distribution of the "Breeding Project Information Exchange" and through a series of highly successful annual meetings. The North American Falconers' Association was also closely allied with many of these activities, and particularly in the early years the memberships of the two organizations broadly overlapped. The Raptor Research Foundation, Inc. has subsequently developed into a large international organization with diverse interests in raptor biology. Today many of its younger members do not know that their organization started out as a small group of people who were intensely devoted to learning how to breed Peregrines and other raptors in captivity.

One of the first accomplishments of the newly organized Raptor Research Foundation was the acquisition in 1966-67 of several pairs of young F. p. pealei from the Queen Charlotte Islands for distribution to private breeding projects. These birds were obtained through the cooperation of the provincial authorities of British Columbia; Canadian falconers Frank Beebe, Brian Davies and David Hancock played an important role in securing the young from their eyries on remote islands. Although the history of this operation is clouded by some unfortunate incidents and "misunderstandings" among its principals, some of these falcons did end up in the hands of men who eventually succeeded in obtaining offspring from them.

One was Frank Beebe, who had been trying to breed Peregrines and other raptors in captivity for a number of years. In 1967 his old pair of F. p. pealei hatched two young from a second clutch of fertile eggs, but the young, unfortunately, were not tended by the parents and died soon after hatching. Nevertheless, Beebe's careful description of his results with this pair provided important insights into captive management, and his paper in Raptor Research News (1967) is still well worth reading, in part to note his clear recognition that the prime reason for propagating Peregrines was because the species was threatened with extirpation over a large portion of its breeding range in North America and Europe.

In 1968, the late Larry Schramm, a falconer and aviculturist in Portland, Oregon became the first American to raise a young Peregrine all the way to the fully fledged, flying stage. He raised it from a captive pair of F. p. pealei (Peterson 1968).

In 1971 and again in 1972, Dr. Heinz Meng in New York achieved international recognition for his successful breeding of one of the pairs of F. p. pealei acquired by the Raptor Research Foundation in 1967. In 1971 he hatched a single chick by artificial incubation, the bird which became famous as "Prince Philip," but in 1972 Meng was able to hatch and rear seven young from two clutches of the same pair

(Kaufmann and Meng 1975). In so doing, he demonstrated the feasibility of greatly increasing above the natural rate the production of young by captive pairs. His result was a great boost to breeders, because it confirmed the notion that large scale production of Peregrines in captivity could be achieved with a relatively small number of breeding pairs, just as Amelie Koehler's earlier work with American Kestrels had shown.

Meng loaned his breeding pair, "Prince Philip" and some of his siblings to The Peregrine Fund at Cornell University after the 1972 breeding season. The original pair produced 23 young in the next five years before going back to New Paltz, and "Prince Philip," a bird imprinted on humans, fathered many young as a voluntary semen-donor for artificial insemination before his death in 1984.

In 1973, The Peregrine Fund at Cornell produced 20 young from just three mating pairs. That same year, Dr. James Enderson at Colorado College raised the first Rocky Mountain *F. p. anatum* Peregrines (three fine females), and John Campbell and Wayne Nelson raised three arctic Canadian "*F. p. anatum*" at Black Diamond, Alberta (Nelson and Campbell 1973). About the same time, the Canadian Wildlife Service program under the direction of Richard Fyfe began raising significant numbers of young at Wainwright, Alberta (Fyfe 1976, Chapter 56). By 1975 sufficient breeding stock was in hand, and the methodology developed for a major production of captive-raised young Peregrines in North America.

A parallel development of captive breeding occurred in Europe, and for the Peregrine especially in West Germany. Koehler (1968, 1969) summarized some of the main efforts in the 1960s in Germany and mentions Herr Röder who had success with a hormone-treated male, obtaining a malformed young from an artificially incubated egg.

Fessner (1970) had a 1961 female eyass from Spain which laid two sets of infertile eggs each year from 1964-70 while paired with different males. In the latter year two veterinarians, Maatsch and Beyerbach (1971), helped Fessner artificially inseminate this female, and he got one fertile egg in the second clutch. It hatched in an incubator, and the chick grew to maturity. This may have been the first successful artificial insemination of a Peregrine; however, since the male and female were always together, it remains uncertain.

Daubert (1971), working with Horst Sander's *F. p. brookei* pair and with help in artificial incubation from Fessner, obtained five chicks from seven fertile eggs in two clutches. His success caused many people to question his reported results, but only a few years later his results were being duplicated and exceeded in the breeding projects of Christian Saar and his associates in the Deutscher Falkenorden.

TABLE 1.   Summary of early efforts to breed Peregrines in captivity.

Year	Name of breeder	Location	Significant results
1942-43	Renz Waller	Dusseldorf, Germany	1 young *F. p. peregrinus* raised each year; natural incubation, etc.
ca. 1967	Herr Röder (*fide* A. Koehler)	West Germany	1 young raised; artificial incubation, hand-reared.
1967	Frank Beebe	Vancouver Island, British Columia	2 young *pealei* hatched; natural incubation, etc., chicks died.
1968	Larry Schramm	Portland, Oregon	1 young *F. p. pealei* raised; natural incubation, parent-reared.
1970	W. Fessner (Maatsch and Beyerbach)	West Germany	1 young *F. p. brookei*; artificial insemination and incubation, hand-reared.
1971	A. Daubert (Horst Sander and W. Fessner)	West Germany	5 young *F. p. brookei*, 2 clutches; natural mating, artificial incubation.
1971-72	Heinz Meng	New Paltz, New York	1 young *F. p. pealei*; artificial incubation, hand-reared and imprinted; 7 young from 1 pair, 2 clutches.
1973	James H. Enderson	Colorado Springs, Colorado	3 young *F. p. anatum* from natural mating pair.
1973	John Campbell and R. Wayne Nelson	Black Diamond, Alberta	3 young from arctic *F. p. anatum*; natural mating, artificial incubation, parent-reared.
1973	The Peregrine Fund, Cornell University	Ithaca, New York	20 young from 3 natural mating pairs; artificial incubation, hand- and parent-reared.
1974	Christian Saar	Berlin, West Germany	6 young from 1 pair.
1975	Canadian Wildlife Service, R. Fyfe	Wainwright, Alberta	18 young from 7 pairs.

CONCLUSION

Table 1 summarizes the attempts to breed Peregrines in captivity from 1942-75. By 1975 more than 200 large falcons, mostly Peregrines, were being produced per year, half by private breeders and half at research centers (Kenward 1977). The stage was set for major attempts to reintroduce captive-produced Peregrines in the United States, Canada, West Germany and Sweden, as the following chapters reveal.

In the late 1970s and in the 1980s, hundreds of Peregrines have been produced each year. More than 2500 have been released to the wild. The development of the techniques, methods, and skills required for propagation and reintroduction in Europe and in North America is almost wholly a contribution of falconers to the conservation of their favorite bird. It is not their only contribution (for example, their presence at the Madison Peregrine Conference in 1965 was conspicuous), but it is their major contribution, the benefits of which, I believe, will extend far into the future.

51 | Peregrine Restoration in the Eastern United States

John H. Barclay

When I was asked to write this report, my first problem was trying to figure out how to condense ten years of research and field work involving the release of Peregrines into a few printed pages. I thought back to the very beginning: how might the idea of raising Peregrines in captivity and releasing them in order to restock the vacant eastern breeding range have sounded 20 years ago at the Madison Conference? Only Nelson (1969c) made specific mention of this possibility in the Madison proceedings, but apparently there was considerable back room and post-conference discussion about breeding Peregrines in captivity. The idea must have sounded pretty farfetched to most at the conference, and I wonder how many imagined that we would be able to talk about breeding success and growth rates of the new eastern United States Peregrine population 20 years later. Just how farfetched an idea it was is characterized by Faith McNulty's statement in a 1972 *New Yorker* article that the captive breeding of Peregrines was a feat "so difficult that it cannot repopulate the wild or provide birds for fanciers." It is reassuring that a number of people did not subscribe to this line of thinking and, instead, took up the challenge. Because of their dedication to this purpose, I am able to report on the progress that has been made towards reestablishing a Peregrine population in the eastern United States.

My intention is to present a brief overview of the eastern United States program: how it has developed, where it stands now, and where it is headed in the next few years. There have been several lengthy publications on this program (Cade and Temple 1977, Sherrod and Cade 1978, Barclay and Cade 1983, Cade and Hardaswick 1985), and I refer the reader to these papers for more detailed discussions of the program.

EXPERIMENTAL RELEASES

The initial experimental phase of our program in the eastern United States began with the release of two captive-reared Peregrines in 1974 in cooperation with Dr. Heinz Meng at the State University of New York at New Paltz. The objective during this phase of the program was to learn how and where to release Peregrines in order to obtain the highest survival during the release process. Work on this phase continued during the next several years as production of captive-bred Peregrines increased. Details of the hacking procedure were worked out, and we began to learn where we might first achieve the goal of having released Peregrines nest in the wild.

These early releases were done at cliff sites where Peregrines historically nested and at specially designed towers in coastal marsh habitats. We discovered that Peregrines released by hacking were extremely vulnerable to predation by the Great Horned Owl, and many of our early attempts at releasing Peregrines at lowland cliffs failed because of predation by owls. We also learned that we could obtain higher survival by hacking falcons from towers and that the birds returned to these towers in subsequent years at a rate that augured well for pair formation and nesting (Barclay and Cade 1983).

The idea of releasing Peregrines and establishing nesting pairs on artificial structures has been a much debated aspect of our program, and I want to summarize briefly the reasons why much of the early effort was toward this end. Arguments both for and against the concept of establishing a tower-nesting population of Peregrines can be fairly convincing, depending upon the strength of one's biological justifications and one's aesthetic perception and appreciation of the idea.

Coastal towers were first used as release sites for several reasons: they were convenient places to hack Peregrines in order to facilitate study of the ontogeny of hunting behavior; the greater availability of prey in the marsh habitats where these towers were located appeared to contribute to the rapid development of hunting behavior (Sherrod 1982); and Great Horned Owl predation could be minimized by constructing the towers away from owl habitat.

The main reason why much of the early emphasis of the program went towards establishing Peregrines on towers was because towers worked better than any other situation we were testing. There was higher survival during hacking from towers, and we saw a much higher rate of return of subadults and adults. In some areas the rate was as high as one returning bird for each three released (Barclay and Cade 1983). We learned that it was possible to modify the Peregrine's traditional choice of nesting sites and that our best chance of getting released Peregrines to nest in the outdoors was on these towers.

Some have argued that it is not appropriate to establish Peregrines in coastal areas where they did not nest historically. While it is true that

Peregrines did not commonly nest in eastern coastal areas, which lack suitable cliff formations, there are two records to show that a few pairs did in fact nest in eastern coastal habitats (New Jersey State Geologist Report 1890, Jones 1946).

RESULTS AND DISCUSSION

Figure 1 shows the temporal and geographical distribution of Peregrines released, sightings of returning subadults and adults, and production of young by nesting pairs from 1975-85. There have now been over 750 Peregrines released in the eastern United States, about 45% of them from towers and urban sites in the mid-Atlantic coastal region, which extends from New York City south to Norfolk, Virginia and includes coastal areas of New Jersey and the Delaware and

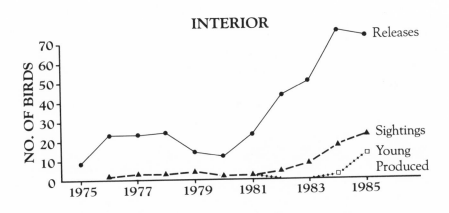

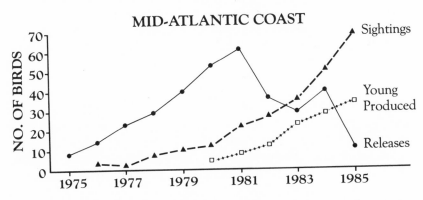

FIGURE 1. Number of releases, sightings and young produced as part of the Eastern Peregrine Recovery Plan, 1975-85.

Chesapeake bays. About 55% of the Peregrines in the eastern United States have been released at interior cliffs and urban sites. Figure 1 shows the trend early in the program (1975-78). Releases were about equally distributed between cliff and tower sites; then they were increased in the coastal region from 1979-81 because of the higher survival during hacking and the increasing numbers of returning falcons there. Releases were de-emphasized at the interior locations during 1978-80, and there were very few sightings of returning birds from the earlier releases at these places.

One of the experimental goals was to prove that captive-raised and released Peregrines would nest in the out-of-doors. Nesting first occurred in 1979 when a pair of released Peregrines bred on a tower in New Jersey. Unfortunately, this attempt failed because of egg predation. The following year, two pairs nested successfully on towers in New Jersey. At this point the program entered the operational phase with the goal of establishing an entire self-maintaining population. It was clear that our best opportunity to accomplish this goal would be by using the coastal towers, and over the next several years the emphasis of our work went towards establishing a population of 20 nesting pairs in the coastal region. We felt that a population of this size could be efficiently established by releasing more Peregrines and constructing enough nesting sites. We also believed that a minimum population of 20 pairs could be self-maintaining and that it could be the nucleus of a founding population whose offspring might disperse and eventually begin to colonize nearby cliff sites.

Figure 1 shows the trend when releases began to be reduced along the coast in 1982 because more of the towers were occupied by adults and the sightings of adults and production of young continued to increase each year. Data indicate that natural reproduction has enabled this regional population to increase despite the reduction of releases.

From the beginning, our program has been committed to the goal of reestablishing Peregrines at cliff sites. Our earlier successes and failures at releasing Peregrines from cliffs made us realize that the best opportunity for success would be to use the cliffs in the mountains of upstate New York and northern New England, where the incidence of Great Horned Owl predation was less severe. Releases began to be emphasized at these sites in 1981 and were increased each year as fewer birds were released in the coastal region. The data in Figure 1 show that sightings of returning birds have increased over the past several years. The rate of increase has not been as great as we saw in the coastal population, where it more closely paralleled the trend in releases. Nevertheless, sightings have been increasing and the releases are paying off. The lower rate of increase in sightings is probably owing in large part to the increased difficulty of finding falcons in mountainous terrain and not necessarily to higher mortality or emigration.

The first nesting of Peregrines at an interior cliff was in 1980, but it was not until 1984 that we knew of any other nesting attempts in this region. It is interesting to note that the members of a pair that nested on a building in Montreal, Canada originated from cliff releases in New York and Vermont. More Peregrines have been seen in the interior over the past few years, but it was not until 1985 that we saw real progress: nine known pairs, five of which nested successfully.

To summarize where the program stands as of 1985 in respect to the recovery goals, we are in a monitoring phase in the mid-Atlantic coastal region where most of our field work goes toward locating additional nesting pairs and documenting nesting success and growth of this regional population. During the past three years, we have discovered several bridge-nesting sites to which Peregrines in the region have dispersed. We are just beginning to see growth of the nesting population in the interior region, and we plan to continue releases until there are 20 nesting pairs in this population. Figure 2 shows the distribution of all Peregrines observed in 1985 in the eastern United States.

Clearly, the many years of releasing Peregrines are paying off (Figure 3). As the combined data on numbers of pairs observed, nesting attempts and production show, the nesting population is growing impressively. There has been an average annual increase of 70% for nesting attempts and 60% for successful nesting attempts over the past three years. Through 1985 there have been 63 documented nesting attempts; 47 (75%) have been successful, and 128 young were produced. Productivity since nesting first started in 1979 has been 2.03 young hatched per nesting attempt and 2.72 young per successful pair, among the highest rates recorded for any Peregrine population. In 1985 there were 40 pairs observed; at least 25 attempted to nest, 16 of which produced 47 young.

These encouraging data accurately quantify the success of the program and satisfy our penchant for scientific evidence. However, there are equally important but less tangible measures of success, measures that do not lend themselves to graphic display but which are nonetheless deserving of mention. I am reminded of certain events that I have had the good fortune to witness. I met 80-year-old Archie Hagar on the cliffs of Mt. Tom in Massachusetts while we were operating a hack site. It was particularly exciting for me to see his undiminished enthusiasm for Peregrines on the cliffs where he had studied them in the 1930s and 1940s, but where they had been absent for some 25 years. It was equally poignant to accompany Jim Weaver while banding young Peregrines at the first reestablished cliff eyrie in New Hampshire

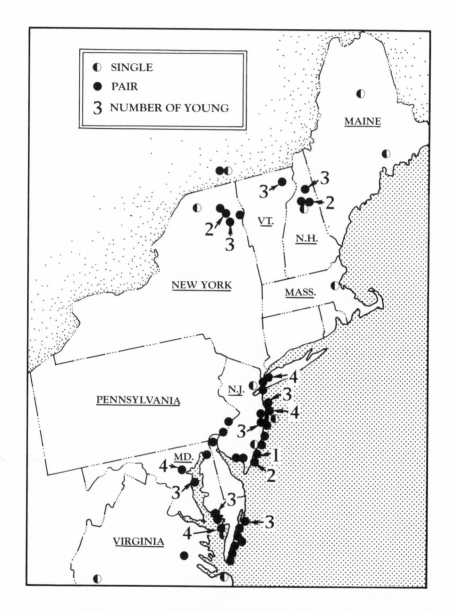

FIGURE 2.   The distribution of Peregrine Falcons observed in spring-summer of 1985.

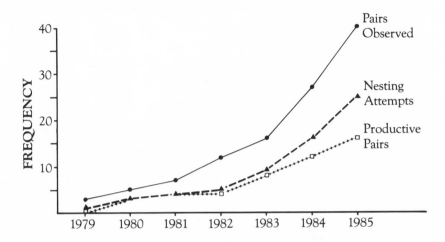

FIGURE 3. Peregrine population growth in the eastern United States.

in 1981, and to see the sense of satisfaction Jim felt at finally being able to rope into an active eastern Peregrine eyrie. And just this past summer I saw how much Tom Cade appreciated the opportunity to tour New England with his wife, Renetta, and once again watch breeding Peregrines and their young at several of the old eyries that have not held nesting falcons for 30 years or more.

RECOVERY GOAL

The original goal of the Eastern Peregrine Recovery Plan (Bollengier 1979) was to restore a breeding population equal to half the number estimated to have occurred in the 1940s, or to a level the present environment will support. A figure of 350 pairs prior to the DDT era (Hickey 1942) means that an "officially" recovered population would consist of 175 nesting pairs. As the entire nesting population in 1985 consisted of only 25 pairs, and only 16 of these pairs produced young, we obviously have some work remaining to reach this goal. The Eastern Peregrine Recovery Team recently defined more specific regional population goals of at least 20 nesting pairs in each of five recovery regions for three consecutive years before downlisting the Peregrine from endangered to threatened status would be recommended and a total of 175 nesting pairs for complete recovery and delisting.

The five eastern recovery regions are shown in Figure 4. The first region is along the mid-Atlantic coast and contains the experimental population nesting on towers, buildings, and bridges. We are very near

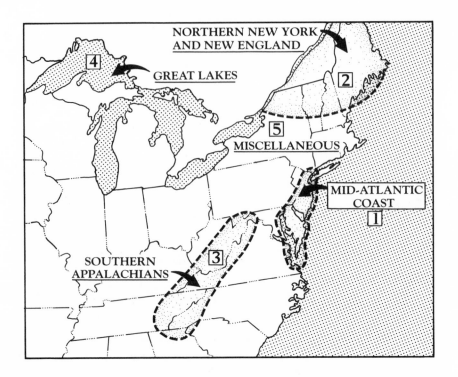

FIGURE 4.   Peregrine Falcon recovery regions in the eastern United States.

the recovery goal of 20 nesting pairs in this region — there were 18 nesting pairs in 1985. The second region is in the mountains of northern New York and New England where releases have been concentrated since 1981. There were six nesting pairs there in 1985, so we are perhaps two or three years away from reaching this regional recovery goal. The third region is in the southern Appalachians. The first releases were carried out there at two sites in 1984, and work was extended to six sites in 1985. We plan to continue releases there as long as there is funding for captive propagation and release work. The fourth region is in the upper Great Lakes, where releases were tried in 1976 and 1977 but discontinued because of Great Horned Owl predation. A release program started in Minnesota in 1982 under the organization of P. Redig and H. Tordoff at the University of Minnesota and the Bell Museum of Natural History has had much better results, and there have been 56 Peregrines released. Although there have been no nesting pairs resulting from these releases as yet, there have been a few sightings of released birds, and the plans are to continue releases during the next few years (Redig and Tordoff Chapter 52). The last region, labeled miscellaneous, has no defined boundaries; it consists mainly of lowland and riverine habitat in several eastern states. No releases are planned in this region, and some different method of releasing Peregrines would have to be devised in order to avoid the problem of Great Horned Owl predation which plagued earlier releases in this region. The best prospect for reestablishing a population there may be to wait for dispersal and colonization by Peregrines from adjacent areas.

How long, then, will it take to achieve these recovery goals? Jim Grier and I have addressed this question in more detail in a paper on the dynamics of founder populations (Chapter 66). The productivity and growth rate data show that the existing population should be capable of increasing by its own reproductive efforts, but the accelerated growth rates we have seen are owing in large part to increases in the numbers of Peregrines released during the past few years. The growth rate will flatten out when releases stop, and any further growth will have to come entirely from autochthonous reproduction. The answer to the question of how long it will take really depends upon how quickly we want to reach the recovery goal. We can reach it sooner, perhaps in another five years, if the present level of releases is maintained; or it could take 10 years or more if releases are discontinued and we have to rely entirely upon the founder populations' own reproduction. Future plans for the eastern United States are to continue raising Peregrines for release as long as there is funding for captive propagation and release work. The complete restoration of an eastern Peregrine population is now a predictable certainty.* It can be achieved as long as there continues to be the dedication to purpose that got this program started and brought it to its present level of success.

ACKNOWLEDGEMENTS

I express appreciation to Dr. T. Cade and J. Weaver for allowing me the opportunity to work on the reintroduction program. The following past and present coworkers with The Peregrine Fund, Inc. deserve credit for their contributions: P. Dague, M. Gilroy, V. Hardaswick,

---

*Editors' Note: The newly reestablished Peregrine population in the eastern states has continued to increase in size pretty much as projected. In 1986, there were 43 pairs and several singles on territory; at least 30 pairs laid eggs, and 25 of them successfully raised 53 young. In 1987, Peregrines were seen at more than 80 locations and included 56 confirmed pairs, 4 unconfirmed pairs, and 27 singles. At least 40 pairs laid, and 27 of them produced 64 young. Production per nesting pair was the lowest recorded since the first pairs began nesting in 1980, but overall it was still high enough to sustain further population increase.

P. Harrity, W. Heck, M. MacLeod, T. Maechtle, S. Sherrod and S. Temple. Thanks also are due the dozens of individuals, too numerous to list, who worked as release site attendants. The eastern Peregrine recovery program is a large cooperative effort which owes much of its success to the varied contributions, both financial and logistical, of numerous federal and state agencies, private organizations, and individuals. These have and will continue to be fully acknowledged in the annual *Peregrine Fund Newsletter* now in its 13th issue.

52 | Peregrine Falcon Reintroduction in the Upper Mississippi Valley and Western Great Lakes Region

Patrick T. Redig and Harrison B. Tordoff

The pre-DDT Peregrine Falcon breeding population in the upper midwestern United States included about 30 pairs along the bluffs of the Mississippi and its tributaries from Red Wing, Minnesota to Dubuque, Iowa; about six pairs along the north shore of Lake Superior; and a few more in the Boundary Waters Canoe Area of Minnesota, the Door Peninsula of Wisconsin, and several localities in Michigan. The breeding population in Michigan, Minnesota, Wisconsin and Iowa probably totaled about 50 pairs, all of which had disappeared by the early 1960s.

Reestablishment of this population began in 1976, with a release by the Minnesota Peregrine Group of five Peregrines from Cornell University on a cliff at Maiden Rock, Wisconsin. Four survived to independence. In 1977, three birds from Cornell were released on a cliff at Nelson, Wisconsin. Two were promptly killed by Great Horned Owls, the third was retrapped and the release program was terminated in the region for five years.

THE RELEASE PROGRAM, 1982-1983

In 1982, a second effort began with the release of five young Peregrines obtained from the University of Saskatchewan. The site chosen for release was Weaver Dunes, an area of unique sand prairie along the backwaters of the Mississippi River 8 km southeast of Kellogg, Minnesota. The 182-ha property, recently purchased for preservation by The Nature Conservancy, includes part of a sand dune prairie that extends upriver for several kilometers. Within a 16-km radius are located more than a dozen historical Peregrine eyries on the dolomite cliffs overlooking the Mississippi River. The area is rich in

559

waterfowl, shorebirds, passerines and other birds that provide a prey base for the Peregrines, as well as Great Horned Owls, a problem whose management is detailed below.

A conventional 12-m high hack tower was erected, courtesy of the Winona, Minnesota office of Northern States Power Company. Two east-facing hack boxes were installed. Three of five Peregrines released that year fledged successfully, one was killed by an owl, and one was injured by a pole trap and subsequently died in captivity. In 1983, a second tower with two hack boxes was installed by Northern States Power about 400 km north of the original tower. Ten Peregrines from Saskatchewan were released; nine survived to independence and again one was killed by an owl. In 1984 and 1985, 11 and 12 Peregrines, respectively, were fledged with no losses to predation.

OWL CONTROL

The loss of falcons to owls in 1982 and 1983 stimulated us to devise a truly effective owl control program. Most Great Horned Owls in the Weaver Dunes area were found nesting in hollow trees, which are abundant. To make owl nests easier to find, we installed 11 artificial stick nests around the area in the fall of 1983. In spring of 1984, two of these were occupied by nesting owls. Prior to fledging of the owlets, the adults were taken by shooting, and the youngsters were relocated and hacked well away from the Peregrine release site. Five more artificial nests were put out in the fall of 1984, but none of the 16 was used in 1985.

To increase protection from owls, in 1984 we adopted owl control techniques used by S. Petersburg and coworkers at Dinosaur National Monument in Colorado. A cassette tape player with a good loudspeaker was used at night to call owls, which were then taken by shotgun. A bright spotlight was sometimes used, but calling from beneath dead snags and shooting at silhouettes against the natural light in the evening sky was most successful. Most owls were taken between sunset and midnight in late June and July. Taped calls of owls, and particularly of squealing rabbits and mobbing crows, were effective. We started intensive control about two weeks before opening the hack box, and continued at least three to four nights per week until the youngest Peregrines had been flying for at least two weeks and were roosting away from the towers. A total of 15 owls was taken within a 1.6-km radius of the hack site in 1984, and another four were taken from the same area in 1985.

RELEASES, 1984-1985

The combination of increased efficiency in finding and/or discouraging owl nesting in the area along with intensive localized control appears to have been entirely successful as no Peregrines were lost to owls in either year. All 23 young falcons released at Weaver Dunes in 1984 and 1985 survived to independence.

We opened a second hack site in 1984, at Mt. Leveaux near Tofte, Minnesota, on the north shore of Lake Superior. The hack site, on a 40-m cliff facing the lake and 1.6 km inland, was developed and supervised by U. S. Forest Service personnel, particularly W. Russ, S. Hoecker, and E. Lindquist. Five Peregrines were released in 1984 and seven in 1985; all survived to independence and dispersal. At least one of the 1984 birds overwintered along with two or three Gyrfalcons in the Duluth harbor, which has abundant pigeons. One of the 1985 birds was spotted near Louisville, Kentucky, 23-25 August 1985, only a month after release about 1160 km to the northwest. This bird, a male, was not seen at the hack site after 22 July, only four days after release.

A third release site was opened in 1985, on the roof of the 51-story Multifoods Tower in downtown Minneapolis, Minnesota. Six Peregrines were released from this site. All survived to independence, providing the metropolitan business community an unparalleled opportunity to watch the falcons and to learn of wildlife conservation. The funds for this site were donations from individuals and businesses in the downtown area. Early in the progress of this release, a subadult falcon was observed in the area on several occasions. Bearing both an aluminum band and a red plastic band, she appeared to be from a Canadian release, but her identity and origins were not confirmed. Eyewitness reports and evidence in the form of fecal stains subsequently found on the parapets of some of the buildings suggested she had been there for some time. She interacted frequently with our youngsters in the air, but was not dangerously aggressive and appeared intimidated by the young falcons at the hack box. She regularly visited the Multifoods Tower, but we never saw her approach closer to the hack box than about 20 m. Following the dispersal of the youngsters from this release site in July 1985, the hack box was removed and a gravel box was installed just below in a large ventilation opening on the side of the building with the hope that the older female or the released young would be attracted to nest there in the coming years. On 28 October 1985, we inspected the box and found evidence of Peregrine droppings and down feathers. Our plans for this site in 1986 are contingent upon the return of any falcons to this site next spring.

DISCUSSION OF RELEASE TECHNIQUES

Most of our release procedures were devised by The Peregrine Fund at hack sites in other parts of the country. We are glad to acknowledge our indebtedness to Peregrine Fund personnel for that assistance.

Because of local circumstances, we developed somewhat different techniques and procedures described below.

Multiple Hack Towers. — We decided to release as many falcons as possible from the Weaver Dunes site because at least 40 historical territories are within 83 km of each other. Accordingly, two towers were placed in view about 250 m apart and each had two hack boxes. This arrangement afforded numerous advantages. Multiple releases required only two or three hack site attendants per summer. The two towers offered familiar and alternate landing sites for the falcons in their early days on the wing, thereby reducing any tendency for them to fly toward owl habitat along the river. Food was delivered to younger birds still confined to a hack box on one tower without adversely affecting older falcons from earlier releases; the latter simply flew to the other tower. Releases of only one or two birds can be made if older young are present. We found that the older birds spend considerable time "socializing" with other young confined in the hack box, and there was less aggression.

Because of the extremely favorable results obtained using the two-tower system at the Weaver Dunes site, we plan to discourage returning adults from adopting the towers as nesting sites by covering them or making them otherwise unsuitable in early spring. Our aim is to divert such birds to nearby cliffs. We hope the adjacent nesting cliffs are sufficiently distant so that aggression of territorial birds towards fledging juveniles will not be a problem. The closest cliff is about 5 km from the towers.

Owl Control. — The Weaver Dunes site required effective owl control. Intensive short-term owl control was accepted by local residents, wildlife agencies in charge, and others interested in the release program. We were open in our discussions of the owl control program, and the necessity for killing them was generally accepted. We believe no longterm harm will come to the local Great Horned Owl population as a result of the control program.

Sources of Peregrines. — Ours was the only release effort in the United States to rely mostly on birds produced by breeders other than The Peregrine Fund. Financial arrangements included an annual subsidy for the cost of the breeding operation (L. Oliphant, University of Saskatchewan), purchase of individual falcons (D. Bird, J. Oar, L. Boyd), and combination of purchase and facility support (D. Hunter, R. Anderson).

Our program depends on favorable state and federal regulations that support private breeders and allow purchase of birds. We feel strongly that private breeders provide flexibility for release programs and insurance against loss of captive breeding birds concentrated in a few large facilities. Other less obvious benefits include genetic diversity, breeding technique innovation, and the provision of birds for falconry independent of wild populations.

Funding. — About 60% of our release program funding was by private contributions, about 20% by private donations channeled through the Minnesota Department of Natural Resources' Non-Game Program, and up to 20% from the U. S. Fish and Wildlife Service. Private support for another 5-10 years is uncertain as the novelty of the program wears off. In 1985 our budget for releasing 25 Peregrines was almost $80,000, well over half of which went to private breeders for falcons. The rest was spent for hack site attendants, release site development, and raising quail for falcon food. We are deeply grateful to all financial contributors to the Minnesota Peregrine Program, and to the devoted hack site attendants and volunteers who made it work.

SUMMARY

From 1982-85, 56 Peregrines were released. Two birds were killed by Great Horned Owls while at towers, one by a pole trap, one was killed by an auto after dispersal from the Tofte site in 1984, and one was injured by an auto but was recovered alive in New Jersey after leaving the Weaver Dunes site in 1983.

Our goal is to establish a population of at least 15-20 pairs of breeding Peregrines in the upper midwestern United States. If we maintain annual releases of 20-30 birds as in 1985, we anticipate reaching this goal by 1990. Beyond that a reduced release program may be needed for a few more years. We are confident of success if public financial support is maintained.

Editors' Note: Three pairs occupied cliffs along the upper Mississippi River in 1986, and one pair hatched a nestling, which disappeared at three weeks of age. In 1987, two of these three pairs laid eggs and hatched young, but later the young were killed by Great Horned Owls; feathers of an adult Peregrine were found in the third eyrie. A fourth pair that set up housekeeping in downtown Minneapolis successfully reared two young (H. B. Tordoff pers. comm.).

53 Recovery Effort for the Peregrine Falcon in the Rocky Mountains

William A. Burnham, William Heinrich,
Calvin Sandfort, Edward Levine,
Daniel O'Brien, and Daniel Konkel

Within an area of about 4,000,000 km², including portions of Montana, Wyoming, Colorado, Idaho, northern Utah, South Dakota, North Dakota, Kansas, Nebraska, Oregon and eastern Washington, over 160 historical Peregrine Falcon breeding territories are known. Only four were known to be occupied by breeding pairs in 1979. Most historical locations were near roads or other places where discovery was likely. Because of the vast amount of remote nesting habitat, Peregrines may have been much more numerous than records suggest. Very conservatively, fewer than half of historical territories were probably known. The same may hold true for southern Alberta, Saskatchewan and portions of British Columbia where Peregrines vanished. Since about 1970, surveys for Peregrines were intensified, but very few eyries were located. Many nest sites were abandoned before extensive use of DDT began. Wetland areas, where prey was abundant, dried up in the 1950s and 1960s according to Nelson (1969a, Chapter 3, Porter and White 1973), or were lost to water containment projects. We believe this effect was probably localized and minor compared to that of chlorinated hydrocarbons. Peregrines have not returned even where increased precipitation has reestablished wetlands. The decline and near total extirpation of the Peregrine occurred and appeared to continue until about 1980, when released falcons began to breed. However, areas much larger than Great Britain remain vacant.

In the early 1970s captive propagation of Peregrines was begun at Cornell University (The Peregrine Fund) by T. Cade, and in Colorado by J. Enderson who had several birds of Rocky Mountain origin. In 1974, The Peregrine Fund in cooperation with the Colorado Division of Wildlife (CDOW), developed a propagation facility at Ft. Collins,

Colorado, with the goal of releasing birds. Peregrines contributed from falconers F. Bond, W. Burnham, J. Enderson and T. Smylie created the nucleus from which the captive population was developed. By trading progeny with the Canadian Wildlife Service and others, by careful pairing, and by acquisition of a few unreleasable or confiscated birds, a genetically diverse stock was developed. The captive population was bred from about 35 Peregrines representing different areas in the Rocky Mountain region. The breeding facility was relocated in 1984 to a new Peregrine Fund facility, the World Center for Birds of Prey, in Boise, Idaho.

This paper reports on the efforts to prevent extinction and facilitate a recovery of the Peregrine Falcon in the Rocky Mountain states by use of propagation and release of falcons. Details on pesticide levels and other aspects of the recovery effort are covered elsewhere (Enderson et al. Chapter 38, Craig et al. Chapter 54).

METHODS

Falcon propagation techniques were described earlier (Weaver and Cade 1983). Procedures for artificial incubation of thin-shelled, wild-laid eggs were also developed (Burnham 1983).

The falcons were released by: (1) fostering, where eggs were removed from wild pairs and replaced by three-week-old young; (2) cross-fostering, where young at Prairie Falcon nests were replaced with Peregrines; and (3) hacking, where attendants released groups of similar-age fledglings without adults (Burnham et al. 1978, Sherrod et al. 1981). The goal was to maximize the production of persisting wild pairs by fostering, to enhance the remnant population through hacking, and to reestablish breeding falcons by hacking in areas where they were once prevalent.

All released falcons were marked with colored and numbered plastic and metal bands. Returning released birds were seen at release sites or in general surveys. Thorough surveys of most release areas were prevented by limited funds. Identification at breeding sites or in wintering areas was by telephoto, spotting scope, or recovery of carcasses. Few birds were captured.

RESULTS

Production of young by The Peregrine Fund's Rocky Mountain program increased from 2 produced by 1 female in 1975, to 147 produced by 39 females in 1985 (Table 1). Of 1671 eggs laid, 59% were fertile, 79% of fertile eggs hatched, and 91% of those hatching survived at least to release. Approximately 53% of the total production of 706 live young resulted from artificial insemination, and 90% of the

TABLE 1.   Production of Peregrines at The Peregrine Fund's Colorado and Idaho facilities.

		1975	1976	1977	1978	1979	1980	1981	1982	1983	1984	1985	Total
Captive Breeding[a]													
No. of laying females	Cop[b]	1	2	2	4	8	7	7	10	13	14	17	20
	AI[c]	0	5	5	10	16	21	17	15	19	20	22	29
	Total	1	7	7	14	24	28	24	25	32	34	39	49
No. of eggs[d]	Cop[b]	12	23	14	33	58	59	67	88	77	92	115	638
	AI[c]	0	29	33	58	81	159	151	100	121	136	165	1033
	Total	12	52	47	91	139	218	218	188	198	228	280	1671
No. of fertile eggs[e]	Cop[b]	4	14	8	25	37	48	48	75	55	67	84	465
	AI[c]	0	12	12	24	38	82	81	50	59	72	95	525
	Total	4	26	20	49	75	130	129	125	114	139	179	990
No. hatched	Cop[b]	2	12	7	17	27	44	12	60	47	58	73	359
	AI[c]	0	5	9	17	31	62	80	37	45	58	74	418
	Total	2	17	16	34	58	106	92	97	92	116	147	777
No. survived	Cop[b]	2	10	4	15	26	38	8	51	47	58	73	332
	AI[c]	0	4	9	13	28	54	58	34	45	55	74	374
	Total	2	14	13	28	54	92	64	85	92	113	147	706
Production in captivity from wild-laid eggs													
No. of pairs			2	6	9	6	4	6	7	7	10	7	64
No. of eggs			11	35	41	38	19	22	26	27	30	25	274
No. fertile			8	32	37	32	18	21	25	27	27	25	252
No. hatched			4	15	24	24	11	16	20	19	18	16	167
No. survived			3	13	24	19	8	16	19	19	18	16	155

[a] Includes production from 2 F. p. pealei whose young were released in eastern United States.
[b] Copulating pairs; some females were also artificially inseminated.
[c] Fertilized through artificial insemination.
[d] Excludes any premature or broken eggs.
[e] Minimum, others died early or were broken.

semen used was supplied by behaviorally imprinted donors. Seventy percent of the production occurred in 1981-85. We also hatched 155 thin-shelled eggs removed from eyries by the CDOW, for a total of 861 young (Table 1).

Between 1976-85, 673 young were released in eight states (Table 2, Figure 1). About 74% of all releases were after 1981. Only 34% of the cross-fostered young survived to flying, 75% of the fostered young survived to flying, and 81% released by hacking survived to disperse normally from release sites after flying for three weeks; together these included 524 Peregrines. Hacking was the most successful release method, especially because success was measured in terms of young that were apparently independent after three weeks of flight rather than young first flying from eyries.

We released an average of 3.4 fostered young per eyrie, of which 2.5 per eyrie survived to flying. Hacking produced 4.6 young released per site and 3.7 survived. Cross-fostering resulted in 3.1 young released per eyrie and 1.3 survived.

Golden Eagles and Great Horned Owls contributed significantly to losses of released young. The losses resulted from direct predation and harassment, especially when young Peregrines were learning to fly. Attacks occurred even when humans or adult Peregrines were present and were frequently repeated at the same location over several days.

Fifty-seven percent of the 673 Peregrines were released in Colorado, and from a low of 4 wild breeding pairs in 1979, 13 pairs were located in 1985, and at least 10 birds bore bands (G. Craig pers. comm.) (Table 3). Released Peregrines also breed in Wyoming, Montana, Idaho, and northern Utah where they were absent for many years. Observations of subadult and adult falcons are increasing in all areas where multiple releases have occurred. Typically, breeding adults were located in an area after four years of multiple releases.

Fall and winter band recoveries of nine female and three male Peregrines were south of release locations (Figure 2). The distances varied from about 100-4600 km. The mean distance traveled was about 1600 km. All were recovered in areas where concentrations of potential prey existed. One released in Idaho was observed during three winters at a marsh near Los Angeles. All other reports were for birds less than one year old. Most recoveries were from areas where DDT is still used.

Most Peregrines in spring and summer were seen defending territories or found dead or injured. Band numbers were read for only a small portion. Adult and subadult females ($n=5$) moved farther from release locations ($\bar{x}=279$ km, range 100-512 km). The mean distance for adult males ($n=4$) was 68 km (range 30-90 km). The farthest movement (840 km) was by an immature female. The adult female

TABLE 2. Release of Peregrines by hacking and fostering, 1974-85.

State		1974	1975	1976	1977	1978	1979	1980	1981	1982	1983	1984	1985	Total
Colorado	P[a]	2		5	14	25	33	28	34	48	52	60	53	354
	I[b]	2		5	7	19	25	25	28	33	44	52	39	279
Wyoming	P							11	8	14	19	21	30	103
	I							9	6	9	18	20	25	87
Idaho	P				3	5	3			8	12	14	20	65
	I				3	2	0			8	9	13	15	50
Utah	P						4	10	9	6	8	13	10	60
	I						3	9	7	3	6	10	6	44
Montana	P								4	8	8	12	25	57
	I								4	6	4	10	22	46
New Mexico	P				8	12	8							28
	I				8	8	0							16
South Dakota	P						3							3
	I						2							2
Nebraska	P						3							3
	I						0							0
Total	P[a]	2		5	25	42	54	49	55	84	99	120	138	673
	I[b]	2		5	18	29	30	43	45	59	81	105	107	524

[a] No. of young placed at release sites.
[b] No. of young succeeding.

TABLE 3.   Number of returning color-banded Peregrines.

State	1979	1980	1981	1982	1983	1984	1985
Colorado	1	2	4	5	4	6	10
Wyoming			2		2	2	4
Idaho						2	3
Utah		2	5	4	2	5	3
Montana					1		
New Mexico					1		
Total	1	4	11	9	10	15	20

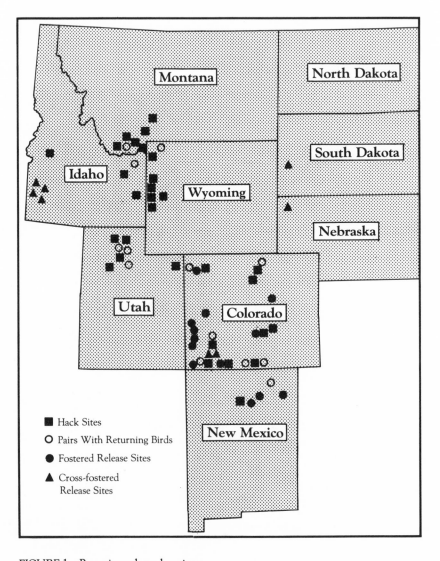

FIGURE 1.   Peregrine release locations.

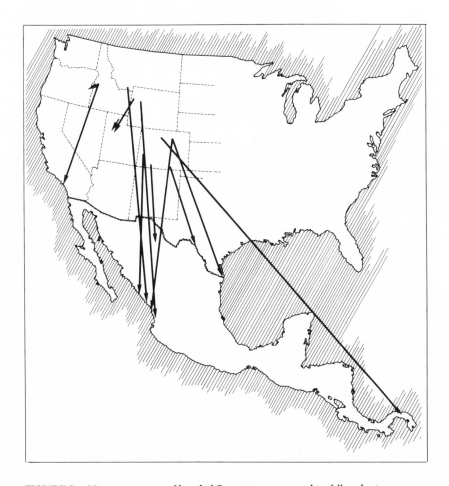

FIGURE 2. Net movements of banded Peregrines recovered in fall and winter.

moving the farthest was found breeding directly south of the release location and may have stopped there on a northward spring movement.

The degree of eggshell thinning varied greatly among eggs within clutches of wild eggs (Burnham et al. 1984). Thin-shelled eggs continue to be laid by many wild females (Enderson et al. 1982, Chapter 38). However, released Peregrines have produced 2.9 young per successful pair (n=8) without intervention in Wyoming, Utah, Montana, and Idaho. Nonaugmented production in Colorado in 1984-85 (n=11) was 2.1 young per successful pair (Enderson et al. Chapter 12), and in southern Utah where populations have persisted unaided, the production in 1984-85 (n=13) was reported as 1.8 young per successful pair (Enderson et al. Chapter 12).

DISCUSSION

The effort to stop the decline of the Peregrine Falcon in the western United States was unorganized until the establishment of The Peregrine Fund facility in late 1974. Several researchers had documented the decline, and J. Enderson had bred the first Rocky Mountain birds in 1973, but no larger commitment of funds or longterm programs existed. The feasibility of large-scale captive propagation was questioned by many, and reestablishment of wild populations doubted by most. There were few Peregrines of western origin in captivity, and the known wild production was near zero. Contributions of Peregrines from falconers, land and support facilities from the CDOW, funds from the National Audubon Society, and a commitment from The Peregrine Fund to construct and operate a facility provided a base for the present program to prevent the extinction of the Peregrine and facilitate a recovery. The first federal agency to participate financially was the Bureau of Land Management. The first corporations to become actively involved were Exxon Company USA, Boise Cascade Corporation and J. R. Simplot Company.

Location of Releases. — For the first four consecutive years of Peregrine releases (1976-79), sites were spread over an area about four times the size of Great Britain (Figure 1). We felt release sites should be concentrated in limited geographical areas until a few breeding pairs were established, from which a regional population could grow. In 1980 isolated releases and cross-fostering were eliminated. A release program was developed in the Teton/Yellowstone National Park area involving Idaho, Wyoming, and Montana wildlife agencies. The number of sites in northern Utah was increased, and hack release sites were established in Colorado to enhance recruitment near eyries receiving fostered young. In 1977-84, eggs were removed from most pairs in Colorado and fostered young were placed in the eyries. As captive production increased, expansion into new areas was minimized, and instead more release sites were added in established release areas. Prior to 1985, at least half of the annual captive production was released in Colorado.

Success of Release Methods. — Although the success of release by hacking and fostering was similar, both techniques have had unique advantages. Fostering allowed falcons to fledge young at historical territories even though thin-shelled eggs were laid, tending to assure use of the location. However, the technique cannot be used without wild breeding falcons. Fostering required frequent observation to determine when eggs were laid so that thin-shelled eggs could be taken before breakage and young of the correct age made available for release.

Hack sites were placed where Peregrines had disappeared. Natural cliffs as well as artificial towers were used. The latter allowed release where prey was concentrated. Predation was minimized by careful selection of release locations. Hacking required two field assistants at each site for 8-10 weeks.

Release by cross-fostering Peregrines into Prairie Falcon eyries was discontinued because of high mortality and the possibility of interspecific imprinting. Mortality resulted primarily from predation and parasite infestations. Cross-fostering in California resulted in less mortality, and a released bird was found paired with another Peregrine (B. Walton pers. comm.).

Fate of Released Falcons. — Although released Peregrines are distinctively banded, they have been difficult to relocate because of the vast area, rough terrain, very large cliffs, and the limited funding for surveys. Most were found near their release locations. When a pair returned it precluded further use by others. Sometimes unbanded immature Peregrines were seen, suggesting reproduction by unknown pairs. In Colorado and Utah, where a remnant population remained, most returning birds bred with unbanded adults. In Wyoming, Montana, and Idaho, where the Peregrine was apparently extirpated, both adults in each pair were banded. Wild-produced young have not been banded in those states, and sightings of immature Peregrines are increasing.

Without extensive surveys, most Peregrines will probably be unbanded as the population increases, and the only criterion for evaluation of population recovery will be the increase of Peregrines at suitable historical sites. At the present level of survey effort, one released Peregrine is positively identified for the release of about 24 (Table 3). We feel that the limited funds should be used to maximize the number of birds released rather than to conduct expensive surveys to locate and/or identify all returning falcons. Those results would be interesting, but since release techniques are proven, the survey results would have less benefit to the restoration program than more falcons in the wild, even were they not relocated.

Population Recovery. — We have seen no evidence of dispersal by Peregrines nesting in Arizona, southern Utah, or even California into Rocky Mountain states. Recolonization of regions of Great Britain was by Peregrines reared nearby (Ratcliffe 1980). Mearns and Newton (1984) found dispersal in Scotland from natal locations to breeding territories averaged 83 km for females and 58 km for males. Even though our data indicate that dispersal on continents is greater than on islands, without further extensive releases we expect only a very gradual expansion of the Rocky Mountain population. Repopulation of the central Rocky Mountains by Peregrines nesting in Arizona and southern Utah would take a very long time.

In the five states where most releases have occurred, excluding southern Utah where Peregrines persisted without augmentation, there is about one known breeding pair per 27,000 km², an area larger than Switzerland. Comparing the average number of young per successful returning pair to those from Peregrines in southern Utah, production may be adequate at least to maintain, if not increase, the population once breeding pairs have been established. Unless production decreases, the critical factor for Peregrine restoration seems to be the number of young successfully released and established as breeders.

Not until 1983 did the release program in the Rocky Mountains reach a significant level. We can now propagate and release about 150 Peregrines each year. We predict that this rate, continued through 1995, will cause Peregrines to breed commonly again through much of the Rocky Mountain region. If the program is reduced or ended before the population has truly recovered and is reproductively viable, it will not be easy to mount another effort to create full recovery in the western or eastern United States. This program is beginning to achieve widespread results, but the goal of population recovery has yet to be attained.

ACKNOWLEDGEMENTS

In the western United States, the Peregrine recovery program has enjoyed cooperation from people with many diverse interests. Such cooperation and dedication, rarely seen in endangered species management, have made all the accomplishments possible. The participants are far too many to list, but include the Congress of the United States of America, state and federal agencies and biologists, conservation groups, corporations and businesses, and thousands of individuals. Also included are dedicated biologists, field assistants, technicians, and office staff. Special thanks are due our coworkers D. Berger, P. Burnham, J. Craig, H. Doty, G. Eitemiller, J. Enderson, J. P. Jenny, and J. Willmarth. Finally, we thank T. Cade for providing the opportunity to contribute to restoration of the Peregrine.

54 | Peregrine Management in Colorado

Gerald R. Craig, Daniel D. Berger, and
James H. Enderson

When the Endangered Species Act was enacted in 1973, Colorado enjoyed several advantages that permitted an aggressive Peregrine recovery program. Early inventories by Enderson (1969a, 1969b) in 1965 established baseline information. The Colorado Division of Wildlife supported research and management efforts. The presence of the western facility of The Peregrine Fund, Inc. at Fort Collins permitted cooperative endeavors to bolster the wild population through captive propagation and release.

Management activities in Colorado have followed those steps outlined in the Recovery Plan for the Rocky Mountain/Southwest Population of the Peregrine Falcon (Craig 1985). We tried to monitor all known breeding territories annually, conduct searches for previously unrecorded sites, collect nonviable eggs and eggshells for pesticide analysis and eggshell thickness measurement, augment poor natural reproduction, and release falcons in vacant territories. The state's goal, to have 20 breeding pairs by 1988, is an interim step toward the recovery plan goal of 31 effective breeding pairs by 1995.

METHODS

Population Monitoring. — Beginning early each April, teams of observers visited recorded breeding territories to look for Peregrines. If falcons were not located within eight hours, the site was tentatively considered unoccupied, but subsequent visits were made to confirm the conclusion. Other escarpments were searched for undocumented sites. Occupied sites were watched intermittently in the breeding season to document reproduction. Broods were watched from near fledging time until they flew.

Hacking. — Hacking is a common method to establish Peregrines in vacant habitats (Barclay and Cade 1983). In Colorado it has been used to release falcons near vacant historical territories. When

575

territories were reoccupied by hacked falcons, hacking efforts were shifted elsewhere. Funding for hack sites was furnished by appropriate land management agencies, and responsibility for their support was distributed among the National Park Service, Bureau of Land Management, and U. S. Forest Service.

Fostering. — Fostering was first attempted in 1974 at an eyrie in the Royal Gorge (Burnham et al. 1978); later it was continued in Colorado to sustain reproduction where pairs were incubating cracked eggs (Enderson et al. 1982). The technique, also termed augmentation, typically involved replacing wild eggs with plastic replicas and returning captive-hatched young to nests when they were 16-21 days old. Wild eggs received special treatment in The Peregrine Fund's incubators, and wild falcons were provided an optimum brood of four half-grown young, thereby circumventing early nestling mortality. When we exchanged young for plastic eggs, four to six dead *Coturnix* quail were placed on the eyrie ledge. This supplement reduced the need for the male to procure additional prey immediately and stimulated parental behavior so that we could determine whether the young had been adopted. After the climber departed, one or both adults visited the ledge to remove and cache the quail. The female usually returned to brood the young. We used hungry young so that they protested being brooded and begged for food. At that point, the falcon retrieved a quail and fed the young. We discovered that if a male was incubating and the female was absent at the time the young were exchanged with the replica eggs, it was best to wait until she returned. Several males became confused when eggs were exchanged for young. They landed repeatedly at the eyrie, screamed at the young, and flew away. When the females returned, the young were accepted, and males settled into their routine of providing prey.

Recycling. — A variation of fostering involved recycling the pair to induce production of a second clutch. If a pair was recycled, the first set of eggs was removed 7-10 days after the clutch was complete. After about 14 days, pairs relocated to another ledge and laid a second clutch. The pair was then given foster young as described above, or permitted to incubate their own eggs. Recycling offered the advantage of augmenting insufficient captive production, relocating a pair to a more secure nest ledge, or delaying early breeding pairs to bring them into synchrony with captive producing pairs.

RESULTS

Population Monitoring. — Known territories with breeding pairs were surveyed annually from 1972-85 to determine occupancy rates and reproduction. By 1972, 27 sites had been observed, but five were deemed unsuitable for occupancy principally owing to human encroachment and habitat change. The 22 suitable sites had suffered a 50% vacancy (Table 1) by 1973 (Enderson and Craig 1974), and occupied sites were further reduced to six by 1975. Vacancies first occurred among the 11 sites along the Front Range, and by 1983 abandonment was complete. Were it not for reoccupancy of three sites by released Peregrines in 1982, 1983 and 1985, all historical sites would have been vacant. In addition to the 27 historical sites on record, potential nesting areas were investigated for previously unrecorded pairs. By 1985, approximately 80% of Colorado had been surveyed, and 18 additional sites were found (Table 1). The presence of scrapes and old whitewash suggested that many of the sites were occupied historically. Attrition has also occurred among the newly found sites as evidenced by vacancy of seven of 14 sites (50%) discovered between 1976-82.

Trends in natural reproduction have been obscured by management actions initiated in 1975 to bolster poor productivity. The productivity of wild pairs prior to 1975 averaged 0.4 young per occupied site, and the overall breeding success of all unmanipulated breeding pairs (1972-85) averaged only 45 young for 32 breeding attempts (1.4 young per attempt).

Egg Condition. — Fostering activities as well as visits to eyries to band young and collect nonviable eggs and eggshell fragments yielded an archive of 284 eggshell samples collected between 1973-85. This archive has provided documentation of eggshell thinning trends that have varied from 12-21% thinner than normal (see Enderson et al. Chapter 38), and it has permitted identification of sites requiring remedial action to succeed.

Each of the 121 first-clutch eggs collected from 1978-85 was considered hatchable in the wild if it was hatched under typical incubator conditions. Cracked eggs or those treated to counter abnormal water loss or gain were considered nonhatchable in the wild. Infertile eggs were deleted from the calculations. Hatchable eggs ($n=56$) averaged 0.322 mm, 10.3% thinner than pre-1947 eggs, and were significantly (t-test, $P<0.01$) thicker-shelled than 65 eggs that required special incubation treatment and averaged 0.310 mm, 13.6% thinner than pre-1947 eggs. The average eggshell thickness of hatchable eggs was depressed by four thin-shelled eggs ($\bar{x}=0.283$ mm) that were considered hatchable in the wild. Average eggshell thickness of unhatchable eggs was elevated by eight nearly normal eggs ($\bar{x}=0.344$ mm) that required artificial incubation.

Hacking. — Since 1978, 32 of 35 hacking attempts have succeeded for a success rate of 93% (Table 2). Failures of two sites were attributed to Great Horned Owl predation that virtually eliminated all

TABLE 1. Territory occupancy and breeding success of Colorado Peregrines.

	1972	1973	1974	1975	1976	1977	1978	1979	1980	1981	1982	1983	1984	1985
Total no. sites on record	27	27	27	27	30	34	36	37	39	39	39	41	44	45
No. new sites located	0	0	0	0	3	4	2	1	2	0	0	2	3	1
No. adult pairs	8	10	7	5	5	11	7	7	7	7	9	10	12	12
No. mixed pairs[a]	0	0	0	2	2	0	2	2	3	1	0	3	2	2
No. lone adults	3	1	2	1	1	1	2	4	3	3	4	1	0	0
Total no. occupied sites	11	11	9	6	8	12	11	13	13	11	11	14	13	14
No. occupied historical sites	11	11	9	6	5	5	4	5	5	5	4	4	3	3
Total no. breeding pairs[b]	0	2	6	5	4	9	6	4	5	6	6	8	12	13
No. successful pairs[c]	0	1	5	2	2	3	1	0	1	0	0	0	2	6
No. wild young fledged	0	2	11	5	2	4	1	0	3	0	0	0	4	13

[a] One member of the pair was in subadult plumage.
[b] Pairs which produced eggs.
[c] Pairs that were not fostered.

TABLE 2. Results of Peregrine hack efforts in Colorado.

	1978	1979	1980	1981	1982	1983	1984	1985	Total
No. hack sites operated	1	2	3	4	5	6	7	7	35
No. successful hack sites	1	2	3	4	3	6	7	6	32
No. young released	5	10	12	13	22	25	32	35	154
No. young achieving independence	4	10	11	13	13	23	27	24	125
Avg. young released/attempt	5.0	5.0	4.0	3.3	4.4	4.2	4.6	5.0	4.4
Avg. young/successful site	4.0	5.0	3.7	3.3	4.3	3.8	3.9	4.0	3.9
Avg. independent young/attempt	4.0	5.0	3.7	3.3	2.6	3.8	3.9	3.4	3.6

the young after they were released. Another site failed after a pair of adults appeared and severe weather followed. Following the storm, no young could be located, and it is possible that the fledglings followed the adults, became disoriented, and could not relocate the hack site. Of 154 Peregrines released by hacking, 125 (81%) achieved independence (Table 2). Causes for failure of 29 young were: premature disappearance ($n=12$), Great Horned Owl predation ($n=9$), Golden Eagle predation ($n=5$), collision with fence ($n=1$), automobile strike ($n=1$), and attack by an adult Peregrine ($n=1$).

It was difficult to document unequivocally the source of most released falcons occupying wild breeding territories since similar marking systems were used on hacked and fostered falcons. Several marked individuals almost certainly originated from hack efforts. One male hacked at a site in 1980 returned as an adult in 1982, attracted a lone wild female from an adjacent territory, and successfully reared young the following three years. Another male hacked in 1981 moved 48 km to a territory that had been vacant since 1976 and courted a wild subadult female in 1983. The pair successfully bred in 1984 and 1985. The only breeding pair of Peregrines on the Front Range since 1982 may also be attributable to an adjacent hack site in operation since 1978.

Fostering. — Fifty-six fostering attempts involving 192 young were made from 1974-85 (Table 3). Only four attempts failed, and they occurred after the young had been adopted by adults. In one case the adult female disappeared, and the young were removed because the male was not supplying sufficient prey. Disappearance of both members of the pair apparently caused the young to starve at three other sites. Single males did successfully rear broods on two occasions. At one site, the female disappeared while the nestlings were less than one week old. Three nestlings were found dead, but the male succeeded in rearing and fledging the remaining two. In another case, the adult female was apparently killed at the eyrie by a Great Horned Owl after four young had been fostered to them. One of the nestlings was killed when it was pushed from the eyrie during the struggle. The adult male was very attentive and continued to care for the young. Rather than remove the brood, we provided the male with live *Coturnix* quail so that he could remain in the vicinity of the eyrie to defend the young. The quail were first tethered to a rock about 4 m from the eyrie, and after the male became familiar with the routine, the attendants would toss the quail to him and he would catch them in the air. All three young successfully reached independence.

Fostering was 78% successful in fledging young (150 fledged of 192 fostered). In addition to loss of 14 young from the failure of four foster attempts, 28 additional fostered young failed to fledge. The causes of

TABLE 3. Results of Peregrine foster efforts in Colorado.

	1974	1976	1977	1978	1979	1980	1981	1982	1983	1984	1985	Total
No. pairs fostered	1	2	6	5	4	4	6	7	7	8	5	56
No. successful pairs	1	2	4	4	4	4	6	6	7	8	5	52
No. young fostered	2	5	13	20	15	16	21	26	27	28	18	192
No. fostered young fledged	2	5	7	15	12	13	15	20	21	25	15	150
Avg. young released/attempt	2.0	2.5	2.3	4.0	3.8	4.0	3.5	3.7	3.9	3.5	3.6	3.4
Avg. young/successful pair	2.0	2.5	1.8	3.8	3.0	3.3	2.5	3.3	3.0	3.1	3.0	2.9
Avg. young fledged/attempt	2.0	2.5	1.2	3.0	3.0	3.3	2.5	2.9	3.0	3.1	3.0	2.7

losses could not be determined for 11 young that disappeared sometime after being placed in eyries and before fledging. Golden Eagle predation usually occurred at the time of fledging when the young called attention to themselves by wing flapping. Although actual predation was not observed, Golden Eagle attack probably caused the demise of four additional young. Eagles nesting several hundred meters away on the same escarpment took two wild fledglings, and an adult Peregrine was photographed among the prey at another eagle nest. Predation by eagles may be a typical mortality among wild nesting Peregrines.

In 1984-85 we successfully fostered young to three subadult females that laid eggs. They appeared more confused than adults about the sudden exchange of eggs for young three weeks old. Although they readily removed the dead quail from the ledge, they took 30-60 minutes to accept the young. Experienced females often entered the eyrie and stood beside or behind the young while the climber was still on the ledge, and several adult females permitted themselves to be touched or even picked up when young were presented to them.

In addition to augmenting productivity of wild pairs, fostering helped to save eggs that probably would not have hatched in the wild. From 1974-85, 191 wild eggs representing 56 first clutches were removed from wild pairs in fostering efforts. It is probable that 11 eggs were damaged in transit, 7 of which were viable and might have hatched in the wild. Judging from the nearly normal incubation conditions under which they hatched in the laboratory, an additional 64 eggs were likely to have hatched in the wild. The remaining 120 eggs probably would not have hatched in the wild owing to infertility, arrested development, or abnormal humidity conditions required to hatch them. In addition to hatching 61 "normal" eggs, The Peregrine Fund salvaged 59 of the eggs deemed unhatchable in the wild. Hence, fostering and subsequent artificial incubation increased the expected hatch rate of wild eggs from 7% to 63%, thereby providing an additional 59 young for release in Colorado, Idaho, Montana, Utah, and Wyoming.

Recycling. — During fostering, 13 attempts were made to recycle pairs, and all efforts successfully produced second clutches. Between 1976-79, recycling served to augment captive production as well as relocate several pairs from inferior eyrie sites. Between 1978-85 one particular pair laid early clutches. They were occasionally recycled to bring them into synchrony with the hatch of captive eggs in order to receive foster young. In all, 43 additional eggs were laid through recycling; 18 young were produced. Eggshell thickness averages were identical between first and second clutches (t-test, P>0.9), and although second clutches averaged 3.2 eggs per attempt compared to an average of 3.5 eggs in first clutches, the difference was not significant (*t*-test, P>0.2).

Recoveries of Released Peregrines. — We have received band recoveries on 13 of the 275 Peregrines (5% recovery rate) released in Colorado. Recoveries were reported on two Peregrines within two months of fledging. The falcons moved 24 and 96 km, respectively, before being found with broken wings after collisions with a tree and a fence. Recoveries were reported for three falcons on their first fall migration. One female hacked in northeastern Colorado was discovered 1450 km away dying of possible pesticide poisoning near Eagle Pass, Texas. A second female from the same site was trapped and released 1770 km away at Brownsville, Texas, and the third, a male, flew 4600 km before he was caught by hand and released at Chilibre, Panama. Based on time of discovery, two falcons were apparently spending their first winter in northern Mexico. A fostered female was reported approximately 960 km away in north-central Mexico, and a fostered male was found dead 1450 km south at La Trinidad, Sinaloa, Mexico. One yearling moved 850 km north from her hack site in southwestern Colorado and frequented a hack site at Yellowstone National Park, Wyoming. A two-year-old male was found dead below a power line in early spring about 112 km south of his foster site. Four individuals established breeding territories after becoming adults at distances of 0 km (returned), 28 km, 48 km, and 560 km from their release sites. The greatest longevity recorded was a seven-year-old male fostered to a wild pair in 1976 and discovered paired with a wild female at an eyrie 30 km away in 1983. He was killed when he struck a single phase power line crossing a meadow near the eyrie. (See Figure 2 of Burnham et al. Chapter 53 for map of Peregrine recoveries described above.)

DISCUSSION AND SUMMARY

A population decline in Colorado was first suggested by Enderson (1969a, 1969b) when he found only seven territories occupied out of 15 known. Annual breeding inventories conducted since 1972 continued to document site vacancies in spite of efforts that nearly doubled the number of recorded territories.

Fostering obscured productivity of 56 breeding attempts between 1974-85, but it is possible to obtain an estimate of wild hatch based on hatchability of the 191 eggs that were artificially incubated. Wild pairs would probably have hatched only 46% (80) of their eggs, yielding an average hatched brood size of 1.6 young per pair. Hagar (1969) and Ratcliffe (1980) cited fledging rates of 80% and 82%, respectively, so the adjusted fledged brood size of all pairs would be 1.3 young. This value is similar to the actual observed value of 1.4 young per breeding wild pair.

Between 1974-85, poor wild production was augmented by 275 Peregrines successfully released to the wild. Hacking introduced 125 Peregrines (3.6 young per attempt) into vacant territories and supplemented production of adjacent wild pairs. Fostering fledged 150 young and doubled the expected wild fledging success to 2.7 young per attempt. Both techniques produced nearly identical success.

Although the majority (60%) of the falcons have been released since 1981, 44% (11 of 25 breeding attempts) of breeding pairs in 1984-85 included at least one banded member that was released through fostering or hacking. In three cases both members of the pair were released birds. Apparently released falcons behave as wild-produced falcons and suffer similar mortalities.

Population variables observed in or thought to represent Colorado Peregrines were fed into a computer model developed by J. E. Hines and J. D. Nichols (U. S. Fish and Wildlife Service, Patuxent, Maryland) and based on Grier's (1980a) work. Simulations were made to project population response to poor productivity (0.48 young per occupied site observed for wild pairs between 1972-84) as well as improved productivity (1.25 young per occupied site considered typical for a stable population) that should result from curtailment of environmental organochlorine pesticide use. Population responses to varying intensities of fostering and hacking were also simulated. The model demonstrated that the population would continue to decline to extinction if poor wild productivity continued and no remedial measures were taken. Simulations also suggested that present enhancement actions involving annual operation of six hack sites and fostering to eight wild pairs was the optimum level necessary to achieve the state's recovery goal even if poor reproduction persisted.

Hacking should be used primarily to introduce falcons into vacant breeding territories while fostering should augment productivity of wild females suffering reproductive impairment. Eggshell conditions of individual wild females of known age have demonstrated deterioration, and similar difficulties have already been documented among introduced falcons.

It will be necessary to monitor eggshell thickness of wild breeding females annually and be prepared to augment production when thinning drops below a critical threshold where hatchability is jeopardized. The exact threshold where eggshell thinning causes significant reproductive impairment has not been demonstrated in the wild. Ratcliffe (1980) suggested that Peregrine populations may be considered self-sustaining with 6-10% eggshell thinning. Cade et al. (1971) cited an Aleutian Peregrine population that was reproducing normally with thickness reductions of 8.5%. Fox and Donald (1980) considered a Merlin population "uncontaminated" at 10% thinning, while Temple (1972) concluded that a 9% reduction in eggshell thickness was sufficient to cause a significant reduction in Merlin brood size. Enderson and Berger (1970) observed a 25% decline in breeding success and a 38% reduction in fledged brood size for Prairie Falcons that experienced eggshell thinning in the range of 9-24%. The Colorado archive of Peregrine eggs demonstrates that there is a significant difference in eggshell thickness between eggs deemed hatchable and those that probably were not hatchable in the wild. This suggests that somewhere within the range of 10-14% thinning, a threshold exists where the population is probably not influenced by reduced reproduction.

In order to treat females with reproductive difficulties, they must be individually identifiable through markers, plumage characteristics, or photographs (see Enderson and Craig Chapter 65), and their eggshell condition must be monitored annually. Remedial actions should be taken when eggshells show more than 10% thinning. This approach was tested by comparing average eggshell thicknesses for nine identifiable females (Table 4). Thickness averages within clutches may be variable (Burnham et al. 1984), but they do provide an overview of a particular female's reproductive history. Based on these thickness trends, six females (A, D, E, G, H and I) were designated as probable candidates for fostering in 1985. Female A was known to be more than six years old, and although her eggs showed improvement, their hatchability had declined. Female D was known to have been hatched in 1979 and had been experiencing cumulative eggshell thinning since she laid her first clutch in 1981. The average eggshell thinning of Female E's clutches fluctuated between 12.7-16.7%, and although Female I was only a yearling, her clutch thickness averaged 17.8% below normal.

In 1985, the eggshell condition continued to deteriorate for two females (D and E) although Female D successfully fledged two young.

TABLE 4. Average percent eggshell thinning of clutches laid by individual Peregrines.

Female	1980	1981	1982	1983	1984	1985
A	16.4		14.0	15.3	11.7	11.7
B				4.5	10.0	8.6
C			8.8	11.4	8.6	18.6[a]
D		2.1	8.5	11.7	12.5	14.5
E	13.8	12.7	14.8	16.7	12.8	14.5[a]
F	9.4	7.0	6.1	9.5		13.1
G				12.3	13.9	10.0
H					17.0	16.2
I					17.8	

[a] Clutch average represented by a single egg.

Eggshell thickness improved for one Female (G), and Female I was replaced. Thickness averages remained 10% below normal for all candidate females.

In summary, our experiences in Colorado may have application to other states endeavoring to restore breeding Peregrines. If reproductive difficulties occur after pairs are reestablished, fostering is a viable means of augmenting productivity. Fostering offers the additional advantage of salvaging eggs that would not hatch in the wild, and it may increase heterogeneity of limited populations by introducing captive-produced young and translocating young among wild sites and hack sites. Hacking and fostering may be the only viable methods of sustaining wild breeding Peregrines as long as the pesticide problem persists.

ACKNOWLEDGEMENTS

We appreciate the assistance provided by W. Burnham, C. Sandfort, W. Heinrich, D. Konkel, E. Freienmuth, S. Petersberg, J. Hogan, D. McVean, B. Grebence, R. Meese, and T. Sisk. We could not have undertaken this effort without them.

55 | Peregrine Falcon Management Efforts in California, Oregon, Washington, and Nevada

Brian J. Walton and Carl G. Thelander

After nearly two decades of widespread and extensive Peregrine population declines in the western United States (as elsewhere), the 1973 Endangered Species Act (ESA) officially listed Peregrines as "endangered," thereby establishing a process for the development, implementation and funding of protection and management efforts. The Pacific States American Peregrine Falcon Recovery Team was soon formed to develop objectives and guidelines for future management activities.

Due to the critical nature of the problem, however, Peregrine Falcon management could not be postponed until a formal Recovery Plan was debated by the newly-appointed Recovery Team, developed as a draft plan, reviewed by a host of government agencies, revised, and finally published. While this lengthy process proceeded, selective management programs were begun under cooperative agreements between state and federal agencies responsible for Peregrine management and in conjunction with programs already developed by the Santa Cruz Predatory Bird Research Group (SCPBRG), located at the University of California, Santa Cruz. The SCPBRG is the west coast facility of The Peregrine Fund, Inc.

In California, where the majority of the early Peregrine management efforts were focused, another committee was formed: the California Peregrine Falcon Working Team. For the most part, the Working Team became a subset of the Recovery Team. Having a local committee helped meet the demand for rapid responses to local needs, better use of resources, and more frequent interactions between the team's members.

For this paper, we separate the efforts to recover Peregrine populations into two fundamental management categories: active and passive. We summarize the activities within each category from 1975 to the present for California, Oregon, Washington, and Nevada. We view all of these programs and activities as collaborative efforts of the Recovery Team, the California Working Team, The Peregrine Fund, Inc., numerous individual and institutional cooperators, and the region's resource management agencies: the U. S. Bureau of Land Management, U. S. Fish and Wildlife Service, U. S. Forest Service, California Department of Fish and Game, Washington Game Department, Oregon Department of Fish and Wildlife, and Nevada Department of Fish and Game.

PASSIVE MANAGEMENT ACTIVITIES

A successful recovery program is based on the systematic implementation of a wide range of well-coordinated activities. Not all activities have as direct or as immediate an impact on the population as placing young Peregrines in a nest where eggs have failed to hatch — an active management activity. By contrast, the indirect or passive management activities include such programs as: (1) developing recovery plans and management priorities, (2) conducting baseline inventories of known nesting sites and previously unsurveyed regions, (3) implementing habitat protection programs, (4) developing and distributing public materials and providing nest site attendants at disturbed nesting areas, and (5) monitoring contamination by DDE and other pollutants.

Federal and state endangered species legislation is the vehicle by which active management efforts can be designed, approved, and implemented. As late as the mid-1960s, Peregrines in most states were considered vermin and were unprotected from shooting, take, or destruction of critical habitat. Protection under the federal Migratory Bird Treaty Act was insufficient. State laws lacked protective measures and failed to recognize the population decline until it was nearly too late.

Since 1973, federal legislation (Endangered Species Act) and several state endangered species protective measures have significantly changed the extent to which Peregrines are protected from disturbance, take, and loss of habitat. But what made the law attractive to wildlife biologists was its emphasis on management programs to "recover" the species to a non-endangered status. This was a significant improvement from the mainly ineffective law enforcement-oriented legislation of the past. The goals of the Recovery Plan approved for this region's Peregrines are achievable and the Plan provides the foundation for collaboration by many cooperators.

The status of Peregrines in the region was relatively unstudied until the late Richard Bond conducted an inventory of nesting sites based on his own field work and information provided to him by many cooperators (Bond 1946). His survey provided a baseline of the number and distribution of nesting sites throughout the western United States. For a review of more recent surveys in the region see Walton et al. (Chapter 14) . Using estimates based on Bond's study and more recent surveys, the Recovery Plan for the region defined the primary recovery objective for Peregrines as 120 pairs in California, 30 pairs in Oregon, 30 pairs in Washington, and 5 pairs in Nevada, with reproduction yielding an average of 1.5 fledglings per year for at least five years.

To effectively monitor the progress of the management effort, annual surveys are required to determine nest site occupancy and productivity. This documentation is done by hundreds of volunteers and minimally paid ornithologists, naturalists, and birdwatchers. They are coordinated by a small contingent of researchers (mostly Working Team/Recovery Team members). These surveys document regional population status, the reoccupation of historical nesting sites, and where active management (see below) efforts should be focused. A reporting system for winter and breeding sightings is established. The centralization of this process has resulted in better and more comprehensive data organization and reporting procedures. The fate of many released Peregrines is determined, the program's effectiveness is quantified, and the recovery process is recorded from year-to-year.

Habitat protection efforts take many forms. The ESA of 1973 includes a mechanism for setting aside "critical habitat" on federal lands, if particular criteria are met. But for such a wide-ranging species as the Peregrine, and with so much suitable cliff-nesting habitat in the region, this concept has not proved feasible. Instead, proposed land developments or other habitat alterations on state and federal lands, or those requiring federal permits or funding, are required to make endangered species habitat assessments. This approach at least recognizes when Peregrines or their habitat may be impacted and some form of protection or mitigation can be required of the project. Regardless, since protection of critical habitat is restricted to only certain instances of loss, each year hundreds, possibly thousands, of acres of important nesting or foraging habitat are destroyed or altered.

Many areas already protected as parks, reserves, or refuges indirectly protect important nesting or wintering habitat for Peregrines. In California, one ecological preserve is dedicated to nesting Peregrines. This is Morro Rock Ecological Preserve, on the central coast (San Luis Obispo County). There are nesting Peregrines within Yosemite National Park, Crater Lake National Park, Castle Crags State Park (California) and several others. A significant effort is made each year in these areas to find new pairs and monitor the existing sites. In one instance in northern California, the National Audubon Society raised funds and purchased an active nesting territory when it was learned the site was in danger of being severely impacted by a proposed development project.

State and federal wildlife refuges help protect essential wintering habitat for Peregrines by concentrating their prey (waterbirds); yet, since refuges usually encourage waterfowl hunting, Peregrines are at risk in such areas. Overall, habitat protection targeted specifically at the recovery of Peregrines has been minimal. Fortunately their recovery has not been dependent on it.

Public education about the plight of Peregrines is greater than ever before. While no public information campaigns were planned, the unintentional newspaper and television exposure generated by public interest in the species has been staggering. National television network news programs have each year reported the dramatic rock climbs in Yosemite National Park "where biologists are attempting to help the endangered Peregrine Falcon."

Several feature documentaries and television "articles" have shown the story of the recovery effort and the research supporting it. The success story associated with Peregrines has raised the public consciousness about all endangered species. When future generations review the Peregrine recovery effort, the impact of the program on public education may be one of its most important legacies.

Taking Peregrines illegally in the region has essentially ceased since captive-bred raptors, including Peregrines, are now available to falconers. Illegal capture and the taking of nestlings were never widespread and it is unlikely that such activities significantly contributed to the Peregrine decline except in the early 1970s, when fewer than 10 active nest sites were known in California. A few successful thefts of nestlings at that time were particularly detrimental to the species since they involved a large percentage of the region's annual production. The well-documented incident at Morro Rock in 1971 (McNulty 1972) and a few other lesser known attempts prompted the California Department of Fish and Game to post nest guards at the few known active nest sites. The program was effective and few, if any, Peregrines (in California) were taken illegally from 1973 to the present. This assessment is based on extensive discussions with falconers and co-operators familiar with their activities, both legal and illegal. We believe that illegal activities in the other states of the region were similarly rare, and not extensive enough to cause even local declines.

The nest "guard" program continues, but now with a biological justification. The observers are responsible for obtaining natural history information such as nesting ledge locations, egg laying dates, clutch size, and behavior data. These data are useful to active management activities such as the manipulation of eggs and young at wild nests. Attendants are stationed at only a few of the nesting sites, particularly those with histories of reproductive failure. It is widely accepted that the primary contributing cause of the Peregrine decline in the region is DDE-caused reproductive failure. If Peregrine populations are to fully recover and be self-sustaining, DDE levels must decline to safe levels. Therefore, DDE monitoring is an essential segment of the Peregrine recovery program. The remains of wild-laid eggs hatched in the laboratory provide excellent samples for determining environmental levels. Eggshell thickness measurements and nest productivity are correlated with DDE levels to develop indices that help predict environmental quality. Through the collaborative efforts of Lloyd Kiff (Western Foundation of Vertebrate Zoology for eggshell measurements) and Robert Risebrough (Institute of Marine Sciences, University of California, Santa Cruz for organochlorine analyses), and their colleagues, an extensive data base now exists on eggshell thinning, DDE and other residue levels, and on Peregrine population status. The results of these efforts are presented in numerous scientific papers on the effects of DDE on Peregrine reproduction, population stability, and the probable origins of the pollution.

DDE residue levels remain high in Peregrines nesting throughout the region, but especially those nesting on the central coast of California. Recent findings indicate that several sources are possible (Hunt et. al 1986). Among these are: (1) residual levels in soils, air, and water; (2) contaminants in other legal pesticides; (3) pollutant residues in migrant prey species; (4) illegal pesticide use in the region; and (5) legal use for emergency applications.

Assuming no new sources of DDE turn up, contamination in Peregrines can be expected to gradually decline as residues are removed from the biosphere (R. W. Risebrough pers. comm.). Meanwhile, active management efforts have been developed and successfully applied to at least partially offset the decline in reproductive output attributed to DDE. The following section describes these techniques and their recent implementation in the region.

ACTIVE MANAGEMENT ACTIVITIES

The techniques used in active management programs have been aptly termed by some as "hands-on" activities. They involve actions intended to offset failed nesting attempts, to stabilize local Peregrine populations, or to help stimulate Peregrine recovery over entire regions. In addition to achieving the intended goals, these activities yield new data that add greatly to our knowledge of natality, mortality, prey utilization, habitat requirements and many other aspects of Peregrine nesting ecology and natural history.

To increase wild Peregrine productivity in the region, a small captive breeding population (13 pairs by 1986) was established at the University of California in Santa Cruz by the SCPBRG and The Peregrine Fund, Inc. From 1977-86, 194 young Peregrines were produced and released in California, Oregon, Washington, and Nevada (Table 1). We estimate that from this source at least 50 young per year will be produced and released through 1990.

A second source of young Peregrines for release has been from the collection and hatching in captivity of 387 thin-shelled eggs. These resulted from 118 wild nesting attempts from 1977-86. The selection of nest sites for egg collection is based upon site-specific evaluations of each previous year's data on productivity, eggshell measurements, and pesticide analyses. If a nest site has had a history of failure it becomes a candidate for yearly egg collections.

When it is believed (or specifically determined) that a new and/or young female is present, no egg collections are made. After the first known nesting attempt is completed, eggshells are collected and measured for thickness. DDE residues are analyzed in most instances. Also, periodic observations are made during the nesting attempt to record behavioral data. If egg failure occurs, or if eggshell measurements or pesticide analyses indicate problems, the site is then considered for egg collection in the following nesting season. If the nesting attempt is successful, no egg collections are planned and the monitoring continues into the next year.

This screening and selection process is intended to result in actions being directed at the most chronically failing nest sites. Since the program began, there have been too many candidates each year with data warranting egg collections for our limited resources to handle. As the Peregrine population increases, which is our intent, so will the number of nesting pairs failing to hatch their eggs.

After collection, the eggs are cared for using established techniques developed for captive propagation (Weaver and Cade 1983) and specifically for hatching thin-shelled, wild-laid eggs (Burnham 1983). In most cases, eggs that would be broken or desiccated during incubation by wild falcons can be saved and hatched in the laboratory. All eggs are hatched in incubators regulating temperature and humidity.

In some instances, "dummy" eggs made of mortar but resembling Peregrine eggs are placed in the nest scrape at the time of collection. This technique keeps the adults on a normal incubation schedule until young Peregrines from the laboratory can later be placed into the nest. An alternative is to not replace the wild eggs with dummy eggs, which stimulates the adults to resume copulation and to lay a replacement set of eggs. This usually occurs about 14 days from the date of egg collection. This replacement set of eggs can also be collected for laboratory hatching.

When young are placed in the nest to replace the eggs of either the first or second clutch, they are readily accepted by the adults and are

TABLE 1. Results of Peregrine egg collections and releases of young by the Santa Cruz Predatory Bird Research Group.

	1977	1978	1979	1980	1981	1982	1983	1984	1985	1986	Totals
No. nest sites where eggs collected	0	2	3	7	10	16	21	28	15	16	118
No. eggs collected	0	6	14	27	38	59	66	81	49	47	387
No. hatchable eggs	0	3	11	20	28	38	54	57	42	31	284
No. eggs hatched	0	2	11	15	26	31	41	46	25	22	219
No. young survived	0	2	5	15	25	30	40	43	21	20	201
No. young released	0	2	5	9	21	30	40	37	21	20	185
No. captive-bred young released[a]	2	0	0	0	6	20	30	44	42	50	194
Total released	2	2	5	9	27	50	70	81	63	70	379

[a] Includes young donated by associates.

reared under wild conditions to fledging and dispersal. This process of placing young from the laboratory into wild nests is termed fostering. Each hatchling is fed for a few days in the laboratory and then reared by captive Peregrine Falcons to the optimum release age of 18 days.

The first fostering effort in California occurred in 1977, when two captive-bred young Peregrines from The Peregrine Fund's Cornell University facility were placed in the Morro Rock (San Luis Obispo County) nest site. The eggs had failed and the effort was an emergency response to a crisis. Later, the adult male was shot and died. One of the young Peregrines died in the nest but, assisted by the resourceful nest site observer Merlyn Felton, the adult female successfully fledged the remaining nestling. From his blind, Merlyn was able to release handicapped birds as prey for the female. This enabled her to minimize the amount time spent away from the immediate area of the nest ledge, thus protecting the nestling. This successful demonstration of placing young, captive-bred Peregrines into the failing nests of wild Peregrines ushered in the era of "hands-on" management activities in California and elsewhere in the region.

Of the 387 eggs collected from wild Peregrines during 1977-85, 284 were alive. Of these, 219 hatched and 201 young survived to fledging. We released 185 of these, plus an additional 9 Peregrines donated from private breeding facilities. The balance were kept for breeding stock and to increase genetic diversity in the captive breeding population.

The 185 young Peregrines described above were hatched from eggs whose shells averaged 18% thinner than normal. Those eggs that died in the laboratory owing to thinning and desiccation problems averaged greater than 20% thinning (L. Kiff pers. comm.). Each year, between 15 and 30 nests with females producing thin-shelled or otherwise defective eggs were manipulated in the manner described. The technique effectively reversed what would have been extremely poor reproductive success for each year it was implemented. There seems to be no choice but to continue this effort for those pairs clearly experiencing reproductive problems associated with DDE in their diet.

A second release technique, cross-fostering, has been used at 2-3 sites per year in California since 1982, and later in Washington. On nine occasions, two young Peregrines have been placed in Prairie Falcon nests (Table 2). All 18 young fledged. Two of these Peregrines are known to have courted and copulated with other Peregrines, indicating no adverse behavioral effects from being reared by adults of another species. A female Peregrine cross-fostered into a Prairie Falcon nest in the central Coast Ranges of California paired with a male that was fostered into a remote nesting site in Napa County; they occupied a nest site on the Oakland Bay Bridge. The female was found shot prior

TABLE 2. Peregrine Falcon releases (including several young donated by associates) in California, Oregon, Washington, and Nevada.

	1977	1978	1979	1980	1981	1982	1983	1984	1985	1986	Totals
No. fostered											
California	2	2	5	9	20	26	34	45	30	28	201
Oregon	0	0	0	0	2	2	0	0	0	0	4
No. cross-fostered											
California						4	4	4	2	6	20
Washington						0	2	2	0	0	4
No. hacked											
California					5	12	24	24	20	24	109
Washington					0	3	3	0	3	0	9
Oregon					0	3	3	3	5	3	17
Nevada					0	0	0	3	3	9	15
Total released	2	2	5	9	27	50	70	81	63	70	379

to egg-laying. A male Peregrine cross-fostered into a Prairie Falcon nest in the same region as the female mentioned above paired with a banded female (nest site unknown); they nested on an offshore rock on California's central coast near Morro Rock, San Luis Obispo County. They successfully produced young.

Fostering and cross-fostering each provide the young Peregrines with protection as nestlings and training at fledging and prior to dispersal. The third release technique provides none of these. Hacking is used to attempt to expand the breeding range of Peregrines into areas where they no longer occur. Limited protection is provided by the human hack site attendants, but upon release from the hack box, the young Peregrines are subject to predation and forced to learn hunting skills on their own. As a result, relatively large numbers of Peregrines must be produced and released for this technique to be effective.

By hacking Peregrines at 10-12 sites per year, with 3 young released per hack site, a total of 114 young have been released since 1981 (Table 2). Approximately 73% reached independence. Some dispersed earlier than preferred and their fates were undetermined, but in most cases the young Peregrines were obviously skilled at hunting and survival when last observed. The most common cause of losses was predation by either Great Horned Owls or Golden Eagles.

Considering the obstacles of releasing Peregrines in the absence of parental care, hacking has proven effective at getting nesting Peregrines established in geographic areas otherwise vacant. But the operation of hack sites is a labor-intensive and relatively costly endeavor. A better understanding of Peregrine dispersal and the process of establishing nesting territories may provide insights for planning future hack site releases in relation to one another. As new pairs become established where hacking was used, a shift to fostering young into their nests to increase productivity and nesting density, until an optimal carrying capacity is reached, may be preferable to maintaining a longterm hacking program.

During the yearly process of handling so many eggs and young Peregrines, we have banded nearly every young Peregrine that has been through the laboratory. The number of Peregrine nest sites has increased dramatically in recent years (see Walton et al. Chapter 14). Not all sites were visited each year, nor could the presence of bands always be confirmed or denied. By 1986, however, one or both of the adults nesting at nearly 50% of the nesting sites in California were banded with blue anodized USFWS bands, indicating they were hatched at our facility. There is little doubt that the releases have had a significant cumulative impact on the recovery of Peregrines, especially in California.

Active and passive management efforts in the Pacific states region have increased by over 300 the number of Peregrines fledged over the past decade. The population has increased in California, where the efforts were concentrated, from just two known pairs in 1970 to over 75 pairs in 1986. But the fundamental cause of the decline, DDE and its effects on reproduction, remains a significant threat to the welfare of Peregrines throughout the region. While these management efforts have been effective, vast areas once used as nesting habitat remain vacant and many of the recently established pairs are failing to hatch their own eggs. As long as the original cause of the Peregrine's decline persists, we remain convinced of the need for continuing with an aggressive management approach.

ACKNOWLEDGEMENTS

The Peregrine management program is a cooperative effort by hundreds of dedicated people, and we feel privileged to have been a part of it. Thanks go to the members of the Pacific States American Peregrine Falcon Recovery Team; California's Peregrine Falcon Working Team members; field personnel of the state and federal resource management agencies who have cooperated so enthusiastically over the years; the University of California at Santa Cruz; the Santa Cruz Predatory Bird Research Group and all of its staff and seasonal employees; Dr. J. Rousch; H. Leach and R. Mallette; E. Harrison, L. and J. Kiff, S. Sumida, and J. Jennings of the Western Foundation of Vertebrate Zoology; Dr. R. Risebrough; S. G. Herman; and the staff of The Peregrine Fund, Inc., especially T. Cade. Special thanks to M. Felton, G. Monk, K. Stolzenburg, R. R. Ramey III, C. Himmelwright, L. Aulman, J. Linthicum, and M. Kirven for their dedication in the field; the recovery of Peregrines in the region is largely the direct result of their efforts to climb into nests, collect eggs, place young, and make the essential observations.

56 The Canadian Peregrine Falcon Recovery Program, 1967-1985

Richard W. Fyfe

In many ways the Canadian Peregrine Recovery Program began when Dr. Joseph Hickey organized the first Peregrine conference in Madison, Wisconsin in 1965. Papers presented at the conference indicated that declines in Peregrine populations had occurred concurrently in widely separated areas; however, they failed to demonstrate any conclusive cause for the declines. Pesticides were implicated by data from England (Ratcliffe 1969). Unfortunately, little additional information on pesticides in raptors was available from the rest of Europe, and virtually no data were available on residues in raptors from the United States and Canada.

In addition to the lack of pesticide data, the conference also pointed out the general paucity of data available on raptor populations. This was particularly true for Canada and its Peregrine populations. One result of the conference was a determined effort to initiate population- and pesticide-monitoring in Canada. This was the beginning of the Canadian Peregrine Recovery Program.

Pesticide monitoring of raptor eggs was increased following the Madison Conference. At the same time, a large cross-section of raptor prey was monitored as part of a general pesticide monitoring program. In the prairie region of Canada, monitoring was carried out on Prairie Falcons, Merlins and *Buteo* species. In general, the levels of organochlorine residues were not alarming; however, some individual birds had high levels of organochlorines and mercury (Fyfe et al. 1969, 1976b, Fimreite et al. 1970).

At a second conference of North American raptor specialists held at Cornell University in 1969, it was recommended that pesticide monitoring should be continued and regular five-year surveys should be initiated throughout the range of the Peregrine Falcon in North America.

SURVEYS

The results of the first survey in 1970 clearly indicated the extent of the decline in the F. p. anatum race and paved the way for initial steps to be taken toward the recovery of these birds. It was agreed that North American Peregrine surveys were to be continued at five-year intervals in cooperation with American researchers. Initially, the Canadian Wildlife Service coordinated and, in large part, funded and carried out the 1970 survey with the help of many Canadian and American volunteers. This format has changed with each survey; there has been more funding from the World Wildlife Fund Canada, and increased involvement (including funding) on the part of provincial and territorial agencies.

During the 1970 survey, an attempt was made to check the occupancy of all known historical eyries of F. p. anatum, F. p. tundrius and F. p. pealei. Before the survey's completion it was obvious that F. p. anatum had all but disappeared from its former range south of the boreal forest and east of the Rocky Mountains. Whereas the initial survey had indicated the severity of the decline for the F. p. anatum population, it also provided a baseline for assessing F. p. tundrius and F. p. pealei populations (Cade and Fyfe 1970). The 1975 survey further documented the decline of F. p. anatum and suggested that the F. p. tundrius population was declining to levels such that it was considered threatened by the Canadian government and listed as endangered by the United States government. In contrast, the F. p. pealei population appeared to be relatively stable (Fyfe et al. 1976a). The 1980 survey showed the first indication of localized recoveries in F. p. anatum populations in Alaska and along the Yukon River in the Yukon (White and Fyfe unpubl. ms.). There was also some suggestion of a population increase in F. p. pealei, and it appeared that the F. p. tundrius population had remained more or less stable since the previous survey; there was even a suggestion of a natural recovery in some areas.

For several reasons it was not possible to carry out a 1985 North American Peregrine survey; nevertheless, several provincial and territorial agencies in Canada carried out surveys in 1985. The remainder have indicated they will do so in 1986. The completion of this survey is particularly important, since it is possible that captive-raised and released birds may have supplemented the wild populations.

CAPTIVE BREEDING

The 1970 survey located only one Peregrine eyrie in Canada south of 67°N and east of the Rocky Mountains (Cade and Fyfe 1970). Two additional eyries were later reported south of 60°N, and a few additional *F. p. anatum* eyries were located in the Yukon and Northwest Territories. The tundra and Pacific Northwest Peregrine populations appeared to have declined in some localities, but no evidence of an overall decline was noted. This situation was reported to the 1971 Federal/Provincial Wildlife Directors' annual meeting, where it was decided that the Canadian Wildlife Service (CWS) should take a small number of the remaining *F. p. anatum* young into captivity.

Following the directive of the wildlife directors in 1970, 12 Peregrine nestlings were taken into captivity from eyries in the Mackenzie Valley, southern Yukon, Labrador, and southern Alberta. These young were taken specifically to preserve a sample of the *F. p. anatum* gene pool, to attempt to find methods of breeding them in captivity, and to determine methods for reintroduction should breeding be successful.

Our Wainwright Peregrine Falcon Breeding Facility was established in 1972. It attempted to gradually increase the gene pool of captive Canadian *F. p. anatum* by taking a small number of young from the wild over a period of several years through the cooperation of the provincial and territorial agencies. These were mostly northern boreal forest Peregrines. Several pairs of Prairie Falcons and Gyrfalcons were also obtained, and Merlins, Cooper's Hawks and Sharp-shinned Hawks which were donated to the project were bred successfully. These species were included specifically for use in initial experimental pairing, breeding, and releases. The larger falcons have also been used extensively as foster parents for *F. p. anatum* eggs and young.

The initial breeding success in the Canadian Wildlife Service Breeding Project came in 1972 with captive Prairie Falcons and was followed in 1974 by the first production of *F. p. anatum* Peregrines at Wainwright. Following the breeding success with the Peregrines, production increased steadily until the 1980s (Table 1). In the peak year, 1981, 99 young were fledged. Production then began to fall off, owing principally, we believe, to the age of the breeding birds. In contrast to the other breeding facilities, we relied totally on mating between paired males and females. We believe that if we can get paired birds to mate, it puts less stress on them than artificial insemination; it also requires much less manpower to achieve the same or better results per pair. By 1981, however, our main breeders were averaging about 11 years of age, and while they were still fertile, fewer of their eggs were viable and fewer of their young survived. In 1983, we began to pair young, inexperienced birds or noncopulating egg-layers with older, experienced birds in an attempt to bring more of our young birds into full breeding potential. Our success rate is currently about 50%, with some indication that the older, experienced females are more successful at bringing in the younger males than are the older males with young or

TABLE 1.   Wainwright Peregrine production, 1971–85.

	No. of laying pairs	No. of copulating pairs	Total eggs	No. of fertile eggs	No. of young hatched	No. of young fledged	No. of young released	No. of young held
1971	1	0	8	0	0	0	0	0
1972	1	0	9	2	1	0	0	0
1973	4	2	18	6	1	0	0	0
1974	6	1	32	6	5	4	0	4
1975	7	5	66	26	18	18	6	12
1976	9	6	100	51	43	42	38	4
1977	10	7	106	51	38	38	33	5
1978	7	6	82	54	46	40	33	7
1979	11	10	121	89	45	39	34	5
1980	16	13	174	115	100	90	88	2
1981	17	14	170	127	104	99	92	7
1982	21	16	208	140	93	77	62	15
1983	20	14	208	109	54	50	46	4
1984	22	14	214	120	90	79	78	1
1985	24	12	230	110	81	68	61	7
Totals			1746	1006	719	644	571	73

nonproductive, egg-laying females. As a consequence of the 50% success rate, we have had difficulty maintaining production levels adequate for releases across the country. We are hopeful that production will increase as more of our young birds breed. If not, we will have to resort to artificial insemination, which will present new problems for our project because it is very labor-intensive.

RELEASES

In 1975, the year following our first breeding success with Peregrines, initial experimental releases were attempted with the fostering of captive-bred young to supplement the production of the few remaining wild *F. p. anatum* pairs in northern Alberta (Fyfe et al. 1977). At the same time, we began exchanging captive-bred for wild young to increase the gene pool in our captive flock at Wainwright. These fostering experiments were then followed in 1976 with experimental hacking in the city of Edmonton and at a historical nest site on the north Saskatchewan River. Other experimental releases were subsequently attempted in both rural and urban areas utilizing such methods as cross-fostering, hacking, and multiple-hack releases. In general, all of these methods have proved feasible. The experimental releases were judged to be successful if the released captive-produced Peregrines bred successfully in the wild. The first documented success occurred in Canada in 1977 (Fyfe et al. 1977); it was followed in subsequent years by others in the United States and Germany, as well as in Canada, and most recently, in Sweden.

The Canadian release program began with the use of fostering and hacking techniques, and these have remained the principal methods of release. Although experiments with cross-fostering have been carried out, the technique has been used sparingly. The release program has been well-received in Canada, and the releases have provided excellent publicity for the Peregrine as well as other endangered species.

The Canadian Wildlife Service facility at Wainwright has produced a total of 644 *F. p. anatum*, of which 571 have been released (Table 1); 418 young were hacked at rural and urban release sites, 155 were fostered, and only 15 were cross-fostered. An additional 217 Peregrines (Table 2) have been produced at the four other Canadian facilities involved in the Peregrine Recovery Program; some of these young have been included in Canadian releases. Available data have been included in the discussion of hacking below.

Young to be released are normally sent from the Wainwright breeding facility at about four weeks of age. They are grouped so that they are as close to the same age as possible, and sexes are divided equally (unless a specific request is received for young of a particular sex). To some extent the young are screened to minimize the number of related birds released at any release site. Close communication is maintained with the contact person at each release site in order to coordinate the releases. The birds are shipped by air in specially designed wooden boxes, and the contact person is advised by telephone of flight times and other details to eliminate potential shipping losses

TABLE 2.   Production at Canadian Peregrine breeding facilities through 1985. [a]

Breeding Facility	No. of years operating	No. of young produced
Private		
Black Diamond	14	76
University		
Macdonald	7	33
Saskatoon	10	93
Government		
Yukon	8	15
Wainwright	15	644
Total		861

[a] Includes only those facilities providing birds for the Canadian Peregrine Recovery Program.

and other problems. Our responsibility ends with the shipping, and the releases are carried out by the respective agencies.

Hack releases have been carried out from both rural and urban release sites. In general, sites have been selected using several criteria: location of suitable release areas, availability of prey, availability of suitable nest ledges, a preliminary assessment of avian predators, and relative proximity to documented historical nest sites of Peregrines. Urban releases have been carried out since 1974 and have been popular because of the excellent opportunity for public relations, the relative absence of predators, and the increased potential for observations on any returning birds. It is of interest to note that the success rates of urban and rural releases are almost identical, with fledging rates of 88% and 89%, respectively (Table 3). This suggests that perhaps the urban advantages are offset to some extent by misadventures (injuries at fledging, hitting glass windows in office towers, etc.). Table 3 includes data on all birds lost and retrapped. "Lost" refers to the 47 birds which disappeared early in the releases plus those known to have been killed by predators or which died from other causes. The 12 retrapped birds include those retrapped and held over the winter for future release, and those retrapped for breeding projects or taken back into captivity because of injury.

The best data available have been collected during hack releases. These data are summarized and the means tabulated in Table 4. The average age of introduction into the hack box varied from 31.5-33 days for different types of releases. Average confinement in the box varied from 11.5-16.3 days (from the day of introduction until the day the door or bars were removed). The resulting average age of release varied from 43.8-48 days. Following release, the young remained in the area and were observed at the release site an average of 22.9-27.7 days for the different categories; their average age at departure was 66.7-75.4 days.

As more provincial agencies have participated in the release program, the role of the CWS has changed to that of a production facility

TABLE 3.   Peregrine hack releases in Canada, 1976-85.

	Rural	Urban
No. of sites	10	10
No. of releases	62	49
No. of birds	234	184
No. fledged (%)	206 (88%)	165 (89%)
No. lost	28	19
No. retrapped	10	2

TABLE 4. Age, confinement, and release date averages for Canadian Peregrines hacked through 1985.

	n	Age placed in hack box (days)	No. of days confined	Age at release (days)	No. of days remained after release	Age at departure (days)
Single release	38	33.0	15.5	48.0	23.2	71.2
Multiple release	73	31.5	12.7	44.3	25.1	69.4
Urban[a]	49	31.8	16.3	47.7	27.7	75.4
Rural	62	32.3	11.5	43.8	22.9	66.7

[a] Urban locations: Arnprior, Brockville, Calgary, Edmonton, Hull, Montreal, Saskatoon, Regina, Toronto, Winnipeg.

providing birds for release. The CWS conducts releases only in those areas where the particular provincial agency does not wish to be involved. Consequently, releases in Canada are carried out mostly by provincial wildlife agencies. For the most part, this arrangement has worked very well; the parties involved have shared data, and it is doubtful that either the CWS or the provincial agencies could have succeeded independently. The major disadvantages have been the absence of experienced personnel to train and direct the biologists, technicians, and students involved in the releases, and the lack of follow-up studies. Nevertheless, the overall response has been positive, with all provinces and territories and some private agencies cooperating in the program.

PESTICIDE MONITORING

Pesticide monitoring of raptors has been carried out in Canada since 1966 and has been expanded in conjunction with the population surveys. However, because of the endangered status of the Peregrine, initial samples consisted almost entirely of dead young or addled eggs.

Extensive pesticide monitoring of raptors was carried out in the prairie region during the late 1960s and early 1970s, and was expanded to include several *Buteo* and *Falco* species and other raptors breeding in the grasslands. Elevated DDE residue levels were the norm in egg samples of Peregrines and Merlins (Fyfe et al. 1976a, Fyfe unpubl. ms.). Considerably lower levels were found in eggs of Prairie Falcons, and most other species monitored had relatively insignificant residue levels (Fyfe et al. 1969, Fyfe unpubl. ms.).

A longterm ecosystem monitoring project was initiated with Prairie Falcons and Merlins as indicator species. They were monitored each year on a random basis to provide an index against which to measure changes in the residue levels in the prairie region. This project was of particular importance to the Peregrine Recovery Program because it provided an indication of residue trends across the prairies, and helped to determine the success of releases. In general, prey species were monitored only coincidentally, e.g., where they were included in other programs such as the specific and extensive monitoring of the effects of seed treatments on wildlife.

When experimental releases of Peregrines began, specific monitoring of their prey was carried out in several potential release areas in an attempt to determine the relative pesticide levels the newly introduced Peregrines would encounter. Also, following the successful release and reestablishment of captive-raised Peregrines in the wild, specific monitoring was carried out to determine what levels had accumulated in the released birds. The results were not encouraging, as it was clear that these birds continued to be exposed to high residue levels of organochlorines in the wild (Fyfe et al. unpubl. ms.). Data from egg analyses suggested that these birds were accumulating significant residue levels. The residue values were comparable to those described by Peakall et al. (1975) as sufficient to affect reproduction. Since the use of organochlorines had been severely restricted in Canada and the United States in the early 1970s, it appeared that the Peregrines and/or their prey were accumulating the residues on the Peregrines' wintering grounds and/or migration routes.

In 1979, the CWS initiated a cooperative project aimed at locating the primary sources of contamination in prey on the wintering grounds. CWS researchers planned to work with colleagues in each of several countries to be monitored. Ten samples of each of ten species of northern migrants were to be collected on their arrival in the wintering areas and then again just prior to their return migration. In addition, provision was made to collect and analyze a limited number of samples of resident species of concern to our coworkers in each country. It was a relatively simple matter deciding which areas should be monitored since many were known through band recoveries of wintering Peregrines. Samples from four countries (Surinam, Peru, Ecuador and Costa Rica) have been analyzed; those from Panama should be analyzed in the current year, and two countries (Mexico and Venezuela) have still to be visited.

BANDING

The CWS coordinated a major raptor banding project in conjunction with the pesticide monitoring and population surveys throughout the Canadian prairies and northern regions. This very successful program was largely performed by interested volunteers, and was particularly significant because it concentrated on the banding of nestlings just prior to fledging. As a result, the age of every recovery was known and could be related to distance moved and direction from the original nest site.

In the 1970s, the banding of birds of prey was well-received at all levels, both by the public and government agencies. In the Canadian prairie region, the CWS coordinated a number of amateur banders who specialized in banding birds of prey. For several years this group annually banded in excess of 1000 birds of prey (Fyfe and Banasch 1981). Unfortunately, this group had to be disbanded owing to changes in the permit system and more rigorous regulations relative to banding.

LAW ENFORCEMENT

With the knowledge of the severity of the decline in Peregrine numbers, one of the principal concerns was the potential loss of birds through illegal activities. Unfortunately, the widespread attitude that birds of prey were pest species had resulted in little or no concern for these birds by enforcement agencies. Consequently, one of the first tasks of raptor biologists was that of educating the public, wildlife agencies and enforcement personnel. CWS biolgists became heavily involved in conducting workshops, adult courses, and field training for the public as well as for provincial and territorial enforcement and technical personnel.

At the same time, CWS biologists encouraged cooperation between enforcement personnel and raptor enthusiasts in an effort to achieve an information network to assist in protecting the birds. This approach was well received, and for several years there was excellent cooperation among the public, enforcement officers and biologists. A measure of the extent of this cooperation is shown by the fact that the only serious illegal activities in the prairie region came from people from other regions.

Unfortunately, a few species of birds of prey have become very valuable in today's international market. Attracted by their value, some entrepreneurs have been totally unscrupulous in their attempts to obtain these birds from the wild. Such activities have resulted in a series of investigations by enforcement agencies in an attempt to enforce the regulations. Their attempts have been widely publicized in what is referred to as "Operation Falcon." A few individuals were caught and given the opportunity to plea bargain. In so doing, these people mentioned the names of most individuals and organizations working with birds of prey. Virtually everyone working with raptors, including those only remotely connected, suddenly found they had been named as suspects on official lists circulated in North America and Europe.

Members of the CWS staff were not exempt, and innuendos resulting from hearsay precipitated an investigation and internal audit of the Wainwright facility in which every egg, chick, and bird ever held had to be accounted for. I am pleased to report that in 17 years of records, only three discrepancies were found, all of which were explained satisfactorily. I do not question that this had to be done; however, the resulting personal trauma experienced by those being investigated was most unfortunate, and time and money was diverted from our primary mission, the recovery of the Peregrine Falcon.

Peregrines and other birds of prey stand to suffer immeasurably because everyone's credibility has been under question, and the entire framework of raptor research and conservation has been shaken. This was very evident at the Sacramento conference. I am concerned that it will take years to repair the damage that has been done and still more time to reestablish the trust and cooperation between raptor workers and enforcement personnel. Yet this rapprochement must be accomplished for the sake of raptor conservation; biologists and researchers need enforcement personnel to enforce the laws which protect these birds and, although they do not appear to understand it, law enforcement officials need the biologists and researchers to provide the necessary information to protect the resource.

SUMMARY

It is now 20 years since the Madison Conference. In some areas, the results of our work have been truly dramatic and have exceeded most expectations. The North American Peregrine surveys were initiated in 1970 (Cade and Fyfe 1970) and carried out in both the United States and Canada in 1975 and 1980 (Fyfe et al. 1976a, White and Fyfe unpubl. ms.). The initial survey had indicated the severity of the decline for F. p. anatum, but merely provided a baseline for assessing the F. p. tundrius and F. p. pealei populations.

The management results have been generally encouraging, and the captive-breeding program particularly so. Several successful breeding attempts of captive-bred birds in the wild have been documented; several others have been recorded but not reported to us. Equally encouraging is the fact that released birds have been reported in subsequent years at every release site. However, one of the disappointments of the program has been the relatively few reports of successful breeding in relation to the number of releases and sightings. This can be explained in part by the lack of observers and the huge area for potential nesting in Canada. However, I believe the real problem is that the necessary follow-up has simply not been done. In my opinion, better follow-up procedures are absolutely essential if we are to evaluate the success of the Canadian program.

Perhaps the most important pesticide monitoring project for the Peregrine Recovery Program was the monitoring of terrestrial ecosystems. This project monitored organochlorine and heavy metal residues in the prairie ecosystem over a 10-year period, providing background data on pesticide residues in our ecosystem (these data are currently being analyzed and a report will be published in the near future). This program provided the information necessary for decisions relative to initiating or continuing Peregrine release projects in the prairie region.

One of the most successful monitoring programs has been the monitoring of Peregrine prey on their wintering grounds. The effort has been successful owing in large part to the excellent cooperation between the scientists from Canada and their counterparts in the host countries. All samples received to date have been analyzed, and it is expected that these data will be published in the near future.

CONCLUSIONS

As reported at Sacramento, the Peregrine Falcon has made dramatic recoveries in some areas, particularly in Great Britain, Switzerland, and parts of France and Germany. There have also been dramatic recoveries of Peregrines in southern Alaska and along the Yukon and Porcupine rivers in the Yukon. F. p. tundrius in the Northwest Territories and northern Quebec appears to be making a somewhat less dramatic recovery, but is doing well in arctic Alaska. There have been some Peregrine pairs reestablished in the eastern United States and in northern Alberta. Boreal Peregrines appear to be holding their own in the Mackenzie District of the Northwest Territories, as are some F. p. anatum populations in the western United States.

Unfortunately, populations remain depressed in other areas, including much of Scandinavia, northern Europe and North America. Over much of the range of F. p. anatum in Canada there has been little improvement, and the Peregrine is still considered endangered. Limited data show poor natural reproduction and medium to high residue levels in eggs which have been sampled.

The Peregrine program has come a long way toward achieving its goals; nevertheless, it has been difficult maintaining the necessary level of support. Clearly we still have a way to go. One major obstacle in Canada continues to be the absence of a National Recovery Plan for this species. Such a plan has been in the works for the past several years, but it has not been totally acceptable to all agencies and is currently being revised once again. This plan is urgently needed to provide goals and guidelines which can be applied across Canada.

ACKNOWLEDGEMENTS

I would like to acknowledge the assistance of my associates, H. Armbruster, P. and H. Trefry, U. Banasch and S. Berry, for helping me to assemble the data presented here. Also, my thanks to those who provided us with their hacking data and who have helped to make the Peregrine program a success.

57 | The Use of Falconry Techniques in the Reintroduction of the Peregrine

Lynn W. Oliphant and W. J. P. Thompson

The release of captive-bred Peregrines to supplement dwindling or regionally extinct populations began just over a decade ago. In areas where Peregrines still nest, these young have sometimes been fostered to wild pairs to supplement natural production. In areas where no Peregrines were nesting, young have been cross-fostered to other species (Prairie Falcons or Gyrfalcons in North America), or more commonly, "hacked" from artificial nest sites (Sherrod et al. 1981). Hacking, the controlled release of young falcons from an artificial eyrie, was developed centuries ago by falconers as a means of building flight skills and strength prior to actual training. It has proved to be a viable reintroduction method as evidenced by the excellent success of the Peregrine restoration program in eastern North America (Barclay and Cade 1983, Cade and Hardaswick 1985, and other chapters in this book).

Hack site attendants fulfill the role of surrogate parents, by providing food prior to the release and for several weeks after the Peregrines fledge. The ability of humans to protect and teach newly fledged falcons is severely limited, however, in comparison to an adult pair of falcons. Mortality of hacked Peregrines both during the hack period and during their first year of independence is normally as high if not higher than that of naturally fledged young. The majority of losses during hacking can be attributed to young not orienting to the hack site and drifting away prior to developing hunting skills, and also to direct losses from predation, primarily by Great Horned Owls.

The mortality for Peregrines during their first year of life is thought to be between 50-70% (Enderson 1969b, Newton 1979). The mortality of birds after their first year is substantially reduced: 20-30% or possibly even lower owing to the bias in banding recovery estimates (see Newton 1979). A total of 775 Peregrines were released in the eastern United States by The Peregrine Fund between 1975-85. In

1985, 38-40 pairs of returning Peregrines were located; 25 of these pairs were known to have attempted nesting (Cade and Dague 1985). The number of Peregrines that attempted to breed represents slightly less than 10% of the total number of birds previously released that would have been two years or older by 1985 (50 out of 534). Although there may have been a considerable number of returning Peregrines that were not seen, it is likely that 70-80% of hacked Peregrines do not live long enough to attempt breeding. Most of this mortality, as in many other species, occurs during the first year of life.

Peregrine releases in Saskatchewan have been handled in a different manner from most of the rest of North America. The reintroduction effort in Saskatchewan has been coordinated by the Saskatchewan Cooperative Falcon Project (SCFP), a rather unique group with input from the Western College of Veterinary Medicine, the wildlife branch of Saskatchewan Parks and Renewable Resources, and the Saskatchewan Falconry Association. Beginning in 1974 with an experimental hack of Prairie Falcons, a variety of falconry techniques were used in an attempt to develop techniques to reduce the losses of birds during the hack and throughout their first year. This paper describes the results of these experiments.

TAME-HACKING

Losses during the hack period owing to predation by Great Horned Owls and disorientation soon after release can be circumvented by a modification of the hacking procedure termed "tame-hacking." Young falcons were taken from their parents at about the same age as for a "wild" hack (4-5 weeks old). Instead of being placed directly into a hack box, however, the young falcons were conditioned to human presence and trained to feed off a lure, which was associated with a whistle. These birds were outfitted with jesses and taken to the hack site just prior to fledging. They could have been placed in a hack box and hacked from a suitable building or camp, but we used a trailer. The birds were given complete freedom during the day but were recalled to the lure (to which a dead quail was tied) each evening. As each bird came in, one lure was thrown down next to a falcon's block (perch). Leashes were attached to the birds while they were eating, and then tied to the blocks. When each bird finished eating it was picked up and taken into a suitable enclosure for the night. In the morning the birds were released again for the day. The birds were generally called to the lure for a half quail when they were taken out in the morning and then allowed to fly off after feeding.

We have tame-hacked only one Peregrine, but we have routinely used this technique to hack other falcons, including 5 Prairie Falcons, 5 Gyrfalcons, 2 Peregrine-Gyrfalcon hybrids and 2 Merlins. The majority of these birds were tame-hacked a short distance from conventionally-hacked Peregrines. Out of the 15 tame-hacked birds, only one was lost during the hack. This bird, a female Gyrfalcon, disappeared after three weeks at hack and was subsequently recovered in excellent shape a week later about 5 km away. In contrast to our 100% survival rate of tame-hacked falcons, we experienced a 14% (6 out of 42 birds) loss in "wild-hacked" Peregrines released in the same location during the same years. The majority of these losses were to Great Horned Owls.

We feel there are two main drawbacks to tame-hacking. First there is the additional effort involved and the need for hack site attendants that are fully qualified falconers. Of more concern is the increased potential for birds being shot that have associated closely with humans and been provided with food. Since the majority of losses to owls occur in the first few days after fledging, a modified tame-hack may solve this potential problem. It would entail shifting the birds to a conventional hack and stopping all human contact after their flight skills were relatively well developed (1-2 weeks). Negative conditioning to humans could then be carried out at a distance from the hack site. Tame-hacking in this way may be a viable method for releasing Peregrines under certain conditions, particularly in areas where they are preyed upon by owls.

HOLDOVER OF HACKED PEREGRINES

Between 1977-83, 20 Peregrines were retrapped after a conventional hack of 2-4 weeks. To facilitate trapping, the birds were habituated to feeding from a hack board (to which their food was tied) as soon as they had become oriented to the site. After a while, the hack board was relocated to a site conducive to trapping. The Peregrines were trapped with a bow net operated from a blind about 10 m from the hack board. Feeding was sometimes skipped the day before trapping was started to ensure that the birds were eager. Birds left at hack longer than about three weeks became increasingly difficult to catch, and sometimes required trapping techniques used for wild birds.

After trapping, the falcons were jessed and hooded and transferred to cooperating falconers as soon as possible. Each falconer signed a contract with the SCFP, modified from the loan agreement drafted by The Peregrine Fund, Inc., which stipulated that the birds must be flown with telemetry gear. Special permits were obtained through the cooperation of the Canadian Wildlife Service; these allowed the Peregrines to be flown on migratory birds all year. The survivorship of Peregrines handled in this manner was substantially greater (Table 1) than that of those in the wild. Only four of these Peregrines were lost while being flown; even if one assumes that all four died, the first-year

TABLE 1.   Fate of 20 Peregrines recaptured following 2-4 week hacking period.

	Frequency	%
No. killed or died while held by falconers	3/20	15
No. lost while being flown	4/20	20
No. released in following year at hack site	13/20	65
No. males released in spring that remained at site	2/3	67
No. females released in spring that remained at site	0/4	0
No. males released in summer that remained at site	2/2	100
No. females released in summer that remained at site	3/4	75

mortality rate was reduced to 35%, about half that of the wild population.

These falconry-trained Peregrines were released at one year of age during the following spring or summer. The actual method of release ranged from simply letting the birds fly from the fist near the hack site to tethering the birds next to the hack site for periods of a week or more. The manner in which the birds were released did not appear to be as important as the time of year (Table 1). All Peregrines released in the summer (usually early July) remained at the hack site for a minimum of several weeks with the exception of one female that was sent to a release site in Alberta rather than being released at the site from which she was hacked. Among the birds released in the spring (usually in April), there was a big difference in the site affinity between males and females. Two out of three males remained at the site for at least a week, while none of the four females remained for more than 24 hours.

Although these birds had not been back to their original release area since being trapped the previous summer, site recognition was sometimes nothing short of amazing. They often flew directly to the hack box, and in several cases, especially when a male and female were released together, courtship activities ensued. Bowing, "eechipping" and nest ledge displays occurred, sometimes within minutes of being released even though the birds had never before been observed to display or vocalize. Again, the males showed a much greater tendency to display than the females. All released birds quickly reverted to a wild state and were generally unapproachable within a week.

Although the details on every released Peregrine would consume far too much space, we would like to transmit a feeling for the potential of this release method by describing the case histories of two birds. Samara was trapped at our release site on a large marsh in the Qu'Appelle Valley in the summer of 1981. She turned out to be a superb duck killer in her first year. She was released at the hack site the following summer with a group of newly fledged Peregrines and later another one-year-old female. She did not interact with the young birds very much and was not aggressive even when she had food and was harassed. She usually took a quail from the hack box and flew over to a far hill where she spent most of the day. She was still at the hack site when the hack was finished, and we decided to retrap her for a second-year holdover. She was again flown on wild quarry daily for the next year. The following spring she was recalled to the project in Saskatoon for potential release in case a male showed up at the hack site. When none did we decided to train Samara to feed young. We had previously been successful in getting falcons that had never bred to feed young (including an injured one-year-old passage male). Samara was slow to start, but after one week was feeding a group of four-week-old Peregrines that were slated for release. The young birds were then placed in a hack box at the release site and Samara was released. She flew immediately to the hack box and remained within a few hundred meters of it for the remainder of the hack. She fed the young sporadically if they came to her and begged, but seldom actively took food to them. At the conclusion of the hack, she was again retrapped to be flown.

In the spring of 1984, the three-year-old Samara and an immature male trapped from the 1983 hack were taken to the release site and turned loose. Within minutes the two birds were courting in the hack box and during that day Samara actively defended the site against other raptors in the area. The following morning only the male was present, and we suspect that Samara was killed by Great Horned Owls that were found nesting about a kilometer away. The male remained at the site for several weeks.

In that same year a male that had been retrapped the previous year was released at our urban release site in Saskatoon. Tinker was a very strong bird that successfully took quarry ranging from a European Starling to several full-grown Mallards. Just prior to release he was on the verge of being out of control when flown. He often had to be pursued using radio telemetry after chasing ducks on passage. Beginning in late April he was tethered in front of the hack box for several hours every few days. On the evening of 2 March he was outfitted with a transmitter and left in the open hack box with a dead quail. He remained in the hack box most of that night but by 0700 he was gone, and we were unable to pick up a signal within 20 km of the city. He was never observed at the hack site the rest of that year.

The following spring (1985) Tinker returned and began roosting on the side of the building where the hack box was located. By mid-May no female had shown up, and we decided to perch at the hack box the only female Peregrine available for release. This bird had been injured at an urban hack site in Manitoba the previous year and was being flown to get her in shape for release. Although immature, she had been moulted during the winter using thyroid and artificial lights, and so was in adult plumage. Tinker responded to her with bowing, "eechipping," high speed stooping over the female while "eechipping" and eventually a nest ledge display. The female did not return his ardor and remained defensive even after she was released. The male adopted and fed young that were put in the hack box and vigorously defended the site. He attacked the female when she was brought back to the site in a last attempt to form a pair bond.

We have released three Peregrines at sites other than those at which they were originally hacked. One female from our 20 retrapped birds was released at a site in southern Alberta and was the only bird of our summer releases that did not remain at the hack site. Likewise the immature female released for Tinker and a two-year-old male from Alberta that was released in the summer at our marsh site in southern Saskatchewan did not seem to orient well to the hack sites, although they both remained in the general area for several days. We feel the difficulty experienced by The Peregrine Fund in attempting to provide a male for Scarlett, the famous female Peregrine that took up residence in downtown Baltimore, was owing, at least in part, to the fact that none of the five males released was originally hacked from that site. The one released male that formed a pair bond with Scarlett was a two-year-old male flown by Dan Cover after being retrapped at a hack site. We feel confident that the success of these releases would have been higher if a male that had fledged from the Baltimore site had been retrapped and flown prior to release.

CONCLUSIONS AND RECOMMENDATIONS

Tame-hacking appears to be of rather limited use except with special problem hacks, such as those that experience heavy predation. Retrapping wild-hacked Peregrines, on the other hand, appears to offer several advantages as a reintroduction technique. Mortality losses during the first year are substantially reduced, with about twice as many birds surviving to one year of age. Based on our experience, we recommend that Peregrines be released during the summer at the same site they were originally hacked from in conjunction with a group of recently fledged falcons. Peregrines released in this way are almost certain to remain at the hack site, potentially increasing site recognition and affinity and also allowing a controlled transition back to the wild state. These falcons are essentially getting a second hack and are returned to the wild with a full year of hunting experience at a time of good weather and high prey density. We feel this combination of factors promotes high survival.

There are other advantages to the holdover technique. Birds are always readily available for release to pair with single birds that have returned to a breeding site. We have also found these birds to be very useful in straightening out problem hacks where the released young failed to orient to the hack site. A tethered bird will bring them in, often within minutes.

The bottom line, however, is the successful establishment of breeding pairs in the wild. Our figures indicate a potential doubling of effectiveness over current approaches: twice the number of Peregrines survive for a given level of production and release, although much greater effort is involved. It is difficult at the present time to assess the overall effectiveness of this technique (as compared to a conventional hack) owing to the limited number of birds we have handled and the high potential for returning birds to disperse and not be located. This is especially true of our marsh site, from which the majority of our birds have been retrapped. We feel that on the basis of the potential demonstrated, a larger-scale trial of this technique should be carried out.

ACKNOWLEDGEMENTS

We thank the Canadian Wildlife Service and Saskatchewan Parks and Renewable Resources for their cooperation with this project and the members of the Saskatchewan Falconry Association who helped with the hacking and/or flew Peregrines for the project: D. Bush, T. Donald, B. Goodhope, D. Guthormsen, J. Jenkins, B. Rafuse, E. Ring, and A. Schmidt.

58 | Reintroducing the Peregrine Falcon in Sweden

Peter Lindberg

The rapid decline of the Peregrine in southern Fennoscandia in the 1960s and 1970s raised the issue of captive breeding as a possible way to reinforce the population. Local extirpation seemed impending in southwestern Sweden, where the known population declined from 65 pairs in 1955 to just a few pairs in the mid 1970s. In the 1960s, the population probably passed a bottleneck that made an increase less probable, if populations were not supplemented with birds from other regions. Nest guarding activities, nest site protection and experiments with double-clutching (Lindberg 1981) perhaps temporarily arrested the decline, but only a few active pairs remained.

A captive breeding program was initiated in 1974 by the Swedish Society for the Conservation of Nature. The project should serve as a gene bank and produce falcons for release following models by Cade and Temple (1977) and Fyfe (1976).

The main reintroduction area is southwestern Sweden (ca. 15,000 km²) and the ultimate goal is to restore a self-maintaining population of about 30 pairs (50% of the pre-1955 population, Lindberg 1983).

The first successful breeding in captivity in Sweden occurred in 1979, and the first hacking took place in 1982. This paper presents results through 1985 and some original data from a private Peregrine project in Denmark.

MATERIAL AND METHODS

Source of Birds. — The captive stock was established with 32 F. p. *peregrinus* collected as downies and 10 as hurt fledglings from both cliff and bog nests in Sweden, Norway, Finland and Scotland. During the years, over 100 falcons have been handled within the program, and the stock consisted of 47 falcons in 1985 (Table 1).

Most of the nestlings collected in the wild were placed together as pairs in breeding chambers at an age of 3-6 weeks. Falcons from

619

TABLE 1. Origin of the captive Peregrine population in 1985.

	No. of males	No. of females	Totals
Southern Sweden	10	7	17
Northern Sweden	4	1	5
Norway	3	4	7
Northern Finland	3	8	11
Scotland	4	3	7
All regions	24	23	47

different nests in the same region were paired. As no other type of selection took place, the pairing was almost random. Several birds were also hatched in incubators, and most of these were hand-fed with siblings before being fostered to pairs in captivity. Birds produced in captivity were paired at an age of 2-5 months. A few birds were imprinted and used for artificial insemination. All others had little human contact.

In Denmark, a private Peregrine project (A. Pedersen) was started in the late 1970s. The falcons produced within this project were offered to the West German falconry market. The breeding stock was legally established with falcons selected from European and North American breeding programs; in 1985 there were 12 birds (7 F. p. peregrinus, 3 F. p. brookei, 2 F. p. pealei).

Facilities. — The birds were kept in outdoor aviaries, with 2-5 cages at six different localities in southern Sweden (latitude 57°N) and at one locality in northern Denmark. Details of cage construction were given by Lindberg (1983). Each cage usually covered an area of 25-35 m² with a maximum height of 5 m. Walls were wood and roofs were of plastic-coated wire netting with a 5 × 5 cm mesh. Two or three alternative nest ledges were placed in each cage. The ground was usually covered with gravel or with grass or small bushes. An observation and entrance corridor was built between cages and sometimes divided into two levels. The lower level provided access to cages and food shelves, and the upper was sound-insulated and equipped with one-way mirrors. To prevent food from freezing in winter, food shelves were heated by a 60-watt lamp. Falcons were exposed to natural temperature and light regimes, and some cages were equipped with TV systems so the falcons could be monitored without disturbance.

In Denmark, Peregrines were kept in a large breeding barn with 12 breeding chambers. Each chamber covered an area of 17 m² with a height of 3.9 and 3.0 m on the sides. The nest ledges were situated in boxes placed in the ceiling of an observation and access corridor. Nests were easy to check and accessible for egg collection or fostering of young. The walls were wooden, their insides painted white to reflect more light. The roof was of plastic-coated wire netting and the ground was filled with gravel. Branch perches and food shelves were covered with coco fiber mats.

Food. — The Swedish Peregrines were mainly fed with thawed 4-5-week-old chickens produced by the project. In the breeding season the Peregrines were provided with fresh 2-4-week-old domestic chickens supplemented with feral pigeons and Japanese Quail. Food was given several times a day to stimulate food transferring activity (cf. Wrege and Cade 1977). Thawed food was supplemented with vitamins and bone calcium powder (trademark Kafomavit), which may have given better eggshell quality for females producing several clutches.

Egg Handling and Incubation Techniques. — All females except first-year layers were subject to double clutching after a week of natural incubation, or eggs were taken fresh. Most eggs from the Swedish facilities were transported to Denmark in a portable incubator operated at 36.5°C and 55% relative humidity.

A total of 412 eggs (158 from the Swedish program, 181 from the Danish program, and 73 from wild Peregrines) were handled between 1979-85. Length (L), breadth (B), weight (W) and eggshell thickness were measured for most eggs. Length and breadth were taken with an accuracy of 0.01 mm using a dial caliper. Volume (V) was calculated by the formula:

$$V = LB^2k$$

where $k=0.51$ (Hoyt 1979). The general k-value given by Hoyt (1979) seems quite accurate for falcon eggs tested for volume calculations by sinking a number of eggs in water. Fresh egg weights (W) were calculated by the formula given by Burnham (1983):

$$W = k_W(LB^2)$$

where $k_W=0.0005474$. Fresh egg weight may also be calculated as $V \times 1.08$.

Most eggs were incubated in forced air incubators (trademark Schumacher, West Germany) using an air temperature of 36.8°C (Lindberg 1981). Each egg was weighed regularly to calculate daily weight loss. We attempted to follow a total egg weight loss of 15% estimated from time of laying to time of pipping. A small sample of eggs that did not loose moisture as required was manipulated by sanding the eggshell over the aircell (cf. Burnham 1983, Heck and

Konkel 1983). All eggs were turned by hand following recommendations of Heck and Konkel (1983). Pipped eggs were removed to a hatcher with a similar temperature as the incubator and a relative humidity of 50-60%.

Hatched young were placed in a forced-air brooder. Most young were returned to foster parents at an age of about 10 days. The remaining young were hand-fed, together with siblings, before being released or taken to the captive breeding stock.

Release Sites and Release Techniques. — A number of historical breeding cliffs in southwestern Sweden were selected for hacking use. By concentrating the release sites in regions where Peregrines still breed, one increases the possibility for future pair formation. We intended to release Peregrines to natural environments, thus excluding city-releases or artificial structures such as hacking towers (cf. Barclay and Cade 1983). Young Peregrines were placed in a hackbox at an age of about four weeks (Sherrod et al. 1981). They were provided food in the hackbox for about 4-6 weeks after release. Wild pairs were used as foster parents and given a maximum brood size of four.

All birds were ringed with a normal metal ring and a color anodized metal ring (height 20 mm, with large engraved figures). Only one color per year was used. The color rings were placed on different legs of captive and wild-produced birds.

RESULTS AND DISCUSSION

Egg-laying Females. — A general problem in Peregrine propagation is that only about half of the mature birds will breed. An important variable for developing reproductive competence is that the young are fed in close association with siblings (Cade and Fyfe 1978). Of less importance is whether young falcons are reared by humans or adult falcons.

Four of our best pairs were caught in the wild as nestlings and had very little contact with humans. The females had the same partners from the beginning. Among low-producing females we changed partners 2-3 times.

Of 14 females older than four years, 12 laid eggs by 1985 but only 7 produced fertile eggs, 5 by natural copulation and 2 by artificial insemination. Average age at first laying was 4.1 years (Table 2).

Age of maturity may vary for different subspecies, sex and possibly also for wild-caught and captive-produced birds (Cade and Fyfe 1978, Burnham et al. 1983). F. p. peregrinus and F. p. pealei appear to mature 1-2 years later than many other races (Burnham et al. 1983). The stock of six females (different subspecies) kept at the Danish project began laying on average at 2.7 years; however, this sample may not be representative as the females were selected as being "good pairs."

TABLE 2. Numbers of eggs laid in the Swedish and Danish Peregrine breeding programs. HY = hatching year.

	S4	S5	S8	S9	S11	S14	S18	S23	S22	S34	S36	S61	Totals
Sweden													
1975	HY	HY											0
1976			HY	HY	HY								0
1977													0
1978	0	0	0	3	0	HY	HY						3
1979	0	0	0	8	0	0	0						8
1980	0	0	0	7	0	0	8	HY	HY				15
1981	4	0	0	7	4	7	8	0	0	HY	HY		30
1982	0	5	7	7	4	7	8	0	0	0	0	HY	38
1983	4	12	9	7	4	9	12	2	0	0	0	0	59
1984	0	6	8	6	0	8	0	0	2	0	0	0	30
1985	5	Died	9	6	4	0	0	2	0	3	4	7	40
No. eggs	13	23	33	51	16	31	36	4	2	3	4	7	223
No. fertile	2	16	14	21	1	0	32	3	0	0	0	0	89
No. young	1	10	8	15	1	0	26	3	0	0	0	0	64

	D2	D4	D11	D5	D6	D8	Totals
Denmark							
1977	HY						0
1978	0						0
1979	0	HY					0
1980	0	2	HY	HY	HY		2
1981	7	4	0	0	0		11
1982	7	12	8	3	0	HY	30
1983	17	14	14	13	0	0	58
1984	15	16	11	12	5	0	59
1985	15	15	0	12	9	4	55
No. eggs	61	63	33	40	14	4	215
No. fertile	54	42	4	27	1	0	128
No. young	39	30	1	20	0	0	90

Time of Egg-laying. — Although all birds were kept under the same light regime (latitude 57°N), the date of first egg-laying varied for females of different origin. Females ($n=11$) breeding for the first time laid eggs later (mean date=5 May) than in subsequent years (mean date=18 April, $n=21$ clutches). Females of north Fennoscandian origin (latitude 66°N) laid significantly later (*mean* date =19 April, $n=10$ clutches, excluding all first-year clutches) than females of south Fennoscandian and Scottish origin (latitude 57°N, mean date=10 April, $n=11$ clutches, Mann-Whitney U-test, $P<0.05$). Peregrines of middle and south European origin (latitude 42°-50°N) laid significantly earlier (mean date=25 March, $n=15$ clutches excluding all first-year clutches, $P<0.05$) than birds of Scottish and south Fennoscandian origin.

Clutch Data. — From most females we got two clutches and, in a few cases, three clutches (Table 2). First clutches ($n=17$) contained on average 3.8 eggs and second clutches 3.4 eggs. Average production per female was 6.0 eggs per year with a fertility rate of 40%. Females that had eggs taken laid on average 7.9 eggs per year. The Danish program showed a lower age at first breeding, higher egg production (mean clutch size=10.2 eggs) as a result of effective egg removal, and higher fertility (60%) (Table 3). Compared to the North American programs, the Swedish project showed a slightly smaller average clutch size and fewer young per laying female (cf. Cade 1980).

Hatchability. — Hatchability of artificially incubated eggs varied slightly between years, but there was no significant difference in hatchability ($\bar{x}=82\%$) between eggs collected in the wild ($n=37$) and eggs from captive birds ($n=67$) in the period 1981-85. Of hatched

TABLE 3. Reproduction of Peregrines within the Swedish and Danish breeding programs.

	1978	1979	1980	1981	1982	1983	1984	1985
Sweden								
No. of laying females	1	1	2	5	6	8	5	8
Total eggs laid	3	8	15	30	38	59	30	40
No. of fertile eggs laid	0	2	6	10	16	28	15	10
% fertility	0	25	40	33	42	71	50	25
No. of eggs hatched	0	1	5	10	14	20	13	6
% fertile eggs hatched	0	50	83	100	88	95	87	60
$\bar{x}$ clutch size	3	8	7.5	6	6.3	7.4	6	5.0
$\bar{x}$ fertile eggs	0	2	3	2	2.7	3.5	3	1.3
No. of fledged young	0	1	5	9	14	19	11	5
% fledged of hatched	0	100	100	90	100	95	85	83
No. of young fledged per laying female	0	1	2.5	1.8	2.3	2.4	2.2	0.6
Denmark								
No. of laying females	0	0	1	2	4	4	5	5
Total eggs laid			2	11	30	58	59	55
No. of fertile eggs			1	5	8	31	44	39
% fertility			50	46	27	53	75	71
No. of eggs hatched			0	5	5	27	32	34
% fertile eggs hatched			0	100	63	87	73	87
$\bar{x}$ clutch size			2	5.5	7.3	14.5	11.8	11
$\bar{x}$ fertile eggs			1	2.5	2	7.8	8.8	7.8
No. of fledged young			0	5	3	26	28	28
% fledged of hatched			0	100	60	96	88	82
No. of young fledged per laying female			0	2.5	0.8	6.5	5.6	5.6

young ($n=150$), 87% survived until fledging. On average 71% of the fertile eggs resulted in fledged young.

Egg Data. — Average length, breadth, volume and fresh weight are given in Table 4 for a sample of captive produced and wild collected eggs. Egg volumes from captive Fennoscandian and middle European birds were close to those of North American eggs (Burnham et al. 1984). Eggs from second and third clutches were narrower and of less volume than eggs from first clutches. Sample size was too small to reveal any trend towards smaller eggs over years of laying as found by Burnham et al. (1984).

Percent volume decrease between first and second clutches of captive birds was smaller (2.9%) than for wild birds (8.5%), which might indicate that wild females are more energy-stressed than captive birds.

Release Results. — Of 82 young in 1979-85, 64 were progeny of captive birds and 18 of wild birds. Fifty-seven were fostered to wild birds and 25 released by hacking at four sites (Table 5). Two fostered birds died prior to fledging, but all hacked birds fledged. One hacked bird was hurt shortly after fledging and was recaptured. All others, to our knowledge, dispersed from the hacking sites after 4-7 weeks. Of fostered and hacked birds, four were found dead during migration and four were found as breeding or territorial birds in southwestern Sweden. One female released in 1982 returned after her first winter migration to a locality with a single territorial male and laid fertile eggs.

In 1985 at least seven wild pairs attempted to breed in southwestern Sweden and southeastern Norway (adjoining the release area). Four historical Peregrine cliffs, empty for decades, were reoccupied in the 1980s, partly as a result of the management and release program. Females of three pairs in southwestern Sweden were color-ringed; they had been released in the 1980s.

Genetic and Demographic Aspects. — The wild population in southwestern Sweden declined from about 65 pairs in 1955 to 1-2 pairs in 1975, indicating a real risk for total extirpation. The population was more or less geographically isolated between the 1960s and 1970s, increasing the risk of inbreeding. Ringing recoveries showed a high fidelity to natal regions. In 1980 it was estimated that the remaining population had an inbreeding coefficient of 0.11; 15 of the fledglings since 1977 were the progeny of two pairs. Thus, new pairs had a 50% probability of being siblings. Uneven reproduction between pairs may rapidly increase the risk of inbreeding. In an island population of Great Tit, Noordwijk and Scharloo (1981) found hatching of eggs was reduced by 7.5% for every 10% increase of the inbreeding coefficient. Similar effects were earlier noted by Greenwood et al. (1978). Poor

TABLE 4. Variation in egg size between sequential clutches of captive and wild Peregrines. Values are means followed by standard deviations.

	No. of clutches	No. of eggs	Length (mm)	Breadth (mm)	Volume (ml)[a]	Initial weight (g)[b]
Captive Sweden						
C_1	28	114	51.20 ± 1.82	40.28 ± 1.12	42.46 ± 3.23	45.54 ± 3.45
C_2	13	44	50.20 ± 2.06	39.97 ± 1.45	41.06 ± 4.28	44.05 ± 4.62
C_1 versus C_2			NS[c]	NS[c]	NS[c]	NS[c]
Captive Denmark						
C_1	17	67	49.63 ± 2.35	40.16 ± 0.98	41.12 ± 1.73	44.03 ± 3.15
C_2	15	58	49.47 ± 2.06	39.96 ± 0.84	40.37 ± 3.15	43.29 ± 3.35
C_3	11	41	49.31 ± 1.30	39.58 ± 0.43	39.45 ± 1.69	42.30 ± 1.85
C_4	6	15	47.81 ± 0.63	39.15 ± 0.50	37.45 ± 1.26	40.20 ± 1.36
C_1 versus C_2			NS[c]	NS[c]	$p < 0.05$	$p < 0.05$
C_1 versus C_3			NS[c]	$p < 0.05$	$p < 0.05$	$p < 0.05$
C_1 versus C_4			NS[c]	$p < 0.05$	$p < 0.05$	$p < 0.05$
Wild						
C_1	14	44	51.15 ± 1.88	40.08 ± 1.46	41.96 ± 3.95	44.68 ± 4.11
C_2	9	29	50.00 ± 2.38	38.73 ± 1.35	38.38 ± 3.85	41.17 ± 4.17
C_1 versus C_2			NS[c]	NS[c]	NS[c]	NS[c]

[a] $V = LB^2 k$; $k = 0.51$ (Hoyt 1979).
[b] $W = k_W (LB^2)$; $k_W = 0.0005474$ (Burnham 1983).
[c] NS = no significance.

TABLE 5.   Number of hacked and fostered Peregrines in Sweden, 1979-85.

Origin	No. hacked	No. fostered	Total
Captive-produced Peregrines			
Southern Sweden	8	10	18
Southern and Northern Sweden	1	1	2
Finland	3	7	10
Finland/Scotland		1	1
Scotland	5	10	15
Total	17	29	46
Wild Peregrines (hatched in incubators)	8	28	36
Total captive-produced and wild	25	57	82
Recoveries			
Dead prior to fledging		2	
Found hurt shortly after fledging	1		
Found dead		3 (Sweden, Belgium)	
Shot	1 (Norway)		

hatching success in many declining Peregrine populations may be an effect of inbreeding as well as of high contaminant levels. Effective management of small populations may require increased genetic diversity.

Lindberg (1983) made some deterministic estimates of population growth using different survival and productivity data. Survival of adult birds was most important and affected population development more than productivity and age of maturity (cf. Grier 1979). Assuming a first-year mortality of 60%, subadult and adult mortality of 20%, production of 1.5 young per breeding female, sexual maturity at two years, equal sex ratio and 100% entry of surviving birds into the population, a release of 200 individuals will result in a population of 32 breeding age pairs after 15 years. This value is probably a maximum value as the calculations do not consider random events and dispersal rate. Barclay and Cade (1983) made similar calculations using a stochastic model and estimated a population of 152-203 breeding age birds after 16 years of release of 1205 falcons (first-year mortality=66.7%, thereafter 20%; productivity=1.5 young; breeding age=2 years).

The Swedish reintroduction program may take longer than previously estimated (Lindberg 1983) owing to increased predation by Eagle Owls (cf. predation from the Great Horned Owl in United States, Barclay and Cade 1983). A reintroduction program of Eagle

Owls was started in southwestern Sweden in 1965, and by 1983 over 600 owls had been released. The Eagle Owl program was highly successful — the wild population has increased from a few pairs in the early 1970s to about 100 pairs in 1985 (Broo 1985). The population is still increasing, and many classic Peregrine cliffs are now occupied by owls. Although the species are sympatric, the use of the same cliff may be detrimental to the falcons. At least one Peregrine pair was probably lost from owl predation in the 1980s. Terrasse and Terrasse (1969) reported from an area in France that Eagle Owls apparently limited the distribution of Peregrines (see also Juillard Chapter 22).

59 Reintroduction of the Peregrine Falcon in Germany

Christian Saar

After the Peregrine population crash in the 1950s and 1960s in central Europe, only a very small population survived in southern Germany. The remaining 40 pairs produced only a few young. North of the river Main in West Germany and in the whole of East Germany the Peregrine Falcon was completely extirpated. At that time many thought that the Peregrine might not survive in Germany without assistance, and so a number of falconers began breeding projects to find out whether it was possible to reproduce this beautiful bird of prey in captivity and give it a chance to survive in this way. A further goal was to create a breeding population in captivity and to release the offspring into the wild to repopulate areas where Peregrines had vanished. Despite the opposition of some members of nature conservation organizations such as the Arbeitsgemeinschaft Wanderfalkenschutz (AGW) in Baden-Württemberg and the Deutschen Bund für Vogelschutz, who postulated that breeding Peregrines and reintroducing them into the wild would be impossible, we set up a captive breeding project in West Berlin.

PRODUCTION OF CAPTIVE PEREGRINES

We had great difficulty obtaining a breeding stock of the regional subspecies, *F. p. peregrinus*, and the first young produced were of the subspecies *F. p. brookei* in 1974. But in the following years young *F. p. peregrinus* were bred also, and we eventually produced more than 300 Peregrines in our West Berlin facilities.

During the early years, we had to develop and use artificial insemination with some imprinted birds, especially those few of middle European origin whose offspring we planned to release. By this method we were able to save some genetic material which otherwise would have been lost forever. Other falconers also had more and more success in reproducing Peregrines in captivity, and we can now proudly state that we are in the position to breed as many Peregrines as we wish (see Saar et al. 1982, Gerriets 1984, Bednarek 1985).

629

RELEASE OF PEREGRINES

Experimental releases were begun in 1977 and proved to be successful (Saar 1978). In West Berlin, four Peregrines fledged from a nest box on the big building of Tempelhof Airport. One of these falcons was lost, but the others reached independence. The one male in the group returned the next summer to the release place!

In this experiment we used *F. p. brookei*, because at that time we did not dare to risk any of the very rare individuals of the nominate form. All subsequent releases in West Berlin and West Germany were undertaken with *F. p. peregrinus*.

In the same year, Trommer (1978) used the fostering method in Bavaria. Young Peregrines were put into a nest of wild Peregrines which had failed to produce for many years. The young were raised and fledged.

After these initial experimental releases we established more release projects both in West Berlin and in West Germany (Hesse, Bavaria and Lower Saxony), using three methods. Releases by hacking continued from nest boxes at former cliff-nesting sites, on suitable buildings, and since 1980, from artificial tree nests (Paasch et al. 1981). Fostering to wild Peregrines could be done only in Bavaria, because in Baden-Württemberg it was not permitted owing to the influence of the AGW; further north not a single breeding pair of Peregrines existed. We have also used Eurasian Kestrels, Northern Goshawks, and Common Buzzards for cross-fostering of Peregrines (Saar et al. 1982, Trommer 1983, 1985).

The most important goal was to repopulate traditional nesting cliffs. On the other hand, we also thought that releases in cities would be promising because the Peregrines would find a suitable range of prey, would be protected from their natural enemies such as the Northern Goshawk and Eagle Owl, and would require fewer people to watch them.

The tree-nesting Peregrine population that once existed in the parts of northern Germany without suitable cliffs has vanished altogether. In this region it is therefore necessary to imprint the Peregrines to tree nests. We believe this goal can be accomplished by releases from artificial tree nests, which we have used since 1980 in West Berlin.

Cross-fostering seems to be a very good method for raising young Peregrines to independent existence. The main role will be played by Northern Goshawks, which may be helpful in establishing a new tree-nesting population. Eurasian Kestrels and Common Buzzards seem to do the job also, but may not be as effective because their prey differs more from that of the Peregrine. We do not have information up to now on the fate of these Peregrines which have been released by cross-fostering.

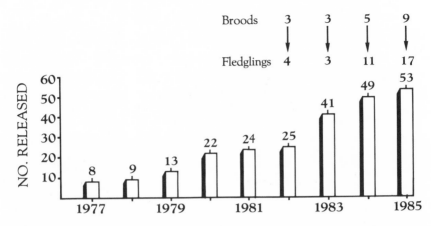

FIGURE 1. Released Peregrine Falcons in West Germany and West Berlin (n=244), breeding pairs and fledglings. In 1985, there were 13 pairs from our projects, and 9 breeding pairs (1 wild bird involved).

From 1977-85 we released young Peregrines in increasing numbers, 244 altogether (see Figure 1). Release site locations are shown in Figure 2.

REOCCUPANCY OF TERRITORIES

In 1982 we received reports from East Germany that a pair of Peregrine Falcons had nested successfully in the Harz Mountains (Saar et al. 1982). The cliff which was repopulated first was the one where the last pair of Peregrines disappeared in 1974. The new birds were identified by their rings and had come from our release programs! That was the first demonstration that our work was successful. The first pair from our releases nested one year later on a building in Frankfurt, West Germany (Anhäuser 1985).

By 1985, we established by releases at least nine breeding pairs in East and West Germany. Four other pairs took over nest sites but were too young to breed. At least 35 young fledged from these pairs (see Figure 1). With five pairs now breeding in the Harz Mountains, we have reestablished local breeding populations in East and West Germany (Figure 2). Peregrines are not restricted by political borders!

These results indicate that continued releases will be successful in the future. We have shown that we can breed large numbers of Peregrine Falcons and release them to the wild to establish new breeding populations. Our main task in the coming years will be to build up a new tree-nesting population in northern Germany.

ACCOUNTS OF SOME RELEASED PEREGRINES

The Tiercel Which Was Released Twice. — In 1978 we initiated our releases in Hessen, West Germany. Three young Peregrines were

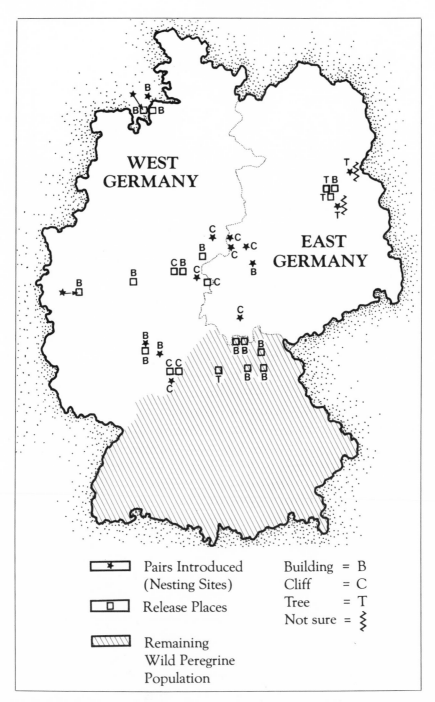

FIGURE 2. Peregrine release sites and introduced pairs in East and West Germany, 1977-85.

put into a nest box at a former nesting cliff near the little town of Eschwege. The release place was situated only 50 m from the East German border. The three Peregrines fledged, became independent, and dispersed without difficulties. In October of the same year, ornithologists who were banding waders and other birds in East Germany observed the released tiercel hunting swifts and catching banded waders just after they were released. Four-and-one-half years later the tiercel was found injured near the town of Sangerhausen in East Germany. The wound, caused by a shot which broke a wing bone, healed well, and the tiercel was handed over to a falconer to give it exercise.

When it was flying strongly enough, the tiercel was released near a former Peregrine breeding cliff not far from the place where it had been found. It spent subsequent winters near a factory but used to disappear each spring. In the early spring of 1985, however, it was joined at the factory by a young female Peregrine, which was an offspring of one of our existing breeding pairs not far away. A few weeks later this young female was replaced by a two-year-old banded female from one of our projects. A big nest box was hung on the chimney of the factory and was immediately occupied by the pair. They did not have eggs that season, but are still on the territory and hopefully will breed successfully in the coming season.

The Peregrines of Cologne Cathedral. — This story is of interest because the failure of our first attempt to bring young Peregrines to this huge building brought negative comments from our critics, who wanted to prove that our way of managing the Peregrine was stupid and had no chance of success. In 1979 we put two young males into a nest box at one of the big towers of the cathedral. They were the last of the lot we had bred that year. When we opened the box to let them free, they were attacked by Eurasian Kestrels from the very first moment. There were about nine pairs of Eurasian Kestrels raising their young in the vicinity, so both members of each pair were very aggressive. The young and inexperienced Peregrines had no chance and were driven away from the cathedral.

In 1984 we repeated the experiment at the same place, but we altered the procedure by using some of the first young Peregrines of the season. In this way we were able to release the Peregrines while the Eurasian Kestrels were incubating their eggs, and only one member of each pair was able to attack the young Peregrines. Also, the Eurasian Kestrels were not as aggressive during incubation as at fledging time. We did not use a box but put the young Peregrines in a room in one of the steeples which had walls 6 m high and opened on all sides at the top. The young Peregrines could not begin to fly about until they could reach the high openings. The birds fledged successfully and became independent. In January 1985 one of the young males returned, and in March one of the females returned. They showed strong territorial behavior, and since that time have remained at the cathedral. We put three captive-bred young in the same place. There was some aggression against the young by the pair, but two of the young fledged; the third was found injured in the streets after perhaps hitting a window. We hope this pair will nest and have young in 1986.

The Lighthouse Peregrines. — There are a few old lighthouses on the coast of the North Sea, situated at the mouth of the river Weser. Depending on the tide, they are surrounded by the sea or by wet ground. Two of these lighthouses are occupied by cormorants, which nest on them because they are no longer used. In 1978, one of our coworkers observed a pair of Peregrines by the lighthouse towers. He suspected a breeding attempt, but no young fledged. In 1981 he showed us slides which revealed very clearly that the female wore jesses and so was a lost hunting falcon; the male wore rings identifying him as a bird released in 1980 from an artificial tree nest in West Berlin. How did he find the isolated female in the North Sea, where there are no Peregrines for hundreds of kilometers? When their eggs did not hatch, we conferred with authorities and obtained permission to put a young Peregrine in their nest. We put a nine-day-old male into the nest in one of the rooms in Lighthouse No. 1 after we had removed the addled eggs. It was adopted with no problems, and two weeks later was ringed with special band No. OEM. It fledged without difficulties. Analysis revealed that the eggs contained very high levels of chlorinated hydrocarbons. We obtained permission for 1983 to try to hatch the entire clutch artificially and then return the young Peregrines to the nest, but were disappointed in the spring of that year to find that the tiercel had gone. Only the old female was there with an infertile clutch, and we were afraid that this Peregrine story was at an end.

In 1984, however, another male joined the female and we were able to collect a clutch of four eggs. We could not immediately determine the origin of the male, but we successfully hatched the eggs even though they had very thin shells. There was a second infertile clutch which we replaced with the four young Peregrines. They were adopted.

In 1985 we did not find a clutch at the time we expected it. When we examined the place weeks later we were very surprised to find two young Peregrines in Lighthouse No. 2. How could that happen, when the old female was too highly contaminated to be successful in our opinion? We then made two exciting discoveries: the female was a young Peregrine whose rings revealed her to be one of the four from the previous year, and the male was No. OEM, which we had fostered in 1983 to the original pair! We obtained permission to foster two more young to this pair; they were adopted without difficulty. Thus we demonstrated that by management, an active eyrie could be continued even though the original mates were lost.

We have also released young Peregrines on the coast not far away from the lighthouses to support the North Sea Peregrines. There are quite a few Peregrines present now, and another pair nested and fledged young about 30 km further north at an artificial nest box which had been fixed to a sea sign (Reilmann 1985).

CONCLUSION

These three accounts show that there are many ways to help the Peregrine Falcon survive in areas where it has vanished. We expect the foundation of small breeding populations of Peregrines in these areas will help the increasing wild population in the south to expand northward. In 10-15 years we will be able to stop our programs because the Peregrine will not need further help. Perhaps by that time the strong antagonism between those who support and those who oppose our programs will diminish. We hope it will be replaced by fruitful and friendly cooperation, for we share the same ideal of helping the Peregrine Falcon to live again in Germany as it did years ago.

ACKNOWLEDGEMENTS

This article should not end without an expression of great gratitude to all the helpers in our projects. Without them we would not be able to work so successfully for the survival of the Peregrine Falcon. They are good people, often from very different walks of life — ornithologists, hunters, and falconers — but they have one feeling in common. They love the Peregrine, and they are devoted to helping this beautiful bird of prey. For all the effort and time they spend to accomplish this work, they are rewarded by the thrill of watching these falcons in flight at the release places and watching them return to nest in areas where their species had been wiped out by human activities in the years before. These people provide information which enables us to understand more about the Peregrine Falcon, and they are the ones who report so many nice events in connection with its management.

Editors' Note: The Peregrines on the Cologne cathedral hatched and reared young in 1987. From the total of 339 Peregrines produced in captivity and released between 1977-87, 20 pairs are known to have become established in East and West Germany, 7 of them in the Harz Mountains. Two pairs in East Germany lost their clutches from eggshell thinning (C. Saar pers. comm.).

60 | Artificial Eyrie Management and the Protection of the Peregrine Falcon in West Germany

Helmut Brücher and Peter Wegner

In conjunction with the loss of Peregrines in many parts of the northern hemisphere 20 years ago (Hickey 1969), the Peregrine population in the Federal Republic of Germany (West Germany) had by 1965 fallen to about 40 pairs producing some 30 fledged young (Mebs 1960, Schilling and König 1980). There were a few isolated breeding pairs in northern and central Germany, but most of the Peregrines were found in a relatively isolated situation in southern Germany where a remnant population was able to maintain itself in the hills of the Swabian Alps and Black Forest (Baden-Württemberg) and in small numbers in the pre-Alps of Bavaria (Rockenbauch 1970, 1975).

After 1955, the tree-nesting population of the north German plains decreased at an increasingly rapid rate, and by 1972 it had become extinct (Kirmse 1970, Kirmse and Kleinstäuber 1977). It may be that residues of pesticides in this population were higher when compared to the south German population, but unfortunately, exact measurements were not made. As the Peregrines of northern Germany fed to a large extent on waders and other waterbirds, they were probably exposed to greater levels of pesticides owing to the considerable concentration of DDE and other pesticides in the marine bioaccumulation cycle (Schnurre 1966). In contrast, the Peregrines of southern Germany prey mainly on thrushes, starlings and pigeons, which have lower residues (Rockenbauch 1971).

In this apparently hopeless situation, a group of idealistic conservationists convened in Baden-Württemberg in 1965 — at the same time as the Madison Peregrine Conference — with the aim of saving the Peregrine Falcon. They founded the Arbeitsgemeinschaft Wanderfalkenschutz (AGW) or "Working Group for the Protection of Peregrines," which recently celebrated its 20th anniversary (Schilling and Rockenbauch 1985). The founding members of the AGW did not sit back fatalistically, but instead started a conservation program for the remnant population in Baden-Württemberg.

CONTROLLING HUMAN PERSECUTION

Year after year, young birds had been disappearing shortly before flying from eyries under observation by the AGW. The losses could not be attributed to an effect of pesticides. A large number of the birds were being robbed from nests. One example among many was an occupied eyrie that had no breeding success over 12 years; in 1966 the three known breeding ledges of this territory were made unusable by the AGW, and the first artificial nest was built in a small, inconspicuous cliff nearby. The pair immediately accepted the artificial nest platform, and young have been raised there every year since.

Encouraged by this success, the AGW began systematic observation of Peregrine nests in Baden-Württemberg. The results of the past 20 years have vindicated the founding members' optimism. Schilling and König (1980) showed, through the analysis of eggs remaining unhatched in nests, that the population in Baden-Württemberg had pesticide residues similar to those of British and Swedish populations (see also Baum and Conrad 1978, Baum 1981, Schilling 1981). The number of fledged young per successful nesting attempt, however, has been similar to that of the "pre-DDT era," because additional factors causing loss of nestlings have been artificially reduced. For this reason, pesticides alone have not accounted for the reduction in the Baden-Württemberg population.

Several additional factors contributing to nestling loss were exacerbated along with the increased pesticide pressure on the environment. For example, falconry experienced a renaissance after World War II in West Germany, and then spread to other countries. When one considers the falconer's requirements, the commercial raptor exhibitions, and the traffic in falcons throughout the world, the uncontrolled take of nestlings loomed as a major factor in the reduction of the Peregrine's reproductive output. In the first few years following the formation of the AGW, only nests in Baden-Württemberg with young birds were guarded (DBV, AGW and AWU 1975). However, when technology made it possible for eggs to be brooded artificially in incubators, it became necessary for the nests to be observed for a period of about five weeks longer — from before the laying of the first egg until the fledging of the young birds. It is sad that this wardening of nests for 80 days has had to be continued to the present. Despite the wardening, certain criminal poachers continue to attempt to rob young birds from the nests. The current market value of a Peregrine Falcon is such that not even the threat of a long prison sentence can stop them. Year after year, this necessity for wardening demands great personal devotion, and ties down manpower that could be used in other conservation projects and basic research.

Rock-climbing is another human disturbance (Rockenbauch 1965). Through seasonal prohibition of climbing (again enforced by the AGW) and by the moving of nests to parts of the same cliffs that are unattractive to climbers, losses owing to this type of disturbance can be avoided completely (Hepp Chapter 61).

CONTROLLING NATURAL LOSSES

Another task for the AGW has been to study natural breeding losses and to devise methods for reducing them. The following mortality factors were identified and reduced, or in some cases completely eliminated.

Predators. — Martens eat both eggs and young birds. The AGW tried to scare the martens away from the nests with acoustic and olfactory methods, but the best deterrent turned out to be a piece of iron painted with a particular varnish and placed next to the eggs (Schilling and Rockenbauch 1985).

Another predator is the Eagle Owl, which has spread as a result of a release program. It preys on both brooding females and nestlings (Rockenbauch 1978). In certain nests the remains of up to five Peregrines (adult and young) have been found. At optimum Peregrine breeding sites in the neighborhood of Eagle Owl nests, we have noticed that adult Peregrines individually recognizable by colored rings disappear regularly and are immediately replaced by other birds. Actions to reduce the impact of Eagle Owls have not been carried out, nor are they anticipated. However, because Peregrine eyries near Eagle Owl nests function like traps, they will be made unusable in order to force the Peregrines to relocate.

Parasites. — Although there is considerable variation from year to year, an average of 10% of young birds are infested by ticks (Schilling et al. 1981). In extreme cases, up to 320 ticks (*Ixodes arboricola*) have been found on one nestling. Death can result through loss of blood, a weakening of the general condition, and through intoxication presumably triggered by allergic reactions. To minimize losses, young infested birds are freed of the ticks, and the nesting ledge is treated chemically. If this treatment is not successful in the long term, then the nest site is made unusable.

Unsuitable Nesting Ledges. — Inferior nesting sites repeatedly result in complete breeding failure or a reduction in the number of fledglings. The following are some examples: (1) after snowfall — particularly wet snow — the female abandons the nest; (2) the breeding hollow fills with water following rain or thawing of snow, resulting in abandonment of the eggs or in the chilling and death of nestlings; (3) eggs become pasted over with mud, and the embryo dies as a result of insufficient gas exchange; (4) nesting ledges that are too small result in nestlings falling out; and (5) easy access for animal predators and humans reduces breeding success. A special subgroup in the AGW oversees the construction of artificial nests, so that these losses caused by weather conditions and other factors can be eliminated (Hepp 1982). Today, about 80% of the Peregrines in the Black Forest successfully breed in artificial nests, as the cliffs there often lack suitable nest sites. Breeding success in artificial nests is distinctly higher than in natural nests.

The improvement of natural nests is carried out by drainage, enlargement of the shelf or cavity, or provision of a roof. New artificial nests were also constructed. Up to 50 m of iron, 2 tons of concrete, and 280 man-hours of work were necessary for the construction of some nests.

RESULTS AND CONCLUSION

After 20 years of conservation work by the AGW in Baden-Württemberg, the Peregrine population has recovered. The Peregrines have increased from 15-20 breeding pairs with 22 fledged young in 1966 to 90 breeding pairs with 160 fledged young in 1985. There are about 30 additional breeding pairs, mainly in Bavaria, and increasing populations in Austria, Switzerland and France. In 1985, the total population for West Germany was over 130 breeding pairs with 190-200 fledged young.

Apart from the raw figures, the population trends in Baden-Württemberg are interesting. It is possible to distinguish three phases in the recovery: (1) an increase in the number of breeding pairs by the occupation of unused cliffs in the core breeding area; (2) the step-by-step replacement of old, established pairs which were driven away by young, mature falcons; and (3) the spread of the population into surrounding regions and an increasing exchange with the populations in Bavaria, Switzerland, Austria, and France.

Also, we suspect that there has been a spread towards the Peregrine-free area in northern Germany. Unfortunately, the natural expansion of Peregrines from the core area in Baden-Württemberg into the area of the former northern population and the reoccupation of old Peregrine territories can be followed only with some difficulty, because the AGW has used some of the same ring color combinations as those placed on captive-produced and released Peregrines from the reintroduction program of the Deutscher Falkenorden (German falconers' organization). This has made identification of individual birds difficult. Even so, the two populations meet together and thus increase the recovery rate.

The AGW has shown that through the consistent protection and intensive management of a remnant population it has been possible to restore the Peregrine in Baden-Württemberg without resorting to release programs. Similar methods have also worked well in other parts of Europe where small breeding populations survived through the worst period in the 1960s and early 1970s (see Juillard Chapter 22, Monneret Chapter 23).

61 | Contributions Toward the Recovery of Peregrine Falcons in West Germany

Karlfried Hepp

This paper is an English version of a report originally published in German (Hepp 1982). It details some of the actions taken by the Arbeitsgemeinschaft Wanderfalkenschutz (AGW) to improve the physical characteristics of Peregrine eyries.

ACTIVITIES IN 1981

The volunteer wardens of the AGW of the German Bird Protection Society (DBV) breathed sighs of relief when, on 31 May 1981, the third young Peregrine Falcon flew safely from its artificial nest on a cliff face. Behind this event lay hard and suspenseful weeks of watching the nest at an altitude of over 800 m in conditions with snow, rain, ice and frost in the very exposed uplands of the Black Forest. In this spot a pair of Peregrine Falcons had bred successfully for the first time since 1948-49.

Thanks to the intensive efforts of the AGW, the population of Peregrine Falcons in Baden-Württemberg had slowly begun to increase, and this cliff was first occupied in the spring of 1980. On 9 March 1980, an adult male and a "brown" female in immature plumage were observed there. As both birds were color-ringed, they were individually recognizable and their origins could be traced. They had clearly been attracted by the single modest but conspicuous square hole in this rocky cliff; they were seen to copulate in the neighborhood of the cliff but, as expected, no eggs were laid. The birds continued to haunt the cliff until mid-May 1980, but only appeared there occasionally thereafter.

That year the AGW specialist group was unable to enlarge the very small cavity in the cliff and protect it against adverse weather conditions. On 28 February 1981, however, at almost the last minute the team spent one whole day hacking into the hard primary rock. Despite heavy snow and frost, they succeeeded in both widening and, in particular, deepening the cavity to over twice its original size. At the same time, as with all cliff eyries constructed by the AGW, the floor of the cavity was provided with adequate drainage: a layer of gravel topped by a bed of fine pine needles in case water infiltrated from outside or from the cliff itself. In this way the Peregrines were provided with suitable accommodation, the benefits of which had already been proven repeatedly at other modified eyries.

On the day this work was carried out, only the tiercel was observed flying past the cliff. By the beginning of March 1981, however, members of the AGW confirmed that, after clearly hesitating between two possible cliffs, the previous year's pair had again decided in favor of this site. By 18 March, eggs had been laid in this artificially-enlarged cavity. Repeated harsh outbreaks of late winter weather during incubation and even after hatching provided ample testimony that, in the face of flying or drifting snow, breeding success would have been out of the question in the original small nest hole. The new deep and roomy hole, however, adequately protected the chicks from snow and rain.

COMPETITION BETWEEN PEREGRINES AND RAVENS

Following the recolonization since 1970 of the southern Black Forest by Common Ravens, the AGW became aware that these birds were once again competing for cliff nest sites with the Peregrines in this region. In the first years, regular contests took place which the Common Ravens tended to win since they start to build their nests in February at the latest and frequently have laid eggs and begun to incubate by the end of the month. Peregrines, on the other hand, usually begin incubation 14 days later (mid-March), even in the highest parts of the Black Forest.

Over the past 12 years, however, the two species have arranged matters such that in many places the Peregrines take over the previous year's Common Raven nests. The two species have bred successfully as close as 20 m apart on the same cliff face.

AN INCREASING THREAT

Increased freedom and mobility have led to a marked expansion of recreational activities among our fellow citizens in the countryside. Of the many varieties of incursion into formerly peaceful areas, by far the most disturbing to Peregrines are the spread of rock-climbing and of falconry. On the once secluded cliff-tops of our highlands, with their wonderful views, there are now paths marked out for hikers, not to mention barbecue pits, and even sausage stalls. A wholly market-oriented holiday industry has sprung up, along with "nursery slopes" and schools for climbers at potential Peregrine breeding sites such as in the neighborhood of Baden-Baden, Freiburg, and the whole cliff region of the southern Palatinate.

Thus, from the early 1950s-70s, the declining native population of Peregrines found an ever more restricted range of suitable breeding sites owing to various human influences. This was particularly so in the primary and volcanic rock cliffs of the Black Forest. The simultaneous "mushrooming" of commercial raptor displays, city-bred falconers, and numerous private collections of birds of prey, led to an increased demand for these much sought-after "commodities," and this demand has resulted in much nest-robbing, both at home and abroad.

The last few remaining pairs of Peregrines in Bavaria and in Baden-Württemberg managed to hang on around cliffs which were still undisturbed but in many cases ill-suited for breeding — often in the most elevated parts of our highlands. Because of the increasing decline in the number of potential nest sites, the birds were in some places forced to occupy cliffs facing northeast or northwest. At the start of the breeding season these sites generally receive little sunlight, and later on only 1-2 hours per day. Many pairs of Peregrines have had to nest on ledges and shelves exposed to weather extremes: snowfalls lasting several days, frost, and icy water streaming down the cliff-face during incubation and rearing.

Losses of eggs and chicks at these inferior eyries have resulted from inclement weather as well as other causes: human interference, martens, ticks, damage to the environment, etc. Also, the lower sloping shelves of the primary rock cliffs in the Black Forest provide ledges and niches that are not flat enough, wide enough, or weather-proof. Daily turning of the eggs by the parents ultimately leads to their rolling over the edge of the cliff.

HELP THROUGH ARTIFICIAL EYRIES

All these distressing factors, together with the concept of "relocating" Peregrine eyries to avoid rock-climbers, led the Sitz Nürtingen branch of the AGW in the early 1970s to begin constructing artificial eyries at sites which Peregrines had not yet abandoned, but where in most cases they failed to breed. In each case the scale and scope of the work depended on the potential and requirements of the site, and the type of rock played a key role. (It should be noted here that Peregrines in southern Germany historically have bred only on cliffs or very rarely on buildings and never in trees as they did, for example, in northern Germany and Poland.)

The Swabian Jura. — Naturally-formed ledges and cavities are numerous in the Jurassic cliffs and offer ideal nesting facilities for

Peregrines. The floors of these cavities typically consist of dry, relatively coarse or fine-grained detritus, and incubation and rearing of young usually proceed without problems. But should there occur a heavy downpour or a late snow storm followed by a sudden thaw in April, these hitherto dependably dry ledges or cavities can suddenly stream with water, resulting in the numbing or drowning of the chicks, or chilling of the eggs with the consequent death of the embryos. Schilling and König (1980) described dramatic rescue operations to save such endangered chicks.

Following identification of the danger, immediate steps have been taken to "defuse" the situation at such nest sites by carefully clearing out the natural substrate and replacing it with a bed of water-absorbent gravel topped by a cushion of dry spruce needles. In some cases a drainpipe has also been installed. In this way future losses owing to water penetration can be wholly prevented.

Quarries and the Black Forest. — Quarries are significant to lasting colonization or recolonization by Peregrines, because they seem to have the largest number of likely rock faces that meet the bird's specific requirements. A quarry worked in terraces and then abandoned holds far less attraction for the Peregrine than a high, vertical wall of rock. The reasons for this are self-evident. One of our tasks has been to persuade the local conservation authorities and owners or tenants to create or maintain high vertical rock faces in conformity with a suitable biotope for Peregrines, preferably before the quarry is dismantled. At the same time, while the quarry is being dismantled, the construction of a number of artificial nest holes can be carried out with comparative ease; these will quickly be occupied by Eurasian Kestrels or Common Ravens, or even by Peregrines.

Usually in these abandoned quarries there are very few cavities or ledges secure from falling stones, humans, martens, weather, and dripping water that can be converted into suitable breeding sites without considerable expense. Of prime importance is the availability of a projecting slab of rock which can serve as a roof to protect the eyrie from rain or excessively strong sunshine. The blasting out of a hole beneath such an overhang saves considerable money, since all that remains to be done is to construct a suitably wide platform out of natural stone, or if necessary, on a specially-made, rust-proof metal framework fixed to the rock wall or into a narrow chimney.

The floor of this platform must be at least 15 cm thick in order to give the birds the requisite security and a feeling of confidence in the structure; then they will breed on it. In general, a platform of thin cement or sandstone over the void does not suffice; evidently it appears too insecure to the birds. Also, it is advisable to provide a permanent drainage system in these structures in the manner already described.

In one instance, the AGW achieved an immediate and lasting success with such a cantilevered concrete platform at an altitude of about 1000 m in the southern Black Forest, by adding to it a 5 cm thick fiberglass mat to prevent loss of heat from below. (At this altitude the temperature at night can regularly fall to $-10°C$.)

In many instances, the special AGW group of Offenburg has managed to transfer eyries from exposed cliff ledges to laboriously carved-out cavities. The construction time of such artificial cavities depends on the hardness of the rock; construction often continues through many weekends with a team of up to 15 people who frequently have to be relieved for safety's sake. In most cases, adequate drainage of the cavity floor against sudden influxes of water cannot be guaranteed.

Such labor-intensive operations are naturally focused on the most suitable places on the cliff — as safe as possible from humans and martens and far from any potential climbing routes. In some instances, from 2-4 different "eyries" have had to be built in the same Peregrine biotope, until one finally hits the "right spot" and catches the bird's fancy. Fresh knowledge is collected in this way every year.

In contrast to the Swabian Jura with its numerous cliff formations, Odenwald and the Black Forest offer a very limited number of possible cliffs. A "switchover" to a more remote and peaceful cliff face which only needs to be lightly worked is seldom possible. Also, the birds themselves may have already announced their preference for some particular cliff by their presence (feeding perch or the like).

Blasting Nest Holes. — For the sake of completeness, an account is also given here of the first and, to date, only blasting operation at a cliff on which a pair of Peregrines had annually tried to breed for at least 10 years (they had been unsuccessful because of snow, damp, frost, falling ice, etc.). Many attempts over successive years with conventional tools such as hammer and chisel had failed to make any impression on the extremely hard rock; members of the AGW could only manage to cut about 1 cm into the cliff.

After it had been decided to abandon the whole idea, the regional Nature Protection Agency provided a welcome solution by suggesting dynamite, and between 1977-80 this project was successfully concluded at a height of 1000 m above sea level. The enterprise was carried out with the help of the pioneer unit of a paratroop regiment in two five-day operations. Our team of 12 soldiers and 15-20 AGW members had managed by the end of their first operation to carve out nothing more than a "recognizable dent" after four days on the cliff. It was most disheartening! During the following summer, however, civilians and soldiers launched an "all-out effort" which led one of the most experienced paratroopers to exclaim: "Ten blasts anywhere else, rather than one here!" Finally, a most efficient, well-drained nest cavity resulted, and in October 1980 was ready for occupation. In March of the very next year (1981), Peregrines bred on this cliff for the first time, fledging three healthy young. In 1982 the same weatherproof site was again occupied, and two young Peregrines flew from it at the end of May.

PROSPECTS AND ACKNOWLEDGEMENTS

In 1982, over 65% of the successful pairs of Peregrines in the Black Forest reared and fledged their young from man-made nests. The view expressed by certain authors that "the availability of suitable nest sites does not constitute a limiting factor for the spread of the Peregrine population" unfortunately does not hold true for the Black Forest. We hope to increase this population still further in the coming years.

Throughout these activities, including the annual wardening of nests, the AGW has maintained excellent relations with the Baden-Württemberg Minister of Agriculture, the local forest officers, wildlife wardens, and owners of cliffs and forests. All have supported us to the full in a nonbureaucratic way. The nature conservation authorities also provided us with considerable assistance.

The AGW's wide-ranging protection measures for Peregrines, from the essential wardening of nests to technical equipment for the task forces, the supply of labor in any form, or concurrent scientific research, were first made possible and considerably advanced by repeated and generous grants from the special "Help Threatened Wildlife" funds of the 1858 Zoological Society of Frankfurt-am-Main. Special thanks are due to their representatives, Prof. Grzimek and Dr. Faust, and also to all the anonymous donors for whom they act!

Thanks are also due to the four major conservation organizations of Baden-Württemberg, which contribute financially to the work of the AGW in conformity with a resolution of the Ministry for the Environment; to the Baden-Württemberg Hunters' Association, to the World Wildlife Fund (Germany), and to the unfailingly loyal donors of the DBV.

We are above all grateful to the personnel of the AGW for their indefatigable, arduous and often dangerous work on the cliffs in snow, rain and blistering heat. The fruits of their tireless labor are documented elsewhere and are their finest reward.

8 | Dynamics and Ecology of Peregrine Populations

62 | Population Ecology of Peregrines in South Scotland

Ian Newton and Richard Mearns

We present here some data on the reproduction, survival, and dispersal of the Peregrine in south Scotland (Mearns and Newton 1984) as a basis for discussing the dynamics of stable and expanding populations and for constructing population models. Previous attempts to model raptor populations (e.g., Young 1969, Henny et al. 1970, Henny 1972) made no allowance for density-dependent change in additions or losses. Yet simple logic shows that the extreme stability normally shown by the breeding populations of the Peregrine and some other raptors must surely involve density-dependent processes.

STUDY AREA AND METHODS

The study population nested on cliffs in a fairly discrete area in southwest Scotland. There were about 38 traditional nesting territories inland and 21 on the coast. Almost all inland cliffs were in the upland zone, where the habitat consisted of large conifer plantations interspersed among areas of open grassland and heather moor. Upland pairs were within a few kilometers of more fertile lowland with small, mixed farms. Coastal cliffs were backed by farmland. The whole region has a mild but damp climate, with annual rainfall in the hills exceeding 100 cm. In winter, snow rarely lies for more than a week or two at a time.

Peregrines were resident in south Scotland, and pairs occupied their nesting cliffs all year (Mearns 1982). They fed principally on feral pigeons, but also took some other avian prey, including a variety of waders and songbirds (Mearns 1983). During the study period, the breeding population was increasing from a lower level, as it recovered from decline imposed by use of organochlorine pesticides. So far as we know, no adults were shot or otherwise removed from breeding cliffs during the study, but some may have been killed away from cliffs. Several sets of eggs or young were taken illegally each year, and a few clutches broke in association with DDE-related eggshell thinning.

651

Each year during 1974-82 an attempt was made to find all pairs, record clutch and brood sizes, and ring young. Beginning in 1976, as many breeding adults as possible were trapped at the nest for ringing and identification. For convenience, the total of territorial birds seen at nesting cliffs each spring is described as the "breeding population," even though in any one year a small proportion of these birds (pairs and singles) did not breed. Those Peregrines that did not defend cliffs or breed could not be counted.

BASIC PARAMETERS

Population. — During 1974-82, the known population of the study area increased from 28 pairs and 6 singles to 67 pairs and 4 singles (Figure 1), a mean increase of slightly over 12% per year. As the coastal population had been depleted most, the increase was more marked on the coast (4 pairs and 3 singles to 21 pairs and 2 singles) than inland (24 pairs and 6 singles to 46 pairs and 2 singles). By 1980, the inland population had become greater than that known before DDT; birds were present in five places not known to have been occupied formerly. These new sites were outside the previous distribution, and represented an expansion into habitat formerly considered marginal. Further increase was attributed to instances of two pairs

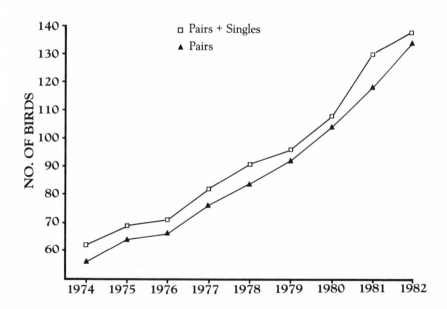

FIGURE 1. Known Peregrine population in the study area, 1974-82. These birds were all present at nesting cliffs. Any birds not occupying cliffs would have been missed.

occupying alternative cliffs formerly occupied by one pair, representing a real (but slight) increase in density. In contrast, by 1982 the coastal population had still not reached its former numbers, and at least two historical sites were reoccupied after the study ended.

Most single birds were seen on newly-occupied territories for up to three years before a pair was seen, but a few occurred as breaks in occupancy of territories by pairs. Once a territory became occupied by a pair, it remained occupied by a pair or single bird for the duration of the study. It was seldom possible to get close to single birds, so their sexes and ages were unknown.

Breeding Success. — Pooling the data from different years gave 397 records of pairs seen on territory in spring, and 48 records of single birds. Eggs were laid in 329 known cases (at 83% of territories with pairs), and young were fledged in 189 cases (47% of territories with pairs, or 57% of clutches). Clutches contained 1-5 eggs, mostly 3-4, with a mean of 3.5. The average number of young in successful broods was 2.3, for a mean overall production of 1.3 young per first clutch or 1.1 young per territorial pair (Table 1).

Nineteen pairs which failed soon after laying produced a second clutch, of which 11 produced young ($\bar{x}=1.7$ young per brood). This brought the overall productivity up to 50% of territorial pairs and 60% of pairs which laid, giving 1.15 young per territorial pair. As these various figures were based on all pairs found each year, including

TABLE 1. Population and breeding performance of Peregrines in south Scotland, 1974-82.

	No. of territorial pairs	No. (%)[a] laid eggs	No. (%)[a] fledged young	Eggs/ clutch	Young/ brood[b]	Young/ clutch	Young/ pair
1974	28	20 (71)	11 (39)	3.67	2.45	1.35	0.96
1975	32	25 (78)	15 (47)	3.62	1.60	0.96	0.75
1976	33	29 (88)	14 (42)	3.50	2.07	1.00	0.87
1977	38	33 (87)	21 (55)	3.67	2.29	1.46	1.26
1978	42	37 (88)	23 (55)	3.48	2.57	1.60	1.41
1979	46	38 (83)	27 (57)	3.65	2.42	1.66	1.38
1980	52	40 (77)	28 (54)	3.35	2.68	1.88	1.45
1981	59	47 (80)	17 (29)	3.21	2.06	0.75	0.60
1982	67	60 (90)	33 (49)	3.64	2.37	1.30	1.16
Overall[c]	397	329 (83)	189 (47)	3.52	2.33	1.33	1.10

[a] % of territorial pairs.

[b] Excludes broods of 0.

[c] The figures exclude 19 repeat nests. If these are included, an overall average of 50% of territorial pairs produced young, or 60% of pairs which laid, and the overall production was 1.15 young per territorial pair.

those which failed at an early stage, they are not biased in any obvious way, and can be taken at face value. The last figure gives the best measure of breeding success, because it accounts for failures at all stages to fledging and for repeat nests.

Besides nonlaying, the main proximate causes of breeding failure included egg-breaking or addling (often associated with high DDE levels in eggs), robbing of eggs and young by people, and mortality of young (Table 2). In some nests, the young died within a day or two after hatching, and in other nests the young died when larger, up to half-grown. Such mortality seemed often to occur during several-day spells of rain and mist when hunting was difficult, and may have been owing to starvation. Other failures, involving the disappearance of eggs and young between our successive nest visits, may also have resulted from human action or from nestling starvation, but we had no direct evidence. Many nests failed around the time of hatching, especially in wet years.

Overall production varied greatly between years; the mean young produced per pair ranged from 0.60 in 1981 to 1.45 in 1980. This was owing more to variations in the proportion of clutches producing young than to variations in brood sizes in successful nests. The proportion of clutches producing young varied in different years according to the rainfall in May (late incubation or early chick stages, Figure 2, $b=-0.130$, $r=-0.792$, $P<0.02$). Breeding production expressed as young per territorial pair did not vary with the size of the breeding population ($b=0.002$, $r=0.134$, NS). Hence, production was not density-dependent at the population levels found.

The male:female ratio among 133 nearly-fledged broods was 148:167 (1:1.1), a ratio not significantly different from unity. The equivalent ratio at the egg stage was examined retrospectively for broods in which all eggs gave rise to large young, and was again close to unity. Within the whole sample the ratio did not vary according to brood size.

Survival of Breeders. — Survival of breeders was estimated from repeated trapping of individuals on the same territories year after year. Females were easier to catch than males, so more information was obtained for females (Table 3). On 61 (81%) of 75 territories where females were caught in successive years it was the same individual the second year, and on 14, a different one. On six of eight (75%) territories where males were caught in successive years, it was the same individual the second year, and on two a different individual. For females alone, annual turnover was 14 of 75 (19%), and for both sexes combined, 16 of 83 (19%). For this analysis, a territory was included more than once if the occupant was caught in more than two years, the unit of observation being one "territory-year."

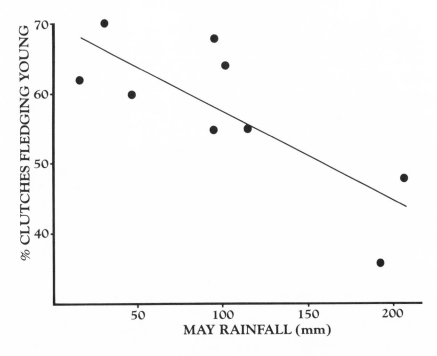

FIGURE 2. Proportion of clutches which produced fledglings, shown in relation to the May rainfall in different years ($b=-0.13$, $r=-0.792$, $P<0.02$).

TABLE 2. Causes of breeding failure by territorial pairs, 1974-82.

Cause of failure	n	% of all failures ($n = 208$)	% of all breeding opportunities ($n = 397$)
Non-laying	68	33	17
Eggs broken/addled	30	14	8
Eggs deserted	3	1	1
Eggs disappeared	8	4	2
Eggs robbed[a]	23	11	6
Young disappeared at hatch	13	6	3
Young died	8	4	2
Young disappeared	20	10	5
Young robbed[a]	13	6	3
Unknown	22	11	6

[a] By human agency, recognized when disappearance of nest contents coincided with signs that the cliff had been climbed. In some cases men were seen at the nest, or later caught with eggs or young. Other nests, when contents disappeared without trace, may also have been robbed.

TABLE 3.   Minimum survival of female Peregrine breeders in different years.

	1977	1978	1979	1980	1981	Overall
No. caught on territory where occupant trapped in next year	13	18	17	13	13	74
No. recaught on same territory in next year	11	15	12	11	11	60
No. recaught on different territory in next year	1	1	1	2	1	6
Total recaught	12	16	13	13	12	66
Minimum survival %	92	89	76	100	92	89

Turnover resulted partly from mortality and partly from movement, for some females changed territories between years. Of 68 females recaptured in a later year, 61 had stayed on the same territory and 7 had moved to a different territory (3-33 km away). Of six males recaptured, all were on the same territory. Allowing for these known movements, the minimum possible survival among those caught was 68 of 75 (91%) for females, and 74 of 83 (89%) for both sexes combined (say 90% as a working figure). The estimate was minimal, because some missing birds may have moved to other territories where no trapping was done, either inside or outside the study area.

Data for females suggest that survival may have varied considerably between years, but the annual samples were small and not amenable to statistical testing (Table 3). Annual survival did not appear to be density-dependent, however, as it did not vary with the size of the breeding population ($b=0.144$, $r=0.274$, NS). It seemed especially low for females handled in 1979. Omitting that year increased the overall estimate from 91% per year to 93%. In this analysis, a bird was included more than once if it was caught in more than two years, as the unit of observation was one "bird-year."

Our estimate of annual survival may have been atypically high, because the known population increased during the study period, when mortality may have been lower than during a period of stability. Also, birds trapped may not have been representative of all breeders. The trapped sample was weighted towards regular inland territories. Inland birds may have survived better than birds on coastal territories where numbers were still depleted and perhaps subject to greater pesticide influence. In addition, it was generally easier to catch females which bred successfully year after year than those which did not lay or which failed soon after laying. If mortality was heavier among the untrapped sector, then our estimate of survival may have been higher than the mean for the whole territorial population. The lack of human persecution of adults at nesting cliffs might also have contributed to high survival, compared with some other populations.

Moreover, our values were considerably higher than previous estimates of adult survival made from ring recoveries. No such general estimate has been made for Britain, but (excluding first-year birds) values of 75% per year have been given for the United States (Enderson 1969b), 81% and 72% for Finland and Germany (Mebs 1971), and 68% for Sweden (Lindberg 1977b). The discrepancy between our result and these others could have resulted partly from genuine differences between populations and time periods, especially since the earlier estimates included some recoveries from the organo-chlorine era, when Peregrine numbers were declining. It could also have been owing partly to the known tendency of general ring recoveries to overestimate mortality, at least as far as breeding birds are concerned (Perrins 1971, Newton 1979). Also, our figures were derived from an elite sector of the population, namely regularly breeding adults, whereas estimates based on general ring recoveries were probably derived from all sectors of the population, including nonbreeders.

Age of First Breeding. — Birds were assumed to be breeding for the first time if they were first to use a territory which was occupied during the study period, or if they replaced another bird on a territory and were not known to have previously nested. Egg laying was taken as the criterion of breeding by females, and egg laying by a mate as breeding by males. Of six trapped males, four were breeding at age 2 years, one at age 3 years and one at age 4 or 5. This last was a bird first caught at age 5 which was not present on that territory two years previously, so had moved in at age 4 or 5. Another male occupied a territory at age 3, but his mate did not produce eggs that year, nor in two previous years. We supposed that with a different female, this male would have bred. Of 16 trapped females, 2 were first breeding at age 1, 13 at age 2 and 1 at age 3. Thus, in both sexes, age at first breeding varied among individuals, but may have been earlier, on average, in females (2.0 years) than in males (2.5 years). Except for yearlings, we could not be absolutely certain that individuals had not bred elsewhere earlier in their lives. However, any such bias was probably slight or nonexistent because movements were found for only 10% of recaptures, all females. Rather, these estimates of mean age of first breeding were almost certainly too low because, in a short study, birds which started at an early age were more likely to be recorded than those that began later, after the study ended.

Yearling birds were recognized, whether trapped or not, by their brown juvenile plumage. Only one yearling male was at a nesting cliff (forming 0.5% of all territorial males), compared with 19 yearling females (5% of territorial females), providing another indication that males occupied breeding cliffs at a later age than females. The one yearling male did not breed, and only seven of the 19 yearling females laid eggs. All yearlings were paired.

The greater mean age of first breeding in males could have resulted from their surplus among Peregrines of breeding age, so that on average males had to wait longer than females to breed. The slight surplus of females at fledging was not significant statistically. However, the ratio of first-year to older individuals among our ringed Peregrines reported dead suggested that males survived longer than females after fledging. This ratio was 6:11 (i.e., 0.55) in males and 13:12 (i.e., 1.1) in females. On such small samples the difference was not significant, but was consistent with a longer mean lifespan in males, resulting in a surplus of males among potential breeders.

Another explanation for the greater mean age of territorial males is that breeding puts more demands on males than on females, making it difficult for young males to attempt it. Both sexes were involved in defense activities, but males also had to provide food for mates and families, whereas females did not. Thus to breed, a greater degree of hunting competence was required of males than of females.

Survival of Prebreeders. — We had no direct measure of survival for individuals not yet breeding. They would have been largely first-year individuals, plus some older birds, at least up to four years old (see above). Most such birds were not regularly at nesting cliffs and thus could not be counted.

Survival in prebreeders, between fledging and recruitment to the breeding population, was estimated indirectly from knowledge of territorial birds present each year, their mean survival (90% per year), mean age at first breeding (2 years in females) and annual production of young. The method entailed estimating numbers of new recruits entering the breeding population each year, and expressing this as a proportion of the young produced two years previously (Table 4). On this basis, some 44% of fledglings entered the breeding population over the study period. This estimate referred to survival over a mean two-year prebreeding period. It unrealistically assumed a closed population, but since Peregrines in neighboring regions showed roughly similar population trend and breeding success (Ratcliffe 1980), errors in the estimate may not have been great. If the breeding population had stayed constant, rather than increasing, while breeder survival and production remained unchanged, then prebreeder survival would have dropped to 22%. Again this is not annual survival, but total survival over the prebreeding period. We know of no comparable figures from other studies, but survival through the first year alone was calculated at

TABLE 4. Calculation of Peregrine survival between fledging and recruitment, with a mean age of first breeding of 2 years (see text).

	(a) No. of territorial adults present[a]	(b) No. of new recruits replacing previous breeders which died[b]	(c) No. of new recruits causing population increase[c]	(d) Total new recruits (b + c)	(e) No. of young produced two years previously	(f) % survival between fledging and recruitment (d/e)[d]
1976	71	7	2	9	27	33
1977	82	8	11	19	24	79
1978	91	9	9	18	29	62
1979	96	10	5	15	47	32
1980	108	11	12	23	59	39
1981	125	13	17	30	63	48
1982	138	14	13	27	75	36
Overall	711	72	69	141	324	44

[a] Pairs plus singles.
[b] Number of territorial birds in previous year × 10% (annual mortality).
[c] Number of territorial birds minus number in previous year.
[d] For purposes of calculation, annual mortality of territorial birds (10%) and age of first breeding (2 years) were assumed to be constant throughout.

30% for North America (Enderson 1969b), 29% and 44% for Finland and Germany (Mebs 1971), and 41% for Sweden (Lindberg 1977b). As these estimates are from general ring recoveries and partly cover a period of population decline, it is hard to assess their relevance to the current scene.

Dispersal Between Hatch Site and Breeding Site. — Thirty-nine breeders (24 males, 15 females) trapped at cliffs had been ringed as nestlings in the study area or elsewhere, enabling us to examine dispersal. Distances involved may not have been typical of the whole population, because ringing effort was geographically uneven in the rest of Britain, but such distances should have been comparable between the sexes. In general, females dispersed farther than males, with median distances of 68 km and 20 km, respectively, and maxima of 185 km and 75 km. These movements occurred in any direction from the hatch site.

Proportions of trapped breeders raised in the study area provided further evidence for differential dispersal between sexes. Of 23 males trapped, 14 (61%) were ringed as nestlings in the study area, while of 64 females trapped, 14 (22%) were ringed as nestlings in the area. The difference in proportions between the sexes was significant ($X^2 = 10.1$, $P < 0.01$), and, as the sex ratio at fledging was almost equal (see above), the difference was consistent with some females dispersing further than males.

In addition, 42 birds ringed as nestlings in south Scotland were reported by others, mostly as found dead. The distances moved by these birds should not have been constrained by areas of ringing, and are therefore not comparable with those for retraps mentioned above; but they should again be comparable between the sexes. Seventeen males moved less far than 25 females, with median distances of 65 km and 87 km, respectively, and maxima of 357 km and 324 km (Figure 3). These differences were not significant.

Some birds ringed as breeders were reported by members of the public. Of three females, one was at the breeding cliff itself (March), another was 11 km from it (December), while the third (at least 7 years old) was found in May 60 km from the territory where it had been trapped four years previously. It had crossed over one intervening territory, but was not near any known breeding cliff; it had an injured foot and, considering the month and locality, was almost certainly not breeding. One male, ringed as a nestling, bred in at least four consecutive years at a territory 23 km from its hatch site, but was then found poisoned (in late March or early April) 28 km from its nesting territory, having moved across one intervening territory. So, excluding the sick female, three firm recoveries of adults were consistent with our own retraps of breeders, most of which were on the same or

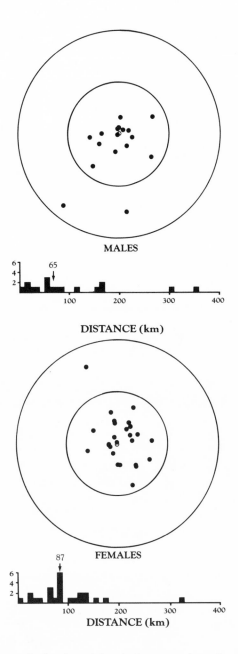

FIGURE 3. Dispersal of male and female Peregrines from the south Scotland study area, as shown by ring recoveries from the general public. Circles at 100 km and 200 km radius.

nearby territories in successive years.

Fifteen birds ringed as nestlings were handled more than once in later life: 11 were trapped on the same territory each time, but had moved 110 km, 110 km, 100 km, 63 km, 53 km, 42 km, 41 km, 28 km, 23 km, 18 km and 16 km from their respective hatch sites; the other four moved distances of 23 km, 68 km, 73 km and 90 km from their hatch sites, and then 33 km, 8 km, 10 km and 32 km between one breeding place and another. Seemingly, then, Peregrines in south Scotland tended to make their longest movements during the first year of life (and in any direction), and having acquired a nesting territory, they tended to remain in the same general area thereafter. We do not extrapolate these generalizations to any "floating" nonterritorial adults in the population, or to territorial Peregrines in other districts, where local food supply for falcons may be more depleted in winter.

DISCUSSION

Our data suggest that this expanding population in south Scotland had a high annual survival of breeders, a low reproductive rate which varied greatly from year to year, an age of first breeding higher in males than in females, and a dispersal in the first year of life in which some females moved farther than males. Measurements of reproduction, mortality, and dispersal made on this increasing population may be inappropriate for application to stable or decreasing populations.

Regulation of Numbers in Stable Populations. — In the absence of pesticides or other human influence, Peregrine breeding populations normally remain relatively stable through time. Breeding numbers in several parts of Britain have fluctuated by no more than 8% of their mean values over periods of 10 or more years, and all instances of greater change are attributable to human influence (Ratcliffe 1980). Similar stability was usual in various parts of continental Europe (e.g., Kleinstäuber 1969, Lindberg 1977b) and North America (Hickey 1942, Cade 1960, Hagar 1969, Hickey and Anderson 1969), or indeed anywhere where pre-DDT Peregrines were studied. Stability could therefore be regarded as the normal state for Peregrine breeding populations. This stability was presumably owing to a constant supply of nest sites and food, the main resources which naturally limit breeding densities (Newton 1979, Ratcliffe 1980).

On the other hand, breeding production is less stable. In many studies, breeding success was depressed by egg collecting in former times and by pesticides in recent times. Yet even in relatively undisturbed populations, mean production per pair often varied greatly year to year, as much as two-fold or more in some areas (e.g., Kleinstäuber 1969 for East Germany, Ratcliffe 1980 for Britain).

Stability of territorial population despite fluctuating breeding success implies the action of density-dependent factors, with greater losses following years when reproduction is high than when reproduction is low. Losses could fall more heavily on breeding adults, or on pre-breeders between fledging and recruitment to the breeding population. By analogy with other birds, density-dependent loss is much more probable in prebreeders than among established breeders, and in south Scotland, where loss among breeders was measured each year, it did not vary with the size of the breeding population. Annual loss, whether from breeders or prebreeders, results from a combination of mortality and movement.

Greater loss between fledging and recruitment could be achieved by either (1) increase in the annual loss of prebreeders, or (2) delay in age of recruitment, so that even with the same annual loss, total loss before breeding is greater, or (3) a combination of both. In other words, with a stable breeding population and adult survival, annual loss of prebreeders and/or age of first breeding will necessarily be lower in years of low total population than in years of high total population. This seems obvious, yet previous attempts to model raptor populations have not allowed for density dependence, or for annual variations in prebreeding mortality or mean age of first breeding.

Density dependence in Peregrine populations results from a relatively fixed number of nesting territories maintaining breeding pairs at a fairly constant level. The annual addition of new recruits is dependent on gaps created by the loss of previously established breeders. The existence of potential recruits is shown by the fact that, when adults are killed at nesting cliffs, they are often quickly replaced by other adults, some of which may breed the same year (Hagar 1969, Newton 1979, Ratcliffe 1980). One male acquired four adult mates in quick succession as each was shot (MacIntyre 1960), indicating in this instance a considerable reserve of potential female breeders.

Regulation of Numbers in Changing Populations. — In recent years, Peregrine populations in much of Europe and North America have not been stable, but increasing, having recovered from the low numbers imposed by use of organochlorine pesticides in the 1950s and 1960s. In populations whose numbers increase as fast as reproduction and mortality will allow, density-dependent factors are unlikely to operate in any significant manner. Reproduction is not necessarily any higher than in stable populations, and may indeed often be lower because of residual DDE contamination. On the other hand, increasing populations are likely to differ in at least two ways from stable ones: (1) mortality may often be lower, because competition is less and mortality which does occur is mostly "inevitable mortality" (owing to old age, accidents, etc.) and not density-dependent (resulting from

competition), and (2) mean age of first breeding may be lower, again
through reduced competition for breeding sites. In studies of stable
populations, made before the introduction of DDT, it was apparently
rare to find birds in first-year plumage at nesting cliffs (Hickey 1942,
Bond 1946, Cade 1960, MacIntyre 1960, White 1969a). In recent
increasing populations, in contrast, the presence of first-year birds at
nesting cliffs has become almost commonplace, but more frequent
among females than males. Hence, parameters appropriate to stable
populations are unlikely to apply in the same way to increasing ones,
in which density-dependent factors are probably slight or nonexistent,
and prebreeder mortality and age of first breeding may be lower.

Age of First Breeding. — Apart from competition for some
limited resource, factors that influence age of first breeding are largely
unknown. One traditional view is that onset of breeding is delayed
because of poor gonad development, and first-year birds are called
"immature." We know of no evidence for this view in Peregrines. In
the easy conditions of captivity, one might expect birds to breed as
soon as their gonads were developed, in their first year. In the breeding
program at Cornell, both sexes have bred in their first year (only one
male, several females), but most individuals waited longer, with a mean
age of first breeding around three years in females and four years in
males (T. Cade pers. comm.). This suggests some intrinsic inhibiting
factor which is partly independent of environmental conditions. In
such captive birds, stress may have been more important in young
than in older birds.

In the wild, other factors may be superimposed to delay breeding
beyond the age set by intrinsic factors. European Sparrowhawks can
breed only if they can obtain enough food (Newton 1986). Only then
can they spare enough time to defend a nesting territory, only then can
the male feed the female, and only then can the female accumulate the
body reserves necessary to breed. Some underweight individuals do
not defend nesting territories, even though unused territories are
available, while other underweight individuals manage to defend
territories but do not produce eggs. In such cases, breeding is postponed because of inability to obtain sufficient food. This is more
frequent in young individuals, owing to their poor foraging skill, or to
their being confined by older birds to habitats where prey are scarce.
The problem can be resolved for the individual if it improves its
foraging skill, if it can move to an area with more prey, or if the prey
itself increases. As Peregrines also need to defend territories, feed
mates, and accumulate body reserves, they may face constraints similar
to those faced by European Sparrowhawks. This might result in
"floating" birds in some areas, even though potential nesting territories
are available for occupation.

Competition with other Peregrines for a limited number of nesting territories could also delay breeding beyond the age at which gonad development and foraging skills allow. This is probably the major factor limiting age of first breeding in stable Peregrine populations that occupy their breeding habitat to the fullest. Since, in increasing populations, some individuals do not breed until their fourth or fifth year, in stable populations the delay in certain individuals may be even greater.

Population Models. — From estimates of survival and age of first breeding, it is a simple matter to calculate the mean production of young necessary to maintain a population. This procedure has become fashionable in raptor studies (e.g., Olsson 1958, Henny 1972, Lindberg 1977b), as a quick check on whether populations are likely to be self-sustaining. The procedure can be misleading, however, because it assumes fixed values for survival and breeding age, both of which may change with breeding density. The procedure may be appropriate for depleted populations, where density-dependent effects are minimal (see Henny and Wight 1969 for successful application of the technique in Osprey), but not for populations near the limit of their resources, where survival or age of first breeding could be strongly density-dependent. Such populations could suffer a very substantial fall in production before any decline in breeding numbers occurred, because poor production could immediately be compensated by improved survival or earlier breeding. In long-lived, slow-to-breed species such as the Peregrine, a fall in production would have much less effect on subsequent breeding numbers than would the same proportionate fall in adult survival, even with no density dependence. Indeed the declines in some breeding populations in the 1950s appeared to be so rapid that they could not have resulted from poor breeding alone, but must have entailed reductions in adult survival (Young 1969).

In conclusion, a priority for future studies is some assessment of the degree of change in Peregrine reproduction, age of first breeding, and survival of prebreeders and breeders, as populations rise. Only then can the effects of reduced production or survival on breeding numbers be more accurately predicted.

ACKNOWLEDGEMENTS

We thank D. A. Ratcliffe for much initial help and advice; G. Carse and R. Roxburgh for help in the collection of field data; J. Enderson, R. Fyfe and F. P. Ward for valuable advice on trapping; F. P. Ward and T. J. Cade of The Peregrine Fund, Inc., for help with funding; and J. P. Dempster and D. A. Ratcliffe for constructive comments on the manuscript.

63 | The Natural Regulation of Peregrine Falcon Populations

W. Grainger Hunt

In large portions of the Peregrine's range, the two classical parameters of population regulation, fecundity and mortality, have changed to the Peregrine's detriment in recent times. This has occurred because of the geometric increase in human populations and the ability of technology to alter the environment adversely for Peregrines. These recent causes of Peregrine population limitation and decline have distracted our attention from an understanding of environmental circumstances under which Peregrines have evolved. In this paper, I will focus on natural limiting factors of Peregrine populations that existed before industrialization. These natural limiting factors are probably operating today in regions where pesticides and similar influences have no effects on the reproduction and mortality of Peregrines.

First, I believe it is now generally accepted that the innate strategy of every organism is to maximize the number of its eventual descendants (or genes identical by descent), and that populational phenomena are merely statistical consequences of the actions of individuals. Natural selection thus results in the tendency of individuals of all species to reproduce as rapidly as possible under existing and historical environmental conditions (see Williams 1966, Gadgil and Bossert 1970, Trivers 1985). Reasoning behind counterarguments to this idea (e.g., Wynne-Edwards 1962, Skutch 1967) involve the unlikely process of group-selection (see Williams 1971).

If birds reproduce as much as they can, then why are their populations not more dense than they are? Lack (1954) solved this problem by proposing that, for many species, there is likely to be density-dependent competition for resources. As population density increases, the scarcity of a resource acts to decrease natality and/or increase mortality. When population size becomes low, reduced competition results in higher reproductive rates and/or lower mortality rates. I will argue that in some geographical regions major elements of population regulation in Peregrines are density-independent.

TERRITORIALITY

A system for population regulation of Peregrines was proposed by Ratcliffe (1962) based on studies of nesting populations in Great Britian. His idea was that nesting densities are limited first by the availability of suitable cliffs and still further through territorial behavior causing a certain spacing of pairs. Territoriality will limit density where suitable cliff sites are close enough to provoke exclusion by near neighbors. Both Hickey (1942) and Cade (1960) made similar suggestions.

A suitable nesting cliff in the British Isles was one with adequate height, security, exposure, altitude, and nesting ledges. Ratcliffe (1962) said that territoriality is the medium through which breeding density has become adjusted to an equilibrium with food supply. In other words, an individual which allows its territory to shrink in size by sharing it with other breeders will have insufficient food for that maximum number of high-quality young it would otherwise be capable of raising; consequently it will tend to leave fewer genes than individuals programmed to defend a more adequate territory.

Ratcliffe (1969) remarked that overt fighting was rarely seen in British Peregrines and suggested that territoriality was of a more subtle nature as in certain passerines. On the other hand, Cade (1960) in his Alaskan studies described some fairly intense encounters between territory-holders and trespassers in Alaska in which there was rather rough bodily contact. Perhaps the arctic Peregrines obliged to vacate their breeding territories in winter are more likely to find themselves in combat with competitors arriving more or less simultaneously in spring.

Ratcliffe (1969, 1980) showed that breeding densities in Britain were greatest where there was the largest overall supply of food. Beebe (1960) found that territories were small (i.e., Peregrines bred in greater densities) in conditions of extraordinary prey abundance on Langara Island, and Nelson and Myres (1976) related increase in territory size to recent declines in prey there.

NONBREEDING ADULTS

What kinds of evidence led Ratcliffe to develop his hypothesis of Peregrine population control? One important observation was that prior to recent decades there was a regular occupancy of practically all historical sites, and the number of pairs in a region tended neither to increase nor decrease with time. These facts suggested an upper limit to the number of suitable cliffs and a constancy of distance between pairs (Ratcliffe 1980).

Another point of evidence was the apparent existence of floating populations of nonbreeding adults. Hickey (1942) observed that if a Peregrine was shot at its eyrie, a replacement would arrive at least by the following spring. He assembled a number of examples of rapid remating and reoccupation, and said:

> There is a British record (Witherington, 1909) of a female replaced within thirty-six hours of her death, and at one Canadian site the adults were replaced so quickly that two new birds eventually raised a brood that neither had parented (Taverner, *in litt*). These and countless less spectacular observations could imply the existence of a mobile non-breeding population of considerable importance to the species. As a rule, missing birds are replaced by at least the start of the next breeding season.

Ratcliffe (1962) also referred to the existence in Britain of a nonbreeding segment of adult Peregrines. His evidence came mainly from the rapidity of reoccupation of areas in southern England where Peregrines had been decimated during the war, and more recently he has reviewed other evidence (Ratcliffe 1980).

What causes these nonbreeding adult populations? If individual Peregrines are indeed trying to maximize their reproductive output, then why would some refrain from breeding? If a Peregrine could not get a high quality cliff because all were occupied by stronger individuals, why would it not instead join another unmated adult at a substandard cliff on the off-chance of raising young? I see two possible explanations. One is a sex difference in mortality or maturation such that all adults of one sex are paired, and the surplus of adults of the other sex cannot find mates; there is little information on this point, although Hickey (1942) has reported remating by both sexes. The other explanation is that attempts at reproduction involve risk, either through direct mortality or bodily wear and tear, or both. Williams (1966), Gadgil and Bossert (1970), Pianka (1974), and many others argue that increases in reproductive effort are accompanied by decreases in survivorship, and that delayed maturity is often a response to risk and/or futility of competition with older individuals in a breeding population. If an adult's chances of surviving to breed in future years are high, the intensity of each breeding attempt may be lowered, especially in early adulthood. Of course, this reduction of reproductive effort is only adaptive if it results, on the average, in the individual producing a greater number of surviving offspring during its lifetime.

THE QUALITY OF BREEDING LOCATIONS

A Peregrine's willingness to make a breeding attempt at a particular site may be based on genetically programmed responses to external cues indicating habitat quality. Peregrines might be expected to forego breeding if the perceived risk from exposure to predation or dangerous competitors is high. Likewise, if conditions do not appear to favor the production and survival of a healthy brood, then normal risk and the additional costs of breeding (e.g., bodily wear and tear) might outweigh the small potential for success. On the other hand, if prey were particularly abundant and easily obtainable at a site, Peregrines breeding there despite moderate risks might leave more eventual descendents than more cautious individuals. Natural selection would favor the development of the Peregrine's ability to perceive and respond to cost/benefit factors in the selection of nesting sites and to regulate the intensity of reproductive effort.

Figure 1 expresses nest site selection as a balance between risk and reproductive potential. The darker areas represent the highest expected degree of reproductive effort, and the triangle shape is considered to be the area in which a Peregrine might be willing to breed. The dots are random cliffs (or clusters of cliffs), some of which fall inside and some outside the "willingness to breed" area. Birds might not be

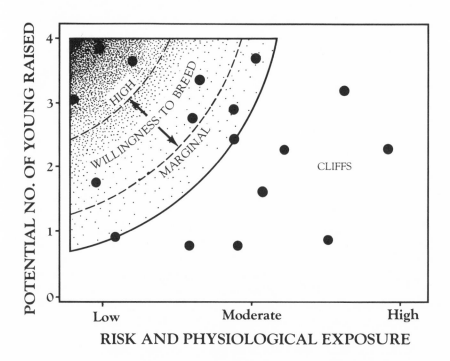

FIGURE 1.   Peregrines select breeding locations in a compromise between risk and
reproductive promise. See text for explanations.

expected to be tenacious to cliffs in the lighter areas of the triangle. The cliffs inside the triangle might be thought of as "serviceable breeding locations" (SBLs).

The quality of an SBL involves all local aspects which influence the probability and extent of nesting success and the well-being of breeders. It therefore includes (1) the actual nesting site, and (2) the entire foraging area. Generally speaking, an SBL is optimal where component variables combine to produce a maximum number of surviving young while minimizing reductions in parental survivorship and future fecundity.

There may be a dozen or so variables affecting the quality of SBLs. Some critical aspects of the nest site may include an adequate substrate for egg incubation and activities of nestlings, an adequate temperature regime, appropriate directional exposure (see Porter and White 1973), defendability, and isolation from predators and parasites. The area of foraging must be characterized by a sufficient abundance of prey and by physiographic features and foliage profiles that result in prey being vulnerable to Peregrine attacks. The presence of competitors or dangerous predators must also affect SBL quality. If the perceptible quality of a location falls below the threshold level, then Peregrines will presumably refuse to breed there.

The probability of the simultaneous occurrence in time and space of all necessary components of a serviceable breeding location may be low. Even single more obvious basic requisites for Peregrine breeding such as cliffs with suitable ledges are in most cases uncommon and often particulate in distribution. Therefore, within any broad geographical region there is a certain limited number of SBLs.

In a hypothetical, otherwise unchecked expanding population of Peregrines (fecundity greater than mortality), pairs tend to fill all SBLs, and then nonbreeding adults will accumulate for a certain period of time. The question of how many nonbreeders will accumulate depends on survivorship. Sooner or later annual productivity approximates the death rate and the population reaches equilibrium.

REGULATION OF A POPULATION AT EQUILIBRIUM

Let us consider a hypothetical population for which there are 100 SBLs. The average productivity is two fledged young, mortality during the first year is 50%, and afterwards, 25%. Under these conditions, the population reaches equilibrium at about 598 individuals (at the time of fledging), and will remain at this size year after year so long as survivorship, fecundity, and the number of SBLs remain constant. If the age at first breeding is three years, then there are 23 individuals three years or older which cannot secure a nesting location in any one year. If the oldest individuals all have territories, then the median age of the breeders is 5 years.

It is interesting to view equilibrium sizes of other hypothetical populations as functions of various adult and juvenile mortality rates. Figure 2 gives fledging-time population sizes (the lower numbers in each cell) at equilibrium for various survivorship values. Here I assume that all 100 SBLs are occupied by pairs producing an average of two fledglings per year and with a maximum physiological longevity of 20 years. The upper figures in each cell indicate the number of surplus adults — in this case, birds over two years old without breeding sites. In some cases there is no surplus of two-year-olds, and yearlings may breed at some of the SBLs. The lower left-hand portion of this table contains values of population size in which there seem to be unreasonably large numbers of nonbreeders. But the unlikelihood of such

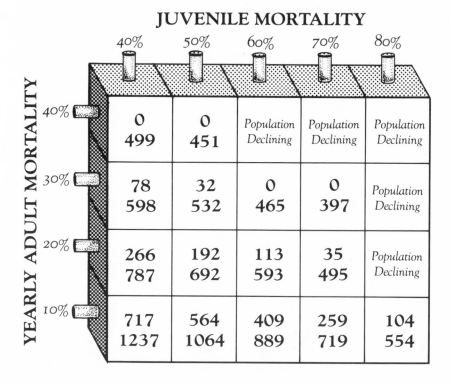

FIGURE 2. The effects of various mortality rates on equilibrium sizes in a hypothetical Peregrine population limited by 100 breeding locations. Assume a mean of 2 fledged young per nest and a maximum longevity of 20 years. The lower numbers in each cell give population sizes at fledging time. The upper numbers indicated floaters 2 years old or older.

a great number of adult nonbreeders is reduced considerably by imagining the average age of first reproduction to be 4-5 years or more. These ages are not unreasonable; for example, among shearwaters (*Puffinus* spp.), some populations of which are believed to be limited by nest sites, the age of first reproduction ranges from 4-8 years (Ashmole 1963).

We know from field studies (Mearns and Newton 1984) and from captive populations that females may begin breeding in their first year and males in their second; but there is little information on the ecological age of first breeding in *stable*, undisturbed populations of Peregrines. There are a number of examples where yearling females have been seen nesting, but this may be in response to the low numbers of Peregrines in recent years and reduced competition. In other species with long-delayed recruitment, individuals may breed much earlier than normal when competition is reduced. The Parasitic Jaeger normally begins breeding at age 4, but in years of lemming abundance it may breed at age 2 (Lack 1966).

Securing an SBL may often be opportunistic owing to the death of one member of an established pair. No doubt a considerable yearly turnover exists, so young individuals at the right place at the right time probably do manage to breed. On the other hand, a young adult might be hesitant to risk a violent encounter with an older, more experienced adult in order to obtain an SBL. Imagine a three-year-old male coming into the territory of a 10-year-old male and trying to displace him! Not only is success unlikely, but he stands a good chance of being injured or killed (see Cade 1960). In any case, time would be wasted that could be used searching for a vacancy during the rather short period of courtship.

It has been shown theoretically that the tendency to make an assertive effort to breed increases with age (see Gadgil and Bossert 1970). It is likely that age and experience provide a bird with the ability to be very aggressive and get away with it. It is relevant to note that there may be progressive plumage changes as adult Peregrines age. The chest bars in some males, for example, become thinner, the patch of light color in the crop region spreads downward, and the color of the feet, cere, and eye-ring go from yellow to deep orange. Does a female respond more readily or is another male more intimidated by a thin-barred, orange-footed male with a deep white throat patch? Are there age-specific elements in Peregrine voices?

THE QUESTION OF
DENSITY-DEPENDENT REGULATION

In a population limited by SBLs, age at first breeding is likely to be a density-dependent phenomenon. The greater the population size relative to the number of SBLs, the more competition takes place for breeding locations, and the less likely young adults are to reproduce.

For density dependence to be cited as a mechanism of population regulation in Peregrines it is necessary to show that the number of territories or reproductive output per territory changes as population size changes within normal limits, or that changes in mortality rate accompany normal changes in population density. Density-dependent checks might occur, for example, where territories are regularly contiguous and there is enough territorial strife or competition for food to depress natality or significantly increase adult mortality. But if the number of such territories remains fairly constant, as is usually the case with Peregrines, and the rate of competition remains constant, then this could not be thought of as a population limited by changes in birth and death rates as functions of density.

The regulation of a Peregrine breeding population by a limited number of SBLs cannot be considered density-dependent because the number of SBLs is determined by physiographic and biotic factors extraneous to Peregrines and would not be expected to increase or decrease in response to changes in total population density. A limited number of SBLs sets an upper limit to the size of yearly cohorts. These cohorts experience a variety of mortalities, some of which may be related to density, but I believe there is little if any feedback on the number of occupied breeding territories as a result of changes in mortality or fecundity.

Density-dependent regulation of nonbreeding segments of Peregrine populations also seems improbable. Peregrines usually eat a rather wide variety of prey. Interacting with a single prey species (on a population level) to a point where Peregrines starve as a result of prey depletion is unlikely over most of the Peregrine's range. Moreover, while most of the terrestrial world is unsuitable for Peregrine breeding because of the absence of cliffs, much of it (e.g., wetlands) is quite appropriate for Peregrine foraging. Nonbreeders and wintering migrants probably achieve sparse enough densities to avoid competition altogether. In pristine times, the Peregrine may have been a common enough and widespread enough predator to influence the evolution of many avian adaptations.

Productivity is the demographic component of a Peregrine population most likely to be affected by density-dependent influences. When the number of nonbreeding adults is large, the disruptive effects of competition for SBLs might be expected to decrease natality. Haller (1982), studying Golden Eagles nesting in the Alps, noted that during this century the species' legal protection resulted in decreased productivity and increased numbers of nonbreeders. He remarked that,

"... pairs frequently confronted with single eagles in spring have no breeding success for years due to their increased territorial activity." Haller observed eagles kill or seriously wound each other in territorial conflicts, but only in conditions of increased population density.

It has yet to be demonstrated whether increasing numbers of adult Peregrines without territories depress productivity, but observations on Peregrines in Baden-Württemberg (Brücher and Wegner Chapter 60) and in the French Jura (Monneret Chapter 23) indicate that interference competition does exist. Territorial intrusion may be more risky among Peregrines than other species. Peregrines, being adapted to kill birds their own size and even larger, are more dangerous to one another than are large raptors adapted to seizing smaller prey. Also, Peregrines use stoop momentum to inflict deadly blows in passing, so it is possible for a Peregrine to injure another without grasping it. A Peregrine attacking an intruder from its perch on a large cliff might well be able to inflict more damage than it would receive. Threat of injury is especially meaningful when mates cooperate in driving away intruders so that food supplies might be insulated within defended spaces at levels where Peregrine productivity is unaffected by food competition.

Rivalry for SBLs should be most intense before and during courtship because a Peregrine displacing another at that time has a chance of producing young that year. But seizure of an SBL is advantageous at any time of year because of the increased likelihood of breeding there in succeeding years. A period when breeding females might be most vulnerable to displacement is just after nesting. Newton et al. (1983) reported that female European Sparrowhawks lose considerable amounts of weight when there are young in the nest, apparently because they feed the nestlings preferentially, depriving themselves of all but surplus food. K. E. Riddle (pers. comm.) found similar weight loss in brooding female Peregrines in Alaska. Interestingly, on Langara Island, British Columbia, Nelson (Chapter 69) observed a tendency for more frequent replacement of female Peregrines having larger-than-average broods the previous year.

Some nesting populations of Peregrines may be more affected than others by density-dependent factors. In the nonmigratory population on Amchitka Island in the Aleutians, where all age classes appear to be resident throughout the year, there is apparently considerable juvenile mortality in winter probably owing to competition for food and to bad weather (White 1975). The nearly extirpated population of Finland might have been regulated by density-dependent checks (Linkola and Suominen 1969). These birds nested on the ground, a habit which presumably rendered their territories movable, compressible, and less defendable, and hence more subject to competition and stress with rises in population density.

On the other hand, in continental regions where suitable cliff locations are often particulate in distribution, and where there are large areas for dispersal of young and a wide and varied food base, it seems likely that the density-independent mechanism imposed by limited numbers of SBLs is paramount in controlling numbers. If cohort survivorship is high then depressed natality owing to interference at nests could reduce the nonbreeding segments of these populations by density-dependent feedback.

CONCLUSION

I have described a mechanism suggested by Ratcliffe (1962) in which each Peregrine breeding population is limited under natural circumstances by a fixed number of "serviceable breeding locations" (nesting territories) selected in compromise between risk and reproductive promise. Because suitable eyries are usually scattered, productivity is unaffected in such situations by density-dependent competition for food between pairs. Food competition among nonbreeders is also thought to be low (i.e., insufficient to cause mortality as a result of density feedback) because of the great numbers of potential prey species exploited and because foraging areas are common on the landscape while suitable nesting locations are rare. Whether increased numbers of nonbreeding adults depress productivity and survivorship of breeders remains to be studied.

ACKNOWLEDGEMENTS

I thank J. Enderson, W. Nelson, T. Cade, D. Ratcliffe and J. Barclay for encouragement and for comments on the manuscript.

64 Population Dispersal, Turnover, and Migration of Alaska Peregrines

Robert E. Ambrose and Kenton E. Riddle

Studies on declining or endangered species generally concentrate on their historical status, present status, and reasons for decline. Many studies of the Peregrine Falcon have taken this approach, but recently, as populations have recovered, more detailed studies on several aspects of the biology of the species have been undertaken.

In Alaska, two threatened or endangered subspecies of the Peregrine occur: *F. p. anatum* in the forested interior and *F. p. tundrius* in the northern tundra region. These birds were the subject of several studies starting as early as the 1950s (Cade 1960) and continuing to the present (Ambrose et al. Chapter 11). For the most part, only the very early and most recent studies have addressed topics other than status and reasons for decline. In 1979, the U. S. Fish and Wildlife Service (USFWS) initiated a survey and banding program in interior and northern Alaska to monitor these populations and determine their migration routes and wintering areas. In 1981, we began trapping adult Peregrines at nest sites to determine dispersal, turnover, movement, and mortality. In this paper, we present the results of these studies.

STUDY AREA, POPULATIONS, AND METHODS

The survey and banding program begun in 1979 was designed to monitor populations with good historical data and to band as many young as possible. Four areas were selected: the Colville and Saga-vanirktok rivers in northern Alaska, and the upper Yukon and Tanana rivers in interior Alaska. These areas were selected as index populations for *F. p. tundrius* and *F. p. anatum*, respectively. Two other areas, the lower Yukon and Porcupine rivers in interior Alaska, were also selected because large numbers of birds were known to breed in these areas, and many young could be banded. All of these areas are for the most part undisturbed, with only occasional river traffic passing near

677

the cliffs. Disturbance such as shooting or the taking of young may occur, but the effects are minimal.

Study areas totaling over 3200 km of river were surveyed annually since 1979. All surveys were made from rafts or small boats, and usually two trips were made annually through each study area. Investigators consisted of personnel from the USFWS, Bureau of Land Management, National Park Service and private research firms, plus individual volunteers.

Populations in all these regions with the exception of the Tanana River have displayed the symptoms of decline and recovery (Ambrose et al. Chapter 11): numbers declined between the mid-1960s and the early 1970s, increased during the late 1970s, and, for the most part, reached or approached their pre-DDT levels in the early 1980s. The Tanana Peregrines have recovered, but to a lesser degree than the others. The number of pairs observed in these areas for the past five years averaged 110 per year. Productivity averaged 1.94 fledged young per total pair and 2.56 fledged young per successful pair since 1981.

Most adults trapped were breeding along the upper Yukon River. Other areas where adults were trapped include the Colville, Porcupine, lower Yukon and Tanana rivers. Trapping was limited to the cliffs and associated floodplains located along the narrow river corridors.

We used a variety of techniques to trap adults. All methods worked well with most birds on the first attempt, but the birds usually became "trap wise" to each method. To overcome this problem, we began putting color bands on adults. The bands were rivet-on, anodized aluminum, with an alpha-numeric code. This method of identifying individuals worked well, and we usually could read bands on adult females. Generally, when one person was at the ledge banding young, a second person at the top or bottom of the cliff could read the band number with a high power (80X) spotting scope when the female landed nearby.

As far as we know, our trapping had no adverse impacts on the birds or on productivity. However, as each bird became "trap wise" to the various techniques used, the time required to catch that bird became longer, and hence the possibility of harm became greater.

RESULTS AND DISCUSSION

Dispersal. — We have trapped 106 different adults since 1981, 78% of them females. Thirty-one of the adults were handled more than once. Of the 106 adults trapped, 26 were banded as nestlings (20 females, 6 males). The females were breeding an average of 121 km (range=2-370 km, S. D.=87) from their natal areas, and the males, an average of 69 km (range=4-206 km, S.D.=74). All of these birds except two returned to breed in the same drainage from which they fledged. Two females moved distances of 140 km and 210 km into a different drainage, less than the distances of some movements within the same drainage. The movements discussed here address only those from natal area to breeding area. Recoveries of Peregrines from the study areas indicate that most of them wintered in South America.

Turnover, Movement, and Mortality. — Since so few males were caught, only the turnover rate for females was determined. In 40 cases we caught females on territories where trapping was also done in the next year, and in 29 cases the bird was the same individual in the same territory (Table 1). In 11 cases the bird caught was a different individual, suggesting a gross annual turnover rate of 28%; however, in at least two cases change in occupancy was owing to movement of the first female to a different territory. Corrected for this movement factor, the mean annual mortality of females does not exceed 23%. This represents a maximum value, since we may not have detected movements of other adults. Mortality rates (corrected for known movements) for the first three years of study were 29%, 30% and 33% respectively. In the fourth year, we detected no mortality. As stated earlier, the trapping took place along the narrow river corridor of the study areas. Although these areas along the river contain the most suitable Peregrine nesting habitat, several territories exist where no trapping was done. The movement of adults we observed consisted of one 5-km move to an adjacent, superior territory, and a move of 226 km from one drainage to another (likely crossing many suitable territories in the process). Although movements by adults to different territories might be expected because of the long migration undertaken by these birds, the majority of females apparently return to the same cliff each year. Since we made many captures ($n=66$) other than the

TABLE 1.   Turnover of female Peregrine Falcons along the upper Yukon and Tanana Rivers, Alaska, 1981-84.

	1981	1982	1983	1984
No. caught on territories where trapping was also done in the next year[a]	7	10	12	11
No. recaptured on the same territories in the next year	5	7	6	11
No. recaptured on different territories in the next or later years	0	0	2	0
Total recaptured	5	7	8	11
Maximum loss (%)	2 (29)	3 (30)	4 (33)	0 (0)

[a] The same female is represented more than once if she was trapped in more than 1 year.

40 which provided a year-to-year comparison, we feel that if movement was a more common event we would have caught more than two birds at different territories.

Age of First Breeding. — Only four females were banded as nestlings and later trapped as breeding adults at cliffs where we know they had replaced the female of the previous year. The mean age of these birds was 3.0 years, but this is not indicative of the age at first breeding. We could not be sure they were breeding for the first time, because in previous years they may have been at a cliff where no trapping was done. Of the 20 females banded as nestlings and later trapped as breeding adults, regardless of known use at the particular cliff the previous year, the mean age was 2.8 years (9 were 2-year-olds). The mean age for five males was 2.6 years (3 were 2-year-olds). Because these birds may have bred at an earlier age, these values of age at first breeding are likely biased on the high side. Furthermore, in several cases where we did not trap, females in subadult plumage were breeding and were usually successful if paired with an adult male. In the few cases where males in subadult plumage were members of a nesting pair, only one was successful (R. Ritchie pers. comm.).

There may be other cases of one-year-old birds attempting to breed which were not detected because of their nearly adult plumage. For instance, one male appeared to be an adult from a distance, but upon trapping we discovered he had been banded as a nestling the previous year. Only a few feathers on the back and about half the flight feathers were brown. In such cases, one-year-old birds may be recorded as adults.

Band Recoveries Outside Alaska. — Since the 1950s, over 1600 Peregrines have been banded in Alaska (Table 2). Just over 200 were banded prior to 1978, and the remainder were banded since that year; 1104 were *F. p. anatum*, 471 were *F. p. tundrius*, and 46 were *F. p. pealei*. Of the 1621 birds banded, 1523 were banded as nestlings, and 98 were banded as adults.

A total of 78 (4.7%) of these birds have been recovered; 42 outside

TABLE 2.   Peregrine Falcons banded in Alaska, 1952-85.

	Pre-1978	1979	1980	1981	1982	1983	1984	1985
No. of adult females	NR[a]	0	0	8	6	19	24	6
No. of adult males	NR[a]	0	0	1	5	2	8	1
Total adults	18	0	0	9	11	21	32	7
No. of nestlings	196	106	148	200	205	237	198	233

[a] NR=no record; sex data not available.

Alaska (Tables 3 and 4) and 40 in Alaska (there were 82 recoveries of 78 birds because 4 birds were handled twice at different locations). Of the 78 birds, 61 were banded as nestlings and 17 were banded as adults. Of the 61 nestlings, 35 were recovered once outside Alaska, 2 were recovered twice at different locations outside Alaska, 2 were recovered outside Alaska and again in Alaska, and 22 were recovered in Alaska. One of the two birds recovered twice outside Alaska was caught in Wisconsin in late September and again on the North Carolina coast in late October of the same year; the other was trapped on the Texas coast in early October and again on the Gulf of Mexico coast in Mexico in mid-October of the same year. In the two cases involving recoveries of birds as migrants outside Alaska and later as adults in Alaska, one was trapped on the Texas coast in the fall of 1979 as a hatch-year bird and later trapped as a breeding adult on the upper Yukon River in Alaska in both 1984 and 1985. The other bird was trapped as a hatch-year migrant in 1982 on the Texas coast and later trapped as a breeding adult on the Colville River in Alaska in both 1984 and 1985.

Fifty-seven of the 76 recoveries were the result of trapping programs either in Alaska or along migration routes. Seventeen recoveries were on North or South Padre Island, Texas; nearly all of these were of hatch-year birds migrating in the fall. This concentration of recoveries along the Texas coast is the result of an intensive trapping program there and may not be representative of the proportion of Alaskan Peregrines that migrate through that area. There are no comparable trapping locations or comparable trapping efforts for Peregrines west of the Texas coast that could yield such a high number of returns; however, a large percentage of Peregrines from Alaska may migrate west of the Texas coast. If the only recoveries considered are those found dead or injured, 9 of the 12 were west of Texas (6 on the west coast) and only 3 of the 12 were recovered near or east of the Texas coast. Although some of the nine recovered west of Texas may have eventually gone to the Texas or east coasts had they lived, the majority were on the west coast, and their migration may have continued on that coast.

All recoveries outside Alaska except one indicate that Alaskan Peregrines winter in South America. The exception was a bird recovered in December on the west coast of Canada. All other recoveries in Canada, the continental United States, and Mexico were during fall and spring months. Eight birds from Alaska were recovered in South America during our winter months: five were in Brazil, two in Argentina, and one in Ecuador. Recoveries by subspecies in South America do not indicate any difference in wintering areas: *F. p. tundrius* has been recovered in Brazil ($n=3$) and Argentina ($n=1$), while

TABLE 3. Recoveries outside Alaska of taiga (*F. p. anatum*) Peregrines banded in Alaska, 1967-85.

Band no.	Age[a]	Sex[b]	Date banded[c]	Location banded	Date recovered	Location recovered
57687953	HY	M	07/14/67	Porcupine River	11/22/67	North-central Argentina
72701617	HY	U	07/13/77	Upper Yukon River	10/23/77	El Salvador
816-39644	HY	M	07/07/83	Middle Yukon River	04/22/84	Padre Island, TX
816-46589	HY	M	07/12/85	Middle Yukon River	10/06/85	Loggerhead Key, FL
987-39734	HY	U	07/11/80	Upper Yukon River	11/??/80	Central Mexico
987-39759	HY	F	07/10/79	Upper Yukon River	10/07/79	Padre Island, TX
987-39767	HY	F	07/17/79	Upper Yukon River	10/06/79	Padre Island, TX
					10/10/79	E. Gulf Coast, Mexico
987-39772	HY	U	07/12/80	Upper Yukon River	01/??/81	Eastern Brazil
987-39774	HY	U	07/12/80	Upper Yukon River	02/15/82	Eastern Brazil
987-47013	HY	U	07/16/81	Lower Yukon River	04/04/82	Padre Island, TX
987-47120	HY	M	07/11/80	Lower Yukon River	09/25/80	Mt. Vernon, WA
987-47140	HY	F	07/16/80	Lower Yukon River	12/10/81	Delta, British Columbia
987-47282	HY	U	07/09/82	Kuskokwim River	10/23/82	Padre Island, TX
987-51006	HY	F	07/12/81	Tanana River	10/21/81	Padre Island, TX
987-62043	HY	U	07/16/83	Upper Yukon River	10/02/83	Padre Island, TX
987-62178	HY	M	07/10/84	Porcupine River	09/25/84	Cedar Grove, WI
					10/31/84	Backbay Refuge, NC
987-62308	HY	F	07/03/83	Middle Yukon River	10/02/83	Padre Island, TX
987-62310	HY	U	07/04/83	Middle Yukon River	10/30/83	Location unknown, LA
987-62357	HY	F	07/19/83	Lower Yukon River	03/15/84	Vancouver, British Columbia
987-62377	HY	U	07/11/84	Lower Yukon River	09/30/84	Cumberland Island, GA
987-62433	HY	U	07/06/83	Charley River	09/28/83	Padre Island, TX
987-62440	HY	U	07/12/84	Charley River	03/15/85	Ecuador
987-71217	HY	F	07/08/84	Upper Yukon River	10/??/84	Padre Island, TX
987-71239	HY	F	07/13/84	Upper Yukon River	10/??/84	Padre Island, TX
987-71318	HY	F	07/07/85	Upper Yukon River	09/30/85	Dunn, ND

[a] Age at banding; HY = hatch year.
[b] Sex: F = female; M = male; U = unknown.
[c] Reference by year banded: 1967: J. Enderson; 1977-1985: USFWS Alaska.

TABLE 4. Recoveries outside Alaska of tundra (*F. p. tundrius*) Peregrines banded in Alaska, 1952-85.

Band no.	Age[a]	Sex[b]	Date banded[c]	Location banded	Date recovered	Location recovered
47709970	HY	U	08/02/52	Colville River	12/13/55	Buenos Aires, Argentina
5299606	HY	F	08/01/59	Colville River	10/15/59	Grays Harbor, WA
61702449	HY	U	07/29/69	Colville River	10/09/69	Location unknown, SW LA
87700847	HY	U	07/31/68	Colville River	08/??/72	Southwest Alberta
87700862	HY	U	08/02/67	Colville River	09/27/67	Southwest Saskatchewan
987-30539	HY	F	07/16/82	Etivluk River	10/11/82	Padre Island, TX
987-30550	HY	U	07/21/82	Colville River	04/17/83	Padre Island, TX
987-30562	HY	M	07/22/82	Colville River	09/29/82	Padre Island, TX
987-30576	HY	U	07/27/82	Kogosukruk River	10/15/82	Padre Island, TX
987-30579	HY	U	07/27/82	Colville River	10/07/83	Padre Island, TX
987-30584	HY	U	07/28/82	Colville River	10/28/82	Rochester, WA
987-30589	HY	U	07/16/83	Colville River	11/18/84	Southeast Brazil
987-39716	HY	U	07/28/79	Colville River	11/??/81	Southeast Brazil
987-47260	HY	U	07/22/81	Colville River	04/??/85	San Miguel Island, CA
987-62217	HY	U	07/21/83	Colville River	04/??/84	Southeast Brazil
987-62238	HY	U	07/28/83	Kogosukruk River	10/09/83	Padre Island, TX
987-70503	ASY	F	06/23/84	Colville River	12/03/84	Leeville, LA

[a] Age at banding; HY = hatch year; ASY = after second year.
[b] Sex: F = female; M = male; U = unknown.
[c] Reference by year banded: 1952, 1959, 1967-1969: T. Cade; 1979-1985: USFWS Alaska.

F. p. anatum has been recovered in Brazil ($n=2$), Argentina ($n=1$), and Ecuador ($n=1$).

There does not appear to be any difference between the migration routes or wintering areas of *F. p. tundrius* and *F. p. anatum* from Alaska. Recoveries of both subspecies are nearly equally dispersed throughout the range of all recoveries.

ACKNOWLEDGEMENTS

Several individuals have participated in the survey and trapping efforts in Alaska: M. Amaral, M. Ambrose, P. Bente, M. Britten, K. Bollinger, T. Cade, B. Dittrick, R. Hunter, C. McIntyre, T. Nichols, R. Ritchie, D. Roseneau, P. Schempf, T. Swem, and S. Ulvi. We appreciate their help. R. Ritchie and R. Hunter reviewed drafts of this paper and made several improvements.

65 | Population Turnover in Colorado Peregrines

James H. Enderson and Gerald R. Craig

Early estimates of mortality in Peregrine Falcons were based on band recovery records that developed gradually with the eventual discoveries of bands on individuals that died from a variety of causes (Enderson 1969b). Until the more recent advent of lock-on bands, the loss of bands after a period of wear may have reduced the likelihood of recovering older birds with bands intact, resulting in a calculated mortality rate biased above the actual. Recently, retrapping of banded adults on territory in subsequent years has provided an estimate of adult mortality in one dense population in Scotland (Mearns and Newton 1984). That work depended upon the strong tendency of Peregrines to return to the same nesting territories every year, or on their discovery at nearby territories when they failed to return.

In Colorado the trapping of adults is impractical because of the tall cliffs chosen for nesting. Plumage color and pattern was reported to vary among individuals allowing identification for periods up to 16 years (Herbert and Herbert 1965). The present paper reports an estimate of adult mortality based on photographs made of breeding adults defending their eyries when young were fostered as a part of a population augmentation program (see Nelson Chapter 69).

METHODS

Both black-and-white and color photographs were made of wild nesting adults at 10 territories with a slide-focus 600 mm lens (Novoflex) on a 35 mm motor-driven camera. Sometimes a similar camera coupled to a stock-mounted 15X spotting scope was also used. The best results were obtained with film speed ASA 200. Normally 2-3 rolls of film were exposed on each visit, and sometimes more than one visit was made to a territory each year.

Photographs were also made of 12 captive adults (5 females, 7 males) in June 1980, and again in June 1981. The ages of the birds ranged from 2-12 years. Photographs taken of each individual in successive years were examined to ascertain the comparability of plumages.

RESULTS

In 11 of 12 cases we obtained usable photographs of captive adults in 1980 and 1981; those of one female were of poor quality because they were made through the one-way glass of the breeding loft. In all 11 instances, the shape of the border of the malar stripe, amount of white on the head behind the stripe, amount of light-colored feathers immediately behind the cere, and the general degree of dark barring on the chest, belly, and flanks were essentially identical after one year. Some slight variation concerning individual feathers was seen, probably relating to the state of the molt. Position of the head affected feather overlap, but did not obscure specific patterns.

In the period of 1981-85 we obtained photographs adequate to determine whether 57 adults returned in subsequent years (Table 1). Included are five instances where the presence of adults was not verified until two years after their earlier identification, in which case they were taken to have been present in each of two years; the unit of observation was one territory per year. In some cases no bird was present a year later, or a replacement was present. In 45 of the 57 cases the same adult returned to the same territory, resulting in a turnover rate by territory of 21% (17% for males, 23% for females).

This turnover was probably owing to mortality and movement to other territories. In three instances adults were found on another territory the next year. These three cases bring to 48 the instances in which adults returned or were seen elsewhere among 57 instances in which their presence was determined in a subsequent year. On this basis the loss rate was 16% (Table 1). This rate is maximum because

TABLE 1. Records of adult Peregrines returning to territories in subsequent years.

	No. (%)		
	Males	Females	Total
Seen on territories where studied in subsequent year	23	34	57
Resighted on same territory[a]	19 (83)	26 (77)	45 (79)
Turnover (territory)[b]	(17)	(23)	(21)
Resighted elsewhere[b]	1	2	3
Total resighted	20	28	48
Maximum loss	3 (13)	6 (18)	9 (16)

[a] Returned to same territory.
[b] On different territory.

some individuals may have dispersed to territories other than those under study.

The yearly sample sizes were not large, and we found considerable yearly variation in maximum loss rate (Table 2). Maximum loss varied between 27% in 1981 and 8% in 1982 (see Ambrose and Riddle Chapter 64).

DISCUSSION

Our overall estimate of 16% maximum annual loss is considerably higher than an estimate of 11% found in a similar study in Scotland involving the retrapping of banded breeding adults (Mearns and Newton 1984). This difference may be owing to the relative ease in the latter locality of finding adults that moved to another territory. In southern Scotland most territories are known, and are much more accessible than those in the rugged interior of Colorado. When movement to other territories was excluded, the return by both sexes to the same territory in a subsequent year was 21% in Colorado and 19% in Scotland.

All three adults that did move to other territories in the present study remained at the new location to breed for four or five years; therefore, turnover on the basis of a given territory is of less interest from the view of survivorship and productivity than is maximum loss rate on the basis of all territories. In Colorado, territories can easily remain undetected and the actual annual mortality rate in this population may have been in the 10-15% range.

This result is markedly lower than values calculated from band recoveries. An average of 25% annual mortality was found for the nonextirpated Peregrine population of the eastern United States banded prior to 1953 (Enderson 1969b). Other estimates included 19% and 28% for Finland and Germany (Mebs 1971) and 32% for Sweden (Lindberg 1977b). Rates determined from band recoveries are probably

TABLE 2.   Maximum losses of adult Peregrines in different years.

	No. (%)				
	1980	1981	1982	1983	1984
Seen on territories where studied in subsequent year	8	11	13	14	11
Resighted on same territory	7	7	10	12	9
Resighted elsewhere	0	1	2	0	0
Total resighted	7	8	12	12	9
Maximum loss	1 (13)	3 (27)	1 (8)	2 (14)	2 (18)

unrealistically high. In any case, the present study suggests a high survivorship among breeding adults in the Rocky Mountain population, and if the normal reproduction seen in 1985 is achieved on a sustained basis, this population may gradually recover to its former density.*

ACKNOWLEDGEMENTS

D. Berger helped with photography and handled banded individuals. R. Enderson helped with photographic processing, and many field workers helped during visits to the eyries. The Colorado Division of Wildlife supported this study.

*Editors' Note: Peregrines occupied 31 cliffs in Colorado during the 1987 breeding season (J. Enderson pers. comm.). See Addendum to Chapter 12 for additional 1986-87 information.

66 Dynamics of Founder Populations Established by Reintroduction

James W. Grier and John H. Barclay

Frank Pitelka, of the Museum of Vertebrate Zoology at the University of California, Berkeley, used to tease Tom Cade by referring to the Peregrine Falcon as a "weed" (Cade 1969b). One of the characteristics of a weed is its resiliency or ability to survive adversity. Even when eliminated from an area, it can make a good comeback if a few propagules can become established.

The history of the Peregrine's decline, the role of toxic environmental contaminants, and details of recent events have been documented and discussed elsewhere, such as in Hickey (1969) and other chapters in this volume. In this chapter we consider the population dynamics of reintroduced populations and make some predictions about their future. Our purpose is to compare theoretical results from mathematical modeling with actual observations of Peregrines reintroduced to the eastern United States.

Grier (1976) developed a stochastic model and predicted that Peregrine releases had a high probability of succeeding. The model is useful for small founder populations in that it incorporates an element of chance for the numbers of young produced by breeding females, sex of each offspring, and yearly survival of particular individuals. The model operates under any given combination of mortality and reproductive rates. Barclay and Cade (1983) subsequently employed this stochastic model for predicting the outcome and growth of the Peregrine population reintroduced to the eastern United States.

Now, after accumulating 10 years of data, we are in a much better position to evaluate the population dynamics of these released birds. We will focus primarily on the Peregrine releases in the eastern United States, using both the stochastic model and related deterministic models. Although we will be discussing the eastern United States Peregrines almost exclusively, the principles should apply to Peregrines reintroduced elsewhere as well as to founder populations of other species.

METHODS, MODELS, AND ASSUMPTIONS

The stochastic model, incorporating chance events, has been published with an accompanying computer program (Grier 1980a), and has been used with a variety of species including the Bald Eagle (Grier 1980b).

A companion deterministic model for population growth has been developed from the stochastic model by removing the random function wherever it occurs and modifying the remainder of the program to accommodate its new, deterministic nature. (Deterministic models provide only one determined outcome for any given set of inputs, unlike the variability introduced by randomness.) The deterministic program provides its output in the same format as the stochastic program and, although less realistic, gives a clearer (less variable) picture of the most likely track of the population. When the two models are used in conjunction with each other, the deterministic gives the basic pattern, and the stochastic provides the probabilities.

The standard deterministic approach to population dynamics involves the life equation or "life table." Life tables have also been used in the past to estimate survival rates, but that use is no longer considered acceptable for most situations (see Brownie et al. 1978). Life tables in general are explained and discussed in Krebs (1985). Grier (1979) published a computer program to calculate avian life tables.

Several different models and assumptions can be used for population growth. The continuous function logistic and its discrete analog, although attractive and intuitively reasonable, do not fit most natural, complex life histories (see Krebs 1985 for discussion). Furthermore, they are awkward to calculate and, when complicated with such things as time lags, may become unpredictable. Simple linear models are too simple and unrealistic, and animal demographers consider them useless. Thus, we have chosen standard exponential growth (including the possibility of negative or zero growth rates) and static schedules of reproduction and survival as being both adequate and realistic. For modeling we have assumed the populations are not limited (within the range of numbers we are considering) by density or genetic considerations (such as inbreeding) and that there are no problems such as the birds having difficulty finding each other or eyrie sites. Any of these assumptions, of course, might be wrong. In particular, reproduction and survival may change even beyond the range of random fluctuations (which are accommodated by the stochastic model) and, if the populations continue to increase, there will likely be density effects sooner or later. Ratcliffe (1962) discussed the effects of territorial behavior in limiting Peregrine density, for example. After carefully considering each assumption, however, we believe that all are reasonable for the present situation.

The exponential model (and the discrete analog) is discussed in detail by Krebs (1985). The basic equation is:

$$n(t)=n(O)(R^t), \text{ or } =n(O)(e^{rt})$$

where n is the number of animals, t is time (in years in this case), O is initial time, R is finite rate of growth (annual), and r is infinite or instantaneous rate of (exponential) growth. To calculate and convert R and r:

$$R = \frac{N(t+1)}{N(t)}, R^t=e^{rt}, \text{ and } r=\ln R \text{ or } R=e^r$$

A stationary population is one in which the numbers remain constant over time. Stationary populations are also sometimes referred to as stable, but the term stable is ambiguous and should be avoided as it also is commonly used for age-stability, which can occur even in nonstationary populations. For a perfectly stationary population, $n(t+1)=n(t)$, $R=1.0000$ and $r=0.0000$. For nonstationary populations, the values of R and r are greater than 1 and 0, respectively, for increasing populations and less than 1 and 0 for decreasing populations.

For simulating releases, we used approximately the same numbers of Peregrines in the models as were actually released in the eastern United States through 1983. After that, as a conservative estimate of sustained releases, a constant number of 80 falcons released per year was used, even though more were actually released in 1984 and 1985.

Rates of reproduction and survival for wild Peregrines can only be estimated. We have better figures for reproduction than for survival, but even when there are good samples and data for the outcomes of known nestings, we generally do not know what proportion of the total adult population is actually attempting to breed and is thus visible at eyrie sites. Nonetheless, it is possible to use a reasonable range of values and simulate what would happen under conditions of different sets of reproductive and survival rates. To obtain such a range of values we consulted numerous estimates for different times and places (and even for closely related species) such as given in Hickey (1969, including Enderson 1969b and Young 1969 and others discussing reproduction), Newton (1979), Cade and Fyfe (1970), Shor (1970a, 1970b, 1975), and our own experiences. We therefore assigned an arbitrary (but we think reasonable) low to high range of values for various parameters such as age of first breeding, percent of adult females attempting to breed, numbers of young per successful female, and first-year versus older mortality rates (Table 1).

TABLE 1. Life table results for Peregrine Falcons under different conditions of survival and reproduction.

Given values	"Stationary"[a]	With reproduction at age 2	EPRP[b]	High survival, high reproduction	High survival, low reproduction	Low survival, high reproduction	Low survival, low reproduction
First year mortality (%)	60	60	67	50	50	70	70
Mortality after first year (%)	20	20	20	15	15	30	30
Age begin breeding (years)	3	2	2	2	3	2	3
Percent of adult females that produce young	66	66	50	80	50	80	50
Average number young/ successful female	2.5	2.5	2.0	3.0	1.5	3.0	1.5
Calculated values							
r^c	0.0028	0.0441	-0.0730	0.2300	-0.0182	-0.0510	-0.2920
R^c	1.0028	1.0450	0.9296	1.2586	0.9820	0.9503	0.7467
Maximum age for cohort of 1000[d]	23[e]	23[e]	22[e]	30[e]	30[e]	14[e]	14[e]
Percent immatures in population[f]	34	38	30	45	22	46	22

[a] Less than 1% population growth/year.
[b] Conditions used in 1979 Eastern Peregrine Recovery Plan.
[c] See text for definition and explanation.
[d] Reflects survival conditions.
[e] This results from an exponential decline with a long, drawn-out tail to the death of the last individual. The cohort is effectively gone at about 2/3 to 3/4 of this age.
[f] Reflects both survival and reproduction. For these conditions where first-year and older survival change together, the values mostly reflect reproduction.

RESULTS AND DISCUSSION

Life Table Calculations. — The calculated life table outcomes that would be expected under various combinations of reproduction and mortality are shown in Table 1. The life table results are deterministic, really applicable only with large populations, and apply only after age-stability has been achieved (usually after two or more generations).

In addition to not having large populations or age-stability, we are faced with two additional problems. First, we do not know what *proportion* of the birds in the wild are being seen, so that we cannot know how data from observations relate to the real situation. That is, how do observed increases relate to biases and variability in observation (numbers of persons looking, experience of observers, times and places of watching, etc.)? Secondly, the populations are not initially growing just on their own; they are being artificially and substantially supplemented by releases of young during the period of reintroduction. Thus, it is difficult to determine what proportion of increase in sightings of Peregrines is a result of natural population growth.

To overcome some problems, we used a combination of deterministic and stochastic modeling. From life table results (Table 1) we found a combination of reproductive and mortality values that led to a nearly stationary population (less than 1% increase per year). (With accumulated rounding error in calculations, the discrete rather than continuous nature of some of the life history variables, and the iterations involved in the models, a perfectly stationary population is difficult to achieve even mathematically.) These values would cause a population to show only slight change on its own. If they are used in conjunction with releases, any resulting change could be interpreted as the result of the continued releases of birds. In a similar manner, we combined actual reintroduction numbers with other values of reproduction and survival.

Table 2 shows for the 20-year period of 1975-95 actual numbers of Peregrines reintroduced to the eastern United States, numbers used in the deterministic model under stationary and slightly increasing (4.5% per year) conditions, and observations to date. Also shown are finite rates of increase (R) for the different columns. Results of the deterministic modeling for these and other sets of productivity and survival rates are plotted in Figure 1.

A number of comments and predictions can be drawn from these results. The finite rates of increase for the deterministic models start large because of large numbers of released birds relative to the number already present, then decline because a relatively constant number is being added each year and that number becomes smaller and smaller relative to the accumulating population. After releases stop (arbitrarily

TABLE 2. Deterministic simulations of Peregrines in eastern United States, based on actual releases and compared to recent observations.

Year	No. released (n=752)	No. used in simulations[a]	No. under "stationary" conditions[b]	No. under conditions of age 2 breeding[b]	No. sighted[c]	No. known nesting attempts	R_P[d]	R_2[e]	R_{KS}[f]	R_{KN}[g]
1975	16	16	6	6	5	0	3.33	3.33		
1976	37	38	20	20	5	0	1.70	1.80	1.00	
1977	46	46	34	36	10	0	1.44	1.53	2.00	
1978	53	52	49	55	14	1	1.31	1.35	1.40	
1979	52	52	64	74	14	2	1.33	1.35	1.00	2.00
1980	65	66	85	100	24	4	1.32	1.33	1.71	2.00
1981	84	84	112	133	31	5	1.21	1.24	1.29	1.25
1982	79	80	135	165	42	9	1.17	1.18	1.35	1.80
1983	79	80	158	199	65	16	1.15	1.16	1.55	1.78
1984	124	80	182	235	94	25	1.13	1.14	1.45	1.55
1985	117	80	206	273	(146)[i]	(39)[i]	1.12	1.13	(1.55)[i]	(1.55)[i]
1986		80[h]	231	312	(226)[i]	(60)[i]	1.10	1.12	(1.55)[i]	(1.55)[i]
1987		80[h]	255	354	(350)[i]	(93)[i]	1.10	1.11	(1.55)[i]	(1.55)[i]
1988		80[h]	280	398			1.09	1.11		
1989		80[h]	304	443			1.08	1.04		
1990		80[h]	329	492			0.98	1.05		
1991			323	511			1.00	1.05		
1992			322	538			1.02	1.05		
1993			327	565			1.01	1.05		
1994			330	594			1.01	1.05		
1995			332	625			1.01	1.05		

[a] Equal nos. for each sex, 1074 birds total through 1990.
[b] Refer to Table 1; no. in population at end of year.
[c] No. of birds sighted in wild (pairs and singles) during spring and summer.
[d] R from previous year via "stationary" model.
[e] R with first breeding at age 2.
[f] R for known sightings.
[g] R for known nesting attempts.
[h] Conservative value based on a number of considerations; see text.
[i] Predictions based on continued R of 1.55 for observations.

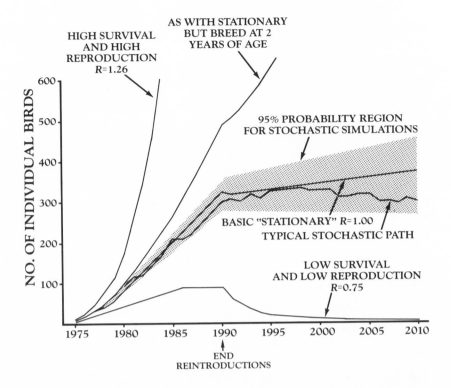

FIGURE 1.   Eastern United States Peregrine population growth under different conditions of survival and reproduction, incorporating releases until 1990. The
figure includes four deterministic plots, a typical stochastic path, and a 95%
probability region for stochastic simulations under "stationary" conditions.

ended here after 1990), the deterministic models yield rates of population growth (*R's*) essentially as expected (that is, as calculated from
the life tables with allowance for accumulated rounding differences).
The finite rates of increase for numbers of Peregrines sighted during
spring and summer and for numbers of known nesting attempts have
shown a fair amount of fluctuation (see two right-hand columns in
Table 2). The average R for sightings is 1.43 and for known nesting
attempts is 1.73. If, rather than taking averages, one smooths the curve
over the whole period of data and then calculates exponentially the
annual finite rate for the period, it is 1.39 ($r=0.33$) for sightings and
1.71 ($r=0.54$) for known nesting attempts.

Because the initial parts of the curves involve smaller numbers and
probably more sampling vagaries, it might be best to concentrate on
the most recent results, which suggest a finite rate of increase (*R*) in

observations of around 1.55. Note that even if this rate roughly reflects the true situation in the population, it is approximately 40% higher than would be predicted at this stage, including releases under either stationary or slightly increasing sets of conditions! Such an increase in sightings could result from an increasing proportion of the population being seen, very good survival and reproduction by the birds in the wild, or both. The size of R for observations would not yet be expected to reflect the increased numbers of releases in 1984 and 1985, except possibly for sightings of birds in 1985.

Under the highest rates of survival and reproduction we modeled (see Table 1 and Figure 1), the maximum R is 1.26. Some increase in the observed number of birds and nesting attempts is undoubtedly a result of better observation and experience, but we think some must be attributed to a Peregrine population that is actually increasing because of its own reproduction. It clearly is not a declining situation even after allowing for increases from additional releases. The only plot that shows a decline after cessation of reintroduction involves low survival and reproduction, conditions which are not supported by field observations.

From these results it is possible to make some tentative predictions for the immediate future. Predicted numbers of future sightings and attempted nestings are included in Table 2 through 1988. As a hint of the possible validity of these estimates, Grier predicted the number of sightings for 1985 before the data were all in. He predicted that 100 Peregrines would be seen. (The calculated number was 100.1.) The actual number turned out to be 92, suggesting that the gap between predicted and observed may be closing.

Stochastic Models. — To consider chance events and the stochastic nature of reality, we applied the stochastic model to releases involving 10-1074 Peregrines occurring until 1990. The simulations were carried out until the year 2010 (Table 3). Similar results were obtained whether the same number of falcons were reintroduced over a period of years or all at once. That is, 1074 falcons introduced to the wild from 1975 to 1990 and followed for the 35 years (last column of Table 3), simulating what has actually been taking place, produced nearly the same outcome as 1074 falcons introduced all at once in 1985 and followed until 2010 (next to last column in Table 3). For the sake of simplicity and efficiency, all remaining simulations with smaller numbers of falcons were conducted with simultaneous releases in 1985 of however many birds were involved.

The reproductive and survival conditions used for the stochastic simulations were those in the second column of Table 1, that is, a slightly increasing population growth ($R=1.045$). Under these

TABLE 3. Stochastic simulations of Peregrine Falcon reintroductions based on a moderate rate of population growth[a] and different numbers of released birds.

	No. of young released[b]								
	10	20	50	100	500	752[c]	1000	1074[d]	1074[d]
No. of simulations	100	100	100	100	100	100	100	100	100
No. that failed[e]	85	61	11	0	0	0	0	0	0
Probability of success[e]	.15	.39	.89	1.00	1.00	1.00	1.00	1.00	1.00
Average population size at end of year 2010[f]	10.3	9.15	24.7	61.6	439	676	942	1014	1021
Standard deviation	14.4	9.9	21.3	33.6	96	120	137	148	153
Coefficient of variation[g]	140	108	86	55	22	18	15	15	15
95% confidence interval	0-39	0-29	0-67	0-129	247-631	436-916	688-1216	718-1310	715-1327

[a] Survival and reproduction as in second column of life tables, Table 1.

[b] Male : female sex ratio 50 : 50.

[c] The number actually released in the eastern United States as of 1985.

[d] The number simulated to be released through 1990 (see Table 2 and Figure 1). In the first 100 simulations of 1074 releases (as well as for all lesser releases to the left) all released birds were released at once during 1985 then followed to the year in 2010. In the second 100 simulations of 1074 birds (last column of this table), the releases were spread out from 1975-90, as in Table 2.

[e] As of the year 2010.

[f] Of successful simulations.

[g] S. D. as a percent of average population size.

conditions two things can be seen. First, as the numbers reintroduced increased, the variability resulting from chance events decreased (note coefficients of variation). With larger numbers the situation thus became more deterministic. Second, after a minimum of 100 falcons was introduced, in 600 repeated stochastic simulations, *not a single case went to extinction*. Through 1985 there have been 752 Peregrines reintroduced into the eastern United States.

In addition to the stochastic simulations involving a slightly increasing set of population conditions, 100 simulations were performed under stationary conditions using birds reintroduced over time as in the deterministic situation, rather than all at once. Those results are indicated in Figure 1 as the 95% probability region around the deterministic plot for a mostly stationary population. After releases end, stochastic paths begin to widen owing to random walking under conditions where increases and decreases are equally likely. (Purely random walking is not something that real populations are likely to do.) Note that even the lowest range of the 95% probability is still well above zero by the year 2010.

A major implied assumption in our computer simulations is that all falcons released in the eastern United States contribute to a single population. In reality, the releases have been separated geographically so that it would have been more accurate to work with several different populations or subpopulations in our modeling. We elected not to do so for the sake of simplicity.

Details of the spatial and temporal distribution of Peregrine releases in the eastern United States are presented elsewhere (Barclay Chapter 51). Briefly, releases were widely scattered in the first few years, concentrated along the mid-Atlantic coast in the late 1970s, and in the mountains of upstate New York and northern New England in the 1980s. A release program was initiated in the southern Appalachians in 1984. A reintroduction program using falcons from sources other than the Cornell facility has been under way in Minnesota since 1982.

The distribution of releases in the eastern United States no doubt influenced the probabilities that adult Peregrines would find one another for pairing. This fact most likely contributed to the trend early in the program where observed results lagged behind predicted results. It should be added that the early years of the program were experimental, and we were trying to learn what worked best.

IS THERE LIFE AFTER REINTRODUCTION?

Based on the preceding results, the answer is almost certainly "yes." In the eastern United States there have already been reintroduced over seven times the number of Peregrines necessary to guarantee survival of the population, based on the conditions and assumptions of this modeling. Even fewer numbers of released falcons would have a good chance of producing a viable population. As few as 50 would have an estimated 89% chance of success.

Nothing done on paper or in a computer can know or predict for sure what is likely to happen. Models at best are only approximations of reality, and they frequently are too rough and not good approximations. The actual reintroduction of Peregrines into the eastern United States had never been done before and obviously had to be done before the results could be known. Assumptions and arbitrary values used in modeling can be grossly inadequate. For example, survival rates of released birds could not be predicted, and the question of the size of the area of release, i.e., the density of the released population, and whether reintroduced birds could find each other for pairing were major unknowns and demanded that adequate numbers be released to the wild. Thus, one can never trust modeling completely, and it is far safer to be conservative and release more birds than predicted to be necessary, if possible. Also, the more birds released, the more rapid is the rate of population growth and recovery.

It is also important to have adequate numbers in the wild to permit a reasonable number of observations, since only a fraction of the falcons actually present will be seen and enter our information as usable data. Thus, in view of the possible risks and inadequacies of modeling, we believe that the number of falcons reintroduced has been appropriate. However, from our calculations it appears that there is already a very comfortable margin of safety and that the number of birds already released is sufficient to ensure growth and survival of the population in the eastern United States.

Unless there are drastic environmental changes or significant new factors emerge, it is virtually 100% guaranteed that there will be Peregrines in the eastern United States in the year 2010, even if there are no further releases. The Peregrine indeed appears to be a "weed," and it is back. Results of both the modeling and field observations of the actual population return merely attest to the impressive power of many living species to persist and to be resilient. The biggest problem many species face appears to be serious environmental changes to which they cannot adapt. For the Peregrine, this change was the introduction of organochlorine pesticides, and no matter how adaptable or how efficient a "weed" species it might be, it is unrealistic to think that it could adapt to chemical pollutants which affected reproductive physiology (and mortality?) so severely.

WHAT LIMITS THE POPULATION — IS THERE A "K"?

Even under the best of circumstances populations cannot increase indefinitely. Sooner or later some factor or set of factors places a limit on further population growth. While the exponential model of population growth appears to be adequate, reasonable, and accurate for Peregrines reintroduced up to the present, it probably will not be adequate or reasonable for much beyond the year 2010.

Although we presume that changes will not put Peregrines into a declining situation again, eventually either survival or reproduction or both will have to decline. As the density of Peregrines increases, for example, the age at which birds first breed will probably become delayed through territorial interactions. As shown in our modeling results, the difference between first breeding at age two versus three causes a difference between a population that is growing at 4.5% annually and one that is nearly stationary. At some point the Peregrine population will certainly either become stationary or simply fluctuate up and down around some mean number above what it is now.

Under logistic models the level at which the population becomes stationary is referred to as "K" or, more generally, the "carrying capacity." Eventually the population will be limited by a set of factors such as the availability of nesting sites, territoriality, availability of prey, other intraspecific competition, various interspecific factors, or increased mortality from human-related actions.

We strongly encourage all efforts to follow and understand the dynamics of reintroduced Peregrine populations in detail. We barely noticed the disappearance of the wild population until after the fact, but we should be able to follow closely the comeback of reintroduced Peregrines. Included in the future population research should be deliberate efforts to reduce observation bias and variability by standardizing sampling procedures in a statistically satisfactory manner. Perhaps, as captive breeding efforts and costs wind down, some of the resources now being spent on those activities can be redirected toward studying the new wild population.

ACKNOWLEDGEMENTS

We give special thanks to three people in particular for their persistence and work through the years in propagating and reintroducing Peregrines. They are T. Cade, P. Dague, and J. D. Weaver. Weaver especially deserves recognition for his insights and experience with the Peregrine.

Special credit is due to the following coworkers with The Peregrine Fund, Inc., who contributed much to the program: M. Gilroy, V. Hardaswick, P. Harrity, W. Heck, M. MacLeod, T. Maechtle, S. Sherrod, and S. Temple.

The reintroduction program owes much of its success to the support and involvement of numerous federal and state agencies and private organizations and individuals. We thank the dozens of individuals who worked as release site attendants for their dedication and hard work.

67 | Prey Availability Limiting an Island Population of Peregrine Falcons in Tunisia

Jean-Marc Thiollay

The decline of Peregrine Falcon populations has been attributed mainly to pesticide contamination or human persecution. Only recently has food availability been suspected as a factor involved in the decrease of populations or failure of some to recover (Ratcliffe 1980). A very dense, but somewhat reduced population of *F. p. brookei* on a small isolated island provided a unique opportunity to study accurately the daily availability and consumption of prey by breeding pairs and to relate their poor breeding success to a recent decrease of some migratory species.

STUDY AREA AND METHODS

The National Park of Zembra Island, off the northeast coast of Tunisia, is a triangle of 390 ha with maximum dimensions of 2.6 km by 2.5 km, rising 435 m above sea level and surrounded by mainly calcareous cliffs up to 200 m high. The island is uninhabited and covered with low macchia, taller in the central area and dominated by *Pistacia, Arbutus, Erica* and *Olea*. Fog, rain and strong winds are frequent especially in spring and winter. Mean daily temperatures range from 10°C in January to 28°C in July.

After most pairs and nest sites were located, I collected field data with my wife, between 0500 and 1930 hours during 43 days in late April and May 1980-81. Only the five most accessible pairs were studied, two of them every day, and the results were pooled without considering the slight individual differences. All movements of one pair at a time were recorded 6-14 hours daily from vantage points overlooking all the territory. The following data were recorded for 318 attacks: territory, date, hour, wind speed, cloud cover, rain, sex of the bird beginning the pursuit and that of the bird doing the catch (if any), hunting method, time spent from the beginning of the chase to the capture or termination, number of strikes, prey size, prey species, position and behavior of the prey, and the size of the flock to which the prey belonged. Observed captures and recent prey remains found around breeding cliffs were used to describe the diet. The total bird population (potential prey) was estimated in three ways in May within the two intensively studied territories: (1) the number of sedentary birds was extrapolated from the density of singing males of the largest, most conspicuous species on four 1-ha plots per territory, twice at two-week intervals; (2) resting migrants were counted daily in the afternoon on the Peregrine territory which was surveyed, along a transect crossing all the patches of particular habitat (old fields and gardens) where most migrants were concentrated; and (3) migrants flying over the sea or the island, within the territory surveyed that day, were counted throughout the watching period.

Residents were mostly a warbler, a tit, a wren, a thrush and several granivorous birds. Among 1140 migrants counted on the transect, 84.1% weighed less than 40 g, 8.7% between 40-90 g and 7.1% weighed more than 100 g (see Thiollay 1982 for a complete list of the avifauna). Migrants flying over the sea in the morning were mostly species of Motacillidae, and those flying over the island throughout the day were mostly swallows and swifts.

RESULTS

Density and Breeding Success. — According to local falconers who took young every year, there were formerly 12 breeding pairs along the 9.5 km of coastline; 11 remained in 1979 (T. Gaultier pers. comm.), and 10 in 1980-81. This is probably the highest density of breeding Peregrines ever recorded in the world (Beebe 1960, Ratcliffe 1980). Only 10-50 ha per territory in the coastal zone were defended, and falcons rarely hunted over or even crossed the central part of the island.

The former breeding success of this population is not known precisely but was presumably higher than today, since every year one to several broods of 2-4 fledglings were taken by local people. In 1977, 11 pairs produced 26 flying young. The five pairs studied closely in 1980-81 produced only two and four young, respectively. This average productivity of 0.4-0.8 young per pair is 2-4 times lower than the mean productivity of holarctic populations (Hickey 1942, Brown and Amadon 1968) and lower than the minimum reproductive rate of a stable population (1.6-2.3 young per pair: Mebs 1960, Enderson 1969b, Lindberg 1977a). Although no chemical analysis was made, a significant influence of pesticide contamination was ruled out because: (1) pesticides have never been used on the island, (2) breeding Peregrines on the nearby mainland in intensively cultivated areas had much higher breeding success (7 pairs fledged 12 young in 1981), (3) the mean clutch size of 1.8 eggs per set was unusually low with a third of the pairs laying no eggs, and (4) all dead young examined obviously died from starvation.*

Hunting Methods. — About 58% of attacks were launched from perches on the tops of coastal cliffs; 41% were from a high soaring flight against the wind when the visibility was poor or the migrants were scarce; and 1% were low, rapid flights over the ground to flush birds. Each method involved an increasing energy expense, but resulted in 0.52, 1.72, and 6.67 attacks per hour, respectively.

A prominent habit of these Peregrines rarely recorded elsewhere (Cade 1960, Glutz von Blotzheim et al. 1971, Cramp and Simmons 1980) was cooperative hunting between male and female, involving 42% of all attacks and up to 92% of attacks by adults feeding young on days with few migrants. This increasingly frequent cooperation when prey become scarcer may have allowed for higher success in fewer attacks.

Hunting Site and Time Budget. — Most birds were hunted over the sea (36%) or along the coast (44%). Falcons detected dove-sized birds at sea at least 4 km from their coastal perch and small passerines at least 2 km away. These distances were calculated from duration of direct flights of attacking falcons (Baker 1967, Hantge 1968, Fox et al. 1976, Treleaven 1977, Monneret and Gowthorpe 1978, Geroudet 1978). When prey was scarce in the morning, adults went hunting on the mainland 15-25 km from their nests, returning 1-6.5 hours later with prey in only three out of 11 instances.

The time budget was similar for days with fine weather (total observation time=574 hours, Figure 1) and for very windy and rainy days (122 hours). Males always hunted more than females, but the difference between them was less than in other populations where a more abundant food supply allows the male to provide enough prey to feed his mate and young (Ratcliffe 1980). Hunting activity was maximum in early morning: 55% of prey was caught before 0830 hours and the percentage steadily decreased thereafter (Figure 2). At least 71% of the day was spent hunting, 22% in flight.

Prey Selection and Hunting Success. — Birds were selected on the basis of their size, behavior and vulnerability. The most profitable prey in terms of energetic return were solitary 100-200 g birds, flying at medium height over the sea, far from cover. Aside from swifts and, to a lesser extent, swallows, which are difficult to catch, most birds were attacked when flying over the sea (Table 1). On the island, only the large species were favored except for residents such as Rock Doves,

---

*Editors' Note: None of these reasons rules out the possibility of DDE-induced effects on reproduction; indeed, small clutches, loss of eggs or failure to lay, and dead downy young in nests are all symptomatic of DDE toxicity.

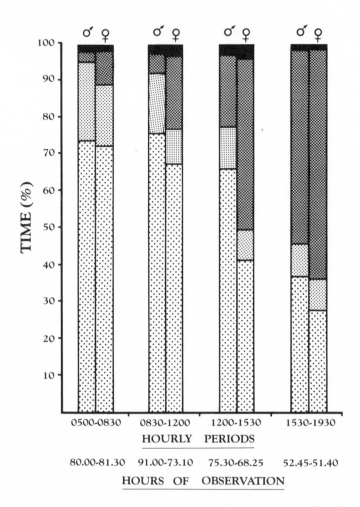

FIGURE 1. Time budget of Peregrine Falcons feeding young on Zemba Island in fine
weather. From bottom to top: perch-hunting, hunting flights, other
activities perched, other flights.

which were either too big or extremely wary and always flew very close
to the slopes (Table 1).

The most preferred prey were pursued with persistence, whereas
nonprofitable ones were often abandoned. Small groups or isolated
birds were strongly preferred over large flocks (Table 2). The well-
known tendency of Peregrines to select odd, rare or abnormal prey
(Rudebeck 1951, Eutermoser 1961, Herbert and Herbert 1965, Baker
1967, Treleaven 1977) was confirmed here. Thirteen species identified
in the diet were apparently very rare, for I never saw them in the field;
76% of the birds caught by these Peregrines behaved in a peculiar way,

TABLE 1. Percent of prey available, attacked, and captured by Peregrines on 2 territories where the breeding pairs were watched 314 hrs over 30 days.

	Prey statistic	n	Swallows	Wagtails, pipits, larks	Other insectivorous passerines	Small granivores	Swifts	Medium-sized species (40-95 g)	Doves, cuckoos, kestrels
Migrants flying over the sea or coast	available	8729	57.2	1.5	0.4		25.2	0.1	0.1
	attacked	130	30.4	8.1	13.7		6.6	3.6	3.6
	caught[a]	40	20.3⁻	12.5⁺	23.4⁺		0⁻	3.1⁺	3.1⁺
Migrants stopped on the island	available	1017		3.2	5.1			0.7	0.8
	attacked	54		4.1	8.6			5.6	9.1
	caught[a]	21		0⁻	14.1⁺			6.3⁺	12.5⁺
Sedentary breeding species	available	587			4.8	0.4		0.3	0.2
	attacked	13			1.5	2.0		0.5	2.5
	caught[a]	3			0⁻	4.7⁺		0ᴺˢ	0ᴺˢ

[a] Significance of positive (+) or negative (−) differences between proportions of prey available in the field and in the actual diet by χ^2 test; $P < 0.05$; NS = no significance.

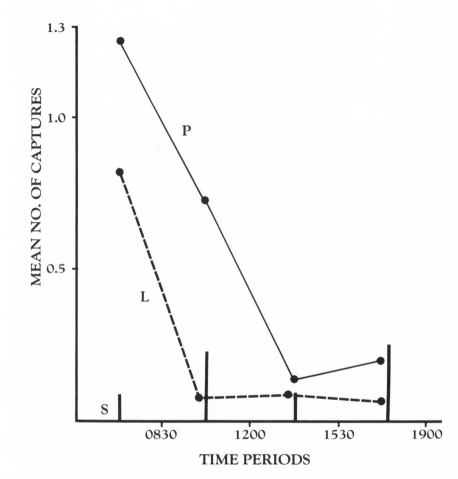

FIGURE 2.   Hourly distribution of the mean number of captures per 3.5 hour period
            per pair of Peregrines. P=small passerines; S=swallows and swifts; L=larger
            birds (over 40 g).

TABLE 2.   Mean size of 264 randomly chosen flocks of migrants and mean size of
           groups actually attacked by Peregrines (both include isolated birds). All
           differences are highly significant (t-tests, $P < 0.001$).

Prey group	Mean size of random flocks	Mean size of flocks attacked by Peregrines
Hirundo spp.	5.1	1.7
Delichon spp.	18.2	6.5
Apus spp.	17.9	2.4
Motacilla spp.	8.1	1.5
Anthus spp.	6.3	1.6

i.e., departed from normal escape behavior (Thiollay 1982), compared to 9% of those which escaped.

Two cooperating adults had a higher success rate (37.8% of strikes) than males (16.5%) or females (23.3%) alone (G-test, P<0.01), but not on a per bird basis (18.9%, P>0.1). Prey was usually shared between the two adults and/or young. The success rate was lowest (0-19%) on swallows and swifts (Table 3), which were by far the most abundant prey (Table 1). It was much higher (30-46%) on other birds, especially over the sea, with no significant difference between the three size classes (Table 3, ANOVA, P>0.05). Success rate was inversely correlated to flock size, decreasing from 22% of isolated migrant swallows to 0% on flocks of more than 20 birds (r_s=−0.97, P<0.001).

TABLE 3. Frequency and success rate of hunting Peregrines on the main prey categories.

Prey category	No. unsuccessful attacks	No. captures	% success
Swallows	57	13	18.6
Other small passerines	53	45	45.9
Swift	13	0	0.0
Golden Oriole	9	3	25.0
Other 40-95 g birds	8	4	33.3
Turtle Dove	13	9	40.9
Other large birds	7	3	30.0

The main prey species in May were the Turtle Dove and the Golden Oriole (18% of the 390 identified catches). Migrants were by far the dominant prey items (87%), local breeding birds being mostly too large (seabirds) or too small and inaccessible (passerines). The proportion of small passerines in the diet (Table 4) was higher than recorded for other populations (Uttendörfer 1952, Cade 1960, Hickey and Anderson 1969, Lindberg 1977a, Ratcliffe (1980), even for *F. p. brookei* (Diaz del Campo 1974), except in western Greenland, where four passerine species make up 90% of the prey (Burnham and Mattox 1984). Males selected significantly (U-test, P<0.001) smaller prey than females (Table 5).

The profitability of a prey may be expressed as the energy expended per unit of prey mass obtained. Energy expenditure can be estimated from duration of hunting flights and mean number of strikes performed before a successful catch. Turtle Doves and other optimal prey were

TABLE 4. Diet of breeding Peregrines on Zembra Island in April-May.

Prey weight	No. of species identified	No. of individuals	% of captures	% of biomass	3 main species
< 40 g	32	216	55.1	14.9	Yellow Wagtail House Martin Barn Swallow
40 - 95 g	17	99	25.7	26.8	Golden Oriole Song Thrush Woodchat Shrike
100 - 500 g	14	75	19.2	58.3	Turtle Dove European Cuckoo Rock Dove

TABLE 5. Prey size of male and female Peregrines in spring on Zembra Island from field observation of attacks by single Peregrines. All differences between male and female are highly significant (Mann Whitney U-test, $P < 0.001$).

Prey category	Male Peregrines		Female Peregrines	
	% of unsuccessful attempts ($n = 89$)	% of captures ($n = 23$)	% of unsuccessful attempts ($n = 16$)	% of captures ($n = 7$)
Small passerines (< 40 g)	92.1	91.3	31.2	42.9
Medium-sized species (40-95 g)	6.8	4.4	25.0	14.3
Larger birds (> 100 g)	1.1	4.3	43.8	42.9

thus 11.3 times more rewarding than swallows (Table 6), but in the field the latter were 500 times more abundant than the former (Table 1). The energy cost of a capture decreased little — or even increased for swallows — with decreasing size of prey, because speed and maneuverability of small birds appeared roughly similar or even greater than that of larger species, as judged from hunting behavior of the Peregrines and duration of strikes or pursuits.

Daily Consumption and Predation Pressure. — The estimated mean daily intake was 4.2 birds per pair per day, based on 14 hunting attempts per day. The rate was 3.7 per family if only full day observations of pairs feeding 1-3 young are considered. With a mean prey live weight of 30 g, each falcon, including fledgings, ate 32-42 g

TABLE 6. Estimate of food yield to Peregrines by 3 prey categories.

	Swallows	Other small passerines	Doves and cuckoos
Mean duration of attacks (sec.)	224	226	333
Success rate (%)	15.6	45.9	37.5
Mean wt. of prey (g)	18	16	125
Pursuit time (sec.) per gram of prey obtained	80	31	7

per day. The figures are well under the observed feeding rates in Europe and the estimated daily requirements for such a raptor (Brown and Amadon 1968, Glutz von Blotzheim et al. 1971, Geroudet 1978, Ratcliffe 1980). Contrary to other Peregrine populations, no caching behavior was seen on Zembra, a fact which may confirm the lack of surplus food. It should be noted that crepuscular hunting has never been seen, and the range of observation covered the whole daylight period. The daily frequency distribution of attacks (Figure 2) was strongly correlated with prey abundance ($r=0.78$) and more strongly with flying migrants ($r=0.87$). If swifts and swallows are excluded, the correlation is excellent ($r=0.98$). From daily censuses on the territories of observed pairs, less than 0.1% of the resident birds were taken per day, compared to 1.4% of swallows, 4.8% of migrants resting on the island, and 21.4% of migrants flying over the sea; and 0.3%, 2.3%, 11.4% and 42.0% of the individuals in these classes, respectively, were attacked.

DISCUSSION

The food of Zembra Island's Peregrines and the cost of obtaining it were mainly correlated with availability and accessibility of avian prey. Medium-sized migrants were preferred and yielded the most food per unit of effort. Preference was determined at least as much by vulnerability (distance from cover, flight speed, escape behavior) as by morphological or taxonomic features. In agreement with the predictions of optimal foraging theory (Pyke et al. 1977, Krebs 1978), Peregrines first devoted their attention to the most profitable prey, attacking all large migrants flying over their territory and often pursuing them in difficult, risky conditions. The rarer these opportunities were, the higher was the proportion of attacks on less profitable prey such as the numerous swallows or the resident, highly concealed passerines. In the process, time and energy expenses increased while energy gain from smaller prey decreased, soon yielding a negative energy balance.

Data strongly support the hypothesis that the reproduction of this population was limited by food: active hunting from dawn to dusk, high proportion of available birds attacked, daily captures well under the estimated requirements, unusual frequency of cooperative hunting, lack of caching behavior, small clutch size, hunting by incubating female, starvation of young, and lack of surplus prey in nests.

The high reliance of this population on a steady spring flow of migrants makes it very sensitive to any disturbance of the migration. Storms and frequent periods of bad weather in March-April at the time of laying and incubation may often reduce both prey abundance and hunting possibilities. But this usual meteorological situation did not prevent former high breeding success with an even higher density of breeding pairs. There is no evidence of a significant reduction in the numbers of the most abundant migrants (*Apus, Hirundo, Delichon, Anthus, Phylloscopus*, etc.), but a widespread decrease of some others in Europe is well documented (*Lanius, Upupa, Coturnix, Streptopelia, Sylvia*, and *Phoenicurus*). The latter are among the most profitable prey for Zembra's Peregrines and may be deeply involved in the food shortage observed here. The only conclusive test would have been a comparison with former conditions, now impossible. Declines in Peregrine population attributed to a decrease in food supply have already been noted for northwest Scotland (Ratcliffe 1980) and for Langara Island, British Columbia (Nelson 1969a, Nelson and Myres 1975).

Another indication of this trend may be the progressive replacement of breeding Peregrines by Lanner Falcons in several localities of inland Tunisia (A. El Hili and T. Gaultier pers. comm.). On the nearby continent, Peregrines rely much more on migrants to feed their young than the more eclectic Lanners, which take advantage of terrestrial birds and even other vertebrates in highly disturbed habitats.

Chemical pollution as well as excessive hunting and environmental changes in both Europe and Africa may threaten the longterm survival of several Mediterranean populations of Peregrines. The Peregrine has been a powerful indicator of changing conditions in its food chains. Now will it also signal still deeper, less reversible degradation of our environment?

ACKNOWLEDGEMENTS

This study received a grant from the UNESCO-MAB Project. A. El Hili and T. Gaultier supported me in various ways. A. Ben Daffer introduced me to each pair of falcons, and my wife Francoise was involved throughout from field work to typing.

68 | Peregrines in Northern Italy: Numbers, Breeding, and Population Dynamics

Paolo Fasce and Laura Fasce

The northern boundary of Italy runs mostly along the Alps' southern watershed, which extends for 700 km and varies between 20-150 km wide. This region consists of limestones and dolomites of Triassic and Cretaceous age, with local outcrops of granite, gneiss, sandstone, and metamorphites formed since the Carboniferous.

The Alps range up to 4000 m or more in elevation and descend to the Po River plain, formed by alluvial drifts during the Quaternary. In the western part many valleys are almost parallel and extend east-west. The valleys are important avian migration routes.

To the south of the Po plain are the Apennines, a mountain chain running along the Italian peninsula like a backbone and having geological, morphological, and climatic features quite different from the Alps. In the northern Apennines rocks are mostly limestone or sandstone, with some scattered ophiolites formed since the Tertiary. Orographically they are more gentle and less complicated than the Alps, with summits seldom more than 2000 m.

OVERVIEW OF PEREGRINE POPULATIONS

Peregrines inhabit both the Alps and Apennines. In the Alps they are widespread in a belt extending from the Po River plain (which they use for hunting) up the slopes to about 1400 m. In the Apennines, cliff-nesting Peregrines occur up to 1000 m, but not abundantly.

Until recently nothing was known about the present distribution of Peregrines in the Alps, their eyries being extremely difficult to locate because of the extensive, hard-to-reach cliffs. Presently the western Alps are becoming well-known, although some valleys still need to be surveyed. Elsewhere in the Alps knowledge of the Peregrine's status is still minimal. Only three territories regularly occupied by Peregrines have been found. The geomorphology suggests that at least 30-35 territories may be there (P. Pedrini unpubl. ms., F. Perco pers. comm.). In the western Alps, however, we are aware of 22 occupied territories plus 3 more in coastal Liguria and 8 in the northern Apennines. Most likely 25-28 pairs are in the western Alps, 4-5 pairs along the Tyrrhenian Sea coast and 10-15 pairs in the northern Apennines. In the whole of northern Italy, therefore, the total population could be 69-83 breeding pairs.

Everywhere in the area Peregrines are mostly sedentary, although both in winter and summer some may move far from their nesting territories in search of food (Chiavetta 1976, Geroudet 1979, Fasce and Mingozzi 1983).

THE SUBSPECIES

It is known that two subspecies live in Italy: *F. p. peregrinus* in northern Italy, and *F. p. brookei*, smaller and slightly different in plumage from the nominate form, in southern Italy, Sardinia, Sicily and Corsica (Vaurie 1961). In Italy, however, natural barriers are absent and geographical boundaries between the two races are not clearcut. Pairs of one subspecies are reported as breeding in the range of the other (Swann 1945, Martorelli 1960, Heim de Balsac *in* Vaurie 1961, Vaurie 1965). Some museum specimens whose wing length is typical of one subspecies show a plumage pattern typical of the other (Mingozzi 1981). The situation becomes more confused by the difficulty in identifying individuals observed in the wild as to subspecies and by the relative scarcity of museum material with reliable collecting data such as sex, date and locality. Furthermore, there is considerable overlap in wing length.

HABITAT AND DENSITY

All eyries are on cliffs, mostly calcareous or sandy. The cliffs are usually high and command a view of the surrounding landscape, but do not face any favored direction. According to the classification proposed by Hickey (1969), cliffs are usually first class in the Alps. In the Apennines, where availability of first class cliffs is lower, Peregrines may also use second class cliffs. In the Alps, eyries are in hollows or on ledges and usually difficult to see and reach; in the Apennines they are more accessible.

Eyrie altitude varies from 20-30 m on the coast up to 1000 m in the Apennines, and between 800-1400 m in alpine areas. However, one alpine pair is known to nest about 2000 m above sea level, which is, as far as we know, the highest in Europe. This nest has more rigorous ecological conditions than those elsewhere in the Alps, marked by persisting snow (November-May), strong local winds and wide temperature variation. The cliff faces south, and prey species in the area reach a high density.

In the Alps, Peregrines use Common Raven nests and possibly those of the Common Buzzard. In the Alps and in the Apennines, unused eyries of Golden Eagles have also been occupied by Peregrines.

Egg laying generally takes place in March, but we do not know exact dates or average clutch size. Fledging normally occurs at the end of May. The earliest fledging date has been 5 May 1985 in the coastal area; the latest has been 10 July 1985 in the Apennines, after a recycled clutch (M. Chiavetta pers. comm.).

Because of different ecological conditions, we prefer to divide the Peregrine population of northern Italy into three units: the "western Alps population" (inhabiting the Alps of Liguria, Piemonte except Ossola Valley, and Aosta Valley); the "northern Apennines population" (in Emilia); and the "Ligurian coastal population" (along the Tyrrhenian Sea).

Western Alps Population. — P. Fasce, L. Fasce and T. Mingozzi started the study in 1979 and continued with the help of F. Bergese, M. Bocca, and occasionally D. Bruzzone and A. Bruzzone, W. Maffei and W. Pieretti. Suitable cliffs were surveyed, and reproductive data were collected from those pairs already known.

Twenty-two territories were known, spread unevenly over the area. In most areas Peregrines appeared to occupy most of the suitable cliffs. Distances between occupied eyries varied from 5 km ($n=3$) to 80 km. The maximum distance may not be accurate, however, as many of the areas between were not completely surveyed. In Aosta Valley, where the landscape is quite homogeneous and suitable, the nearest neighbor's average distance was 11.7 km ($n=6$).

During eight years, 79 occupied territories were checked: 54 pairs reared 135 young. The average net reproduction (fledged young per pair) was 1.99; the average brood size (young per successful pair) was 2.5. The breeding success (successful pairs per checked pairs) was 79%.

Every reproductive pair consisted of adults. Only six territories were held by pairs where the male was adult and the female juvenile; none of these laid eggs, but copulations were observed. We never observed pairs with juvenile male and adult female.

On eight occasions we observed an adult pair defending a territory and showing courtship displays, but could not ascertain whether young were raised. These are not included in the calculations of breeding rate (Table 1).

Ligurian Coastal Population. — The study was started in 1979 with data also from U. and S. Ricci and D. and A. Bruzzone. The

Ligurian coast has little habitat for Peregrines. Towns, cottages, and beaches are continuous; suitable cliffs are infrequent.

We know of three territories on sea cliffs, and their reproduction is given in Table 2. Two were occupied during survey years but the third, mentioned by Martorelli (1960), was not used consistently. A pair of Peregrines was present there in 1980, in January and February 1981, and in February 1982. In 1983 and 1984 an adult female and a lone juvenile were observed, respectively. In 1985 no birds were at the cliff. The repeated desertion may result from the presence of Eagle Owls on the same cliff.

Northern Apennines Population. — Data for this area were provided by M. Chiavetta since 1971. Eight territories were held in 1985, and 60 nesting attempts have been checked in the last 14 years (Table 3). Thirty-four nestings produced a total of 73 young. Reproduction averaged 1.2 young per pair (range: 0.5-1.83); brood size averaged 2.1 (range: 1.6-2.75); and breeding success was 57% (range: 25-71%).

The Peregrine in this area is sympatric with the Lanner Falcon, and competition for nesting sites is likely. Both species have bred on the same cliff or very close to one another (shortest distance: 90 m on the

TABLE 1.   Reproduction and breeding success for 68 breeding attempts by Peregrines in the western Alps of Italy, 1978-85.

	1978	1979	1980	1981	1982	1983	1984	1985	Total
No. of checked pairs	2	5	9	8	11	11	15	18	79
No. of fledged young	1	7	13	11	23	16	36	28	135
No. of successful pairs	1	3	5	4	9	6	13	13	54
Young/pair	0.5	1.4	1.4	1.4	2.1	1.5	2.4	1.6	2.0
Average brood size	1	2.3	2.6	2.8	2.6	2.7	2.8	2.2	2.5
Breeding success	50%	60%	56%	50%	82%	55%	87%	72%	68%

TABLE 2.   Reproduction and breeding success for 15 breeding attempts by Peregrines along the Ligurian coast of Italy, 1979-85.

	1979	1980	1981	1982	1983	1984	1985	Total
No. of checked pairs	1	2	2	2	2	3	3	15
No. of fledged young	0	2	0	0	3	1	7	13
No. of successful pairs	0	1	0	0	1	1	2	5
Young/pair	0	1	0	0	1.5	0.3	2.3	0.9
Average brood size	0	2	0	0	3	1	3.5	2.6
Breeding success	0	50%	0	0	50%	33%	67%	33%

TABLE 3. Reproduction and breeding success for 60 breeding attempts by Peregrines in the northern Apennines of Italy, 1971-85.

	1971	1972	1973	1974	1975	1976	1977	1978	1979	1980	1981	1982	1983	1984	1985	Total
No. of checked pairs	1	1	1	2	2	4	4	4	5	6	6	5	7	7	6	60
No. of fledged young	0	1	2	7	4	4	2	2	6	5	11	7	8	7	9	73
No. of successful pairs	0	1	1	2	2	2	1	1	2	3	4	3	5	3	4	34
Young/pair	0	1	2	3.5	2	1	0.5	0.5	1.2	0.8	1.8	1.4	1.1	1	1.5	1.2
Average brood size	0	1	2	3.5	2	2	2	2	3	1.7	2.8	2.3	1.6	2.3	2.3	2.1
Breeding success	0	100%	100%	100%	100%	50%	25%	25%	40%	50%	67%	60%	71%	43%	67%	57%

same cliff). At other times, however, the presence of one of the two species has pushed away the other from the nesting cliff. In 1980 Peregrines occupied an eyrie where, until the previous year, Lanner Falcons had nested.

POPULATION DYNAMICS

Few Peregrine nest sites were known in northern Italy until our surveys. The species was considered rare or uncommon in the Alps prior to this century (Mingozzi 1981). Recent surveys, together with the topographic features of the region, suggest that this population has changed little since the last century. We suggest that much of the decline of the 1960s and 1970s in central and northern Europe never happened in Italy.

Western Alps. — Without ring data we make hypothetical calculations on the basis of Mebs' (1971) formula, assuming 11% adult mortality as found by Mearns and Newton (1984) in south Scotland and using the reproductive rate of 1.99 from our data. The formula suggests a critical reproductive value for population stability when we use an 88% mortality of young based on our data. This hypothetical mortality is much higher than shown from recoveries in other countries: 59% in Sweden, 56% in Germany, 71% in Finland (Lindberg, Mebs, and Mebs, respectively, *in* Ratcliffe 1980) and 70% in North America (Enderson 1969b). Mortality of young is likely to vary annually, however.

A rough assessment of the lowest possible juvenile mortality may be obtained using our survey data. At least 135 young fledged in eight years, or about 17 young per year. At least six of them (4%) became part of a pair at one year of age (out of the 86 pairs for which we know the age composition). Thus mortality in the first year of life cannot have been higher than 96%. This is certainly too high a value.

If a juvenile mortality rate as high as 96% occurred in the western Alps population with an adult mortality rate of 11%, the result would be about a 10% drop in total population in one year and 50% in seven years. On the other hand, a juvenile mortality reduced to 80% would increase the total population by about 5% per year and 50% within nine years. But, in the last eight years we never observed the desertion of any eyrie or any territory held by a single adult. (We could not collect evidence of reproduction in four eyries in 1985: at two we think the pair moved to another cliff, not yet known; one was not checked; one was found after possible fledging.) In fact, in 1982 a cliff was used which previously had been abandoned.

From Mebs' formula and an increased adult mortality rate of 25% (a value similar to those of Lindberg, Mebs, and Mebs *in* Ratcliffe

1980, Enderson 1969b), we get a critical juvenile mortality rate of 60% to maintain a population. That value is similar to the value from band recoveries.

Using the lowest reproduction rate obtained in the last eight years, we also obtained a reasonable value for juvenile mortality of 72% (with adult mortality at 11%), or 52% (with adult mortality at 25%).

Reproduction has ranged from 1.38 in 1981 (not counting 1979 because of a small sample size) to 2.09 in 1982 (Table 1). Brood size has ranged from 2.15 in 1985 to 2.77 in 1984, with the lowest breeding success in 1981 (50%) and the highest in 1984 (87%). All these values are in the range of values for other parts of Italy (Schenk et al. 1983) and Europe (Glutz von Blotzheim et al. 1971, Newton 1979, Ratcliffe 1980, Meyburg 1981) where populations are believed to show little influence from pesticides. We think, therefore, that the western Alps population is healthy and stable or perhaps slightly increasing.

Northern Apennines. — Breeding rates in the Apennines are significantly lower than in the western Alps, and close to values noticed by Ratcliffe (1980) in Great Britain from 1961-71; average reproduction was 1.2, brood size 2.1, and breeding success 57%.

To maintain population stability with an adult mortality of 11%, juvenile mortality must be no more than 80%. However, adult mortality in the 1950s and 1960s was likely higher because shooting and poaching were frequent. If it was 25%, for instance, juvenile mortality must have been 44% to maintain a constant population, an almost unbelievable value.

Actually, only one pair of Peregrines was present at the beginning of the 1970s in the northern Apennines, where the population was reported to have been 20-25 pairs in the 1940s (Chiavetta 1981b). After 1970 shooting and poaching became rarer. There were seven occupied territories in 1981 and eight in 1985. Nevertheless, the population is still endangered by persistent human persecution.

THREATS AND CONSERVATION

Regions inhabited by Peregrines in northern Italy are not intensively cultivated, and even if individuals move to the cultivated Po River plain it does not seem likely that they would be heavily poisoned. The main factor limiting the population appears to be human persecution.

In the Apennines, where eyries are easily seen and accessible, shooting and robberies were frequent; in the western Alps such incidents were only occasional. Human persecution occurs in many different ways. Rock-climbing is becoming more important, to such an extent that authorities, made aware by protectionists' associations, have forbidden climbing on some cliffs.

Another threat, chiefly in the Apennines, is that of careless photographers, self-styled biologists, and rash protectionists who, in different ways, cause irretrievable losses. Furthermore, some robberies of eggs or nestlings for illicit falconry and shooting have been noticed, even though the Peregrine has been protected throughout Italy since 1978.

Lastly, urbanization and competition with the Eagle Owl play important roles in limiting the possible spread of the Peregrine Falcon population.

ACKNOWLEDGEMENTS

We are grateful to Dr. C. Violani for the useful discussion about subspeciation.

69 Do Large Natural Broods Increase Mortality of Parent Peregrine Falcons?

R. Wayne Nelson

Efficient hunters that they are, Peregrine Falcons must still experience an additional cost for raising an additional nestling. The cost may be borne in a number of ways. In a larger brood, nestlings (and fledglings) may be lighter in weight, show slower growth, or remain longer in the nest because less food per nestling is provided by the parents. With a larger brood, the parents may experience additional wear and tear because of many more hunting flights and food deliveries; aggressive nestlings and fledglings may add to this stress. The cost of a larger brood may be measurable in terms of increased mortality or decreased productivity of the offspring, the parents, or both. Possibly the cost is masked by other mortality factors, or it may not measurably decrease reproduction or increase mortality under normal circumstances, but only under unusual stress. For theoretical discussions of these life history relationships see Charnov and Krebs (1974), Stearns (1976), Ricklefs (1977) and Reznick (1985).

This investigation sought to find the way in which the cost of a larger brood is expressed in Peregrines, by (1) comparing the weights of nestlings in large and small broods, and (2) comparing the turnover rates of adults after having reared large broods versus small broods. This appears to be the first bird study to demonstrate that a large natural brood size is associated with higher apparent mortality (disappearance) of the parents before the next breeding season.

METHODS

The Study Population. — The Peregrines (*F. p. pealei*) studied lived on Langara Island, Queen Charlotte Islands, British Columbia (54°N, 113°W). Adults were present on the island through the winter and were paired on territories at least as early as mid-February. The history of the population is rather well-known. Since I first visited the island in 1968 it has held 5-7 territorial pairs (Nelson and Myres 1975,

719

1976, Nelson 1977), although in earlier years there were more (Beebe 1960).

Age, Sex and Weight of Nestlings. — Nestlings were aged by comparison with photos of Peregrines of known age (Heinroth and Heinroth 1967, Hall 1970, Nelson 1970).

Sexing of nestlings was not difficult when both sexes were present in the nest and the nestlings were more than 10 days old. If only one nestling was in the nest, characteristics such as the general size and age, the size of the head and the feet relative to the body, shape of the head, and behavior were used as guides to the sex; the bird was compared to similarly aged, known-sex birds in photos. Very young birds were sometimes sexed at a later visit to the nest. At banding, nestlings were weighed in a bag using Pesola spring scales. Two nestlings also were weighed once prior to banding.

Identification of Adults. — The pattern of black and white on the head of an adult Peregrine is unique and consistent year to year. Major features used were the presence or absence, length, width and shape of the malar stripe, the auricular white area, the band over the cere, the eyebrow patches, marks on top of the head and the ocelli on the nape. Important fine details were recorded in the patterns of white on black and vice versa in these areas. Comparison with photos of captives and of the Sun Life female with her unusual breast indentation (Hall 1970) showed this method to be reliable.

Binoculars (20-40X) or a telescope (15-45X) were used to see details of head markings. These were sketched onto standard outline drawings of the various views of the head. The drawings were compared against Peregrines seen in later years. Beginning in 1983, a camera attached to the telescope was used to supplement the sketches with annual color photos of each bird.

When a known adult was not found at its territory, it was presumed dead. It is possible that a missing adult was in the floating population of nonbreeders. In no instance was a known adult discovered at another eyrie on the island, or at the original eyrie after another bird of the same sex was in residence there.

Time Periods. — Adults were individually identified from 1968-75 and 1980-85. Brood sizes from 1968-74 and 1980-84 were used with the respective adult survival data. These periods are referred to as the "early years" and the "recent years," respectively.

Statistics. — The Chi-square test was used to test for statistical significance of observed differences at the 95% level. Some suggestive lesser levels (e.g., 90%) are noted, as larger sample sizes may show these tendencies to be statistically significant also.

In order to have sufficiently large samples to carry out statistical tests, data from broods of 0-2 were pooled as small broods, and data from broods of 3-4 were pooled as large broods.

RESULTS

The mortality rates of territorial adults in the 12 months following the rearing of 0, 1, or 2 nestlings were similar. Broods of three young were associated with a much higher level of adult mortality, and broods of four with a somewhat higher level (Table 1). Similar differences in these mortality rates were seen when males alone, or females alone, were considered.

When data for the early and recent years were combined, the mortality of adults following the rearing of large broods was much higher (almost significant, $P=0.94$). In 1980-85 the difference was not significant, and for 1968-75 the expected distributions were inadequate to test by Chi-square (Table 1).

For females, the mortality rate and brood size were strongly positively related ($0.90<P<0.95$). For males, this relationship was almost significant at the 0.90 level (Figure 1a).

The male mortality rate was significantly higher in the recent years, but the female mortality rate and the mortality rates of the sexes combined were not significantly different between the two time periods.

The mortality rate of males in 1968-75 was significantly lower than that of females, but for 1980-85 and for both time periods combined, the mortality rates of the sexes were not significantly different. Brood size was significantly smaller in the early period ($P>0.99$) (Figure 1b).

Similarly, preliminary data from banded female Peregrines on the upper Yukon River and Tanana River, Alaska (R. E. Ambrose pers. comm.) show a positive relationship between brood size and parent mortality before the next summer. Twenty-five percent of mothers of broods with 3-4 nestlings were not found in the following year ($n=20$), whereas only 15% of mothers with broods of 0-2 were missing ($n=27$). The sample sizes were not adequate to test by Chi-square. The combined Langara Island and Alaska data indicate that, following the production of a large brood versus a small brood, Peregrines in these populations disappear at a significantly higher rate in the following 12 months ($P>0.95$).

Nestlings were weighed at a variety of ages, providing a rough growth curve for the Langara population (Figure 2). Visual inspection showed that a few broods were considerably underweight for their age. Most of these were broods of 3-4; however, rather few broods of 1-2 were weighed. At least some broods of 3-4 contained nestlings as heavy as similarly aged nestlings from broods of 1-2.

TABLE 1. Brood size and the loss of breeding adult Peregrines before the next nesting season, Langara Island, British Columbia.

	1968-74			1980-84			All Years		
	No. adults[a]	No. lost[b]	% lost[c]	No. adults[a]	No. lost[b]	% lost[c]	No. adults[a]	No. lost[b]	% lost[c]
Brood size (n)									
4	2	1	50	12	3	25	14	4	29
3	5	2	40	25	13	52	30	15	50
2	19	4	21	9	2	22	28	6	21
1	8	2	25	4	1	25	12	3	25
0	9	2	22	6	2	33	15	4	27
Unpaired	5	1	20				5	1	20
Totals	48	12	25	56	21	38	104	33	32
Summary									
$n = 3, 4$	7	3	43	37	16	43	44	19	43
$n = 0, 1, 2$	41	9	22	19	5	26	60	14	23
	NA[d]			NS[e]			$0.90 < P < 0.95$		

[a] No. of adults known in both years.
[b] No. of adults lost before next breeding season.
[c] Percent of adults lost before next breeding season.
[d] NA = data not adequate to test by Chi-square.
[e] NS = not significant.

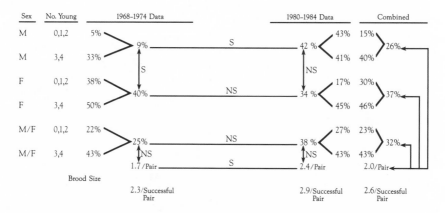

FIGURE 1a. Adult mortality of Peregrines on Langara Island, B. C., comparing differences in sex, brood size, and sampling periods. N=significant difference; NS=no significant difference. See text for details.

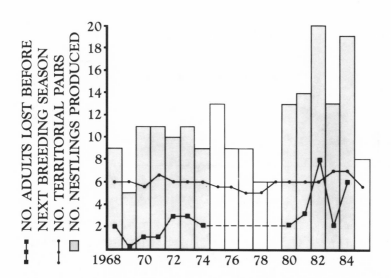

FIGURE 1b. Number of nestlings produced (bars) by Langara Island, B. C., Peregrines in relation to the number of territorial pairs and adult mortality. Non-shaded bars represent years lacking adult mortality data.

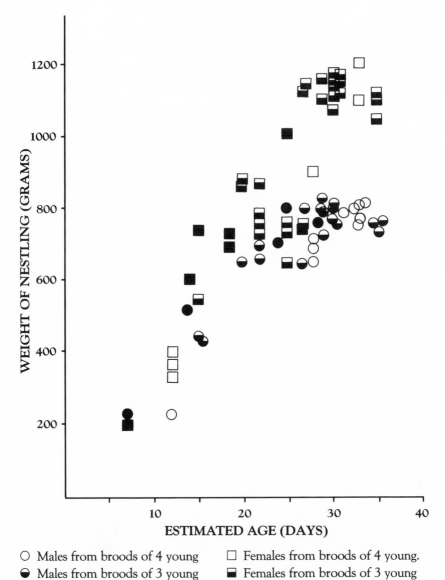

FIGURE 2. Weights and estimated ages of nestling Peregrines at Langara Island, British Columbia.

DISCUSSION

Despite much theoretical speculation, a positive relationship between reproductive effort and parent mortality has been weakly supported by field studies. Indeed, several studies found the opposite relationship, that the raising of large unmanipulated broods was associated with less parental mortality (Kluyver 1963, Högstedt 1981, Smith 1981). In several species larger broods were associated with increased weight loss by the parent birds (Hussell 1972, Askenmo 1977), an indication that those adults may have been at greater risk; increased weight loss of adult Glaucous-winged Gulls with enlarged broods was not associated with a difference in survival to the next year (Reid 1985).

Askenmo (1979) reported a lower rate of return for male Pied Flycatchers which had reared experimentally enlarged broods in the previous year. However, Högstedt (1981) noted that such losses may not be the result of higher mortality but probably were owing to the fact that the enlarged broods had higher rates of nesting failure, and unsuccessful breeders of that species change nest sites at a much higher rate before the next season. A cost of reproduction was clearly demonstrated in Adelie Penguins; adults which did not breed experienced 22% annual mortality, whereas those which did breed had 39% mortality (Ainley and DeMaster 1980). Finally, although in House Martins brood size was not significantly related to adult mortality, females which reared second broods in a summer were much less likely to return than females which reared only one brood (Bryant 1979). It appears that prior to my study there have been no investigations which showed that different natural brood sizes were positively related to subsequent loss of the parent birds.

The particular reproductive strategy of a population may depend on such factors as the life expectancy of the average breeder, the likelihood that the brood size will be reduced naturally, the relative effects of shifting some reproductive costs from the parents onto the offspring, the severity of the stress on the breeding adult, and the amount of "recovery time" between the breeding effort and the first substantial stresses of fall-winter. It must be noted that a brood size/parent mortality relationship opposite to that observed in the Langara Island and interior Alaska Peregrines has been detected in preliminary data from the *F. p. tundrius* population at Rankin Inlet, Northwest Territories (G. S. Court pers. comm.). Only 11% of Rankin Inlet parents rearing broods of 3-4 failed to return in the next breeding season ($n=28$), whereas 38% of parents rearing broods of 0-2 failed to return ($n=32$) (sample sizes not adequate for Chi-square test). Does *F. p. tundrius* shift more of the cost of large broods onto the nestlings?

If a parent of a small brood is more likely to survive and breed again than a parent of a large brood, this might have a dramatic effect on its overall reproductive output. A mortality rate of 10% means that the average life expectancy of the breeding bird is 9.5 more years, whereas a mortality rate of 20% gives the average bird only 4.5 more years, 30% gives 2.8 years, and 40% gives only 2.0 more years (formulae of Lack 1954, von Haartman 1971). However, the brood sizes found in Peregrines appear to bear little relationship to the clutch sizes of the respective Peregrines; rather, they seem to result from winter-spring weather effects acting upon a relatively uniform clutch size in all nests in the same population (see Figure 1). Note that in its lifetime the average breeder at Langara in the early years fledged almost exactly the same number of offspring as the average breeder in the recent years. Therefore, it seems unlikely that the increased mortality found in parents of larger broods would cause selection favoring one clutch size over another.

Small brood sizes appear to favor the survival of the male parent (see Figure 1a). This may occur because a female has to produce a similar output of energy for incubation and brooding and nest protection regardless of brood size. On the other hand, a male with a small brood has his hunting efforts considerably reduced for 2-3 months, a somewhat longer period than for the female.

The relatively high mortality rate of the Langara Island adult Peregrines probably results from their year-round residence on the island, their dependence upon seabird prey whose populations are greatly reduced from earlier times (Nelson and Myres 1976), and the hostile winter conditions the Peregrines face. For other populations, subtle differences can be expected in the weighting of the factors which determine the average brood size, the nourishment of the brood, and the average breeding adult mortality rate.

Larger broods of Peregrine Falcons in interior Alaska were fed more often, but individually, the nestlings in larger broods received fewer feedings per day (Enderson et al. 1972). Such nestlings might be lighter in weight, as has been found in other species (e.g., Askenmo 1977).

Some of the Langara broods were considerably lighter in weight than others of the same age. Because of the small number of broods with 1-2 nestlings during the 1980-85 period when weights were obtained, it is not clear whether the occasional low-weight brood was a result of brood size, harsh environmental conditions of a particular year, or other factors. It is also unknown whether the smaller body weight is retained through life or is made up sometime later. In some species, heavier fledglings have higher survival rates (Perrins 1965, Thomsen 1971, Perrins et al. 1973). At Langara the nestlings from larger broods tended to fly at younger ages than small-brood nestlings, not older (Nelson 1977). This is additional evidence that the larger broods in this population usually are adequately nourished.

The Peregrine's reproductive and territorial strategies are based on the production of only somewhat more offspring than are necessary for the eventual replacement of breeders (Nelson 1977, 1983). That is, an adequate quantity (but not an excess) of nonbreeding adults or floaters is produced. Captive-breeding and release efforts have shown that Peregrines can produce relatively large numbers of eggs consecutively, can incubate five or six eggs adequately, and can rear five or six foster nestlings in the wild. Why aren't the average clutch size and brood size five or six? When the Peregrine's brood size surpasses four nestlings, the additional costs to adults, nestlings, or both must far override any benefits, for larger broods in nature are a rarity.

CONCLUSION

The following primary relationships are apparent in the Peregrines of Langara Island. Environmental factors, which the Peregrines cannot compensate for, act upon the relatively uniform clutch sizes in the population to produce the substantial year-to-year variations in brood sizes. The parent Peregrines usually are able to respond to these brood sizes by providing for the maximum growth of the nestlings. As a result, in years with small broods the parents (especially males) are less stressed by the breeding effort and experience lower mortality over the following winter. In years with large broods, breeding stresses are particularly significant and mortality of breeders over the winter is higher. The average breeder produces approximately the same number of well-nourished offspring whether its reproductive life spans a period which has small broods, large broods or a mixture of both.

A variety of experiments are suggested by these findings. Conspicuously missing from the published literature are documented growth curves for well-nourished nestling Peregrines from hatching to fledging and beyond. Based on such growth curves, comparisons should be made of the growth of individuals in different-sized broods of captive-bred and wild pairs. It could be determined, for example, whether adults with an abundance of food "protect themselves" by working less hard to feed nestlings in large broods. Are there territories with such abundant food supplies that foster broods of 5-6 young can be well-nourished without significantly endangering the survival of the parent Peregrines? It would also be valuable to know whether members of larger hacked broods are lighter in weight through some factor inherent in brood size. Finally, because of the immediate value to the Peregrine reintroduction effort, it should be determined whether the light-weight nestling Peregrine is just temporarily affected, or whether its asymptotic weight, fledgling weight, adult weight, chance of recruitment, and survival rate are permanently diminished.

ACKNOWLEDGEMENTS

In my 15 visits to Langara Island my studies have been aided by too many kind people and agencies to be individually acknowledged here. I thank them all, and am especially indebted to the following: M. T. Myres and the Department of Biology of the University of Calgary, R. Fyfe and the Canadian Wildlife Service, W. Munro and B. van Drimmelen of the British Columbia Wildlife Branch, the Ministry of Transport, the Prince Rupert Fishermen's Co-op, the Frank M. Chapman Memorial Fund of the American Museum of Natural History, the National Research Council of Canada (grants to M. T. Myres), K. Hodson, R. E. Ambrose, D. Pitt-Brooke, and A. Nelson.

ADDENDUM

Harsh Winter Weather and Increased Mortality of Langara Island Breeding Peregrines. — For the 12 years in which data are available, Figure 1b shows that the number of banding-age nestlings in each year was roughly paralleled by the number of breeding adults lost before the next breeding season. Based on the production of eight nestlings in 1985, it was predicted that 1-2 of the 1985 breeders would be missing in 1986. Further, the 1986 data were expected to provide sufficient samples to make the Langara brood size/parent mortality relationship statistically significant on its own at $P>0.95$.

In 1986, 5 adult pairs reared 11 nestlings. Of the 11 territorial adults present in 1985, 6 were lost (1 was not replaced) by late May-early June 1986. Weather records from the Langara light station show a week in February with temperatures of $-15°C$, extremely hostile conditions in which the Peregrines had to hunt seabirds offshore. Apparently the other 12 winters under consideration were "average" in their selective effects upon the Peregrines, whereas the 1985-86 winter was severe. Analyses of the local weather data may indicate which aspects of the weather are particular threats to these over-wintering falcons.

70 | The Population Biology of Peregrine Falcons in the Keewatin District of the Northwest Territories, Canada

Gordon S. Court, D. Mark Bradley,
C. Cormack Gates, and David A. Boag

Peregrine Falcons have been studied intensively since 1981 on a small study area (450 km²) in the southern Keewatin District of the Northwest Territories. The research has dealt with many aspects of the breeding biology of this northern population (*F. p. tundrius*), including population limitation, population dynamics, and the extent of pesticide contamination; the results have been extensively documented elsewhere (Court 1986). In this paper we summarize our observations on the density and reproductive success of this population and discuss those factors which were shown to have had a profound short-term effect on these variables.

STUDY AREA

This research was conducted on a study area near the community of Rankin Inlet, Northwest Territories, on the western coast of Hudson Bay (62°49'N, 92°05'W). The summers in this region are typically short and cool with mean high and low temperatures in July of 13.1°C and 4.5°C, respectively. Spring thaw begins in mid-May, reaching a peak by the first week of June. Ice cover on small lakes and ponds begins to melt at this time; however, landfast sea ice persists until the second week of July. Average annual precipitation figures include 118.0 cm of snow and 16.0 cm of rain, giving a liquid total of 27.8 cm.

The study area encompassed approximately 450 km². The landscape is typical of the barrenlands of Canada with low rolling hills separating numerous tundra ponds and lakes. Geologically the area is dominated by altered intermediate volcanic rock and derived amphibole schist and gneiss (Wright 1967). Rock outcrops of up to 53 m in height are a prominent feature of the landscape and are particularly well-developed as offshore islands in Rankin Inlet. Outcrops with rock faces large enough for cliff-nesting raptors are smaller and less numerous as one moves inland. Nest cliffs occur as much as 6 km inland and on islands up to 4 km out to sea.

Ridge tops, upland areas, and well-drained slopes are covered with associations of lichens, mosses and low shrubs. Labrador tea (*Ledum palustre*), mountain cranberry (*Vaccinium vitis-idaea*), and crowberry (*Empetrum nigrum*) are the dominant vascular plants. Bell heather (*Cassiope tetragona*) occurs in moist low-lying areas and rock crevices. Vegetation on most slopes and hillsides consists of combinations of heaths with *Dryas integrifolia*, *Carex* spp., *Cassiope*, and lichens (Maher 1980).

METHODS

Beginning in mid-May the entire study area was surveyed for arriving Peregrines. In all years but 1981, these ground surveys were followed up in mid-June (during early incubation) and again in early July (during late incubation) by helicopter surveys of all known and potential nesting sites. Data on total egg production, nest failures, and egg losses were obtained on these surveys. The entire study area was surveyed each time, thus eliminating any bias that could occur when surveying an unfamiliar nesting area, such as looking only at "apparently suitable" nesting habitat or traditionally-used cliffs. Such survey techniques were necessary in detecting some of the "ephemeral" nesting territories in this population. Furthermore, all occupied nest sites were visited on foot at least three times during each field season. Clutch size data were available for only nine of 14 laying pairs in 1981. Mean brood size was calculated using the number of young present at the nest when nestlings were three weeks of age.

The actual size of the study area and the density of nesting pairs therein were calculated using the method of Ratcliffe (1980). The 19 nesting territories occupied in 1982 were used to calculate the size of the study area and the mean distance between nests (for density comparisons). Although originally suggested as a means of measuring density in inland areas where nesting habitat is relatively homogenous in dispersion, this method serves adequately to establish the study area size for the Rankin Inlet population.

RESULTS AND DISCUSSION

Population Density. — The number of occupied territories in the Rankin Inlet study area varied from 17 in 1981 to 26 in 1985 and 1986. The smaller number is probably the least accurate as observers were new to the study area that year and no helicopter surveys were undertaken. Consequently some territorial pairs may have been overlooked. It is extremely unlikely that any territorial pairs were overlooked in the study area from 1982-86. The cliff faces used for nesting varied between 4-30 m in height. The lowest nest was 2 m from the base of a 4-m face, and the highest was 26 m from the base of a 30-m face. Actual nest locations, in the form of natural rock ledges or abandoned Rough-legged Hawk nests, were superabundant in the study area: of 112 breeding attempts recorded between 1981-86, precisely the same ledge was reused on only seven occasions. Eggs were laid on broad, open ledges as large as 2 × 4 m and as small as the flattened remains of a stick nest (less than 1 m²).

A mean distance between nests of 3.3 km (± 2.0 S. D.) was calculated for the breeding population (range: 0.7-9.8 km). The mean distance between nests was used to delimit the 450 km² area occupied by the breeding population, giving a density of approximately one pair of Peregrines per 17 km². Approximately one-half of the area, however, consisted of ocean surface.

In terms of mean distance between nests, the density of Peregrines in the study area is the second highest recorded in North America. A mean distance between nests of 1.6 km was calculated for populations of *F. p. pealei* on the Queen Charlotte Islands (Beebe 1960). Both in terms of mean distance between nests and pairs per unit area, the density at Rankin Inlet is higher than at all other arctic locations yet recorded. Fyfe (1969), for example, estimated a density of one pair per 50 km² for "optimum" habitat on the Northwest Territories mainland and the arctic islands; Burnham (1975) estimated one pair per 200 km² in his study area in west Greenland; Falk and Møller (Chapter 5) estimated one pair per 240 km² in south Greenland; and Hickey (1942) estimated a density of one pair per 1364 km² for the eastern United States. Density at Rankin Inlet approaches the highest densities recorded for populations of the Peregrine in Great Britain — those nesting in association with seabird colonies on the sea cliffs of southeast England and some Scottish islands (Ratcliffe 1969).

There can be little doubt that Rankin Inlet represents an exceptional breeding area for Peregrine Falcons. However, it is most unlikely that this extraordinary density can be extrapolated to any other section of the Keewatin mainland or coastline. The study area at Rankin Inlet is relatively small and, as Ratcliffe (1980) pointed out, local concentrations of cliffs in a region where they are otherwise sparse can produce unusually close clustering of pairs. This may be the case at Rankin Inlet, where the local cliffs have attracted a high density of pairs which, unlike some other dense populations, show no strict feeding specialization on a single superabundant prey species.

Territory Use and Variability in Population Size. — The number of territorial pairs was relatively constant from 1981-84, but increased by about one-third to 26 pairs in 1985 and 1986 (Table 1). Some territories were occupied by pairs every year, others in most years, and some territories only once in six years. Of the 29 nesting territories used between 1981-86, only 10 were occupied in all six years. Records of banded birds have shown that this pattern is not always explainable by use of alternate nest sites or movements of adults between territories. Some pairs occupying territories for as long as three years simply disappeared, and the territories were then left vacant. At other territories, pairs of birds appeared and often bred successfully but were absent the following year. These territories were often occupied by completely new pairs in later years. Hickey (1942) suggested that there are different "grades" of nesting cliffs, identified by their dimensions and history of use. He noted that "first class" cliffs were often very high and were always occupied, even if pairs using them were continually persecuted and suffered poor productivity. The occupancy pattern at Rankin Inlet suggests a similar situation, in which cliffs with the highest vacancy rate are somehow less suitable for nesting.

At territories used only once in the six years, there was nothing to suggest that the occupants had previously nested in the area. Such birds were particularly evident in 1985, when "new" pairs established territories at the alternate nest sites of pairs in regularly occupied territories or on available nesting habitat between such territories. Ratcliffe (1980) noted that "new" pairs could occupy alternate nest sites and occasionally contribute to an increase in population density. He concluded, however, that such pairs were usually unsuccessful and sooner or later disappeared. At Rankin Inlet, however, there was no significant difference between the mean number of young fledged at nest sites occupied in only one year and the mean at sites occupied in

TABLE 1.   Breeding success of Peregrine Falcons on the Rankin Inlet study area, 1981-86.

	1981	1982	1983	1984	1985	1986
No. of occ. territories	17	19	19	20	26	26
No. of pairs with eggs	16	17	17	16	25	21
No. of eggs produced	unknown	63	60	58	92	77
No. of pairs with young	15	14	14	14	20	12
No. of pairs fledging young	15	14	13	12	20	8
No. of young hatched	unknown	39	42	43	(68-74)	(28-32)
No. of young fledged	36	35	36	37	61	13

all five years (Court 1986). A peculiar trait of these "new" pairs in Rankin Inlet was that, although often successful, they frequently failed to return to the cliff the next year. Some members of these pairs were color-banded, yet were never recorded in the breeding population in subsequent years. The overall results suggest that a certain percentage of the breeding population in any one year will occupy territories the location of which cannot be predicted from year to year.

A noteworthy aspect of the breeding biology of Peregrines at Rankin Inlet was the variability in the number of pairs attempting to breed each year. Other well-studied populations of the Peregrine have shown remarkable constancy in size in the absence of organochlorine pesticides (summary in Newton 1979). Yet, in 1985, the Rankin Inlet population increased by six pairs (30%), and the total number of young Peregrines produced in the study area was nearly double that in any of the previous four years (Table 1).

Initially, it might be suspected that this increase represented a recovery from pesticide-induced decline. However, results of pesticide residue analyses of eggs collected from this population in 1981 and 1982 do not suggest a pesticide problem. The generally high reproductive success of this population, relative to others, also supports this contention. Furthermore, in the early stages of recovery one would have expected to see younger birds, possibly yearlings, attempting to breed, as seen in other populations recovering from pesticide problems (Mearns and Newton 1984). But all of the birds that obtained territories at the Rankin Inlet study area between 1981-86 were adults; of the 12 new birds (6 pairs) in 1985, only 1 was recruited from the 142 young produced in the previous 4 nesting seasons.

The noticeable increase in the proportion of laying pairs and the slight increase in the average brood size in 1985 suggest that food supply was more abundant in that year. The experiments of Newton and Marquiss (1981) showed that the proportion of "nonlaying" pairs in a population of European Sparrowhawks can be reduced to zero if food is abundant enough in the prelaying phase of the nesting cycle. It is possible that the increase in the population of Peregrines at Rankin Inlet was in response to an increase in prey abundance, in a manner similar to other raptor species that feed upon prey with fluctuating populations (Lockie 1955, Pitelka et al. 1955, Village 1983).

Subjective appraisal of prey abundance on the study area did not suggest a dramatic increase in the numbers of any avian prey species. Although Rock Ptarmigan are known to fluctuate greatly in abundance from year to year, they rarely breed in the study area and are preyed upon by the Rankin Inlet Peregrines only in the very early spring. Rock Ptarmigan appeared even less numerous in the spring of 1985 than in the previous four years. The only potential prey species known to have increased dramatically in abundance in 1985 were mammalian.

Studies at Eskimo Point, Northwest Territories, 240 km south of Rankin Inlet, established that populations of four microtine species (*Lemmus sibricus, Dicrostonyx groenlandicus, Clethrionomys gapperi* and *Microtus pennsylvanicus*) peaked in 1985. Not only were the populations of all four species substantially greater than in the previous four years, but individuals in 1985 were of larger body size than those of previous summers. Researchers responsible for these findings suggest that this peak in microtine abundance was synchronized over an area large enough to include Rankin Inlet (Dr. F. Mallory, Laurentian University, pers. comm.). The dramatic increase in the population of Rough-legged Hawks breeding in the study area (Figure 1) supports this assumption, as this species is known to show fluctuations in population size and reproductive performance synchronous with microtine cycles (Hagen 1969, White and Cade 1971).

Peregrine Falcons nesting at Rankin Inlet commonly took mammalian prey, although in most years the remains of juvenile Arctic Ground Squirrels (*Spermophilus parryii*) were most often encountered. In 1985, however, the remains of lemmings, including whole carcasses, were commonly found at the nests. In view of the use of these species as prey, it is not unreasonable to suggest that the Peregrine population

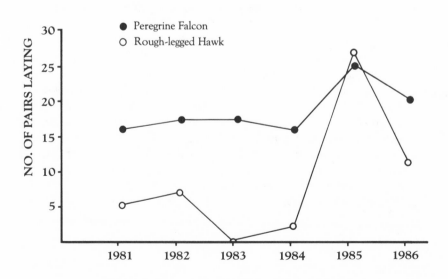

FIGURE 1.   Number of Peregrine Falcons and Rough-legged Hawks that initiated breeding each year on the Rankin Inlet study area, 1981-86.

responded to the abundance of these microtines in 1985. Relative to the preceding four years, more pairs attempted to breed, a larger proportion of territorial pairs laid eggs and there was a sharp increase in total number of young fledged (Table 1).

Although the Peregrine preys primarily on birds (Ratcliffe 1980, Cade 1982), and mammals usually make up an insignificant part of its diet (Hickey and Anderson 1969), there are references — most of them from studies on the tundra — which relate heavy predation upon mammals by Peregrines. Fischer (1967) quoted two studies from Siberia that placed the contribution of mammals to the Peregrine diet at 28.5-50%. Bertram et al. (1934) suggested that Peregrines show an increase in density of breeding pairs during microtine peaks. However, Cade (1960) summarized information from several arctic studies and concluded that while Peregrines do catch microtine rodents in peak years, there was little evidence to indicate that breeding density and reproductive performance are influenced by the numbers of these rodents. At Rankin Inlet, it is easy to see how Peregrine predation on mammals might evolve, as there are no trees, and a great proportion of prey taken during the summer consists of fledgling passerines which are caught on or near the ground (see Sherrod 1983 for similar observations in Greenland).

From what is known of microtine rodent fluctuations (Krebs 1964), we predicted that the abundance of these mammals in the study area would decline precipitously in 1986, followed by a decrease in the population density and breeding success of both Peregrines and Rough-legged Hawks. The number of Rough-legged Hawks that laid eggs in 1986 declined (Figure 1); however, the breeding population was larger than in all other years of the study except 1985. This observation suggests that microtines were less numerous in 1986, but were not as scarce as in the "pre-peak" years, 1981-84. Unexpectedly, the number of Peregrines observed on territory in the spring of 1986 did not decrease from the 1985 total, but the number of laying pairs did decline (Table 1, Figure 1). Three of the five Peregrine pairs that did not lay in 1986 were at irregularly occupied nesting sites between more regularly used territories. Although these Peregrines were territorial during the early spring, their defense behavior dropped off as the season progressed, and in July and August single birds or pairs, often nondefensive, were only seen occasionally.

Unfortunately, poor spring weather affected hatching success of the Peregrines in 1986, preventing a comparison between reproductive output in 1985 and 1986 based only on relative prey abundance. However, circumstantial evidence obtained in 1985 and in the early spring of 1986 suggests that periodic fluctuations in populations of small mammals can affect the number of Peregrine pairs attempting to breed and, consequently, the total reproductive output of the population. Continued study involving detailed documentation of prey use over a series of microtine peaks will clearly determine the relative importance of these mammals as prey for the Peregrines nesting at Rankin Inlet.

Reproductive Performance. — In 1986, extraordinarily poor weather during early incubation in mid-June appeared to have a profound effect on the reproductive success of the Peregrines at Rankin Inlet. As 1986 was a very abnormal year (Table 2), data on reproduction are discussed separately from other years in the following summary of reproductive success.

At Rankin Inlet, 10% (10 out of 101) of Peregrine pairs occupying nesting territories between 1981-85 failed to lay (Table 1). The proportion of pairs failing to lay in any one year varied from as high as 20% in 1984 to 4% in 1985. Although failure to lay contributed significantly to the total of all nesting failures, losses of entire clutches and broods were significant. Of the 91 pairs that produced a clutch, 77 hatched young, and 74 fledged young. Thus, about 74% of all pairs to initiate a breeding attempt were successful in fledging young. Loss of clutches (13, or 48% of all failures) was more than four times as common as loss of entire broods. Of those failed nests with eggs, seven involved desertion of entire clutches, in three cases eggs were lost through breakage, and in three cases the details of loss were unknown. Nest predation was unrecorded in this population of Peregrines and seemed to be rare or nonexistent. Indeed, clutches abandoned for weeks were untouched by scavengers or potential nest predators such as Arctic Ground Squirrels (as noted by Cade 1960), Herring Gulls, and jaegers.

Besides loss of entire clutches, another significant factor contributing to reduced reproductive output was partial nest failure or infertility of eggs. All eggs hatched in 44% of the clutches laid in 1983 and 1984, indicating that some eggs were lost through breakage, embryo death or infertility in about half of all clutches. Using samples from North American populations, Hickey (1942) addressed the importance of loss of Peregrine eggs during incubation by calculating the difference between the mean number of young fledged and the mean clutch size. He noted a "drop" of 23.3% from mean clutch size to mean fledging number. The Rankin Inlet population produced a ratio of 2.79/3.62, or 0.77, similar to that obtained using data from Hickey (1942). Detailed investigation of hatching success in 1983 and 1984 suggested, however, that not all of this loss was related to problems of hatchability. As might be expected, much of the loss came from unrecorded mortality of very young chicks (Court 1986). The ratio of total eggs hatched to total eggs produced in these years was 85/98, giving a hatching success of about 87%.

TABLE 2. Clutch size, brood size, and young produced per territorial pair (mean ± S. D.) of Peregrine Falcons in the Rankin Inlet study area, 1981-86.

	Clutch size (n)	Brood size (n)	No. young/ territorial pair (n)
1981	3.44 ± 0.73 (9)	2.40 ± 0.83 (15)	2.12 ± 1.11 (17)
1982	3.71 ± 0.77 (17)	2.79 ± 0.70 (14)	1.84 ± 1.30 (19)
1983	3.53 ± 0.51 (17)	2.71 ± 0.73 (14)	1.89 ± 1.45 (19)
1984	3.63 ± 0.62 (16)	2.93 ± 0.83 (14)	1.85 ± 1.66 (20)
1985	3.68 ± 0.47 (25)	3.05 ± 0.76 (20)	2.35 ± 1.47 (26)
1986	3.62 ± 0.80 (21)	1.75 ± 1.16 (8)	0.54 ± 1.03 (26)

Pairs with young that totally failed accounted for 11% (3 out of 27) of all failures. All of these losses occurred before the young were one week old. The entire brood disappeared at one nest; dead, emaciated young were found at two other abandoned nests. Some young were also lost from successful nests, although these losses could only be quantified in 1983 and 1984. In these years, 85 young were hatched but only 73 fledged, a nestling mortality of 14%. Hagar (1969), studying a population of Peregrines in Massachusetts, found that nestling mortality varied from as low as 14% at "superior" nest sites to as high as 26% at "poorer" sites. Ogden and Hornocher (1977), in their study of Prairie Falcons, found that 17% of all young hatched did not fledge. At Rankin Inlet, six of the 12 Peregrine chicks that died were lost in complete nest failures. The remaining six were the last-hatched young in six asynchronous broods, and presumably died of starvation. Detailed investigation of the effects of hatching asynchrony in this population showed that the last-hatched young died in about half of all broods of four chicks (Court 1986).

During most years of this study, successful pairs produced about 35 young, or about two young per occupied territory per year (Table 1). Annual production added about the same number of males as females to the population. Of the 108 young produced between 1982-84, 56 were males and 52 females. Male:female ratios varied from 16:20 in 1983 to 23:14 in 1984, neither of which is significantly different from an equal sex ratio (Chi-square analysis, $P>0.05$). This result agrees with nestling sex ratios previously reported for the Peregrine (Hickey 1942, Ratcliffe 1980) and for other raptors (Newton 1979).

The mean clutch size of 3.62 ±0.59 (1981-85, n=84) for the study population was similar to that of many populations from both arctic and mid-temperate latitudes and is only slightly greater than clutch sizes reported from Alaska (Cade 1960, Haugh 1976). The mean brood size of 2.79 ±0.78 (1981-85, n=77) is most similar to that reported by Kuyt (1980) for Peregrines nesting along the Thelon River in the Keewatin District of the Northwest Territories, and by Burnham and Mattox (1984) for a population in Greenland. The number of young produced per territorial pair ranged from 0.54 ±1.03 to 2.35 ±1.47 (Table 2); however, 1.9 young fledged per territorial pair is the representative figure for a normal year at Rankin Inlet.

Between 1981-84, year-to-year figures were strikingly consistent in terms of the number of pairs that produced eggs, the number that produced young, and the total number of young fledged (Table 1). The increase in the size of the breeding population in 1985 altered the impression of constancy to some extent, but although brood size was greater in 1985, there was no significant difference between 1985 and the previous four years in the clutch size, brood size, or number of fledged young per occupied site (Court 1986).

In 1986, however, there were significant declines in mean brood size and the mean number of young fledged per territorial pair (Table 2). The consistently high reproductive output of pairs during the first five years of the study and the significant decline during the sixth year are noteworthy, as speculation exists that climatic vagaries and associated changes in food availability might result in sharp fluctuations in the reproductive success of northern Peregrines (Cade 1960). This possibility poses a potential problem for studies that purport to show that pesticide-induced reproductive failure has caused measurable population declines in arctic Peregrines over the last two decades (Cade and Fyfe 1970, Fyfe et al. 1976a). Particularly where surveys documenting the decline were performed only once every five years, it is possible that poor reproduction or a reduced number of productive pairs may simply represent normal fluctuation rather than a major population decline.

Justification for this interpretation was obtained in 1986 at Rankin Inlet. A severe storm (high winds and snow) occurred in the area in mid-June, shortly after clutch completion. Prevailing winds out of the northwest deposited snow on south- and southwest-facing cliffs, covering many Peregrine nests. Some of the nests were abandoned immediately, but other pairs continued to incubate. Hatching success was reduced considerably. Although not measured precisely, success could not have been more than about 45%. Nestling mortality was also high. Although the absolute number of young that hatched is not known, only 46% (13 of 28) of the nestlings counted a few days after hatching survived to fledging. Higher-than-average nestling mortality may have been related to a decrease in prey abundance. There was evidence of mortality among adult passerines during the June storm, and passerines appeared, subjectively, to be less abundant than in previous years. The poor productivity in 1986, plus increases in population size and reproductive yield in 1985, indicate that some arctic populations of the Peregrine are not as stable as populations in other parts of the world.

ACKNOWLEDGEMENTS

Logistical support and funding for research was provided by: the Department of Renewable Resources, Government of the Northwest Territories; Natural Sciences and Engineering Research Council of Canada (operating grant to D. A. Boag and postgraduate scholarship to G. S. Court); the Science Advisory Board of the Northwest Territories; the Boreal Institute for Northern Studies (Northern Science Training Grant 55-51799); the Canadian Wildlife Service, Environment Canada; the World Wildlife Fund, Canada; and a Max and Marjorie Ward Scholarship, University of Alberta. The authors gratefully acknowledge the laboratory and field assistance of P. Kolit, R. Mulders, M. Sawatsky, H. Armbruster, G. Erickson, G. Stenhouse, R. Bromley, D. Turnbull, D. Bigelow, and F. Ayaruak.

Editors' Note: Reproduction by the Rankin Inlet Peregrines was again late and reduced by a June storm in 1987: 23 pairs were on territory, 18 of them laid, and 13 pairs hatched 18 young that reached near fledgling age. Apparently in 1986 there were 22 pairs that laid, and 9 pairs that fledged 15 young, 1 more successful pair than reported in Table 1. (Data provided by Chris Shank, Raptor Biologist, Renewable Resources, Yellowknife, Northwest Territories.)

71 | Behavioral Differences in Peregrine Falcons

Steve K. Sherrod

This paper is based on over 4000 hours in the field observing the behavior of wild Peregrine Falcons. The observations were conducted over a period of 20 years, especially but not exclusively during the nesting and post-fledging seasons. Observations of Peregrines trained for falconry have also influenced my thoughts as have discussions with Peregrine students too numerous to mention. I further introduce this paper by mimicking White (1969b) in saying that ideas stated here are at best suggestive, and I present them for what they may be worth in stimulating further study. I make no passionate defense of the data because of the conjectural nature of the subject and the lack of definitive proof based on a sample of adequate size; at the same time I make no apologies. Many more hours of behavioral observations by qualified observers are necessary to test these ideas thoroughly.

That the Peregrine Falcon enjoys a cosmopolitan distribution has led systematists to divide the species into as many as 22 different races (Dementiev and Gladkov 1951) or as few as 12 or 13 (see Hickey 1969). When envisioning the differences among populations or races of Peregrines, the first characteristics that come to mind are morphological — slight color differences (Weick 1980), variations in body size (Brown and Amadon 1968, White 1968a, 1968b, Weick 1980) including seemingly minor differences in beak size, toe length, tail length, wing shape, skull shape, and proportions, as well as the geographical boundaries of subspecies. In reality the precise geographical boundaries for many of these subspecies are rather hazy, and if a truly detailed comprehensive study could be conducted, it would probably show clinal gradation from one race to another especially where several races occur on a single continent such as North America (see Beebe 1974 for discussion). According to evolutionary principle, those races which are isolated to the greatest extent geographically, or reproductively to be more exact, and those populations inhabiting environments which select for special traits, are the most likely to show distinctive differences.

The fact that some morphological characteristics of certain races have differentiated in varied environments is, in some cases, no doubt a result of zoogeographical principles such as Bergmann's Rule, Gloger's Rule and Allen's Rule. Other differentiations such as beak size, tail length and wing shape may be adaptive from other perspectives of survival. It is possible that subtle behavioral differences also may have arisen in conjunction with these morphological modifications.

Brown (1975) indicates that behavioral differences within a species often tend to be rather subtle and unstudied. Consequently, it is necessary to look at those differences which are most obvious in order to find any differences at all.

Theoretically those broad categories of behavior that differ the most would be the ones affected initially in Peregrines founding a new population. Such founders must be able to make a living by successfully hunting in the new area utilizing the available prey, and they must reproduce successfully there. Naturally many variables influence aspects of these behaviors such as competitors, predators, terrain and climate.

POPULATIONS STUDIED

I am most familiar with western Greenlandic Peregrines (*F. p. tundrius*), Australian Peregrines (*F. p. macropus*) in Victoria, and Aleutian Peregrines (*F. p. pealei*) on Amchitka Island, Alaska. These geographical populations of Peregrines are relatively well-isolated from neighboring races, occur in quite different environments, and should theoretically exhibit behavioral differences if such differences exist among subspecies.

If one were to compare hunting behavior and reproductive behavior for these three populations, the latter would be more difficult. Extremely detailed studies which examine behavior during the entire nesting season in the wild, as conducted by Nelson (1970, 1977) on the Peregrines of Langara Island, British Columbia, have not been made for *F. p. macropus*, *F. p. tundrius* or Aleutian *F. p. pealei*; however, less detailed observations in captive breeding projects and from other studies (White 1975, White et al. 1978, Burnham and Mattox 1984, Hovis et al. 1985) suggest that all three races exhibit extremely similar reproductive behavior. Subtle differences may well exist, such as flexibility in use of nest sites (Ratcliffe 1980) or incubating behavior in relation to eggshell porosity, but I do not feel qualified to examine these behaviors in detail.

Many facets of hunting behavior exhibited by these three populations are similar to each other and are common to typical Peregrine hunting behavior, but at the same time other aspects seem to differ.

VARIATION IN HUNTING BEHAVIOR

Aleutian *F. p. pealei* is large, relatively dark colored, with a long, broad wing and long tail. It is adapted to flying in almost constant, sometimes strong wind and at times in fog. It tends to have a large, powerful beak and large, heavily-toed feet. This Peregrine at times can be seen hunting over land and lakes and along the tidal zone. There it may catch prey such as teal, ptarmigan, longspurs, Rosy Finches, Rock Sandpipers and Snow Buntings (White 1975) from shallow stoops and by using fast-flying, low approaches just above the tundra in the manner of a Gyrfalcon. (In fact, its build and behavior are very Gyrfalcon-like.) However, Aleutian *F. p. pealei* preys primarily on alcids such as auklets and murrelets and other seabirds by flying in a manner as just described, but over the ocean surface. It flies 10–20 m above the sea and makes short shallow stoops at flying alcids, or approaches low and fast just above the swells, surprising alcids and catching those that flush in front of it. I have observed far too few *F. p. pealei* hunting flights on alcids to draw solid conclusions, but Wayne Nelson (pers. comm.) states that in more than 200 observed captures, he has very rarely seen an adult Langara *F. p. pealei* bind to the prey. Prey is nearly always hit from a shallow stoop, killed or stunned and then plucked from the surface of the water. Aleutian *F. p. pealei* is a year-round resident of the Aleutian Islands as far as present knowledge shows.

The west Greenlandic *F. p. tundrius* Peregrine is a medium to medium-small race usually light in color with a proportionately long, narrow wing and medium-length tail. Though it is fully capable of killing large ducks such as drake Mallard, it is smaller-framed than *F. p. pealei*, with a small to medium-sized beak and medium-sized feet. In west Greenland it feeds almost exclusively on small passerines and shorebirds (Burnham and Mattox 1984). It catches these over the open tundra, over small lakes and along river drainages by stooping from a height of fifty to several hundred meters or by flying low to the ground in Gyrfalcon fashion and pursuing those that fly up in front of it. It will sometimes pursue on foot passerines which take cover in the stunted trees and brush of the tundra over which it hunts. It is a transequatorial migrant which must deal with a variety of habitats and prey species on its migration routes and wintering grounds. It is assumed that passerines and shorebirds provide much of the winter diet; some west Greenlandic *F. p. tundrius* winter along coasts (Schoonmaker et al. 1985) and in cities, where they feed on doves and pigeons (Jones and Bren 1978, Albuquerque Chapter 73).

The Australian *F. p. macropus* race is a nonmigratory, year-round resident. It is compact, relatively heavy-bodied, and medium to medium-small, with a solid black head, short tail and a proportionally broader wing than F. p. tundrius. It has a proportionally large, heavy beak and thick, relatively heavy-boned tarsi with large feet. It catches its prey by using combinations of the same tactics described for the other two races. Australian Peregrines catch some prey from a stoop, other prey by direct pursuit or in surprise attacks, and still other prey by isolating them over water. While I observed both Greenlandic and Australian pairs hunting cooperatively, the Australian birds did so to a much greater extent. Australian Peregrines feed primarily on pigeons, psittacines and passerines (White et al. 1978). Not only does this Peregrine pursue prey over open space such as lakes, fields and the tops of forest canopies, but the pairs which I studied followed prey into and through relatively dense "open woodlands" and "semi-open woodlands."

I would like to discuss woodland hunting in more detail. Individuals of the F. p. macropus race which I observed pursued much of their prey over open terrain as noted above, but they also habitually hunted the open woodlands surrounding the general area of their eyries. I did not see them flying through the woodlands as if searching in the manner of an accipiter; rather, adults flew over wooded areas as do most other Peregrines. Once in pursuit, however, they showed no reluctance whatsoever to follow fleeing prey through and into relatively dense woodlands. On several occasions I observed young falcons crash through the foliage of trees when pursuing birds which had taken refuge there. Not only did adults and young pursue prey into these woodlands, but adults frequently flew into woods where food transfers were made to offspring that followed the adults there. Adults also attempted to "hide" from their persistent and aggressive offspring by flying into the woods and perching deep in the tree foliage.

I do not mean to imply that the Australian Peregrine has completely converged upon the niche of a goshawk. When I could observe birds, most of their activity occurred in open areas, but such observations are biased because I could not see them once they were in woods. This subject needs more study. I was surprised when I first witnessed this behavior. Having observed many wild and trained Peregrines alike, I fully expected Australian Peregrines to flare away as they reached the forest edge rather than pursue the prey or parent Peregrines (an occurrence that became rather common as the young ranged out from the eyrie) into the woodlands. F. p. tundrius trained for falconry rarely if ever follow prey into woodland.

Utilization of the forest in this manner is apparently not peculiar to the pairs of F. p. macropus I observed. Richard Weatherly (pers. comm.) has assured me that he has also observed Australian Peregrines flying into the forest, and he regularly flies rehabilitated F. p. macropus being exercised for release at prey in open woodlands. Czechura (1984a), in writing of Peregrines in southeastern Queensland, stated that vegetation type appeared to exert little or no influence on the overall distribution there since closed forests, open forests, woodlands, wetlands and agricultural areas were all frequented by falcons. He also referred to Dwyer et al. (1979) and Longmore (1978) as indicating occupation by Peregrines of a wide spectrum of vegetation types including vine forest, various forms of open forest and woodland, heath, herb and sedgeland. Clunie (1972), in discussing hunting methods and prey of Fijian Peregrines (*F. p. nesiotes*), professed puzzlement over the high incidence of the Golden Whistler, a forest-dwelling bird, in the diet of this "open space" predator. Clayton White and Dan Brimm (pers. comm.) report that in their recent survey of Fiji (White et al. Chapter 29), they watched an adult Peregrine flying under their aircraft drop below the forest canopy and disappear. One suspects that the Fijiian race might also pursue prey into forested areas. The African Peregrine (*F. p. minor*) reportedly hunts similarly, and it is likely that all the forest-dwelling races of Peregrine are adapted to pursuit below the canopy.

It seems logical that young *F. p. tundrius* Peregrines would avoid forests because they are not familiar with them. Nesting *F. p. anatum* Peregrines are often associated with boreal forests; however, they show no tendency to pursue prey through the trees or spend any appreciable time there. Instead, they hunt birds flying high above forest or over large rivers (Cade 1960).

The parent *F. p. macropus* which I studied spent a great deal of time interacting with their young in the forest, a fact that would undoubtedly introduce offspring to that type of habitat. In contrast, Richard Weatherly (pers. comm.) related that the several "zoo raised" *F. p. macropus* youngsters he had flown back to the wild regularly chased and captured prey in the "semi-open" forest although they had never had any parental association there. Tom Cade (pers. comm.) relates similar behavior by a young *F. p. macropus* hybrid he flew with falconry techniques. In other words, these birds seemed to display no natural avoidance of forested areas.

Although each race of Peregrine considered in this report captured a different type of prey on its breeding ground, each used very generalized techniques to catch them, albeit over different types of terrain: water, tundra, mixed pastures and woodlands.

Having observed a variety of races flown in falconry, I used to consider their hunting behavior similar. Falconry birds, however, enjoy a very special situation in which prey is flushed for them at precisely the right moment, making it vulnerable to their attack. They are conditioned to expect prey to be flushed if the falcon performs or "waits on" in a certain manner. The capture of prey by a wild Peregrine in its own environment is a very different situation. It involves finding vulnerable prey and making a successful approach followed by a successful attack. One wonders just how specialized these populations of Peregrines are at capturing a particular type of quarry in a given environment, particularly nonmigratory Peregrines.

HUNTING IN RELATION TO BODY FORM

With its slighter frame, *F. p. tundrius* is efficient in capturing small passerines. Its long, narrow wing may be adapted for fast pursuit above the tundra as well as for long distance migrations. White (1968b) has suggested that *F. p. tundrius* does not follow Bergmann's Rule because of selection pressures on the wintering ground. Cade (1982) presents information derived by Andersson and Norberg (1981) which suggests that small raptor body size relative to prey should be selected for, and the more agile the prey, the closer the raptor should approach that size below which subduing and transport of prey become counterselective. Perhaps this is another pressure resulting in the small size of *F. p. tundrius*, as it feeds on passerines and small shorebirds. That it has not converged closer in size to these prey species probably results from the fact that as a migrant it must remain generalized enough to capture varied prey in different areas while migrating and wintering.

Although falconers have often trained and used *F. p. tundrius* "beach birds" to capture ducks as large as Mallards on a daily basis, I doubt that prey that large is taken regularly by wild *F. p. tundrius*. Instead, smaller birds are the usual fare. Trained *F. p. tundrius* usually show much more zeal for large ducks and other large prey during their first year of life (Sherrod 1983). After the first year many *F. p. tundrius* prefer to take smaller species of ducks. This probably happens because the exertion involved in daily capture of large ducks and other large prey is enough to "wear out" Peregrines in the wild and reduce their future breeding fitness.

I interpret *F. p. pealei* as being the Peregrine's counterpart of a Gyrfalcon. With its long, broad wings and long tail it is adapted to swift and direct low-level pursuit of seabirds, to ruddering and maneuvering in strong winds, and to hovering over the water momentarily to pluck a stunned alcid from the water just as the long-tailed kestrels, or even on occasion the Gyrfalcon, do so well while searching for hiding prey. Wayne Nelson (pers. comm.) confirms my observations of the low-flying tendency of *F. p. pealei* by indicating that in all of his observations of the Peregrines at Langara Island, he has rarely if ever seen the birds flying at heights greater than approximately 150 m. This race of Peregrine does not follow the principle of convergence toward prey size suggested by Andersson and Norberg (1981). In fact it is a large Peregrine catching small prey. Perhaps its hostile winter environment dictates a larger body and consequently a smaller corresponding surface area from which heat may be lost as suggested by White (1968b). Perhaps it is as specialized as a Peregrine can become, as dictated by its isolation, resident status, and primary dependence on alcid prey.

The Australian Peregrine appears to me to be a generalized race utilizing a wide diversity of prey but with proportionally large beak, foot, and heavy tarsus apparently adapted to frequent catching of psittacines (White et al. 1981). Psittacines are a potentially dangerous prey which must be dispatched immediately upon capture. *F. p. macropus* does that effectively.

Peter Jenny (pers. comm.) has found that the Orange-breasted Falcon, which has a similarly large beak, foot, and heavy tarsus, catches both bats and psittacines which must be dispatched quickly. The fact that *F. p. macropus* also catches prey in the open and semi-open forests is perhaps made possible because, as Richard Weatherly (pers. comm.) has suggested, Australia is inhabited by no large, powerful goshawk.

FLYING STYLES

If in fact morphological changes such as body size, wider wings, longer tails, heavier tarsi and bigger beaks can be selected in a subspecies of Peregrine that specializes on a particular type of prey, then it seems likely that certain behavioral traits such as flying styles may be selected too. I would like to point out that, in only a few generations, artificial selection has produced a great variety of different flying performances in strains of feral pigeons such as homers, tumblers, tipplers, and high fliers (Levi 1941). Given the time and number of generations during which natural selection has operated on Peregrines, it is reasonable to expect that there have been genetic modifications of behavior as well as of morphology, modifications which adapt different populations to their particular environmental conditions.

It seems logical that in a given population such as that found in Britain (*F. p. peregrinus*), which has apparently evolved feeding upon pigeons and doves, such a trait as high flying (at several hundred meters) might be selected. This likelihood assumes that high flight allows an advantageous position from which to launch successful attacks on pigeons. At the same time, in a population of *F. p. pealei*, selection might be made for relatively low, Gyrfalcon-like flight since the majority of prey is found at or around water and is in fact aquatic. Naturally, neither situation results in selection to the complete exclusion of other flight styles. As a bird predator, it is disadvantageous to become too specialized.

After studying post-fledging behavior in Peregrines (Sherrod 1983), I am convinced that early association with parents, individual experimentation, and learning play major roles in the development of flight style, prey selection, and habitat utilization. It is easy to understand, however, that especially in nonmigratory populations, those young with a genetic predisposition for searching and attacking behavior adapted to the predominant prey species and habitat would have the greatest chance for survival.

CONCLUSION

It is intriguing to ponder the results of a giant, imaginary experiment. If it were possible to remove all of the approximately 17 resident pairs of *F. p. pealei* from Amchitka Island and replace them with the same number of pairs of resident *F. p. tundrius* from west Greenland, would the latter rely primarily on the passerines of Amchitka as they do in their native nesting territories, or would they be able to utilize the alcids by hunting out over the windy seas as the native *F. p. pealei* residents do? And at what numbers could the newly founded *F. p. tundrius* population exist? Would a *F. p. pealei* population transplanted to the "bush" of Victoria be able to utilize effectively the psittacines and columbiforms in order to maintain a successful breeding population? Probably not, but on the other hand a number of *F. p. pealei* Peregrines released in the eastern United States are now successfully breeding there in the complete absence of alcids as prey (Barclay and Cade 1983).

In short, the discussion boils down to the "nature/nurture" argument. As Ratcliffe (1980) has rightly and repeatedly commented concerning a variety of biological subjects relating to the Peregrine, the truth is probably somewhere between the two extremes.

ACKNOWLEDGEMENTS

I thank M. A. Jenkins and T. J. Cade for reading this paper and offering suggestions.

72 | Aspects of Breeding and Feeding Behavior of Peregrine Falcons in Guayllabamba, Ecuador

Nancy Hilgert

Throughout the world, the Peregrine Falcon breeds in a considerable diversity of habitats. It occurs in all countries of South America, either as a breeding species or as a migrant from arctic and subarctic breeding grounds in North America and Greenland (Bloom et al. 1980, Gochfeld 1977). The biology of the Peregrine is known principally from northern temperate areas, and detailed information from the tropics and southern latitudes is lacking or preliminary. The importance of data from southern latitudes lies in their comparative value. Data on ecology and general selective pressures on seasonality and breeding phenology of Peregrines can be compared with those of northern populations (Pruett-Jones et al. 1981a).

In Ecuador we have *F. p. tundrius* and *F. p. anatum* migrants from the northern hemisphere and *F. p. cassini* migrants from the southern hemisphere (cf. Chapman 1926, Ortiz and Valarezo 1975). Many specimens of each subspecies have been collected since 1917 (Albuquerque 1978). In this study, I present a brief history of breeding and observations on feeding behavior of a pair of nonmigratory Peregrines located in the inter-Andean region in Ecuador. Peregrines at this location appear to have a variable breeding season (June-December), and young may remain near their eyries for nine weeks. Similar data are reported for northern Peru (Schoonmaker et al. 1985, P. Schoonmaker pers. comm.). I suspect there are nesting sites other than the one studied here because of the copious amounts of fecal material observed on some cliffs in surrounding areas.

STUDY AREA

The pair of Peregrines in this study has several alternate eyries in a deep wash close to the town of Guayllabamba (00°04'S, 79°46'W) approximately 30 km northwest of Quito (Figure 1). This location is

749

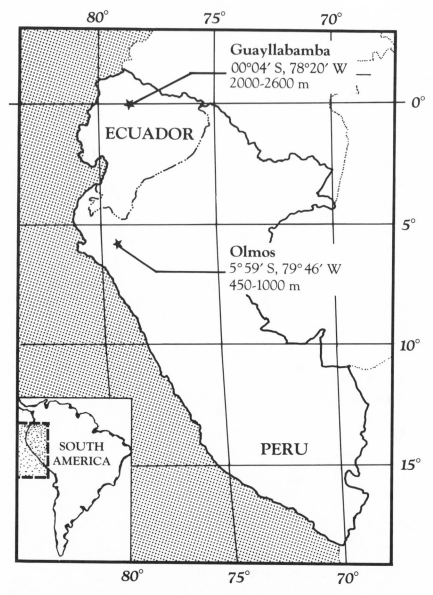

FIGURE 1. Map and geographical locations of Peregrine Falcons breeding in Peru and
          Ecuador.

at the junction of the foothills of the eastern cordillera and the floor of
the inter-Andean basin of the Guayllabamba River, at 2380 m elevation
(Jenny et al. 1981). The wash is approximately 300 m wide with

vertical sedimentary cliffs on both sides. The cliffs have soft sections, and slides are frequent in rainy seasons. The wash has a small stream running its entire length from south to north and flowing into the Guayllabamba River. The west wall of the wash is approximately 50 m high; the east wall is approximately 100 m high and slightly divided into two slopes. Vegetation on the cliff top is mainly dry thorn scrub characterized by *Acacia pelalcantha, Agave americana, Bromelia* spp., *Cereus* spp., and *Opuntia* spp. At the base of the hill, vegetation is mainly thorn scrub steppe characterized by *Acacia pelalcantha, Acacia macralcantha, Agave americana, Percea americana, Anona chirimoya,* and some agricultural plants.

The area is dry and warm, with annual rainfall of 38-69 cm and annual average temperatures of 10°C at night and 21°C at midday. During the summer months (June-August) the area is windy.

METHODS

This study was conducted in different stages, depending on available time (Hilgert 1984). Observations were first made from October 1981-February 1982 for a total of 60 hours. Occasional observations were made in October-November 1982 and January-February 1983. Two observations were made in April 1984. From July 1984-January 1985 there were a total of 224 hours. Finally, two observations were made in August and October 1985.

Observations were made from different sites in the wash, depending on the stage of breeding. Distances were approximately 50 m, 100 m, and 300 m, respectively, during copulation, courtship, and the nestling stage. Climatological data for Ecuador are scarce. For this location information was only available up to 1982. Nest Site 1 and Nest Site 2 were visited in 1982 (Jenny et al. 1983) and 1983, and I collected all remains of prey. Prey was identified either in the field or in the laboratory at the Pontificia Universidad Catolica del Ecuador, Quito. In 1981, two unhatched eggs were removed in order to measure eggshell thickness and analyze their contents for chlorinated hydrocarbons (Jenny et al. 1983). In 1982, the fate of two unhatched eggs was unknown.

During November 1983 and March 1984 I collected prey samples for a study on toxic chemical residues. Guayllabambean birds were also collected for the Canadian Wildlife Service.

RESULTS

Nesting Sites. — This Peregrine territory has two cliffs in an east-west plane. The pair used several ledges and cracks in successive years. Sites were classified as sandstone and limestone. Nest Site 1 and Nest

Site 2 were in the upper half of the cliff; Site 3 was in the lower half. The three sites were on the eastern cliff, and Site 1 was used twice. All three sites received full afternoon sun. Their characteristics are shown in Table 1. Although there is agricultural land at the cliff base and there are homes about 500 m away, disturbance by humans was minimal.

Breeding Cycle. — Peregrines were first observed at this location in March 1979 when Jenny et al. (1981) found a pair with two fledglings. A pair (including a subadult male) was also seen in February 1980, but did not seem to be nesting then. I found a pair in an incubation exchange on 10 October 1981. The eyrie had three eggs and the ledge was heavily whitewashed, suggesting longterm occupancy. On 31 October, I observed a one- or two-day-old young. The remaining two eggs did not hatch. Fledging occurred in early December. The immature female remained near the eyrie until February 1982.

In 1982, breeding was about one week earlier than in 1981. I found a one-week-old young and two eggs on 27 October in a second nest site. The remaining two eggs did not hatch, and the fledgling female remained near the eyrie until February 1983.

I observed copulations from August 1983-April 1984. The pair showed courtship behavior as described by Nelson (1970, 1977). Copulations occurred from 2-12 times per day with a duration of 2-8 seconds. Cloacal contacts could not be determined.

The exact laying date was not recorded, but on 20 July 1984 I found four eggs in the same nest site used in 1981. Both male (40%) and female (60%) incubated during the day for 1-2 hours at a stretch. The male did most of the hunting. I could not observe which adult incubated at night. The first young hatched on 14 August, and the other two hatched on 15 August and 16 August, respectively. The

TABLE 1.   Characteristics of the three Peregrine eyrie sites used at Guayllabamba. Site 1 was used in 1981 and 1984, Site 2 in 1982 and Site 3 in 1985.

	Site 1	Site 2	Site 3
Altitude, cliff top (m)	2500	2500	2500
Height, cliff (m)	100	120	120
Distance of nest below cliff top (m)	12	5	35
Substrate location	crack	crack	cavity
Eyrie ledge length (m)	6	3.5	1
Eyrie ledge depth (m)	0.9	0.6	0.7
Height of opening (m)	0.3	0.2	0.2
Orientation of opening	E	NNE	NNE
Means of human access	rappeling	rappeling	rappeling

fourth egg did not hatch. After hatching, the female behaved aggressively toward the male, but they started copulating two weeks later on 31 August.

The immatures consisted of two males and one female. The males fledged on 25 September and the female on 27 September. The males remained in the area until November, while the female stayed until 16 December, my last date of observation for 1984.

I observed copulation in January 1985. On 27 August, I observed three unsexed recently-fledged young begging for food and practicing food exchange with the adults. The adults copulated twice in four hours of observation. On 11 October, I observed copulation again but did not see an immature near the eyrie. This was my last observation in 1985.

The "breeding season" (Figure 2) of Ecuadorean Peregrines can be summarized as: (1) courtship: any time of the year except during laying and part of the nesting phase; (2) laying: late June into December; (3) hatching: early August into January; (4) fledging: August into February; and (5) independence of the young: October-March. The juveniles may remain near the eyries for approximately nine weeks. The adult pair remained in their territory throughout the year, and I suspect it is the same pair found in March 1979.

Food. — The most abundant species in the area were the Blue-and-white Swallow, Brown-bellied Swallow, Eared Dove, Common Ground Dove, Vermilion Flycatcher, and Sierra Finch (Ortiz 1975).

During the long courtship period in 1983-84, I observed the pair feeding mostly on two species of swallows. In 15 days of observations during the nestling phase in August-September 1984, I recorded 71 prey items; all but 14 were identified (Table 2). The most important source of food during this phase was the Eared Dove, an abundant species that is easy to identify in the field. I observed the female Peregrine plucking Eared Doves in the eyrie, as well as Blue-and-white Swallows, the second most important food species.

Results of chemical analyses showed that the eggs contained relatively low pesticide concentrations. The low contamination level may be related to the Peregrine's feeding habits rather than location (Jenny et al. 1983). Results of chemical analysis on Peregrine prey in Guayllabamba are not yet available.

Breeding Cycle. — The most important factor regulating the breeding schedule of raptors, as well as other birds, is abundance of food (Newton 1979, Pruett-Jones et al. 1981a). In Ecuador, plant growth and productivity and the abundance of breeding birds are more or less stable, but linked to the rainy season-dry season cycle (Figure 2).

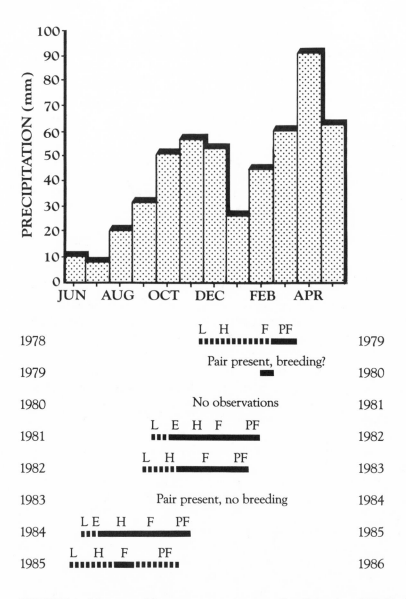

FIGURE 2.* Mean monthly precipitation (mm) at Guayllabamba, 1978-82 (top) and the corresponding breeding schedules (bottom). Solid lines indicate periods of observation; dashes are extrapolations. L=laying; E=eggs; H=hatching; F=fledging; PF=post-fledgling period.

*Editors' Note: There appears to have been a regular shift to earlier breeding each succeeding year, as though there is some internal rhythm independent of environmental events.

TABLE 2. Peregrine prey items recorded during 108 hours of observations over a 15-day period during the nestling phase at the Guayllabamba eyrie in 1984.

Species	n	%
Spotted Sandpiper	4	5.6
Blue-and-white Swallow	9	12.7
White-collared Swift	1	1.4
Eared Dove	27	38.0
Band-tailed Pigeon	2	2.8
Common Ground Dove	6	8.5
White-fronted Dove	1	1.4
Vermilion Flycatcher	1	1.4
Fringillidae (finches)	6	8.5
Not identified	14	19.7
Total	71	100.0

The nesting of Ecuadorean Peregrines begins any time from June to December. The only other known region with a comparably wide range of beginning dates is Kenya (Thomsett Chapter 30). It would be interesting to learn something about the Peregrine's breeding schedules near the equator in other parts of the world.

Food. — While most Peregrines worldwide feed on birds, some feed on bats and other small mammals (Cade 1982). The Eared Dove appears to be the favorite prey of Peregrines in South America (Albuquerque 1978, Jenny et al. 1983, Vasina and Straneck 1984). In Guayllabamba, Eared Doves and Blue-and-white Swallows are abundant year-round. The Peregrine pair in Guayllabamba fed mainly on these two species, as well as on other doves and swallows, depending on the season.

ACKNOWLEDGEMENTS

"Thanks to You, Father, for allowing me to cooperate with You in the mystery of nature." . . . Richard Armstrong.

I thank my husband, V. Benavides, for patience and support during this project and help in the field. I gratefully thank the Canadian Wildlife Service (CWS) for supporting this research program since 1983, and R. Fyfe and U. Banasch (CWS) for their friendship and advice. J. Ruos, M. Fuller, K. Titus, and M. Howe from the Patuxent Wildlife Research Center helped with literature.

P. Schoonmaker helped me to improve my data. I thank my professor, Dr. T. de Vries, for his encouragement. M. Cullen assisted me in proof-reading and gave suggestions. Last but not least, the Hinojosa Family permitted me to use their property for my observations.

73 | Behavior and Feeding Habits of Coinhabiting Peregrine Falcons Wintering in Brazil

Jorge L. B. Albuquerque

Knowledge about the behavior of the nearctic Peregrine Falcon wintering in South America is very limited (Albuquerque 1978, 1982, 1984, Sick 1960, 1961, 1985, White and Cade 1971). Among the many questions that need to be answered are whether courtship begins on the wintering grounds, and whether there are differences in feeding habits between males and females wintering contiguously. It is important to know whether any of the courtshiplike behaviors displayed by Peregrine males on the wintering grounds are really associated with pairing or whether these behaviors are linked to some other function. The following observations add to the information on the winter ecology of Peregrine Falcons in South America and may serve to stimulate more research on the intrasexual and intersexual interactions of the species.

INTRASPECIFIC INTERACTIONS

Although many Peregrines winter alone (Newton 1979, Ratcliffe 1980), a considerable number winter together in large cities in South America (Albuquerque 1978, Sick 1985). In Australia, the Aleutian Islands and elsewhere, resident pairs may remain together throughout the year (Jones and Bren 1978, N. Birks and C. M. White pers. comm.). Several may congregate at one particular point to hunt bats (e.g., in Brazil) or other concentrated prey (Albuquerque 1984). Territorial and social behavior can be observed in such situations.

During my studies on the winter ecology of Peregrine Falcons in Porto Alegre City, Rio Grande do Sul, Brazil (Albuquerque 1982, 1984), I recorded several intrasexual and intersexual interactions. A pair of Peregrines established their hunting ranges approximately 800 m apart along the port, facing the Guaiba River. Territorial interactions were usually near food concentrations such as bat (mainly *Tadarida braziliensis*) roosts and feral pigeon nests. Early in the morning I heard Peregrine vocalizations over the Guaiba River and its islands; they were similar to vocalizations heard in the city in territorial encounters. On several occasions, passage falcons flew through the territory of the pair. The female showed stronger territorial aggressiveness toward passing females than toward the resident male. One immature male passed over the female's territory without eliciting any response from her.

The interactions between the male and the female are summarized as follows: (1) On 16 January 1979 at 1805, I saw the adult female soaring in large circles and the adult male soaring in small circles close to her. The male was vocalizing "chuuueeck." The female did not show any aggression toward the male. (2) On 20 January 1979 at 0755, the male pursued the female until she perched. He did a pendular (shallow, U-shaped) stoop over her and flew away. (3) On 8 February 1979 at 1725, the female pursued the male vocalizing "clee . . . clee . . . cleee . . ." The male, flying at high speed, made a spiral flight vocalizing "clee . . . chip." (4) On 5 February 1979 at 0740, the male was perched at the center of his hunting range. Later, he took wing, made a long pendular flight over the street, gained height, and twice made a helicoid maneuver. (5) On 19 March 1979, the female was perched on a ledge close to the river when the male appeared and made a pendular flight over her. She responded to the male with a vocalization of a hard "cleerr . . . shuuuck . . . cleerr . . . shuuck." Some behaviors observed in Porto Alegre were clearly agonistic (e.g., pendular stoops, "clee-chip" vocalizations) whereas others (e.g., helicoidal or figure-8 flight) were more typical of courtship displays. The interactions between the male and the female showed a range from aggressive and territorial behaviors to general social and courtship behaviors. These behaviors may have a socializing function; they may inhibit potential aggression by the larger female (Cade 1960), allowing individuals of both sexes to overlap hunting ranges and better exploit prey resources.

FEEDING BEHAVIOR OF COINHABITING FALCONS

In Porto Alegre, the pair showed two periods of activity: early in the morning and late in the afternoon. Most (67%) of the female's activities were concentrated within a 300-m radius of her hunting range center (Albuquerque 1984). Eighty-five percent of the morning activities were foraging flights. This decreased to 53% in the afternoon, when she used the remaining time to soar over the city. In late afternoon the female performed long soaring flights over the city center. These constituted about 13.5% of her daily activities. The female showed one overall pattern in the use of her hunting range: she foraged along the river early in the morning and soared over the city in late afternoon and evening.

My sampling of the male's activities was not as complete as that of the female's, but it suggests that the male foraged over the river more often than the female. He used alternative ledges far from the center of his hunting range and closer to the river than did the female. There he intercepted passerines crossing the river during the day and bats in the evening (Albuquerque 1984).

There was considerable overlap in the hunting ranges of the male and female in Porto Alegre, but prey remains indicated a different use of resources. The female foraged mostly on feral pigeons, while the male used passerines and bats (Albuquerque 1982, 1984).

In conclusion, the observations on intraspecific interactions between wintering Peregrines in Porto Alegre suggest that males perform elements of courtship displays outside the breeding grounds. These behaviors may have a socializing function. The large concentration of feral pigeons, doves, and bats in South American cities creates a strong attraction for Peregrines and other raptors. For the Peregrine male, it is advantageous to evolve behaviors that minimize aggressive conflicts with the larger Peregrine female. The indirect result of these socializing behaviors is the ability of the males to share hunting ranges with the females, thus exploiting abundant food resources. The association of the above behaviors with their usual mating functions needs further study.

ACKNOWLEDGEMENTS

I thank my parents, A. Albuquerque and T. Albuquerque, for the financial and moral support for my field work at Porto Alegre. The manuscript benefited from comments by C. M. White and J. Parrish. I thank my wife Annette for her editing of the English in this paper. My graduate work at Brigham Young University was supported by the Conselho Nacional de Pesquisas of Brazil.

Commentary

Population Regulation in Peregrines: An Overview

Ian Newton

As certain Peregrine populations recover from the crash caused by organochlorine pesticides, they are again likely to come up against other limiting factors. My aim here is to set out an hypothesis of population regulation, based largely on historical data, in the hope that it will stimulate collection of further information. The paper overlaps with that of Hunt (Chapter 63), but makes some additional points and differs, in places, in interpretation. My thinking on this subject has been greatly influenced by Ratcliffe (1962, 1980) and Hickey (1942), and also by my own findings on European Sparrowhawks (Newton 1986), which resemble Peregrines in several relevant respects.

Over much of their range, Peregrines nest on cliffs. This habit restricts their breeding distribution, as prey are available in many areas lacking cliffs. Once they have left the nest, Peregrines are almost immune to predation, and are not known to suffer greatly from disease.

BREEDING POPULATION

The only segment of the total population which has traditionally been measured is the territorial component; those birds present at potential nesting places in spring. Normally all (or almost all) such individuals are paired. These constitute the breeding population, even though in any one year not all such individuals may nest. Peregrines which do not hold nesting territories and do not breed are not normally counted. They probably live singly. Their existence can be inferred from other information, as will be discussed later.

The density of territorial pairs varies from one region to another, apparently according to the availability of nest sites or food. In some regions, shortage of potential nesting sites limits the breeding population below the level that food would permit. Pairs are thus spaced irregularly, depending on the occurrence of cliffs or other suitable nesting sites; if additional sites are made available, for example by quarrying, they are then occupied, leading to an increase in density. In regions with surplus nest sites, breeding pairs are usually spaced regularly at densities which correlate with food supplies (Newton 1979, Ratcliffe 1980). High densities are found in coastal areas, where seabirds abound, or inland, where pigeons or other prey are numerous. Territorial behavior is apparently the proximate mechanism whereby densities are adjusted to local food supply, with pairs spacing themselves more widely in districts where prey are sparse. Moreover, in districts which have experienced a longterm decline in food supply, breeding densities of Peregrines have also declined. Thus, Ratcliffe (1980) linked the longterm decline of Peregrines in northwest Scotland with poor land management, which gradually reduced the prey population, while Nelson and Myres (1975) attributed the marked decline of the Peregrines on Langara Island, British Columbia to known reduction in seabird populations, which provided their food. Similarly, a recent increase of breeding density in parts of Britain to levels higher than before the DDT-era has been associated with an increase in the amount of pigeon-keeping, and hence in the numbers of pigeons available as prey (Ratcliffe 1984a). In general, however, the historical data indicate longterm stability in the numbers of Peregrines breeding in particular regions (Hickey and Anderson 1969, Ratcliffe 1980). This stasis is presumably linked with longterm stability in habitat, and hence in prey numbers. It further implies some regulation of breeding density. In both Europe and North America, territorial Peregrine populations that were measured fluctuated by no more than about 10% of the mean value over long periods of years, and the idea of stability was implicit in the writings of all Peregrine workers earlier this century. Hence, stability can be regarded as the normal state of Peregrine breeding populations, though it would not be expected in areas where food supply changed markedly in the long term (or from year to year, if sufficiently extreme situations existed).

BREEDING PRODUCTION

In the absence of serious pesticide contamination or other human influence, production is usually in the range of 1.0-1.5 young per pair per year (Newton 1979). However, while breeding numbers remain fairly constant from year to year, breeding success (the number of young per pair) may vary greatly. In the past, production was often poor in certain areas because of continual human interference, with eggs taken for collections and young for falconry. But even where human disturbance was slight or nonexistent, production sometimes varied markedly from year to year. This was especially true of populations inhabiting cold or wet regions, including those in the Alps

(Kleinstäuber 1969), arctic Alaska (White and Cade 1971), or in the oceanic climate of the Aleutians (White 1975) and western Britain (Ratcliffe 1984, Newton and Mearns Chapter 62).

Poor years are usually associated with cold or wet springs, which reduce prey availability or hinder hunting. The effect on reproduction is perhaps through the food supply, but also by direct impacts on survival of eggs and young nestlings (Court et al. Chapter 70). Cold or wet spells result in reduced egg production if they occur during egg-laying and by reduced hatching and chick survival if they occur later. Other natural breeding failures have been attributed to predation on chicks, most notably by the Eagle Owl in Europe and the Great Horned Owl in North America, but also by a wide range of other raptors, including the Northern Goshawk and Golden Eagle. In central Europe, additional chick mortality has been attributed to martens and ticks (Schilling and Rockenbauch 1985, Brücher and Wegner Chapter 60). However, while production normally varies substantially from year to year, the annual variations are less great than in certain owls and other species which depend on cyclic prey (Pitelka et al. 1955, Hagen 1969, Newton 1979).

NONBREEDERS

Evidence for the existence of nonbreeders is fourfold. First, it may be inferred from the age structure of the breeding population, which is usually deficient in younger age-classes, especially first-year birds. Second, when a pair is disturbed at the nest, their calling sometimes attracts one or more extra birds. As this occurs even at isolated sites and often involves first-year birds, not all such extra birds can be dubbed as breeding neighbors; rather, most must be from a nonbreeding segment. Third, when Peregrines of either sex have been removed from their sites, they have often been replaced within days by other individuals which then bred (Hickey 1942, MacIntyre 1960, Newton 1979, Hunt Chapter 63). The most reasonable explanation is that these replacement birds were nonbreeders that were suddenly presented with an opportunity to nest. Finally, the presence of a second or even third female at an active eyrie has been recorded several times (Spofford 1947, Ratcliffe 1980, Cugnasse 1984, Monneret Chapter 23).

The nonbreeding segment of the population thus consists of individuals which have not yet started to breed (i.e., mainly birds in their first few years of life), and possibly also some older birds which have bred previously but no longer hold a nesting territory. Input to the nonbreeding segment may therefore be in the form of young resulting from reproduction, or in the form of adults resulting from "demotion" from the breeding sector (Mearns and Newton 1984 reported one such probable incident in Scotland). Loss from the nonbreeding segment can be from mortality of nonbreeders or from "promotion" of nonbreeders to the breeding sector. Local densities of nonbreeders may of course be modified by their movements. Some nonbreeders live in the breeding areas, but, because they do not require nest sites, they also live in areas denied to breeders.

Theoretically, the number of nonbreeders could be determined in two ways. If the areas of suitable habitat were restricted, this could limit the number of nonbreeders that could persist there, with competition for space or food as the likely proximate mechanisms. In this case, mortality among nonbreeders would be density-dependent. Alternatively, if the area of potential habitat were so vast that the nonbreeders could never fill it, their numbers would be set instead at whatever point the annual inputs equaled the losses, as described by Hunt (Chapter 63). Because input from reproduction is inevitably limited by the numbers and productivity of breeders, the input of young to the nonbreeding sector must also be limited. There will come a point when the numbers of birds added each year will equal the numbers lost. This point will set the numbers of nonbreeders below the habitat limit, but it may well vary from year to year owing to variation in breeding success and survival. In this system, nonbreeders might be limited in density in particular areas, but as their numbers rose, the excess could simply spread elsewhere with no constraint on total numbers. This could hold true in regions where cliffs restricted the distribution of breeders, but where nearby cliffless areas with abundant food provided unlimited habitat for nonbreeders.

While no attempts have been made to count the nonbreeders in any given region, they could outnumber the breeders by several fold, as a result of high reproductive rates and subsequent survival. If the figures on reproduction and survival in an expanding Scottish population (Newton and Mearns Chapter 62) held in a stable one, and no environmental factor was limiting, then the nonbreeding sector would stabilize at a minimum of three birds per breeding pair.

At breeding time, nonbreeders may prefer to live near nesting areas because their chances of obtaining a breeding territory are greatest there. This could lead to competition for well-placed localities, and to unsuccessful birds being relegated to more distant terrain. There the prospects of eventually breeding may be less promising, but those of survival no different. Where nonbreeders are numerous, individuals perhaps move to progressively better-placed localities as they age, before eventually obtaining a nesting territory.

Losses from the nonbreeding sector are influenced partly by the number of gaps which become available each year in the breeding population. If the annual mortality of breeders were 10% (Newton and

Mearns Chapter 62), then about 10% of places in the breeding population would become available each year. Some individuals will be prevented from breeding in any one year simply through shortage of nesting places, as confirmed by the facts that all or most sites are normally occupied by breeders in any one year, and that if birds of either sex are removed from sites, they are often swiftly replaced by other individuals. Replacement birds may even help to incubate eggs and feed chicks that are not their own. By helping to rear an existing brood, the replacement bird gains parental experience, a territory and a mate, and thereby enhances the prospect of future reproduction. Selection for this behavior could be applied by the widowed bird, which accepts as a mate only an individual which will help to rear the existing brood.

Another factor which may prevent certain individuals from taking up a breeding territory is shortage of food. To my knowledge, this has not yet been demonstrated in the Peregrine, but may well occur in the closely related Gyrfalcon (Cade 1960). Data from Rankin Inlet, Northwest Territories, Canada are indicative (Court et al. Chapter 70). In the European Sparrowhawk, food shortage is an important factor which leads some individuals not to breed, even though potential sites are available (Newton 1986). To defend a breeding territory, a European Sparrowhawk (like a Peregrine) has to be present for most of the day. Hence, only a bird which can obtain its food in a small part of each day can afford a territory. In order to breed, a male must also be able to feed a female, as well as himself, for she could not otherwise produce and incubate the eggs. The reason that the female does not hunt for herself while laying is perhaps to prevent damage to the eggs within her body. This risk is especially great in raptors, because of the way they get their food (Walter 1979a). Moreover, these heavy needs for food occur in early spring when most prey species have not started to breed and are still scarce. Occupancy of a territory also puts demands on the female, as she has to defend the territory against other females as well as against potential predators. It follows logically that a well-fed female in good physical condition probably has a better chance of defending a territory than does one in poor condition.

While an inability to obtain sufficient food may prevent individuals of both sexes from breeding, it is probably more crucial to the male, which has the threefold task of feeding himself and the female, as well as defending the site against other males. In contrast, perhaps almost any female could take on defense duties and breed if she received enough food from the male. The ability of an individual Peregrine to obtain sufficient food will depend on prey availability in the surrounding hunting range, and on the foraging skill of the bird itself, which will presumably improve with age and experience. The important point is that even in an area with vacant sites, nonbreeders may occur if they cannot meet the physical demands of defending a territory.

Since habitat varies, some localities can provide more prey than others. Also, the birds themselves may vary in their foraging skills. Thus, any given individual may be able to breed if it can acquire a good territory with abundant prey, but not if it can acquire only a poor territory. Similarly, some highly skilled individuals might produce young on almost any territory, even the poorest, where less competent ones fail. In European Sparrowhawks, replacements have been observed in certain favored territories, while others nearby remain unoccupied. This is partly because individuals move from poor territories to nearby good ones that become vacant, leaving the poorer territories to be reoccupied sporadically, and mainly by first-time breeders (Newton unpubl. ms.). Observations by Hagar (1969) suggest that the same may happen in Peregrines.

ROLE OF HABITAT AND CLIFF TYPE IN INFLUENCING BREEDING DENSITY

Despite longterm stability of breeding populations, numbers of sites occupied do vary slightly from year to year within regions (Ratcliffe 1962). But breeding cliffs are not occupied at random. Usually certain territories are occupied every year, or almost every year, while others are occupied irregularly. In Britain, Ratcliffe (1980) formally recognized this with his classification of British nesting territories into regular, irregular and occasional; Hickey (1942) and Hagar (1969) had earlier adopted a similar classification for eastern North America. This grading of territories is usually associated with cliff height and aspect: large, imposing cliffs that offer a wide view are used more frequently than smaller cliffs. The interpretation has been that large cliffs are more attractive to Peregrines because they offer greater protection from mammalian predators than small cliffs. The occupancy of small cliffs is attributed to individual Peregrines showing different thresholds in what they will accept, so that while all individuals will accept a big cliff, only certain birds will accept a small cliff. The occupancy of small cliffs is thus dependent upon appropriate "low threshold" birds being available in the vicinity.

Large cliffs may also be favored because they facilitate hunting and defense in a way that small cliffs do not. A bird perched on a large, imposing cliff can do much of its hunting from the energy-saving perched position, can keep watch over a wide area, and has the advantage of great height and good updraft when it starts a chase. At the same time it can advertise its presence and guard the nesting place. There are many observations of Peregrines hunting in this way (Hagar 1969, Treleaven 1977, see Cade 1982 for comments). In contrast, a bird on a low cliff, or at a low point in the landscape such as a gully, has none of these advantages. Its view is restricted, and many of the potential prey it sees will be at a higher level than the cliff itself. It must, therefore, sit elsewhere to hunt, or else hunt from the wing — an energy-demanding method which may entail long absences from the cliff, and hence greater defense costs. To summarize, it is very possible that the size and position of the nesting cliff affect the availability of food for the birds. Tall cliffs which offer a wide view serve to increase food availability, and thus tend to be occupied more regularly and show better breeding production than small cliffs. To put it another way, for Peregrines to occupy a small hidden cliff and breed success-fully, the number of prey in the vicinity must be greater than around a large cliff. A link between food availability and cliff type may explain why Peregrines in forested country generally use only very large cliffs, whereas those in open country use small ones too (Cade 1960 comparing data from the Colville and Yukon rivers, Mendelsohn Chapter 31 for Africa). Only by observing birds on different types of cliffs and calculating their energy budgets can these ideas be checked. They are of course irrelevant in tree-nesting or ground-nesting populations.

The variation in habitat quality owing to prey availability could also provide the mechanism by which breeding density is limited. If the best places (best food supply, biggest cliffs) are occupied preferentially, then as numbers rise and less preferable sites become occupied, the quality of the remaining vacant places will decline progressively to the point of unsuitability, where territorial behavior and reproduction are not fruitful. The availability of prey will be greater in some years than others, permitting more sites to be occupied. The number occupied could also depend on the competence of the Peregrines available as potential settlers each year. A large total population is likely to contain more birds able to breed on inferior territories than is a small total population, thus increasing the chance of poor sites being used. Ratcliffe (1980) attributed the occupancy of territories in Britain formerly considered marginal partly to improved food supply allowing increased breeding density and partly to "population pressure" and the increasing numbers of potential recruits resulting from improved nesting success.

DENSITY DEPENDENCE

I use this term for any population parameter which varies with the density of breeders or density of the total population (breeders plus nonbreeders). Such parameters may include age of first breeding, breeding rate, recruitment, mortality, and/or dispersal. Since recruitment in a stable population is limited to whatever gaps become available in the breeding population each year, some density-dependent process must occur. The numbers of recruits are limited, yet more birds are available for recruitment following years of good breeding success than following years of poor success. Hence, a smaller percentage of total birds is recruited in years of high total population than in years of low total population. The density dependence could be manifested by a greater annual mortality among the nonbreeders in years when their numbers are high or by a delay in their age of recruitment to the breeding population. The longer birds wait to be recruited, the greater the percentage that die between fledging and breeding, even with a constant annual mortality. In increasing populations, some individuals do not breed until their fourth year (Newton and Mearns Chapter 62), so in stable populations the delay could be even greater. Density-dependent annual mortality among nonbreeders is likely only if habitat and food resources for nonbreeders are limited, leading to competition among themselves or with breeders. If resources for nonbreeders are not limited, i.e., if any number of such birds can persist, then the density dependence is likely to occur at age of recruitment, with a later mean age of first breeding when the nonbreeding population is high. Although in theory density dependence could also occur in other population parameters, no evidence was found in an expanding population in south Scotland (Newton and Mearns Chapter 62). In fact, based on the data available, all aspects of population dynamics were independent of density except for age of recruitment. Cases of female Peregrines breeding in their first year have been recorded frequently in depleted or increasing populations, but may be rare in "full" populations near the limit of their resources.

CONCLUSIONS

I have described a means by which Peregrine breeding populations could be regulated in terms of their resources, and nonbreeding populations either limited by resources or, probably more commonly, set at whatever point restricted inputs equaled losses in unlimited habitat. The story has been developed in terms of cliff-nesting populations, but there is no reason why it should differ substantially for bog-nesting or tree-nesting ones. Nor should it differ greatly between resident and migrant populations, though in the latter any competition for nesting territories may be concentrated into a brief period each spring when the birds arrive. Also, habitat for migrants is even less likely to be limiting in winter, when breeders and nonbreeders alike have greater freedom to search out the better places.

While the ideas described are, I believe, consistent with established facts, further information on several aspects is desirable. This is especially true of the nonbreeders, for we know little of their numbers, distribution, and behavior. So far, the nonbreeding segment has remained such an intangible entity that the theoretical possibilities assume far greater weight than the hard data. Yet it may be among the nonbreeders that the most intense competition occurs, not necessarily for survival, but for the opportunity to breed. We also need more information on age of first breeding as populations expand. Understanding the dynamics of nonbreeders and first-breeders centers on questions of recruitment and the maintenance of breeding numbers. However, the rest of the story is still based on circumstantial evidence, and some experimental testing of ideas is required. Careful removal experiments of both sexes from both good and poor territories would help to confirm the existence of surplus birds and the extent to which their recruitment depends on territory quality. Food provision experiments may be expensive or impractical, but it might be possible to provide a continuous supply of pigeons at some sites in order to check effects on occupancy. Also, if a population could be found that depended on a prey base which fluctuated greatly from year to year, then it could be seen whether Peregrine breeding numbers depended on food supplies, i.e., the number of pairs should also fluctuate from year to year in parallel with the prey. However, note that in other raptor species the fluctuations in the prey base have to be extreme before they affect pair numbers, otherwise they merely affect breeding success (Newton 1979).

One further point is apparent. To breed, both Peregrine sexes require a mate, a nesting place, and a sufficient food supply. However, because of the different roles of the sexes in breeding, the key resource permitting reproduction is likely to differ between them. For males, whose job it is to provide the food during the breeding cycle, the quality of the home range is paramount, for males must have an abundance of prey to feed their females and young. Hence, landholding ability is more important to males than to females, competition between males is likely to be primarily for home ranges containing good food and nesting places, and it is the males which are likely to determine breeding density. For females, on the other hand, the crucial resource is a competent male on territory, for only with a male capable of feeding her can a female reproduce. Hence the most important competition among females is likely to be for competent males. The greater demands put on males for breeding may help to explain why there are far fewer records of first-year males breeding than of first-year females (Ratcliffe 1984a; for a successful first-year male, see Plate 8 *in* Hickey 1969).

SUMMARY

(1) Peregrine breeding densities are naturally limited either by nesting sites or food supplies. Where nesting sites are in short supply, they may limit breeding densities below the level that food would permit. Where nesting sites are surplus to needs, pairs are usually spaced regularly, at distances that vary from district to district according to the food supply. Natural longterm changes have been associated with changes in food supply. Otherwise, in the absence of human influence, breeding densities are normally stable over long periods, linked with constancy in nest sites and food supplies.

(2) Nonbreeders consist mainly of birds in their first few years of life not yet recruited to the breeding population. Nevertheless, as shown by removal "experiments," many such birds are capable of breeding if a place is made available to them by removal of a territorial bird.

(3) The numbers of nonbreeders could be limited in either of two ways, depending on region. They could be limited by food supplies, in competition with one another or with breeders, leading to density-dependent regulation; or with limitless food supplies, their numbers could be set at whatever point inputs (mainly fresh youngsters) equaled losses (mortality and recruitment to breeding sector). The input of young is limited each year because the number of breeding pairs is limited. An unlimited food supply seems the likeliest in most regions, and could result in a nonbreeding sector greater than the breeding population.

(4) As well as providing greater protection from predators, large cliffs may facilitate hunting by Peregrines in a way that small cliffs do not, and thus increase the availability of prey. This advantage may account for the preference that Peregrines show for large cliffs over small ones.

(5) As production of young varies more than does the normally stable breeding population, some density-dependent process must inevitably be involved in the regulation of breeding numbers. Based on present data, age of first breeding is the most likely variable to act in a density-dependent manner, with more delay occurring when total population is high.

ACKNOWLEDGEMENTS

I would like to reiterate my debt to Dr. D. Ratcliffe for his influence on my thinking, and also to many others with whom I have discussed Peregrines in recent years, notably T. Cade, J. Enderson, W. G. Hunt, M. Marquiss, R. Mearns, W. Nelson, and C. White. I am also grateful to T. Cade, J. Dempster, J. Enderson and D. Ratcliffe for constructive comments on the manuscript.

9 | Geographic Variation in Peregrine Populations

74 | Biochemical Genetic Variability in Peregrine Falcon Populations

Donald C. Morizot

The first extensive raptor genetic studies of Bald Eagles (Morizot et al. 1985) documented a pattern of small genetic divergence among widespread populations (Alaska to Arizona) characterized by relatively gradual north-to-south changes in allele frequency at polymorphic loci. The common allele at each locus surveyed appeared to be present at high frequency throughout the United States. These results suggested that if enough polymorphic loci could be identified, individual raptors could be assigned to their natal populations with considerable confidence.

Genetic markers would be of considerable utility in several ongoing studies of Peregrine Falcons. From a management perspective, captive breeding projects producing birds for reintroduction into the Peregrine's historical range could avoid inbreeding in their stocks by monitoring variability at polymorphic loci. If clinal geographic variation were demonstrated, original allele frequencies could be predicted and matched with the most genetically similar captive birds. Monitoring allele frequencies in migrant populations could allow assessment of changes in proportions contributed by various natal populations or suggest differential mortality in wintering areas. Finally, detection of sufficient numbers of variable genes would allow highly precise paternity and maternity testing of birds used in falconry or traded on world markets.

The preliminary results of a survey of approximately 60 genetic loci expressed in blood samples from nearly 300 Peregrines are presented here to show geographic distribution of alleles at three polymorphic enzyme loci well resolved in the present study. Estimates of the proportions contributed by various natal populations to migration flocks passing through Assateague Island, Virginia and Padre Island, Texas are compared to those obtained from band recoveries.

773

MATERIAL AND METHODS

Blood samples were drawn from brachial veins. Samples from most falcons in captive breeding colonies at Ithaca, New York, Ft. Collins, Colorado, Santa Cruz, California, and Wainwright, Alberta, Canada were provided by F. Prescott Ward, Aberdeen Proving Grounds, Maryland. Sampling from wild birds from Greenland and Assateague Island, Virginia was coordinated by Ward, and sampling from wild birds in Alaska and Padre Island, Texas by Kenton E. Riddle, University of Texas Science Park, Bastrop, Texas.

Sample preparation and vertical starch gel electrophoresis were performed using methods described by Siciliano and Shaw (1976), Brewer (1970) and Morizot et al. (1985). Histochemical stain recipes are slightly modified from Siciliano and Shaw (1976) and from Harris and Hopkinson (1977). Two buffers, TVB (or TEB), pH 8.0, and TC, pH 7.0, of Siciliano and Shaw (1976) were used routinely to resolve proteins (Table 1). Electrophoretic alleles and allozymes were designated by number according to decreasing anodal mobility.

RESULTS AND DISCUSSION

Electrophoretic variability was observed in at least 10 of approximately 60 gene products surveyed. The genetic basis for seven variable

TABLE 1.   Protein coding loci routinely typed from blood.[a]

Acid phosphatase	Hexosaminidase
Adenosine deaminase	Inosine triphosphatase
Adenylate kinase	Isocitrate dehydrogenase
Albumin[b]	Lactate dehydrogenase
Aldolase	Malate dehydrogenase
Carbonic anhydrase	Malic enzyme
Creatine kinase	Mannosephosphate isomerase
Enolase	Nucleoside phosphorylase
Esterases 1, 2, and 3	Peptidases A and B
Galactose-1-phosphate uridyltransferase	Phosphoglucomutase
Glucose-6-phosphate dehydrogenase	6-phosphogluconate dehydrogenase
Glucosephosphate isomerase	Phosphoglycerate kinase
Glutathione reductase	Phosphoglyceromutase
Glyceraldehyde-3-phosphate dehydrogenase	Pyruvate kinase
Glycerate-2-dehydrogenase	Superoxide dismutase
Glyoxalase I	Transferrin[b]
Guanylate kinase	Triosephosphate isomerase
Hemoglobin	Uridine monophosphate kinase

[a] Based on adequate resolution in blood specimens from Peregrine Falcons.
[b] Plasma proteins.

proteins (a tripeptidase, guanylate kinase, glutamate-pyruvate trans-aminase, lactate dehydrogenase-2, phosphoglucomutase, and at least two plasma proteins) remains to be documented. The geographic variability of the three best resolved enzyme polymorphisms, lactate dehydrogenase-1 (*LDH1*), mannosephosphate isomerase (*MPI*), and nucleoside phosphorylase (*NP*) will be considered below.

Table 2 presents allele frequencies for the three loci estimated by gene counting of presumably unrelated birds. It should be emphasized that in sampling captive populations, 10 or more related birds may permit the use of only 2-4 independent genes in population allele frequency estimation. Thus, only samples from the Colville River, Alaska, and Yukon-Tanana Rivers, Alaska-Canada, and Greenland are comprised of 10 or more independent individuals from wild populations. The allele frequencies presented in Table 2, therefore, must be viewed as preliminary estimates.

The geographic distribution of the *MPI-1* allele remains to be determined. It has been observed only in Colville River residents and in Padre Island migrants at very low frequencies. The usefulness of *MPI-1* as a genetic marker is minimal unless specific populations exhibiting appreciably higher allele frequencies are identified.

The two remaining polymorphic enzymes, *LDH1* and *NP*, are much more informative. Among resident populations the *LDH1-1* allele has been observed only in Alaskan birds, at highest frequencies in *F. p. pealei* and at lower frequencies in Colville River falcons. The appreciable frequencies of the *LDH1-1* allele in Padre Island samples presumably reflect substantial proportions of Alaskan birds in the migrant population.

The four alleles identified at the *NP* locus convey by far the most information concerning geographic origin. The *NP-1* allele is virtually absent in North and South American samples but reaches very high frequencies in Europe and Australia. (The single apparent *NP-1* heterozygote from Alaska could easily be a reading error; the sample was weak and the *NP-0* and *NP-1* allozymes differ only slightly in anodal mobility.) If the moderate *NP-1* allele frequency in Greenland is indicative of an east-to-west cline, the *NP-1* allele may occur in eastern Canada, undetected as yet because of small sample size. The high *NP-1* frequency in Australian *F. p. macropus* suggests that the -1 allele may be present throughout Europe and Asia. Variability in allele frequencies of *NP-2* and *NP-3* is as yet of uncertain utility.

The salient result of this preliminary survey of genetic variability in Peregrines is that the common alleles at most, if not all, loci sampled occur virtually worldwide. This result implies a very recent evolutionary origin of Peregrines and/or extensive gene flow presently or in the recent past. The lack of population-specific fixed allelic differences

TABLE 2.   Allele frequencies of three polymorphic loci in Peregrine Falcon populations.

Race if known or locality[a]	NP				LDH1		MPI	
	0	1	2	3	1	2	1	2
Colville River (n = 22)	0.023	0.023	0.932	0.023	0.045	0.955	0.026	0.974
F. p. pealei (n ≤ 5)			0.75	0.25	0.125	0.875		1.00
Yukon-Tanana Rivers (n = 20.5)			0.854	0.146		1.00	Unfinished	
Alberta (n ≤ 8)			0.94	0.06		1.00		1.00
Colorado (n ≤ 11)	0.045		0.773	0.136		1.00		1.00
Quebec (n ≤ 4)			1.00			1.00		1.00
Greenland (n = 13)		0.208	0.792			1.00		1.00
F. p. peregrinus (n ≤ 3)		1.00				1.00		1.00
F. p. brookei (n ≤ 3)		0.125	0.375	0.50		1.00		1.00
F. p. macropus (n = 2)		0.750	0.250			1.00		1.00
F. p. cassini (n = 2)			1.00			1.00		1.00
Assateague Island (n = 24)		0.083	0.854	0.063	0.039	0.961		1.00
Padre Island: Fall 1982 (n = 51)		0.041	0.918	0.041	0.021	0.979	0.020	0.980
Padre Island: Spring 1984 (n = 47)		0.011	0.936	0.053	0.021	0.979		1.00
Padre Island: Fall 1984 (n = 39)		0.048	0.935	0.016	0.026	0.974		1.00

[a] Colville River, Alaska; Yukon River and Tanana River, Alaska; province of Alberta, Canada; Assateague Island, Maryland; South and North Padre Islands, Texas; F. p. pealei – Aleutian and Queen Charlotte Islands, Alaska and British Columbia; F. p. peregrinus – Scotland; F. p. brookei – Spain; F. p. macropus – Australia; F. p. cassini – Argentina and Chile.

necessitates sampling of larger numbers of loci to provide the variability in allele frequencies needed to generate an adequate set of genetic markers for population-of-origin determination.

Even with these presently meager data, estimates of the composition of the Padre Island and Assateague Island migrants can be compared to those derived from band recovery data. Band recovery data from birds trapped on Padre Island during migration and as residents have yielded estimates that some 58% of the migrants originate from Alaska and an additional 10% from Greenland (Yates et al. Chapter 44). Similar data from Assateague Island result in estimates that 50% or more of the individuals migrate from Greenland to South America (Yates et al. Chapter 44). How do allele frequencies in the Padre Island and Assateague Island samples compare with these estimated compositions? The *LDH1-1* allele provides a rough estimator of the Alaskan contribution to Padre Island migrants, since *F. p. pealei* individuals have been recovered only in west coast flyways (Anderson et al. Chapter 47). North Slope Alaskan birds therefore must provide most of the *LDH1-1* alleles observed in the Padre samples. The average *LDH1-1* allele frequency in fall Padre Island migrant samples is 0.0325, or about 70% of the frequency estimated in Colville River populations, in relatively close agreement with band recovery estimates. Similarly, the average frequency of the *NP-1* allele of 0.0445 in Padre Island fall migrants (presumably contributed by Greenland birds since no continental European bands have been recovered on Padre Island) is about 21% of the estimated Greenland allele frequency, over twice the proportion suggested by band recoveries. Several explanations other than sample inadequacy could explain such a discrepancy: (1) unsampled Greenland populations may have substantially higher *NP-1* frequencies, (2) the *NP-1* allele may occur at appreciable frequencies in unsampled North American populations, or (3) the Padre Island samples may have been taken in years with unusually large proportions of Greenland migrants. Additional geographically and temporally separated samples should distinguish among these possibilities. The *NP-1* allele frequency in Assateague Island samples agrees closely with band recovery estimates: 50% of Greenland birds estimated from band recoveries, 40% from allele frequency data.

The above results exemplify the utility of genetic markers in identifying the breeding populations of migrants. Several ongoing approaches promise to increase the precision with which individual Peregrines can be assigned to natal populations or even to specific parents in the case of parental testing. First, it is apparent that breeding birds from many more localities worldwide must be sampled. Reliably accurate allele frequency estimates require sampling at least 30 unrelated individuals per population. The immense effort required to sample very large numbers of individuals of a cosmopolitan threatened or endangered species should be easily appreciated; data usually trickle in a few individuals at a time. Ongoing banding programs in nesting areas are essential to expand the data base for genetic studies; tracking trapped migrants to breeding grounds could add immeasurably to the data base. A second, albeit time consuming, approach is optimization of electrophoretic conditions for proteins which exhibit variability inadequately resolved for confident genetic interpretation. The behavior of falconid enzymes on gel is surprisingly quirky; even electrophoretic conditions which beautifully resolve accipitrid genetic variation often produce much less than optimal resolution in Peregrine samples. The paucity of published avian electrophoretic studies compounds this problem and necessitates exhaustive trials of different gel and buffer compositions. The third approach is simply to increase the number of different gene products analyzed. The number of specific visualization procedures available has expanded dramatically during the last decade but very few laboratories sample more than the products of 30-50 genes. Though the restriction of sampling only blood proteins and enzymes hinders expansion of the Peregrine gene product data base, resolution of over 100 different proteins should be feasible in the near future. Identification of particularly fast-evolving genes hopefully will provide a maximally informative set of genetic markers for application in solving a variety of evolutionary and management problems.

ACKNOWLEDGEMENTS

This research was supported by the U. S. Army, Department of Defense, through National Institute of Health contract NO1-RS-4-2104 and U. S. Fish and Wildlife Service contract 14-16-0002-81-227. I am indebted to far too many persons for their cooperation in obtaining samples to recognize them individually; to all of you, my heartfelt thanks. For spearheading the assembly of logistical and funding support, I especially am grateful to F. P. Ward, W. S. Seegar and K. E. Riddle, and to R. C. Whitney and S. W. Hoffman for administrative support. I extend my thanks to J. P. Hoolihan, Jr., L. Limmer and R. Schmidt for technical support.

75 | Identification and Development of Breeding Population-Specific DNA Polymorphisms within the Genome of the Peregrine Falcon

Jonathan L. Longmire

By the 1960s, Peregrine Falcon populations had declined dramatically on the North American and European continents (Hickey 1969, Ratcliffe 1969, Cade and Fyfe 1970, Fyfe et al. 1976a). These declines were thought to have resulted from widespread use of DDE and other chlorinated pesticides (Cade et al. 1971, Lincer 1975, Peakall and Kiff 1979), and clearly predicate the need to monitor the dynamics of various populations of Peregrine Falcons. This paper describes a new and powerful tool that can be used to supplement traditional methods of population study such as nest site surveys and banding efforts.

Because Peregrine Falcons migrate along certain routes in spring and fall, a means of determining natal origin of Peregrines trapped during migration would be useful in identifying and managing geographic demes. Several approaches aimed at this goal are being explored, including the search for population-specific isozyme polymorphisms by Morizot (Chapter 74) and for differences in feather trace elements displayed by Peregrines originating from distinct geographical areas. Parrish et al. (1983) demonstrated that neutron-activation analysis of feather-trace elements allowed accurate discrimination of Peregrine Falcons originating from three geographical regions: the Colville and Yukon rivers in Alaska, and west Greenland.

My coworkers and I are searching for breeding population-specific DNA restriction fragment length polymorphisms (RFLPs) within the genomic DNA of the Peregrine Falcon. We may also identify DNA polymorphisms which will serve as markers for species and individuals. Species-specific markers would allow study of naturally occurring interspecific hybridizations, such as the Peregrine/Prairie Falcon cross reported in Saskatchewan in the spring of 1985 (Rafuse 1985). Individual "fingerprints" would be useful to federal and state law enforcement agencies which regulate captive propagation of falcons, and may allow study of genetic family lineages of wild Peregrines.

This paper provides a generalized background of concepts and techniques involved in this investigation and presents a preliminary analysis of a highly polymorphic set of loci which have been identified within the Peregrine genome.

METHODS

Figure 1 outlines the analysis of Peregrine DNA for RFLPs. Such analysis involves the isolation and digestion of high molecular weight DNA (>50 kilobase pairs) with restriction endonucleases, agarose gel electrophoresis, Southern blotting, and filter hybridization using radio-labeled DNA sequence probes. High molecular weight genomic DNA was isolated from small quantities of peripheral blood using standard nucleic acid purification techniques (Crawford et al. 1985). Because the red blood cells of birds are nucleated, large masses of DNA were obtained from small volumes of blood, and 0.5 cc of Peregrine blood commonly yielded about 500 μg of DNA. The loss of this volume of blood is not deleterious to the birds, and the mass of DNA obtained is sufficient for approximately 500 independent restriction analyses.

Purified high molecular weight Peregrine DNA was digested to completion (all recognition sites cleaved) by commercial restriction endonucleases using reaction conditions recommended by the supplier (New England Biolabs, Beverly, MA). Resulting DNA restriction fragments were size-resolved by agarose gel electrophoresis (Maniatis et al. 1982).

Following electrophoresis, the DNA restriction fragments were alkaline denatured and transferred to a nucleic acid binding membrane, using a blotting technique developed by Southern (1975). When bound to the membrane, the denatured, single-stranded DNA was probed with cloned DNA sequences made highly radioactive (>1 x 10^8 cpm/μg) by techniques that substitute [α^{32}P] deoxytriphosphates for bases within the DNA being labeled. During hybridization the probe will anneal to membrane-bound restriction fragments that contain complementary base sequences. Following this treatment, membranes were washed free of all radiolabeled material except for those molecules which annealed specifically to homologous sequences bound to the filter. The washed membrane was then used to expose X-ray film to produce an autoradiograph. The series of bands seen upon development of the film represent the "restriction pattern" that a given DNA sample consistently produced when digested with a

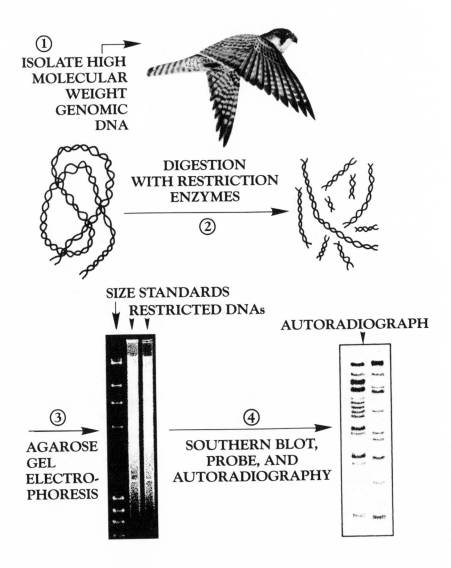

① ISOLATE HIGH
MOLECULAR
WEIGHT
GENOMIC
DNA

DIGESTION
WITH RESTRICTION
ENZYMES
②

SIZE STANDARDS
RESTRICTED DNAs

AUTORADIOGRAPH

③
AGAROSE
GEL
ELECTRO-
PHORESIS

④
SOUTHERN BLOT,
PROBE, AND
AUTORADIOGRAPHY

FIGURE 1.   Method of analysis for detecting DNA polymorphisms within the genome
of the Peregrine Falcon (see text).

particular restriction enzyme followed by hybridization to a specific
DNA sequence probe. In the development of breeding population-
specific "fingerprints," it was these restriction patterns that were
analyzed for intraspecific polymorphic loci.

RESULTS AND DISCUSSION

Restriction Patterns. — At the least sensitive level of analysis, restriction patterns can serve as species-specific markers. As shown in Figure 2, when DNAs isolated from a variety of raptors are analyzed with the same restriction enzyme and probe combination, the resulting pattern for each species is unique, even though slight variations (polymorphisms) may appear among conspecific individuals.

Because restriction patterns are, in general, species-specific, this methodology can be used to determine the genetic derivation of hybrids, if hybrids have restriction patterns that are either complete or partial composites of both parental patterns. The completeness of a hybrid's composite restriction pattern will depend on which parental chromosomes are retained in the hybrid progeny. Although I am unaware of studies on the chromosomal content of hybrid falcons, even a partial hybrid karyotype should reveal restriction patterns which would confirm the hybrid's genetic origin.

Restriction Fragment Length Polymorphisms. — When individuals or groups of individuals display hybridizing fragments of different sizes upon analysis with the same restriction enzyme and probe combination, these differences, if inherited in Mendelian fashion, are known as restriction fragment length polymorphisms. Thus, RFLPs are inherited intraspecific restriction-pattern variants.

At present two distinct types of RFLPs have been described. "Simple RFLPs" are generally dimorphic variants usually occurring at a single set of genetic loci. These polymorphisms are predominantly identified with single-copy gene probes and result from base substitutions, insertions, and deletions (Botstein et al. 1980). In the last decade, simple RFLPs have provided a valuable tool for human gene mapping (Botstein et al. 1980, Drayna et al. 1984), antenatal diagnosis (Weatherall 1982), and studies of inherited genetic disorders (Botstein et al. 1980, Murray et al. 1982, Gusella et al. 1983). Restriction patterns displayed by mitochondrial DNAs of the cricetid rodent *Peromyscus* have also been used to distinguish natural breeding populations (Advise et al. 1979).

My coworkers and I recently began screening Peregrine DNA for simple RFLPs to find a large number of genetic polymorphisms to establish a set of population-specific markers. We believe that future analyses will reveal enough variant loci for this purpose.

Recently, a new and very exciting class of restriction fragment length polymorphism, the "hypervariable RFLP," has been described in humans (Wyman and White 1980, Higgs et al. 1981, Bell et al. 1982, Proudfoot et al. 1982, Capone et al. 1983, Goodbourne et al. 1983). Hypervariable RFLPs are multimorphic variants of dispersed tandemly

Pst QR-12

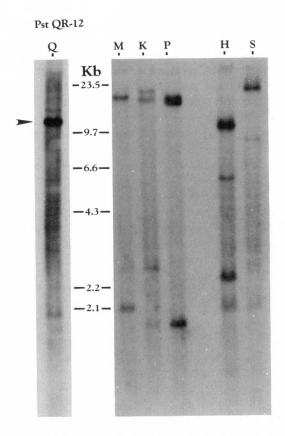

FIGURE 2. Southern filter hybridization of PstI digested DNAs to a 12 kilobase pair quail sequence probe. Ten μg each DNA was digested to completion with PstI, and then electrophoresed within a 0.8% agarose gel. Following electrophoresis the gel was Southern blotted onto a Zeta Bind membrane (AMF Corporation) and subsequently hybridized to 10×10^6 cpm of the gel purified 12 Kb quail probe (indicated by arrow) for 30 hours at 42°C in 5X SSC (1X=0.15 M NaCl; 0.015 M Na citrate); 1X Denhardt's solution; 0.02 M NaPO$_4$ pH 6.7; 100 μg/ml sonicated and denatured salmon sperm DNA; 10% Dextran sulfate; and 40% formamide. Following hybridization the filter was washed twice in 2X SSC, 0.1% SDS 22°C; one in 0.1X SSC, 0.1% SDS 22°C; and twice in 0.1X SSC, 0.1% SDS 50°C, and then autoradiographed –70°C using Kodak XAR-5 film. Lanes include: Q, quail (*Coturnix*); M, Merlin; K, American Kestrel; P, Peregrine Falcon; H, Harris' Hawk; and S, Swainson's Hawk. Size markers, as indicated in kilobase (Kb) pairs, derived from Hind III restricted bacteriophage λ DNA.

repeated "satellite" DNA sequences. They are thought to be the result of large-scale genetic alterations, such as unequal crossing-over and DNA slippage during replication (Jeffreys et al. 1985). Perhaps the most pronounced feature of hypervariable RFLPs is the high degree of sensitivity they afford in revealing genetic differences between even very closely related individuals. Unlike single copy gene probes, which allow the analysis of DNA segments within and around a single set of loci on a single pair of chromosomes, hypervariable probes allow examination of multiple copies at a variety of independently segregating loci. The sensitivity of these sequences is due to their dispersed nature coupled with a propensity for recombination. Hypervariable regions in human DNA have proved useful in maternity and paternity testing, in certain aspects of forensics, and in segregation analysis of both normal and disease-associated genetic markers (Jeffreys et al. 1985).

Probe for Hypervariable Peregrine Loci. — Considering the level of sensitivity, a probe for hypervariable regions in Peregrine DNA would be of substantial value in the development of individual finger-prints and, possibly, population markers. We have cloned a 175-base pair repetitive element from the Merlin and have found that this sequence, when used as a probe, reveals hypervariable loci in the Peregrine.

Although the complete molecular characterization of this cloned Merlin repeat is in progress (Longmire et al. unpubl. ms.), we have found that the 175-base pair monomeric unit is highly reiterated in a tandem fashion, genomically dispersed, and apparently specific to falcons. Filter hybridization experiments have shown this sequence to be present within all falconids examined including American Kestrels, Peregrines, Gyrfalcons and Merlins, but absent in all accipitrids tested including Harris' Hawks, Swainson's Hawks, Ferruginous Hawks and Golden Eagles. The apparent distribution of this repeat throughout the Falconidae indicates that this probe would be useful in similar studies on other species of falcons. Data from preliminary in situ hybridization show that clusters of the cloned repeat are located at the centromeres of at least one-half of the 40 Merlin chromosomes. The estimated high copy number of this sequence within Merlin DNA is based on the speed of signal development following filter hybridization.

Presently we are using the cloned Merlin repeat to screen DNA samples isolated from migrants, and from captively propagated families of Peregrines. A typical family unit analysis is shown in Figure 3. The Merlin probe revealed a high degree of polymorphism within this family of Peregrines. By this single analysis, at least six RFLPs (bands A-F) can be used to distinguish genetically not only the adult female (F. p. tundrius, Alaska) from her mate (F. p. peregrinus, Scotland), but also most of the offspring. In addition to these six RFLPs where fragments present in one adult were simply lacking in the other, there were also copy number variations detectable between these two individuals at other positions. For example, although both adult Peregrines had fragments Z and Z′, the signal intensity at both of these positions was greater in the male than in the female. Since 2 μg of DNA from each individual were analyzed, these differences may be the result of different fragment copy numbers. Thus the cloned Merlin probe detected both qualitative and quantitative polymorphisms in Peregrine DNA.

Another important result of the family analysis shown in Figure 3 is the demonstration that all polymorphic fragments within the adults were inherited in a Mendelian fashion by their offspring. This result confirms the utility of this probe for the identification of heritable markers in Peregrine Falcons.

Hypervariable Testing for Genetic Relatedness. — Owing to the large number of heritable polymorphisms which the cloned Merlin repeat revealed in Peregrine DNA, it is possible to develop the use of this probe to determine relatedness among individuals. When DNAs from parents were compared with unknown combinations of offspring and unrelated young samples, the samples from unrelated birds were always identified (Figure 4). This determination was based upon the assumption that, barring a recombinatory event which gave rise to novel bands, all fragments within the restriction patterns of real offspring should be traceable back to at least one parent. In contrast, unrelated birds should display fragments which could not have been inherited from either parent. The presence of bands A and B within the restriction patterns of the three samples marked X identify these individuals as unrelated to this adult pair. The sensitivity of this assay can be further enhanced with additional restriction enzymes and could become a very powerful "paternity test" for falcons.

CONCLUSIONS AND FUTURE DIRECTIONS

Using molecular biological techniques, my coworkers and I have begun screening the genome of the Peregrine Falcon for restriction fragment length polymorphisms. Initial results indicate this to be a viable approach to the development of population-specific markers. These results include the molecular cloning of a repetitive sequence that, when used as a probe, enabled detection of genetic variation among siblings of a captively propagated family of Peregrines. This result demonstrates that the level of sensitivity afforded by restriction analysis should be sufficient for the identification of genotypic differences among inbreeding populations of this species.

Analysis with the Merlin probe can be adapted to provide a very

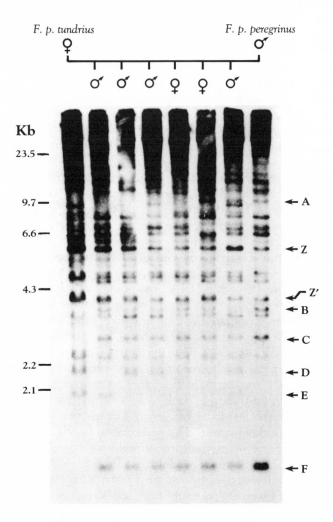

CPF-1
Hind III
MR-1

FIGURE 3. Hypervariable family analysis using a cloned Merlin tandem repeat probe. Two μg each DNA were digested with Hind III, followed by eletrophoresis within a 0.8% agarose gel. The resulting Southern blot was hybridized to 10×10^6 cpm of a primer extended probe derived from a recombinant M-13 clone containing the 175-nucleotide Merlin repetitive DNA insert. Hybridization and washing conditions were the same as described in Figure 2. Lanes include male and female offspring (as indicated) flanked by the mated adult pair (adult male F. p. peregrinus, Scotland; adult female F. p. tundrius, Alaska). Size markers (in Kb) derived from Hind III restricted bacteriophage λ DNA. Eight RFLPs identified (bands A-F and Z, Z').

Hind III, MR-1

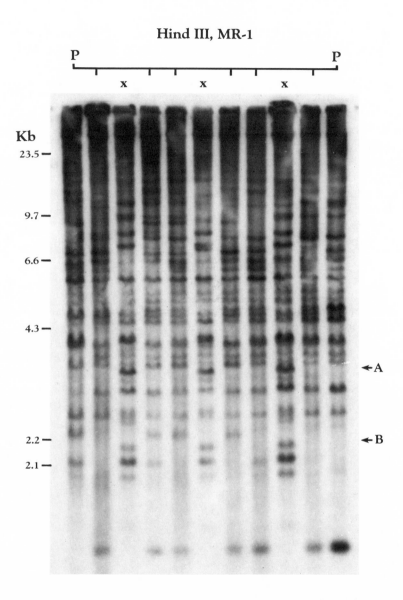

FIGURE 4. Hypervariable analysis to determine relatedness. Two μg each DNA were digested to completion with the restriction endonuclease Hind III, followed by eletrophoresis within a 0.8% agarose gel. The resulting Southern blot was hybridized to a radiolabeled Merlin repeat probe as described in Figure 3. Post-hybridization washes were carried out as described in Figure 2. Outside lanes include DNAs from an actual mated pair of Peregrines (designated P). Inside lanes include DNA samples isolated from offspring and unrelated young (designated x). Size markers (in Kb) derived from Hind III restricted bacteriophage λ DNA. Bands A and B show RLFPs not found in either adult.

powerful "paternity test" for falcons. Such a test has applications in the area of wildlife law enforcement and in genetic investigations of inheritance patterns through multigeneration family lineages.

Another result was the discovery of several restriction patterns which are diagnostic for Peregrines and for other falcons. These species-specific "fingerprints" can reveal natural interspecific hybrids.

We hope to identify a large number of heritable variant loci to serve as breeding population-specific markers for the Peregrine. This will be accomplished through continued restriction analyses, using both single copy and repetitive sequence probes, and through correlation of variant forms with specific inbreeding groups. Once established, these markers will greatly enhance our ability to investigate several aspects of Peregrine biology, including population dynamics, migratory patterns, and the possible existence of population-specific wintering sites.

ACKNOWLEDGEMENTS

The author is grateful to: N. Brown for excellent and dedicated technical assistance, to M. Fink for manuscript preparation, to F. P. Ward (Aberdeen Proving Grounds) for encouraging this work, to D. Morizot and T. Cade for generously supplying migratory and family Peregrine blood samples, respectively, and to R. K. Moyzis and C. E. Hildebrand for many helpful discussions. This work was supported by the Life Sciences Division of the Los Alamos National Laboratory.

76 | An Overview of Peregrine Falcon Subspecies

Clayton M. White and Douglas A. Boyce, Jr.

This paper presents a particular point of view rather than an exhaustive examination of systematic questions pertaining to the Peregrine Falcon. Our view is that the geographic variation seen in Peregrines has biological meaning, is useful in evaluating evolutionary processes, and can be summarized by the use of trinomials. First, the concept of subspeciation (throughout, the term geographic race or simply race equals subspecies) and what it means or does not mean requires comment. Second, we review the nature of morphological variation currently shown by Peregrines and relate it to geography and to presumed selection forces acting to produce such variation. Finally, we will summarize the available information and try to make it useful, given our current knowledge and scientific methodology.

BACKGROUND

Historically, the concept of race has undergone many changes. In fact, in the early and mid-1800s each of several races recognized today was thought to be a distinct species. For example, the Peregrine of Europe, called *F. communis*, was thought to be a different species than the Indian subcontinent representative, called *F. atriceps*, or the Australian representative, called *F. macropus*.

Next, in the late 1890s and early 1900s, look-alikes from various continents were lumped together as conspecific, but then local variations were split out and formally named as races. During that time, Peregrines in Europe alone were divided into 4-5 races. Examples of names were *F. p. germanicus*, *F. p. scandinaviae*, and *F. p. britannicus*. The names reflected local variations on a regional basis, what might be called expanded demes (local inbreeding units), or perhaps the names merely mirrored nationalistic ardor.

Finally, by the mid-1900s, the naming of subspecies was on the decline, as it tended to conceptually isolate those units as distinct genetic populations and obscured the real nature of the variation and the evolutionary reasons for it (cf. James 1970, Power 1970, Selander 1971). In recent times, variation has been analyzed in terms of multivariate trends or clines in character change within and between populations rather than by description of distinct racial types (Wilson and Brown 1953). Racial names for the Peregrine are still widely used, however, because the species has a worldwide distribution and some insular subspecies are well-differentiated.

Diverse views exist today about the subspecies concept, as indicated by a recent series of commentaries in the *Auk* (American Ornithologists' Union 1982). Eleven authors participated in the forum, and opinion ranged from the idea that subspecies were useful mainly as a sorting and cataloging device in museum collections (Mayr 1982) to the idea that subspecies remain basic systematic (evolutionary?) units in ornithology (Phillips 1982). Some argued (Mayr 1982) that subspecies are not an evolutionary concept, while others maintained that subspecies provide a useful tool in discussing evolutionary models of speciation (Monroe 1982, O'Neill 1982) and in focusing attention on the process of natural selection.

The subspecies concept is based on the idea that certain recognizable traits are present in 75% of a given population ("the 75% rule"), such that they can be distinguished from 75% of the individuals of another population (Amadon 1949, Mayr 1969). Seldom can one separate 100% of one population (race) from 100% of another population of the same species using genetic information or morphology unless the two populations have been geographically isolated for some time. Subspecies are usually separated by a steep character gradient or cline over a small geographic space (Endler 1977) and may be correlated with some environmental factor(s), past or present. In continental Peregrine races, the gradients are gradual because ranges abut and intergradation occurs.

Peregrines show considerable geographic variation in external morphology, and some populations are well-differentiated. This variation results from where the falcons live geographically, what they hunt, their migratory habits, and their degree of isolation from other breeding populations. Because Peregrines are strongly philopatric, local variations which are apparently genetically controlled become fixed in a population and may render it quite different from another (Corbin 1983). Subspecies designations may impart information about the evolutionary biology of members of a recognized group because they are more similar to each other than they are to members of another phenotypic group, i.e., there is more commonality in the history shared by each of the group's members.

A convenient test for accepting the validity of races is to demonstrate that there is a concordance among various traits and that morphological boundaries generally follow boundaries of other differences and are correlated with geography (see Barrowclough 1980, Corbin 1981). Evolution, however, is opportunistic; it seldom works neatly in clear categorical fashion. For example, some of the selection pressures molding behavior, or simple random changes in behavior that become fixed in a population, may be totally independent of size, color, or other genetic variation. In fact, lack of total concordance seems to be the rule rather than the exception.

MATERIALS AND METHODS

Statistical Analyses. — We investigated two major questions. First, among the North American races, can 75% of the individuals of one race be statistically separated from the other races? To examine this question we used discriminate function analysis (SPSSX software). Second, what is the phylogenetic relationship among all Peregrine races? To examine this question we used PAUP (Phylogenetic Analysis Using Parsimony, version 2.3, Swofford 1985).

Variables used in discriminate function analysis were standard museum measurements of wing chord, tail length, tarsus length, middle toe length less claw, and bill culmen length from cere. Facial measurements were width of dark color between eye and upper end of paler auricular, width of auricular at a midpoint, and length of malar from distal tip to upper end of auricular. Sex and age categories were analyzed separately. Specimens were analyzed by taxonomic race and by locality, but only results of the former are given because of larger sample sizes.

In our phylogenetic analysis we wanted to establish hypotheses of juxtaposition(s) of races. Males were analyzed separately from females. Twenty-one characters were used; they included standard museum measurements of mean wing length and range, tail length and range, tarsus and toe lengths; ratios of toe:tail, tail:wing, tarsus:wing, and toe:wing; color or marking of auricular, malar (including size), and forehead band; breast barring size and density; dorsal color and ventral color; and finally, a geographic component. Each character was given equal weighting. The continuous characters were gap-coded (Archie 1985) to locate subgroups of a similar range of numerical values within the group. Parsimonious trees that minimized the number of character transformations within the data set were produced.

We view kestrels as ancestral to large falcons. We therefore used the Eurasian Kestrel as the taxonomic outgroup in order to generate hypotheses of character polarity. The Eurasian Kestrel and the Peregrine shared only eight derived traits or characters. The resulting cladogram identified *F. p. brookei* as most closely related to the outgroup, suggesting that it is the oldest among Peregrine races. We then used *F. p. brookei* as the functional outgroup to root other races. In this procedure we were able to use 12 additional derived traits common to all Peregrine races. Tables of cladogram synapomorphies are not presented owing to space constraints, but are available from the senior author.

EXTERNAL MORPHOLOGY AND PHENOTYPE

To date, most studies on geographic variation of Peregrines have been neither broad enough nor sophisticated enough to examine many traits that vary geographically. While most have been restricted to external morphology, we realize that there is also geographic variation in clutch and egg size. Little else has been determined about geographic variation with respect to physiology, biochemistry or genetics, although there was an attempt with respect to temperature regulation (Mosher and White 1978). We therefore restrict our remarks to morphological variation in subspecies that have been described in greater detail elsewhere (Vaurie 1961, Porter et al. 1987), especially for North America (White 1968a, 1968b). Other reports describing geographical variation in some detail are Fischer (1972, 1973) and D. Schmidl (1985 Peregrine Conference, Sacramento, CA).

The Subspecies. — There are two distinct races with rufous head or neck markings, *F. p. pelegrinoides* and *F. p. babylonicus*, which are sometimes classified as a separate species, the Barbary Falcon (*F. pelegrinoides*). Whether or not they form a separate species (Brosset 1986), they are certainly more closely related to Peregrines than to any other falcons (Mayr and Short 1970). We provisionally include them here as Peregrines, but the true status of these short-tailed desert forms may only be settled by field work and biochemical studies. The 15 individuals that we have had in captivity were like Peregrines in vocalization, behavior, and superficial looks, but Dementiev and Iljitschew (1961) considered the skeletons of *F. p. babylonicus* to differ significantly from those of Peregrines. Some would argue that the first three traits are of little value in evaluating species. Using those same traits, however, one would be tempted to say that the stocky, heavy-breasted, short-tailed Australian Peregrine is as different from the long-tailed, cantankerous Aleutian Peregrine as is *F. p. peregrinus* from *F. p. pelegrinoides*. A quick comparison of tail:wing, tarsus:tail, tarsus:wing and toe:tarsus ratios in *F. p. peregrinus*, *F. p. pealei*, *F. p. macropus*, *F. p. anatum* ("western" type) and *F. p. pelegrinoides* showed that, depending on the sex examined, the magnitude of difference could be of the same order between any pair of forms depending upon which ones were compared.

Of the more than 66 names that have been applied to various populations of Peregrines, we here refer to only 19 as being valid morphological races (Table 1); these are also listed by Stresemann and Amadon (1979). Figure 1* shows the type localities of these accepted subspecies. The map of subspecies' ranges in Hickey and Anderson (1969) was little more than a copy of the map of Dementiev and Gladkov (1951). Fischer's (1973) maps are considerably better. Cade's (1982) range maps were not intended to show the subspecies limits. Note in Figure 1 how uniformly the type localities of the races are spread over the globe.

Overall Variation. — Morphological variation takes several forms and is expressed differently. First, there is individual variation within populations. Variation in color extremes is clearly shown in immature *F. p. pealei* ("Queen Charlotte" type): pale individuals may be as pale as the lightest of the *F. p. tundrius* race and dark individuals are among the darkest of all Peregrines. Color morphs are a special kind of individual variation. *F. p. cassini* from South America has a very dark and very pale morph in immature plumage and this difference persists into adulthood. The "pallid" morph of *F. p. cassini* is now well-known (see McNutt et al. Chapter 26). Occurrence of color morphs or variants is usually but not necessarily geographically distributed, e.g., pale individuals of *F. p. pealei* have not shown up in the Aleutians, and the pale morph of *F. p. cassini* has not shown up in the central or northern part of its range or in the Falkland Islands. A second kind of variation that adds confusion is local or regional variation. This is usually represented as "family" or demic variation. It is one of the forms of variation that Longmire (Chapter 75) may be able to analyze with DNA polymorphism techniques. Four small regions in western Europe were once thought to contain four different subspecies, but their differences are best understood as demic variation caused by rather small, largely self-contained breeding populations. The final kind of morphological variation is geographic, and it is this kind that is best reflected by the presently recognized races.

Size. — The pattern in size (Figure 2) generally is: large Peregrines are in the north Pacific rim, smaller ones are in the western United States and Mexico, but they become larger eastward. Through Eurasia westward from the Pacific they become smaller. Peregrines also become smaller toward the equator and in the southern hemisphere, especially in the Old World (Table 1). These sizes generally follow Bergmann's ecogeographical rule (Zink and Remsen 1986). It has been suggested that the rule correlates with factors associated with body mass and temperature regulation. Several degrees of size difference are shown in Figure 3. Using wing length as the standard of measure, these size

* Editors' Note: Figure 1 is on the inside front cover of this volume.

TABLE 1. Comparison of adult Peregrines in relative size, generalized gestalt appearance (color and markings) and general breeding locations. The largest based on wing length, F. p. pealei, represents 100% body size and others are percents of it (see text).

Subspecies (largest to smallest)	Body size	Dominant color dorsal/ventral	Breast barring size[a]/density[b]/spots[c]	Breeding latitudes[d] (region)
F. p. pealei	100	black/black	W/M-S/Sp	NL-I (North America)
F. p. calidus	98	blue/white	M-C/M-S/Sp	NL (Eurasia)
F. p. japonensis	98	black/blue-buff	W-M/M/Sp	NL (East Asia)
F. p. anatum	97	blue/rust	M-N/N/Sp	NL (North America)
F. p. furuitii	97	black/black-buff	W/M/Sp	NL-I (Volcano-Bonin Island)
F. p. peregrinus	97	blue/white-buff	M/M/Sp	NL (Eurasia)
F. p. madens	96	blue-brown/buff	M/M	ML-I (Cape Verde Island)
F. p. tundrius	96	blue/white	M-C/M-S/Sp	NL (North America)
F. p. cassini	96	blue/buff (blue/white)	M-N,(C)/D-M,(S)	SL (South America)
F. p. brookei	92	blue/buff	M/M/Sp	ML (Mediterranean)
F. p. babylonicus	90	blue-brown/buff-white	N-C/M-S	ML (Mideast - South Asia)
F. p. nesiotes	89	black/black-rust	M-N/M-D/Sp	SL-I (Southwest Pacific islands)
F. p. ernesti	89	black/black-blue	M-N/M-D/Sp	ML/SL (Indonesia-Papuan)
F. p. macropus	88	blue/rust	M-N/D-M	SL (Australia)
F. p. submelanogenys	88	blue/rust	M-N/D-M	SL (Australia)
F. p. minor	88	blue/black-white	M/M/Sp	SL (Africa)
F. p. peregrinator	88	black/rust	M-C/M-S	ML (India - South Asia)
F. p. radama	86	blue/black-white	M/M/Sp	SL-I (Madagascar)
F. p. pelegrinoides	85	blue-brown/buff-white	N-C/M-S	ML (North Africa - Arabia)

[a] Dark breast cross-barring represents size of bar: W=wide; M=medium; N=narrow; C=clear (without conspicuous barring).
[b] Bar density: D=densely barred; M=moderately dense; S=sparse or widely spaced.
[c] Sp=presence of spots (or bars becoming circular) on breast, usually in crop or midline.
[d] NL=northern latitudes; ML=middle latitudes; SL=southern latitudes; I=insular forms. Compare with Figures 1 and 2.

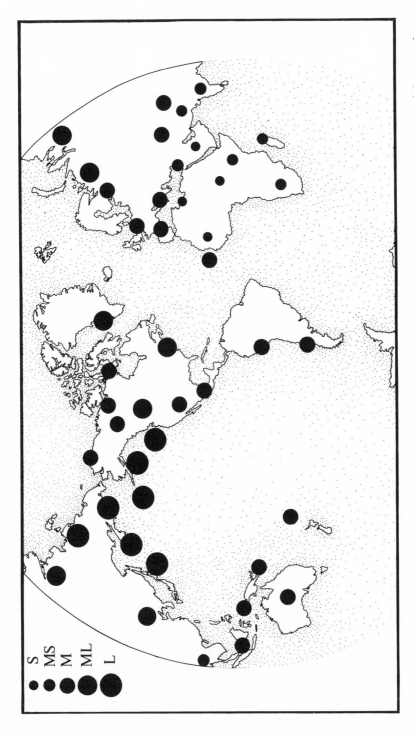

FIGURE 2. Trends in size differences in Peregrines. Sizes are based only on average wing length. Symbols given are relative and determined as a percent of the largest Peregrine, *F. p. pealei*.

SIZE VARIATION

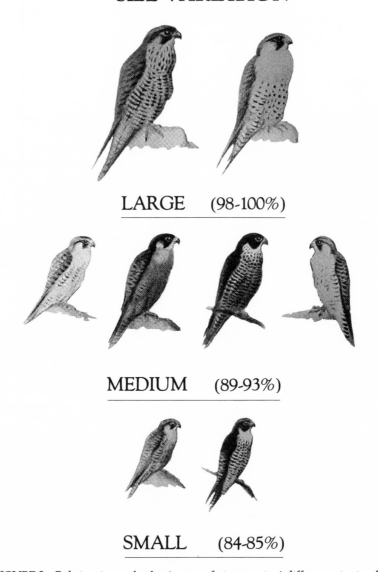

LARGE (98-100%)

MEDIUM (89-93%)

SMALL (84-85%)

FIGURE 3. Relative sizes and color (extent of pigmentation) differences in size classes of Peregrines. *F. p. pealei* is the largest (based on average wing length) and equals 100%. Other values are percentages of *F. p. pealei*. Races represented from left to right: top, *F. p. pealei*, *F. p. calidus*; middle, *F. p. babylonicus*, *F. p. peregrinator*, *F. p. ernesti*, *F. p. cassini* ("pallid morph"); bottom, *F. p. pelegrinoides* (Arabian population), *F. p. radama*. Figure from Kleinschmidt (1958).

differences are shown in Table 1, although they are somewhat misleading. For example, the wing length of male *F. p. brookei* averages 92% of male *F. p. pealei* while female *F. p. brookei* averages 89% of female *F. p. pealei*, and in *F. p. pelegrinoides* the males average 86% of male *F. p. pealei*, while females average 83% of female *F. p. pealei*. In contrast, male and female *F. p. macropus* differ nearly equally in size, respectively, from their *F. p. pealei* counterparts. Weight, tail length and wing shape (thus wing-loading) modify the entire situation shown in Table 1 and the races would undoubtedly line up differently. There are not enough data on weights and wing areas to make such an analysis.

Migrant races or populations tend to have longer, narrower, more attenuated wings than resident nonmigrants. This is particularly evident when comparing highly migratory tundra-breeding birds to resident *F. p. pealei* from the west coast of North America (cf. White 1982).

Color. — Color variation follows Gloger's rule (Zink and Remsen 1986): Peregrines are pale in dry climates, dark in humid climates (Table 1). Red hues predominate in hot, dry climates, while pale creams and blues predominate in cold climates. These colors correlate best with the breeding rather than wintering ranges (if they are different). Ventral barring is usually more dense in humid or tropical climates.

Problematic Areas. — While the subspecies mentioned in Table 1 have been described generally, there are few areas within their ranges where variation has been thoroughly and quantitatively documented. Even Vaurie (1961), who worked extensively with the Palearctic populations, did not do so. Except for insular forms, range boundaries are poorly delimited and intergradation between adjacent subspecies has not been studied in detail.

We have referred to races as though each represents a homogeneous taxon. This is generally not the case except with some island forms. More often there are recognizable subpopulations within the range of named subspecies. Some examples are: (1) Members of *F. p. cassini* from central and northern Chile are generally paler overall with defined pale auriculars compared to southern Argentine birds, many of which are very dark with a grizzled overwash to the breast and with essentially no pale auricular area. Extreme darkness is seen in the Falkland Island birds. Then, there is the *F. p. pelegrinoides*-like "pallid" morph of *F. p. cassini* in the extreme southern and coastal part of South America — an apparent exception to Gloger's rule. (2) Individuals of *F. p. peregrinus* from central Europe (Germany, for example) are uniformly barred right across the breast while those of England have different, more irregular barring, and many are spotted in the central breast. (3) Adults of *F. p. pealei* from the British Columbia-southeastern Alaska region have a crop area almost without spots in some, especially males where it is almost clear and white, as compared to heavily streaked and spotted Aleutian birds. (4) Individuals of *F. p. anatum* from western North America have a wing length that averages 10-15 mm less than those formerly in eastern North America. (5) Representatives of *F. p. peregrinator* from India and Ceylon typically have a clear unmarked rufous breast and unbarred back, while Asian Peregrines to the east of them are barred like *F. p. macropus* on the breast and barred on the back (D. Schmidl unpubl. ms.).

Peregrines from Fiji are incredibly uniform in color and markings suggesting no immigration of genes from other races. In this lack of variation they differ from other populations we have studied, including the highly uniform Aleutian population. Specimens that we have seen from the South Pacific area suggest that those from Fiji may differ significantly from those in Vanautu and New Caledonia (currently assigned to the same race), but this possibility requires more study. In this case, and some mentioned above, one must decide how important the differences are and what to do with nomenclature. If they are isolated breeding units, should a new race be named for one of the populations or should these differences be noted simply as interdemic variation within a highly variable race? Such decisions are sometimes arbitrary, but there are some guidelines involving the 75% rule as shown below.

Variation in North America: A Case Study. — Where they are well-known, trends in the color, markings (Figure 4), and size of North American Peregrines can provide a case study in the nature of variation within the species. As mentioned earlier, Amadon (1949) suggested that, on average, one race should be distinguished from another (usually an adjacent one) in at least 75% of the cases. Does this comparison hold? Clearly not enough traits have been analyzed (skeletal, internal anatomy, behavior, biochemical) to give a clear indication of the concordance of traits, but those that have been examined can be informative.

Discriminate function analysis of five mensural characters and three facial color patterns in museum specimens suggests that overall the three North American races can be separated or identified at about the 79% level (Table 2). Differences were significant in most cases at $P<0.05$ based on F and Chi-square tests. Using only morphological traits or only facial measurements reduced discriminating power (Table 3). In some cases, usually adults, adding primary length (primaries 10 to 5) increased discriminating power a few percent while in others, usually immature, discriminating power was lowered. Primaries were not used alone because of small sample sizes. Had we coded color or body markings into the analysis, the level of discrimination would probably have risen. Males of different races were easier to separate

FIGURE 4. Adult breeding male Peregrines from North America exclusive of Greenland. Peregrines from Greenland are somewhat intermediate between the right hand head top row and the center head bottom row. Breeding locations are left to right: Top row, *F. p. tundrius* (pale), Colville River, Alaska; *F. p. tundrius* (average), Colville River, Alaska; *F. p. anatum* (pale "interior taiga" subgroup), Yukon River, Alaska. Middle row, *F. p. pealei* ("Queen Charlotte" subgroup), British Columbia, Canada; *F. p. pealei* ("Aleutian" subgroup), Aleutian Islands, Alaska. Bottom row, *F. p. anatum* ("western" subgroup), Baja California, Mexico; *F. p. anatum* ("western" subgroup), Utah; *F. p. anatum* (*sensu stricto*—"eastern" subgroup), New York. Painting by William Dilger.

than females, and immature plumaged birds, except in *F. p. pealei*, were more easily separated than adults.

Note that *F. p. pealei* was the easiest to discriminate (Table 2) on measurements alone and that *F. p. anatum* and *F. p. tundrius* were confused in 20-35% of the cases, probably because the "western"

TABLE 2. Results of discriminant analysis of 5 body and 3 facial color mensural variables from museum specimens for 3 North American subspecies of Peregrines (see text for methods). Among adults, only those collected during the breeding season or while wintering in continental United States or northward were used. The "western" and "eastern" *F. p. anatum* groups, "Aleutian" and "Queen Charlotte" *F. p. pealei* groups, and the "Greenland" and remaining "tundra," *F. p. tundrius* groups were lumped by subspecies.

Sex	Age	Race	n	Mean % correctly identified birds	Predicted group membership (%)		
					F. p. tundrius	F. p. pealei	F. p. anatum
male	adult	F. p. tundrius	47		76.6	2.1	21.3
male	adult	F. p. pealei	24		0.0	95.8	4.2
male	adult	F. p. anatum	40		20.5	0.0	75.0
Total:			111	80.0			
female	adult	F. p. tundrius	65		84.6	4.6	10.8
female	adult	F. p. pealei	23		4.3	95.7	0.0
female	adult	F. p. anatum	74		24.3	14.9	60.8
Total:			188	75.3			
male	juvenile	F. p. tundrius	42		95.2	2.4	2.4
male	juvenile	F. p. pealei	38		0.0	89.5	10.5
male	juvenile	F. ·p. anatum	63		9.5	9.5	81.0
Total:			143	87.4			
female	juvenile	F. p. tundrius	45		80.0	6.7	13.3
female	juvenile	F. p. pealei	49		0.0	83.7	16.3
female	juvenile	F. p. anatum	68		20.0	10.3	69.1
Total:			162	76.5			
Overall total, all groups			604	79.8			

TABLE 3. Results of discriminant analysis of the same measurements of Peregrines as those in Table 2. The first value in each duplex is for the 5 body measurements, the second value is for the 3 facial measurements. Percents are rounded to the nearest value.

Sex	Age	Race	n	Mean % correctly identified birds	Predicted group membership (%)		
					F. p. tundrius	F. p. pealei	F. p. anatum
male	adult	F. p. tundrius	47/40		72/79	5/6	28/15
male	adult	F. p. pealei	24/32		3/29	97/58	0/13
male	adult	F. p. anatum	40/40		35/18	8/13	58/71
Total:				74/71			
female	adult	F. p. tundrius	65/43		67/63	5/26	28/11
female	adult	F. p. pealei	23/30		0/52	90/48	10/0
female	adult	F. p. anatum	74/49		31/19	8/18	61/64
Total:				71/61			
male	juvenile	F. p. tundrius	42/25		76/83	4/5	20/12
male	juvenile	F. p. pealei	38/41		0/8	90/34	10/56
male	juvenile	F. p. anatum	63/49		12/18	10/29	78/54
Total:				82/57			
female	juvenile	F. p. tundrius	45/28		75/64	4/22	21/13
female	juvenile	F. p. pealei	49/58		0/12	91/57	9/31
female	juvenile	F. p. anatum	68/47		23/25	11/25	66/50
Total:				79/56			

population of *F. p. anatum* has a mean wing and tail measurement smaller than the mean of *F. p. tundrius*, while the tarsus, toe, and bill are larger. The formerly extant "eastern" *F. p. anatum* was larger than either the "western" *F. p. anatum* or *F. p. tundrius*, and closer to *F. p. pealei* in some traits with more extensive malar measurements. The majority of the sample of *F. p. anatum* was "western," a fact that contributed to the high discriminating power between *F. p. anatum* and *F. p. pealei*.

Other Cases. — Other races of Peregrines have not been as thoroughly examined as those in North America, but some data are instructive when comparing certain geographic regions or size classes. The combined range of wing measurements of adult breeding males (259-334 mm) is about the same as for adult females (297-375 mm). Tails are more variable in length (males: 118-162 mm, females: 139-189 mm) than wings. Measurements by themselves may not indicate a racial affinity; however, there are 11 races in which male wing measurements are smaller than 290 mm. Most of these races are in the southern hemisphere or at least from "southern" continents. These males fall into three morphological groups based on the configuration of the malar relative to the normally paler auricular area (Table 4). Those with malars nearly confluent with the back and with essentially no distinct auricular can be easily identified by only 2-3 traits taken together (Table 4). Females are generally more difficult than males to allocate to a race. To illustrate the point (Table 5), we have excluded males by using large females (those with wings over 350 mm). The females are northern hemisphere forms, and many intergrades occur where the races' ranges are adjacent. Many of the traits characteristic of one race are often shared by numerous individuals of another and frequently adjacent race. There tend to be fewer differences between races in the northern hemisphere than between those in the southern hemisphere, probably because the latter are more geographically isolated.

A HYPOTHETICAL RELATIONSHIP

We believe that some races fall into more closely related groups than others. For example, *F. p. peregrinus*, *F. p. calidus*, *F. p. japonensis*, *F. p. furuitii* (commonly misspelled as *F. p. fruitii*), *F. p. pealei*, *F. p. tundrius*, and *F. p. anatum* form a northern group. In this group, *F. p. pealei* and *F. p. furuitii* or *F. p. japonensis* and *F. p. furuitii* are the most closely related. *F. p. brookei* may or may not belong within the northern group. *F. p. macropus*, *F. p. submelanogenys*, *F. p. ernesti*, and *F. p. nesiotes* form a tropical and southern group, with *F. p. ernesti* and *F. p. nesiotes* or *F. p. macropus* and *F. p. nesiotes* the most closely related. *F. p. peregrinator* may be distantly attached with the latter cluster or may

TABLE 4. Data on adult male Peregrines with wings under 290 mm. This table concentrates on those with heavy malars ("full helmets"), as they are distinctive. Most of the races here are from the southern hemisphere and the ranges tend to be widely separated.

Race	Thin malar, wide auricular	Malar and auricular about equal	Malar wide, "no" auricular	Dorsal color	Crop color	Breast bar width (mm)	Spacing of breast bars (mm)	Overall breast wash
F. p. cassini (some)	no	no	yes	blue	grizzled	5-8	5-10+	gray/grizzled
F. p. nesoites	no	no	yes	black	orangish	5-8	<5	orangish
F. p. ernesti	no	no	yes	black	buff	1-2	<5	blue/gray
F. p. macropus	no	no	yes	blue	white	3-5	5-8	buff
F. p. submelanogenys	no	no	yes	blue	buff	3-5	5-8	orangish
F. p. cassini (some)	no	yes						
F. p. minor	no	yes						
F. p. radama	no	yes						
F. p. brookei	no	yes						
F. p. peregrinator	no	yes						
F. p. cassini ("pallid" morph)	yes							
F. p. babylonicus	yes							
F. p. pelegrinoides	yes							

TABLE 5. Data on adult female Peregrines with wings over 350 mm. They all happen to be from the northern hemisphere. Note that the distinctions between them are not clear. They occupy breeding ranges that are continental and may merge with one another. Percentage figures indicate frequency within each race.

Race	Malar average narrower than auricular	Malar average wider than auricular	Overall color dark and saturate [a]	Overall color intermediate [b]	Overall color pale or light [c]	Heavy markings [d]	Intermediate markings [e]	Sparse markings [f]	Marked crop area	Clear crop area	Breast wash buff to orangish
F. p. pealei	no	yes	yes	10-15%	no	yes	10-15%	no	yes	10-15%	10-15%
F. p. furuitii	no	yes	yes	10-15%	no	yes	no	no	yes	no	no
F. p. japonensis	15-20%	75%	10-15%	75%	10-15%	75%	10-15%	no	yes	no	10-15%
F. p. peregrinus	15-20%	75%	no	75%	10-15%	15-20%	10-15%	10-15%	75%	10-15%	10-15%
F. p. anatum	15-20%	75%	no	75%	10-15%	15-20%	75%	10-15%	75%	10-15%	yes
F. p. calidus	yes	no	no	10-15%	yes	10-15%	10-15%	yes	10-15%	yes	no
F. p. tundrius	yes	10-15%	no	10-15%	yes	no	10-15%	yes	10-15%	yes	10-15%

[a] Back deep blue/slaty black; breast reddish or with grays, with dense or wide markings.

[b] Back blue/slaty; breast buff to orangish, barred on sides tending to spots in mid-breast.

[c] Back blue/pale bluish; breast whitish to buff, with wide spacing between narrow bars, center clear.

[d] Ventral cross bars wide (5-8 mm), may be dense (<5 mm apart), large spots frequent.

[e] Ventral cross bars moderately wide (3-5 mm), may be 5-8 mm apart, much barring in breast, center takes form of spots.

[f] Ventral cross bars narrow (<3 mm) and sparse (8-10 mm apart), spotting infrequent and scattered.

be an early offshoot from the northern group. *F. p. minor* and *F. p. radama* seem closely related, with *F. p. minor* perhaps being derived from the northern group or perhaps from *F. p. brookei*. *F. p. pelegrinoides* and *F. p. babylonicus* are probably allied and constitute at least a sister species to *F. peregrinus* (sensu stricto); they are perhaps closest to *F. p. brookei*. *F. p. cassini* is probably an offshoot of a Nearctic form. It is most like *F. p. anatum* overall, but has taken on some color traits common to southern hemisphere races. *F. p. madens* is difficult to place, but if it is not related to *F. p. pelegrinoides*, then it is probably related to *F. p. brookei*.

The use of available morphological measurements (Table 6) to construct cladograms gave results with a low consistency index (0.46-0.54). Thus, we were unable to construct relationships lacking extensive homoplasy (similarity owing to convergence or parallelism). This problem can be resolved with biochemical characters because they have a much higher consistency index.

Some important traits may have been overlooked or are not available from the literature, while others (for example, geographic) perhaps should not be included. Eight cladograms were generated for males and nine for females. A cladogram based on similarity for adult males shows a hypothetical presumed relationship (Figure 5). Overall, the relationships are similar to our subjective expectations. There are two separate subclades evident (Figure 5). They originate from nodes 30 and 34 (one may choose to use nodes 31 and 35 to define the subclades). One subclade identifies a northern group of Peregrines as already indicated, except for *F. p. madens*, which is included based on a toe measurement. The true relationships of *F. p. madens* may indeed lie with this group, but it is probably not as close to *F. p. peregrinus* as the size-based conclusion would indicate. *F. p. minor* was placed as shown (Figure 5) based on a forehead band trait and tarsus measurement.

The second subclade is basically a southern group, but at least two races merit comment. *F. p. cassini* should seemingly have rooted closer to the northern group, but emerged as it did based on four traits. Among these traits were auricular and ventral barring characteristic of southern hemisphere races, but probably independently derived. *F. p. radama* was removed from *F. p. minor* on the basis of mensural traits (no color traits were included at node 26), whereas at node 32 the density of breast barring was an important trait. *F. p. peregrinator* clustered where it did based once again on five traits, all measurements. We are comfortable that those races arising from nodes 23 and 30 represent a true relationship as do those from node 33 except for *F. p. radama*.

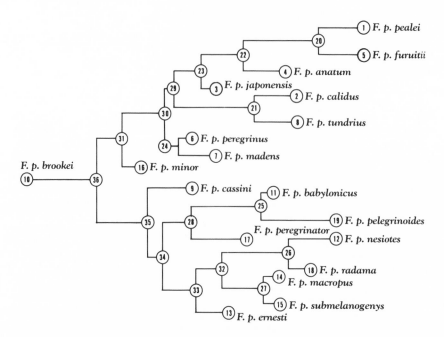

FIGURE 5. A cladogram showing the hypothetical phylogentic relationship of subspecies using adult males that are rooted to a functional taxonomic outgroup (*F. p. brookei*). The phylogeny was generated using 21 taxonomic characters, with the PAUP program (see text for variables). Numbers are called nodes. Those nodes not followed by a name represent hypothetical ancestors having shared traits leading to the taxa derived from that node and that contain certain suits of character.

CONCLUSIONS

The subspecies concept has existed for over 200 years. Its application has waxed and waned as different analytical techniques have come into vogue. It has often been said to be of little value, and has been abused by those trying to assign each individual they have in the hand to a given geographic race.

On the other hand, the concept has been beneficial in numerous ways. For example, wildlife managers or conservationists have used it in dealing with endangered species (see Cade 1983), although they could accomplish the same thing by considering the status of regional populations rather than formally named races.

The subspecies concept has also been useful in indicating evolutionary trends and limits of gene flow between or within populations. For example, specimens of *F. p. macropus* we have seen from the Cape York Peninsula, Australia, differ markedly (as does *F. p. macropus* in general) from *F. p. ernesti* of New Guinea just 160 km across the Torres Straits. Although an adequate sampling of specimens from the most adjacent regions of both land masses is lacking, the suggestion is that essentially no gene flow occurs across the Torres Straits.

For a geographic race to develop in the first place, gene flow into a given area must be slower and of less importance than the selection pressures forcing certain morphological traits (local alleles) to become fixed. The problem of genetic fixation of traits and its meaning to evolutionary biology is by no means totally settled, as suggested by studies of James (1983) on passerines. Nonetheless, evolutionary biologists can order information meaningfully from the subspecies concept.

We are encouraged about the biological utility of subspecies designations when we compare the Peregrine to other geographically variable birds such as the Common Barn-Owl, a species nearly as widespread as the Peregrine. Concordance between the geographical limits of traditional subspecies in the Common Barn-Owl and Peregrine suggests commonality of selection pressures on a geographic basis, producing change. For example, the Common Barn-Owl in sub-Saharan Africa is all one race (as is the Peregrine), but the Common Barn-Owl of Madagascar and the Comoro Islands is different (as is the Peregrine race, *F. p. radama*). The race of Common Barn-Owl in Australia extends into Tasmania (as does the Peregrine), but a different race occurs in New Guinea and Indonesia (as with the Peregrine). The Common Barn-Owls on New Caledonia, the Loyalty Islands, and Fiji form a separate race (as in the Peregrine) except that Common Barn-Owls on Vanuatu are a different race, whereas the same Peregrine occurs there as in the aforementioned locations. The Common Barn-Owl race of India, Pakistan, and Ceylon extends eastward in southern Asia, and another race has been named from Burma eastward. Taken together, the two races correspond with the kind of variation and limits shown by *F. p. peregrinator* (D. Schmidl unpubl. ms.), although separate races are not named in the Peregrine. Further comparisons can be made, but these details illustrate the point.

Currently we see a strong relationship between morphology and geography. Because little genetic work has been done, the relationships between genetics, morphology, behavior, and geography remain to be established. Even though we have no genetic information on Peregrines, except that forthcoming from Morizot (Chapter 74) and Longmire (Chapter 75), we do not expect to see many gene duplication events (i.e., major, gross differences), but we do expect to see change in allele frequencies (i.e., subtle differences) along clines. We also expect island forms, which tend to be most morphologically distinct and are sometimes few in numbers, to have fixed allelic differences because of their isolation and the general nature of Peregrine fidelity to nesting locations.

TABLE 6. Character-state data for male Peregrine races.

Race	Fore-head band[a]	Auri-cular area[b]	Breast bar width[c]	Breast bar density[d]	Mid-breast spots[e]	Dorsal color aspect[f]	Ventral color aspect[g]	Hemi-sphere[h]	Mean wing length[i]	Min. wing length[j]
F. p. pealei	1	2	3	3	1	3	4	1	1	1
F. p. calidus	1	1	1	1	1	2	1	1	1	1
F. p. japonensis	1	2	2	2	1	2	2	1	1	2
F. p. anatum	1	2	2	2	1	2	2	1	1	2
F. p. furuitii	2	3	3	3	1	3	4	1	1	1
F. p. peregrinus	1	2	2	2	1	2	2	1	1	2
F. p. madens	1	2	2	2	1	1	2	1	1	1
F. p. tundrius	1	1	1	1	1	2	1	1	1	2
F. p. cassini	2	3	2	3	1	2	2	2	2	3
F. p. brookei	2	2	2	2	1	2	2	1	2	3
F. p. babylonicus	2	1	1	1	1	1	2	1	3	3
F. p. nesiotes[k]	2	4	3	2	2	3	3	2	3	3
F. p. ernesti	2	4	2	3	2	3	4	2	3	3
F. p. macropus	2	4	2	2	2	2	2	2	3	3
F. p. submelanogenys	2	4	2	2	2	2	2	2	3	3
F. p. minor	1	2	2	2	1	2	2	2	3	3
F. p. peregrinator	2	3	1	1	1	3	3	1	3	3
F. p. radama	2	2	2	2	2	3	2	2	3	3
F. p. pelegrinoides	1	1	1	1	1	1	2	1	3	3

[a] 1 = present; 2 = absent.
[b] 1 = large; 2 = moderate; 3 = small; 4 = none.
[c] 1 = thin; 2 = moderate; 3 = wide.
[d] 1 = sparse; 2 = moderate; 3 = dense.
[e] 1 = present; 2 = absent.
[f] 1 = brownish; 2 = bluish; 3 = blackish.
[g] 1 = whitish; 2 = buffish; 3 = reddish; 4 = blackish.
[h] Breeding hemisphere (deleted character from tree length calculation): 1 = northern; 2 = southern.
[i] 1 = 308-318 mm; 2 = 295-300 mm; 3 = 285-290 mm; 4 = 277-280 mm.
[j] 1 = 305-315 mm; 2 = 290-295 mm; 3 = 255-283 mm.
[k] Some measurements are from live birds rather than from museum specimens, and may not be entirely comparable with measurements for other races.

The reality of Peregrine races in light of morphology, geography, and genetics remains a fascinating question that could lead to experimentation. For instance, there is a marvelous outdoor experiment in progress that may elucidate the value of genetic versus morphological variation in subspecies allocations (cf. James 1983). If the passerine rates of change are a gauge (Selander and Johnston 1967, Johnston and Selander 1971), it may take 30-50 Peregrine generations to obtain enough quantifiable data to analyze. The experiment involves the release of Peregrine stocks from F. p. cassini, F. p. brookei, F. p. anatum, F. p. pealei, F. p. peregrinus, F. p. tundrius, and F. p. macropus into the eastern United States (Barclay and Cade 1983). These races vary from the largest Peregrine, a dark and heavily pigmented falcon, to smaller ones that are browner or pale blue. A good portion of the total range of variation in Peregrine Falcon size and color is represented. If our cladograms reflect true phylogenies, then the oldest and most derived

TABLE 6. (cont.)

	Characters										
	Max. wing length[l]	Mean tail length[m]	Min. tail length[n]	Max. tail length[o]	Mean tarsus length[p]	Mean middle toe[q]	Toe: tail[r]	Tail: wing[s]	Tarsus: wing[t]	Toe: wing[u]	Area[v]
F. p. pealei	1	2	1	1	2	1	3	3	2	2	6
F. p. calidus	1	3	2	1	4	2	1	3	3	2	3
F. p. japonensis	1	3	1	1	2	2	2	3	2	2	5
F. p. anatum	1	1	2	1	5	2	3	2	3	2	5
F. p. furuitii	2	1	1	1	?	?	?	2	?	?	5
F. p. peregrinus	2	3	2	1	2	3	2	3	2	2	2
F. p. madens	2	2	?	?	?	?	?	3	?	?	3
F. p. tundrius	1	3	2	1	6	4	2	3	3	3	4
F. p. cassini	1	3	2	1	5	5	2	3	2	2	4
F. p. brookei	2	3	2	1	1	2	2	2	1	2	1
F. p. babylonicus	3	3	2	2	5	?	?	3	2	?	2
F. p. nesiotes[w]	4	2	1	1	4	1	2	1	2	1	6
F. p. ernesti	3	3	2	1	4	?	?	3	2	?	4
F. p. macropus	3	3	2	1	4	5	3	1	2	2	5
F. p. submelanogenys	3	3	?	?	?	?	?	1	2	2	5
F. p. minor	2	3	2	1	3	4	2	3	2	2	3
F. p. peregrinator	3	3	2	1	3	5	2	2	1	2	3
F. p. radama	4	?	?	?	?	?	?	?	?	?	3
F. p. pelegrinoides	4	4	3	2	6	6	1	3	2	2	2

[l] 1 = 328-334 mm; 2 = 309-320 mm; 3 = 298-302 mm; 4 = 238-290 mm.
[m] 1 = 155-157 mm; 2 = 150-152 mm; 3 = 130-147 mm; 4 = 123 mm.
[n] 1 = 140-150 mm; 2 = 124-138 mm; 3 = 118 mm.
[o] 1 = 144-162 mm; 2 = 131-136.
[p] (rounded): 1 = 50 mm; 2 = 49 mm; 3 = 47 mm; 4 = 46 mm; 5 = 45 mm; 6 = 44 mm.
[q] Length less claw (rounded): 1 = 49 mm; 2 = 48 mm; 3 = 47 mm; 4 = 46 mm; 5 = 45 mm; 6 = 43 mm.
[r] 1 = 34.9-35.2; 2 = 32.1-33.8; 3 = 30.6-30.9.
[s] 1 = 51.3-52.6; 2 = 48.9-49.8; 3 = 43.3-47.7.
[t] 1 = 16.8-17.2; 2 = 15.2-16.3; 3 = 14.2-14.6.
[u] 1 = 17.0; 2 = 15.2-16.0; 3 = 14.9.
[v] Approximated nearest geographic range from center of functional outgroup range: 1 = functional outgroup; 2 = 500-3500 km; 3 = 4000-6500 km; 4 = 7000-9000 km; 5 = 9500-13,500 km; 6 = 14,000-18,000 km.
[w] Some measurements are from live birds rather than from museum specimens, and may not be entirely comparable with measurements for other races.

forms are among them. The original F. p. anatum (sensu stricto) that occurred in that region was a heavy, dark, and extensively marked bird with a rufous suffusion on the breast. Size and color reflected trends that occur in residents in a somewhat humid temperate environment with cold winters and warm summers. These same morphological patterns appear several times in different populations that occur in similar environments (i.e., some F. p. cassini, some F. p. macropus, and F. p. furuitii from the Pacific Ocean). Stocks that have been released into the United States will undoubtedly prove to have different allelic ratios consistent with the preliminary data of Morizot (Chapter 74).

Passerine data demonstrate that color, size, and structure of species introduced into a new environment mirrored the changes that theory predicted. Introduced passerines acquired characteristics of other geographically variable passerines native to those regions in accordance with biogeographical rules (Johnston and Selander 1971). Once sufficient random mating has occurred in the introduced Peregrine population and after several episodes of severe selection, some uniformity in phenotype should begin to appear. At this point, we may witness the beginning of a concordant trend in protein variation.

It will be most interesting to see whether the resulting Peregrine product takes on characteristics similar to the original population. One concept suggests it will; another suggests it may not because the former population reflected a long history of occupancy, while the introduced Peregrines will be subject only to recent history in a rather different environment, and perhaps also be subject to different random changes. Hopefully there will be students of Peregrines interested enough to chronicle this event.

ACKNOWLEDGEMENTS

We have profited from and been stimulated by discussions regarding geographic variation in Peregrines with R. M. Mengel, R. C. Banks, J. W. Aldrich, F. L. Beebe, W. R. Spofford, J. D. Rising, D. Amadon, E. Mayr, W. H. Behle, S. A. Temple, K. H. Voous, T. J. Cade, W. G. Hunt, S. K. Sherrod, D. J. Brimm, G. E. Watson, and the late C. Vaurie, J. Delacour, G. P. Dementiev, F. Salomonsen, B. Stegmann, K. D. Smith, A. Wetmore, and L. A. Portenko. R. W. Murphy gave advice on PAUP and gap coding procedure. C. "Bud" Anderson has been a continuous source of questions which have kept us interested in the problem of geographic variation and its meaning. So many people have discussed the Peregrine subspecies concept with us that it is not possible to list them all, but we are no less appreciative to those not listed.

10 | Humanity and the Peregrine

77 | Human Impacts on the Environment in Relation to the History and Biological Future of the Peregrine

Derek A. Ratcliffe

DIRECT INFLUENCE OF HUMAN ACTIVITIES

Although to many people the Peregrine is the very embodiment of wild Nature, its story is inextricably interwoven with human affairs. For many centuries, or in some regions for thousands of years, humanity has had a quite direct influence on this bird. The Peregrine has become an ally and friend through the ancient art of falconry and, in some countries, has been protected accordingly. Yet, on the whole, it has had the misfortune to be seen more often as a competitor, drawing for its prey on bird populations which some people regard as a source of food or sport. For this reason it has suffered relentless persecution in some regions, but has proved to be a resilient species, holding its own in the face of much destruction by game preservers and pigeon fanciers. Not even the inroads made by "that most efficient of mortals, the Scottish gamekeeper" have had any permanently depressing effect on its numbers in Britain — evidently there remained enough remote and inaccessible eyries to produce a supply of replacements. Air Ministry "control" during World War II showed that regional eradication was possible, but only by sustained removals year after year. In general, it seems that persecution has caused no more than local reduction in numbers or contraction of range, but with much depending on the nature of the terrain and accessibility of the breeding haunts.

In both Europe and North America, the erstwhile vogue pastime of egg collecting had still less effect on Peregrine populations, though it reduced breeding success locally and may have been a contributory factor in holding down the expansion of range. It is an activity which dies hard but seems nevertheless to be on the decline. Local hazards such as the shooting of Peregrines on well-known migration routes have ceased in some places, notably at Hawk Mountain, Pennsylvania, but continue elsewhere, such as in parts of the Mediterranean region. The taking of young, as part of the general cropping of wild bird populations for food by native peoples living at subsistence level, has been another local hazard for the species.

INDIRECT HUMAN INFLUENCE

All of these direct human interferences have been far less influential factors in the Peregrine's ecology than the indirect and unintentional effects implied by the term "environmental." Humanity is a destroyer of forests on a gigantic scale, and while this has had a disastrous effect on many forms of wildlife, it has been of benefit to some types which are adapted to open, nonwooded country. The Peregrine is one of these with a mode of hunting and choice of prey evolved to match open or, at most, only partially wooded conditions. Large areas of dense, closed forest seem to be one of the few habitats where the species is absent, although the Peregrines of Africa and Australia live in the dry, open forests of those continents. Where it habitually and widely nests in trees, the Peregrine needs substantial breaks in the tree cover for hunting. It is difficult to know just how much of an effect forest clearance has had on the distribution of the species around the world. In Britain, it seems likely that the scale of this effect, which by 1900 left only 5% of the country wooded, certainly allowed an increase in the breeding population during the last 3000 years. Given that most of the land was wooded up to at least 650 m elevation until deforestation became significant in late Stone Age times, there would have been less scope for Peregrines inland because of unavailability of suitable habitat. In some parts of the world where forest clearance went further and contributed to the advance of deserts, the changes may have been less favorable for Peregrines. We have heard how in North America, Prairie Falcons may have taken the place of Peregrines as conditions became more arid (Nelson Chapter 3). It seems likely that in the Old World, related falcons better adapted to desert conditions, such as the Lanner and Saker, may similarly have replaced the Peregrine as deserts advanced.

The effects of human impact in reducing suitable nesting habitat appear to have been minor; any limitations are mainly the natural ones of geological processes. Draining and afforestation of open bogs in Finland, where Peregrines were once widespread as ground nesters, is one example of a major loss of nesting habitat. Effect on food supply usually appears to be a key human impact: where intervention has reduced its amount, there may have been a parallel drop in Peregrine numbers. There is very limited evidence for such an effect, but it seems to have occurred in the west of the Scottish Highlands and the west of Ireland. In these highly oceanic regions with their prevalence of acidic rocks and poor soils, extractive use as grazing range for sheep and deer has further reduced the land's carrying capacity. Populations of wild prey for Peregrines, such as Red Grouse and shorebirds, have declined to low densities, and there is documentary evidence of the desertion of once-regular Peregrine eyries during the period 1880-1930 in the western highlands and islands (Ratcliffe 1980). In some localities, Golden Eagles replaced Peregrines, for they had an abundant food supply in the form of carcasses of sheep, which had helped to cause the decline in carrying capacity. Perhaps up to 100 pairs of Peregrines were replaced by Golden Eagles in Scotland. Modern arable farming may also have reduced prey populations to critically low levels in some areas, but such effects are perhaps masked by those of pesticides.

Yet there also appear to have been quite appreciable benefits which humanity has conferred upon the Peregrine, however unwittingly. Domestication of the wild Rock Dove, first as a source of food and later for the sport of pigeon fancying and racing, has given the Peregrine a prime prey species in many regions of the world. In many parts of Britain where the Peregrine is now flourishing, it could scarcely exist at present breeding density but for the ready availability of this favorite prey. Earlier, I gave reasons for supposing that the increase in Peregrine numbers to unprecedented high levels in certain parts of Britain during the last 10 years is at least partly connected with an increase in pigeon fancying (Ratcliffe Chapter 17). Another factor is that the quarrying of stone has provided numerous additional nesting places, in some cases where there was previously no suitable habitat for long distances. This provision of new breeding haunts has lately extended to industrial waste tips, and the Peregrine's propensity for nesting on buildings has been utilized in the captive breeding management work in the ways we have heard. Regarding both food supply and nesting habitat, the Peregrine has the potential to adapt to an urban environment, though it has so far done so only to a very limited extent. The natural ecological resilience of the species has also led to the beginnings of a return to both ground-nesting and tree-nesting in Britain and Ireland, as the population has built up, thereby greatly expanding the potential breeding range.

PESTICIDE PROBLEMS

The impact of persistent, synthetic toxic chemicals, especially the organochlorine insecticides, on Peregrine populations is a unique event and one of staggeringly widespread occurrence and overwhelming importance. Since this has been the central theme of our concern with this species over the past 20 years or so, some further reflections on its significance seem appropriate. One important aspect is that the effect was largely unforeseen and so took us by surprise. Some far-sighted biologists, including Bill Vogt and Vincent Wigglesworth, were warning of the potential hazards of the indiscriminate use of DDT and lindane when these "wonder" insecticides were released for general use after 1945. But few if any saw the ramifications of this group of compounds' action via food chains and ability to affect predators through secondary contamination. It is a sobering thought that another 20 years elapsed before onset of the DDE effect on eggshell thinning came to light and that the evidence for such an event should lie around for so long, in the form of residue traces in eggshells more than 20 years old.

Also important is the role that chance — or luck, if you prefer — has played in the story. In the first place, there is the unfortunate biochemical chance that the cyclodiene insecticides should be so toxic to birds, and perhaps especially raptors, and that DDT/DDE should happen to cause eggshell thinning. And then there is the ecological/ geographical accident that some falcon populations should be heavily and completely exposed to organochlorine contamination, while others were relatively shielded. Whether or not this circumstance could be viewed in terms of evolutionary strategy, the Peregrine has maintained its reputation for resilience through a wide-spectrum ecological adaptability, which has allowed survival beyond this worst-yet crisis. We just do not know whether, or to what extent, a capacity for developing physiological resistance to organochlorines has been part of the survival process.

Survival and recovery of threatened Peregrine populations have, however, not been only a matter of good luck and natural resilience. They have been considerably assisted by human attempts to make amends by reducing the hazards which caused the problem. The work of biologists and other concerned people to restrict the use of harmful toxic chemicals has been a major factor. The process of achieving this objective has become a major issue of the ecopolitics which so occupies the wildlife conservation scene. It has involved competition of interests and related behavior which should ring bells with all students of animal ecology. The case of the persistent pesticides and their effects on wildlife was at the forefront of the great wave of environmental concern which has developed over the last 30 years. This concern has passed its peak and, to some extent, subsided and been overtaken by other issues, such as acid deposition and destruction of the tropical moist forests. But it is time now for a reassessment of the problem that remains and what we should be doing.

Some countries have dealt with the issue by banning the use of most or all of the persistent organochlorine pesticides. Britain, in its usual way, has clung to the voluntary principle and avoided mandatory withdrawals, believing that persuasion and staged restrictions would achieve the desired results, in combination with the search for alternative chemicals. This seems to have worked in the case of the cyclodiene compounds but not for DDT, for which voluntary restrictions were less rigorous. There is still unauthorized use of these chemicals, including dieldrin, obtained from sources which are widely believed to include Ireland. A year ago, Britain had to conform with a European Economic Community (EEC) regulation requiring the withdrawal of all persistent organochlorine pesticides, and the results are being awaited. Domestic legislation to ensure that the EEC regulation is legally enforced has been enacted, but it consists of broad provisions within which the details are later worked out by the agriculture departments. Residue monitoring will have to be maintained to determine the practical effectiveness of the restrictions.

Another possible problem is that there is now so much of certain persistent organochlorine residues in environmental circulation that even a total ban on new additions will not reduce the load. It may take many years for the recycling residues to diminish substantially. The more crucial point is that wildlife-pesticide problems remain. Despite great improvements in control of pesticide use in the developed countries, the problem has been widely exported, especially to developing countries. As the sophistication of their agriculture has developed, which it must if their food and economic problems are ever to be resolved, so has their demand for pesticides. This trend can only be expected to continue. Use of pesticides has become an enormous problem for human health in the developing countries. Their continued use underlines the difficulty of persuading those involved that wildlife is a matter of any concern. It becomes part of the truly daunting difficulty of obtaining even rudimentary gestures to nature conservation in the tropics and subtropics, where nature has so much to lose but where the common distress of humanity eclipses all other issues.

The Peregrine may hold out against the wave of environmental destruction and degradation better than many species, judging by what we know of its ability to persist. In Europe, pesticide problems linger for the species, and the exposure of the Scandinavian population on its wintering grounds south of the Baltic is evidently a continuing problem. Organochlorine problems remain in regions of North America through transfer of residues by migratory birds which ingest them in Central and South America. In Britain, the failure of the Peregrine to recover, or even reappear, in some of its southeastern and eastern haunts is difficult to explain other than as a lingering pesticide effect. There is concern that a close relative of the Peregrine, the Merlin, has now replaced it as the most threatened of our more common raptors. Although the evidence is less clear-cut, many ornithologists believe that pesticides must be a contributing factor to the Merlin's decline. I alluded earlier (Ratcliffe Chapter 17) to the rather anomalous and mysterious failure of coastal Peregrines in northern Scotland to match the recovery of many areas further south, and of the reasons for linking this fact to marine pollution, of which the persistent PCBs are one main indicator. This pattern points to both a need for vigilance over marine pollution and a need for further research and conservation action. There is also a question mark about the as yet unknown potential effects from the galaxy of synthetic pesticides besides those of the organochlorine group.

THE PRESENT POSITION

At this point it is tempting to discuss future needs for research and conservation, but that subject is the prerogative of the final participants at this conference. I shall say only that there remain a number of aspects concerning Peregrines and pollutants, from fairly complete mysteries to only half-understood things, that only further research can unravel. We are at present stating an interim position, but one in which we can feel satisfaction that the past effort has achieved very worthwhile results. We understand immensely more about pesticides and pollution than we did 20 years ago, and more about Peregrine biology and ecology than ever before. Research into the effects of toxic chemicals on wildlife has been the key to moderating the conservation problem by controlling the substances involved. Remedial action has depended very largely on producing convincing evidence of cause and adverse effect, sufficient to override — at least eventually — the vested interests and political pressures which create and maintain the hazards.

The success of captive breeding and reintroduction in the restoration of a wild Peregrine population after regional extinction is a vindication of both philosophy and method. It has been demanding, both technically and in resources, and not without its own political problems. If purists and doubters still remain, they should try to see that in a real world increasingly molded by human drive, ambition and need, the survival of nature in a desirable form will also depend increasingly on the conscious intervention of human planning and management. Humans have to adapt their beliefs and outlook, unless they wish to emulate the late King Canute. The scale of the Peregrine's recovery in Britain has also owed a good deal to the direct protection of the birds and their nests by the Royal Society for the Protection of Birds, as well as many dedicated local enthusiasts. Robbery of eggs for collections and of eggs and young for falconry has increased again, but has been contained.

The present position could probably not have been achieved without large inputs and gains on the educational and public relations fronts, some of these not directly involving Peregrines. In various western countries, the Peregrine has benefited from the great increase in environmental concern and enthusiasm for wildlife and countryside. In Britain there has been a huge growth in the nature-minded public since World War II. It now forms a powerful constituency and lobby of which the politicians are keenly aware. Its support and pressure have become a political force which has helped to influence government to make appropriate legal and administrative provisions for wildlife conservation and which has persuaded both commercial and land (or other natural resource-using) interests to pay similar heed. Changed public opinion appears to have been an important factor in inducing game preservers to treat Peregrines as a protected species. The same trend is observable in many other countries. Nevertheless, wildlife and its habitat remain threatened almost everywhere by the relentless advance of human progress, economic growth and the demand for development of natural resources. We should remember that the pesticide problem is largely one stemming from agricultural advance.

The Peregrine has won a reprieve from the predicted possible fate of some two decades ago. It is a species better able than many to cope with modern trends such as spreading urbanization and habitat modification. Continuing attrition of habitat will adversely affect Peregrines in some places, we can be sure. Yet the devastating level of change (such as intensive agricultural development) needed to reduce the Peregrine's food supply below critical levels over large areas of presently suitable habitat is at present incomprehensible.

We must not, however, be complacent. Not only do serious pesticide problems remain in many parts of the world, but we cannot dismiss the possibility of new ones. If past experience has any lesson, it is that our track record in prophesies is not particularly good and that future threats tend to be unforeseen. We can at least try to ensure, through pesticide approval and experimental testing, that all new compounds are carefully screened for their environmental effects before being released for use, and that the routine monitoring of both populations and residues maintains an early warning system for hazards. In Britain there is a certain perennial anxiety that as the Peregrine recovery proceeds, the homing pigeon predation issue could again erupt. So far, it has grumbled away in the background. Beyond this, in many parts of the country, the Peregrine is now so dependent on the homing pigeon as to be vulnerable in principle. Any species is at risk whose fortunes are geared so largely to those of another. The consequences of epidemic disease or change in economic circumstances for the prey species could be disastrous for the predator.

On a global basis, the Peregrine as a species seems well set to maintain its evolutionary success. With the devotion to its welfare which is evident from this conference, it will not fail from lack of human concern. Our urge to think about the future is nevertheless clouded by the dominant anxiety — that a nuclear Armageddon could not only extinguish all human concerns, including those for environment and wildlife, but could also produce a "winter" of such apocalyptic severity as to destroy all higher forms of life on earth. Whether this now somewhat trite reflection has anything to do with this conference is a matter for individual judgement.

78 The Peregrine Falcon in Relation to Contemporary Falconry

James D. Weaver

I am going to digress completely from a scientific format and certainly from the more scholarly presentations of this conference. I will attempt to explain some attitudes, ideas and ideals, all relating one way or another to the Peregrine Falcon and falconry. Along the way I will be assuming your general acceptance of hunting and falconry as reasonable pastimes of real and rational human beings and not crimes against nature and humanity. If you are anti-hunting, you will, by definition, be anti-falconry.

I will go so far as to describe what, in my mind, is the *art* of falconry and describe why the Peregrine is essential to this art. Art is defined in the Merriam-Webster Dictionary as: the systematic use of knowledge or skill in making and doing things; skill acquired in making and doing things; skill acquired by experience or study; a branch of learning; or, finally, the use of skill and imagination in the production of things of beauty. My final remarks will touch briefly on the current status of the Peregrine in captivity and the continuing commitment of falconers to its general welfare.

Three weeks ago I found myself in the midst of the Peregrine migration on an island 90 miles offshore in the Gulf of Mexico. In 11 days I saw hundreds of falcons come ashore on this tiny island and spend a day or so feeding, resting, and flying in what can only be described as devilish pursuit of anything that dared to show itself in the air. Their squealing sounds during mock battles could be heard all through the daylight hours, rain or shine. Squadrons of as many as nine Peregrines would fly out to sea to intercept incoming passerines, stooping in formation as these tiny travelers tried to reach the safety of the island's trees.

It occurred to me there that a true wizard in his wildest imagination could conjure up no better place or time to ponder the power of the Peregrine. It was in the midst of this abundance of falcons that I tried valiantly to put to paper answers to some very important questions, the most basic and most difficult being: Why is the Peregrine so important to falconry?

The question is difficult not because the answer is elusive but, rather, because of the problem I face in expressing myself adequately on a subject so close to me. If I should fall short of the mark here, please forgive me and accept my sincere wish that each of you could see and, perhaps more importantly, feel the perfection in the art of falconry that it has been my privilege to witness during the past 25 years.

The Peregrine Falcon has been the premier bird in classical falconry for the last several centuries for which we have written records. Classical falconry is defined here as limited to larger falcons flown against upland game and waterfowl. Flights at herons and cranes, never having been popular or feasible in the United States, will be left to the imagination.

Art enters into falconry when the falconer endeavors to do more than merely hunt. After weeks or months of work and preparation, it becomes his duty, above all else, to provide an opportunity for his falcon to demonstrate its natural abilities to the fullest extent possible. He will realize any and all reward for his meticulous preparation only within the tiny window of time when the falcon is in control. Satisfaction lies in knowing that he has done his job well and that he alone has set in motion the events of the day. It is the successful orchestration of all the variables of the field that becomes the falconer's burden and purpose.

The burden is substantial. There must be quarry in suitable, safe terrain with adequate cover. Well-trained and talented dogs are almost a necessity and complement a well-trained and properly conditioned falcon. The falconer must have a complete understanding of how these animals will interact under given wind and weather conditions, and he must determine the proper moment and manner for flushing the quarry. At that point, it is left to the skill, experience, and natural athletic abilities of the falcon and its quarry to determine the outcome of the flight.

Hours, days, weeks, months in preparation, minutes in performance, but, if all goes well, a lifetime of remembrance. It is the vivid recollection of the best of these experiences and the desire to duplicate or better them that motivate the falconer.

Where does the Peregrine come in? Why is this species so revered? Simply stated, the Peregrine is the best possible bird with which to practice classical falconry. There are several reasons, none complicated. The bird is widely distributed throughout the world, is strikingly beautiful, and is capable of taking all species of upland game. It is very tractable and even docile relative to other falcons, it is easy to keep and maintain in good health, it has a natural hunting method which lends itself to what falconers seek, it is not easily discouraged and, therefore, is not prone to going off to hunt on its own. Finally, the general athletic ability of the Peregrine sets it apart from all others.

Everything else being equal, the simple fact is that the falconer seeking perfection in his art will achieve more consistent satisfaction with the Peregrine than with any other long-winged falcon. I do not mean that perfection cannot be attained with other birds; nothing could be further from the truth. It is just that the Peregrine will, by its nature, behave more predictably and more spectacularly in any given situation.

Just as hunters have used pointing dogs rather than less specialized breeds, and just as the dressage rider prefers the thoroughbred horse, so falconers for centuries have recognized the contribution this most perfectly suited species, the Peregrine, can make to the art of falconry. There simply is no substitute. The fact that the Peregrine can inflame the passions of so many people from such diverse backgrounds is evidence enough. If there were an adequate challenger, fewer would be at this conference.

We can take the thoroughbred from the dressage rider, we can deny the salmon fisherman his flyrod, we can lift a primary color from the palette of the artist and we can outlaw the use of the Peregrine in falconry, as some suggest; but by doing so, we would effectively prohibit the attainment of the highest level of expression in all these endeavors. To what purpose? There is no benefit to be derived from thwarting those aspiring to excellence in any activity that materially harms no one. Falconry, with its use of the Peregrine, materially affects no one. It can, however, measurably enrich the lives of all those who come in contact with it either accidentally or by design. The real value of falconry lies in that fact.

When we look at what has happened to falconry during the past 15 years, there are really no surprises. Complete protection of the Peregrine in the United States during the early 1970s was naturally reflected in the numbers being flown in falconry. Many who held birds at that time made them available to The Peregrine Fund, Inc., or developed their own breeding facilities. Since eyasses were the most desirable as breeders, many intermewed passage-taken Peregrines continued to be flown for years; in fact, a few are still being flown today. It was, of course, these eyasses in the various projects that formed the nucleus of the breeding and release programs that have proved so successful in the United States. The progeny from those birds account for about 70% of releases to date.

It is all too often discounted, but must be pointed out again, that these falconers came forward of their own volition and offered up their prized falcons for use in this work. There were no guarantees; they expected nothing more than to be treated fairly when (not if) the problems facing the Peregrine became known and population declines reversed. The necessity of success in captive breeding and even the ultimate recovery of some populations of Peregrines were perhaps closer to the hearts of this group than to any other. I feel that it was the optimism within the falconry community that provided the drive and enthusiasm to see these programs through and was largely responsible for what we are seeing today in this country both in the wild and in the mews.

Success in breeding Peregrines is responsible for the influx of birds back into the hands of falconers today. Most of these birds are being kept for further breeding, but many are flown in falconry as well. Figures supplied by Robert Berry of the North American Raptor Breeders' Association indicate that the number of Peregrines held privately for breeding has increased from 90 in 1981 to approximately 330 in 1985. Predictions of production by private breeders run as high as 500 young birds per year by 1989.

Attendance records at field meets from the North American Falconers' Association (NAFA) reflect a similar increase in the numbers of Peregrines being flown, i.e., 4 in 1974 versus 25 in 1984. Information on the actual number of Peregrines being held under falconry licenses is currently unavailable. NAFA estimates that number at around 100 birds.

In North America today, there appear to be more Peregrine Falcons than at any time since the 1950s. The trend is very clear, and along with the recovery of Peregrines in the wild, we will continue to see the species returned to its rightful place in the traditions of falconry.

Article I, Section 2 of the NAFA constitution reads in part: " . . . to promote conservation of the birds of prey and an appreciation of their value in nature and wildlife conservation programs; to urge recognition of falconry as a legal field sport; and to establish traditions which will aid, perpetuate, and further the welfare of falconry and the raptors it employs."

It must be clear that we cannot succeed in any of these endeavors without healthy wild raptor populations. The very essence of that which falconers hold most dear depends entirely on the survival and abundance of the Peregrine Falcon.

There is no group of people who have a better understanding of what the Peregrine is, does, and means than do the falconers of the United States. I would ask that all devotees of the bird accept this fact both as an expression of falconers' sincerity and also as a guarantee, if you wish, of their continued commitment to this species and its survival for all time and for all people.

79 | An Overview of Arab Falconry, Its Medical Lore, and the Introduction of Avian Medicine in the Arabian Gulf

J. David Remple

Traditional concepts of falconry and medical care of falcons vary considerably between the Middle East and the West. The geographical location and unique climate of the Arabian Gulf make it possible to examine falcon diseases infrequent or absent in the West. The frequencies of several disease conditions seen in the Arabian Gulf differ because of different conditions. The Dubai Falcon Hospital was created in 1983 to provide the first modern medical care for the captive falcons of the Arabian Gulf. Thus far the hospital has accommodated over 950 falcons, and our research group at the hospital is trying to create hematological and serological diagnostic profiles for several disease conditions common to falcons worldwide.

Humanity's long sporting association with falcons has provided insights into their diseases. Any culture whose ancient history includes an association of humans and falcons also describes ailments afflicting falcons and colorful descriptions of treatment. Owing to the separation of cultures, little is known in the western world of the Arabs, their falconry, or their medical practices. The Bedouin (nomadic Arabs) still practice the same medicine their ancestors did a thousand years ago. Some of the ancient Arab treatments have practical value. This paper briefly explores traditional Arab falconry, its medical lore, and the impact modern medicine is having on ancient customs.

ARAB FALCONRY

Approximately 3000 falcons are employed for falconry on the Arabian Peninsula each year. Between two-thirds and three-fourths are used in the Arabian Gulf region. Most of these falcons are trapped as migrants in Pakistan, Iran, Afghanistan and the Arabian Peninsula, and the vast majority are immature. Saker Falcons represent at least 70%

of the captive falcon population throughout Arabia. Peregrine Falcons are commonly encountered in the Arabian Gulf region but diminish toward the interior of Saudi Arabia. Other falcons such as the Lanner Falcon form less than 2% of the total captive raptor population.

The fall capture of migratory falcons in and around Arabia has continued for centuries. It is difficult to assess the impact this removal has had on wild populations. Those trapped represent a wide and scattered sampling of populations from immense and diverse breeding ranges. About 60% are released each spring on natural migratory flyways as fattened and experienced hunters (Butti pers. comm.).

It is well known that falconry in the Middle East is practiced differently than in most regions of the world. The enduring popularity of falconry in the Arab world may relate to cultural ties to the past. Falconry is also a source of immense enjoyment to the Arabs. It provides a means of social integration between all economic and social levels, and Arab camaraderie reaches its highest level in the activities of many people with one common interest. However, the Arabs do not regard falconry as a sport in the same sense that westerners do. Allen (1982) wrote: "In Arabia, even more than was the case in medieval Europe, which was so much richer in food supplies, game taken by the Arab's trained hawk was an important addition to his thin diet. Wild hawks were trapped by rich and poor alike and were flown through the winter months when quarry became available. The Arabs flew their hawks because they wanted to hunt and eat. They did not go hunting because they wanted to see their hawks fly. This is an important distinction to bear in mind, because it underlies the techniques and apparent ruthlessness of desert hawking." The style of Arab falconry is still practical, even though it has long ceased to be utilitarian for the sheikhs and princes. Its technique and style are also influenced by available quarry.

The quarry consists mainly of the Houbara Bustard and the Stone Curlew. Both are relished as food by Arab falconers. The latter, although unrelated, resembles a miniature Houbara, and is hunted with male and female falcons. Female Sakers and Peregrines are preferred for falconry because their size and strength enable them to cope with the larger Houbara.

As a rule, falcons used by the Arabs can outfly and usually outmaneuver Houbaras and Stone Curlews. Once well on the wing, however, both quarries can prove challenging. A direct chase by the falcon is the quickest and most efficient means of capture. Waiting-on flights with the falcon circling high overhead are unknown to most Arabs. Knowledgeable falconers consider waiting-on flights impractical for the Houbara, or they interpret such flights to be indicative of inferior falcons that "dive and strike" compared to those that possess the "strength" to climb and the "courage" to bind. Therefore, climbing or ringing flights are held in the highest regard. Since both types of quarry are generally larger than the pursuing falcons, the emphasis in training is placed on aggressiveness.

Because migrating falcons become available at about the same time as migrating quarry, training methods must be fast. Aggressiveness and tameness are quickly instilled by constant handling and by a reduced diet. Daily exercise typically consists of a single flight, usually directly from a release point to a food-garnished lure. The distance is typically 100-300 m. Endurance conditioning is unnecessary with newly caught, well-muscled, migratory falcons. Once conditioned over this distance, the falcon is entered to the prey and training is complete.

DISEASE AND MEDICAL LORE

Stress appears to precede many diseases observed in captive falcons of the Arabian Gulf. From a medical standpoint stress is any influence which upsets the physiological homeostasis of an organism, causing an overproduction of adrenal hormones which act to suppress the immune system, rendering the organism susceptible to disease (Nickel et al. 1977). Examples of stressful conditions are excessive psychological or physical discomfort, extremes in environmental conditions and poor nutrition (Cooper 1978). The association between stress and disease is widely accepted. Many potential pathogens are borne as normal biota within an organism where they are symbiotic or commensal with the host. For example, low numbers of coccidia and possibly the spores of *Aspergillus* spp. may serve to stimulate the host's immune system against the diseases they produce (C. Hibler pers. comm.). However, stress-weakened immune systems may permit low numbers of normally innocuous organisms to proliferate, creating disease.

A common stress in captive falcons of the Arabian Gulf appears to be insufficient food. The initial reduction in a falcon's weight during training can be carried too far by inexperienced trainers, especially in the absence of a scale to show the precise loss of weight or in the absence of sustained flights to show the falcon's endurance and strength. Since demanding training flights are unnecessary, and the use of a scale was unknown to most Arab falconers until recently, a falcon's fitness was judged on subjective observation of the bird at rest or under mild exercise conditions. Also, the same hunger in a falcon trained in a hot environment compared to a more temperate one requires a greater reduction in caloric intake, so that birds trained by those less than astute and conscientious are occasionally weakened.

Diseases I saw in the falcons of the Arabian Gulf are similar to those in the West, but frequency and degree are different. Classic aspergillosis seems as frequent as in temperate climates; however, an *Aspergillus*-related disease appears at the end of the hot summer molting period. Falcons exhibit chronic, exudative air sac infections. A falcon with this syndrome (which Arabs refer to as "Hiatha") eats well and remains bright and alert for an indefinite period of time, but exhibits profound shortness of breath with the slightest exertion. Although bacteria have been incriminated as the cause of air sac infections in raptors (Cooper 1978), I feel excessive heat, certain bacteria, lungworms, and *Aspergillus* may play a combined role in the etiology of this disorder.

Coccidiosis and capillariasis are the chief digestive disorders. Of all healthy falcons I examined, 10% had small numbers of coccidial oocysts in their feces, and 5% displayed *Capillaria* eggs. Both parasites are transmitted to falcons by the ingestion of infested prey. Stress appears to precipitate fulminating infestations in falcons, but parasite load can be independent of stress and relate to food source directly.

Lungworms of the genus *Serratospiculum* are common in healthy large falcons, both wild and captive, throughout the world (Cooper 1978). The life cycle is unknown, but arthropods are thought to serve as intermediate hosts (Davis et al. 1971). Stress and clinical signs of lungworm disease appear directly correlated. With heavy lungworm infestations the presence of another parasite, *Tetrameres* sp., previously undescribed in falcons, has been observed in the Arabian Gulf (I. Keymer pers. comm.). A direct relationship between *Tetrameres* sp. and *Serratospiculum* sp. has yet to be determined (L. Khalil pers. comm., G. Nelson pers. comm.).

Avian pox is common and results from pox virus gaining entry through abraded skin. Cases involving eyelids often result from unhygienic seeling procedures, while those involving feet may result from self-inflicted scratches or bloodsucking arthropods, both of which can introduce virus into breaks in the skin. It appears that stress during procurement and training of falcons occasionally combines with pox to produce an intense itching in the distal extremities of the toes. Such birds may eat their own toes from the talons inward. Psychological and/or physical distraction may correct this condition.

Most falcons of the Arabian Gulf are inexplicably infested heavily with lice, which are known to proliferate in sick birds (Davis et al. 1971). However, nearly all the healthy falcons I examined were infested. Biting lice may provide entry for pox virus by inducing self-mutilation. Louse flies (Hippoboscidae) and possibly feather lice (Mallophaga) may act as intermediate hosts for *Haemoproteus*, a blood sporozoan parasite of birds (Davis et al. 1971). Although not previously considered pathogenic for falcons (Remple 1980), *Haemoproteus* may cause functional anemia. We have witnessed up to 10% of red blood cells parasitized in heavily lice-infested falcons.

Bumblefoot, an infection of the foot, is not uncommon to captive falcons worldwide. Most cases in the Arabian Gulf arise from self-inflicted punctures by sharp or badly overgrown talons. Coping to reduce beak or talon length is largely unknown to the Bedouin, who believe that needle-sharp talons are necessary for a falcon's hunting success.

The differences between modern medical practices and those of a society isolated until recently are profound. Because they do not understand physiology, Bedouin falconers recognize only obvious symptoms and combine them into single diseases of the mouth, feet, or breathing. Some folk treatments provide at least visual improvement. For example, conditions associated with foot swelling are often treated, but not cured, by placing the bird in hot sand, thereby providing heat to improve circulation and reduce pain. Furthermore, sea sand, rich in salts, may osmotically reduce edema.

Some ailments are treated by "smoking" the patient with alum thrown over a campfire. This practice is thought to have powers of warding off the "evil eye," which they frequently associate with illness (Kanafani 1983).

The most widely used treatment is "branding," the application of a red-hot iron to an affected part. If a falcon suffers from a breathing difficulty, the cere is burned; if from lameness, a joint is burned. Branding was common to early western medicine also, and was called "firing." It creates an acute inflammation that may promote healing of a chronic or degenerative lesion by arousing natural defenses.

The poor success of most ancient remedies creates an underlying sense of futility about medicine. The Bedouin are impatient with long-term treatment. Unless something looks better almost immediately, treatment is usually abandoned. Also, the sight of illness, deformity, and pain in falcons is not easily tolerated by Arab falconers. For cultural reasons many Arab falconers find it difficult to accept euthanasia as a humane solution in hopeless situations. When remedies fail and suffering becomes too painful, the ailing falcon may simply be released "to Allah's will." Fortunately, this philosophy is gradually being replaced by more pragmatic viewpoints.

MODERN AVIAN MEDICINE

The wealth of the Middle East has thrust it into the 20th century and provided technology that was virtually unknown 20 years ago. Through the progressive thinking of the rulers of Dubai, the Maktoum family, and most notably H. H. Shaikh Hamdan bin Rashid Al Maktoum, an avian medical facility was recently created to provide first-of-its-kind modern medical care for hunting falcons of the region. In Abu Dhabi a similar facility will follow, to be directed by K. Riddle,

DVM. Since the Arabian Gulf region alone may have as many as 2000-2500 trained falcons (with Peregrines representing 10-30% of the population), the opportunity exists to obtain normal physiological as well as pathological data from many falcons. Knowledge of health and disease in falcons is proportional to the number of cases examined by veterinarians in many regions. For this reason we plan to add to the rapidly growing information on the Peregrine Falcon. Although Peregrines and other falcons are susceptible to many of the same pathological conditions worldwide, the special climate and location of the Arabian Gulf provide the opportunity to study endemic diseases absent or infrequently observed elsewhere.

Our immediate goals are threefold: (1) to provide medical care for the falcons of the Arabian Gulf region, (2) to acquaint the local people with the diseases that affect their falcons and to promote early recognition of diseases, their effective treatment, and most importantly, their prevention, and (3) to accumulate physiological data from normal and unhealthy falcons in order to create diagnostic clinical profiles for specific diseases. Presently there is little information on hematological and serological profiles from normal and diseased falcons in spite of a growing wealth of diagnostic profiles for other avian species. Unfortunately, profiles from falcons differ from nonraptorial species (Campbell and Dein 1984). In one year we treated more than 450 cases and made hematological and/or serological profiles on 128 cases. Abnormal profiles included various infections, toxemias, necrotic conditions, post-surgical stress, and molting irregularities.

We do not know whether the alterations in falcon blood arising from disease will be diagnostically useful as in mammalian medicine, but all available means will be explored to find out. It is our aim, therefore, to gather and catalogue clinical data on Peregrines and other falcons in a part of the world where these species are encountered frequently in captivity.

ACKNOWLEDGEMENTS

I acknowledge H. H. Shaikh Hamdan bin Rashid Al Maktoum, whose concern for the welfare of falcons and understanding for the need of continuing research has provided the foundation for our work. H. H. Shaikh Hamdan and H. E. Shaikh Butti Al Maktoum and their falconers have shared their camaraderie and passion for desert hawking, for which I am grateful.

80 | "Operation Falcon" and the Peregrine

Williston Shor

"Operation Falcon" was an undercover "sting operation" carried out by the Division of Law Enforcement of the U. S. Fish and Wildlife Service (USFWS). Its primary targets were falconers and raptor breeders, mainly breeders of the Peregrine Falcon. Hence, Operation Falcon is of interest to all who are concerned with the biology and conservation of this species. In my role as editor of *Hawk Chalk* for the North American Falconers' Association, much of my time in the past 17 months has been spent investigating and reporting on Operation Falcon to our members. I have developed some perspectives that I would like to share on the impact of stings on conservation and on the conduct of biological research.

Although this paper demonstrates that the number of Peregrines taken illegally for falconry in the United States and Canada is very small compared with the numbers that are otherwise removed from the population, this comparison should not be misinterpreted as condoning the illegal take. The North American Falconers' Association considers illegal taking and sale of even a single wild raptor to be ethically and morally wrong, and its Board of Directors has voted to drop any members found guilty of such activities. On the other hand, the use of so-called "sting operations" in law enforcement appears morally wrong to much of the public. It has had such destructive effects on relationships among groups that should work together to preserve the Peregrine that it is obviously poor public policy, and would be so even if it could be justified as an effective law enforcement tactic.

HISTORY OF OPERATION FALCON

Operation Falcon was made possible by the 1972 annex to the United States' Migratory Bird Treaty with Mexico, which added raptors to the list of birds granted federal protection, and by the Endangered Species Act of 1973. Shortly after these laws came into effect, the USFWS started enforcement activity. It included as a major accomplishment in its Fiscal Year (FY) 1975 annual report the development of a master file "on all known parties interested in raptors, including all known dealers in eagle feathers or their parts." Its FY 1976 annual report includes the statement: "Some Americans find it very lucrative to smuggle [endangered Peregrine Falcons] out of the country to wealthy Middle East monarchs who have paid up to $25,000 for the birds." Prices in the Middle East for legal birds were in fact far less. (See Cade's letter to Herbst, 1977, *in* Cade 1985b.)

Shortly thereafter, the Federal Bureau of Investigation greatly expanded its use of stings. Its undercover operations climbed from 53 in 1977 to over 300 in 1983 (House Judiciary Committee 1984). The USFWS followed suit, and by 1985 it had carried out at least seven such investigations (Bavin 1985).

Begun officially in early 1981, Operation Falcon was centered about the USFWS "informant," John Jeffery McPartlin of Great Falls, Montana. McPartlin was a falconer with a history since the mid-1960s of possessing and trading many more raptors than any single falconer could use. He was convicted in 1972 of violating the Lacey Act by attempting to ship to Saudi Arabia two Gyrfalcons, which missed the plane and were seized at McPartlin's home, then in Cheyenne, Wyoming. No later than 1975 he became a government informant on a part-time basis, reporting on violations of the law by several falconers (Hester 1985).

When the USFWS began Operation Falcon, it assigned agents to operate under cover with McPartlin from his home. During its first 18 months, the sting concentrated on infractions of the regulations by American falconers attempting to obtain or exchange birds for their personal use in falconry. Typically, McPartlin would invite a falconer to visit him and would then help him obtain a bird illegally. On one occasion he even climbed a tree to remove a nestling Northern Goshawk when the falconer proved physically unable to do so (Schmidt and Hart 1983). Infractions included the taking of a raptor in Montana by a nonresident (legal only for a Montana resident) and then reporting that the bird had been taken in a state where it was legal for him to do so; concealment of illegal acquisitions by re-using bands from birds that had died; and concealment by placing two wild Northern Goshawk nestlings from Montana in a breeding project in Illinois and claiming they had been hatched from eggs of a captive bird.

The USFWS could find no existing illegal commercial traffic in wild North American raptors in the United States. However, they were able to set up foreign trade. In August of 1982 Lothar Ciesielski, a member of a German family that had been actively trading in large falcons obtained illegally in Scandinavia and possibly in Canada and Alaska, heard of McPartlin and wrote him a letter inquiring about the possibility of visiting. McPartlin immediately invited him to come to Montana.

As a result of this and ensuing visits, McPartlin trapped 12 immature and adult Gyrfalcons and three Prairie Falcons in Montana and sold them to Ciesielski. The Gyrfalcons each brought $4000-$6000, and the Prairie Falcons each brought $1000. McPartlin then bought seven Gyrfalcons for $41,000 from Glen Luckman, a Canadian who smuggled them into the United States (Zimmerman 1984a). He resold them for $49,000 ($7000 each) to the Ciesielskis, who illegally transported them from the United States (Zimmerman 1984b). Later, McPartlin bought or traded for eight Peregrines and three European Northern Goshawks smuggled from Canada by the same Canadian operator. McPartlin was also involved in initiating the smuggling of Northern Goshawk eggs from Europe into the United States.

Until almost the end of its undercover phase, the sting's involvement with Peregrine Falcons was essentially limited to birds originating in Canada. However, in May of 1984 McPartlin and Special Agent John Gavitt of the USFWS engineered an expedition to Lake Powell on the Colorado River, where Gavitt helped a falconer descend a cliff to remove three eggs from a Peregrine eyrie. The eggs went to an incubator at McPartlin's home; only one hatched despite the late stage of incubation. The population from which the eggs were taken is a particularly endangered one. Gavitt's and McPartlin's involvement in this episode appears to be a violation of the Endangered Species Act, which requires a government agent to obtain a federal permit before disturbing the nest (such a permit was never obtained). At the same time, McPartlin persuaded two other falconers to take three young Peregrines from a nest in Capitol Reef National Park, Utah, and turn them over to him. He placed them in what appeared to be a breeding project at his home (under cross-examination later he admitted that he had never bred any birds). From there he sold them to falconers through a sales operation that was so aggressive that two of the falconers involved in the purchase of these birds and one other Peregrine were acquitted later on the basis that McPartlin had entrapped them into violating the law. A third person accused of conspiracy was acquitted because no conspiracy was proved, a fourth who declined to use the entrapment defense was convicted, and a fifth pleaded no contest.

On 29 June 1984, Operation Falcon was made public with the execution of 54 search warrants in the United States and a number more in Canada. About 30 individuals were arrested in the United States. Searches without warrants were made of facilities of other individuals against whom there was no evidence of wrongdoing, and they were questioned under the federal rule that permits on-demand government inspection of facilities for compliance with regulation.

Most of the approximately 30 people initially arrested in the United States were charged with felonies under the Lacey Act. Only three of them actually came to trial. The remainder made plea bargains resulting in fines and, in two cases, prison terms. Most of the charges were reduced to misdemeanors in the plea bargaining process. After the initial searches, about 30 more individuals were charged with less serious misdemeanors and one with a civil violation; most pleaded guilty and paid small fines.

QUESTIONABLE JUSTIFICATION FOR USE OF STINGS

Sting operations have many undesirable consequences: potential violations of civil rights, generation of crime that otherwise would not occur, suspension of normal law enforcement to avoid alarming potential sting victims, and erosion of trust between the people and their government. In justifying USFWS use of stings, its Chief of Law Enforcement, Clark Bavin, said in September 1985: "The prices people are willing to pay for wildlife are astonishing. With the increase in profits, more money and resources are available to the criminal . . . In order to meet [this challenge] attention has been shifted away from large numbers of smaller violations . . . to fewer, large-scale violations often carried out by persons or organized groups intent on commercial gain . . . As part of this refocusing of limited law enforcement resources on large-scale or commercial violations, the use of undercover techniques has increased many fold." Bavin then went on to describe five sting operations. It is possible to ascribe a dollar size to the first two he discussed. He described "Operation Gillnet" as "an eighteen-month covert operation involving illegal commercial dealings in Great Lakes fish, featuring the use of a Chicago wholesale fish business as a 'cover' . . . It revealed that as many as 60,000 pounds of fish were illegally taken from the Great Lakes and sold each year . . . To date, 90 individuals have been convicted" (Bavin 1985). We may put an upper bound on the value of these fish, primarily lake trout but including less valuable fish as well, by estimating $3.33 per lb. as an average wholesale price. With this generous estimate, "as many as 60,000 pounds a year" translates into "up to $200,000 a year." After costs are subtracted the profit is less. This hardly seems enough to support an organized group of 90 people intent on commercial gain.

The amounts Operation Falcon found being paid for *wild* raptors in the United States were small even in comparison with those in Operation Gillnet. Except for McPartlin's transactions with the foreigners, Luckman and Ciesielski, *documented* payments, almost all to

McPartlin, averaged less than $10,000 per year. Expenses were much higher than sales, so that a commercial operation was not even realistically simulated by the USFWS scam.

In contrast, there was some commercial activity in wild North American raptors (both legal and illegal) in Canada independent of that generated by the USFWS sting. Legal and illegal sales combined by those Canadian residents engaged in illegal activities appear to have amounted to an average of about $350,000 per year before deduction of expenses. Had it taken place in the United States rather than Canada, most of the illegal portion of that commercial traffic could have been stopped by ordinary law enforcement practice, i.e., without a sting. A simple inspection in January 1984 found the principal suspect in possession of 19 raptors including Peregrines, Red-tailed Hawks, Northern Goshawks, and Gyrfalcons in apparent violation of an Ontario law, but action was delayed by a challenge to the law's applicability to raptors (P. Meerveld pers. comm.).

NUMBER OF PEREGRINES TAKEN OR SOLD ILLEGALLY

While the USFWS originally claimed that it knew of 181 Peregrines illegally taken or smuggled (Anon. USFWS report circa 1984), by July 1985 its claim of the number taken illegally in the United States during the 3.5 years of Operation Falcon had shrunk to 71 (Lambertson 1985). Even this number has not been substantiated. When checked against USFWS evidence made available through the Justice Department it appears to be high by a factor of two or three. Table 1 covers all allegedly illegal Peregrines described in publicly available legal documents on Operation Falcon. (The public documents consist of indictments, affidavits describing alleged offenses that were presented to magistrates by USFWS Special Agents requesting search warrants, and so-called "Rule 11 Statements" which are summaries of the evidence that the prosecutor would have presented had a case settled by plea bargain actually come to trial.) Data in Table 1 are consistent with the nonpublic evidence that prosecutors are required to provide to defendant's counsel in those cases where such evidence has been made available to the author. Altogether, it lists only 35 Peregrines held illegally in the United States, and 11 of these appear to be based on information from sources of dubious validity; only 24 appear to be credible allegations. Thirty-five Peregrines in a 3.5-year period is 10 Peregrines per year allegedly involved in illegal activities (many of which constituted noncommercial taking, transfer, or band manipulation). The smaller and more believable number of 24 over 3.5 years averages to only 7 birds per year.

The number of Peregrines allegedly sold illegally in the United States was much smaller. Table 1 shows a total of 16 Peregrines allegedly

TABLE 1. Wild Peregrines involved in Operation Falcon in the United States.

Case	Indictment or other charge	State	Data source	No. and age of wild birds[a]	Allegations
A	CR84-42-GF	UT	Rule 11 statement	5 fully grown	5 people bought 5 *F. p. anatum* from McPartlin who earlier had bought 8 smuggled from Canada by Luckman, a Canadian[d]
B	CR84-41-GF	UT	Rule 11 statement	1 fully grown	2 people exchanged bands between 2 Peregrines and placed band from 1 dead Gyrfalcon onto live one
C	Not charged	UT	Affidavit	1 nestling	Removed *F. p. anatum* from eyrie
D	CR84-51-GF	TX	Trial evidence	1 nestling, 1 passage[b]	3 people bought 2 *F. p. anatum* from McPartlin; transported them to Texas
E	CR84-44-GF	TX	Indictment	1 unknown	2 people bought 1 Peregrine from McPartlin; transported it to Texas
F	CR84-45-GF	IL	Rule 11 statement	1 passage or older	2 people placed band from dead Peregrine on an illegal *F. p. tundrius* and shipped it to McPartlin
G	CR84-230	AZ	Judgement and order	1 passage (flying immature)	Illegally possessed and transported 1 *F. p. anatum* he had trapped in Arizona
H	CR84-123	MO	Plea agreement, affidavit	1 grown[c]	Possessed illegal wild *F. p. anatum* allegedly obtained through chain of owners, the second of whom placed a black (wild-bred) marker on it
I	CRR-85-43-ECR	NV	Plea agreement, affidavit	3 nestlings	Banded 3 wild *F. p. anatum* nestlings (1 alleged to be later possessed by defendant in Case H)
J	Not charged	NV	Affidavit	6 eggs	Sold 6 *F. p. pealei* hatched from wild eggs to C. Ciesielski, father of Lothar Ciesielski; no data on how exported
K	2 convicted of misdemeanors	UT	Statements by Gavitt in trial; affidavit	3 eggs	2 people and 2 agents removed 3 *F. p. anatum* eggs from eyrie; McPartlin hatched 1 of them
L	1 convicted of misdemeanors; 1 acquitted	MT	Affidavit; defendant statement	2 nestlings	2 people purchased 2 young *F. p. anatum* from McPartlin (allegedly from same nest as bird in Item D)
M	Not charged	UT	Affidavit	5 eggs	Broke 5 wild *F. p. anatum* eggs while trying to take them from Utah eyrie
N	Convicted of misdemeanor	IL	Affidavit	2 passage	Trapped 1 *F. p. tundrius* and 1 other Peregrine (subspecies unknown); released them within 2 weeks
O	Not charged	UT	Affidavit	1 passage	Flew illegal *F. p. tundrius* received from another person
P	Not included in charges (pleaded guilty to other offenses	IL	Affidavit	2 passage	Trapped 2 passage *F. p. tundrius* on fall migration; gave both away

[a] Total listed judged credible: 24.
Total listed judged not credible: 11.
[b] Same bird as in Case G.
[c] Same bird as 1 of nestlings in Case I.
[d] Other 3 Peregrines appear to have been given away.

TABLE 1 (cont.).

Case	Appraisal of evidence	Apparent source of Peregrines	Allegedly laundered through breeding project?	Allegation of how "covered"	Type of bands	No. allegedly bought or sold in U.S.[g]
A	Guilty Plea	Canada via McPartlin	No	Applied 4 bands intended for captive-bred hybrids	4 yellow nylon and 1 Canadian)	5 bought from sting
B	Conviction	Utah eyrie	No	Exchanged bands; misused band issued for captive-bred	1 black & 1 yellow nylon	None
C		Utah eyrie	?	Unknown	Unknown	None
D	1 conviction; 2 not guilty	Utah eyrie, Arizona	1 McP,[f] 1 No	McPartlin placed bands for captive-bred birds on wild birds	Yellow nylon	2 bought from sting
E	1 guilty plea; charges dropped on other	Unknown	No	Buyer provided band which McPartlin placed on bird	Yellow nylon	1 bought from sting
F	Guilty plea	Trapped in Illinois	No	Reported transfer of pre-act bird	Black nylon	None
G	Guilty plea	Arizona	No	Used band intended for captive-bred hybrid	Yellow nylon	None
H	Assumed to be true because of plea bargain	Utah eyrie	No	Used band intended for captive-bred young	Yellow nylon	None
I	Assumed to be true because of plea bargain	Utah eyrie	Yes	Used 1 band intended for captive-bred, 2 for wild birds	1 yellow nylon, 2 black nylon	None
J	Not credible	Canada	Yes	No attempt to appear legal	None	6 sold to Ciesielski
K	Guilty pleas	Utah eyrie	McP[f]	McPartlin placed band for captive-bred bird on wild young	Yellow nylon	None
L	Conviction	Utah eyrie[e]	McP[f]	McPartlin placed bands for captive-bred birds on wild young	Yellow nylon	2 bought from sting
M	Not credible	Utah eyrie	No	None	None	None
N	Conviction	On migration in Illinois	No	No cover (released)	None	None
O	Credible	On migration?	No	Not stated	Unknown	None
P	Credible	On migration in Illinois	No	1 not covered, 1 not stated	1 bird had none, 1 not stated	None

[e] Allegedly taken from eyrie by defendants in Cases A and G.

[f] McP = McPartlin's.

[g] No. alleged bought or sold judged credible: 10.
(All were sold by McPartlin, sting operator; those birds he bought from Canada not counted: 5 of them would be duplications of birds listed here, remainder not relevant to sales by other American falconers.)
No. alleged bought or sold judged not credible: 6.

sold. The evidence for six of the 16 consists of uncorroborated statements by Lothar Ciesielski, who has a reputation for untruthfulness. Even if all of the allegations are accepted as true, they amount to less than five Peregrines per year sold in the United States during the period of the sting.

There could be a legitimate concern that the illegal exports from Canada might have provided a major leakage of Peregrines from North America; however, the USFWS reported to Congress that the total illegal take of Peregrines in Canada during Operation Falcon was only 40, or about 12 per year (Lambertson 1985). This figure is consistent with export data reported in accordance with the Convention on International Trade in Endangered Species (CITES). It shows an annual average of 30 Peregrines apparently exported legally from 1980-83 (*Traffic* 1985). Since the illegal birds were all (or nearly all) exported with falsified papers showing them to be legal, they were included in the CITES count. Their total must have been substantially fewer than 30 per year since many birds known to have been legally produced through captive breeding were exported (for example, to Minnesota for release to the wild).

ILLEGAL TAKE COMPARED WITH OTHER CAUSES OF ATTRITION

Table 2 lists significant known causes of losses from the North American population of Peregrines and provides rough estimates of their magnitude. The Law Enforcement Division placed priority in Operation Falcon on work to "stop the unlawful take from the wild of protected raptors, particularly endangered Peregrine Falcons" (Anon. USFWS report circa 1984). It is evident that Operation Falcon concentrated attention and public resources on the least significant listed cause of attrition — illegal taking in the United States and Canada for falconry.

HARASSMENT OF BREEDERS OF CAPTIVE PEREGRINES

McPartlin questioned many individuals with whom he became involved during the sting as to their knowledge of the activities of raptor breeders, whose supply of young Peregrines and Gyrfalcons was envied by many who wanted birds. Some of the questioned individuals were willing to conjecture that major breeders were obtaining young or eggs from the wild and passing them off as captive-bred. Equally often, they alleged that the breeders were illegally selling some of their output. There was another motive beyond envy. When Lothar Ciesielski visited McPartlin, he admitted that he and his father had been smuggling nestlings from the Swedish wild and passing them off as captive-bred. He clearly wanted to believe others were doing what he was doing — a common desire of those outside the law. His taped conversations include conjectures of illegal behavior by most of the important breeders in the United States and Canada.

Despite major errors that even a cursory check would have found (e.g., that a prominent Canadian had been fired from a job which he in fact still held), the USFWS included many of the conjectures elicited by McPartlin in a briefing it provided to hundreds of its own agents and state agents to prepare them for the 29 June 1984 search and arrest operation (Anon. USFWS report circa 1984). Later someone used hard copies of the slides employed in that briefing in what appears to have been an attempt to influence the Washington State Game Commission to disapprove proposed regulations that would permit sale of captive-bred Peregrines. Copies of the briefing report quickly passed into the hands of others from the state of Washington.

Using the same dubious information, the USFWS developed a questionnaire whose preamble alleged that a major nonprofit organization had been involved in taking birds and eggs from the wild and selling birds illegally. During the searches and "inspections" carried out when Operation Falcon was made public, agents across the United States read this preamble to individuals who chanced to be at the facilities which were searched or "inspected" and then solicited corroboration through a series of questions, the answers to which were recorded. The questionnaire also made the novel assumption that if the organization gave a surplus (e.g., nonbreeding) bird to anyone who either before or after made a donation to support the breeding program, the donor had bought a raptor illegally. This was hardly likely to inspire donations by falconers, who have furnished nearly all of the labor and much of the private financing for captive breeding of Peregrines both for falconry and for release to the wild.

After Operation Falcon was made public, the USFWS and its Canadian counterparts also conducted detailed audits of the records of the major captive breeding projects in the United States and Canada because they suspected that discrepancies between their own records and those of the projects indicated diversion of birds to illegal channels. This protracted accounting was disruptive and extremely costly to the breeding programs, particularly to the Canadian Wildlife Service program in Alberta. It did demonstrate that the government records contained so many errors as to make their use counterproductive and that breeder record-keeping systems should contain the kind of self-checking provisions found in good accounting systems.

TABLE 2. Rough estimates of attrition of Peregrines from various causes.

Cause of attrition	No. Peregrines/year	Basis of estimate
Illegal take in United States	7-20	Lower limit — analysis of legal documents (Table 1); upper limit — USFWS claims (Lambertson 1985)
Illegal take in Canada (primarily for export)	12	USFWS statement to Congress (Lambertson 1985)
Killing for taxidermy in Latin America	10-200	CITES reports of more dead raptors in international trade than live ones, apparently for taxidermy use in Europe and Asia (*Traffic* 1985)
Illegal take in Mexico for pet trade and falconry	Approx. 100	Letters from Mexican falconers reporting birds sold in public markets and illegal exports
Random shooting by hunters	> 200	Over 2% of an estimated 10,000 birds alive at end of breeding season are shot based on conservative evaluation of pre-1964 band recoveries (Shor 1970b) plus recent reports of recoveries of birds banded in Greenland (Mattox and Seegar Chapter 4) and Sweden (Lindberg et al. Chapter 18)
Electrocution on power poles	> 300	High frequency of electrocution of falconers' birds indicates more important than random shooting
Natural attrition	3000-3750	Assume minimum 10,000 at end of breeding season, half just fledged, half adult. Assume 50% attrition of immatures, 10% to 25% of adults
Pesticides, used legally in Latin America and illegally in the United States and Canada	5000	Assume current population at end of breeding season half that in pre-DDT era; then number not being produced equals number now produced

IMPLICATIONS FOR MANAGEMENT OF THE USFWS

The direct impact of the Operation Falcon sting on the Peregrine was clearly negative. There was essentially no illegal commerce in live Peregrines in the United States to be stopped. The adverse effects of mounting a sting operation to encourage, catch, and punish a few amateurs willing to involve themselves in illegal taking was a high price to pay for reducing a small threat to the Peregrine population. None of the few professional poachers and traffickers caught by Operation Falcon received punishment commensurate with their crimes, and at least one of them is still trading in raptors. The gratuitous attacks on captive breeders were damaging. Even more important, Operation Falcon diverted resources and attention from the more important problems listed in Table 2.

The reason for this state of affairs on matters involving the Peregrine can be found in a shift of authority within the USFWS from experts on wildlife biology and management to the Division of Law Enforcement. Like any bureaucracy, the Division of Law Enforcement is interested primarily in what it is authorized and funded to do, which is not the preservation of wildlife populations but the enforcement of laws and regulations. The public has never heard anything from the Chief of Law Enforcement describing the needs of any raptor population and what his organization has done to meet them. Rather, his speeches contain many statistics on the number of convictions obtained and the dollars in fines and months of imprisonment, probation and community service imposed on persons who have violated the law.

There is another, less obvious impact of the shift from wildlife management to police work. Because of the nature of their work, police forces tend to become closed communities with a "we against them" attitude. Outsiders are treated with suspicion, and communication becomes difficult. The Law Enforcement Division has the outward trappings and the inner sociology of a police force. The locked and guarded offices of its Chief are physically isolated from the rest of the USFWS. It therefore could, under the best of circumstances, have difficulty working with private organizations as well as other government organizations. When this inherent handicap is complicated by the sour relations with most groups involved in raptor conservation resulting from Operation Falcon, it is easily understood how the spirit of cooperation that formerly existed between both the falconry and raptor breeding communities and the USFWS has been eroded.

It would be unfortunate to end with the thought that mismanagement and misdirection of resources will inevitably continue, since there is a good possibility that it will be brought under control. The Congress has been informed of the abuses in Operation Falcon through a series of hearings culminating in a hearing before the House Subcommittee on Fisheries and Wildlife Conservation and the Environment. That hearing, nominally on the extension of the Endangered Species Act, became effectively a brief oversight hearing on Operation Falcon, in which the USFWS Division of Law Enforcement was subjected to much criticism by the Subcommittee members. The directorate of the USFWS should by now be concerned about the behavior of its law enforcement division. It therefore seems likely that the authority to set priorities will move above the Division of Law Enforcement, and the priorities will be directed more towards the needs of wildlife. For the longer term, however, it will be essential that power move laterally from the Division of Law Enforcement to the people in USFWS who have responsibilities in population dynamics, ecology, biology, and wildlife management.

Editors' Note: Operation Falcon eventually turned into a joint U.S.-Canadian law enforcement fiasco. Concerned citizens should read Paul McKay's (1987) series of articles in The Whig-Standard of Kingston, Ontario for a detailed analysis of the Canadian side of the story.

81 | Future Goals and Needs for the Management and Conservation of the Peregrine Falcon

Stanley A. Temple

Whatever I say about the future must remain clouded by uncertainties, for environmental conditions affecting the Peregrine Falcon and other raptors can and do change rapidly in today's world. Imagine how wrong my comments on the future would probably have been if a symposium had been held in 1945, and I had been given the same charge I now have. Nonetheless, my crystal ball — murky as it is — still provides some tantalizing clues about how the Peregrine's future may unfold. Indulge me while I engage in a bit of augury on what we now understand about the biology of the Peregrine Falcon.

PRESENT AND FUTURE GOALS FOR PEREGRINE MANAGEMENT

Almost all conservation programs for endangered species have established their goals on the basis of the past, inasmuch as they typically try to restore depleted populations to some former size or distribution. With Peregrines it is typically the pre-DDT population status that sets the standard (e.g., Bollengier 1979). Much hope for the future of Peregrines has been placed on the fact that the impact of one limiting factor, toxic chemicals, has now been reduced over many temperate portions of the Peregrine's cosmopolitan range. With removal of this one factor Peregrine populations seem likely to recover their numbers gradually until some new limiting factor exerts its effect.

Limiting Factors in the Future. — Size and distribution of future Peregrine populations will be determined by new limiting factors which, given the magnitude of environmental changes in recent times, are not likely to be identical to those in the late pre-DDT environment. Nest sites and food supplies are factors most likely to become limiting. Peregrine nest sites, especially artificial ones, can be readily manipulated. Prey populations, on the other hand, are less easily managed to

843

specifically benefit the Peregrine, and indeed we have not had examples of this approach.

Future populations, therefore, will eventually be limited by availability of nest sites where natural prey populations are adequate. This would be similar to the pre-DDT situation in which preferred nesting sites on cliffs were important limiting factors in most areas. There is, however, likely to be an important difference. The ultimate number and distribution of nest sites for future Peregrine populations will almost certainly be influenced in several regions by the availability of artificial ledges on buildings, bridges, towers, other artificial structures, and improved natural sites.

The future size and distribution of some Peregrine populations will, therefore, probably be determined by the ability of conservation-minded friends of the Peregrine Falcon to provide adequate nest sites. We have already learned how it is possible to encourage Peregrines to live in areas of North America previously unavailable to them by imprinting fledglings on artificial nest sites in areas with adequate prey.

In the more settled portions of the temperate zone the future size and distribution of Peregrine populations may, therefore, be very different from the pre-DDT situation. In less developed portions of the temperate zone and certainly throughout most of the rest of the Peregrine's vast range, manipulations of nest sites will probably be impossible. This dictates that Peregrines in these parts of the world will continue to be limited by the number and distribution of preferred natural nest sites with adequate prey nearby. These areas are crucial limiting resources that, in the absence of artificial sites, must be protected and managed for the benefit of the Peregrine.

Possible Modifications of Recovery Efforts. — We have been given a generally encouraging picture of the recovery of Peregrine populations in North America and Europe. The recovery is, however, still in progress, and Peregrine populations have not yet reached recovery goals in most areas. Is there anything that can be done now, while recoveries are in midstream, to better ensure the eventual attainment of goals?

As I listened to the many excellent reports on the courses of the recoveries of various populations, a few unexpected patterns emerged. I would like to expand on one of these, for it may play an important role in the Peregrine's future.

As we all know, *Falco peregrinus* literally means the wandering falcon, and one is generally given the impression in the literature that Peregrines are capable of migrating and dispersing over great distances and typically do so. Despite this reputation, the reports given at this symposium have revealed a bird that, at least in terms of dispersal, is something of a "homebody," showing consistently strong philopatry to natal areas. Although this tendency for Peregrines to breed as close as possible to their natal areas has probably always been the case, the pattern becomes particularly noticeable in closely monitored, small, isolated populations.

Natural recoveries, particularly the closely monitored ones in the British Isles and Europe, seem to have been narrowly restricted to areas within or immediately adjacent to regions where remnant populations or breeding pairs survived the pesticide era. There seems to have been little tendency for young birds to disperse to areas where local populations were extirpated. This pattern seems to hold even when, for example in the British Isles, densities around these pesticide-era refugia reach such high levels that competitive exclusion from nest sites occurs (Ratcliffe Chapter 17, Newton and Mearns Chapter 62). Similarly, in North America reintroduced Peregrines have stayed remarkably close to the areas in which they were released (Barclay Chapter 51). This tendency has certainly helped Peregrines, which might otherwise have scattered widely, to find each other and form breeding pairs. Strong philopatry is not uncommon in birds, but I am a bit surprised that Peregrine Falcons are apparently not aggressive dispersers that can recolonize vacant habitat over a wide area.

If this pattern is as real as the reports seem to imply, it has some potential implications for recoveries of remnant populations. Strong philopatry in small, isolated, recovering populations suggests that each of these local populations (or demes) is expanding intrinsically without much demographic or genetic input from other local populations. In the population geneticists' parlance, they are passing through separate genetic bottlenecks, and the outcome of each bottleneck becomes an independent issue with little relationship to what might be happening genetically and demographically in the other isolated populations. Some of these remnant local populations became very small during the pesticide era; in some cases apparently only a handful of pairs remained in a region. These small, semi-closed, local populations reached such critically small sizes that stochastic genetic changes are almost certain to have occurred in their respective gene pools. Strong philopatry always leads to elevated rates of inbreeding, and all of the attendant risks of close inbreeding become disproportionately great if the population is small.

Because many of these recovering populations are already closely monitored and managed, an additional management strategy could mitigate against possible genetic problems that might eventually hinder the recovery of some populations in future generations. I suggest that it would be prudent and relatively straightforward to force gene flow between isolated populations by exchanging eggs or nestlings among eyries, thereby ensuring a degree of outbreeding that might otherwise not be achieved for many generations in isolated populations. I was encouraged to learn that at least in Sweden such prophylactic measures are already under way (Lindberg Chapter 58). They should probably begin elsewhere.

Furthermore, if recolonization of vacant range is likely to be a slow process — as strong philopatry suggests — it might be desirable to use reintroduction techniques to establish released birds in areas which are unlikely to be colonized naturally for some time. The logic of doing such work now is that there is still much momentum for managing Peregrine Falcons. Much of that momentum is likely to wane as recoveries proceed and Peregrines become less threatened.

Genotypes and Phenotypes in Future Populations. — From what I have just said about philopatry and reduced gene flow between recovering local populations or populations that have been reintroduced into different areas, we can speculate about the genotypes and phenotypes of future Peregrine populations. At present, our best understood evidence of genotypic differences between regional Peregrine populations comes from the study of phenotypic differences among the various subspecies, although more recent work on biochemical systems is yielding increasingly sophisticated results (cf. Morizot Chapter 74, Longmire Chapter 75). The phenotypic characteristics that allow us to segregate regional populations into recognizable subspecies clearly have a genetic basis. Regional subspecies, in fact, retain their unique phenotypes because philopatry and resulting inbreeding have fixed certain alleles in the local populations.

With many Peregrine populations now recovering from small remnant pesticide-era populations, there have almost certainly been substantial changes in gene frequencies as a result of stochastic events while populations were passing through major bottlenecks. These changes in gene frequencies are known collectively as genetic drift, and they may result in birds in a recovered population having markedly different gene frequencies — and phenotypes — from those in the pre-bottleneck populations on which we based our subspecific designations. In the future, therefore, it is likely that systematists will be able to describe new "subspecies" that will be the evolutionary products of the genetic bottlenecks of the pesticide era and of new selective pressures from an altered environment.

Another intriguing genetic issue involves the gene pool of Peregrine populations being formed from individuals bred in captivity and released into vacant habitat, as is the case in the eastern United States. The pedigree records of The Peregrine Fund, Inc. show that the founders of this new population come from diverse genetic backgrounds (Figure 1). Thus the gene pool for the population that is eventually reestablished will certainly be unlike that of the original

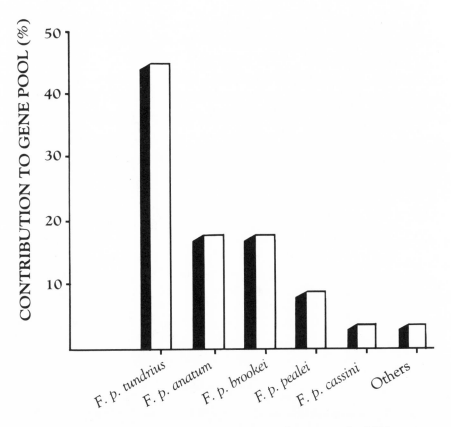

FIGURE 1. Contributions of various subspecies to the gene pool of 758 captive-reared Peregrines released to the wild in the eastern United States, 1975-85; based on pedigree records maintained by The Peregrine Fund, Inc.

gene pool of the eastern population of *F. p. anatum*. A novel regional gene pool will have been created, and individuals in this population will eventually have a new phenotype that reflects relatively stable and adaptive gene frequencies. A new "subspecies" will have been produced.

No "closet" taxonomist — and I count myself as one — could resist the temptation of applying a name to such a new "subspecies." Although I may be jumping the gun by several generations, I suggest that an appropriate subspecific designation for this new eastern North American population of Peregrines, a name that truly reflects its origin, would be: "*Falco peregrinus cadei*." If the future of this population continues to be as encouraging as it appears now, it may be only a few decades before such a nomination could become a reality. I hope future systematists remember my suggestion!

PRESENT AND FUTURE NEEDS FOR PEREGRINE
CONSERVATION

One could easily become complacent about the future of the Peregrine after learning of all the success stories reported during this symposium. Indeed, the future looks bright for some Peregrine populations that only a few years ago seemed headed for extinction. In fact, some populations have now recovered to the point where they can no longer be considered endangered or threatened.

Nonetheless, despite all of the encouraging successes, one must put the Peregrine's recent recovery into perspective. The Peregrine is a cosmopolitan species, one of only four living bird species to achieve a worldwide distribution without the help of human beings. We have heard much about Peregrine populations in North America and Europe (about 20% of the species' range), but relatively little about populations in the remainder of the world. An urgent present need for the conservation of the Peregrine Falcon is basic information on the status and ecology of populations in the rest of its range, where threats to its continued existence have not been reduced as they have in Europe and North America. There is a particular need for information on its status in Japan, China, the Soviet Union, and the Indian subcontinent. In an era in which Peregrine populations have been eliminated in some areas, it is remarkable that we have recently discovered previously unknown breeding populations in areas such as the central Andes of South America (Ellis and Glinski 1980, Jenny et al. 1981, Schoonmaker et al. 1985). Much more pioneering work in new areas needs to be done.

Once the present need for basic information has been satisfied, there is certain to be a future need for Peregrine conservation in regions of the world where falcon biologists have rarely ventured. Whether or not conservation in these areas can be closely modeled after the successful approaches in Europe and North America remains to be determined; more traditional conservation approaches, such as habitat preservation and control of toxic chemicals, may be more appropriate than such radical approaches as captive breeding.

The immediate future of the Peregrine Falcon seems secure, but its continued preeminence as a globally successful, cosmopolitan species may be in jeopardy. The global distribution and relative sizes of regional populations that existed prior to the pesticide era are not likely to be duplicated by Peregrines of the future. Still, I hope, a new symbiosis between humanity and the Peregrine will ensure that this remarkable falcon has a guaranteed place in the future.

Summary and
Conclusion

Summary

Ian C. T. Nisbet

At the Madison Conference in 1965, it was established that many regional populations of Peregrine Falcons had declined rapidly and that the species appeared headed for widespread extirpation (Hickey 1969). The North American Peregrine Surveys of 1970 and 1975 showed that the population declines had continued and had extended to arctic populations (Cade and Fyfe 1970, Fyfe et al. 1976a). Retrospective studies by Peakall and Kiff (1979, Chapter 34) have further shown that populations throughout much of the Peregrine's world range experienced significant levels of DDE contamination and eggshell thinning during the 1950s and 1960s.

The papers presented at this symposium in 1985 show that most of these trends have been reversed within the past 10-15 years and that many regional populations have started to recover. Among the 48 regional or local populations for which recent data are presented, only a few appear still to be in serious trouble. Local populations in northern Germany (Mebs Chapter 19), southern England (Ratcliffe Chapter 17), parts of Yukon Territory (Mossop Chapter 9), and probably the northern Rocky Mountains (Enderson et al. Chapter 12) are still absent or virtually so. Local populations in parts of Spain (Heredia et al. Chapter 25), the Northwest Territories (Bromley Chapter 7), Colorado (Enderson et al. Chapter 12), and Texas (Hunt et al. Chapter 16) are reported to have declined within the past 10 years. Local populations in parts of Sweden (Lindberg et al. Chapter 18), Alberta and Yukon Territory (Bromley Chapter 7, Bromley and Matthews Chapter 8), and Oregon and California (Walton et al. Chapter 14) appear to be stable at markedly reduced numbers. Some of these populations (e.g., those in Colorado and central California) have begun to respond favorably to reintroductions and are no longer critically endangered. Apart from these populations, however, most reports presented in this symposium describe local or regional populations that are reproducing well and are either increasing or stable at relatively high densities (see Kiff's Commentary on Part 1

851

and Newton's Commentary on Part 2). In North America and Germany, Peregrines have been successfully established in cities, and many are now breeding on buildings or bridges.

This remarkable reversal in the fortunes of Peregrine Falcon populations has been the central theme of this symposium. Recovery of these populations has resulted from a series of successful measures to protect and manage the species. These include: (1) recognition of the severity of the problem and prompt initiation of research into its causes; (2) identification of organochlorine pesticides as the primary cause of the declines (despite initial scepticism by academic scientists and organized opposition by industry consultants); (3) partial or complete bans on uses of DDT and other organochlorines in most developed countries (despite vigorous promotion of these pesticides by agricultural and industrial interests); (4) enhanced legal protection of the Peregrine in many countries; (5) active protection of many eyries and hack sites; and (6) striking success in breeding the species in captivity and reintroducing it into parts of its lost range.

These achievements required arduous field work, skillful scientific analysis, determined political and regulatory activity, and imaginative and dedicated management. Success in so remarkably short a time reflects great credit on all concerned — not only the individuals who led the effort but also the army of enthusiasts who promoted the Peregrine's cause in the field, aviary, laboratory, and courtroom.

Before we indulge in self-congratulation, however, I want to point out one major qualification and to pose four questions. The qualification is that most of our stories of successful management and recovery of Peregrine populations come from a limited number of developed countries in Europe, North America, and Australia. We know little or nothing about the current status or trends of Peregrine populations in Asia, Africa, and South America — areas which comprise more than half the species' range. The work of Peakall and Kiff (1979, Chapter 34) has shown that many of these populations were contaminated with DDE and experienced substantial eggshell thinning, and it is well-known that DDT and other organochlorines continue to be used in many developing countries. Charting the extent and consequences of contamination, working to limit uses of organochlorines, and restoring depleted Peregrine populations in these countries will be major tasks for the 20 years until the next Peregrine conference.

FOUR IRREVERENT QUESTIONS

What Caused the Population Crashes? — Workers in North America have attributed the declines in North American Peregrine populations to reproductive impairment induced by DDE. British workers, however, have pointed out that Peregrines and other birds of prey were able to maintain or increase their populations despite severe reproductive impairment; these workers have attributed the population declines primarily to excessive adult mortality caused by dieldrin poisoning. In the original conference version of this overview paper, I pointed out this divergence of opinion and challenged North American workers to produce critical evidence for the role of DDE. This challenge led to the preparation of two detailed reviews included in this volume (Nisbet Chapter 35, Risebrough and Peakall Commentary on Part 5). The evidence summarized in these reviews suggests that both reproductive impairment and excess adult mortality occurred in Peregrine populations in the 1950s and 1960s, and that population declines would not have been as rapid as was observed in the absence of either. The relative importance of DDE, dieldrin, and other pesticides may have varied from area to area and from time to time, but the critical evidence — direct measures of exposure during the periods of decline — is lacking for nearly all areas.

What Is Known About the Population Dynamics of Peregrines? — Despite extensive fieldwork on Peregrine populations, the only population model based on detailed data is that of Newton and Mearns (Chapter 62). This study indicated an adult mortality rate not exceeding 10%, about 12% of pairs holding territory but not laying, about 47% of territory-holding pairs raising young with an average of 1.15 young per pair, an average age at first breeding of 2-2.5 years, and 44% survival from fledging to adult breeding age. This combination of parameters led to a 12% annual increase in the local breeding population. Other data reported in this book, however, suggest wide variability in these population parameters. Estimates of annual adult mortality vary from 5% in Australia (Olsen and Olsen Chapter 28) to more than 30% in the Queen Charlotte Islands, Canada, increasing to 43% among females that raised young (Nelson Chapter 69). The data presented by these and other contributors suggest great variability in the Peregrine's population parameters, especially in adult mortality and age at first breeding. This flexibility has enabled some populations to persist for many years despite very low productivity (as in central California), and other populations to recover very rapidly when stresses were relieved (as in northern England and Wales); it should be taken more fully into account in population modeling. It should also be recognized that some commonly reported parameters, such as the number of fledged young per successful nest, are not very useful in assessing population status and viability.

What Is Being Learned About the Biology of the Peregrine from Captive Breeding Programs? — Although extensive captive breeding programs in several countries have produced thousands of young Peregrines, very little information on the biology of captive-bred Peregrines has been reported, even in this symposium. Important aspects of breeding biology that are difficult to study in the field, but would be easy to study in the aviary, include the following: age-related breeding performance; differential growth and viability of young according to sex, brood size, and hatching order; physiological costs of breeding; eggshell structure; clutch size; and growth rates. Little systematic information has been reported on the characteristics (parentage, egg and eggshell characteristics, fledging weight, etc.) of the captive-raised birds that have survived to enter the wild breeding population. I suggest that we may be losing two important opportunities: to collect important biological data on the species, and to identify the characteristics that lead to survival of captive-bred birds in the ecological conditions into which we release them.

Where Have All the Captive-reared Birds Gone? — Despite success in reestablishing breeding pairs in several areas, the number of captive-reared birds known to be nesting in the wild in 1985 was only a small fraction of the number that had been released (Table 1). After excluding birds released in 1984 and 1983 (many of which would have been too young to breed in 1985), I estimate that 10-15% of the birds released through 1982 had survived to enter the known breeding population. In comparison, about 44% of wild Peregrines fledged in Scotland returned to breed 2-3 years later (Newton and Mearns Chapter 62). Perhaps, then, we should not be so eager to congratulate ourselves on our success in reestablishing approximately 100 breeding pairs; instead, we might ask why we do not have twice that number. More thorough study of the parentage and other pre-fledging characteristics of the birds that succeed in the wild might lead to a better understanding of why the majority do not succeed. Such study might lead to improvement in our captive breeding programs and to production of birds that are better matched to the environments into which we release them.

TABLE 1. Reported results of programs to reintroduce Peregrine Falcons into 7 areas (source: this book, Chapters 51-59).

Area	No. of birds released	No. of breeding pairs found in 1985
Eastern United States	511	25
Canada	588[a]	7+
Minnesota	23	0
Rocky Mountains (U. S.)	415	45+
California	147	62
West Germany	142	9+
Sweden	64[a]	3

[a] Includes birds released through 1985.

CONCLUDING REMARKS

By asking these questions, I am not seeking to detract from our success in reversing the declines in many Peregrine populations; I am merely drawing attention to the fact that many important questions about the biology of the Peregrine and about its decline and recovery are still incompletely answered. If we had better answers to these questions, we could manage the species better. But if we had waited for complete answers before starting to manage it, many more local and regional populations would have disappeared. Practical management of a wild species must always be based on incomplete information. In the case of the Peregrine, our success has resulted from taking action on a number of fronts, even before we had conclusive information on the factors causing the decline or on the measures required to reverse it. Our task over the next 20 years is to learn enough from our successes and failures to maintain the recovery of the species in Europe and North America, and to promote its recovery in the rest of the world. At present, we can justifiably congratulate ourselves on the successes achieved since the Madison Conference in 1965. I would particularly like to express appreciation to the leaders of this effort during the past 20 years — Joe Hickey, Derek Ratcliffe, Richard Fyfe, and Tom Cade.

Conclusion

The Editors

Ian Nisbet originally posed his four "irreverent questions" at the Sacramento Conference in order to stimulate discussion and research. We wish to comment briefly on them in closing.

What Caused the Population Crashes? — This question has already received a great deal of attention. We wish to add only that exposure to organochlorine pesticides was measured directly during the decline of the arctic Alaskan Peregrines between 1967-73 (Cade et al. 1971, Peakall et al. 1975). The studies revealed high DDE residues in egg contents in association with abnormally thin eggshells and lowered reproductive rate, but there was no indication of increased adult mortality from pesticide toxicity. Since the mid-1970s, the reverse trends in DDE contamination and related reproductive parameters have been evident (Ambrose et al. Chapter 37). A similar pattern was also reported in the Rocky Mountains (Enderson and Craig 1974), and wild Prairie Falcons experimentally fed substantial amounts of dieldrin in the breeding season experienced no apparent mortality (Enderson and Berger 1970).

What Is Known About the Population Dynamics of Peregrines? — As Nisbet has implied, much more needs to be learned about the dynamics of Peregrine populations. At the same time, several contributors to this book have made significant clarifications, either from a theoretical modeling approach (Hunt Chapter 63, Grier and Barclay Chapter 66, Newton Commentary on Part 8) or from a factual, empirical approach (Monneret Chapter 23, Newton and Mearns Chapter 62, Enderson and Craig Chapter 65). Enough is known about Peregrines to place them among those species whose *breeding* populations are normally buffered against wide annual variations in both mortality and natality rates because the number of breeders is limited by the fixed distribution and occurrence of specific nesting biotopes or "serviceable breeding locations" (Hunt Chapter 63), which Hickey (1942) likened to "ecological magnets." This limitation on breeders produces a surplus of nonbreeding adults

857

when natality exceeds mortality for n years. Thus, while vacancies in the breeding population are quickly replaced from this "floating" adult population, overall numbers are basically controlled by density independent factors associated with the environment.

What Is Being Learned About the Biology of the Peregrine from Captive Breeding Programs? — While captive breeding has been geared primarily toward producing as many young Peregrines as possible for reintroduction, a good deal of significant biological information has been accumulated nevertheless. Only some of this information has been published: for example, on courtship and mating behavior (Wrege and Cade 1977; see also sections on behavior in Cramp and Simmons 1980 for the Peregrine, Gyrfalcon, and Lanner), on incubation and hatching (Burnham 1983, Weaver and Cade 1983), on the physical characteristics of eggshells (Burnham 1983, Burnham et al. 1984) and characteristics of semen (Hoolihan and Burnham 1982), on sexual imprinting (Cade 1980, 1982, Weaver and Cade 1983), and on parental behavior and development of behavior in young Peregrines (Sherrod 1982, 1983). In addition, Temple et al. (unpubl. ms.) have analyzed data on the geographic and genetic backgrounds of released Peregrine Falcons that have become established as breeders in the eastern United States (see also Barclay and Cade 1983).

One of the most important questions at the outset of the restoration effort was whether or not young birds released by hacking (Sherrod and Cade 1978, Sherrod et al. 1981) would be able to develop self-maintaining capabilities and normal intraspecific social responses in the absence of parental care. This question, which has many interesting theoretical aspects, was the subject of a doctoral dissertation by Sherrod (1982). He demonstrated that, even though interactions between fledgling falcons and their parents involving the manipulation and pursuit of prey are a conspicuous part of normal experience (see Sherrod Chapter 71), self-sufficiency and hunting capability developed on the same schedule and in the same basic ways among parentless young at hack as among those with parents at wild eyries.

Where Have All the Captive-reared Birds Gone? — According to one widespread rumor they have mostly gone to Saudi Arabia, and according to a "working hypothesis" developed by Canadian law enforcement officials they never existed (McKay 1987). In fact, by 1985 some 2000 captive-produced Peregrines had been released in North America, and there is little doubt that such birds are not recruited into the breeding segment of the population as effectively as wild Peregrines. However, the difference may not be as great as Nisbet has indicated. First, the population of south Scotland which

Nisbet cites (Newton and Mearns Chapter 62) is not an "average" population. It has been increasing at a remarkable rate for a number of years, and so its natality and survivorship reflect unusually favorable environmental conditions. Second, while we can state precisely how many captive-produced birds have been released, we can only talk meaningfully about the number of *known* pairs that have become established as breeders. Certainly the *actual* number of reestablished pairs is larger than the known number, but there is no reliable way to estimate the difference. Particularly for the western United States and Canada, the known number could be a small fraction of the actual, conceivably no more than 50%. In the eastern states we may be failing to locate 10% of the breeders each year.

If we focus just on the eastern United States, which is the most thoroughly known region as well as a region where the recovery began with no known remaining wild birds, then Table 1 shows the actual number of falcons released ($n=511$) and estimated to have reached independence ($n=402$) from 1975-83. The table presents two simplified estimates of survival for all cohorts; one assumes 50% survival of first year birds and 90% per year thereafter (similar to the Newton and Mearns figures for south Scotland); the other estimate uses the Barclay and Cade (1983) life table, which assumes 45% survival of the birds reaching independence in the first year and 80% thereafter. Both models assume breeding at two years of age. The table extends both models to 1985 in order to show the predicted number of breeding age birds for that year.

The higher survival rate of the Newton and Mearns model indicates that there should have been about 171 breeding age birds in the 1985 population, or a potential for 85 pairs, while the less favorable assumptions of mortality in the other model give only 84 breeding age birds or potentially 42 pairs. In 1985 we actually recorded 40 pairs and 12 single birds, at least 6 of which were adults (Barclay Chapter 51). The observed results conform remarkably well to the predictions of the Barclay and Cade (1983) model, which derives from Young's (1969) model and which does not differ much from assumptions about mortality, age of first breeding, and other parameters for some wild populations. Obviously these birds reintroduced into eastern North America perform differently from the Peregrines in south Scotland; but the two populations also exist under rather different ecological conditions. There really is no unbiased way to judge how well the reintroduced eastern Peregrines are doing in their environment in comparison to wild birds. The Scottish breeding population has been increasing at an annual rate of about 12% during its recovery phase, while the newly established eastern United States breeding population has been growing at a rate of nearly 50% per

TABLE 1. Estimated survival of Peregrine Falcons released in the eastern United States, 1975–83. Case A is based on 45% survival of the birds reaching independence during the first year and 80% thereafter, as in Barclay and Cade (1983). Case B uses 50% survival of the birds released during the first year and 90% thereafter, similar to Newton and Mearns (Chapter 62). Both models are extended to 1985 in order to show the projected number of breeding birds, assuming breeding begins at age 2.

	No. released	No. reaching independ.	Case A: no. surviving									
			1976	1977	1978	1979	1980	1981	1982	1983	1984	1985
1975	16	12	5	4	3	2	1	0	0	0	0	0
1976	37	25		11	9	7	6	5	4	3	2	2
1977	46	35			16	13	10	8	6	5	4	3
1978	53	34				15	12	10	8	6	5	4
1979	52	40					18	14	11	9	7	6
1980	65	55						25	20	16	13	10
1981	84	60							27	22	17	14
1982	79	72								32	25	20
1983	79	69									31	25
Projected total at breeding age												84

	No. released	No. reaching independ.	Case B: no. surviving									
			1976	1977	1978	1979	1980	1981	1982	1983	1984	1985
1975	16	12	8	7	6	6	5	5	4	4	3	3
1976	37	25		18	17	15	13	12	11	10	9	8
1977	46	35			23	21	19	17	15	14	12	11
1978	53	34				26	24	21	19	17	16	14
1979	52	40					26	23	21	19	17	15
1980	65	55						32	29	26	24	21
1981	84	60							42	38	34	31
1982	79	72								39	36	32
1983	79	69									39	36
Projected total at breeding age												171

year; but again, these are not really fair comparisons because most of the serviceable breeding locations in the eastern United States remain vacant, while in Scotland they must be largely occupied.

In conclusion, Nisbet's questions and our responses reveal that not all desired data on Peregrines are contained in this volume despite its size. However, this book does make available, to a wide audience, a summary of current knowledge about the species and its conservation. There are still inadequacies, particularly in our understanding of the Peregrine in vast areas of the developing world. We believe that the efforts of the researchers whose papers appear here provide for a better understanding of this fascinating bird, point out the value of single-species conservation programs, and will inspire new research. Especially needed are studies aimed at developing broad, widely applicable theoretical and biological concepts like those posed by Newton and Mearns (Chapter 62), Hunt (Chapter 63), Nelson (Chapter 69), and Sherrod (Chapter 71); in other words, studies that seek to answer Nisbet's "irreverent questions." The answers to these questions are not limited to Peregrine biology but may be applicable to a growing number of global ecological issues.

Appendices

Laws and Regulations: Their Current Relevance to Peregrine Management

James L. Ruos

The Peregrine has been "managed" as a species of special interest for more than a thousand years. Depending upon time and place, goverments have provided for its protection and authorized its destruction. Early protection was based upon the need to conserve the Peregrine for falconry. Where falconry did not flourish, the Peregrine was considered little more than vermin. There is now ample evidence that these early conservation efforts served more as an expression of social morality than as an effective management program. In spite of harvest by falconers, persecution by game-keepers and egg collectors, the use of this species by humanity has had little impact on healthy populations. In the mid-20th century, DDT and other chemicals were recognized as a threat to the Peregrine in parts of Europe and North America. Environmental laws were enacted to encourage its protection and restoration including actions that prohibited the take of Peregrines for falconry. By 1980, these efforts resulted in the significant recovery of the Peregrine throughout most of its affected range. As a consequence, falconers were joined by a new and much larger group of conservationists who now share a strong emotional interest in the welfare of the Peregrine but who often differ as to its use in falconry. Incumbent upon governments is the responsibility to support such groups by providing for the interests of all citizens as well as the needs of the resource. Where Peregrine populations are no longer in jeopardy, governments should be responsive to the traditional and legitimate needs of falconers by providing biologically sound and realistic laws for the Peregrine's use in falconry.

Peregrine Falcon Recovery Plans: Concept, Implementation, and Utility

John. L. Spinks

Four teams appointed by the U. S. Fish and Wildlife Service developed regional recovery plans for the Peregrine Falcon in Alaska, the Pacific states, the Rocky Mountains/Southwest, and eastern North America. This paper discusses the efficacy of each plan relative to achieving stated recovery goals and objectives and the manner in which each plan is used by the USFWS to identify, fund, and carry out recovery tasks. The team approach to recovery plan development, in particular the integration of ideas from federal, state, and private agencies, has proven successful in achieving agency approval of the plans and support for implementing identified recovery tasks.

Factors Affecting Peregrine Concentrations in Coastal Areas

William W. Cochran

Radio-tagged migrant Peregrine Falcons were followed to and along Atlantic and Gulf of Mexico coastal areas and over the Atlantic Ocean. Hatch-year (HY) Peregrines turned west at sundown when migrating over the ocean, avoided continuously forested areas, and loitered when they encountered markedly new habitat. In particular geographic areas, each of these behaviors can cause a concentration of HY Peregrines. The Assateague Island, Maryland area is unique in that all three behaviors cause HY Peregrine concentrations there by a combined factor on the order of 1000:1.

The Shaheen Falcon, *F. p. peregrinator*, in the Indian Subcontinent

T. Suresh Kumar

A general survey was made and information was collected on *F. p. peregrinator* from various parts of India. Information on the illegal trapping and selling of these birds in recent years is considered. Conservation measures are described. The method used in catching these birds is illustrated in detail. Trapped birds were kept in cages after stitching their eyelids together. Later these birds were taken possibly to Bombay, Calcutta, or other port cities and transported illegally along with pet birds. Reports say that birds were usually taken via sea route and sometimes by air.

Feather Trace Element Studies with Nearctic Peregrine Falcons: A Summary

Jimmie R. Parrish and F. Prescott Ward

In 1978 a study was begun to investigate the trace element content in Peregrine Falcon feathers in North America. The technique of Instrumental Neutron Activation Analysis (INAA) was determined the most expedient method of analyzing feather samples for trace element quantity. Initial results identified 14 trace elements in feathers of nestling Peregrines from the Yukon and Colville rivers in Alaska, and western Greenland. In addition to determining the most useful method of analysis, initial work was designed to test the disparate nature of feather trace element concentrations from various Nearctic nestling localities. Preliminary results indicated that feather trace element quantities are useful in separating Peregrine breeding localities (*Auk* 100(3):560-567). Subsequent studies have been designed to test further trace element quantities as a means of determining geographic origins of migrant Peregrines in the Nearctic. An update of this ongoing research is provided. Concentrations of mercury in Peregrine feathers from western Greenland populations represent the lowest levels isolated thus far and thereby provide a basis for comparison with other populations.

APPENDIX B: Scientific names of all bird species mentioned in text by common name. The common names are listed alphabetically with some synonyms provided. See Appendix C for names of Peregrine subspecies.

Abyssinian Roller
  Coracias abyssinica
Adelie Penguin
  Pygoscelis adeliae
African Crowned Eagle
  Stephanoaetus coronatus
  (often placed in *Spizaetus*)
African Fish Eagle
  Haliaeetus vocifer
African Goshawk
  Accipiter tachiro
African Harrier Hawk
  Polyboroides typus
African Hawk-Eagle
  Hieraaetus spilogaster
African White-backed Vulture
  Gyps africanus
African White-necked Crow
  Corvus leucognaphalus
American Black Duck
  Anas rubripes
American Coot
  Fulica americana
American Kestrel
  Falco sparverius
American Robin
  Turdus migratorius
American Woodcock
  Scolopax minor
Andean Condor
  Vultur gryphus
Aplomado Falcon
  Falco femoralis
Augur Buzzard
  Buteo rufofuscus
  (may be full species, *B. augur*)
Australian Kestrel
  Falco cenchroides
Australian Raven
  Corvus coronoides

Azure-winged Magpie
  Cyanopica cyana
Bald Eagle
  Haliaeetus leucocephalus
Band-tailed Pigeon
  Columba fasciata
Barking Pigeon
  (also called Peale's Pigeon)
  Ducula latrans
Barn Swallow
  Hirundo rustica
Bateleur
  Terathopius ecaudatus
Bat Falcon
  Falco rufigularis
Bearded Vulture
  Gypaetus barbatus
Belted Kingfisher
  Ceryle alcyon
Black-billed Magpie
  Pica pica
Blackbird
  (also called Common Blackbird)
  Turdus merula
Black-crowned Night-Heron
  Nycticorax nycticorax
Black Falcon
  Falco subniger
Black Guillemot
  Cepphus grylle
Black Kite
  Milvus migrans
Black-legged Kittiwake
  Rissa tridactyla
Black-shouldered Kite
  Elanus caeruleus
Black Sparrowhawk
  (also called Great Sparrowhawk)
  Accipiter melanoleucus

Black Stork
  Ciconia nigra
Black Storm-Petrel
  Oceanodroma melania
Black-winged Stilt
  Himantopus himantopus
Blue-and-white Swallow
  Notiochelidon cyanoleuca
Blue Jay
  Cyanocitta cristata
Bonaparte's Gull
  Larus philadelphia
Bonnelli's Eagle
  (also spelled Bonelli's)
  Hieraaetus fasciatus
Booted Eagle
  Hieraaetus pennatus
Brambling
  Fringilla montifringilla
Broad-winged Hawk
  Buteo platypterus
Brown-bellied Swallow
  Notiochelidon murina
Brown Falcon
  Falco berigora
Brown Pelican
  Pelecanus occidentalis
Calandra Lark
  Melanocorypha calandra
California Condor
  Gymnogyps californianus
Canada Goose
  Branta canadensis
Cape Vulture
  Gyps coprotheres
Carolina Parakeet
  Conuropsis carolinensis
Carrion Crow
  Corvus corone
Cassin's Kingbird
  Tyrannus vociferans
Chaffinch
  Fringilla coelebs
Chough
  Pyrrhocorax pyrrhocorax

Cinereous Vulture
  Aegypius monachus
Citril Finch
  Serinus citrinella
Collared Lory
  Phigys solitarius
Collared Petrel
  Pterodroma brevipes
Common Barn-Owl
  Tyto alba
Common Black-headed Gull
  Larus ridibundus
Common Buzzard
  Buteo buteo
Common Grackle
  Quiscalus quiscula
Common Ground Dove
  Columbina passerina
Common Moorhen
  Gallinula chloropus
Common Murre
  Uria aalge
Common Myna
  Acridotheres tristis
Common Poorwill
  Phalaenoptilus nuttallii
Common Quail
  Coturnix coturnix
Common Raven
  Corvus corax
Common Redpoll
  Carduelis flammea
Common Roller
  (also called European Roller)
  Coracias garrulus
Common Sandpiper
  Actitis hypoleucos
Common Snipe
  Gallinago gallinago
Common Swift
  Apus apus
Cooper's Hawk
  Accipiter cooperii
Crag Martin
  Hirundo rupestris

Craveri's Murrelet
  Synthliboramphus craveri
Crimson-crowned Fruit Dove
  Ptilinopus porphyraceus
Curlew Sandpiper
  Calidris ferruginea
Dark Chanting Goshawk
  Melierax metabates
Dunlin
  Calidris alpina
Eagle Owl
  (also called Northern or
  Eurasian Eagle Owl)
  Bubo bubo
Eared Dove
  Zenaida auriculata
Eared Grebe
  Podiceps nigricollis
Eastern Bluebird
  Sialia sialia
Eastern Meadowlark
  Sturnella magna
Eastern Red-footed Falcon
  Falco amurensis
Eastern Reef Heron
  Egretta sacra
Eastern Screech-Owl
  Otus asio
Egyptian Vulture
  Neophron percnopterus
Eleonora's Falcon
  Falco eleonorae
Eurasian Kestrel
  Falco tinnunculus
Eurasian Skylark
  Alauda arvensis
European Bee Eater
  Merops apiaster
European Cuckoo
  (also called Common Cuckoo)
  Cuculus canorus
European Sparrowhawk
  Accipiter nisus
European Starling
  Sturnus vulgaris

Fan-tailed Raven
  Corvus rhipidurus
Ferruginous Hawk
  Buteo regalis
Fiji Goshawk
  Accipiter rufitorques
Fulvous Whistling-Duck
  Dendrocygna bicolor
Gabar Goshawk
  Melierax gabar
Galah
  Cacatua roseicapilla
Glaucous-winged Gull
  Larus glaucescens
Golden Dove
  Ptilinopus luteovirens
Golden Eagle
  Aquila chrysaetos
Golden Oriole
  Oriolus oriolus
Golden Plover
  (properly called Greater
  Golden Plover)
  Pluvialis apricaria
Golden Whistler
  Pachycephala pectoralis
Goldfinch
  (properly called European
  Goldfinch)
  Carduelis carduelis
Gray Catbird
  Dumetella carolinensis
Great Blue Heron
  Ardea herodias
Greater Kestrel
  Falco rupicoloides
Greater Short-toed Lark
  Calandrella cinerea
Greater Spotted Eagle
  Aquila clanga
Great Horned Owl
  Bubo virginianus
Great Spotted Cuckoo
  Clamator glandarius

Great-tailed Grackle
  Quiscalus mexicanus
Greenfinch
  Carduelis chloris
Green Woodpecker
  (also called European
    Green Woodpecker)
  Picus viridis
Griffon Vulture
  Gyps fulvus
Gyrfalcon
  Falco rusticolus
Harris' Hawk
  Parabuteo unicinctus
Heermann's Gull
  Larus heermanni
Helmeted Guineafowl
  Numida meleagris
Herring Gull
  Larus argentatus
Hoopoe
  (properly called Common Hoopoe)
  Upupa epops
Houbara Bustard
  Chlamydotis undulata
House Martin
  Delichon urbica
House Sparrow
  Passer domesticus
Imperial Eagle
  Aquila heliaca
Indian Roller
  Coracias benghalensis
Jackal Buzzard
  Buteo rufofuscus
Jackdaw
  Corvus monedula
Jack Snipe
  (also called European Jack Snipe)
  Lymnocryptes minima
Japanese Quail
  Coturnix japonica
Jay
  (properly called Eurasian Jay)
  Garrulus glandarius

Jungle Myna
  Acridotheres cristatellus
Killdeer
  Charadrius vociferus
Laggar Falcon
  Falco juggar
Lanner Falcon
  Falco biarmicus
Lapland Longspur
  Calcarius lapponicus
Lappet-faced Vulture
  Aegypius tracheliotus
Leach's Storm-Petrel
  Oceanodroma leucorhoa
Least Storm-Petrel
  Oceanodroma microsoma
Lesser Kestrel
  Falco naumanni
Levant Sparrowhawk
  Accipiter brevipes
Linnet
  (also called Eurasian Linnet)
  Acanthis cannabina
Little Eagle
  Hieraaetus morphnoides
Little Owl
  Athene noctua
Little Sparrowhawk
  Accipiter minullus
Little Stint
  Calidris minuta
Lizard Buzzard
  Kaupifalco monogrammicus
Long-crested Eagle
  Lophaetus occipitalis
  (often placed in *Spizaetus*)
Long-legged Buzzard
  Buteo rufinus
Mallard
  Anas platyrhynchos
Many-colored Fruit Dove
  Ptilinopus perousii
Masked Owl
  Tyto novaehollandiae

Merlin
Falco columbarius
Mistle Thrush
Turdus viscivorus
Montagu's Harrier
Circus pygargus
Mourning Dove
Zenaida macroura
Northern Bobwhite
Colinus virginianus
Northern Goshawk
Accipiter gentilis
Northern Harrier
Circus cyaneus
Northern Hobby
Falco subbuteo
Northern Lapwing
Vanellus vanellus
Northern Mockingbird
Mimus polyglottos
Northern Saw-whet Owl
Aegolius acadicus
Northern Shrike
Lanius excubitor
Northern Wheatear
Oenanthe oenanthe
Orange-breasted Falcon
Falco deiroleucus
Osprey
Pandion haliaetus
Ovampo Sparrowhawk
Accipiter ovampensis
Pacific Pigeon
(also called Pacific Fruit Pigeon)
Ducula pacifica
Pacific Swallow
Hirundo tahitica
Pallas' Fish Eagle
Haliaeetus leucoryphyus
Pallid Harrier
Circus macrourus
Palm-nut Vulture
Gypohierax angolensis
Parasitic Jaeger
Stercorarius parasiticus

Passenger Pigeon
Ectopistes migratorius
Pel's Fishing Owl
Scotopelia peli
Peregrine Falcon
Falco peregrinus
Pied Flycatcher
Ficedula hypoleuca
Pin-tailed Sandgrouse
Pterocles alchata
Polynesian Starling
Aplonis tabuensis
Polynesian Triller
Lalage maculosa
Prairie Falcon
Falco mexicanus
Purple Sunbird
Nectarinia asiatica
Razorbill
Alca torda
Red Avadavat
Amandava amandava
Red-billed Quelea
Quelea quelea
Red-breasted Merganser
Mergus serrator
Red-breasted Sparrowhawk
(also called Rufous-breasted
Sparrowhawk)
Accipiter rufiventris
Red Crossbill
Loxia curvirostra
Red Grouse
Lagopus lagopus
Red-headed Falcon
Falco chicquera
Red-headed Parrot Finch
Erythrura cyanovirens
Red-legged Partridge
Alectoris rufa
Red-necked Nightjar
Caprimulgus ruficollis
Red-necked Phalarope
Phalaropus lobatus

Redshank
Tringa totanus
Red-shouldered Hawk
Buteo lineatus
Red-tailed Hawk
Buteo jamaicensis
Red-winged Blackbird
Agelaius phoeniceus
Ring-billed Gull
Larus delawarensis
Ringed Turtle Dove
Streptopelia risoria
Ring-necked Pheasant
Phasianus colchicus
Rock Dove
Columba livia
Rock Ptarmigan
Lagopus mutus
Rock Sandpiper
Calidris ptilocnemis
Rock Sparrow
Petronia petronia
Rook
Corvus frugilegus
Rosy Finch
Leucosticte arctoa
Rough-legged Hawk
Buteo lagopus
Ruddy Turnstone
Arenaria interpres
Ruppell's Griffon
Gyps rueppellii
Saker Falcon
Falco cherrug
Say's Phoebe
Sayornis saya
Shag
(also called Common Shag)
Phalacrocorax aristotelis
Sharp-shinned Hawk
Accipiter striatus
Shikra
(also called Shikra Goshawk)
Accipiter badius

Short-toed Eagle
Circaetus gallicus
Snow Bunting
Plectrophenax nivalis
Snow Goose
Chen caerulescens
Song Thrush
Turdus philomelos
Sooty Falcon
Falco concolor
Sooty Tern
Sterna fuscata
Spotless Starling
Sturnus unicolor
Spotted Dove
Streptopelia chinensis
Spotted Sandpiper
Actitis macularia
Stock Dove
Columba oenas
Stone Curlew
Burhinus oedicnemus
Swainson's Hawk
Buteo swainsoni
Swamp Harrier
Circus approximans
Taita Falcon
(also spelled Teita)
Falco fasciinucha
Tawny Eagle
Aquila rapax
Turtle Dove
Streptopelia turtur
Vanikoro Broadbill
Myiagra vanikorensis
Vermillion Flycatcher
Pyrocephalus rubinus
Verreaux's Eagle
Aquila verreauxii
Verreaux's Eagle Owl
(also called Milky Eagle Owl)
Bubo lacteus
Wahlberg's Eagle
Aquila wahlbergi
(sometimes placed in *Hieraaetus*)

Wandering Tattler
  Heteroscelus incanus
Wattled Honeyeater
  Foulehaio carunculata
Wedge-tailed Eagle
  Aquila audax
Western Honey Buzzard
  Pernis apivorus
Western Kingbird
  Tyrannus verticalis
Western Marsh Harrier
  Circus aeruginosus
White-breasted Sea Eagle
  Haliaeetus leucogaster
White-capped Noddy
  Anous minutus
White-collared Kingfisher
  Halcyon chloris
White-collared Swift
  Streptoprocne zonaris
White-faced Ibis
  Plegadis chihi

White-fronted Dove
  Leptotila verreauxii
White-tailed Eagle
  Haliaeetus albicilla
White-tailed Tropicbird
  Phaethon lepturus
White-throated Swift
  Aeronautes saxatalis
White-winged Dove
  Zenaida asiatica
Woodchat Shrike
  Lanius senator
Wood Lark
  Lullula arborea
Wood Pigeon
  Columba palumbus
Wood Sandpiper
  Tringa glareola
Yellow Wagtail
  Motacilla flava

References:

Amadon, D. and J. Bull. In press. Hawks and Owls of the World: An Annotated List of Species. Proc. Western Foundation of Vertebrate Zoology, vol. 3 no. 4.

American Ornithologists' Union. 1983. Checklist of North American Birds, 6th Edition. AOU, Washington, D. C.

Clunie, F. and P. Morse. 1984. Birds of the Fiji Bush. Fiji Museum, Suva.

Gruson, E. S. 1976. Checklist of the World's Birds. Quadrangle/The New York Times Book Co.

Howard, R. and A. Moore. 1980. A Complete Checklist of the Birds of the World. Oxford Univ. Press, Oxford.

Paynter, R. A. Jr. 1987. Checklist of Birds of the World. Volume XVI, Comprehensive Index. Museum of Comparative Zoology, Cambridge, Mass.

Peters, J. L. 1931–1972. Checklist of Birds of the World. Harvard University Press, Cambridge, Mass.

Scott, S. L. (Ed.). 1983. Field Guide to the Birds of North America. National Geographic Society, Washington, D. C.

Slater, P., P. Slater, and R. Slater. 1986. The Slater Field Guide to Australian Birds. Rigby Publishers, Griffin Press, Adelaide.

APPENDIX C: Common names of the 19 Peregrine Falcon (*Falco peregrinus*) subspecies referred to in the text.

Scientific Name	Common Names
F. p. anatum	Duck Hawk, Great-footed Hawk, American Peregrine Falcon, Rock Peregrine
F. p. babylonicus[a]	Red Shaheen, Red-capped Shaheen
F. p. brookei	Lesser Peregrine, Mediterranean Peregrine, Spanish Peregrine
F. p. calidus	Siberian Peregrine, Eurasian Tundra Peregrine
F. p. cassini "kreyenborgi"	Cassin's Falcon, Austral Peregrine Kleinschmidt's Falcon, Tierra del Fuego Falcon, Pallid Falcon, Patagonian Falcon
F. p. ernesti	Ernest's Falcon, Hose's Falcon
F. p. furuitii	Volcano Islands Peregrine, Iwo Peregrine
F. p. japonensis	Japanese Peregrine
F. p. macropus	Black-cheeked Falcon, Australian Peregrine
F. p. madens	Cape Verde Islands Peregrine
F. p. minor	African Peregrine, Lesser Peregrine
F. p. nesiotes	Island Peregrine, Fiji Peregrine
F. p. pealei	Peale's Falcon, Peale's Peregrine
F. p. pelegrinoides[a]	Barbary Falcon, Red-naped Shaheen
F. p. peregrinator	Black Shaheen, Indian Peregrine
F. p. peregrinus	Peregrine Falcon, European Peregrine
F. p. radama	Madagascar Peregrine
F. p. submelanogenys	Black-cheeked Falcon
F. p. tundrius	Tundra Falcon, Tundra Peregrine, Arctic Peregrine, Beach Peregrine

[a] *F. p. pelegrinoides* and *F. p. babylonicus* are sometimes referred to as *F. pelegrinoides*.

874

APPENDIX D: Abbreviations of U. S. states and Canadian provinces.

AK	Alaska		MT	Montana
AL	Alabama		NC	North Carolina
AR	Arkansas		ND	North Dakota
AZ	Arizona		NE	Nebraska
CA	California		NH	New Hampshire
CO	Colorado		NJ	New Jersey
CT	Connecticut		NM	New Mexico
DC	District of Columbia		NV	Nevada
DE	Delaware		NY	New York
FL	Florida		OH	Ohio
GA	Georgia		OK	Oklahoma
HI	Hawaii		OR	Oregon
IA	Iowa		PA	Pennsylvania
ID	Idaho		RI	Rhode Island
IL	Illinois		SC	South Carolina
IN	Indiana		SD	South Dakota
KS	Kansas		TN	Tennessee
KY	Kentucky		TX	Texas
LA	Louisiana		UT	Utah
MA	Massachusetts		VA	Virginia
MD	Maryland		VT	Vermont
ME	Maine		WA	Washington
MI	Michigan		WI	Wisconsin
MN	Minnesota		WV	West Virginia
MO	Missouri		WY	Wyoming
MS	Mississippi			

ALB	Alberta		NWT	Northwest Territories
BC	British Columbia		ONT	Ontario
MAN	Manitoba		PEI	Prince Edward Island
NB	New Brunswick		QUE	Quebec
NS	Nova Scotia		SASK	Saskatchewan
NWF	Newfoundland		YUK	Yukon Territory

George Allez
Cedar Grove Ornithological
  Research Station
Route 1
Cedar Grove, WI 53013

Jorge Albuquerque
Department of Zoology
Brigham Young University
Provo, UT 84602

Stefano Allavena
Ministry of Agriculture and
  Forests
Via Carducci, 5, 00100
Roma, Italy

Robert E. Ambrose
U. S. Fish and Wildlife Service
1412 Airport Way
Fairbanks, AK 99701

Clifford M. Anderson
Falcon Research Group
P. O. Box 248
Bow, WA 98232

Daniel W. Anderson
Department of Wildlife and
  Fisheries
University of California
Davis, CA 95616

John H. Barclay
The Peregrine Fund, Inc.
Cornell University
Laboratory of Ornithology
Ithaca, NY 14850

Peter J. Bente
802 Alice Road
Fairbanks, AK 99701

Daniel D. Berger
1806 Grevelia Street
South Pasadena, CA 91030

David M. Bird
MacDonald Raptor Research
  Center
McGill University
Ste. Anne de Bellevue, QUE
Canada H9X 1C0

David A. Boag
Department of Zoology
University of Alberta
Edmonton, ALB
Canada T6G 2E9

Douglas A. Boyce, Jr.
Department of Zoology
Brigham Young University
Provo, UT 84602

D. Mark Bradley
Department of Veterinary
  Anatomy
University of Saskatchewan
Saskatoon, SASK
Canada S7N 0W0

Daniel J. Brimm
2411 Vallecitos
La Jolla, CA 92037

Robert G. Bromley
Department of Renewable
  Resources
Government of the NWT
Box 1177
Yellowknife, NWT
Canada X1A 2L9

Helmut Brücher
Arbeitsgemeinschaft
  Wanderfalkenschutz
Sternenburgstr 89
53 Bonn 1
West Germany

William A. Burnham
The Peregrine Fund, Inc.
World Center for Birds of Prey
5666 West Flying Hawk Lane
Boise, ID 83709

Ashley C. Butler
National Institute of Water
  Research
P.O. Box 17001
Congella 4013, South Africa

Tom J. Cade
The Peregrine Fund, Inc.
Cornell University
Laboratory of Ornithology
Ithaca, NY 14850

Fergus Clunie
Fiji Museum
Suva, Fiji

Gordon S. Court
Department of Zoology
University of Alberta
Edmonton, ALB
Canada T6G 2E1

Gerald R. Craig
Colorado Division of Wildlife
317 W. Prospect
Fort Collins, CO 80526

John A. Crawford
Department of Fisheries and
  Wildlife
Oregon State University
Corvallis, OR 97331

Robert Dittrick
Biological Investigative Research
  Studies
Box 4-1740
Anchorage, AK 99509

David H. Ellis
U. S. Fish and Wildlife Service
Patuxent Wildlife Research Center
Laurel, MD 20708

James H. Enderson
Department of Biology
The Colorado College
Colorado Springs, CO 80903

Knud Falk
University of Roskilde
P. O. Box 260
DK-4000 Roskilde
Denmark

Laura Fasce
Via di Brera, 2-25
16121 Genova
Italy 76121

Paolo Fasce
Via di Brera, 2-25
16121 Genova
Italy 76121

Mark R. Fuller
U. S. Fish and Wildlife Service
Patuxent Wildlife Research Center
Laurel, MD 20715

Richard W. Fyfe
P. O. Box 3263
Ft. Saskatchewan, ALB
Canada T8L 2T2

Cesar Peres Garat
1647 Montevideo
1021 Buenos Aires, Argentina

C. Cormack Gates
Renewable Resources
Government of the Northwest
  Territories
Fort Smith, NWT
Canada X0E 0P0

Martin J. Gilroy
The Peregrine Fund, Inc.
Cornell University
Laboratory of Ornithology
Ithaca, NY 14850

Jose L. González
Museo Nacional de Ciencias
  Naturales
Jose Gutierrez Abascal 2
28006 Madrid, Spain

Luis M. González
ICONA
Subdirección General de Recursos
  Naturales Renovables
Gran Via de S. Francisco 35
28005 Madrid, Spain

James W. Grier
Zoology Department
North Dakota State University
Fargo, ND 58105

David L. Harlow
U. S. Fish and Wildlife Service
Office of Endangered Species
2800 Cottage Way
Sacramento, CA 95825

William Heinrich
The Peregrine Fund, Inc.
World Center for Birds of Prey
5666 West Flying Hawk Lane
Boise, ID 83709

Charles J. Henny
U. S. Fish and Wildlife Service
Pacific Northwest Field Station
480 S. W. Airport Road
Corvallis, OR 97333

Karlfried Hepp
Lindenstr. 18
7530 Pforzheim
West Germany

Borja Heredia
ICONA
Subdirección General de Recursos
Naturales Renovables
Gran Via de S. Francisco 35
28005 Madrid, Spain

Joseph J. Hickey
Department of Wildlife Ecology
University of Wisconsin
Madison, WI 53705

Nancy Hilgert
Departmento de Biologia
Pontificia Universidad Catolica del
  Ecuador
Casilla 2184
Quito, Ecuador

Fernando Hiraldo
Museo Nacional de Ciencias
  Naturales
Jose Gutierrez Abascal 2
28006 Madrid, Spain

Mark A. Hitchcock
524 Linda Vista
Las Cruces, NM 88005

Karel Hudec
Institute for Vertebrate Research
Czechoslovakia Academy of
  Research
Brno, Czechoslovakia

Craig S. Hulse
U. S. Fish and Wildlife Service
Patuxent Wildlife Research Center
Laurel, MD 20708

W. Grainger Hunt
BioSystems Analysis, Inc.
303 Potrero Street, Suite 203
Santa Cruz, CA 95060

Robin E. Hunter
1830 N. 37th Street
Phoenix, AZ 85008

Walter M. Jarman
Institute of Marine Sciences
University of California
Santa Cruz, CA 95064

M. Alan Jenkins
George Miksch Sutton Avian
  Research Center, Inc.
P. O. Box 2007
Bartlesville, OK 74005

Brenda S. Johnson
Department of Zoology
University of California
Davis, CA 95616

Michel Juillard
Foundation Suisse Pour Les
  Rapaces
Clos Gaspard
2946 Miécourt
Switzerland

James O. Keith
Denver Wildlife Research Center
P. O. Box 25266
Denver, CO 80225-0266

Lloyd F. Kiff
Western Foundation of Vertebrate
  Zoology
1100 Glendon Avenue, Suite 1400
Los Angeles, CA 90024

Wolfgang Kirmse
Am Bogen 43
Leipzig, 7030
East Germany

Monte N. Kirven
Bureau of Land Management
555 Leslie Street
Ukiah, CA 94982

Gert Kleinstäuber
Stollnhausgasse 13
Freiberg, 9200
East Germany

Daniel Konkel
11 Beaver Drive
Sheridan, WY 82801

Dirk V. Lanning
5014 Guadalupe Trail NW
Albuquerque, NM 87107

Edward Levine
The Peregrine Fund, Inc.
5666 West Flying Hawk Lane
Boise, ID 83709

Jeffrey L. Lincer
4718 Dunn Drive
Sarasota, FL 33583

Peter Lindberg
Department of Zoology
University of Göteborg
Box 25059
S-40031, Göteborg, Sweden

Jonathan L. Longmire
Genetics Group, MS-M886
Los Alamos National Laboratory
Los Alamos, NM 87545

Thomas C. Maechtle
University of Texas
System Cancer Center
Science Park — Research Division
P. O. Box 389
Smithville, TX 78957

Steven B. Matthews
Department of Renewable
  Resources
Government of the Northwest
  Territories
Box 1177
Yellowknife, NWT
Canada X1A 2L9

William G. Mattox
Greenland Peregrine Falcon Survey
P. O. Box 29403
Columbus, OH 43229

J. Weldon McNutt
Graduate Group in Animal
  Behavior
Department of Psychology
University of California
Davis, CA 95616

Richard Mearns
Connansknowe, Kirkton
Dumfries, Scotland

Theodor Mebs
Schwalbengrund 43
D-4630 Bochum 1
West Germany

John M. Mendelsohn
Durban Natural History Museum
P.O. Box 4085
Durban 4000, South Africa

Søren Møller
University of Roskilde
P.O. Box 260
DK-4000 Roskilde
Denmark

J. Geoffrey Monk
6 Dale Court
Walnut Creek, CA 94595

René-Jean Monneret
Fonds d'Intervention Pour les
  Rapaces
Moulin du Haut
39160 Arlay, France

Donald C. Morizot
University of Texas
System Cancer Center
Science Park — Research Division
P. O. Box 389
Smithville, TX 78957

David Mossop
Department of Renewable
  Resources
Government of Yukon
Box 2703
Whitehorse, YUK
Canada Y1A 2C6

Helmut C. Mueller
Department of Biology
University of North Carolina
Chapel Hill, NC 27514

William T. Munro
Ministry of Environment
Victoria, BC
Canada V8V 1X5

Morlan W. Nelson
73 East Way
Boise, ID 83702

R. Wayne Nelson
4218 — 63rd Street
Camrose, ALB
Canada T4V 2W2

Ian Newton
Institute of Terrestrial Ecology
Monks Wood Experimental
  Station
Abbots Ripton
Huntingdon PE17 2LS, England

Ian C. T. Nisbet
72 Codman Road
Lincoln, MA 01773

Daniel O'Brien
The Peregrine Fund, Inc.
World Center for Birds of Prey
5666 West Flying Hawk Lane
Boise, ID 83709

Joseph C. Okoniewski
New York State Department of
  Environmental Conservation
Wildlife Resources Center
Game Farm Road
Delmar, NY 12054

Lynn W. Oliphant
Department of Veterinary
  Anatomy
University of Saskatchewan
Saskatoon, SASK
Canada S7N 0W0

Penny D. Olsen
CSIRO Division of Wildlife and
  Rangelands Research
P.O. Box 84
Lyneham, A. C. T. 2602
Australia

Jerry Olsen
RMB 1705, Read Road
Sutton, New South Wales 2602
Australia

David B. Peakall
National Wildlife Research Center
Canadian Wildlife Service
Ottawa, ONT
Canada K1A 0E7

Roger Tory Peterson
Neck Road
Old Lyme, CT 06371

Joseph B. Platt
Dubai Wildlife Research Center
P. O. Box 11626
Dubai, United Arab Emirates

Richard D. Porter
325 North 300 West, RR #1
Mapleton, UT 84663

Derek A. Ratcliffe
Nature Conservancy Council
Northminster House
Peterborough, Cambs
Great Britain PE1 1UA

Patrick T. Redig
Department of Veterinary Biology
University of Minnesota
St. Paul, MN 55108

J. David Remple
Dubai Falcon Hospital
P. O. Box 13919
Dubai, United Arab Emirates

Robert J. Ritchie
Alaska Biological Research
Box 81934
Fairbanks, AK 99708

Kenton E. Riddle
University of Texas Cancer Center
Veterinarian Resources Division
Bastrop, TX 78602

Robert W. Risebrough
Institute of Marine Sciences
University of California
Santa Cruz, CA 95064

David G. Roseneau
P. O. Box 80810
Fairbanks, AK 99708

Terry B. Roundy
607 South 1400 West
Salt Lake City, UT 84104

Christian Saar
Deutscher Falkenorden
Eickoffweg 25
2000 Hamburg 70
West Germany

Calvin Sandfort
The Peregrine Fund, Inc.
World Center for Birds of Prey
5666 West Flying Hawk Lane
Boise, ID 83709

Peter J. Schei
Ministry of Environment
Myntgat. 2, Oslo Dept.
Oslo 1, Norway

Philip F. Schempf
U. S. Fish and Wildlife Service
P. O. Box 1287
Juneau, AK 99802

William S. Seegar
U. S. Department of Defense
Aberdeen Proving Ground
Aberdeen, MD 21010

Steve K. Sherrod
George Miksch Sutton Avian
  Research Center, Inc.
P. O. Box 2007
Bartlesville, OK 74005

Williston Shor
North American Falconers'
  Association
318 Montford Ave.
Mill Valley, CA 94941

Ron R. Sibbald
National Institute of Water
  Research
P. O. Box 17001
Congella 4013, South Africa

Ward B. Stone
New York State Department of
  Environmental Conservation
Wildlife Resources Center
Game Farm Road
Delmar, NY 12054

Ted Swem
Biological Investigative Research
  Studies
Box 4-1740
Anchorage, AK 99509

Stanley A. Temple
Department of Wildlife Ecology
University of Wisconsin
Madison, WI 53706

Carl G. Thelander
BioSystems Analysis, Inc.
303 Potrero Street, Suite 203
Santa Cruz, CA 95060

Jean-Marc Thiollay
Department of Zoology
E.N.S., 46 rue d'Ulm
75005 Paris, France

W. J. Patrick Thompson
Department of Veterinary
  Anatomy
University of Saskatchewan
Saskatoon, SASK
Canada S7N 0W0

Simon Thomsett
P. O. Box 42818
Nairobi, Kenya

Kimberly Titus
Virginia Polytechnic Institute
Patuxent Wildlife Research Center
Laurel, MD 20708

Harrison B. Tordoff
6 Chickadee Lane
St. Paul, MN 55110

Benjamin van Drimmelen
Ministry of Environment
Smithers, BC
Canada V0J 2N0

W. Guillermo Vasina
Museo Argentino de Ciencias
  Naturales
Avenida Angel Gallardo 470
Casilla Correo 230 — Sucursal 5
1405 Buenos Aires, Argentina

Wayman Walker II
2711 Piedmont Avenue
Berkeley, CA 94705

Brian J. Walton
The Peregrine Fund, Inc.
Predatory Bird Research Group
University of California
Santa Cruz, CA 95064

F. Prescott Ward
U. S. Department of Defense
Aberdeen Proving Ground
Aberdeen, MD 21010

James D. Weaver
The Peregrine Fund, Inc.
North American Falconers'
  Association
159 Sapsucker Woods Road
Ithaca, NY 14850

Peter Wegner
Arbeitsgemeinshaft
  Wanderfalkenschutz
Geibelstr. 3
509 Leverkusen 1
West Germany

Clayton M. White
Department of Zoology
Brigham Young University
Provo, UT 84602

Marcus Wikman
Finnish Game and Fisheries
  Research Institute
Pitkansillanranta 3 A
SF-00530 Helsinki, Finland

Michael A. Yates
7818 Woodyard Road
Clinton, MD 20735

LITERATURE CITED

Ackerman, L.B. 1980. Overview of human exposure to dieldrin residues in the environment and current trends of residue levels in tissue. Pestic. Monitor. J. 14:64-69.

Advise, J. C., R. A. Lansman, and R. O. Shade. 1979. The use of restriction endonucleases to measure mitochondrial DNA sequence relatedness in natural populations. I. Population structure and evolution in the genus *Peromyscus*. Genetics 92:279-295.

Ainley, D. B., and D. P. DeMaster. 1980. Survival and mortality in a population of Adélie Penguins. Ecology 61:422-530.

Albuquerque, J. L. B. 1978. Contribuicao ao conhecimento de *Falco peregrinus* Tunstall, 1971 na America do Sul (Falconidae, Aves). Rev. Brasil. Biol. 38:727-737.

Albuquerque, J. L. B. 1982. Observations on the use of rangle by the Peregrine Falcon (*Falco peregrinus tundrius*) wintering in southern Brasil. Raptor Res. 16:91-92.

Albuquerque, J. L. B. 1984. The Peregrine Falcon (*Falco peregrinus*) in southern Brazil: aspects of winter ecology in an urban environment. M.S. thesis, Provo, Utah, Brigham Young Univ.

Alerstam, T. 1978. Analysis and a theory of visible bird migration. Oikos 30:273-349.

Allen, M. 1982. Falconry in Arabia. Brattleboro, Vermont, The Stephen Greene Press.

Allen, R. P., and R. T. Peterson. 1936. The hawk migrations at Cape May Point, New Jersey. Auk 53:393-404.

Alliston, W. G., and L. A. Patterson. 1978. A preliminary study of Peregrine Falcon populations in the polar gas area, districts of Franklin and Keewatin, N.W.T. Polar Gas Project Report. Toronto, LGL Ltd.

Alvarez, J., A. Bea, J. M. Faus, E. Castien, and I. Mendiola. 1985. Atlas de los Vertebrados Continentales de Alava, Vizcaya y Guipuzcoa. Bilbao, Gobierno Vasco.

Amadon, D. 1949. The seventy-five percent rule for subspecies. Condor 51:250-258.

American Ornithologists' Union. 1931. Check-list of North American birds, 4th ed. Lancaster, Pennsylvania, Amer. Ornithol. Union.

American Ornithologists' Union. 1982. Forum: avian subspecies in the 1980s. Auk 99:593-615.

Ames, P. L. 1966. DDT residues in eggs of the Osprey in the northeastern United States and their relation to nesting success. J. Appl. Ecol. 3:87-97.

Ames, P. L., and G. S. Mersereau. 1964. Some factors in the decline of the Osprey in Connecticut. Auk 81:173-185.

Anderson, C. M., P. M. DeBruyn, T. Ulm, and B. Gaussoin. 1980. Behavior and ecology of Peregrine Falcons on the Skagit Flats, Washington. Olympia, Washington State Dept. of Game.

Anderson, C. M., and D. H. Ellis. 1981. *Falco kreyenborgi*: a current review. Raptor Res. 15:33-41.

Anderson, D. W. 1976. The Gulf of California, Mexico. Pp. 270-271 *in* The 1975 North American Peregrine Falcon survey (R. W. Fyfe, S. A. Temple, and T. J. Cade, Eds.). Can. Field-Nat. 99:228-273.

Anderson, D. W., and J. J. Hickey. 1972. Eggshell changes in certain North American birds. Proc. 15th Intern. Ornithol. Congr.: 514-540.

Anderson, D. W., and J. J. Hickey. 1974. Eggshell changes in raptors from the Baltic region. Oikos 25:395-401.

Andersson, M., and R. A. Norberg. 1981. Evolution of reversed sexual size dimorphism and role partitioning among predatory birds, with a size scaling of flight performance. Biol. J. Linnean Soc. 15:105-130.

Anhäuser, H. 1985. Frankfurter Wanderfalken. Deutscher Falkenorden 1984:49-53.

Anon. ca. 1984. "Operation Falcon," a three year undercover investigation by the Division of Law Enforcement of the United States Fish and Wildlife Service. Material apparently used by the USFWS to brief state and federal agents prior to the coordinated searches and arrests on 29 June 1984.

Anon. 1955. Chemical sprays. Maryland Conservationist 32:29.

Anon. 1966. Report of a new chemical hazard. The New Scientist 32:612.

Anon. 1979. Snake River birds of prey special research report to the Secretary of the Interior, June 1979. Boise District, Idaho, U. S. Dept. of the Interior, Bureau of Land Mgmt.

Anon. 1985. Tätigkeitsbericht der Arbeitsgruppe "Wanderfalkenschutz" im Landesbund für Volgelschutz. Vogelschutz, Zeitschrift des LBV in Bayern, Heft 1:27-28.

Aragüés, A., and J. Lucientes. 1980. Fauna de Aragon. Las Aves. Ed. Guara. Zaragoza.

Archie, J. W. 1985. Methods for coding variable morphological features for numerical taxonomic analysis. Syst. Zool. 34:326-345.

Aro, M. 1973. Suomen muutohaukat v. 1972. Suomen Luonto 32:50-59.

Asay, C. E., and W. E. Davis. 1984. Management of an endangered species in a national park, the Peregrine Falcon in Yosemite. San Francisco, California, Western Region, National Park Service, Cooperative National Park Resources Studies Unit, Tech. Rep. No. 16.

Ashmole, N. P. 1963. The regulation of numbers of tropical oceanic birds. Ibis 103:458-473.

Askenmo, C. 1977. Effects of addition and removal of nestlings on nestling weight, nestling survival, and female weight loss in the Pied Flycatcher *Ficedula hypoleuca* (Pallas). Ornis. Scandinavica 8:1-8.

Askenmo, C. 1979. Reproductive effort and return rate of male Pied Flycatchers. Amer. Natur. 114:748-753.

Aspelin, A. 1975. Statement of testimony in public hearings on suspension of registrations of heptachlor and chlordane. Washington, D. C., U. S. Environmental Protection Agency.

Association of Official Analytical Chemists. 1984. Official methods of analysis, 14th ed., Section 29. Washington, D. C.

Aston, A. R. 1984. The effect of doubling atmospheric CO_2 on streamflow: a simulation. J. Hydrology 67:273-280.

Awender, E. 1980. Modern falconry mourns a leader: Renz Waller 1895-1979. J. N. Amer. Falconers' Assoc. 18/19:60-61.

Baker, J. A. 1967. The Peregrine. London, Collins.

Bancroft, G. 1927. Notes on the breeding coastal and insular birds of central Lower California. Condor 29:188-195.

Banks, R. C. 1969. The Peregrine Falcon in Baja California and the Gulf of California. Pp. 81-91 *in* Peregrine Falcon populations: their biology and decline (J. J. Hickey, Ed.). Madison, Univ. of Wisconsin Press.

Barclay, J. H., and T. J. Cade. 1983. Restoration of the Peregrine Falcon in the eastern United States. Bird Conservation 1:3-37.

Barrowclough, G. F. 1980. Genetic differentiation in *Dendroica coronata* complex. Ph.D. dissertation, Minneapolis, Univ. of Minnesota.

Baum, F. 1981. Chlorierte Kohlenwasserstoffe in wildlebenden Tieren und Nahrungsnetzen: Vorkommen, Bedeutung und Nachweis. Ökol. Vögel 3 (Sonderh.): 5-71.

Baum, F., and B. Conrad. 1978. Greifvögel als Indikatoren für Veranderungen der Umweltbelastung durch chlorierte Kohlenwasserstoffe. Tierarztl. Umschau 33:661-668.

Bavin, C. L. 1985. Paper presented at the business meeting of the International Association of Fish and Wildlife Agencies by the Chief, Division of Law Enforcement. Sept. 12, 1985, Sun Valley, Idaho, U. S. Dept. of the Interior, Fish and Wildl. Serv.

Beason, R. C. 1978. The influences of weather and topography on water bird migration in the southwestern United States. Oecologia 32:153-169.

Beck, R. H. 1899. Tropical expedition wrecked. Bull. Cooper Ornithol. Club (Condor) 1:55.

Bednarek, W. 1985. Greifvögelzucht im DFO 1984. Deutscher Falkenorden 1984:23-24.

Beebe, F. L. 1960. The marine Peregrines of the northwest Pacific Coast. Condor 62:154-189.

Beebe, F. L. 1967. Experiments in the husbandry of the Peregrine. Raptor Res. News 1:61-86.

Beebe, F. L. 1969. The known status of the Peregrine Falcon in British Columbia. Pp. 53-60 *in* Peregrine Falcon populations: their biology and decline (J. J. Hickey, Ed.). Madison, Univ. of Wisconsin Press.

Beebe, F. L. 1971. The myth of the vanishing Peregrine. Revised version. Privately distributed from Saanighton, British Columbia.

Beebe, F. L. 1974. Field studies of the Falconiformes of British Columbia. British Columbia Prov. Mus. Occ. Pap. No. 17.

Beecham, J. J., and M. N. Kochert. 1975. Breeding biology of the Golden Eagle in southwestern Idaho. Wilson Bull. 87:506-513.

Bell, G. I., M. J. Selby, and W. J. Rutter. 1982. The highly polymorphic region near the human insulin gene is composed of simple tandemly repeating sequences. Nature 295:31-35.

Benedict, S. H. 1973. Statement of testimony in public hearings on cancellation of registrations of aldrin/dieldrin. Washington, D. C., U. S. Environmental Protection Agency.

Benson, P. C., and J. C. Dobbs. 1984. Causes of Cape Vulture mortality at the Kransberg colony. Pp. 87-93 *in* Proceedings of the 2nd Symposium on African Predatory Birds (J. M. Mendelsohn and C. W. Sapsford, Eds.). Durban, Natal Bird Club.

Bent, A. C. 1938. Life historics of North American birds of prey. U. S. Natl. Mus. Bull. No. 170.

Berger, D. D., D. W. Anderson, J. D. Weaver, and R. W. Risebrough. 1970. Shell thinning in eggs of Ungava Peregrines. Can. Field-Nat. 84:265-267.

Berger, D. D., and H. C. Mueller. 1969. Nesting Peregrine Falcons in Wisconsin and adjacent areas. Pp. 115-122 *in* Peregrine Falcon populations: their biology and decline (J. J. Hickey, Ed.). Madison, Univ. of Wisconsin Press.

Berger, D. D., C. R. Sindelar, Jr., and K. E. Gamble. 1969. The status of the breeding Peregrines of the eastern United States. Pp. 165-173 *in* Peregrine Falcon populations: their biology and decline (J. J. Hickey, Ed.). Madison, Univ. of Wisconsin Press.

Bernis, F. 1966. Aves Migradoras Ibericas. Fasc. 2. Vol. Esp. Sociedad Española de Ornitologia.

Bertram, G. C. L., D. Lack, and B. B. Roberts. 1934. Notes on east Greenland birds, with a discussion of the periodic non-breeding among arctic birds. Ibis 76:816-831.

Bezzel, E. 1969. Zum Stand quantitativer Greifvogeluntersuchungen in Bayern. Deutsche Sektion Internat. Rat f. Vogelschutz 9:31-36.

Bijleveld, M. 1974. Birds of prey in Europe. London, MacMillan Press Ltd.

Binford, L. 1979. Fall migration of diurnal raptors at Pt. Diablo, California. Western Birds 10:1-16.

Bishop, L. B. 1900. Annotated list of birds. Pp. 47-96 *in* Results of a biological reconnaissance of the Yukon River region (W. H. Osgood, Ed.). N. Amer. Fauna No. 19.

Bitman, J., H. C. Cecil, S. J. Harris, and G. F. Fries. 1969. DDT induces a decrease in eggshell calcium. Nature 224:44-46.

Bloom, P. H., R. W. Fyfe, M. N. Kirven, R. W. Risebrough, D. G. Roseneau, N. J. Schmitt, A. M. Springer, S. A. Temple, C. G. Thelander, W. W. Walker, C. M. White, J. L. B. Albuquerque, A. Luscombe, M. Perez, and W. G. Vasina. 1980. Observations of the Peregrine Falcon, *Falco peregrinus* spp. in South America. Report to U. S. Fish and Wildl. Serv. Berkeley, California, Bodega Bay Institute.

Blus, L. J. 1982. Further interpretation of the relation of organochlorine residues in Brown Pelican eggs to reproductive success. Environ. Pollut. A28:15-33.

Blus, L. J., C. D. Gish, A. A. Belisle, and R. M. Prouty. 1972. Logarithmic relationship of DDE residues to eggshell thinning. Nature 235:376-377.

Blus, L. J., C. J. Henny, and A. J. Krynitsky. 1985a. The effects of heptachlor and lindane on birds, Columbia Basin, Oregon and Washington, 1976-1981. Sci. Total Environ. 46:73-81.

Blus, L. J., C. J. Henny, and A. J. Krynitsky. 1985b. Organochlorine-induced mortality and residues in Long-billed Curlews from Oregon. Condor 87:563-565.

Blus, L. J., C. J. Henny, D. J. Lenhart, and T. E. Kaiser. 1984. Effects of heptachlor- and lindane-treated seed on Canada Geese. J. Wildl. Mgmt. 48:1097-1111.

Blus, L. J., T. E. Kaiser, and R. A. Grover. 1983a. Effects on wildlife from use of endrin in Washington state orchards. Proc. 48th N. Amer. Wildl. and Nat. Resources Conf.: 159-174.

Blus, L. J., B. S. Neeley, A. A. Belisle, and R. M. Prouty. 1974. Organochlorine residues in Brown Pelican eggs: relation to reproductive success. Environ. Pollut. 7:81-91.

Blus, L. J., O. H. Pattee, C. J. Henny, and R. M. Prouty. 1983b. First records of chlordane-related mortality in wild birds. J. Wildl. Mgmt. 47:196-198.

Bogan, J. A., and J. Mitchell. 1973. Continuing dangers to Peregrines from dieldrin. Brit. Birds 66:437-439.

Bollengier, R. (Ed.). 1979. Eastern Peregrine Falcon recovery plan. Washington, D. C., U. S. Dept. of the Interior, Fish and Wildl. Serv.

Bond, R. M. 1946. The Peregrine population of western North America. Condor 48:101-116.

Borg, K., H. Wanntorp, K. Erne, and E. Hanko. 1969. Alkyl mercury poisoning in terrestrial Swedish wildlife. Viltrevy 6:301-379.

Botstein, D., R. L. White, M. Skolnick, and R. W. Davies. 1980. Construction of a genetic linkage map using restriction fragment length polymorphisms. Amer. J. of Human Genet. 32:314.

Bowdler, S. 1984. Hunter Hill, Hunter Island: archeological investigations of a prehistoric site. Dept. Prehistory, School of Pacific Studies, Canberra, Australia National Univ.

Boyce, D. A., Jr., and C. M. White. 1979. Peregrine Falcon nesting habitat survey of the Mendocino, Six Rivers, Klamath, Shasta, and Trinity National Forests, 1979. San Francisco, California, U. S. Forest Service.

Boyce, D. A., Jr., and C. M. White. 1980. Peregrine Falcon nesting habitat survey on the Fremont National Forest, 1980. U. S. Forest Service, Wilderness Res. Inst., Contract No. 00-0485-0-0875.

Brabourne, L., and C. Chubb. 1912. The birds of South America, vol. 1. London, R. H. Porter.

Bray, R. (with Comments By T. H. Manning). 1943. Notes on the birds of Southampton Island, Baffin Island, and Melville Peninsula. Auk 60:504-536.

Brewer, G. J. 1970. An introduction to isozyme technique. New York, Academic Press.

Brewster, A. B. 1922. The hill tribes of Fiji, a record of forty years intimate connection with the tribes of the mountainous interior of Fiji. London, Seeley, Service & Co., Ltd.

Bromley, R. G. 1983. 1982 raptor survey. Northwest Territories Wildl. Serv. File Rep. No. 35.

Broo, B. 1985. Reflektioner Kring Berguvens (*Bubo bubo* L.) nedoch uppgang i Sydvastra Sverige. Nat. Hist. Mus. Gothenburg, Yearbook 1984.

Brosset, A. 1986. Les populations du Faucon Pélerin *Falco peregrinus* Gmelin en Afrique du Nord: un puzzle zoogeographique. Alauda 54:1-14.

Broun, M. 1939. Fall migrations of hawks at Hawk Mountain, Pennsylvania, 1934-1938. Auk 56:429-441.

Brown, D. E. (Ed.). 1982. Biotic communities of the southwestern United States and Mexico. Desert Plants 4:1-342.

Brown, J. L. 1975. The evolution of behavior. New York, W. W. Norton and Co.

Brown, L. F., Jr., J. L. Brewton, T. J. Evans, J. H. McGowen, W. A. White, C. G. Groat, and W. L. Fisher. 1980. Environmental geologic atlas of the Texas coastal zone: Brownsville-Harlingen area. Austin, Univ. of Texas, Bureau of Economic Geology.

Brown, L. F., Jr., J. H. McGowen, T. J. Evans, C. G. Groat, and W. L. Fisher. 1977. Environmental geologic atlas of Texas coastal zone: Kingsville area. Austin, Univ. of Texas, Bureau of Economic Geology.

Brown, L. H., and D. Amadon. 1968. Eagles, hawks and falcons of the world, vol. 2. New York, McGraw-Hill Book Co.

Brown, L. H., E. K. Urban, and K. Newman. 1982. The birds of Africa. London, Academic Press.

Brownie, C., D. R. Anderson, K. P. Burnham, and D. S. Robson. 1978. Statistical inference from band recovery data: a handbook. U. S. Fish and Wildl. Serv. Resource Publ. 131.

Brüll, H. 1984. Das Leben europäischer Greifvögel, 4 Auflage. Stuttgart und New York, Gustav Fischer Verlag.

Bruun, B. 1985. Raptor migration in the Red Sea area. Pp. 251-255 *in* Conservation studies on raptors, ICBP Tech. Publ. No. 5 (I. Newton and R. D. Chancellor, Eds.). London, Intern. Council for Bird Preservation.

Bryant, D. M. 1979. Reproductive costs in the House Martin (*Delichon urbica*). J. Anim. Ecol. 48:655-675.

Bue, C. D. 1963. Principal lakes of the United States. U. S. Geol. Survey Circular 476.

Bunck, C. M., R. M. Prouty, and A. J. Krynitsky. 1987. Residues of organochlorine pesticides and polychlorinated biphenyls in Starlings (*Sturnus vulgaris*), from the continental United States, 1982. Environ. Monit. Assess. 8:59-75.

Bunck, C. M., J. W. Spann, O. H. Pattee, and W. J. Fleming. 1985. Changes in eggshell thickness during incubation: implications for evaluating the impact of organochlorine contaminants on productivity. Bull. Environ. Contam. Toxicol. 35:173-182.

Burgers, J., P. Opdam, G. Muskens, and E. De Ruiter. 1986. Residue levels of DDE in eggs of Dutch Sparrowhawks *Accipiter nisus* following the ban on DDT. Environ. Pollut. B11:29-40.

Burnham, W. A. 1975. Breeding biology and ecology of the Peregrine Falcon in Greenland. M.S. thesis, Provo, Utah, Brigham Young Univ.

Burnham, W. A. 1983. Artificial incubation of falcon eggs. J. Wildl. Mgmt. 47:158-168.

Burnham, W. A., J. Craig, J. H. Enderson, and W. R. Heinrich. 1978. Artificial increase in reproduction of wild Peregrine Falcons. J. Wildl. Mgmt. 42:626-628.

Burnham, W. A., J. H. Enderson, and T. J. Boardman. 1984. Variation in Peregrine Falcon eggs. Auk 101:578-583.

Burnham, W. A., and W. G. Mattox. 1984. Biology of the Peregrine and Gyrfalcon in Greenland. Meddr. Grønland. 14:1-30.

Burnham, W. A., B. J. Walton, and J. D. Weaver. 1983. Management and maintenance. Pp. 10-19 *in* Falcon propagation: a manual on captive breeding (J. D. Weaver and T. J. Cade, Eds.). Boise, Idaho, The Peregrine Fund, Inc.

Butler, A. C., R. R. Sibbald, and B. D. Gardner. 1983. Gas chromatographic analysis indicates decrease in chlorinated hydrocarbon levels in northern Zululand. S. Afr. J. Sci. 79:162-163.

Cade, T. J. 1960. Ecology of the Peregrine and Gyrfalcon populations in Alaska. Univ. California Publ. Zool. 63:151-290.

Cade, T. J. 1968. The Gyrfalcon and falconry. Living Bird 7:237-240.

Cade, T. J. 1969a. The status of the Peregrine and other Falconiformes in Africa. Pp. 289-321 *in* Peregrine Falcon populations: their biology and deline (J. J. Hickey, Ed.). Madison, Univ. Wisconsin Press.

Cade, T. J. 1969b. The northern Peregrine populations. Pp. 502-505 *in* Peregrine Falcon populations: their biology and decline (J. J. Hickey, Ed.). Madison, Univ. of Wisconsin Press.

Cade, T. J. 1974. Plans for managing the survival of the Peregrine Falcon. Raptor Res. Rep. 2:89-104.

Cade, T. J. 1975. Current status of the Peregrine in North America. Raptor Res. Rep. 3:3-12.

Cade, T. J. 1976. The Charley River, Alaska. Pp. 254-261 *in* The 1975 North American Peregrine Falcon survey (R. Fyfe, S. A. Temple, and T. J. Cade, Eds.). Can. Field-Nat. 90:228-273.

Cade, T. J. 1980. The husbandry of falcons for return to the wild. Intern. Zool. Yearbook 20:23-35.

Cade, T. J. 1982. The falcons of the world. London, William Collins Sons.

Cade, T. J. 1983. Hybridization and gene exchange among birds in relation to conservation. Pp. 288-309 *in* Genetics and conservation (C. M. Shonewald-Cox, S. M. Chambers, B. MacBryde and L. Thomas, Eds.). Menlo Park, California, Benjamin/Cummings Publ. Co.

Cade, T. J. 1985a. Peregrine recovery in the United States. Pp. 331-342 *in* Conservation studies on raptors, ICBP Tech. Publ. No. 5 (I. Newton and R. D. Chancellor, Eds.). London, Intern. Council for Bird Preservation.

Cade, T. J. 1985b. Statement of Dr. Tom Cade, Professor of Ornithology, Cornell University, and President, the Peregrine Fund, Inc. Pp. 497-503 and 549-555 *in* Endangered Species Act hearings before the Subcommittee on Fisheries and Wildlife Conservation and the Environment of the Committee on Merchant Marine and Fisheries. House of Representatives, Captive Raptors H.R. 2767, July 10, 1985. Serial No. 99-10, Washington, D. C., Government Printing Office.

Cade, T. J. 1986a. Reintroduction as a method of conservation. Raptor Res. Rep. 5:72-84.

Cade, T. J. 1986b. Propagating diurnal raptors in captivity: a review. Intern. Zool. Yearbook 24/25:1-20.

Cade, T. J., and P. R. Dague. 1980. The Peregrine Fund Newsletter. No. 8.

Cade, T. J., and P. R. Dague. 1984. The Peregrine Fund Newsletter. No. 12.

Cade, T. J., and P. R. Dague. 1985. The Peregrine Fund Newsletter. No. 13.

Cade, T. J., and R. Fyfe (Eds.). 1970. The North American Peregrine survey, 1970. Can. Field-Nat. 84:231-245.

Cade, T. J., and R. W. Fyfe. 1978. What makes Peregrine Falcons breed in captivity? Pp. 251-262 *in* Endangered birds: management techniques for preserving threatened species (S. A. Temple, Ed.). Madison, Univ. of Wisconsin Press.

Cade, T. J., and V. J. Hardaswick. 1985. Summary of Peregrine Falcon production and reintroduction by The Peregrine Fund in the United States, 1973-1984. Avicul. Mag. 91:79-92.

Cade, T. J., J. L. Lincer, C. M. White, D. G. Roseneau, and L. G. Swartz. 1971. DDE residues and eggshell changes in Alaskan falcons and hawks. Science 172:955-957.

Cade, T. J., and S. A. Temple. 1977. The Cornell University Falcon Programme. Pp. 353-368 in Proceedings of the ICBP World Conference on Birds of Prey (R. D. Chancellor, Ed.). London, Intern. Council for Bird Preservation.

Cade, T. J., and C. M. White. 1976. Colville River watershed, Alaska. Pp. 245-248 in The 1975 North American Peregrine Falcon survey (R. Fyfe, S. A. Temple, and T. J. Cade, Eds.). Can. Field-Nat. 90:228-273.

Cade, T. J., C. M. White, S. Ambrose, and B. Ritchie. 1976. The central Yukon River, Alaska. Pp. 251-254 in The 1975 North American Peregrine Falcon survey (R. Fyfe, S. A. Temple, and T. J. Cade, Eds.). Can. Field-Nat. 90:228-273.

Cade, T. J., C. M. White, and J. R. Haugh. 1968. Peregrines and pesticides in Alaska. Condor 70:170-178.

Cain, B. W., and C. M. Bunck. 1983. Residues of organochlorine compounds in Starlings (*Sturnus vulgaris*), 1979. Environ. Monit. Assess. 3:161-172.

Cain, B. W., and E. A. Pafford. 1981. Effects of dietary nickel on survival and growth of Mallard ducklings. Arch. Environ. Toxicol. 10:737-745.

Calef, G. W., and D. C. Heard. 1979. Reproductive success of Peregrine Falcons and other raptors at Wager Bay and Melville Peninsula, Northwest Territories. Auk 96:662-674.

Campbell, R. W., M. A. Paul, M. S. Rodway, and H. R. Carter. 1977. Tree-nesting Peregrine Falcons in British Columbia. Condor 79:500-501.

Campbell, T. W., and F. J. Dein. 1984. Avian hematology. In The veterinary clinics of North America: symposium on caged bird medicine (G. J. Harrison, Ed.). Philadelphia, W. B. Saunders Co.

Campos, F. (Ed.). 1982. Avifauna no passeriforme de al cuenca del Duero. Salamanca.

Capone, D. J., E. Y. Chen, A. D. Levinson, P. H. Seeburg, and D. V. Goeddel. 1983. Complete nucleotide sequence of the T24 human bladder carcinoma oncogene and its normal homologue. Nature 302:33-37.

Cawkell, E. M., and J. E. Hamilton. 1961. The birds of the Falkland Islands. Ibis 103:1-27.

Cerny, W., K. Hudec, B. Matousek, Mosansky A., and K. Stastny. 1977. *Falco peregrinus*, distribution in CSSR. In Fauna CSSR, Ptaci II (K. Hudec and W. Cerny, Eds.). Praha, Academia.

Chapman, F. M. 1926. Distribution of bird-life in Ecuador. Bull. Amer. Mus. Nat. Hist. 55:1-784.

Charnov, E. L., and J. R. Krebs. 1974. On clutch size and fitness. Ibis 116:217-219.

Chiavetta, M. 1976. Il Falco Pellegrino ed il Falco Lanario nell'Appennino emiliano-romagnolo con riferimenti alla situazione italiana generale. SOS fauna-Animali in periocolo in Italia. WWF ed. Camerino.

Chiavetta, M. 1981a. I rapaci d'Italia e d'Europa. Milano, Rizzoli.

Chiavetta, M. 1981b. Undici anni di osservazioni sul Falco Pellegrino (*Falco peregrinus*) e sul Falco Lanario (*Falco biarmicus*) in un'area dell'Appennino settentrionale. Considerazioni sulla dinamica delle loro popolazioni. Pp. 51-57 in Atti I Convegno Italiano di Ornitologia. Aulla.

Choudbury, B., and G. Kukla. 1979. Impact of CO_2 on cooling of snow and water surfaces. Nature 280:668-671.

Clark, D. R., Jr. 1981. Bats and environmental contaminants: a review. Washington, D.C., U.S. Dept. of the Interior, Fish and Wildl. Serv., Special Scientific Report, Wildl. No. 235.

Clark, D. R., Jr., and A. J. Krynitsky. 1983. DDT: recent contamination in New Mexico and Arizona? Environment 25:27-31.

Clark, D. R., Jr, R. K. LaVal, and D. M. Swineford. 1978. Dieldrin-induced mortality in an endangered species, the Gray Bat (*Myotis grisescens*). Science 199:1357-1359.

Clark, D. R., Jr., C. O. Martin, and D. M. Swineford. 1975. Organochlorine insecticide residues in the Free-tailed Bat (*Tadarida brasiliensis*) at Bracken Cave, Texas. J. Mammal. 56:429-443.

Clark, D. R., Jr., and M. A. R. McLane. 1974. Chlorinated hydrocarbon and mercury residues in Woodcock in the United States, 1970-71. Pestic. Monitor. J. 8:15-22.

Clawson, S. G., and M. F. Baker. 1959. Immediate effects of dieldrin and heptachlor on Bobwhites. J. Wildl. Mgmt. 23:215-219.

Clement, R. C. (Ed.). 1974. Proceedings of a conference on Peregrine Falcon recovery. Audubon Conservation Rept. No. 4.

Clunie, F. 1972. A contribution to the natural history of the Fiji Peregrine. Notornis 19:302-322.

Clunie, F. 1976a. A Fiji Peregrine in an urban-marine environment. Notornis 23:8-28.

Clunie, F. 1976b. Long-tailed Fruit Bats as Peregrine prey. Notornis 23:245.

Clunie, F. 1980a. Ducks of the rocks (Fiji Peregrines). Fiji Heritage, October:2-10.

Clunie, F. 1980b. Kill remains from a falcon's nest. Fiji Heritage, February:1-2.

Clunie, F. 1984. Birds of the Fiji bush. Suva, Fiji Museum.

Clunie, F. (Ed.). 1986. Letters from the highlands of Vitilevu, 1877, by J. A. Boyd. Domodomo 4:20-46.

Cochran, W. W. 1985. Ocean migration of Peregrine Falcons: is the adult male pelagic? *In* Proceedings of Hawk Migration Conference IV (M. Harwood, Ed.). Hawk Migration Assoc. of North America.

Compton, C. C. 1951. The status of dieldrin for fly control in 1951. Pest Control April 1951:10-11.

Condy, J. B. 1973. Peregrine Falcons in Rhodesia. Honeyguide 75:11-14.

Conrad, B. 1977. Die Giftbelastung der Vogelwelt Deutschlands. Vogelkundliche Bibliotek, vol. 5. Greven, Kilda Verlag.

Conrad, B. 1981. Zur Situation der Pestizidbelastung bei Greifvögel und Eulen in der Bundesrepublik Deutschland. Ökol. Vögel. 3:161-167.

Cooke, A. S. 1975. Pesticides and eggshell formation. Symp. Zool. Soc. London 35:339-361.

Cooke, A. S. 1979. Changes in eggshell characteristics of the Sparrowhawk (*Accipiter nisus*) and Peregrine (*Falco peregrinus*) associated with exposure to environmental pollutants during recent decades. J. Zool. London 187:245-263.

Cooke, A. S., A. A. Bell, and M. B. Haas. 1982. Predatory birds, pesticides and pollution. Cambridge, Institute of Terrestrial Ecology.

Coon, N.C., L. N. Locke, E. Cromartie, and W. L. Reichel. 1970. Causes of Bald Eagle mortality, 1960-1965. J. Wildl. Diseases 6:72-76.

Cooper, J. E. 1978. Veterinary aspects of captive birds of prey. Saul, Gloucestershire, U. K., Steadfast Press.

Corbin, K. W. 1981. Genetic heterozygosity in the White-crowned Sparrow: a potential index to boundaries between subspecies. Auk 98:669-680.

Corbin, K. W. 1983. Genetic structure and avian systematics. Current Ornithol. 1:211-244.

Costa, L., O. Llamas, and I. Tirados. 1982. Persecucion de aves de presa en Leon. Quercus 6:70-72.

Court, G. S. 1986. Some aspects of the reproductive biology of tundra Peregrine Falcons. M. S. thesis, Edmonton, Univ. Alberta.

Craig, G. R. (Ed.). 1985. American Peregrine Falcon recovery plan, Rocky Mountain southwest populations, first revision. U. S. Dept. of the Interior, Fish and Wildl. Serv.

Cramp, S. 1962. The second report of the Joint Committee of the British Trust for Ornithology and the Royal Society for the Protection of Birds on toxic chemicals. London, Royal Society for the Protection of Birds.

Cramp, S. 1965. The fifth report of the Joint Committee of the British Trust for Ornithology and the Royal Society for the Protection of Birds on toxic chemicals. London, Royal Society for the Protection of Birds.

Cramp, S. 1967. The sixth report of the Joint Committee of the British Trust for Ornithology and the Royal Society for the Protection of Birds on toxic chemicals. London, Royal Society for the Protection of Birds.

Cramp, S., and K. E. L. Simmons (Eds.). 1980. The birds of the western Palearctic, vol. 2. Oxford, Oxford Univ. Press.

Crawford, B. D., M. D. Enger, J. K. Griffith, J. L. Hanners, J. L. Longmire, A. C. Munk, J. G. Tesmer, R. L. Stalliongs, R. A. Walters, and C. E. Hildebrand. 1985. Coordinate amplification of metallothionein I and II genes in cadmium-resistant Chinese hamster cells. Application to studies on the regulation of metallothionein gene transcription. Mol. Cell Biol. 5:320-325.

Cromartie, E., W. L. Reichel, L. N. Locke, A. A. Belisle, T. E. Kaiser, T. G. Lamont, B. M. Mulhern, R. M. Prouty, and D. Swineford. 1975. Residues of organochlorine pesticides and polychlorinated biphenyls and autopsy data for Bald Eagles 1971-72. Pestic. Monitor. J. 9:11-14.

Cugnasse, J.-M. 1984. Le Faucon Pélerin *Falco peregrinus* dans le sud du Massif Central de 1974 a 1983. Alauda 52:161-176.

Czechura, G. V. 1984a. The Peregrine Falcon (*Falco peregrinus macropus*) Swainson in southeastern Queensland. Raptor Res. 18:81-91.

Czechura, G. V. 1984b. Notes on an insular raptor community. Sunbird 14:15-19.

Dabbene, R. 1902. Fauna Magallanic, mamiferos y aves de la Tierra del Fuego e islas adyacentes. Anales del Museo Nacional de Buenos Aires, Seria 3. 1:341-409.

Dall, W. H. 1873. Notes on the avifauna of the Aleutian Islands, from Unalaska eastward. Proc. California Acad. Sci. 5:25-35.

Daubert, A. 1971. Successful breeding of Peregrine Falcons and some ethical considerations. Captive Breeding Diurnal Birds of Prey 1:12-15.

Davis, J. W., R. C. Anderson, L. Karstad, and D. O. Trainer. 1971. Infectious and parasitic diseases of wild birds. Ames, Iowa State Univ. Press.

Dawson, W. L., and J. H. Bowles. 1909. The birds of Washington, vol. II. Seattle, Occidental Publ. Co.

DBV, AGW, and AWU. 1975. 3. Denkschrift zur Situation des Wanderfalken in der Bundesrepublik Deutschland. Sonderheft 1-35 (Selbstverlag).

de Juana, E. 1980. Atlas Ornitologico de la Rioja. Logrono, Instituto de Estudios Riojanos.

Dekker, D. 1979. Characteristics of Peregrine Falcons migrating through central Alberta, 1969-1978. Can. Field-Nat. 93:296-302.

Dekker, D. 1984. Spring and fall migrations of Peregrine Falcons in central Alberta, 1979-1983, with comparison to 1969-1978. Raptor Res. 18:92-97.

Dementiev, G. P., and N. A. Gladkov (Eds.). 1951. The birds of the Soviet Union, vol. 1. Moscow, Soviet Science.

Dementiev, G. P., and V. D. Iljitschew. 1961. Bemerkungen über die morphologie der wusten Wanderfalken. Der Falke 8:147-154.

Dewey, K. F., and R. Heim Jr. 1982. A digital archive of Northern Hemisphere snow cover, November 1966 through December 1980. Bull. Amer. Meterol. Soc. 63:1132-1141.

DeWitt, J. B., C. M. Menzie, V. A. Adomaitis, and W. L. Reichel. 1960. Pesticidal residues in animal tissues. Proc. 25th N. Amer. Wildl. Conf.: 277-285.

Diaz del Campo, F. 1974. Unos comentarios sobre la alimentación del Falcon Peregrino (*Falco peregrinus*). Ardeola 19:351-357.

Dietzen, W., and W. Hassmann. 1982. Der Wanderfalke in Bayern: Rückgangsursachen, Situation und Schutzmöglichkeiten. Ber. Arb. gem. Natursch. u. Landsch. pflege 6:6-30.

Dobson, S., P. Howe, E. E. C. Wade, and N. J. Westwood. 1984. Review of toxicity and environmental hazard assessment for chlorothalanil, endosulphan, hexachlorobenzen, quintozene and tetradifon. Huntingdon, Institute of Terrestrial Ecology.

Draffan, R. D. W., S. T. Garnett, and G. L. Malone. 1983. Birds of Torres Strait: an annotated list and biogeographical analysis. Emu 4:207-234.

Drayna, D., K. Davies, D. Hartley, J. L. Mandel, G. Camerino, R. Williamson, and R. White. 1984. Genetic mapping of the human X chromosome by using restriction fragment length polymorphisms. Proc. Natl. Acad. Sci. USA 81:2836-2839.

Dunlap, T. R. 1981. DDT: scientists, citizens, and public policy. Princeton, New Jersey, Princeton Univ. Press.

Dwyer, P. D., J. Kikkawa, and G. J. Ingram. 1979. Habitat relations of vertebrates in subtropical heathlands of coastal southeastern Queensland. Pp. 281-299 *in* Ecosystems of the world, 9A: heathlands and related shrublands: descriptive studies (R. L. Specht, Ed.). Amsterdam, Elsevier.

Dyck, J., J. Eskildsen, and H. S. Moller. 1977. The status of breeding birds of prey in Denmark 1975. Pp. 91-96 *in* Proceedings of the ICBP World Conference on Birds of Prey (R. D. Chancellor, Ed.). London, Intern. Council for Bird Preservation.

Early, T. J. 1982. Abundance and distribution of breeding raptors in the Aleutian Islands, Alaska. Pp. 99-111 *in* Raptor management and biology in Alaska and western Canada (W. N. Ladd and P. F. Schempf, Eds.). Anchorage, U. S. Dept. of the Interior, Fish and Wildl. Serv., Alaska Regional Off.

Eastin, W. C., Jr. and T. J. O'Shea. 1981. Effects of dietary nickel on Mallards. J. Toxicol. Environ. Health 7:883-892.

Ebert, J. 1967. Wanderfalk tragt Ei aus dem Horst. Zool. Abh. Staatl. Museum Tierkunde Dresden 29 6:65-69.

Edelstam, C. 1972. The visible migration of birds at Ottenby, Sweden. Var Fagelvarld, Suppl. 7.

Ellenberg, H., and J. Dietrich. 1981. The Goshawk as a bioindicator. Pp. 69-87 *in* Understanding the Goshawk (R. E. Kenward and I. M. Lindsay, Eds.). International Assoc. for Falconry and Conservation of Birds of Prey.

Ellis, D. H. 1976. Arizona [Peregrine Falcon survey]. Pp. 268 *in* The 1975 North American Peregrine Falcon survey (R. W. Fyfe, S. A. Temple, and T. J. Cade, Eds.). Can. Field-Nat. 90:228-273.

Ellis, D. H. 1982. The Peregrine Falcon in Arizona: habitat utilization and management recommendations. Oracle, Arizona, Inst. for Raptor Studies Res. Rep. No. 1.

Ellis, D. H. 1985. The Austral Peregrine Falcon: color variation, productivity, and pesticides. Nat. Geog. Res. 1:388-394.

Ellis, D. H., C. M. Anderson, and T. B. Roundy. 1981. *Falco kreyenborgi*: more pieces for the puzzle. Raptor Res. 15:42-45.

Ellis, D. H., and R. L. Glinski. 1980. Some unusual records for the Peregrine and Pallid Falcons in South America. Condor 82:350-352.

Ellis, D. H., and R. L. Glinski. 1987. Population estimates for the Peregrine Falcon in Arizona: a habitat inventory approach. Washington D.C., National Wildl. Fed., Proc. Southwestern Raptor Symposium.

Ellis, D. H., and C. Peres G. 1983. The Pallid Falcon *Falco kreyenborgi* is a color phase of the Austral Peregrine Falcon (*Falco peregrinus cassini*). Auk 100:269-271.

Ellis D. H., and G. Monson. 1987. A historical review of Peregrine Falcon summer records for Arizona. Washington D.C., National Wildl. Fed., Proc. Southwestern Raptor Symposium.

Elosegui, J. 1985. Atlas de aves nidificantes en Navarra. Pamplona, Caja de Ahorros de Navarra.

Emison, W. B., and W. M. Bren. 1981. Banding of Peregrine Falcon chicks in Victoria, Australia. Emu 80:288-291.

Enderson, J. H. 1964. A study of the Prairie Falcon in the central Rocky Mountain region. Auk 81:332-352.

Enderson, J. H. 1965. A breeding and migration survey of the Peregrine Falcon. Wilson Bull. 77:327-339.

Enderson, J. H. 1969a. Population trends among Peregrine Falcons in the Rocky Mountain region. Pp. 73-79 *in* Peregrine Falcon populations: their biology and decline (J. J. Hickey, Ed.). Madison, Univ. of Wisconsin Press.

Enderson, J. H. 1969b. Peregrine and Prairie Falcon life tables based on band-recovery data. Pp. 505-508 *in* Peregrine Falcon populations: their biology and decline (J. J. Hickey, Ed.). Madison, Univ. of Wisconsin Press.

Enderson, J. H. 1969c. Coastal migration data as population indices for the Peregrine Falcon. Pp. 275-278 *in* Peregrine Falcon populations: their biology and decline (J. J. Hickey, Ed.). Madison, Univ. of Wisconsin Press.

Enderson, J. H., and D. D. Berger. 1968. Chlorinated hydrocarbon residues in Peregrines and their prey species from northern Canada. Condor 70:149-153.

Enderson, J. H., and D. D. Berger. 1970. Pesticides: eggshell thinning and lowered production of young in Prairie Falcons. BioScience 20:355-356.

Enderson, J. H., and J. Craig. 1974. Status of the Peregrine Falcon in the Rocky Mountains in 1973. Auk 91:727-736.

Enderson, J. H., G. R. Craig, W. A. Burnham, and D. D. Berger. 1982. Eggshell thinning and organochlorine residues in Rocky Mountain Peregrines, *Falco peregrinus*, and their prey. Can. Field-Nat. 96:255-264.

Enderson, J. H., D. G. Roseneau, and L. G. Swartz. 1968. Nesting performance and pesticide residues in Alaskan and Yukon Peregrines in 1967. Auk 85:683.

Enderson, J. H., S. A. Temple, and L. G. Swartz. 1972. Time-lapse photographic records of nesting Peregrine Falcons. Living Bird 11:113-128.

Enderson, J. H., and P. H. Wrege. 1973. DDE residues and eggshell thickness in Prairie Falcons. J. Wildl. Mgmt. 37:476-478.

Endler, J. A. 1977. Geographic variation, speciation and clines. Princeton, New Jersey, Princeton Univ. Press, Monog. Pop. Biol. No. 10.

Eng, R. L. 1952. A two-summer study of the effects on bird populations of chlordane bait and aldrin spray as used for grasshopper control. J. Wildl. Mgmt. 16:326-337.

Escalante, R. 1961. Occurrence of the Cassin race of the Peregrine Falcon in Uruguay. Condor 63:180.

Eutermoser, G. 1961. Erlauterungen zur Krähenstatistik. Deutscher Falkenorden: 49-60.

Evans, P. R. 1966. An approach to the analysis of visible migration and a comparison with radar observations. Ardea 54:14-44.

Evans, P. R., and G. W. Lathbury. 1973. Raptor mgiration across the Straits of Gibraltar. Ibis 115:572-585.

Faber, R. A., and J. J. Hickey. 1973. Eggshell thinning, chlorinated hydrocarbons, and mercury in inland aquatic bird eggs, 1969 and 1970. Pestic. Monitor. J. 7:27-36.

Faber, R. A., R. W. Risebrough, and H. M. Pratt. 1972. Organochlorines and mercury in Common Egrets and Great Blue Herons. Environ. Pollut. 3:111-122.

Falk, K., and S. Møeller. 1986. Vandrefalken *Falco peregrinus* i Sydgrønland. M. S. thesis, Roskilde Univ.

Falk, K., S. Møller, and W. A. Burnham. 1986. The Peregrine Falcon *Falco peregrinus* in South Greenland: nesting requirements, phenology and prey selection. Dansk Orn. Foren. Tidsskr. 80:113-120.

Fasce, P., and T. Mingozzi. 1983. Il Falco Pellegrino (*Falco peregrinus*) sulle Alpi Occidentali. Parte II: censimento e primi dati sulla biologia riproduttiva. Riv. Ital. di Orn. Milano 53:161-173.

Feilberg, J. 1984. A phytogeographical study of South Greenland. Vascular plants. Meddr. Grønland, Biosci. 15:1-70.

Ferguson, A. L., and H. L. Ferguson. 1922. The fall migration of hawks as observed at Fishers Island, N.Y. Auk 39:488-496.

Fessner, W. 1970. Success breeding Peregrine Falcons. Captive Breeding Diurnal Birds of Prey 1:22.

Fimreite, N., R. W. Fyfe, and J. A. Keith. 1970. Mercury contamination of Canadian prairie seed-eaters and their avian predators. Can. Field-Nat. 84:264-276.

Finch-Davies, C. G., and A. C. Kemp. 1982. The birds of prey of southern Africa. Johannesburg, South Africa, Winchester Press.

Fischer, W. 1967. Der Wanderfalk (*Falco peregrinus* und *Falco pelegrinoides*), 2nd ed. A. Ziemsen Verlag, Wittenberg Lutherstadt.

Fischer, W. 1972. Einige bemerkengen zum unterartenstatus nordamerikanischer Wanderfalken (*Falco peregrinus*). Beitr. Vogelkd. Leipzig 18:214-248.

Fischer, W. 1973. Der Wanderfalk: *Falco peregrinus* und *Falco pelegrinoides*. Die Neue Brehm-Buchereir, A Zremsen Verlag. German Democratic Republic, Wittenberg Lutherstadt.

Fisher, C. H. 1901. Reminiscences of a falconer. London, John C. Nimmo.

Flemming, W. J., M. A. R. McLane, and E. Cromartie. 1982. Endrin decreases Screech Owl productivity. J. Wildl. Mgmt. 46:462-467.

Flickinger, E. L., and K. A. King. 1972. Some effects of aldrin-treated rice on Gulf Coast wildlife. J. Wildl. Mgmt. 36:706-727.

Flickinger, E. L., and D. L. Meeker. 1972. Pesticide mortality of young White-faced Ibis in Texas. Bull. Environ. Contam. Toxicol. 8:165-168.

Flint, V. E. (Ed.). 1978. Krasnaga Kniga CCCP (Red data book of USSR). Part II. Birds. Moscow, Lesnaya Promyshlennost Publishers. (In Russian).

Forberg, S., and T. Odsjö. 1983. An X-ray back scatter method for field measurements of the quality of bird eggshells during incubation. Ambio 12:267-270.

Formont, A. 1969. Contribution a l'etude d'une population de Faucons Pélerins dans l'Est de la France. Nos Oiseaux 30:109-139.

Fox, G. A. 1971. Recent changes in the reproductive success of the Pigeon Hawk. J. Wildl. Mgmt. 35:122-128.

Fox, G. A., and T. Donald. 1980. Organochorine pollutants, nest defense behavior and reproductive success in Merlins. Condor 82:81-84.

Fox, G. A., A. P. Gilman, D. B. Peakall, and F. W. Anderka. 1978. Behavioral abnormalities of nesting Lake Ontario Herring Gulls. J. Wildl. Mgmt. 42:477-483.

Fox, R., S. W. Lehmkuhle, and D. H. Westendorf. 1976. Falcon visual acuity. Science 192:263-265.

Fuchs, P., J. Rooth, and R. H. De Vos. 1972. Residue levels of persistent chemicals in birds of prey and owls in the Netherlands in the period from 1965-1971. TNO-Nieuws 27:532-541.

Fyfe, R. 1972. Canadian Wildlife Service involvement with birds of prey. Trans. 36th Federal-Provincial Wildl. Conf.: 69-76.

Fyfe, R. W. 1969. The Peregrine Falcon in northern Canada. Pp. 101-114 in Peregrine Falcon populations: their biology and decline (J. J. Hickey, Ed.). Madison, Univ. Wisconsin Press.

Fyfe, R. W. 1973. Dieldrin and heptachlor epoxide in Alberta wildlife. Canadian Wildl. Serv., Pesticide Section, Manuscript Rep. No. 18.

Fyfe, R. W. 1976. Rationale and success of the Canadian Wildlife Service Peregrine breeding project. Can. Field-Nat. 90:308-319.

Fyfe, R. W., H. Armbruster, U. Banasch, and L. Beaver. 1977. Fostering and cross-fostering of birds of prey. Pp. 183-193 in Endangered birds: management techniques for preserving threatened species (S. Temple, Ed.). Madison, Univ. of Wisconsin Press.

Fyfe, R. W., and U. Banasch. 1981. Raptor banding in western Canada. Pp. 57-62 in Bird banding in Alberta (M. K. McNicholl, Ed.). Alberta Naturalist, Special Edition No. 2.

Fyfe, R. W., J. Campbell, B. Hayson, and K. Hodson. 1969. Regional population declines and organochlorine insecticides in Canadian Prairie Falcons. Can. Field-Nat. 83:191-200.

Fyfe, R. W., R. W. Risebrough, and W. Walker II. 1976b. Pollutant effects on the reproduction of the Prairie Falcons and Merlins of the Canadian prairies. Can. Field-Nat. 90:346-355.

Fyfe, R. W., S. A. Temple, and T. J. Cade. 1976a. The 1975 North American Peregrine Falcon survey. Can. Field-Nat. 90:228-273.

Gabrielson, I. N., and S. G. Jewett. 1940. Birds of Oregon. Corvallis, Oregon State College.

Gadgil, M., and W. H. Bossert. 1970. Life historical consequences of natural selection. Amer. Natur. 104:1-24.

Gallagher, M., and M. Woodcock. 1980. The birds of Oman. London, Quartet Books.

Galushin, V. M. 1977. Recent changes in the actual and legislative status of birds of prey in the U.S.S.R. Pp. 152-159 *in* Proceedings of the ICBP World Conference on Birds of Prey (R. D. Chancellor, Ed.). London, Intern. Council for Bird Preservation.

Gargett, V. 1977. A 13-year population study of the Black Eagles in the Matopos, Rhodesia, 1964-1976. Ostrich 48:17-27.

Garrett, R. L., and D. J. Mitchell. 1973. A study of Prairie Falcon populations in California. California Dept. of Fish and Game, Wildl. Mgmt. Branch, Admin. Rep. No. 73-2.

Garzón, J. 1973. Contribucion al estudio del status, alimentacion y proteccion de las Falconiformes en España Central. Ardeola 19:279-330.

Garzón, J. 1977. Birds of prey in Spain, the present situation. Pp. 159-170 *in* Proceedings of the ICBP World Conference on Birds of Prey (R. D. Chancellor, Ed.). London, Intern. Council for Bird Preservation.

Garzón, J., and J. Araujo. 1972. El clima y su posible influencia sobre las aves de presa. Ardeola 16:193-213.

Gauthreaux, S. A., Jr. 1971. A radar and direct visual study of passerine spring migration in southern Louisiana. Auk 88:343-365.

Genelly, R. E., and R. L. Rudd. 1956. Effects of DDT, toxaphene, and dieldrin on pheasant reproduction. Auk 73:529-539.

Geroudet, P. 1979. Les rapaces diurnes et nocturnes d'Europe, IV ed. Delachaux et Niesté, Neuchâtel.

Gerriets, D. 1984. Untersuchungen am Wanderfalken im Rahmen eines Artenschutzprojektes. Inaug. Diss. Veterinärmedizin FU Berlin.

Gesell, G. G., R. J. Robel, and J. Frieman. 1979. Effects of dieldrin on operant behavior of Bobwhites. J. Environ. Sci. Health B14:153-170.

Gilbertson, M., and L. Reynolds. 1973. A summary of DDE and PCB determinations in Canadian birds, 1969 to 1972. Can. Wildl. Serv. Occ. Pap. No. 19.

Glasier, P. E. B. 1978. Falconry and hawking. London, B. T. Batsford Ltd.

Glutz von Blotzheim, U. N., K. M. Bauer, and E. Bezzell. 1971. Handbuch der Vögel Mitteleuropas, vol. 4. Frankfurt am Main, Akademische Verlagsgesellschaft.

Gochfeld, M. 1977. Peregrine Falcon sightings in eastern Peru. Condor 79:391-392.

Goldberg, E. D. 1975. Synthetic organohalides in the sea. Proc. Roy. Soc. London 189:277-289.

González, L. M., and F. Hiraldo. 1985. Estudio preliminar del efecto de los contaminantes organochlorados sobre la reproduccion del Aguila Imperial Iberica. ICONA. Monografia 36, parte II:47-59.

Goodbourne, S. E. Y., D. R. Higgs, J. B. Clegg, and D. J. Weatherall. 1983. Molecular basis of length polymorphism in the human γ-globin gene complex. Proc. Natl. Acad. Sci. USA 80:5022-5026.

Gordon, A. C. H. (Lord Stanmore) (Ed.). 1897-1912. Fiji: records of private and of public life, 1875-1880, vol. I-IV. Edinburgh, private printing.

Govortchenko, V. I. 1983. DDT. Pp. 39 _in_ Scientific Reviews of Soviet Literature on Toxicity and Hazards of Chemicals (N. F. Izmerov, Ed.). Moscow, Centre of International Projects, GKNT.

Graber, R. R., S. L. Wunderle, and W. N. Bruce. 1965. Effects of a low-level dieldrin application on a Red-winged Blackbird population. Wilson Bull. 77:168-174.

Greenburg, R. R., R. W. Risebrough, and D. W. Anderson. 1979. _p,p'_-DDE-induced changes in the organic and inorganic structure of eggshells of the Mallard, _Anas platyrhynchos_. Toxicol. Appl. Pharmacol. 48:279-286.

Greenwood, P. J., P. H. Harvey, and C. M. Perrins. 1978. Inbreeding and dispersal in the Great Tit. Nature 271:52-54.

Grier, J. W. 1976. Predicting the success of raptor reintroductions through deterministic and stochastic models. Paper presented at the Raptor Research Foundation 1976 Annual Meeting, 29 Oct-1 Nov 1976. Ithaca, New York.

Grier, J. W. 1979. Caution on using productivity or age ratios alone for population inferences. Raptor Res. 13:20-24.

Grier, J. W. 1980a. Ecology: a simulation model for small populations of animals. Creative Computing 6:116-121.

Grier, J. W. 1980b. Modeling approaches to Bald Eagle population dynamics. Wildl. Soc. Bull. 8:316-322.

Grier, J. W. 1982. Ban of DDT and subsequent recovery of reproduction in Bald Eagles. Science 218:1232-1235.

Gunn, D. L. 1972. Dilemmas in conservation for applied biologists. Ann. Appl. Biol. 72:105-127.

Gusella, J. F., N. S. Wexler, P. M. Conneally, S. L. Nalor, M. A. Andersen, R. T. Tanzi, P. L. Watkins, K. Ottina, M. R. Wallace, A. Y. Sakaguchi, A. B. Young, I. Shoulson, E. Bonilla, and J. B. Martin. 1983. A polymorphic DNA marker genetically linked to Huntington's disease. Nature 306:234-238.

Haegele, M. A., and R. H. Hudson. 1977. Reduction of courtship behavior induced by DDE in male Ringed Turtle Doves. Wilson Bull. 89:593-601.

Hagar, J. A. 1969. History of the Massachusettes Peregrine Falcon population, 1935-1957. Pp. 123-131 _in_ Peregrine Falcon populations: their biology and decline (J. J. Hickey, Ed.). Madison, Univ. of Wisconsin Press.

Hagen, Y. 1952. Rovfuglene og viltpleien. Oslo, Gyldendal Norsk Forlag.

Hagen, Y. 1969. Norwegian studies on the reproduction of birds of prey and owls in relation to micro-rodent fluctuations. Fauna 22:73-126.

Hair, J. F., Jr., R. E. Anderson, R. L. Tatham, and B. J. Grablowsky. 1979. Multivariate data analysis with readings. Tulsa, Oklahoma, Petroleum Publ. Co.

Hall, G. H. 1955. Great moments in action: the story of the Sun Life falcons. Montreal, Mecury Press.

Hall, G. H. 1958. Eggs disappearing from Peregrine eyries. Brit. Birds 51:402-403.

Hall, G. H. 1970. Great moments in action: the story of the Sun Life Falcons. Can. Field-Nat. 84:209-230.

Hallamore, C. 1972. Observations on the African Peregrine by a falconer. Honeyguide 69:13-16.

Haller, H. 1982. Populationsokologie des steinadlers in den Alpen. Ornithol. Beob. 79:168-211.

Hallman, B. 1985. Status and conservation problems of birds of prey in Greece. Pp. 55-59 _in_ Conservation studies on raptors, ICBP Tech. Publ. No. 5 (I. Newton and R. D. Chancellor, Eds.). London, Intern. Council for Bird Preservation.

Hantge, E. 1968. Zum Beuterwerb unserer Wanderfalken. Ornithol. Mitt. 20:211-217.

Harrington, R. W., Jr., and W. L. Bidlingmayer. 1958. Effects of dieldrin on fishes and invertebrates of a salt marsh. J. Wildl. Mgmt. 22:76-82.

Harris, H., and D. A. Hopkinson. 1977. Handbook of enzyme electrophoresis in human genetics. New York, American Elsevier Publ. Co.

Harris, J. T., and D. M. Clement. 1975. Greenland Peregrines at their eyries. Meddr. Grønland 205:1-28.

Hartley, R. 1983. Successful breeding of the African Peregrine in captivity. Bokmakierie 35:75-77.

Haugh, J. R. 1972. A study of hawk migration in eastern North America. Cornell Univ. Agric. Exp. Stn. Search 2:1-60.

Haugh, J. R. 1976. Population changes in Alaskan arctic Peregrines. Can. Field-Nat. 90:359-361.

Hayes, R., and D. H. Mossop. 1982. The recovery of an interior Peregrine Falcon population in the northern Yukon Territory. Pp. 234-243 in Raptor management and biology in Alaska and western Canada (W. N. Ladd and P. F. Schempf, Eds.). U. S. Dept. Interior, Fish and Wildl. Serv., Alaska Regional Off.

Hayes, W. J., Jr. 1959. Pharmacology and toxicology of DDT. Pp. 9-247 in DDT, the insecticide dichlorodiphenyltrichloroethane and its significance (P. Mueller, Ed.). Birkhauser Verlag, Basel.

Hazeltine, W. 1972. Disagreements on why Brown Pelican eggs are thin. Nature 239:410-411.

Hazelwood, D. 1850. A Feejeean and English and an English and Feejeean dictionary: with examples of common and peculiar modes of expression, and uses of words. Vewa, Feejee, Wesleyan Mission Press.

Heath, R. G. 1969. Nationwide residues of organochlorine pesticides in wings of Mallards and Black Ducks. Pestic. Monitor. J. 3:115-123.

Heath, R. G., and S. A. Hill. 1974. Nationwide organochlorine and mercury residues in wings of adult Mallards and Black Ducks during the 1969-70 hunting season. Pestic. Monitor. J. 7:153-164.

Heath, R. G., J. W. Spann, and J. F. Kreitzer. 1969. Marked DDE impairment of Mallard reproduction in controlled studies. Nature 224:47-48.

Heath, R. G., J. W. Spann, J. F. Kreitzer, and C. Vance. 1972. Effects of polychlorinated biphenyls on birds. Proc. 15th Intern. Ornithol. Congr.: 475-481.

Heck, W. R., and D. Konkel. 1983. Incubation and rearing. Pp. 34-76 in Falcon propagation: a manual on captive breeding (J. D. Weaver and T. J. Cade, Eds.). Boise, Idaho, The Peregrine Fund, Inc.

Heinroth, O., and M. Heinroth. 1967. Die Vögel Mitteleuropas, 2 vols. Leipzig.

Heinz, G. H. 1976a. Methylmercury: second-year feeding effects on Mallard reproduction and duckling behavior. J. Wildl. Mgmt. 40:82-90.

Heinz, G. H. 1976b. Behavior of Mallard ducklings from parents fed 3 ppm DDE. Bull. Environ. Contam. Toxicol. 16:640-645.

Heinz, G. H. 1979. Methylmercury: reproductive and behavioral effects on three generations of Mallard Ducks. J. Wildl. Mgmt. 43:394-401.

Hellmayr, C. E. 1932. The Birds of Chile. Publ. No. 308, Field Mus. of Nat. Hist. 19:282-283.

Hellmayr, C. E., and B. Conover. 1949. Catalogue of birds of the Americas, Part 1, No. 4. Field Mus. Nat. Hist. Ser. Vol. 13.

Henny, C. J. 1972. An analysis of the population dynamics of selected avian species. Washington, D. C., U. S. Bureau of Sport, Fish. and Wildl. Res. Rep. 1.

Henny, C. J. 1977. Research, management and status of the Osprey in North America. Pp. 199-222 *in* Proceedings of the ICBP World Conference on Birds of Prey (R. D. Chancellor, Ed.). London, Intern. Council for Bird Preservation.

Henny, C. J., L. J. Blus, and R. M. Prouty. 1982b. Organochlorine residues and eggshell thinning in Oregon seabird eggs. Murrelet 63:15-21.

Henny, C. J., L. J. Blus, and C. J. Stafford. 1983. Effects of heptachlor on American Kestrels in the Columbia Basin, Oregon. J. Wildl. Mgmt. 47:1080-1087.

Henny, C. J., and W. S. Clark. 1982. Measurements of fall migrant Peregrine Falcons from Texas and New Jersey. J. Field Ornithol. 53:326-332.

Henny, C. J., A. J. Krynitsky, and C. M. Bunck. 1984. Current impact of DDE on Black-crowned Night-Herons in the intermountain west. J. Wildl. Mgmt. 48:1-13.

Henny, C. J., C. Maser, J. O. Whitaker Jr., and T. E. Kaiser. 1982a. Organochlorine residues in bats after a forest spraying with DDT. Northwest Sci. 56:329-337.

Henny, C. J., and D. L. Meeker. 1981. An evaluation of blood plasma for monitoring DDE in birds of prey. Environ. Pollut. A25:291-304.

Henny, C. J., and M. W. Nelson. 1981. Decline and present status of breeding Peregrine Falcons in Oregon. Murrelet 62:43-53.

Henny, C. J., and J. C. Ogden. 1970. Estimated status of Osprey populations in the United States. J. Wildl. Mgmt. 34:214-217.

Henny, C. J., W. S. Overton, and H. M. Wight. 1970. Determining parameters for populations by using structural models. J. Wildl. Mgmt. 34:690-703.

Henny, C. J., F. P. Ward, K. E. Riddle, and R. M. Prouty. 1982c. Migratory Peregrine Falcons, *Falco peregrinus*, accumulate pesticides in Latin America during winter. Can. Field-Nat. 96:333-338.

Henny, C. J., and H. M. Wight. 1969. An endangered Osprey population: estimates of mortality and production. Auk 86:188-198.

Henny, C. J., and H. M. Wight. 1972. Red-tailed and Cooper's Hawks: their population ecology and environmental pollution. Pp. 229-250 *in* Population Ecology of Migratory Birds. Patuxent Wildl. Res. Center.

Henriksson, K., E. Karppanen, and M. Helminen. 1966. High residue of mercury in Finnish White-tailed Eagles. Ornis Fennica 43:38-45.

Hepp, K. F. 1982. "Kunsthorstbauten" für Wanderfalken in Baden-Württemberg. Veroff. Naturschutz Landschaftspflege Bad.-Württ. 55/56:23-26.

Herbert, R. A., and K. G. S. Herbert. 1965. Behavior of Peregrine Falcons in the New York City region. Auk 82:62-94.

Herbert, R. A., and K. G. S. Herbert. 1969. The extirpation of the Hudson River Peregrine Falcon population. Pp. 133-154 *in* Peregrine Falcon populations: their biology and decline (J. J. Hickey, Ed.). Madison, Univ. of Wisconsin Press.

Herman, S. G. 1971. The Peregrine Falcon decline in California. Amer. Birds 25:818-820.

Herman, S. G., and J. B. Bulger. 1981. The distribution and abundance of shorebirds during the 1981 spring migration at Grays Harbor, Washington. Seattle, Washington, U. S. Army Corps of Eng. Rep. No. DACW67-81-0939.

Herman, S. G., M. N. Kirven, and R. W. Risebrough. 1970. The Peregrine Falcon decline in California: I. A preliminary review. Audubon Field Notes 24:609-613.

Hernández, L. M. 1982. Contaminacion de las aves por pesticidas. Quercus 3:24-25.

Herren, H. 1962. *Falco peregrinus*. Pp. 226-229 *in* Die Brutvogel der Schweiz (U. Glutz von Blotzheim, Ed.). Sempach, Schweizerischen Vogelwarte.

Hester, F. E. 1985. Remarks of the Acting Director, U. S. Fish and Wildlife Service, at award ceremony honoring Jeff and Anne McPartlin. Washington, D. C., November 6, 1985.

Hickey, J. J. 1942. Eastern population of the Duck Hawk. Auk 59:176-204.

Hickey, J. J. 1943. A guide to bird watching. New York, Oxford Univ. Press.

Hickey, J. J. (Ed.). 1969. Peregrine Falcon populations: their biology and decline. Madison, Univ. of Wisconsin Press.

Hickey, J. J., and D. W. Anderson. 1968. Chlorinated hydrocarbons and eggshell changes in raptorial and fish-eating birds. Science 162:271-273.

Hickey, J. J., and D. W. Anderson. 1969. The Peregrine Falcon: life history and population literature. Pp. 3-42 *in* Peregrine Falcon populations: their biology and decline (J. J. Hickey, Ed.). Madison, Univ. of Wisconsin Press.

Hickey, J. J., and L. B. Hunt. 1960a. Initial song bird mortality following Dutch elm disease control program. J. Wildl. Mgmt. 24:259-265.

Hickey, J. J., and L. B. Hunt. 1960b. Songbird mortality following annual programs to control Dutch elm disease. Atl. Nat. 15:87-92.

Higgs, D. R., S. E. Y. Goodbourne, J. S. Wainscoat, J. B. Clegg, and D. J. Weatherall. 1981. Highly variable regions of DNA flank the human alpha globin genes. Nucleic Acids Res. 9:4213-4224.

Hilgert, N. 1984. Historia Natural del Halcon Peregrino (*Falco peregrinus*) en el Valle de Guayllabamba. Soc. Ecust. de Biologia, VIII Jornadas de Biologia, vol. 1, Ambato.

Hiraldo, F., J. Andrada, and F. F. Parreno. 1975. Diet of the Eagle Owl (*Bubo bubo*) in Mediterranean Spain. Donana Acta Vertebrata 2:161-177.

Hitchcock, M. A. 1976. A breeding survey of Peregrine Falcons in northeastern Mexico, 1975-1976. Chihuahuan Desert Res. Inst. Contrib. No. 5.

Hitchcock, M. A. 1978. A nesting survey and ecological study of the Peregrine Falcon in the western Chihuahuan Desert, 1976-1978. M. S. thesis, Alpine, Texas, Sul Ross State Univ.

Hofslund, P. B. 1966. Hawk migration over the western tip of Lake Superior. Wilson Bull. 78:79-87.

Högstedt, G. 1981. Should there be a positive or negative correlation between survival of adults in a bird population and their clutch size? Amer. Natur. 118:568-571.

Hoolihan, J., and W. A. Burnham. 1982. Peregrine Falcon semen: a qualitative and quantitative examination. Raptor Res. 19:125-127.

Hovis, J. T., D. Snowman, V. L. Cox, R. Fay, and K. L. Bildstein. 1985. Nesting behavior of Peregrine Falcons in West Greenland during the nestling period. Raptor Res. 19:15-19.

Howell, A. B. 1917. Birds of the islands of the coast of southern California. Pacific Coast Avif. No. 12.

Hoyt, D. F. 1979. Practical methods of estimating volume and fresh weight of birds eggs. Auk 96:73-77.

Hudson, R. H., R. K. Tucker, and M. A. Haegele. 1984. Handbook of toxicity of pesticides to wildlife. Washington D. C., U. S. Dept. of Interior, Fish and Wildl. Serv. Resource Publ. 153.

Humphrey, P. S., D. Bridge, P. W. Reynolds, and R. T. Peterson. 1970. Birds of Isla Grande (Tierra del Fuego). Preliminary Smithsonian Manual, Univ. of Kansas Mus. of Nat. Hist.

Hunt, W. G. 1966. Observations of Peregrines on the Texas coast. M. S. thesis, Alpine, Texas, Sul Ross State Univ.

Hunt, W. G. 1977. The significance of wilderness ecosystems in western Texas and adjacent regions in the ecology of the Peregrine. *In* Transactions of the Symposium on the Biological Resources of the Chihuahuan Desert: United States and Mexico (R. H. Wauer and D. H. Riskind, Eds.). National Park Serv. Trans. and Proc. Series No. 3.

Hunt, W. G., B. S. Johnson, C. G. Thelander, B. J. Walton, R. W. Risebrough, W. M. Jarman, A. M. Springer, J. G. Monk, and W. Walker II. 1986. Environmental levels of p,p'-DDE indicate multiple sources. Environ. Toxicol. Chem. 5:21-27.

Hunt, W. G., F. P. Ward, and B. S. Johnson. 1981. Peregrine Falcon migrations: continuing studies. U. S. Army Report.

Hunt, W. G., F. P. Ward, B. S. Johnson, C. M. Anderson, and G. P. Vose. 1980. A study of the spring passage of Peregrine Falcons at Padre Island, Texas, using radio telemetry. BioSystems Analysis, Inc. for U. S. Fish and Wildl. Serv. (Contract No. 14-16-0002-80-220) and National Park Serv. (Contract No. I-126).

Hunt, W. G., R. R. Rogers, and D. J. Slowe. 1975. Migratory and foraging behavior of Peregrine Falcons on the Texas coast. Can. Field-Nat. 89:111-123.

Hunter, D. V., Jr., and B. E. Harrell (Eds.). 1967. Raptor Research News, vol.1.No.1.

Hussell, D. J. H. 1972. Factors affecting clutch size in Arctic passerines. Ecol. Monogr. 42:317-364.

Hussell, D. J. H. 1981. The use of migration counts for monitoring bird population levels. Pp. 92-102 *in* Estimating numbers of terrestrial birds (C. J. Ralph and J. M. Scott, Eds.). Stud. Avian Biol. No. 6.

Hustler, K. 1983. Breeding biology of Peregrine Falcons in Zimbabwe. Ostrich 54:161-171.

Idso, S. B. 1983. Carbon dioxide and global temperature: what the data show. J. Environ. Quality 12:159-163.

Idso, S. B. 1984. CO_2 greenhouse effect: the big scare. Fusion Sept.-Oct. 1984:6-8.

Irwin, M. P. S. 1981. The birds of Zimbabwe. Salisbury (Harare), Zimbabwe, Quest Publ.

Ito, M. 1986. Peregrine Falcon. Tokyo, Yama-kli Publishers Co. Ltd. (In Japanese).

Jacknow, J., J. L. Ludke, and N. C. Coon. 1986. Monitoring fish and wildlife for environmental contaminants, the national contaminant biomonitoring program. U.S. Dept. of Interior, U. S. Fish and Wildl. Serv., Fish and Wildl. Leaflet 4.

James, F. C. 1970. Geographic size variation in birds and its relationship to climate. Ecology 51:365-390.

James, F. C. 1983. Environmental components of morphological differentiation in birds. Science 221:184-186.

Jefferies, D. J. 1969. Induction of apparent hyperthyroidism in birds fed DDT. Nature 222:578-579.

Jefferies, D. J. 1973. The effects of organochlorine insecticides and their metabolites on birds. J. Reprod. Fert. 19:337-352.

Jefferies, D. J., and M. C. French. 1972. Changes induced in the pigeon thyroid by *p,p'*-DDE and dieldrin. J. Wildl. Mgmt. 36:24-30.

Jefferies, D. J., and J. L. F. Parslow. 1972. Effect of one polychlorinated biphenyl on size and activity of the gull thyroid. Bull. Environ. Contam. Toxicol. 8:306-310.

Jefferies, D. J., and I. Prestt. 1966. Post-mortems of Peregrines and Lanners with particular reference to organochlorine residues. Brit. Birds 59:49-64.

Jeffreys, A. J., V. Wilson, and S. L. Thein. 1985. Hypervariable "minisatellite" regions in human DNA. Nature 314:67-73.

Jehl, J. R., and M. A. E. Rumboll. 1976. Notes on the avifauna of Isla Grande and Patagonia, Argentina. Trans. San Diego Soc. of Nat. Hist. 18:145-154.

Jenkins, M. A. 1978. Gyrfalcon nesting behavior from hatching to fledging. Auk 95:122-127.

Jenkins, M. A. 1984. A clutch of unusually small Peregrine Falcon eggs. Raptor Res. 18:151-153.

Jennings, M. J. 1981a. Birds of the Arabian Gulf. London, George Allen and Unwin Ltd.

Jennings, M. J. 1981b. The birds of Saudi Arabia: a checklist. Private printing.

Jenny, J. P., W. A. Burnham, T. De Vries, N. Hilgert, and F. Ortiz. 1983. Analysis of Peregrine Falcon eggs in Ecuador. Condor 85:502.

Jenny, J. P., F. Ortiz, and M. D. Arnold. 1981. First nesting record of the Peregrine Falcon in Ecuador. Condor 83:387.

Johnson, A. W. 1965. The birds of Chile and adjacent regions of Argentina, Bolivia, and Peru, Part I. Buenos Aires, Platt Establecimientos Graficos.

Johnson, A. W. 1967. The birds of Chile and adjacent regions of Argentina, Bolivia, and Peru, Part II. Buenos Aires, Platt Establecimientos Graficos.

Johnson, L. D., R. H. Waltz, J. P. Ussary, and F. E. Kaiser. 1976. Automated gel permeation chromatographic cleanup of animal and plant extracts for pesticide residue determination. J. Assoc. Off. Anal. Chem. 59:174-187.

Johnston, D. W. 1974. Decline of DDT residues in migratory songbirds. Science 186:841-842.

Johnston, R. F., and R. K. Selander. 1971. Evolution in the House Sparrow. II. Adaptive differentiation in North American populations. Evolution 25:1-28.

Johnstone, W. G. 1853. The Peregrine Falcon (*Falco peregrinus*) laying eggs in confinement. The Naturalist 3:106-107.

Joiris, C., J. Dejaegher, and K. Delbeke. 1979. Changes of eggshell thickness in Belgian birds of prey. Le Gerfaut 69:195-210.

Jones, F. M. 1946. Duck Hawks of eastern Virginia. Auk 63:592.

Jones, S. G., and W. M. Bren. 1978. Observations on the wintering behaviour of Victorian Peregrine Falcons. Australian Bird Watcher 7:198-203.

Judiciary Committee, House of Representatives. 1984. FBI undercover operations. Report of the Subcommittee on Civil and Constitutional Rights of the Committee on the Judiciary, House of Representatives, April 1984. House Doc. 98-267, Washington, D. C., U. S. Government Printing Office.

Jung, C. S. 1964. Weather conditions affecting hawk migrations. Lore 14:134-142.

Kaiser, K. L. E. 1978. The rise and fall of mirex. Environ. Sci. Technol. 12:520-528.

Kaiser, T. E., W. L. Reichel, L. N. Locke, E. Cromartie, A. J. Krynitsky, T. G. Lamont, B. M. Mulhern, R. M. Prouty, C. J. Stafford, and D. M. Swineford. 1980. Organochlorine pesticides, PCBs, PCB residues, and necropsy data for Bald Eagles from 29 states: 1975-77. Pestic. Monitor. J. 13:145-149.

Kanafani, A. S. 1983. Aesthetics and ritual in the United Arab Emirates. Beirut, Lebanon, American Univ. of Beirut.

Kaufmann, J., and H. Meng. 1975. Falcons return. New York, William Morrow and Company.

Keck, G., P. Paubel, and R.-J. Monneret. 1982. Organochlorine and mercury residues in Peregrine Falcon eggs in France. Bull. Environ. Contam. Toxicol. 28:705-709.

Keith, A. R. 1970. Bird observations from Tierra del Fuego. Condor 72:361-363.

Keith, J. A., and I. M. Gruchy. 1972. Residue levels of chemical pollutants in North American birdlife. Proc. 15th Intern. Ornithol. Congr.: 437-454.

Keith, J. O. 1966. Insecticide contaminations in wetland habitats and their effects on fish-eating birds. J. Appl. Ecol. 3 (suppl):71-85.

Keith, J. O., and E. G. Hunt. 1966. Levels of insecticide residues in fish and wildlife in California. Proc. 31st N. Amer. Wildl. Conf. 150-177.

Kendall, H. 1968. Breeding Prairie Falcons in captivity. J. N. Amer. Falconers' Assoc. 7:57-64.

Kenward, R. 1977. Captive breeding: a contribution by falconers to preservation of Falconiformes. Pp. 378-381 in Proceedings of the ICBP World Conference on Birds of Prey (R. D. Chancellor, Ed.). London, Intern. Council for Bird Preservation.

Kenward, R. E. (Ed.). 1972. Captive breeding of diurnal birds of prey, vol. 1. No. 3.

Kerlinger, P. 1985. Water crossing behavior of raptors during migration. Wilson Bull. 97:109-113.

Kerlinger, P., V. P. Bingman, and K. P. Able. 1985. Comparative flight behaviors of migrating hawks studied with tracking radar during autumn in central New York. Can. J. Zool. 63:755-761.

Kesteloot, E. J. J. 1977. Present situation of birds of prey in Belgium. Pp. 85-87 in Proceedings of the ICBP World Conference on Birds of Prey (R. D. Chancellor, Ed.). London, Intern. Council for Bird Preservation.

Kiff, L. F. 1980. Historical changes in resident populations of California Islands raptors. Pp. 651-673 in The California Islands: proceedings of a multidisciplinary symposium (D. M. Power, Ed.). Santa Barbara, California, Santa Barbara Mus. Nat. Hist.

Kiff, L. F., D. B. Peakall, and D. P. Hector. 1980. Eggshell thinning and organochlorine residues in the Bat and Aplomado Falcons in Mexico. Proc. 17th Intern. Ornithol. Congr.: 949-952.

Kiff, L. F., D. B. Peakall, M. L. Morrison, and S. R. Wilbur. 1983. Eggshell thickness and DDE residue levels in vulture eggs. Pp. 440-458 in Vulture biology and management (S. R. Wilbur and J. A. Jackson, Eds.). Berkeley, Univ. California Press.

Kiff, L. F., D. B. Peakall, and S. R. Wilbur. 1979. Recent changes in California Condor eggshells. Condor 81:166-172.

Kimball, B. A. 1983. Carbon dioxide and agricultural yield: an assemblage and analysis of 430 prior observations. Agronomy J. 75:779-783.

Kimball, B. A., and S. B. Idso. 1983. Increasing atmospheric CO_2: effects on crop yield, water use and climate. Agricul. Water Mgmt. 7:55-72.

Kirmse, W. 1970. Beobachtungen an einheimischen Wanderfalken, Falco p. peregrinus Tunstall. Beitrage z. Vogelkunde XV:320-332.

Kirmse, W., and G. Kleinstäuber. 1977. Die Kalculation der Populationsentwicklung von Wildtierarten, Dargestellt am Beispiel der Felsbruten Wanderfalken (*Falco p. peregrinus* Gmel.) in der DDR. Mitt. Zool. Mus. Berlin, Bd. 53, Suppl., 1977: Ann. Orn. 1:137-148.

Kirven, M. N. 1982. Peregrine Falcon inventory and management recommendations for the Ukiah BLM District, 1982. Ukiah District Office, California, U. S. Bureau of Land Mgmt.

Kirven, M. N. 1983. Peregrine Falcon inventory and management recommendations for the Ukiah BLM District, 1983. Ukiah District Office, California, U. S. Bureau of Land Mgmt.

Kirven, M. N. 1984. Peregrine Falcon inventory and management recommendations for the Ukiah BLM District, 1984. Ukiah District Office, California, U. S. Bureau of Land Mgmt.

Kirven, M. N. 1985. Peregrine Falcon inventory and management recommendations for the Ukiah BLM District, 1985. Ukiah District Office, California, U. S. Bureau of Land Mgmt.

Kirven, M. N. 1986. Peregrine Falcon population monitoring and management in the Ukiah BLM District, 1986. Ukiah District Office, California, U. S. Bureau of Land Mgmt.

Kitchin, E. A. 1930. Fall observations at West Point. Murrelet 11:71-73.

Klaas, E. E., and D. M. Swineford. 1976. Chemical residue content and hatchability of Screech Owl eggs. Wilson Bull. 88:421-426.

Kleinschmidt, O. 1958. Raubvögel und eulen der heimat. A. Ziemsen Verlag. German Democratic Republic, Wittenberg Lutherstadt.

Kleinstäuber, K. 1963. Bestandskontrolle und Horstsicherungsmassnahmen fur unsere Felsen-Wanderfalken (Stand 1962). Falke, Publ. A, Berlin 10 3:44-46.

Kleinstäuber, K. 1969. The status of cliff-nesting Peregrines in the German Democratic Republic. Pp. 209-216 *in* Peregrine Falcon populations: their biology and decline (J. J. Hickey, Ed.). Madison, Univ. of Wisconsin Press.

Kleinstäuber, K., R. Zimmermann, and R. Marz. 1938. Das Vorkommen von Wanderfalk, *Falco peregrinus* Tunst., und Uhu, *Bubo bubo* (L.), in Sachsen. Tharandter Forstliches Jahrbuch 89:714-739.

Kluyver, H. N. 1963. The determination of reproductive rates in Paridae. Proc. 13th Intern. Ornithol. Congr.: 706-716.

Koehler, A. 1968. Über die Fortpflanzung einiger Greifvö gelarten in Gefangenschaft. Falkner 18:28-33.

Koehler, A. 1969. Captive breeding of some raptors. Raptor Res. News 3:3-18.

Koeman, J. H., C. F. van Beusekom, and J. J. M. de Goeij. 1972. Eggshell and population changes in the Sparrow Hawk. TNO-Nieuws 27:542-550.

Koeman, J. H., and H. van Genderen. 1966. Some preliminary notes on residues of chlorinated hydrocarbon insecticides in birds and mammals in The Netherlands. J. Appl. Ecol. 3(Suppl):99-106.

Koeman, J. H., J. A. J. Vink, and J. J. M. de Goeij. 1969. Causes of mortality in birds of prey and owls in The Netherlands in the winter of 1968-1969. Ardea 57:67-76.

König, C. 1977. The situation of the Peregrine Falcon (*Falco peregrinus*) in South-Western Germany. Pp. 115-118 *in* Proceedings of the ICBP World Conference on Birds of Prey (R. D. Chancellor, Ed.). Intern. Council for Bird Preservation.

König, C., and F. Schilling. 1970. Beeinflussen Pestizide die Populationsentwicklung des Wanderfalken (*Falco peregrinus*) in Baden-Württemberg? Vogelwelt 91:170-176.

Krantz, W. C., B. M. Mulhern, G. E. Bagley, A. Sprunt, IV, F. J. Ligas, and W. B. Robertson, Jr. 1970. Organochlorine and heavy metal residues in Bald Eagle eggs. Pestic. Monitor. J. 3:136-140.

Krebs, C. J. 1964. The Lemming cycle at Baker Lake, Northwest Territories, during 1959-62. Arctic Institute of North America, Tech. Paper No. 15.

Krebs, C. J. 1985. Ecology, 3rd ed. New York, Harper and Row.

Krebs, J. R. 1978. Optimal foraging: decision rules for predators. Pp. 23-63 *in* Behavioral ecology: an evolutionary approach (J. R. Krebs and N. B. Davies, Eds.). Sunderland, Massachusetts, Sinauer.

Kreitzer, J. F. 1974. Residues of organochlorine pesticides, mercury and PCBs in Mourning Doves from eastern United States, 1970-71. Pestic. Monitor. J. 7:195-199.

Kreitzer, J. F. 1980. Effects of toxaphene and endrin at very low dietary concentrations on discrimination acquisition and reversal in Bobwhite Quail, *Colinus virginianus*. Environ. Pollut. 23:217-230.

Kreitzer, J. F., and J. W. Spann. 1968. Mortality among Bobwhites confined to a heptachlor contaminated environment. J. Wildl. Mgmt. 32:874-878.

Kruyfhooft, C. 1964. Serious decrease of the Peregrine Falcon in Belgium during the autumn migration. Pp. 70-73 *in* Working conference on birds of prey and owls. Caen, 10-12 April 1964. Intern. Council for Bird Preservation.

Kuhk, R. 1969. Weiteres über Bruten des Wanderfalken (*Falco peregrinus*) an menschlichen Bauwerken. Deutscher Falkenorden 1968:65-66.

Kumari, E. 1974. Past and present of the Peregrine Falcon in Estonia. Pp. 230-252 *in* Estonian wetlands and their life (E. Kumari, Ed.). Estonian contribution to IBP, No. 7. Acad. Sci. Estonian S.S.R.

Kumlien, L. 1879. Contributions to the natural history of Arctic America made in connection with the Howgate Polar Expedition: 1877-1878. U. S. Natl. Mus. Bull. No. 15.

Kuyt, E. 1980. Distribution and breeding biology of raptors in the Thelon River area, Northwest Territories, 1957-1969. Can. Field-Nat. 94:121-130.

Labisky, R. F., and R. W. Lutz. 1967. Responses of wild pheasants to solid-block applications of aldrin. J. Wildl. Mgmt. 31:13-24.

Lack, D. 1954. The natural regulation of animal numbers. Oxford, Clarendon Press.

Lack, D. 1966. Population studies of birds. Oxford, Oxford Univ. Press.

Lamb, C. C. 1927. The birds of Natividad Island, Lower California. Condor 29:67-70.

Lambertson, R. E. 1985. Statement of Ronald E. Lambertson, Associate Director for Wildlife Resources, U. S. Fish and Wildlife Service, U. S. Dept. of the Interior. Pp. 461-465 *in* Endangered Species Act hearings before the Subcommittee on Fisheries and Wildlife Conservation and the Environment of the Committee on Merchant Marine and Fisheries, House of Representatives. Captive Raptors H. R. 2767. Serial No. 99-10, Washington, D. C., U. S. Government Printing Office.

Lanning, D. V., and P. W. Lawson. 1977. Ecology of the Peregrine Falcon in northeastern Mexico, 1977. Chihuahuan Desert Res. Inst. Contrib. No. 41.

Lanning, D. V., P. W. Lawson, and W. G. Hunt. 1985. Ecology of the Peregrine Falcon in northeastern Mexico. Pp. 377-388 *in* National Geographic Society Research Reports, 1977, vol. 18 (W. Swanson, Ed.). Washington, D. C., National Geographic Society.

Lehmann, V. W., and R. G. Mauermann. 1963. Status of Attwater's Prairie Chicken. J. Wildl. Mgmt. 27:713-724.

Lesheim, Y. 1985. Israel: an international axis of raptor migration. Pp. 243-255 *in* Conservation studies on raptors, ICBP Tech. Publ. No. 5 (I. Newton and R. D. Chancellor, Eds.). Cambridge, Intern. Council for Bird Preservation.

Levi, W. M. 1941. The Pigeon. Sumter, South Carolina, Levi Publ. Co.

Lincer, J. L. 1972. The effects of organochlorines on the American Kestrel (*Falco sparverius* Linn.). Ph.D. dissertation, Ithaca, New York, Cornell Univ.

Lincer, J. L. 1975. DDE-induced shell thinning in the American Kestrel: a comparison of the field situation and laboratory results. J. Appl. Ecol. 12:781-793.

Lincer, J. L., T. J. Cade, and J. M. Devine. 1970. Organochlorine residues in Alaskan Peregrine Falcons (*Falco peregrinus* Tunstall), Rough-legged Hawks (*Buteo lagopus* Potoppidan), and their prey. Can. Field-Nat. 84:255-263.

Lincer, J. L., and J. A. Sherburne. 1974. Organochlorines in Kestrel prey: a north-south dichotomy. J. Wildl. Mgmt. 38:427-434.

Lindberg, P. 1975. Pilgrimsfalken i Sverige. Stockholm, Swedish Society for the Conservation of Nature.

Lindberg, P. (Ed.). 1977a. Ringmarkning av Pilgrimsfalk i Sverige. Pilgrimsfalk. Report from a Peregrine conference held at Grimso Wildlife Research Station, Sweden 1-2 April 1977. Stockholm, Swedish Society for the Conservation of Nature.

Lindberg, P. 1977b. The Peregrine Falcon in Sweden. Pp. 329-338 *in* Proceedings of the ICBP World Conference on Birds of Prey (R. D. Chancellor, Ed.). London, Intern. Council for Bird Preservation.

Lindberg, P. 1981. Insampling och maskinruvning av agg fran pilgrimsfalk *Falco peregrinus*. Var Fagelvarld 40:327-340.

Lindberg, P. 1983. Captive breeding and a programme for the reintroduction of the Peregrine Falcon (*Falco peregrinus*) in Fennoscandia. Proc. Third Nordic Congr. Ornithol. 1981:65-78.

Lindberg, P. 1985. Population status, pesticide impact and conservation efforts for the Peregrine (*Falco peregrinus*) in Sweden, with some comparative data from Norway and Finland. Pp. 343-351 *in* Conservation Studies on Raptors, ICBP Tech. Pub. No. 5 (I. Newton and R. D. Chancellor, Eds.). London, Intern. Council for Bird Preservation.

Lindberg, P., and R. Mearns. 1982. Occurrence of mercury in feathers from Scottish Peregrines (*Falco peregrinus*). Bull. Environ. Contam. Toxicol. 28:181-185.

Lindberg, P., and T. Odsjö. 1983. Mercury levels in feathers of Peregrine Falcon *Falco peregrinus* compared with total mercury content in some of its prey species in Sweden. Environ. Pollut. B5:297-318.

Lindberg, P., T. Odsjö, and L. Reutergardh. 1985. Residue levels of polychloro-biphenyls, ΣDDT, and mercury in bird species commonly preyed upon by the Peregrine Falcon (*Falco peregrinus* Tunst.) in Sweden. Arch. Environ. Contam. Toxicol. 14:203-212.

Linde'n, H., T. Nygård, and M. Wikman. 1984. On the eggshell thickness and reproduction of the Peregrine Falcon (*Falco peregrinus*) in Finland. Ornis Fennica 61:116-120.

Linkola, P., and T. Suominen. 1969. Population trends in Finnish Peregrines. Pp. 183-191 *in* Peregrine Falcon populations: their biology and decline (J. J. Hickey, Ed.). Madison, Univ. of Wisconsin Press.

Lockie, J. D. 1955. The breeding habits and food of the Short-eared Owl after a Vole plague. Bird Study 2:53-69.

Loft, J. 1978. The Skoole for a young ostringer or faulkener. (Mus. Brit. Bibl. Sloane 2721 Plut. XCVC). Falconer 7:112-117.

Longcore, J. R., F. B. Sampson, and T. W. Wittendale, Jr. 1971. DDE thins eggshells and lowers reproductive success of captive Black Ducks. Bull. Environ. Contam. Toxicol. 8:485-490.

Longmore, N. W. 1978. Avifauna of the Rockhampton area, Queensland. Sunbird 9:25-53.

Lopez Beiras, Z., and J. Guitian. 1983. Atlas provisional de los vertebrados terrestres de Galicia. Parte II. Aves nidificantes. Univ. Santiago de Compostela, Instituto Desarrollo de Galicia.

Maatsch, I., and U. Beyerbach. 1971. Über die Oinstrumentelle Samennubertragung bei einem Wanderfalken paar. Der Prakt. Tierarzt 4:140.

MacDonald, I. A. W., and V. Gargett. 1984. Raptor density and diversity in the Matopos, Zimbabwe. Proc. 5th Pan-African Ornithol. Congr.: 287-308.

MacIntyre, D. 1960. Nature notes of a highland gamekeeper. London, Seeley, Service and Co. Ltd.

MacPherson, A. H., and I. A. McLaren. 1959. Notes on the birds of southern Foxe Peninsula, Baffin Island, Northwest Territories. Can. Field-Nat. 73:63-81.

Maher, W. J. 1980. Growth of the Horned Lark at Rankin Inlet, Northwest Territories. Can. Field-Nat. 94:405-410.

Maniatis, T., E. F. Fritsch, and J. Sambrook. 1982. Molecular cloning: a laboratory manual. Cold Spring Harbor, New York, Cold Spring Harbor Laboratory.

Martin, W. E. 1969. Organochlorine insecticide residues in Starlings. Pestic. Monitor. J. 7:62-66.

Martin, W. E., and P. R. Nickerson. 1972. Organochlorine residues in Starlings, 1970. Pestic. Monitor. J. 6:33-40.

Martorelli, G. 1960. Gli Uccelli d'Italia (ed. riveduta da E. Moltoni and C. Vandoni). Milano, Rizzoli.

Matsumura, F. 1985. Toxicology of insecticides, 2nd ed. New York, Plenum Press.

Mayr, E. 1941. Geographic variation of *Falco peregrinus* in the Papuan and Australian region. Amer. Mus. Novit. 1133:1-2.

Mayr, E. 1945. Birds of the southwest Pacific. New York, The Macmillan Co.

Mayr, E. 1969. Principles of systematic zoology. New York, McGraw-Hill.

Mayr, E. 1982. Of what use are subspecies? Auk 99:593-595.

Mayr, E., and L. L. Short. 1970. Species taxa of North American birds: a contribution to comparative systematics. Publ. Nuttall Ornithol. Club No. 9.

McArthur, M. L. B., G. A. Fox, D. B. Peakall, and B. J. R. Philogene. 1983. Ecological significance of behavioral and hormonal abnormalities in breeding Ring Doves fed an organochlorine chemical mixture. Arch. Environ. Contam. Toxicol. 12:324-353.

McEwan, E. H. 1957. Birds observed at Bathurst Inlet, Northwest Territories. Can. Field-Nat. 71:109-115.

McEwen, L. C., C. E. Knittle, and M. L. Richmond. 1972. Wildlife effects from grasshopper insecticides sprayed on short-grass range. J. Range Mgmt. 25:188-195.

McGregor, R. C. 1899. The Duck Hawk in lower California. Oologist 16:181-182.

McKay, P. 1987. Criminal justice. Operation Falcon: a special report. The Whig-Standard Magazine. Kingston, Ontario. October 31:2-31.

McKelvie, C. L. 1973. The distribution and breeding success of the Peregrine Falcon *Falco peregrinus* in Northern Ireland 1970-73. Hawk Trust Annual Report: 20-27.

McLane, M. A. R., E. H. Dustman, E. R. Clark, and D. L. Hughes. 1978. Organochlorine insecticide and polychlorinated biphenyl residues in Woodcock wings, 1971-72. Pestic. Monitor. J. 12:22-25.

McLane, M. A. R., L. F. Stickel, E. R. Clark, and D. L. Hughes. 1973. Organochlorine residues in Woodcock wings, 11 states, 1970-71. Pestic. Monitor. J. 7:100-103.

McLane, M. A. R., L. F. Stickel, and J. D. Newsom. 1971. Organochlorine pesticide residues in Woodcock, soils and earthworms in Louisiana, 1965. Pestic. Monitor. J. 5:248-250.

McLaren, M. A., and W. G. Alliston. 1981. Summer bird populations on western Victoria Island, N.W.T., July 1980. Polar Gas Project Report. Toronto, LGL Ltd.

McNulty, F. 1972. Falcons of Morro Rock. New Yorker, December 23:67-74.

McNutt, J. W. 1981. Seleccion de presa y comportamiento de caza del Halcon Peregrino (*Falco peregrinus*) en Magallanes y Tierra del Fuego. Anales del Instituto de la Patagonia 12:221-228.

McNutt, J. W. 1984. A Peregrine Falcon polymorph: observations of the reproductive behavior of *Falco kreyenborgi*. Condor 86:378-382.

Mearns, E. D. 1890. Observations on the avifauna of portions of Arizona. Auk 7:45-55.

Mearns, R. 1982. Winter occupation of breeding territories and winter diet of Peregrines in south Scotland. Ornis Scandinavica 13:79-83.

Mearns, R. 1983. The diet of the Peregrine *Falco peregrinus* in south Scotland during the breeding season. Bird Study 30:81-90.

Mearns, R., and I. Newton. 1984. Turnover and dispersal in a Peregrine *Falco peregrinus* population. Ibis 126:347-355.

Mebs, T. 1960. Probleme der Fortpflanzungsbiologie und Bestandserhaltung bei deutschen Wanderfalken. Vogelwelt 81:47-56.

Mebs, T. 1969. Wanderfalkenbruten an menschlichen Bauwerken. Deutscher Falkenorden 1968:55-65.

Mebs, T. 1971. Todesursachen und Mortalitätsraten beim Wanderfalken (*Falco peregrinus*) nach den Wiederfunden deutscher und finnischer Ringvögel. Die Vogelwarte 26:98-105.

Mehner, J. F., and G. J. Wallace. 1959. Robin populations and insecticides. Atl. Nat. 14:4-10.

Mendenhall, V. M., E. E. Klaas, and M. A. R. McLane. 1983. Breeding success of Barn Owls (*Tyto alba*) fed low levels of DDE and dieldrin. Arch. Environ. Contam. Toxicol. 12:235-240.

Menzie, C. 1969. Metabolism of Pesticides. U. S. Dept. of the Interior, Fish and Wildl. Serv., Special Scientific Report, Wildl. No. 127.

Merikallio, E. 1958. Finnish birds: their distribution and numbers. Fauna Fennica 5:1-181.

Metcalf, R. L. 1974. Statement of testimony in public hearings on cancellation of registrations of aldrin/dieldrin. Washington, D. C., U. S. Environmental Protection Agency.

Meyburg, B. U. 1981. Newsletter No. 4. World Working Group on Birds of Prey. ICBP.

Meyburg, B. U. 1985. Die Situation des Wanderfalken in Deutschland. Rundbrief Nr. 2 der Weltarbeitsgruppe für Greifvögel des Internat. Rats f. Vogelschutz 4-5.

Mikkola, H. 1976. Owls killing and killed by other owls and raptors in Europe. Brit. Birds 69:141-154.

Miller, D. S., W. B. Kinter, and D. B. Peakall. 1976. Enzymatic basis for DDE-induced eggshell thinning in a sensitive bird. Nature 259:122-124.

Milstein, P. Le S., I. Prestt, and A. A. Bell. 1970. The breeding cycle of the Grey Heron. Ardea 58:171-257.

Mindell, D. P. 1983. Nesting raptors in southwestern Alaska: status, distribution, and aspects of biology. Anchorage, U. S. Dept. Interior, Bureau of Land Mgmt. Rept. BLM/AK/TR-83/08.

Mingozzi, T. 1981. Il Falco Pellegrino (*Falco peregrinus*) sulle Alpi Occidentali. Parte I: analisi storico-bibliografica della distribuzione sull'arco alpino italiano. Riv. Ital. di Orn. Milano 51:179-190.

Monk, J. C. 1979. Peregrine Falcon inventory, data evaluation and management recommendations, 1979. Ukiah District Office, California, U. S. Bureau of Land Mgmt.

Monk, J. C. 1980. Peregrine Falcon inventory, data evaluation and management recommendations, 1980. Ukiah District Office, California, U. S. Bureau of Land Mgmt.

Monk, J. C. 1981. Peregrine Falcon inventory, data evaluation and management recommendations, 1981. Ukiah District Office, California, U. S. Bureau of Land Mgmt.

Monk, J. G., and D. L. Harlow. 1984. California Peregrine Falcon reproductive outcome and management effort in 1982 and 1983. Sacramento, California, U. S. Dept. of the Interior, Fish and Wildl. Serv., Endangered Species Office.

Monneret, R.-J. 1973. Etude d'une population de Faucons Pèlerins dans une region de l'Est de la France: Analyse de causes possibles de regression. Alauda 12:121-128.

Monneret, R.-J. 1987. Le Faucon Pèlerin. Editions du Point Veterinaire, Maisons-Alfort, France.

Monneret, R.-J., and P. Gowthorpe. 1978. Le Faucon Pèlerin. FRIR Monts du Jura-Alpes du Nord.

Monroe, B. L., Jr. 1982. A modern concept of the subspecies. Auk 99:608-609.

Mooney, N. J., and N. P. Brothers. 1987. The Peregrine Falcon, *Falco peregrinus macropus* S., in Tasmania. I. Distribution, abundance and physical characteristics of nests. Australian Wildl. Res. 14:81-93.

Moore, N. W., and D. A. Ratcliffe. 1962. Chlorinated hydrocarbon residues in the egg of a Peregrine Falcon (*Falco peregrinus*) from Perthshire. Bird Study 9:242-244.

Moore, N. W., and J. O'G. Tatton. 1965. Organochlorine residues in the eggs of sea birds. Nature 207:42-43.

Moore, N. W., and C. H. Walker. 1964. Organic chlorine insecticide residues in wild birds. Nature 201:1072-1073.

Morillo, C. 1984. Guia de las Rapaces Ibericas. Madrid, ICONA, 2nd Ed.

Morizot, D. C., R. G. Anthony, T. G. Grubb, S. W. Hoffman, M. E. Schmidt, and R. E. Ferrell. 1985. Clinal genetic variation at enzyme loci in Bald Eagles (*Haliaeetus leucocephalus*) from the western United States. Biochem. Genet. 23:337-345.

Morris, J., and R. Stevens. 1971. Successful cross-breeding of a Peregrine tiercel and a Saker Falcon. Captive Breeding Diurnal Birds of Prey 1:5-7.

Morrison, A. 1939. The birds of the Dept. of Huancavelica. Ibis 81:453-486.

Mosher, J. A., and C. M. White. 1978. Falcon temperature regulation. Auk 95:80-84.

Mossop, D. H., and G. Baird. 1985. Peregrine Falcon recovery project. *In* 1985 annual report, birds of prey and non-game birds, inventory, population studies and management projects. Yukon Dept. Renewable Resources Report.

Mossop, D. H., and R. Hayes. 1980. 1980 North American Peregrine Falcon survey: Yukon Territory. Pp. 10-18 *in* 1980 annual report, inventory, population studies and management projects, birds of prey. Yukon Dept. Renewable Resources Report.

Mueller, H. C., and D. D. Berger. 1961. Weather and fall migration of hawks at Cedar Grove, Wisconsin. Wilson Bull. 73:171-192.

Mueller, H. C., and D. D. Berger. 1967a. The relative abundance of species caught in mistnets during fall migration at Cedar Grove. Passenger Pigeon 29:107-115.

Mueller, H. C., and D. D. Berger. 1967b. Fall migration of Sharp-shinned Hawks. Wilson Bull. 79:397-415.

Mulhern, B. M., W. L. Reichel, L. N. Locke, T. G. Lamont, A. Belisle, E. Cromartie, G. E. Bagley, and R. M. Prouty. 1970. Organochlorine residues and autopsy data from Bald Eagles, 1966-68. Pestic. Monitor. J. 4:141-144.

Mundy, P. J., K. I. Grant, J. Tannock, and C. L. Wessels. 1982. Pesticide residues and eggshell thickness of Griffon Vulture eggs in southern Africa. J. Wildl. Mgmt. 46:769-773.

Muntaner, J., X. Ferrer, and A. Martinez-Villalta. 1984. Atlas dels ocells nidificants de Catalunya i Andorra. Barcelona, Ed. Ketres.

Murie, O. 1959. Fauna of the Aleutian Islands and Alaska Peninsula. N. Amer. Fauna No. 61.

Murphy, J. E. (Compiler). 1987. 1985-86 Canadian Peregrine Falcon Survey. Ottawa, Canadian Wildl. Serv.

Murray, J. M., K. E. Davies, P. S. Harper, L. Meredith, C. R. Mueller, and R. Williamson. 1982. Linkage relationship of a cloned DNA sequence on the short arm of the X chromosome to Duchenne muscular distrophy. Nature 300:69-71.

Myers, N. 1986. Tackling mass extinction of species: a great creative challenge. The Horace M. Albright Lectureship in Conservation, XXVI. Univ. of California, College of Natural Resources, Dept. of Forestry and Resource Mgmt.

Nagy, A. G. 1977. Population trend indices based on 40 years of autumn counts at Hawk Mountain. *In* Proceedings of the ICBP World Conference on Birds of Prey (R. D. Chancellor, Ed.). London, Intern. Council for Bird Preservation.

Neill, D. D., H. D. Muller, and J. V. Schutze. 1971. Pesticide effects on the fecundity of the Gray Partridge. Bull. Environ. Contam. Toxicol. 6:546-551.

Nelson, M. W. 1969a. The status of the Peregrine in the Northwest. Pp. 61-72 *in* Peregrine Falcon populations: their biology and decline (J. J. Hickey, Ed.). Madison, Univ. of Wisconsin Press.

Nelson, M. W. 1969b. The Peregrine Falcon in Western North America and Mexico. Pp. 93-97 *in* Peregrine Falcon populations: their biology and decline (J. J. Hickey, Ed.). Madison, Univ. of Wisconsin Press.

Nelson, M. W. 1969c. Research needs in reestablishing local raptorial bird populations. Pp. 403-407 and plate 59 *in* Peregrine Falcon populations: their biology and decline (J. J. Hickey, Ed.). Madison, Univ. Wisconsin Press.

Nelson, R. W. 1970. Some aspects of the breeding behavior of Peregrine Falcons on Langara Island, British Columbia. M. S. thesis, Calgary, Alberta, Univ. of Calgary.

Nelson, R. W. 1976. Langara Island, Queen Charlotte Islands. Pp. 261-262 *in* The 1975 North American Falcon Survey (R. W. Fyfe, S. A. Temple, and T. J. Cade, Eds.). Can. Field-Nat. 90:228-273.

Nelson, R. W. 1977. Behavioral ecology of coastal Peregrines, (*Falco peregrinus pealei*). Ph.D. disseration, Calgary, Alberta, Univ. of Calgary.

Nelson, R. W. 1983. Natural regulation of raptor populations. Pp. 126-150 *in* Natural Regulation of Wildlife (D. S. Eastman, F. L. Bunnell, and J. M. Peek, Eds.). Moscow, Idaho, Univ. of Idaho Press.

Nelson, R. W., and J. A. Campbell. 1973. Breeding and behavior of Arctic Peregrines in captivity. Hawk Chalk 12:39-54.

Nelson, R. W., and M. T. Myres. 1975. Changes in the Peregrine population and its seabird prey at Langara Island, British Columbia. Raptor Res. Rept. 3:13-31.

Nelson, R. W., and M. T. Myres. 1976. Declines in populations of Peregrine Falcons and their seabird prey at Langara Island, British Columbia. Condor 78:281-293.

New Jersey State Geologist Report. 1890. Final report of the state geologist: mineralogy, botany, zoology, vol. 2. Trenton, New Jersey, J. L. Murphy Co.

Newton, I. 1974. Changes attributed to pesticides in the nesting success of the Sparrowhawk in Britain. J. Appl. Ecol. 11:95-101.

Newton, I. 1976. Raptor research and conservation during the last five years. Can. Field-Nat. 90:225-226.

Newton, I. 1979. Population ecology of raptors. Berkhamstead, England, T & A D Poyser.

Newton, I. 1984. Effects of organochlorine pesticides on birds. Pp. 151-159 *in* Proceedings of the 2nd Symposium on African Predatory Birds (J. M. Mendelsohn and C. W. Sapsford, Eds.). Durban, Natal Bird Club.

Newton, I. 1986. The Sparrowhawk. Calton, England, T & A D Poyser.

Newton, I., and J. Bogan. 1974. Organochlorine residues, eggshell thinning and hatching success in British Sparrowhawks. Nature 249:582-583.

Newton, I., and J. Bogan. 1978. The role of different organochlorine compounds in the breeding of British Sparrowhawks. J. Appl. Ecol. 15:105-116.

Newton, I., J. Bogan, E. Meek, and B. Little. 1982. Organochlorine compounds and shell thinning in British Merlins *Falco columbarius* Ibis 124:328-335.

Newton, I., and R. D. Chancellor (Eds.). 1985. Conservation studies on raptors, ICBP Tech. Publ. No. 5. London, Intern. Council for Bird Preservation.

Newton, I., and M. B. Haas. 1984. The return of the Sparrowhawk. Brit. Birds 77:47-70.

Newton, I., M. Marquis, and A. Village. 1983. Weights, breeding, and survival in European Sparrowhawks. Auk 100:344-354.

Newton, I., and M. Marquiss. 1981. Effect of additional food on laying dates and clutch size of Sparrowhawks. Ornis Scandinavica 12:224-229.

Nicholson, E. M. 1932. The art of bird watching. New York, Charles Scribener's Sons.

Nickel, R., A. Schummer, E. Seiferle, W. G. Siller, and P. A. L. Wright. 1977. Anatomy of the domestic birds. Berlin Hamburg, Verlag Paul Parey.

Nickerson, P. R., and K. R. Barbehenn. 1975. Organochlorine residues in Starlings, 1972. Pestic. Monitor. J. 8:247-254.

Nie, N. H., D. H. Bent, and C. H. Hull. 1970. Statistical package for the social sciences. New York, McGraw-Hill.

Noordwijk, A. J. van, and W. Scharloo. 1981. Inbreeding in an island population of the Great Tit. Evolution 35:674-688.

Norris, D. W., and H. J. Wilson. 1983. Survey of the Peregrine *Falco peregrinus* breeding population in the Republic of Ireland in 1981. Bird Study 30:91-101.

Norris, D. W., H. J. Wilson, and D. Browne. 1982. The breeding population of the Peregrine Falcon in Ireland in 1981. Irish Birds 2:145-152.

Norstrom, R. J., D. J. Hallett, F. I. Onuska, and M. E. Comba. 1980. Mirex and its degradation products in Great Lakes Herring Gulls. Environ. Sci. Technol. 14:860-866.

North, A. J. 1912. Nest and eggs of birds found breeding in Australia and Tasmania, vol. 3. Sydney, F. W. White.

Noval, A. 1976. Aves de Presa. Oviedo, Ed. Naranco.

Nygård, T. 1983. Pesticide residues and shell thinning in eggs of Peregrines in Norway. Ornis Scandinavica 14:161-166.

Odsjö, T., and P. Lindberg. 1977. Reduction of eggshell thickness of Peregrines in Sweden. Pp. 61-64 *in* Pilgrimsfalk, Report from a Peregrine Conference held at Grimso Wildlife Research Station, Sweden 1-2 April 1977 (P. Lindberg, Ed.). Stockholm, Swedish Soc. for the Conservation of Nature.

Odsjö, T., and J. Sondell. 1982. Eggshell thinning and DDT, PCB and mercury in eggs of Osprey (*Pandion haliaetus* (L.)) in Sweden and their relations to breeding success. *In* Eggshell thickness and levels of DDT, PCB and mercury in eggs of Osprey (*Pandion haliaetus* (L.)) and Marsh Harrier (*Circus aeruginosus* (L.)) in relation to their breeding success and population status in Sweden (T. Odsjö). Ph.D. dissertation, Stockholm, Univ. Stockholm.

Ogden, V. T., and M. G. Hornocher. 1977. Nesting density and success of Prairie Falcons in southwestern Idaho. J. Wildl. Mgmt. 41:1-11.

Ohlendorf, H. M. 1981. The Chesapeake Bay's birds and organochlorine pollutants. Trans. Wildl. Nat. Resour. Conf. 46:259-270.

Ohlendorf, H. M., D. M. Swineford, and L. N. Locke. 1979. Organochlorine poisoning of herons. Pp. 176-185 *in* Proceedings of 1979 Conference of the Colonial Waterbird Group (W. E. Southern, Compiler). Ithaca, New York, Lab. Ornithol., Cornell Univ.

Ohlendorf, H. M., D. M. Swineford, and L. N. Locke. 1981. Organochlorine residues and mortality of herons. Pestic. Monitor. J. 14:125-135.

Olrog, C. C. 1948. Observaciones sobre la avifauna de Tierra del Fuego y Chile. Acta. Zool. Lilloana 5:437-531.

Olrog, C. C. 1968. Las Aves Sudamericas. Tucuman, Argentina, Instituto Miguel Lillo.

Olsen, P. D. 1982. Ecogeographic and temporal variation in the eggs and nests of the Peregrine, *Falco peregrinus*, (Aves: Falconidae) in Australia. Australian Wildl. Res. 9:277-291.

Olsen, P. D. 1985. Population studies of the Peregrine in Australia. Pg. 381-388 *in* Conservation studies on raptors, ICBP Tech. Publ. No. 5 (I. Newton and R. D. Chancellor, Eds.). London, Intern. Council for Bird Preservation.

Olsen, P. D., and J. Olsen. 1979. Eggshell thinning in the Peregrine, *Falco peregrinus* (Aves: Falconidae), in Australia. Australian Wildl. Res. 6:217-226.

Olsen, P. D., and J. Olsen. 1985. Preliminary report on changes in eggshell thickness of Australian *Falco*. Pg. 389-392 *in* Conservation studies on raptors, ICBP Tech. Publ. No. 5 (I. Newton and R. D. Chancellor, Eds.). London, Intern. Council for Bird Preservation.

Olsen, P. D., and D. B. Peakall. 1983. DDE in eggs of the Peregrine Falcon in Australia, 1949-1977. Emu 83:276-277.

Olsson, O. 1958. Dispersal, migration, longevity and death causes of *Strix aluco, Buteo buteo, Ardea cinerea* and *Larus argentatus*. Acta Vertebratica 1:91-189.

O'Neill, J. P. 1982. The subspecies concept in the 1980s. Auk 99:609-612.

Ortiz, F. 1975. Checklist of the most common birds of Quito and its surroundings. P. U. Catolica del Ecuador.

Ortiz, F., and S. Valarezo. 1975. Lista de Aves del Ecuador. Plub. Scc. Francisco Campos, No. 2, Quito.

Paasch, B., C. Spaeter, and C. Saar. 1981. Gezüchtete Wanderfalken fliegen aus künstlichem Baumhorst aus. Deutscher Falkenorden 15-16.

Palma, L. 1985. The present situation for birds of prey in Portugal. Pp. 3-14 *in* Conservation studies on raptors, ICBP Tech. Publ. No. 5 (I. Newton and R. D. Chancellor, Eds.). London, Intern. Council for Bird Preservation.

Parellada, X., and A. De Juan. 1981. Les Accipitriformes des milieux alpins des Pyrennees catalanes. Pp. 34-43 *in* Rapaces Mediterraneens. Parc Naturel Regional de Corse. Centre de Recherche Ornithologique de Provence.

Parrish, J. R., D. T. Rogers, Jr., and F. P. Ward. 1983. Identification of natal locales of Peregrine Falcons (*Falco peregrinus*) by trace element analysis of feathers. Auk 100:560-567.

Paton, J., J. Menz, and P. Bowie. 1981. Peregrine Falcons along the Murray River in South Australia. Australasian Raptor Assoc. News 2:5-6.

Pattee, O. H. 1984. Eggshell thickness and reproduction in American Kestrels exposed to chronic dietary lead. Arch. Environ. Contam. Toxicol. 13:29-34.

Pattee, O. H., W. G. Mattox, and W. S. Seegar. 1984. Twin embryos in a Peregrine Falcon egg. Condor 86:352-353.

Peakall, D. B. 1967. Pesticide-induced enzyme breakdown of steroids in birds. Nature 216:505-506.

Peakall, D. B. 1970. *p,p'*-DDT: Effect on calcium metabolism and concentration of estradiol in the blood. Science 168:592-594.

Peakall, D. B. 1974. DDE: its presence in Peregrine eggs in 1948. Science 183:673-674.

Peakall, D. B. 1975. Physiological effects of chlorinated hydrocarbons on avian species. Pp. 343-360 *in* Environmental dynamics of pesticides (R. Hague and V. Freed, Eds.). New York, Plenum Press.

Peakall, D. B. 1976. The Peregrine Falcon (*Falco peregrinus*) and pesticides. Can. Field-Nat. 90:301-307.

Peakall, D. B., T. J. Cade, C. M. White, and J. R. Haugh. 1975. Organochlorine residues in Alaskan Peregrines. Pestic. Monitor. J. 8:255-260.

Peakall, D. B., and A. C. Kemp. 1976. Organochlorine residue levels in herons and raptors in the Transvaal. Ostrich 47:139-141.

Peakall, D. B., and A. C. Kemp. 1980. Organochlorine levels in owls in Canada and South Africa. Ostrich 51:186-187.

Peakall, D. B., and L. F. Kiff. 1979. Eggshell thinning and DDE residue levels among Peregrine Falcons *Falco peregrinus*: a global perspective. Ibis 121:200-204.

Peakall, D. B., T. S. Lew, A. M. Springer, W. Walker II, R. W. Risebrough, J. G. Monk, W. M. Jarman, B. J. Walton, L. M. Reynolds, R. W. Ryfe, and L. F. Kiff. 1983. Determination of the DDE and PCB contents of Peregrine Falcon eggs: a comparison of whole egg measurements and estimates derived from eggshell membranes. Arch. Environ. Contam. Toxicol. 12:523-528.

Peakall, D. B., J. L. Lincer, R. W. Risebrough, J. B. Pritchard, and W. B. Kinter. 1973. DDE-induced eggshell thinning: structural and physiological effects in three species. Comp. Gen. Pharmacol. 4:305-313.

Peakall, D. B., and M. L. Peakall. 1973. Effect of a polychlorinated biphenyl on the reproduction of artificially and naturally incubated dove eggs. J. Appl. Ecol. 10:863-868.

Peakall, D. B., L. M. Reynolds, and M. C. French. 1976. DDE in eggs of the Peregrine Falcon. Bird Study 23:183-186.

Perrins, C. M. 1965. Populations and clutch size in the Great Tit, *Parus major* L. J. Anim. Ecol. 34:601-647.

Perrins, C. M. 1971. Age of first breeding and adult survival rates in the Swift. Bird Study 18:61-70.

Perrins, C. M., M. P. Harris, and C. K. Britton. 1973. Survival of Manx Shearwaters *Puffinus puffinus*. Ibis 115:535-548.

Peters, J. L. 1931. Check-list of birds of the world, vol. 1. Cambridge, Harvard Univ. Press.

Petersen, R. S. 1968. The domestic raising of the Peale's Peregrine Falcon. J. N. Amer. Falconers' Assoc. 7:64-68.

Peterson, J. E., K. M. Stahl, and D. L. Meeker. 1976. Simplified extraction and cleanup for determining organochlorine pesticides in small biological samples. Bull. Environ. Contam. and Toxicol. 15:135-139.

Phillips, A., J. Marshall, and G. Monson. 1964. The birds of Arizona. Tucson, Univ. of Arizona Press.

Phillips, A. R. 1982. Subspecies and species: fundamentals, needs, and obstacles. Auk 99:612-615.

Pianka, E. R. 1974. Evolutionary ecology. New York, Harper and Row.

Piper, S. E., P. J. Mundy, and J. A. Ledger. 1981. Estimates of the survival in the Cape Vulture *Gyps coprotheres*. J. Anim. Ecol. 50:815-825.

Pitelka, F. A. 1981. The Condor case: an uphill struggle in a downhill crush. Auk 98:634-635.

Pitelka, F. A., P. Q. Tomich, and G. W. Treichel. 1955. Ecological relationships of Jaegers and owls as Lemming predators near Barrow, Alaska. Ecol. Monogr. 25:85-117.

Platt, J. B. 1983a. Falcon breeding as a conservation tool in Arabia. Intern. Zool. Yearbook 23:84-88.

Platt, J. B. 1983b. Pakistan hawk bazaars and Arab falconers. Hawk Chalk 22:38-42.

Poole, K. G., and R. G. Bromley. 1985. Aspects of the ecology of the Gyrfalcon in the Central Arctic, Northwest Territories, 1983 and 1984. Yellowknife, Northwest Territories Wildl. Serv. File Rep. No. 52.

Porter, R. D., M. A. Jenkins, and A. L. Gaski. 1987. Working bibliography of the Peregrine Falcon. Wildlife Federation Scientific and Technical Series No. 9. Washington, D. C., Inst. for Wildl. Res., Natl. Wildl. Fed.

Porter, R. D., and C. M. White. 1973. The Peregrine Falcon in Utah: emphasizing ecology and competition with the Prairie Falcon. Brigham Young Univ. Sci. Bull. 18:1-74.

Porter, R. D., and S. N. Wiemeyer. 1969. Dieldrin and DDT effects on Sparrow Hawk eggshells and reproduction. Science 165:199-200.

Porter, R. D., and S. N. Wiemeyer. 1970. Propagation of captive American Kestrels. J. Wildl. Mgmt. 34:594-604.

Porter, R. D., and S. N. Wiemeyer. 1972. DDE at low dietary levels kills captive American Kestrels. Bull. Environ. Contam. Toxicol. 8:193-199.

Post, G. 1952. The effects of aldrin on birds. J. Wildl. Mgmt. 16:492-493.

Postupalsky, S. 1974. Raptor reproductive success: some problems with methods, criteria and terminology. Raptor Res. Rep. 2:21-31.

Potts, G. R. 1968. Success of the Shag on the Farne Islands, Northumberland, in relation to their content of dieldrin and p,p'-DDE. Nature 217:1282-1284.

Power, D. M. 1970. Geographic variation of Red-winged Blackbirds in central North America. Univ. Kansas Publ. Mus. Nat. Hist. 19:1-83.

Prestt, I., and D. Ratcliffe. 1972. Effects of organochlorine insecticides on European birdlife. Proc. 15th Intern. Ornithol. Congr.: 486-513.

Prestt, I., D. J. Jefferies, and J. W. MacDonald. 1968. Post-mortem examinations of four Rough-legged Buzzards. Brit. Birds 61:457-465.

Proudfoot, N. J., A. Gil, and T. Maniatis. 1982. The structure of the human zeta-globin and a closely linked, nearly identical pseudogene. Cell 31:533-563.

Prouty, R. M., O. H. Pattee, and S. K. Schmeling. 1982. DDT poisoning in a Cooper's Hawk collected in 1980. Bull. Environ. Contam. Toxicol. 28:319-321.

Pruett-Jones, S. G., C. M. White, and W. R. Devine. 1981a. Breeding of the Peregrine Falcon in Victoria, Australia. Emu 80:253-269.

Pruett-Jones, S. G., C. M. White, and W. B. Emison. 1981b. Eggshell thinning and organochlorine residues in eggs and prey of Peregrine Falcons from Victoria, Australia. Emu 80:281-287.

Pyke, G. H., H. R. Pulliam, and E. L. Charnov. 1977. Optimal foraging: a selective review of theory and tests. Q. Rev. Biol. 52:137-154.

Rafuse, B. 1985. Directors' reports. Hawk Chalk 24:26-27.

Ratcliffe, D. A. 1962. Breeding density in the Peregrine *Falco peregrinus* and Raven *Corvus corax*. Ibis 104:13-39.

Ratcliffe, D. A. 1963. The status of the Peregrine in Great Britain. Bird Study 10:56-90.

Ratcliffe, D. A. 1967. Decrease in eggshell weight in certain birds of prey. Nature 215:208-210.

Ratcliffe, D. A. 1969. Population trends of the Peregrine Falcon in Great Britain. Pp. 239-270 in Peregrine Falcon populations: their biology and decline (J. J. Hickey, Ed.). Madison, Univ. of Wisconsin Press.

Ratcliffe, D. A. 1970. Changes attributable to pesticides in egg breakage frequency and eggshell thickness in some British birds. J. Appl. Ecol. 7:67-115.

Ratcliffe, D. A. 1972. The Peregrine population in Great Britain in 1971. Bird Study 19:117-156.

Ratcliffe, D. A. 1973. Studies of the recent breeding success of the Peregrine, *Falco peregrinus*. J. Reprod. Fert. (Suppl.) 19:377-389.

Ratcliffe, D. A. 1980. The Peregrine Falcon. Vermillion, South Dakota, Buteo Books.

Ratcliffe, D. A. 1984a. The Peregrine breeding population of the United Kingdom in 1981. Bird Study 31:1-18.

Ratcliffe, D. A. 1984b. Tree-nesting by Peregrines in Britain and Ireland. Bird Study 31:232-233.

Real, J. 1981. Aproximacio a l'estudi dels Rapinyaires (Falconiformes) dels Massissos de Sant Llorenc del Munt-Serra de L'Obac, Montserrat i zones envoltants. Butll. Inst. Cat. Hist. Nat. 47:155-164.

Real, J. 1983. Addicions a l'estudi dels Rapinyaires (Falconiformes) dels Massissos de Sant Llorenc del Munt-Serra de L'Obac, Montserrat i zones envoltants. Butll. Inst. Cat. Hist. Nat. 49:155-158.

Reichel, W. L., E. Cromartie, T. G. Lamont, B. M. Mulhern, and R. M. Prouty. 1969b. Pesticide residues in eagles. Pestic. Monitor. J. 3:142-144.

Reichel, W. L., T. G. Lamont, E. Cromartie, and L. N. Locke. 1969a. Residues in two Bald Eagles suspected of pesticide poisoning. Bull. Environ. Contam. Toxicol. 4:24-29.

Reichel, W. L., L. N. Locke, and R. M. Prouty. 1974. Peregrine Falcon suspected of pesticide poisoning. Avian Diseases 18:487-489.

Reid, W. 1985. The cost of reproduction in Glaucous-winged Gulls. Pacific Seabird Group Bull. 12:27.

Reidinger, R. F., Jr. 1976. Organochlorine residues in adults of six southwestern bat species. J. Wildl. Mgmt. 40:677-680.

Reilmann, F. 1985. Wanderfalkenbrut auf Leuchttürmen im Nordseewatt und ihre Hege. Deutscher Falkenorden 1984:40-49.

Remple, J. D. 1980. Avian malaria with comments on other haemosporidia in large falcons. *In* Recent advances in the study of raptor diseases. Keighly, West Yorkshire, U. K., Chiron Publications, Ltd.

Reynolds, L. M. 1969. Polychlorobiphenyls (PCBs) and their interference with pesticide residue analysis. Bull. Environ. Contam. Toxicol. 4:128-143.

Reynolds, L. M., and T. Cooper. 1975. The analysis of organochlorine residues in fish. Pp. 196-205 *in* Water quality parameters. Philadelphia, American Society for Testing and Materials.

Reynolds, P. W. 1934. Apuntes sobre aves de Tierra del Fuego. El Hornero 5:339-353.

Reznick, D. 1985. Costs of reproduction: an evaluation of the empirical evidence. Oikos 44:257-267.

Rice, J. N. 1969. The decline of the Peregrine population in Pennsylvania. Pp. 155-163 *in* Peregrine Falcon populations: their biology and decline (J. J. Hickey, Ed.). Madison, Univ. of Wisconsin Press.

Richardson, W. J. 1978. Timing and amount of bird migration in relation to weather: a review. Oikos 30:224-272.

Richardson, W. J. 1979. Southeastward shorebird migration over Nova Scotia and New Brunswick in autumn: a radar study. Can. J. Zool. 57:107-124.

Ricklefs, R. E. 1977. On the evolution of reproductive strategies in birds: reproductive effort. Amer. Natur. 111:453-478.

Risebrough, R. W. 1972. Effects of environmental pollutants upon animals other than man. Pp. 443-463 in Proceedings Sixth Berkeley Symposium Mathematical Statistics and Probability (L. Le Cam, J. Neyman, and E. L. Scott, Eds.). Berkeley, Univ. of California Press.

Risebrough, R. W. 1986. Pesticides and bird populations. Current Ornithol. 3:397-427.

Risebrough, R. W., and D. W. Anderson. 1975. Some effects of DDE and PCB on Mallards and their eggs. J. Wildl. Mgmt. 39:509-513.

Risebrough, R. W., G. L. Florant, and D. D. Berger. 1970. Organochlorine pollutants in Peregrines and Merlins migrating through Wisconsin. Can. Field-Nat. 84:247-254.

Risebrough, R. W., R. J. Huggett, J. J. Griffin, and C. E. D. Goldberg. 1968a. Pesticides: transatlantic movements in the northeast trades. Science 159:1233-1235.

Risebrough, R. W., W. M. Jarman, A. M. Springer, W. Walker II, and W. G. Hunt. 1986. A metabolic derivation of DDE from Kelthane. Environ. Toxicol. Chem. 5:13-19.

Risebrough, R. W., P. Reiche, D. B. Peakall, S. G. Herman, and M. N. Kirven. 1968b. Polychlorinated biphenyls in the global ecosystem. Nature 220:1098-1102.

Risebrough, R. W., F. C. Sibley, and M. N. Kirven. 1971. Reproductive failure of the Brown Pelican on Anacapa Island in 1969. Amer. Birds 25:8-9.

Ritchie, R. J. 1976. A suggested management approach for the upper Yukon River, Alaska. M. S. thesis, Fairbanks, Univ. of Alaska.

Ritchie, R. J., and R. E. Ambrose. 1978. Status of the Peregrine Falcon, Falco peregrinus, in the central Kuskokwim River region, Alaska. Can. Field-Nat. 92:293.

Rockenbauch, D. 1965. Kletterverbot wegen Vogelschutz. Nachr. dt. Alpenver. (DAV), Sekt. Schwaben (Sonderh. Naturschutz):8-9.

Rockenbauch, D. 1970. Vom Ruckgang und Schutz des Wanderfalken (Falco peregrinus). Ornithol. Mitt. 22:35-38.

Rockenbauch, D. 1971. Die Ernährung südwestdeutscher Wanderfalken (Falco peregrinus). J. Ornithol. 112:43-60.

Rockenbauch, D. 1975. Hat unser Wanderfalkenbestand noch Zukunft? Beih. Veroff. Naturschutz Landschaftspflege Bad.-Württ. 7:42-53.

Rockenbauch, D. 1978. Untergang und Wiederkehr des Uhus Bubo bubo in Baden-Württemberg. Anz. orn. Ges. Bayern 17:293-328.

Rogers, H. H., J. F. Thomas, and G. E. Bingham. 1983. Response of agronomic and forest species to elevated carbon dioxide. Science 220:428-429.

Romanoff, A. L., and A. J. Romanoff. 1949. The avian egg. New York, John Wiley and Sons.

Rosene, W., Jr. 1958. Whistling-cock counts of Bobwhite Quail on areas treated with insecticide and on untreated areas, Decatur County, Georgia. Proc. 12th Ann. Conf. S.E. Assoc. Game Fish Comm.: 240-244.

Rosene, W., Jr. 1965. Effects of field applications of heptachlor on Bobwhite, Quail and other wild animals. J. Wildl. Mgmt. 29:554-580.

Roseneau, D. G., H. Reynolds, and C. M. White. 1976a. Northeastern Alaska. Pp. 243-245 in The 1975 North American Peregrine Falcon survey (R. Fyfe, S. A. Temple, and T. J. Cade, Eds.). Can. Field-Nat. 90:228-273.

Roseneau, D. G., A. M. Springer, and L. G. Swartz. 1976b. The western coast of Alaska. Pp. 257-259 *in* The 1975 North American Peregrine Falcon survey (R. Fyfe, S. A. Temple, and T. J. Cade, Eds.). Can. Field-Nat. 90:228-273.

Rosenfield, R. N., and D. L. Evans. 1980. Migration indices and sequence of age and sex classes of the Sharp-shinned Hawk. Loon 52:66-69.

Rudd, R. L., and R. E. Genelly. 1955. Chemicals and wildlife: an analysis of research needs. Proc. 20th N. Amer. Wildl. Conf.: 189-198.

Rudd, R. L., and R. E. Genelly. 1956. Pesticides: their use and toxicity in relation to wildlife. California Dept. Fish and Game, Game Bull. 7.

Rudebeck, G. 1950. Studies on bird migration based on field studies in southern Sweden. Var Fagelvarld, Suppl. 1.

Rudebeck, G. 1951. The choice of prey and modes of hunting of predatory birds with special reference to their selective effect. Oikos 3:200-231.

Rufino, K., A. Araujo, and M. V. Abreu. 1985. Breeding raptors in Portugal: distribution and population estimates. Pp. 15-28 *in* Conservation studies on Raptors, ICBP Tech. Publ. No. 5 (I. Newton and R. D. Chancellor, Eds.). London, Intern. Council for Bird Preservation.

Ryckman, R. E., C. T. Ames, and C. C. Lindt. 1953. A comparison of aldrin, dieldrin, heptachlor and DDT for control of plague vectors on the California Ground Squirrel. J. Econ. Entomol. 46:598-601.

Saar, C. 1970. A breeding attempt with Peregrine Falcons. Captive Breeding Diurnal Birds of Prey 1:10.

Saar, C. 1978. Die Auswilderung von gezüchteten Wanderfalken in Berlin. Deutscher Falkenorden 4-14.

Saar, C. 1985. The breeding and release of Peregrines in West Germany. Pp. 363-365 *in* Conservation studies on raptors, ICBP Tech. Publ. No. 5 (I. Newton and R.D. Chancellor, Eds.). London, Intern. Council for Bird Preservation.

Saar, C., G. Trommer, and W. Hammer. 1982. Der Wanderfalke, Bericht über ein Artenschutzprogramm: Methoden, Ziele und Erfolge. Bonn, Deutscher Falkenorden.

Saar, C., G. Trommer, and W. Hammer. 1985. Auswilderungsbericht 1984. Deutscher Falkenorden 1984:25-33.

Salminen, P., and M. Wikman. 1977. Pilgrimsfalkens populations-trend och status i Finland. Pp. 25-30 *in* Pilgrimsfalk, Report from a Peregrine Conference held at Grimso Wildlife Research Station, Sweden 1-2 April 1977 (P. Lindberg, Ed.). Stockholm, Swedish Soc. for the Conservation of Nature.

Salomonsen, F. 1950. Grønlands Fugle. Copenhagen, Munksgard.

Salomonsen, F. 1981. Grønlands Natur. *In* Grønlands Fauna (B. Muus, F. Salomonsen, and C. Vibe, Eds.). Copenhagen, Gyldendal.

Saurola, P. 1985. Persecution of raptors in Europe assessed by Finnish and Swedish ring recovery data. Pp. 439-448 *in* Conservation studies on raptors, ICBP Tech. Publ. No. 5 (I. Newton and R. D. Chancellor, Eds.). London, Intern. Council for Bird Preservation.

Schei, P. J. 1984. Siste nytt om Vandrefalken i Norge. Var Fuglefauna 7:217-223.

Schenk, H., M. Chiavetta, S. Falcone, P. Fasce, B. Massa, T. Mingozzi, and U. Saracino. 1983. Il Falco Pellegrino: indagine in Italia. Milano, Lega Italiana Protezione Uccelli.

Schilling, F. 1981. Die Pestizidbelastung des Wanderfalken in Baden-Württemberg und ihre Rückwirkungen auf die Populationsdynamik. Ökol. Vögel 3 (Sonderh.): 261-274.

Schilling, F., M. Bottcher, and G. Walter. 1981. Probleme des Zeckenbefalls bei Nestlingen des Wanderfalken. J. Ornithol. 122:359-367.

Schilling, F., and C. König. 1980. Die Biozidbelastung des Wanderfalken (*Falco peregrinus*) in Baden-Württemberg und ihre Auswirkung auf die Populationsentwicklung. J. Ornithol. 121:1-35.

Schilling, F., and D. Rockenbauch. 1985. Der Wanderfalke in Baden-Württemberg: gerettet! Beih. Veroff. Naturschutz Landschaftspflege Bad.-Württ. 46:1-80.

Schmidt, D., and R. Hart. 1983. Report of investigation R-60 INV 7-49459, June 27, 1983. U. S. Dept. of the Interior, Fish and Wildl. Serv.

Schnurre, O. 1966. Zur Ernahrung markischer Wanderfalken. Beitr. Vogelkde. 11:368-378.

Schoonmaker, P. K., M. P. Wallace, and S. A. Temple. 1985. Migrant and breeding Peregrine Falcons in northwestern Peru. Condor 87:423-424.

Schriver, E. C. 1969. The status of Cooper's Hawks in western Pennsylvania. Pp. 356-359 in Peregrine Falcon populations: their biology and decline (J. J. Hickey, Ed.). Madison, Univ. of Wisconsin Press.

Schröder, H. 1969. The decline of tree-nesting Peregrines in the German Democratic Republic. Pp. 217-224 in Peregrine Falcon populations: their biology and decline (J. J. Hickey, Ed.). Madison, Univ. of Wisconsin Press.

Scott, T. G., Y. L. Willis, and J. A. Ellis. 1959. Some effects of a field application of dieldrin on wildlife. J. Wildl. Mgmt. 23:409-427.

Selander, R. K. 1971. Systematics and speciation in birds. Pp. 57-147 in Avian biology, vol. 1 (D. S. Farner and J. R. King, Eds.). New York, Academic Press.

Selander, R. K., and R. F. Johnston. 1967. Evolution in the House Sparrow. I. Intrapopulation variation in North America. Condor 69:217-258.

Serventy, D. L., and H. M. Whittell. 1976. Birds of western Australia. Perth, Univ. of Western Australia Press.

Sharpe, R. B. 1873. On the Peregrine Falcon of the Magellan Straits. Ann. and Mag. Nat. Hist. XI:220-224.

Sheldon, M. G., E. G. Wellein, M. H. Mohn, R. A. Wilson, and G. H. Ise. 1962. Evaluation of local pesticide-wildlife problems in the western United States. Pp. 1-9 in Annual Progress Report. U. S. Dept. of the Interior, Fish and Wildl. Serv., Denver Wildl. Res. Center.

Shell Chemical Co. (USA). 1974. Estimated annual liftings or sales of aldrin/dieldrin in U.K. (tonnes). Exhibit 141Z in public hearings on suspension of registrations of aldrin/dieldrin Washington, D. C., U. S. Environmental Protection Agency.

Sherrod, S. K. 1982. Behavior of young Peregrine Falcons after leaving the nest. Ph.D. dissertation, Ithaca, New York, Cornell Univ.

Sherrod, S. K. 1983. Behavior of fledgling Peregrines. Ithaca, New York, The Peregrine Fund, Inc.

Sherrod, S. K., and T. J. Cade. 1978. Release of Peregrine Falcons by hacking. Pp. 121-136 in Birds of prey management techniques (T. A. Geer, Ed.). Oxford, British Falconers' Club.

Sherrod, S. K., W. R. Heinrich, W. A. Burnham, J. H. Barclay, and T. J. Cade. 1981. Hacking: a method for releasing Peregrine Falcons and other birds of prey. Fort Collins, Colorado, The Peregrine Fund, Inc.

Shor, W. 1970a. Banding recoveries of arctic migrant Peregrines of the Atlantic coast and Greenland populations. Raptor Res. News 4:125-131.

Shor, W. 1970b. Peregrine Falcon population dynamics deduced from band recovery data. Raptor Res. News 4:49-59.

Shor, W. 1975. Survival rate of wild adult Prairie Falcons deduced from band recovery data. Raptor Res. 9:46-50.

Siciliano, M. J., and C. R. Shaw. 1976. Separation and visualization of enzymes on gels. Pp. 185-297 *in* Chromatographic and electrophoretic techniques (I. Smith, Ed.). London, William Heineman Publ. Co.

Sick, H. 1960. Notas sobre *Falco peregrinus anatum* Bonaparte no Brasil. Museu Nac. Rio de Janeiro, Publ. Avuls. 34.

Sick, H. 1961. Peregrine Falcon hunting bats while wintering in Brasil. Auk 78:646-648.

Sick, H. 1985. Ornitologia Brasileira. Editora Universidade de Brasilia. Brasilia, DF, Brasil.

Siegel, S. 1956. Nonparametric statistics for the behavioral sciences. New York, McGraw-Hill.

Sileo, L., L. Karstad, R. Frank, M. V. H. Holdrinet, E. Addison, and H. E. Braun. 1977. Organochlorine poisoning of Ring-billed Gulls in southern Ontario. J. Wildl. Disease 13:313-322.

Simkiss, K. 1967. Calcium in reproductive physiology. New York, Reinhold Publ. Co.

Skutch, A. F. 1967. Adaptive limitation of the reproductive rate of birds. Ibis 109:579-598.

Slack, R. S., and C. B. Slack. 1981. Fall migration of Peregrine Falcons along the Rhode Island coast. J. Field Ornithol. 52:60-61.

Sládek, J. 1977. The status of birds of prey in Czechoslovakia. Pp. 87-91 *in* Proceedings of the ICBP World Conference on Birds of Prey (R. C. Chancellor, Ed.). London, Intern. Council for Bird Preservation.

Sloan, M. J. 1973. A United States historical account, aldrin/dieldrin registrations, uses and sales. Statement of testimony in public hearings on cancellation of registrations of aldrin/dieldrin. Washington, D. C., U. S. Environmental Protection Agency.

Smart, N. A., A. R. C. Hill, and P. A. Roughan. 1974. Chlorinated hydrocarbon pesticide residues in foodstuffs: comparison of methods. J. Assoc. Off. Anal. Chem. 57:153-164.

Smith, J. N. M. 1981. Does high fecundity reduce survival in Song Sparrows? Evolution 35:1142-1148.

Smith, R. D., and L. L. Glasgow. 1963. Effects of heptachlor on wildlife in Louisiana. Ann. Conf. Southern Assoc. Game Fish Comm. 17:140-154.

Snelling, J. C., A. C. Kemp, and J. L. Lincer. 1984. Organochlorine residues in southern African raptor eggs. Pp. 161-168 *in* Proceedings of the 2nd Symposium on African Predatory Birds (J. M. Mendelsohn and C. W. Sapsford, Eds.). Durban, Natal Bird Club.

Snyder, N. F. R., H. A. Snyder, J. L. Lincer, and R. T. Reynolds. 1973. Organochlorines, heavy metals, and the biology of North American accipiters. BioScience 23:300-305.

Sokal, R. R., and F. J. Rohlf. 1981. Biometry. San Francisco, W. H. Freeman.

Soler, M., J. M. Zuñiga, and I. Camacho. 1983. Alimentacion y reproducion de algunas aves de la Hoya de Guadix (Sur de España). Trab. Monogr. Dep. Zool. Univ. Granada 6:27-100.

Soper, J. D. 1946. Ornithological results of the Baffin Island expeditions of 1928-1929 and 1930-1931, together with more recent records. Auk 63:1-24, 223-239, 418-427.

Southern, E. M. 1975. Detection of specific sequences among DNA fragments separated by gel electrophoresis. J. Mol. Biol. 98:503-517.

Speer, G. 1985. Population trends of the Peregrine Falcon (*Falco peregrinus*) in the Federal Republic of Germany. Pp. 359-362 *in* Conservation studies on raptors, ICBP Tech. Publ. No. 5 (I. Newton and R. D. Chancellor, Eds.). London, Intern. Council for Bird Preservation.

Spitzer, P. R., R. W. Risebrough, W. Walker II, R. Hernandez, A. Poole, D. Puleston, and I. C. T. Nisbet. 1978. Productivity of Ospreys in Connecticut-Long Island increases as DDE residues decline. Science 202:333-335.

Spofford, W. R. 1947. A successful nesting of the Peregrine Falcon with three adults present. Migrant 18:49-51.

Spofford, W. R. 1969a. General discussion: the Peregrine Falcon in eastern North America. Pp. 175-178 *in* Peregrine Falcon populations: their biology and decline (J. J. Hickey, Ed.). Madison, Univ. of Wisconsin Press.

Spofford, W. R. 1969b. Extra female at a nesting site. Pp. 418-419 *in* Peregrine Falcon populations: their biology and decline (J. J. Hickey, Ed.). Madison, Univ. of Wisconsin Press.

Springer, A. M., W. Walker II, R. W. Risebrough, D. Benfield, D. H. Ellis, W. G. Mattox, D. P. Mindell, and D. G. Roseneau. 1984. Origins of organochlorines accumulated by Peregrine Falcons, *Falco peregrinus*, breeding in Alaska and Greenland. Can. Field-Nat. 98:159-166.

Springer, P. F. 1956. Insecticide, boon or bane? Audubon Mag. May-June:128-130, July-August:176-178.

Stearns, S. C. 1976. Life-history tactics: a review of the ideas. Quart. Rev. Biol. 51:3-49.

Stevens, R. 1953. Laggard. London, Faber and Faber.

Stevens, R. 1956. The taming of Genghis. London, Faber and Faber.

Stevens, R. 1964. Breeding hawks in captivity. The Falconer 4:151-157.

Stevens, R. 1967. An attempt to breed hawks under controlled conditions. The Falconer 5:45-48.

Stevenson, H. M. 1957. The relative magnitude of the trans-gulf and circum-gulf migrations. Wilson Bull. 69:39-77.

Steyn, P. 1982. Birds of prey of southern Africa. Cape Town, David Philip.

Stickel, L. F. 1968. Organochlorine pesticides in the environment. Washington, D. C., U. S. Dept. of the Interior, Fish and Wildl. Serv., Special Scientific Report, Wildl. No. 119.

Stickel, L. F. 1973. Pesticide residues in birds and mammals. Pp. 254-312 *in* Environmental pollution by pesticides (C. A. Edwards, Ed.). London, Plenum Press.

Stickel, L. F., W. H. Stickel, R. D. McArthur, and D. L. Hughes. 1979. Chlordane in birds: a study of lethal residues and loss rates. Pp. 387-396 *in* Toxicology and occupational medicine (W. B. Deichmann, Ed.). New York, Elsevier/North Holland.

Stickel, L. F., S. N. Wiemeyer, and L. J. Blus. 1973. Pesticide residues in eggs of wild birds: adjustment for loss of moisture and lipid. Bull. Environ. Contam. Toxicol. 9:193-196.

Stickel, W. H., L. F. Stickel, and F. B. Coon. 1970. DDE and DDD residues correlated with mortality of experimental birds. Pp. 287-294 *in* Pesticides Symposia. Seventh Inter. Am. Conf. Toxicol. Occupational Med. (W. B. Deichmann, Ed.). Miami, Florida, Hale and Assoc., Inc.

Stickel, W. H., L. F. Stickel, R. A. Dryland, and D. L. Hughes. 1984. Aroclor 1254 residues in birds: lethal levels and loss rates. Arch. Environ. Contam. Toxicol. 13:7-13.

Stickel, W. H., L. F. Stickel, and J. S. Spann. 1969. Tissue residues of dieldrin in relation to mortality in birds and mammals. Pp. 174-204 *in* Chemical fallout: current research on persistent pesticides (M. W. Miller and G. G. Berg, Eds.). Springfield, Illinois, Charles C. Thomas.

Stone, W. 1937. Bird studies at Old Cape May. 2 vols., Philadelphia, Pennsylvania, Delaware Valley Ornithol. Club.

Stone, W. B. 1981. An American Kestrel killed by organochlorine pesticides in Dutchess County, New York. Kingbird 31:79-81.

Stone, W. B., and J. C. Okoniewski. 1983. Organochlorine toxicants in Great Horned Owls from New York, 1981-82. Northeast. Environ. Sci. 2:1-7.

Stresemann, E., and D. Amadon. 1963. What is *Falco kreyenborgi*, Kleinschmidt? Ibis 105:400-402.

Stresemann, E., and D. Amadon. 1979. Order Falconiformes. Pp. 271-425 *in* Check-list of birds of the world, vol. 1, 2nd ed. (E. Mayr and G. W. Cottrell, Eds.). Cambridge, Massachusetts, Mus. Comp. Zool.

Strickland, A. H. 1965. Amounts of organochlorine insecticides used annually on agricultural, and some horticultural, crops in England and Wales. Ann. Appl. Biol. 55:319-325.

Strickland, A. H. 1966. Some estimates of insecticide and fungicide usage in agriculture and horticulture in England and Wales, 1960-64. J. Appl. Ecol. 3(Suppl):3-14.

Sultana, J., and C. Gauci. 1977. The situation of birds of prey in Malta 1975. Pp. 136-139 *in* Proceedings of the ICBP World Conference on Birds of Prey (R. D. Chancellor, Ed.). London, Intern. Council for Bird Preservation.

Svensson, S. E. 1978. Efficiency of two methods for monitoring bird population levels: breeding bird censuses contra counts of migratory birds. Oikos 30:373-386.

Swann, H. S. 1945. A monograph of the birds of prey (order Accipitres), vol. II. London, Wheldon & Wesley, Ltd.

Swarth, H. S. 1933. Peale falcon in California. Condor 35:233-234.

Swofford, D. C. 1985. PAUP, phylogenetic analysis using parsimony, version 2.3, program manual. Urbana, Illinois Nat. Hist. Sur.

Tamame, J. M., and A. Barbero. 1983. Estudio sobre las matanzas de aves de presa en Zamora. Quercus 8:45.

Tannock, J., W. W. Howells, and R. J. Phelps. 1983. Chlorinated hydrocarbon pesticide residues in eggs of some birds in Zimbabwe. Environ. Pollut. B5:147-155.

Tarboton, W., and D. Allan. 1984. The status and conservation of birds of prey in the Transvaal. Pretoria, South Africa, Monog. No. 3, Transvaal Mus.

Tarboton, W. R. 1984. Behaviour of the African Peregrine during incubation. Raptor Res. 18:131-136.

Temple, S. A. 1972. Chlorinated hydrocarbon residues and reproductive success in eastern North American Merlins. Condor 74:105-106.

Temple Lang, J. 1968. Peregrine Falcon Survey 1967-68. Irish Bird Report 16:3-4.

Terrasse, J.-F. 1969. Essai de recensement de la population Francaise de Faucon Pélerin *Falco peregrinus* in 1968. Nos Oiseaux 30:149-155.

Terrasse, J.-F., and M. Y. Terrasse. 1969. The status of the Peregrine Falcon in France in 1965. Pp. 225-230 *in* Peregrine Falcon populations: their biology and decline (J. J. Hickey, Ed.). Madison, Univ. of Wisconsin Press.

Thelander, C. G. 1976. Distribution and reproductive success of Peregrine Falcons in California during 1975 and 1976. Calif. Dept. of Fish and Game, Admin. Report 76-3.

Thelander, C. G. 1977. The breeding status of Peregrine Falcons in California. M.S. thesis, San Jose, California, San Jose State Univ.

Thelander, C. G., and B. Walton. 1980. Evaluation of cliff-nesting raptor habitat, Angeles, San Bernadino, Los Padres National Forests in California. U. S. Forest Service (Los Padres National Forest), Admin. Report.

Thiollay, J. M. 1966. Essai sur les rapaces du Midi de la France: distribution and ecologie: tentative de delnombrement. Alauda 3:210-227.

Thiollay, J. M. 1968. Notes sur les rapaces diurnes de Corse. L'Oiseau et la Revue Francais 38:87-208.

Thiollay, J. M. 1982. Les ressources alimentaires, facteur limitant la reproduction d'une population insulaire de Faucons Pélerins, *Falco peregrinus brookei*. Alauda 50:16-44.

Thomasson, K. 1947. Nagot om Pilgrimsfalkens boplatsval. Var Fagelvarld 72-81.

Thomsen, L. 1971. Behavior and ecology of Burrowing Owls on the Oakland Municipal Airport. Condor 73:177-192.

Thomson, W. R. 1984a. Comparative notes on the ecology of Peregrine, Lanner and Taita Falcons in Zimbabwe. Pp. 15-18 *in* Proceedings of the 2nd Symposium on African Predatory Birds (J. M. Mendelsohn and C. W. Sapsford, Eds.). Durban, Natal Bird Club.

Thomson, W. R. 1984b. Captive breeding of Peregrine Falcons *Falco peregrinus minor* in Zimbabwe. Pp. 241-244 *in* Proceedings of the 2nd Symposium on African Predatory Birds (J. M. Mendelsohn and C. W. Sapsford, Eds.). Durban, Natal Bird Club.

Thomson, W. R. 1984c. DDT in Zimbabwe. Pp. 169-171 *in* Proceedings of the 2nd Symposium on African Predatory Birds (J. M. Mendelsohn and C. W. Sapsford, Eds.). Durban, Natal Bird Club.

Titus, K., and J. A. Mosher. 1982. The influence of seasonality and selected weather variables on autumn migration of three species of hawks through the central Appalachians. Wilson Bull. 94:176-184.

Tori, G. M., and T. J. Peterle. 1983. Effects of PCBs on Mourning Dove courtship behavior. Bull. Environ. Contam. Toxicol. 30:44-49.

Traffic (U.S.A.). 1985. The international raptor trade. Washington, D. C., World Wildl. Fund (U.S.).

Train, R. E. 1974. Shell Chemical Co., et al., consolidated aldrin/dieldrin hearing. Fed. Reg. 39:37246-37272.

Trap, J. P. 1970. Danmark. *In* Grønland, vol. 14 (N. Nielsen, P. Skautrup, and C. Vibe, Eds.). Copenhagen, G. E. C. Gad.

Treleaven, R. B. 1977. Peregrine: the private life of the Peregrine Falcon. Penzance, Headland Publ.

Trevor-Battye, A. 1903. Lord Lilford on birds. London, Hutchinson and Co.

Trivers, R. 1985. Social evolution. Menlo Park, California, Benjamin Cummings Pub.

Trommer, G. 1978. Zucht und Auswilderung von Wanderfalken. Voliere 21:18-19.

Trommer, G. 1983. Habichte als Adoptiveltern für Wanderfalken. Deutscher Falkenorden 1983:56-58.

Trommer, G. 1985. Turmfalken ziehen jungen Wanderfalken auf. Deutscher Falkenorden 1984:54-56.

Trowbridge, C. C. 1895. Hawk flights in Connecticut. Auk 12:259-270.

Turk, A. 1981. Birds of prey kept at Lilford Park, Peterborough. Avicult. Mag. 87:276-277.

Turner, L. M. 1886. Contributions to the natural history of Alaska. Washington, D. C., U. S. Government Printing Office.

Turtle, E. E., A. Taylor, E. N. Wright, R. J. P. Thearle, H. Egan, W. H. Evans, and N. M. Soutar. 1963. The effects on birds of certain chlorinated insecticides used as seed dressings. J. Sci. Fd. Agric. 14:567-577.

Tyler, C. 1966. A study of the eggshells of the Falconiformes. J. Zool. London 150:413-425.

U. S. Environmental Protection Agency. 1975. DDT, a review of scientific and economic aspects of the decision to ban its use as a pesticide. Washington, D. C., U. S. Environmental Protection Agency, EPA-540/1-75-022.

U. S. Fish and Wildlife Service. 1982. Peregrine Falcon recovery plan: Alaska populations. Anchorage, Alaska Regional Office, U. S. Dept. of Interior, Fish and Wildl. Serv.

U. S. Fish and Wildlife Service. 1983. Proposal to reclassify *F. p. tundrius* from endangered to threatened. *Federal Register* (1 March 1983) 48(41):8796-8801.

Uttendörfer, O. 1952. Neue Ergebnisse über die Ernahrung der Greifvögel und Eulen. Stuttgart, Eugen Ulmer.

Valverde, J. A. 1967. Estructura de una comunidad mediterranea de vertebrados terrestres. Monografia 1. Estacion Biologica de Donana. Madrid, CSIC.

Van Horn, D. G., G. McDonald, and G. Ravensfeather. 1982. Breeding populations of the Peregrine Falcon in southeast Alaska. Pp. 154 *in* Raptor management and biology in Alaska and western Canada (W. N. Ladd and P. F. Schempf, Eds.). Anchorage, U. S. Dept. Interior, Fish and Wildl. Serv., Alaska Regional Off.

Vasic, V., B. Grubac, G. Susic, and S. Marinkovic. 1985. The status of birds of prey in Yugoslavia, with particular reference to Macedonia. Pp. 45-53 *in* Conservation studies on raptors, ICBP Tech. Publ. No. 5 (I. Newton and R. D. Chancellor, Eds.). London, Intern. Council for Bird Preservation.

Vasina, W. G. 1975. Algunas consideraciones sobre *Falco peregrinus* en nuestro pais. El Hornero 11:281-284.

Vasina, W. G., and R. J. Stranek. 1984. Biological and ethological notes on *Falco peregrinus cassini* in central Argentina. Raptor Res. 18:123-130.

Vaurie, C. 1961. Systematic notes on Palearctic Birds No. 44. Falconidae: the genus *Falco* (Part I. *Falco peregrinus* and *Falco pelegrinoides*). Amer. Mus. Novitates 2035:1-19.

Vaurie, C. 1965. The Birds of the Palearctic Fauna. Non-Passeriformes. London, Witherby.

Vegas, R., and E. Banda. 1982. Tectonic Framework and Alpine Evolution of the Iberian Peninsula. Earth Evol. Sci. 4:320-343.

Venegas, C., and J. Jory. 1979. Guia de campo para las aves de Magallanes. Publ. del Instituto de la Patagonia Monografias No. 11. Punta Arenas, Chile, Instituto de la Patagonia.

Vermeer, K., and L. M. Reynolds. 1970. Organochlorine residues in aquatic birds in the Canadian prairie provinces. Can. Field-Nat. 84:117-130.

Village, A. 1983. The role of nest site availability and territorial behavior in limiting the breeding density of Kestrels. J. Anim. Ecol. 52:635-645.

von Haartman, L. 1971. Population dynamics. Pp. 391-459 in Avian Biology, vol. 1 (D. S. Farner and J. R. King, Eds.). New York, Academic Press.

Voous, K. H. (Ed.). 1972. Proceedings of the 15th International Ornithological Congress. The Hauge, The Netherlands, 30 August-5 September 1970. Leiden, The Netherlands, E. J. Brill.

Walker, W. II. 1977. Chlorinated hydrocarbon pollutants in Alaskan Gyrfalcons and their prey. Auk 94:442-447.

Walker II, W., W. G. Mattox, and R. W. Risebrough. 1973a. Pollutant and shell thickness determinations of Peregrine eggs from west Greenland. Arctic 26:256-258.

Walker II, W., R. W. Risebrough, J. T. Mendola, and G. W. Bowes. 1973b. South American studies of the Peregrine, an indicator species for persistent pollutants. Antarctic J. 8:29-31.

Waller, R. 1962. Der wilde Falk ist mein Gesell. Melsungen, J. Neumann-Neudamn.

Wallin, K. 1984. Decrease and recovery patterns of some raptors in relation to the introduction and ban of alkyl-mercury and DDT in Sweden. Ambio 13:263-265.

Walter, H. 1979a. The Sooty Falcon (*Falco concolor*) in Oman: results of a breeding survey, 1978. J. Oman Studies 5:9-59.

Walter, H. 1979b. Eleonora's Falcon: adaptions to prey and habitat in a social raptor. Chicago, Univ. of Chicago Press.

Warburton, S. 1925. Birds at Westport. Murrelet 6:62.

Ward, F. P. 1975. Colored and numbered tarsal bands as an aid to raptor demographic studies. Pp. 98-102 in Proceedings of the North American Hawk Migration Conference. Syracuse, New York.

Ward, F. P., S. J. Belardo, and S. Williams. 1978. Report on 1978 spring migration studies of Peregrine Falcons at South Padre Island, Texas. U. S. Dept. of the Interior, Fish and Wildl. Serv.

Ward, F. P., and R. B. Berry. 1972. Autumn migrations of Peregrine Falcons on Assateague Island, 1970-71. J. Wildl. Mgmt. 36:484-492.

Ward, F. P., and R. C. Laybourne. 1985. A difference in prey selection by adult and immature Peregrine Falcons during autumn migration. Pp. 303-309 in Conservation studies on raptors, ICBP Tech. Publ. No. 5 (I. Newton and R. D. Chancellor, Eds.). London, Intern. Council for Bird Preservation.

Warren, R. L. M. 1966. Type-specimens of birds in the British Museum (Natural History), vol. 1, Non-passerines. London, Brit. Mus. (Nat. Hist.).

Watling, D. 1982. Birds of Fiji, Tonga, and Samoa. Wellington, New Zealand, Millwood Press Ltd.

Watling, D. 1985. The distribution of Fijian land and freshwater birds, based on the collections and observations of the Whitney south sea expedition. Domodomo 3:130-152.

Wauer, R. 1974. Birds of the Big Bend National Park. Austin, Univ. of Texas.

Weatherall, D. J. 1982. The new genetics and clinical practice. London, Nuffield Provincial Hospitals Trust.

Weaver, J. D., and T. J. Cade (Eds.). 1983. Falcon propagation: a manual on captive breeding. Ithaca, New York, The Peregrine Fund, Inc.

Webster, J. D. 1977. The avifauna of the southern portion of the Chihuahuan Desert. *In* Transactions of the Symposium on the Biological Resources of the Chihuahuan Desert: United States and Mexico (R. H. Wauer and D. H. Riskind, Eds.). National Park Serv. Trans. and Proc. Series No. 3.

Weick, F. 1980. Birds of prey of the world. Hamburg, Germany, Parey.

Weir, R. D., F. Cooke, M. H. Edwards, and R. B. Stewart. 1980. Fall migration of Saw-whet Owls at Prince Edward Point, Ontario. Wilson Bull. 92:475-488.

Weise, B. R., and W. A. White. 1980. Padre Island National Seashore: a guide to the geology, natural environments, and history of a Texas barrier island. Univ. Texas, Austin, Bur. Econ. Geology.

White, C. M. 1968a. Diagnosis and relationships of the North American tundra-inhabiting Peregrine Falcons. Auk 85:179-191.

White, C. M. 1968b. Biosystematics of the North American Peregrine Falcons. Ph.D. dissertation, Salt Lake City, Univ. of Utah.

White, C. M. 1969a. Breeding Alaskan and arctic migrant populations of the Peregrine. Pp. 45-51 *in* Peregrine Falcon populations: their biology and decline (J. J. Hickey, Ed.). Madison, Univ. of Wisconsin Press.

White, C. M. 1969b. Is there a genetic continuity concerned in eyrie maintenance? Pp. 391-397 *in* Peregrine Falcon populations: their biology and decline (J. J. Hickey, Ed.). Madison, Univ. of Wisconsin Press.

White, C. M. 1972. *Falco peregrinus pealei* in Ohio: an error. Ohio J. Science 72:153-154.

White, C. M. 1975. Studies on Peregrine Falcons in the Aleutian Islands. Raptor Res. Rep. 3:33-50.

White, C. M. 1976. Aleutian islands. Pp. 262-263 *in* The 1975 North American Peregrine Falcon survey (R. Fyfe, S. A. Temple, and T. J. Cade, Eds.). Can. Field-Nat. 90:228-273.

White, C. M. 1982. Food and other habits in relation to the evolution of the Peregrine Falcon in Alaska. Pp. 174-186 *in* Proc. symposium, raptor management and biology in Alaska and western Canada (W. H. Ladd and P. F. Schempf, Eds.). Anchorage, Alaska Regional Office, U. S. Dept. of the Interior, Fish and Wildl. Serv., FWS/AK/PROC-82.

White, C. M., and D. A. Boyce. 1978. A profile of various rivers and their raptor populations in western Alaska, 1977. Anchorage, U. S. Dept. Interior, Bureau Land Mgmt. Rep. BLM/AK/TR-78101.

White, C. M., and T. J. Cade. 1971. Cliff-nesting raptors and ravens along the Colville River in Arctic Alaska. Living Bird 10:107-150.

White, C. M., and T. J. Cade. 1977. Long term trends of Peregrine populations in Alaska. Pp. 63-71 *in* Proceedings of the ICBP World Conference on Birds of Prey (R. D. Chancellor, Ed.). London, Intern. Council for Bird Preservation.

White, C. M., W. B. Emison, and F. S. L. Williamson. 1971. Dynamics of raptor populations on Amchitka Island, Alaska. BioScience 21:623-627.

White, C. M., W. B. Emison, and F. S. L. Williamson. 1973. DDE in a resident Aleutian Island Peregrine population. Condor 75:306-311.

White, C. M., S. G. Jones, and W. R. Devine. 1978. Distribution and ecology of the Peregrine Falcon in Victoria. Melbourne, Australia, Ministry for Conserv., Fisheries and Wildl. Div.

White, C. M., S. G. Pruett-Jones, and W. B. Emison. 1981. The status and distribution of the Peregrine Falcon in Victoria, Australia. Emu 80:270-280.

White, C. M., D. G. Roseneau, and M. Hehnke. 1976. Gulf of Alaska coast and southeast Alaska. Pp. 259-261 *in* The 1975 North American Peregrine Falcon survey (R. Fyfe, S. A. Temple, and T. J. Cade, Eds.). Can. Field-Nat. 90:228-273.

White, D. H. 1976. Nationwide residues of organochlorines in Starlings, 1974. Pestic. Monitor. J. 10:10-17.

White, D. H., and M. T. Finley. 1978. Effects of dietary cadmium in Mallard Ducks. Pp. 220-223 *in* Trace substances in environmental health, XII (D. D. Hemphill, Ed.). A symposium, Columbia, Univ. Missouri.

Whitwell, A. C., R. J. Phelps, and W. R. Thomson. 1974. Further records of chlorinated hydrocarbon pesticide residues in Rhodesia. Arnoldia 6:1-7.

Widmark, G. 1967. Residue analysis of pesticides with the aid of gas chromatography. Abstracts Intern. Congr. of Plant Protection, 30 August-6 September 1967, Vienna.

Wiemeyer, S. N., T. G. Lamont, C. M. Bunck, C. R. Sindelar, F. J. Gramlich, J. D. Fraser, and M. A. Byrd. 1984. Organochlorine pesticide, polychlorobiphenyl, and mercury residues in Bald Eagle eggs, 1969-79, and their relationships to shell thinning and reproduction. Arch. Environ. Contam. Toxicol. 13:529-549.

Wiemeyer, S. N., T. G. Lamont, and L. N. Locke. 1980. Residues of environmental pollutants and necropsy data for eastern United States Ospreys, 1964-1973. Estuaries 3:155-167.

Wiemeyer, S. N., B. M. Mulhern, F. J. Ligas, R. J. Hensel, J. E. Mathisen, F. C. Robards, and S. Postupalsky. 1972. Residues of organochlorine pesticides, polychlorinated biphenyls, and mercury in Bald Eagle eggs and changes in shell thickness, 1969 and 1970. Pestic. Monitor. J. 6:50-55.

Wiemeyer, S. N., and R. D. Porter. 1970. DDE thins eggshells of captive American Kestrels. Nature 227:737-738.

Wiemeyer, S. N., P. R. Spitzer, W. C. Krantz, T. G. Lamont, and E. Cromartie. 1975. Effects of environmental pollutants on Connecticut and Maryland Ospreys. J. Wildl. Mgmt. 39:124-139.

Wier, D. N. 1982. Cliff-nesting raptors of the Kisaralik River, western Alaska. Pp. 138-152 *in* Raptor management and biology in Alaska and western Canada (W. N. Ladd and P. F. Schempf, Eds.). Anchorage, U. S. Dept. Interior, Fish and Wildl. Serv., Alaska Regional Off.

Wikman, M. 1985. The Peregrine population in Finland. Pp. 353-358 *in* Conservation studies on raptors, ICBP Tech. Publ. No. 5 (I. Newton and R. D. Chancellor, Eds.). London, Intern. Council for Bird Preservation.

Wille, F. 1977. Pilgrimsfalken in Danmark. Pp. 31 *in* Pilgrimsfalk (P. Lindberg, Ed.). Stockholm, Swedish Soc. for the Conservation of Nature.

Willgohs, J. F. 1977. Birds of prey in Norway. Pp. 143-148 *in* Proceedings of the ICBP World Conference on Birds of Prey (R. D. Chancellor, Ed.). London, Intern. Council for Bird Preservation.

Williams, G. C. 1966. Adaptation and natural selection. Princeton, New Jersey, Princeton Univ. Press.

Williams, G. C. 1971. Group selection. Chicago, Aldine-Atherton.

Williamson, M. 1981. Island populations. Oxford, Oxford Univ. Press.

Willoughby, E. J., and T. J. Cade. 1964. Breeding behavior of the American Kestrel (Sparrow Hawk). Living Bird 3:75-96.

Wilson, E. O., and W. L. Brown, Jr. 1953. The subspecies concept and its taxonomic application. Syst. Zool. 2:97-111.

Wilson Ornithological Society. 1961. Some effects of insecticides on terrestrial birdlife in the Middle West. Wilson Bull. 73:398-424.

Wood, C. A., and A. Wetmore. 1926. A collection of birds from the Fiji Islands. Ibis 12:91-136.

Woodward, P. W. 1972. The natural history of Kure Atoll, northwestern Hawaiin Islands. Atoll Res. Bull. No. 164:1-318.

Woodwell, G.M., P. P. Craig, and H. A. Johnson. 1971. DDT in the biosphere, where does it go? Science 174:1101-1107.

Wrege, P. H., and T. J. Cade. 1977. Courtship behavior of large falcons in captivity. Raptor Res. 11:1-27.

Wright, G. M. 1967. Geology of the southeastern barren-grounds, parts of the districts of Mackenzie and Keewatin. Geological Survey of Canada, Dept. of Energy, Mines, and Resources. Ottawa, Queens Printers.

Wurster, C. F., D. H. Wurster, and W. N. Strickland. 1965. Bird mortality after spraying for Dutch elm disease with DDT. Science 148:90-91.

Wüst, W. 1981. Avifauna Bavariae: Die Vogelwelt Bayerns im Wandel der Zeit. Ornithologische Gesellschaft in Bayern, München 430-435.

Wyman, A., and R. White. 1980. A highly polymorphic locus in human DNA. Proc. Natl. Acad. Sci. USA 77:6745-6758.

Wynne-Edwards, V. C. 1962. Animal dispersion in relation to social behavior. Edinburgh, Oliver and Boyd.

Yarrell, W. 1871. A history of British birds, vol. 1, 4th ed. London, John van Voorst, Paternoster Row.

Yegorov, O. V. 1959. Material on the ecology of the Yakutsk sapan *Falco peregrinus*. Zool. J. 38:112-122.

Yelisyeev, N. V. (Ed.). 1983. Krasnaya Kniga RSFSR. Moscow, Rossyel'khozizdat.

Young, H. F. 1969. Hypotheses on Peregrine population dynamics. Pp. 513-519 *in* Peregrine Falcon populations: their biology and decline (J. J. Hickey, Ed.). Madison, Univ. of Wisconsin Press.

Zar, J. H. 1974. Biostatistical analysis. Englewood Cliffs, New Jersey, Prentice-Hall, Inc.

Zimmerman, R. L. 1984a. Rule 11 statement concerning Case CR-84-43-GF, U. S. A. vs. Glen Luckman. U. S. District Court, Great Falls, Montana, November 15, 1984.

Zimmerman, R. L. 1984b. Rule 11 statement concerning Case CR-84-43-GF, U. S. A. vs. Marcus Ciesielski. U. S. District Court, Great Falls, Montana, August 28, 1984.

Zink, R. M., and J. V. Remsen, Jr. 1986. Evolutionary processes and patterns of geographic variation in birds. Current Ornithol. 4:1-69.

INDEX

Concepts such as mortality and productivity, and subjects such as prey refer to the Peregrine Falcon unless otherwise indicated; pf = Peregrine Falcon.

DATE DUE

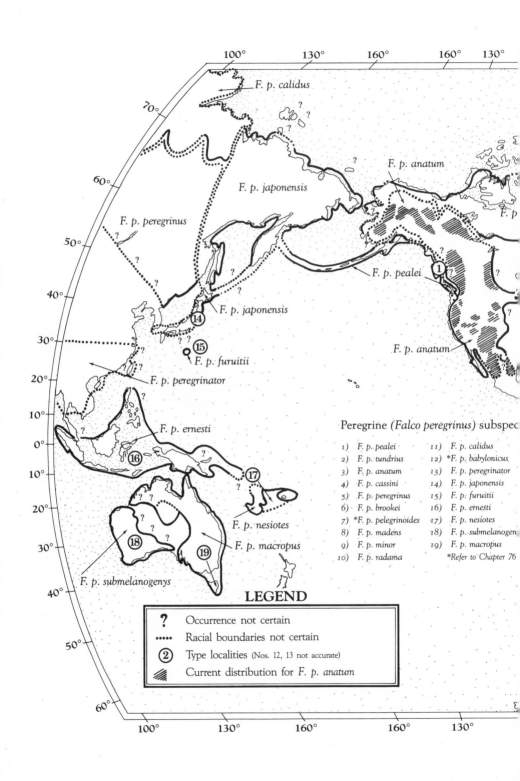

Peregrine (*Falco peregrinus*) subspec

1)	*F. p. pealei*	11)	*F. p. calidus*
2)	*F. p. tundrius*	12)	**F. p. babylonicus*
3)	*F. p. anatum*	13)	*F. p. peregrinator*
4)	*F. p. cassini*	14)	*F. p. japonensis*
5)	*F. p. peregrinus*	15)	*F. p. furuitii*
6)	*F. p. brookei*	16)	*F. p. ernesti*
7)	**F. p. pelegrinoides*	17)	*F. p. nesiotes*
8)	*F. p. madens*	18)	*F. p. submelanogen*
9)	*F. p. minor*	19)	*F. p. macropus*
10)	*F. p. radama*		**Refer to Chapter 76*

LEGEND

?	Occurrence not certain	
·····	Racial boundaries not certain	
②	Type localities (Nos. 12, 13 not accurate)	
▨	Current distribution for *F. p. anatum*	